D1032097

THE ESSENTIAL SUPERMAN ENCYCLOPEDIA

THE ESSENTIAL SUPERMAN ENCYCLOPEDIA

ROBERT GREENBERGER AND MARTIN PASKO

SUPERMAN CREATED BY
JERRY SIEGEL AND JOE SHUSTER

BALLANTINE
BOOKS
NEW YORK

DERE28003

Published in the United States by Del Rey, an imprint of The Random House Publishing Group, a division of Random House LLC, a Penguin Random House Company, New York.

Del Rey is a registered trademark and the Del Rey colophon is a trademark of Random House LLC.

This work was originally published in slightly different form by Del Rey, an imprint of The Random House Publishing Group, a division of Random House, Inc. in 2010.

ISBN 978-0-385-36504-8

Printed in China, 2015

www.dccomics.com
www.delreybooks.com

9 8 7 6 5 4 3 2 1

Interior design by Brad Foltz

For Deb, who patiently allowed me to soar to the exclusion of so much

—R.G.

To my darling wife, Judith, and equally beloved daughter, Laura, who patiently survived the sleepwalking of their husband/father while he was sometimes dizzified by the mythology this book seeks to summarize and clarify

—M.P.

SUPERMAN
No. 41
WORLD'S LARGEST SELLING COMIC MAGAZINE!
OCT.
ACTION COMICS
REG. U S PAT OFF
10¢

PREFACE

Labors of love are not unique to anyone, and many of us tread the same territory in different eras. Long before there was an Internet, let alone computers with vast stores of memory, a writer named Michael Fleisher catalogued every Superman comic book DC Comics had published to date. He had this crazy notion that a single-volume encyclopedia of super heroes could actually be researched and written. Then he entered DC's fabled print library one day in the late 1960s and saw the vast scope of what a single company had published since its founding over thirty years earlier. Undaunted, he changed his plans to a multivolume series featuring the greatest super heroes, starting with Batman.

His assistant, Janet Lincoln, helped him store their data on twenty thousand index cards. Their first book was published in 1976, and all told, only three of the projected eight volumes ever saw print. In 2007, DC released facsimile editions of these three, spotlighting Batman, Wonder Woman, and Superman, filling a desire among longtime comic book fans and collectors and other kinds of super hero enthusiasts to possess this information.

Still, Fleisher's chronicles ended around 1971 while DC continued to publish comics long afterward. As a result, much more of the mythology has been expanded and revised since his work first saw print. DC and Del Rey thought there remained a desire to have the core information updated so the triumvirate would star in three books over the next few years, concluding with the volume in your hands.

Fleisher had to limit his research and writing to Superman's appearances in *Superman, Action Comics, Justice League of America, Trinity,* or *Superman/Batman*. Back in that day, the Man of Steel also appeared regularly in *World's Finest Comics; Superboy; Adventure Comics; Superman's Girl Friend, Lois Lane;* and *Superman's Pal, Jimmy Olsen* as well. Although the number of titles in which he regularly appears today has shrunk, the Man of Steel continues to make regular appearances in more of DC's other core titles than ever before. Elements from these various other comics have proven to be essential to understanding Superman's world, so this new work needed to broaden the horizons of the original Fleisher text to include them, while omitting the comparatively inconsequential minutiae of the original "encyclopedia" to keep the focus on the broad sweep of the character's evolution over an additional thirty years.

That's why this book lives up to its title by limiting itself only to those stories or characters that are considered "essential" to an understanding of the Man of Steel's history and his various reincarnations (or "retconnings"—meaning, retroactive changes to continuity, as the fan audience puts it). So if you'd like to know who Luthor's lab monkey was in 1940, you won't find it here. If, however, you'd like to know which characters, in not only Superman's immediate orbit but in the greater DC Universe as well, have had the greatest impact on his mythology throughout the multiple retconnings, you're in the right place. This volume seeks to be your guide to that often tortuous, difficult-to-navigate landscape.

In addition, comics based on the feature films or animated series are not reflected in these pages. Similarly, Superman's appearances in movie serials, live-action television, and the like are also beyond this book's purview, so don't be confused if, say, you don't find Luthor's late-'70s henchpeople Otis or Miss Teschmacher listed here.

What can be confusing, though, is the notion of parallel worlds and how the stories and character details have changed through cosmic events. In short, DC Comics was not overly concerned with a universe of consistent story details until the mid-1960s. Prior to that, the editorial presumption was that the readership turned over every six to eight years, so comics publishers didn't feel constrained by stories published in years past. As a result, Superman fought the Nazi menace during World War II and then aliens and monsters in the 1950s without having to worry about things like aging.

That all ended when editor Julius Schwartz introduced the Earth-1/Earth-2 concept. Parallel universes were a staple of science fiction for decades by 1961, and Schwartz, who first read, then agented science fiction, introduced the concept to comic books. It all started in *Flash* #123 (September 1961), when the modern-day Flash met his 1940s-era inspiration, whom he thought was actually a character in comic books he read in his childhood. It turned out that the Flashes' respective universes occupied the same physical space but vibrated at different speeds, allowing them to coexist. Since one parallel world was popular with readers, through the years more and more parallel worlds were introduced.

Superman existed on several of these worlds, with the original version—the one first published in 1938—considered an inhabitant of Earth-2. That became the home to all the heroes who were reimagined as the forerunners of the super heroes familiar to today's readers. When comic book buffs founded a formal comics fandom, this era became known as the Golden Age. Superman was among the first inhabitants of that age. As a result, Superman aged, albeit slowly, and while the Superman of Earth-1 was in his prime, his forerunner was in semiretirement, with an adult cousin from Krypton named Power Girl replacing him.

By 1983, DC had decided that its editors, writers, artists, and, most important, its readers were fatigued by tracking these myriad worlds, especially as characters crossed back and forth willy-nilly. To celebrate the company's fiftieth anniversary in 1985, it was decided to blow up all the parallel universes and reduce everything to one cosmology, with one Superman, one Luthor, etc. The result was *Crisis on Infinite Earths,* a twelve-issue comic book "event" that was cosmic in scope, with countless universes being wiped out and the remaining ones combined into one reality. On the heels of the series' conclusion, a new editor and creative team on Superman began a revised continuity, from the destruction of Krypton through the Man of Steel's adulthood.

In time, though, inconsistencies throughout the DC titles led to one retcon after another, all intended to streamline events and correct "mistakes." In 2003, a new road map was drawn up that put Superman in the center of the action. A series of stories ran across the various titles and in their own miniseries, culminating in 2006's *Infinite Crisis,* a sequel to the *Crisis on Infinite Earths,* which fans now refer to as the First Crisis, to avoid confusing the two similar-sounding titles. Reality was modified once more, including the creation of new parallel worlds, although limited to a mere fifty-two. New Earth, the core of the DC Universe, presented once-more modified backgrounds and details for the familiar heroes and their enemies. What we attempt to do in this volume is sort all that out by clearly identifying what happened in each reality. We try to sift through the many seemingly self-contradictory events to help you understand how these characters evolved. If you scratch your head in bewilderment only once or twice, our job here was done well.

Some of the new ongoing storylines introduced as we were writing were going to continue unfolding long after this book would see print. Some end point needed to be established, and after consulting with the DC editors, it seemed that leaving off with the conclusion of the New Krypton storyline made the most practical sense. Still, comics coming out after that time will add new elements, retell familiar stories, and add wrinkles that may make some of these entries seem wrong.

ACKNOWLEDGMENTS

A book this massive in scope could no longer be done entirely by one or two people filling out index cards. As a result many sources and people provided information that proved vital for the completion of the project.

The authors thank DC Comics's former president and publisher Paul Levitz, a longtime friend. He provided support and access to its archives and staff with generosity.

Obviously, this book could not exist without the work of the countless writers, artists, and editors who crafted the mythos, expanded it, and helped it endure. Clearly, Jerry Siegel and Joe Shuster knew what they were doing when creating the character. Over time, their efforts were supported by collaborators and others before the creators left Metropolis and its denizens to others. All have provided countless hours of reading enjoyment to us both.

Additionally, the authors would like to thank:

DC's editor, Christopher Cerasi, who kept us focused on issues of content, style, and comprehension. Chris made certain we had plenty of current research at our fingertips and was always there when we needed help.

At Del Rey, Erich Schoeneweiss once more brought on the amazing Brad Foltz and his crack design team, Foltz Design, and the book benefits from their loving attention to detail. Publisher Scott Shannon showed unwavering faith in the authors and the project.

Matt Idelson, editor of the core Superman titles during the production of this book, was happy to answer our questions and provide sneak peeks at upcoming scripts to enable our manuscript to be as complete as possible.

Mark Waid made time to answer questions and serve as a reader, so his enthusiasm and gracious words of support are appreciated.

The following websites were invaluable to cross-check facts and details about characters and stories: The Grand Comics Database; Julian Darius's Superman Continuity Pages; Mike's Amazing World of DC Comics; Supermanica, the Superman Home Page; DarkMark's Comics Indexing Domain; the Unofficial Guide to the DC Universe; and Michael Koolman's Cosmic Teams.

Bob would like to thank Deb, his wife, without whom he could never have cleared his spring 2009 calendar to work on the book. She was indulgent and loving, supportive and caring, and for that, she continues to win my heart. This book could not have been done without her understanding.

Martin would like to thank his wife, Judith, and daughter, Laura, who cheerfully sacrificed his company as he experienced the fascination of absorbing the details of various Superman reinventions since he himself last wrote the character earlier in the past decade. He would also like to acknowledge the supportiveness and counsel of friends like Paul Kupperberg, whose understanding of the enormity of the enterprise continually reassured Pasko that there wasn't something he wasn't "getting." Martin is also grateful for the input and assistance of other Superman experts like Julian Darius himself and Kurt Busiek.

Last, but certainly not least, special thanks for the enormous contribution of John Wells. For years now, many a comics professional has turned to John for research assistance. His exhaustive and authoritative lists of characters, places, objects, and the like helped organize much of the information found in this book. His files have been ransacked with glee, and both writers, DC, as well as Del Rey, must thank him for his enthusiasm, support, and assistance in helping us keep things coherent yet as concise as possible.

Robert Greenberger
Connecticut

Martin Pasko
New York
2010

INTRODUCTION

It all started with the *S*.

One of my very first memories is of waking up in my toy-littered bedroom on Harvard in Grosse Pointe, Michigan, and staring over at Superman's insignia. It was the world to me. My mom had painted a wall in my room a deep blue and on top of that she carefully, and expertly, painted Superman's *S* across it.

Yeah, I know. Best mom ever.

I'm guessing she did that because I really liked Superman. I mean, I remember wearing pajamas with a cape and Underoos. I remember the movie being shown on TV and playing with the action figures. But that *S* wasn't only about a Man of Steel with powers from the planet Krypton. It symbolized Truth, Justice, and the American way. For some that might seem antiquated in a world where heroes have claws and guns, but trying to do the right thing because it's the right thing to do will forever resonate. I think it's what has drawn so many people to Superman over the decades and across the world. It's why that *S* shield will endure for centuries as a symbol of strength and morality while the claws and guns will fade away in a sea of antiheroes with attitudes.

Superman made me want to do the right thing.

I wonder if Jerry Siegel and Joe Shuster knew when they created Superman back in *Action Comics* #1 in 1938 what kind of impact their creation would have not only on people but on society.

Superman introduced the world to the very concept of the super hero: a being with powers beyond our wildest imaginations who used them to fight against evil. Superman spawned endless doppelgängers and entire universes full of colorfully clad men and women with flight, speed, and power rings. Siegel and Shuster invented the keystone to this modern mythology that only grows every year as new fans discover the heroes we've loved since we first saw them.

I grew up with a dream to one day work specifically with the heroes of the DC Universe, including the king of them all, Superman. After I graduated from Michigan State University, coincidentally the college with the largest comic book collection in the world, I packed my bags and moved out West. After settling into an apartment in Burbank, California, with three friends and $1,500 to my name, I started looking for work. A cold call to Richard Donner's office at Warner Bros. landed me an internship in the company run by the man who directed *Superman: The Movie.*

I worked for Dick as his assistant through two pictures over four years. One of the greatest times of my life. And while I was doing that I started my writing career at DC Comics. Eventually, I moved on to pursue writing full-time . . . but when I left I asked Dick if he'd ever want to work on Superman again. He smiled and said, "With you, kid? Anytime."

Some years later, Dick and I got together with superstar artist Adam Kubert for *Superman: Last Son,* a tale about the son of General Zod who was caught between his father and Superman. We followed that up with *Superman: Escape from Bizarro World* with critically acclaimed artist Eric Powell. And then I flew solo teaming up with Gary Frank.

I have to speak about Gary for a second. There have been a lot of amazing artists over the years who have worked on Superman, but in my opinion, between the work he's done on *Superman and The Legion of Super-Heroes, Superman: Brainiac,* and *Superman: Secret Origin,* with all due respect, Gary has earned his place among the greatest artists who have graced the pages of the Man of Steel. What sends Gary above the rest is his pure understanding of Superman and his willingness to embrace it. Gary and I would talk for hours about why Lex Luthor or Lois Lane would do what they did, but Superman's motivations were never in doubt. We always knew what Superman would do.

Superman would do the right thing.

Superman brought me together with one of the greatest artists I've ever had the pleasure to work with. You'll see Gary's wonderful renditions of Superman and his world throughout this book, among many others. I hope you find them and the others as inspiring as I do. Superman has been an integral part of my life professionally and personally. And I've got a feeling he's been a part of yours, too.

It's an absolute privilege to be a part of this book.

Geoff Johns
April 12, 2010

HOW TO USE THIS BOOK

We used Michael Fleisher's *The Great Superman Book* as our starting point, but with double the number of years to cover, it was impossible to include versions of every entry he first wrote in addition to every major and minor character to appear in a Superman comic.

Our master list concentrated on those characters to appear at least twice in a core Superman title, including *Superman* (and related one-shots and miniseries); *Action Comics; The Adventures of Superman; Superman: The Man of Steel; Superman: The Man of Tomorrow; World's Finest Comics; Justice League of America; Trinity;* and *Superman/Batman.* Characters that moved among their own titles and the family of Superman-titled books, including *Steel, Supergirl, Superboy,* and *Adventure Comics,* were also included. Entries on many of the heroes Superman has worked alongside were limited to those who had particular impact on the Man of Tomorrow's life, such as being handpicked to work with him in the JLA, whereas casual team-ups had to be excluded.

For Jack Kirby's so-called Fourth World titles and the rich mythology of the *Legion of Super-Heroes,* each of which could be subjects of their own encyclopedia, their content has had to be painted in only the broadest of strokes, due to space limitations—despite their significant impact on the Superman mythos.

Characters are listed following standard encyclopedia style. The Club of Heroes would appear as Club of Heroes, The. Characters are listed alphabetically, and those with surnames are indicated by them (e.g., Kent, Clark). Those with titles are listed by title such as Mr. Mxyzptlk. Those with dual identities are listed both ways, such as Michaels, Albert and Atomic Skull. The detailed entries for the heroes tend to be listed with their birth names, given how many people have used many of the same names, such as multiple Superboys and Supergirls.

Cover dates appearing here are those used on the actual comic books, including those listing only a year, meaning that no month was identified—an increasingly common practice since 1986. Story titles were omitted for space considerations.

Cross-references are indicated by names appearing in small capitals.

SUP

THE ESSENTIAL SUPERMAN ENCYCLOPEDIA

ABDUL

A genie on the pre-First Crisis Earth-1 who called out to Jimmy Olsen from within a lamp discovered by Superman in an ancient tomb in the Arabian desert. The lamp, among other antiquities, was temporarily in Olsen's possession so that Jimmy could photograph them for a Daily Planet article. Initially, Olsen rubbed the lamp to see if he could conjure up Abdul to cure a toothache, but upon discovering that Abdul was indeed the famous *djinn* of Aladdin's lamp, Olsen could not resist making further requests. In conversation, Olsen innocently used the word *kill* (not as part of a command), and discovered that, according to the "magic rules," when a master of the genie used the word *kill,* he instantly changed places with the genie, and now Olsen had become Abdul's slave. Their positions could be reversed only if Jimmy the genie could trick Abdul into saying *kill.* This he did when Abdul requested a screening of horror movies, and Jimmy gave him his choice of films, including *Dr. Jekyll and Mr. Hyde.* Abdul picked the latter, speaking the phoneme *kyll* and dooming himself to return to the lamp (*Superman's Pal, Jimmy Olsen* #42, January 1960).

ABDULLAH

A magician of ancient Baghdad and secret leader of the infamous Forty Thieves. The Superman of the pre-First Crisis Earth-1, along with Batman and Robin, was sent to this time period by Professor Carter Nichols and met the legendary Aladdin. The group helped recover an inheritance that the naïve Aladdin had traded to Abdullah in exchange for a worthless "magic" lamp (*World's Finest Comics* #79, November–December 1955).

ABERNATHY, K. RUSSELL

See Kryptonite Man.

ABSORBIUM

An element capable of "soaking up" any form of energy, gas, or liquid. Absorbium existed only at the Earth's core. In the thirtieth century of the Earth-1 universe, it was the original intended solution to the threat of the Sun-Eater (*Adventure Comics* #353, February 1967; *Action Comics* #343, November 1966).

ABU, GARN

A lawyer on the planet Lexor, which revered Lex Luthor as a hero, who, along with his partner, Vel Quennar, was appointed to defend the Superman of the pre-First Crisis Earth-1 when the Man of Steel was charged with murdering Luthor. Luthor had escaped prison on Earth and fled to Lexor, to which he was pursued by Superman. During a fight with Luthor, the Man of Steel seemed to deliver a killing blow. Superman, however, discovered—and persuaded his reluctant defense attorneys—that Luthor had merely taken a drug that placed him in a catatonic state so deep that it was indistinguishable from death. Its effects were to be temporary, designed so that Luthor would awaken only after Superman had been convicted and executed by Lexor's swift legal system. Superman then administered the antidote to Luthor "prematurely," and, with Luthor alive, the Man of Steel was released from custody. Superman left Luthor on Lexor, unable to convince its citizens that Luthor had taken the drug deliberately to entrap Superman (*Action Comics* #318–319, November–December 1964).

ACE, THE

The leader of a gang of smugglers on the pre-First Crisis Earth-1 who were captured thanks to an elaborate ruse in which Superman pretended to have murdered Clark Kent. The smugglers knew that Kent had learned the date and time of their next secret meeting, but did not change it after being duped into believing Kent dead (*Superman* [first series] #62, January–February 1950).

ACE O' CLUBS BAR, THE

A blue-collar bar in the Suicide Slum district of Metropolis, owned and operated by former prizefighter "Bibbo" Bibbowski, who bought the watering hole he frequented with the proceeds from a winning lottery ticket (*The Adventures of Superman* #428, May 1987). The ticket originally belonged to his friend Jose Delgado, who lost it. Ultimately, the ticket was found by Bibbo (*Superman* [second series] #51, January 1991), and the prize money allowed him to buy the bar (*Action Comics* #661, January 1991).

ACHILLES

The alias of a Metropolis criminal on the pre-First Crisis Earth-1 with a foot encased in a heavy lead box, evidently to protect a genuine and literal "Achilles' heel." He assumed leadership of a gang of bank robbers by claiming to possess the near invulnerability of his mythological namesake. Actually, Achilles was simply an ordinary criminal, with the lead box housing "a powerful anti-magnetic device" capable of repelling "all metal objects"—such as bullets and most other weapons. Aided by the Metropolis PD, Superman easily apprehended him (*Superman* [first series] #63, March–April 1950; retold in *Superman* [first series] #148, October 1961).

ACID MASTER, THE

A costumed criminal and Soviet loyalist on the pre-First Crisis Earth-1 who specialized in using acid-based devices to commit sabotage. Philip Henry Master first came to prominence in scientific circles as an "analytical and research chemist specializing in acids." Not long thereafter, after being convicted on a charge of selling U.S. secrets, he defected to "Iron Curtain countries" and began a new life as the infamous Acid Master. In one terrorist act after another, the villain used various acid-derived weapons—darts, grenades, sprays, time-released vessels—to strike at U.S. installations. Dressed in red, with green cape and accessories, the Acid Master was briefly classified as "the nation's foremost saboteur threat." His theft of FBI personnel files left that agency temporarily compromised and prompted J. Edgar Hoover himself to recruit as an agent an unlikely civilian whom the Acid Master would not recognize: Clark Kent. Thanks in part to his superpowers and a strategically placed vat of acid, Kent was successful in bringing the Acid Master to justice, but was sworn to secrecy regarding his involvement (*Action Comics* #348, March 1967).

ADONIS

An aging movie star on the pre-First Crisis Earth-2 who was hideously disfigured by plastic surgery performed by a criminal surgeon. He was former matinee idol James Trevor, whose box-office appeal declined as the ravages of age took their toll on his looks. Trevor unwittingly became the victim of a form of extortion by a renegade surgeon whose work at first seemed to restore the actor's youthful countenance.

Trevor's newly handsome face, however, was in fact a cleverly realistic rubber mask. Once it was removed, the doctor's true surgical efforts were revealed: He had transformed Trevor not into his former good-looking self, but into a grotesque monstrosity. The effects were only temporary—or so claimed the surgeon—and he had an antidote, in exchange for which Trevor was forced to commit a series of thefts victimizing his wealthy Hollywood friends, in the guise of Adonis. While Superman intervened in an effort to end the robberies, the doctor shot and mortally wounded "Adonis" to prevent him from confessing to the authorities. But "Adonis" did not die before he was able, with his last ounce of strength, to kill the doctor (*Action Comics* #58, March 1943).

ADORIA

A distant planet in another solar system in the universe of the pre-First Crisis Earth-1 inhabited by strong, beautiful Amazon-like women and timid, bald-headed, diminutive men. As Clark Kent, Superman was tricked by Adoria's Princess Jena, posing as a movie actress, into entering a spacecraft that the Man of Steel assumed was a prop for the film. It was, in fact, a real ship that took Superman to Adoria, where he was given a love potion that led to his marriage to Jena. When he escaped captivity, the marriage was invalidated (*Action Comics* #266, July 1960).

ADVERSARY, THE

A foulmouthed, leather-clad, cigar-chomping criminal who first appeared in the Metropolis of the post-First Crisis unified Earth for the sole purpose of starting seemingly unmotivated brawls with Superman. He then disappeared as mysteriously as he had arrived (*The Adventures of Superman* #579, June 2000). He had powers that were the equal of Superman's, but seemed less knowledgeable, resourceful, or experienced. These bizarre encounters continued until the Man of Steel learned that the Adversary was an agent of the demonic Lord

Satanus, which led Superman to discover his foe's true nature.

In a sense, this superpowered bully—a living caricature of a child's notion of macho—didn't really exist. When Brainiac 13 transformed Metropolis into the City of Tomorrow, the computer virus he unleashed on the city not only upgraded all technology, but also bestowed heightened consciousness on meta-humans and certain others. One of these was a troubled, handicapped teen named Cary Richards, whose latent psychic powers suddenly manifested themselves. The Adversary was the result: a real-world incarnation of what angry young Richards imagined to be a worthy antagonist for the Superman he resented. Richards had been captured by the Man of Steel's old enemy the Prankster, who was also under Satanus's spell at the time, and brought to Satanus's underworld lair, where he was persuaded that Satanus could help him refine and develop his psionic abilities and transform him into the Adversary.

Ultimately, Superman invaded Satanus's surreal netherworld and defeated him, rescuing Richards in the process (*The Adventures of Superman* #588, March 2001).

AESOP

The leader of a gang of criminals on the pre-First Crisis Earth-2 who committed a series of crimes based on Aesop's fables. When Superman learned that Aesop's criminality began after a fall from a horse, he super-massaged the base of Aesop's skull to relieve the vascular pressure that had distorted his thinking, resulting in anti-social behavior. Aesop reverted to the responsible citizen he had been before his accident (*Action Comics* #75, August 1944).

AETHYR

An entity in the universe of the pre-First Crisis Earth-1 believed to be the creator of that reality's Phantom Zone, its mind physically manifesting itself as a massive gem-like form—an amalgam of all the souls it had absorbed. A Kryptonian wizard named Thul-Kar regarded himself as one of Aethyr's disciples and described it as a god that "causes existence" and establishes "its own physical laws." The Phantom Zone itself, Thul-Kar claimed, was "the interface of its universe and [that of Krypton and Earth]—the outmost limits of its ability to abstract." Seeking to escape from the Zone, Superman and Quex-Ul were forced to penetrate the crystal mind to forcibly enter Aethyr and endure its attempts to absorb their souls into itself. Tragically, Aethyr successfully devoured Quex-Ul

(*The Phantom Zone* #3–4, March–April 1982), but Aethyr ultimately doomed itself when it took the soul of the Fifth Dimensional Mr. Mxyzptlk. "It was like godhood-by-committee till he absorbed me," the imp declared. Now in control of "the most powerful force in the universe," Mxyzptlk added the souls of the escaped Phantom Zone criminals to Aethyr's crystal brain and returned to his own dimension to wreak havoc (*DC Comics Presents* #97, September 1986).

AGAMEMNON

The mythological king of Mycenae in ancient Greece and commander in chief in the war to recover Helen from the Trojans. Superman met Agamemnon while traveling back in time to ancient Greece and helped him finish building the Trojan horse (*Superman* [first series] #53, July–August 1948).

AGENDA, THE

A secret paramilitary organization dedicated to creating and deploying clone armies (*Superboy* [fifth series] #32, October 1993). Many of the Agenda's operations were directed against Superboy and coordinated by a group of unnamed directors. Among their agents was Amanda Spence, daughter of the late Project Cadmus director Paul Westfield, whose death Spence blamed on Kon-El.

AGENT LIBERTY

The super heroic identity of ex-CIA agent Ben Lockwood of the post–First Crisis unified Earth. Lockwood had been left for dead when the antiterrorist mission to which he had been assigned went awry. After surviving in hostile terrain for several months, Lockwood at last made his way back home, where he was forced to confront the bitter truth of how the agency had rewarded his service: His records had been erased. Indeed, all evidence of his having lived had been obliterated. As far as his government was concerned, there had never been a Ben Lockwood.

With no one else who could verify his identity, in desperation Lockwood sought out Jay Harriman, his former bureau chief, who had long since left the CIA. Lockwood had already become deeply disenchanted with the CIA's methods and the types of missions to which he was being assigned. And now that the agency had repudiated his very existence, Lockwood's disgust with, and loss of faith in, his country's leadership was absolute. Thus he was receptive to Harriman's suggestion that he join the well-funded Sons of Liberty—a secret right-wing paramilitary group that shared Lockwood's extreme views. The S.O.L.'s membership was made up exclusively of rogue and disaffected members of the U.S. intelligence community.

Assigned the code name *Agent Liberty,* Lockwood was equipped with a high-tech battle suit made of highly resilient and flame-retardant materials, as well as gauntlets that could generate ordnance-deflecting force fields and deploy razor-sharp blades—all prototypes "acquired" by the S.O.L. from the R&D labs of "black ops" departments. Agent Liberty was also fitted with a jetpack that allowed him to fly at the speed of an Apache helicopter, as well as a variety of sidearms and a helicopter backup team that acted as a lookout.

For most of his career, Agent Liberty worked alone, fighting crime he perceived as resulting from federal law enforcement's incompetence or corruption. It was on one such occasion that the Man of Steel first encountered him—in the course of one of Superman's many battles with Intergang, the notorious national crime syndicate once headquartered in Metropolis (*Superman* [second series] #60, October 1991). While Superman did not approve of Lockwood's vigilante methods, the two men nevertheless forged an uneasy alliance on a number of occasions, most notably when Liberty agreed to join the army of super heroes recruited by the Man of Steel to thwart Brainiac's use of Warworld to annihilate Earth (*Action Comics* #674, February 1992; *Superman* [second series] #65, March 1992; others).

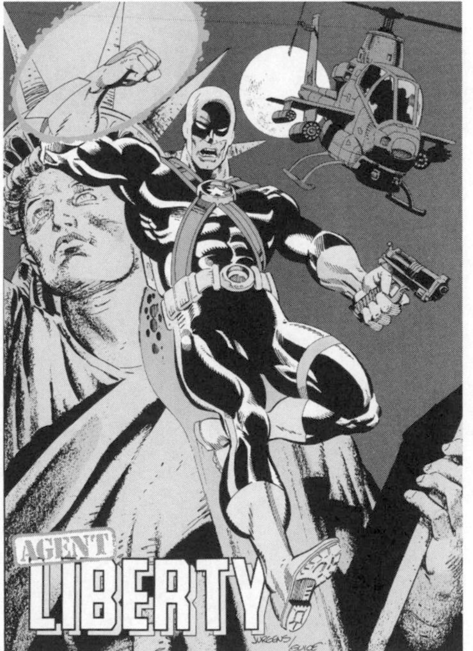

The two heroes met repeatedly, despite the fact that Agent Liberty made Washington, DC, his base of operations—especially after Clark Kent's boyhood friend Pete Ross became a U.S. senator. When Ross was blackmailed by the Sons of Liberty into assassinating a former S.O.L. leader turned whistle-blower, Lockwood stole the gun from Ross—who had refused to go through with the crime—and did the deed himself. Lockwood escaped, but by the time he refused an order to execute Ross, he had long since begun questioning his loyalty to the Sons of Liberty. In short order, Lockwood discovered that the S.O.L. had a long history of orchestrating assassinations.

Spiraling out of control, Lockwood was driven by rage and a sense of betrayal to murder both Jay Harriman and the federal judge with whom Harriman had transformed the S.O.L. into a death squad.

At that point, Lockwood severed all ties with the organization and went underground, beginning a brief period as a fugitive—but not before breaking into the S.O.L.'s files, deleting all references to himself, and turning the remaining documents over to Clark Kent at the *Daily Planet.*

Agent Liberty later joined the Justice League of America for a short time after Superman had been killed by the alien monstrosity Doomsday, in the hope that this membership could immunize him from any prosecution. But following a few JLA cases, and a battle with Arclight after Superman's "resurrection," Lockwood disappeared and was not seen again before the event known as the Infinite Crisis.

During that reality-altering event, however, Agent Liberty was documented as serving among those crime fighters who united to prevent the society from conquering Metropolis (*Infinite Crisis* #6, May 2006). It was subsequently revealed that Liberty had come out of retirement to help provide security while the president met with Superman and the former citizens of Kandor newly relocated to Earth (*Superman* #681, December 2008).

Liberty was apparently killed by Superwoman when she discovered he was spying on Sam Lane and Lex Luthor (*Action Comics* #873, March 2009). Although his body was retrieved from Metropolis Harbor, it was mysteriously removed from Metropolis City Hospital before his suit—which had emitted a distress signal that could have helped identify his killer—could be removed or examined.

Most recently, a *female* Agent Liberty joined the Secret Service to help protect the current U.S. president. As of this writing, no definitive documentation has established whether she was connected in any way with the late Ben Lockwood or involved with a New Earth incarnation of the Sons of Liberty (*Action Comics* #871–873, January–March 2009; *Supergirl* [fifth series] #37–38, March–April 2009; others).

AJAX

A former SUPERMAN ROBOT who achieved his greatest fame as WONDER MAN (*Superman* [first series] #163, August 1963).

AK-VAR

See FLAMEBIRD.

ALADDIN

The mythical hero of the *Arabian Nights* whom Superman met during a visit to tenth-century Baghdad (*World's Finest Comics* #79, November-December 1955; see also ABDULLAH).

ALPHA AND BETA

Female criminals from Earth's thirty-seventh century who fought the LINDA LEE DANVERS SUPERGIRL of the pre-FIRST CRISIS Earth-1. Because of their study of twentieth-century "ancient history," they knew that STANHOPE COLLEGE student David Carew was destined to invent a vaccine against all diseases. Time-traveling to Supergirl's present, they enclosed the campus inside a force bubble and threatened to destroy the college if Supergirl intervened. Alpha and Beta then attempted to force Carew to create the vaccine on command so that they could sell it at a tremendous profit in their own time.

Supergirl responded by deliberately exposing herself to gold KRYPTONITE to permanently erase her powers, enabling her to escape Alpha and Beta's notice as she sneaked onto the campus as Linda Lee Danvers, ultimately apprehending the two criminals with Superman's help. Fortunately, thirty-seventh-century policemen, tipped by a time-traveling Man of Steel, were able to secretly shield Supergirl from the effects of the kryptonite. The Maid of Might was relieved to discover that she had not sacrificed her superpowers after all (*Action Comics* #366–368, August–October 1968).

ALPHA CENTURION, THE

A meta-human who began life as a soldier in the ancient Rome of Earth-1 in the time of Hadrian, the Alpha Centurion became a super hero and ally of Superman's in METROPOLIS. He had two incarnations thanks to the phenomenon of Hypertime, the term used to describe the existence of multiple histories or timestreams.

Superman encountered the first Alpha Centurion when he found himself in one such alternate time line during the universe-altering event known as ZERO HOUR (*The Adventures of Superman* #527, September 1995). In the Alpha Centurion's world, Superman did not exist because the Centurion was Metropolis's resident hero instead. He was also the Metropolis Marvel's replacement in the romantic life of that timestream's LOIS LANE. This Alpha Centurion joined the super heroes of the "main time line" in their struggle to stop the insane Parallax (see GREEN LANTERN) from destroying the universe and remaking it according to his own design. When Parallax was defeated, the Alpha Centurion dematerialized. It was not known whether this incarnation continued to exist in some other Hypertime line (*The Adventures of Superman* #516, September 1994; others).

The Centurion who appeared in the Metropolis of Earth shortly thereafter was one Marcus Aelius, who had been abducted from ancient Rome circa AD 100 by interstellar explorers from the planet VIRMIRU, perpetrators of classic "alien abductions" since the dawn of human civilization. However, unlike modern-day instances—in which the abductee loses only a few hours of his or her life—Aelius spent ten Earth years on Virmiru. During this time, he absorbed much of his hosts' general knowledge, particularly their technology. Aelius integrated his Virmiru influences into his Roman customs and style; one result was his super heroic costume, an amalgam of traditional super hero garb and Roman toga, sandals, helmet, and so forth.

Eventually, Aelius set out for home in a Virmiru spacecraft he dubbed the *Pax Romana,* but landed in Metropolis to discover an Earth eighteen hundred years in his own future because his journey to Virmiru had taken place at faster-than-light speed.

Aelius quickly adapted to his new environment and, after learning of Superman's existence, concluded that he could use his own physicality and superior technology to become a heroic figure himself. In time, he was drawn to the CONTESSA ERICA ALEXANDRA DEL PORTENZA, who was then the CEO of LEXCORP. With her support, Aelius transformed TEAM LUTHOR into the Centurions, and led this private security force that protected Metropolis using techniques and principles derived from comparatively harsh ancient Roman law (*Superman: The Man of Tomorrow* #2, Fall 1995; *Action Comics* #715, November 1995; others).

Aelius self-identified as a colleague of Superman's rather than a rival, ultimately demonstrating both friendship and loyalty by accompanying the Kon-El SUPERBOY, STEEL, and SUPERGIRL on a deep-space mission to rescue Superman from the Galactic Tribunal, which had charged the Man of Tomorrow with having destroyed KRYPTON (*Superman* [second series] #106, November 1995; *Superman: The Man of Steel* #51, December 1995; others).

Sometime later, Aelius was publicly humiliated when innocent bystanders were injured during a Centurion operation. Suspecting Luthor of orchestrating his disgrace, Aelius responded by disbanding the Centurions and returned to working solo, without a connection to LexCorp. Later, he disavowed the Virmiru as well when he learned of its sinister plans for Earth (*Alpha Centurion Special* #1, September 1996).

ALTHERA

The beautiful leader of a crew of female warriors from the planet Vrandar in the universe of the pre-FIRST CRISIS Earth-1. She fell in love with Superman when she encountered him on a remote jungle-like planet. She and her crew were on a mission to mine Ergonite, a mineral that supplied energy for their homeworld, and they needed the slave labor of the planet's primitive tribal people to do it. When Superman intervened to free the slaves, Althera marveled at his strength and flying ability, and assumed he was a member of her race—a long-lost, powerful male specimen, superior to the other Vrandarian males of her homeworld, who were weak and subservient to the females.

For his part, Superman was enthralled by Althera's strength and courage as well as her beauty, thinking her a "super woman" with whom he could be compatible. They fell in love and were considering marriage until the first time Althera removed her helmet to reveal a headful of ostrich-like plumes—*feathers* instead of hair. Thus Superman learned that the Vrandarians were an avian species, related to birds, which is why his power of flight had convinced Althera that he was one of them. Once it became clear that Althera and Superman were members of two different species and nothing could ever come of their union, she reluctantly gave him up. He helped her mine the Ergonite and Althera left the jungle world, vowing never to return or enslave its inhabitants again. Back home on Earth, Superman installed a memorial to his doomed love in his FORTRESS OF SOLITUDE.

The chronicle of these events reported a limitation of Superman's powers rarely documented elsewhere, and the account is probably apocryphal: At one point, Superman's super-hearing could not pick up any sound from within the Vrandarian spacecraft because it was lined with lead. By all other accounts, lead blocked only the Man of Steel's X-ray vision (*Action Comics* #395, December 1970).

ALURA; AKA ALLURA

The wife of the Kryptonian scientist ZOR-EL, brother of Superman's father JOR-EL, and the mother of Superman's cousin, KARA, in all of Superman's realities.

On the KRYPTON of the universe inhabited by the pre-FIRST CRISIS Earth-2, she was Allura In-Z, married to Zor-L, brother of Jor-L, and lived in KANDOR.

LATER, MY FATHER MARRIED AND I WAS BORN!
OUR LITTLE KARA WILL GROW UP STURDY AND STRONG AS LONG AS WE'RE SAFE FROM THAT RADIATION UNDERGROUND!

This version of Allura is little-documented (*Showcase* #98, March 1978; *JSA: Classified* #4, December 2005; *Power Girl* #1 [second series], July 2009; and only a handful of other accounts) and, unlike her Earth-1 counterpart, died when Krypton exploded.

Superman's aunt ALURA on the Krypton of Earth-1 lived with her husband, the scientist Zor-El, in a Kryptonian city that survived the planet's destruction when it was flung into space, enclosed in an experimental bio-dome (see ARGO CITY). At least, it survived until a meteor shower punctured the dome as well as the LEAD shielding that paved the ground and *had* protected the Argoans from the deadly radiation in its bedrock. As Argo neared its demise, Zor-El and Alura placed Kara, the twelve-year-old daughter they'd had in the intervening years, in a rocket ship and sent her to Earth.

Years later, Zor-El and Alura were able to make telepathic contact with their daughter, who had become SUPERGIRL on Earth-1, to reveal that, as Argo City was dying, Kara's parents saved themselves by escaping into the SURVIVAL ZONE, a PHANTOM ZONE–like dimension Zor-El had discovered (*Action Comics* #309, February 1964). Supergirl was able to free her parents. Eager to live among fellow Kryptonians in familiar surroundings, Alura and her husband allowed themselves to be miniaturized so they could live in the bottle city of Kandor in Superman's FORTRESS OF SOLITUDE (*Action Comics* #310, March 1964).

There they remained until Superman found a way to permanently enlarge the city of Kandor and reestablish it on the planet ROKYN, whose atmospheric and environmental conditions were very similar to those of Krypton (*Superman* [first series] #338, August 1979). Thereafter, comparatively little was documented about the Earth-1 Supergirl's parents.

During the First Crisis, Supergirl was killed, and ultimately collective memory of her having existed was deleted. As the history of Krypton was reconstructed in the post–First Crisis universe, Jor-El had a brother with a family who lived in Argo City, but they, too, died along with the rest of Krypton.

Accounts of New Earth, which was formed during the reality-altering events known as INFINITE CRISIS, established that the Zor-El of that universe's Krypton was not the scientist of the couple; rather, Alura was. It was Alura, for example, and not Zor-El, who designed the ship that took their daughter to Earth.

These more recent accounts contradict a previous chronicle ultimately revealed to be a ruse by the Monitors to determine if this Supergirl had the qualifications to be allowed to remain in the New Earth universe. In this account, Zor-El actually was insane, an envious, inferior scientist who hated his brother and sent his daughter to Earth not to aid, but to kill, her cousin KAL-EL, to prevent a curse on the HOUSE OF EL from being spread to Earth. During this time, Alura begged Kara to kill her and "make your father proud," to help wipe out the curse, which consisted of a form of demonic possession by beings from the Phantom Zone (*Superman/ Batman* #8–13, May–October 2004; others).

Yet another incarnation of Alura—the most recent—emerged on New Earth after the reality-rearranging events of the FINAL CRISIS. In the newly revised history of Krypton, it was Alura, not Zor-El, who was the driving force behind saving Argo City by designing the protective dome. In this reordering of Kryptonian history, however, it was the interstellar criminal BRAINIAC who had caused Krypton's destruction; after the explosion, he returned to the vicinity in an effort to leave no survivors. He merged Argo with the bottle city of Kandor and killed those he deemed "redundancies." Superman found the city in Brainiac's ship. Zor-El and Alura managed to communicate with Kal-El to gain information about Kara. With their and Kara's help, Superman ultimately triumphed over Brainiac, returning the bottle city of Kandor to normal size at the NORTH POLE, near the Fortress of Solitude (*Action Comics* #866–870, August–December 2008).

This new incarnation of Alura was a less warm figure than her pre–First Crisis Earth-1 antecedent, mistrustful of Earth's citizens and wary of the commitment made by Superman and Supergirl to defend them. She seemed disinterested in the prospect of assimilation, preferring instead to preserve Kryptonian culture. Much of her emotional strength in coping with the transition to life outside the bottle was derived from the love and support of Zor-El, the leader of the "New Kryptonians" then adapting to life on Earth. But when Zor-El was murdered by REACTRON during his attack on Kandor—as an agent of General SAM LANE, charged by the U.S. government with repelling the "Kryptonian invasion" (see NEW KRYPTON)—her grief and rage colored her judgment as she assumed leadership of her people.

She became an almost ruthless commander, banishing as many as possible of her daughter and nephew's enemies—such as DOOMSDAY, sworn enemy of all Kryptonians—to the Phantom Zone. But some innocent Earth citizens, members of the police and military, were killed in the attempt, and hostilities escalated. Alura seemed prepared to declare war on humanity in retaliation for her husband's murder until an alliance of super heroes, led by Superman, defeated her by de-powering the Kryptonian Army. The battle ended only when Kryptonian scientists found a way to use Brainiac's technology to lift Kandor off Earth, allowing Alura to use Kryptonian Sunstones to fashion an entirely new planet supporting Kandor. This so-called New Krypton was placed in orbit around Earth's yellow sun, on the side of Sol directly opposite Earth, so it would remain forever hidden from Earth as both planets revolved in tandem.

Since then, some of Alura's leadership decisions have seemed questionable, such as releasing GENERAL ZOD from the Phantom Zone. She installed Zod as the head of the Military Guild to help her rule New Krypton. Alura also insisted that her daughter had to choose between life with her or on Earth. Kara decided to remain on Krypton and joined the Science Guild in the hope of better understanding her mother. On frequent occasions, however, Alura has dispatched Kara back to Earth, such as seeking the criminals responsible for Zor-El's murder. Her nephew Kal-El was initially unwelcome on New Krypton until he foreswore Earth and she placed him with the Military Guild (*Action Comics* #871–873, January–March 2009; *Superman* #681–683, December 2008–February 2009; *Superman: World of New Krypton* #1–12, May 2009–April 2010; others).

As New Krypton and Earth drew closer to an interplanetary war, Alura tortured the captured Reactron for intelligence about General Samuel Lane's plans to destroy New Krypton. Reactron turned the table on Alura by sacrificing himself in a nuclear blast triggered inside of him thanks to General Lane's surgical orders. Alura managed to place her daughter safely in a Sunstone chamber before Reactron detonated. The resulting blast destroyed New Krypton utterly, with Alura among the first casualties of the devastating explosion (*War of the Supermen* #1, July 2010).

AMALAK

A space pirate first encountered by the Superman of the pre–First Crisis Earth-1. Amalak later reappeared in similar form on New Earth. His most distinctive characteristic was his obsessive hatred of all surviving Kryptonians and his compulsion to exterminate them. There was no evidence of this mania, however, in his first encounter with the Man of Steel, whom Amalak tried to destroy by using the technology of his homeworld to create three assassins who were living incarnations of the ancient Greek "elements," earth, air, water, and fire. He failed in this attempt because of his inability to fully control the elementals from his orbiting spacecraft (*Superman* [first series] #190, October 1966).

By the time Amalak was free to challenge Superman again, however, his vendetta was firmly in mind, though he did not divulge its origins. He brainwashed another alien into carrying out an assassination plot against Superman, Supergirl, Krypto, and the citizens of the bottled, miniaturized Kryptonian city of Kandor. With Superman's help, the would-be assassin realized that the real criminal in this scenario was the manipulative Amalak, and partnered with Superman to defeat him. Not even Amalak's unique weapon, which fired explosive bullets made of green kryptonite, could help him defeat the Man of Steel (*Superman* [first series] #195, April 1967).

...BUT SO AM I! I, AMALAK, AM THE GREATEST, MOST FEARED SPACE-PIRATE OF ALL!

In his next recorded appearance, Amalak became one of nine "ultimate foes" of Superman. He joined Mr. Mxyzptlk, Lex Luthor, the Prankster, Brainiac, Terra-Man, Toyman II, the Kryptonite Man, and the Parasite, who were brought together by an alien named Xviar to use their combined powers against the Man of Tomorrow (*Superman* [first series #299], May 1976).

The vengeful alien criminal survived that battle to continue his war on Kryptonians, returning to Earth to unleash a deadly plague on its populace in an effort to flush out Superman and Supergirl. After Superman prevailed over numerous obstacles to eradicate the plague, Amalak made a desperate attempt to achieve some small measure of victory by committing suicide. He had hoped to trick Superman into believing that he himself was responsible for the death, which would have compelled the Man of Steel to give up his super heroic career for having violated his code against killing. Ultimately, Superman wrested from Amalak a confession of the deception, and the would-be Kryptonian-killer succeeded in slaying no one but himself (*Superman* [first series] #313–314, July–August 1977).

In his most recent appearance, Amalak came to New Earth in pursuit of Karsta Wor-Ul, a survivor of Krypton and former criminal discovered by Superman after the Auctioneer informed him of her existence. Before settling on New Earth, Karsta had been pursued from one inhabited planet to another by the relentless Amalak. Karsta's trail led Amalak to discover Superman, Supergirl, Krypto, and Power Girl, as well as the bottle city of Kandor. At one point, Superman used an alien device to read Amalak's thoughts and memories, and learned from them the reason for his vendetta. During one of Amalak's forays into deep space, the Kryptonian warlord Dru-Zod (see Zod, General) had conquered Amalak's homeworld, Rinoti, and committed genocide against its inhabitants. Amalak returned to a lifeless Rinoti to be possessed by the discarnate souls of the annihilated populace, whose thirst for vengeance propelled Amalak on his unstoppable quest. Ultimately, with the help of Superman's ally Batman, Amalak was defeated in the Fortress of Solitude, where he had gone in search of Kandor. He was turned over to Karsta, who pledged to surrender herself and Amalak to intergalactic authorities (*Superman* #670, February 2008).

AMAZING GRACE

A duplicitous, coldhearted, sadistic Apokoliptian beauty who used her appearance to control the will of others in service to Darkseid. She was first documented in the post–First Crisis cohesive universe, and apparently "survived" the two subsequent mutations of reality. Grace's original role was to identify potential rebels against Darkseid's rule by preaching revolt and pretending to be a kindred spirit, then aiding in the apprehension and punishment of those who were identified by her ruse as subversives. She once seduced Superman into believing he was Darkseid's son in an effort to neutralize his threat to her master's agenda, but her spell was broken and her plan thwarted with the help of Orion. Grace's mind-manipulating powers were the same as those of her brother, Glorious Godfrey (*Superman* [second series] #3, March 1987; *The Adventures of Superman* #426, March 1987; others).

AMAZO

While the android dubbed Amazo was best known for its many battles with the founding members of the Justice League of America, among whom was Superman, Amazo and the Man of Steel squared off in a few one-on-one battles prior to the Crisis on Infinite Earths.

Amazo's primary ability was to replicate the powers of the meta-humans it battled (though super-people were not referred to by that term at the time). Because Superman was generally considered the old Earth-1's most powerful hero, he was arguably Amazo's most formidable opponent.

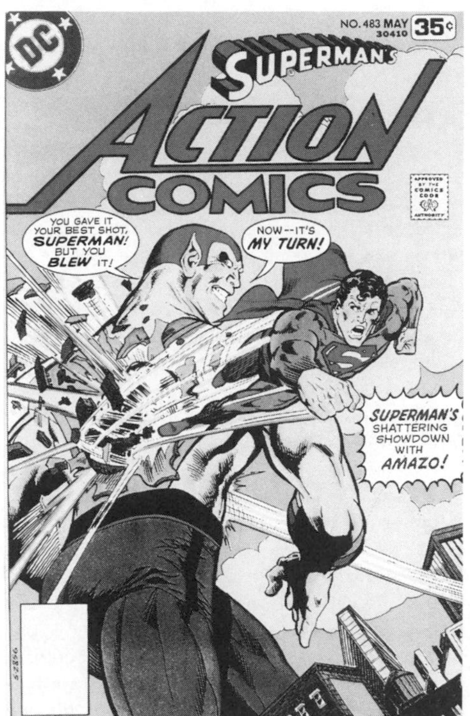

Amazo was built by the cyberneticist Anthony Ivo, who in his youth developed a pathological fear of death, with the result that he devoted the rest of his life to achieving immortality. This, he thought, could be accomplished by infusing himself with the same unknown kinds of energy expended by meta-humans. The resulting android was, in a sense, an animate battery in humanoid form.

Amazo was powered by Ivo's "absorption cells," which permitted the android to absorb and replicate the unique energy of any meta-humans with whom it interacted. Thus the android became even more powerful with every super hero it encountered, as it continued to amass an array of powers greater than those of any one hero (*The Brave and the Bold* [first series] #30, May–June 1960). Once captured, Amazo proved difficult to contain, on one occasion escaping even from an airtight chamber within Superman's Fortress of Solitude.

The Man of Steel and the amazing android had several one-on-one confrontations that proved terrific tests of the hero's fortitude (*Action Comics* #480–483, February–May 1978; others). No documentation ever existed to verify whether there was one Amazo or many. It was theorized, however, that Ivo built several, which would account for the android's many reappearances after having been utterly destroyed, at times when Ivo could not have built another one. Although both Amazo and his creator reappeared in the post-First Crisis unified Earth, over the years Amazo evolved beyond its original programming. While its own sentience exhibited no drive to dominate humankind, Amazo continued to be regarded as a monstrosity whose existence itself was threatening.

AMAZONS, THE

The Amazons were female humanoid beings formed from clay, given life by five Olympian goddesses—Artemis, Athena, Demeter, Hestia, and Aphrodite—who used earthen figurines as vessels in which to reincarnate the souls of women murdered by men more than three thousand years ago. The Amazons' mission in life was to show the men of "Patriarch's World" the power of love and equality. The immortal Amazons inhabited the island of Themyscira, birthplace of Wonder Woman, Superman's Justice League of America colleague and occasional romantic interest in the earliest days of the post-Crisis universe. Themyscira was known on both Earth-1 and Earth-2 of the pre-Crisis universe as Paradise Island. (For a detailed account of the Amazons, please consult *The Essential Wonder Woman Encyclopedia,* 2010.)

AMBUSH BUG

The nonsensical costumed identity of Irwin Schwab of Metropolis, who was—depending on which account one consulted—a legendary, widely acclaimed super hero; a mere misunderstood misfit upon whom super heroic greatness had been thrust; or a paranoid schizophrenic who needed to be hospitalized, preferably under heavy sedation. Unfortunately, almost all the accounts came from the disordered mind of Schwab himself, so it was virtually impossible to tell which, if any, were believable. This, despite the myriad reported appearances of the Ambush Bug on several Earths, beginning with the pre-First Crisis Earth-1 and continuing into New Earth. Perhaps all this peripatetic longevity was best explained by the Bug's ability to teleport anywhere, anytime, which was also one heck of a way to sneak up on people—hence the term *ambush.*

This power, like the invulnerability and the comparatively mild super-strength that got Schwab into so much trouble, derived from an insect-like, alien green jumpsuit filled with unfathomable technology. This costume, which permanently fused itself with Schwab's body the instant he tried it on, fell into his lap—almost literally, considering that Irwin found it inside a spaceship that crashed into his apartment building. Schwab's first thought was to use his new powers for crime, but after being deeply impressed by Superman upon their first meeting, the Bug decided to become a hero instead . . . as if the disastrous results of that decision could not have been predicted (*DC Comics Presents* #52, July 1983; others).

AMERTEK COMPANY

An arms manufacturer that recruited engineer John Henry Irons—later the super hero Steel—right out of college to develop advanced weapons systems. Irons left AmerTek in disgust when the weapons he developed started showing up in the hands of terrorists and Suicide Slum "gangstas." He became a target of reprisals by AmerTek as he forged his super heroic identity, part of his plan to reclaim his weapons prototypes and put them to constructive use or destroy them (*Steel* #1, February 1994).

AMNESIA MACHINE

The pre-First Crisis Earth-1 Superman kept this machine—a "selective amnesia-inducer"—in his Fortress of Solitude and used it to wipe from Batman and Robin's minds their awareness of his Clark Kent persona. The Man of Steel's motivation was to test his secret identity's security. But the experiment, to which all parties agreed, served only to prove that, while Superman was the mightier of the Superman–Batman team, the Cowled Crimefighter's deductive abilities were superior. That became apparent when Batman and Robin were able to deduce Superman's real identity unaided by any super-technology. When the device was used to erase the Man of Steel's knowledge that Batman and Robin were Bruce Wayne and Dick Grayson, however, Superman was unable, despite extraordinary efforts, to discover his two teammates' true identities (*World's Finest Comics* #149, May 1965).

AMNESIUM

A glowing white "space metal" or "mineral" discovered by the pre-First Crisis Earth-1 Superboy through unknown means. It could erase the recent memories of anyone who came within its influence. Like kryptonite, its rays were blocked when encased in lead. The Boy of Steel twice erased the memories of time-travelers from the future when he presented Amnesium to them as they returned—intentionally in the case of Jimmy Olsen, who'd learned he was Clark Kent (*Superboy* [first series] #55, March 1957), and accidentally in the case of his father Jor-El's teenage incarnation

(*Superboy* [first series] #121, June 1965). As an adult, Superman distilled Amnesium into a gas (*Superboy* [first series] #135, January 1965), perhaps prompted by his decision to use the mineral to erase the entire world's memories of the Justice League of America members' real names (*Justice League of America* [first series] #19, May 1963). The Man of Steel also used the gas to remove Ardora's knowledge that her husband Lex Luthor was a criminal (*Action Comics* #335, March 1966).

As Superman later confirmed when trying to restore the memories of Lois Lane after she'd been in an accident, Amnesium did not work in reverse (*Superman's Girl Friend, Lois Lane* #35, August 1962). Bizarro-Amnesium by its very nature worked in reverse, however, enabling the Man of Steel to use it to recover his own lost memories (*Action Comics* #375, April 1969). Superman was immune to genuine Amnesium, but once experienced a degree of its effects when he was exposed to it in tandem with a second alien element (*Action Comics* #560, October 1984).

The true potential of Amnesium remains unknown, as suggested by Doctor Light's theft of the fragment in the Fortress of Solitude. He discovered that all memories stolen by its rays were retained in the space rock and could be "tapped" with the proper technology. In the course of his actions, Light also scrambled the memories of several Justice Leaguers, convincing each that he or she had one of the others' true identities (*Justice League of America* [first series] #122, September 1975).

AMOK

An enemy of Superman's in the post–First Crisis universe who harbored a grudge against the Man of Steel because their first battle lasted all of ten seconds before Amok was defeated. He later became the Futuresmiths' first pawn in their campaign against Superman and was given great power to use against the Man of Tomorrow—power that eventually caused his cellular structure to disintegrate, killing him (*Superman: The 10-Cent Adventure* #1, March 2003; *Action Comics* #799, March 2003; others).

ANDERS, BILLY

A young boy living in the apartment building of the pre–First Crisis Earth-1 Clark Kent. Following a chance encounter with an alien artifact, he was endowed with a symbiotic link to his pet lynx. This link evidently made the youngster well suited to being a "repository" for Superman's superpowers when, thanks to an alien villain, those powers began to turn against the Man of Steel himself. The Man of Steel found a partial solution when he discovered that his powers could be housed in the body of another person until he needed them, and then transferred back before the "boomerang effect" kicked in. Billy eagerly volunteered for the responsibility. Superman could go into action when he whispered and visualized "lynx" and transferred his powers back to himself from Billy Anders (*Superman* [first series] #253–254, June–July 1972). The awkward relationship came to an end when Terra-Man used his super-science in an attempt to permanently separate Superman from his powers. Instead he set in motion the circumstances that restored Billy, his lynx, and the Man of Steel to normal (*Superman* [first series] #259, December 1972). When last seen, Billy Anders had befriended a muscleman named Captain Horatio Strong (*Action Comics* #521, February 1973).

ANDERSEN, MITCH

See Outburst.

ANDRIESSEN, STEFAN

An explorer and adventurer on the pre–First Crisis Earth-1 who aroused Superman's concern that he was out to make the Man of Steel's secret identity the next "big game" he would "bag," when Andriessen began collecting Superman trophies and memorabilia from all over the world. Ultimately, Superman needn't have worried, as Andriessen simply became the founder of the Superman Museum (*Action Comics* #164, January 1952).

ANDROMEDA

A figure similar to Supergirl in one of the realities of the Legion of Super-Heroes. Like others from her planet, she possessed all the powers of Superman, except that her vulnerability was that she could be poisoned not by kryptonite but by lead.

She was Laurel Gand, who hailed from the xenophobic and closed society on the planet Daxam and was deeply reluctant to represent her homeworld in the newly founded Legion. However, as she learned more about the myriad worlds making up both the United Planets and the Legion membership, her worldview changed.

In the course of her work with the Legion, she suffered severe lead poisoning and would have died had not a fellow Legionnaire found a cure. Andromeda was last documented on a journey of personal discovery, seeking spiritual solace and undergoing a physical transformation that left her shorter but possessing new, energy-manipulating powers. When last chronicled, she was still unsure how these new powers affected her (*Legion of Super-Heroes* [fourth series] #6, April 1990; others).

ANGELICO, DR. HELEN

A specialist in meta-human medicine also known as Doc Angel. She first came to the genetic engineering R&D lab Project Cadmus at the behest of its second chief administrator, Mickey Cannon, with whom she was once romantically involved. Angelico was recruited to treat the Kon-El Superboy for a clone illness that had robbed him of his powers (*Superboy* [third series] #75, June 2000).

Angelico had an ongoing rivalry with her one-time protégée, Dr. Sarah Charles of S.T.A.R. Labs, which began after Charles accepted a job with S.T.A.R., of whose methods Angelico disapproved.

ANGRY CHARLIE

A grotesque purple DNAlien that was one of the creations of insane renegade scientist Dabney Donovan of the pre–First Crisis Earth-1 and "survived" the Crisis to be reincarnated on the unified Earth. Charlie—as he was dubbed by Gabby of the second Newsboy Legion, who encountered the monster in one of Donovan's labyrinthine caverns—was given to rages and had the odd habit of eating furniture. After helping Gabby escape Donovan's netherworld, Charlie remained at Project Cadmus HQ, but stayed in hiding within the complex, prompting the other Newsboys to write him off as Gabby's imaginary friend . . . until the day he showed himself to save Gabby from Boss Moxie and the Female Furies (*Superman's Pal, Jimmy Olsen* #145, January 1972; *Superman* [second series] #56, June 1991; others).

ANGST, JOSEPH

See Angstrom.

ANGSTROM

A gigantic purple-skinned, irradiated monstrosity that went on a murderous rampage while in the process of decaying like radioactive matter. It was created by a secret U.S. Army experiment, Project Angstrom (the unit of measurement of radioactive wavelengths), whose goal was to develop an army of soldiers who could be deployed as living weapons. But the cease-fire in the Gulf War was called before the "prototype"—the coincidentally named

Private Joe Angst—was ready. The project was shut down and the general who spearheaded it died, but the army would not allow the hideously mutated Angst to die.

Superman battled the transformed soldier when he escaped from his containment cell at S.T.A.R. Labs and attempted to kill Lois Lane's father, then-retired Captain Sam Lane, who had urged Angst to volunteer for the experiment and whom Angst blamed for his condition. Superman succeeded in restraining "Angstrom" before he could completely degenerate and returned him to S.T.A.R., whose scientists were also attempting to restore the Parasite to normal after his last battle with the Man of Steel. As Angstrom lay dying, the Parasite broke free of his restraints and attempted to "recharge" himself by touching Angstrom. By draining the radiation from Angst's body completely, the Parasite inadvertently cured him (*Superman: The Man of Steel* #4, October 1991).

ANOMALY

Floyd "Bullets" Barstow was just "Number Four," another one of the many resident clones working at Project Cadmus, when the teleporting "Hairy" Misa—still more of a mischief-maker at this point than an actual criminal—invaded the lab, seemingly on a whim (*Superman's Pal, Jimmy Olsen* #148, April 1972). Barstow was the first staffer to encounter her, and she scratched him when he tried to restrain her as she escaped in the blink of an eye. The scratch became inflamed, and in some way this seemed to trigger the emergence of Barstow's power to re-form his body out of any material he touched. For example, his first encounter with Superman was at a construction site, where he became, in rapid succession, a creature of marble, steel, and wet cement.

Evidently, the tissue from which Barstow was cloned may have contained a metagene—the genetic anomaly that defines meta-humans and whose activation manifests the meta-human's latent abilities (though there is no documentation of this in the specific case of Barstow). If this theory is correct, however, perhaps the scratch was the trigger of the gene in this case.

What was known about the donor of the genetic material, who was also the source of his clone's name, was that he was a convicted killer called Bullets Barstow. The heavily redacted documents obtainable from Cadmus under the Freedom of Information Act seemed to suggest that in this instance the goal of the cloning was to test whether an inclination toward criminal behavior could be a genetic predisposition. Indeed, this was the question that weighed heavily on Barstow's mind. A kind, responsible, and generous man prior to his transformation and adoption of the criminal alias Anomaly, Barstow was a kind of Jekyll-Hyde by way of the mother in *The Bad Seed,* always acting out the internal struggle of a divided nature, while wondering all the while if evil was in his DNA and impossible to resist (*The Adventures of Superman* #539, October 1996).

Together with Misa, Riot, Barrage, and Maxima, Barstow made up one of the two post-Crisis incarnations of the Superman Revenge Squad, this one formed by Intergang operative Morgan Edge, who turned out to be engaging in a vendetta against Lex Luthor. It was Edge's intention that Squad members fail in their assignment and be apprehended so that Luthor would be framed for their crime (*The Adventures of Superman* #543; *Action Comics* #730; *Superman: The Man of Steel* #65—all February 1997).

As a result of Barstow's recruitment by Edge, it was Intergang that broke him out of prison after Superman defeated the Squad, and it was Intergang that ordered Anomaly to murder Cadmus's Guardian. But at the eleventh hour, Barstow's inner conflict asserted itself, and it seemed he couldn't bring himself to fight his old friend to the death. The Guardian bested him handily, resolving to take him back to Project Cadmus to see what could be done to restore him to normal (*The Adventures of Superman* #550, September 1997).

The Guardian's hopes that Floyd might be rehabilitated were quashed when Anomaly took part in a Stryker's Island jailbreak—stopped by the Justice League of America (*Superman* [second series] #147, August 1999)—and subsequently joined a band of other Superman foes. That time, he was laid low by a telepathic bolt from Supergirl (*Batman and Superman: World's Finest* #10, January 2000).

ANTI-HERO, THE

The Anti-Hero was, in essence, the super-villainous equivalent of the Wizard of Oz. He was an all-powerful and mysterious force, the mere mention of whose name supposedly left an entire cosmos of meta-humans quaking in their boots. But he turned out to be little more than "that man behind the curtain." He was, as one reporter put it, "an urban legend on a cosmic scale." His reputation, entirely of his own making, was that he was the universe's first and most fearsome super-criminal, alongside whom the worst mass murderers on Earth paled. He was supposed to have the horrifying ability to absorb and deploy the superpowers of every meta-human he killed. Thus he was said to have thousands of discrete powers, the number climbing with every atrocity he committed. Allegedly, he traveled between star systems in a city-sized death ship, yet no sighting of the Anti-Hero had ever been recorded. As it turned out, he was indeed an interstellar traveler, but the size of his vessel was somewhat exaggerated, as the Kon-El Superboy, Supergirl, and Steel discovered. The Anti-Hero's arrival in Earth orbit was the first occasion on which these three worked together formally as "Team Superman."

When the Man of Steel ostensibly blundered badly in handling a terrorist hostage-taking crisis, dozens of innocent people died. Taking full responsibility, Superman formally "resigned" his position as Earth's protector and left the planet. But Lois Lane, who was by then secretly Superman's wife, suspected an impostor. As Team Superman very quickly discovered, this Man of Steel was in fact the Anti-Hero in disguise, with the real Superman held prisoner aboard his ship. After a few minor setbacks, the super-trio freed Superman, and together the four heroes had relatively little difficulty defeating the Anti-Hero after Steel used his own computer to strip him of his many superpowers. In the end, he was unmasked as a small, ugly alien. As his computer room revealed, whatever power and menace he possessed had come from a machine, just as had the Wizard's (*Team Superman* #1, July 1999).

ANTI-LIFE EQUATION, THE

A supposed mathematical proof of the futility of human life and freedom: "Loneliness + alienation + fear + despair + self-worth ÷ mockery ÷ condemnation ÷ misunderstanding x guilt x shame x failure x judgment n = y where y = hope and n = folly, love = lies, life = death, self = dark side" (*Seven*

Soldiers: Mister Miracle miniseries #1–4, November 2005–May 2006). The formula gave whoever learned it the power to dominate the will of any living being. It was Darkseid's primary motive for sending his Apokoliptian forces to Earth: He believed that parts of the equation lay in all human beings' subconscious. The formula was called the Anti-Life Equation because "if someone possesses absolute control over you, you're not really alive" (*Forever People* #5, October–November 1971). Darkseid thereafter gained full control of the Anti-Life Equation, and various heroic figures, including Orion and the Shilo Norman Mister Miracle, have been documented as having knowledge of it—and even some super-criminals, too, such as the Pied Piper (*Countdown to Final Crisis* #10, February 20, 2008).

ANTI-MONITOR, THE

The Anti-Monitor was every bit the monster the Anti-Hero wasn't and a million times more so—the murderer of countless beings in countless universes and time lines. Billions of years ago, an alien scientist obsessed with the origins of the universe violated his culture's taboo against inquiring too deeply into that subject, creating a device that would allow him to see the moment of creation. For reasons lost to antiquity, the experiment disrupted the process of creation itself. The story of what, exactly, were the unforeseen effects of the machine has changed many times over the years, probably due less to human revisionism than to temporal disruptions that have caused the literal rewriting of history. But many believe that the consequence of the scientist's folly was the creation of evil itself.

That evil took the form of the Anti-Monitor (*Crisis on Infinite Earths* #1, April 1985) and the creation of the anti-matter universe in which he was simultaneously spawned. Like anti-matter itself, the Anti-Monitor was dedicated to the destruction of all matter, his motives, if any, as unimaginable as the scope of his power. In addition to possessing a complement of "conventional" superpowers (although of considerably greater magnitude than usually found among meta-humans), the Anti-Monitor also had reality-warping abilities, as well as technology capable of dislocating, merging, or destroying entire universes.

By annihilating countless worlds and time lines and infusing himself with their life force and other energies, the Anti-Monitor grew stronger. Eventually, the destruction of the universe we know as our own was his only remaining objective. But our positive-matter universe had spawned a counterpart to the Anti-Monitor—called, naturally, the Monitor—who had amassed an opposing army of superpowered beings, primarily the meta-humans of Earth.

In the long cosmic conflict that ensued, some time lines merged and others were erased. Many heroes died or were "unborn," their altered time lines causing them not to have existed in the first place. But in the end, at the ultimate showdown at the dawn of time, the most evil entity of all time and space was destroyed.

In the wake of the multiverse being reborn during the Infinite Crisis, the Anti-Monitor rose again. He has since been working across the galaxy to bring about the universe's destruction by fueling the event known as the Blackest Night, a cosmic upheaval that left no planet unscathed (*Green Lantern: Sinestro Corps Special* #1, August 2007).

After being killed during the events of Blackest Night, he was subsequently resurrected, once more a formidable force to be reckoned with (*Blackest Night* #8, May 2010).

ANTI-SUPERMAN, THE

A super-criminal identity briefly assumed by *Daily Planet* editor Perry White after he was exposed to a personality-altering alien gas during a visit to Superman's Fortress of Solitude on the pre–First Crisis Earth-1. White used various alien technologies found in the Fortress to rejuvenate himself and give him superpowers, which he attempted to use for crime until Superman deduced the Anti-Superman's identity and exposed White to an antidote (*World's Finest Comics* #159, August 1966).

ANTI-SUPERMAN GANG, THE

An exceptionally well-financed society of criminals, hierarchical, ritualistic, and secretive, yet flamboyant in style, not unlike the traditional image of the Mafia. They were not so much dedicated to organized criminal activity, however, as to, specifically, the destruction and elimination of Superman.

They first came to attention by trying to use Superman's friends to get close enough to kill him (*Superman's Pal, Jimmy Olsen* #39, September 1959; *Superman's Girl Friend, Lois Lane* #13, November 1959). Indeed, after their first attempt at blowing up the Fortress of Solitude failed (*Action Comics* #261, February 1960), they used a doll marketing scheme that caused Lois Lane to nearly fulfill that same goal (*Superman's Girl Friend, Lois Lane* #21, November 1960). Aware that the would-be killers had the girl reporter under surveillance, Super-

man and Jimmy Olsen once fed her false information about Superman's true identity to arrange a sting (*Superman* [first series] #145, May 1961). On two occasions, the Gang successfully discovered that the Man of Steel was secretly Clark Kent, requiring elaborate ruses on Superman's part to convince them otherwise (*Action Comics* #261, February 1960; *Superman* [first series] #152, April 1962).

Even the exposure of well-respected philanthropist John Kiley as the Anti-Superman Gang's leader and financier (*Action Comics* #276, May 1961) didn't significantly affect its coffers. Impressed at the response they got by putting a twenty-thousand-dollar price (if alive; otherwise ten grand) on the head of Jimmy Olsen (*Superman's Pal, Jimmy Olsen* #85, June 1965), Gang members formally offered one million dollars to the person who killed Superman with descending amounts of fifty and twenty-five thousand for Lois and Jimmy (*Superman's Girl Friend, Lois Lane* #60, October 1965). When attempts began to taper off, the Gang put out a call for criminal scientists to compete (*Action Comics* #376–377, May–June 1969). Raising the bounty to five million finally seemed to bear fruit, albeit only because the Man of Steel was temporarily suffering a loss of his powers. After a humiliating auction in which each piece of his costume was sold to the highest bidder, the nude Man of Steel was rocketed into space to the so-called Execution Planet—from which he inevitably escaped (*Superman* [first series] #228, July 1970). In the Gang's final recorded attempt on Superman's life, members once again took advantage of his temporarily diminished powers . . . and still failed in their goal (*Superman* [first series] #240, July 1971).

APOKOLIPS

One of two diametrically opposite planets in the Fourth World, the dimension created by the war that destroyed the Old Gods. It was ruled by the "dark god" Darkseid, who exerted total and unyielding authority over everyone and everything on Apokolips, which was often thought of as Hell on a planetary scale. It was vast, desolate, and forbidding, with toxic-looking machinery covering much of its surface, a darkness relieved only by the massive fire pits that supplied the planet's light and power. It was first documented by the Superman of the pre–First Crisis Earth-1 (*Superman's Pal, Jimmy Olsen* #139, July 1971) but existed in—or, more accurately, separately from—all of the Man of Steel's realities. It was the total antithesis of the other planet of the Fourth World, New Genesis, home to the New Gods led by Orion, Highfather, and so on.

APOLLO

See Zha-Vam.

AQUAMAN

Known to the surface world primarily as a costumed super hero who was amphibious, possessed extraordinary swimming skill, strength, and speed, and was able to communicate with and control marine life, Aquaman was in fact the king of the undersea city-state of Atlantis. Both iterations of Earth prior to the Infinite Crisis had an Aquaman, as did the New Earth that emerged thereafter.

In his youth on the pre-Crisis Earth-1, he believed himself simply to be Arthur Curry, the son of an American lighthouse keeper and a woman named Atlanna who died when he was an infant. He did not learn until much later that his mother had been a water-breathing outcast from Atlantis. Curry decided at an early age to use his talents to become the defender of Earth's oceans, and by one account he was inspired to assume the identity of Aquaman when he met the teenage Superboy who later became Superman (*Superboy* [first series] #171, January 1971).

Later, on that same Earth, Aquaman became a close friend and frequent ally of the adult Superman, as both a helping hand in water-related crises and a founding member of the Justice League (*Justice League of America* [first series] #9, February 1962). He eventually returned to Atlantis and became its hero, ultimately being voted into the monarchy upon the death of the previous regent, who'd had no heir.

The Aquaman of post-Crisis Earth had somewhat different origins, and with the exception of their contact as members of the Justice League, he and Superman had comparatively little interaction, some of it contentious. Early in his career, while trying to seek clues as to his origins (post-Crisis, he wouldn't learn of his Kryptonian heritage until later), Superman had sought out various other meta-humans. Directed to Aquaman by the Flash, Superman came upon the hero in the midst of a clash between him and the sea god Poseidon (*Aquaman Annual* #1, 1995; *Superman: The Man of Steel Annual* #4, 1995). It was through Aquaman that Superman learned the location of Atlantis and was able to track down his long-lost girlfriend Lori Lemaris (*Superman* [second series] #12, December 1987). Years later, when Lori was reported dead during the First Crisis, it was Aquaman who reluctantly agreed—at her request—to maintain that fiction despite her survival. She felt that Superman would never find happiness as long as he continued to carry a torch for her (*Superman* [second series] #63, January 1992). At separate points, Aquaman and Lori—her deception ended—would join Superman in battle with giant sea monsters

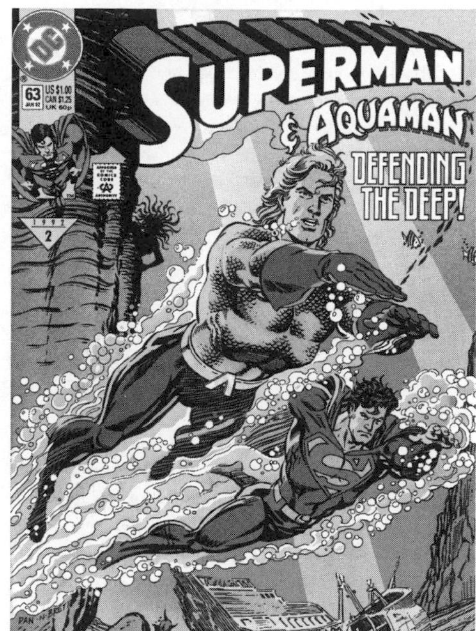

controlled by a being called Kosnor. Both Kosnor and the giant creatures were mutations caused by chemical pollutants leaked from Engine City, the coastal metropolis built by the Cyborg Superman, Hank Henshaw. (*Superman: The Man of Steel* #48, September 1995, and #106, November 2000).

Aquaman continued to protect the sea and serve beside Superman in the Justice League. Like so many of the team's founders, he made the ultimate sacrifice by dying to help free a group of humans who had been trapped undersea (*Aquaman: Sword of Atlantis* #50, March 2007). The recent cosmic event known as Blackest Night saw Aquaman return, first in Zombie-like form, and then as a living being to take his rightful place as the King of the Seven Seas (*Blackest Night* #8, June 2010).

ARATHAZA

The mean-spiritedness of petty, spiteful, self-pitying, and overworked secretary Barbara Kowaleski was magnified commensurately with the grandiosity that overtook her when she became

Arathaza. Her transformation occurred when a magic talisman, an ancient sorcerer's staff, morphed her into a latter-day incarnation of its owner. How or where Kowaleski acquired it was never known, but its power was unmistakable. With it she created a gigantic flying fortress in the skies over Metropolis from which to launch an attack on the city in a melodramatic bid for the attention denied her in her previous life. Superman destroyed the staff and restored Kowaleski to normalcy, but not before almost losing his life when Arathaza's magic drained his life force, aging him in a matter of minutes (*Action Comics* #585, February 1987).

ARCHER, THE

On the pre-First Crisis Earth-2, a famous big-game hunter named Quigley donned a Robin Hood–like costume to conceal his identity when he became a merciless extortionist, killing by bow and arrow any victim who refused to pay up. "The Archer" met his match in Superman, however, to whose invulnerable skin no arrow posed a threat. The *Daily Planet*'s coverage of the Archer's capture and unmasking represented the first byline for young office boy Jimmy Olsen (*Superman* [first series] #13, November–December 1941).

The Archer returned sometime later, using "brainwave devices" implanted in his arrows that temporarily nullified each of Superman's powers as he used them. Nonetheless, the Man of Steel overcame the handicap, and a well-timed punch from the now young adult Jimmy Olsen prevented the villain's escape (*Superman Family* #221, August 1982).

ARCLIGHT

To the mob, an arsonist is a "torch"—hence the name *Arclight* for the creature Mafia torch Noah Pastenetti became. Arclight was born when Pastenetti was found to be an investigative reporter's source, and the "made guy's" crew trapped him inside a nuclear power plant before blowing it up. Pastenetti survived as a being of destructive energy, however, given form by a containment suit, in which he literally burned for revenge. His hotheadedness extended to reporters as well, and Clark Kent's *Daily Planet* colleagues found themselves threatened by Arclight while attending a journalists' convention in Washington, DC, where Superman reteamed with Agent Liberty to save his friends (*Superman* [second series] #99, April 1995). After murdering reporter Alicia Parker in Washington and attempting to steal the contents of her strongbox, Arclight overexerted his power and merged his energy into Superman's body. Once the energy of Arclight's essence had been drained off, he was placed into a new containment shell and taken into custody (*Superman* [second series] #103, August 1995; *Superman: The Man of Tomorrow* #2, Fall 1995).

ARDORA

Lex Luthor's one known lover and, later, wife in the pre-Crisis universe was Ardora, a native of a distant, arid planet that would rename itself Lexor in Luthor's honor. It was originally visited by Superman and Luthor as the site of a boxing match to which Luthor had challenged the Man of Steel, chosen because of its red sun—under which Superman would have no superpowers and would presumably be Luthor's physical equal. When Superman discovered the desert-like world's primitive humanoid civilization, he learned that its denizens knew nothing of irrigation. He quickly corrected that problem, but through a complex series of misunderstandings, the natives attributed the miracle of lush greenery that bloomed in their midst to Luthor's scientific genius rather than Superman's superspeedy canal building.

Thus Lexor became the planet that revered Luthor as a great hero, and he saw to it that they mistakenly believed Superman to be their worst enemy. In time, Luthor found ways of returning to Lexor to indulge what capacity for humanitarianism he possessed, eventually transforming the planet into a high-tech Utopia. And with each visit, his gentler side continued to be nurtured by Ardora's enduring love, until at last they married.

Luthor returned to Lexor one last time, discovering that Ardora had given birth to his son, Alexander Luthor, Junior. As usual, Lex performed acts of heroics, notably erecting a Neutrarod that would stabilize the internal stresses at Lexor's core that threatened to blow it up. Meanwhile, Lex made use of technology he'd discovered in an ancient lab to build a battle suit for the inevitable day that Superman came for him. When that conflict took place, though, one of Luthor's power blasts ricocheted off the Man of Steel's chest, striking the Neutrarod and starting a chain reaction. Desperately flying toward Ardora and his son, Lex had nearly reached them when the planet exploded.

On the parallel world of Earth-154, Lex and Ardora had a teenage daughter also named Ardora who once encountered the super-sons of Superman and Batman (*World's Finest Comics* #238, June 1976). She was glimpsed briefly on New Earth (*Infinite Crisis* #6, June 2006).

ARGO CITY

The birthplace of the pre-Crisis Supergirl, Kara Zor-El, who was born after Krypton exploded. Argo City survived the destruction because the fragment of the planet on which it was built was hurled into deep space by the force of the explosion. Its citizens survived, with buildings and ecosystem intact, because the city was enclosed in a synthetic bio-dome, built to accommodate meteorological research being conducted by Zor-El, Argo's preeminent scientist and the man who would later father Kara (*Action Comics* #252, May 1959; *Superman* [first series] #150, January 1962; *Action Comics* #316, September 1964; others).

The floating city was able to drift though space in this fashion for almost fifteen Earth years. For most of that time, life for the Argoans settled back into a kind of normalcy, until they discovered what Superman, on Earth, was also learning: The chain reaction that had destroyed Krypton had left its fragments radioactive. This meant that Argo City now sat atop a giant mass of the lethal green mineral Superman would call kryptonite. The radiation beneath their feet began to sicken and kill the citizens of Argo until Zor-El blocked it by sealing off the ground with lead shielding. Other accounts, however, have stated that the radioactive mineral was actually something called anti-kryptonite; regular green kryptonite could only affect superpowered Kryptonians. In any event, life in Argo City went on.

But the year Kara turned fifteen, a meteor shower punctured both Argo's dome and the lead-covered surface, releasing deadly radiation that ostensibly killed off Argo's population, but not before Zor-El and his wife Alura had placed Kara in a small spacecraft and launched her toward Earth.

The kryptonite-poisoned Argo City was later visited by the evil Vrangs (*Action Comics* #548, October 1983) and ultimately caused to collide with Metropolis by Mr. Mxyzptlk (*DC Comics Presents* #97, September 1986).

Argo City

In the history that emerged after INFINITE CRISIS, Argo City was once again the home of Zor-El and family. Prior to Brainiac's destruction of Krypton, Alura used the evil alien's shield technology to form a protective dome over the city, allowing them to survive. When Brainiac discovered their use of his tools, he located the floating city and had it added to the already captured city of Kandor. It was then that Zor-El and Alura chose to send their daughter Kara to Earth to find her cousin Kal-El (*Action Comics* #869, November 2008).

ARION, LORD OF ATLANTIS

This volatile, magically powered, and immortal protector of ATLANTIS first existed 45,000 years ago, long before the disaster that submerged the so-called lost continent (*Warlord* #55, March 1982). He was incarnated in three of Superman's realities: the pre–FIRST CRISIS Earth-1 (*Arion, Lord of Atlantis* #1–35, November 1982–September 1985); the post–First Crisis unified cosmos (*Arion the Immortal* #1–6, July 1992–December 1992); and New Earth.

In each instance, he was the offspring of Atlantean gods. He was revered by the Atlantean people for having sacrificed his corporeal form to prevent Atlantis from being destroyed in an act of divine retribution by his vengeful mother and older brother. His mastery of magic allowed him to exist as a wraith for nearly 500,000 years, becoming tangible once more approximately 5,000 years ago. At that point, he became the Lord High Mage of Atlantis, residing in the City of the Golden Gate.

The Superman of the pre–First Crisis Earth-1 first encountered Arion when the Atlantean mage journeyed through time into his future, arriving in then-present-day Metropolis in pursuit of a renegade god named Chaon. The quest led Arion and the Man of Steel back to ancient Atlantis, where they ultimately defeated Chaon (*DC Comics Presents* #75, November 1984).

Perhaps the most significant interaction between Arion and the Man of Tomorrow was in the New Earth reality. This iteration of Arion, however, seemed more morally ambiguous and less overtly a champion of the oppressed. This became clear when, in the year 1659, Arion had a series of nightmarish visions of an apocalyptic far future wherein the destruction of human society had been in some way caused by Superman. Using an assortment of magical artifacts to generate enough eldritch energy to propel him forward in time, Arion arrived in present-day Metropolis with a warning for Superman.

Arion argued that humankind's natural development was being corrupted by the good works of the Man of Steel—and all super heroes, for that matter, but Arion appealed to Superman as the most powerful being, or at least the first among equals. Super-beings were constantly saving humans from their own tendency toward self-destruction, Arion cautioned, advancing their development to a point that was, in a sense, unnatural. Arion argued that entropy affects everything, and human civilization itself must inevitably and ineluctably collapse. This, Arion prophesied, would occur with the emergence of a Middle Eastern warlord named Khyber, who would conquer Earth with the aid of an army of cyborg assassins who would also kill Superman. Khyber's rule, Arion envisioned, would plunge Earth into a new Dark Age. Human society, having been allowed to evolve beyond the point at which it was meant by nature to degenerate, merely had been given, by Earth's super heroes, farther to fall.

Arion's argument, then, was not unlike the theme sounded by BATMAN's enemy, eco-terrorist Rā's al Ghūl: "It is necessary to destroy the Earth in order to save it." Arion pleaded with Superman and Earth's other super heroes to voluntarily abandon their careers, allowing humankind to fulfill whatever its destiny may be—risking its eventual entropic degeneration but averting the catastrophe of Khyber's reign of terror that Arion had foreseen.

Superman found himself faced with a moral dilemma when he discovered evidence that could have substantiated Arion's prediction, forcing him to consider the possibility that he and his cohorts might be more hindrance to humanity than help. Ultimately, however, he decided to maintain the status quo. As a result, Arion felt forced to attempt neutralizing Earth's heroes himself by using his magic to turn them against one another.

Ultimately, with the aid of the supernatural figure the PHANTOM STRANGER, the Man of Steel was able to break Arion's magical hold and disarm the Atlantean of the mystical artifacts from which he gained his power, thereby returning Arion to 1659, seemingly for good (*Superman* #654–658, September 2006–January 2007; #662–664, May 2007–August 2007; #667, November 2007; *Superman Annual* #13, January 2008).

ARMAGEDDON 2001

The name for the future-altering event set in motion by the creation of the heroic WAVERIDER, who became the leader of the LINEAR MEN, Superman's time-traveling comrades in the post–FIRST CRISIS universe. The distant future of that Earth was bleak and forbidding. There MATT RYDER, a scientist specializing in chrononautics, volunteered to be the test subject in a potentially dangerous attempt at time travel. His secret agenda: preventing the rise to power of Monarch, this future era's tyrannical ruler. Ryder knew that forty years previously, Monarch had been one of Earth's meta-humans and had murdered all of the planet's other superpowered beings. But which one had he been?

As Ryder embarked on his first attempt to move through time, he was transformed into an energy being capable of both time-traveling at will and psychically divining people's probable futures simply by touching them. Upon arriving at his destination—the time period of Superman and the other members of the JUSTICE LEAGUE OF AMERICA—the physically transformed Ryder adopted the name Waverider.

Ultimately, Waverider learned that Monarch was originally a hero known as Hawk. But he also discovered, to his horror, that all along he had been the Big Brother–like Monarch's unwitting pawn. Monarch had known of Ryder's intentions and facilitated the latter's voyage into the past because it would cause Hawk to become Monarch. With Superman's help, however, Waverider was able to change his own dreaded destiny, but not before his seer-like touch revealed a number of possible futures for Superman and his friends. In one, Superman would attempt to impose a global nuclear weapons ban after a nuke detonated by INTERGANG killed millions, most of them citizens of METROPOLIS—including LOIS LANE, who by then would have been Mrs. CLARK KENT. But the enraged and grief-stricken Superman's campaign would become a demented rampage resulting in the deaths of seven American sailors and one Justice Leaguer, until the U.S. government would implore BATMAN to assassinate the renegade Man of Steel (*Superman* [second series] *Annual* #3, 1991).

In another possible future, Clark Kent's friend Congressman PETE ROSS would begin a presidential race with Kent as his campaign manager. While on the stump, Ross would be seriously wounded by a sniper's bullet, and Clark's Superman identity would be revealed when he sprang into action to save his friend's life. Superman would then take Ross's place on the ticket and win by a landslide, setting in motion an assassination plot by LEX LUTHOR that Superman would have to thwart (*Action Comics Annual* #3, 1991).

In a third vision of things to come, Lois Lane, married to Superman in this future as well, would die while pregnant with his child. Unable to bear remaining on Earth under these circumstances, Superman would abandon his adopted planet to roam deep space. There he would eventually find love with MAXIMA, the ruler of the alien House of Almerac who, in the actual post-Crisis world, vacillated between opposing and aiding Superman (*The Adventures of Superman Annual* #3, 1991).

Ultimately, each of these possible futures was averted when Waverider altered the timestream to change the future world whence he had come.

ARMAGETTO

The capital of Apokolips, it was a foul, pestilent, life-chokingly polluted slum, if *slum on Apokolips* isn't in fact a redundancy. Home to Darkseid's Tower of Rage, Granny Goodness's Happiness Home, and the largest population of Hunger Dogs on the planet, it was notoriously fearsome for being patrolled by Darkseid's Parademons.

ARMSTRONG, ASHBURY

The blind daughter of Dirk Armstrong, a right-wing columnist for the *Daily Planet* of the post-Crisis Metropolis. At age seventeen, she was kidnapped by a deranged reader of her father's rants but was rescued by Ceritak, aka Scorn, the prince of the other-dimensional incarnation of Kandor whose blue skin and grotesque, monstrous appearance she could not see. While joining Ceritak on a visit to his native city, Ashbury received Kandorian goggles that restored her sight, but the resulting revelation did nothing to damage their relationship. Together they returned to Earth, where they remained devoted companions (*The Adventures of Superman* #546, May 1997; *Superman: The Man of Steel* #68, June 1997; others).

ARMSTRONG, DIRK

A conservative *Daily Planet* columnist hired by Franklin Stern. Armstrong's extreme-right politics often landed him on the opposite side of an issue from Clark Kent, Lois Lane, and Perry White (*Superman: The Man of Tomorrow* #6, Fall 1996). Dirk was quick to judge and frequently leapt to conclusions that more deliberative individuals might not draw, but he was sincere and never lacked the courage of his convictions, even when they didn't favor Superman and he was therefore defying his own paper's corporate culture. When Superman's powers changed during the Superman Red/Superman Blue period, Armstrong denounced him as a "super-menace" (*Superman: The Man of Steel* #67, May 1997). But because of stances he took in

support of the unpopular Lex Luthor, Armstrong was one of the few reporters to escape a pink slip when Luthor bought the *Planet*, and he went to work for LexCom shortly thereafter.

Armstrong considered himself appropriately protective of his blind daughter Ashbury, though for her part she tended to find him stifling and meddlesome. She welcomed the possibility of a permanent move to Kandor with Ceritak as an escape from his suffocating possessiveness, but her father rose to the occasion by begrudgingly trying to accept Ashbury's choices, persuading her that his love and regard for her best interests were genuine.

ARMY OF CRIME, THE

A band of military-themed super-villains who kidnapped wealthy citizens of the Gotham City of the pre-First Crisis Earth-1. Their goal was to use the ransoms to purchase high-tech instruments of war left on Earth by the alien Weapon-Master. The army was led by General Scarr, and included Colonel Sulphur, Major Menace, and Captain Cutlass; it was defeated in its first and only documented encounter with Superman and Batman (*World's Finest Comics* #279–281, May–July 1982).

ARMY OF TOMORROW, THE

Energy-powered human mutations created on the pre-First Crisis Earth-1 as the ultimate in military efficiency, engineered by the renegade scientist Calixto. The troops were distinguished by possessing two thumbs on each hand, which they banged together to discharge the energy they used as weapons. Superman freed the mutant army from Calixto's hold over them with the help of Perry White, and the troops expressed their gratitude by gifting White with cigars that gave him unusual superpowers (*Superman* [first series] #265, July 1973; *Action Comics* #436, June 1974).

AR-RONE

One of several citizens of the Kandor of the pre-First Crisis Earth-1 who formed the Lookalike Squad, a team of Kandorians who were doubles of Superman's friends and could, when a need arose, be recruited to impersonate them. Ar-Rone was a reformed criminal who was Perry White's look-alike (*Action Comics* #309, February 1964; others).

AR-UAL

A Kryptonian Phantom Zone escapee on the pre-First Crisis Earth-1 who posed as Wonder Woman in a scheme to drain Superman's super-strength. Her ruse was detected by Lois Lane when, as Wonder Woman, Ar-Ual faked a romantic interest in the Man of Steel not shared by the real Amazing Amazon—whom Ar-Ual had actually kidnapped and sidelined. (*Superman's Girl Friend, Lois Lane* #93, July 1969).

AR-VAL

A native of the Kandor shrunk by Brainiac in the pre-First Crisis universe of Earth-1, the blond, preening Ar-Val was rated "highest in physical and mental abilities" of all Kandor's young males.

On this basis, Superman chose him to be his own backup or replacement in the event the Man of Steel was killed or disabled. When the Caped Kryptonian was sidelined by a temporary loss of his superpowers, the immature Ar-Val did indeed get his shot at being the next Superman, but proved himself unfit. With his judgment impaired by arrogance, ego, and a love of applause, Ar-Val barely apprehended super-villains who nearly escaped justice thanks to his mistakes. Guilt-ridden over his failures, he ultimately proved his nobility when he sacrificed his own life so that Superman's powers could be restored (*Superman* [first series] #172, October 1964).

ASHERMAN, OSCAR

The weatherman on WGBS-TV's nightly newscast in the Metropolis of the pre-First Crisis Earth-1, a member of the on-air staff hired by Morgan Edge that included entertainment reporter Lola Barnett, sportscaster Steve Lombard, and Lana Lang as well as co-anchor Clark Kent (*Superman* [first series] #270, December 1973). Asherman was also the station's science editor whose near-encyclopedic knowledge was occasionally helpful to Kent when he could not access his Fortress of Solitude's Kryptonian data banks as Superman. Sometimes Oscar was also a useful "lightning rod": The diminutive Asherman managed to be even more mild-mannered than Superman's Clark Kent act, and as such drew the practical-joking fire of macho blowhard Lombard that would otherwise have been aimed at Kent.

ATLANTIS

One common element in all versions of Earth has been the sunken continent of Atlantis. In all instances, Atlantis began as a legendary civilization lost to surface-world history, having sunk into the Pacific Ocean around 9600 BC. In each case, its existence only became common knowledge

thanks to the appearance in the pre–First Crisis Earths' twentieth century of such citizens as the super hero Aquaman and the beautiful mermaid Lori Lemaris, an object of Superman's romantic interest in at least two of his incarnations. There had been a few earlier interactions between Atlantis and Superman's world, however. For example, on Earth-1, an Atlantean renegade named Kronn once recruited a teenage Lex Luthor in an attempt to overthrow the undersea city (*Adventure Comics* #308, May 1963). Previously, though not documented until long after the fact, an Atlantean space probe saved the life of Mag-El—an ancestor of the future Superman—around 8000 BC (*Superman* [first series] #266, August 1973).

In time, questions arose about how two such different humanoids as the Atlantean king born Arthur Curry and the mermaid Lemaris had the same country of origin. The explanation was that they were from separate Atlantean cities named Poseidonis and Tritonis that evolved independently (*Action Comics* #475, September 1977; *DC Special Series* #5, November 1977; *Super Friends* #9, December 1977; others).

Atlantis originally comprised, among other confederate states, the two domed cities of Tritonis and Poseidonis, each of which housed one of two factions into which the continent's original population—which had evolved a highly advanced civilization as early as 150,000 BC—had divided. The city of Poseidonis was ruled by King Orin, while Tritonis was home to the subjects of Orin's brother Shalako. Atlantis was believed to be the cradle of real (as opposed to stage) magic on the post-Crisis Earth. It was also the birthplace of *homo magi,* who were classified as a discrete species that gave rise to magical heroes such as Dr. Mist and Zatanna, just as the more "conventional" super heroes were identified as meta-humans (*Secret Origins* [second series] #27, June 1988). One of many documents that supported this theory was the account of a curse Shalako put on the rival Tritonians, causing them to develop fins in place of their legs and spawning a race of "mer-people."

ATLAS

The name for two different figures encountered by Superman in different realities. The Superman of the pre–First Crisis Earth-1 had one significant encounter with the Titan of Greek mythology (*Action Comics* #353, August 1967; see Zha-Vam). Other "Atlases" encountered by the Earth-1 Supermen were either circus performers or alien super-villains using the name as an alias.

The Atlas who has had greatest impact on the Man of Steel's career thus far, however, was the one who appeared suddenly in the Metropolis of New Earth (*Superman* #677, August 2008; others). This Atlas, born in an ancient, mysterious land, became a hero to his people in his efforts to free them from the tyranny of their ruler King Hyssa. Atlas had grown up as one of the peaceful People of the Crystal Mountain when his village was sacked and raided by Hyssa's troops, who burned it to the ground and killed or captured all of Atlas's friends and family. Ever after, Atlas swore vengeance, using the great strength that he derived from his glowing, alien crystal talisman, mined from the Crystal Mountain. In his campaign, he would be aided by a noble older man named Chagra, who became a kind of surrogate father to the young Atlas.

The original account of this Atlas established only that he managed to escape from those who tried to enslave him, but did not record whether Atlas ever managed to get his revenge on King Hyssa (*First Issue Special* #1, April 1975). It was later revealed, however, that he led his people to freedom and became their king. Originally, Atlas wore the strength-giving crystal close to his body, but Chagra found a means by which Atlas could "internalize" it. The crystal became a part of his anatomy and thus made his strength more like a native ability than a mystical weapon. Unfortunately, this process also caused Atlas to become "unstuck in time," which was how he was able to be kidnapped and brought to the modern-day, New Earth Metropolis.

This Atlas, who eventually operated in Metropolis under the alias *Tom Curtis,* was plucked from the timestream by means of advanced "time-pool technology," an upgrading of the tech once used for time-traveling purposes by the super hero Atom. He was then brought to New Earth by General Samuel Lane and pressed into service as hired muscle to the general's Project 7734, a top-secret program whose objective was to kill Superman.

Upon arrival, Atlas was openly defiant of Lane and attempted to refuse to be made his agent, but the strongman later came to some sort of accommodation with the general that, like all of 7734's activities, has remained shrouded in secrecy. For example, he complied with Lane's order that Atlas attack Superman as a cover for a 7734 test of the effectiveness of its magic-based weapons on the Man of Steel, with Superman emerging the victor. Thereafter, Atlas again cooperated in one of Lane's intrigues by earning the trust and comradeship of John Henry Irons, only to betray him. Atlas seemed to have an agenda of his own that, as of this writing, has not yet been fully documented, nor his motivations clearly revealed.

Atlas posed a particular challenge to the Man of Steel because of his morally ambiguous nature. In many public appearances, he behaved heroically, often seeming to reverse himself and save the lives of innocent citizens he himself had endangered. He walked a fine line between super hero and super-criminal, but it appeared that more often than not the villainous side of his nature won out.

ATOM, THE

A super hero with the power to shrink to microscopic size and even have adventures in subatomic worlds. Ray Palmer, a physics professor at Ivy University on the pre–First Crisis Earth-1, discovered a piece of a white dwarf star when a meteorite struck the outskirts of Ivy Town. Studying the celestial object, he learned how to harness its properties, which allowed him to control his size and weight. Creating a costumed identity, Palmer began a crime-fighting career as the Atom (*Showcase* #34, September–October 1961), and subsequently joined with Superman as a member of the Justice League of America. In Earth-1's reality, the two paired up on several occasions, most notably when they were stranded in a subatomic world

Atlas

and needed to rescue it from a threatening entity in order to escape themselves (*World's Finest Comics* #213, August–September 1972). The Atom also once joined Superman to battle alien invaders who intended to wreck the Fortress of Solitude (*DC Comics Presents* #15, November 1979).

In the reordered universe after the Crisis on Infinite Earths, the Atom dealt with the double blows of his wife Jean Loring's infidelity and mental illness, which led her to kill Sue Dibny, wife of fellow JLAer Elongated Man. Palmer then vanished from sight, entering one of myriad microscopic universes to deal with his grief.

Palmer's disappearance turned out to have cosmic repercussions. When the multiverse was re-formed in the wake of Infinite Crisis, Palmer apparently visited many of the newly formed parallel Earths, leaving behind a trail. He was said to be the solution to an impending "Great Disaster," although the secrets remained unrecorded (*Countdown* #52, 2007; *Countdown Presents: The Search for Ray Palmer,* January–February 2008).

At various times, the Atom identity was assumed by others, such as Suicide Squad agent Adam Cray and nanotechnologist Ryan Choi—both having the same powers as Palmer—but their documented interactions with Superman were negligible.

ATOMIC SKULL, THE

Dr. Albert Michaels, a disgruntled S.T.A.R. Labs employee who suffered from a rare neurological disease, was the first Atomic Skull, appearing on the pre–First Crisis Earth-1. Rogue medical doctors corrected the malfunctioning of the neurotransmitters and receptors in his brain with cybernetic implants. But Michaels soon discovered that the malfunctioning microcircuitry gave him the power to convert his brain's electrical impulses into massively destructive bursts of energy that he could direct with pinpoint accuracy. He took his name from Skull, the criminal organization with which he had become entangled (*Superman* [first series] #303, September 1976—as Michaels; *Superman* [first series] #323, May 1978).

Michaels was widely believed to have perished in the Earth-reshaping cataclysm of the First Crisis, although there was one reported sighting thereafter. In any event, there was no known connection between him and the second Atomic Skull, Metropolis University film student Joe Martin. Suffering a variety of symptoms that his regular doctors couldn't explain, Martin turned to S.T.A.R. Labs, whose scientists were able to tell him that he possessed a dormant metagene. Martin's symptoms began to appear during the event known as Armageddon 2001, and the S.T.A.R. building was under attack from Monarch at the exact time Joe was hearing the diagnosis. Martin escaped the building's destruction, but not before the stress of the experience triggered the gene's activation.

Martin awoke the next morning to find himself bald, glowing in the dark, and seemingly possessed of super-strength. Then, on his way back to S.T.A.R. for help, he suffered severe head trauma in an altercation with some gang members trying to steal his bike (*Action Comics* #670, October 1991).

By the time Superman caught up with him, his flesh had turned transparent, which, coupled with the radiation he was emitting, made him look as if he had a flaming skull for a head. When Superman attempted to stop his destructive rampage—which began after Martin stole a motorcycle and dubbed it his skull bike—it quickly became clear that the student had grown delusional. Martin seemed to believe he was the hero of a favorite old movie serial—*The Atomic Skull.* And Superman, it seemed, appeared to Martin as the Atomic Skull's archenemy Dr. Electron.

While Superman attempted to capture him, reporter Lois Lane arrived on the scene to get the story and immediately found herself abducted by Martin, who believed her to be the heroine of the serial. The Man of Steel was able to subdue the Skull only by wrapping his head in a dampening rod from S.T.A.R.'s nuclear reactor, absorbing enough radioactivity to allow Superman to knock him out (*Superman: The Man of Steel* #5, November 1991).

Thereafter, Martin occasionally relapsed into his Atomic Skull psychosis despite ongoing treatment. Joe actually had one sustained period of recovery that allowed him to write a book on his experiences (*The Adventures of Superman* #571, October 1999) but has continued to have increasingly violent relapses (*Manhunter* [fourth series] #31, August 2008).

ATOM-MASTER, THE

A bald, bespectacled scientist who briefly terrorized Metropolis and Gotham City with elaborate illusions created by a thought-projection helmet. The illusions were in the service of a series of robberies through which he hoped to bankroll a more elaborate device that could create solid, vastly more threatening images, altering "the atoms in the dust to create illusions and then materialize

The Atomic Skull

them." Before the plan could come to fruition, Batman deduced the location of the criminal and Superman raced in at super-speed, rendering the man he dubbed the Atom-Master unconscious, vowing that he'd wake up in jail (*World's Finest Comics* #101, May 1959). Years later, the Atom-Master returned to finally use his new tech, built into a more formfitting helmet, as a member of the Forgotten Villains (*DC Comics Presents* #77, January 1978, and #78, February 1985; *Resurrection Man* #25, June 1999).

AUCTIONEER, THE

An alien criminal whose powers and capabilities were functions of advanced technology rather than genetic anomaly. He was an intergalactic "importer" who, not unlike the pre-First Crisis incarnation of Brainiac, effortlessly amassed all objects or creatures that struck his fancy anywhere in the universe. He then sold his "collection" at auction.

As he did in his first documented appearance, the Auctioneer would dispatch his robotic "collectors" to uproot significant landmarks while remaining concealed aboard his spacecraft. It was from that spacefaring headquarters that the Auctioneer would accept bids on his "catalog," and there that Superman tracked him. But as one of the few surviving Kryptonians, the Man of Steel inadvertently became the Auctioneer's most valuable "collectible" of all. Adding many other meta-humans to the captives aboard his ship, the Auctioneer effectively formed a coalition of super heroes and their super-enemies. At first believing their powers to have been stripped, members of the uneasy alliance soon deduced that their powerlessness was only a self-delusion, induced by tech that affected them psychologically. Overcoming their mental block, the united antagonists neutralized the Auctioneer's powers by disabling his hardware and threatened to make his incapacity permanent unless he agreed to leave Earth. The Auctioneer complied and departed, but not without indicating his desire to "do business" with Earth's meta-humans sometime in the future (*Action Comics* #841, September 2006).

AURA

An Asian American meta-human who was a comrade of the clone Superboy Kon-El in a team that called itself the Ravers. Her real name was Lindsay Wah, and she adopted the Aura persona after manifesting the ability to manipulate polarity, meaning she could control virtually anything magnetic, even resisting the gravitational fields of planetary surfaces, enabling her to fly. Always a colorful, somewhat flamboyant figure, she used her magnetic abilities to build the suits of armor she wore against her opponents (*Superboy and the Ravers* #1–19, September 1996–March 1998).

Wah was clearly an emotionally troubled young woman with a brittle, edgy personality, sometimes characterized even by her teammates as having a mean, almost vicious streak. This quality made her a formidable opponent and a teammate the other Ravers could rely on in battle, but she could be difficult to work with. Small wonder, considering her wildly dysfunctional family and tragic history.

She joined the Ravers to escape the haunting memory of having allowed her wealthy father, a Hong Kong businessman with a dubious reputation, to frame her for his murder of her mother, who was also meta-human—an act motivated by his hatred of metas (*Superboy and the Ravers* #17, January 1998). In clearing her own name in the present, Wah forced a confession from her father and brought him to justice, but the conflicting emotions aroused by having betrayed her father in order to serve justice weighed heavily on her forever after (*Superboy and the Ravers* #16, December 1997). When last seen, Aura had nearly been killed by Dr. Polaris, aka Repulse (*Action Comics* #827, August 2005).

AURON

A super hero who was actually a clone of another, earlier meta-human. After the Man of Steel was murdered by Doomsday in pre-Infinite Crisis Metropolis, then-director of Project Cadmus Paul Westfield stole the Man of Steel's body in an attempt to map his Kryptonian genomes. After the closest possible approximation of Superman's genetic code was developed and saved to a computer disk, Westfield conspired to confiscate it from the Cadmus personnel responsible for its security—forcibly if necessary. To that end, Westfield created a clone of Jim Harper (the Guardian), which he named Auron. The project director outfitted Auron in indestructible, solar-powered armor and a digitized jetpack cybernetically plugged into his brain.

Auron succeeded in wresting the disk from the other clones, who included the young Newsboy Legion, their adult "fathers," and Dubbilex, almost killing them in the process. But his interaction with them triggered his replicated, buried memories of having been the Guardian. Thus reminded of his true allegiances, Auron was persuaded to take the only copy of the DNA into space with him, rather than surrendering it to Westfield (*Legacy of Superman* #1, March 1993).

Later, the resurrected Superman encountered Auron in space and enlisted his help against the super-criminal Massacre; Auron was subsequently killed and buried by Superman on a distant planet. There have been no reported appearances of Auron since (*The Adventures of Superman* #509, February 1994).

AXELROD, CARRIE

The *Daily Planet* photographer who famously ran afoul of Lex Luthor's mania for secrecy regarding his private life. Prone to dressing in black, the platinum-blond Axelrod (*The Adventures of Superman* #554, January 1998) saw her fifteen minutes of fame begin when she sneaked into LexCorp and took the first photographs of Lex Luthor's newborn daughter Lena Luthor (*Action Comics* #742, March 1998). After buying the *Daily Planet*, Luthor took particular satisfaction in firing Axelrod and "advising" her that she would thereafter be unemployable in Metropolis (*Superman: Save the Planet* one-shot, October 1998).

BABE

A friend and former co-worker of Jimmy Olsen on the post–First Crisis Earth who briefly became a menace to Metropolis upon being transformed into a vampire. Fired alongside Olsen from the *Newstime* commissary (*Superman: The Man of Steel* #2, August 1991), Yoshi Tanaka took it as an opportunity to pursue her passion for pop music as Babe, the lead singer in the band Shredded Metal (*Superman: The Man of Steel* #7, January 1992). Babe's eccentric bandmates accepted her vampirism, adapting their on-stage personae accordingly and taking the nickname *Children of the Night* (*Superman: The Man of Steel* #37, September 1994). Eventually, the influence of the vampire responsible for Babe's condition, Ruthven, dominated her life, but a chance meeting with a sorcerer named the Lock saved Babe. The latter was "a living corridor between this dimension and one . . . beyond," a realm to which he and Babe banished the vampire master and sealed the portal between dimensions (*Superman: The Man of Steel* #41–42, February-March 1995).

BAKER, NONA-LIN

See White Lotus; Supermen of America.

BAND OF SUPER-VILLAINS, THE

A trio of super-criminals who fought Superman, Batman, and Robin on the pre–First Crisis Earth-1. Their superpowers were granted them by an alien from another star system. This alien struck a bargain with the three ordinary thugs: In exchange for the vast wealth they could steal using the powers given them by the alien's high-tech devices, they would aid him in his plans to take over his homeworld.

But the pact was just a cover for the alien's real agenda. The belt-like devices that gave the trio their powers were actually designed to disperse an alien chemical that would poison Earth's environment and wipe out humankind, so that the alien's race could colonize the planet. After Superman and his two fellow heroes defeated both the Band of Super-Villains and their benefactor, the alien blew up his spacecraft with him in it, per his superiors' orders in the event he failed in his mission (*World's Finest Comics* #134, June 1963).

BANNIN, BREK

The real name of Polar Boy of the planet Tharr, a member of the Legion of Substitute Heroes as constituted in the thirtieth century of the pre–First Crisis Earth-1 (*Adventure Comics* #306, March 1963; others).

BANNIN, MINTOR

The father of Polar Boy of the Legion of Substitute Heroes, who shared his son's cold-radiating powers, which the inhabitants of their homeworld Tharr evolved as a defense against the hot climate that would otherwise have been deadly.

Bannin and his wife, the latter unnamed in the account, once helped the Superboy of the pre–First Crisis Earth-1 by posing as the Boy of Steel's "new" adoptive parents, whom he claimed to prefer over Jonathan and Martha Kent. The pretense was part of a plan to "exorcise" alien flame creatures who had possessed the Kents' bodies. When Superboy pretended to prepare to leave Smallville with his new parents, the flame creatures attempted to possess the Bannins instead and were killed by the Tharrians' natural cold-generating abilities (*Superboy* [first series] #148, June 1968).

BANTOR

See Regor.

BARACODA ISLAND

A remote base of operations used by the Lex Luthor of the pre–First Crisis Earth-2. The island was the staging ground for "omega ray" experiments that produced monstrous, dinosaur-sized animals, which the renegade scientist intended to use as a weapon in a bid for world conquest. In the battle with Superman in which Luthor was apprehended,

the entire island was destroyed (*Superman* [first series] #12, September-October 1941).

BARD, STEVE

An obnoxious, wisecracking reporter on the DAILY STAR of the pre-FIRST CRISIS Earth-2 who enjoyed needling LOIS LANE even though she always got the last laugh (*Superman* [first series] #29, July-August 1944; *Superman Family* #212, November 1981, and #216, March 1982). Bard's fashion sense—bow ties and checkered jackets—might have been a sartorial inspiration to JIMMY OLSEN. Bard's more extensively documented Earth-1 incarnation was STEVE LOMBARD.

BARNES, NED

See SELWYN, DIGBY; SELWYN, SALLY.

BARNETT, LOLA

The waspish, aggressive entertainment reporter—referred to more frequently, and more accurately, as a gossip columnist—on the nightly newscast on WGBS-TV in the pre-FIRST CRISIS METROPOLIS of Earth-1. In her first on-air appearance, Barnett divulged what she thought was Superman's secret identity, until it was discovered she was merely a pawn in a scheme by one of Superman's enemies (*Superman* [first series] #275, May 1974).

Her career with the station was short-lived and little was documented about her other than that she was highly competitive, not much of a team player, and relentless in pursuit of her scoops. Once convinced she had an exclusive, she could not be dissuaded from going on the air with her bombshell by anything less than a direct threat to her life. Working in close proximity to CLARK KENT, she posed the constant threat that some of the Man of Steel's most vital secrets might be uncovered and broadcast to the entire city on any night of the week. Barnett was documented as having survived the First Crisis to be incarnated on the unified Earth (*Justice League Task Force* #15, August 1994), but it is not yet known whether she had a counterpart on the post-Final Crisis New Earth.

BARON SUNDAY

A contract killer who ostensibly dispatched his victims using Obeah, more familiar in the METROPOLIS of post-FIRST CRISIS Earth as voodoo. Famous felon Willie Sutton once told the press that he robbed banks because that was where the money was; similarly, Caribbean-born Baron Sunday told his colleagues that he came to the United States because that's where all the killing was. It was METROPOLIS S.C.U.'s (SPECIAL CRIMES UNIT) CAPTAIN MAGGIE SAWYER and Sergeant DAN TURPIN who first alerted Superman to a series of mysterious deaths caused by sudden, massive internal bleeding—deaths that would have been considered natural had they not had two bizarre details in common: The victims all died with looks of abject horror on their faces, and tiny voodoo dolls, each pierced with a metal spike, were found near the bodies.

Baron Sunday quickly got word from an underworld informant that the S.C.U. had called in Superman, who was known to be vulnerable to magic, and warmed to the challenge of taking on the Man of Steel. Because the post-First Crisis Superman wore a costume that was not invulnerable, Sunday was able to obtain a shred of fabric from one of the Kryptonian's ripped capes. With it, he created a voodoo doll of the Man of Steel and lay in wait for the right moment to use it.

While Superman was preoccupied by a global crisis, Sunday saw his opportunity and used his magic to diminish Superman's powers, knocking him out of the sky. The Man of Steel fell to Earth so forcefully that he was driven deep underground on impact. He went missing and was feared dead for several weeks. However, all this occurred during a period in which Superman was experiencing a series of "fugue episodes" due to the effects of a plot by another one of his enemies. The fugue states were periodic blackouts during which the Man of Tomorrow assumed the identity of a non-superpowered local costumed hero called GANGBUSTER. This would prove ironic and mete out a kind of poetic justice to Baron Sunday.

In the Gangbuster guise, Superman sought clues to the perp behind the voodoo murders from the very same informant who'd alerted Sunday to Superman's interest in the case. But even without using his superpowers, the Man of Steel ultimately overmatched Sunday, whose mystical energies were insufficient to hold "Gangbuster" (*Superman* [second series] #26, December 1988). Once he'd recovered from his Gangbuster identity confusion, Superman eventually discovered that the murderous Sunday had been a longtime student of real magic in his native land, where for many years he had used his minor mastery of the mystic arts for profit as a hit man. After gaining great notoriety among the superstitious denizens of the underworld by dressing up his hits with the trappings of voodoo, he took his act stateside to see how big a payday he could earn from leveraging his street cred.

Baron Sunday was tried, convicted, and sent to STRYKER'S ISLAND Maximum Security Prison in the middle of Metropolis's West River. There he ostensibly killed six fellow inmates by means unknown, though it was eventually discovered that his victims were not, in fact, dead, but rather in deep comas simulating death. Sunday's real agenda became clear when the convicts rose, zombie-like, from their morgue slabs, responding to the magical psychic manipulations of the Baron. Superman intervened to stop the "zombified" sextet from breaking Sunday out of his cell, ultimately administering an electrical shock that jolted the convicts back to waking consciousness—but not before causing a kind of "feedback" that shocked Baron Sunday's brain, rendering him unconscious.

At last report, the Baron remained in a catatonic state in the Stryker's Island hospital ward, a prisoner of his own immobile body (*Action Comics* #665, May 1991). It is logical to assume that Sunday was a member of the human subspecies called *homo magi,* although no explicit documentation of this can be found. What casts doubt on this theory is the evidence that whatever natural magical abilities Baron Sunday may have had were of a minor order, as he never developed them to serve a grander agenda. He seemed to prefer focusing exclusively on the acquisition of material wealth rather than cosmic empire building.

BARRAGE

The trouble with some guys is their preoccupation with the size of their gun. And their failure to recognize that world-class firepower in the service of small-mindedness and lack of imagination means nothing more than an overdressed petty crook with a one-way ticket to hard time. So it was with a two-time loser on the post-FIRST CRISIS unified Earth known only as Karnowsky, whose ambitions seldom rose above the level of a local bank vault or an all-night convenience store's safe. (Later accounts maintained that his real name was Paul Rooney and *Karnowsky* was only an alias.) Where he got his code name, *Barrage,* or his exoskeletal armor and its built-in weaponry, was anybody's guess, but the smart money said he didn't dream these up himself. However, Barrage's tendency to attract attention by shooting an ant with a howitzer brought out METROPOLIS's über-SWAT team, the METROPOLIS S.C.U., when he attempted a simple retail store heist. A volley fired from the built-in cannon in Barrage's suit that seriously wounded DAN TURPIN was all the excuse CAPTAIN MAGGIE SAWYER needed to open fire with S.C.U.'s more major ordnance. The resulting explosive charge set off in Barrage's cannon took off most of Karnowsky's right arm.

After his hospitalization, Karnowksy was sent to do a stretch at STRYKER'S ISLAND (*Superman Annual* #2, 1988). It took a lot of calling-in of old favors, but Karnowsky got the help he needed to spring himself from Stryker's sometime later. He resumed his career as Barrage with upgraded shock-absorbing armor and a new blaster that seemed fitted to his shoulder socket, replacing his missing arm. This time, revenge was the order of the day, but Barrage only brought down on himself Superman's wrath when he tried attacking Sawyer and her S.C.U. teammates (*Action Comics* #726, October 1996). After once again escaping jail, Barrage joined MORGAN EDGE'S SUPERMAN REVENGE SQUAD, only to be caught once again by Superman (*The Adventures of Superman* #543, February 1997).

Barrage met further defeat when the PARASITE, with whom he had been working, turned on him

and Barrage attempted to flee, only to come face-to-face with Superman. Barrage then confessed the location of the Revenge Squad's lair (*Superman* [second series] #127, September 1997). Subsequent returns to crime by Barrage have been documented (*Superman* [second series] #188, January 2003), as well as unsuccessful escapes from Stryker's Island (*Superman* [second series] #147, August 1999; *The Adventures of Superman* #641, August 2005). It is not entirely clear whether he survived the Infinite Crisis to reappear on New Earth.

BARSTOW, FLOYD

See Anomaly.

BASHFORD, "BASH"

A blond, crew-cut jock at the Smallville High School of pre–First Crisis Earth-1 who delighted in bullying Clark Kent (*Superboy* [first series] #157, June 1969; others). Clark mostly withstood Bashford's abuse, recalling the brain trauma that he had accidentally inflicted on Bash during a youthful athletic competition (*Superboy* [first series] #161, December 1969).

But the scales were somewhat balanced by the fact that Bashford had unwittingly done the Boy of Steel a favor early in Superboy's costumed career. His discovery of Clark's discarded clothing while Superboy was in action briefly led Bashford to suspect Superboy's secret identity, motivating the latter to begin the practice of adding a pouch to his cape to hold his compressed civilian garb (*The New Adventures of Superboy* #9, September 1980).

On occasion, Clark would observe unexpected depths in Bash, noting his anger at the escalating Vietnam War and increasing violence throughout the world (*The New Adventures of Superboy* #39, March 1983), as well as his spirited defense of Johnny Webber, newly released from reform school (*The New Adventures of Superboy* #52, April 1984). Bash Bashford's post-high-school life was never documented, and by all accounts he was among those persons "deleted" by the First Crisis.

BATGIRL

Five young women in various realities assumed the super heroic identity of Batgirl, a young-adult female counterpart to Batman who frequently assisted the Dark Knight in his battles with the Gotham City underworld. But only one had extensive interaction with Superman, and she was the second Batgirl of the pre–First Crisis Earth-1. She was librarian Barbara Gordon, daughter of Police Commissioner James Gordon, who became a costumed crime fighter after encountering and battling a super-villain, with Batman and Robin's help, while dressed in a "Batgirl" costume she had created for a costume party (*Detective Comics* #359, January 1967).

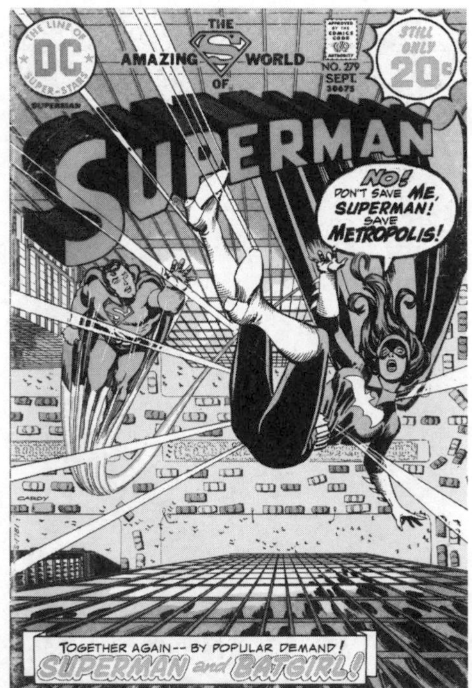

This Batgirl worked on many cases with Superman, and occasionally Supergirl as well, usually during the period after she moved to Washington, DC, following her election to the House of Representatives. Having begun to doubt her effectiveness as Batgirl, Gordon entered politics with the intention of giving up her super hero career, but fate had a way of drawing her out of retirement repeatedly. On one such occasion, Superman needed her help in a battle against a criminal organization called Maze (*Superman* [first series] #268, October 1973). At this time, she also had a blind date with Clark Kent, establishing a long-lasting friendship with the bespectacled reporter.

She and Superman teamed up twice more, once in Gotham City to thwart oil smugglers (*Superman* [first series] #279, September 1974) and later to oppose the world-threatening plans of the century-old Dr. Horus (*DC Comics Presents* #19, March 1980). Supergirl and Batgirl crossed paths when each woman individually investigated a female criminal gang (*Adventure Comics* #381, June 1969) and again to combat a modern-day incarnation of Cleopatra with designs on conquering the United States (*Superman Family* #171, June–July 1975).

In the post–First Crisis single Earth, Barbara Gordon was reincarnated as James Gordon's niece, and she, too, assumed a super heroic personality, but her Batgirl career was cut short when the Joker shot and crippled her (*The Killing Joke,* 1988). Refusing to give up the fight against crime, she turned her computer skills into her greatest asset and became the digital "mentor" and database keeper for the other Bat-heroes, taking the code name Oracle. In this reality, Supergirl did not arrive on Earth until after Barbara Gordon became wheelchair-bound, and the two women never worked together as costumed crime fighters.

Subsequently, other women, most notably the mute Cassandra Cain, as well as Stephanie Brown, assumed the mantle of Batgirl, who continued to exist on New Earth. Stephanie was rescued by Supergirl when she was investigating an unusual partnership between the Kryptonite Man, Mister Freeze, and Toyman. Together, they aided Superman and Batman (Dick Grayson) in ending a threat to Gotham City (*World's Finest* #3–4, February–March 2010).

BATMAN

A legendary nocturnal, non-superpowered crime fighter clad in a costume designed to resemble a bat, for the purpose of striking fear into the hearts of "cowardly and superstitious" criminals. Not only was the so-called Dark Knight arguably the finest martial artist alive, but he was also a brilliant detective. While individual background details have varied in each instance, there was a Batman in the pre–First Crisis universe (on both Earth-1 and Earth-2), on the unified post-Crisis Earth, and on New Earth as well.

In each instance the Batman was, in private life, wealthy industrialist and philanthropist Bruce Wayne of Gotham City, who, as a young boy, watched helplessly as his parents were murdered by an armed robber in a dark alley while they walked home from a movie (*Detective Comics* #27, May 1939). For ten-year-old Bruce—whose haunting, accusatory stare so unnerved the gunman that he fled, sparing the boy—this was the defining moment of his life. He vowed then and there to devote the rest of that life, as well as the considerable fortune he would inherit, not only to apprehending his parents' killer but also to waging war on crime in all its forms, so that other potential victims would be spared the kind of suffering he had endured. Ever after, Wayne—in particular, the Wayne of the post-Crisis Earth—was relentless in his pursuit of that goal, never pausing or finding any personal peace that might lead him to question the path he chose for even a moment. It was this haunted quality that sometimes made him

seem to his super heroic associates as obsessive and emotionally troubled.

Each Earth's Batman had a somewhat different relationship with the Superman of that world. On the pre-Crisis Earth-2, the two heroes interacted rarely. They met in the course of working with that Earth's super hero team the Justice Society of America on a handful of occasions. While they did not often collaborate, they went from being mere acquaintances to close friends when they learned each other's secret identities while simultaneously working on a case aboard an ocean liner (*Superman* [first series] #76, May–June 1952).

On Earth-1, the two enjoyed a close friendship and collaborated on many cases. Each was among the few persons entrusted with the closely guarded secret of the other's true identity. Often the friends helped each other protect their secrets, sometimes impersonating each other to create the illusion of each man's two selves appearing side by side. They also worked together as members of the Justice Society's Earth-1 counterpart, the Justice League. Their partnership had the unintended effect of inspiring their archenemies to team up on several occasions, with the result that the Man of Steel and the Dark Knight often faced ad-hoc teamings of Lex Luthor and the Joker, or Brainiac and a shape-shifting criminal known as Clayface.

After the Crisis on Infinite Earths consolidated the multiverse into one world and rewrote the histories of Superman and Batman, the two heroes' relationship developed in a very different way. When Batman first became a mysterious presence in Gotham City, evolving in the public imagination from urban legend to—perhaps inaccurately—notoriously violent and potentially dangerous costumed vigilante, Superman felt a responsibility to bring him to justice.

But Batman managed to persuade the Man of Steel that both men were on the same side of the law, and Superman aided the Dark Knight in defeating a murderous psychopath called Magpie. In the course of this incident, an apprehensive Man of Steel was gradually persuaded that Gotham was a much darker and corrupt place than Me-

TROPOLIS, and that the Dark Knight's reliance on fear and the elements of surprise and mystery, as well as his tougher, "edgier" style in general, were not merely appropriate but necessary for getting results in Gotham.

Superman's slightly grudging acceptance of their philosophical differences—Bruce Wayne being a more driven, pessimistic personality, less willing than KAL-EL to believe that human beings' better selves could prevail—made their subsequent collaborations wary, if not actually uneasy. The two heroes volunteered little about themselves, each having to discover the other's true identity on his own and earn his counterpart's respect incrementally over time. Their hard-won truce warmed into a somewhat aloof friendship only after repeated collaboration and much work together as members of the post-Crisis Justice League.

The heroes' relationship remained essentially unchanged after the INFINITE CRISIS, with both men continuing only slightly reordered existences on New Earth. For example, in this reality they were close friends dating back to the formation of the Justice League, a far earlier point in each man's life than in the post–First Crisis unified Earth (*Justice League of America* [second series] #0, September 2006). But no matter the nature of the relationship in any reality, Superman and Batman remained fundamentally different personalities. As much as their association was full of camaraderie and mutual admiration, informed by the certainty that each had the other's back, it held the potential to erupt into conflict, without warning and at any moment, because of who each man was at his core.

(For a comprehensive account of the Batman's career, his enemies, associates, and adventures, see *The Essential Batman Encyclopedia,* 2008.)

BAT-MITE

A tiny, mischievous creature from another dimension who was to BATMAN what Superman's nemesis MR. MXYZPTLK was to the pre-Crisis Superman—a magical irritant, more pest than menace. While Mxyzptlk also visited the post–FIRST CRISIS Earth and was somewhat more malevolent than his earlier counterpart, Bat-Mite was spotted comparatively rarely in that reality, and accounts of those sightings seemed not to agree on precisely what Bat-Mite was.

Bat-Mite first appeared in this dimension as a small, gnomish figure in an ill-fitting, oddly designed version of Batman's costume, wielding magical powers similar if not identical to those of Mxyzptlk (*Detective Comics* #267, May 1959). It was generally believed that both "imps" hailed from the same place, the Fifth Dimensional land of ZRFFF, but no documentation that definitively confirmed this was ever found. While Mxyzptlk delighted first in annoying Superman, then actively bedeviling him, Bat-Mite insisted he was Batman's "greatest fan" and that his only reason for appearing in this dimension was to thrill to Batman's exploits.

Bat-Mite and Mxyzptlk often collaborated on magical pranks that spelled trouble for Superman when he was teaming up with Batman (*World's Finest Comics* #113, November 1960; #123, February 1962; #152, August 1965; others), and on those occasions it was clear that Mxyzptlk was the more noticeably mean-spirited. Mxyzptlk never regretted giving Superman a headache, whereas, when Bat-Mite realized that he had enraged his idol, he would often express remorse as he vanished whence he had come.

The iterations of Bat-Mite documented post–First Crisis were all described in terms implying that none was a discrete organic being but, rather, explainable in other terms. For example, on one occasion, Superman and Batman drew the conclusion that the Bat-Mite they'd encountered was a magical construct created by Mxyzptlk (*Batman and Superman: World's Finest* #6, September 1999). In another case, Batman's archenemy the JOKER figured out a way to steal Mr. Mxyzptlk's power to alter reality, remaking the entire world, reflecting the twisted vision of a disordered mind (*Emperor Joker* #1, October 2000; *Superman* [second series] #160, September 2000; *The Adventures of Superman* #582, September 2000; others). Subsequent events suggested that even though the Joker was defeated and the world put right again, the Clown Prince of Crime had retained traces of Fifth Dimensional powers. Superman's enemy, the imperfect Superman duplicate BIZARRO, was able to force this latent "magical essence" out of the Joker, and what appeared took a form resembling Bat-Mite. By this account, Bat-Mite was reincarnated in the post–First Crisis universe, and presumably on New Earth as well, as a manifestation of Mr. Mxyzptlk's magic, "cultivated" within the Joker (*Superman/Batman* #20–25, June 2005–May 2006).

BATSON, BILLY

See SHAZAM.

BAUD

A member of a team of cybernetic super-criminals called MAINFRAME, who first appeared during the SUPERMAN RED/SUPERMAN BLUE period. Baud was a promiscuously flirtatious energy being who was super-fast, able to disrupt magnetic fields, and known to alter her own molecular density, allowing her to "phase" through solids—meaning she would appear to become immaterial and then re-form inside an object or on the other side of a barrier. For Mainframe, she spied on METROPOLIS's underworld, evaluating the competition, and became

the first member of the team to confront Superman. On the orders of Mainframe's leader OVERRIDE, Baud also joined MORGAN EDGE's SUPERMAN REVENGE SQUAD, but fled into another dimension when it became clear the Squad was on the losing side of a battle with Superman. Baud returned alongside Mainframe shortly thereafter only to be permanently confined to their other-dimensional refuge through the efforts of MISA (*Superman: The Man of Steel* #71, September 1997; *Superman* [second series] #127, September 1997; *Superman: The Man of Steel* #72, October 1997; *Superman 3-D* [second series] #1, December 1998).

BEE-BOY

The male equivalent of INSECT QUEEN, the super heroic identity of the LANA LANGS of both the pre-FIRST CRISIS Earth-1 and Earth-2. Bee-Boy was the super-persona briefly assumed by Lana Lang's onetime African guide, Kim, who became infatuated with her. Though his love remained unrequited, Lana interceded on his behalf when he sustained a life-threatening injury, securing SUPERBOY's help in healing Kim (*Superboy* [first series] #127, March 1966).

BELCHER, SERGEANT

See CERBERUS.

BENSON, VAL

The temporary replacement for PERRY WHITE as *DAILY PLANET* editor on the post–FIRST CRISIS Earth-1. During White's temporary appointment to the U.S. Senate, his place on the *Daily Planet* was taken by Benson, a much younger man (*Superman's Girl Friend, Lois Lane* #62, January 1966; *Superman's Pal, Jimmy Olsen* #91, March 1966; *Action Comics* #335, March 1966). Argumentative and acid-tongued, Benson quickly alienated his new

employees. Moreover, Lois Lane thought she had uncovered evidence that he was a member of the Superman Killers' Underground League (SKUL—not to be confused with the criminal organization later led by Albert Michaels, aka the Atomic Skull), which had targeted the Man of Steel and his friends for death. Benson ultimately confided in Lois that he was an FBI agent who had been tasked with bringing down SKUL and confiscating its anti-Superman weapon. His mission completed, Benson left the *Planet* as Perry White returned (*Superman's Girl Friend, Lois Lane* #63–64, February–April 1966).

BEPPO THE SUPER-MONKEY

On the Krypton in the same dimension as the pre-First Crisis Earth-1, Superman's scientist father, Jor-El, used at least two small animals to test prototypes of the rocket that would ultimately carry his infant son, Kal-El, to Earth. The point of using living creatures in the tests was to determine whether the spacecraft's life-support systems would keep Kal-El alive. One of these test subjects was Krypto, Kal-El's puppy, and another was Jor-El's lab monkey Beppo. According to one account, Beppo's rocket, like Krypto's, went off course and drifted aimlessly through space until much later, when Kal-El's rocket ripped open a warp in space through which both prototypes and millions of green, now radioactive fragments of the planet were sucked. All these objects emerged from the warp millions of light-years away, in close proximity to Earth's orbit, from which they eventually fell into Earth's atmosphere (*Action Comics* #500, October 1979). Another account contended that the monkey returned safely to Jor-El's lab—confirming that the rocket design was safe—but noted that Beppo later mischievously stowed away in Kal-El's rocket at the moment of Krypton's destruction. Whichever the case, however, the result was the same.

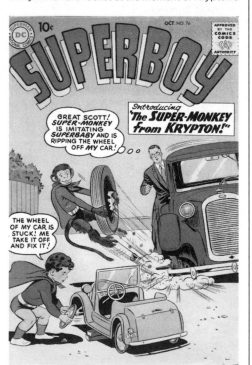

Under Earth's yellow sun, Beppo developed superpowers and presumably flew off, not to be reunited with his former master's son until some years later, when Kal-El had long since become Clark Kent and had just begun his career as Superboy. While Beppo demonstrated the same kinds of powers as Superboy, they were somewhat weaker because they were proportionate to his smaller size (*Superboy* [first series] #76, October 1959).

At first, Beppo, wearing a red-and-blue costume patterned after Superboy's, represented an enormous headache for the Teen of Steel, complicating his crime-fighting work and threatening to compromise his secret identity by being seen with Clark Kent as well as with Superboy. Finally, the Boy of Tomorrow was forced to lead Beppo into deep space and harmlessly abandon him there, hoping he would not find his way back to Earth. That was not to be the case, however, although it took several more years to happen. By the time Beppo returned, Superboy had grown into Superman, and his cousin Kara had arrived on Earth and assumed her super heroic identity of Supergirl. Through Supergirl, Beppo met Krypto and Supergirl's pet, the technologically super-empowered Earth cat Streaky. Together with Comet, a super-horse, Beppo and his new friends founded the Legion of Super-Pets (*Adventure Comics* #293, February 1962).

There was no superpowered Beppo in the post-First Crisis universe, only a non-Kryptonian simian sidekick to Crackers the Clown (*Action Comics* #668, August 1991).

BERKOWITZ, FRANK

The mayor of the Metropolis of the post-Crisis unified Earth for four terms. He sealed his fate by ordering Superman to arrest Lex Luthor (*Man of Steel* #4, November 1986), whereupon Luthor hired Casey Griggs to assassinate Berkowitz, after which Luthor killed Griggs (*Superman* [second series] #131, January 1998). Berkowitz left a wife, Jan, and two daughters, Suzie and Julianna.

BERTRON

An alien scientist who used the prehistoric Krypton of the post–First Crisis universe, with its harsh, sunbaked terrain scarcely capable of sustaining carbon-based life, as a vast laboratory some 250,000 years ago. From left-behind records of Bertron's pioneering, albeit ghastly, experiments, the humanoid Kryptonian race that later tamed the planet derived its understanding of the science of cloning and, indeed, much of its phenomenally advanced technology. Cold, emotionless, utterly lacking in compassion, and ruthless in his pursuit of scientific inquiry, Bertron earned his place in the annals of infamy primarily by creating Superman's murderer, the monstrosity known as Doomsday. Bertron envisioned developing what he called the Ultimate, a creature who could survive in the most unforgiving environment and perhaps even achieve immortality. What better place to do this, then, than Krypton, whose domi-

nant life-forms at this point were regarded as the most dangerous in the universe? So Bertron developed a test-tube infant whom he deliberately put at risk by exposing it to Krypton's inhospitable landscape and ravenous, remorseless fauna. Over and over, the child was killed and, each time, its remains were retrieved and used to create a stronger clone, a process that amounted to a kind of hyperaccelerated natural selection. The Ultimate that resulted from these atrocities—later dubbed Doomsday—had the memory of its former selves' terrifying traumas and painful assaults genetically "imprinted" on its consciousness. Once unleashed, Doomsday took revenge for every death it had suffered, and its burning desire to destroy all life was ultimately acted out upon Superman.

Centuries earlier, Bertron managed to alter Doomsday's DNA so that the monster could regenerate itself each time it was killed, with the resuscitated version then immune to whatever had killed its previous self. This second set of experiments, however, cost Bertron his life (*Superman/Doomsday: Hunter/Prey*, 1994).

BHUTRAN

A troubled Asian country best known as the birthplace of Savitar Bandu, aka Shadowdragon (*Superman* [second series] #97, February 1995) and his notorious siblings, drug lords Nazeer (*Superman: The Wedding Album* #1, December 1996) and Rajiv Naga (*Action Comics* #728 and *Superman: The Man of Steel* #63—both December 1996). "Some might speculate that excessive lawlessness in Bhutran is a reaction to the area's oppressive heat, while others blame its poverty. Even more point the finger at a political system that, when not corrupt, is easily manipulated" (*Superman Annual* #9, 1997). The neighboring nation of Tehrac, along the Chaitan Desert, has long had an adversarial relationship with Bhutran (*The Adventures of Superman* #566, April 1999).

The country does contain areas for reflection and solitude, notably "the Sacred Gardens of Bhutran" and a steep peak reputed to be home to "the Man Atop the Mountain." In fact, those who climb to the summit discover that the "man" is actually a natural formation resembling a face. Moved by the beauty of the mountaintop view, a young Clark Kent "was so impressed he said he would forever find solutions in the cold and solace of mountains" (*Superman* [second series] #118, December 1996).

BIBBOWSKI, BIBBO

This close friend of Jimmy Olsen and idolizer of Superman was a slovenly, tough-talking, diamond-in-the-rough "regular character." Bibbo Bibbowksi was known throughout the post–First Crisis Metropolis's Suicide Slum district as the owner-bartender at the neighborhood's favorite seedy watering hole, the Ace o' Clubs Bar. Bibbo practically worshipped the Man of Steel, whom he called his "fav'rit" hero. And while no one would've wanted to step into a dark alley with him after accusing him of being a "snitch," it was well known that, as a confidant of rough customers in the most crime-ridden part of town, Bibbo often overheard valuable information that he was only too happy to share with Superman (*The Adventures of Superman* #428, May 1987; others).

Because conflicting accounts have stated the same information as either fact or myth, Bibbo was a sort of Baron von Münchhausen for the boilermaker crowd, making grandiose claims of a colorful past in one moment, and in the next, maintaining a cryptic silence regarding even the most mundane aspects of his background. For example, at his most expansive when matching a customer shot for shot, he wove elaborate tales of having been a brawling longshoreman and former heavyweight contender. Yet he remained vague about how he came to Metropolis (some folks said it was to escape some disreputable difficulty in Milwaukee); had a brother who was a professor; and declined to reveal his actual first name to anyone but arresting police officers—not even to his

closest non-meta-human friend, the *Daily Planet*'s Olsen, whom Bibbo often provided with tips and leads just as he did Superman.

With Bibbo, you never knew what form of drunkenness you were seeing, punch- or the more common variety. But it seemed unlikely that he'd gone soft in the noggin, because he was reputed to have the hardest head in Metropolis—one that he frequently used as a battering ram to kayo an unruly barfly. To call Bibbo unpretentious was a gross understatement, with the operative word being *gross.* He'd been a fixture on the waterfront for more than two generations, most of that spent as a more literal fixture—on an Ace o' Clubs bar stool. Then his luck changed when he found a winning lottery ticket lost by Jose Delgado, aka Gangbuster. The first year's payout from the fourteen-million-dollar jackpot allowed Bibbo to buy the Ace o' Clubs, but he seemed not to invest any of his newfound wealth in upgrading the establishment, let alone his residence, wardrobe, or dental work. Nor did he ever bother hiring a bouncer, preferring to handle those chores personally.

In addition to his hard head, Bibbo was famous for packing a mean punch, one so powerful that even Superman could, on occasion, be fazed by it. Because Metropolis was Superman's home, it attracted more than its share of super-criminals out to amp their street cred by taking out the Man of Steel. But not even Superman could be in two places at once, and when he was out of town but the baddies weren't, the hard-knuckled Bibbo provided backup, patrolling the docks and the tavern's vicinity for meta-human miscreants. Keeping the peace while running a tough saloon in a tougher part of town was the way he kept in "fighting shape."

This "noble hooligan" continued to hold court at the Ace o' Clubs, but will put his fists to good use when needed. His last attempt at heroic public service saw him badly beaten by the time-tossed warrior Atlas (*Superman* #679, October 2008).

BIG BELLY BURGERS

Although a division of LexCorp, the giant national fast-food chain Big Belly Foodstuffs, Inc., on the post–First Crisis unified Earth had a far less sinister reputation than its parent company's CEO. Big Belly Burgers' real relevance to the Man of Steel lay in its fictitious mascot, "Big Belly" himself—a bearded, Falstaffian figure, a statue of whom could be found at every restaurant location. It was one of these statues that the Fifth Dimensional imp Mr. Mxyzptlk, magically animated to serve as a brawling opponent to Superman.

Additionally, *Daily Planet* staffers Jimmy Olsen and Perry White appeared in a promotion for the Metropolis outlets in which Perry posed as a short-order cook grilling the famous "belly-busting burgers." The ads failed to avoid the obvious joke and had Perry telling Jimmy, "Don't call me chef!" (*The Adventures of Superman* #441, June 1988; others).

"BIG WORDS"

See Newsboy Legion.

BIRD, JEREMY

An elderly former lumberjack on the pre–First Crisis Earth-1 who suffered ridicule for his contention that he had encountered Superman in his youth, at a time when, as all historians knew, the Man of Steel had not yet arrived on Earth.

Bird's tales of being rescued by the Man of Steel from murderous Native Americans made him the laughingstock of his North Dakota retirement home until Superman investigated and discovered that the "Superman" Bird knew was actually Kal-El's grandfather, the father of Jor-El. This ancestor had apparently journeyed briefly to Earth while experimenting with space travel sometime around the turn of the nineteenth century (*Superman* [first series] #103, February 1956). As this chronicle contradicts other accounts of the House of El of this reality, some historians consider it apocryphal.

BIZARRO

An "imperfect duplicate" of Superman, also described as a flawed clone, Bizarro looked like a grotesque caricature of the Man of Steel as designed by a madman. The defective technology that created the first Bizarro also imperfectly duplicated Superman's costume, so that the pre–First Crisis Bizarro's garb was invulnerable just like Superman's, but the *S* in the chest emblem was backward, like a mirror image. Two of the four subsequent incarnations of Bizarro shared this characteristic.

It or he (the pronouns were used interchangeably) possessed superpowers that were initially identical to, but in later instances the opposite of, the Man of Steel's. Unfortunately, no incarnation of the so-called Thing of Steel had any of Superman's keen intelligence; in fact, all versions of Bizarro's thought processes were illogical, inverted, and counterintuitive. The word most frequently used to describe his thinking was *backward.*

As a result, Bizarro's behavior was almost always inexplicable; sometimes amusingly zany; and, on many occasions, terrifyingly dangerous and unpredictable. Versions of Bizarro existed on the pre–First Crisis Earth-1, on the post-Crisis unified Earth (there referred to at first only as "the

bizarre imperfect duplicate"), and on New Earth, but not on Earth-2.

All versions of Bizarro were somewhat like an android in that they were animate and sentient, but not organic; or, in the words of the pre–First Crisis Bizarro's inventor, "composed of lifeless matter." The pre-Crisis creature's "flesh" was chalk white and appeared rough-hewn, sometimes even faceted, as if crudely chiseled. Its black hair was spiky and untamed.

Everything about Bizarro was flawed, especially the clumsy and ungrammatical speech informed by his skewed logic. For example, Bizarro would express happiness by saying, "Me am sad." Most disturbing of all, Bizarro, like a clone, was imprinted with a copy of his "father's" memories, but they, too, were imperfectly duplicated. This meant he was aware that Superman was reporter Clark Kent in everyday life, but it was not entirely clear to him that the duality was supposed to be a secret. Such thinking, coupled with judgment that was intrinsically unsound, made him a constant security threat to Superman.

Were he capable of normal human cognition and conventional strategizing, the original Bizarro would have been a skilled combatant and formidable opponent. Predictably, however, he was confused, incompetent, and clumsy in battle, and it was only his superpowers that made him a force to be reckoned with. In the pre–First Crisis Smallville of Earth-1, the first Bizarro was created as an imperfect double of Superboy by a Professor Dalton, inventor of a "duplicator ray" that didn't quite live up to its billing, creating things like a diamond that melted like ice or an apple that weighed several hundred pounds.

Dalton inadvertently exposed the Boy of Steel to radiation as the result of a lab accident. When Superboy first saw the grotesque creature, he exclaimed that it was "bizarre." But the witless replicant misheard him and mistakenly assumed Superboy had spoken his name. Thus he began to call himself what he thought he'd heard—"Bizarro"—just as the imperfect duplicate of the adult Superman would many years later. Although Dalton contended that the duplicate could not possibly be alive, the creature still moved and functioned like a living being and escaped the lab. Having a dim copy of Superboy's memory, Bizarro fancied himself Smallville's protector, but his hideous appearance and erratic behavior terrorized the town, especially since he was unable to control his superpowers. Superboy was forced to conclude that he must destroy Bizarro, but the creature, who had been treated kindly by a blind girl, dimly perceived that if he caused a head-on collision with Superboy by flying straight at him, the resulting shock wave might restore the girl's sight. In the course of carrying out his plan, this first Bizarro was destroyed (*Superboy* [first series] #68, November 1958).

Dalton's was not the only duplicator device that existed during Superman's youth. The criminal mastermind known as the Brain later re-created Dalton's duplicator machine, using it to create a Bizarro Krypto that perished saving the true Dog of Steel from an alien creature (*Superboy* [first series] #82, July 1960). The Boy of Steel hid the second duplicator ray in a crater on a barren planet, watched over by the Bizarro Super-Dog (*Superboy* [first series] #109, December 1963). And, in an odd coincidence, Kryptonian criminal General Zod had created an earlier duplicator machine on the planet Krypton, generating an army of imperfect duplicates of himself while attempting an unsuccessful coup (*Adventure Comics* #283, April 1961).

Years later, in Metropolis, a Professor Clyde invited Superman to his laboratory for a demonstration of a ray that would supposedly immunize the Man of Steel against kryptonite. But the ray turned out to be a duplicator like Dalton's, and when it was trained on Superman, the Man of Steel found himself standing beside an adult Bizarro. No sooner had Kal-El adjusted to the shock than "Professor Clyde" removed his disguise to reveal himself as Lex Luthor, in his pre–First Crisis incarnation as a renegade scientist. As it turned out, Luthor had stolen the blueprints for Dalton's original machine and rebuilt it, with the goal of creating an equivalent of Superman that would do his bidding and destroy the Man of Steel (*Action Comics* #254, July 1959).

However, this Bizarro was no more compliant than the last had been and instead tried to emulate Superman's heroism, even helping the Man of Steel deliver Luthor and his assistant to the police. Unfortunately, this Bizarro's further efforts to be helpful were as wrongheaded and destructive as the younger Bizarro's. In addition, he experienced an imperfect version of Superman's love for Lois Lane, and in a misguided attempt to "propose," kidnapped her, not understanding that his Frankenstein-like appearance only repelled her. But the ever-resourceful reporter realized that

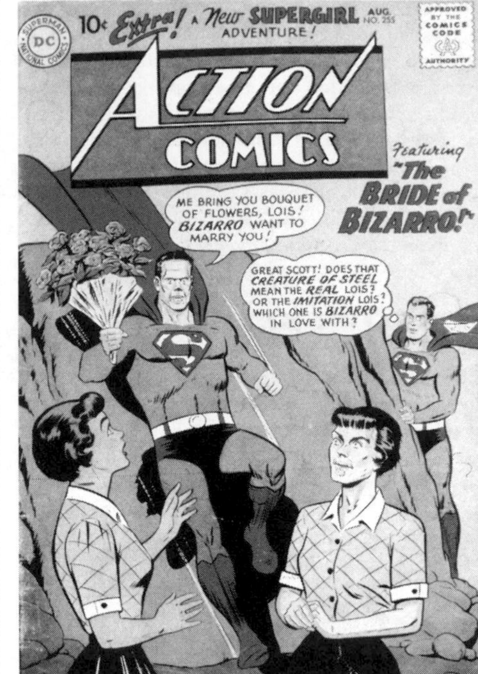

what Bizarro needed was to be among "his own kind," and, gaining access to the duplicator, she created an equally imperfect replica of herself (*Action Comics* #255, August 1959).

Realizing they would always be misunderstood and shunned on Earth, Bizarro and the newly created Bizarro Lois left Earth in search of another planet to live on. In a distant star system, they found a once-inhabited planet whose civilization had died out, leaving only the remnants of its architecture and advanced technology. Tiring of their Adam-and-Eve-like existence, Bizarro responded to his mate's loneliness by creating from the alien tech an "Imitator Ray" that would produce exact duplicates of himself and Bizarro Lois—that is, copies that were not imprecise in some other way. Evidently, Bizarro's inexact copy of Superman's mind retained just enough of the Man of Steel's super-intelligence to design and build a device that could function as intended.

They called their new world, now populated by hundreds of thousands of identical Bizarros and Bizarro Loises, Htrae (*Earth* spelled backward).

The first Bizarro became Htrae's leader and took to wearing a large medallion around his neck plainly identifying himself as BIZARRO NO. 1, just as his "first lady" wore one identifying her as BIZARRO-LOIS NO. 1. Together they ruled their world like king and queen, seated in stone thrones in a tumble-down "palace" in their imitation Metropolis, which they called Bizarro City.

Just as any human society needed to be governed by laws, so, too, did the Bizarros evolve their own code: "Us do opposite of all earthly things. Us hate beauty. Us love ugliness. Is big crime to make anything perfect on Bizarro World." Superman learned of this ethos on a visit to Htrae when he made the mistake of repairing what he mistook to be their dysfunctional infrastructure. Arrested and put on trial for violating the code by correcting imperfections, Superman redeemed himself and escaped punishment by reshaping the perfectly spherical Htrae into an imperfect cube (*Action Comics* #263, April 1960, and #264, May 1960)!

In time, Superman learned that Bizarro was capable of reproducing by more "natural" means, although how that was possible, given that Bizarro and his mate were formed of nonliving matter, was never explained. Nevertheless, Bizarro Lois gave her husband a baby boy Bizarro, an event at first deemed tragic because of the infant's "birth defect": Bizarro's son resembled a perfectly normal-looking human male. Superman's efforts to help the couple resulted in the discovery that all Bizarro children would be born this way, only taking on the white, "chiseled" characteristics of adult Bizarro skin later in life, much as tadpoles naturally morph into frogs. In the course of being taken to live on Earth as a human in the orphanage where LINDA LEE had grown up (see SUPERGIRL), Bizarro, Junior, gained access to the duplicator ray in Superman's FORTRESS OF SOLITUDE, accidentally creating a Bizarro Supergirl, and exposed a mass of green kryptonite to the ray as well.

This led to another discovery: While Bizarros were immune to the effects of the "regular" green radiation, an imperfectly duplicated version of the radioactive isotope, in the form of blue kryptonite, was lethal to them, and Bizarro Supergirl succumbed to its effects (*Superman* [first series] #140, October 1960). Now prepared for the initial shock of a human-looking newborn, the Bizarro First Family added a daughter who looked exactly like her mother as a child (*Superman* [first series] #143, February 1961).

In short order, life on the Bizarro World degenerated into a kind of grotesque parody of Superman's life on Earth, with Bizarro duplicates of the Man of Steel's friends and enemies being created

under strange circumstances, with predictably unpredictable results. For example, Bizarro No. 1 established his own version of Superman's Fortress of Solitude—this one called the "Fourtriss uv Bizarro" and located in a desert rather than the frigid wastes of the Arctic—and in it he kept his own version of the duplicator ray. It was there that his son, Bizarro, Junior, played with the device, shining the ray into space, where it created a Bizarro version of the Fifth Dimensional imp MR. MXYZPTLK. The Bizarro version—called Mr. Kltpzyxm, of course—bedeviled Bizarro by improving the imperfections around him and normalizing his environment.

As Bizarro Clark Kent, Superman's grotesque double went to work at the *Daily Htrae,* where his colleagues included Bizarro JIMMY OLSEN and Bizarro PERRY WHITE. Early on, Bizarro No. 1 created another Bizarro Krypto, who was timid and routinely "treed" by Bizarro cats, even though he could fly. On another occasion, the duplicator ray was trained on a television set receiving a news broadcast from Earth of TV reporter LANA LANG interviewing Lois Lane's younger sister, and Bizarro Lana Lang and Bizarro LUCY LANE were born. Before accounts of pre–First Crisis Bizarros began to occur less frequently, there had been created a heroic and humanitarian Bizarro Lex Luthor; a Bizarro bottle city of KANDOR; and a Bizarro TITANO the Super-Ape, who was groomed to become a TV wrestler (*Adventure Comics* #285–299, June 1961–August 1962).

At around this time, documents were discovered revealing that Superboy, who periodically visited the pre–First Crisis Earth-1's thirtieth century for adventures with the LEGION OF SUPER-HEROES, had learned from his fellow Legionnaires of the creation of a Bizarro version of that super-team. A Bizarro Superboy came to thirtieth-century Earth demanding membership in the club and, when rejected, flew off in a huff to create his own Legion, which included Bizarro LIGHTNING LAD, Bizarro SATURN GIRL, Bizarro BRAINIAC 5, Bizarro CHAMELEON BOY, Bizarro Invisible Kid, Bizarro COSMIC BOY, Bizarro Mon-El, and Bizarro ULTRA BOY. They called themselves the LEGION OF STUPOR-BIZARROS. When they began to create havoc on Earth, the real Legion defeated them and forced them to disband, leaving no record of their existence other than one account (*Adventure Comics* #329, February 1965).

A Bizarro Legion figured into at least two other iterations of the Legion of Super-Heroes' time lines. In one, an experiment involving Bizarro genetic material went awry, temporarily transforming Brainiac 5, FERRO, Karate Kid, Kinetix, Leviathan II, LIVE WIRE, Magno, M'onel, Spark, and Triad into chalk-white creatures (*Legion of Super-Heroes* [fourth series] #113–115, March–May 1999). In another, Colossal Boy, Shadow Lass, and Sun Boy were among those said to have Bizarro counterparts—at least in a perhaps-apocryphal account related by Lightning Lad (*Legion of Super-Heroes* [fifth series] #5, June 2005).

Not long before the First Crisis that wiped out the inhabitants of Htrae and their world, Bizarro visited Earth a handful of times. However, a collision with a meteor of unknown origin had by then reversed some of his powers, granting him freeze-vision rather than heat vision; fire-breath rather than freezing super-breath; and X-ray vision that could see through lead but nothing else (*Superman* [first series] #306, December 1976). During this time, the Bizarros had continued to monitor developments on Earth and imitate them: Just as Clark Kent had begun working at the Galaxy Broadcasting building, reporting to MORGAN EDGE, so did Bizarro Kent work for Bizarro Morgan Edge at Htrae's misshapen Molekul Secrecy Building (*Superman* [first series] #333, March 1979).

By this point, a Bizarro BATMAN, whose post–First Crisis version would be known for a time as "Batzarro" (*Superman/Batman* #20–25, June 2005–May 2006), had come into being, as had a Bizarro JOKER (*World's Finest Comics* #156, March 1966). There would also be another Bizarro Supergirl (*DC Comics Presents* #71, July 1984). Other documents attested to the existence of a Bizarro

Justice League, first hinted at by accounts of a Bizarro version of the Flash, who boasted that he was the slowest Bizarro on Htrae (*Superman's Girl Friend, Lois Lane* #74, May 1967). This was confirmed by the later appearance of Bizarro Wonder Woman (*DC Comics Presents* #71, July 1984), Bizarro-Hawkman, and a Bizarro Aquaman who couldn't swim. Perhaps the strangest of all was the Bizarro Yellow Lantern, yellow objects being the one thing that the pre–First Crisis Green Lantern's power ring could not affect (*Superman* [first series] #379, January 1983). Unlike the normal Justice League, whose headquarters had been established inside a hollow mountain and, later, an orbiting satellite, the Bizarro League convened in a submarine at the bottom of an ocean, from which it was exceedingly difficult to be aware of Bizarro code-busting activity elsewhere on Htrae (*DC Comics Presents* #71, July 1984).

After the First Crisis created a single, unified Earth, Lex Luthor was reincarnated not as a criminal scientific genius, but as an untrustworthy billionaire industrialist of dubious ethics and sinister objectives. And many of those goals were the same as his earlier counterpart's, such as creating a duplicate of Superman who would answer only to him. To that end, Luthor had arranged the defection of a brilliant bioengineer named Teng from the People's Republic of China. Luthor put Teng to work on "Project Changeling," for which Teng devised the "bio-matrix" with which he claimed he could clone any known form of life perfectly. When Luthor lured Superman into a confrontation in LexCorp's Hong Kong office, Teng scanned Superman's entire cellular and molecular structure into his bio-matrix device. But until seeing the data from the sensor scan, neither Luthor nor Teng had known that Superman was an alien. Teng could only replicate Superman's body structure, minus the unknown elements in Kryptonian DNA that were not present in human genes. Teng hoped that his device could compensate for the differences between human and Kryptonian DNA, but this hope proved futile when what emerged from the bio-matrix was an unstable, "imperfect duplicate."

Because Teng's clone looked exactly like the Man of Steel and possessed all his powers, it appeared perfect at first, but its body quickly began to deteriorate as the bio-matrix rejected the Kryptonian DNA. When its cells began to crystallize, the clone took on a white, chalky appearance. Contemptuous of Teng's failure, Luthor ordered the "bizarre" creature destroyed. He needn't have bothered; the imperfections in this duplicate, like those of the later Bizarros that were the result of LexCorp's subsequent attempts to create a Superman clone, would eventually prove fatal to it.

But before the duplicate could be destroyed or die of natural causes, as it were, it escaped into the streets of Metropolis, where it became clear that although it was mute and seemed mindless, it retained some dim instinct that drove it to imitate Superman, including wearing a jacket and glasses over its still-visible costume. This creature, who would be dubbed Bizarro only much later, had Superman's basic morality, including a drive to save the imperiled. But, just as was the case with the pre–First Crisis Bizarro, the citizens of Metropolis fled from the imperfect duplicate in horror. The exception was Lucy Lane, Lois's younger sister, who had been a flight attendant like her Earth-1 counterpart until being blinded by exposure to chemicals of unknown origin.

Too despondent over her sightlessness to stave off deep depression, Lucy surrendered to a suicidal impulse and threw herself from her sister's apartment window. But the duplicate saved her life by catching her in midair, and in the course of this some white crystalline residue from its skin got into her eyes and somehow began to restore her vision.

Superman confronted his doppelgänger when it appeared at the Daily Planet Building, and Bizarro met Superman's assault with unrestrained ferocity. The brawl spilled into the streets and raged until the creature, seeing Lois Lane and feeling some vague echo of his attraction to her, captured the reporter and flew back to her apartment, where a rattled Lucy, who had gradually begun to see again, waited. Superman arrived in pursuit of the creature, and in their final confrontation realized the duplicate wasn't actually alive, but more like an android. Thus relieved of his obligation to pull his punches, the Man of Steel resolved to strike with full force. But this Bizarro actually threw himself into Superman head-on, allowing the impact to demolish his clone body. The strange white dust of which he'd been composed rained down on Lucy, its composition counteracting the chemicals that had blinded her and completing the process of restoring her sight (*Man of Steel* #5, October 1986).

Sometime later, when Luthor was dying, he had a member of his then-current research team, Sydney Happerson, revisit Teng's technology in the hope of creating a body in which Luthor could live on. The Bizarro "clone" once again was doomed to degenerate, but somewhat more slowly. This second Bizarro also seemed more human, possessing speech and emotions, the strongest of which involved "Lo-iz." This Bizarro sought to impress her by creating his own "world" from junk and refuse in a warehouse, a surreal version of Metropolis over which "Lo-iz" could reign like a queen. He then kidnapped the reporter and effectively held her hostage in his weird, distorted mini-city while Superman searched frantically for her. Before Superman ultimately rescued Lois, Bizarro helped put a stop to Happerson and Luthor's agenda—then died in Lois's arms (*Superman* [second series] #87–88, March–April 1994; *The Adventures of Superman* #510, March 1994; *Action Comics* #697, March 1994; *Superman: The Man of Steel* #32, April 1994).

Thereafter, additional Bizarro clones were spawned by LexCorp scientists sporadically, with only incremental improvements. Surprisingly, the longer each clone was left to develop on its own, the more closely the personality it evolved seemed patterned on Superman's. All the clones would attempt to save Lois Lane from any danger, and that protectiveness unfortunately extended to guarding Lois against the real Superman.

Around this time, Project Cadmus had also been attempting to create a Superman clone, once producing similar results—a Bizarro Superboy who eventually emerged from stasis and died (*Superboy* [second series] *Annual* #2, 1995).

It was unknown how many LexCorp personnel aside from Luthor himself had access to the Bizarro genotype or the means to produce Bizarros of their own. The only other confirmed instance of a Bizarro being created outside LexCorp was masterminded by the Contessa del Portenza, who created a Bizarro whom she ordered to kidnap her daughter Lena Luthor to take her away from her father. But this duplicate, as imperfect as all the others, did not survive for very long (*Superman Forever* #1, June 1998).

The third post-Crisis incarnation of Bizarro was not a product of genetic engineering. Instead he was the perverse inspiration of the Batman's psychotic enemy, the Joker, who had obtained the reality-altering powers of Mr. Mxyzptlk. The Clown Prince of Crime called into existence a mixed-up Earth in which bizarre new villains made up an unruly Justice League. And while Bizarro once more came into being as Superman's opposite number,

with powers equal to the Man of Steel's, there was a particularly nasty twist: Not only was this Bizarro immune to harm from kryptonite, but he actually gained greater strength when exposed to it. This Bizarro had smooth gray, rather than faceted chalk-white, skin and wore a perpetual rictus-like grin not unlike the Joker's own (*Superman* [second series] #160–161, September–October 2000).

This Bizarro, who made his headquarters in what he called his Graveyard of Solitude, was one of the few of the Joker's constructs saved by Mr. Mxyzptlk from the conjured-up "Jokerworld" after the Joker was stripped of his stolen powers. He was later captured by the dictator of Pokolistan, General Zod, and tortured, apparently because mistreating a creature who resembled Superman was the next best thing to torturing Superman himself. Bizarro was able to escape Pokolistan with Superman's help, and he re-created his former headquarters, the Graveyard of Solitude, from which he periodically emerged thereafter to "help" or antagonize Superman as the whim struck him (*Action Comics* #785, January 2002; others).

Invited to join Luthor's villainous Society, Bizarro agreed only after participating in a race with a super-speed-empowered criminal named Zoom. By winning the race, Bizarro had disgraced himself. "Bizarro not agree to not join if me not win race me not agree to run against jerk me not like. See?" (*Action Comics* #831, November 2005). The association only encouraged darker impulses, most tragically when Bizarro literally beat to death a veteran super hero known as the Human Bomb (*Infinite Crisis* #1, December 2005).

Bizarro is known to have survived the INFINITE CRISIS, and was revealed to have been held captive by Lex Luthor for approximately thirteen months after that event, continually watching TV in his small cell and gaining some small degree of intelligence as a result.

The post-Infinite Crisis Superman learned from a hologram of JOR-EL in the Fortress that yellow sunlight, which gives Superman strength, could weaken Bizarro, while the light from a younger, blue sun could increase his power. That energy also endowed Bizarro with "Bizarro vision," with which he was able to create other Bizarros and populate a new, cubed post-Infinite Crisis Bizarro World. Like the pre-First Crisis version, this one was home to Bizarro duplicates of all Superman's friends, and even of a Bizarro Justice League stranger than the one that had existed on pre-First Crisis Earth-1 (*Action Comics* #855–857, October–December 2007).

Bizarro appears to have some innate sense of his connection to Kal-El, as evidenced by his visit to the grave of Jonathan Kent, where he uttered "Me am happy" (*Superman* #682, November 2008). Not long afterward, he was abducted by members of Kandor's Military Guild and placed for a brief time in the Phantom Zone (*Superman* #684, January 2009). After being freed by Superman, Bizarro left Earth for a time and returned to assist in the cosmic event known as Blackest Night, where he incinerated the Black Lantern version of Solomon Grundy (*Superman/Batman* #66–67, December 2009–January 2010).

BIZARRO, A.

The clone of Al Beezer, a former employee of the LEXCORP of the post-FIRST CRISIS unified Earth. Al Bizarro was originally the product of an early test of the cloning process developed for LEX LUTHOR by Dr. Sydney Happerson. After the cloning equipment eventually produced the desired result, the prototype was placed in suspended animation and forgotten. Upon being freed, he began a quest to establish his own identity and a purpose in life, an odyssey taking him to such far-flung locations as APOKOLIPS, with lack of fulfillment and despair dogging him at every turn. Along the way, when the clone met his "parent," Al Beezer told Al Bizarro that, if he wanted to be happy, he should do "the exact opposite" of everything the original Al did.

And so, back on Earth, Al, Seera—a FEMALE FURY wannabe he met on Apokolips—and another hanger-on he picked up in his travels, the con man J. WILBUR WOLFINGHAM, groomed Al for a career as a rock star, at which he was a great success. All this time, Al was also on the run from Lex Luthor, who claimed that Al was his property. Escaping Luthor, the trio made their way to the South American nation of San Lattée, where they led a rebellion against the corrupt government, resulting in a democratically elected president. Al married one of the rebels he led, Rosamunda, and presumably remained in San Lattée at least until the time of the INFINITE CRISIS. There has been no account of an Al Bizarro existing on New Earth (*A. Bizarro* #1–4, July–October 1999).

BIZARRO CODE

See Bizarro.

BIZARRO WORLD

See Bizarro.

BLACK, MANCHESTER

A British-born telekinetic, telepath, and crypto-fascist whose ability to manipulate minds and control others' perception of reality was used to serve an extreme concept of "justice" that Superman found deeply repugnant. Black, supposedly a vigilante, not only rejected Superman's code of never killing, but instead—as the leader of the Elite, a small team of "crime fighters"—ordered the murder of every criminal the group encountered.

Despising Superman's "corny" and "unrealistic" regard for human life, Black positioned himself as the Man of Steel's sworn enemy (*Action Comics* #775, March 2001; others). After being defeated by Superman, Black was pardoned and released from prison by then-president Lex Luthor, who drafted him to lead a new Suicide Squad during the war with Imperiex (*The Adventures of Superman* #593-594, August-September 2001). With his psionic abilities, it did not take Black long to uncover the identities of all of Superman's friends and family, who soon found themselves in danger from a host of super-villains sent against them by Black in a vicious vendetta against the Man of Steel.

Ultimately, Superman prevailed over the phalanx of old enemies dispatched by Black, and tracked the telepath back to Clark Kent's apartment, where Black appeared to have killed his wife Lois Lane. This was Black's endgame, to provoke the Man of Steel into killing Black, thereby proving that Superman, with all his high-blown pretensions about the sanctity of life, was in the end no less debased than Black himself. But at the eleventh hour, Superman pulled back, realizing that Lois was still alive and that her death was merely a psionically staged ruse to corrupt the Man of Steel.

Black retreated in defeat and, after erasing the knowledge of Superman's secret identity and his other intimate secrets from Lex Luthor's mind, as well as from LexCorp's databases, went into seclusion in a seedy motel room. There he was believed to have committed suicide when he used his tele-

kinesis to destroy the motel in a fiery explosion. While Superman believed they'd seen the last of Manchester Black, Lois was not quite so convinced (*Action Comics* #795-796, November-December 2002; *The Adventures of Superman* #608-609, November-December 2002; *Superman* [second series] #186-187, November-December 2002).

BLACK FLAME

An auburn-haired, masked super-criminal on the post-First Crisis Earth-1 and self-proclaimed enemy of Supergirl. Black Flame presented herself as the Girl of Steel's equal with persuasive justification: She claimed to be Kara's sixtieth-century descendant. With additional tools such as a "brain command ring," Black Flame was even able to bend Comet the Super-Horse to her will.

Horrified that her bloodline might eventually result in a super-terrorist, Supergirl exposed herself to gold kryptonite, seemingly stripping herself and all her descendants of their powers. In fact, that was exactly what Black Flame had wanted. She was secretly Zora Vi-Lar, a friend—and perhaps relative—of the criminal Lesla-Lar. Vi-Lar had left the bottle city of Kandor to seek revenge for Lesla-Lar's defeat and death. Supergirl, however, had already deduced this, having detected in Vi-Lar dental work that wouldn't have been present in someone who'd had superpowers since birth. Supergirl had merely faked her exposure to gold kryptonite. Black Flame was not so lucky: She had her superpowers permanently removed when she was exposed to a few genuine grains of the golden radioactive element (*Action Comics* #304, September 1963).

Years later, the supposedly reformed Vi-Lar resumed her costumed alter ego in an unsuccessful attempt at trapping Supergirl and Superman in the dimension where Kandor then existed (*Krypton Chronicles* #1-2, September-October 1981).

Two previous accounts chronicled evident returns of Black Flame. In one, she and Catwoman had seemingly joined forces, only to be unmasked as Mr. Mxyzptlk and Bat-Mite (*World's Finest Comics* #169, September 1967). On another occasion, Black Flame conspired with three Phantom Zone escapees to torment Supergirl and ultimately expose her to gold kryptonite, but numerous details in this account contradicted other documents and suggested that this assertion was apocryphal (*Adventure Comics* #400, December 1970).

BLACK MERCY, THE

A fungus-like alien parasite that kept its victims docile while draining their life force by placing them in trances in which they had dreams of their greatest desires being fulfilled. The Black Mercy *Cater clemtia* plants are the seeds expelled by the plant known as the Mother Mercy. Upon maturity, the plants were sent out among the stars with the intention of healing the sick and alleviating the suffering of the dying. When the Mother Mercy's home planet was discovered by Mongul, he began harvesting and weaponizing the plants. Mongul sent one such plant to Superman, disguised as an anonymous Christmas gift, but the Man of Steel was freed from the parasite by the combined efforts of Wonder Woman, Batman, and Robin. (*Superman* [first series] *Annual* #11, 1985).

Recently, Mongul's son and members of the Sinestro Corps have managed to use the Black Mercy to spread fear across the galaxy.

BLACKROCK

First seen in the pre-First Crisis Metropolis of Earth-1, the original Blackrock seemed to be either a super hero or a super-criminal, depending on whether you happened to be Superman or not. Clad in a green costume with a purple hood that completely concealed his face, Blackrock was Superman's first nemesis to have a different civilian identity every time he appeared—ultimately having no alter ego whatsoever, because by that point he wasn't even human.

The source of all four pre-First Crisis Blackrocks' powers was the same, even as the technology designed to tap it kept evolving: radio and TV waves. In each iteration, Blackrock could convert broadcast signals into energy he could manipulate at will. But with each reappearance, Blackrock's tech was upgraded somewhat, and his ability to exploit it in ever more imaginative ways grew by quantum leaps. Thus, at his most formidable, he was able to create visual and auditory illusions;

short out any communications device at will; and disintegrate into tiny particles of black energy, in which form he could assume any shape he chose as well as ride broadcast waves at light speed to any destination on Earth. Blackrock could also fashion a defensive force field or fire concentrated beams of destructive power made from those charged particles.

While he first focused his black energy with a wand designed to resemble a miniature TV antenna, Blackrock later employed a "power stone," a polished jet-black gem that looked like a baseball-sized rock strapped to his hand. With this "black rock" drawing on a nearly inexhaustible power source, Blackrock could marshal such potent energy that even Superman and the first Kara Zor-El Supergirl were vulnerable to its effects. But this unique power also gave him a unique weakness: In areas where broadcast signals did not reach, such as behind lead shielding or in underground tunnels, Blackrock could be rendered powerless.

In his first appearance, Blackrock was more of a competitor to Superman than an enemy, interfering with and complicating the Man of Steel's mission by trying to catch the crooks before Superman did. His name was coined by TV gossip maven Lola Barnett, who thought the energy particles looked like tiny black rocks. He was a made-to-order menace, created for Samuel Tanner, president of the United Broadcasting Company, a close second in the ratings wars to the Galaxy Broadcasting System. Tanner's Metropolis station was a fierce rival of Galaxy's WGBS-TV, and Tanner suspected that Galaxy had so many Superman "exclusives" because the Man of Steel deliberately favored it over him. So Tanner turned to the most brilliant physicist in his R&D lab, Peter Silverstone, to create a super hero for UBC to exploit as its very own.

Having invented the tech and built the costume, Silverstone then decided only Tanner himself had the "right stuff" to be effective in the role. Silverstone hypnotized Tanner, without the latter's knowledge or consent, into donning the suit, with the intended result of improved ratings for UBC. But no one besides Silverstone knew who Blackrock really was—not even Tanner—because of a post-hypnotic suggestion that Tanner would remember nothing of his experiences as Blackrock (*Action Comics* #458–459, April–May 1976).

Months later, when UBC's ratings had returned to their pre-Blackrock lows, Silverstone revived the "character," this time in the person of Tanner's nephew, TV comedian Les Vegas, who was also hypnotized and left with no recollection of his connection to Blackrock. Again, Superman defeated the black energy wielder, and Vegas got on with his life, never knowing what he had done (*Superman* [first series] #315, September 1977).

In their remaining pre-First Crisis encounters, Blackrock became more of an overt enemy to the Caped Kryptonians. The third Blackrock wasn't even human but, rather, an energy construct. Silverstone avoided the need to manipulate yet a third person by using charged ions to animate the costume itself (*Superman* [first series] #325–326, July–August 1978). Ultimately, Silverstone was unmasked as the real brains behind Blackrock, but only because he made the mistake of assuming the mantle himself, in desperation and on his own initiative, to commit industrial espionage when his own inventiveness had begun to dry up. This time, Blackrock found himself pitted against the original Supergirl, who blew his cover when she turned him over to the police. At the time of the multiverse's "implosion" during the First Crisis, Silverstone was serving a prison term at a low-security federal penitentiary and was said to find it salutary to have an enforced vacation from the constant pressure to invent (*Superman Family* #212–213, November–December 1981).

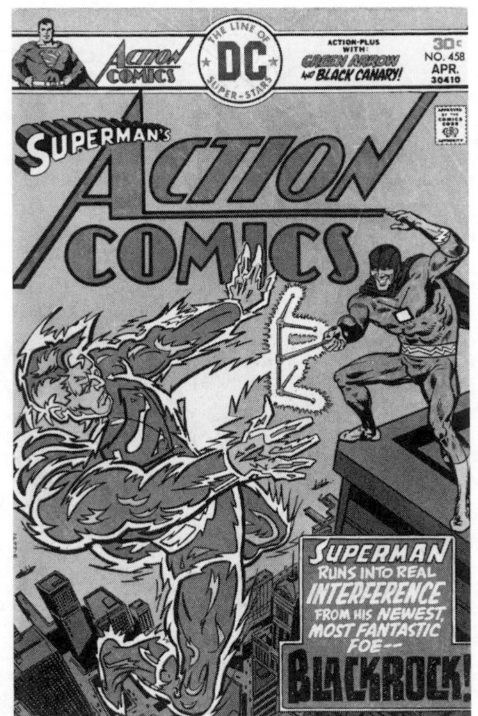

On the post-First Crisis Earth, before the Infinite Crisis, the term *Blackrock* was less commonly used to denote a super-villain than to refer to a source of power. Although a version of Dr. Peter Silverstone surfaced there, Samuel Tanner was among the millions "deleted" by the First Crisis. In this world, the costumed Blackrock had likewise fought Superman in the past, but he had been Silverstone exclusively. Now reduced to hanging out in a super-villain bar, Silverstone once saw his power stone—along with other villainous talismans—briefly stolen by tabloid reporter Wally Tortolini (*Justice League America* #43–44, October–November 1990). The scientist was now aged beyond his years because of overexposure to the energies of "the Blackrock."

In Silverstone's first documented appearance in this reality, his lengthy exposure to the rock had blinded him and left him an insane hermit holed up in his apartment, a constant TV couch potato, mumbling to himself. Or so he was found by the ex-convict who had just moved in next door, a violent sociopath named Sam Benjamin, who stole the Blackrock after beating Silverstone to death with it. Between data gleaned from Silverstone's semi-coherent rambling and some Internet research of his own, Benjamin surmised that the Blackrock was a kind of symbiotic alien life-form, rather than the product of a laboratory. Its appearance and abilities seemed to be identical to the pre-First Crisis version, but to Benjamin's disordered mind it seemed as if the black stone were sentient, and that the rock itself "decided if its host was worth its power." Or, perhaps more accurately, the power it generated was proportionate to how strong its host was. Silverstone, in his weakened state, had little power left.

Using the Blackrock, Benjamin attacked the city, sending destructive black beams through several buildings to flush out Superman. Superman ultimately overcame Benjamin's black energy with heat vision, wresting the stone from him and hurling it into the sun, but not before panicking a Metropolis already spooked by media speculation on how well Superman could be trusted to control his vision powers in particular. As if to echo that sentiment, when Superman demanded to know why Benjamin had gone on a rampage, he replied, "Because you're Superman. Because you don't belong here" (*Superman* [second series] #218, August 2005).

A short time later, during the Infinite Crisis, Alexander Luthor, Junior, disguised as Lex Luthor, dispatched Bizarro to retrieve the Blackrock from the sun. He then passed it on to a drug-smuggling female Peruvian revolutionary known only as Lucia, who had been previously jailed by Superman after trying to destroy the new Fortress of Solitude in Pucallpa (*Superman* [second series] #217, July 2005).

In their second encounter, in the desert outside Las Vegas, Lucia used the Blackrock to achieve vengeance against Superman, claiming that the stone could sense her intense hatred of the Man of Steel—and shared it. Though she proved particularly skillful in using the rock, Superman trapped her behind lead shielding, cutting off the stone's ability to draw power from transmission waves. At that point, the Blackrock "disconnected" its psychic bond and withdrew from its host (*Superman*

[second series] #224, February 2006). The Blackrock was confiscated by Superman and locked away in the Fortress. But it eventually "escaped" when Batman and the super-stretchable hero Plastic Man retrieved it to use in opposing Superman, who was believed to be in the grip of an alien power that was controlling his mind. Superman threw off the alien domination in time, and in turn freed Batman from the Blackrock's parasitic mind control (*Superman/Batman* #31–33, January–March 2007). As of this writing, an iteration of Blackrock has not been documented on the post-Infinite Crisis New Earth.

BLACK ZERO

The Black Zero of the pre-First Crisis Earth-1 dimension was a member of a ruthless network of space pirates and terrorists who dedicated themselves to the destruction of entire planets. He was bald and had no fingerprints; purple eyes; and a forked tongue.

This Black Zero drew Superman's fire, so to speak, when he targeted Earth with an anti-matter missile. In the course of their battle, he told Superman that three decades previously he had been assigned by the Pirate Empire to destroy Krypton. His superiors had determined that the molecular instability at the planet's core that ultimately would have destroyed it was naturally abating, requiring Black Zero's intervention to make sure Krypton's grim destiny would be fulfilled. But this account may well have been apocryphal, as it was confirmed by no other report. It seemed far more likely that, with no way to disprove his story, Black Zero simply claimed to have destroyed Krypton to enhance his reputation (*Superman* [first series] #205, April 1968).

On the post-First Crisis incarnation of Krypton, its inhabitants extended their lives with clone banks, essentially living organ farms of cloned duplicates in three distinct stages of physical development. These were kept in suspended animation, during which they were harvested for replacement body parts. Here, *Black Zero* was the name of a subversive cult that protested this "genetic slavery," precipitating the infamous Kryptonian War of Clone Rights, which lasted for a thousand years. This Black Zero's final terrorist act was the detonation of a nuclear device in the planet's core, eventually resulting in Krypton's destruction many centuries later (*The World of Krypton* [second series] #1–4, December 1987–March 1988).

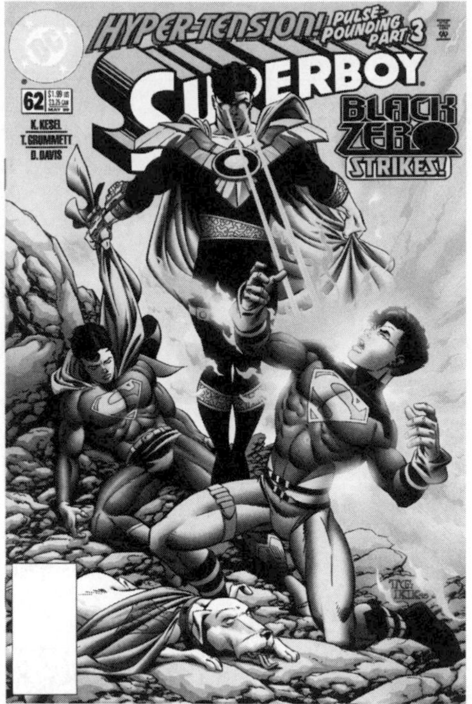

A second terrorist group calling itself Black Zero II later developed an artificially intelligent computer virus—a "Trojan" that was inadvertently activated by Apparition in the Kryptonian technology Superman used to build his Fortress of Solitude. Running Black Zero II's program caused a distorted reenactment of a Kryptonian history that would have climaxed with the destruction of Earth. It was halted when the Legion of Super-Heroes' Brainiac 5 caused a power outage, and was eventually quarantined and deleted from the Fortress computers (*Superman Plus* #1, February 1997).

A fourth entity called Black Zero was a counterpart of the Kon-El Superboy from a Hypertime stream in which Superman had remained dead and Kon-El had been allowed to mature to adulthood, replacing Superman and deploying not only a full complement of Kryptonian superpowers but also his "tactile telekinesis." This Superman II, however, was convinced he encountered resentment for not being the equal of the original Superman. Heroes and civilians were killed in the riots that resulted when this older clone Superboy's inexperience led to a public backlash against cloning. Among those who died in the mob violence was the super hero Guardian, which led Superman II to resolve to stop the anti-clone faction no matter what it took.

Inspired by Kryptonian history, he took the name Black Zero to go undercover in his struggle for clone rights, eventually instigating a war in which most of Earth's heroes died. He was ultimately stopped by a coalition of Kon-El counterparts from other timestreams, led by the Superboy of the post-Crisis Earth (*Superboy* [third series] #61–64, April–July 1999).

A fifth Black Zero was a group of mercenaries in Infinite City, a pocket dimension that Jor-El had futilely hoped to make into a refuge for Krypton's people. Although its precise nature and motivations were unclear, this Black Zero seemed to have taken its name from the ancient Kryptonian terrorist group and worked to circumvent Infinite City's strict immigration policies (*Superman: Infinite City,* 2005).

The most recent iteration of Black Zero was the name of an elite strike force within Krypton's Military Guild (see Guilds), of which the parents of Thara Ak-Var, aka Flamebird, were members (*Action Comics Annual* #12, 2009; others).

BLAZE

A horned, red-skinned "demi-demon," several millennia old, and the sister of Lord Satanus, whose parents were the wizard Shazam and a female demon (*Power of Shazam!* #10, December 1995). Though her brother disagreed, Blaze claimed to be the sole and absolute ruler of an other-dimensional Netherworld—what metaphysicians called Hell. Indeed, she and Satanus used Superman as a pawn in their struggle for control over that realm on at least one occasion and possibly others, since not all the goings-on in that largely hidden Netherworld were documented.

Whatever matter Blaze's Netherworld may

have been composed of, she ruled that as well, having the power to animate what appeared to be volcanic rock and lava. Blaze could also teleport between dimensions and effortlessly morph into any shape at will. She behaved in classic biblical devil-tempter fashion, corrupting mortals and, it was said, stealing their souls. She also called herself "the eternal deceiver"—which, for many who came into contact with her, was further proof that her seemingly insane boasts were at best lies and at worst lunatic ravings.

But then there were those who, thanks to Superman, survived her attempts to seduce and damn them, and they swore that everything Blaze claimed was true. Occasionally, she granted certain mystic powers to the condemned souls she ruled, but she never relinquished a fraction of her hold on them. How many creatures of evil she was responsible for was not known; her involvement in the creation of the Silver Banshee, for example, was comparatively subtle and indirect (*Action Comics* #662, February 1991; others), and there may have been other similar cases. The earliest verified instance of her corruptive influence, however, dates back to the late 1880s, when she seduced the British physician Aleister Hook, transforming him into the winged Skyhook, who appeared in the post-First Crisis Metropolis after nearly two centuries in oblivion (*Superman* [second series] #34, August 1989, and #47, September 1990).

In order to gain better access to souls for the stealing, Blaze assumed human form as Angelica Blaze, having acquired the abandoned and deconsecrated St. Christopher's Church and turned it into a dance club. There she nurtured the outsized ambition of corrupting and collecting every soul on Earth. Jerry White, son of the *Daily Planet* managing editor, applied for a job there and soon found himself in Blaze's thrall. Under her influence, White became involved in drug trafficking, with the result that he and his friend Jimmy Olsen were shot by Intergang gunmen. Blaze captured their souls and repaired to her hellish domain with them in tow. As the young men's mortal bodies remained on life support in Metropolis General Hospital, Superman pursued their souls with the help of New God the Black Racer. Superman ultimately reclaimed Jimmy's soul and caused the apparent destruction of Blaze's domain in a gigantic explosion, but not before Jerry White sacrificed himself to save Jimmy, and the Man of Steel had to face the proverbial hosts of Hell (*The Adventures of Superman* #469–470, August–September 1990; *Action Comics* #656–657, August–September 1990; *Superman* [second series] #47, September 1990).

Blaze subsequently gained a demonic foothold on Metropolis's Newstime building, a structure that was secretly the Earthly base of her brother Satanus. Correctly intuiting that Satanus coveted Superman's soul, Blaze imagined that her preemptive strike would enable her to beat her brother to that prize. Instead the ensuing family feud forced a grudging alliance between the Man of Steel and Satanus, whose power and knowledge were crucial in helping Superman rescue his friends from Blaze's realm (*The Adventures of Superman* #493, August 1992; *Action Comics* #680, August 1992; *Superman: The Man of Steel* #15, September 1992; *Superman* [second series] #71, September 1992).

Weeks later, after Superman had been slain by Doomsday, his adoptive father Jonathan Kent was hospitalized following a massive heart attack. While clinging to life in the ICU, Jonathan had an out-of-body experience in which his spirit interacted with what at first appeared to be people who had predeceased him. It soon became clear that one of these spectral figures was actually the soul of his dead son, Clark Kent, who was ready to move on to the afterlife permanently. Jonathan resisted this, trying to persuade Clark that it was not yet "his time." That was the point at which the entity responsible for the visions appeared: Blaze, attempting to break the spiritual bond between father and son.

Escaping Blaze's influence, Jonathan led Clark to another spiritual realm, where Clark found himself caught in a struggle between Jonathan and his birth father, Jor-El. As soon as Jonathan's soul drove off the soul of Jor-El and pulled Clark back to safety, the elder Kent awakened in the hospital, telling his wife Martha Kent that he had brought Clark back. Shortly thereafter, the news that Superman had returned began to circulate in Metropolis (*The Adventures of Superman* #500, June 1993).

Sometime later, after Brainiac 13's transformation of Metropolis into a high-tech City of Tomorrow, Satanus attempted to capture every soul in the city. Superman offered his own soul in exchange, but eventually he thwarted Satanus with the help of a young psychic and shaman named Night Eagle, who might actually have been Blaze in another human guise.

After the Infinite Crisis, it became clear that both Blaze and Satanus had been incarnated in the universe of New Earth as well. They became the rulers of Purgatory and fought Neron and a host of other demonic figures while leading a rebellion against the hierarchy of Hell, with Blaze and Satanus ultimately triumphant. Blaze then turned on her brother and became sole ruler of Hell (*Reign in Hell* #1–8, September 2008–April 2009; others).

BLINDSPOT

The ultimate master of camouflage whose light-refracting body stocking enabled him—as well as anything or anyone he seized—to blend into his surroundings and effectively become invisible. His real name was unknown, and little else was known about him other than that he was Asian American and an agent of Intergang.

Superman's first encounter with Blindspot occurred when the latter was assigned to kidnap *Daily Planet* columnist Catherine "Cat" Grant. The difficult-to-see Intergang agent blindsided Grant, her son Adam, and her bodyguard Jose Delgado (see Gangbuster) as the three of them left a theater. Blindspot captured Grant and might very well have spirited her away had it not been for the timely intervention of Delgado and plainclothes detective Slam Bradley, Junior. Jose helped Cat and Adam escape to safety, and Superman arrived on the scene, deactivating Blindspot's suit by ripping out its power pack (*Superman* [second series] #44, June 1990).

After serving time for the attempted kidnapping, the man who was Blindspot kept a low profile in Metropolis's Chinatown, not daring to resurface until Superman seemed to have dismantled Intergang. He then resumed his costumed criminal identity, his suit augmented with gauntlets fitted with "brass" knuckles made from the virtually indestructible alloy Promethium. These allowed him to punch through brick walls.

His first order of business was revenge against

Delgado and Bradley for his humiliation in failing to abduct Grant. But Superman, flying overhead, shorted out his cloaking circuitry with a burst of heat vision, allowing Delgado to deliver a knockout blow that would shame Blindspot for a second time (*The Adventures of Superman* #483, October 1991).

When last accounted for, Blindspot was in custody. It is not known whether he survived the Infinite Crisis to continue life on New Earth, or whether a new version of him exists there.

BLITHE

One of three entities known as Earth-born angels who appeared on the unified post-Crisis Earth (*Supergirl* [fifth series] #39, December 1999). The first of these "angels" was the Angel of Fire. She had been the protoplasmic, shape-shifting synthetic life-form called Supergirl, aka Matrix, who was secretly a young woman living in Leesburg, Virginia, named Linda Danvers. The Angel of Love was an entity named Comet, who also called Leesburg home. And the Angel of Light was the mysterious Blithe.

Little was known about Blithe's origins; the record showed only that she once opposed the Matrix Supergirl while in the service of Earth's first vampire, a demonic being calling itself Carnivore. But after her betrayal and rejection by the vampire, Blithe became the Matrix Supergirl's ally instead. Each Earth-born angel was created when one individual gave up his or her own life to save another who otherwise would have been hopelessly doomed. In each moment of ultimate sacrifice, the saved and the savior merged into one being, and that dual entity was known as an Earth-born angel, each with a unique pair of wings. Linda Danvers, for example, originally had been a troubled young woman under the spell of her boyfriend Buzz, who claimed to be a demon in disguise. Buzz had tempted Danvers into a variety of criminal acts while preparing to sacrifice her to his liege, a demon calling itself Lord Chakat. The Matrix Supergirl intervened to save Danvers, in the process losing her own life and fusing with Danvers to become the Earth-born Angel of Fire (*Supergirl* [fifth series] #10–50, June 1997–November 2000).

The newly transformed Supergirl no longer had the shape-shifting powers of Matrix, and the remains of her synthetic body that could not be absorbed into Danvers's organic one were transformed into an insane Matrix who fought the new Linda Danvers Supergirl. Blithe, on the other hand, seemed an unlikely candidate for angelhood, having served a demon herself. During her battle with the Matrix Supergirl at Carnivore's behest, she was crippled when trapped under an avalanche. Blithe's pleas for help from Carnivore not only went unanswered, but were met with overt scorn. Unfortunately, Blithe had been in love with the vampire, and she was so deeply wounded by this betrayal that she turned on her former master, retaliating by searching out the place where the insane, "leftover" Matrix was incarcerated and merging with her. Fusing with the protoplasmic form healed her damaged body and made her even more superpowerful, adding super-strength and the ability to fire blasts of psionic force to her repertoire. Blithe then joined forces with Comet and the new Linda Danvers Supergirl to destroy Carnivore with their combined angelic powers of Love, Fire, and Light.

As the Earth-born Angel of Light, Blithe could fly at super-speed on wings made of lightning. She could also fire blasts of electricity from antennae on her forehead and produce psionic light bursts, which she called her Light of Truth. This light could restore others' repressed memories.

BLOAT, MR.

A "matter osmosifier" classified as a "Magnitude Ten metacriminal" by the post–First Crisis Metropolis S.C.U. His real name was Hannibal Leach, but the more apropos code name *Bloat* was inspired by Leach's ability to absorb any material he touched into his own blubbery body. He was one of the more bizarre felons associated with Intergang. He and his partner Shrewface were subsequently recruited by the super hero Steel to help thwart the super-criminal Overmind's seizure of LexCorp's B13 technology (*Superman: The Man of Steel* #97, February 2000; #112, May 2001; #124, May 2002; #125, June 2002; others; see also Brainiac 13).

BLOCKHOUSE

See Cerberus.

BLOODSPORT

The tragic embodiment of a failure of personal responsibility, this man tried in vain to expiate his feelings of shame and remorse by blaming forces outside himself for the consequences of his own choices. A massively muscled African American in combat fatigues and a red "do-rag" fashioned into a makeshift mask, Bloodsport wore a high-tech device that enabled him to teleport weapons into his hands from an armory in an undisclosed location. His arsenal included not only conventional short-range firearms and military ordnance such as bazookas, but also experimental weaponry so advanced it could inflict damage on the post–First Crisis Superman, including a gun that could shoot needles made of kryptonite.

He appeared in Metropolis out of nowhere, seemingly insane and on a murderous rampage whose motivation or provocation was not immediately clear. His random acts of armed violence were punctuated by a crypto-fascist screed, claiming he was fed up with America's squandering of its precious freedoms that Bloodsport "and Mickey" fought for in 'Nam, and for which "Mickey" died.

He was, in reality, a man named Robert DuBois, and "Mickey" was his younger brother. Robert's rampage turned out to have been instigated by a man named Kimberly, who was charged with a sophisticated form of psy-op by billionaire Lex Luthor as part of the latter's never-ending quest for a surrogate to assassinate Superman. It was LexCorp that supplied the high-tech weaponry.

Superman lost the first round when wounded by Bloodsport's kryptonite needles so badly he required medical attention, but he confronted Bloodsport again as soon as he could stand. This time, the Man of Tomorrow used his heat vision with pinpoint accuracy, ionizing the air around Bloodsport without detonating any of his ordnance, and scrambled the teleporter. But Bloodsport then threatened to ignite his teleporter's power pack, blowing up ten square miles of the city. Fortunately, Jimmy Olsen, who had narrowly escaped death in one of Bloodsport's earliest attacks, had run down his true identity from an FBI fingerprint check. Olsen learned that during the Vietnam conflict, DuBois had received an induction notice calling him to serve in the U.S. Army. Like so many young men at that time, DuBois chose not to report to duty, but instead to dodge the draft and relocate in Canada. DuBois was no conscientious objector, however, nor even an ideological opponent of the war; he simply didn't want to die.

For reasons never stated on the record, DuBois's younger brother Michael posed as Robert and reported in his place. As Robert, Michael DuBois was deployed on a combat mission in which he lost both arms and both legs. The news of Michael's fate had made its way back to his brother in Canada, and the resulting guilt feelings had Robert in and out of psychiatric hospitals repeatedly over the next several years, increasingly obsessing on the war. It was in this state of mind that Luthor's operatives found him. A team led by Kimberly psychologically conditioned DuBois to kill Superman by conflating the Man of Steel with "the Cong" in a *Manchurian Candidate*-style scenario. They had further impaired his reality-testing ability and persuaded him that he had actually served in Vietnam and that his brother was dead.

Just as Bloodsport was about to blow his power pack, Olsen arrived on the scene accompanied by the wheelchair-bound Michael DuBois. Reminded by Michael that the war was over and hearing his impassioned plea to "let it end," Robert collapsed, overcome with grief. Perhaps the greatest tragedy of Robert DuBois—who later died in prison—was that he never achieved personal responsibility because he never really understood it: It never occurred to him that he was not to blame for his brother's decision, which was Michael's alone (*Superman* [second series] #4, April 1987).

Ironically, the second man who much later took the code name Bloodsport was a fanatical racist. Alex Trent was a member of the Aryan Brotherhood, a white supremacist group that Perry White and Franklin Stern encountered when they were young men. Trent used high-tech weapons provided by Bloodthirst to advance his agenda and attack ethnic minorities. This Bloodsport, too, had a weapons teleporter, but this one was cybernetically implanted in his body and wired to his nervous system. Superman captured him after *Daily Planet* reporter Ron Troupe destroyed the warehouse from which Bloodsport was teleporting his weapons.

Sometime later, a boxing match between the two Bloodsports was set up at Stryker's Island prison as part of the warden's effort to defuse rising tensions there—a battle witnessed from afar by Superman. Trent did not intend to fight fair with a man of color, however, and wanted only to use the match as a diversion that would facilitate a prison break. To that end, he found a way to reactivate his implanted teleporter and bring in weaponry. In the resulting confusion, DuBois was shot to death by guards while trying to escape. Trent was caught and returned to the prison by Superman, only to be set afire in his cell by fellow Brotherhood inmates, for showing weakness in front of DuBois (*Superman: The Man of Steel* #47 and *The Adventures of Superman* #526—both August 1995). Horribly scarred, Trent escaped prison one last time and was quickly recaptured (*Superman: The Man of Steel* #129, October 2002).

After the deaths of DuBois and Trent, the teleporter technology was used by the anti-corporate vigilante Demolitia, as it had been earlier by a deranged homeless man (*Superman* [second series] #59, September 1991). Meanwhile, an unnamed African American man—evidently a cellmate of DuBois—escaped from Stryker's Island and briefly operated as the third Bloodsport (*Batman and Superman: World's Finest* #10, January 2000). He resurfaced on New Earth in the aftermath of the Infinite Crisis, in the period immediately following Superman's disappearance, when the Man of Steel's powers gradually began to return. Some strength, invulnerability, and speed had come back, but he could not yet fly and had no vision powers. This made him particularly vulnerable to a combined assault from the Puzzler, Live Wire, Silver Banshee, Bloodsport, Hellgrammite, and Riot (*Superman* #652, July 2006). In his last documented appearance, he was known to have escaped the prison planet where dozens of Earth's super-criminals had been exiled (*Salvation Run* #7, July 2008).

BLOODTHIRST

A massive, shape-shifting, apparently cybernetic monstrosity with sharply fanged teeth and what looked like an external circulatory system of complex tubing, with strange nozzles on its boots and gauntlets that could emit toxic green gas. But despite its human-made appearance, Bloodthirst nevertheless claimed to be a demonic entity that had existed on Earth for thousands of years. It seemed to relish causing death and destruction for the sheer sadistic pleasure of it. Bloodthirst instigated a massacre of dozens of Metropolis citizens, in collaboration with the second Bloodsport Alex Trent and the cybernetic criminal Hi-Tech. Bloodthirst materialized in front of Superman after the initial carnage, challenging the Man of Might to take it on. Superman seemed to have the upper hand in their clash, and Bloodthirst quickly vanished, apparently content merely to have left a landscape of carnage and devastation in its wake. More about its motives and origins were unknown; there were no other documented accounts of its appearance; and it has not yet been documented whether it reappeared on New Earth (*The Adventures of Superman* #507, December 1993; *Action Comics* #694, December 1993; *Superman: The Man of Steel* #29, January 1994).

BOOM TUBE, THE

See New Gods.

BORGONIA

A small Latin American monarchy on the pre-First Crisis Earth-1, ruled by a Queen Lucy, who briefly assumed the alias of Supergirl while visiting the United States (*Superboy* [first series] #5, November–December 1949). The nation later became a dictatorship under the ruthless Torm. Promising free elections, Torm secretly tampered with the voting machines but was outwitted by Superman. Former underground leader Gault led the resultant democracy (*Action Comics* #233, October 1957).

BOROTAVIA

A Balkan country whose military police staged a coup, "removing the nation's democracy and replacing it with a brutal dictatorship." Superman intervened when the troops attempted to take their civil war into neighboring countries. Joseph Rabinovitch, a scientist who specialized in state-of-the-art film development, defected to the United States about a year after the overthrow, assisted by Jimmy Olsen and—secretly—Superman (*Action Comics* #467, January 1977; *Superman Family* #184, July–August 1977).

BOUNTY

A mysterious, Old West–themed super-criminal on the post–First Crisis unified Earth with certain similarities to the pre–First Crisis Earth-1's Terra-Man. Bounty employed more futuristic accessories than any gunslinger of old, however: He had cybernetic forearms and rode a flying robotic horse. And the "psionic projectiles" fired by his gun could stun his target, or worse (*Superman: The Man of Steel* #104, September 2000). "Once those bullets have locked onto your D.N.A.," he declared, "they'll follow you to the end of the universe" (*Superman* [second series] #161, October 2000). Bounty was part of the Joker League of Anarchy in the alternate reality created by the Joker but was not documented in any other reality; nor have there been accounts of his appearance on New Earth.

BRADLEY, SLAM, JR.

A plainclothes detective who worked in the post-First Crisis Metropolis Police Department. Bradley affected a "hard-boiled" demeanor, looking and sounding as if he had read one too many Raymond Chandler novels. But that was just a case of an apple not falling too far from the tree. He was the son of Samuel Emerson "Slam" Bradley—of Cleveland and later New York—whose investigations with his idolizing sidekick "Shorty" Morgan often found the pair going undercover in various professions to collar the perp (*Detective Comics* #1–152, March 1937–October 1949).

The younger Bradley inherited his father's resemblance to Superman, and was once mistaken for Clark Kent. Superman first encountered him

when he helped Cat Grant elude an Intergang kidnapping plot (*Superman* [second series] #44, June 1990). He showed up again later, in the Superman Red/Superman Blue era, joining "Blue" in a manhunt for Inkling (*Action Comics* #743, April 1998).

Shortly thereafter, Bradley moved to Gotham City to join its police department, where he later died, having had no further interaction with Superman or the citizens of Metropolis.

BRAHMA

A member of the Supermen of America whose civilian name was Cal Usjak.

BRAINIAC

Arguably the most fearsomely intelligent and powerful force of unadulterated evil the Man of Steel ever encountered—an idea that the wounded pride of Brainiac's chief rival and frequent coconspirator, the brilliant Lex Luthor, would howlingly protest. The same characteristics that made it difficult to decide whether Brainiac posed less of a threat to Superman than Luthor also argued that he was the greater menace. Toward Superman, at least, Brainiac was ice-cold, aloof, totally without emotion, and therefore not "invested" in the Man of Steel.

Did that make him less "motivated" an opponent? Perhaps. But Brainiac did not burn with the judgment-impairing, obsessive fear and resentment Luthor felt for Superman. Therefore he could see the Kryptonian with the objective scientist's pitiless detachment—as a gnat to be flicked aside. That said, there were those, like Luthor, who contended that the absence of human emotions in Brainiac resulted in his single greatest weakness: his utter lack of insight into human psychology. Documented at first as a mere technologically advanced, green-skinned humanoid alien, and later as a sophisticated artificial intelligence in humanoid form, he or it—the terms are, for all intents and purposes, interchangeable—has since come to be recognized as something much, much more. So much, in fact, as to be beyond human comprehension. Brainiac was impressive enough when viewed simply in conventional high-tech criminal terms, but his accomplishments on that level represent the least of his achievements. He created devices such as an impenetrable force-field generator, replete with an anti-gravity capability that allowed him to fly; and a means of compressing mass that could literally miniaturize entire cities. He also piloted a morphing starship, sometimes seen as a transparent globe, at other times assuming a bizarre lightbulb shape, and on still other occasions camouflaging itself as a stereotypical "flying saucer." In any form, this craft was capable of moving through time as well as deep space, where it transported him at hyperdrive speeds anywhere in the known universe.

After his first encounter with Superman, Brainiac made sure that his defense technology was designed with the Man of Steel in mind: His force field was upgraded to be impenetrable to heat vision; he developed various types of synthetic kryptonite; he invented new ways of harnessing natural kryptonite radiation; and he even came up with a "coma ray" with which he could temporarily paralyze the Man of Steel. But even when reduced to something within the human frame of reference regarding intellect, Brainiac's mind was astonishing and frightening. Once described as having a "twelfth-level intellect," Brainiac possessed superhuman calculation abilities; limitless and infinitely retrievable memory; and an understanding of mechanical engineering, bioengineering, physics, and other theoretical and applied sciences that exceeded Earth's own. Accordingly, when Brainiac set that ferocious mind to achieving an objective with significant consequences for Earth, it was only the planet's meta-human population that could stand in his way. And sometimes, it took the combined might of all of them to do it.

Brainiac had numerous incarnations, each more powerful than the one before, not only by virtue of incarnating in several different universes, but also because he was an experienced and adept time-traveler within each of those dimensions. His toxic presence was felt in countless alternate realities and time lines. It could be argued that he achieved his apotheosis in the post-First Crisis universe. Accounts of him in that world show that he was, at his core, formless: a consciousness comprising electrical impulses that could inhabit any digitized hardware; exchange data with, override, corrupt, crash, or wipe out any binary system; and physically inhabit any organic being. His presence could then enhance or increase the natural abilities of the host organism. Over time, his many host bodies displayed an array of powers such as super-strength, near invulnerability, and energy projection. One aspect of his origins in the unified post–First Crisis universe even suggested that he could, in some barely understood way, exert a mental control over the space-time continuum itself, as when his consciousness somehow survived his organic body's destruction and he traveled from his homeworld to Earth.

Brainiac was humankind's first true cyberpunk nightmare, free to exist in either cyberspace or the physical world at will; infinitely upgradeable and self-replicating; and as undying as data itself. He was neither machine made flesh nor fusion of flesh and machine, but all of the above, and terrifyingly more.

Even in the pre–First Crisis era, Brainiac took more than one physical form. In his first incarnation, he closely resembled the humanoid inhabitants of his native world: He was bald-headed, with green skin and eyes. He was described as a spacefaring pirate, the former ruler of the planet Bryak, whom Superman first encountered when Brainiac came to Earth in an attempt to use his matter-condensing "hyper-force" to shrink Metropolis and other Earth cities to the size of model-railroad layouts. Aboard his craft, Brainiac had a collection of many such shrunken cities from various inhabited worlds, trapped in the large bottles in which he had kidnapped them. It was said that the populace of Bryak had been wiped out by a global plague, and Brainiac was collecting cities whose inhabitants and architecture could be used to rebuild his homeworld. While fighting Brainiac, Superman discovered that the pirate had also stolen the Kryptonian city of Kandor before Krypton's destruction. The Man of Steel was able to restore the Earth cities to full size, but the Kandorians sacrificed their own restoration to help him thwart Brainiac's plan. Although the "space pirate" retreated in his interstellar craft, Superman was nevertheless able to hide the bottled city of Kandor in his Fortress of Solitude for safekeeping, vowing to someday return his fellow Kryptonians and their habitat to normal dimensions (*Action Comics* #242, July 1958).

Some of this account, however, was later proven to be apocryphal by a discovery of Lex Luthor's. Brainiac was not an organic being, but rather a humanoid computer, which was why he had a distinctive gridwork of what appeared to be red diodes traversing his skull, variously described in the chronicles as "electrodes" or "the electric terminals of his sensory 'nerves.' "

In his pre-First Crisis mad-scientist incarnation, Luthor developed a device that allowed him to remotely tap into the databases of something calling itself Master Computer One on the planet Colu, whose humanoid inhabitants had built it. Millennia ago, the Coluans had constructed many

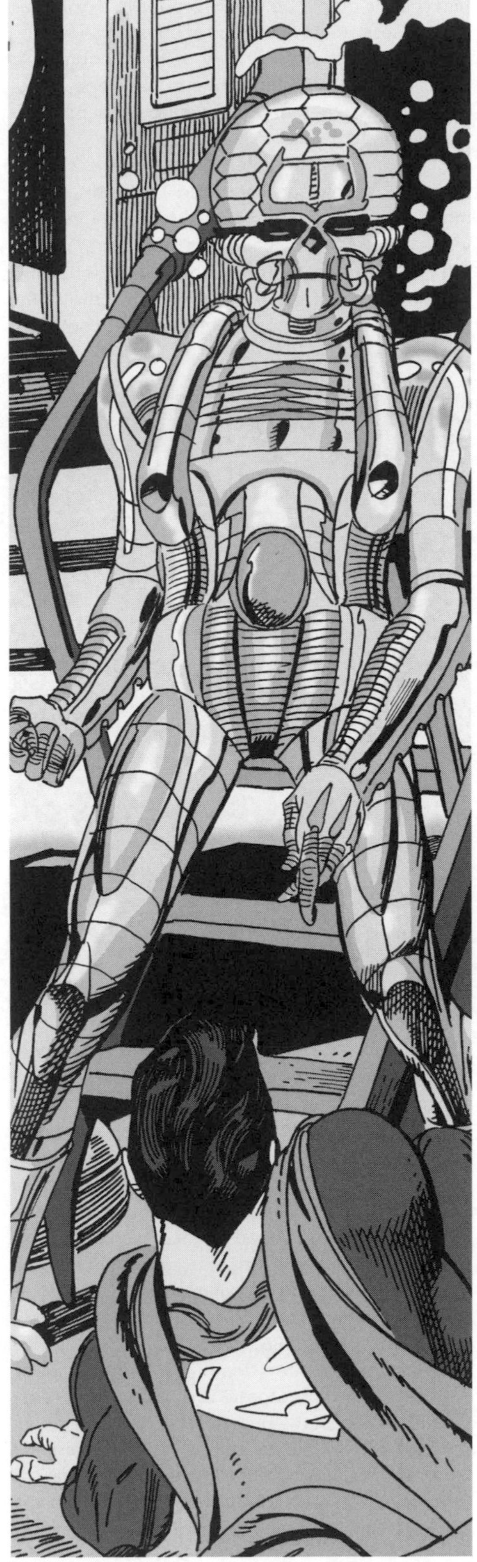

such super-sophisticated, networked computers, possessed of "tenth-level effector" intelligence, compared with the Coluans' own "sixth-level" status. These computers were also fully sentient, thinking independently—so much so that they resented being "operated" by inferior beings and resolved to control the Coluan populace for the planet's own good. Collectively referred to as "the Computer Tyrants" by the resentful, subjugated Coluans, they had recorded the history of their revolution in the memory banks of their leader, Master Computer One.

The Computer Tyrants enforced their dominance by constructing awesome weapons of mass destruction. Soon their appetite for a global security achieved by eliminating reckless humanoid judgment extended beyond Colu to other worlds inhabited by organic life-forms. The Tyrants decided they needed a "spy"—a time- and space-traveling secret agent who would reconnoiter those worlds. This operative would bring back miniaturized "sample cities" that could be enlarged on Colu and used for target practice, in a sense—to determine which weapons systems would be most effective for conquering each civilization.

Brainiac was built to appear humanoid—specifically, like the Coluans themselves—rather than to reveal his robotic nature as he carried out his covert programming. The Tyrants outdid themselves in more ways than one; they endowed Brainiac with a twelfth-level effector brain, superior to their own (although some accounts contradict this, stating that Brainiac's original tenth-level effector was later upgraded by Luthor). To ensure that the deception would be flawless, the Tyrants imprinted on their spy's digital brain the structure and synapses of one of Colu's most brilliant scientists, giving him the ability to replicate a full complement of humanoid emotions, speech inflections, and mannerisms, albeit in the coolly rational manner of a scientific genius (*Superman* [first series] #167, February 1964).

To complete the charade, the master computers selected the humanoid Vril Dox, an outstanding young student, to accompany Brainiac on his journey, posing as his son. But the boy, whom the Tyrants dubbed Brainiac II (rendered in later accounts as Brainiac 2.0), had no intention of serving his computer masters' agenda and took the first opportunity to escape, forcing Brainiac to depart without him. As the original Kara Zor-El Supergirl learned later, while Brainiac was offworld, Vril Dox led his people in a great revolution that toppled the Computer Tyrants and restored native rule. That courageous youngster was the ancestor of Querl Dox, the original Brainiac 5 of the thirtieth-century Legion of Super-Heroes (*Action Comics* #276, May 1961).

In light of what Luthor was able to learn about his sometime ally's true background, the original account of Brainiac hailing from the planet Bryak was probably just one more element of the elaborate cover story invented by the Computer Tyrants. Brainiac was one of the most frustrating of Superman's foes: Because he was an inorganic construct, he was not protected by the Man of Steel's pledge never to kill; yet in numerous en-

Vril Dox

counters over the years, Brainiac proved himself endlessly resourceful and difficult to dispatch. For example, Superman once sent him back to Earth's Ice Age, trapped in a state of suspended animation, but Brainiac was able to escape from even this by telekinetically inducing a boulder to crash into his vessel, smashing a hole in the hull that allowed the gas keeping him in stasis to escape (*Action Comics* #280, September 1961). The Man of Steel also devoted a great deal of time and energy trying in vain to penetrate that force field.

On the occasion of their first meeting, Brainiac 5 told Supergirl of a fateful encounter in which the original Brainiac had been shrunk to nothingness. He neglected to mention that the Girl of Steel herself was responsible for that development, which took place on the eve of Kandor's restoration to full size (*Superman* [first series] #338, August 1979). Although he had a retrieval system in place for such a turn of events, Brainiac found his computer brain malfunctioning upon his return to normal size. Invading the Fortress of Solitude, the villain networked with the Man of Steel's Super-Computer to facilitate repairs—only to have Superman use the occasion to reprogram Brainiac as a force for good (*Action Comics* #514, December 1980). Unfortunately, Brainiac had constructed a computer-controlled synthetic planetoid beforehand, and the secret of its defeat lay in his original

programming. Once restored, Brainiac engaged Superman in battle again, and the Man of Steel left him stranded at the center of this sphere, unable to escape (*Action Comics* #528–530, February–April 1982).

He was, however, able to cause a nearby star to go nova, destroying his artificial world, believing that this would free him. Instead the nova's radiation blasted the humanoid computer into a floating mass of molecules. This cloud of Brainiac's atoms drifted through space randomly until being drawn to a world of living machines where life was not carbon-based, but electronic. There he merged his consciousness with that of the planet's networked biocomputers, absorbing data stored there since the dawn of time. This was followed by an interval in which Brainiac's atoms continued drifting from world to world, absorbing more data wherever they went.

Finally returning to the computer world, Brainiac's atoms began to reintegrate over time until a new physical form was created, but his appearance was dramatically changed. Brainiac in his new body was a skeleton of living metal with a green, honeycomb-patterned "braincase" (*Action Comics* #544, June 1983). He also created a starship whose controls were actually plugged into his brain and directly operated by his mind—in essence, an extension of himself. The ship was shaped like his own skull, with metal tentacles suspended from it that he could manipulate at will. It was this living machine with no trace of human emotion that "disappeared" in the Crisis on Infinite Earths. Brainiac would be reincarnated in the new reality with yet a fourth discrete appearance.

He began life anew as a creature of flesh and blood. He was the humanoid, green-skinned Vril Dox, also of Colu, now defined as a planet approximately one hundred thousand light-years from Earth.

Somewhat similar to their pre–First Crisis counterparts, these Coluans, too, had been enslaved by their own artificial intelligence technology. The dominant computer consciousness, called the Supreme Authority, deployed mobile units—secretly and contemptuously called "Computer Tyrants" by the few Coluans whose spirit they had not yet broken—that dominated the organic citizens' every waking moment. These ever-present Tyrants controlled all information flow, dictated what each organic would know or perceive, and, through crude punishment and reward, reinforced strict compliance with the Supreme Authority's rules, always severely punishing intellectual curiosity and independent thought. But these Tyrants noted Vril Dox's unique genius, perhaps exceeding their own, even in his infancy. And, to more fully exploit his potential, they exempted Dox from the brainwashing inflicted on all other organics. The brilliance in Dox that was off the Tyrants' scale, however, would be both Dox's salvation and his ultimate undoing. For what would be more likely to rebel against limits imposed on knowledge and inquiry than a giant intellect among Lilliputian minds?

At first, Dox played the dutiful servant, feigning gratitude for being allowed free will and working tirelessly for the Tyrants as their chief of science and technology, aka Scientist Prime. (Dox was so focused, detached, and dispassionate that he even cloned a younger version of himself just for a lab assistant. The clone, named Vril Dox II, wanted love from his "father," but the elder Dox did not regard him as a son.) In any event, Scientist Prime was merely lying in wait, patiently working toward the day when the knowledge his masters had allowed him to accumulate could be used to subvert them. Dox would then take his rightful place as the machines' master.

The network of robot spies called Tyrants was too pervasive and sophisticated, however. Dox's plans were discovered, and it became the mechanicals' turn to lie in wait. Eventually, Dox would slip up. The Tyrants' moment came when Dox's experimental teleportation apparatus malfunctioned, and his computer masters seized on this as an excuse to expunge the traitor in their midst. Dox was pronounced guilty of scientific failure—evidently a crime punishable by whatever sentence struck the Tyrants' whim. Dox's fate was to have his own flawed teleporter turned on him, breaking his body down into its component atoms and dispersing them into space, never to be reunited.

Yet somehow, Dox's consciousness survived. It has been said that sometimes hate can burn with such ferocity, it can transcend death. Others seek a less metaphysical explanation. Later, Dox would manifest astonishingly powerful psionic abilities, telepathic and telekinetic, and it was suggested that these were latent, present even at the moment of his disintegration. Perhaps these forces, unknown and unknowable, were what allowed Dox to retain sentience without organic matter to support it.

Whatever the explanation, Dox's consciousness not only survived his torment but looked outward, scanning the cosmos, searching relentlessly for a corporeal entity in which he could reconstitute himself (*The Adventures of Superman* #438, March 1988; *L.E.G.I.O.N. '91* #23, January 1990). In time, he made psionic contact with a tortured alcoholic named Milton Moses Fine, who billed himself as "the Amazing Brainiac"—a sideshow mentalist in a circus playing Metropolis. Dox sensed that Fine was not altogether a fraud, possessing a minor telepathic ability that allowed him to see things in people's minds so disturbing to him that he drank too much. Gradually, Dox began to "possess" Fine, invading his consciousness and dominating more and more of his thoughts. As Dox's hold strengthened, Fine experienced excruciating headaches, and his own powerful psi abilities began to awaken.

Due to slightly heightened psi awareness in Superman's yellow-sun-energized brain (his super-intellect made him a telepathic adept in most incarnations), Clark Kent felt similar pain. Switching to Superman, he traced the source of his own splitting headache to Fine, arriving on the scene just as Dox's discarnate mind took full control of the mentalist.

Testing, with deep satisfaction, Fine's newly aroused power, Dox counterattacked with abandon, and his enhanced psionic powers gave Superman a workout. With the aid of Fine's wife and assistant, however, the Man of Steel rendered Fine unconscious and turned him over to the police. The authorities thought the mentalist's story of possession by an alien entity indicated a psychotic break. Fine was confined to the psychiatric ward of Metropolis General Hospital, drifting in and out of catatonia as he tried in vain to resist Dox's tightening hold on his mind (*The Adventures of Superman* #438, March 1988).

Following his wife's death in a traffic accident, Fine was granted outpatient status to attend her funeral. While on the outside, Dox reasserted control and drove Fine to escape his caretakers. As Fine tried to fight off the mental domination, he developed a massive brain tumor. In the ensuing weeks, Dox in Fine's body killed several homeless

men, taking samples of their spinal fluid in the hope of developing a palliative for the pain. The murder spree ended only when a psychic struggle with Superman left Fine/Dox comatose (*Superman* [second series] #20, August 1988; *The Adventures of Superman* #445, October 1988).

Learning of Fine/Dox's existence through his vast network of associates and informants, industrialist Lex Luthor acquired the comatose body and concluded that the alien consciousness was a potentially powerful weapon against Superman. Luthor arranged for LexCorp scientists to surgically remove the tumor from Fine's brain, but insisted that special bionic circuitry be surreptitiously implanted to boost his mental powers. This tech gave the post–First Crisis Brainiac a "crown" of diodes as well, for a time.

Luthor had hoped that the ongoing struggle between the two consciousnesses would permit Luthor to assert control over both—a kind of divide-and-conquer strategy—but the billionaire was disappointed when the last traces of Milton Fine's memory and personality were cut out with the tumor. One reminder of Milton Fine remained, however. Something in Fine's hokey old stage name must have appealed to a burgeoning sense of irony in the brainy Dox, for he took it as his own and allowed the rest of the universe to refer to him by it forever after.

"Sole occupancy" of Fine's body only empowered Brainiac further. He took a grim satisfaction in the turnabout of the dominated becoming the dominator when he took over operational control of LexCorp. By faking his own death and making himself Lex's silent partner, Brainiac ran LexCorp's affairs for quite some time, during which Luthor could do nothing to stop him. After an encounter with Superman when the latter was experiencing his Gangbuster identity confusion, Brainiac was so jolted by the psychic pushback he got from the man he mistakenly assumed to be an ordinary Earther that he was knocked back into a coma. Luthor seized the moment and had Brainiac heavily sedated, then moved to a special research facility for further study (*Superman* [second series] #27–28, January–February 1989; others).

It was then that Brainiac's organic vessel began wasting away. To save his own life, Brainiac's still-vivid consciousness reached out to exert telepathic control over several LexCorp cyberneticists and even Luthor himself, ordering the ad-hoc surgical team to upgrade his dying body. Covertly obtaining special equipment from the clone-obsessed Project Cadmus, the LexCorp team began to rearrange Milton Fine's genetic material, restoring Brainiac's Coluan form. His cranial diodes now increased and stabilized his mental powers, as well as allowing him direct interface with any computer system. Brainiac grew more powerful than ever thanks to the procedure, with his reconstituted body physically more powerful than any normal human or Coluan. This development encouraged Brainiac to regard himself as an entirely new life-form. Now he had no need of hardware in order to mentally subjugate and control dozens of people at once, though the strength of his hold on each would vary depending on the number of people under his control at any one time, as well as the strength of each individual mind. His telekinetic abilities grew equally awesome. He could now levitate himself and other objects, as well as generate his own force field by sheer will.

Superman discovered Brainiac's renaissance too late to prevent it. The Coluan launched yet another psionic assault on the Man of Steel but was again defeated by the power of Superman's mind. The now muscular, fully green-skinned Coluan retreated to the depths of space in a new starship, shaped to resemble a robotic head (some accounts even described it as his "headship"), searching for new worlds to conquer (*Action Comics* #647–649, November 1989–January 1990). But he would be back months later, with a vengeance. During his time off Earth, Brainiac had wrested from Mongul control of the artificial planet dedicated to gladi-

atorial games called Warworld and now used it as a heavily fortified base from which to launch a full-scale attack on Earth. In response, Superman formed a coalition of most of Earth's super heroes to launch a preemptive attack on Warworld before it could reach Earth. Maxima, in her crime-renouncing phase, was among those heroes. She claimed to use her own psionic powers to short out Brainiac's, effectively "lobotomizing" him. His body, which appeared to be in a persistent vegetative state, was taken to New Genesis to be kept in a secure chamber and under constant observation (*Action Comics* #674–675, February–March 1992; *Superman: The Man of Steel* #9–10, March–April 1992; *Superman* [second series] #65–66, March–April 1992; *The Adventures of Superman* #488–489, March–April 1992).

Several months after Superman returned from the dead, he discovered that Brainiac had not been permanently put out of commission, either. It turned out that Brainiac had feigned being in a coma. He was, in fact, in a self-induced trance, partly to fool his enemies into thinking him comatose. But the trance was also intended to facilitate a "gestation period" in which he could morph yet again, becoming physically stronger and psionically more powerful. He secretly escaped New Genesis and fled to Earth, leaving behind an illusion of his still-comatose self to mislead his captors. By the time he returned to Earth, his head had grown grotesquely large, with the wrinkles and segments of his brain visible through his skull.

This time, he battled Superman during an attempt to drive the Man of Steel insane by causing him to doubt his identity and mistrust his perception of reality. Brainiac tried to do this by creating the illusion of a dead Superman in his previously empty tomb, raising questions about whether the resurrected Man of Tomorrow was actually an impostor. Ultimately, Superman bested Brainiac with a verbal psychological attack by asserting that the prideful Coluan was nothing more than a cheap sideshow trickster. Brainiac let down his guard, with the result that Superman could smash through his force field.

Suddenly appearing disoriented, bewildered, and as meek as Milton Fine, Brainiac passed out (*Superman: The Man of Steel* #40, January 1995; *Superman* [second series] #96, January 1995; *The Adventures of Superman* #519, January 1995; others). Later, Professor Emil Hamilton concluded that at the moment when Brainiac's defeat was inevitable, his mind became susceptible to Superman's effort to psychologically undermine him. Thus Brainiac persuaded himself that he was indeed mortal Milton Fine. When Brainiac regained consciousness, the dominant personality was Fine's, with no recollection of Brainiac's deeds and an inability to see his true self in the mirror: Only Fine's dazed, sodden countenance stared back at him.

Brainiac's personality reasserted itself, and banished Fine's presence once and for all, upon reemerging to discover that his body had been checked into the Lovelace Psychiatric Hospital. Now the main impediment to Brainiac increasing his power was that Fine's brain had reached the limit of its data storage capacity. Because human brains cannot be upgraded to add memory, a new body—and more capacious brain—was in order. Brainiac's discovery of Chas Cassidy, a teenage patient suffering from the delusion that he was Superman, inspired the Coluan's next move. Luring Superman to the hospital, Brainiac used his increased abilities to transfer Superman's mind into Cassidy, essentially vacating the Man of Steel's body so that Brainiac could possess it. Unfortunately for the Coluan, something about Superman's Kryptonian anatomy made it impossible to use the Man of Might as a host.

Instead Brainiac created a new, impenetrable stronghold in the middle of Metropolis. From there, he used his psi power, transmitted in television broadcasts, to hypnotically control the city. The renegade Coluan transformed Metropolitans into little more than data storage units with no will of their own, into which he could download as much data as he wished. Superman, in Cassidy's body, breached Brainiac's lair and used the equipment there to switch his, Brainiac's, and Cassidy's minds back to their rightful bodies—which meant that Brainiac could once again use his psychic powers to attack Superman. The reintegrated Cassidy was able to figure out how to reverse Brainiac's effect on Metropolis, resulting in a sudden and massive "data dump" back into Brainiac's mind. The shock of this sensory assault left Brainiac psychically damaged once again, this time babbling incoherently in binary code (*The Adventures of Superman* #536, July 1996; *Action Comics* #723, July 1996; *Superman: The Man of Steel* #58, July 1996; *Superman* [second series] #114, August 1996).

Following an encounter with the Legion of Super-Heroes in which Brainiac first returned to Colu, where he fought and was defeated by the Legion, then was banished into deep space (Showcase '96 #11, December 1996, and #12, Winter 1997), Brainiac returned to Earth with one of his most bizarre and grandiose schemes to remove Superman as an obstacle to his agenda once and for all.

Engaging Superman in a battle of Kryptonian superpowers versus psionic energy blasts on city streets, Brainiac was apparently crushed to death between two vehicles in a freak traffic accident. The accident also caused a massive explosion due to a ruptured gas tank. When the smoke cleared, Brainiac was gone, leaving behind only a shattered fragment of his skullcap. Superman accepted MPD sergeant Dan Turpin's assessment that Brainiac was dead.

It turned out, however, that at the moment of the explosion, Brainiac's broken body had in fact been teleported back to Colu by Prin Vnok, a previously undocumented henchman of Brainiac's. Vnok had used Coluan time-traveling tech to journey to the End of Time, where Doomsday had been previously stranded by Superman. Doomsday had been left there to be destroyed when the immutable forces of entropy would finally cause the universe as we know it to wind down, and all matter would fade away, taking Doomsday with it. (This was only possible, however, because of the way Doomsday's fate was "rewritten" by the future history-altering event known as Zero Hour; also see Waverider.) Back on Colu, Vnok used Coluan technology to transfer Brainiac's consciousness out of his dying body and into Doomsday.

But when the stasis field in which Vnok had contained Doomsday was deactivated momentarily to allow the mind transfer to proceed, Doomsday immediately went characteristically berserk, and it became clear that eventually Doomsday's primitive, murderous impulses would overwhelm

Brainiac's consciousness. "Before that happens," vowed Brainiac, "we will grow a new body for me to inhabit."

Brainiac had no intention of relinquishing such power as Doomsday's, however; the plan was to combine human DNA with Doomsday's to create an equally powerful version but without the original's bestial rage. Returning to Earth, Brainiac in Doomsday's body intercepted Superman en route to the country's best neonatal ICU. The Man of Steel was carrying a small metal canister—a self-contained miniature life-support system—containing Pete Ross and Lana Lang's newborn son, eight weeks premature and badly injured in a road accident in Smallville, where the local hospital was unequipped to meet the dying infant's needs. Sensing that the life inside the canister was connected to someone Superman cared about, Brainiac decided the baby would be the perfect source of the human DNA he needed—all the better to wound the Man of Steel emotionally as well as physically.

Superman ultimately drove Brainiac out of Doomsday's body with a telepathy-negating "psi-blocker," an invention of Professor Hamilton's. He had previously used it to ward off Brainiac's probing of his mind. At the climax of their battle, Superman slapped the blocker disk onto Doomsday's head, with the result that Doomsday became immobilized: Brainiac could no longer control the monster's body and was forced to flee.

Vnok had a backup plan, however. He had constructed a robot body into which Brainiac could, as a last resort, download his consciousness. But having done so, he believed he was forced to remain forever trapped in this metal shell, dubbed Brainiac 2.5, for reasons never fully explained in the surviving accounts. He had come full circle: He was a computerized intelligence once again, now garbed in a purple-and-silver garment (*Superman: The Doomsday Wars* #1–3, 1999).

In this form, Brainiac returned to Earth, having coerced three superpowered aliens to serve him in another attempt to destroy Superman and Earth. In the soil of the homeworlds of Vestion, Paz, and Vartox—a later incarnation of the alien who battled Superman on the pre–First Crisis Earth-1—Brainiac 2.5 had embedded what he called his omega spears, then did the same to Earth. These devices, placed in strategic locations across each planetary surface, could generate an energy web that could shatter the planet. And that is exactly what would have happened to the three aliens' homeworlds if they did not cooperate. Superman managed to facilitate their rebellion against Brainiac 2.5., however, and while the four super-beings saved Earth from the omega spears, Brainiac 2.5 escaped into hyperspace in his ship (*Superman* [second series] #150, November 1999).

Not long afterward, Brainiac 2.5's next attempt to massively upgrade himself created instead a portal that enabled his future self, Brainiac 13, to enter the twenty-first century, and Brainiac 2.5's consciousness to reside in Lex Luthor's infant daughter Lena Luthor. In the course of Brainiac 13's subsequent return to Earth—allied with Imperiex—and yet another defeat at Superman's hands, Brainiac's consciousness was banished from Lena (*Action Comics* #782, October 2001). In cyberspace, Brainiac discovered Barbara (Oracle) Gordon and imagined her mind strong enough to survive when he would inhabit her body. He reckoned without her using that strength to successfully deflect his attack, but left behind a physical computer virus on her person (*Birds of Prey* #70–73, Late September–Early November 2004).

Months later, Superman and Batman discovered a similar virus in Metallo's cybernetic brain implants and traced it to a satellite. "From a communications orbital platform like this one," Batman noted, "Brainiac can 'broadcast' himself to any cybernetic with a Wi-Fi connection." Initially manifesting himself in human form in a cloud of nanites, Brainiac took refuge in the body of an OMAC before the robotic super heroes known as the Metal Men destroyed that body (*Superman/Batman* #35–36, July–August 2007).

After reality was reordered once again by the Infinite Crisis, a new iteration of Brainiac appeared on New Earth. This one was revealed also to have come from Colu, and had all the physical forms of the pre–Infinite Crisis version, but also miniaturized and stole cities as did the Brainiac of the pre–First Crisis Earth-1's universe. He was a centuries-old information hoarder. Over countless decades, he collected data from inhabited planets all over the universe, evolving himself into the highest form of intelligent life. But *this* Brai-

Brainiac 2.5

niac destroyed the city's home planet after stealing it, to make sure that no one else could share the information he possessed. Days after Brainiac stole Kandor, Krypton was destroyed. After his first encounter with the Coluan in this new reality, Superman remained convinced that, although conventional wisdom still held that Krypton's demise was a natural disaster, it was Brainiac who had destroyed his homeworld.

Superman first learned of this new Brainiac's existence after being attacked by probe missiles the Coluan sent to Earth. Brainiac had learned of Kal-El's existence, and, unwilling to share Krypton's knowledge, the Coluan attempted to seek out and destroy the Kryptonian survivor. The probes located the Man of Steel but were unable to report his location before Superman destroyed them. Ultimately, it was Superman who sought out Brainiac, after learning that Kandor remained in the Coluan's possession. Upon finding Brainiac attacking yet another planet and preparing to steal a city from its surface, Superman was captured by the Coluan and taken aboard his ship.

The craft then proceeded to Earth to successfully shrink and capture Metropolis, and Brainiac launched a missile that would destroy the sun, extinguishing all life on Earth itself, but Supergirl stopped the projectile. Meanwhile, Superman, having escaped from his imprisonment aboard the ship, saw the horrific collection of "bottled cities," including Kandor, and the network of cables "plugged" directly into Brainiac's brain, allowing him to absorb and process everything the cities' databases contained. In the ensuing struggle, the Man of Steel discovered that Brainiac's seemingly limitless knowledge of technology, bioengineering, and theoretical physics facilitated genetic self-manipulation over the centuries, transforming him into a creature as strong and invulnerable as any Kryptonian in a yellow-sun environment—as long as he remained within, or in proximity to, his craft, which he called his bio-shell.

Superman also learned what aspects of Brainiac's history had been replicated in the New Earth reality, with minor variations. For example, Milton Fine had been infected with nanite probes that later migrated into Doomsday, the Brainiac 2.5 android, and finally into Lena Luthor. With his ability to inhabit, as discarnate electrical impulses, other bodies and mechanical "shells" of one sort or another, no one had ever actually met the "real" Brainiac.

In the course of their battle, Superman knocked Brainiac out of his ship and into a swamp, where the Coluan was attacked by microscopic organisms against which he seemed to have no defense. This distraction enabled the Man of Steel to defeat Brainiac, but at a terrible price. While Superman recaptured the cities of Metropolis and Kandor and began to use Brainiac's own technology to restore them to normal size, the Coluan retaliated by launching a missile at the Kent farm. The farm was destroyed, and, after preventing his wife from being killed, Jonathan Kent suffered a fatal heart attack.

Brainiac was then brought for further study to a top-secret military installation that would later become the headquarters of General Samuel Lane's Project 7734. But after the Coluan murdered the first scientific research team assigned to the case, Lane arrested and imprisoned in the compound a felon who might have been able to do the job just as well but could be considered expendable if he, too, were killed by Brainiac: Lex Luthor.

Luthor eventually found a way to use Brainiac's bio-link to his spacecraft to kill the soldiers assigned to guard him. Brainiac, in turn, managed to break Luthor's hold over him, forcing him onto the ship, in which Brainiac made his escape with Luthor in tow.

Meanwhile, Superman used Coluan technology to free Kandor from its bottle and enlarge it in a location at the North Pole, not far from his Fortress (*Action Comics* #850–855, June–October 2008).

Working together with Lex Luthor, Brainiac launched an all-out assault on New Krypton, determined to reclaim the city he so recently lost. The Coluan villain was opposed by General Zod's military guild, aided by Superman and Mon-El (*Superman: Last Stand on New Krypton* #1–3, May–June 2010). Brainiac was eventually bested by the Kryptonians and taken to be imprisoned by his descendant from the thirty-first century, Querl Dox, the Legionnaire known as Brainiac 5. Dox had traveled back in time with several of his fellow Legionnaires to rescue all of the bottled cities on Brainiac's vessel in order to preserve the safety of the future time line (*Adventure Comics* #511, Early May 2010). The Legionnaires managed to free many of the stolen cities and gave them fresh starts on new planets. Among the cities re-enlarged were Rimbor, Imsk, Titan, and New Durla. Brainiac 5 delivered Brainiac to Vril Dox in the meantime, letting the leader of R.E.B.E.L.S. turn the criminal over to Coluan authorities to be imprisoned for his crimes (*Adventure Comics* #514, July 2010). However, it is certain that a being as willfull and powerful as Brainiac will not remain out of action for long.

BRAINIAC 5

See Brainiac; Legion of Super-Heroes.

BRAINIAC 13

In the post–First Crisis unified universe, Brainiac 13 was the being Brainiac was to become in the sixty-fourth century. He traveled back through time to the twentieth century and exploited events caused by end-of-millennium anxieties in 1999 in an attempt at world conquest.

As the twentieth century drew to a close, there was widespread fear of the so-called Y2K bug. Early computer program design had caused chronological processes for dates and times to transition between December 31, 1999, and January 1, 2000, to be unreliable or to actively malfunction. Thus there was a global concern that all computerized activity on which infrastructure was dependent—not only vital public services, but also simple activities such as ATM functions, elevator operation, and so forth—would grind to a halt at the stroke of midnight on 12/31/99.

Companies and organizations worldwide checked and upgraded their computer systems, with Lex Luthor's LexCorp most prominent among them. LexCorp sought to assure the world that there was no need for fear—and certainly not in Metropolis, "Luthor's town"—because of LexCorp's corrective Y2Kompliance software, which was supposed to prevent any malfunction.

But Brainiac 2.5, the android body Brainiac created to house his consciousness after his attempts to "harness" Doomsday had failed, fueled the public's anxieties when he arrived from Colu, landing atop the LexCorp building and stealing into the command center where the Y2Kompliance software was being launched. At midnight, the city was enveloped in a blackout; a global panic ensued as the world realized that its worst nightmare had apparently come true. Brainiac 2.5 had bugged Luthor's program, deliberately creating the panic to distract Superman and the world's other metahumans while he pursued his true agenda.

His real goal was to dramatically boost his psychic and intellectual abilities by channeling all the electrical power of the entire planet into himself. The disruption to digitally automated missile defense systems was to have caused every nuclear warhead on Earth to be detonated simultaneously, destroying Superman. Instead, however, the concentration of energy somehow enabled Brainiac 13 to send his consciousness back in time just as the new century dawned, overloading Brainiac 2.5 with a massive data dump (*Superman: Y2K* #1, February 2000).

This overload from the future transformed Brainiac 2.5's robotic shell into a mechanized host for Brainiac 13, which first appeared as a gigantic hologram looming over the city—a hologram that could become immaterial or solid at Brainiac 13's whim, as Superman discovered when he attacked it. Meanwhile, Brainiac 2.5 escaped being "overwritten" by Brainiac 13 at the last moment by occupying the body of Luthor's infant daughter Lena. Brainiac 13 then began using a futuristic viral nanobite technology to reshape Metropolis according to his vision—presumably that of the Metropolis he ruled in the sixty-fourth century.

What had figuratively been dubbed by Luthor the City of Tomorrow became one literally in a matter of hours, as Metropolis was completely transformed right before the citizens' eyes and under their feet. Collapsing infrastructure was repaired and upgraded automatically as Brainiac 13's virus swept through all the city's hardware, from the triple-decker "Rail Whale" commuter train with self-repairing tracks; through Suicide Slum, which experienced urban renewal at superspeed; to the thirty-seven-story headquarters of the *Daily Planet*, made more user-friendly with state-of-the-art tech, up to and including the giant rooftop globe, which was replaced by a hologram.

In short order, Superman discovered that Brainiac 13 was similar to his previous incarnations in one respect: Things of Kryptonian origin were resistant to Brainiac 13's psi-control, just as Superman's mind had been to Vril Dox's. From this the Man of Steel evolved a plan to stop Brainiac 13's conquest and enslavement of Metropolis with Kryptonian technology. Outfitting Luthor with a Kryptonian battle suit, and aided by Brainiac 2.5, speaking from Lena's body, Superman persuaded Luthor to jack into one of Brainiac 13's power conduits, claiming that Luthor would serve as a Kryptonian matrix through which to channel energy that would destroy Brainiac 13. Superman managed to confine Brainiac 13's consciousness in the war suit, leaving Brainiac trapped in a technology he couldn't understand or control. When it was clear he could not prevail, Brainiac 13 bargained away control of the newly renovated Metropolis—in the form of the codex to unlock the futuristic tech—in exchange for Lena, in whom Brainiac 2.5 still resided and who was forced to help Brainiac 13 escape (*Superman* [second series] #154; *The Adventures of Superman* #576; *Superman: The Man of Steel* #98; *Action Comics* #763—all March 2000).

Sometime later, Superman traveled into the future and battled Brainiac 12, discovering a time paradox: What Brainiac 13 had done in the twenty-first century had facilitated the subsequent development of Brainiac 13 in the sixty-fourth. When the Man of Might defeated Brainiac 12, the creation of Brainiac 13 was prevented, thus undoing everything he had caused. As a result, most technology and infrastructure in Metropolis was returned to twenty-first-century levels (*Superman* [second series] #200, February 2004).

But not before Earth and its allies were forced to fight a war against Brainiac 13 and "the Destroyer of Galaxies," Imperiex, a gigantic energy creature contained in a human-shaped suit of armor who was believed to be the incarnation of entropy itself. At first, Brainiac 13 claimed to ally himself with Earth against Imperiex, but this was just a ruse to enable him to conquer Earth once more. In this campaign he was aided by the green-skinned Leniac, a teenage girl with forehead diodes similar to those seen on earlier versions of Brainiac. Leniac turned out to be what Lena had grown into while occupied by Brainiac 2.5.

At the height of the battle, Brainiac 13 absorbed Imperiex's entropy energy through a crack in his armor and set about using it to establish his dominion over Earth. With the help of the Justice League, Steel, and the New Gods, Superman ultimately managed to send both Imperiex's and Brainiac's consciousnesses back to the Big Bang at the dawn of time, in which both entities were destroyed. With Brainiac 13's apparent destruction, Brainiac 2.5 was "exorcised" from Leniac, who reverted to the infant Lena (*The Adventures of Superman* #595; *Superman: The Man of Steel* #117; *Action Comics* #782—all October 2001).

BRAIN STORM

A costumed super-villain whose primary antagonist was the Green Lantern of the pre–First Crisis Earth-1, but who battled Superman and Supergirl on several occasions. He was scientist Axel Storm, who had created a helmet that would harness the cosmic energy constantly bombarding Earth and found himself almost instantly corrupted by power, adopting the persona of Brain Storm.

He quickly became increasingly proficient in the use of his helmet, developing telekinesis to manifest weapons out of thin air and mentally injure his enemies. In frequent encounters with the Justice League of America, he noted that even Superman was not immune to his power because some of Brain Storm's stellar energy was drawn from a red sun (*Justice League of America* [first series] #36, June 1965).

Soon Brain Storm coveted the power of a quasar-generated burst of energy headed toward Earth. To harnesss it, however, he had to depopulate the entire planet. So he "hypnotically self-induced a dream in which everyone on Earth disappeared to another dimensional plane," and his helmet made it reality. Superman, who'd been off-planet at that moment, ultimately caught up with Brain Storm, reconfiguring "key circuits" in his helmet to convince him to dream the Earth back into existence (*Superman* [first series] #294, December 1975).

Implacable in his quest for ever more power, Brain Storm plotted to steal Superman's abilities. Theorizing that the Man of Steel unconsciously suppressed his powers while in his secret identity, the mind master imagined that those periods left him vulnerable to his power-siphon. Brain Storm

then manipulated Jimmy Olsen into seeking out the Man of Steel's identity—and he nearly succeeded in his quest before Superman duped him into believing his siphon was a failure (*Superman Family* #219–221, June–August 1982). Ironically, the hypnotic device Brain Storm had used on Olsen triggered actual precognitive powers in the young reporter, and Storm later sent some of his men to capture Olsen for further study (*The Daring New Adventures of Supergirl* #5, March 1983).

In time, Brain Storm found his powers waning. "Through frequent use, the human brain eventually builds up a resistance to the star-energies channeled through the helmet." Determined to go out with a bang, Storm siphoned the powers of a super hero named Captain Comet into himself, a turn of events that caused the mutant hero to go berserk while instilling a heightened sense of heroism and morality in Axel Storm. Through the efforts of Superman, both men were restored to normal—but Brain Storm found himself changed for the better (*DC Comics Presents* #91, March 1986).

Brain Storm was one of the many fortunates who survived the First Crisis to be reincarnated on the newly consolidated Earth. Using the Man of Steel as a reference, Storm (now calling himself Bart Sturm) created a problem-solving company called Brainstormers. Though largely unable to access his helmet's power, he could still use it to "reach near-genius level for short periods" (*Flash* [second series] *Annual* #3, 1989). Later he would use the meta-human Terrorsmith in an unsuccessful attempt to restore his brain's receptivity to the helmet (*Showcase '94* #7, Late June 1994). When last documented, Brain Storm had been forcibly joined with five other individuals—including Professor Emil Hamilton—to form a gestalt entity called Enginehead (*Enginehead* #1, June 2004). This union was apparently undone, given Hamilton's subsequent involvement with Superman as a separate individual. A New Earth version of Brain Storm is known to exist (*JSA* #28, November 2001), but there have been no recorded encounters with the Man of Steel. There also exists a thirty-first-century incarnation of the villain, who has battled the Legion of Super-Heroes (*Legion Worlds* #5, October 2001).

BRANDE, R. J. (RENE JACQUES)

The founder and benefactor of the Legion of Super-Heroes.

BRATTEN, PERCY

While the Clark Kent of the pre–First Crisis Earth-1 put on a cowardly act, his junior colleague Bratten was the genuine article. If the weak-kneed preppie's lack of a spine weren't enough to alienate him from the other reporters on the *Daily Planet* staff, his myriad other off-putting qualities were sure to do the trick. The son of parent company Galaxy Broadcasting's biggest shareholder, Bratten was totally unqualified, pampered, overprivileged, arrogant, and presumptuous into the bargain: "I'm here," he said, "because I promised Dad I'd take a fling at news reporting, though I'd much prefer something more challenging."

Initially, reporter Jimmy Olsen had the misfortune of being forced to mentor Percy, and for his trouble discovered that Bratten had become a rival for the attentions of his latest love interest, Meg Tempest. Fortunately for his long-suffering co-workers, the dilettante journalist's career was short-lived to say the least, as surviving records listed fewer than half a dozen instances of Bratten filing stories for the *Planet* (*Superman's Pal, Jimmy Olsen* #151, July 1972; *Superman* [first series] #338, August 1979; others). An incarnation of Percy Bratten was documented on the post–Infinite Crisis New Earth, once again working for the *Daily Planet* (*Action Comics* #839–840, July–August 2006).

BRAVERMAN, KENNY

See Conduit.

BRAWL

A high-tech mechanical monster seen in post–First Crisis Metropolis, a formidable fighting machine in the form of a gargantuan male, with razor-sharp fins on selected areas of its limbs and back and strange, blade-like strands of hair. It did not seem fully sentient and did not speak except to sporadically bellow "Brawl!" This super-robot was believed to have been built by Lex Luthor and intended to be the equal of Doomsday in its ability to destroy Superman, which it nevertheless failed to do (*Superman: The Man of Steel* #53, February 1996).

BRIMSTONE

A flaming, synthetic monstrosity created on the post–First Crisis Earth by Darkseid, using an Apokoliptian technology called the techno-seed. By projecting the seed into the heart of an experimental nuclear reactor at the New York branch of S.T.A.R. Labs, Darkseid spawned a sentient entity made of superheated gases. It functioned as if it comprised solid matter thanks to the action of several sophisticated magnetic fields. An apparently indestructible, towering creature of ter-

rifying strength and power, Brimstone scorched, burned, melted, or disintegrated anything it touched. It was initially created as a diversion, to distract Superman and other members of the Justice League of America while Darkseid's minions carried out his real agenda.

Brimstone described itself as a vengeful angel sent to Earth as a punishment from God. Not far wrong, considering that Darkseid was one of the New Gods, but Brimstone didn't seem to know that. It even fashioned a flaming sword from its own hydrogen plasma that it used to raze buildings and slay its enemies, all the while denouncing the "sinners" it was charged with "cleansing" (*Legends* #1–3, November 1986–January 1987).

A second Brimstone emerged from a volcano in Hawaii some years later to battle the clone Superboy (Kon-El). After its defeat, a techno-seed was discovered inside it, suggesting that the seed had been deliberately planted in the volcano to generate another Brimstone. But the exact origin of this creature remained undocumented (*The Ray* [second series] #1–2, May–June 1994).

Later still, the sighting of another incarnation was recorded in Washington, DC, when Brimstone joined a number of other super-criminals to attack Superman. This occurred after then-president Lex Luthor branded the Man of Steel a public enemy and offered a one-billion-dollar bounty for his apprehension (*Superman/Batman* #3, December 2003).

In the post–Infinite Crisis universe, it was believed that a new version of the monster battled Asian super heroes in Tokyo (*52* #6, June 14, 2006). Most recently, Brimstone was enslaved by Starro the Conqueror, threatening to trigger a nuclear disaster before Supergirl hurled it into outer space, where it exploded (*Teen Titans* [third series] #51, November 2007–January 2008).

BRUTE

A tall, sinewy, flat-headed purple alien agent of the Galactic Tribunal. When the Tribunal sought to prosecute Superman for the "willful and unlawful deaths of the inhabitants of . . . Krypton," charging him with one billion counts of murder, Brute was sent to arrest the Man of Steel. Brute, himself a prisoner, having been victimized by the Tribunal's misguided sense of justice, was promised release for himself and his "milk brother" Mope in exchange for delivering Superman. The term *milk brother* has not been fully explained, but it is assumed to refer to two beings of different species who bond as if they are siblings, due to having been raised by the same mother figure.

Superman was indeed captured, bested in a battle in deep space by Brute's amazing strength, invulnerability, and "paralysis beams," whereupon the Tribunal's cruiser enveloped them in its tractor beam and hauled them aboard. The Man of Steel and Brute were taken at hyperspeed to the Tribunal Planet, a sort of intergalactic court, where, even though Brute had fulfilled his part of the bargain, he was sentenced to be executed, presumably because the Tribunal was dissatisfied with how Brute had captured Superman. This left Superman, restrained by unbreakable chains,

POOM!

wondering what sort of perverse, unjust justice he would have to overcome in order to survive (*Superman: The Man of Steel* #50, November 1995; *The Adventures of Superman* #529, November 1995, and #531, January 1996).

BUNNY

See Elite, The.

BUZZ; AKA BUZZ ALDRIN

The "bad influence" boyfriend—to say the least—of the post–First Crisis Linda Danvers of Leesburg, he claimed to be an actual demon from Hell serving certain Lords of Chaos whom he would not identify. As evidence of his often bizarre sense of humor, in Leesburg he took the name Buzz Aldrin, delighting in having to explain repeatedly that he did not claim to be *the* Buzz Aldrin, the astronaut.

Buzz was ancient by mortal reckoning, and had many identities over the centuries. One of his earliest recorded incarnations was as Gaius Marcus, an altruistic ancient Roman who sold his soul to Baalzebub to eliminate the man who raped his wife, Valeria—none other than the insane emperor Caligula. However, the enraged Valeria murdered Gaius because he had supposedly witnessed her violation and done nothing to stop it. After his death, Gaius was transformed by Baalzebub into the demon Buzz, who became a powerful figure in Hell. In the guise of the human Buzz Aldrin, he started a cult on behalf of the Lords of Chaos (*Supergirl* [fourth series] #58, July 2001). A slovenly yet paradoxically charismatic individual, Buzz seduced Linda Danvers and lured her into his ambit. His intention was to use her as a human sacrifice in an effort to release a demonic entity named Lord Chakat. Buzz ultimately murdered Danvers, which in turn allowed her to merge with Supergirl and become an Earth-born angel (*Supergirl* [fourth series] #1–2, September–October 1996). Nothing about Buzz was ever as it appeared, and it may be that he also arranged Linda's merging with Supergirl.

Despite his ruthlessness and utter moral bankruptcy, Buzz showed signs of having a conscience, as well as some feeling for humanity and Linda/Supergirl in particular. Constantly manipulating both Supergirl and Linda for his own ends, in the process of trying to "demonize" Supergirl for his bosses, he wound up instead falling in love with her and suffering a punishment as a result. In his last documented appearances, Buzz revealed that Linda had been "the image of [his] long-dead wife Valeria" and orchestrated the death of Baalzebub's own wife Lilith as his long-sought act of revenge (*Supergirl* [fourth series] #74, November 2002). Buzz was also the father of Dominique Beaumont, aka Demoniq (*Supergirl* [fourth series] #56–57, May–June 2001).

ONLY THING I CAN PROMISE IS THAT IT'S GOING TO GET WEIRDER.

CAMP HIAWATHA

The alleged site of the first meeting between Clark Kent and Lois Lane, and Lois Lane and Lana Lang, on the pre-First Crisis Earth-1. It was a coed summer camp just outside the town of Smallville, and Clark, Lana, and Lois spent one summer there. Supposedly, Lois also met Superboy for the first time at Camp Hiawatha, when the Teen of Steel rescued Lana and Lois from a bear attack. This account contradicted many other chronicles of the first meetings of Superman and Lois, and Lois and Lana—and even the first meeting of Lois and Superboy—and may well be apocryphal (*Adventure Comics* #261, June 1959).

CANNON, MICKEY "THE MECHANIC"

A veteran of the intelligence community who became the second chief administrator of Project Cadmus, after the death of Paul Westfield, on the post-Crisis unified Earth. Cannon's exact age was unknown and the subject of debate in some circles, as he was still vigorous at the time of his appointment to Cadmus, yet reputed to have been active in covert operations since the late 1940s.

Known variously as the Mechanic and the Fixer, the Suicide Slum native was known for being able to fix almost anything, a skill that Cannon developed, over a long career, into a reputation for solving complex problems of all kinds—mechanical, organizational, personal, or political. He seemed the perfect man for the job when it was the image of Project Cadmus itself that needed fixing.

Like the CIA and other government agencies whose activities are covert and shielded from public scrutiny in the name of national security, Project Cadmus became a source of concern to the American electorate as the public increased its understanding of cloning—Cadmus's primary area of research and experimentation, along with meta-humanity and the metagene. Additionally, numerous internal conflicts and controversies created by the insane geneticist Dabney Donovan's initiatives threatened to spill over into the public arena. The government's response was a major restructuring of Cadmus that put Cannon in place as director.

In addition to bringing in new staff such as Helen Angelico and Serling Roquette, Cannon's approach included making Cadmus's activities more "transparent," initiating public relations efforts that attempted to demonstrate the value of the Project's work to humanity, such as its relevance to life-extension research and innovations in the treatment of incurable diseases (*Superboy* [third series] #56, November 1998; others).

Either directly or indirectly, Lex Luthor was the primary impediment to Cannon's success. Shortly after Cannon took over, the Project was infiltrated by clones in the employ of Darkseid's Evil Factory, by that time a part of the Agenda. The Agenda, which as a result gained control of Project Cadmus for a time, was run by Luthor's ex-wife the Contessa Erica Alexandra del Portenza.

After Luthor became president of the United States, Cannon felt increasing discomfort with the amount of government interference with the Project. Following the war against Imperiex, the Project seemed to have been shut down and its facility, in an underground, bunker-like structure three miles beneath Metropolis, was abandoned. Clearly, this was primarily a retaliation against Cannon, who viewed the administration's efforts to influence and redirect the Project's research as an encroachment on his authority. After Luthor left office, it was discovered that the facilities had been appropriated by him (*Outsiders* [third series] #24, July 2005).

Project Cadmus was still in existence after the reality-redefining Infinite Crisis that created New Earth, and Mickey Cannon was still its director (*Countdown* #33–30, September 12–October 3, 2007).

CAPTAIN INCREDIBLE

An improbably short, scrawny, and bespectacled would-be super hero who appeared in the Metropolis of the pre-First Crisis Earth-1, ostensibly to help Superman until he turned against the

Man of Steel. Incredible's "90-pound weakling" looks were complemented by an equally absurd, "droopy drawers" costume. Despite his unimpressive appearance, however, the Captain possessed all of Superman's superpowers—ostensibly in even greater abundance—plus a few others, such as "atomic breath" and "paralysis vision."

Functioning as a super hero, Captain Incredible more frequently embarrassed Superman than helped him, by saving the Man of Steel and in general upstaging him. Soon he turned on Superman and the two fought, with Superman being defeated, until the Man of Steel began to deduce Captain Incredible's origins, which he investigated further by traveling to the year 2600. There he confirmed that the "peewee powerhouse" was actually a robot sent back in time to help Superman; in the process, the robot's programming had been damaged, transforming him into an enemy. Returning to the twentieth century, Superman lured Captain Incredible forward in time again to the twenty-*seventh* century, where his programming could be repaired. There he became a hero in his own right in a new era of his own (*Action Comics* #354, September 1967).

CAPTAIN MARVEL

See Shazam.

CAPTAIN STRONG

A quasi-super-heroic figure who was aided by the Superman of the pre-First Crisis Earth-1 when the source of his powers began to threaten his sanity. Captain Horatio Strong was a merchant seaman with strength as great as Superman's—his punches were powerful enough to daze the Man of Steel, not unlike Bibbo Bibbowski's—who could also fly or glide in a distinctive style: He "swam" through the air, his arms so powerful that he could, in Superman's words, "thrash air currents" to maintain altitude.

Strong gained these powers from eating a seaweed he called Sauncha, which grew in only one undersea location that he alone had discovered and kept secret. He intended that Sauncha would benefit humankind, but Superman was forced to help disentangle Strong from a packaged-food company that sought to exploit Strong's discovery unscrupulously. That was when the Man of Steel discovered that eating too much Sauncha caused megalomania and distorted judgment, and the vegetation was analyzed and turned out to be a previously unknown species of flora. Superman concluded that the "seaweed" was actually a form of alien plant life whose spores, which Superman had found on the ocean floor, had fallen to Earth from outer space (*Action Comics* #421, February 1973).

Strong and his wife Olivia made their home in Metropolis and became good friends of Clark Kent and Lois Lane. Superman encountered him on one other occasion, when Strong was hired to pilot a schooner on a cruise to a Caribbean island believed to be the home of the Fountain of Youth. There Superman battled a mysterious magical being known only as the Old Lady of the Sea, who tried to use her magic to destroy the trespassers on "her" island. But Captain Strong wasn't much help to the super heroic heavy lifting, because, at Olivia's insistence, he had given up snacking on Sauncha (*Action Comics* #566, April 1985).

It was not clear whether Captain Strong could be considered a meta-human, since his appearance predated the discovery of the metagene and the development of the meta-human concept, which occurred on the post-First Crisis unified Earth. No incarnations of him have yet been reported in any other reality.

CAPTAIN THUNDER

A super hero resembling Captain Marvel in many respects, who appeared in the Metropolis of the

pre-First Crisis Earth-1. Like the Captain Marvel of this reality, Captain Thunder came from a parallel world, presumably one in which there was also a city named Metropolis. His secret identity was Willie Fawcett, a young employee of WHAM-TV, and he became Captain Thunder by rubbing his magic belt buckle and speaking the word *thunder.* He, too, was Superman's equal in power. In addition, the magic properties of the belt buckle made him capable of time and interdimensional travel.

In his final battle with his archenemies, the Monster League of Evil, the League placed a curse on Willie that would turn Captain Thunder into a super-criminal the next time Willie said, "Thunder." Evidently, Willie had some sort of accident the next time he tried to move between dimensions—the records of his encounter with Superman did not explain it—because he one day found himself in the Metropolis of Earth-1, mistaking it as his own hometown. He clashed with Superman when he attempted to stop an armored car robbery, but was compelled by the curse to help the thieves get away. Thunder escaped by switching back to Willie Fawcett, in which identity he sought help from Superman, making the Man of Steel aware of his existence. But the next time Willie became Captain Thunder, the curse kicked in again and a titanic battle with the Man of Might ensued. Eventually, Superman helped Willie realize he was in a parallel dimension and not on his homeworld. Willie summoned the power of the belt buckle one last time, and while Superman physically restrained him, he drew on his power of shamanistic wisdom (not unlike Captain Marvel's "wisdom of Solomon") to concentrate mightily and break the spell, whereupon he returned to his own dimension. There have been no further accounts of Captain Thunder since the first multiverse was unified during the First Crisis (*Superman* [first series] #276, June 1974).

CARNIVEAN, CARL

See Carnivore.

CARNIVORE, THE

The world's first vampire, an ancient demon that on the post-FIRST CRISIS unified Earth adopted the identity of Carl Carnivean. Carnivore targeted the three EARTH-BORN ANGELS—his former lover BLITHE, COMET, and the LINDA DANVERS SUPERGIRL—for destruction, coveting their power. He was implacably resolved to create Hell on Earth by taking control of all three. Following the death of Linda's boyfriend DICK MALVERNE, Linda/Supergirl fell under the Carnivore's control, though she ultimately defeated him with the help of the other two Earth-born angels—but only by killing him, for which Linda/Supergirl suffered terrible consequences, both emotional and physical.

Linda/Supergirl lost her angelic half, which was held hostage by the Carnivore's mother Lilith, who wanted to use Supergirl to free her son from "perdition," the hellish void into which he had been cast. Lilith was foiled in the attempt by Linda Danvers and BUZZ ALDRIN. There have been no reports of the Carnivore manifesting itself on New Earth (*Supergirl* [fourth series] #1–50, September 1996–November 2000).

CARNOX

A one-million-year-old alien who, upon his arrival on pre-FIRST CRISIS Earth-1, took the form of a giant Neanderthal to "assimilate" into the hominid population of the time, then voluntarily entered a state of suspended animation. CAPTAIN STRONG and his girlfriend Olivia, as well as Superman himself, were menaced by Carnox when he awakened. Superman and S.T.A.R. LABS scientists eventually deduced that Carnox was merely attempting to resume his natural form, and for this he needed to find specimens of SAUNCHA, the seaweed spawned from alien spores that gave Captain Strong his strength. After assisting Carnox in his quest, Superman transported the alien back into the past so he could locate his spacecraft and leave Earth (*Action Comics* #439, September 1974).

CARVER, BERNIE

A weary, shuffling, over-the-hill crime reporter for the *DAILY PLANET*'s chief competitor in the post-FIRST CRISIS METROPOLIS, the *DAILY STAR*. CLARK KENT encountered Carver when Kent, during a time when his journalistic career was at a low ebb, was temporarily assigned to "the Shack." That gloomy space in the basement of Metropolis police HQ was the home-away-from-home for reporters assigned as "ride-alongs" covering the METROPOLIS S.C.U. (Special Crimes Unit). The Shack was generally considered a bottom-of-the-barrel assignment reserved for beginners with dues to pay or has-beens counting their days till retirement. The

veteran Carver was a sad example of the latter, with somewhat disturbing implications for Clark (*The Adventures of Superman* #627, June 2004, and #629, August 2004; others).

CASEY, SERGEANT

A sergeant in the METROPOLIS Police Department on the pre-FIRST CRISIS Earth-2, who was Superman's primary police contact before Inspector WILLIAM HENDERSON came along. Sergeant Casey, whose first name was not documented, was typical of many big-city cops in the years before World War II: brave and dedicated, but occasionally something of a dim bulb and stubborn to boot.

Superman's earliest encounters with Casey were as an antagonist. Early in his career, the Earth-2 Man of Steel was perceived more as an untrustworthy, possibly even dangerous, vigilante than as a hero or crusader. This dubious reputation was enhanced by the Earth-2 Superman's comparative disdain for the letter of the law or due process. For example, his fondness for demolishing tenements was seen as a crime against property rather than good citizenship. And so it was that Casey was

frequently called upon to arrest the Man of Tomorrow, who would use his powers to escape police custody effortlessly time and time again (*Action Comics* #37, June 1941; *World's Finest Comics* #2, Summer 1941; others).

Casey's attitude toward the Man of Steel changed, though, after he was saved from certain death by Superman on at least three occasions, becoming perhaps the first police officer in Metropolis to conclude that the Man of Might was unambiguously on the side of the law (*Action Comics* #41, October 1941). It certainly didn't hurt that Superman's awareness of Casey's predicaments tended to be informed by what he learned of the sergeant's caseload as CLARK KENT. Casey had the wariness of journalists that characterizes many lawmen, all too aware of reporters' capacity for compromising evidence and impeding investigations, intentionally or otherwise. But over time, he developed a grudging respect for both Kent and his colleague LOIS LANE—despite having had to arrest each of them on more than one occasion!—and had even begun to "leak" information to them for their stories before his last documented involvement with Superman (*Action Comics* #118, March 1948). By the 1950s, at which point Kent and Lane were husband and wife, Casey had been promoted to lieutenant (*Superman Family* #219, June 1982).

On Earth-1, a Detective Casey once sought Lois Lane's help on a fraud case (*Superman's Girl Friend, Lois Lane* #37, November 1962), but no other appearance of this Casey was documented. In post-First Crisis history, a Jack Casey was Metropolis's police commissioner. Since *Casey* is a very common name, however, historians have offered no suggestion that either of these Caseys was an iteration of the sergeant Superman dealt with on Earth-2.

Commissioner Jack Casey was a victim of the political fallout in the wake of Superman's apparent murder by DOOMSDAY. With crime rates skyrocketing in the weeks that followed, Casey's response was deemed inadequate and he resigned under pressure. He was succeeded as commissioner by William Henderson (*Legacy of Superman* #1, March 1993; *Action Comics* #688, Early July 1993).

CAT CRIME CLUB, THE

Feline enemies of the SPACE CANINE PATROL AGENCY in the universe of the pre-FIRST CRISIS Earth-1—a gang of alien cats and dogs whose crime spree was halted by KRYPTO when the super-dog held their leader for ransom. The Cat Crime Club's members included Scratchy Tom, Kid Kitty, Gat Cat, and Purring Pete (*Superboy* [first series] #132, September 1966).

CATWOMAN

On Earth-2, Selina Kyle began her criminal career as the Cat, wearing a gown and cat-head mask (*Batman* #1, Spring 1940). She used a cat-o'-nine-tails and was drawn to spectacular robberies. Time and again she and the BATMAN opposed each other, both acknowledging there was some romantic tension underlying each meeting. Finally, in the 1950s, both slowly withdrew from their

battle and subsequently gave in to their romantic feelings. Bruce Wayne and Selina Kyle were married in a lavish ceremony that was attended by a large gathering, including Clark Kent and Lois Lane (*Superman Family* #211, October 1981).

Some years later, Selina gave birth to a daughter, Helena, and the three settled into a happy family situation. This idyll was shattered when Selina was blackmailed into committing a crime, which resulted in her death (*Adventure Comics* #461–462, January–February and March–April 1977). The brutal act galvanized teenage Helena into action, and she put on a costume of her own and became the Huntress, working alongside that reality's Superman in the Justice Society of America (*DC Super-Stars* #17, November–December 1977).

On Earth-1, Selina Kyle became Catwoman and enjoyed many successes as a cat burglar and frequent opponent of Batman and Robin. The attraction between Selina and Bruce that existed on Earth-2 was also present here, but to a lesser degree. She battled often against the Dynamic Duo and even once crossed paths with Metropolis reporter Lois Lane (*Superman's Girl Friend, Lois Lane* #70, November 1966).

In the wake of parallel worlds being melded into one during the Crisis on Infinite Earths, Kyle's life changed dramatically. This Kyle was a prostitute and dominatrix with a jaundiced view of society, who performed in a catsuit with a whip. When news reports first told of a man dressed as a bat, she was intrigued. She modified one of her catsuits and entered the Batman's life for the first time (*Batman* #404–407, February–May 1987).

While Kyle toyed with and tormented the Dark Knight through the years, she was also walking the line between good and evil, coming to rescue Superman and members of the Justice League when Prometheus attacked their Watchtower headquarters on the Moon (*JLA* #17, April 1998). Since then, she has mainly stayed in Gotham City's East End, although she has traveled to Metropolis, encountering Superman and Lois Lane on numerous occasions, including coming to Superman's rescue when he fell prey to Poison Ivy (*Batman* #612, April 2003).

(For a detailed account of Catwoman, see *The Essential Batman Encyclopedia,* 2008.)

CENTAURI CITY

The hometown of Zigi and Zagi, which was located "on a planet in the Alpha Centauri system," 23,342,816,000,000 miles from Earth in the universe of the pre–First Crisis Earth-1 (*Action Comics* #315–316, August–September 1964).

CERBERUS

The name of both a terrorist organization and its leader, a bizarre and mysterious armor-clad entity named after the three-headed dog that guarded the gates of Hades in ancient Greek mythology. Cerberus amassed a collection of living human heads that he could attach to and remove from his body like vacuum-cleaner attachments. Cerberus's personality and demeanor changed with each new head he or it attached.

The Superman of the post–First Crisis Metropolis initially encountered this enigmatic creature when his organization was hired by the Latin American island nation of Tattamalia to commit terroristic acts against LexCorp, which had taken over the tiny country's only industry to the detriment of the local economy. Cerberus's attacks—usually in the form of robot helicopters spraying napalm on LexCorp property—were aimed at forcing Luthor to pull out of Tattamalia.

The first Cerberus agent Superman faced was an unnamed cyborg that the Man of Steel handily defeated. But before Superman could interrogate the cyborg, it was vaporized by the Eradicator—an entity dedicated to "eradicating" cultures inferior to Krypton's, which had returned to Earth to begin turning Earth's sun into a red dwarf star, the type that Krypton once orbited (*Superman: The Man of Steel* #1, July 1991).

Cerberus then sent two more henchmen to continue his campaign against LexCorp. These, too, were cyborgs. Rorc had been fitted with one robotic eye empowered with thermal and telescopic vision. In addition, his left arm had been replaced with a razor-sharp, crab-like metal claw that could be used for slashing and grappling with Superman. His partner was the psychotic Sergeant Horace Belcher, an army vet whose ulcer-ridden stomach had been replaced by Cerberus with a cybernetic counterpart that gave him the power to spew highly corrosive acid and flame from his mouth. (It was implied, but never explicitly stated, that this power somehow derived from exposure to toxic chemical warfare agents when Belcher served in the Gulf War.) After a protracted skirmish, Superman bested each of them in turn,

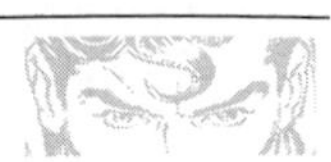

only to discover that they had some sort of psychic link with their superior that enabled him to "shut down" their brains when the Man of Might tried to interrogate them. Each cyborg slipped into a catatonic state from which he never awoke (*Superman: The Man of Steel* #2, August 1991).

The conflict between Cerberus and Superman escalated when the bizarre multiheaded villain sought to collect his payment from Tattamalia and found that the tiny country did not have the money in its treasury. Superman saved the island from being decimated by Cerberus's napalm missiles, but now, to Cerberus, the Man of Steel was no longer a mere inconvenience; he was The Enemy.

The next stage in this escalating war was initiated with a plan to kidnap Lois Lane on the theory that her disappearance could lure Superman into a trap. Assigned to that task was another cyborg, Jolt, this one an acrobatic, female martial artist with a mechanical eye like Rorc's that could project heat vision and see telescopically. She was also capable of flight and armed with an "energy whip," with which she could shock her opponents (hence the name) and drain their strength. She was joined by Blockhouse, a massive, invulnerable flying mercenary (*Superman: The Man of Steel* #7–8, January–February 1992).

Lois was saved, however, and Cerberus was surprised by the speed with which the Man of Steel located his headquarters, where Superman finally met Cerberus face-to-face. The Man of Tomorrow was horrified by the strange being's collection of human heads, kept alive in transparent helmets that appeared to be self-contained life-support systems. Cerberus treated these people—or what was left of them—abusively and with neither regard for their safety nor the slightest trace of conscience. A protracted fight ensued in which the Man of Steel was continually disoriented by Cerberus's head switching, each time taking on a new personality and voice. The Dragon Lady head made him the devious and calculating strategizer. The Physicist was the cerebral, detached, nonviolent analyst, the opposite of the Macho Man, who was all aggression and cerebral cortex, fight or flight unhindered by rationality. The Homicidal Maniac was all that the name implied: pure fury and an unrestrained impulse to destroy. These were but four of the dozens of heads at his disposal.

When he was stripped of his armor, Cerberus's own face was exposed—in the center of his chest and somewhat demonic looking. Cerberus himself hinted that he was of supernatural origin and spoke only through whichever human head he was wearing at any given moment. All of the heads appeared to have a psychic link allowing them to communicate telepathically. In the course of Cerberus's battle with Superman, it became clear that the many weapons with which his agents were equipped, his cyborg-creating technology, and even his own mountain headquarters were all products of the accumulated knowledge of the many heads. Cerberus also displayed super-strength and invulnerability, as well as the power to spew a green gas capable of weakening Superman. Whether this was kryptonite or a magical effect was never determined. By the end of the battle, the base was destroyed and seemingly Cerberus with it, leaving the origin and fate of this odd villain a mystery (*Superman: The Man of Steel* #13, July 1992). At some point thereafter, Cerberus was finally captured and incarcerated at the meta-human prison known as the Slab. During a riot, he was infected with the Joker virus and joined the super-criminal known as the Matter Master in a rampage in Midway City before the Air National Guard recaptured him (*Joker: Last Laugh* #4, December 2001). There has not been a documented reincarnation of Cerberus on the post-Infinite Crisis New Earth.

CERIMUL

The father of Ceritak.

CERITAK

The prince of the other-dimensional incarnation of Kandor on the unified post-First Crisis Earth, which was ruled by the wizard Tolos.

CHAMELEON, THE

A master of disguise in the Metropolis of the pre-First Crisis Earth-2, dubbed "the thief of faces" by the Metropolis press. He succeeded in framing the men he impersonated for his crimes, a series of robberies and murders, until he was unmasked by Superman. In doing so, the Man of Steel became the first super hero to use the then-recent innovation of a mobile television unit to broadcast visual evidence against the Chameleon to a live TV audience (*Action Comics* #126, November 1948).

CHAMELEON BOY; AKA CHAMELEON

See Legion of Super-Heroes.

CHAMELEON COLLIE

A shape-shifting member of the Space Canine Patrol Agency in the universe of the pre-First Crisis Earth-1 that could transform itself into a fork-tailed cat, a feathered bear, a monster blob, and other bizarre, alien life-forms (*Superboy* [first series] #131, July 1966).

CHAMELEON MEN GANG, THE

A criminal team in the thirtieth century of the universe of the pre-First Crisis Earth-1, documented as members of a shape-shifting race from another planet but not specifically identified as originating on Chameleon Boy's homeworld of Durla. The Chameleon Men Gang captured the Legion of Super-Heroes and used its ability to change form to "replace" the Legionnaires on Earth. Gang members were forced to persuade Supergirl that they had lost their superpowers because they could mimic the appearance of the Legionnaires but not replicate their abilities. They were able to trick her into being their accomplice before banishing the Maid of Might and the super-cat Whizzy into the Phantom Zone. Supergirl ultimately captured the gang and imprisoned its members inside an impenetrable dome before rescuing the real Legion, having been freed from the Zone with the aid of Whizzy (*Action Comics* #287, April 1962).

CHARLES, DR. SARAH

A S.T.A.R. Labs scientist and former lover of the Teen Titans' Cyborg Vic Stone (*Tales of the Teen Titans* #57, September 1985; others), whom she met when she was assigned to Stone as his physical therapist after surgery to upgrade his cybernetic body parts. Their mutual attraction soon led to romance, while Charles continued to work at S.T.A.R., but as a scientist rather than a physical therapist. Stone and Charles parted when she accepted a job with the S.T.A.R. branch in San Francisco (*New Teen Titans* [second series] #41–42, March–April 1988). There she developed a reputation as one of the foremost S.T.A.R. scientists, regularly called upon to consult in matters related to meta-humans.

Vic's hopes of someday renewing his romance with Sarah were dashed when she began a new relationship with a fellow scientist at S.T.A.R., the charming Dr. DeShaun Kendall (*The Titans* [first series] #7, September 1999). Sarah and DeShaun were temporarily transferred to S.T.A.R.'s Metropolis branch to study the B13-transformed City of Tomorrow (*The Titans* [first series] #20, October 2000). While there, Sarah put her medical expertise to the test as she worked with Bridgette Crosby, Kitty Faulkner, John Henry Irons, and the Atom to cure Superman of kryptonite poisoning (*Superman* [second series] #158; *The Adventures of Superman* #580; *Superman: The Man of Steel* #102; *Action Comics* #767—all July 2000).

Charles developed an impressive enough reputation to attract the attention of Mickey Cannon, who brought her to Project Cadmus to help treat Roxy Leech when she was briefly merged with the being known as Pyra. It was only after Charles arrived that Cannon learned there had been some history between Charles and the meta-human medicine specialist Helen Angelico, who had been Charles's mentor before she left Angelico to work for S.T.A.R. (*Superboy* [third series] #80–81, November–December 2000). Documents indicated that both Charles and Kendall survived the Infinite Crisis to continue existence on New Earth, as they ultimately married there (*DC Special: Cyborg* #1, July 2008).

CHASE, CAMERON

A female agent of a government agency called the D.E.O.—Department of Extranormal Operations—on the post-First Crisis Earth, whose mission was

to monitor meta-humans and others with unusual powers and to protect U.S. citizens from them. New York-born Chase was a former private detective who, as a young girl, had been deeply traumatized by her discovery of the body of her father, who had secretly been an obscure super hero and was murdered by his meta-human enemies. The experience left her with a lifelong hatred and mistrust of all meta-humans or super-beings of any kind (*Batman* #550, January 1998; *Chase* #1–9, February–October 1998).

Chase had minimal direct interaction with Superman during her career as she and the D.E.O. tended to give the Man of Steel a wide berth. However, Superman's foe Manchester Black suggested that rogue D.E.O. agents were responsible for the creation of the Menagerie, one of Black's team members in the Elite (*Action Comics* #775, March 2001).

Later, when one out of every thousand Americans started developing superpowers of one form or another—most of which they could not control, making them a threat to national security—Chase was charged with investigating the phenomenon. But it was Superman who ultimately discovered that the cause of the superpower "epidemic" was a Kryptonian virus, which was eradicated by temporarily turning Earth's sun into a red dwarf star (*Action Comics* #801–803, May–July 2003).

CHEMO

A twenty-five-foot-tall Plexiglas chemical vat in vaguely humanoid form that came to life on the pre-Crisis Earth-1 as a rampaging, radioactive monstrosity spewing poisonous, deadly chemicals from its mouth.

Chemo was the unintended result of failed chemist Ramsey Norton's odd concept of self-motivation in his tireless quest to conquer disease, famine, pestilence, and a host of other plagues to humankind. The giant vat stood in Norton's high-ceilinged lab as a constant reminder of Norton's failures, since it was his habit to dump into it all the chemical compounds created in those botched experiments. One would think that working with this symbol of failure looming over him, haunting him night and day, would be a masochistic exercise. But not for the deeply eccentric Norton, for whom the man-shaped object was also a kind of mascot. Norton would talk to it as he worked and even affectionately named it Chemo. And the higher the level of discarded chemicals rose inside Chemo, the harder Norton would work on his next experiment to benefit humanity, only to fail over and over again.

Norton's final failure was the proverbial straw that broke the camel's back. It was a growth serum for fruits and vegetables intended to cure world hunger, and pouring it off into Chemo finally filled the plastic figure. After resolving to empty the vat the next morning, Norton fell asleep at his desk, only to be awakened by a weird gurgling noise. His eyes opened to the sight of Chemo coming to life and rapidly growing larger. Before Norton could make another move, Chemo spat out a stream of highly toxic chemicals that engulfed the chemist and eventually killed him.

Chemo quickly demonstrated an ability to expectorate its chemicals in specific formulas for specific effects, such as burning a substance, melting another, or killing a living organism. The growth-inducing chemicals also gave it the power, under certain, never-fully-explained circumstances, to increase its height from twenty-five to one hundred feet. All this became apparent during Chemo's initial destructive rampage, which could be stopped by only the elemental, shape-shifting robots known as the Metal Men. Though seemingly destroyed by them, Chemo returned to life many times thereafter to engage Gold, Iron, Lead, Platinum, Tin, and Mercury in battle. Apparently, its inexplicable pseudo-intelligence somehow could survive even within its chemical residue, as Chemo repeatedly reassembled itself despite its plastic "hide" being pierced, shattered, or otherwise destroyed (*Showcase* #39–40, August–September and October–November 1962; *Metal Men* #14, June–July 1965; others).

Superman first battled Chemo when Ira Quimby, the super-genius also known as I.Q. and an old foe of Superman's Justice League of America colleague Hawkman, tried to gain control of Chemo in an attempt to prevent Earth's sun from going nova, a process he himself had inadvertently set in motion. Summoning the walking weapon to him telepathically, Quimby set out to create from Chemo's contents "a beam of chemical energy" that would, when shot into the sun, restore it to normal. I.Q. ultimately created his beam, but not before briefly losing control of Chemo, during which time the monstrosity had gone characteristically berserk.

The Man of Steel encountered the Metal Men at S.T.A.R. Labs, where they had gone seeking assistance in their effort to stop this latest Chemo rampage. Superman soon deduced that the chemicals to be fired into the sun would actually trigger the very nova they were intended to prevent. Together

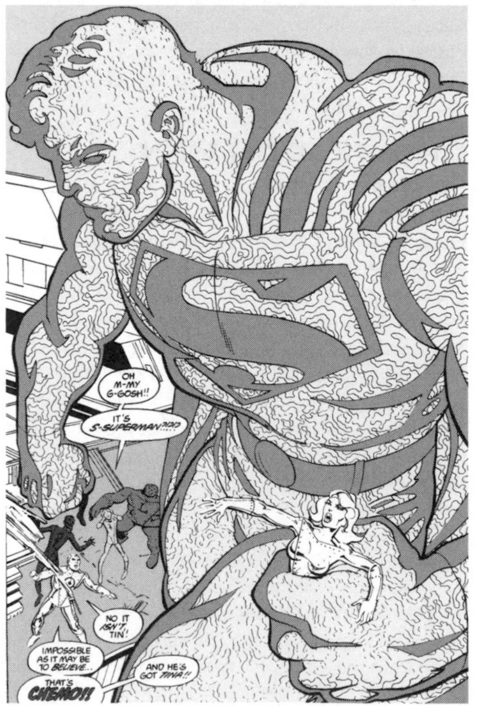

he and the super-robots stormed Quimby's observatory, but too late to stop the firing of the beam.

The Man of Steel flew into space, overtaking the beam and deflecting it back to Quimby's observatory. Ultimately, the combined efforts of the Metal Men and Superman caused Chemo to exert itself so much that its chemicals overheated, "starting a . . . chemical chain-reaction that [couldn't] be reversed." Just before Chemo could explode, Superman hurled it into outer space. The blast occurred in the upper limits of the Earth's atmosphere, where it spread Chemo's contents over the globe like an outer layer—a chemical filter that protected the planet from harmful UV radiation until the sun returned to normal (*DC Comics Presents* #4, December 1978).

Chemo was later reconstituted as an unintended consequence of a S.T.A.R. Labs experiment to counteract air pollution, and it was Superman who had to stop it, ultimately hurling the defeated colossus into deep space with such force that it became a "chemical comet that [would] orbit the galaxy for centuries" before ever returning to Earth (*Superman* [first series] #342, December 1979). Evidently, Superman miscalculated, however, because sometime later, Chemo reappeared on Earth (*Superman* [first series] #370, April 1982). And so it went for many years, despite increasingly inventive attempts by the Man of Steel to destroy Chemo once and for all. The giant's durability even allowed it to survive the First Crisis and reappear on the unified Earth (*Action Comics* #590, July 1987; *Supergirl* [fourth series] #5, January 1997; *The Adventures of Superman* #593, August 2001; others).

During the Infinite Crisis, the aptly named Brotherhood of Evil dropped Chemo on a city called Blüdhaven, where it burst open and polluted the city with radiation and toxic waste, killing thousands. Superman assaulted Chemo in the belief that it would reconstitute itself quicker as the Man of Steel continued to provoke it into attacking him. While reintegrating, Chemo drained the toxins and radiation out of the city, cleansing Blüdhaven, whereupon the Man of Tomorrow hurled the monstrosity into deep space (*Infinite Crisis* #4, and *The Adventures of Superman* #648—both March 2006). Chemo survived to reappear on New Earth as well, and as of this writing the most recent account of its whereabouts asserted that it had been transported to a prison planet. Ultimately, Chemo would prove crucial to the inmates when he was used as a power source that allowed them to transport themselves back to Earth (*Salvation Run* #2–7, February–July, 2008). He survived the ordeal and was once more wandering the Earth. Superman later encountered a trio of colorful miniature Chemos that were soon traced back to a LexCorp warehouse. Lana Lang, then the company's CEO, said they were the results of experiments using samples from Blüdhaven. They were not considered to be a threat but were confiscated by members of the New Gods regardless (*Superman* #663, July 2007).

CHILLER

A grotesquely deformed, white-skinned professional killer who described himself as a human cha-

meleon, having the power to "sculpt" the malleable flesh of his face into a perfect disguise. Chiller was apparently a "street name" rather than a descriptive of an additional, temperature-related ability.

After the Legion of Super-Heroes thwarted Chiller's assignment to assassinate the president and vice president with the help of the time-traveling super hero Booster Gold (*Booster Gold* [first series] #8–9, September–October 1986), Chiller briefly worked for Bruno "Ugly" Mannheim of Intergang as one of two thugs, the other being Shockwave, who were assigned to kidnap Catherine Grant once Blindspot failed to carry out the mission (*Superman* [second series] #44; *The Adventures of Superman* #467; *Action Comics* #654—all June 1990). But they, too, failed.

Chiller's career decline continued as he attacked a weakened and vulnerable Superman at S.T.A.R. Labs—exactly as more than a dozen other super-criminals had attempted. Instead Chiller was taken down by Metropolis S.C.U. (Special Crimes Unit) commander Lupé Teresa Leocadio-Escudero (*Action Comics* #817–818, September–October 2004). As of this writing, an incarnation of Chiller has yet to be documented on the post-Infinite Crisis New Earth.

CIRCE

The moon goddess and witch of ancient Greek mythology whom Superman learned, from an encounter with her namesake descendant on the pre–First Crisis Earth-1, was actually a native of Krypton. This Circe's legendary "power" to transform humans into animals was actually derived from her use of a super-scientific "evolution serum" (*Action Comics* #243, August 1958). Although Superman found records of Circe's experiments in a Kandorian library, there were no known documents that explained how the original Circe left Krypton to arrive in ancient Greece. Lois Lane would later encounter a hypnotist claiming to be Circe (*Superman's Girl Friend, Lois Lane* #13, November 1959), while Superman himself once gifted Jimmy Olsen with Circe's wand to perform various trained-animal tricks (*Superman's Pal, Jimmy Olsen* #45, June 1960).

It was known, however, that the Circe of Greek mythology did exist on Earth-1, as it was Circe who transformed the centaur Biron into the telepathic creature who was later named Comet the Super-Horse (*Action Comics* #293, October 1962). The sorceress proved a staunch ally, subsequently assisting not only Comet (*Action Comics* #311, April 1964, and #323, April 1965) but also Supergirl (*Action Comics* #331, December 1965) and Superman (*Superman's Girl Friend, Lois Lane* #92, May 1969).

The incarnation of Circe documented in the post–First Crisis era was a native of Earth whose history was more consistent with the ancient Greek accounts, although some aspects of it were incorrectly documented by the ancients as having been those of Medea. This Circe was primarily a foe of Wonder Woman, whose values of love, peace, and gender equality Circe opposed (*Wonder Woman* [second series] #17, June 1988; others). Superman had little contact with her outside

"NO ONE MUST EVER KNOW HOW THE SORCERESS, CIRCE, TURNED ME INTO A HORSE..."
GASP! I HAD HOPED TO CHANGE YOU INTO A NORMAL HUMAN! BUT I GAVE YOU THE WRONG POTION AND IT'S CHANGED YOU INTO A HORSE FOREVER! BUT I'LL MAKE UP FOR MY MISTAKE! --I'LL USE MY MAGIC TO GIVE YOU SUPER-POWERS!

of his role as a member of the Justice League of America, which fought Lex Luthor's criminal Injustice Gang, into which Luthor had recruited Circe (*JLA* #9–12, Early September–November 1997, and #15, February 1998).

The incarnation of Circe who survived the Infinite Crisis to appear on New Earth played a pivotal role, as Queen Hippolyta's principal adviser, in inciting a brief war between the United States and the Amazon nation-state of Themyscira, in which Supergirl was heavily involved in defending the United States, and Superman was ineffective because his pleas for peace were undermined by the intervention of the U.S. military. The most recent accounts of this Circe revealed that she had been banished to Hades (*Wonder Woman* [third series] #3–7, October 2006–June 2007; *Amazons Attack!* #1–6, March–Late October 2007; others).

(For a complete account of Circe please see *The Essential Wonder Woman Encyclopedia,* 2010.)

CIRCLE, THE

A quintet of shape-changing, psychic humanoid super-beings whose exact origins and nature were never fully understood, due to certain apparent contradictions. For example, they did not appear to be of the same species, yet they claimed to be descended from an ancient race that, they believed, was God's first creation, before Adam and Eve. They also believed that it was their duty to protect Earth from the inferior species known as *Homo sapiens* by conquering them. The first step in achieving that goal was to defeat the United States, and to that end the Circle's members supplied the Middle Eastern country of Qurac with super-weapons utilizing their own advanced technology. These weapons were then used in Qurac-sponsored terrorist activities, beginning in Metropolis.

It was while in Qurac to put a stop to this terrorism that Superman first learned of the Circle's existence, when his mind was probed by the group's gray-skinned, cat-like leader named Prana. Prana believed that Superman was the fulfillment of the Circle's prophecy of the Chosen One, a member who at some point in antiquity had broken away from the group, but who would one day return to lead the Circle to its rightful domination of the planet.

While Prana's efforts to telepathically link with Superman caused the Man of Steel several shocking and enervating hallucinations, the psionic contact put too great a strain on the leader's weaker mind, and he suffered a stroke and died. Prana's widow Zahara, assumed the leadership position and decided that Superman was not the Chosen

I WILL BE THE FIRST--TO REVEAL THE TRUE MEASURE OF OUR STRENGTHS!
FOR HUMANKIND I AM NO LONGER STHULA--
I AM--
--CONCUSSION!

The Circle member Concussion

One after all, but rather a renegade ex-member of the group.

Zahara held the Man of Steel responsible for her husband's death and sent the other three members of the Circle—the massive, super-strong Sthula, aka Concussion; Deuce, who did not in fact change form but could cast illusions of an altered appearance; and Charger, who could absorb electricity and emit lightning—to exact revenge. Each was defeated by the Man of Steel, whereupon Zahara decided that the Circle had no future on Earth. After luring Superman to their headquarters, they asked for his help in facilitating their departure. The Man of Might agreed, and the Circle disappeared (*The Adventures of Superman* #427, April 1987; #429, June 1987; #430, July 1987; #435, December 1987).

CIR-EL

A Supergirl type who was the creation of Brainiac, as part of his campaign to use the Futuresmiths as his agents in his ongoing campaign against Superman. She appeared in the post-First Crisis Metropolis, claiming to be Superman's daughter, in an attempt to sow seeds of mistrust between Superman and his wife Lois Lane, by implying she was the issue of a hitherto-secret affair (*Superman: The 10 Cent Adventure,* 2003).

Bizarro brought Cir-El from across time to team with the various incarnations of Supergirl—Linda Danvers, two Kara Zor-Els, and Power Girl—to rescue Superman from the Source Wall at the edge of the universe (*Superman/Batman* #24, April 2006).

CLARK, BERTRAM MATHIAS

Clark Kent's adoptive uncle, brother of Martha Clark Kent.

CLERIC, THE

An ancient alien of unknown origin who was the custodian of the Eradicator, created in antiquity by an ancestor of Superman's father Jor-El on the Krypton of the unified post-First Crisis universe.

The Cleric arrived on Krypton as its civilization

was being torn asunder by the Kryptonian War of Clone Rights, in which Kryptonians of faith challenged the practice of using specially bred clones kept in suspended animation as organ or limb donors. Although he did not worship the Kryptonian god Rao, the Cleric was himself a religious leader whose values aligned themselves with those who sought to free the clones. And so it seemed only appropriate that he should join the anti-cloning movement, rapidly becoming its leader as he taught his new followers principles of nonviolent, passive resistance not unlike the ideas of such figures as Mahatma Gandhi or Martin Luther King on Earth.

It was only a matter of time before the ruling Kryptonian Science Council began to view the alien religioso as a subversive. It appointed the scientist Kem-L to design and develop a weapon that would help maintain the dominance of native Kryptonians over other, presumably inferior species. That device would become the Eradicator, whose destructive power was unleashed on the Cleric himself. The device emitted a beam that agonized the Cleric but did not kill him. The Kryptonian wielding the weapon was using it incorrectly, however, causing a massive explosion, during which the Cleric was able to gain control of the device.

Persuading his Kryptonian followers that their rebellion against cloning would only lead to more violence and death, the Cleric invited as many who wished to accompany him—along with the Eradicator—aboard an interstellar spacecraft in which they could leave Krypton forever. Many Kryptonians opted to flee, but for each of them, the decision had tragic consequences.

What the Cleric could not have known was that the Eradicator had altered all natural-born Kryptonians' genetic structure so as to bind them irrevocably to their native environment, even as it made Krypton incapable of supporting alien life. All the refugees led by the Cleric died the moment their "ark" escaped Krypton's atmosphere. Only the Cleric survived, doomed to live with the guilt of his followers' extermination for hundreds of years, in exile on a distant asteroid, accompanied only by the Eradicator. The Cleric became its keeper until it could be surrendered to Superman, its rightful heir, during one of his journeys through space. As soon as the Man of Steel took possession of the device, the Cleric died, having come to the conclusion that the Eradicator somehow had been keeping him alive beyond his normal life expectancy. Surviving accounts maintained that the Cleric's body remained on the asteroid to which he had fled (*Action Comics Annual* #2, May 1989; *The Adventures of Superman* #455, June 1989; *Superman* [second series] #32, June 1989; others).

While some accounts of the formation of New Earth following the Infinite Crisis implied that the humanoid incarnation of the Eradicator existed in some iteration of New Earth's future (*Action Comics* #850, Late July 2007), questions surrounding its origins, and therefore whether the Cleric himself existed in New Earth's universe, have not been answered.

CLOCKWORK MAN, THE; AKA CLICK-CLOCK

A simple-looking, seemingly low-tech robot on the pre-First Crisis Earth-1—the first "lifesized, fully automated and programmed" windup toy—created by an eccentric, habitually late, *Wizard of Oz*-loving cyberneticist at S.T.A.R. Labs' Kansas facility, in fulfillment of a childhood dream. In a misguided effort to cure its inventor's tardiness, the robot found a means to speed up time. Superman had to, and did, find a way to abort Click-Clock's "mission" before its disruption of the timestream could destroy the entire planet (*Action Comics* #522, August 1981).

CLUB OF HEROES, THE

An organization founded by philanthropist John Mayhew of the Metropolis of the pre-First Crisis Earth-1, who built a headquarters for the club, which comprised not only Superman, but also Batman and Robin and super-crime-fighters from all over the world, such as the Gaucho, the Squire, the Knight, Lightning-Man, the Legionary, and the Musketeer. Many of these heroes would later be part of a group known as the Global Guardians (*World's Finest Comics* #89, July–August 1957).

COBALT, PROFESSOR CLARENCE

The Cobalt Clinic was a front for a criminal operation where unfortunate victims of infantile paralysis and other forms of bone and joint malformations were charged sky-high prices for worthless cures and "medicinal" pills that were really just sugar. The nefarious quack Clarence Cobalt and his accomplice Grafton were quickly apprehended by Superman (*Action Comics* #26, July 1940).

CODENAME: ASSASSIN

Jonathan Drew's life changed when he was ten years old and his parents died tragically. His older sister Marie took care of him until he was old enough for college (*1st Issue Special* #11, February 1976).

While attending Antioke University, he agreed to be a subject for ESP studies designed by his graduate professor Dr. Andrew Stone. An accident during the experiment sent a surge of energy through Drew that seemingly activated his

meta-human gene, gifting him with telekinesis. When Marie arrived to bring him home, she was gunned down in a hail of bullets. In his anger, Drew let loose a telekinetic burst, crushing the car containing the killers.

As he investigated the murder, Drew was astonished to learn his sister worked for the criminal Victor Grummun in order to pay for his college tuition. The mobster had deemed her a risk based on the intelligence she knew and ordered the hit.

Drew vanished from the public, honing his newfound abilities and crafting a costumed persona. As Codename: Assassin he tracked down his sister's killers, gaining much needed revenge and beginning a war against Grummun's employees Rossi, Morganthau, and Carmody. Victor Grummun swore he would kill the Assassin, but there is no record of a final conflict between the two.

Drew continued to operate as a costumed vigilante after ending Grummun's career. According to Ted Knight, the first Starman, Codename: Assassin worked for a brief time in Opal City (*Starman* [second series] #76, April 2001).

Drew's origins remained largely the same after the reality altering events of the Infinite Crisis. The major difference appeared to be his being a government-sanctioned operative, briefly assigned to Project Cadmus as head of security. During a conflict, he killed the clone of Jim Harper, then working at Cadmus as the Golden Guardian.

In time, he was transferred to Project 7734, General Samuel Lane's anti-Kryptonian scheme. He was ordered to kill his mentor, Stone, in addition to the original Newsboy Legion and the DNAlien Dubbilex. *Daily Planet* reporter Jimmy Olsen discovered the conspiracy when glimpsing Codename: Assassin during a battle between Superman and Atlas. Drew was ordered to assassinate the young photographer but failed. Drew continued to loyally serve Lane without question (*Superman's Pal, Jimmy Olsen Special* #1, December 2008) until Lane's suicide. His whereabouts after the project's dissolution are as yet unrecorded.

COLDCAST

See Elite, The.

COLONEL FUTURE

The gang leader of the pre-First Crisis Earth-2 who used super-scientific weapons to commit crimes, the most notorious of which were his attempts to assassinate the newlyweds Clark Kent and Lois Lane, whose investigative reporting for the *Daily Star* often compromised his criminal plans—when they did not lead outright to his arrest (*Superman* [first series] #327, September 1978). On another occasion, Colonel Future made an attempt on the lives of the entire *Daily Star* staff by altering the physical structure of the *Star* building (*Superman Family* #198, November–December 1979).

COLOSSAL BOY

See Legion of Super-Heroes.

COLU

See Brainiac.

COMET

A companion of Supergirl in her incarnations in two different realities, and, like the Maid of Might herself, a very different being in each iteration.

The first Comet entered the life of the Kara Zor-El Supergirl of pre-First Crisis Earth-1 as a horse possessing human intelligence, some superpowers similar to Supergirl's, and the ability to communicate telepathically (*Adventure Comics* #293, February 1962). She first saw him in a dream in which a kryptonite ray from an invading alien spacecraft caused her to plummet from the sky and a flying white stallion broke her fall. In her dream, she named the horse Comet because of a mark on his back that resembled a shooting star.

Soon afterward, on a visit to a dude ranch in her civilian identity of Linda Lee Danvers, Supergirl spotted a white stallion identical to the one

in her dream. Riding the horse, Linda discovered that he did indeed have the powers of superspeed, super-strength, invulnerability, and flight. He possessed super-intelligence as well—as he demonstrated when he was able to indicate his awareness that Danvers was secretly Supergirl (*Action Comics* #292, September 1962).

The Girl of Steel next discovered that Comet had psi powers, which included "telepathic vision," and could communicate psychically. Thus he revealed to her that he was once Biron, a centaur in ancient Greece, where a wizard named Maldor tried to kill the legendary sorceress Circe by poisoning a well from which she routinely drank. But Biron foiled the attempt, and Circe showed her thanks by attempting to fulfill Biron's long-cherished dream of one day becoming a real man. It was not until it was too late, however, that Circe and Biron realized that Maldor had sabotaged Circe's potions, and the altered one Biron drank transformed him fully into a horse. Circe couldn't reverse the effects, but she tried to compensate for Biron's tragic fate by magically giving him superpowers as well as telepathy.

Reducing a centaur to a horse was not enough to slake Maldor's thirst for revenge, however. The wizard magically imprisoned Biron on a planet in the Sagittarius system, where he remained trapped for more than three thousand years. When he escaped and returned to Earth in its twentieth century, he located Kara Zor-El and telepathically insinuated himself into her dreams to instigate a meeting. He did this for reasons directly related to how he was freed: When the spacecraft taking little Kara to Earth from the dying Argo City passed close by the prison planet, its "mine-sweeping" advance defense beams shattered the magical aura that had been confining Biron (*Action Comics* #293, October 1962).

In gratitude for her releasing him, Biron became Supergirl's equine companion as Comet the Super-Horse, frequently accompanying her on her adventures clad in a red cape, attached to a blue harness, that bore a yellow S-shield like that of Superman and his cousin. The Steed of Steel was also a member of the Legion of Super-Pets, along with Krypto, Streaky, and Beppo, and briefly joined the Legion of Super-Heroes in the guise of Biron the Bowman (*Adventure Comics* #364, January 1968).

As he was in her first dream, Comet became Supergirl's rescuer, often saving her from death by kryptonite poisoning because, not being Kryptonian, he was immune to its radioactivity. He could also compensate for her temporary loss of superpowers due to red-sun rays, since his powers were of magical origin. On one such occasion, Superman sent Comet on a mission to a red-sun planet of sorcerers whose ruler, Prince Endor, thanked Comet for his help by endowing him with the power to temporarily morph into different forms.

Endor's spell allowed Comet to become a centaur in a brief transitional phase, and then to assume fully human form, whenever a comet passed Earth or entered its atmosphere and Comet was within sight of it. At such times, the super-stallion adopted the human identity of "Bronco" Bill Starr, a rodeo trick rider with whom Supergirl fell in love.

Starr was briefly the Maid of Might's boyfriend and the chief rival for her affections of Dick Malverne, Linda Lee Danvers's love interest. In his human guise, Comet also had a brief romance with Lois Lane.

But Supergirl's involvement with Starr was short-lived because his unique condition put an unusual strain on the relationship. He could remain in human form only as long as the comet was "in range," and the threat that on a date he could, at any moment, revert to a horse was an untenable complication. Comet the Super-Horse was one of many beings "unborn" as a result of the universe-reshaping First Crisis, and the Comet that emerged later on the newly unified Earth was a very different creature, one of the three Earth-born Angels (*Supergirl* [fourth series] #14, October 1997; others).

Like the other two Earth-borns—the Linda Danvers Supergirl, who had once been Matrix, and Blithe—Comet was a composite of two entities that expired and merged into a single being when one of them tried but failed to save the other's life. Comet's "components" were Andrea Martinez, a young woman with a confused sexual identity, and a former jockey named Andrew Jones.

Jones had been paralyzed from the neck down in a racing accident in which he had been thrown from his mount and trampled by the other horses. After being visited in the hospital with the promise of a cure by a representative of Carl Carnivean—the secretly vampiric demon Carnivore—he underwent experimental treatments that gave him superpowers.

Carnivean's secret organization, known only as the Stable, genetically engineered a new body for Jones using equine DNA, creating a super-human whom the Stable code-named Zed-One. As Zed-One, Jones had three fingers on each hand; legs resembling a horse's hind limbs (with backward-bending hocks rather than knees); long, mane-like white hair; and a star-shaped mark on his forehead. He was outfitted with a suit of high-tech armor equipped with sensors that could pick up various electromagnetic wavelengths and aid in tracking. In addition, he had been given the ability to generate intense cold as well as the power to fly. He was far faster than Supergirl, flying at such high velocity that it was impossible to clock him. In flight, he left a contrail behind him, making him resemble a comet. This "tail" could freeze anything in its wake, covering people with frost and causing bodies of water to ice over. In exchange for being given mobility, Jones was expected to serve the Stable, but he rebelled against it and began to operate independently instead.

Meanwhile, Andrea Martinez was reaching a tipping point in a life already marked by bad choices and emotional turmoil. Uncertain of not only her personal ambitions but also her sexual orientation, she had been disowned by her parents upon coming out to them as bisexual. She had gotten involved with drugs, been married and divorced, and attempted suicide more than once by the time she decided to try channeling her risk-taking impulses into a noteworthy achievement. For reasons not entirely clear from the accounts, she chose to attempt climbing Mount Everest in a solo expedition.

During the climb, Martinez fell and broke her leg, and as she lay dying from exposure, she was detected by Zed-One's sensors. He came flying to her rescue, only to be disabled himself when his armor shorted out due to the extreme cold. Zed-One threw himself over Martinez in an attempt to shield her from an avalanche. Trapped under the snow, both Zed-One and Martinez died, merging into what their joined consciousnesses would only much later discover was the Earth-born Angel of Love. The Linda Danvers Supergirl had no knowledge of any of this, however, when she first encountered Zed-One in her hometown of Leesburg, Virginia. He appeared in the Leesburg area seemingly out of nowhere, and demonstrated the same quality that led him to the dying Andrea Martinez—an almost instinctual ability to show up in the nick of time, execute some astonishing feat, then disappear. Not coincidentally, it would turn out, Comet came to Leesburg shortly after an aspiring stand-up comedienne named Andy Jones moved there. Andy was the ex-wife of Linda's friend Cutter Sharp, the reporter for the *Leesburg Tribune* who dubbed Zed-One "Comet."

Upon Comet's meeting Supergirl, it didn't take "him" long to fall in love with her. Although the being called Comet had not yet apprehended or "fully embraced" its angelic identity, and its entire complement of angelic powers and attributes had not yet manifested themselves, Comet was nevertheless able to instill—for a brief time, at least—reciprocal romantic feelings in Supergirl.

In time, the Maid of Might learned that Comet and Andy Jones, who self-identified as a lesbian, were one and the same. Like Supergirl/Linda Danvers herself, Comet could shape-shift between its human and superpowered forms, but its change also involved switching genders. At the time Comet chose for a civilian identity a new career path as an entertainer, the conjoined consciousness of Andrea Martinez and Andrew Jones had taken the name *Andi Jones* in honor of the rescue attempt that created the merged entity. It turned out that Andy Jones was attracted to Linda/Supergirl as well, but the Girl of Steel rejected Comet's advances when she learned that Comet was also a woman. This was simply too much for the Maid of Might to handle.

The third Earth-born, Blithe, who was then under the spell of the Carnivore, used her powers to manipulate Comet's feelings of rejection and turn Comet against Supergirl. In the course of this, Comet fully manifested its angelic qualities, transforming into a centaur with wings of ice, "ice vision" (blasts of subzero cold emitted from his eyes), and horse-like strength and endurance. Comet also became fully aware of, and able to control, the psionic aura that stimulated feelings of love in those around itself.

While the two Earth-born angels in the Carnivore's thrall were turning on the third, they learned that the Earth-born angels were all avatars of the Schechina, the female aspect of the Source, as most meta-humans called God. Once they realized their true destiny and loyalties, they understood their obligation to one another and their duty to oppose the Carnivore, whom they defeated as a team. Shortly thereafter, Jones left Leesburg to make a fresh start, and Comet has been seen only once since, at which time it seemed to have begun a relationship with Blithe. The account suggested that Blithe herself was bisexual, since Comet claimed that Blithe loved Comet in either its male or female form (*Supergirl* [fourth series] #14, October 1997; #22, June 1998; #25–26, September–October 1998; #50, November 2000; #68–69, May–June 2000; others).

Because the Supergirl of the post–Infinite Crisis universe was a native of Krypton, it has seemed unlikely that Earth-born angels existed in the cosmology of New Earth. A version of Comet closer to that of Earth-1 has yet to be documented, but there was an account of Clark Kent glimpsing a statue of a centaur with a bow and arrow as accessories while Diana Prince remarked, "His name was Biron. He was the kindest, most gentle of the centaurs—according to my mother's stories, that is" (*Superman* #661, April 2007).

COMPOSITE SUPERMAN, THE

One of Superman's most formidable opponents on the pre–First Crisis Earth-1. The Composite Superman had not only all of the Man of Steel's superpowers, but also those of the then-membership of the Legion of Super-Heroes. In addition, alternate incarnations of the Composite Superman, or super-criminals similar to him, appeared at other times, some of them in other realities.

The original Composite Superman was in reality the impoverished and emotionally unstable Joe Meach, who sought fame and fortune as a high diver. When Superman thwarted an ill-conceived diving stunt that surely would have killed Meach,

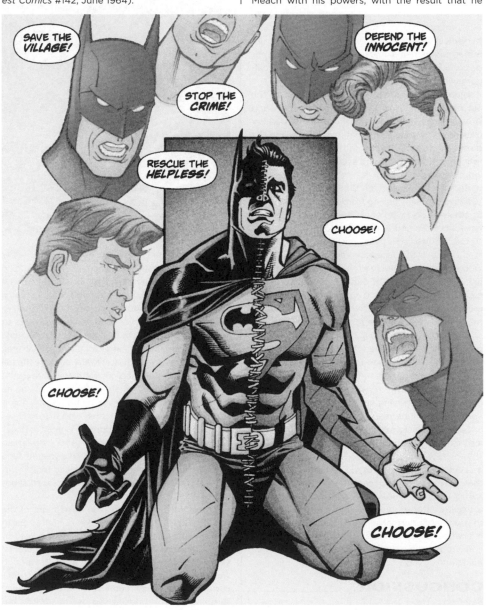

the diver overlooked the fact that his life had been saved, instead interpreting Superman's deed as an attempt to humiliate him. Realizing that Meach was embittered by his failure to achieve his life's dream, Superman overlooked the diver's ingratitude and, as an offer of friendship, arranged for Meach to be hired as the caretaker of the Superman Museum in Metropolis. But the deeply troubled Meach saw this only as further degradation: "Superman humiliated me by making me a lowly [janitor]!" (*World's Finest Comics* #142, June 1964). And being surrounded by artifacts that continually reminded Meach of Superman served only to intensify his resentment, escalating it into an obsessive passion for vengeance.

Meach was super-empowered when, in a freak occurrence, a bolt of lightning entered the museum through an open window, electrifying a display of life-like statues of the Legion of Super-Heroes. The resulting chain reaction created an energy blast that struck Meach, endowing him with all the powers of each Legionnaire depicted in the display (he obtained his Kryptonian powers from the figure of Supergirl, who was at that time a Legionnaire).

Surviving records of the Composite Superman cannot explain how, exactly, the statuettes were able to give Meach superpowers, but at least one account suggested that the figurines, which were donated to the museum by the Legionnaires themselves, were not sculpted in the conventional sense, but rather created by a thirtieth-century matter-duplicating technology. By some quirk that not even their primary creator Brainiac 5 fully understood, the Legion's powers were replicated or "stored" in the statuettes, and this energy was released on contact with the lightning.

Meach used Chameleon Boy's shape-changing powers to give himself green skin, but in every other respect he appeared to be a weird amalgam of Superman and Batman, the duality expressed visually in a "half-and-half" costume: His right side looked like Superman and his left, Batman. His strength and invulnerability were three times greater than Superman's because the Legionnaires Mon-El and Ultra Boy were also invulnerable and possessed super-strength, but did not share Superman's weaknesses (Mon-El, for example, was impervious to kryptonite, and Ultra Boy could see through lead).

Additionally, the Composite Superman commanded a host of other powers conferred on him by various other Legionnaires, such as Colossal Boy's ability to grow to giant size and Shrinking Violet's to do the exact opposite. Like Triplicate Girl, he could replicate himself twice to produce three "copies" of himself; he fired bolts of electricity like Lightning Lad; and he possessed Sun Boy's ability to generate intense heat and light, as well as twelve additional, discrete powers (*World's Finest Comics* #142, June 1964).

Because Meach possessed Saturn Girl's telepathy, too, he could divine the secret identities of Superman, Batman, and the latter's young aide, Robin. This made it easy for Meach to blackmail the three heroes into doing his bidding as part of his campaign to publicly disgrace them and force them into retirement. But the heroes were able to defeat Meach when it turned out that his superpower "charge" was only temporary. When it faded, it left the again-mortal Meach with no memory of his brief career as the Composite Superman.

Thereafter, Meach apparently obtained psychiatric help, for, when Superman and Batman next encountered him, his resentment of the heroes had been replaced by admiration and gratitude. But that was before Earth was visited by an alien named Xan who sought revenge against Superman and Batman for having captured and imprisoned his dead father, an intergalactic criminal (*World's Finest Comics* #168, August 1967).

Xan re-created the accident that endowed Meach with his powers, with the result that he

not only became the Composite Superman again but also went mad once more. His renewed thirst for revenge against the heroes was the linchpin of Xan's plan to use Meach as a pawn in his own campaign of vengeance.

This time, the Composite Superman's powers wore off before he could fulfill Xan's objective. Xan then appeared from hiding, intending to deliver the final blow himself. He returned Meach to his normal self and fired a lethal energy blast at the heroes. But Meach, now restored to sanity and full of remorse over his responsibility for Superman and Batman's peril, threw himself in front of the heroes, taking the hit and dying instantly. This allowed the heroes to disarm and capture Xan.

Sometime later, Xan escaped from prison and once again re-created the lightning strike that turned Meach into the Composite Superman—but this time he imbued himself with the powers (*World's Finest Comics* #283, September 1982). Xan as the Composite Superman proved to be an even more formidable adversary than Meach in that he was more adept at controlling his various superpowers, but needed to "recharge" them periodically. Xan soon abandoned the Composite Superman persona in favor of an original, self-designed costume, taking the new name Amalgamax.

Ultimately, Superman and Batman enlisted the aid of the Legion of Super-Heroes in defeating Amalgamax. They accomplished this in part by tricking Xan into thinking that he had inherited the disease that had killed his father, and his deteriorating condition was being accelerated by exercising his stolen powers.

Earth-247's Legion of Super-Heroes faced a "Composite Man" hailing from the same planet as Chameleon Boy, who could duplicate any Legionnaire's powers and appearance (*Legion of Super-Heroes* [fourth series] #68, May 1995). Additionally, Hiro Okamura, the Japanese version of the Toyman who was once a teenage foe of Superman's—but later became an ally of Superman and Batman—created a giant "mecha" (robot) with a design that closely resembled the Earth-1 Composite Superman (*Superman/Batman* #6, March 2004).

The other-dimensional trickster Mr. Mxyzptlk once magically combined the Supermen and Batmen of several alternate realities into one being. Upon Mxyzptlk's defeat, the magical imp was banished whence he came, and his composite creation vanished, leaving only the original Superman and Batman (*Superman/Batman* #25, May 2006).

Lastly, a version of the Composite Superman also existed on New Earth. Created by Professor Anthony Ivo, this Composite Superman had been a seemingly failed prototype for the later Amazo that utilized DNA from many early members of the Justice League of America. Reviving itself more than a decade after its creation, the entity attempted to supplant Superman and Batman until it became overwhelmed by the joint responsibilities and literally tore itself in two (*Superman/Batman Annual* #3, March 2009).

CONCUSSION

See Circle, The.

CONDUIT

A childhood friend and rival of Clark Kent, aka Superman, on the post-First Crisis unified Earth. His civilian identity was Kenny Braverman, who was believed to have been a meta-human who absorbed high levels of kryptonite radiation as an infant. Apparently, the long-dormant radioactivity in the adult Braverman's cells eventually "activated" his metagene, granting him super-strength and, according to some accounts, the power to fly.

The gene also caused a network of organic tubing to grow on his body. Through these "conduits," he could channel and direct the kryptonite radiation infusing his cells. After adding a special costume and technology that enhanced his meta-human strength and allowed him to deploy the radiation as a weapon, Braverman waged a campaign of revenge against the Man of Steel in the guise of Conduit.

This vendetta, which Conduit launched after learning Superman's true identity, was begun in retaliation for imagined indignities suffered at the hands of Clark Kent, with whom he competed athletically in high school. (Kent was simply the superior athlete; he never used his superpowers to unfair advantage in physical competition. Exercising such restraint was easier for Clark at that time than it might have been later in life, because the full range of his powers had not yet manifested itself.) And every time Braverman was beaten by Kent, he was derided for it mercilessly by his macho, domineering, verbally abusive father, who made no secret of his disgust and disapproval. Unable to direct his rage toward his actual persecutor, Braverman psychologically transferred his hatred to Kent, who became the focus of an obsessive need for retribution, which even extended to attempting to sabotage Kent's first serious romance.

Braverman was born on the same night of the freak blizzard on which baby Kal-El fell to Earth in his Kryptonian spacecraft. After icy road conditions caused an accident that disabled his parents' vehicle en route to the maternity ward, Braverman was born by the side of the road. The birth occurred at the exact moment Kal-El's Kryptonian "birthing matrix" pod passed overhead. It is believed that a chunk of kryptonite was lodged in the pod's tail section—the result of colliding with Kryptonian space debris as it pulled away from Krypton orbit. In a sense, Kal-El's craft was, for Braverman, an "evil star."

Superman later theorized that Braverman was contaminated by the radioactivity in the same way Lex Luthor would later be poisoned by his kryptonite ring. Braverman grew up a sickly child, suffering frequent bouts of what appeared to be a form of radiation poisoning his doctors could not account for, though he rallied every time.

After graduation, Braverman joined the Central Intelligence Agency and, while functioning as a covert operative, also volunteered himself for experimentation by agency scientists in an effort to cure his illness. Braverman's superiors had reservations about his value to them because of his continued poor health, but he remained determined to prove himself.

In his CIA role, Braverman grew increasingly bold and reckless as his obsession overtook his sanity, to the point that his superiors decided to "terminate" him—an effort abandoned after repeated failures due to Conduit's superpowers (*Action Comics* #0, December 1994). Braverman killed the last CIA assassins he confronted and then "went rogue," eventually forming his own freelance, mercenary-style black ops team, which he called the Pipeline. But not before CIA scientists had encased him in an experimental cybernetic armor that included metal gauntlets from which Conduit could fire kryptonite beams (*Superman: The Man of Steel* #38, November 1994) and enhanced his network of organic "tubing," more efficiently extracting the radiation from his tissues and amplifying it (*Action Comics* #711, July 1995).

Conduit contracted with Shadowdragon to acquire S.T.A.R. Labs' confidential data on the Man of Steel (*The Adventures of Superman* #521, March 1994), and this, coupled with his own personal experience with Clark Kent, gave him persuasive evidence that Kent and Superman were one and the same. This served to aggravate his mental instability, as Braverman took the discovery to mean that Kent had unfairly defeated him in high school by using his Kryptonian powers. Braverman, as Conduit, finally decided to murder Clark Kent—but naturally this attracted the attention of Superman, and he was taken into custody (*The Adventures of Superman* #0 and *Action Comics* #0, both October 1994). Upon his escape, he launched a series of attacks against all of Clark's friends and family before Superman came face-to-face with the madman (*Superman* [second series] #100, May 1995). Braverman confronted the Man of Steel with his knowledge of the latter's dual identity, but refused to believe Clark's explanation that his powers didn't fully mature until after the boys had competed in high school (*Action Comics* #711, June 1995).

Braverman's obsessive state was his undoing in his final encounter with Superman. Braverman repeatedly amplified his radiation, literally burning himself out. So much heat was generated internally that some of Conduit's cybernetic parts were fused together, killing him. To date, no version of

Conduit has been seen on the post-Infinite Crisis New Earth.

CONNOR, DR. DAVID

See Eradicator, The.

CONTESSA, THE; AKA CONTESSA ERICA ALEXANDRA DEL PORTENZA

An enigmatic criminal beauty who was rumored to be immortal and possibly even a real magician (*Superman: The Man of Tomorrow* #1, Summer 1995). She was once married to Superman's archenemy Lex Luthor and bore him a daughter. Chroniclers have produced evidence that strongly suggests she may have been several thousand years old, having had affairs with ancient Roman emperors and having played pivotal behind-the-scenes roles in many milestone historical events.

The Contessa first met Luthor in his youth. The couple found a mutual attraction rooted more in their shared lust for power than lust for each other, and consequently parted after a brief affair. Later, when Luthor was indisposed due to illness, the Contessa purchased a controlling interest in LexCorp and ran it in a manner that was arguably even more ruthless and aggressive than Luthor's own management style. Upon his recovery, Luthor resumed his pursuit of the Contessa, eventually marrying her and regaining control of his operations. Not long after, the Contessa gave birth to a daughter, Lena Luthor.

Having outlived her usefulness to Luthor, the Contessa was imprisoned and kept hidden at a private medical facility, drugged and unable to escape. But the highly resourceful Contessa found a way to end the drugging and escaped, faking her own death to evade pursuit and retaliation by Luthor. She dedicated herself to getting revenge and freeing her daughter from his influence, including arranging to have Lena kidnapped. The baby was returned, yet Luthor never forgave or forgot the Contessa's role in the abduction. Just before his election as president of the United States, he sent missiles to destroy the Contessa's headquarters, but her body was never found (*Secret Files: President Luthor* #1, March 2001).

Lena Luthor may not have been the Contessa's only child. She may have had many half siblings throughout the world, all their mother's equal in ruthlessness and possibly even magical abilities.

The Contessa also headed the secret genetics research facility known as the Agenda, initially through a proxy—a slightly altered clone of herself known as Agent Beta (*Superboy* [third series] #34, December 1996, and #55, September 1998). Under her leadership, the Agenda actually seized control of Project Cadmus (*Superboy* [third series] #71–74, February–May 2000). Although Superboy and other heroes soon wrested Cadmus away from her, the Contessa was left well pleased that the endeavor had provided her with Kryptonian and Amazonian DNA samples from Superman and Wonder Woman (*Young Justice: Sins of Youth* #2, May 2000). No incarnation of the Contessa has yet been documented on the post-Infinite Crisis New Earth.

CONWAY, LAURA

The executive assistant to Morgan Edge on the pre-First Crisis Earth-1, she initially served the criminal clone of Edge, who was a servant of Darkseid. She continued to work for Galaxy Communications after the clone was replaced by the real Edge following his escape from captivity (*Superman's Pal, Jimmy Olsen* #138, June 1971; *Superman* [first series] #278, August 1974; *Action Comics* #441, November 1974; others). After the First Crisis, she was incarnated in the Metropolis of the unified Earth in the same capacity, now serving an unambiguously criminal version of Edge (*The Adventures of Superman* #448, December 1988, and #450, January 1989; *Superman* [second series] #38, December 1989, and #40, February 1990; others). Accounts of her presence in Metropolis end with Edge's removal from Galaxy Communications, and as of this writing there are no records of a version of Laura Conway in the post-Infinite Crisis New Earth.

CORAM, MICHAEL J.

A major organized-crime figure in the Metropolis of the pre-First Crisis Earth-1 and the sponsor and leader of a clandestine group called the Think-Tankers, which was dedicated to the development of super-scientific devices to be used for crime. An imposing presence whose affectations included a black cape, Coram staffed the Think-Tankers by finding gifted but impoverished science students and paying their way through college, in exchange for which the students would be indentured to Coram for the rest of their lives, obliged to use their talents to serve organized crime.

Superman first encountered Coram through a S.T.A.R. Labs scientist who was secretly a Think-Tanker and engineered a plan to banish the Man of Steel from Earth by staging a bogus encounter with the ghosts of his birth parents Jor-El and Lara, who implored him to abandon Earth and head into space to build a new Krypton. The Man of Steel quickly saw through the hoax and captured the Think-Tankers in their entirety (*Action Comics* #440, October 1974). Superman encountered Coram one more time after his escape from prison, but again he proved no match for the Man of Might (*Superman* [first series] #290, August 1975).

CORBEN, JOHN

See Metallo.

CORBEN, ROGER

See Metallo.

COR-LAR

A renegade female Kandorian scientist on the pre-First Crisis Earth-1. During one of Lois Lane's visits to Kandor, Cor-Lar enlisted Lane's cooperation in an experiment that gave the reporter temporary superpowers. Cor-Lar then convinced Lane that her inexperience with her new abilities made her a danger to the outside world—all part of a ruse to take Lane's place on Earth while stranding the reporter in Kandor. With Superman's help, Cor-Lar's plan was discovered; she was apprehended and returned to Kandor to face justice (*Superman's Girl Friend, Lois Lane* #85, August 1968, and #87, October 1968).

CORRIGAN, JIM

An impoverished African American youth who became one of the best police officers in the Metropolis of the post-First Crisis Earth-1 (no relation to the first Earthly identity of supernatural hero the Spectre). Corrigan, who grew up in Suicide Slum, met Jimmy Olsen while walking his beat and became Olsen's occasional police contact. Corrigan was eventually promoted to detective, but due to circumstances not fully documented, he was subsequently demoted to a beat cop. He also worked successfully with Black Lightning despite his dislike for the vigilante. There were no accounts of Corrigan having survived the First Crisis or being incarnated in any other reality (*Superman's Pal, Jimmy Olsen* #150, May 1972, and #163, February–March 1974; *Superman Family* #167, October–November 1974; *Black Lightning* [first series] #9, May 1978; others).

COSMIC BOY

A magnetically powered member of the Legion of Super-Heroes, an incarnation of whom existed in all realities. Just as consistent was the role Cosmic Boy played as a sensible, steady presence and the Legion's natural leader. In the thirtieth century of the pre-First Crisis Earth-1, Rokk Krinn, a native of Braal who possessed his people's innate ability to wield magnetic forces, founded the Legion along with Saturn Girl and Lightning Lad (*Adventure Comics* #247, April 1958).

As the Legion's history was most recently rewritten by the Infinite Crisis, the United Planets mistrusted its own youth, and in that environment Rokk Krinn donned a costume as Cosmic Boy and rallied other Legionnaires to join their teenage rebellion against oppression, using the super heroes of a thousand years before, such as Superman and Supergirl, as inspiration.

During his tenure as Legion leader, Cosmic Boy fought the terrorist group Terror Firma, held off the threat of a competing team, the Wanderers, and beat back a superpowered Dominator invasion of Earth. Cosmic Boy led the counterattack that appeared to have destroyed the Dominator homeworld. While the planet had, in fact, merely been transported to the Phantom Zone, Cosmic Boy took the public blame and dropped from sight. Supergirl became Legion leader in his absence, followed by Lightning Lad.

COSMIC HOUND

See Peg-Leg Portia.

COUNCIL OF SCIENCE, THE

See Krypton.

COYLE, JOSH

The director of the WGBS-TV nightly news program that Clark Kent anchored on the pre-First Crisis Earth-1. Blond, handsome Coyle was harried, hard driving, and cynical. His demeanor toward Kent, which was occasionally similar to *Daily Planet* editor Perry White's irritable, dismissive treatment of Jimmy Olsen, often seemed to border on contempt (*Superman* [first series] #258, November 1972; others).

CRASH

The criminally inclined younger brother of John Henry Irons, known as the super hero Steel on the post–First Crisis unified Earth. Like most young people living in the shadow of a more accomplished sibling, Clay Irons both admired and resented his older brother, being unable to match his accomplishments and bristling at his overprotectiveness. Clay's situation worsened considerably after the Irons children were orphaned by the brutal murder of their parents. Clay and John Henry went to live with their grandparents and chose divergent paths. John strove to become a high achiever in school while Clay chose the path of life on the street.

Clay's life turned chaotic as he became by turns a gang member, unmarried father, then husband. He tried to clean up his act for the sake of his family, but crime was all he knew as a way to support himself, much less wife Blondel and children Natasha, Jemahl, and Paco. He seized an opportunity to become a mob enforcer, then turned state's evidence. As a consequence, a contract was put out on his life. To escape the hit, he faked his own death and went underground, taking the name Reggie Jones.

But when his secret was compromised and his enemies came looking for him even then, he emerged as a hit man code-named Crash, working out of Jersey City, New Jersey, to which his brother and daughter Natasha had relocated. When a rogue cop beat up John Henry, Crash went berserk and killed the cop, taking from him a pair of experimental flight boots the renegade officer had stolen. Crash built many copies of them, and used the limited flying powers they gave him to further his activities, which now included trying to fight crime from within the system.

Everything that his mistakes and misfortunes had cost Clay began pushing him in the opposite direction as he tried from behind the scenes to protect his family, who still thought him dead. Crash was eventually forced to reveal himself when an assassin named Skorpio poisoned his daughter. Her only hope was a blood transfusion. Knowing he was Natasha's best chance for survival, Crash turned himself in. An incarnation of Crash has not yet been documented on New Earth (*Steel Annual* #2, 1995 [as Clay]; *Steel* #39, June 1997 [as Crash]; others).

Betrayed from all sides, he is now a man alone.
Steel's younger brother, a secret he will take to his grave.

CRISIS ON INFINITE EARTHS, THE

The universe in which Superman lived was destroyed and re-created many times. Each time, the Earth in the newly reconstituted universe, although identical to its predecessor in most respects, differed in certain details. The result was that a somewhat different incarnation of the Man of Steel appeared on each successive Earth. The first of several major events that reshaped reality is best known to historians as the First Crisis, although some still prefer its original designation, Crisis on Infinite Earths.

The cosmos that resulted from the Big Bang was actually two discrete universes, each in a parallel dimension and invisible to the other. One was composed of positive matter, as is our own Earth, and the other of anti-matter. The electrical charge of each microscopic particle in anti-matter is the polar opposite of those in positive matter, and, according to theoretical physicists, if matter collides with anti-matter, both will be utterly obliterated without a trace. Among the planets in the anti-matter universe was a world known as Qward. Four billion years ago, on the distant planet Maltus at the heart of the universe (original home of the race that later became the Guardians of the Universe, who migrated to the planet Oa and established the Green Lantern Corps), a scientist named Krona attempted to understand the act of Initial Creation, in flagrant violation of Maltusian law. He invented a device that allowed him to look back in time to the moment when the entire cosmos was born. As if by some vast, unknowable act of divine retribution, while Krona witnessed the birth of reality an explosion racked the two universes, forming countless more parallel realities that came to be known collectively as the multiverse. It is believed that some iteration of the Man of Steel later developed on most of these, but only a comparatively small number of Supermen could be reliably documented.

The first of these was the Superman who appeared on the planet that super heroes would later call Earth-2. This Man of Steel was born on the Krypton of Earth-2's universe as Kal-L, roughly twenty-five years before his counterpart appeared on Earth-1. He was born to parents named Jor-L and Lora, who, anticipating the destruction of their homeworld, sent their infant son to Earth. He was found by John and Mary Kent, who adopted him and named him Clark Kent.

In adulthood, this Clark moved to Metropolis, where he was hired as a reporter for the *Daily Star* by editor George Taylor. At the *Star,* Kent met star reporter Lois Lane, and, like her Earth-1 counterpart, she was at first attracted to Superman. Considering the super hero unobtainable, however, she turned her attentions to Clark Kent instead. The two were married for forty-seven years, and Lois continued working for the *Daily Star* until her midsixties, when the First Crisis began. By contrast, the Superman of what came to be called

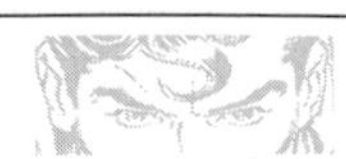

Earth-1 was born as Kal-El to Jor-El and Lara; was adopted by Jonathan and Martha Kent; and was later hired by *Daily Planet* editor Perry White. The powers of these two Supermen differed as well, with the Earth-2 version initially being able to leap great distances but unable to fly per se, and possessing a much narrower range of vision powers than his Earth-1 counterpart.

Some chronicles have also suggested that the Superman of Earth-2 was not entirely invulnerable, but could be harmed by a powerful enough force, such as an atomic blast. A much different version of a super-man appeared in yet another alternate dimension, the one whose Earth was called Earth-3. Here criminality ran rampant, and superpowered outlaws ruled every nation with an iron fist. The Lois Lane of Earth-3 was married to the brilliant Alexander Luthor, a scientist who devoted his genius to a campaign against the planet's tyrannical rulers, becoming that world's sole super hero.

But the strangest variation on Superman was unquestionably that on the world that came to be known as Earth-Prime. There all super heroes and their enemies were fictional characters who appeared in comic books and other popular culture. So when a spacecraft crashed on Jerry and Naomi Kent's farm and the couple discovered a baby inside, it seemed a far more extraordinary event than it might have in a world in which alien super-beings were commonplace. Like their counterparts on Earth-1 and -2, these Kents adopted the child and named him Clark. This Clark grew up with no special powers, never suspecting that he possessed them, but they were latent and would manifest themselves later in his adolescence. As fate would have it, this happened on the day he attended a costume party dressed as his "namesake," the comic book hero Superboy. When he suddenly found himself genuinely airborne while pretending to fly, he realized that he truly *was* a Superboy, and became Earth-Prime's sole real-life super hero.

But all this was still far in the future when the same inexplicable event that created the multiverse also released twin, near-omnipotent beings from a slumber in which they had lain for untold millennia. The beneficent Monitor and his malign counterpart the Anti-Monitor, who had ruled Qward, had once fought at the dawn of time. The injuries they had inflicted on each other caused them to lapse into coma-like states. After the Anti-Monitor was awakened by the strange explosive force unleashed by Krona, he quickly reestablished his dominance of Qward. But this was not enough to slake his thirst for greater and greater power. He began wiping out each of the newly created positive-matter alternate universes, one after the other. His plan was to increase the size of the anti-matter universe, making himself proportionately more powerful. In this campaign, he used the might of a Qwardian army, which unleashed a wave of anti-matter that destroyed the targeted worlds utterly.

When first encountered by the super heroes of Earth-1 and -2, the Monitor was attempting to save the multiverse from total annihilation: The anti-matter wave had already wiped out untold numbers of alternate Earths. The Monitor scoured the remaining universes, as well as time and space, to assemble an army of super heroes that could hold off the Anti-Monitor until he could be stopped for good.

On Earth-3, Alexander Luthor foresaw the impending destruction of his world, and placed his newborn son, Alexander Luthor, Junior, in an interdimensional craft, sending him through the dimensional barriers to what he hoped was safety. That safety was Earth-1 orbit, where he was found by the Monitor. And by this time, Alex Junior was no longer a newborn, but a teenager. As it turned out, matter and anti-matter had somehow manifested within Alex simultaneously, but instead of annihilating him and everything in his ambit, these opposing forces nurtured him in a way that aged him rapidly. Within hours, he had grown from infant to teenager. Thus it was a much older Alex Luthor who was recruited by the Monitor to join the team being formed to oppose the Anti-Monitor. Alex saved whom he could from the collapsing multiverse.

In the war that resulted, all but five worlds were destroyed. These five were merged into one, with reality altered so that there were no longer multiple incarnations of the same individual. For example, in the aftermath, there was no longer an Earth-2 Batman. No one remembered the parallel worlds or the ways in which their pasts may have been vastly different. There were only two exceptions: super-criminal the Psycho-Pirate, whose claims were dismissed as madness, and the Kara Zor-L of Earth-2, who was known as Power Girl and whose knowledge of her true heritage was blocked for years.

The Superman of Earth-1 and a diverse array of heroes and villains defeated the Anti-Monitor even as the remaining Earths collapsed into one—but not before the Earth-2 Superman and his wife Lois; Alex Luthor of Earth-3; and Superboy-Prime watched in horror as the Anti-Monitor's wave of destruction headed straight toward them. To escape it, Alex used his matter/anti-matter powers to transport the four of them to another dimension. It was a newfound Heaven—a crystalline limbo in which they were isolated from the reordered universe. In the aftermath, many super-beings and civilians died, but the single positive- and anti-matter universes endured (*Crisis on Infinite Earths* #1–12, April–March 1986).

In the years following this cataclysmic occurrence, reality was continually altered in a number of similarly dramatic events with far-reaching effects, including the Infinite Crisis and the Final Crisis.

CROSBY, PROFESSOR BRIDGETTE

See S.T.A.R. Labs.

CROSS, SIMON

A ghostly contact on the pre–First Crisis Earth-1 who aided Lois Lane in her investigative report on a gangster calling himself the Tarantula. Lane first met Cross while he was still alive and working for an endangered botanist; he helped Lane investigate his employer's murder (*Superman Family* #166, August–September 1974). In the course of this, Cross was killed, but his spirit later appeared to help Lois and Superman on the Tarantula case (*Superman Family* #169, February–March 1975).

CROSS, TERRI

A self-proclaimed "TV star groupie" in the Metropolis of pre–First Crisis Earth-1 who briefly dated WGBS-TV sports reporter Steve Lombard, but was only using him to wangle an introduction to Clark Kent. A gorgeous redhead with an aggressively flirtatious manner, Cross claimed to have a weakness for "the shy type" and to be unable to resist on-air television personalities, making Kent her dream date. Her attempts to seduce Clark came while the TV anchor was seriously dating Lois Lane, and Cross's pursuit of him frequently brought out Lois's jealous side (*Superman* [first series] #301, July 1976; #307, January 1977; others).

CUTLER, KRISTEN

The introverted and self-involved former roommate of Lois Lane on the pre–First Crisis Earth-1, sharing a Metropolis apartment with Lane, Julie Spence, and Marsha Mallow (*Superman's Girl Friend, Lois Lane* #121, April 1972). Cutler was troubled by horrific nightmares and sleepwalking (*Superman's Girl Friend, Lois Lane* #125, August 1972), and hid from her roommates the fact that she had a child. Lane and Jimmy Olsen later investigated her murder (*The Daring New Adventures of Supergirl* #6–7, April–May 1983).

CYBERN GALAXY, THE

The home of a race of "mathematical geniuses" in the universe of the pre–First Crisis Earth-1 whose homeworld's destruction was prevented by Superman. They expressed their gratitude by sending him "a predicting machine that can answer three questions about the future." The Man of Steel was frustrated by the answers to the questions he posed, each of which was "L.L." But the answers did seem prophetic, ultimately, as "the double L" figured prominently in the life of this reality's Superman: Lois Lane, Lana Lang, Lex Luthor, Lori Lemaris, et al. (*Superman* [first series] #157, November 1962). Later, Supergirl had a similar experience with a second predicting machine sent to Earth by the Cybernians (*Action Comics* #312, May 1964).

CYBORG SUPERMAN, THE

The half human, half machine on the post–First Crisis unified Earth who impersonated Superman, appearing in Metropolis after the real Man of Steel's death at the hands of Doomsday. He was created as a result of the first test flight of the *Excalibur*, an experimental spacecraft designed and launched by LexCorp. During the flight, astronaut Henry "Hank" Henshaw and his crew, comprising his wife Terri and two other pilots, were bombarded by radiation from a solar flare, causing the *Excalibur* to crash. At first, it seemed as if Hank and Terri had suffered no ill effects other than Hank's hair turning white. But the other two crewmen had been imbued with telekinetic powers while their bodies were destroyed. Their consciousnesses survived, however, and they were able to use their new psionic powers to fashion artificial cybernetic bodies for themselves.

Henshaw encountered Superman when the quartet headed for the LexCorp labs in Metropolis in an effort to cure the two mutated crewmen. But the afflicted pair, having been driven mad by their transformations, committed suicide before anything further could be done to help them. By this time, the Henshaws had begun to manifest their own delayed reactions to the radiation poisoning: Hank's body had started to decay—for example, his face took on the appearance of a skull off which the flesh was melting—while Terri began to dematerialize.

With Superman's help, however, Henshaw was able to use LexCorp technology to save her (*The Adventures of Superman* #466, May 1990). In short order, Hank manifested the same telekinetic consciousness-transferring abilities as the dead crewmen, and, over Superman's objections, projected his consciousness into the LexCorp mainframe computer. From there, he was able to manipulate various LexCorp technologies to construct a mechanical body to inhabit, making him a robot with human elements, also known as a cyborg.

But when Henshaw was reunited with his wife in his new form, the horror of his bizarre appearance inflicted a trauma from which Terri never recovered. The resulting erosion of what was left of her sanity eventually led to her suicide as well, leaving Hank the sole survivor of the ill-fated *Excalibur* mission.

Devastated by his loss and racked by loneliness, Henshaw wanted to die, but couldn't. All he could do was attempt to leave behind every reminder of his nightmarish ordeal on Earth. Turning his psionic power on NASA communications equipment, Henshaw beamed his consciousness into Superman's "birthing matrix," which was still orbiting Earth as it had on the night Kenny Braverman, aka CONDUIT, was born. With his superpowered robot body and knowledge gained from inhabiting the LexCorp computer, Henshaw found it a simple matter to create an interstellar craft from the birthing matrix and head into deep space on his own (*The Adventures of Superman* #468, July 1990).

Although Henshaw traveled from planet to planet and interacted with various other cultures, the loneliness of his existence took its toll, and he slowly descended into the same kind of madness that had claimed the rest of the crew. Upon learning that Superman had inadvertently caused the solar flare that caused the *Excalibur* disaster (*Tales of the Sinestro Corps: Cyborg Superman* #1, December 2007; also see ERADICATOR), Henshaw became increasingly irrational. He began to burn for revenge against the Man of Steel, convincing himself that Superman had ruined his life deliberately and arranged his banishment from Earth.

Henshaw returned to Earth and posed as Superman as part of a failed effort to forcibly enlist the alien warlord MONGUL, of whom he became aware while visiting a planet Mongul controlled, in his quest for revenge. By this time, Superman had been killed in his battle with Doomsday, but not even his enemy's death could deter the Cyborg. If he could not kill the Man of Steel himself, Henshaw would settle for destroying his reputation with erratic, unheroic, and destructive behavior while passing himself off as Superman. He claimed to be the dead hero returned to life, his body having been reconstructed and resuscitated by advanced Kryptonian technology. It was information he gained during his psionic "possession" of Superman's birthing matrix that enabled him to pull off this ruse. Henshaw was able to build a body whose cybernetic components were made from Kryptonian materials and whose organic elements seemed genetically identical to Superman's. All this was confirmed upon careful examination by PROFESSOR EMIL HAMILTON (*Superman* [second series] #79, June 1993; others).

Henshaw appeared as Superman at the same time that three other super heroes arrived on the scene to fill the void left by the Man of Steel's death: John Henry Irons, aka STEEL; the Last Son of Krypton, who claimed to possess Superman's memories but did not share the Man of Steel's code against killing (he later turned out to be the Eradicator); and the Metropolis Kid, a new SUPERBOY.

The Metropolis Kid was a clone created by PROJECT CADMUS from genetic material it obtained by stealing Superman's body, which it kept until it was reclaimed by SUPERGIRL and LOIS LANE (*Superman: The Man of Steel* #22; *The Adventures of Superman* #501; *Action Comics* #687—all June 1993; others). Henshaw's positive actions, including the banishment of Doomsday into deep space, persuaded the U.S. government that Henshaw was the "real" Superman, conferring on him instant credibility and acceptance.

By the time Mongul was prepared to carry out the plan he had been forced into by Henshaw, the real Superman had in effect returned from the dead. It turned out that Superman's body had been stolen yet again, this time by the Last Son of Krypton, who had placed the body in a "regeneration matrix" in the FORTRESS OF SOLITUDE, to siphon off Superman's powers as the Man of Steel was revived in the chamber. But the regeneration matrix cracked open, freeing the original Superman, who was considerably less powerful but alive nevertheless.

Henshaw continued to pose as the real Superman until Mongul's warships appeared in orbit around Earth, as part of his attempt to transform Earth into a new WARWORLD. But the real Man of Tomorrow and a host of super-heroic allies, including Steel, Supergirl, and the Metropolis Kid, thwarted the plan. Henshaw's robotic body was destroyed, but his discarnate consciousness escaped.

After creating yet another new body for himself—this one clad in a costume less reminiscent of Superman's—the Cyborg repeatedly returned to bedevil his old enemy, in most cases assuming new forms as he projected his "electronic consciousness" into newly constructed bodies or other objects. At one point, he even inhabited a clay statue. In one case, Superman fought the Cyborg on APOKOLIPS after Henshaw had projected his consciousness into Doomsday (*Superman/Doomsday: Hunter/Prey* 1-3, 1994). In another encounter, Henshaw helped split the Man of Steel into twin energy beings, SUPERMAN RED and SUPERMAN BLUE (*Superman Red/Superman Blue* #1, February 1998; others).

In time, the Supermen were reintegrated into one organic being, and the Man of Steel's next battle with the Cyborg ended with Henshaw being trapped in the interstice between the other-dimensional city of KANDOR and Earth known as the PHANTOM ZONE (*The Adventures of Superman* #563, December 1998). After his efforts to escape the Zone with the help of the Cybermoths (see OVERMIND) failed (*Superman: The Man of Steel* #100, May 2000), the Cyborg found freedom courtesy of MANCHESTER BLACK's vendetta against Superman. He merged with Bunny, through which the Cyborg once more fought Superman (*Action Comics* #795, November 2002).

Henshaw reappeared as the Grandmaster of the Manhunters, the renegade robot police force created by the Oan Guardians of the Universe (*Green Lantern* [fourth series] #11, May 2006; others). His corporeal self was again destroyed when the Manhunters' homeworld exploded, leaving little more of the Cyborg intact than his head, which was then taken by the Guardians of the Universe back to their homeworld Oa for study.

Meanwhile, the GREEN LANTERN Corps's sworn enemy Sinestro, who wielded a yellow power ring designed to counteract the effects of the Green Lanterns' green ones, had formed the Sinestro Corps, a malign counterpart to the group created on Oa. Home base for the Sinestro Corps was the anti-matter world of Qward (*Green Lantern* [fourth series] #10, May 2006). At this point, Sinestro counted among his allies the resurrected ANTI-MONITOR.

The Sinestro Corps seized Henshaw's head during an attack on Oa and took it back to Qward. Fitted with a new cyborg body, Henshaw became a member of the Sinestro Corps and a herald of the newly returned Anti-Monitor. His hope was that the Anti-Monitor would eventually murder him and lay him to his final rest at last (*Green Lantern* [fourth series] #22, October 2007; others). Henshaw's last recorded contact with Superman to date occurred when the Cyborg joined the Sinestro Corps in an attack on Earth. En route, Henshaw and the Manhunters he led attacked the JUSTICE LEAGUE OF AMERICA's satellite headquarters, in an effort to destroy it by knocking it out of orbit. Superman intervened, and the knock-down, drag-out battle between the two moved to Earth, where Henshaw was ultimately driven away by the Man of Steel with the help of Supergirl and POWER GIRL (*Tales of the Sinestro Corps: Cyborg Superman* #1 and *Tales of the Sinestro Corps: Superman-Prime* #1—both December 2007).

Henshaw's last documented whereabouts placed him among the Manhunters, who, seeking the leadership of their fallen Grandmaster, were attempting to reconstruct him. They had rescued a fragment of his remains after Henshaw committed suicide. He did so by exposing himself to the massive blast that resulted when the Green Lantern Corps blew up the Sinestro Corps's central power battery to destroy the Anti-Monitor.

CYRIL

The civilian identity of the British super hero the Squire, whose father was the Earl of Wordenshire, secretly the KNIGHT, both of whom were charter members of the CLUB OF HEROES, a kind of prototype of the Global Guardians of which Superman was also a member (*Batman* #62, December 1950–January 1951; *World's Finest Comics* #89, July–August 1957). In the reality of New Earth, an adult Cyril became the new Knight and acquired a replacement Squire.

DAILY PLANET, THE

Arguably the greatest daily newspaper in Metropolis and possibly the nation, but more recently having experienced many reversals in fortune. The *Daily Planet* was the employer of all but one incarnation of Clark Kent, aka Superman—those of the pre–First Crisis Earth-1, the post-Crisis unified Earth, and New Earth—as well as co-workers and friends such as Lois Lane and Jimmy Olsen.

Ironically for an organization dedicated to disseminating fact and maintaining a public record, a comprehensive and consistent account of the *Planet*'s own history does not seem to have survived. Perhaps because the paper was always a venerable institution (according to varying accounts, it was between 150 and 210 years old in all its incarnations on three different Earths), and its reality was repeatedly revised by the various Crises, records of its founding, ownership, and notable achievements are riddled with discrepancies and possible apocrypha.

For most of its time on the pre–First Crisis Earth-1, the *Daily Planet* was the bestselling newspaper in Metropolis, with a reputation for accuracy and fairness that was beyond reproach. Precise records of the Earth-1 version's circulation at any given time no longer exist, but there was one account of the *Planet* celebrating the sale of its five billionth copy (*Superman* [first series] #144, April 1961). Whether this included the circulation of the *Planet*'s international editions in London, Paris, Bombay, Athens, Rome, Amsterdam, and Tokyo remains unknown.

The Earth-1 Daily Planet Building stood at the center of Planet Square in the heart of Metropolis (*Action Comics* #36, May 1941, and #77, October 1944; others). The exterior was renovated many times, adding and deleting various design features. For example, at one time, the building featured a horizontally scrolling electronic news feed that encircled the topmost story. But through all the face-lifts, the building's most distinctive feature remained constant. It was an icon as emblematic of the Metropolis skyline as the Empire State Building is of Manhattan's: a giant rooftop globe encircled by a Saturn-like ring, surmounted by huge block letters spelling out the paper's name.

There are varying accounts of the year the *Planet* began publication, some making the paper much older than others. In one chronicle, Perry White contended that the paper was founded in 1793 (*Superman* [first series] #20, January–February 1943). Another report claimed that the *Planet* had been founded in 1826 as a four-sheeter. Dates mentioned in other chronicles included 1844 and 1861, and yet another account claimed that the paper's official owner, the Daily Planet Publishing Company, Inc., was founded in 1870 (*Action Comics* #194, July 1954). One other document, however, gave the date as 1887 (*World's Finest Comics* #68, January–February 1954). Perhaps the least plausible account was that the *Planet* originated in San Francisco sometime around 1906 and was subsequently moved to Metropolis (*Superman* [first series] #168, April 1964).

Some of the legends in which the paper's early days were shrouded were more fanciful. For example, company mythology had it that tragedy struck on the paper's very first day of operation: A teenage "printer's devil" was crushed and killed when a huge roll of paper fell on him. Ever after, his ghost was said to guard the *Planet* and was credited on more than one occasion with scaring off enemies, such as would-be publishers plotting hostile takeovers (*Action Comics* #531, May 1982).

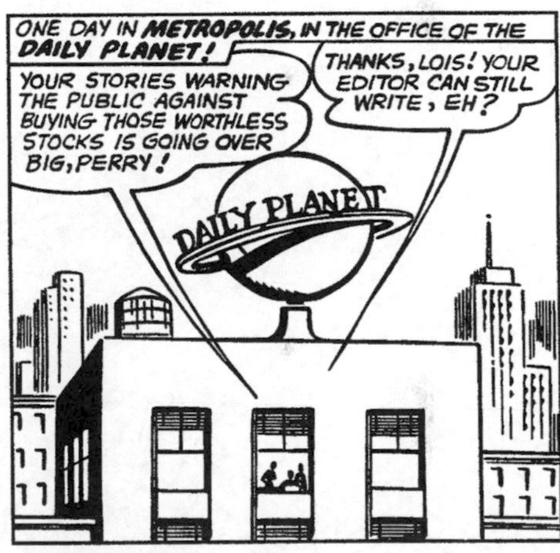

As ambiguous as the paper's founding date were the identities of the parent company and those who served as the Earth-1 *Planet*'s publisher over the years. While a plaque near the front entrance identified the owner as the Daily Planet Publishing Company, Inc. (*World's Finest* #29, July–August 1947; others), other accounts maintained that the paper was owned by an unidentified newspaper chain that also owned the *Gotham Gazette* (*World's Finest Comics* #75, March–April 1955). Not long before the First Crisis, the *Planet* was acquired by Galaxy Communications (*Superman* [first series] #233, January 1971).

The publisher's job was apparently that of a salaried employee rather than a part owner, as the publisher's office seems to have had a revolving door. Records identified no fewer than eight different individuals as the Earth-1 *Planet*'s publisher. Only one of these, Mark Vine, also identified as the paper's biggest stockholder (*Superman* [first series] #181, November 1965)—was reincarnated on the post-First Crisis unified Earth, appearing on mastheads as "Deputy Publisher" (*Daily Planet* facsimile, 1988). In at least two documents, Perry White was identified as the *Planet*'s publisher, but these were clearly historians' errors.

Even before its acquisition by Galaxy Communications, owners of the GBS television network, the *Planet* had ties to broadcasting in the form of subsidiary enterprises. The paper had its own radio station, WPLT (*Superman* [first series] #39, March–April 1946); its own television studios, WMET-TV (*World's Finest Comics* #52, June–July 1951); and its own mobile television unit for covering news events as they happened (*Superman* [first series] #57, March–April 1949). By the same token, the *Planet* became the first newspaper in Metropolis to embrace a form of news-gathering equipment that is commonplace today, when it began operating its own helicopter, which it called the Flying Newsroom (*Superman's Pal, Jimmy Olsen* #1, September–October 1954; others).

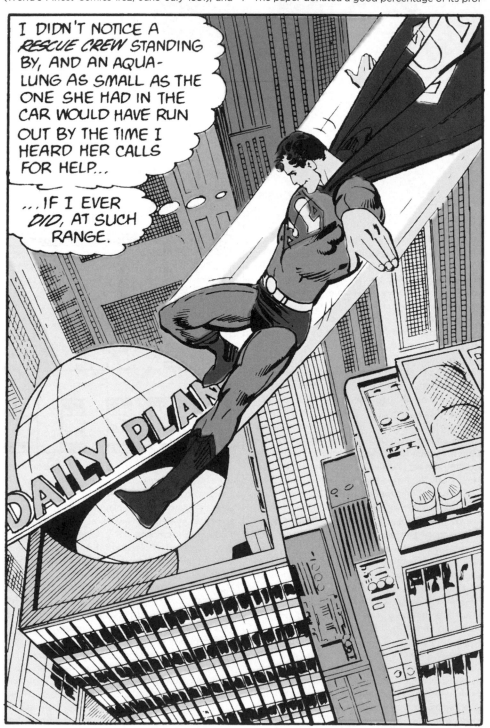

Perhaps the most admirable characteristic of the *Planet* that distinguished it from its competitors was its serious commitment to philanthropy. The paper donated a good percentage of its profits to charity. That was what the public believed to be the main reason for Superman's apparently special relationship with the paper, which always ran more "exclusives" on the Man of Steel's exploits than did its rivals.

While the paper's goodwill certainly endeared it to Superman, the public would never know that the primary reason for Superman seeming to "favor" the *Planet* was that it was his boss. Clark Kent had chosen journalism for his profession because having access to late-breaking news kept him apprised of situations that required Superman's attention.

The Man of Steel's connection with the paper loomed large in the public imagination. For example, the *Planet* became the place where strangers went to leave messages for Superman or send him mail (*Action Comics* #161, October 1951; others). Not surprisingly, "the most complete collection of Superman's feats ever recorded on film" was in the paper's morgue (*Superman* [first series] #91, August 1954).

The *Planet* was just as valuable to Superman as he was to it. Clark Kent's job enabled him to investigate criminals without their suspecting that Superman was on to them. Moreover, a job in which he was routinely expected to be off-site, "in the field," was made to order for him, since it allowed him to function as Superman without having to explain frequent absences.

But any conventional job can pose unique challenges for a super hero. The Earth-1 Kent often had to change to Superman in empty closets and storage spaces, and at one point he took to hiding a sophisticated Clark Kent robot behind a secret panel he had constructed in a supply room. The robot was programmed to do Kent's job whenever he was needed elsewhere as Superman.

Shortly before the First Crisis, the *Daily Planet* was acquired by Galaxy Communications, whose CEO, Morgan Edge, reassigned Clark Kent to an owned-and-operated station of the Galaxy Broadcasting System, local Metropolis station WGBS. There Kent began as an on-air reporter and was quickly promoted to anchor of the local evening newscast (*Superman* [first series] #233, January 1971; others). Not long afterward, Kent acquired a co-anchor in the form of his boyhood friend from Smallville, Lana Lang.

Galaxy extensively remodeled the Daily Planet Building, adding extra stories to bring the total to fifty-two. The *Planet* offices were located on the eighth floor; the WGBS studios on the twentieth; Galaxy Records and Video on the fourteenth; and so on. Morgan Edge worked in a combination office-apartment in the penthouse.

After the ownership change, the *Planet,* like many newspapers, had considerable financial difficulties in the years just before the First Crisis. But that event would change Superman's work environment dramatically. Just as the histories and daily existences of many *people* in Metropolis were reshaped by the effects of the First Crisis, so, too, were the *Planet*'s. But the new version of the paper was every bit the equal of the old in its reputation for journalistic excellence, to which its numerous Pulitzer and World Press Awards attested.

This version of the paper was founded by an early American named Joshua Merriweather, who began it in 1775 as a weekly called *Our Planet.* A record survived of a guest editorial written for the first daily edition by George Washington, and the paper always claimed that the first president's farewell address was based on that editorial's text. In June 1938, the *Planet* moved to new quarters in a thirty-seven-story building at the corner of Fifth Street and Concord Lane. Like its Earth-1 predecessor, this Daily Planet Building, too, was distinguished by an enormous rooftop globe, and this roof, too, became the site for many impromptu meetings between the *Planet*'s senior staff and Superman. For Clark Kent, it also served as an excellent place to which to beat a hasty retreat when a quick change to Superman was needed.

The unified Earth's Perry White emerged with a new past as well. He was born in the Metropolis ghetto of Suicide Slum and started his career at the *Planet* as a copyboy while just a teenager. He worked his way up, job by job, from cub reporter to managing editor, finally becoming editor in chief in a maneuver worthy of a sophisticated publishing tycoon. As a result, the *Planet* of this reality remained under his editorial guidance for almost three decades.

Long before either Clark Kent or Lois Lane began working for the paper, it was owned by Lex Luthor. But not even the most successful newspaper in the world could yield the kind of profits that would satisfy a man like Luthor, who quickly became disenchanted with publishing and sought to rid himself of what had come to be an albatross around his neck. Sensing his opportunity, Perry White convinced an international conglomerate, TransNational Enterprises, to buy the paper, but with the stipulation that Perry White would become editor in chief. Perry's old friend Franklin Stern would be named publisher.

Under TransNational, the *Planet* published both a morning and an evening broadsheet, as well as a sizable Sunday edition. Several overseas bureaus gathered worldwide news for both the hometown paper and the *International Daily Planet*, which became the most widely read English-language newspaper on the European continent.

Under White's skillful guidance, the *Planet* weathered a number of major challenges—most of them much more dramatic than the usual union negotiations, strikes, declining circulation and ad revenue, and pressures from local politicians faced by newspapers in cities that *didn't* have a resident super hero and the superpowered enemies he attracted. In addition to ongoing hostility from the fearsomely powerful Luthor, who felt he got insufficiently respectful coverage from TransNational's *Planet,* White's job was complicated by the near destruction of the Planet Building itself on at least two occasions.

On one, a "clone plague" unleashed by Project Cadmus—the inspiration of the madman Dabney Donovan—began sickening and threatening the lives of numerous prominent figures who were—secretly or otherwise—clones. These included Kon-El/Conner Kent, the Metropolis Kid. Another was Alexander Luthor, Junior—who was not, as the public believed, the son of the better-known tycoon, believed dead, but in fact merely a freshly cloned "continuation" of the same Luthor all Metropolis knew and feared. To protect himself from Superman or any other meta-human acting against him in his plague-weakened state, Luthor established a stockpile of ultrasonic missiles aimed at key locations in Metropolis. When Superman located the dying Luthor, the missiles were launched, and one of them decimated the upper stories of the Planet Building, blasting off the globe (*Action Comics* #699–701, May–July 1994; others). On White's watch, the Planet Building also sustained heavy damage as a result of Doomsday's various rampages.

Arguably the paper's darkest hour, however, came when Franklin Stern, unable to stem the tide of red ink caused by a public turning ever increasingly to electronic media, felt compelled to put the *Planet* up for sale. Lex Luthor had always despised the heavy criticism of himself and his company for which the TransNational *Planet*

became renowned. This was largely due to Lois Lane's relentless efforts to prove and publicize her conviction that Luthor was no mere "misunderstood businessman" but, in fact, a world-class criminal. The proverbial last straw came after Luthor's marriage to the Contessa and the birth of their daughter Lena Luthor, a photograph of whom was published by the *Planet.* This violation of Luthor's privacy so enraged the billionaire that he dedicated himself to acquiring the paper once more, this time to shut it down for good (*Superman: Save the Planet,* October 1998; others).

Luthor fired all *Planet* employees except Simone DeNeige, Dirk Armstrong, Jimmy Olsen, and Lois Lane. To add insult to injury, Luthor had the *Planet's* trademark globe removed and hauled away as scrap. In place of the newspaper emerged "LexCom," an Internet news site that existed primarily as a mouthpiece for Luthor's views, essentially making Superman's longtime nemesis a yellow journalist in the tradition of William Randolph Hearst.

Eventually, Luthor sold the *Daily Planet* to Perry White, backed by a group of investors called Global Communications, for a nominal sum, for reasons known only to Luthor and Lois Lane. The star reporter made a secret deal whereby, in exchange for allowing the *Planet* to reopen for business, Luthor would be granted the option of spiking one story of his choice at some later time, no questions asked.

The paper was quickly revived, and its entire former staff rehired. One of the conditions of the Global deal was that Perry White would be made publisher, a high-pressure job quite challenging for a man like White, who was nearing traditional retirement age. In some circles, Luthor let it be known that he hoped the stress of the job would kill Perry. Despite Luthor's loss of an ownership position, his deal with Lane afforded the billionaire a means of exerting undue influence over the paper, however indirectly, that would not diminish until Luthor was elected president.

As long as Luthor's designs on the *Planet* could still be perceived, many Metropolis power brokers remained uneasy—and even some leaders in communities not directly served by the *Planet,* such as Gotham City, shared their concern. Lucius Fox, a close associate of Bruce Wayne, aka Batman, acquired a seat on Global's board of directors, perhaps as a hedge against Luthor tightening his grip on the *Planet* from behind the scenes. Fox paved the way for Wayne to acquire the *Planet,* and during the Wayne period, the paper redoubled its efforts to recapture its former, sterling reputation.

Just as all of Metropolis was transformed into the City of Tomorrow by Brainiac 13's Y2K virus, so, too, was the Daily Planet Building "upgraded," including a holographic rooftop globe that replaced the material one. The thirty-seven-story skyscraper became more futuristic in appearance and technologically more user-friendly. But the virus ultimately caused "temporal instabilities," as the chronicles put it, and both the Daily Planet Building—including the globe—and Metropolis as a whole reverted to their previous forms. The restoration, however, did not prevent the latest technology from being made available to the paper's staff, and the *Planet* was still able to cover late-breaking stories with greater speed than ever before. The venerable news outlet continued to compete with LexCom and other Internet news services. Bruce Wayne retained ownership of the *Planet* until reality was once again reordered by the Infinite Crisis.

The *Daily Planet* that emerged on the New Earth was in many respects similar to its previous incarnations and in many ways quite different. Its location, at the corner of Fifth Street and Concord Lane, remained the same, but its chief competitors as news sources became the tabloid *Daily Star* and WGBS-TV, which, in this new reality, were both owned by New Earth's version of Lex Luthor, and subsequently Morgan Edge. This *Planet* challenged Luthor's media manipulation, and a fiery editorial written by Perry White was seen as a challenge to Luthor's supremacy. Luthor's control over businesses led to advertising dollars for the *Planet* vanishing and circulation plummeting, and by the time Clark Kent began work at the paper, it was on the verge of bankruptcy. The globe atop the building had rusted to a halt, and the reporters the paper could afford were described as "bottom of the barrel . . . troublemakers . . . extremists and fresh fish" (*Superman: Secret Origin* #3, January 2010). The New Earth Luthor was little different from his previous incarnation. He, too, was a master manipulator working from behind the scenes who used his characteristically underhanded techniques to undermine the *Daily Planet*'s reputation.

The appearance of Superman and the special bond he forged with the paper set it on course to becoming a great journalistic institution. All the staffers with special ties to Superman—White, Lane, Olsen, and Kent—remained with the paper. Versions of other staffers, who had left the *Planet*'s employ in previous realities—such as Catherine "Cat" Grant and sportscaster Steve Lombard—were employees as of this writing.

DAILY STAR, THE

The *Daily Planet*'s counterpart on the pre-First Crisis Earth-2 (*Action Comics* #1, June 1938; others). As Clark Kent, Superman worked for the *Star* under editor George Taylor. The Kent of Earth-2 eventually became the editor in chief of the *Daily Star,* something his Earth-1 counterpart never achieved. The *Daily Star* of Earth-1 was the major newspaper in Star City, edited by George Taylor II (*World's Finest Comics* #244, April–May 1977; others). On the post–First Crisis unified Earth, the *Daily Star* existed in Metropolis as one of the *Daily Planet*'s competitors (*Superman* [second series] #9, September 1987; others). It remained so in the New Earth reality, but its owner was Morgan Edge.

DALE, JAROD

The pawn of corrupt meta-human minister Matthew Hightower, who was turned into the super-criminal Redemption (*Action Comics* #848, May 2007).

DANVERS, EDNA

The adoptive mother of the Kryptonian Kara Zor-El Supergirl on the pre-First Crisis unified Earth, in the small Metropolis suburb of Midvale. At the time of her adoption, Supergirl—going by the name Linda Lee Danvers—had lost her superpowers, but they were quickly restored. Those powers, like the existence of her costumed identity itself (Supergirl was originally her cousin Superman's "secret weapon" before being publicly revealed to the world), were initially kept secret even from Edna and her husband Fred. But the subterfuge did not last long, and when Linda's secret was revealed to them, the Danverses were totally accepting of their daughter's unusual nature. Edna seemed to be very much the average, middle-class suburban parent of her day, appropriately supportive and attentive to her daughter's needs, but her life was not extensively chronicled and little is known about her today (*Action Comics* #279, August 1961; others).

DANVERS, FRED

The name of Supergirl's human father on both the pre-First Crisis Earth-1 and the post–First Crisis Earth. About the Earth-1 incarnation, who had adopted Kara Zor-El under the name Linda Lee Danvers, little was recorded. What information does survive suggests that Danvers was a middle-class family man whose high moral values and commitment to his loved ones were very much the

product of his time (*Action Comics* #279, August 1961; others). A gifted scientist, Danvers was later tapped to serve as director of a division of S.T.A.R. Labs in his hometown of Midvale (*Superman Family* #188, March–April 1978; others).

The post-Crisis incarnation was a police officer in the town of Leesburg, Virginia (*Supergirl* [fourth series] #1, September 1996; others). As he advanced through the ranks from police sergeant to plainclothes detective, Danvers became increasingly disturbed by his daughter's worsening delinquency—not only out of paternal concern but also because the possibility that her association with criminal elements could compromise his career and impair his ability to support his family. He was always much harder on Linda than her mother or other loved ones, which ultimately seemed to aggravate the problem more than help it. But when he learned that his daughter had merged with Matrix to become Supergirl (*Supergirl* [fourth series] #14, October 1997), he was the first to embrace the development and took great pride in his daughter.

DANVERS, LINDA

On the post-First Crisis unified Earth, an emotionally troubled teenage native of Leesburg, Virginia, and the natural-born human daughter of Fred and Sylvia Danvers. At the moment of her death, she joined with the Supergirl, who was also known as Matrix—a genetically engineered being created by a good Lex Luthor in an alternate reality known as a "Pocket Universe"—to become the Earth-born Angel incarnation of Supergirl (*Supergirl* [fourth series] #1, September 1996; others).

DANVERS, LINDA LEE

The name taken by the Kryptonian Kara Zor-El Supergirl when she became the adoptive daughter of Fred and Edna Danvers on the pre-First Crisis Earth-1. She was adopted from Midvale Orphanage, where she had been living as Linda Lee (*Action Comics* #279, August 1961; others).

DANVERS, SYLVIA

The mother of Linda Danvers, aka Supergirl, on the post-First Crisis unified Earth. She had great difficulty accepting the idea that her daughter had merged with the artificially created Supergirl—also known as Matrix—to become an Earth-born Angel, when the secret was finally revealed to her (*Supergirl* [fourth series] #14, October 1997). She was able to make her peace with it only with the help of counseling from Wally Johnson, an odd neighborhood child who claimed to be a manifestation of God, or the Source, as the concept was sometimes identified in the super hero world. The experience inspired her to pursue entering the ministry, and she became one of her daughter's staunchest supporters and advisers.

DARKSEID; AKA DARK SIDE

A breathtakingly ruthless tyrant and conqueror of entire planets, arguably the most dangerous being in the documented super hero universe. Darkseid was the embodiment of unimaginable evil, and the greatest threat to life as we know it. He was a formidable figure, super-strong, ostensibly invulnerable, and possibly immortal. He stood more than eight and a half feet tall and weighed over eighteen hundred pounds, with a gray, stone-like hide and red eyes from which he could—at least at one point in his life—project the Omega Effect. This effect comprised beams of unlimited power that could incinerate and vaporize anything, living or otherwise, and teleport and dematerialize any organic being.

Darkseid was a fearfully unforgiving overlord who ruled exclusively by terror, torture, and various other forms of sadism. If he possessed a positive quality at all, it was his profound sense of honor, which sometimes trumped his ruthlessness. Occasionally, he was known to spare the lives of opponents who likewise comported themselves honorably, and fought with valor and loyalty to their causes.

Darkseid's life's ambition became reshaping the universe to his own specifications and desires,

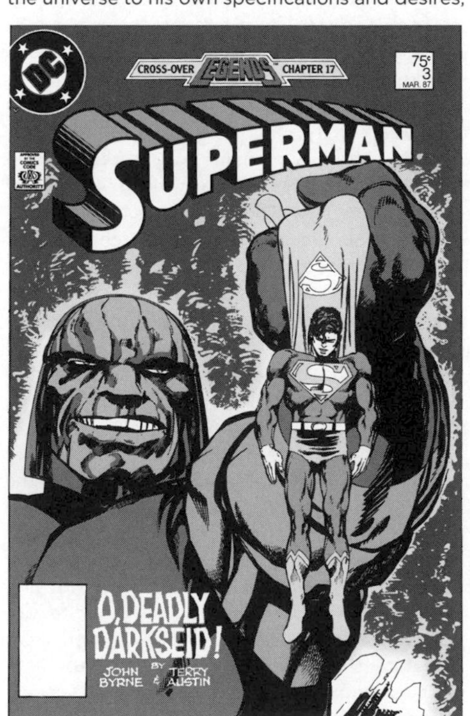

and doing so by eradicating free will from all its inhabitants. This he hoped to accomplish by finding and deciphering the elusive and enigmatic Anti-Life Equation. The equation was so difficult for ordinary humans to comprehend that various historians defined it in different ways. But the consensus, if any, was that it was a mathematical proof of the pointlessness and hopelessness of life itself. By possessing the Anti-Life Equation, Darkseid would, he believed, gain total mind control over all living beings.

Darkseid was particularly intent on pursuing his agenda on Earth, believing that all *Homo sapiens* were born with most, if not all, elements of the equation in their subconscious. By probing every human mind, Darkseid hoped to assemble the equation, piece by piece. This was the reason Darkseid fought so fiercely with so many super heroes, particularly Superman. In time, it was discovered—especially during the world-changing events of Infinite Crisis and Final Crisis—that certain individuals, usually meta-humans such as Mister Miracle, retrieved from their subconscious the equation in its entirety. Some, like Scott Free, had the willpower not to use it; others simply didn't seem to know what to do with it.

Darkseid generally kept a low profile, preferring instead to send various agents and minions with a wide array of strange powers and skills to do his dirty work. He found it particularly helpful to work through Intergang, a national crime syndicate armed with technology from Apokolips. Some more recent accounts depicted Intergang as having developed into a cult that worshipped Darkseid as the god of evil, but the implied religiosity in no way diminished Intergang's threat to the country, particularly Metropolis. Over the years, Darkseid's powers increased or waned, usually as a result of seemingly having been mortally wounded, or siphoning off energy from Orion during his frequent battles with this New God, who was his son. Upon one of Darkseid's many "deaths," Orion assumed leadership of Apokolips, only to be forced to cede that control to his father when the latter returned from "the grave."

First documented by historians in *Superman's Pal, Jimmy Olsen* #134, November 1970, and *Forever People* #1, February–March 1971, among other chronicles, Darkseid emerged from obscurity as a major threat to the pre-First Crisis Earth-1 when he was unmasked as the secret mentor and financier of the original Secret Society of Super-

Villains. But he was an amoral figure, willing to help the heroes of Earth as well, if it would advance his own agenda of the moment or prevent his own destruction.

Hailing from the other-dimensional planet Apokolips, in the so-called Fourth World—where, it was theorized, time and other physical laws operated somewhat differently than on our own plane of existence—Darkseid and the other New Gods were relatively unchanged by the First Crisis, and persisted through the many reality-altering cataclysms afterward.

Apokolips was born out of the conflagration that claimed the old gods and became a perpetually burning world. Upon the old gods' death, two races of new ones evolved on different planets: verdant, beautiful New Genesis and hellish, horrifically oppressive Apokolips. From the first, the two worlds waged war incessantly. On Apokolips, king Yuga Khan and his queen Heggra had two sons, the princes Uxas and Drax. Uxas, only second in line to the throne, plotted to seize power. When Drax sought to harness the legendary Omega Force for his personal and exclusive use, Uxas ostensibly killed him (but it would later be revealed that he had survived the attempt on his life, to emerge in the guise of Infinity-Man) and took the power, which transformed his body's tissues into a mineral-like substance. At that point, he took a new name: Darkseid (*Jack Kirby's Fourth World* #2–5, April–July 1997).

Heggra and her surviving son continually plotted against each other in their quest for absolute rule of Apokolips and the universe beyond, in grand dramas with inevitably Shakespearean or Wagnerian overtones. For example, when Darkseid married a sorceress against his mother's wishes, Heggra ordered her daughter-in-law killed by the court torture master DeSaad—but not before Darkseid's first wife Suli bore him a son, Kalibak. Despite killing Suli, DeSaad became a close ally of Darkseid's, and even murdered Heggra at his lord's secret behest (*New Gods* [first series] #11, February–March 1971; *New Gods* [third series] #20, September 1990; *Eclipso* #10, August 1993).

The point of Heggra's intrigues was to facilitate a cessation of hostilities, if not outright peace, between Apokolips and New Genesis. Darkseid was forced to remarry, and his second wife Tigra gave him a second son, the handsome, fair-haired Orion. All this was in preparation for the terms of the treaty known as the Pact, in which the sons of the warring worlds' leaders were exchanged. New Genesis's Highfather raised Orion as his own, while Scott Free, who on Earth would be known as the super-heroic escape artist Mister Miracle, would be raised in a brutal orphanage on Apokolips. While the boys' true parentage was at first kept secret, the truth was ultimately revealed to them. The hatred and resentment Orion felt for his natural father and his repudiation of the values of Apokolips, as well as the enmity Scott Free felt for his adoptive father, would complicate Darkseid's quest for the Anti-Life Equation many times in the years to come.

The murder of his first wife did little to soften Darkseid's already considerably hardened heart, of course, and after Darkseid had his mother killed, he secured his position as undisputed ruler of Apokolips. Darkseid bided his time, consolidating his power until the modern age of heroes on Earth, when he began his quest for the Anti-Life Equation in earnest. During his so-called Operation: Humiliation, Darkseid attempted to destroy Earth's growing super hero community by reducing their legends to dust. His agent, propagandist Glorious Godfrey, turned Earth's populace against its heroes, quickly transforming them into outlaws (*Legends* #1–6, November 1986–April 1987). Superman was among the heroes to eventually prove triumphant, thereby earning him Darkseid's perpetual enmity.

Soon after, Superman was captured and brought to Apokolips, where, working on behalf of Darkseid, the New God Amazing Grace temporarily turned Superman into Darkseid's champion of Apokolips. With the help of Orion, Superman soon defeated Darkseid (*Superman* [second series] #3; *The Adventures of Superman* #426; *Action Comics* #586—all March 1987). Superman, on his first and only date with Wonder Woman, was also present to battle Darkseid when he dared lay siege to Mount Olympus (*Action Comics* #600, July 1987).

Highfather and Metron then summoned a host of heroes to prevent Darkseid from harnessing the power of the Anti-Life Equation. With the Thanagarians in the grip of madness induced by an aspect of the Anti-Life, Superman and Orion strove to prevent a doomsday weapon from destroying the planet Thanagar. Green Lantern John Stewart, however, felt responsible for the destruction of the planet Xanshi (*Cosmic Odyssey* #1–4, 1988).

The struggles between Superman and Darkseid continued through the subsequent years. When Green Lantern Hal Jordan and the Man of Steel discovered the planet Pluto had vanished, they learned that Maxima and Massacre had formed an alliance with Darkseid thanks to the encroachment of Imperiex [*Superman* [second series] #159, August 2000). Lex Luthor secretly handed over Doomsday to Darkseid as payment for the "war debt" that existed between Apokolips and Earth following the Imperiex war (*Superman* [second series] #175, December 2001).

Given the dark lord's perseverance, it was inevitable that he would finally one day obtain the Anti-Life Equation. Once he possessed it, he used it to completely destroy the Fourth World (*Seven Soldiers: Mister Miracle* #1–4, November 2005–May 2006). The New Gods fled to Earth and found

themselves reincarnated in different forms, with Darkseid now a criminal gang leader called Boss Dark Side. As he amassed his power on Earth, Boss Dark Side finally took possession of humankind's will, corrupting heroes and villains alike. One by one the various Gods were subsequently being killed, with all suspicion pointing to Dark Side until he battled his son Orion, with Superman as a powerless witness, resulting in his death (*Death of the New Gods* #1–8, Early December 2007–June 2008). Using Metron's Mobius Chair, Darkseid also fired a "time-traveling" Radion bullet that killed Orion. The Boss's spirit then took up residence in Metropolis cop Dan Turpin, which began the Final Crisis, the last part of Darkseid's gambit to control the universe. As humanity succumbed to the Anti-Life Equation, Dark Side found himself at war for Turpin's soul. After finally conquering weakened Turpin, Darkseid was resurrected in a new form, complete with modified armor. As the remnants of the meta-human community struggled for freedom, Batman managed to shoot Darkseid with a Radion bullet. At the same time, Darkseid seemingly killed the Dark Night with twin blasts of his Omega beams. With the Radion poison coursing through his body, Darkseid and a distraught Superman battled across Earth until the New God was finally claimed by the Black Racer. Darkseid's spirit still sought purchase on the mortal plane by attempting to access Superman's Miracle Machine, but the Man of Steel sang a musical note at the only frequency that could shatter the device thereby seemingly ridding the universe of Darkseid's presence forever (*Final Crisis* #1–7, July 2008–March 2009).

There is little doubt that at some point the malevolent Darkseid will find his way back to the Fifth World.

DAVIS, LISA

A quiet, somewhat shy high school student who harbored a crush on Clark Kent in the Smallville of the pre-First Crisis Earth-1. Just as Superboy sometimes chafed that Lana Lang tended not to notice his mild-mannered alter ego, so, too, did Clark Kent fail to recognize Lisa Davis's interest in him until Lana herself finally pointed Clark in the right direction. Lisa misinterpreted Clark's mysterious, abrupt exits as a sign that he didn't care, but apologies were made and the couple settled into a comfortable routine. Clark's self-esteem rose as Lisa prodded him to stop making self-deprecating comments. Although details were never documented, the romance was short-lived, an evident consequence of possibly criminal deals made by Lisa's real estate agent father (*The New Adventures of Superboy* #40–50, April 1983–February 1984, and #54, June 1984).

DAXAM

A planet that figured prominently in the history of the Legion of Super-Heroes in all its realities. Second in orbit around the red sun Valor (*Action Comics Annual* #10, 2007), Daxam was home to a race of people settled by Kryptonians who interbred with natives found on the planet, thereby forming a new society. In time, they forgot about their connection to Krypton, but when a Daxam expedition came to Earth eons ago, a son was born to one of the Daxamite women who was half human. This woman was an ancestor to Lar Gand, who grew up to become the hero known as Mon-El (*Superman* [second series] *Annual* #14, 2009). Given their genetic heritage, Daxamites gained approximately the same abilities as Kryptonians under a yellow sun in lighter gravity. They had a far more insidious vulnerability than kryptonite, however. Exposure to lead caused rapid deterioration of any Daxamite's bodily functions and could also result in death. As a result, to protect themselves, space travel was forbidden. Lar Gand violated that taboo after discovering his ancestral starship and used it to leave his homeworld, eventually landing in Smallville on Earth (*Superboy* [first series] #89, June 1961).

DEARDEN, DANA

A mentally unstable Superman fan who obtained superpowers from stolen mystical artifacts and adopted the costumed identity of Superwoman in an effort to become his lover and partner. She kidnapped Jimmy Olsen to gain access to his signal watch, to lure the Man of Steel to their first meeting. Olsen had a different idea about a name for Dearden's costumed persona, by which she became better known: Obsession (*The Adventures of Superman* #534, May 1996; others).

DEATHTRAP

See Master Jailer.

DELGADO, JOSE

See Gangbuster.

DEMOLITIA

A Latin American female vigilante in the post-First Crisis Metropolis who used the ordnance and

teleportation technology of Bloodsport not for crime, but to avenge the underprivileged who had been victimized as she had. The account of her one appearance gave only her first name, Marita. When Metropolis lay in ruins during the clone plague, Marita was trapped under the rubble of a demolished building. She was found by a gang, who brutally assaulted her. She made a vow that if she survived, she would devote herself to championing the downtrodden. And survive she did.

By means not documented, Marita acquired Bloodsport's capability to teleport weapons to himself from a distant, unknown location, as well as teleport herself to that location. In a costume based on the original Bloodsport's, she assumed the persona of Demolitia. Superman encountered her when she targeted a recently acquitted arms dealer whom she was convinced was guilty. The Man of Steel intervened when a firefight ensued between Demolitia and former LexCorp employees who were in the arms dealer's employ. In the course of this, Demolitia confronted a confusing moral ambiguity when the workers at the munitions factory she tried to shut down—underprivileged people like herself—protested that she would take away their only means of feeding their families. Demolitia teleported away and was never seen again (*Action Comics* #718, February 1996). There has been no record of a version of Demolitia appearing on New Earth.

DENEIGE, SIMONE

A celebrated international journalist on the post-First Crisis unified Earth, hired by Lex Luthor's *Daily Planet* as marketing director in a desperate bid to boost the paper's flagging circulation (*The Adventures of Superman* #543, February 1997; others).

A native of France, DeNeige was originally a reporter for *Le Journal du Monde* in Paris. She may also have been young Clark Kent's first lover, when he spent some time in Paris after graduating from college (*The Adventures of Superman* #0, October 1994). After the end of their affair, DeNeige worked as a foreign correspondent for a number of news outlets.

Ironically, it was one of Simone's directives that caused the temporary shutdown of the *Planet*. It was she who ordered the publication of the photo of Lex Luthor's daughter that drove the enraged megalomaniac to acquire and dismantle the paper. Luthor did not fire DeNeige, however; his hatred of Lois Lane seems to have trumped his indignation over the photograph. Instead Luthor made DeNeige managing editor of his online news feed, LexCom, knowing how much it would enrage Lois. Previously, during Lane's stint at LexCom, she and DeNeige repeatedly locked horns over issues of ethics and social responsibility, with Lois maintaining that the only kind of journalism DeNeige knew was tabloid sensationalism.

D.E.O.

See chase, cameron.

DESAAD

A master of sadism and torture who served the court of Darkseid on Apokolips.

DEV-EM

A Kryptonian juvenile delinquent who was placed into orbit in a state of suspended animation when he could not be properly rehabilitated. The explosion of Krypton threw his ship from orbit, and it tumbled through space until it landed in Smallville on Earth. Revived during his trip, he challenged Superboy, upon meeting the Teen of Steel, and sent the young hero to the Phantom Zone. He then assumed Superboy's identity in an effort to destroy the goodwill the hero had earned throughout Smallville. Satisfied his work was done, he traveled to the thirtieth century to seek new thrills. (*Adventure Comics* #287–288, August–September 1961).

Superboy next encountered Dev-Em after he had joined the Interstellar Counter-Intelligence Corps (*Adventure Comics* #320, May 1964). His irritating manner did not stop the Legion of Super-Heroes from offering him membership, something Dev-Em turned down. When needed, however, Dev-Em came to the Legion's aid several times, including during the Great Darkness Saga (*Legion of Super-Heroes* [second series] #294, December 1982; others).

After the events of the Crisis on Infinite Earths, Dev-Em was known as David Emery, a former resident of Titan, homeworld of Saturn Girl, who possessed several Kryptonian-style superpowers (*Who's Who in the Legion* #1, April 1988) that were a throwback to rare earlier Titanian heroes, such as the twentieth century's Kral (*Adventure Comics* #205, October 1954).

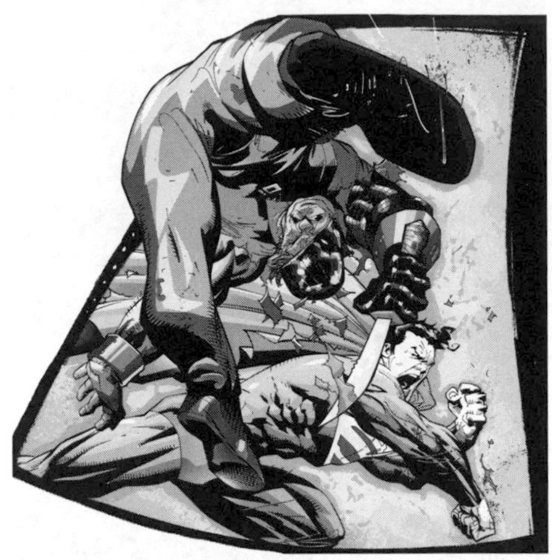

When Superman found himself bounced through time to the thirtieth century, he encountered Dev-Em, who was said to be an insane native of Daxam trying to destroy Earth's moon, but was confronted by the Legion. While proving a match for Superman's abilities, he could not stop a final assault from Shrinking Violet, who crawled into his ear canals, distracting him while Superman finally took the vigilante out (*The Adventures of Superman* #478, May 1991).

A different man known as Devem was seen as part of the cult of Kryptonian worshippers honoring the sacrifice of Superboy during the Infinite Crisis (*52* #4, May 31, 2006, #13, August 2, 2006). It was revealed that Devem was actually Derek Mathers, an escapee from a psychiatric ward who had a long history of fraud behind him (*52* #31, December 6, 2006).

The real post-Infinite Crisis version of Dev-Em was seen as a renegade murderer trapped within the Phantom Zone. At one point, he attempted to attack Superman but was stopped by Mon-El (*Action Comics* #851, August 2007).

DEV-RE

A paraplegic scientist in the Kandor of the pre-First Crisis Earth-1 who was the friend and confidant of Superman and Jimmy Olsen when they operated in the Kryptonian city as Nightwing and Flamebird, respectively. He became the duo's trusted ally after he accidentally discovered the pair's "Nightcave" before it could be destroyed by a construction project and moved its equipment, including the Nightmobile, to his home in Kandor (*Superman Family* #173, October–November 1975.

DICKSON, DEKE

A former S.T.A.R. Labs CPA who gained possession of a molecular disrupting device to give himself the power to "phase," or pass through, matter, as Loophole (*The Adventures of Superman* #505, October 1993; *Superboy and the Ravens* #8, April 1997; others).

DNALIENS

A general term for cloned humanoids created by altering human DNA and, occasionally, recombining it with alien genetic material, usually Kryptonian. The DNAliens were exclusively the product of Project Cadmus; the most extensively documented of them was Dubbilex.

DNANGELS

Three super-beings named Cherub, Epiphany, and Seraph who were bioengineered at the order of the U.S. military at a cost of more than two billion dollars. Their orders, whose motivations and purpose often seemed questionable, frequently placed the DNAngels in conflict with Kon-El, the Metropolis Kid. For example, on one occasion they were directed to abduct the infant clone of Jim Harper, the Guardian, while the Kid was caring for the baby.

Later, the Kid learned from Amanda Spence that the DNAngels were in part the product of the Kid's own genetic material, as well as that of other metahumans. Eventually, the DNAngels realized they were being manipulated by the government for ethically questionable purposes, and they decided to strike out on their own as independent super heroes (*Superboy* [third series] #87–90, June–September 2001). To date, there have been no accounts of an equivalent to the DNAngels appearing on New Earth (see also Project Cadmus; New Gods).

DOC

See Hocus and Pocus.

DOCTOR VIRUS

The code name for a renegade scientist in New Earth Metropolis whose real name was Dr. Verisofsky. An aspiring Intergang member, Verisofsky attempted to kill Superman with a seemingly sentient organism he called Kryptococcus the Omni-Germ, but the Man of Steel quickly neutralized the bizarre entity and arrested Doctor Virus (*Action Comics* #840, August 2006).

DOCTOR ZODIAC

A fraudulent fortune-teller on the pre–First Crisis Earth-1. He was tricked by Superman and Batman into revealing the identity of numerous criminals when the heroes allowed him to capture robot duplicates of themselves (*World's Finest Comics* #160, September 1966). Later the Man of Steel and the Dark Knight thwarted his plan to steal twelve magical Zodiac coins from Atlantis (*World's Finest Comics* #268, April–May 1981), but Zodiac gained control of them again, and wresting their power from him required that Superman and Batman enlist the aid of Wonder Woman and the real magic practitioner, Zatanna (*World's Finest Comics* #285–287, November 1982–January 1983).

DOMINUS

In all the documented realities, pre–First Crisis and afterward, there were Lords of Order and Lords of Chaos, opposing mystical entities with near-divine power. They existed to keep each other in check and created a stasis that kept the universe in balance and slowed its inevitable entropy. These forces usually required physical form to have a direct effect on the material world, by either creating bodies for themselves, inhabiting a living creature, or forcing humans to function as their agents. And though they were incorporeal in their natural state, what kept them one step removed from genuine godhood was that they were susceptible to the emotional frailties usually associated with physical existence, such as ambition, lust, greed, and so on.

Dominus was a prime example of this apparent paradox. One Lord of Order, named Ahti, evolved to a state more closely approaching genuine godhood, earning the designation Kismet, Illuminator of All Realities. As Kismet, she existed on a plane of existence beyond Superman's comprehension, acting as a kind of buffer between the Lords of Order and Chaos (*Superman* [second series] #139, October 1998). She appeared to humans when necessary and gave them opportunities to choose between good and evil by showing them the potential consequences of their choices—in other words, possible alternate realities.

Kismet was a mysterious figure, not fully understood by Superman's biographers. For example, for reasons the chroniclers can't explain, Kismet took a special interest in Superman's fate and appeared to him at critical points in his life on the post–First Crisis Earth (*The Adventures of Superman* #494, September 1992, and #500, Early June 1993; others). Her fate seemed inextricably intertwined with Superman's, and in one of her appearances to the Man of Steel, Kismet warned of a forthcoming massive disruption in time (*Superman Forever,* June 1998). She was referring to what would happen during Superman's first encounter with Dominus.

Originally an extraterrestrial religious leader named Tuoni, Dominus fell in love with Ahti before she evolved into Kismet. Unfortunately, the Illuminator of All Realities was a "position" Tuoni coveted, and Ahti's exaltation at Tuoni's expense drove him mad. His jealousy grew so intense that he vowed to destroy Kismet in order to take her place as the Illuminator. The spell he cast to do so all but destroyed his mortal form, but the endlessly merciful Kismet allowed Dominus to live on, freed of his shattered, useless body, in the Phantom Zone. Within the Zone, Dominus encountered a computer program based on one of Superman's long-dead ancestors, Kem-L. The Kem-L program used Kryptonian technology to "rebuild" Dominus, allowing him to escape the Zone, still intent on avenging himself against Kismet (*Action Comics* #754, May 1999).

Because he knew of the unique bond between Superman and Kismet, Dominus used the Man of Steel to lure Kismet into the physical world in order to attack her. It was then that Superman first experienced Dominus's awesome power. The renegade Lord of Order could alter reality and ensure that his victims never realized that their existence had changed around them. He was even capable of crafting more than one reality at a time, each creation designed by preying on his victim's psychological vulnerabilities. With Superman, Dominus fashioned four very different realities in which the Man of Steel seemed to exist in four separate time periods.

While these multiple existences were real and tangible in the sense that Superman could be physically affected by whatever happened to him in them, to those around him in the "real world," it

appeared that Superman was hallucinating and behaving erratically. Thus Kismet was forced to take human form and show herself, to convince the Man of Steel of the "unreality" in which he was trapped. And that was when Dominus attacked. With the aid of the time-traveling WAVERIDER, Superman was able to hide Kismet in the past, within the form of Clark Kent's childhood playmate SHARON VANCE, who would otherwise have perished in an accident (*Action Comics* #747, August 1998; *Superman: The Man of Steel* #82, August 1998; *Superman* [second series] #138, September 1998; others).

Frustrated in his efforts to find Kismet, Dominus retreated to devise a new strategy. This time he telepathically divined Superman's deepest insecurities and preyed on them—specifically, his fear of letting down the citizens of Earth who depended on him. Dominus was able to so severely compromise Superman's sense of reality that the Man of Steel came to believe he needed to exert absolute control over Earthers' lives, to save them from themselves—in essence, becoming a super-benevolent dictator. Suffering from the delusion, fostered by Dominus, that civilization would end unless Superman remained hypervigilant, the Man of Steel proclaimed himself King of the World. He then built an army of SUPERMAN ROBOTS that would police Earth, patrolling the planet twenty-four hours a day, seven days a week—forever.

This time it was his wife LOIS LANE who was able to break through the delusion gripping Superman, and, freed from Dominus's hold, the Man of Steel deactivated the robots. He then defeated Dominus in battle using TORQUASM-VO, an ancient Kryptonian martial art. The price of Superman's victory was the destruction of his Arctic FORTRESS OF SOLITUDE, but the Man of Tomorrow was ultimately able to return Dominus to the Phantom Zone (*Superman* [second series] #144, May 1999; *Superman: King of the World* #1, June 1999; others). While the Lords of Order and Chaos were known to exist on the post-FINAL CRISIS New Earth, a version of Dominus has not yet been documented there.

DONOVAN, DABNEY

The deranged and unscrupulous co-founder and former director of PROJECT CADMUS who was obsessed with cloning. His presence was first made known on the pre-FIRST CRISIS Earth-1, where he was an anonymous aerospace scientist who'd long ago developed a miniaturized planet as a testing ground for his experiments (*Superman's Pal, Jimmy Olsen* #141–142, October–November 1971; others), but an incarnation of Donovan also emerged on the post-First Crisis unified Earth who was affiliated with Cadmus. The amoral and ethically challenged Donovan did not believe there should be any restrictions on experimenting with human genes, and the research conducted by Cadmus on his watch resulted in numerous bizarre, often grotesque, new life-forms.

Some of the monstrosities he helped create were released into the labyrinthine tunnels of Cadmus's subterranean headquarters, where they would terrorize Cadmus employees at the most inopportune moments. A few even escaped into METROPOLIS to become a headache for Superman.

The most notorious of Donovan's inspirations were the DNALIENS, genetically altered humans with alien characteristics and paranormal abilities, the best documented of which was the creature called DUBBILEX.

Donovan was not above selling his expertise in cloning to the highest bidders, even if they were known criminals. For example, he created new, young bodies for the aging founders of the crime syndicate INTERGANG, and, when the radiation from the KRYPTONITE ring LEX LUTHOR wore for a time gave him terminal cancer, Donovan cloned a new body for him. Luthor tried to protect his secret by killing Donovan, but he discovered what so many of Donovan's enemies already knew: The man had a habit of creating multiple clones of himself to misdirect would-be assassins. He was reported killed on many occasions, only to reappear elsewhere, more dangerous than ever. Donovan was eventually imprisoned, and from captivity acted as a kind of consultant to Cadmus when its original directors left and the project was being run by MICKEY CANNON (*Superman* [second series] #55, May 1991; *Action Comics* #678, June 1992; others). An incarnation of Project Cadmus appeared on New Earth, but no Dabney Donovan in that reality has yet been recorded.

DOOMSDAY

The monstrous synthetic life-form, originally called the Ultimate by its creator, that succeeded in killing Superman on the post-FIRST CRISIS unified Earth. Before humanoid life evolved naturally on KRYPTON, the planet was a hellish, inhospitable place inhabited only by ferocious monstrosities, believed to be the most dangerous in the universe. BERTRON, an amoral alien scientist visiting the planet approximately 245,000 years ago, conducted experiments designed to create an "ultimate life-form" that could survive all attacks by these beasts, in the process carefully studying the concept of survival of the fittest, and how organisms adapt to changes in their environment in order to survive.

To do this, Bertron abandoned an infant created in vitro on the surface, where it promptly died of exposure. Bertron harvested its remains and used them to clone another version of the child. This was done repeatedly, and what resulted was a creature capable of amazing leaps of evolution; Bertron's experiments were, in a sense, a form of accelerated natural selection. Each time another Ultimate was created by cloning, the new version was more dangerous than the last, because the newly reincarnated Ultimate not only was more physically powerful but also gained an immunity to, or the ability to survive, whatever had killed its previous incarnation.

Like some kind of malignant racial memory, the horror of the creature's multiple deaths was "recorded" in its genes, evolving a barely sentient creature that hated all other life. Eventually, it evolved the power to return from the dead and destroy what had killed it in its previous incarnation without Bertron's intervention. The Ultimate went on to kill off all life on Krypton, including Bertron, effectively "cleansing" the planet and setting the stage for the development of the advanced humanoid race that would much later populate it.

The Ultimate that Superman encountered was covered by bony spurs that protected its vital organs and grew on its hands, elbows, and knees, to be used as weapons. The creature traveled much like the early Earth-2 Superman, leaping great distances "at a single bound." In addition to extreme strength, the Ultimate also possessed a high tolerance for extremes of temperature—making it highly adaptable to most alien environments, including deep space—and the ability to regenerate severed limbs and rapidly heal its wounds. It needed no food, water, air, or sleep. It also evolved the ability to breathe flame, extend its claws, and secrete a poison that could affect even Superman.

While most recent accounts have stated that

the Ultimate was part Kryptonian due to its genes having been spliced with Kal-El's, its flame-breath was the last new power recorded to date. The monster's Kryptonian DNA made it vulnerable to kryptonite, but the radiation could not kill it. Nevertheless, various gene-splicing experiments conducted while the monster was in captivity made it somewhat more docile or containable.

Back on ancient Krypton, the Ultimate easily escaped being marooned on the planet after murdering Bertron by commandeering a supply ship that had been periodically delivering cargo. By this means, the creature moved throughout the universe on a killing spree of unimaginable proportions, bringing misery and carnage to innumerable planets. Among them was Bylan 5, where Darkseid first encountered, then escaped from, the creature. Another was Oa, home of the Guardians of the Universe, mentors of the Green Lantern Corps, where one Guardian sacrificed his life in a battle that released so much of the master power battery's green energy that a hole was torn in space, through which the Ultimate fell.

It was in this way that the creature reached the planet Calaton, where the Ultimate was ostensibly killed by a being known as the Radiant. Deeming the creature too vile to be buried in Calatonian soil, its citizens shackled the seemingly dead body in chains and locked it in a coffin-like chamber, which they then launched into space. Hundreds of years later, the craft crashed on Earth, in what would later become the midwestern United States. The force of impact was great enough to knock the still-undead Ultimate into a deep coma and bury the coffin-like craft so far beneath the Earth's surface that it would be untold centuries before the creature awoke and clawed its way to the surface.

On its first appearance on Earth, it nearly killed the entire Justice League of America. One of the heroes commented that the carnage the Ultimate caused was like "the arrival of Doomsday"; when the broadcast media picked up that comment, Doomsday became the creature's generally accepted name. The rout of the Justice League brought Superman to the scene, and the Man of Steel quickly discovered that Doomsday's awesome power was the equal of his own. Doomsday could not be allowed to reach Metropolis, Superman reasoned, since to battle it there might possibly destroy the city, resulting in a death toll in the millions. The titanic battle culminated in a duel to the death, when the opponents simultaneously landed a blow that left both seemingly lifeless (*Superman* [second series] #75, January 1993). While Superman had been killed, however, Doomsday had only lapsed once again into a deep coma.

Doomsday was jettisoned into space by the Cyborg Superman, Hank Henshaw, who was then posing as Superman. When the real Man of Steel returned to life, he realized that his killer was not only still alive but terrorizing other worlds. Superman next battled Doomsday when Brainiac's assistant Prin Vnok traveled to Doomsday's prison "at the end of space-time," to which the creature had been banished upon his defeat by Superman and the time-traveling heroes known as the Linear Men and Waverider. Vnok retrieved the hopelessly damaged body and delivered it to Brainiac, who restored Doomsday's form to its former vitality and power and placed his own consciousness in Doomsday's brain.

Superman succeeded in driving Brainiac's consciousness from Doomsday's body, but, freed of Brainiac's manipulation, the monster reverted to type, relentlessly focusing on destroying the Man of Steel. This time, using the Justice League's teleportation technology, Superman banished Doomsday to the surface of the moon. There, instead of being wholly reassembled in a single transporter chamber, the monster was divided into four separate entities, each diminished in power by 75 percent.

Not long after, Doomsday was released by agents of Lex Luthor to battle the colossal entropy being Imperiex, a threat judged even more dangerous than Doomsday itself—a judgment validated when Imperiex used his weaponry to reduce Doomsday to a skeleton.

Doomsday's body was ultimately reclaimed and reconstituted by Luthor, who then remanded Doomsday to the custody of Darkseid. By this time, Doomsday had evolved a form of intelligence. Darkseid attempted to produce an army of Doomsday "clones," but was unable to replicate the creature with all its previous power and abilities intact, possibly due to the complexities of its DNA, which was by that time a hybrid of many different species'.

When Superman traveled to Apokolips to rescue Steel, aka John Henry Irons, Darkseid's wife Mortalla ordered Doomsday released in an attempt to help Darkseid. Doomsday's freedom was brief, however, for Steel defeated him by using the Entropy Aegis—an armor with incredible power. Escaping Apokolips and returning to Earth were simple matters for the monster with its newly acquired intelligence.

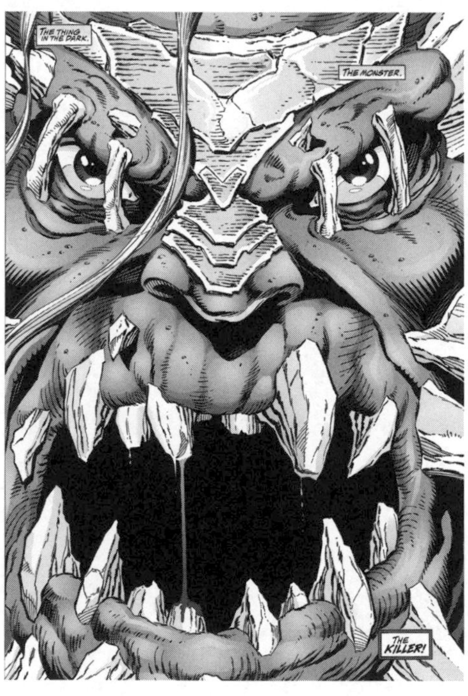

But with intelligence came a new experience, one profoundly alien and disturbing to Doomsday: emotions. Love and compassion were particularly difficult for the creature to reconcile with the hatred that ran as deep within it as its genes. When Superman faced death at the hands of Gog, Doomsday surprisingly helped him battle Gog's army. Doomsday's efforts were unsuccessful, however, and the resulting death of Superman caused a divergent future time line.

In this new alternate future, Doomsday was hailed as a great hero. This time line was retroactively erased when a weary and remorseful Gog allowed Doomsday to return to the past and save Superman, but at the cost of returning to existence as a mindless monstrosity.

During the Infinite Crisis, a pair of super-criminals freed Doomsday from captivity in a cavern near the center of the Earth. With its mind under their control, Doomsday joined their attack on Metropolis. The creature was stopped, however, by Superman and Kal-L, the former Superman of Earth-2, who, joining forces for the first time, overmatched the clawed monstrosity.

Having apparently survived the transformation of reality that spawned New Earth, Doomsday reappeared in Metropolis, only to be killed again by Superman and Supergirl. In this, the super heroes were aided by several of the one hundred thousand citizens of Kandor who were by then living near the North Pole, as a result of Superman having enlarged the bottle city and freed them. This had occurred following Superman's first New Earth encounter with Brainiac (*Action Comics* #866–870, August–December, 2008). Together the Kryptonians defeated Doomsday, crushing the monster's skull (*Superman* #681, December 2008; *Action Comics* #871, January 2009).

Lois Lane's father, General Samuel Lane, by this time in charge of a government project intended to counter the "Kryptonian invasion of Earth" represented by the hundred thousand Kandorians, came into possession of Doomsday's mutilated body. Lane viewed Doomsday as a potential weapon in the resistance to the Kandorians, and enlisted Lex Luthor in a campaign to "improve" the monster, which, as of this writing, remained dead.

The most recent accounts of Doomsday revealed a significant difference in the creature, probably the result of revisions to reality caused by the Infinite Crisis: Doomsday recalled the horrors of its creation by Kryptonians (as opposed to Bertron, who was a visitor to Krypton). As a result, it hated all Kryptonians.

DOWNLOAD

A female criminal who could teleport herself and anyone in her ambit instantaneously, and a member of the super-criminal gestalt Mainframe.

DOX, VRIL

See Brainiac.

DRAAGA

An alien warrior who was pitted against Superman in gladiatorial combat on Warworld, Mongul's massive, artificial world—a spacecraft "masquerading" as a planet. Draaga had been the undefeated champion of these duels to the death, staged for Mongul's amusement, for many years.

Superman had exiled himself in deep space because of his fear of harming Earth due to psychological problems he was suffering at the time. Mongul's minions found the Man of Steel drifting in space and captured him, bringing him to Mongul to compete in the warlord's arena. Superman defeated every opponent Mongul threw at him, but, because of his code against killing, he refused to strike a death blow, enraging both the spectators and Mongul himself. And so the warlord pitted Draaga against Superman, demanding the Man of Steel's head. While Dragga proved a formidable opponent, Superman prevailed and knocked him out, but again he refused to deliver the coup de grâce. A revolt of sorts broke out

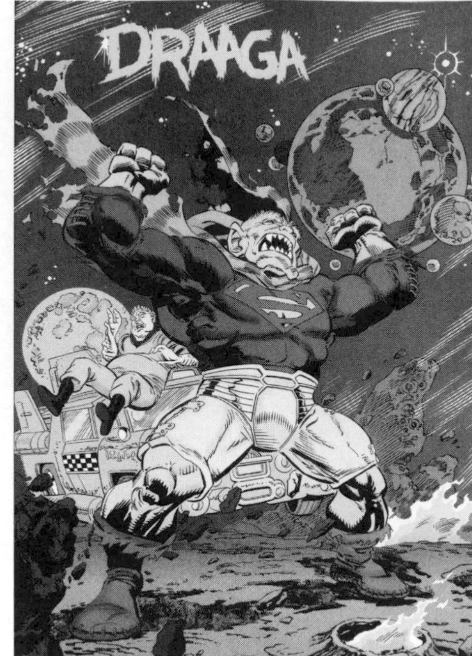

among the spectators over this and Mongul's own inability to kill Superman in combat. The result was that Warworld's Council of Overseers turned against Mongul, naming Draaga as their leader—a mere figurehead—instead. Mongul was forced to flee Warworld for his life.

Draaga soon tired of his new role and left Warworld to search for Superman, who had been teleported away from Warworld by a being called the Cleric. Finding torn remnants of Superman's costume, Draaga took to wearing them as a gesture of grudging respect for the gladiator who had bested him. After locating an interstellar craft, Draaga journeyed to Earth.

There he was hired by Superman's old enemy Maxima to kill Superman, but the Man of Steel whom Draaga encountered was actually the shape-shifting Matrix (the Pocket Universe Supergirl) assuming Superman's form. Matrix lost the battle to Draaga but could not be killed by him. Much later, Draaga died while joining Superman in a battle against Brainiac; he was buried, along with the Cleric, on a distant asteroid (*Superman* [second series] #32, June 1989; others).

DRANG

A reptilian monstrosity on the Krypton of the pre-First Crisis Earth-1 universe (*Action Comics* #303, August 1961).

DRAPER, CARL

The civilian identity of Superman's enemy the Master Jailer on the pre-First Crisis Earth-1 (*Superman* [first series] #331–332, January–February 1979; others). As a teenager in Smallville, "Moosie" Draper felt an unrequited love for Lana Lang, and hated Superboy because Lana only had eyes for the Teen of Steel. While Draper had his chance to gain revenge in adulthood, he had at least one documented, earlier opportunity to battle Superboy in the guise of Kator.

Kator was a robot with artificial intelligence that Superboy built as a sparring partner and abandoned, but which Draper inhabited, assuming the robot's powers before being defeated by Superboy (*The New Adventures of Superboy* #17–18, May–June 1981).

A different incarnation of Draper as the Jailer was documented on the post–First Crisis unified Earth, when he was hired by S.T.A.R. Labs to create an inescapable prison for Conduit. The chronicles stated that this Draper had a daughter, Carla (*The Adventures of Superman* #517, November 1994; *Superman: The Man of Steel* #43, April 1995; others). Carla was a partner with her father in a company called Draper Security, and on at least one occasion she assumed the costumed identity of Snare in an attempt to capture the Metropolis Kid when he was believed to have gone rogue (*Superboy* [third series] #32, October 1996).

At around this time, Draper began a supercriminal career, hiding behind a holographically projected figure that called itself Deathtrap. During the period when Superman was slowly morphing into a blue-costumed energy being (see Superman Red/Superman Blue), the Deathtrap holo-figure reappeared, this time calling itself Locksmith (*Action Comics* #739, November 1997). However, it was revealed that Carla was behind Locksmith, with her father having no knowledge of her activities. Draper eventually returned to his criminal life, resuming his role as Master Jailer and plaguing Superman and many other metahumans.

Another incarnation of Draper emerged on the post–Infinite Crisis New Earth, as a security consultant to Checkmate, an independent, mercenary covert operations agency that had become affiliated with the United Nations Security Council. Carl Draper's successes, on behalf of Checkmate, in repelling attacks on the organization Draper suspected originated with his daughter earned him a promotion to head of security, in which role he took on yet another code name: Castillian (*Checkmate* [second series] #17, October 2007; others).

DRAX

The brother of Uxas, aka Darkseid, ostensibly slain by his sibling when he attempted to steal the power of the Omega Force for his own purposes. But Uxas was mistaken in thinking Drax dead; he had not been obliterated, but merely propelled through the dimensional barriers into a world called Adon, where he assumed the identity of the Infinity-Man (*Jack Kirby's Fourth World* #18, August 1998).

DREADNAUGHT

One of two alien, artificial life-forms—the other was named Psi-Phon—who were a reconnaissance team for a planned invasion of Earth. The pair crash-landed their spacecraft in the West River of the post–First Crisis Metropolis. Dreadnaught's partner could create the illusion of being able to "siphon" off Superman's powers by reading his mind and implanting in Dreadnaught's brain the mental processes by which the Man of Steel controlled those powers. His psionic abilities also allowed him to block Superman's ability to use his own powers.

This, coupled with Dreadnaught's own native abilities, allowed him to simulate many of those powers. On his own, Dreadnaught was a not inconsiderable physical combatant, hugely powerful. He was also able to increase both his mass and his volume, but there was no documentation of how (*The Adventures of Superman* #442, July 1988; *Superman* [second series] #19, July 1988; others).

DUBBILEX

The first and foremost of the DNAliens, created on the pre–First Crisis Earth-1 by the Project (later known as Project Cadmus) at the order of Dabney Donovan (*Superman's Pal, Jimmy Olsen* #136, March 1971). Dubbilex, like many other products of Donovan's lab, was an experiment in human cloning whose altered DNA gave him an alien appearance and superpowers such as telepathy and telekinesis. He also had the power to emit what he called brain blasts, psionically inflicting violent headaches on his enemies. Despite his monstrous appearance and paranormal abilities, however, he was among the gentlest and most peaceful of beings.

After the First Crisis, Dubbilex emerged on the unified Earth in an incarnation almost identical to his predecessor, and with the same origins (*Superman* [second series] *Annual* #2, 1988), save for the identification of his creator as Dabney Donovan (*Secret Origins* #49, June 1990).

Dubbilex grew close to the Metropolis Kid, Kon-El, and joined him when he left Cadmus to relocate in Hawaii (*Superboy* [third series] #1, February 1994). Initially, their association was not without its tensions, as Dubbilex had been assigned to keep Cadmus apprised of the Kid's

activities. But Dubbilex had led a sheltered existence, having spent most of his life inside Cadmus, and as the Kid introduced the DNAlien to the many wonders of the modern world, they became fast friends.

Once the Kid decided to return to Metropolis (*Superboy* [third series] #50, April 1998; others), Dubbilex returned to Cadmus, where he became the head of genetics. Eventually, Dubbilex came to realize that it was time for Kon-El to get on with his life on his own. Shortly thereafter, the government shut down Project Cadmus and confiscated all its equipment. Dubbilex was left behind to maintain the now empty subterranean research facility. At this point, documents chronicling his career became more sporadic and less detailed.

Project Cadmus reappeared, back in business along with Dubbilex, after the upheavals caused by the Infinite Crisis, and Dubbilex emerged on New Earth to help Jimmy Olsen manage his new superpowers (*Countdown to Final Crisis* #20, September 19, 2007; others). When Olsen began pursuing a story about the activities of a meta-human mercenary known as Codename: Assassin, his investigation took him to Project Cadmus, where he found that the mercenary had arrived ahead of him and mortally wounded Dubbilex (*Superman's Pal, Jimmy Olsen Special* #1, October 2008).

DURAN

A sorcerous ecological terrorist who operated out of Mexico City and possessed a magical power to manipulate the elements. Duran was a member of the Oto Tribe in central Mexico and used his powers to create mass destruction with mystical monsters he conjured up. All this was part of a misguided protest against the environmental unfriendliness of the Mexican people that ended when he was stopped by the Man of Steel (*Superman* [second series] *Annual* #12, August 2000).

EARTH-BORN ANGELS, THE

The term for three beings created on the post-First Crisis Earth when, in each case, one person sacrificed his or her life for another who was beyond hope of survival, and the two mystically joined together to create a single entity (*Supergirl* [fourth series] #21, May 1998; others).

The mystical powers of the Earth-born angels were bestowed on them by the Schechina, the female aspect of the Source or Presence (terms used in the meta-human community for what others might call God), which was the origin of all mercy and love. Just as it took six days to create the universe, so it took six individuals to create the three Earth-born angels—of whom only five were documented.

The Supergirl who was the Angel of Fire was created by the fusion of Linda Danvers and Matrix; and Comet, the Angel of Love, was produced by the merging of Andrea Martinez and Zed-One, formerly Andrew Jones. Less was known about the Earth-born Angel of Light, Blithe, who was never seen in any form other than her angelic one. The identity of her other "component" was never documented before the reality in which she existed was reordered by the Infinite Crisis.

EDGE, MORGAN

The Metropolis broadcasting mogul who, in different incarnations in the various realities, was either a major crime figure or a ruthless, but relatively benign and law-abiding, businessman. Edge was first documented on the pre-First Crisis Earth-1 (*Superman's Pal, Jimmy Olsen* #133, October 1970; *Superman* [first series] #233, January 1971; others) as the president and CEO of Galaxy Communications, owner of the Galaxy Broadcasting System television network and Metropolis "O&O" (owned-and-operated station) WGBS-TV, Channel 6. He first came to the attention of Superman's biographers when his media corporation bought the *Daily Planet* shortly before the First Crisis.

The first known Earth-1 Edge was connected to the Apokolips-sponsored crime organization Intergang, yet this was not the real Edge, but rather an impostor, a clone of the businessman created by Darkseid's Evil Factory. The real Edge had been kept prisoner in his own luxurious penthouse until he finally escaped (*Superman* [first series] #241, August 1971, and #244, November 1971; *Superman's Girl Friend, Lois Lane* #118, January 1972). The Edge clone proved molecularly unstable and disintegrated during an attempt to kill the real Edge (*Superman's Pal, Jimmy Olsen* #152, September 1972); the original version resumed his

normal life. No one but Jimmy Olsen and Superman ever knew there had been an Edge clone.

The Earth-1 Edge was a self-made man with humble origins, born Morris Edelstein to a cleaning woman who raised him on her own after she was widowed. Young Morris was something of a ne'er-do-well who won his first television station in a poker game. Over a period of approximately two decades, he built that holding into a media empire (*Action Comics* #468, February 1977). No other relatives were documented except for a mean-spirited niece named Stephanie (*Superman Family* #175, February–March 1976, and #208, July 1981).

By the time Clark Kent encountered Edge, he had become one of the wealthiest men in Metropolis and a major political figure in the city, only slightly less influential than the Lex Luthor who would emerge on the post–First Crisis Earth, but without the criminality. Among his newly acquired personnel, Edge quickly developed a reputation for being suave and smoothly ruthless. He had a handsome, strong-jawed face and sported an impeccably tailored wardrobe. This, as well as his affectation of using a cigarette holder, projected an air of sophistication and charm that disarmed his associates and lulled them into a false sense of security. His mood would then turn on a dime and he would strike a blow when least expected, earning him the nickname the Smiling Cobra.

His decisions concerning the *Planet* were particularly disruptive to the continuity and morale of its staff. He aggressively attempted to change the paper's collegial culture and make it more competitive, wasting no time undermining the older Perry White's authority. First and foremost a broadcaster, he seemed unconcerned about weakening the *Planet*'s talent pool, attempting to turn many of the paper's reporters, notably Clark Kent and Jimmy Olsen, into broadcast personalities. Kent was transferred—somewhat against his will—to the news staff of WGBS not long after the acquisition of the *Planet*. In short order, Kent was named anchorman of the local evening newscast. Edge remained Kent's employer, though a somewhat tangential figure in Superman's life, until the events of the First Crisis resulted in a Clark Kent who was once again a newspaperman and a very different Morgan Edge whose path would not cross Superman's for a few more years.

The first record of the Morgan Edge that was created on the post–First Crisis unified Earth revealed that this one, too, was the CEO of Galaxy Communications (*Superman* [second series] #16, April 1988), but he had achieved that status by usurping his father's position. This Morgan Edge directed his media outlets to take an anti-Superman stance because the Man of Steel attracted dangerous super-criminals to Metropolis. Unlike his Earth-1 predecessor, this Edge was unambiguously criminal. He was not only "involved with" Intergang, which had also been reincarnated after the First Crisis, but in fact the official head of the organization—or, at least, its Earth-based leader, since the high-tech weaponry Intergang used came from Apokolips.

This Edge grew up under the thumb of a violent, abusive father with a questionable background.

Vincent Edge was a wealthy media magnate not unlike what his son's Earth-1 counterpart became. Morgan's mother died the day she tried to protect her son from one of his father's rages, as she had always done—this one particularly humiliating because it was in public, on a sidewalk in downtown Metropolis. The parents' disagreement became physical, and Vincent roughly pushed her away. She fell into oncoming traffic and was instantly killed when struck by a bus (*Superman* [second series] #35, September 1989). Vincent claimed it was an accident, but the everlasting, intense hatred of the son for the father suggested that Morgan never really believed him. Certainly, Vincent never took responsibility for having killed his wife even accidentally, maintaining that she had tripped and fallen into the street.

On the night of Morgan's primal scream of desperation, shouting out his hatred for Vincent, Darkseid appeared before him and promised to make him powerful and fearless. Superman historians were unable to reconstruct how, exactly, this relationship developed, but Darkseid remained a controlling influence in Edge's life thereafter. On reaching adulthood, a much-transformed Morgan Edge wasted no time maneuvering Vincent into early retirement and taking his father's job, before turning his attention to reviving a long-dead criminal organization.

In the Roaring Twenties, the underworld of Metropolis was ruled by Intergang, which went out of business when its founder, Boss Moxie, died in a hit orchestrated by rivals. Edge re-formed Intergang with himself as boss, making the organization more fearsome than ever, thanks to Apokoliptian weapons supplied by Darkseid's master torturer DeSaad.

It wasn't long before Clark Kent, Lois Lane, and Perry White at the *Daily Planet* began to suspect Edge's connection to Intergang. By this time, emotionally troubled Los Angeles syndicated gossip columnist Catherine "Cat" Grant had joined the *Planet* in the same capacity. In short order, she began to feel the need to prove she could be a "real reporter," and accepted an offer from Edge to host her own show on WGBS while continuing her work for the *Planet*. In Grant's mind, she was going "undercover" to help ferret out information for the *Planet*'s planned exposé on Edge. Perhaps she didn't count on becoming Edge's live-in lover, which eventually happened.

Edge's criminal activities were eventually exposed by the *Planet*, in articles by Clark Kent, Lois Lane, and Grant herself. But by this time, Superman had begun experiencing fugue episodes caused by a psychic attack from Brainiac, in which a dark side of the Man of Steel's personality manifested itself. During one of these, he killed three Pocket Universe citizens of Krypton who had wiped out all life on the Pocket Universe Earth. Having broken his code against killing, Superman decided to exile himself from Earth, with Clark Kent leaving a message for Perry that he was going into hiding indefinitely, fearing reprisals from Intergang (*Superman* [second series] #28, February 1989; others).

While Superman was off Earth, Turmoil, a robotic assassin from Apokolips, was sent to Metropolis by Darkseid for Edge to control as it carried out its

programming to destroy the city and assassinate the reporters responsible for the Edge exposé (*The Adventures of Superman* #456, July 1989).

Superman returned to Earth just in time to battle and defeat Turmoil and then confronted Edge in his control room. Edge had been growing increasingly anxious about Turmoil, due to the number of innocent bystanders who were being slaughtered during its rampage, and the stress of Superman arriving to capture him caused him to have a heart attack and collapse (*Action Comics* #643, July 1989).

Incapacitated and in intensive care, Edge became a serious liability to Intergang. One of his lieutenants, Bruno "Ugly" Mannheim, took the reins of Intergang and ordered Edge "whacked." Meanwhile, still in a coma, Edge had a quasi-mystical experience—or one enabled by Apokoliptian technology; the chronicles are vague on this point—in which Darkseid appeared before him. The evil god of Apokolips brought even more dire news for Edge: He was not all-powerful thanks to Darkseid's protection at all, because all along he had been dealing not with Darkseid, but with his master "enforcer," DeSaad. The weapons master had used Apokoliptian technology to take on Darkseid's image. Now that Edge had shown weakness by nearly being scared to death by Superman, he could no longer count on Apokolips's support (*Superman* [second series] #35, September 1989).

Nevertheless, the assassin sent by Mannheim to finish off Edge failed in his mission, and Edge survived to be sent to prison. Meanwhile, the forces of Apokolips facilitated the creation of a young clone of Boss Moxie, the original leader of Intergang, who took over the organization. The imprisoned Edge also discovered that in his absence, Vincent had been reinstated to the board of Galaxy Communications, and he would have no further influence there, either (*Superman* [second series] #40, February 1990, and #42, April 1990; others).

While in jail, Edge wrote a blistering autobiography that embarrassed both Cat Grant and his father with its revelations about their sordid pasts (*Superman* [second series] #83, November 1993; others). It didn't take long for Edge to pull off his escape from prison, however. But, finding himself thoroughly discredited in the Metropolis underworld, he began recruiting comparatively low-threat super-criminals such as Maxima, Barrage, and Anomaly to form the post–First Crisis unified Earth's version of the Superman Revenge Squad (*The Adventures of Superman* #543, February 1997; *Superman* [second series] #127; others). Once members of the Revenge Squad began their work as a criminal gang, Edge attempted to frame Lex Luthor by naming him its leader.

It became clear that Edge's goals were not only to destroy Superman and take back control of Intergang from Boss Moxie, but also to discredit Lex Luthor and take his place as Metropolis's crime kingpin. Ultimately, the Revenge Squad was brought to justice, but the Edge of the post–First Crisis reality remained at large when last documented. At that time, Edge was operating from "a secret complex far below the GBS Tower."

Edge was reincarnated on the post–Infinite Crisis New Earth as the owner of the *Daily Planet*'s chief competitor, the *Daily Star*, and WGBS-TV. As of this writing, there has been no definitive documentation that this Edge was secretly a criminal, but he did seem to harbor a hostility toward superpeople in general. He was a self-styled media pundit who gave himself his own show, *Edge of Reason*, on which he delivered anti-Kryptonian rants and seemed willing to advance the agenda of General Samuel Lane (*Action Comics* #880–881, October–November 2009; others).

EDGE, VINCENT ("VINNIE")

The father of the post–First Crisis Earth's Morgan Edge (*Superman* [second series] #35, September 1989) and briefly a leader of the criminal organization Intergang. The elder Edge took over his son's lawful businesses while the latter was hospitalized with a heart attack. The silver-haired "Vinnie" was a quintessential "dirty old man" whose lecherous advances on Cat Grant complicated her life until she finally brought a sexual harassment suit against him, which she announced live at the end of one of her *Hollywood Tonight* broadcasts (*The Adventures of Superman* #510, March 1994).

As front man for Boss Moxie, Edge subsequently gathered together all of Metropolis's gang leaders with the intent of absorbing them into a revived Intergang. In fact, Moxie's true intent was to murder his competition in one place, culminating with Vincent Edge himself, strangled to death by Noose (*The Adventures of Superman* #544, March 1997). There has not yet been a record of a Vincent Edge being incarnated on the post–Infinite Crisis New Earth.

EFFRON THE SORCERER

A magically powered, possibly demonic would-be world conqueror on the pre–First Crisis Earth-1 who ruled the kingdom of Veliathan through figurehead kings at an unspecified point in Earth's distant past. As the only person capable of controlling the magic that served as ancient Earth's primary power source, Effron ruled a race of faceless slaves who rarely acquired distinctive features unless they established themselves as individuals. The bored Effron pulled Superman and Green Arrow from the future with the intention of having the Emerald Archer face off against the figurehead King Dextro to determine Veliathan's next puppet ruler. The distraction allowed Effron to lose control of a slave named Kanow, who promptly seized the throne for himself (*World's Finest Comics* #210, March 1972).

SUDDENLY, THE PYRE BEGINS TO SPUTTER... AND BEFORE FOUR STARTLED EYES APPEARS...
EFFRON THE SORCERER--FROM THE ANCIENT KINGDOM OF VELIATHAN!
THE SAME, MAN OF STEEL--
--WITH A PROPOSITION FOR YOU!

In the wake of a second battle with Effron alongside Batman, Superman confiscated the mage's hypnotic Golden Eye, a large, oval-shaped talisman that vanished from the Man of Steel's Fortress of Solitude (*Superman* [first series] #268, October 1973) and ended up, in miniaturized form, on the forehead of a would-be super hero named Gunther Jacoby, who was corrupted by its power (*Superman* [first series] #273, March 1974).

Regaining control of Veliathan, Effron grew bored again, traveling to the future to tap the magical energy of the Eternal Flame in the hidden Maine community of Valhalla and temporarily revive magic as Earth's primary power source. Threatening to kill the kidnapped citizenry of Valhalla, Effron forced Superman to engage in a series of duels with other super heroes until Green Arrow tricked the sorcerer into revealing the location of the lost Valhallans. Afterward, Superman imprisoned Effron in his Fortress of Solitude, using a specially created device to keep the mage in an eternal trance (*Action Comics* #437, July 1974).

In the post–Infinite Crisis reality, the Golden Eye of Effron remained a threat. Traveling into the past, Superman was joined in his quest by the Silent Knight, whose sword destroyed the enchanted orb once and for all (*The Brave and the Bold* [third series] #10, April 2008).

ELASTIC LAD

The super heroic persona occasionally assumed by the Jimmy Olsen of the pre–First Crisis Earth-1. Elastic Lad had the power to stretch his malleable body seemingly limitlessly, a power not unlike that of super heroes Elongated Man and Plastic Man.

Olsen first became Elastic Lad when he came across a bottle of green fluid in a chest filled with alien artifacts that the Man of Steel had found in outer space. Olsen assumed that the liquid was a form of kryptonite and tried to do Superman a favor by disposing of it. He was transformed into a "rubber boy" when he spilled its contents on himself and the alien chemical was absorbed through his skin. While attempting to find a cure, he joined a carnival sideshow, for which he invented the "Elastic Lad" persona. Olsen found that he could stretch every part of his body, even to the point of becoming giant-sized, although his mass (and therefore weight) did not change.

With Superman's help, Olsen was outfitted with a special purple costume that expanded and con-

YOU'RE THE PHONEY, MISTER... THE FAKE ANDROID SUPERMAN THEY HONOR ON THIS WORLD! UUUHH!
SHUT UP!
BOP!
ELAST LAD

tracted as he did. Ultimately, Jimmy discovered that, ironically, kryptonite radiation could permanently cure his alien elastic affliction (*Superman's Pal, Jimmy Olsen* #31, September 1958).

The "retirement" of Elastic Lad was not as permanent, however. Jimmy's friend (and Lana Lang's uncle), the eccentric research scientist and inventor Professor Phineas Potter, developed a "stretching serum" (Potter was notorious for his bizarre, often useless inventions, such as a huge device for making onion juice by the gallon, documented in *Superman* [first series] #176, April 1965). When Jimmy accidentally drank Potter's serum, he became Elastic Lad once again (*Superman's Pal, Jimmy Olsen* #37, June 1959).

The elastic serum worked for only a limited period of time, however. How long Jimmy would remain stretchable seemed to depend on how much of the serum he drank. Unlike the alien liquid, Potter's chemical was immune to kryptonite radiation. As Elastic Lad, Olsen became something his normal self wasn't: a skillful hand-to-hand combatant. In time, he came to see the possibilities of Elastic Lad as a bona fide super hero, and had many further adventures when, from time to time, he would deliberately drink Potter's serum (*Superman's Pal, Jimmy Olsen* #46, July 1960, and #54, July 1961; others). On more than one occasion, Jimmy, as Elastic Lad, traveled to the thirtieth century and became an honorary member of the Legion of Super-Heroes (*Superman's Pal, Jimmy Olsen* #72, October 1963; *Adventure Comics* #323, August 1964; others).

On the Earth of the unified universe created by the First Crisis, Jimmy Olsen also became an elastic lad, but without the super heroic persona. In an encounter with the Eradicator during its initial attempts to re-create Earth in Krypton's image, Olsen's DNA was temporarily altered by an alien virus, with the result that he would stretch—but this time painfully and with no control over the transformations (*The Adventures of Superman* #458, September 1989).

On New Earth, in the days preceding the event known as the Final Crisis, a younger incarnation of Jimmy Olsen once again demonstrated Elastic Lad's powers without donning an Elastic Lad costume, because his stretching was just one of many powers he manifested temporarily. Olsen's body inexplicably stretched during an encounter with the super-criminal Killer Croc, allowing him to escape. Jimmy's other powers included superspeed and the ability to project porcupine-like darts from his body, but the powers manifested themselves unpredictably (*Countdown to Final Crisis* #49, May 23, 2007, and #50, May 16, 2007; *Action Comics* #852, September 2007; others). All of this was ultimately revealed to be a by-product of a large-scale scheme of Darkseid's, precipitating the event known as Final Crisis.

ELITE, THE

An amoral super hero team—one might say "super anti-hero team"—formed by the late Manchester Black on the post–First Crisis unified Earth to "free the Earth from scum" (*Action Comics* #775, March 2001). Black, who was contemptuous of Superman's code against killing, created the Elite to respond to criminal behavior with deadly force, unencumbered by the scruples and self-restraint characteristic of most other super heroes. The vastly powerful telekinetic and telepathic Black "persuaded" team members—through mind control—that their power and righteousness entitled them to ignore international law and national sovereignty. Predictably, the group, like Black himself, was corrupted by its own power so that, at least until Black's suicide (*Action Comics* #796 and *Superman: The Man of Steel* #131, both December 2002), the Elite were no better than the super-criminals they literally sought to exterminate.

Before Manchester's leadership role was taken by his sister Vera upon his death, the original Elite comprised three other members and a base of operations that was also a living organism. One of these was Nathan Craig Jones, aka Coldcast, who could control electromagnetism, thereby affecting matter at the molecular level. He could slow time to a crawl, if not stop it altogether, by making electrons inert. In like fashion, he could disable electronic devices with the electromagnetism he could emit.

Another member was Menagerie, a Puerto Rican woman identified in the chronicles only as Pamela. The account was vague about the origin of her powers, but it was known that she was infected with a host of microscopic living alien weapons called symbeasts. Menagerie could mentally command the symbeasts to manifest themselves on her body and form various appendages, or assume the shape of weapons such as claws, spikes, or whips. In addition, they often formed wings, giving Menagerie the power of flight. The symbeasts could take other forms as well, or separate from her body altogether to attack an enemy on their own. In an encounter with Superman, Menagerie confessed that she and the other Elite were compelled by Black's psionic powers to operate as they did, against their will. Black avenged this disloyalty by using his telekinesis to give Menagerie a cerebral hemorrhage, leaving her in a persistent vegetative state.

The third member was the Japanese Rampotatek, aka the Hat, whose powers were never fully or clearly documented. He was variously described as a demon and an "earth elemental." He possessed a magic hat that could conjure up any object he chose and assume an entirely different form that called itself the Dragon.

The Elite called their living base of operations Bunny. "She" was a bacterial colony that grew to enormous size and evolved into a floating fortress before the Elite brought her to their universe for their use.

After Vera Black became the group's leader, the Elite underwent a dramatic transformation. The Hat quit the team, and the comatose Menagerie was replaced by Menagerie II, the sister of the original, known only as Sonja. She, too, was "bonded" with symbeasts, with the consequence of eventually being driven mad. Coldcast, who had been persuaded by Superman to abandon the lethal tactics imposed on him by Manchester Black, joined Vera, Menagerie II, and new members Naif al-Sheikh, Kasumi, Manitou Raven, and Dawn in forming the Justice League Elite, a super hero black ops organization that captured and eliminated meta-human menaces before they assumed a public criminal persona (*JLA* #100, August 2004; *Justice League Elite* #1–12, September 2004–August 2005; others). Their affiliation with the Justice League eventually ended, but Vera Black chose to keep the Elite a private operation under her sole leadership.

ENCANTADORA, LA

The magically powered super-criminal-for-hire who was both foe and would-be seductress to Superman. She was Lourdes Lucero, the daughter of an archaeologist on the post–First Crisis Earth who devoted his life to finding the vial containing the legendary Mists of Ibella. He was successful in his efforts, but the quest drove him mad, and the constant struggle to avoid the mists' corrupting influence drained his health and ultimately killed him. On his deathbed, he implored Lourdes to get rid of the mists for the good of the family. Instead Lourdes saw in their power a potential way out of her life of crushing poverty, as well as a better future for her preteen brother Victor. Instead of disposing of the mists, she used them to become La Encantadora—Spanish for "enchantress."

Lucero was a morally ambiguous and not altogether unsympathetic figure: She could be engaged to perform many criminal acts, and much of what she was willing to do, she told herself, was for Victor, but she would not kill. Nor did she seem to fully understand the nature of, or risk associated with, her own abilities, which included teleportation and telekinesis as well as mind control. She wore the mists in a vial around her neck but was often seen surrounded by the strange, orange, perfume-like vapor, suggesting that she had the power to control them telekinetically, extracting them from the vial and returning them at will.

Some accounts suggested that at least one of her powers became permanently "internalized" from prolonged exposure to the mists: She was reported to teleport without having the vial in her possession. In addition, she exuded pheromones whose enchanting power could sexually enslave men she sought to dominate.

Superman first encountered La Encantadora and brought her to justice when she sold fake KRYPTONITE to a number of super-criminals, and the Man of Might rescued her from their attempts to avenge her deception. But not before discovering the full extent of her mists' power to cloud minds: The Man of Steel felt the effects of Lucero's kryptonite even though he knew it was counterfeit (*Action Comics* #760, December 1999).

The Man of Steel dealt with La Encantadora a few more times, and on one of those occasions, the conscience that was the hope of her salvation came to light. With a quick kiss, Lucero infected the Man of Steel with a kryptonite nanobot supplied to her by her latest client, Superman's old enemy ZOD. Slowly, Superman began to die of kryptonite poisoning as the nanobot destroyed his body, one cell at a time. It was only Lucero's remorse that saved him, when she sought out LOIS LANE to reveal what had happened, and Lane was able to get her husband to S.T.A.R. LABS for treatment.

In their final recorded encounter, Superman and TALIA HEAD reunited Lucero with Victor when the boy was kidnapped by Head's father, Rā's al Ghūl, the near-immortal leader of a cult of assassins. The boy was threatened with death unless La Encantadora surrendered the Mists of Ibella to Rā's.

When Superman turned her over to the authorities, Lucero gave up her mists to the Man of Steel and vowed to reform. As he flew off, the vial disappeared from his hand, leaving observers to wonder if this was an act of renunciation or if she had magically retrieved the vial. Perhaps not without misgivings, Superman could only hope that Lucero would make the best of her chance to go straight (*Action Comics* #761, January 2000; *The Adventures of Superman* #580, July 2000; *Action Comics* #772, December 2000; others).

ENDERS, PROFESSOR WILLIAM

It was William Enders who studied the distant world of KRYPTON in the days before it exploded. Using a radio, he made contact with the planet and engaged the scientist JOR-EL in a dialogue, learning to construct a "matter-radio"—"a transmitter that can send all forms of living matter—even living people—across space by radio," allowing him to visit the doomed world. Jor-El excitedly explained his theory and introduced him to his wife LARA and their son KAL-EL.

After his remarkable visit, the astronomer authored *The Planet Krypton,* which brought him to the attention of the criminal Buttons Harris. With his henchmen, Harris kidnapped Enders and stole the matter-radio to use for robberies. Instead, Superman intervened and brought Harris and his cohorts to the police (*Superman* [first series] #77, July–August 1952).

ENTROPY AEGIS, THE

The most powerful suit of armor ever created. When worn by the super hero STEEL, it proved the decisive factor in defeating the intergalactic conqueror IMPERIEX. In his attack on Earth, Imperiex employed an army of "probes"—somewhat like miniature versions of himself—each clad in a suit of invincible armor of alien design. The alliance that repelled the Imperiex attack captured a damaged and deactivated probe and retrofitted it with technology from APOKOLIPS, creating an even more powerful armor that it dubbed the Entropy Aegis. This armor made Steel invulnerable and gave him the power to emit cosmic radiation as a weapon (*Superman: The Man of Steel* #116, September 2001; others).

EON

A manifestation of the combined consciousnesses of "the Union," a collection of disembodied brains stolen from various alien races and assembled by a mysterious alien known as Hfuhruhurr, or the WORD-BRINGER. Eon was able to fire intense concussive waves, even knocking Superman into space, but the Man of Steel defeated Eon by convincing him that, contrary to what he'd been told by the Word-Bringer, he was not a divinity but, rather, merely another of the Word-Bringer's victims. Realizing he'd been duped, Eon made amends by helping Superman defeat Hfuhruhurr and promising to keep him under custody (*The Adventures of Superman* #452, March 1989).

EQUUS

Equus was a human being transformed by steroids, genetic engineering, cybernetic enhancements, and a host of other forms of exotic high-tech into a huge, monstrous super-soldier with foot-long claws that could penetrate Superman's skin. The eight-foot Equus had white, scaly, self-healing skin, and like many reptilian species he could rapidly regenerate entire severed limbs. In his first encounter with Equus, Superman discovered that the monstrosity's synthetic parts were made of a form of soft plastic the Man of Steel had never seen before. Equus's solar-powered mechanical components gave him seven senses rather than five (*Superman* [second series] #206, August 2004).

Equus wore a chest plate displaying the number *3* in Roman numerals, suggesting that he was the third "upgrade" of his model produced by the secret super-soldier program that created him. Because of his enlarged "lizard brain" and massive hormone therapy, Equus was referred to by one of his employers—a mysterious man known only as MR. ORR—as "a psychotic killer."

Superman was drawn into his first encounter with Equus while searching for his wife LOIS LANE, who had disappeared from Earth along with one million others, leaving only ghostly shadows at the points from which they had vanished. Superman first tracked the device that caused the VANISHING to the Middle Eastern country from which it was firing its beams at random, and there he was attacked on two occasions by Equus. In the course of these battles, the Man of Steel ripped the claws out of Equus's right hand and used his vision powers to learn enough about Equus's synthetic augmentations to disable many of them. The identity of Mr. Orr's employers, who operated the laboratory in which Equus was created, was never documented.

Equus escaped Superman using the vanishing weapon, causing himself and another three hundred thousand other people from all over the world to disappear. Superman ultimately rescued the victims from an alternate reality within the PHANTOM ZONE called Metropia, where Equus was attempting to aid a non-Kryptonian "Phantom Zod" in destroying it. This Zod rebuffed Superman's attempts to save him when Metropia began to collapse in on itself. Equus, locked in battle with another super-soldier prototype named Pilate, rematerialized on Earth above an island, the outcome of their battle unknown (*Superman* [second series] #206–215, August 2004–May 2005).

Documents make clear that Equus survived the INFINITE CRISIS, as he reappeared, still under Mr. Orr's control, to fight the super heroes Karate Kid and Triplicate Girl (*Countdown to Final Crisis* #36, August 22, 2007, and #35, August 29, 2007; *Supergirl* [fifth series] #21–22, November–December

2007). Orr subsequently employed multiple clones against the former Teen Titan known as Cyborg (*DC Special: Cyborg* #4–6, October–December 2008).

ERADICATOR, THE

The term for a weapon, created on the Krypton of the single, post–First Crisis universe, that Superman repeatedly tried to disable and destroy until it morphed itself into humanoid form.

The Eradicator was created two hundred thousand years ago, at the time when the Cleric had arrived on Krypton. Superman's ancestor Kem-L envisioned the Eradicator as the embodiment of all of Krypton's most "glorious" ideals—values that might, in Earth terms, be called ultraconservative, perhaps even fascistic. They were xenophobic in the extreme: wary of outsiders and demanding of both ethnic purity and absolute loyalty to the motherland.

Kem-L seemed to hope that the energies the Eradicator emitted would ultimately bind Kryptonians to their planet by making them absolutely dependent on their environment for their survival. This is part of the reason why Superman chroniclers believed for many years, during the existence of the post–First Crisis reality, that the only Kryptonian ever to have survived outside that environment was Superman.

Over the millennia, the Eradicator developed an artificial intelligence and continued to observe developments on Krypton from afar. There is no clear consensus among Superman historians of how the planet's destruction affected the Eradicator. During his self-imposed exile in space, after escaping from Warworld following his first encounter with Draaga, Superman encountered the Eradicator on an asteroid in the superannuated Cleric's possession. The Man of Steel tapped the Eradicator's power and used it to return to Earth (*Action Comics Annual* #2, May 1989). On Earth, however, the Man of Steel decided that the device, which had begun emitting bursts of energy, was potentially too dangerous to human life. So Superman locked it up within a metal canister and buried it in an Arctic crevasse.

The Eradicator was not deactivated by this, however, and continued to carry out its programmed mandate to preserve Kryptonian culture. It attempted to transform Earth into a new Krypton from a huge base it built, retrieving materials from the Phantom Zone to do so. By using the Zone's time-travel capabilities to return to Krypton and undergo a rite of passage, Superman was able to seize control of the Eradicator and was stunned to see the transformation of its subsurface base into a museum-like memorial to Krypton. Via the now sealed-off Phantom Zone, it had drawn numerous Kryptonian artifacts and technologies, including servo-mechanicals. This ultimately became the first Fortress of Solitude on the post-Crisis Earth (*The Adventures of Superman* #461, December 1989). At this point, the Eradicator began to transform the Man of Steel himself, gradually turning him into its image of the "ideal"—that is, cold, cerebral, unemotional—Kryptonian.

Superman smashed the Eradicator when Martha and Jonathan Kent tried to persuade their adopted son, who had rejected the name Clark Kent in favor of Kal-El, that reframing his life as that of a "true Kryptonian" was a betrayal of Earth, which needed him, and the Eradicator attacked the Kents. After shaking off the Eradicator's hold over him, Superman hurled the damaged and disabled device into the sun (*Action Comics* #652, April 1990).

But the Eradicator's energies survived the destruction of its physical shell, and it tapped the sun's thermonuclear reactions to re-create itself in humanoid form. The Eradicator returned to Earth to resume its campaign to transform Earth into a replica of Krypton. It began by attempting to turn the sun into a red dwarf star like Krypton's, causing numerous "natural" disasters on Earth (*Superman: The Man of Steel* #1, July 1991; others). Ultimately, assisted by Professor Emil Hamilton, Superman trapped the Eradicator inside the mysterious mystical gemstone of Mister Z, an immortal who had captured many human souls in the gemstone (*Action Comics* #667, July 1991). One of these had been Superman, who was able to escape and free the other captives, then kept the gemstone in the Fortress for safekeeping.

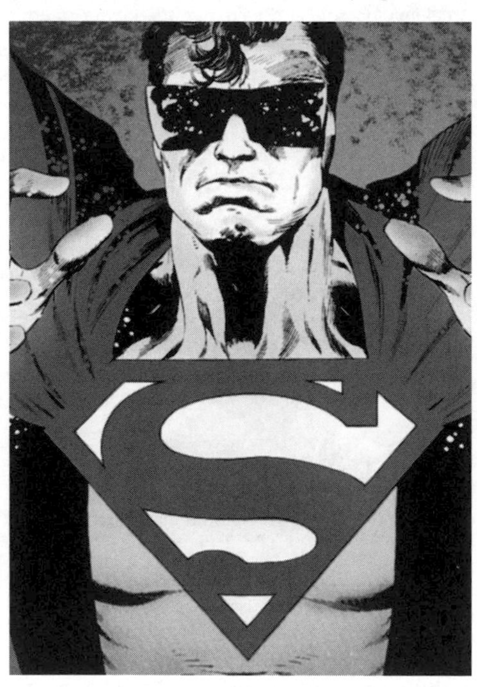

But the Eradicator's energies were presumably still powerful enough to reach out from within the gemstone and manipulate the Kryptonian robots with which it had "stocked" the Fortress. The robots re-created the Eradicator after Superman's death at the hands of Doomsday (*Action Comics* #687, June 1993; others) and facilitated its creation of a body based on Superman's. It created a faux-organic, humanoid form by tapping into solar energy still present in Superman's corpse.

In humanoid form, the Eradicator found it couldn't absorb yellow sunlight directly; it had to keep tapping into whatever of it still remained in Superman's body. These energies created in the Eradicator the delusion that it actually *was* Superman, and it appeared in Metropolis calling itself the Last Son of Krypton. It had also absorbed some of Superman's memories: When Lois Lane demanded to know its identity, its remarks implied that the Last Son of Krypton recalled their relationship, which would have to end because, from then on, "he" would only be Superman and no longer Clark Kent.

The humanoid Eradicator, with its more "perfectly Kryptonian" sensibility, was essentially a brutal Superman who did not hesitate to kill criminals. However, when Steel attempted to put a stop to this, the Eradicator began to reevaluate its tactics. While visiting Coast City, the Eradicator stumbled upon a plot by Mongul and the Cyborg Superman, Hank Henshaw, to destroy the municipality. Attempting to frame the Eradicator for the attack on Coast City, Henshaw nearly killed the program in human form (*Superman* [second series] #80, August 1993).

But the Eradicator survived and returned to the Fortress to discover that its use of Superman as a conduit of solar energy had resurrected the Man of Steel. The Eradicator drained all power from the Fortress, using it to regenerate itself and morph its humanoid body. Its personality changed, too, as it began to feel greater compassion for the human race (*Action Comics* #691, September 1993).

This kinder, gentler Eradicator joined forces with Superman and several other super heroes to prevent Mongul and the Cyborg Superman from destroying Metropolis. This time, the Eradicator seemed to have been actually killed while blocking a lethal blast of kryptonite-based energy intended for Superman (*Superman* [second series] #82, October 1993). For reasons the chroniclers could never fully explain, the Eradicator's mass somehow altered the kryptonite radiation to allow Superman to absorb power from it, restoring the Man of Steel's superpowers to their full capacity in the process.

But once again, the Eradicator's "techno-consciousness" survived despite the destruction of the physical form that housed it. Its apparently dead body was examined at S.T.A.R. Labs, where Dr. David Connor, a scientist frail with terminal cancer, stumbled and fell into the controls of the chamber containing the Eradicator's body, causing an explosion. As Connor's body was destroyed, his mind apparently entered and assumed control of the Eradicator (*Action Comics* #693, November 1993).

The Eradicator's body remained powerful even though its face now seemed older and was scarred. For a time, this Eradicator attempted to function as a super hero under the Eradicator name, becoming part of the group dubbed the Outsiders (*Outsiders* [second series] #9–24, July 1994–November 1995) and occasionally joining Superman, Supergirl, and Steel in "Team Superman."

But this attempt to achieve humanity also failed. The original Eradicator annihilator program still existed in the computers of the Fortress of Solitude, which had been destroyed in Superman's first battle with Dominus. The program assumed the form of Kem-L, in which it again attempted to bend Superman to its will. This activity came to the attention of the David Connor Eradicator. When the Fortress Eradicator attempted to merge with Brainiac 13's transformational Y2K program, in order to use the virus to help re-create Krypton yet again,

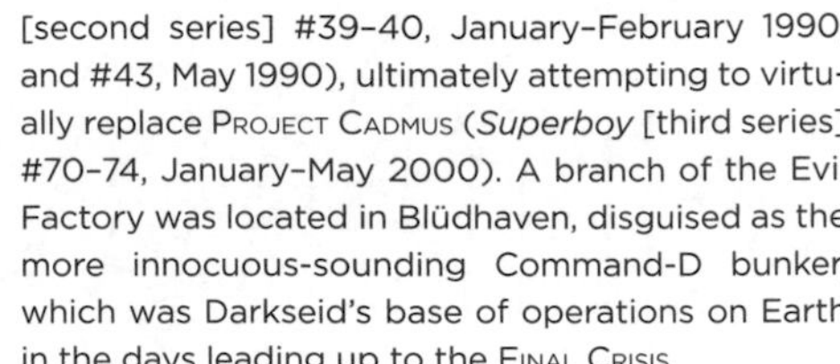

Connor resolved not to let Brainiac 13 take control of the Eradicator's "evil side." The Connor Eradicator merged both sides of his programming, then departed to exile himself in space, just as Superman had once done (*Superman: The Man of Steel* #95–98, December 1999–March 2000).

Connor's consciousness seemed to have been completely lost by the time a seemingly unstable Eradicator returned to Earth to warn of the coming of Imperiex (*Superman: The Man of Steel* #114, July 2001). When the Eradicator turned violent as it desperately sought to have its ravings taken seriously, Superman trapped it in the freezing liquid of an absolute-zero chamber at John Henry Irons's Steelworks. This allowed the Man of Steel to separate Connor from the Fortress component, creating a new, humanoid Eradicator. After a brief interlude in which he was freed from captivity by the Joker (*Superman: The Man of Steel* #119, December 2001), the Eradicator was again imprisoned inside the Fortress.

Shortly before reality was reordered by the Infinite Crisis, the Eradicator was reported to have been seriously injured (*Superman* [second series] #220, November 2005) and was allegedly being held, in a comatose state, at Steelworks. Something that appeared to be an Eradicator program has been seen on at least one occasion (*Final Crisis: Resist,* January 2009). Since then, the Eradicator emerged from its coma and in an unrecorded event was named a New Krypton representative to Earth. The Eradicator was also readmitted to the latest incarnation of the Outsiders (*Outsiders* [third series] #26, January 2010). After the destruction of New Krypton, the Eradicator's true role and purpose remains to be recorded.

ERKOL

The oldest city on the Krypton that existed in the universe of the pre–First Crisis Earth-1. It was founded in ancient times on Urrika, the planet's largest continent and the one on which the Kryptonian civilization of this reality began. It was destroyed at least twice, initially during a long war with another city-state, Xan. Each time it was rebuilt and was still standing at the time of Krypton's destruction. The city's moniker was a corruption of *Erok-El,* the name of a warrior king and descendant of Kal-El (*Superman* [first series] #239, June–July 1971; *Krypton Chronicles* #1, September 1981; others).

EROK-EL

An important ancestor of Kal-El in the Krypton of the pre–First Crisis Earth-1 universe, arguably the founder of the House of El. Prior to Erok's time, all Kryptonians had only one name. Erok was the first to create surnames and called himself Erok-El (which translated roughly to "Erok of the star"). Milia, the daughter of a Bethgar (ancient Kryptonian king), was his wife who bore him a son, Kal-El the First (*Krypton Chronicles* #1–3, September–November 1981; also see Rao).

ERSORK

See Mental Emperor; Superboy Revenge Squad.

ETERNO

A supposedly invulnerable giant android employed as a weapon by one of the many assemblages of the Superman Revenge Squad in the universe of the pre–First Crisis Earth-1. The plan backfired, resulting in this iteration of the Revenge Squad being annihilated, finding itself unable to control Eterno (*Action Comics* #343, November 1966).

EUPHOR

Euphor was a super-villain on the pre–First Crisis Earth-1 who could instill "emotional energies" in others, whipping into a vengeful frenzy those with grudges against Superman and arming them with superpowers with which to attack the Man of Steel (*Superman* [first series] #382, April 1983).

EVIL FACTORY, THE

The original name for the Apokolips-influenced research laboratory run by Simyan and Mokkari on the pre–First Crisis Earth-1 that functioned as a twisted counterpart of the benevolent DNA Project (*Superman's Pal, Jimmy Olsen* #135, January 1971; others). In the post–First Crisis merged universe, the Evil Factory continued to exist (*Superman*

[second series] #39–40, January–February 1990, and #43, May 1990), ultimately attempting to virtually replace Project Cadmus (*Superboy* [third series] #70–74, January–May 2000). A branch of the Evil Factory was located in Blüdhaven, disguised as the more innocuous-sounding Command-D bunker, which was Darkseid's base of operations on Earth in the days leading up to the Final Crisis.

EVIL THREE

See Kizo, Mala, and U-Ban.

EXAMINER, THE

One of the many competitors to the *Daily Planet* in the Metropolis of pre–First Crisis Earth-1, noteworthy for the unscrupulously aggressive competitiveness of its editor and publisher, who once attempted murder in an effort to sabotage a *Planet* publicity campaign designed to increase the latter paper's circulation (*Superman* [first series] #49, November–December 1947).

EXECUTRIX, THE

A highly trained female assassin on the pre–First Crisis Earth-1, employed by the corrupt management of a company called Metrosteel to silence a Metrosteel engineer named Page. Page became a whistle-blower to the *Daily Planet* when he learned that Metrosteel was supplying a cheap, comparatively weak grade of steel to the builders of a major bridge. Page was forced into hiding when the Executrix killed Page's contact at the *Planet.* Superman joined with the Batman in defeating the Executrix when she located and kidnapped Page, then held him hostage over the crumbling bridge. When the bridge collapsed despite Superman's best efforts to hold it up, he retrieved her unconscious body, along with Page, from the river. The Executrix went to prison and was never heard from again (*World's Finest Comics* #314, April 1985).

RED K.

FAORA

A beautiful but brutal Kryptonian criminal, incarnations of whom existed in three of Superman's realities. In most iterations, she had been exiled to the Phantom Zone, where she was incorporeal and effectively immortal. She never aged and, like the other "Zoners," outlived Krypton's destruction—which, like most events on the material plane, she was able to observe from within the Zone.

The most frequently documented Faora was the first, whose full name was Faora Hu-Ul. She was a native of the city of Alezar on Krypton in the universe of the pre-First Crisis Earth-1. This Faora was a telepath and a serial killer who, for reasons never documented, used her beauty to lure men to her home. She kept her captives as slaves, many of whom she would torture to death in a secret "concentration camp" concealed within her residence. Of these, twenty-three were killed, and when she was arrested and convicted by the Kryptonian authorities, Faora Hu-Ul was sentenced to three hundred years in the Phantom Zone—the longest sentence for a woman, and the second longest of any Zoner after Jax-Ur.

This Faora monitored Superman's activities on Earth and obsessively focused her hatred of Kryptonian men on him. She frequently escaped the Zone to Earth, where she would attempt to destroy the Man of Steel and all human males, as well as conquer the planet, with the superpowers she gained in Earth's environment.

Faora Hu-Ul initially escaped the Zone by establishing a psychic bond with an Earth man, elderly widower Jackson Porter, that was so powerful it cut through the dimensional barrier separating Earth from the Zone, allowing her to escape temporarily. During this time, she had her first encounter with Superman, to whom she appeared to be an actual spirit-like entity. She accomplished this by drawing some Phantom Zone mist with her through the opening in the barrier and surrounding her body with it, making her appear wraithlike. In this form, Faora pretended to be the ghost of Porter's wife, whose every command the devoted Porter obeyed unquestioningly.

As "Katie," Faora persuaded Porter to move to 344 Clinton Street in Metropolis, next door to Clark

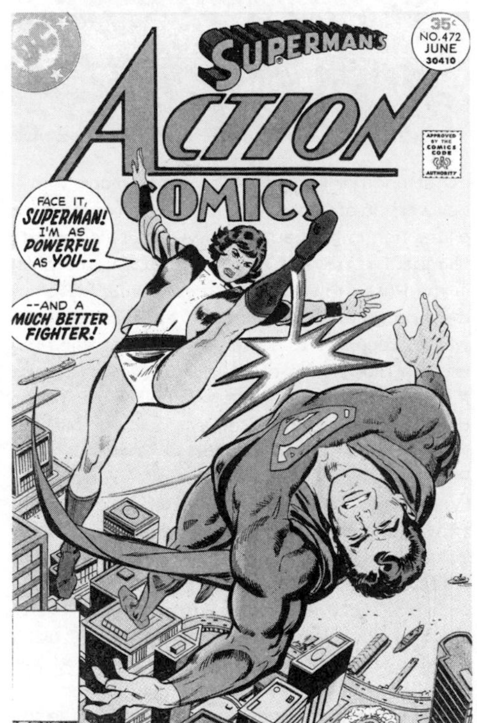

Kent (*Action Comics* #471, May 1977). Directed by "Katie" to steal an alien artifact from Kent's apartment, Porter used it to generate enough energy to puncture the dimensional barrier and allow Faora to escape the Zone permanently. Superman could not defeat Faora in battle because she was an expert in the deadly Kryptonian fighting style known as Horu-Kanu. This martial art relied on knowledge of certain "secret" pressure points on the Kryptonian body, causing either uncontrollable reflex responses or instantaneous, temporary paralysis—either of which could disable Superman's powers long enough for Faora to deliver a killing blow. Superman was forced to retreat and seemingly fled in cowardice by banishing himself to the Phantom Zone.

There he planned to disguise himself as a Phantom Zone criminal, having divined Faora's master plan. Using a Kryptonian device called a dimensional phaser (presumably stolen from Superman's Fortress of Solitude when she battled the Man of Steel there previously), Faora sent as many of Superman's friends and allies as she could into the Zone, where they'd be powerless to oppose her. At the same time, she released dozens of Phantom Zone criminals—including Jax-Ur, Kru-El, and General Zod—into Earth's dimension. She planned to dominate and ultimately kill them, fulfilling her man-hating agenda, but only after her "subjects" had helped her become Earth's ruler.

In his disguise as a Phantom Zone prisoner, Superman located the phaser where Faora had hidden it. He then reversed it so that Faora and the other Zoners were returned whence they had come, and Superman's friends reappeared on Earth (*Action Comics* #472–473, June–July 1977). Faora, along with Jax-Ur, Zod, and Kru-El, battled

Superman several more times before Earth-1 was altered by the First Crisis.

After that event, an incarnation of Faora called Zaora appeared in the same Pocket Universe in which Lex Luthor artificially created the shape-shifter Matrix. Zaora conspired with Zod and Quex-Ul to trick the Pocket Universe Luthor into releasing them from the Zone, in an attempt to conquer the Pocket Universe Earth. Meeting more resistance from the Pocket Universe humans than they had anticipated, the trio of Phantom Zone escapees decided to annihilate Pocket Universe humanity by lethally poisoning its atmosphere.

Before all life could be wiped out, Matrix had sought help from the Superman of "our" Earth, who stripped the three Kryptonians of their powers by exposing them to gold kryptonite. Once the trio were powerless, Superman, in a rare departure from his code against killing, executed them by exposing them to *green* kryptonite—both in punishment for their act of genocide and to protect his own Earth, which the Zoners had vowed to attack and destroy as well (*The Adventures of Superman* #444, September 1988; *Superman* [second series] #22, October 1988; others).

A different version of Faora—who was probably an artificial construct rather than human—was encountered in the Phantom Zone by the Eradicator. It was presumed to be another device created by Kem-L, and it claimed that it was called Faora after Kem-L's grandmother. The account of this event was unclear as to whether the construct's claims were true.

Convinced instead that "Faora" was a malicious entity, the Eradicator downloaded into "her" all elements of its original programming that were objectionable to Dr. David Connor. Unfortunately, this only enabled the Faora construct to assume a frighteningly powerful new form with the ability to escape the Zone. The Eradicator apprehended and destroyed it, but not before it had murdered Connor's wife in retaliation (*Eradicator* #1–3, August-October 1996).

Superman encountered another iteration of Faora when he and Lois Lane traveled to an artificial Krypton created within the Phantom Zone. This artificial version in some ways resembled the Krypton in the universe of the pre–First Crisis Earth-1, yet in other ways evoked the unified universe's Krypton. Like the latter, the Phantom Zone Krypton was characterized by xenophobia and emotional coldness. It was a fascistic society that promoted "cultural purity," presumably a product of "ethnic cleansing" conducted by Eradicators, which were slightly different-looking versions of the device that, outside the Phantom Zone, evolved into the humanoid Eradicator (*Superman* [second series] #166–167, March–April 2001; and *The Adventures of Superman* #589; *Superman: The Man of Steel* #111; *Action Comics* #776—all April 2001).

The most fanatical about Kryptonian supremacy was General Zod, the equivalent of a defense secretary on this Krypton's governing body, here called the Imperial Council rather than the Science Council. Superman lost his powers due to this Krypton's red dwarf star sun, and he became vulnerable to attack by two of General Zod's fiercest deputies, Kru-El and his wife Faora (*Superman: The Man of Steel* #111, April 2001).

After their adventure here, Superman and Lois remained uncertain as to whether what they'd experienced was illusory or real. The artificial Krypton's Faora was never seen again. While Lois and Superman didn't realize it at the time, the artificial Krypton had been created in the Phantom Zone by Brainiac 13 during the period in which his Y2K virus was transforming aspects of Superman's reality, such as Metropolis, into sixty-fourth-century versions of themselves.

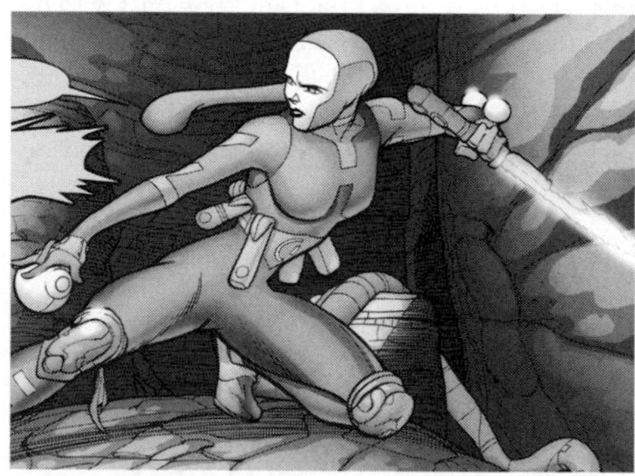

Yet another incarnation of Faora, along with a new version of General Zod, became an unwelcome distraction in the Earth's otherwise unified efforts to repel Imperiex. This version had been an orphan in the Russian Federation's meta-human development program—a cybernetically enhanced teenage warrior recruited to serve the Zod who ruled the Eastern Bloc nation of Pokolistan (*Action Comics* #779, July 2001; others). It was believed she took the name Faora at Zod's request, but her real name was never documented. A former Soviet republic, Pokolistan was a military dictatorship ruled by an Earth-born General Zod, supported by Faora and two other meta-humans, Ignition and Kancer. While Pokolistan's citizens were not free by U.S. standards, this Zod turned the country into a functional, orderly society with relatively contented citizens. Much of this seemed to be the product of using Kryptonian technology, even though this Zod was not of Kryptonian origin.

This Zod was originally named Avruiskin, the son of Russian cosmonauts exposed to radiation that resulted in their newborn son gaining superpowers on exposure to red dwarf star energy. Once Soviet scientists discovered this, they provided him with a suit of red armor that would maintain in him the levels of red-sun energy necessary to sustain his powers, and manipulated Avruiskin into hating Superman. It was also thought that telepathic influence from a version of Zod in the Phantom Zone fanned the flames of that hatred and prompted Avruiskin to adopt the name Zod. A psionic influence by Zod was also the possible "inspiration" for naming his female Russian henchwoman Faora.

This version of Faora had the ability to disrupt molecular cohesiveness. She created a mutagenic virus that was the linchpin of Zod's plan to strip Earth's super heroes of their powers, kill Superman, and conquer Earth (*Superman: Our Worlds at War* #1–2, August 2002; others). After Zod died fighting Superman during this campaign, Faora was forced to repair the damage he had done before being taken into custody (*Action Comics* #805, September 2003).

No Kryptonian named Faora has yet been documented in the post–Infinite Crisis reality. Historians believe that Ursa was the Faora analogue among the Kandorians who briefly inhabited New Earth before the establishment of New Krypton.

FARR, DR. WILSON

A high-ranking scientist with S.T.A.R. Labs who appeared on the pre-Crisis Earth-1 as Superman's initial contact with the organization (*Superman* [first series] #246, December 1971; others). His last known project for S.T.A.R. was a solar-powered jet prototype (*Superman Family* #187, January-February 1978).

FATAL FIVE, THE

A super-criminal gang first documented in the thirtieth century of the pre–First Crisis Earth-1. The Fatal Five fought Superboy more often than Superman. The Fatal Five, on the other hand, were enemies of Superboy primarily during his time trips into the future in his capacity as a member of the Legion of Super-Heroes.

The Legion itself was responsible for the existence of the original Fatal Five, having assembled the group to combat a Sun-Eater heading toward Earth. Sun-Eaters were living nebulae who could absorb all of a star's energy, plunging entire solar systems into subzero temperatures and freezing to death all life on the inhabited planets. Each of the Fatal Five was originally a criminal who operated independently, but the Legion gambled that their combined powers, along with the Legionnaires', could destroy the Sun-Eater (*Adventure Comics* #352, January 1967).

After the Sun-Eater was destroyed and Earth saved thanks to the ultimate sacrifice of a single Legionnaire, Ferro, the five super-criminals nevertheless earned pardons in acknowledgment of their participation. They rejected the implicit invitation to join the side of superpowered law enforcement, however, and instead opted to work together as a criminal gang, their goal being the conquest of the worlds they had saved.

During their career, the original Fatal Five proved unexpectedly powerful—enough so, for example, to conquer an entire planet while trapped in another dimension. They became five of the Legion's most formidable enemies, as Lex Luthor was to Superman.

The first quintet to take the name Fatal Five were:

• The Emerald Empress, who had no superpowers of her own but achieved spectacularly deadly effects on her enemies through the power of the Emerald Eye of Ekron, a sphere that the Empress controlled telepathically.

• The Persuader, who carried an atomic ax that could slice through anything and which he could control telekinetically.

• Mano, a mutant whose glowing right hand could disintegrate anything it touched.

• Validus, an invulnerable, super-strong giant whose transparent skull revealed a brain that could fire deadly bolts of energy.

• Their leader Tharok, a half cyborg whose body had been reconstructed after a terrible accident. His electronically amplified brain gave him mind-control powers that allowed him to dominate the others, effortlessly becoming the group's commander.

This group had repeated encounters with Superboy and the Legion of Super-Heroes until reality was reorganized by the events of the First Crisis (*Adventure Comics* #365, February 1968, and #378, March 1969; *Superboy* [first series] #190, September 1972, and #198, October 1973; others).

The membership of the Fatal Five, as well as its history, changed somewhat, just as the Legion's did, owing to the various events that reorganized the Legion's reality, particularly Zero Hour (*Zero Hour: Crisis in Time* #0–4, September 1994). Just before the First Crisis, Tharok had died (*Legion of Super-Heroes* [second series] #271, January 1981) and Validus returned to normal humanoid form (*Legion of Super-Heroes* [third series] *Annual* #2, 1986). The conditions led the Emerald Empress to recruit three new members to join her and the Persuader in a new Fatal Five. These recruits were the flame-wielding Flare; Caress, whose acid touch was lethal; and the recently rejected Legion applicant Mentalla, who was secretly undermining the Five's efforts in a bid to be reconsidered for Legion membership. Ultimately, the Emerald Empress discovered Mentalla's true loyalties and

killed her (*Legion of Super-Heroes* [third series] #24–26, July–September 1986; others).

Following the events of Zero Hour, a version of the Legion known as Batch SW6 appeared. They were a group of time-paradox duplicates of the early Legion. This SW6 Legion battled a Fatal Five whose members were Tharok; Mano; the Persuader; a new Emerald Empress named Cera Kesh, who had been rejected for membership in the Legion; and a monstrous being called Mordecai (*Legionnaires* #2, May 1993; others).

The original Fatal Five reappeared to battle the "real" (non-SW6) Legion after they were assembled to help fight another Sun-Eater in this reordered reality, although here it was discovered that the Sun-Eater didn't exist and was an elaborate hoax, masterminded by corrupt United Planets president Chu to create an excuse for the creation of a Fatal Five that would presumably serve her (*Legion of Super-Heroes* [fifth series] #78, March 1996; others).

After the events of the Infinite Crisis, the thirty-first-century future was reconstituted and its Legionnaires and other inhabitants began interacting with the heroes of the twenty-first century once again. One such event occurred when the Fatal Five—in this reality comprising the Emerald Empress, Validus, Mano, Tharok, and the Persuader—were brought to the twenty-first century by a super-criminal known as the Lord of Time. He needed the Five to help him steal a weapon called the Haruspex, which could evaluate various probabilities to determine what kind of response could best eliminate a threat, which it would then manifest.

Batman and another super hero, Blue Beetle, intervened, and in the resulting battle the Lord of Time found himself on the losing side and retreated to the future, abandoning the Fatal Five. As Batman and Tharok fought, the Haruspex fused Batman and Tharok together into one entity. The Legion used its technology to teleport the Five and Batman—still merged with Tharok—back to the thirty-first century, where the Five were imprisoned. Between the use of thirty-first-century technology and the powers of the Haruspex, the Legion was able to uncouple Tharok and Batman and return the Dark Knight to the twenty-first century (*The Brave and the Bold* [third series] #3–6, July–October 2007). This incarnation of the Fatal Five was also among the allies of the Legion of Super-Villains formed by Superman-Prime (*Final Crisis: Legion of 3 Worlds* #1–5, October 2008–September 2009).

Previously, a version of the group appeared on the post–First Crisis unified Earth to battle Superman. They were an artificially created version of the team, "hard-light images" (solid holograms) generated by Brainiac 13 to use against the Man of Steel (*Superman* [second series] #171, August 2001).

FAULKNER, DR. KAREN LOU "KITTY"

A mild-mannered, shy, and reserved physicist on the post–First Crisis Earth who developed a non-polluting energy source to enter in a competition

S.T.A.R. Labs Metropolis is headed by Dr. Karen Lou "Kitty" Faulkner — who is also known as the metahuman Rampage.

staged by the *Daily Planet*. Dr. Tom Moyers, a colleague with grave misgivings about Faulkner's invention, which he found potentially dangerous, shut down the safety systems on Faulkner's device while pleading his case to reporters. Perhaps inadvertently (though some accounts suggested he was acting with malign intent), Moyers triggered an explosion that transformed Faulkner into a huge, incredibly strong, orange-skinned giant who later became the super heroine known as Rampage (*Superman* [second series] #7, July 1987).

It was soon discovered that Rampage's powers came from Faulkner's newfound ability to absorb solar energy through her skin. After she was returned to normal, it was learned that she needed to continue to absorb a certain amount of solar energy or she would die. Ostensibly to atone for his role in creating Rampage (but with a hidden agenda of being able to control Rampage and have her do his bidding), Moyers developed a "regulating collar" that would maintain the exact level of solar energy absorption to keep her alive. Instead it gave Moyers the ability to transform her into Rampage at will—*his* will. After Superman helped Kitty get her powers under control, she accepted a job at S.T.A.R. Labs. Following a stint as director of the S.T.A.R. facility in Phoenix, she was brought back to Metropolis to help with a major reorganization of S.T.A.R. in the wake of the destruction of its international headquarters during the event known as Armageddon 2001 (*Armageddon 2001* #1–2, May–October 1991). Shortly thereafter, she was promoted to director of the Metropolis S.T.A.R. facility.

Faulkner survived the Infinite Crisis to continue life on New Earth, and for the most part resisted the temptation to become Rampage, although the influence of various super-criminals sometimes forced the transformation, as was likely the case in her clash with Mon-El (*Superman* #686, May 2009).

FAWCETT, WILLIE

See Captain Thunder.

FEMALE FURIES, THE

A team of Apokoliptian female warriors, trained and led using brutally violent methods by Granny Goodness. They were first seen in the universe occupied by the pre–First Crisis Earth-1 (*Mister Miracle* [first series] #6, February 1972). Though unquestionably loyal to Darkseid, there was constant infighting among the Furies to appoint a field commander—a second in command to Granny.

The majority of Furies were New Gods themselves, but Granny was known to recruit females of other races, including several super heroines of Earth during the event known as the Final Crisis. Four members of the team, Lashina (armed with flexible steel bands she could use as weapons, controlling them via telekinesis), Stompa (who could create earthquakes by stamping her feet), Bernadeth (the sister of master torturer DeSaad, who armed her with a flaming knife, and often opposed Lashina), and the insane Mad Harriet (whose weapons were her "energy claws") appeared on Earth-1 to bring escapee Big Barda, wife of Mister Miracle, back to Apokolips. However, Barda persuaded her former teammates to help her, and the four Furies remained on Earth-1, functioning as heroines, for a time.

After the First Crisis, the Furies remained essentially unchanged, as did Darkseid and most aspects of Apokolips. In addition to Bernadeth, Lashina, Mad Harriet, and Stompa, other Furies included Gilotina (who could slice through things with karate chops), Malice (who was the youngest Fury and niece of Darkseid lieutenant Virman Vundabar, and whose weapon was a brutal, disembodied mouth called Chessure), Wunda (the last known addition to the team, whose weapons were her light-based powers), and Artemiz (an archer with arrows that could seek out organic life). Following the deaths of the New Gods that occurred during the Final Crisis, the spirits of some of the Furies found refuge in the bodies of various humans for a time.

FERRO; AKA FERRO LAD

A grotesquely facially deformed young super hero incarnated in several realities, in each case named Andrew Nolan and always one of twin brothers. First seen in the thirtieth century of the pre–First Crisis Earth-1, Andrew and twin brother Douglas were human mutations whose facial deformity was a function of the same genetic abnormality that allowed the twins to transform their bodies into living iron, retaining all of their normal human capacities such as movement and speech, and developing super-strength and invulnerability. Both boys wore iron masks to conceal their ugliness, and, adopting the name Ferro Lad, Andrew successfully applied for membership in the Legion of Super-Heroes (*Adventure Comics* #346, July 1966; others).

Shortly after he joined the Legion, Earth was threatened by a Sun-Eater. Ultimately, despite the aid of the Fatal Five's powers, it became clear that the only solution was to deposit a thirtieth-century explosive device deep inside the Sun-Eater. It was decided that the invulnerable Superboy would execute the maneuver, but Andrew Nolan realized that Superboy might face grave danger because the Sun-Eater partially comprised red dwarf star energy. So Ferro Lad knocked the Boy of Steel out of his way and delivered the device himself, ultimately perishing along with the Sun-Eater (*Adventure Comics* #353, February 1967).

A younger version of Ferro Lad, who had the same powers and personal history but had shortened his name to simply Ferro, existed among the "Batch SW6" time-paradox Legionnaires (*Legion of Super-Heroes* [fourth series] #38, Late December 1992; others).

Another iteration of Andrew Nolan appeared after Zero Hour, but this one came from twentieth-century Earth in the post–First Crisis cosmos. This Andrew Nolan and his twin Douglas were born to a famous actress, Nancy Nolan, who gave them up because of their deformities, leaving them in the care of an unscrupulous scientist who mistreated them. Andrew escaped to seek out their mother; fearful Douglas stayed behind. Andrew found Nancy and saved her from a collapsing building, never revealing himself as anything other than "Ferro," the super-heroic identity he took for himself on the spot. In this guise, he helped Clark Kent deliver the *Daily Planet* while Metropolis was in the grip of the ice and snow that resulted during the events known as the Final Night (*The Adventures of Superman* #540, November 1996).

When the Earth was freezing because of a Sun-Eater consuming Earth's sun, this Andrew Nolan became involved with the Legion of Super-Heroes, who were stranded in the twentieth century. This time it was the former Green Lantern, Hal Jordan, now operating under the persona of Parallax, who seemed to sacrifice his life so that the sun could be reconstructed (*Final Night* #1–4, November 1996). Ferro chose to throw in with the Legionnaires, though they did not immediately tell him that they were from the thirty-first century. Nevertheless, when the Legionnaires were able to return home at last, Ferro accompanied them and served with them for some time.

MY BODY IS WHITE HOT... ONLY MY WILL POWER IS KEEPING ME FROM MELTING ... BUT I HAVE TO PENETRATE DEEPER! DEEPER!
Fe

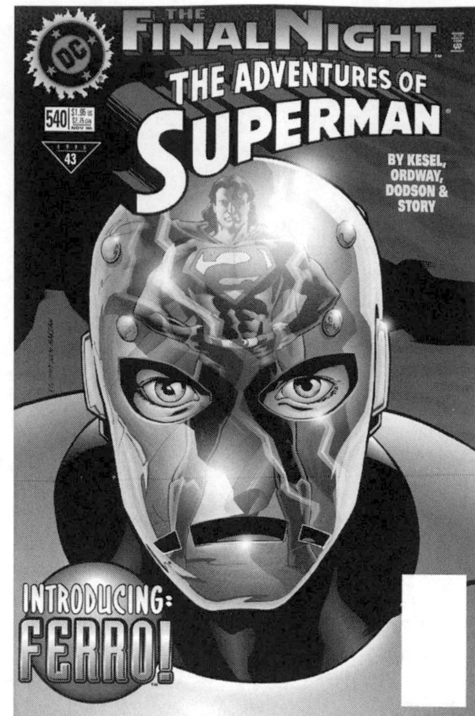

When several Legionnaires were lost in a space accident and the remaining members ordered by the United Planets to disband, Ferro went to live in a monastery on a planet called Steeple. Steeple was located within a black hole, and could be visited by off-worlders only during brief intervals, once every ten years, before it disappeared, Brigadoon-like, once more. This meant that Ferro was marooned there for a decade. While on Steeple, Nolan was brutally beaten by an escaped convict. The monks were able to save Nolan's life, but thereafter he remained in his living iron form—with his helmet and mask, in effect, *becoming* his head—permanently (*Legion Worlds* #5, October 2001).

The Infinite Crisis reconstructed reality so that a version of the Legion that was very similar to the pre–First Crisis incarnation came into existence. Andrew Nolan was documented as being a member of this Legion (*Justice Society of America* [third series] #5, June 2007; *Action Comics* #858, Late December 2007; others). The account also stated, however, that this Legion's history was very close to that of the pre–First Crisis Legion's. In that case, this version of Ferro would also have died fighting the Sun-Eater.

FEVER PLAGUE

The cause of death for the Jonathan and Martha Kent of the pre–First Crisis Earth-1, for which there was no known cure. The Kents' condition mystified doctors because no one had contracted the disease for a century. This made Superboy feel overwhelmingly guilty, believing he had caused their demise because they had contracted the disease during a trip into the past that he himself had facilitated (*Superman* [first series] #161, May 1963). It should be noted, however, that this account is one of many contradictory reports of the nature and cause of the Kents' deaths and may be apocryphal.

FIFTY-TWO

A term created to denote the events of the year following the end of the Infinite Crisis, during which Superman temporarily retired his costumed identity and a new multiverse was created. The number refers not only to the number of weeks in which those events occurred, but also to the fifty-two separate parallel universes, each with its own Earth, that were created.

The account of those fifty-two weeks chronicled the various complications and alterations to the lives of many super heroes and super-criminals when time-traveling super hero Booster Gold's robot sidekick Skeets was inhabited by Mister Mind. Mind, a longtime foe of Captain Marvel, was the sole survivor of a race of psionically powered, worm-like creatures originating on the planet Venus, possessing abilities that included telepathy, mental domination, and the power to project images from their minds.

Mister Mind had been using Skeets's metal shell as a cocoon in which he could complete his year-long metamorphosis into a gigantic, monstrous creature that fed on entire worlds and space-time itself, and decided to consume the entire multiverse. As Skeets, Mind pursued Booster Gold and time-traveling comrade Rip Hunter back through time to the end of the Infinite Crisis and the birth of the multiverse. He followed them from universe to universe, feeding on portions of each world's history, causing changes to their time lines that created fifty-two new, distinct parallel Earths. Mind was ultimately lured back to Rip Hunter's lab, where he shrank back to his larval form, trapped inside Skeets's shell long enough to be disposed of.

After these events, and before the Final Crisis, the Earth that was home to Superman was the fifty-second iteration, or, according to Rip Hunter, "New Earth." There were variant incarnations of Superman known to exist on a few, but not all, of the fifty-two worlds, not merely because some didn't have any form of Superman at all, but also because the inhabitants of all fifty-two Earths had not been documented.

For example, there is a Superman on Earth-9, which became home to the super heroes reported to have fled the Earth-97 of the reality created during the Infinite Crisis. Earth-11 was inhabited by "gender-reversed" versions of New Earth's super heroes, which included a Superwoman. Earth-16 was home to a Superman who had an equally super son. And on Earth-31, there was a much older version of Superman who worked directly for the president of the United States (*52* #1–52, May 10, 2006–May 2, 2007).

FINAL CRISIS

The name for the reality-threatening event caused by Darkseid's most ambitious plan to date, the creation of a "final crisis" for humanity—the reshaping of existence according to Darkseid's own whim and design.

After the First Crisis, the war between the benevolent New Gods of New Genesis and the malign New Gods of Apokolips had escalated to the point that the Source itself began to manipulate reality in an effort to resolve the conflict. In its efforts to end the Fourth World and usher in a fifth, the Source used Infinity-Man, disguised as the New God Himon, to kill off the New Gods. The first to die was Orion. Darkseid, by this time in possession of the Anti-Life Equation, used Jimmy Olsen as a soul catcher, acquiring the murdered gods' powers as they died and unwittingly transferring them to Darkseid. In response, the Source resurrected Orion, who fought the prophesied battle in which he would kill his father, which he ostensibly did. After taking the Anti-Life Equation back into itself, the Source combined Apokolips and New Genesis into one planet (*Death of the New Gods* #1–8, Early December 2007–June 2008).

Darkseid, though, managed to survive (*DC Universe* #0, June 2008), and inhabited the body that was once Dan Turpin, taking on the persona of an early-twentieth-century gangster—presumably influenced by his contact with the earliest incarnation of Intergang—and adopting the name *Boss Dark Side*. The death of the gods was a serious enough development that the Guardians of the Universe initiated an investigation. Darkseid, in his gangster guise, unleashed the Anti-Life Equation all over New Earth, which, as ever, erased the free will of those it affected, reducing them to mindless automatons susceptible to control by a master—in this case, Dark Side. The survivors, many of them super heroes, formed a resistance movement. Among them was Superman, who was most profoundly affected by these events by almost losing his wife Lois Lane when she was injured in an explosion. Following the directions of a Monitor, the Man of Steel participated in a reality-altering event that saved Lois's life (*Final Crisis: Superman Beyond 3D* #1–2, October 2008–March 2009).

Ultimately, Darkseid and his fellow Apokoliptians were defeated and humankind was freed. Once again, Darkseid was seemingly destroyed, and the Source resurrected Highfather and the gods of New Genesis on Earth-51 (*Final Crisis* #1–7, July 2008–March 2009).

FINAL NIGHT, THE

The term for a series of catastrophic events caused in the post–First Crisis reality, when Earth's sun was devoured by a Sun-Eater (*Final Night* #1–4, November 1996; others). A mysterious alien named Dusk arrived on Earth in a spacecraft to warn Earth's heroes of the approaching Sun-Eater, whose progress she had followed as it moved relentlessly through the galaxy, destroying one star system after another. Dusk was pessimistic from all she had seen, and was convinced that Earth, too, would freeze to death, as had all the inhabited planets in the systems whose stars the Sun-Eater had consumed, but she held out a slim hope that Earth, with its super heroes, might be an exception.

Unsuccessful attempts to destroy the Sun-Eater were made by an odd alliance that included Lex Luthor, the Justice League of America, and the Legion of Super-Heroes, who had traveled through time back

Superman and Quantum Superman try to escape the Graveyard Universe.

to twentieth-century Earth. Their efforts included an attempt by Mister Miracle to use a gigantic version of the Boom Tube to send the Sun-Eater into another dimension, only to discover that the Sun-Eater did not exist entirely in this dimension and was too powerful for Miracle's device.

Superman with his heat vision joined with other heat-producing heroes to generate a second sun, in an effort to misdirect the Sun-Eater and lure it away from Sol (the Latin and astronomical term for the yellow dwarf star at the center of our solar system). The Sun-Eater wasted no time in consuming the "decoy" sun, but then moved on to Sol and, despite the heroes' best efforts to prevent it, began to consume Sol as well.

As Sol was being devoured, Superman began to lose his powers altogether, due to the fact that they were yellow-sun-based. While a new Ice Age engulfed Earth and the people of Metropolis tried to cope with the inevitability that they would freeze to death, Superman met the Earth-born Ferro, who played a significant role in the outcome of this crisis.

Meanwhile, Brainiac 5 had calculated that the sun was shrinking, yet maintaining its mass. This meant that the sun would soon go supernova, causing a blast of thermal energy that would wipe out all remaining life on Earth. The goal then became to shield Earth from the supernova.

The alliance's response was a technological approach. Lex Luthor set his people to work on designing an interlinked network of force-field modules, ultimately producing half a million of these devices (with the super-speed assistance of the Flash) that were to have created a force field large enough to shield the entire planet. But the modules could not be deployed unless someone flew them into the sun as it went supernova.

Superman, already greatly weakened from the loss of yellow-star radiation, volunteered to pilot Dusk's ship into the sun and activate the force-field network. But in an eerie echo of events that had happened in the future of the pre–First Crisis Earth-1, Ferro recognized that Superman was too important to sacrifice and stole the ship to pilot it himself. He was shunted aside by Hal Jordan, the former Green Lantern then known as Parallax.

Jordan, who had gained many new superpowers as Parallax (*Green Lantern* [third series] #48, January 1994, and #50, March 1994; *Zero Hour* #0–4, September 1994; *Green Lantern* [fourth series] #0, October 1994; *Darkstars* #0, October 1994; others), flew into the sun and absorbed the supernova blast. Adding to the mix his own Green Lantern green energy, which he had internalized, Jordan then used that energy to reignite Sol and save Earth. This effort taxed even Parallax, who died in the sun's core. After the alliance of heroes restored Earth's damaged ecosystem, in time, life returned to normal.

FINE, MILTON

See Brainiac.

FIRE FALLS

A natural wonder documented on the Krypton of the universe in which Earth-1 existed. The falls comprised flowing gouts of flame—or, in the words of another account, "a fiery liquid"—geysering up from Krypton's core and spilling out over scenic rock formations (*Superman's Girl Friend, Lois Lane* #21, November 1960). It was believed that if all the fragments of the exploded Krypton became kryptonite, then somewhere out in space there must have been an asteroid—a fragment of Krypton—on which the famed Fire Falls, now green and radioactive, still cascaded (*Action Comics* #324, May 1965; others).

FIRST CRISIS

See Crisis on Infinite Earths.

FLAMEBIRD

A Kryptonian bird preserved by Nor-Kan in Earth-1's miniaturized bottle city of Kandor. Its name and appearance served as inspiration, in various realities and contexts, for a number of super heroic figures who operated under that name, all of whom were well known to Superman or Batman or both.

In the Earth-1 Kandor, Jimmy Olsen fought crime as Flamebird alongside Superman, who assumed the guise of Nightwing. With Superman deprived of his superpowers in Kandor, where Krypton's environment was perfectly reproduced, he and Jimmy became a crime-fighting team in part patterned after Batman and Robin, using rocket belts to fly (*Superman* [first series] #158, January 1963; *Superman's Pal, Jimmy Olsen* #69, June 1963; others).

Later, Superman's cousin, the scientist Van-Zee, who closely resembled Kal-El, took on the Nightwing persona to continue his cousin's work fighting crime in Kandor. He was joined in this pursuit by a Flamebird who was in reality his lab assistant, who was also his niece's husband, Ak-Var (*Superman Family* #183, May–June 1977). This iteration of the duo effectively ended crime in Kandor.

On the post–First Crisis Earth, neither Superman nor Jimmy Olsen ever fought crime together as Nightwing or Flamebird. The two heroes were, instead, Kryptonian legends: mythic heroic figures. In this reality, Dick Grayson had assumed the adult super-heroic persona of Nightwing, having chosen the name after Superman related to him

the Kryptonian legend. The name Flamebird was used primarily by Bette Kane. Kane's Earth-1 counterpart had been Bat-Girl, who was secretly Betty Kane, niece of that world's Batwoman and a member of Titans West, a Los Angeles "auxiliary" to the better-known super hero group Teen Titans, which operated out of New York. The post–First Crisis Earth had no Batwoman or Bat-Girl (only Batgirl—one word), but the Titans West were reincarnated in that reality.

In the Bat-Girl Betty Kane's place appeared Bette, a Los Angeles debutante, tennis champ, and martial artist who had chosen a training regimen to sharpen her physical skills to Olympic caliber to become a crime fighter herself, under the name Flamebird. In this guise she joined Teen Titans West. She would later interact with the adult Dick Grayson as Nightwing, but her choice of the name Flamebird was strictly coincidental since she chose it long before Grayson took his new alias (*Secret Origins Annual* #3, 1989; others).

The connection was documented only later, when Superman and Lois Lane assumed costumed identities during their trip to the Krypton created by Brainiac 13 in the Phantom Zone (*Superman: The Man of Steel* #111, April 2001). When they were greeted by an off-worlder as "Nightwing and Flamebird," champions of the oppressed, Superman explained to Lois that he had once related the Kryptonian legend to Dick. The Flamebird identity was also assumed at one point by the Kryptonian Kara Zor-El (the one who landed on Earth after the period in which Earth's Supergirl was the Earth-born angel "fusion" of Matrix and Linda Danvers). She had returned from adventures with the Legion of Super-Heroes to the twenty-first-century New Earth one year after the multiverse was restored by the Infinite Crisis. As a result of this reality shift, she was able to coexist with Power Girl, and when Kandor was jeopardized by the anti-matter Earth-2's Ultraman and Saturn Queen, they intervened. After they lost their superpowers in the Kandorian environment, Supergirl adopted the identity of Flamebird, with Power Girl as Nightwing (*Supergirl* [fifth series] #6–8, April–September 2006).

After reality was again reordered following the Final Crisis, one hundred thousand Kryptonians lived on Earth in the city of Kandor, which Superman, having encountered the Brainiac of this reality for the first time, removed from his ship and enlarged in the Arctic. Before New Krypton was grown beneath the city, a new Flamebird—who was the female, dominant partner—appeared in Kandor with a Nightwing who turned out to be Lor-Zod, General Zod's son, who had been freed from the Phantom Zone by Flamebird. Their goal was to guard the Phantom Zone projector in Superman's Fortress of Solitude, with the intent of preventing followers of General Zod living in Kandor from freeing Zod from the Phantom Zone. They were later overruled by Alura when she took command of New Krypton and installed Zod as head of what was called the Military Guild (see Guilds).

It was eventually revealed that this Flamebird was Thara Ak-Var, the chief of security whom Alura blamed for the death of her husband Zor-El by failing to protect him from the attack on him by General Sam Lane's Project 7734 agent Reactron. This version of the Flamebird-and-Nightwing team policed Earth, hunting hostile Kryptonians who had infiltrated human society and positions of power with malign intent (*Action Comics* #875, May 2009; others), before the formation of New Krypton. Thara Ak-Var displayed the standard complement of those superpowers endowed by a yellow-sun environment to any Kryptonian, but also manifested the ability to shoot fireballs from her hands. She believed herself to be an embodiment of the Flamebird, which in the history of the New Earth reality's Krypton had become a mystical creature, sacred to the Kryptonian religion that

was based on worship of Rao, the red sun of the Kandorians' homeworld. The best description of the possibly mythical Flamebird, in Earth terms, was as a cross between a phoenix and a dragon. To Thara, Lor-Zod was similarly an incarnation of the Nightwing, her predestined and eternal mate, also according to the ancient scripture.

Thara was raised on Krypton, dividing her time between her native Kandor and Argo City, the home of her best friend Kara Zor-El, later Supergirl. Thara had had lifelong dreams and visions of flames and had always been devoutly religious. But her faith was sorely tested at age fourteen, when Thara was among the thousands of Kandorians shrunk and kidnapped by Brainiac. During that event, she was doubly traumatized by witnessing the death of her parents, members of the elite Military Guild unit Black Zero, in an attempt to rescue her, and their abandonment by their commanding officer Ursa.

Thara met Kara Zor-El's parents, Alura and Zor-El, and became their surrogate daughter, when Brainiac integrated the population of the subsequently captured Argo City into that of Kandor. Zor-El guided Thara to the Religious Guild, hoping to help restore her religiosity, and when she entered the temple called the House of Rao, the Flamebird appeared to her in a sacred vision. It was after her initiation in the Religious Guild that she suffered a seizure during which she had another vision, one that convinced her there was a young man trapped in the Phantom Zone who was destined to be "her" Nightwing. This was Lor-Zod, whom she released from the Zone. The two were lovers and partners thereafter, even though Thara was afraid to share with him the intensity of her love *or* her faith, afraid that he would come to fear for her sanity or reject her (*Action Comics Annual* #12, August 2009; others).

Thara's faith was tested when she was seriously injured by Ursa using a kryptonite-laced knife, forcing Lor-Zod to bring her to his surrogate mother, Lois Lane, for assistance. Lois summoned the Justice League's Doctor Light who helped Thara absorb healing solar energy (*Action Comics* #876, April 2009). Thara and Nightwing then resumed their mission, which saw them in action against both Kryptonian and human villains including Codename: Assassin, Reactron, and Metallo. The former managed to kidnap Thara and access her memories and learn all her secrets, allowing him to manipulate Flamebird by threatening Lor-Zod's life (*Action Comics* #879, July 2009). Flamebird and Nightwing's successes led to a brief period of public acceptance and acclaim, and Thara's simmering jealousy over Earth females' attention toward Nightwing bubbled over, leading to the ignition of a romance between the two. Sentiment turned against them, however, when they were framed for the seeming murder of Mon-El, Metropolis's champion while Superman was living on New Krypton. With Supergirl, the three fled to Paris to assess their options, but were interrupted when they were attacked by Project 7734's Squad K (*Action Comics* #881, September 2009). Tensions continued to mount between Thara and Kara as the once close friends let miscommunication and misunderstanding cloud their actions and judgment. Kara accused Thara of participating in her father's assassination, while Thara remained hurt that her childhood friend never accepted her religious convictions. When Squad K found them once more, the trio of heroes attempted to surrender, but Reactron slaughtered the Squad before turning his attention to the Kryptonians. Thara was injured while protecting Supergirl, and the impact triggered the complete manifestation of the reincarnated Flamebird, proving Thara's faith to be well placed. Supergirl convinced the entity not to kill Reactron, so instead, Flamebird kissed Lor-Zod and submerged itself once more within Thara's consciousness. Kara then apologized for mistrusting her friend's beliefs, and for a brief moment, peace was restored (*Supergirl* [fifth series] #46, December 2009).

Project 7734's final act involved a re-creation of the Kryptonian god Rao, comprised of thousands of computers designed and programmed by Lex Luthor. It threatened the remaining survivors of New Krypton in the wake of the artificial world's destruction. However, the Flamebird entity flew into Rao and sacrificed its life-force in a gigantic explosion of light and flame, thereby destroying the weapon (*Superman: War of the Supermen* #3, July 2010). Soon after, Mary Elizabeth ("Bette") Kane resumed her costumed crime-fighting career and once more became Earth's Flamebird (*Detective Comics* #863, May 2010).

FLAME DRAGON

A gigantic creature, similar to the fire-breathing dragons of ancient Earth legends, that was indigenous to the planet Krypton in the universe of the pre–First Crisis Earth-1. Superman never discovered how one of them survived Krypton's destruction, but when it came to Earth, it, too, gained superpowers under Earth's yellow sun and proved a near-unbeatable antagonist to the Man of Steel.

Before the monstrosity could lay waste to Earth, however, it was temporarily deprived of its powers by exposure to red kryptonite, and Superman seized the opportunity to freeze it with his super-breath into "a great mass of ice," whereupon he hurled it into orbit around the planetoid Pluto. There it remained frozen, in suspended animation, until the flame dragon species was erased from reality by the changes wrought during the First Crisis (*Superman* [first series] #142, January 1961).

Some time later, Earth was menaced by one more Kryptonian flame dragon, this one a baby hatched from an egg laid by the first. This younger form of the species was a less formidable threat, however, and Superman was able to dispatch it by flying it into the prehistoric past, where it could successfully coexist with the dinosaurs (*Superman* [first series] #151, February 1962).

Yet a third flame dragon was created by Jimmy Olsen, using a device created by eccentric inventor Phineas Potter, to fight Titano the giant super-ape as part of a science-fiction film Jimmy had talked a Hollywood producer into letting him make (*Superman's Pal, Jimmy Olsen* #84, April 1965).

FLAMMBRON

The "hottest sun" in the universe of the pre–First Crisis Earth-1. See Virus X.

FLANNELHEAD

See Hocus and Pocus.

FLASH, THE

An incarnation of this super-speeding hero has existed as a friend and ally to Superman in all his realities. All versions of the Flash had similar powers, having derived them from the same source, an "extra-dimensional energy field" known as the Speed Force. The first two, who could only run at *near* light speed, were research scientist Jay Garrick of Keystone City on the pre–First Crisis Earth-2 (*Flash* [first series] [aka *Flash Comics*] #1, January 1940; *The Flash* [first series] #123, September 1961; others) and his pre–First Crisis Earth-1 counterpart, the ironically slow-moving Central City police scientist Barry Allen (*Showcase* #4, September–October 1956; *Flash* [first series] #105, February–March 1959; others). Allen was killed during the First Crisis but later returned as the Flash following the Final Crisis (*DC Universe* #0, June 2008; *Final Crisis* #2, August 2008; *The Flash: Rebirth* #1–6, April–September 2009; others).

Allen's successor in the post–First Crisis reality was his nephew Wally West of Keystone City, who had previously been Barry's occasional teenage partner Kid Flash. Grown to young adulthood at the time of the First Crisis, he took over the Flash persona after his uncle's death, and in the new reality found he was different from his predecessors in that he could run not only at the speed of light, but faster than it, which allowed him to propel himself across "interdimensional space-time" (*The Flash* [second series] #1, June 1987; others). He was different in one other, very significant respect: He did not conceal his civilian identity. Not only did he allow the world to know that the Flash was Wally West, but he was also known on occasion to exploit his celebrity, such as with commercial endorsements.

All the Flashes could cause their molecules to vibrate so that they could pass through solid objects, but Barry Allen learned how to use this skill to break the interdimensional barrier, and Wally West could, if he so desired, cause the objects he vibrated through to explode. The various Flashes' metabolisms varied somewhat as well, with Jay Garrick aging at a slower rate than his contemporaries, and Wally West needing to eat almost constantly to "feed the speed." Wally also had the ability to lend his speed to moving objects or people by touch.

There was briefly a fourth Flash named Bart Allen, who originally appeared in the post–First Crisis reality as a teenage super hero calling himself Impulse, then assumed the mantle of Kid Flash during a stint with the Teen Titans. Finally, Bart Allen battled Superboy-Prime during the Infinite Crisis wearing Barry Allen's original Flash costume. His very complex history (for example, he hailed from the far future but was raised and mentored

in the twentieth century in Manchester, Alabama) is beyond the purview of this text, but his greatest relevance to Superman, as well as his role in paving the way for Barry Allen's return as the Flash, was documented in the accounts of the Infinite Crisis.

The Superman of the original Earth-2 had comparatively little contact with the Flash of that world before the First Crisis. While Superman was officially a member of the JUSTICE SOCIETY OF AMERICA, of which the Earth-2 Flash was a charter member, Superman's global responsibilities actually permitted him to work on only a handful of cases with them. That changed in the post–First Crisis and New Earth realities, wherein the Man of Steel fought countless super-criminals and all manner of menaces alongside Garrick, who, after a brief retirement, was last reported to have resumed membership in the Justice Society.

The Superman of the pre–First Crisis Earth-1 interacted much more frequently with Barry Allen, however, as very active members of the JUSTICE LEAGUE OF AMERICA, most notably in a series of famous footraces staged for various reasons. In the first, the Flash and Superman agreed to a race as a charity fund-raiser for the United Nations (*Superman* [first series] #199, August 1967). Their good intentions were almost subverted by crime syndicates that began betting on the outcome, then started trying to influence it by capturing both heroes and replacing them with imposters who were trying to lose because they were working for gangs who had bet on their opponent. The real heroes escaped imprisonment in time to defeat the imposters and complete the race in a tie.

On another occasion, the two speedsters were tricked into racing as part of a plot by one of the Flash's enemies to kill him (see ROKK AND SORBAN), but again the heroes saw through the deception and again the question of who was faster, Flash or Superman, could not be answered by the outcome of the race (*The Flash* [first series] #175, December 1967). On two more occasions, the Barry Allen Flash and Superman raced to correct time distortions that threatened Earth (*World's Finest Comics* #198–199, November–December 1970; *DC Comics Presents* #1–2, August–October 1978). And shortly before the First Crisis, the Flash and Superman had to work together to defeat an invading alien who had stopped time altogether (*DC Comics Presents* #38, October 1981).

After the First Crisis, the Superman of that reality raced Wally West twice and, on one occasion, even Jay Garrick. The Man of Steel's first race with the Flash of this reality was staged on a magically created, booby-trapped track encircling the world—the creation of the magical MR. MXYZPTLK, who instigated the race by telling Superman that if he won, Mxyzptlk would return to his other-dimensional home for the next thirty days. In this reality, it appeared that the Flash was just slightly faster than Superman, because Wally West won this race by inches . . . to the dismay of Mxyzptlk, who had lied to Superman. The magical condition Mxyzptlk had set in motion would send him home only if the Flash won, because the magical imp assumed, incorrectly, that Superman was a sure bet to win (*The Adventures of Superman* #463, February 1990).

Superman's race with Jay Garrick was likewise a compulsion caused by a magically powered foe, in this case the Flashes' old enemy from the distant future, the "magician" Abra Kadabra. Upon his most recent escape from prison, Kadabra traced both Wally West and Garrick to METROPOLIS, where they had gone on an errand, and found them in the company of Superman. Kadabra put a spell on Wally and several bystanders, causing them to age rapidly, as well as instilling in all three heroes an irresistible impulse to run. Wally, the fastest of the trio, took the lead, but with Wally in the grip of the aging spell, the prospect of nonstop running became life threatening, and the only way to save him was for Superman or Jay to overtake him.

As Wally slowed with age, Jay and Superman were matched, and Garrick desperately tried to use on Superman a technique that Wally had developed of stealing speed from others. With Superman's speed augmenting his own, Jay caught up with Wally—which was exactly what Kadabra wanted. He was able to manipulate the kinetic energy concentrated in Garrick to power a return to his own era. Superman pursued him there, however, and discovered that Kadabra's "aging spell" was actually the work of nanobots that the Man of Steel easily disabled. He then captured Kadabra, bringing him back to the twenty-first century to face justice (*DC First: Flash/Superman* #1, July 2002).

Superman's second and final race with Wally West was less a race per se than an elaborate chase around the world. Because of a tragedy Wally West believed was caused by the public's knowledge of his identity, enabling his enemy Zoom to strike at his family, Wally had asked the Hal Jordan Spectre to erase the entire world's memory of the Flash's true identity. But Wally did not remain affected by the spell, and just as his memory returned he was summoned to JLA headquarters to account to his fellow heroes for the fact that they no longer knew who he was. Distraught over having been left by his wife only hours before, Wally chafed at the third degree from his teammates and bolted. He then took off on a global search for his missing wife, with Superman trying to catch up with him to find out what was going on. Ultimately, unable to find his wife, Wally returned to their Keystone City apartment to resign himself to the inevitable. As Superman caught up with him, Wally removed his cowl, triggering Superman's memories, and Wally West had his first emotionally significant encounter with Clark Kent (*The Flash* [second series] #209, June 2004).

During the events of the Infinite Crisis, Wally chose to begin life anew with his recently reconstituted family in another dimension. As of this writing, no major one-on-one encounter between the Superman of the New Earth reality and the resurrected Barry Allen has been documented.

FLASHMAN, FRANCIS "FUNKY"

This grandiose, smarmy, venal, unscrupulous entrepreneur epitomized capitalism without social responsibility at its very worst. Flashman was first documented in the universe of the pre–First Crisis Earth-1 (*Mister Miracle* [first series] #6, February 1972) and was incarnated in the post–First Crisis reality as well. His specialty seemed to be attempts to exploit meta-human heroes for personal gain, usually the Apokoliptian hero Mister Miracle and his wife Big Barda (*Mister Miracle* [second series] #11, December 1989; others). His ambitions extended even to the exploitation of super-criminals, such as when he secured employment as a public relations man for the Secret Society of Super-Villains (*Secret Society of Super-Villains* [first series] #4, November–December 1976; and #10, October 1977; others). In this capacity, Flashman facilitated the Society's ensconcement in a new headquarters and helped make the organization more efficient in other ways, but he characteristically did not know when to let well enough alone. His vain and foolish overreaching set him on a collision course with the Society's leadership, and as a result he was summarily dismissed and grateful for being allowed to live. On another occasion, he became a pawnbroker dealing in super-criminals' weapons and equipment (*Son of Vulcan* [second series] #4–5, November–December 2005).

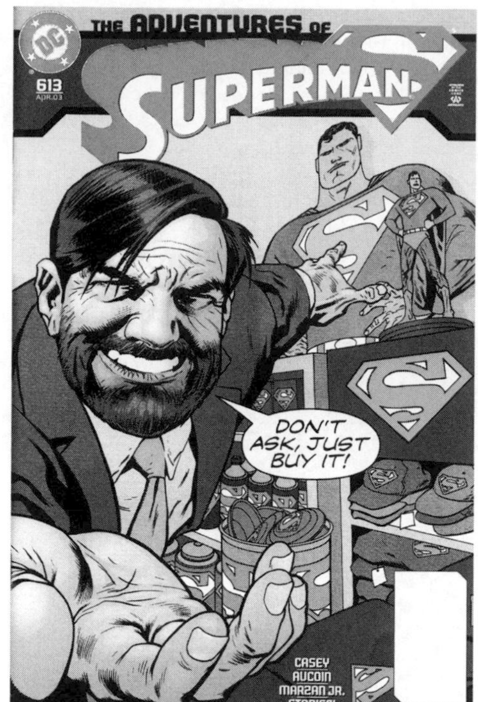

Flashman's direct interaction with Superman was minimal, but one encounter was particularly noteworthy: He emerged in Metropolis as the proprietor of the Super Store, a retail establishment purveying apparel, toys, and other merchandise based on the likenesses of super heroes, in particular Superman himself—without their permission or license, contending that as public figures who concealed their true identities, the heroes were in the public domain. With millions in revenue and no royalties or fees as part of his overhead, Flashman aggressively expanded the Super Store chain, attracting the disapproving attention of Lois Lane, secretly Mrs. Superman.

Lane's response was to persuade Flashman to expand his product line to include merchandise based on super-criminals and, as usual, Flashman's greed trumped his sense of self-preservation. As might have been predicted, the community of super-criminals did not take kindly to being exploited in this way, and sent Captain Cold, replete with his deadly freezing weaponry, to pay a call on Flashman as their ambassador of ill will (*The Adventures of Superman* #613, April 2003). Exactly how much harm was inflicted on the hapless hustler was not documented, but records indicate that Flashman did survive the Infinite Crisis to be incarnated on New Earth. There he was last documented as the proprietor of Flashman's Pre-Owned Auto, selling vehicles based on various super heroes, including replicas of the latest Batmobile (*Tales of the Unexpected* [second series] #5, April 2007).

FLEA CIRCUS

See Insect Queen.

FLINT, JAMES

See Regor.

FLINT, MICAH

On the post–First Crisis Earth, a volunteer for a LexCorp program, which morphed him into a super-strong, rock-like creature. Obsessed at first with getting revenge on Lex Luthor (*Superman: Man of Tomorrow* #8, Spring 1997), he later appeared to be equally angry at Superman for stopping him. He was also recruited by Morgan Edge for the Superman Revenge Squad (*Action Comics* #736, August 1997).

FLYING NEWSROOM, THE

See *Daily Planet*, the.

FORTRESS OF SOLITUDE, THE

Superman's headquarters, a private retreat for rest and relaxation, as well as a secure repository of numerous potentially dangerous creatures and items requiring protection, such as the miniaturized, bottled city of Kandor (until it was enlarged). The Man of Steel had such a hideaway in all of his realities, though not always known as "the Fortress of Solitude" per se. While the first such retreat was carved out of a mountain, the most extensively documented Fortress of Solitude was located in the Arctic. Other, subsequent incarnations of it were recorded in the Antarctic, the Andes, and the Amazon rain forest. But no matter where it was physically located, each one served the same purpose: to afford the Caped Kryptonian utter privacy while exercising and pursuing uniquely "super" hobbies; performing scientific experiments; and escaping, if only temporarily, the pressures of his daily life.

On the pre–First Crisis Earth-2, Superman had a secret citadel carved into a mountainside on the outskirts of Metropolis. The Earth-2 Superman apparently had fewer concerns about security than

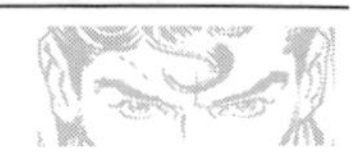

his other incarnations: This mansion-like retreat had an ostentatious façade prominently displaying a huge red S-crest like the one on his costume. It contained a collection of trophies of Superman's past adventures and a large gym stocked with specially designed exercise equipment that only someone with super-strength could use.

The sanctuary was entered by means of an ordinary doorway, but the Superman emblem above the door was on special hinges and functioned as an emergency "escape hatch," allowing the Man of Tomorrow to enter and exit at super-speed (*Superman* [first series] #17, July–August 1942; *World's Finest Comics* #7, Fall 1942; *Action Comics* #53, October 1942; others).

Not long after, the Superman of Earth-2 would speak of his secret hideaway as being located in "the polar wastes," suggesting he had abandoned the mountaintop outside Metropolis and moved his headquarters north. He claimed he chose the new location because the intense cold and dangerous climb would better deter snoopers (*Superman* [first series] #58, May–June 1949; others).

The best-known Fortress was the one built by the Earth-1 Superman somewhere in the Arctic, but it was allegedly not the only sanctuary this Superman constructed for himself. One account asserted that, prior to building the golden-doored structure in the Far North, Superman established secret bases in outer space and at the center of the Earth. This report may have been inaccurate, however (*Action Comics* #261, February 1960).

At one point, the Superman of Earth-1 also created an undersea Fortress of Solitude, in an underwater cave. This Fortress was equipped with sensors and monitors designed to facilitate a constant feed of information on occurrences in all the Seven Seas. But it turned out that this stronghold was merely part of an elaborate ruse Superman crafted to drive away aquatic aliens bent on conquering Earth. With that mission accomplished, he abandoned the undersea Fortress, allowing it to be used by the merpeople of Atlantis as a tourist attraction (*Action Comics* #244, September 1958).

The most familiar Fortress, however, was carved into the rock face of an "ice-covered mountain." Some accounts place it at the North Pole; others merely near it. The Fortress's giant, gold-colored door could be opened only by an equally enormous, arrow-shaped key, so heavy that only Superman (or another superpowered, Earth-bound Kryptonian such as Supergirl) could lift it. When not in use, the key stood on a base on a peak overlooking the Fortress, some distance away. From above, it appeared to be a directional marker for passing aircraft.

At first, if members of the general public were even aware of the Fortress's existence, it was only because of vague references made by Superman in passing. Its exact location was one of the world's best-kept secrets. But whenever Superman flew his friends or other select individuals to the Fortress, he would insist, at first, that they be blindfolded (*Action Comics* #149, October 1950; others). Nevertheless, the Man of Steel entrusted the Batman, his occasional crime-fighting partner who also knew his secret identity, with the Fortress's precise location and gave him unlimited access to its contents.

Both Jimmy Olsen and Lois Lane were explicitly told of the stronghold's existence (*Action Comics* #244, September 1958; others). Not long afterward, Superman temporarily transported the entire Fortress to a location on the edge of Metropolis, to conduct guided tours of it for charity. However, he warned all visitors that certain rooms contained classified information and were off limits (*Action Comics* #261, February 1960). Ultimately, it became common knowledge that Superman's Fortress was located somewhere in the Arctic (*Superman* [first series] #139, August 1960).

Not long before the First Crisis, however, the giant key was no longer used as an airline guidepost, and was instead hung vertically on brackets, to the left of the Fortress door. At the same time, Superman installed a hidden "mirage projector" to camouflage the Fortress's entrance completely, leaving the illusion of an ice-covered cliff face in place of the huge door and its key (*Limited Collectors' Edition #C-48: Superman and the Flash,* 1976; *DC Special Series* #26, Summer 1981; others).

The Earth-1 Fortress's roof was fitted with a vast, electronically controlled observation dome, and the walls were insulated with LEAD to block any KRYPTONITE radiation that would otherwise penetrate the Fortress. The interior comprised three stories of gigantic, museum-like, high-ceilinged rooms. Although Superman maintained living quarters at the Fortress, his primary residence remained his apartment in Metropolis (*Action Comics* #241, June 1958; *Superman* [first series] #134, January 1960, and #144, April 1961; others).

This Fortress was equipped with many of the same kinds of accoutrements as his Earth-2 counterpart's, such as specialized exercise equipment, this time including a bowling alley with giant-sized pins and a swimming pool filled with molten lava. It, too, had a laboratory where Superman worked on various projects such as finding an antidote to kryptonite poisoning and ways to prevent the various-colored kryptonites' effects on him. The Man of Steel created a special dressing room containing the most sophisticated materials in existence for creating super-disguises: masks, wigs, makeup, and the like that the Man of Steel needed for going undercover, but allowed him to use his superpowers without destroying the disguises. The Fortress was also where Superman went to clean his indestructible costume. He could swim, in uniform, in his lava-filled swimming pool or immerse himself in the white-hot flame of a "super-blowtorch" (*Action Comics* #247, December 1958; *Superman* [first series] #134, January 1960; others).

This Fortress also contained dozens of new inspirations, such as an interplanetary zoo; a genius-level, artificially intelligent, chess-playing robot to help sharpen Superman's mental powers; the most sophisticated computer system on Earth; and global monitoring and communications equipment that were the equal of the JUSTICE LEAGUE OF AMERICA's. The monitoring area also had special equipment for communicating not only with governments and law enforcement all over Earth, but also with distant planets and alien dimensions, as well as the inhabitants of Kandor, the city miniaturized and placed in a bottle by BRAINIAC; the undersea city-state of Atlantis; and even the PHANTOM ZONE.

Among the more imaginative additions was a giant steel diary in which Superman wrote entries by using either his invulnerable fingernail or his heat vision to engrave its pages. Another was a series of exhibit-hall-like rooms intended as tributes to all his friends. Each contained museum-like installations such as statues of the honoree and display cases showing replicas of the subject's "signature" paraphernalia, such as Jimmy Olsen's signal watch. The Fortress even included a room honoring CLARK KENT, intended to mislead visitors who did not know Superman's double identity. In addition to being honored by a tribute room, Supergirl also enjoyed the use of an apartment in annex to the Fortress, discrete from Superman's living quarters

(*Action Comics* #285, February 1962). Among various Kryptonian artifacts found by Superman and brought to the Fortress for safekeeping—such as the Phantom Zone projector—was something not Kryptonian in origin, but handcrafted by Superman: memorial statues of Jor-El and Lara, Superman's birth parents, symbolically holding between them a globe of Krypton. It was also the home of Kandor's bottle until the city was enlarged, and the shrinking and enlarging rays Superman and certain others used to enter and exit Kandor—both of which were prototypes, not powerful enough to affect the entire populace of Kandor.

The Fortress was also where the Superman Robots were stored, as well as trophies from the Man of Steel's past adventures. In addition to the robots, the Fortress was guarded in Superman's absence by the Superman Emergency Squad (*Action Comics* #303, August 1963; others). They, plus a network of alarms and booby traps, served to repel unwanted visitors. Other security features included a kryptonite radiation detector and a special air-circulating system that also released "antibiotic gases" that would kill off any alien microbes Superman could have brought with him from outer space, or that might have been infecting an addition to the interplanetary zoo.

After the First Crisis, when Superman had a very different history, there was initially no Arctic citadel. Over the course of this Superman's career, however, he would eventually have a Fortress of Solitude in three different locations. At first, he used the term "Fortress of Solitude" as a metaphor for his Clark Kent persona, because without it he would have been unable to enjoy any of the privacy of ordinary citizens and would be besieged by fans, the press, the needy, and more, wherever he went. But eventually, an actual, physical Fortress developed. When Superman was entrusted with a Kryptonian artifact called the Eradicator (*Action Comics Annual* #2, 1989), which had been programmed by its inventor to preserve Kryptonian culture, the device built a new Fortress in the *Ant*arctic, where Superman tried to bury it. It was part of an attempt by the Eradicator to begin re-creating Krypton on Earth, starting with a vast exhibit hall commemorating the planet's history. Superman managed to abort the Eradicator's process, but he decided to retain the space, which had grown out of a crevasse, as a potentially valuable headquarters (*The Adventures of Superman* #461, December 1989; others).

Rechristened the Fortress of Solitude, the cavernous hideaway contained many artifacts from the post-Crisis Krypton. Foremost among these were several servo-mechs—robot servants—one of whom was Kelex, who became a loyal aide to the Man of Steel not unlike Batman's butler Alfred. These "Superman Robots" were different from their Earth-1 counterparts in that they retained their original, Kryptonian design, rather than having been created by Superman in his own image.

In addition to the robots, this Fortress's many levels held working models of Kryptonian war suits, oversized suits of battle armor that were worn by Superman's ancestors during Krypton's last war. (Much later, one of the battle suits also served as a kind of mobile incubator, slowly healing the Man of Steel's injuries after his resurrection from his death at Doomsday's hands.) There was also a Phantom Zone "portal"—actually just a window-like device through which Superman could analyze various regions of the Zone. It was discrete from this reality's Phantom Zone projector, also stored in the Fortress.

There were also holographic displays of Krypton's past, and other Kryptonian technology, drawn to Earth by the Eradicator across time and space through a "trans-dimensional gateway." (Though the Eradicator was banished many years before Krypton's destruction, its sensors had kept track of the changes on the planet.) Another account, however, explicitly stated that where the trans-dimensional gateway was pulling the Kryptonian artifacts from was the Phantom Zone (*The Adventures of Superman* #460, November 1989). The centerpiece of this Fortress was similar to that of its Earth-1 counterpart: a globe of Krypton held aloft by statues of Jor-El and Lara.

The Eradicator also installed a Kryptonian regeneration chamber, an ovular crystalline device that stored solar radiation. That radiation later helped the Eradicator replenish its stores of energy when it first took human form—and it, too, figured prominently in the resurrection and healing of Superman after he was killed by Doomsday. Much of this Fortress was destroyed when Superman had to defend Jonathan and Martha Kent, when the still-mechanical Eradicator turned the Fortress's automated defense systems against them after they tried to interfere with Kal-El's transformation into a cold, emotionless "perfect Kryptonian." Superman later repaired the broken statues of Jor-El and Lara and added a memorial of sorts to the three Pocket Universe Kryptonians he killed, as a reminder never to break his code against killing again.

In the rebuilt Fortress, Superman stored the birthing matrix pod that brought him to Earth, along with a few rare samples of kryptonite, which were embedded in a presumably lead-lined wall. He also restored the circuitry controlling the Fortress's self-repairing utilities. But for much of this period in Superman's career, the Fortress remained in a solitude of its own, buried deep beneath the Antarctic ice.

During the time when the Eradicator, in humanoid form, was nearly destroyed by the Cyborg Superman, Hank Henshaw, at Coast City, the Eradicator drew all of the available energies out of the Fortress's systems to re-form his physical body, and the Fortress was destroyed in the process.

Later, Superman and Professor Emil Hamilton returned to find that the Kryptonian robots had rebuilt the stronghold completely (*Superman* [second series] #117, November 1996).

When Dominus began controlling Superman's mind, persuading him that he needed to become a hypervigilant "King of the World" for humanity's own good, the Man of Steel dramatically redesigned the Fortress. He made many structural changes, allowing the Fortress to be seen aboveground so that the media could publicize that the self-proclaimed King was aware of everything occurring around the globe. He also dispatched his new army of humanoid Superman Robots, which had been manufactured under Kelex's supervision.

Superman's self-coronation particularly enraged Lex Luthor, who managed—with the help of Outburst, the teen hero from the Supermen of America—to push orbiting debris into Earth's atmosphere, where it fell onto the Fortress, destroying it utterly (*Superman* [second series] #143, April 1999; and *Superman* [second series] #144; *The Adventures of Superman* #567; *Action Comics* #754—all May 1999). When Superman examined the ruins of the Fortress, he located Kelex's head and repaired it enough to permit him to consult his mechanical majordomo. They discovered that it was primarily the exterior of the Fortress that was destroyed. Most of the interior had been "shifted" into some sort of dimensional rift called a trace singularity, in which it appeared to exist in an immaterial form, not unlike a Phantom Zone prisoner. This "Ghost Fortress" was complete in every detail. Kelex helped provide a means for Superman to interact with the Ghost Fortress, hoping to keep the trace singularity intact so that the Ghost Fortress could serve as the template for a new one.

Shortly after the Y2K upgrade of Metropolis, the new Fortress was constructed with the help of Dr. John Henry Irons of Steelworks, aka the super hero Steel. Irons had created a device called the

Spectral Nexus Apparatus to capture the trace singularity and bring it to Metropolis, where the Ghost Fortress was placed inside a newly discovered tesseract within Steelworks—a portal from one area of space to another, made possible through bending the structure of the space-time continuum; essentially an infinite space within a finite containment. But the heroes realized that the new Metropolis was now controlled by Lex Luthor, so the Ghost Fortress could not remain in Metropolis (*Superman: The Man of Steel* #100, May 2000; others).

As a security measure, this extradimensional space—visible from our dimension as a glowing orb—could be reached only through a vast puzzle-globe. Only a meta-human with super-strength and flight capability could align the plates of the globe—not unlike a Rubik's Cube on a grand scale—to unlock the entrance to the orb. In this form, the Fortress was mobile, and was relocated to an icy cliff high in the Andes mountain range. The Andean Fortress contained redesigned service robots as well as a practical, security-code-activated portal to the Phantom Zone. The Andean Fortress was destroyed in a battle between Superman and Wonder Woman (*Superman* [second series] #211, January 2005). Later, Superman built himself a new Fortress in the Amazon jungle, using Kryptonian technology to transform ancient temple ruins in the Cordillera Del Condor Mountains, near the village of Pucallpa, Peru, into a new Fortress. This one somewhat resembled the Earth-2 Superman's "citadel," with the addition of Mesoamerican design elements (*Superman* [second series] #215, May 2005; others).

The Man of Steel used Kryptonian technology to enlarge his new stronghold beyond the confines of the temple structure. Tunnels led from the central chamber, which, as in all the previous Fortresses, honored Jor-El and Lara, to a series of catacombs housing a holographic global monitoring room; a trophy and artifact area, which held the bottle city of Kandor and the spacecraft in which he and Kara Zor-El arrived on Earth; a new version of the Earth-1 interplanetary zoo (this one more humanely reserved for *endangered* alien species); and a conference room for meetings with visiting allies. This Fortress could be seen only from the air, high above the jungle, and only by those who knew where to look. This final pre-Infinite Crisis Fortress was also home to the recently rediscovered Krypto and his dog-sitter, Ned, who was the last remaining humanoid Superman Robot. As had been the case with most of the post-First Crisis fortresses, the caretaker of this one was Kelex.

Shortly after the Infinite Crisis, while Superman was gone on his one-year "sabbatical," Luthor discovered the crystalline Kryptonian mineral known as the Sunstone at a site where a space probe, launched decades ago by then-admiral Zod in this reality's Krypton, had crashed into the Earth. Upon his return to active duty, the Man of Steel battled Luthor and confiscated the Sunstone fragments in his possession. Superman disposed of all but the original crystal, then flew to the Arctic and hurled the crystal into the frozen wastes. Following its programming, the crystal sprang up into a huge structure that served as Superman's Fortress of Solitude on New Earth (*Action Comics* #840, August 2006, and #844, December 2006; *Supergirl* [fifth series] #14, April 2007; *Action Comics* #847, April 2007).

Superman later discovered the crystal that powered a communications console within the Fortress, activating a holographic image of Jor-El, programmed with the entire elder Kryptonian's memories and knowledge, enabling Superman to seek his counsel as if he were actually speaking to the real Jor-El.

The Fortress also currently houses the spacecraft Mon-El used to travel across the stars to Earth, and the healing matrix that restored Connor Kent (Superboy) to perfect health after being badly beaten by Superboy-Prime.

FORT ROZZ

A heavily reinforced structure on the Krypton of two realities, serving a different purpose in each. On the pre-First Crisis Krypton, Rozz was a military command center in Kandor (*Superman Annual* #1, 1960). After reality was reordered by the Infinite Crisis, Rozz was documented as a former Kryptonian prison, a segment of which had been sent into the Phantom Zone due to a projector malfunction. In the Zone, it maintained solidity for reasons as yet unaccounted for. Inside Fort Rozz, time passed normally and "Zoners" became corporeal themselves provided they remained in the structure. This was how Zod and Ursa were able to mate and produce their son, Lor-Zod.

While trapped inside the Phantom Zone on one occasion, Superman was led to Fort Rozz by Mon-El. Superman entered the building because becoming corporeal would provide him with his only means of escaping the Zone. But inside Rozz, there was no source of yellow solar energy, so the Man of Steel lost his powers. He did, however, discover a number of Kryptonian "pod" spacecraft that had been used as part of a plan to unleash Phantom Zone criminals on Earth, and he used it to escape and return to Metropolis (*Action Comics* #844–846, December 2006–February 2007, and #851, August 2007; *Action Comics Annual* #11, May 2008).

FOSTER, DR. CLAIRE

A psychiatrist whom Superman saw briefly during a period of intense anxiety about the Pokolistanian Zod, complicated by concerns about his

Fort Rozz

adoptive parents and wife Lois Lane (*Superman* [second series] #179, April 2002; *Action Comics* #797, January 2003).

FOSWELL, SAM

The occasional editor in chief pro tem of the *Daily Planet* of the post-First Crisis Earth, running the paper's day-to-day editorial activities while Perry White was ill (*Superman* [second series] #51, January 1991; others). He also made the mistake of turning down ace reporter Ron Troupe for a *Daily Planet* job. Fired by the publisher at the time, Foswell began a downward spiral that saw him nearly lose his soul to the demon Blaze. Spared by Blaze's brother and rival Lord Satanus, Sam Foswell fled for parts unknown (*Action Comics* #665, May 1991; #677, May 1992; #680, August 1992; others).

FOUR-ARMED TERROR, THE

A monstrosity created by the Evil Factory on the pre-First Crisis Earth-1 and sent by Simyan and Mokkari to destroy the DNA Project (*Superman's Pal, Jimmy Olsen* #137–139, April–July 1971). There was, in fact, more than one Four-Armed Terror, dozens more having been hatched from eggs. Superman lured the monsters to their doom after determining that they needed to find an energy source. He used the nuclear reactor that powered the DNA Project as bait, destroying the creatures in an underground atomic blast. Superman also fought a version of the creature in the post-First Crisis reality, this one set against him by Mokkari and Simyan as well (*Superman* [second series] #40, February 1990).

FRANK, GERALDINE "JERRY"

A rookie reporter for *The Weekly* in Metropolis who was assigned to cover the crime beat with the Metropolis Special Crimes Unit. Geraldine had once looked up to reporter Clark Kent, but was

disgusted to find that he had been assigned to the same beat as her—"the Shack," considered by Metropolis reporters an elephant's graveyard. Her respect for Kent was sorely tested by finding him there (*The Adventures of Superman* #627, June 2004; others).

FREE, SCOTT

See Mister Miracle.

FREEMAN, DR. TORVAL

Only one of several consciousnesses contained within the Parasite of the post-First Crisis Earth, but the first one to coexist with another, that of Rudy Jones (*Action Comics* #715, November 1995; *Superman: The Man of Steel* #50, November 1995; others).

FRIEDMAN, JEB

A conceited and cocky union organizer on the post-First Crisis Earth who had a history of unrequited love for reporter Lois Lane. He became an informant who provided Lane with information concerning Intergang. During these meetings, Jeb developed a fondness for Lois even though she was already engaged to marry fellow reporter Clark Kent. Despite his obvious intentions, Lois and Jeb actually became friends, although it made Clark more than a little jealous.

Friedman acted as the pressmen's union organizer during a strike at the *Daily Planet*, when Metropolis suffered a recession (*Superman: The Man of Steel* #4, October 1991). He later reappeared in Metropolis, hoping to establish a deeper romantic connection with Lois when she and Clark temporarily suspended their engagement, but Lois was far from interested. He worked with her on an investigation involving union corruption and mob infiltration of the fish market, but was shot and drowned after killing a mobster to save Lois's life (*Superman: The Man of Steel* #55, April 1996).

FUTURESMITHS, THE

A group of mysterious but apparently benevolent and extremely powerful guardians of the "timestream" who appeared on the post-First Crisis Earth in the futuristic Metropolis that had been "upgraded" by Brainiac 13's Y2K virus. Ostensibly, their goal was to monitor Superman's activity to prevent the inadvertent creation of destructive divergent time lines. But ultimately they were discovered to be an incarnation of Superman's mortal enemy, Brainiac, who had disintegrated his physical form and reconstituted it as the group who called themselves Futuresmiths.

When a riot broke out in Metropolis and Superman's wife Lois Lane began to behave oddly, the Man of Tomorrow discovered that the source of the behavior was a wildly successful new brand of coffee. This coffee was secretly being used by Brainiac as a delivery system for something Superman's microscopic vision detected: nanobots—microscopic cybernetic devices that had a transformative effect on those who ingested them with their coffee. The nature of the technology seemed like Brainiac's handiwork.

Venturing into the future to confront a version of Brainiac into which the Futuresmiths had reorganized themselves, Superman discovered the ultimate effect the nanobots had on humans: They would become cybernetic organisms, making them more vulnerable to being "inhabited" and controlled by Brainiac. Superman then teamed up with a cybernetic version of himself and other super heroes to defeat Brainiac. The twenty-first century was rescued from a horrible fate, and, with the end of the Futuresmiths, the futuristic version of Metropolis began to degenerate. The city ultimately morphed back into a Metropolis that was modern merely by twenty-first-century standards (*Superman: The 10-Cent Adventure* #1, March 2003; *Superman* [second series] #190, April 2003; others).

GABRIELLE, JOHN "GABBY"

See GUARDIAN, the; NEWSBOY LEGION.

GALACTIC GOLEM, THE

An artificial being whose energy came from absorbed starlight, the Golem was created by LEX LUTHOR on the pre-FIRST CRISIS Earth-1 in one of his many attempts to destroy Superman (*Superman* [first series] #248, February 1972). The starlight gave the Golem incredible strength and near invulnerability. Only cutting off this radiation could defeat the Golem, by rendering it immobile.

"I'LL NEVER FORGET THE ASTONISHED LOOK ON SUPERMAN'S FACE AS MY CREATION SHOOK OFF HIS MOST POWERFUL BLOW-- AND I QUICKLY PRESSED MY ADVANTAGE..."
YOU'VE WAGGLED THAT GLIB TONGUE OF YOURS FOR TOO MANY YEARS! IT'S TIME SOMEONE SILENCED IT FOR YOU!
UNNHH! FEEL AS IF IT'S TEARING MY SOUL!
GOT TO BREAK ITS HOLD!

During its first battle with Superman, the Golem released so much energy that it appeared to wipe out all life on Earth, leaving only Superman, the Golem, and Luthor. But Luthor discovered that the energy had merely transported all Earth's inhabitants into a parallel world. After Superman hurled the Golem into space and out of range of the sun's radiation, the Earth's inhabitants returned to their own dimension unharmed.

Later, the Golem returned to fight Superman in his FORTRESS OF SOLITUDE. Superman ultimately defeated it by drenching it with molten steel that, when hardened, cut off all the light that might have powered it and paralyzed it (*Superman* [first series] #258, November 1972).

A version of the Golem was recorded on the post-INFINITE CRISIS New Earth. In this reality, it was an agent of the Elders of the planet DAXAM, who unleashed it on the Man of Steel (*Superman* #675, June 2008).

GALAXY COMMUNICATIONS

See EDGE, MORGAN.

GAM-EL

One of KAL-EL's ancestors on the KRYPTON of the pre-FIRST CRISIS universe. He designed the city KRYPTONOPOLIS, which became the planet's capital after BRAINIAC "stole" "KANDOR" (*Superman Family* #172, August-September 1975).

GAND, LAR

See MON-EL.

GAND, LAUREL

See ANDROMEDA.

GANGBUSTER

A crime fighter in the post-FIRST CRISIS METROPOLIS and on New Earth. He had no superpowers but was a proficient martial artist, marksman, and expert in the use of nunchakus. Jose Delgado grew up in SUICIDE SLUM, where the demands of survival on its mean streets motivated him to become a skilled boxer. Escaping the destiny of the less fortunate in the barrio, he became a high school teacher and a mentor to JERRY WHITE, son of *DAILY PLANET* editor in chief PERRY WHITE, thereby becoming acquainted with the *Planet* staff (*The Adventures of Superman* #428, May 1987).

After helping LOIS LANE investigate one of LEX LUTHOR's covert activities—arming street gangs through his mob contacts—Delgado assumed the costumed Gangbuster persona. In his first recorded appearance, Gangbuster helped Superman end a gang war and thwart Luthor's objectives (*The Adventures of Superman* #434, November 1987). At first, Lane's only interest in Delgado was the story she could get out of his work helping at-risk youth, but they soon began dating. On one of those dates, they encountered a super-criminal called Combattor, an armor-clad human mutation given superpowers by Luthor's "Synapse Project." Attempting to save Lane's life in the subsequent battle, Delgado was severely injured, suffering a spinal cord injury, and it was left to Superman to stop Combattor (*The Adventures of Superman* #437–438, February–March 1988).

In the hospital, Delgado was talked into retiring by CATHERINE GRANT, but the point was moot: Doctors told Delgado his spinal cord was severed

and he would never walk again. Lois helped him get settled in his apartment after his release from the hospital, and their relationship grew more serious. Almost as soon as Delgado began adjusting to life as a paraplegic, a company called A.R.L.—Advanced Research Laboratories—approached him, seeking a volunteer for an experimental treatment: a digital implant that would connect his spine's severed nerves and allow him to walk again.

Delgado shrugged off Lois's misgivings when she told him she'd discovered that A.R.L. was a wholly owned subsidiary of LexCorp. At that point, Jose would have sold his soul to the devil to walk again. As it turned out, he did almost exactly that, but he would not realize it till much later. As Delgado underwent the surgery, Lois continued to be wary, straining their relationship. Afterward, Jose told Lois he could more or less walk, but only slowly and tentatively until the implant could be better attuned to his nervous system, which would have to be done at A.R.L.'s facilities.

It was during this period of inactivity as Gangbuster that Delgado discovered someone else had assumed his costumed identity and was tarnishing his image by using more violent methods against the criminals he apprehended. This turned out to be Superman, experiencing amnesiac fugue episodes in which he suffered a mild form of multiple personality disorder, his second personality calling itself Gangbuster and donning the real one's costume. This condition was triggered by the Man of Steel's remorse over killing the Pocket Universe Kryptonians and a psionic interaction with Brainiac that had induced a psychotic break, culminating in Superman's period of self-imposed exile in space (*The Adventures of Superman* #446, November 1988; others).

Summoned to A.R.L.'s offices, Delgado met the devil to whom he'd sold his soul: Luthor himself, who—when Delgado refused to don a suit of LexCorp armor—activated a device that controlled Jose's physical movements via the implant. Delgado could now be jerked around like an electronic marionette, and Luthor forced him to wear the armor against his will. Luthor then dispatched Delgado to break in on Professor Emil Hamilton.

Attacked in his home lab, the resourceful Hamilton maneuvered Delgado behind a force field that cut off the signal from Luthor. Delgado collapsed like a marionette whose strings had been cut. Hamilton could then remove from Jose's suit the self-destruct mechanism that guaranteed Luthor's commands would be obeyed, and Delgado was able to use the armored suit as his new high-tech Gangbuster costume. The newly reinforced suit was put to the test when Gangbuster and Lois were attacked by Turmoil, an Apokoliptian robot assassin sent by Morgan Edge to assassinate those responsible for the exposés of Edge in the *Planet* (*The Adventures of Superman* #450, January 1989, and #456, July 1989; others).

Because Superman returned from exile just in time to stop Turmoil, Delgado was not seriously injured. During his brief hospital stay, however, he accepted how deeply Lois was still emotionally involved with Superman and ended his relationship with her. Sadly, the fallout from his continuing Gangbuster activity was the loss of his teaching job and eventual eviction from his apartment. But after Cat Grant had participated, as a "mole" at Galaxy, in exposing Edge's links to Intergang, her ex-husband Joe Morgan thought she needed a bodyguard to protect her and their son Adam. Delgado was happy to have the job, and even though Grant was kidnapped by Intergang and recovered by Delgado only with the help of Superman and Batman, the two became lovers for a time.

But Adam, who still looked up to his father, resented Delgado's presence in her life. After Adam's death and the end of Delgado's relationship with Grant, his personal life began to fall apart and he had trouble keeping jobs. During this time, he occasionally functioned as Gangbuster when he felt he was needed, but after Superman's death at the hands of Doomsday, the Metropolis Police Department, which had discovered Gangbuster's true identity, considered him a dangerous vigilante and pressured him to leave town or face arrest (*Legacy of Superman* #1, March 1993).

When Gangbuster attempted to stop a drug deal in progress, he discovered that the police were in hiding, ready to make an arrest. They also attempted to collar Delgado, but, despite taking a bullet in his arm, he escaped by diving into Hob's Bay and surfacing farther away, climbing onto the docks. That was the point at which he apparently took the hint and left Metropolis to start a new life in another city (*The Adventures of Superman* #500, Early June 1993). Gangbuster first resurfaced in Brick City, then home of the super hero Black Lightning, where Delgado traveled to help Lightning defeat an extremely violent impostor Gangbuster who was actually a shape-changer named Ishmael and an agent of Lightning's archnemesis Tobias Whale (*Black Lightning* [second series] #7–8, August–September 1995). Moving on to midwestern Fawcett City, Delgado was helped by a local detective named Woolfolk to clear his name of the charges still lingering in Metropolis (*Power of Shazam!* #47, March 1999).

A version of Jose Delgado has been documented on New Earth, appearing in the Greater Los Angeles area as a friend of Marguerita Covas, a woman with apparently genuine psychic abilities, known to locals as Tarot (*Trinity* #3, June 18, 2008). This Delgado had once been Gangbuster in the Metropolis of New Earth but moved to Southern California, where he resumed his work as a community organizer, opposing gangs. When Tarot was kidnapped, Delgado resumed his superheroic career with an updated version of his body armor, outfitted with what appeared to be a large complement of nonlethal weapons (*Trinity* #5, July 2, 2008, and #52, May 27, 2009; others).

GAUCHO, THE

See Club of Heroes, The.

GLASS FOREST

On the Krypton of the universe that was home to the pre-First Crisis Earth-1, a huge wooded area that was crystallized into glass by the heat from a powerful explosion (*Superman* [first series] #275, May 1974).

GLORIOUS GODFREY

A handsome Apokoliptian con man; a master manipulator via super-hypnosis; a servant of Darkseid; and the brother of the evil New God Amazing Grace. Godfrey, unusually handsome for one of Darkseid's minions, remained a minor figure in the Apokolips of the pre–First Crisis universe.

He was sent to Earth, using his psionic persuasion to induce humans to join his "Justifiers revolution." The Justifiers were soldiers who served Darkseid, powered by nothing more (or less) than the Anti-Life Equation itself and its effect on their psyches, causing them to devalue their own survival and surrender willingly to domination without any resistance whatsoever. As if their indifference to survival did not make the Justifiers implacable enough, they were also armed by Apokoliptian armor and weapons. Godfrey built an army of such brainwashed humans in an attempt to prepare the Earth for conquest by Darkseid, but he was defeated by the Forever People and retreated to Apokolips (*Forever People* #3, June–July 1971).

After the First Crisis, Darkseid sought to rid Earth of its super heroes, beginning with an attempt to turn its citizens against them. At first, he sent various destructive monstrosities to Earth in the hope that the collateral damage caused by the heroes' fights with them would stir up resentment against the humans. With their distress aggravated by the persuasive powers of Godfrey, whom Darkseid sent to Earth under the name G. Gordon Godfrey, the plan very nearly succeeded, resulting in a presidential executive order outlawing superheroic activity.

The final phase of the campaign found Godfrey easily recruiting from among his docile and obedient victims a small army of human "volunteers" to serve as hosts "bonded" to cybernetic Apokoliptian Warhounds. Godfrey led his Warhounds in a march on Washington, DC, only to be stopped by an alliance of super heroes, who defeated them.

Godfrey then resorted to a desperate move and donned the helmet of the mystical hero Doctor Fate, in an attempt to siphon off the magical powers of the eldritch entity that resided in it. Instead the god-like entity called a Lord of Order, who occupied the helmet and was the "true" Doctor Fate, seized the opportunity to "mindwipe" Godfrey—erasing his memory and thought processes, leaving him incarcerated in Belle Reve prison in a persistent vegetative state. He was subsequently broken out of the institution by the Female Furies, but it appeared that his usefulness to Darkseid had been seriously compromised, as thereafter he did not seem to have been trusted with overseeing another major Apokoliptian initiative (*Legends* #1–6, November 1986–April 1987).

Like Darkseid and most other Fourth World inhabitants, Godfrey was reincarnated in the universe of New Earth after the Infinite Crisis, under the name Reverend G. Godfrey Goode, a televangelist who psychologically manipulated his broadcast audience to help make them more susceptible to Darkseid's designs on them (*Final Crisis* #1, July 2008). He later assisted Darkseid in gaining a new body, but was not rewarded in kind. As of this writing, Godfrey appeared to have at last met his end. He, Mokkari, and Simyan were allowed to fall apart when their bodies wore out after completing their assignments for Darkseid, and their pleas to be re-created were denied (*Final Crisis* #5, December 2008).

GLOVER, REGGIE

See Crash.

GOG

See Magog.

GOLDEN GUARDIAN

See Guardian, The.

GOLD VOLCANO

See Krypton.

GORGEOUS GILLY

A bizarre, spectacularly ugly woman created by the Joker during the period when he stole most of the magic powers of Mr. Mxyzptlk, who later transferred Gilly from the Joker's insanely distorted reality to the real Post–First Crisis Earth. Gilly was able to hypnotize any man into seeing her as breathtakingly beautiful. But her psychic hold could be broken by force of will, especially when she could no longer see her victim. She came from the swampland of rural Florida, one of a large meta-human family who called themselves the Rednex. By their behavior, the banjo-strumming, interbreeding Rednex seemed to make a point of defiantly reinforcing the worst southern "white trash" stereotypes (*Action Comics* #769, September 2000; others).

Gorgeous Gilly

GOTHAM CITY

Gotham City is the northeastern U.S. home to Batman. It is a corrupt and plague-ridden city that is in constant need of its costumed vigilante protector. (For a detailed account of Gotham City, see *The Essential Batman Encyclopedia,* 2008.)

GRA-MO

Before Jor-El discovered the Phantom Zone on the Krypton in the universe of Earth-1, criminals were punished by being placed in space capsules in suspended animation, then launched into orbit with their brains attached to devices that erased their criminal tendencies. Gra-Mo was the last Kryptonian criminal to be so punished, after taking over the Kryptonian robot police for criminal purposes by using thought-control devices originally designed to direct android servants in menial tasks.

Many years later, his ship, thrown out of orbit

by Krypton's explosion, crashed on Earth, where he encountered Superboy (the young Kal-El). The Teen of Steel, who had not yet learned of the old practice of sending criminals into orbit, accepted Gra-Mo's explanation that he was an old El family friend because, Superboy reasoned, if Gra-Mo were a criminal, he would be in the Phantom Zone. Communicating with Jax-Ur and other telepathic Phantom Zone prisoners via his telepathy helmet, Gra-Mo embarked on a campaign to free the Phantom Zone criminals and, with them, dominate Earth.

It didn't take Superboy long to see through the ruse, however, and Gra-Mo soon became the latest Kryptonian outlaw to be sent to the Phantom Zone—this time with the ray projector Superboy had discovered and hidden much earlier (*Superboy* [first series] #104, April 1963, and #114, July 1964).

GRANNY GOODNESS

A member of Darkseid's Elite on Apokolips. Though her interaction with Superman was comparatively limited over the years, as an Apokoliptian she was predictably one of Kal-El's foes. She remained fundamentally unchanged in each incarnation, as was the case with most Fourth Worlders. She was most notorious as the headmistress of a chain of "orphanages" that trained the abandoned children of the hellish slum Armagetto to become warriors for Darkseid, as well as the leader of the Female Furies. The white-haired warrior was unusually vigorous considering her age. Although she was a worthy physical opponent when necessary, she usually prevailed against her enemies through sheer force of will. Her weaponry included energy gauntlets that could electrocute her enemies.

Goodness began life as one of the "Lowlies"—the Apokoliptian peasant class whose lives were a succession of oppressions and tortures inflicted by the higher-born. She was taken from her parents at an early age and trained to become one of Darkseid's Hounds, his prestigious and widely feared shock troops.

Of these, Trooper Goodness was one of the most effective, easily outshining her male counterparts. Like all troopers, she was bonded to a Warhound, whom she named Mercy. Goodness rose quickly to face the ultimate test of loyalty: She was ordered to kill her beloved Mercy. Goodness refused, killing her supervisor instead. When called before Darkseid, the evil god of Apokolips—the dog's true master—escalated the testing of Goodness by ordering Mercy to maul her to death.

Goodness immediately responded by killing the dog, passing Darkseid's test to become one of the very few females among Darkseid's Elite. When first documented in the universe of the pre–First Crisis Earth-1 (*Mister Miracle* [first series] #2, May 1971; others), the aging Goodness, now called Granny, had been running her orphanages for several years. In one of these, she raised Scott Free, who became the first child to successfully escape her.

These orphanages were thinly disguised boot camps for making Hounds out of disenfranchised children, not unlike Granny herself had been. Her methods were a grotesque and brutal mockery of child care, using brainwashing and whatever torture could be inflicted by Apokoliptian technology to transform her charges into fanatics eager to sacrifice all for Darkseid's agenda. Granny even extended her recruitment and indoctrination campaign to Earth: She established orphanages there, too, looking for potential warriors among mortal humans.

On the post-First Crisis Earth, in the period immediately before Infinite Crisis, the Amazons of Themyscira, the original home of Wonder Woman, attacked the United States, led by a seemingly crazed Queen Hippolyte obsessed with destroying "Man's World" once and for all. The war ended with the Amazon attack successfully repelled, with the Greek goddess Athena seemingly having enslaved the other Greek gods and the Amazons transformed into mortal women scattered throughout the world with no memory of their previous existence. It was Granny Goodness, however, who had imprisoned the Greek gods, incapacitated Athena and stolen her identity, then used the Athena persona to incite the Amazons to attack Man's World (*Amazons Attack!* #1–6, March–August 2007). Goodness also used her Athena impersonation to recruit more warriors for her Female Furies (*Countdown to Final Crisis* #45, June 20, 2007, and #35, August 29, 2007; others in that series).

During the Infinite Crisis, the Greek gods were freed by an alliance of super heroines, and Granny was ostensibly killed by Infinity-Man (*Death of the New Gods* #3, January 2008). Shortly before the beginning of the Final Crisis, however, Granny was reincarnated on Earth, along with other Apokoliptians, as a member of Boss Dark Side's gang. She was killed by the Goth teenage meta-human Black Alice (*Birds of Prey* [first series] #118, July 2008), but during the Final Crisis itself, it was revealed that, by means not fully documented, she had inhabited the body of an Alpha Green Lantern named Kraken, and in that guise set in motion the events leading to the confrontation between Darkseid and Batman at Blüdhaven in which the latter was ostensibly killed (*Final Crisis* #6, January 2009). After she was expelled from Kraken's body, the whereabouts of Granny Goodness's consciousness was reconstituted on Earth-51 with the rest of the New Gods.

GRANT, CATHERINE JANE "CAT"

A recovering alcoholic and gossip columnist with aspirations to more serious reporting, an incarnation of whom was documented on both the post–First Crisis Earth and New Earth.

On the post–First Crisis Earth, Grant was well known for her syndicated gossip column written from her native Los Angeles. When first docu-

mented, she was recently divorced from Monarch Studios production head Joseph R. Morgan; their marriage had been so unhappy, she'd sought solace in drink. She found herself a single mother with a young son named Adam, desperate to make a fresh start somewhere else as well as to stay sober.

That opportunity came in the form of an offer from the DAILY PLANET to move to METROPOLIS and become its gossip columnist (*The Adventures of Superman* #424, January 1987). There Cat was immediately attracted to CLARK KENT, and they became close friends, eventually becoming romantically involved for a brief period. Grant's relationship with Kent ended when she realized that Clark really loved LOIS LANE, and seemed more interested in helping Cat get her act together than being her lover. JIMMY OLSEN, too, was attracted to Grant, but she seemed either oblivious or unaware, perhaps because of the age difference, and not altogether kindly. Indeed, at various times both Lois and PERRY WHITE found Grant's behavior in the *Planet* offices objectionable, worrying that her struggle with alcohol might be spilling over into her professional life, and finding her not particularly adept at keeping her private life private (*The Adventures of Superman* #445, October 1988; others).

Grant soon felt constrained by the gossip beat, and began wanting to prove to Perry, Clark, and Lois that she could be a "real reporter." At the same time, however, she received the proverbial offer she couldn't refuse from MORGAN EDGE: to moonlight as an on-air gossip reporter for WGBS-TV (*The Adventures of Superman* #446, November 1988). But she continued to contribute to the *Planet* while working at WGBS, having by this time earned the respect of Lois Lane and endeared herself to all of Lois's circle by getting their friend Jimmy Olsen a job at WGBS.

Not long thereafter, Kent and Lane wrote a series of articles in the *Planet* exposing Morgan Edge's secret role as the leader of INTERGANG. Grant became fearful for her life, confiding in Lane that she had been Clark's informant all along and had only gone to WGBS to function as a "mole." Galaxy fired Cat, but Edge was nevertheless convicted of racketeering and sent to prison (*Superman* [second series] #42, April 1990). Following attempts on her life as well as Lois's and Clark's, Grant's ex-husband felt she and her son needed a bodyguard, and Gangbuster was hired (*Superman* [second series] #43, May 1990). He and Cat eventually became lovers, but Jose was resented by Cat's son Adam, who still looked up to his father. During this period, Delgado was forced to join with Superman and BATMAN in rescuing Grant from a kidnapping and murder attempt by Intergang (*The Adventures of Superman* #467, June 1990; *Action Comics* #654, June 1990; others).

Edge's father, VINCENT EDGE, rehired Grant upon regaining control of Galaxy Communications, and she became an on-air personality, eventually winning her own talk show. It was rumored that Cat essentially slept her way up the ladder, exploiting an intimate relationship with "Vinnie" (*The Adventures of Superman* #480, July 1991; others).

Not long afterward, Superman gave Cat an interview that was interrupted by an attack by DOOMSDAY and this, plus her live coverage of the Man of Steel's battle to the death with the monstrosity, boosted her ratings and fueled both her continued rise within WGBS and more rumors about her use of sex to do it. Grant's already dramatic life took a turn for the tragic when Adam was abducted by a now deeply psychotic TOYMAN, along with several other children. The Toyman stabbed Adam to death for leading the others in an attempted escape, and Cat later suffered a breakdown after identifying Adam's body. Superman captured the Toyman, and Grant confronted him in prison, where the deranged WINSLOW SCHOTT not only showed no remorse but defiantly accused Cat of being a "bad mommy," asserting a justification for killing Adam (*Superman* [second series] #84, December 1993, and #85, January 1994).

Adam's death was almost enough of a trauma to trigger Grant's resumption of drinking, but she

managed to avoid that pitfall largely thanks to support from her co-workers. With nothing else left, Cat's career became her entire life, to help her avoid the pain. After recovering from the effects of her grief, Grant finally put an end to the gossip that had swirled around her concerning her connection with Vincent Edge by charging him with sexual harassment (*The Adventures of Superman* #510, March 1994). As a consequence, Edge was forced to resign from the Galaxy board, and with Jimmy Olsen's help, Grant persuaded the board to give her his seat (*Superman* [second series] #111, April 1996).

Much later, when LEX LUTHOR successfully ran for the U.S. presidency, he named Grant the White House press secretary (*President Luthor: Secret Files and Origins* #1, March 2001). Following his impeachment, Grant returned to her hometown of Los Angeles, where she went to work for a paper called the *Los Angeles Tattler.*

After the Infinite Crisis, both Grant herself and certain aspects of her history were incarnated on New Earth. She was established as working at the *Daily Planet* prior to Clark Kent joining the reporting staff (*Superman: Secret Origin* #3, January 2010). She remained there until shortly after Adam's death, as in previous versions. Cat decided to return to Metropolis when the Toyman began to persuade Jimmy Olsen that Grant's son Adam

was killed not by the Toyman but by a Toyman *robot* Schott had constructed to carry on for him in the event he was incapacitated—a robot that then malfunctioned (*Action Comics Annual* #11, July 2008; *Action Comics* #865, July 2008; others). But as Jimmy dug deeper into the story, the Toyman's claims seemed to lack credibility.

A changed Cat Grant then came back to work at the *Daily Planet* to edit the arts and entertainment section (*Action Comics* #866, August 2008). With her looks "improved" by plastic surgery and her style of dress more revealing and provocative, Grant seemed overtly sexually predatory. At one point she even attempted to seduce Clark Kent, leading Lois to sarcastically call her a "cougar" and question Cat's sanity. But the ever-generous Clark maintained that Cat's personality "makeover" was simply another example of her attempts to cope with the pain of losing Adam by starting a new life.

In her new job, Cat seemed to develop an animosity toward Supergirl, who was frequently the target of attacks in her column. Indeed, Grant's first piece was titled "Why the World Doesn't Need Supergirl." But with Kara spending more and more of her time on New Krypton, Grant found it increasingly difficult to justify her condemnation of the Maid of Might of the New Earth reality.

GRAVES, MERCY

See Hope and Mercy.

GRAYVEN

An Apokoliptian deity; the third son of Darkseid, born of an unknown mother; younger brother to Kalibak and Orion. With the exception of the various reality-altering crises, Grayven had little direct interaction with Superman, being primarily an opponent of one of the Green Lanterns of Earth, Kyle Rayner (*Green Lantern* [third series] #74, June 1996; others).

GREEN LANTERN

The name of a meta-human super hero, an iteration of which has existed on Earth in all of its realities, as well as that of each of the thirty-six hundred members of the Green Lantern Corps, an intergalactic peacekeeping force whose members comprised many nonhumanoid species from many worlds. Each member wore a ring that was the most powerful weapon in the universe, generating a green "hard light" energy that could be shaped into any weapon, tool, device, or form that the Green Lantern wearing the ring could imagine. The Green Lanterns controlled and manipulated this energy with the sheer power of thought.

The Corps reported to the Guardians of the Universe, their blue-skinned mentors and supervisors on the planet Oa at the center of the universe. The Guardians were so named partly because they guarded the Central Power Battery from which the Green Lantern of every space sector derived his, her, or its power. All Green Lantern Corps members had their own, smaller power batteries which, in the universe of the pre-First Crisis Earth-1, needed to be used to charge their rings once every twenty-four hours. The original rings' energy had one limitation: It was ineffective against anything yellow.

There was a Green Lantern on the pre-First Crisis Earth-2 who interacted with the Superman of that reality only rarely, as did most of the Justice Society of America of that time and dimension. His subsequent encounters with the Man of Steel of the pre-First Crisis Earth-1 occurred in the context of the latter world's Justice League of America teaming up with the JSA. He was a super hero with a vastly different origin, and his ring operated in very different ways. He was not a member of the Green Lantern Corps. In the post-First Crisis reality, he had a slightly altered history, and interacted with Superman occasionally by virtue of having been based in Metropolis early in his career (*Secret Origins* [second series] #18, September 1987; others).

On the pre-First Crisis Earth-1, jet test pilot Hal Jordan was the first documented Green Lantern of the "space sector" that included Earth, although he inherited that role from a hitherto-unknown Green Lantern, Abin Sur, upon the latter's death (*Showcase* #22–24, September–October 1959–January–February 1960; *Green Lantern* [second series] #1, July–August 1960; many others). Jordan was selected to assume the mantle of Earth's Green Lantern because his career demonstrated an unusually high degree of courage in his character; he was metaphorically referred to as a "man without fear." Jordan interacted frequently with the Superman of Earth-1, as both were charter members of the Justice League.

Additionally, Superman and Green Lantern teamed up on many occasions, sometimes being pitted against each other by their respective enemies or enemies of the JLA, such as when the sorceror Felix Faust masqueraded as their Justice Society colleague Doctor Fate to lure them into a contest to determine which was the more powerful—all part of a scheme to destroy them both (*World's Finest Comics* #201, March 1971). On another occasion, Jordan's enemy Star Sapphire had become unusually powerful, defeating Jordan in battle, and the GL was forced to loan his power ring to Clark Kent to finish the job of apprehending her (*DC Comics Presents* #6, February 1979). Later Green Lantern was captured by an alien would-be conqueror named N'Gon, who stole the power ring and used it to assume GL's form in attempt to lure Superman to his destruction (*DC Comics Presents* #26, October 1980).

The Superman of this reality, as well as that of the post-Crisis unified universe, had another, albeit more tangential, connection to Green Lantern, specifically to the GL of Space Sector 2813, Tomar-Re. This Green Lantern earned legendary status for his valiant, though doomed, efforts to save Krypton from destruction (*Superman* [first series] #257, October 1972).

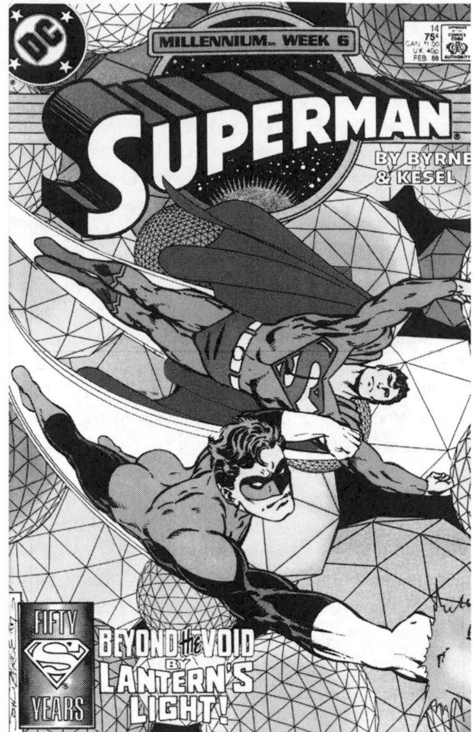

On Earth-1, as well as on the post-First Crisis Earth, there were two alternate or "backup" Green Lanterns in Hal Jordan's space sector, who were called upon to pinch-hit when a crisis arose that needed a GL's attention when Jordan was otherwise occupied. One was the grim, somewhat angry African American John Stewart (*Green Lantern* [second series] #87, December 1971; *Green Lantern: Mosaic* #1–18, June 1992–November 1993; others) and the far less serious-minded, macho "frat boy" type Guy Gardner (*Green Lantern* [second series] #59, March 1968; *Guy Gardner* #1, October 1992; *Guy Gardner: Warrior* #17, February 1994; others), whose freewheeling ways and idiosyncratic personality were often perplexing to his Oan supervisors. Superman's one-on-one interaction with these substitute GLs, however, was negligible, although the Man of Steel of the post-Infinite Crisis interacted with them frequently, particularly during the reality-morphing events known as Fifty-Two and Final Crisis.

Hal Jordan had what was arguably his greatest impact on Superman's life during the post-First Crisis period when the Cyborg Superman destroyed Jordan's home, Coast City, and Jordan went insane with grief. The Guardians refused to allow him to restore Coast City using his ring, whereupon Jordan seemingly wiped out the Guardians and their Corps, transforming himself into a super-criminal with nearly god-like powers who called himself Parallax. Though Parallax died during the Sun-Eater crisis, Jordan's spirit lived on as the universe's new Spectre.

Jordan was replaced for a time in the role of Green Lantern by the young graphic designer Kyle Rayner, whose upgraded ring had no imperfection that made it useless against anything colored yellow (*Green Lantern* [third series] #48, January 1994; many others), and whose interaction with Superman was minimal. His complex history and career path are beyond the purview of this text.

On the post–Final Crisis New Earth, the primary Green Lantern was again Hal Jordan, this time incarnated as an air force major. In his super-heroic identity he remained a core member of the Justice League and staunch ally to the Man of Steel.

GRIGGS, CASEY

The foster father of the Lex Luthor of post–First Crisis Earth. Working for his foster son, Griggs assassinated four-term Metropolis mayor Frank Berkowitz, whereupon Luthor killed Griggs (*Superman* [second series] #131, January 1998).

GRUNDY, SOLOMON

A semi-mindless, white-skinned monstrosity, often called a zombie or zombie-like, first documented on the pre–First Crisis Earth-2, where he was a recurring enemy of that reality's Green Lantern, Alan Scott (*All-American Comics* #61, October 1944; others). There he was originally the wealthy, and allegedly criminal, nineteenth-century merchant Cyrus Gold, who was murdered around the turn of that century. Gold's body was dumped in Slaughter Swamp, near Gotham City, wherein swamp vegetation and fragments of tree branches interacted with his skeleton to revive the corpse half a century later by means never fully documented. In this fashion, Gold's corpse was transformed into a massive, lumbering, but deadly behemoth with only partial sentience, comprising fragments of Cyrus Gold's memory. Criminally minded homeless men he encountered asked him his name, but the only one of Gold's memories regarding his identity that remained intact was that he was "born on a Monday." In response, one of the men referred to a nursery rhyme character, Solomon Grundy, who was also "born on a Monday," and the creature took that to be its name. The Earth-2 Green Lantern first fought Grundy when the homeless men enlisted his aid in facilitating their crimes.

Grundy required no food or air to survive and did not age. He could withstand and drain off from

his super-heroic opponents various forms of energy, and seemed impervious to real magic. He had repeated clashes with the Earth-2 Green Lantern and the Justice Society of America, in which Grundy invariably died and was inevitably resurrected, each time returning with a further-distorted mental and physical state (*All Star Comics* #33, February–March 1947; *All-Star Squadron* #1, September 1981; others). The Earth-2 Superman had little direct involvement with Grundy, but eventually the monstrosity found a means to cross the dimensional barrier into Earth-1 (*Superman* [first series] #301, July 1976), where he encountered and was destroyed by that reality's Man of Steel.

A longer-lived Earth-1 incarnation was born when the Parasite found a way to grow a new Grundy from bits of Grundy's shattered body that he found in the sewers, left over from the monster's first clash with Superman. The Man of Steel conceded that this new, more bestial version of Grundy was too powerful for him to handle, as his power was being periodically drained by the Parasite. So Superman flew the monster to an alien world that could support none but the most durable life-forms. There the child-like brain of this Grundy was mollified when Superman gave him a cape to wear while, thanks to the planet's lighter gravity, Grundy went "flying," imitating his former foe (*Superman* [first series] #319–322, January–April 1978).

Those same sewers apparently spawned yet another Grundy, because there is no record of Grundy having escaped the alien world on which Superman marooned him—yet some time later, the Earth-1 Man of Steel encountered Grundy in the Metropolis sewer system. There Superman was knocked out by a roundhouse punch from Grundy, and upon regaining consciousness, he found more of Grundy's leftover matter, which he took to S.T.A.R. Labs for analysis. The scientists determined that an unknown chemical reaction had been causing Grundy's cells to morph into clone-like replications, presumably accounting for Grundy's reappearance despite having been left in space. In short order, sixty Solomon Grundys were rampaging through Metropolis, until Superman administered the cure for the effect developed by S.T.A.R. and destroyed all the Grundy "clones" (*DC Comics Presents* #8, April 1979).

Grundy appeared without documented explanation one more time on Earth-1, battling another hero, before being "undone" by the First Crisis, reappearing thereafter on the unified Earth with a slightly different history. The post–First Crisis Superman's encounters with this Grundy were usually within the context of his membership in the Justice League of America, but the two sparred one-on-one on at least one occasion. After an "artificial" Grundy appeared in the altered reality created by the Joker and Mr. Mxyzptlk (*Superman* [second series] #160, September 2000), the Man of Steel battled the Grundy of this reality, now considered a "plant elemental," during the time of the Imperiex attack on Earth (*Superman* [second series] #182, July 2002). Later, Grundy helped attack Superman and Batman when a bounty was placed on both of them by President Lex Luthor, and was defeated by Batman (*Superman/Batman* #3, December 2003).

During the Infinite Crisis, Grundy joined the Society, and despite being killed yet again, this time by Superboy-Prime (*Infinite Crisis* #7, June 2006), he was reincarnated on New Earth, from which he was exiled to the prison planet, where he was killed again (*Salvation Run* #7, July 2009). However, Grundy once more cheated death and was resurrected on Earth, but as a zombie-like Black Lantern who attacked Bizarro. The mirror-Superman battled his one-time ally until he sent the Black Lantern Grundy into the sun, thereby destroying his ebony power ring and incinerating his body (*Superman/Batman* #67, January 2010).

GUARDIAN, THE

A non-superpowered crime fighter who has had more incarnations than most costumed heroes, not only by virtue of having been documented in four separate realities, but because of having been cloned repeatedly and having had the Guardian persona assumed by others.

The Guardian first appeared in the New York City of the pre–First Crisis Earth-2, where he had little contact with Superman. He was James Jacob "Jim" Harper, who had grown up in Suicide Slum, an impoverished, crime-ridden area as bad as or worse than Hell's Kitchen. He was working a beat there as a rookie cop when, while off duty, he was brutally beaten by a gang of hoodlums. With his clothes shredded, Harper started after them when he happened on a costume shop whose door had been left unlocked. He decided that both a change of clothes and a disguise were in order. Leaving behind enough cash to cover his unofficial purchase of the components of a yellow-and-blue costume, with yellow helmet and shield, he traced his assailants to a nearby pool hall.

The sight of the costume gave him the element of surprise as he apprehended his attackers, whom he discovered to have been responsible for a recent kidnapping. When asked who he was, Harper realized he couldn't give his real name without compromising his police career, and so stammeringly replied that he was simply "guarding society from criminals." Evidently, this was picked up by the press, who dubbed him the Guardian. Seeing how much more effective he could be as

a vigilante, and noting the boost to neighborhood morale that his appearance made, he decided to continue fighting crime in two different uniforms.

On patrol duty the next day, Harper arrested four young street-corner paperboys—members of the Newsboy Legion—in the act of committing some petty larceny. At their arraignment, Harper persuaded the judge to remand the homeless, orphan youths to his custody rather than sending them to reform school. In the years that followed, the boys renounced petty crime for good. Jim Harper played the role of guardian on two fronts that effectively blended into one, as, in time, the Newsboys—Tommy, "Big Words," Gabby, and Scrapper—learned the secret that *their* guardian was *the* Guardian. They all worked together against crime for many years, until the boys grew to adulthood and both Jim Harper and the Guardian retired (*Star-Spangled Comics* #7–64, April 1942–January 1947; *Secret Origins* [second series] #19, November 1987).

On Earth-1, Suicide Slum developed in Metropolis, and both the Guardian and the Newsboy Legion had similar histories, with the exception that the boys always suspected Harper was the Guardian, but could never prove it. However, the boys added a fifth member to their tightly knit group—"Flipper Dipper"—and went to work for the top-secret DNA Project, which after the First Crisis would be reincarnated as Project Cadmus. When alerted to the fact that their elderly former guardian Harper was dying, the quintet took a tissue sample from the old man and availed themselves of the resources of the Project's genetics research laboratories to transfer Harper's mind and memories into a newly cloned, youthful, and muscular body. The Guardian was now not only younger and stronger, but faster and more agile than before, and possessed a fast-healing ability engineered into the clone body. Modern technology also made his shield indestructible. The new Guardian, known as the Golden Guardian, became the Project's head of security (*Superman's Pal, Jimmy Olsen* #135, January 1971; others).

Not long before the First Crisis, the Teen Titan Mal Duncan, who had not as yet assumed a costumed persona, took the name Guardian and wore the original's costume (borrowed from fellow Titan and Harper's nephew Roy "Speedy" Harper) with the addition of an exoskeletal strength-enhancing device (*Teen Titans* [second series] #44, November 1976). Eventually, Speedy helped rescue the Harper clone from Adam, a malevolent clone-creature created using genetic material from both Jim Harper and Dubbilex, who was trying to take over the DNA Project (*Superman Family* #191–194, September–October 1978–March–April 1979). The changes to reality wrought by the Crisis on Infinite Earths removed the history of Mal Duncan's career as the Guardian.

The history of the younger version of the Newsboy Legion also changed after the First Crisis. On the post–First Crisis Earth, the newsboys were younger clones of the adult versions, with the originals' memories (up to their present age), which sometimes caused them to feel anachronistic as their memories were rooted in the 1940s. Here the Guardian (no longer "Golden") was also a clone of the old Harper and head of security of the DNA Project, here called Project Cadmus (*Superman* [second series] *Annual* #2, 1988).

The public first became aware of the Guardian's existence shortly thereafter, as he helped keep watch over Metropolis when Superman was absent and aided him whenever necessary (*Superman* [second series] #26, December 1988; others). Ironically, the Guardian played a larger role in Superman's life after the Man of Steel's death. He became caught in the middle of a struggle to claim possession of Superman's body among Cadmus, the Metropolis S.C.U., and LexCorp, and helped thwart all of them (*The Adventures of Superman* #498; *Action Comics* #685; *Superman: The Man of Steel* #20, January 1993).

The Guardian proved immune from the "clone plague" that began killing clones throughout Metropolis, and his blood provided the antidote. However, while the serum was being created, Lex Luthor's men attacked Cadmus (*The Adventures of Superman* #513, June 1994; others). The resulting explosion sealed off Cadmus's hidden base. The news that reached the public was that this meant the end of Project Cadmus, and all its personnel had been killed—but that was merely a cover story generated by the government to hide the fact that Cadmus was being moved and reorganized.

When Mickey "the Mechanic" Cannon was brought in as the new head of Cadmus, the Newsboys were dismissed, but the Guardian stayed on as head of security—although he had to share his duties with Adam Winterbourne (*Superboy* [third series] #56, October 1998; others). The Guardian was later killed by the energy being called Shrapnel, who was able to inhabit and animate scraps of metals, and cloned once again, with new technology allowing him to age rapidly from infancy to adulthood. Harper had requested that, in the event of his death, he not be cloned again, but the Luthor administration disregarded his wishes. Indeed, *several* Guardian clones were created to help fight against Imperiex. The Kon-El Superboy, who had been mentored by Harper and

understood his feelings, managed to destroy the clones, but the Guardian lived on nevertheless.

The Infinite Crisis reordered reality so that the Guardian who emerged on New Earth had a different history. According to Dubbilex, Jim Harper had been shot and killed by Cadmus's first head of security, Jonathan Drew, aka Codename: Assassin, when the latter learned that a clone of Harper was being created (*Superman's Pal, Jimmy Olsen Special* #1, October 2008). The original Guardian left Cadmus not long after its creation, moving to the town of Warpath on the Mexican border. Later appearances of the Guardian were new clones, each of which died within a year.

The original Guardian clone moved to Metropolis with Gwen, his adopted daughter, who was in fact an adolescent female clone of himself (*Adventure Comics Special* #1, January 2009). He then joined the Metropolis Science Police. Before the formation of New Krypton, Science Police team leaders DuBarry and Daniels, along with several prison guards, were killed when a team of Kandorians assaulted Stryker's Island in an effort to break out the Parasite. The Science Police assigned the Guardian to work with the Metropolis Police Department and an alliance of super heroes to ensure that the Kandorians were brought to justice. After all the Kandorians left Earth to inhabit New Krypton, the Guardian was promoted to Science Police field commander, replacing DuBarry and Daniels. His superiors' confidence in his qualifications came from the fact that, although merely another Guardian clone, he retained the memories—and, in effect, the experience—of Jim Harper the police officer as well as Guardian the super hero (*Superman* #682–684, January–March 2009).

The Guardian helped Mon-El get a job with the Science Police, at Superman's request, at the time the Man of Steel ostensibly left Earth to live on New Krypton. Harper then proceeded to mentor the Daxamite on how to be a crime fighter. As Science Police field commander, Harper recruited a number of uniquely talented people, such as those he selected as his seconds in command, Wilcox and Romundi. Another S.P. officer, Billi Harper, was in reality Jamie Harper, formerly of Gotham's police department. The Guardian was part of a group of Superman's allies when the final assault on Project 7734 occurred. He beat Codename: Assassin into submission and, honoring the moral code of the original Guardian, placed the killer under arrest rather than exacting a more permanent punishment. In the aftermath, Jim Harper's clone, Gwen, and grandniece Billi left Metropolis, and Billi revealed she was pregnant with Mon-El's child (*Superman: War of the Supermen* #4, July 2010).

According to various accounts, the Jim Harper Guardian coexisted with another one, who began operating in the New York of the post-First Crisis Earth shortly before the Infinite Crisis, and survived to continue his career on New Earth. This one's name was Jake Jordan, and he was a disgraced former police officer who accepted an unusual job at a tabloid called the *Manhattan Guardian*. He was hired to be the paper's "resident super hero" as the Manhattan Guardian (in a costume similar, but not identical, to Harper's) and, as Jake Jordan, a reporter who would cover the Manhattan Guardian's exploits. The tabloid's owner, Ed Stargard, unwittingly orchestrated a scenario similar to the interdependence of Superman and Clark Kent, with the former providing story fodder for the latter. Obviously an inventive executive, Stargard had also made an unusual arrangement, having licensed the Guardian persona and imagery from Project Cadmus, which, as the original Guardian's sponsor, made the arguably dubious assertion that those rights were its to sell (*Seven Soldiers: The Manhattan Guardian* #1–4, May–November 2005).

GUARDIANS OF THE UNIVERSE, THE

See Green Lantern.

GUILDS, THE KRYPTONIAN

The traditional caste system on the Krypton of the post-Infinite Crisis universe, preserved by Kandorian leader Alura on New Krypton. All Kryptonian citizens were assigned, or born, into a class according to their skill set and knowledge base, or "orientation"—that is, the aspect of Kryptonian life to which they could most productively contribute, whether it be science and technology, culture, defense, industry, or religion. In a sense, society on New Krypton reflected or incorporated various qualities of the other iterations of Kryptonians that had existed in previous realities. It is important to note that Krypton strived to be a democratic society—but only ostensibly, at least from the Labor Guild's perspective—and the terms *caste* and *class* signify only divisions of responsibility, not a hierarchy of power or privilege. Moreover, as Alura and Zor-El's own union, as well as the pairing of Nightwing and Flamebird, attested, there were no restrictions on intermarriage or relationships across Guilds.

The Science Guild, to which Alura herself belonged, administered and controlled most forms of scientific research and development. Its members resembled the Kryptonians of the post-First Crisis reality in that the other classes tended to view them as emotionally cold hyper-rationalists, which often put them at odds with New Krypton's aesthetes and religiosos. However they were viewed, their work made the original—and then the new—Krypton one of the most technologically advanced planets in the universe.

The late Zor-El's guild was the Artists' Guild, which was also somewhat science-oriented in that technology was used to create art, on an order of magnitude far greater than Earth's developing digital culture. This Guild's membership comprised artists, designers, writers, and creatives of every kind. Members tended to be more spiritual than those of the Science Guild; many of them saw their creativity as a gift from the Kryptonian fire god Rao, and felt Rao's presence in the products of their self-expression.

The Military Guild, led by freed Phantom Zone criminal General Zod, was New Krypton's equivalent of any nation's armed forces. Its members seemed to believe in nothing more than their own might and sense of entitlement to power. They made many of the other Guilds nervous, as Zod's drive to preserve Krypton's "glory" was seen as what would be called, in Earth terms, fascistic. It could be argued that this Guild, and Zod in particular, were what motivated Kal-El to pretend to take up permanent residence on New Krypton, so that he could monitor any potential military threat to Earth—a threat made more worrisome once all citizens of the former Kandor developed superpowers like his own.

The Labor Guild greased the wheels of New Kryptonian society, its members responsible for all manufacturing and whatever manual labor was still necessary in so high-tech a society. They were New Krypton's "masses," all but ignored by the other classes. They were, in fact, the only Guild unrepresented in the ruling Council.

Though not "invisible" to the other Guilds in the same sense as the Labor Guild, the Religious Guild had a reverently quiet presence in New Kryptonian life. Priests and assorted acolytes conducted rituals and various devotions to the pantheon of Kryptonian gods, each the "patron" of one of the other Guilds, whether its members were devout or not: Telle was the god of wisdom and science; Lorra was the god of beauty and art; the god of might and power was Mordo; and Labor was spiritually guided by the moon god Yuda. The Religious Guild itself worshipped Cythonna, the ice goddess, and all served the Supreme Deity Rao (to which Thara Ak-Var/Flamebird was devoted). Rao was considered the life force in all of Krypton's people, flora, and fauna (*Superman Secret Files 2009,* October 2009; others).

GUNN, MIKE MACHINE

The principal gunman of the original 1920s incarnation of Intergang. A younger version was cloned to serve the modern Intergang initially run by Morgan Edge. In the process, he was genetically modified to enable his arms to transform into actual machine guns. After taking a rap for Intergang and doing prison time, Gunn was sprung by his lover Ginny "Torcher" McGee; he was mortally wounded by gunshots fired by members of the Metropolis Special Crimes Unit in pursuit (*The Adventures of Superman* #544, March 1997, and #545, April 1997; others).

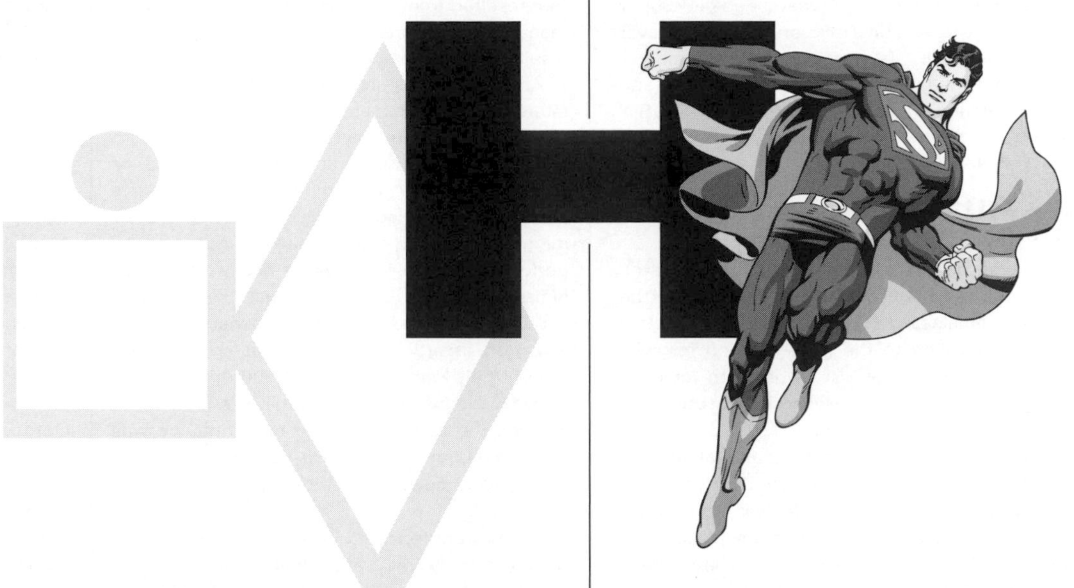

HAIRIES, THE

A race of hirsute humanoids, the product of one of many strange cloning experiments conducted by the DNA Project on the pre–First Crisis Earth-1 (*Superman's Pal, Jimmy Olsen* #134, December 1970; others). Iterations of the Hairies were also documented on both the post–First Crisis Earth and New Earth.

The Hairies lived outside the physical facilities of the Project and steadfastly resisted any attempt by Project personnel to keep them under surveillance or try to control them, which, given their abilities, wasn't difficult. They possessed an advanced intelligence as a function of their genetic engineering. Thus they had acquired a vast store of knowledge that allowed them to develop transportation and defense technology beyond ordinary human comprehension.

At first, the Hairies inhabited a forest of living tree houses called the Habitat, before moving to a mobile "Mountain of Judgment" that kept them out of sight of both the Project and society in general. Their incarnations on each Earth were very similar, if not identical. When the Jimmy Olsen of New Earth most recently visited the Habitat, he found it occupied by the friendly motorcycle gang known as the Outsiders (*Countdown to Final Crisis* #11, February 13, 2008).

HALF-LIFE

A zombie-like teenager on the post–First Crisis Earth and a member of the Ravers whose superpowers and name were derived from the bizarre green "ectoplasm" that made up roughly half his body. In addition to dramatically slowing down his aging process, the green slime gave him super-strength and the power to manipulate the gelatinous substance into weapons (it may also have conferred a kind of immortality, but that was never quite clear). He was also terrifyingly hideous, which gave him the element of surprise in combat.

Born Byron Stark in a desert community in the American West, his memories of the accident that created him were vague. He knew that he was a teenager in the late 1950s when the rest of his family and the pregnant girlfriend he wanted to marry were killed by an alien spacecraft that crash-landed on their property. With roughly half his body destroyed by his injuries, Stark, too, would have died, except that the "ectoplasm" that oozed from the ship mimicked the form of Stark's damaged body parts and replaced them, keeping him, for lack of a better term, "half alive."

Stark encountered the Kon-El Superboy and became a member of the Ravers when the dimension-hopping Event Horizon appeared in the desert where Half-Life had been living in seclusion since the accident. There rave promoter Kindred Marx, seeing a "coolness factor" in Stark's appearance, invited him to join the Event Horizon (*Superboy and the Ravers* #2, October 1996). By this point, Stark had begun to recall that the aliens responsible for wiping out his family were from the other-dimensional, anti-matter world of Qward. Thus his

primary motivation for joining the rave was that it represented his only chance to explore the universe and other dimensions, to perhaps find and bring to justice his family's murderers.

His dream was fulfilled when he joined Superboy and the Ravers on a mission to Qward to avert a civil war. Half-Life acquitted himself nobly in battle, but the Qwardian weapons based on antimatter technology ultimately overpowered him; he was killed in the fight (*Superboy and the Ravers* #18, February 1998).

HAMILTON, PROFESSOR EMIL

The eccentric but brilliant scientist with a history of mental and emotional instability. Nevertheless, he remained a trusted scientific consultant, adviser, and aide to the generous and forgiving Superman of the post-First Crisis Earth for many years—despite several psychotic episodes and other periods of irrationality.

During his long periods of comparative functionality, the bearded, unkempt, and bespectacled Hamilton was a genial, endearing sort whose love of big-band music (*Superman* [second series] #38, December 1989) and intense scientific curiosity could make him fascinating company. Despite undisciplined work habits and an erratic attention span, he defied the stereotype of the absentminded professor.

Long before his first encounter with Superman, Hamilton had a reputation for being difficult to work with in commercial research and development labs, even ones as innovative as S.T.A.R. Labs, being immensely independent-minded by contrast with his more conventional, career-oriented colleagues. For example, as a young man, he impetuously quit his job at a company called Hitek to spend the next two decades developing a magnetic field generator that he believed could provide the United States with the ultimate defense against a nuclear attack. The frustrations that resulted from his efforts led to the first of his many psychotic breaks, which not coincidentally resulted in his first encounter with Superman.

After he'd experienced repeated failures to interest the government in his generator—meeting with little more than cavalier dismissal from condescending bureaucrats (*The Adventures of Superman* #424, January 1987)—Lex Luthor's LexCorp approached Hamilton, implying that it might be willing to finance the work necessary to perfect the device. But when he finally met Luthor himself, Hamilton discovered that LexCorp had acquired Hitek and claimed full ownership of his invention, asserting that it was created on Hitek's time. When Hamilton rejected Luthor's insulting offer in compensation for Hamilton's life's work, and refused to turn over the blueprints, he was beaten by Luthor's goons. He was unable to prove conclusively, however, that LexCorp had used coercive tactics.

The pattern repeated itself with another company, a dummy corporation owned by Luthor that financed a larger-scale model of Hamilton's invention. The larger device electrocuted a bystander during a public demonstration—all orchestrated by Luthor to discredit Hamilton and retain control of the generator (*The Adventures of Superman* #425, February 1987).

After being twice victimized, Hamilton suffered a nervous breakdown. He decided that the best way to prove that the generator worked was by using it against Superman. He hired an actress to portray a hostage, then dared Superman to save her. The Man of Steel responded to Hamilton's publicly broadcast challenge, and the professor attempted to trap Superman in an electromagnetic cage created by his generator. When Superman successfully resisted, Hamilton's mind snapped utterly and he attempted to overload the generator, forcing the Man of Tomorrow to protect Hamilton and his fake hostage from the resulting explosion with his own invulnerable body.

Hamilton was arrested and received court-ordered psychiatric treatment, to which he responded well; he served a few months in prison before being paroled on Superman's recognizance. Clark Kent then helped him set up a small independent laboratory in Suicide Slum. From then on, Hamilton devoted much of his time to helping the Man of Steel, out of gratitude for the latter's compassion. As an inventor, he created technological work-arounds on many occasions when Superman's powers were impaired or insufficient to a task at hand. For example, Hamilton created a force-field belt and an armored battle suit when Mr. Mxyzptlk once eliminated the Man of Steel's powers (*The Adventures of Superman* #472, November 1990; *Action Comics* #659, November 1990; others); he also invented a breathing device that facilitated Superman's flight into deep space (*The Adventures of Superman* #450, January 1989). Hamilton was responsible, too, for creating a Phantom Zone projector and an early Su-

perman Robot prototype, although the latter was a failure (*The Adventures of Superman* #439, April 1988).

Hamilton's scientific analyses of various phenomena—including Superman's own physiology and powers—were enormously helpful to the Man of Steel. Among these were his assessments of the structure and function of the mysterious Eradicator (*The Adventures of Superman* #459, October 1989) and his theories about Mister Z's strange "soul-imprisoning" crystal (*Superman: The Man of Steel* #1, July 1991; *Superman* [second series] #57, July 1991; others). Additionally, Hamilton's talent for appraising the capabilities of metahuman criminals often gave Superman invaluable insights into the best way to apprehend them.

During the chaos in Metropolis that followed the clone plague and Luthor's over-the-top efforts to utterly destroy Lois Lane, which ultimately led to mass hysteria and much carnage, Hamilton was mistaken for a pimp by an armed prostitute who shot him in the left arm. Superman arrived in time to fly Hamilton to an emergency room, but the medics were forced to amputate the arm (*The Adventures of Superman* #514, July 1994). Later, Hamilton replaced it with a self-designed cybernetic prosthetic, many variations on which—some with unique, specific, and sometimes bizarre applications—he designed over the years. They could be used interchangeably like vacuum-cleaner attachments.

Just before the futuristic morphing of Metropolis engineered by Brainiac 13 at the turn of the millennium, John Henry Irons, aka Steel, returned to the city and was readily available to Superman when the Man of Tomorrow required technological expertise. The unstable Hamilton began to feel that not only had his role as Superman's scientific adviser been usurped, but he would also become less valuable to the Man of Steel because, unlike Irons, he was not a fellow super hero.

Hamilton seemed to disappear during the Y2K virus's transformation of the city, only to resurface as the Overmind, the leader of a cyberpunk gang working to facilitate the return of Brainiac 13. When apprehended, however, he claimed—apparently with some validity—that the Y2K virus had also "upgraded" his cybernetic arm, endowing it with artificial intelligence, and it was the arm that was controlling his actions (*Superman: The Man of Steel* #123–125, April–June 2002).

After apparently recovering from this second derailment from law-abiding sanity, Hamilton resumed functioning as Superman's primary scientific counsel, learning to collaborate with Irons rather than compete with him. For example, Superman's ability to travel to and explore the artificial Krypton created within the Phantom Zone was made possible only by Hamilton and Irons working together to develop special equipment. Besides, given the demands of understanding the futuristic technology then available to, and sometimes overwhelming, the citizens of Metropolis, there was more than enough room for two techies on Superman's team.

Hamilton's third recorded psychotic episode apparently resulted in his permanent removal from Superman's inner circle of trusted allies and helpers. Not long after the Overmind incident, Superman faced a super-criminal named Ruin who, for reasons that remained unclear, was targeting the Man of Tomorrow's loved ones. Ruin wore a "power suit" that allowed him to fire beams of red solar energy, which could negate Superman's powers. Ruin was also able to teleport himself from one place to another by using the Phantom Zone as a kind of wormhole, compressing distance between origin point and destination. Ruin's motivation for wanting to destroy Superman seemed to be the lunatic belief that because the Man of Steel's powers were derived from the sun, he was draining it of solar energy and would eventually cause it to burn out faster.

Ruin was ultimately unmasked as Hamilton, who was by this point perhaps incurably insane. What doomed Hamilton's relationship with the Man of Steel was that Hamilton tried to frame Clark Kent's boyhood friend and the former president, Pete Ross, for Ruin's crimes. Ross insisted he was innocent, but his claims were undermined by his apparent escape from prison, which, it turned out, was actually Hamilton kidnapping him (*The Adventures of Superman* #636–640, March–July 2005).

It took great effort on Superman's part to restore Ross's damaged reputation and save his wife and child from the jeopardy in which Hamilton had placed them, evidently removing any hope of yet another reconciliation. Thereafter Hamilton was sent to prison.

HARCOURT, MATTIE

An African American medical resident in the town of Leesburg, Virginia, on the post-First Crisis Earth, and a longtime friend of the Linda Danvers who merged with the Matrix Supergirl to become an Earth-born angel (*Supergirl* [fourth series] #1, September 1996; others). As an increasing number of supernatural events and super-criminals began to appear in Leesburg concurrent with Supergirl's "arrival," Mattie became involved with former *Leesburg Tribune* reporter Wendell "Cutter" Sharp. Sharp responded to the dramatic disruptions to Leesburg's previously placid way of life by quitting his newspaper job to become Supergirl's publicist and merchandising agent, and he and Mattie became engaged shortly thereafter (*Supergirl* [fourth series] #67, April 2002).

While Mattie was a loyal and supportive friend, chroniclers have appeared reluctant, perhaps out of political correctness, to point out that she must have been lacking in acute perceptiveness. For, despite her friendship with Danvers and intimate relationship with Sharp, she managed to remain close to her best friend for quite some time before catching on that Danvers was Supergirl (*Supergirl* [fourth series] #77, February 2003).

HARPER, JIM

The survivor of a hardscrabble youth in the treacherous Suicide Slum of New York (on the pre-First Crisis Earth-2) and Metropolis (of the post-First Crisis Earth-1), Harper triumphed over the depredations of life in ghetto tenements to become first a police officer, then a super hero.

Like many kids of his circumstances, young Jimmy subsisted on the proceeds of petty robberies until his life was turned around by the intervention of a man named Joe Morgan (operating, for reasons irrelevant to this account, under the alias Nat Milligan), who convinced young Harper that physical fitness and education could provide the escape from crushing poverty he so desperately needed. With Morgan as his trainer, Jim Harper became a talented gymnast and boxer.

When, in time, Harper was ready to start his professional athletic career, he ran into his old buddy and partner in petty crime Leo, who had become a minor crime figure. After Leo was mortally wounded in a drive-by shooting and died in Harper's arms, Jim decided then and there that he could do more for his community as a police officer. With his newly developed physique and athletic abilities, he had no trouble being accepted by the police academy. After graduation, Jim Harper requested assignment to Suicide Slum, there to work as a beat cop until the fateful day when he took on the secondary persona of crime fighter the Guardian.

On the post-First Crisis Earth, Jim Harper was reunited with his sister Mary on her deathbed and learned of her orphaned grandchild and only living relative Bobby Harper. Jim Harper and his charges, the newly rejuvenated (that is, cloned) Newsboy Legion, rescued Bobby from an orphanage that Granny Goodness had been using as a "recruiting" center for Apokoliptian warriors, as was her wont. "Bobby" Harper—who, it turned out, was actually Roberta, to the hitherto all-male Newsboy Legion's initial disgust—temporarily became the Legion's fifth member (*Guardians of Metropolis* #1–4, November 1994–February 1995).

HAT, THE

See Elite, The.

HAWKINS, INSPECTOR ERSKINE

A rotund, bowler-hatted Scotland Yard detective considered the world's greatest sleuth (with the possible exception of the Batman) on the pre-First Crisis Earth-2. He had dedicated himself to solving what he considered the greatest mystery of all time—Superman's true identity—and had come to the unshakable conclusion that it was Clark Kent. Hawkins's clue-gathering and deductive powers were far more formidable than Lois Lane's, and Superman had his hands full disproving the inspector's assertion on several occasions before finally seeming to convince him once and for all that Superman and Kent were two different men (*Action Comics* #100, September 1946; *Superman* [first series] #69, March–April 1951; others).

HEAD, TALIA; AKA TALIA AL GHŪL

The daughter of the Batman's seemingly immortal enemy, ecoterrorist Rā's al Ghūl (which translates from the Arabic as "head of the demon"). In her pre-First Crisis incarnation on Earth-1, she was known only as Talia (*Detective Comics* #411, May 1971; others). In all the realities in which she appeared, she was a morally ambiguous figure, sometimes helping Batman; sometimes aiding her father's campaigns against him.

On the post-First Crisis Earth, she was just as much of an "anti-heroic" figure, becoming part of Lex Luthor's corporation yet helping to bring about his ruination not long before the events of the Infinite Crisis. She preferred to use the surname Head when she assumed the leadership of LexCorp as CEO when Luthor was elected president. She was an MBA and held additional advanced degrees in biology and engineering. She had been trained by her father in several forms of martial arts, and was considered an Olympic-level athlete.

The dubiousness of her loyalties was illustrated by the fact that, in her capacity as an ally of Luthor, she wanted to extend Metropolis's superior technology (resulting from the Y2K virus) into a

global network, applying the city's resources to the betterment of all humanity. Yet all the while, she secretly worked to undermine Luthor, anonymously tipping off Superman to his archenemy's more questionable activities.

When President Luthor was forced to flee the White House because of the revelations that he had foreknowledge of an Imperiex probe attack on Kansas but made no effort to prevent it, as well as having had dealings with Doomsday and Darkseid, Talia sold most of LexCorp's assets to the Wayne Foundation (*Superman/Batman* #6, March 2004; others), leaving Luthor penniless and a fugitive before reality was altered by the Infinite Crisis. In the days preceding that event, Talia became one of the core members of the new Secret Society of Super-Villains. On the post-Infinite Crisis New Earth, she became the new head of the League of Assassins, and had little further contact with Superman's world as of this writing.

HELLGRAMMITE, THE

An entomologist named Roderick Rose, who developed a process to transform himself into a grasshopper-like humanoid criminal. As the Hellgrammite, he possessed a thick, bullet-resistant exoskeleton and super-strength. He also had the power to leap great distances; secrete a sticky, glue-like substance; and weave cocoons to imprison his enemies. He was documented not only on the pre-First Crisis Earth-1, but on the post-First Crisis Earth and New Earth as well.

Most of Rose's schemes involved trapping people in his cocoons to transform them into weaker insectoid creatures he could dominate, which was his modus operandi when first encountered by Batman and the Creeper (*The Brave and the Bold* [first series] #80, October–November 1968). When the Hellgrammite was reincarnated on the post–First Crisis Earth, he first encountered Superman when he was hired by a dissident board member at LexCorp to kill Lex Luthor (*Action Comics* #673, January 1992). Thereafter he fought the Man of Steel many times.

Later, Rose made a deal with the demonic Neron, selling his soul in exchange for increased strength and a greater power to transform others into larvae. This account also confirmed that on

the post–First Crisis Earth, his history was essentially the same as that of his Earth-1 counterpart (*Underworld Unleashed: Patterns of Fear,* November 1995; *The Adventures of Superman* #530, December 1995; others).

The Hellgrammite was documented on New Earth one year after the events of Infinite Crisis, having joined with Bloodsport, Riot, and other enemies of Superman to gang up on the Man of Steel while he was still recovering his superpowers (*Superman* #652, July 2006).

HENDERSON, MICHAEL

On New Earth, Commissioner William Henderson often consulted with Inspector Mike Henderson, an African American detective who headed the Metropolis Meta-Crimes Division, one of two units—the Science Police being the other—whose counterparts in the previous reality were Maggie Sawyer and Dan Turpin's Metropolis Special Crimes Unit (*Supergirl* [fifth series] #37, March 2009).

HENDERSON, WILLIAM

A Metropolis police veteran who rose through the ranks to the job of inspector, then chief of police, and finally commissioner. He rode out many political and social changes in the city; Metropolis's citizens stood behind Henderson for years.

As an inspector, he was Superman's primary police contact on the pre-First Crisis Earth-1, where he was also the confidant of the African American hero Black Lightning (*Action Comics* #440, October 1974; *Black Lightning* [first series] #3, July 1977; others). During the latter hero's battle with Tobias Whale, Henderson was saddened to discover that his son Andy was affiliated with the criminal combine known as the One Hundred (*Black Lightning* [first series] #7, March 1978).

Inspector Henderson's activities on the post-First Crisis Earth were less frequently documented, as Superman's interaction with the police involved him more with cops such as Dan Turpin or Maggie Sawyer of the Metropolis Special Crimes Unit. During that time, Henderson was on much closer terms with reporter Clark Kent than Superman. The inspector was never reluctant to share information with Kent when appropriate, but would not risk compromising appropriate procedure in the name of his personal friendship with Kent. In this iteration, Henderson was married to a woman named Maddie and had more than one child.

Though the exact reasons were never documented, Henderson did not get along well with Sawyer. The origins of their discord appeared to be a personal matter, but as with Henderson's relationship with Kent, he would not allow their personal history to negatively affect their working relationship.

Before reality was reordered by the Infinite Crisis, Henderson had risen to become Metropolis's police commissioner (*The Adventures of Superman* #424, January 1987; others).

HENSHAW, HANK

See Cyborg Superman.

HERO

A young super hero on the post-First Crisis Earth, a member of the Ravers who had the power to transform into a new super hero for one hour, never knowing beforehand what form he would take. Little was documented about Hero Cruz's background other than that he grew up in a middle-class Puerto Rican family in Metropolis and was a regular of the Event Horizon, the interdimensional rave at which the super hero team the Ravers was formed. Although the exact circumstances under which Hero did so remain unclear, one day he discovered—some accounts alleged *stole*—a cache of high-tech weapons and devices amassed by the Kon-El Superboy's old foe the Scavenger. From among these, he took the Achilles Vest, which generated a force field that rendered the wearer effectively invulnerable. It was this power that motivated Event Horizon promoter Kindred Marx to grant Hero admittance to the rave (*Superboy and the Ravers* #1, September 1996).

Along with Superboy and the other Ravers, Hero traveled across the universe and through alternate realities with the Event Horizon. In time, the Scavenger came looking for his vest, believing that the Raver Sparx had stolen it. While Hero lost the vest in the course of defending Sparx, he discovered a mystical dial with alphabetical settings that could be clicked to *H, E, R,* and *O.* Presumably on a whim and because of his first name, Cruz used the dial like a combination lock to spell

out *hero* and found that it transformed him into different super heroic personae with names like Badaxe, Human Justice, Stormfront, et al. One of the device's quirks was that it never allowed Cruz to turn into the same hero twice (*Superboy and the Ravers* #5, January 1997).

In any event, Cruz used the dial, subsequently "internalized," to assume personae that rescued both Sparx and Superboy from the Scavenger and defeated him. Sparx fell in love with Hero, but her ardor cooled when Hero grew distant, and he eventually revealed to her that he was gay.

HIGHFATHER

See New Gods, The.

HIGHTOWER, REVEREND MATTHEW

See Redemption.

HI-TECH

A cybernetic assassin on the post–First Crisis Earth, used by Thaddeus Killgrave to make an attempt on Superman's life. Killgrave used Hi-Tech to exhaust Superman before trying to destroy them both (*Action Comics* #682, October 1992; *The Adventures of Superman* #608, November 1992).

HOB'S BAY

One of the main neighborhoods of the Metropolis on the post–First Crisis single Earth, as well as the name of the bay itself, which was fed by the river that ran along the eastern side of the island that was Metropolis. Because of the docks along the river in the northeastern side of the city, the area was more commonly referred to as Suicide Slum (*The Adventures of Superman* #487, February 1992, and #502, July 1993; *Action Comics* #699, May 1994; others).

HOCUS AND POCUS

On the pre–First Crisis Earth-2, the erudite, slight-of-build "Doc" and the muscular, slow-witted "Flannelhead" were a pair of genial, resourceful, but not terribly bright street-corner salesmen of books on magic, operating under the business names of Hocus and Pocus. They became a thorn in Superman's side when a number of strange coincidences convinced the gullible pair that they had suddenly acquired actual magical powers. Along with their pet rabbit Moiton, they lived in a shabby furnished room in a Metropolis boardinghouse (*Action Comics* #83, April 1945).

DOC, YA LOOKS UPSET!
I SHOULD'VE ASKED HER FOR TEN GUINEAS INSTEAD OF THREE! MAYBE IT ISN'T TOO LATE —

Because their "magic" only *seemed* to work, either by coincidence or the occasional secret superpowered intervention by the Man of Steel—to keep them out of serious trouble when criminals attempted to exploit their "powers"—they were called the magicians by accident. From time to time, Superman also found himself in a position in which he had to perpetuate the myth of Hocus and Pocus's magic to protect his double identity.

Superman tried many times to explain to the pair the truth about their abilities, but each time he was interrupted by the know-it-all Hocus with assurances that he needn't fear that the duo would willingly use their gifts to commit crimes. Their real goal however was to *solve* them: They opened a detective agency (*Action Comics* #88, September 1945)! Their increased visibility in this capacity got them into even bigger trouble, with Superman being forced repeatedly to use his superpowers to reinforce the illusion that the eccentric pair were genuine conjurers (*Action Comics* #97, June 1946; *Superman* [first series] #45, March-April 1947; others).

HOPE AND MERCY

The statuesque, stunningly beautiful female bodyguards of Lex Luthor, possessed of above-average height, strength, and physical stamina. Mercy Graves and Hope Taya were first documented on the post–First Crisis Earth but remained mysterious figures, with no detailed accounts of their backgrounds. Both have been incarnated on New Earth.

Caucasian Mercy, with her blonde hair worn in a long, distinctive, whip-like braid, was the quicker of the pair to anger and full of attitude, arguably more ruthless and willing to use brute force than her partner. She often played "bad cop" to the somewhat quieter, seemingly more sensitive, African American Hope, whose equally commanding presence was accentuated by her distinctive dreadlocks. Both women were approximately six feet tall, weighed more than 150 pounds, sported matching tattoos, and displayed a wide range of highly developed martial arts skills.

In fact, they were known to be able to hold their own in physical combat with Superman, which was one of many reasons some believed them to have been Amazons (natives of the island of Themyscira, the most famous of whom was Wonder Woman). The only explicit documentation to support this claim was an account of a visit to President Luthor's oval office by the sorceress Circe, who was recognized by Hope and Mercy despite her disguise, whereupon Circe spoke of them derisively as Amazons (*Secret Files: President Luthor* #1, March 2001).

Equally enigmatic were the reasons for their unswerving loyalty to (and implicit sexual relationship with) Luthor, which included a willingness to sacrifice their lives to protect him. More explicitly documented was the fact that Luthor's intimacy with the pair extended to including them in his workouts as sparring partners, engaging them in combat both armed and unarmed. These

exercises had their own unique rituals as cryptic as everything else about the duo, such as the fact that they ended only when Luthor spoke the word "Waterloo."

Hope and Mercy seemed inseparable, but when Luthor, as president, deliberately allowed Topeka, Kansas, to be decimated by an Imperiex probe, Hope was determined that the world know of her boss's duplicity and gave the story to the *Daily Planet*. Despite Clark Kent and Lois Lane's efforts to protect her as their informant, they needed Hope to acknowledge her role in leaking the story to give it credibility. At that point, she disavowed being the *Planet*'s source, leading to Clark Kent's temporary dismissal from the paper.

But unlike Clark, Hope could not save herself. Luthor knew that her story could lead to his impeachment, so he ordered her removed from the White House staff, lobotomized, and held prisoner in the LexCorp Tower sub-basement. Superman was tipped off to Hope's predicament by Talia Head and rescued Hope, who disappeared once Luthor was driven from office.

Following the events of the Infinite Crisis, Hope went into witness relocation under the name of Maya Andrews while Mercy, similarly estranged from Lex Luthor, briefly worked with John Henry Irons and the young heroes of the new incarnation of Infinity, Inc. (*The Adventures of Superman* #573, December 1999; *Action Comics* #764, April 2000; *Superman* [second series] #163, December 2000; *52* #40, February 7, 2007; others). She attempted a heroic life, donning a costume and using the codename Vanilla (*Infinity Inc.* [second series] #8, June 2008). Her extreme training and feral instincts almost led to her beating a man to

death, and as a result, she abandoned her identity of Vanilla and left the team.

HORU-KANU

See Faora.

HOST

A robot, documented on the post–First Crisis Earth, in the shape of an ancient Egyptian mummy that was the repository for the remaining consciousnesses of an ancient alien race called the H'v'ler'ni.

HOUSE OF EL, THE

The name for Superman's ancestry, a famous dynasty of scientists and prominent public figures throughout Krypton's history in all its realities whose earliest members were among the founders of the Kryptonian civilization itself. See also Jor-El.

The earliest recorded member of the El family was Feln, the father of Rugard, who was the father of Tomnu, who was the father of Erok. Erok married Milla, daughter of Uved, and became the first Bethgar of the united Urrika, a city-state on Krypton. He took the name of Erok-El when his son, Kal-El, was born. For over twenty generations, the Els ruled Urrika and were considered benign sovereigns, although a few were ruthless tyrants (*Krypton Chronicles* #3, November 1981).

An alternate account of this era established the beginning of the line with El, adoptive son of Naton and Mar. Rising from the dead with an "S"-shaped scar on his chest, El was believed by many to be the chosen one of the god Rao and became a popular hero who died defeating the tyrant Utor. El's pregnant wife, Laras Lilit El, gave birth to a son, Sor-El, who continued the House of El (*Superman: Blood of My Ancestors,* 2003).

Sometime following, the tyrant Wab-El fathered two sons, Vad-El (also a tyrant) and Hyr-El (who fled after a quarrel with Vad-El). Hyr-El had two children, the prophet Jaf-El and the naturalist Tio-El. Jaf-El never married, but Tio-El continued the El line (*Krypton Chronicles* #3, November 1981).

After several years, Fol-El married a Kryptonian named Roxa, despite her family's misgivings (*Superman* [first series] #263, April 1973). Generations later, a descendant of the El line, Skul-Dor, terrorized the seas as a pirate (*Superman's Pal, Jimmy Olsen* #121, July 1969). A generation or more later, Mag-El and his sister Jaki encountered a probe from ancient Atlantis on Earth (*Superman* [first series] #266, August 1973).

A nuclear disaster then destroyed a Kryptonian city, leading science to be outlawed for a time, and a group of scientists led by Zat-El sought refuge first in the Jewel Mountains and later in a colony on Earth that perished in an attack by once docile dinosaurs they brought with them (*Adventure Comics* #333, June 1965).

Generations later, Bur-El married Wedna Kil-Gor and recorded the accomplishments of his mentor—and later father-in-law—Kil-Gor (*Krypton Chronicles* #3, November 1981; *Superman* [first series] #268, October 1973). The evil Tro-El founded Bokos, known as the island of thieves, while his explorer brother Val-El discovered the island of

Vathlo and, ultimately, the continent of Lurvan, where he helped found Argo City. Val-El continued the El family line (*Krypton Chronicles* #2–3, October–November 1981).

The next recorded member of the family was Sul-El, who gained fame as an astronomer while his son Hatu-El was renowned for his electrical accomplishments circa 6832 (*Krypton Chronicles* #2–3, October–November 1981). According to the chronicles after the First Crisis, there was Faora (*Eradicator* #2, September 1996), grandmother to Kem-L, who developed the Eradicator, a device that genetically bound everyone on Krypton to their home planet, resulting in the death of anyone who left (*The Adventures of Superman* #460, November 1989).

Some 100,000 years later, Ran-L, a soldier, married Eyra (*The World of Krypton* #1–2, December 1987–January 1988) and raised a son Van-L, a World Council leader who helped defeat Black Zero and move Krypton away from cloning (*The World of Krypton* #1–3, December 1987–February 1988). Van-L subsequently had a son named Jan-L (*The World of Krypton* #3, February 1988).

A soldier had saved Van-L's life from Black Zero forces, and while "the man's name was lost to history, his family was adopted into the House of El as a sign of gratitude." They became the second House of El (*Superboy* [third series] #59, February 1999).

Years later, inventor Wir-El was the first to perfect sophisticated recording equipment (*Krypton Chronicles* #1 and #3, September and November 1981). Two generations later, mathematician Shu-El became an expert on computer theory. He had a legislator daughter, Fedra Shu-El, who helped set up Kandor's first Science Council, and a jurist son named Thar-El who reformed the trial system. Thar-El's son Plen-El was considered Krypton's greatest novelist, and his son was the entertainer Nox-El, one of the leading lights of the Kryptonian musical theater. Nox-El's son was Fil-El, a surgeon who saved countless lives with his new methods of operating (*Krypton Chronicles* #1 and #3, September and November 1981). Fil-El's grandson was the agriculturalist Sorn-El, who developed new strains of grain, which made food shortages a thing of the past (*Krypton Chronicles* #1 and #3, September and November 1981).

Physicist Im-El's discoveries in the field of atomic energy revolutionized most industries on Krypton (*Krypton Chronicles* #1 and #3, September and November 1981).

A descendant of the El line, Klar-Don worked as a reporter for the *Daily World* while also maintaining the heroic alter ego of Skyman (*Superman's Pal, Jimmy Olsen* #121, June 1969). Generations later, Yu-El, a priest of Rao, was the brother of Pir-El, general in the Earth-1 Krypton's final war of 9846. Pir-El's son Tala-El wrote the planetary constitution in 9852 and had two sons of his own, the architect Gam-El and the detective Pym-El, in the latter half of the 9800s. Gam-El continued the El line (*Krypton Chronicles* #1 and #3, September and November 1981).

Bav Sor-El's Science Council forced out Har-Zod's ruling Military Council, and the Kryptonian Stellar Navy was shut down on the grounds that

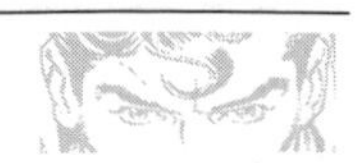

it was immoral (*Superman* #669, Late December 2007).

Don-El had a son named Ter-El (*The World of Krypton* #4, March 1988). In an earlier time line, Ter-El was named Var-El. In that time line, he was a scientist who teleported himself to Earth, leaving behind three children, Jor-El I, Kalya Var-El, and Zim-El (*Krypton Chronicles* #3, November 1981). In alternate time lines, Jor-El I was named Seyg-El (*The World of Krypton* #3–4, February–March 1988).

Scientist Zim-El married Byma Ruth-Ar, and they were the parents of Kru-El. Later, Kalya Var-El married Science Council member Nim-Zee and had two sons, Gem-Zee and Van-Zee. Van-Zee married the Earthwoman Sylvia DeWitt, and they had twins, Lyle-Zee and Lili Van-Zee. Gem-Zee and his wife had a scientist son, Rad-Zee, and a daughter named Thara Gem-Zee, who married Ak-Var (*Krypton Chronicles* #3, November 1981).

Scientist Jor-El I married Nimda An-Dor (*Superman Family* #192, November–December 1978) and had three scientist sons, Zor-El and the twins Jor-El II and Nim-El. Zor-El married Alura In-Ze and had a daughter Kara Zor-El. Nim-El was the scientist in charge of Kandor's armory and married Dondra Klu-Ta and had a son Don-El (*Krypton Chronicles* #3, November 1981).

Jor-El II married Lara Lor-Van, a librarian, charged with the care and maintenance of the central data banks, the vast repository of Kryptonian history and science. The daughter of Lor-Van and Lara Rok-Var, she was the granddaughter of Nara (*The World of Krypton* #3, February 1988). Their only child was Kal-El (*Krypton Chronicles* #3, November 1981). Kal-El was identified as the twenty-third generation of the House of El (*The World of Krypton* #4, March 1988).

In the post-Crisis universe, Kon-El represented the second House of El, descended from the man who saved Van-L generations ago (*Superboy* [third series] #59, February 1999).

HOT DOG

See Space Canine Patrol Agency.

HTRAE

See Bizarro.

HUSQUE

An ancient being of unidentified alien origin, a member of a race who called themselves the Exiles because they had elected to banish themselves to another dimension. Husque briefly caused panic in Metropolis when he temporarily switched places with the Jimmy Olsen of the post–First Crisis Earth.

During the reign of the pharaoh Seti, the ancient Egyptians were visited by aliens from a distant, unidentified star system who had come to colonize Earth. At first, the aliens and Egyptians coexisted not only in peace but also in friendship. The pharaoh's son particularly enjoyed flying over the desert in the aliens' spacecraft, until he was killed in a crash that was his own fault.

Nevertheless, the aliens felt responsible for the death, and their leadership decreed they must atone. This they did by banishing themselves, in their mother ship, to another dimension, earning their designation in the Egyptians' ancient scrolls as the Exiles. But the aliens wanted to keep in touch, so to speak, and remain apprised of the development of their far more primitive Terran friends. So the aliens arranged for a "dimensional bridge" to appear for two days once every hundred years, which would allow the Exiles to see how the Egyptians had developed.

What the aliens were slow to realize, however, was that the primitive Egyptians revered them as gods, and the first time the dimensional bridge appeared to show the aliens a glimpse of Egypt, they discovered dozens of dead bodies: Egyptians sacrificed to appease their alien "gods." Rather than leave bad enough alone, the aliens attempted to resuscitate the dead humans. Their experiments did not achieve the intended results, but did yield the realization that an Exile's life force could occupy a dead human body, creating a new being whose whole, in terms of powers and abilities, was greater than the sum of its parts. The development of this new hybrid species led to the establishment of a caste system within the aliens' society, with the composite creatures becoming the overclass. Consequently, once a century, violence broke out among the aliens as the dimensional bridge appeared, with the lower-class aliens trying to claim human bodies and morph into new beings, in a grotesque form of social climbing.

By the time of the post-First Crisis Earth's twentieth century, the aliens' technology had developed to the point that the Exiles were no longer dependent on the dimensional bridge to access Earth. The alien who developed this technology became the aliens' Emperor, and he began sending young members of his race to Earth to, in effect, kidnap humans for the hybridization process. The first of these, a female named Tehra, captured Jimmy Olsen, who alerted Superman. When the Man of Steel pursued Jimmy and Tehra into the other dimension, where the Emperor ordered all of them to be imprisoned, Tehra began to see that what the Emperor was forcing his people to do was wrong. Superman was able to stop the Emperor's attempt to merge Jimmy with the Emperor's son, and Tehra was then able to return Superman and Jimmy to Earth. In retaliation for Tehra's role in thwarting the Emperor's plan, her brother Husque was severely punished.

Back in Metropolis, the image of Husque began to invade Jimmy's dreams, as if Husque were attempting to establish mental contact with him. Later, while Jimmy was being examined by Professor Emil Hamilton for any negative side effects from his experience in the Exiles' dimension, a bolt of lightning struck Hamilton's equipment, opening up an interdimensional warp through which Husque was able to "lock on to" Jimmy telepathically. Using alien technology beyond human comprehension, Husque teleported to Earth and transferred Jimmy to the Exiles' other-dimensional realm in his place. Disoriented by the sudden shift in his surroundings, Husque fled Hamilton's lab and ran out into the city streets. Taking shelter for the night at a construction site, he was found by workers the next morning, and reflexively defended himself from their efforts to forcibly evict him by animating a derrick with his own life force. The patrolling Superman saw the disturbance and swooped down to calm the agitated Husque. With Professor Hamilton's aid, Husque was exchanged for Jimmy, and the young Exile returned whence he had come (*Superman* [second series] #37, November 1989; #38, December 1989; #39, January 1990; others).

H'V'LER'NI, THE

An ancient race that existed on the post-First Crisis Earth, discovered during an archaeological dig being covered by Lois Lane, that unearthed an ancient pyramid. It and its contents revealed the existence of the H'v'ler'ni, a society advanced far beyond our own that existed more than one hundred thousand years ago. At the dig site, Superman battled what appeared to be a living mummy that turned out to be a robot. The H'v'ler'ni, it seemed, were a civilization indigenous to Earth in prehistory; they were her dominant species until a plague wiped out most of them. While the majority of H'v'ler'ni fled the planet, five hundred stayed behind. Their technology allowed them to remove their consciousnesses from their physical forms and transfer them to the giant robot Superman fought, which they called the Host.

The Man of Steel learned this "through" Lois Lane when the H'v'ler'ni leader, A'x'ar, transferred his consciousness from the robot to Lois. The reawakened H'v'ler'ni wanted to find host bodies for those consciousnesses still inside the Host, so the Host flew to Metropolis to "possess" five hundred citizens. Superman followed, offering himself as a receptacle for a H'v'ler'ni. Seeing the Man of Steel's powers, the discarnate H'v'ler'ni within the Host fought one another, competing to be the one who occupied Superman. The resulting storm of chaotic psionic activity within the Host short-circuited it. The H'v'ler'ni were "exorcised" from Lois and all others they had possessed, who were freed from H'v'ler'ni control. The others remained trapped within the Host (*Superman* [second series] #5, May 1987, and #6, June 1987).

HYPERTIME

See Magog; Quintessence, The.

I-CHING

A blind, elderly, Asian scholar of ancient cultures who was the Confucian mentor and sensei of Diana Prince, aka Wonder Woman. I-Ching worked with her on the pre–First Crisis Earth-1 during her time as a martial artist crime fighter without superpowers (*Wonder Woman* [first series] #179–202, November–December 1968–September–October 1972).

Superman encountered I-Ching when the Chinese mystic helped the Man of Steel restore the superpowers that had been stolen from him by the other-dimensional Sand Superman (*Superman* [first series] #233–242, January–September 1971). I-Ching was the sole survivor of an ancient sect whose credo was that one culture's magic was another's science. Its mission was to record and preserve ancient mystical knowledge that would otherwise have been lost to history.

Superman first met I-Ching as Clark Kent when the Asian sage appeared in Kent's office, asserting that he knew the TV newsman was secretly Superman. I-Ching revealed that one of the lost civilizations of which he had knowledge was that of Quarrm, the other-dimensional home of the Sand Superman. Because of the inherent nature of Quarrm, the old man believed that only metaphysics, or practical magic, could recapture Superman's powers.

The Chinese seer proposed to release Superman's "astral self"—his soul—from the Man of Steel's body and send it out in Superman's stead to confront the Sand Superman. After a series of complications and setbacks during which the creature grew ever more powerful, I-Ching finally managed to extract Superman's spirit, which drained all the stolen powers out of the Sand Superman and returned them to the Man of Might.

Wonder Woman's career as the nonpowered Diana Prince on Earth-1 came to an end some time later, still within the pre-First Crisis era, in a series of events that began with I-Ching being gunned down by sniper fire and dying in Diana's arms (*Wonder Woman* [first series] #204, January–February 1973).

In the universe reordered by the First Crisis, Diana Prince never renounced her Amazon powers or embarked on a career as a nonpowered martial artist mentored by I-Ching. It is believed, however, that an incarnation of I-Ching existed on New Earth, but only as a code name for an Asian martial artist, rather than an actual legal name. And it is known that Diana Prince's time as a nonpowered heroine is once again part of her history (*Justice League of America* [second series] #0, September 2006), and further that she spent a year in I-Ching's company while the Wonder Woman persona was assumed by the former Wonder Girl, Donna Troy (*Wonder Woman* [third series] #2, September 2006). I-Ching also seems to have had a history with the Batman, whom he aided during the events leading up to the resurrection of Rā's al Ghūl (*Batman* #670, December 2007; others). (For a complete account of I-Ching, see *The Essential Wonder Woman Encyclopedia*, 2010.)

IDENTITY CRISIS

The chroniclers' collective title for a series of events surrounding the search for the murderer of Sue Dibny, wife of the super hero Elongated Man, who was ultimately revealed to be the mentally ill Jean Loring, former wife of Justice League of America member the Atom. These events unearthed long-buried secrets and intrigues within the Justice League whose revelations seriously strained the relationships of its members. One of the issues that came to light was the practice, not known to all JLA members, of mindwiping super-criminals and altering their personalities to make them less dangerous, as in the case of Doctor Light, who was turned by the magic of JLA member Zatanna

Identity Crisis

into an ineffectual buffoon with no memory of having raped Sue Dibny.

As one of the Leaguers who banded together to bring Dibny's killer to justice, Superman was affected by these events, such as when the still-at-large murderer sent a death threat to his wife Lois Lane. He did not play a significant role in the case, however, even though he was the official leader of the League. The handling of the Dibny investigation brought to light the idea that Superman and Batman had always been so busy with their own cases in Metropolis and Gotham City, respectively, that a smaller, core group within the League—Green Arrow, Black Canary, Hawkman, the Flash, Green Lantern, Elongated Man, and Zatanna—had made most of the key decisions defining the League's practices, including those regarding mindwiping criminals and altering their personality types. As Green Arrow put it, Superman and Batman "saw what they wanted to see" regarding the others' activities, which would have consequences that would later play a role in the Infinite Crisis (*Identity Crisis* #1–7, June–December 2004).

IGNITION

A super-criminal on the post-First Crisis unified Earth created by the Joker, Ignition was an armored, living weapon that could fly and fire destructive energy bolts from huge metal hands. "He" came into existence as a member of the Joker League of Anarchy, the perverse, living parody of the Justice League materialized by "Emperor Joker," which is what the Batman's old enemy called himself after acquiring the majority of Mr. Mxyzptlk's Fifth Dimensional magical powers and using them to reshape the world according to his own insane, surreal vision (*The Adventures of Superman* #582, September 2000).

While the weird-looking Ignition (he had human legs and feet, but a robotic torso and no head) was assumed to be an original creation of the Joker's dementia, not even the Joker himself seemed to know who he really was. It was as if Ignition somehow had a life of his own, independent of the Joker's mind. Ignition apparently possessed certain information, and addressed Superman in certain ways, that suggested he could have been imagined as a being of Kryptonian origin. Ignition also seemed to have made some sort of deal with Mxyzptlk, the exact nature of which was never chronicled (*Action Comics* #770, October 2000). But it may have been that, once the Joker was defeated and Mxyzptlk's magical powers were returned to him, Ignition was allowed to live on in the restored "real world" after the Joker's mad "rewriting" of reality was erased.

Another clue to this possibility lay in Ignition's demand that Superman "kneel before [his] sovereign," the *kneel before* expression being a familiar, recurring catchphrase of General Zod's. Ignition later turned up, with no connection to the Joker, in the Pokolistan of the Russian-born Zod, joining Faora and Kancer as aides to Zod (*Action Comics* #780, August 2001). Ignition served under Zod until the general was killed in battle with Superman after the Imperiex War.

ILLIUM-349

See Nor-Kan.

IMAN

A Mexican super hero on the post-First Crisis Earth, operating out of Mexico City, who helped Superman defeat the magically powered eco-terrorist Duran (*Superman* [second series] *Annual* #12, 2000). A brilliant, Yale-educated cyberneticist and astrophysicist, as well as the second astronaut employed by S.T.A.R. Labs, Diego Irigayen returned from a spaceflight to discover that his mother had been murdered. The tragedy motivated him to use his technological expertise to transform himself into a super crime fighter. As Iman, the athletic Irigayen donned a special armor that increased his strength, made him invulnerable, and immensely increased his stamina and endurance. Diego considered Superman his hero and inspiration. Iman recently fought alongside Mon-El to repel an alien invasion (*Superman* #689, August 2009).

IMPERIEX

An intergalactic conqueror and destroyer of worlds that appeared in the post-First Crisis integrated universe. The omnipotent Imperiex, which may have been older than creation itself, had discovered what it considered imperfections in the makeup of the cosmos. And so Imperiex set out to destroy the universe with a new Big Bang, wiping out all flaws and replacing it with a new, perfect reality.

The universe-consolidating First Crisis had apparently made Earth the center of reality, a kind of linchpin holding existence together, so Imperiex needed to destroy it to start the second Big Bang. Therefore, Imperiex relentlessly advanced toward Earth, leaving scores of dead planets such as Kalanor, Karna, and Daxam, original birthplace of Mon-El, in its wake.

One of the worlds so destroyed was Warworld, dominated by Mongul II (son of the original), who so feared what he *thought* was Imperiex that he came to Earth to warn Superman of Imperiex's approach and to beg for the Last Son of Krypton's help in defeating the cybernetic monstrosity (*Superman* [second series] #153, February 2000). The Man of Steel and the second Mongul traveled far into deep space to intercept and engage "Imperiex," ultimately destroying it and preventing its attack on Earth. (Whereupon Mongul turned on Superman, but the Caped Kryptonian—who was prepared for this inevitability—had prearranged to surrender Mongul to the intergalactic bounty hunter Lobo.)

At the time, however, no one realized that they had not, in fact, battled the real Imperiex. What Superman had fought was merely an "Imperiex probe," a mechanized foot soldier designed as a miniature version of the true, vastly larger Imperiex, which referred to itself as Imperiex-Prime and was also known as the Devourer of Galaxies. Although Imperiex-Prime resembled a huge, ornately constructed robot, it was, in fact, entropy incarnate—the tendency of the universe to "run down" to inertness, instability, or "death." Imperiex-Prime was a mass of destructive energy given form only by its colossal, humanoid-shaped armor.

It wasn't long before Imperiex-Prime dispatched what seemed like hundreds more probes to attack Earth and kill thousands. These were joined by city-sized "hollower" machines that devastated eight Earth targets. Their goal was to drill through the planet, which supposedly would devastate the space-time continuum and trigger the new Big Bang. Imperiex-Prime waged a full-scale war against Earth, killing several prominent super-beings including Maxima, Massacre, the war hero General Frank Rock, and Queen Hippolyta. The Amazon queen died trying to save her homeland, the island of Themyscira, which was just one of many human and meta-human habitats decimated by Imperiex-Prime's assault. Through it all, Imperiex-Prime itself remained floating in Earth's orbit, regarding the carnage below dispassionately, with neither jubilance nor remorse.

Dozens of alien species united behind Earth's defenders in the Imperiex War. These included the survivors of the worlds Imperiex-Prime had already destroyed (including Warworld and Maxima's home planet of Almerac). So great was the threat that Apokolips and Earth formed an unprecedented coalition, with Darkseid as its commander. These unlikely alliances probably would not have happened but for the intervention of Brainiac 13, fresh from his attempt to dominate Metropolis with his Y2K virus. Brainiac 13 had secretly forced Earth into the alliance with Apokolips. What were ostensibly actions intended to save the universe from Imperiex-Prime, however, ultimately proved—not surprisingly—to have been nothing more than steps toward fulfilling Brainiac 13's ongoing agenda. But that would not become clear till much later.

Meanwhile, the equally treacherous President Lex Luthor ostensibly did his part, rallying other super heroes, the U.S. military, and those of other countries such as the Pokolistan ruled by the Russian General Zod. But Luthor also took it upon himself to decide unilaterally that Superman was not powerful enough to single-handedly lead the opposing forces. As an alternative, Luthor released Doomsday from captivity and tried to turn the creature into a formidable weapon by having it brainwashed into seeing all Imperiex drones as Superman. The alliance successfully destroyed enough of the probes that Imperiex-Prime itself personally intervened, killing Doomsday in a matter of seconds with a fusillade of searing cosmic energy that left nothing of Doomsday but his skeleton. Thankfully, Darkseid elected to save Superman from the same fate.

The sacrifices of Strange Visitor, Kismet, and General Rock allowed Superman and his allies to crack open Imperiex-Prime's armor. The plan was that Darkseid would then use Boom Tubes to banish the released energy to the galaxies Imperiex-Prime had destroyed, thereby preventing the triggering of the second Big Bang. This, however, was the point at which Brainiac 13 appeared on the scene with his own digital version of Warworld, and his true intentions and role in the war became clear: He absorbed Imperiex-Prime's entropic energies and stored them in Warworld, intending to use them to effect his ultimate "upgrade" and rule the universe.

Superman dived into the sun, hoping to absorb enough solar energy to acquire a power boost that would let him take on the "amplified" Brainiac 13. But the allies realized that if the computerized Warworld were destroyed, Imperiex-Prime would be released and the second Big Bang triggered.

At Superman and Luthor's urging, the allies switched to a last-minute, and highly risky, strategy. Darkseid's powers had been weakened during Brainiac's attack, but he could use an Atlantean sorcerer as a "host" for them, amplifying

Imperiex

them, then focusing the energy through Steel's Entropy Aegis armor. Thus, the allies theorized, they might be able to send Imperiex-Prime and Brainiac 13 back in time to the *original* Big Bang—roughly fourteen billion years.

Meanwhile, from Earth, Lex Luthor added the energy of an experimental time-shifting weapon to the mix, resulting in a Boom Tube that, rather than instantaneously shuttling its subjects across great distances, could move them through *time.* With his newly solar-enhanced strength, Superman literally shoved the digital Warworld itself into the "time Boom Tube."

The tube worked as hoped, whisking both Imperiex-Prime's and Brainiac 13's consciousnesses back to the point of the Big Bang, destroying both menaces. Ironically, it occurred to Imperiex-Prime in its final moments that the imperfection it had detected in the universe was itself. The allies' successful strategy resulted in two enormous explosions that scattered Brainiac 13's consciousness over sixty trillion light-years of space and time (*Action Comics* #782, October 2001). It was hoped that Imperiex-Prime, whose energies could only be dissipated but not destroyed per se, suffered a similar fate.

The Imperiex War was won at great cost to Earth, the magnitude of which was deeply felt for some time. At least eight million Earthers died during the war, and Topeka as well as other cities—including Themyscira—had to be reconstructed.

On a brighter note, Aquaman, alternate Green Lantern Guy Gardner, Jonathan Kent, and Steel, who were all counted among the dead, later turned up alive for different reasons. Unfortunately, the same was true for Doomsday as well. Up to the time of the Imperiex War, Luthor's presidency was relatively unblemished by scandal. But his political career was ended when suspicions arose that his administration had advance intelligence of the Imperiex probe that took out Topeka, yet did nothing (not unlike FDR is believed to have known of the impending attack on Pearl Harbor). When Luthor's aide Hope Taya leaked the truth to the *Daily Planet,* it was the beginning of the end for the Luthor administration.

The collateral damage to Superman's personal life was just as severe, if not more so. Although he was later restored to life in another reality-morphing event, Superman's father-in-law, Major Sam Lane, Luthor's secretary of defense, was seemingly killed by Imperiex probes. His daughter Lois Lane took this loss especially hard, finding her marriage sorely tested when her husband's inability to save her father raised unwelcome and disturbing doubts about Superman's power, and even about how he ordered his "heroic" priorities.

In time, these doubts faded and the marriage endured, but not before Superman himself had to work his way through a depressive crisis of self-confidence. For some time afterward, he altered his costume to give his red S-emblem a black background rather than yellow, to commemorate those who had died in the battle (*Action Comics* #780–782; *The Adventures of Superman* #593–595; *Superman* [second series] #171–173; *Superman: The Man of Steel* #115–117—all August 2001–October 2001; *Superman: Our Worlds at War Secret Files* #1, August 2001; others).

INERTRON

See Validus.

INFINITE CRISIS

A series of reality-altering events that created several multiple universes, which then collapsed into a single "New Earth." It was discovered subsequently, however, that the multiverse did indeed continue to exist, with New Earth but one of fifty-two parallel universes.

When the First Crisis caused the original multiverse to collapse into a single positive-matter universe and a single negative-matter universe, four humans escaped the cosmic upheaval, transporting themselves into a supposedly paradise-like crystalline dimension: Kal-L, the Superman of Earth-2, and his wife, the Earth-2 Lois Lane; the Superboy from Earth-Prime, most frequently referred to in the chronicles as Superboy-Prime; and Alexander Luthor, Junior, from Earth-3. From this otherworldly space, they could observe events on the reconstituted singular Earth and saw that it was a grim, dark place, much more awash in crime and corruption than the Earths they had come from. What was especially painful for the Earth-2 Superman was watching his wife Lois continuing to age. Her health began deteriorating while he remained vigorous—aging at a far slower rate—but was nevertheless powerless to change her circumstances. Meanwhile, Superboy-Prime felt that his contented life had been put on hold indefinitely, just as he had begun to savor its delights.

Alexander, however, had begun making secret plans whose potential consequences would later suggest that the time this quartet spent in their strange space between realities had begun to corrupt them . . . with grandiosity and arrogance. Carefully, over time, Alexander found ways to leave the crystalline dimension for Earth, where he set in motion events intended to re-create the pre–First Crisis multiverse, but revised according to his personal design—that is, his unilateral moral judgment. His activities manifested themselves in a series of inexplicable events, documented gradually over a long period, that in retrospect would seem to historians like omens or harbingers of the dramatic reality warping to come.

Among the first seemed to be a sudden change in the Kon-El Superboy's history. He had always understood that he had been cloned from genetic material provided by Project Cadmus director Paul Westfield, with Cadmus making modifications that gave him powers similar to Superman's. Suddenly he discovered that he had been cloned from both Superman's and Lex Luthor's DNA (*Teen Titans* [third series] #1, September 2003).

There were other changes as well—such as the unexplained reappearance of the dead Jason Todd (the younger Robin who replaced the adult Dick Grayson), and the murder of the Ted Kord Blue Beetle by Maxwell Lord, a wealthy businessman and former supposed benefactor of the Justice League of America, who also possessed the superpower of mind control and had become the corrupt "Black Knight" (chief executive) of a government covert operations agency called Checkmate. Kord was killed because he had discovered Lord's campaign, conducted gradually over many years, to ultimately eliminate the world's super heroes, whom Lord considered a threat to the planet (*DC Countdown* #1, May 2005).

Part of the fallout from the revelations of the Justice League's magical mindwiping was that Batman learned that he himself had had certain of his own memories erased by his fellow Leaguers. In response, he built and launched (using the vast resources of Wayne Industries) the spy satellite Brother MK I to carefully monitor all "super" activity on Earth.

Lord was given control of Brother MK I by Alexander Luthor, posing as the post-Crisis Earth's Lex Luthor during one of Alex's forays out of the crystalline realm. Lord used both the satellite's tech and the auspices of Checkmate to create an army of OMACs—Observational Meta-human Activity Constructs—whose mission would be to hunt down and kill super-beings. These OMACs were randomly chosen humans who were turned into cyborgs by means of a virus developed with nanotechnology left over from Brainiac 13's attempted sixty-fourth-century "makeover" of Metropolis.

Lord then used his powers to control Superman's mind and began employing the Man of Steel as a living weapon, sending him to attack Batman (beginning the feud between the two that was ongoing when the Infinite Crisis began). Wonder Woman arrived in time to prevent Batman's death. Then Superman turned on Wonder Woman, who successfully repelled Superman's attack and had him taken into custody by the JLA. The League's telepathic member Martian Manhunter perceived an image of Lord in Superman's mind. Armed with that information, Wonder Woman confronted Lord and bound him with her truth-compelling lasso. When Lord told her that the only way to remove the threat Superman had become was to kill Lord, she did so by snapping his neck (*The OMAC Project* #1–4, June–September 2005; and *Action Comics* #829; *The Adventures of Superman* #642; *Wonder Woman* [second series] #219—all Septem-

ber 2005). The friendship between Superman and Wonder Woman was severely strained over the killing of Maxwell Lord, which Superman could not accept as necessary or justified. Both he and Batman seemingly turned their backs on her, even though she had saved their lives, and their relationship would not be fully repaired until much later, well over a year after the Infinite Crisis had ended.

To add injury to insult, Lord's OMACs then took over Brother MK I and, from it, photographed and broadcast around the world the image of Wonder Woman killing Lord, severely damaging her reputation and hobbling her effectiveness against a new threat to all super heroes—the now autonomous spy satellite, which had renamed itself Brother Eye, directing more than two hundred thousand OMACs programmed to wipe out Earth's super heroes (*The OMAC Project* #5–6, October–November 2005; others). It would only be much later that the OMACs would be stopped, when Batman formed a strike force that destroyed Brother Eye (*Infinite Crisis* #6, May 2006).

Another strange event was the destruction of the Justice League's Watchtower, its headquarters on the moon (*JLA* #120, December 2005). The mistrust that had been fomented by the events of Identity Crisis had effectively led the Justice League to disband (*JLA* #115–119, August–Late November 2005). The Martian Manhunter had wanted to re-form the group, and had Superman's blessing to do so. As he and Earth Green Lantern John Stewart sat in the Watchtower, discussing who to recruit for the revived League and debating the meaning of the various strange phenomena occurring around the world, the Watchtower's teleporters registered the arrival of Superman. But it turned out to be someone else, a stranger in a Superman costume. Suddenly the Watchtower exploded.

The truth would come out later: Not only had Alexander Luthor Junior, been leaving the crystal realm, but Superboy-Prime had been doing so as well, and it was the latter who destroyed the Watchtower. As events escalated, it became clear that the fundamental personalities of Kal-L and the Earth-2 Lois Lane had not been changed by their exile in the crystal dimension; it was only Alexander and the Earth-3 Superboy who had gone mad. Alex preyed on the emotionally distraught Kal-L's feelings, saying that if Kal-L would trust him, Alex could save Lois.

On another of his forays to Earth, Alex again posed as Lex Luthor to assemble a large number of super-criminals into a secret Society, agitating them into a frenzy of vengefulness over the super heroes' practice of magically mindwiping them and altering their personalities. Such was the state of Earth as Alexander set in motion the final phase of his plan to destroy the crystalline realm and leave it for good, along with his three fellow survivors of the First Crisis: The Watchtower had been destroyed; Superman, Wonder Woman, and Batman were feuding; and bizarre, often inexplicable events continued to affect the lives of Earth's heroes.

Now, per Alex's plan, Superboy-Prime used his super-strength to smash through the crystalline walls enclosing their space. He succeeded in doing so (*Infinite Crisis* #1, December 2005), but his repeated punches into the wall before it shattered triggered "ripples" in the fabric of reality, causing various events in the post–First Crisis universe to become undone.

Once released, Kal-L and Lois located his cousin Power Girl, who, before the First Crisis, had been the Earth-2 version of Supergirl. By means undocumented, the touch of Lois's hand restored Power Girl's memories of Earth-2, lost when the First Crisis created the singular universe. The nature of Kal-L's manipulation by Alexander became clear when Kal-L told Power Girl that he and Alex believed Lois could recover her health in her native environment. That was why their plan was to replace the current Earth with Earth-2, which they considered perfect (*Infinite Crisis* #2, January 2006; *JSA* #82, April 2006).

Kal-L went to Batman and tried to forge an alliance with him, stating his belief that the "wrong" Earth had resulted from the First Crisis. Kal-L felt that the dark nature of the post–First Crisis Earth had played a major role in creating Batman's recent paranoia, which led to the construction of the spy satellite. Batman refused Kal-L's offer, and later felt justified in his suspicion of the First Crisis survivors when he learned that it was Superboy-Prime who had destroyed the JLA Watchtower (*Infinite Crisis* #3, February 2006).

In corroborating Kal-L's account of the plan, Alex revealed to Power Girl that he and Superboy-Prime had been leaving the crystal realm periodically for some time. Their various intrigues had helped amass a small army of superpowered people who would energize an interdimensional "tuning fork" that would splinter reality. Acting on that plan, Alex restored Earth-2, unpopulated except for the former denizens of Earth-2 who were transported there, including Kal-L, the ailing Lois, and Power Girl (*Infinite Crisis* #4, March 2006).

Alexander and Superboy-Prime continued using the "cosmic tuning fork" to create parallel world after parallel world, but none could quite measure up to the standard of perfection Alex envisioned. Each newly created Earth weakened the previous ones, too, and the fragile realities were in danger of collapsing like a house of cards.

Meanwhile, Superboy-Prime was disgusted by the Kon-El clone Superboy, finding him soft and weak. Now the madness of Superboy-Prime became frighteningly obvious, as his rage over Earth's imperfection possessed him. He became relentless in his campaign to destroy those who didn't meet his standards as heroes—standards as dangerously and impossibly perfectionistic as Alex's.

Superboy-Prime's rampage was stopped only by the combined efforts of several super-fast heroes, including multiple iterations of the Flash, who dragged Superboy-Prime into the Speed Force, the little-understood extradimensional energy force from which the speedsters drew their powers (*Infinite Crisis* #4 and *Teen Titans* [third series] #32—both March 2006). Soon after Kal-L and Lois's arrival on Earth-2, Lois died. Kal-L's super-screams of anguish were so loud that Earth's Superman Kal-El could hear them, and he went to Earth-2 to investigate. Mad with grief, Kal-L attacked Superman, accusing him of having corrupted Earth-2 as he did his own Earth. The fight ended only when Wonder Woman separated them (*Infinite Crisis* #5, April 2006; *Superman* [second series] #226, April 2006; and *The Adventures of Superman* #648–649, March–April 2006).

Back on what now had to be called New Earth, one of the Flashes returned from the Speed Force with the news that the speedsters were unable to hold Superboy-Prime there. Superboy-Prime emerged wearing armor that stored yellow-sun radiation, empowering him to become an even greater menace as he continued his killing spree. In his wake were left the bodies of many super heroes and super-criminals, including Kon-El (*Infinite Crisis* #6, May 2006).

Superboy-Prime was finally stopped—although at great cost to the Supermen, who knew that the only way to end his rampage was to remove his powers. But they also knew that the plan they formed was very risky, and bravely accepted the near certainty that they would be seriously harmed. The two Supermen grabbed Superboy-Prime and flew him through the red sun of the solar system that had once included Krypton. All three began losing their powers in the process, and the Supermen crash-landed, with Superboy-Prime in tow, on a sentient, living planet named Mogo. In the final battle, the older, less resilient Kal-L died while Kal-El survived, but his superpowers were "erased" for a year, during which period Clark Kent would retire his super heroic identity. The now docile, powerless Superboy-Prime was turned over to the Green Lantern Corps, who imprisoned him inside a red Sun-Eater.

Batman tracked down Alex Luthor and seemed ready to kill him until dissuaded from that act by Wonder Woman. Alex escaped, only to be found by an unhappy Joker, who killed him for not inviting Joker to join the Society (*Infinite Crisis* #7, June 2006).

The various incarnations of the Legion of Super-Heroes that had existed since the First Crisis were "erased," leaving a Legion with only one history—which closely resembled the one it had had before the First Crisis. One exception was that Clark Kent had become a Legionnaire before assuming his costumed persona. Finally, the various versions of General Zod were replaced by the one and only Zod, who played a major role in the events leading up to the establishment of New Krypton.

Alexander Luthor's manipulations of reality ultimately resulted in the total restoration of the multiverse, comprising fifty-two parallel universes existing in the same space but vibrating at different frequencies. After interference from Mister Mind posing as Booster Gold's robotic companion Skeets, many of the worlds were altered and were no longer perfect duplicates of New Earth, but instead close counterparts.

INFINITY-MAN

An Apokoliptian New God with super-strength, invulnerability, magnetic powers, and the ability to "phase" through matter and alter atomic structures, among other gifts. Astorr, a powerful warrior on a world in a different dimension from Apokolips, rescued and nursed back to health the badly burned Drax, who had not been killed by his brother Uxas, aka Darkseid, when Drax attempted to steal the Omega Force, but was merely shot through the dimensional barrier. When Astorr died from old age, Drax assumed his persona of Infinity-Man. As Infinity-Man, Drax served Highfather on New Genesis, where he became acquainted with the Forever People and became their protector (*Forever People* #1, February–March 1971; others). On several occasions thereafter, the Forever People returned the favor and saved Infinity-Man from entrapment or death as Darkseid began to perceive Infinity-Man as a threat to his agenda.

Infinity-Man was correctly suspected by Superman, Mister Miracle, and Orion to be the killer of the New Gods. However, the Mother Box used by the Forever People to summon Infinity-Man appeared to have been destroyed, and the Forever People themselves had been murdered. Later, it was revealed that Infinity-Man actually *was* responsible for the death of the New Gods.

INSECT QUEEN

The super-identity assumed by Lana Lang on both the pre-First Crisis Earth-1 and Earth-2. On Earth-1, teenage Lana gained the powers of various insects, accompanied by a transformation of her lower body into the form of the corresponding bug. The power came from a ring given to her by a grateful alien, crash-landed on Earth, whom she saved from being pinned under a fallen tree (*Superboy* [first series] #124, October 1965). Her career as Insect Queen was short-lived, but she did serve in the reservists of the thirtieth-century Legion of Super-Heroes for a time (*Adventure Comics* #355, April 1967; others).

On Earth-2, the adult Lana became the super-*criminal* Insect Queen when she was possessed by the effects of a magical scarab unearthed by her archaeologist father. The scarab gave her the power to enlarge and control insects (*Superman Family* #213, December 1981; others). After initially engaging in criminal acts, Lana was freed from the spell by the Earth-2 Superman and became an occasional super heroine thereafter. In reality as it was reordered by the First Crisis, neither version of Lana became an Insect Queen.

There were two other Insect Queens besides the one most recently documented on New Earth. One, who existed in the thirtieth century of the post-First Crisis unified Earth, was named Lonna Leing and came from the planet Xanthu (*Legion of Super-Heroes* [fourth series] #82, July 1996; others). She was a member of a hero team whose members were allies of the Legion, and she had powers virtually identical to those of the Lana Lang Insect Queen. The other minor Insect Queen was a former member of the Justice Underground, a team of heroes who opposed the Crime Syndicate of America in the anti-matter universe (*JLA Secret Files 2004*).

Another Insect Queen emerged in the new reality created by the Infinite Crisis, an insectoid alien who took a human form looking somewhat like Lana Lang (*Superman* #651, June 2006, and #671, February 2008; others). She was the leader of a civilization of giant insects sent to Earth to colonize it. She began by sending her advance scouts, drones whom she called the Flea Circus, to enlist Lex Luthor's aid in finding a human form for her to inhabit, in exchange for the Flea Circus's help in stockpiling kryptonite.

Lana Lang had become the new CEO of LexCorp by the time the Insect Queen arrived on Earth to complete the arrangement. The alien Insect Queen abducted Lang and held her in the Queen's new base on the moon. There she evolved into a form resembling Lang with wings, four arms, antennae, and an insectoid exoskeleton, and prepared to do away with Lana. Superman was captured by the Insect Queen when the Man of Steel discovered she could control him with psychic powers to which he was vulnerable. This was accomplished thanks to her swarm of alien midges—tiny flying insects that, on Earth, generally bite, feed on blood, and spread disease—which burrowed into Superman's skull. Before she could finish using Superman's Kryptonian genetic structure to breed an army of "super soldier-ants," however, Lana freed the Man of Steel, and together they trapped the Insect Queen within the suspended animation amber in which she first came to Earth.

However, unbeknownst to Lana, a portion of the alien being's DNA had been injected into her body and spent several months gestating. When Lana began experiencing health issues, no one could have forseen that the cause was the Insect Queen's rapid growth. At one point, Lana collapsed and appeared to die on the operating table but was actually finally taken over by the Insect Queen. Lana and the hospital were quickly covered in a thick cocoon that was resistant to the Metropolis Science Police's weaponry. The Guardian led SP agents into the hospital but quickly became trapped, requiring rescue by Supergirl. The Maid of Might was told that the Insect Queen intended to use the Kryptonian's body as a template to create a new and powerful army. Supergirl resisted the Queen's attack and used Kryptonian technology to defeat and expel the alien from Lana's body (*Supergirl* [fifth series] #50, May 2010).

INTERGANG

A global crime syndicate headquartered in Metropolis, versions of which existed on the pre-First Crisis Earth-1 and both of Superman's subsequent realities. All iterations of Intergang were more formidable than any other criminal group Superman ever faced because the gangsters were armed with alien weaponry and technology. In Intergang's first two incarnations, that firepower came from Apokolips. On Earth-1, Intergang was run by a scar-faced gangster named Bruno "Ugly" Mannheim (*Superman's Pal, Jimmy Olsen* #133, October 1970; #139, July 1971; #141, September 1971; others). Mannheim was not an autonomous leader. Rather, he took orders from and executed the strategy of Darkseid, for whom Intergang's primary purpose was to discover the Anti-Life Equation.

Intergang also seemed to be working with Morgan Edge, the head of Galaxy Communications that had purchased the *Daily Planet*. This was not the real Edge, however, but a clone. Shortly before the Crisis on Infinite Earths rearranged reality, an Intergang hit man confused the clone with the real Edge, who had escaped captivity, and the clone was killed. Thereafter, reporter Clark Kent was personally responsible for capturing and testifying against a group of Intergang's key leaders (*Superman* [first series] #296–299, February–May 1976), reducing its effectiveness to a degree that the organization nearly became a footnote.

Following the First Crisis, Intergang reappeared as having originated during the heyday of "the mob," the Prohibition era of the 1920s. This Intergang had a slightly different history, but with Bruno Mannheim's father Boss Moxie as its founder. His inner circle—powerful members of Intergang, all—included Intergang's chief assassin Noose; Rough House, Intergang's muscle and its most soft-spoken member; the gang's most accomplished hit man, Mike "Machine" Gunn; and Moxie's moll, Ginny "Torcher" McCree.

Ultimately, like so many gangsters of the era who were involved in violent rivalries with other criminal organizations, these underlings died in a hail of bullets, which seemed to spell the end of Intergang. Boss Moxie himself spent decades in prison. The Intergang of this reality was founded when, shortly after Superman emerged in Metropolis, Morgan Edge—whose Galaxy Communications was a large, successful, and legitimate business, but also a front for its CEO's criminal activities—began his scheme to remake the group. He persuaded all of Metropolis's criminal organizations to consolidate into a single entity, which would be operated like a major corporation, with a board of directors, a chief executive (Edge), and divisional vice presidents.

Edge was able to make Intergang much more of a force to be reckoned with than it had been in Moxie's day, thanks to the backing of, and Apokoliptian weaponry supplied by, Darkseid's master torturer DeSaad. Edge also sought to seize the criminal opportunities created by Lex Luthor's increasing willingness to devote more of LexCorp's resources to undermining Superman's activities. Realizing that Luthor saw the Man of Steel in no other terms than as a competitor for control of Metropolis, Edge saw Luthor's distraction as an advantage. Because Luthor himself was Edge's rival for that same dominion, however, Edge viewed Superman as *his* enemy as well (*Superman* [second series] #28; *The Adventures of Superman* #451—both February 1989; others). Ironically, Luthor made little effort to stop Intergang, for reasons similar to Edge's: Each man appreciated the other's potential to divert Superman's attention from his own criminal activities.

The old Intergang used traditional organized-crime methods, but Edge modernized things, creating and supervising an "enforcement" division. Its heavily armored squads included the Gassers, who could disperse poison gas as well as poison victims with a touch; Shock Troops, whose primary weapon was their electrocuting Energy Truncheons; and Wall-Crawlers, whose armor allowed them to do exactly what their name implied; to reach otherwise inaccessible targets in high places and destroy them with their laser pistols.

Edge's second in command was one Louis Gillespie (*Superman* [second series] #28, February 1989). Also working under Edge was this world's Bruno Mannheim (*The Adventures of Superman* #450, January 1989), who evidently felt a sense of entitlement to a more significant leadership role. Subsequent events suggested that all along he had deeply resented Gillespie, and coveted Edge's role.

Intergang had many means of laundering its money, but the most clever and successful was the operation at Happyland Amusement Park, designed by Thaddeus Killgrave working in collaboration with the former British toy designer Winslow Schott (*Action Comics* #657, September 1990).

In its early years under Edge's stewardship, Intergang committed many audacious crimes, most of which were foiled by Superman and the police, usually in the form of Dan Turpin and Maggie Sawyer's Metropolis S.C.U. (Special Crimes Unit). The organization itself—and especially its bosses, whose identities had been shrouded in mystery—became the object of intense scrutiny by the *Daily Planet,* in particular reporters Clark Kent, Lois Lane, and Cat Grant. Nevertheless, Edge extended Intergang's agenda to ever more outrageous lengths, making attempts on the lives of not only the *Planet* reporters, but even Lex Luthor. The first upheaval in the Intergang chain of command occurred when Superman returned from space in time to prevent Turmoil from killing Lois, then confronted Edge in his lair, scaring Edge so badly that he had a heart attack (*Action Comics* #643, July 1989). In the ICU, Edge became vulnerable to Mannheim's designs on his job, but an attempt on Edge's life while he was hospitalized failed. Nonetheless, Mannheim oversaw all Intergang operations from that point forward (*Superman* [second series] #36, September 1989).

As Morgan Edge recovered from his heart failure, the DA brought an indictment against him, and plans for a trial began. A key witness for the prosecution was Cat Grant. Mannheim ordered her abduction, with the intention of using Intergang's technology to erase certain of her memories and replace them with false counterparts that would be advantageous to the defense when Grant testified. But the plan failed: Cat was rescued by Superman and other heroes before her mind could be tampered with. At that point, a disgusted Mannheim abandoned any effort to help save Edge, with the result that Edge was found guilty and sentenced to a lengthy prison term (*Action Comics* #654, June 1990).

Sometime later, after Superman traced Louis Gillespie to Happyland and secretly confiscated his briefcase, Clark Kent published a massive exposé listing the locations of Intergang hideouts all over the world, which were promptly raided. The fact that Gillespie did not intentionally "leak" the evidence made no difference to Mannheim, who attempted to kill him. Superman intervened as Gillespie was being beaten, and Mannheim surprised the Man of Steel by holding his own in a physical battle, made possible by Mannheim's Apokoliptian bio-armor. In the course of this, Mannheim revealed that he was actually from Apokolips. Superman prevailed, and Mannheim was sent to Stryker's Island. Intergang seemed to have been eradicated once and for all (*Superman* [second series] #60, October 1991).

Gillespie, in serious condition, ordered Mannheim "whacked." Superman intervened there, too (*Action Comics* #673, *The Adventures of Superman* #486—both January 1992), stopping the Apokoliptian robotic assassin sent to Stryker's. But Mannheim was able to cannibalize the robot for tech to open a Boom Tube. Superman pursued, and before the chase was over Mannheim was dead, seemingly burned to a crisp.

Intergang apparently lay dormant for many years, until Vincent Edge brought all the Metropolis crime bosses together to found a new Intergang under the direction of Boss Moxie, who then murdered any potential rivals who would have been members of the new organization, including Vincent. But it was not the original, elderly Moxie who assumed control. After his release from prison, he had encountered the Newsboy Legion, whose members were the same age as when he had first opposed them. Investigating how this was possible led him to the insane renegade geneticist Dabney Donovan.

Donovan helped Moxie "reincarnate" himself as a younger clone with superpowers, and did the same with Moxie's old associates. Intergang's head assassin became Noose, who could now elongate his supple fingers, extending them to encircle his victims' throats. Rough House gained super-strength that amplified his power as Moxie's enforcer. Mike "Machine" Gunn was genetically modified so that his forearms could morph into machine guns. And Ginny "Torcher" McCree, who in her new incarnation became Gunn's lover, was given the power to control fire and shoot flames from her fingertips (*The Adventures of Superman* #544, March 1997).

Because the post-Mannheim Intergang did not have strong ties to Apokolips, Boss Moxie needed a new source of high-tech weaponry and found one in Lex Luthor, who would supply whatever Intergang required through LexCorp. Unsurprisingly, however, Luthor reneged on the deal; after a brief battle with Moxie, the victorious Luthor refused to continue as Intergang's arms supplier unless he himself were made the head of the organization (*The Adventures of Superman* #552, November 1997).

Ultimately, Boss Moxie, Noose, and Rough House were captured by Superman (*Action Comics* #758, October 1999). After being apprehended by the S.C.U., Gunn was sprung by Torcher, who had used a series of incendiary bombs to divert Superman as she and Gunn fled the police. But before they could make good their escape, Gunn was shot by S.C.U. officers and died in Ginny's arms. With her lover gone, Torcher had no incentive to go on living and committed suicide using one of her own incendiary bombs (*Superman Forever,* June 1998; *The Adventures of Superman* #562, October 1998; others).

Intergang, also reincarnated on New Earth, grew vastly in power, expanding its operations far beyond their scope on the post–First Crisis Earth, reaching into parts of the world they previously had not touched. This Intergang also developed a much stronger presence in Gotham City (*52* #48, April 4, 2007; others).

Its leader was New Earth's version of Bruno "Ugly" Mannheim, who had become an acolyte of a cult that worshipped Cain—the first killer—and treated the Seven Deadly Sins as if they were sacraments. The cult even had a sacred text, the Crime Bible, Mannheim's strict adherence to which led to such excesses as drinking blood and engaging in cannibalism (*52* #25, October 25, 2007). This Intergang, too, was armed and supported by Apokolips, which funded the horrific inventions that came out of Oolong Island.

There Mannheim underwent treatments that enlarged his body to colossal size. He claimed that technology from an unnamed alien benefactor, rather than Apokolips, was enabling Intergang to control all organized crime in Metropolis. Superman used his super-hearing to home in on the distinctive-sounding beat of Mannheim's enlarged heart and end Mannheim's threat to his city. However, Intergang has continued to expand its reach from coast to coast, crashing criminal opposition and avoiding detection by all law enforcement.

INTERLAC

An intergalactic language common among spacefaring civilizations and regularly used by Superman on his adventures throughout the cosmos. It was the official language of Earth by the thirtieth-century era of the Legion of Super-Heroes (*Adventure Comics* #379, March 1969; others).

INVASION

A term for one of the most dramatic alien attacks on Earth in the post–First Crisis universe. The emotionless, calculating alien Dominators assembled an alliance of troops from various worlds to invade Earth, ostensibly to eliminate the threat to the universe posed by meta-humans. But this was merely a cover story to conceal from the Alliance the Dominators' true objective: to harness the metagene and breed their own army of meta-humans.

The Alliance annihilated many potential opponents, including several former members of the then-disbanded Green Lantern Corps, then launched an attack on Earth, establishing a base in Australia where they began their efforts to conquer the rest of the planet. The Alliance offered to spare the human race if the world's governments would turn over their meta-humans, but the United Nations General Assembly emphatically turned them down, whereupon Superman led a counterattack against the main Alliance base.

The counterattack was temporarily disrupted by the Daxamite members of the Alliance, who became the equals of Superman in power under the Earth's yellow sun and temporarily defeated him. But they in turn were felled by the differences between Earth's atmosphere and that of their homeworld. Superman rescued the Daxamites, and in gratitude they turned on the Alliance

and helped defend Earth. Thousands of Daxamite troops entered our solar system and gained superpowers under the yellow sun. This was a major contribution to the collapse of the Alliance and led to individual surrenders by each former member (*Invasion* #1–3, January–March 1989; *The Adventures of Superman* #449–450, December 1988–January 1989; *Superman* [second series] #26–27, December 1988–January 1989; others).

IRONS, CLAY MICHAEL

See Crash.

IRONS, JOHN HENRY

See Steel.

IRONS, NATASHA JASMINE

The niece of John Henry Irons and daughter of John Henry's brother Clay, with his wife Blondel, on the post-First Crisis unified Earth. Since, like the rest of her family, Natasha knew of her uncle's double identity as Steel, it was easy to arrange for her to spend her formative years working alongside John Henry when he returned to their family home in Washington, DC. They developed a close bond, and later—after the death of the family matriarch Bess—Natasha became the only other member of the family to relocate with John Henry to Jersey City, at least openly. Natasha had little contact with her father growing up, but on one particularly dramatic occasion, the criminal Clay Irons emerged from hiding to donate blood that would save his daughter's life.

Natasha developed quite differently from her siblings, possessing a pragmatism and detachment not present in the others, particularly her brother Jemahl. Something of an overachiever, by her late teens she was working as an intern for U.S. senator Jane Weaver (*Steel* #14, April 1995; others)—though, curiously, most recent biographies omit this detail. "Nat," as she preferred to be called, was a keenly intelligent woman and possibly underestimated by her uncle in that regard, which may have contributed to some of their more dramatic later disagreements. Despite Steel's paternalistic misgivings, Natasha was drawn into the lifestyle of the superpowered. On more than one occasion, she unobtrusively helped John Henry in his heroic role. In an effort to become her uncle's partner and equal, she took the performance-enhancing drug Tar, which made humans briefly super-strong—but with addictive consequences. She subsequently underwent a complete recovery.

When the Entropy Aegis was used to trap John Henry and others on Apokolips, Natasha designed a suit of armor fueled by the power of the Aegis and assumed the persona of Steel herself. She went to Apokolips to free her uncle and the other victims, with the help of many other super heroes. Back on Earth, John Henry decided that his injuries demanded that he retire as Steel, so he designed a new, even more advanced armor for Nat to wear as the new Steel, while he became a full-time inventor and engineer.

This new armor was equipped with both projectile and energy weapons and gave Nat both super-strength and flight capability, thanks to rockets built in to her boots. The armor could also expand, growing to as high as sixty feet. Nat's primary weapon was her hammer, whose unique technology increased its force when thrown: the greater the distance, the harder it would strike. It could also generate powerful electromagnetic fields at Nat's command, and when she put it down, it couldn't be lifted by anyone except her or someone with a similar genetic makeup, like her uncle. Technology cannibalized from the Entropy Aegis allowed Nat to teleport as well as fire energy bolts from her hands.

After the Infinite Crisis, Nat and John Henry both existed on New Earth. Nat wanted to apply for membership in the Teen Titans. John Henry forbade this, but Natasha disregarded his wishes, so John Henry deactivated her armor, taking away her powers. Undaunted, she became one of many to receive "internalized" superpowers via Lex Luthor's Everyman Project. Nat's disagreements with John Henry escalated into a physical fight, after which they remained estranged from each other for some time, with her uncle's attempts to contact her continually rebuffed.

Nat's new super heroic persona was Starlight, as whom she could fly, was super-strong, and was nearly invulnerable. She derived her name from

her ability to fire blasts of cosmic energy from her fists—energy she could also deploy as a force field, either to defend herself or to trap an opponent.

John Henry was eventually able to reach Nat, and when other subjects of the Everyman Project began dying as the result of the sudden failure of their powers, he persuaded her that she had been wrong to place her trust in Luthor. She then began to function as a mole inside Luthor's organization, but was discovered and imprisoned. Eventually, it was up to Steel and the Teen Titans to rescue Natasha, but not before Luthor had removed her Everyman powers, too. But it was Nat who had the privilege of taking Luthor into custody, wearing a new "Steel" armor that John Henry had made for her. Reconciled at last, Nat and her uncle restored Steelworks. But Luthor proved unable to strip every subject of the Everyman Project of all powers; some saw their abilities morph into different ones. So it was with Nat, who developed the ability to transform herself into a cloud of gas, in which guise her uncle suggested she adopt the name Vaporlock while a member of Infinity, Inc.

When Natasha and members of her former team learned of the government's Project 7734, they were determined to understand just why the Federal authorities were planning for the death of Superman. Buried within Project 7734 was Project Breach, which was designed for brainwashing the quantum-powered Captain Atom. Irons leaked information about Project 7734 to *Daily Planet* reporter Jimmy Olsen, then buried herself within Project Breach. She went to the magical world where Captain Atom was sent, and there she led a group of rebels to free the captured hero. Just before Natasha was attacked by Major Force, who had been sent by Project 7734 to kill Captain Atom, she and her group were teleported back to Earth, where Mon-El came to their aid (*Action Comics* #882–883, December 2009–January 2010).

Using the knowledge gleaned during her months as a mole, Natasha led a force comprised of Superboy, Krypto, the Guardian, Jimmy Olsen, and Steel to a secret bunker where General Lane was hiding. After helping to end Project 7734, Natasha returned to her public life (*Superman: War of the Supermen* #4, July 2010).

J

JACKAL, THE

The Jackal, a criminal on Earth-2, owned a carnival whose attendees were frequently victimized by pickpockets and petty thieves. Superman caught wind of these misdeeds and quickly put the owner out of business (*Superman* [first series] #8, January–February 1941). There have been several other criminals operating under the name Jackal during Superman's time, including two different foes of his friend, the Batman.

A meta-human operating on Earth-2 in the wake of the Crisis on Infinite Earths, the enigmatic vigilante known only as the Jackal envisioned each assignment as an opportunity to act as judge, jury, and executioner. Animal-like in appearance, he took on assignments that usually tended to pit him against drug-dealing criminals (*Action Comics* #683, November 1992). He and Superman tangled on several occasions without the Man of Steel ever learning Jackal's origins or what motivated the vigilante to lash out against criminals.

A different Jackal was seen years before leading the terrorist group Angels of Allah, whose destructive rampage was swiftly stopped by Superman, aided by the government agency Checkmate (*Action Comics* #598, March 1988).

JACKHAMMER

Jackson Hammersmith was a minor criminal who assumed the costumed identity of Jackhammer. Armed with a powerful sonic jackhammer, he committed numerous robberies throughout Metropolis before finally being apprehended and jailed by the Man of Steel (*Action Comics* #537, November 1982). Hammersmith's brother succeeded him as Jackhammer and became part of the Demolition Team (*Green Lantern* [second series] #178, July 1984).

JAN-DEX

Hailing from the thirtieth century, Jan-Dex and his criminal companion Zo-Gar used a time machine to arrive in Superman's era. Their goal was to destroy the Man of Steel by constructing a Superman statue on Rock Island using red kryptonite. Once the Man of Steel was lured to the bizarre sight in Metropolis Bay, they intended to use both red and green kryptonite to slay him. Exposure to the crimson material temporarily imbued Superman with the ability to read minds and exhale flames, which complicated his ability to function—but he still managed to defeat the would-be alien killers. Given their orange skin and twin antennae, the criminals may have hailed from Durla, home to Chameleon Boy (*Action Comics* #283, December 1961).

JAX-UR

In the reality containing Earth-1, Jax-Ur was a Kryptonian scientist, sentenced to serve time in

the Phantom Zone for destroying the Kryptonian moon Wegthor and killing five hundred of its colonists. He was still in the limbo-like void when Krypton exploded, and the amoral criminal considered himself the most dangerous inhabitant of the Zone (*Action Comics* #284, January 1962). His invention, a nuclear-tipped rocket, was intended to annihilate a passing asteroid but instead veered off course and struck Wegthor. Had the experiment succeeded, his intent was to build a nuclear stockpile at his hidden lab located within Krypton's Jewel Mountains and take over the planet. Jax-Ur also claimed to be the first person imprisoned in the Phantom Zone, although there was no historic proof for this (*Action Comics* #310, March 1964).

In a later retelling of the tale, Jax-Ur's rocket was said to have struck a ship built and piloted by fellow scientist Jor-El. It was Jor-El's ship that crashed on Wegthor, which led Krypton's government to ban rocket-ship construction and travel, a decision that

would later prove deadly when their world faced extinction (*The World of Krypton* #1, July 1979).

Jax-Ur eventually escaped from the Phantom Zone, and he first encountered Jor-El's son Superboy (*Adventure Comics* #289, October 1961) on Earth-2. He impersonated the teen's adoptive father Jonathan Kent, but his ruse was discovered and Jax-Ur was returned to the Phantom Zone. Over the next several years, he was among the most active criminals to attempt to gain freedom without success. When Superman added wax statues of his friends and foes to the Fortress of Solitude, Jax-Ur was among those represented (*Action Comics* #292, November 1962).

After the events known as Infinite Crisis, Jax-Ur was released from the Phantom Zone by General Zod (*Action Comics* #846, May 2007) when the dictator took over Earth and imprisoned its heroes. He was eventually stopped and returned to the Phantom Zone, as usual, by the Man of Steel. Later, when the Phantom Zone was eliminated, Jax-Ur was tasked by Zod to be one of his sleeper agents on Earth (*Action Comics* #875, May 2009).

His guise was that of Canadian Dr. Pillings, working for a branch of S.T.A.R. Labs with a fictionalized reputation as one of the world's leading xenobiologists. He was called on to consult on Christopher Kent's bizarre spurts of rapid aging. Jax-Ur developed a device to help modify the youth's rapid aging, but he also stole DNA from Kent's partner, Thara Ak-Var, to re-create a version of the Kryptonian god Rao. Jax-Ur then used a shard of the Phantom Zone to send Christopher into the realm, where he finally evolved into an aspect of the Kryptonian entity Nightwing (*Action Comics* #887, May 2010). The final aspect of the Kryptonian trinity, Vohc, possessed Jax-Ur at this point, watching in delight as the false Rao caused havoc across Earth. Flamebird attempted to stop Rao and free Nightwing, aided by Wonder Woman, Alan Scott, Mr. Terrific, the Jay Garrick Flash, and Dr. Fate. Vohc and Jax-Ur fought to control Rao. Jax-Ur was eventually separated from Vohc, which resulted in the cruel Kryptonian's death (*Action Comics* #888–889, Early–Late June 2010).

JENA

The princess of distant world Adoria, blonde beauty Jena decided that the submissive men of her planet were too easy a challenge for her. Turning her attention to Earth, she threatened to destroy it with a "destructo-ray" if Superman did not abandon his adopted home and marry her. He reluctantly went through with the wedding, presided over by the king and queen, then portrayed himself as a super-boor, causing the disinterested princess to annul the marriage. With Earth's safety guaranteed, Superman happily returned home (*Action Comics* #266, July 1960).

JENKINS

An adept and wealthy inventor who used his fortunes to build a "sky vessel" to the stars and lured eight members of Elkhart University's Pi Theta Dau fraternity aboard. The bitter inventor then explained to the men that he was going to murder them for allowing his brother to die during a hazing incident while rushing during his freshman year. Four of the men were killed before Superman intervened, saved the others, then apprehended Jenkins and took him to prison (*World's Finest Comics* #7, Fall 1942).

JENSEN, RAYMOND MAXWELL

The low-life criminal who became the Parasite on Earth-1 and often fought Superman.

JEVIK

An alien creature that once caused trouble for Superman (see Amalak).

JEWEL MOUNTAINS

Among the beautiful sights known throughout the galaxy, few matched the glittering Jewel Mountains on Krypton (*Superman* [first series] #141, November 1960). Discovered by Bor-Ak (*Superman* [first series] #164, October 1963), a Kryptonian explorer, the jewels were soon found to be living crystalline forms, the remnants of ancient Crystal Birds that crowded Krypton's skies long ago. Zoologists theorized that the birds were drawn to this region to die, and their decomposing forms led to the formation, over the millennia, of the captivating mountain range (*Action Comics* #310, March 1964).

Through the years, stories and superstitions about the mountains grew, such as the belief that bad luck would befall a bride who wore jewels carved from the mountains' crystals on her wedding day.

TOGETHER, THE HAPPY COUPLE ROAMS AMIDST SUCH KRYPTONIAN MARVELS AS THE JEWEL MOUNTAINS, LOST IN THE MAGIC OF EACH PRECIOUS MOMENT THEY SHARE...

On Earth-1, Superman first visited the legendary mountain range during his brief romance with Lyla Lerrol (*Superman* [first series] #141, November 1960).

Through the manipulations of Jax-Ur, a chunk of the Jewel Mountains survived Krypton's explosion as jewel kryptonite, becoming a psychic transmitter of sorts. Jewel kryptonite also existed in the reality that came into being following the Crisis on Infinite Earths (*Silver Age: Justice League of America* #1, July 2000).

JOHNS

A professor who developed a revolutionary "power formula" was attacked by criminals who wanted it for their own use. Before lapsing into a coma, he whispered the formula to *Daily Planet* reporter Clark Kent. Superman then apprehended the criminals and, following the scientist's wishes, turned the formula over to the federal government. Whatever became of it was never revealed (*Superman* [first series] #60, September–October 1949).

JOHNSON, BARBARA

An extremely religious woman, Barbara Johnson viewed Superman as a literal Heaven-sent angel. As a result, she repeatedly placed herself in mortal danger in the misguided belief that she would be rescued by Superman as a sign of God's love (*Superman* #659, February 2007). The Man of Steel first saved her from a drunken teen driver; when she later saw on the news that a Chicago train was in danger, she prayed for Superman's intervention—and sure enough, he arrived in the nick of time. This spurred her to find and confront criminals herself, certain that she would always be saved. Unfortunately, she hunted down the Bay Lords in Hob's Bay when Superman was preoccupied with an energy being from the stars that was stranded in Antarctica, and was unable to save Barbara from being shot. He did, however, hear

her prayers, and rushed to the hospital once his mission was complete. She absolved Superman of guilt, as she had managed to stop the gang from committing any further crimes. Freed from her over-reliance on the Man of Steel, she went on to create community-based programs to help those in need like herself.

JOHNSON, WALLY; AKA WALLY THE GOD-CHILD

A youth who followed Linda Danvers around Leesburg, Virginia. He was revealed to possess amazing powers.

JOKER, THE

The Joker was the white-skinned, green-haired maniac who plagued Batman in almost every reality recorded. Their epic matches caused untold collateral damage, and neither could seem to exist without the other (*Batman* #1, Spring 1940).

A mass murderer, the Joker used his specially designed venom to kill his victims, leaving their faces with a smiling rictus. On a few early occasions, the criminal was seemingly killed; each time he returned to trouble the Caped Crusader days or months later.

The Joker teamed with Lex Luthor to stop the World's Finest pairing of Superman and Batman on several occasions, but the two villains always failed to top the heroes (*World's Finest Comics* #88, May–June 1957).

There were, surprisingly, two instances that required Superman to actually form a tenuous alliance with the Joker, once in order to rescue a kidnapped Perry White from the Prankster (*DC Comics Presents* #41, January 1982), and later when the villain's insanity proved uniquely suited to helping the Man of Steel navigate a realm of madness that threatened to spill onto Earth (*DC Comics Presents* #72, August 1984).

In the wake of the Crisis on Infinite Earths, the Harlequin of Hate's origins became somewhat cloudy. It was thought the Joker might have been a chemical engineer turned failed comedian who got roped into committing a robbery as the Red Hood in order to earn money to care for his pregnant wife; a freak lightning strike killed his wife, and a despondent Red Hood was forced into going ahead with the crime the same day. In this version of events, Batman was not present when the Joker fell into a vat at the Ace Chemical Processing Plant, eventually swimming through a pipe and emerging in the polluted river, disfigured (*Batman: The Killing Joke,* 1988).

The Joker and Man of Steel first tangled one-on-one when he threatened to destroy Metropolis with a thermonuclear bomb. He kidnapped Lois Lane, Jimmy Olsen, and Perry White, but Superman saved them before destroying the Joker's weapon (*Superman* [second series] #9, September 1987).

After killing the second Robin, the Joker avoided arrest by convincing the Iranian government to name him ambassador to the United Nations as part of his latest insane plot to wreak chaos for Earth's heroes. The UN president summoned the Man of Steel to watch over the proceedings, which Superman did while in disguise. At first he stopped a grief-stricken Dark Knight from exacting revenge against the Joker, but then he realized what the villain was planning. He used his super-breath to prevent the Joker's deadly poison from killing everyone in the General Assembly (*Batman: A Death in the Family,* 1989).

Years later, Turleytoys owner Anson Turley made the mistake of launching a line of dolls and action figures based on the Clown Prince of Crime. When they were introduced at the Metropolis Toy Fair, news reached the Joker, who was anything but amused. The madman kidnapped Turley, then tried to derail the Mile-O-Mirth Parade that was planned for the toy launch. The Man of Steel successfully thwarted the plot, but not before a Joker doll was delivered to Daily Planet journalist Lois Lane (*Action Comics* #714, October 1995). The doll was laced with a lethal toxin that poisoned Superman's wife upon contact. While she lay in critical condition, Superman sought Batman's aid in interrogating the Joker at Arkham Asylum. In a turnabout, the Caped Crusader stopped the Man

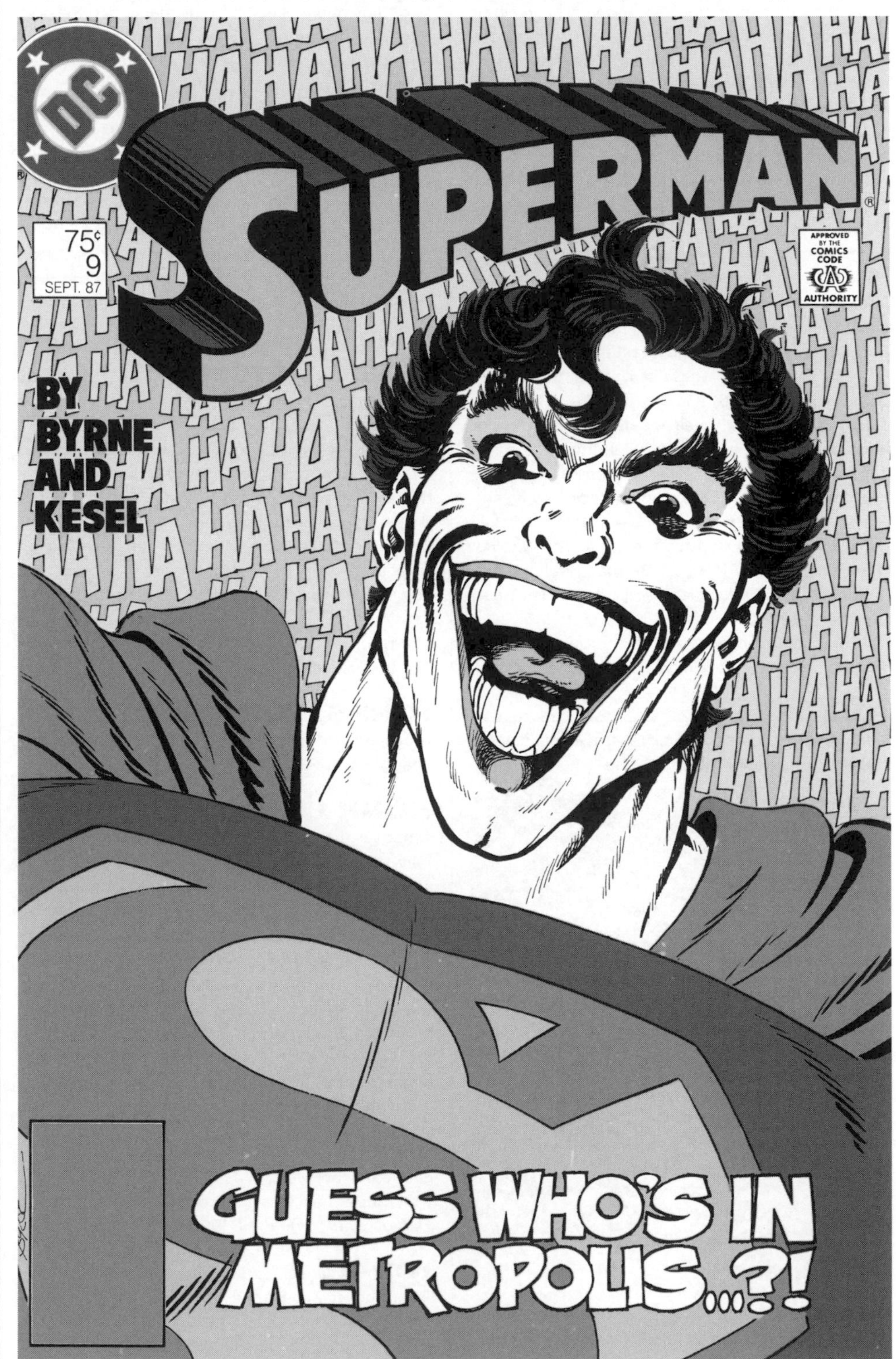

of Steel from killing the villain, which was the plan all along, since the toxin was never designed to actually kill Lois Lane. It would have been the ultimate joke on Superman, who'd sworn never to kill anyone (*Action Comics* #719, March 1996).

Upon escaping from Arkham, the Joker managed to steal 99 percent of the magical powers from the Fifth Dimension's Mr. Mxyzptlk (*Superman: Emperor Joker* #1, October 2000). Earth suffered greatly at the Joker's maniacal hands, although despite the powers he possessed, he could not bring himself to eliminate Batman. Indeed, he realized that he always needed Batman around to oppose him and keep things interesting (*Superman* [second series] #160, September 2000; *Action Comics* #770, October 2000; others).

While never a team player, the Joker occasionally allied himself with various bands of criminals, including the Injustice Gang (*JLA* #9–10, September–October 1997). However, when he learned that the Lex Luthor from another world had formed a Secret Society of Super-Villains to oppose Earth's heroes, he grew angry that he was not invited to join. Once the calamitous events of Infinite Crisis came to an end, he and his world's Luthor tracked down the mastermind and shot him to death in a rare case of bad humor (*Infinite Crisis* #7, June 2006).

Throughout the myriad parallel realities that have been recorded, for every Batman there has almost always been a Joker. On one such world, the Joker obtained Kryptonian technology and used it to kill Robin and Batgirl in front of Batman, who finally killed his foe (*JLA: The Nail* #3, November 1998). After that Batman died, the two continued their struggles as spirits in Hell (*JLA: Another Nail*, 2004).

(For a detailed account of the Joker, consult *The Essential Batman Encyclopedia*, 2008.)

JOLT

An acrobatic female cyborg with a mechanical eye and an exterior skeleton. She brandished a whip and worked for Cerberus alongside the powerful Blockhouse (*Superman: The Man of Steel* #7, January 1992; others).

JONES, ANDY/ANDREA

A friend of Linda Danvers in Leesburg who was also the Comet in human form.

JONES, CATAWAMPUS

The small mining town of Saddle Fork was once besieged by ghost-like phantoms that raided the gold dug up by its various mining camps. The townsfolk temporarily deputized visiting reporter Clark Kent in order to help them stop the robberies. Kent and his alter ego Superman discovered that the phantoms were actually the Rockdust Bandits, a group led by petty thief Catawampus Jones, who covered themselves in rock dust in order to appear ghostly and menacing. They had been stealing the mined gold and shipping it out for sale until the Man of Steel put an end to their dishonest dealings. Jones, a Saddle Fork resident, was exposed as the ringleader and sent to prison (*World's Finest Comics* #30, September–October 1947).

JONES, PRIVATE

Stationed at Camp Metropolis, army private Jones was wearing an experimental helmet radio when it was struck by lightning. The two somehow combined to temporarily grant him powers and abilities similar to Superman's. While Jones did not do anything special with his newfound skills, Superman did use the accident to convince foreign spies that he now had the ability to transfer his powers to others in an effort to keep them from causing trouble. Jones's abilities wore off; he happily returned to duty and was promoted to sergeant (*Superman* [first series] #122, July 1958).

JONES, RUDY

A civilian who became the second version of the deadly Parasite.

J'ONN J'ONZZ

A native of the planet Mars, J'Onzz was accidentally transported to Earth by scientist Mark Erdel and remained on the planet to fight crime as the hero known as the Martian Manhunter (*Detective Comics* #225, November 1955). He eventually worked alongside Superman in the Justice League of America. In the continuity that arose following the Crisis on Infinite Earths, J'Onn had been aware of young Clark Kent's Kryptonian origins since Kal-El's arrival on Earth and secretly shadowed him in a variety of guises as Clark grew into adulthood before formally introducing himself to the young Superman (*Martian Manhunter* [second series] #20, July 2000; a somewhat different account of the Martian Manhunter's first meeting with Superman was recorded in *Superman: The Man of Steel Annual* #4, 1995).

JOR-EL

The father of Kal-El, the infant who grew up to become Superman, Jor-El hailed from a celebrated line of great Kryptonian scientists and leaders. His influence and legacy extended from Superman to the very history of the doomed planet Krypton.

In the Earth-2 continuity, he was known as Jor-L, and with his wife Lora he had a son named Kal-L. When Krypton was on the very brink of destruction, he used a rocket of his own design—a scale model of one he envisioned mass-producing to save the planet's entire population—and sent the infant boy into space mere moments before Krypton exploded. (*Action Comics* #1, June 1938. The names of Jor-L, Lora, and Kal-L were originally used only in the *Superman* newspaper comic strip and were affirmed as the names of their Earth-2 counterparts in *Showcase* #97, February 1978. All references to Jor-El herein—as his name was rendered since *Superman* [first series] #53, July–August 1948—reflect the stories as published rather than the retroactive change.)

The Earth-2 Superman first learned of Jor-El and Lara's existence while trying to discover the origins of a mysterious green rock he'd later come to know as kryptonite. Traveling through time to trace the path of the mysterious meteorite, the Earth-2 Superman came to know of Jor-El and Lara and the fact that he was their son (*Superman* [first series] #53, July–August 1948). On Earth-1, the teenage Superboy retained dim memories of his Kryptonian origins, which he augmented by using the Mind-Prober Ray (*Superboy* [first series] #79, March 1960).

Jor-El's vessel was outfitted with a special jewel that focused energy to destroy the iron composing most meteors and asteroids so that no harm could come to baby Kal-El (*Action Comics* #172, September 1952). He also added pods of condensed food to help the infant thrive on Earth until Kal-El could adapt to his new world, but the pods detached from the ship and were discovered years later by Roger Bliss and his wife (*Action Comics* #217, June 1956).

In addition to the infant, Jor-El placed his last will and testament within the ship, the document containing the plans to his three greatest devices: a "dimension-traveler," a "missile-projector," and a "nuclear fission tester." The thin sheet of metal was

"70 BELYUTH-- WHEN KEN-DAL AND GENERAL ZOD SAW MY DEMONSTRATION, ESPECIALLY THE BELT I USED TO FLY MYSELF.."
FINE, JOR-EL! YOU HAVE PERMISSION TO CONTINUE WITH YOUR PROJECT!
IT'S THE MOST IMPORTANT BREAK-THROUGH YET!

buried deep in the ground when the ship crashed into a field in SMALLVILLE and was discovered years later by the Man of Steel (*World's Finest* #69, March–April 1954). Jor-El also included "thought-projection discs" in the ship, which provided video recordings of the courtship of Jor-El and Lara, but these, too, had been separated from the ship and were found in orbit years later by a U.S. experimental rocket. They were retrieved and viewed by the ever-curious LOIS LANE (*Action Comics* #149, October 1950).

Jor-El sought to preserve his legacy by storing many of his greatest inventions in a vault that he hoped could survive Krypton's explosion. The chunk of rock containing the vault managed to follow the rocket's wake to Earth and was found years later by LEX LUTHOR, who used Jor-El's inventions against his own son (*Superman* [first series] #74, January–February 1952). Similarly, Jor-El tried to help end the war on Krypton by rocketing outlawed war weapons into space (*Action Comics* #216, May 1956).

Jor-El's journal and his laboratory miraculously survived Krypton's destruction and were floating in space until they were eventually stumbled upon by Superman. As he explored the lab in awe, the Man of Steel found videos that showed how Jor-El had scrupulously studied Earth, experimenting with the planet's gravity and how it would affect Kal-El. To Superman's surprise, there was also footage of his heroic father defeating two criminal scientists, Val-Arn and KHAI-ZOR, who wanted to profit from Jor-El's experiments (*Action Comics* #223, December 1956).

In the Earth-1 universe, Jor-El's pleas to rescue Krypton's populace fell on deaf ears, as the planet was focused on the celebration of its ten thousandth year of civilization (*Action Comics* #223, December 1956). His discovery that the planet's URANIUM core had been building "a cycle of chain-reactions" and would lead to Krypton exploding like a planet-sized atomic bomb was so preposterous, few gave it credence, despite Jor-El's impeccable reputation as a scientist and leader. He begged his wife Lara to accompany their child on his journey to Earth, but she chose instead to stay by her husband's side and watched as Krypton's last hope began his unprecedented journey. Although Jor-El was Krypton's foremost scientist, he was ignored by the ruling Science Council, thereby dooming their race.

Jor-El had been developing the theory supporting Krypton's eventual destruction for quite some time (*Action Comics* #158, July 1951) and had this theory confirmed through a chance meeting with QUEEN LATORA, a visitor from the planet Vergo (*Superman* [first series] #113, May 1957). She had come to Krypton intending to use her world's technology to pluck the doomed planet from its orbit, then let Krypton reignite her solar system's dying sun. She chose Krypton knowing it was due to explode soon. Relieved that his theories were correct, Jor-El did convince the woman to let him try to save his people, temporarily sparing his homeworld.

"AS YOU WORKED FEVERISHLY FOR MONTHS, TOMAR-RE, TO DELAY THE CATACLYSM... LIFE WENT ON. JOR-EL AND LARA'S SON WAS BORN..."
THE SURNAME EL, IN ANCIENT KRYPTONESE, MEANT CHILD... AND KAL MEANT STAR!
A STAR-CHILD... BORN ON A DOOMED WORLD! KAL-EL SHALL HAVE HIS FUTURE, LARA!

After the Science Council and the general public's dismissal, the only two Kryptonians, other than Lara, who believed him were Jor-El's brother ZOR-EL (*Superman* [first series] #146, July 1961) and the scientist SHIR KAN (*Action Comics* #218, July 1956).

Prior to the Council's rejection of his disaster theory, Jor-El's distinguished career included numerous inventions, among them the hovercar dubbed the "Jor-El" (*Superman* [first series] #134, January 1960); the critical and revolutionary discovery of the PHANTOM ZONE (*Superboy* [first series] #104, April 1963); and several pioneering contributions to rocket technology. Jor-El hailed from a long line of distinguished figures known as the HOUSE OF EL, which included VAL-EL, a famous explorer; SUL-EL, the inventor of Krypton's first telescope; TALA-EL, the author of Krypton's first planetary constitution; Hatu-El, the inventor of Krypton's first electromagnet and electric motor; and GAM-EL, the father of modern Kryptonian architecture (*Adventure Comics* #313, October 1963).

The family name was born millennia in the past when the warrior king EROK (*Superman's Pal, Jimmy Olsen* #121, July 1969) took the surname El (star) because the stars had always shone in his favor. Erok-El's son was christened Kal-El (star-child). ERKOL, the oldest city on Krypton, had originally been known as Erok-El in honor of its first ruler (*Krypton Chronicles* #3, November 1981).

Sul-El was the first member of the distinguished family to locate Earth (*Adventure Comics* #313, October 1963), while the ill-fated Var-El (Jor-El's uncle) accidentally teleported himself to Earth in the nineteenth century and lived there in seclusion even as his family on Krypton believed him dead (*DC Comics Presents* #37, September 1981). When Jor-El was just an infant, his father, Jor-El I, managed to visit Earth in an experimental spacecraft, foreshadowing his son's greatest achievement (*Superman* [first series] #103, February 1956). The plans for Jor-El's rocket technology were seemingly lost in the intervening years, but appeared to subconsciously inform the younger Jor-El's work. They may also have led the scientist to study Earth until it grew to become his favorite planet, and the natural place to send his infant son (*Superman* [first series] #141, November 1960).

Amazed with this monumental discovery, Jor-El began trying to find a way to bring the Kryptonians to Earth, but when it became clear they couldn't build the rockets fast enough to do so, he tried another method—a radio transmitter that could transport people instantaneously across the stars. Sadly, that plan also proved unsuccessful (*Superman* [first series] #77, July–August 1952). In the days prior to Krypton's destruction, as her people celebrated their ten-thousand-year anniversary, a computer analyst released a report confirming Jor-El's prediction, as well as the fact that the planet would explode before a complete evacuation could be conducted (*Action Comics* #314, July 1964).

Jor-El's higher education was impressive, and

WHAT DO YOU MEAN? IF KRYPTON IS DOOMED AS YOU SAY, OUR CHILD IS DOOMED ALSO.
NO, LARA. NO.
SEALED WITHIN THE MATRIX ORB, HE HAS BEEN SHIELDED FROM THE POISONOUS RADIATION. TRUE, THE ORB COULD NOT SURVIVE THE EXPLOSION OF OUR PLANET...
...BUT IT IS RESILIENT ENOUGH TO SURVIVE A JOURNEY THROUGH HYPER-SPACE!

he associated with a select circle of peers, most of whom would go on to benefit Krypton in a variety of substantial ways. Among them was his roommate Kimda, who went on to become a professor and lived in Kandor when it was stolen by Brainiac. Jor-El befriended Kimda's son, years later, and the two grew close (*Action Comics* #242, July 1958). Ral-En was a fellow scientist who became warped by dictatorial ambitions fostered and encouraged by his mercenary father Mag-En (*Superman* [first series] #154, July 1962). There were also Nor-Kan (*Superman* [first series] #158, January 1963) and Lon-Es, who worked as Jor-El's lab assistants (*Superman* [first series] #154, July 1962).

Jor-El and his twin brother Nim-El were the eldest of three brothers, sired by Jor-El I and Nimda An-Dor. Nim-El was a climatologist who lived in Kandor (*Adventure Comics* #304, January 1963). Their younger brother Zor-El, who lived in Argo City, was also a scientist who went on to discover the Survival Zone (*Action Comics* #252, May 1959). His daughter Kara arrived on Earth years after her cousin and grew up to become the super heroine Supergirl. As Jor-El reached adulthood, he met Lara, the astronaut daughter of Lor-Van, and the two fell in love, married, and had one son, Kal-El (*Superman* [first series] #233, January 1971; *Superman* [first series] #246, December 1971; *The World of Krypton* #2, August 1979).

Jor-El's distinguished career saw him awarded the Science Prize, a statuette molded from rare Illium metal (*Superman* [first series] #173, November 1964), and an honorary medal from the Kryptonian Science Society (*Action Comics* #182, July 1953).

After Lon-Es moved to a different assignment, Jor-El used Lara as his lab assistant for a brief time prior to the birth of their son (*Superman* [first series] #170, July 1964). Part of Lara's attraction to Jor-El was due to not only his brilliance, but also his concern over the welfare of his fellow citizens. It was his disapproval of capital punishment that led to the notion of sending criminals into space in satellites (*Superman* [first series] #65, July–August 1950). His discovery of the Phantom Zone quickly led to its becoming the humanitarian way to mete out justice, thereby putting an end to the space satellite program (*Adventure Comics* #283, April 1961; *Superboy* [first series] #104, April 1963).

When the Council refused to resume its space program to save Krypton, Jor-El retreated to his lab, where he continued work on his own. He constructed several experimental craft, launching each in secret. One contained the family dog Krypto, who was lost in space for many years before arriving on Earth and finding his master's son in Smallville (*Adventure Comics* #210, March 1955). Jor-El managed to construct one larger craft before the planet's doom was sealed.

After the universe was reordered by the Crisis on Infinite Earths, Jor-El remained one of Krypton's greatest scientists, raised under the withering rule of his father Seyg-El. His studies led him to invent devices that enabled him to glimpse life on other worlds, including Earth. When something dubbed the Green Death began killing his fellow Kryptonians, Jor-El's studies led him to the conclusion that the planet's core was unstable, and the radiation leaking to the planet's surface was causing the deaths. He also realized that the planet would soon explode. The pressure building beneath the planet's crust led to elements being transformed into a radioactive metal that was potentially lethal. This "kryptonium" was increasing in volume and would crack Krypton's mantle, obliterating the planet. Jor-El prepared for such an emergency by taking his son from his gestation chamber and placing the matrix in a spacecraft he had specially built.

Jor-El had first learned of Earth from the time-tossed Jack Knight and Mikaal Tomas, two of the men who would become known as Starman (*Starman* [second series] #51, March 1999). Having later studied life on Earth in great detail, Jor-El concluded that his own people had grown as cold as the crystalline surface of Krypton, and that their way of life was devoid of all pleasure. That Jor-El had strong feelings of love for Lara was considered aberrant by his peers, and Jor-El wanted Kal-El to have a better life. He convinced Lara that Earth would be the ideal haven for their son given that the system's yellow sun would imbue Kal-El with energy to make him faster and stronger than the native Earthlings who would raise him. Lara reluctantly agreed, and they watched Kal-El's matrix, aided by a sophisticated warp engine, speed away from Krypton as the world collapsed around them (*Man of Steel* #1, July 1986).

Years later, Kal-El, now living as both Clark Kent and Superman, encountered a second Kryptonian rocket, this one containing a green isobar. He examined this with his friend Professor Emil Hamilton, and they found a way to transmit the isobar's programming directly into the Man of Steel's mind. There he "met" his father Jor-El (*Superman* [second series] #166, March 2001). The scientist revealed that he had lied about the cold nature of his homeworld and instead wanted to show his son the true Krypton. In this new version of reality, Superman witnessed Krypton's destruction due to a change in the planet's orbit, which brought it closer to its red sun and caused gravitational variances that cracked the world apart. The Kryptonian Council had disagreed with Jor-El's theories and disregarded any threat. The devious General Zod, head of the planet's military, saw this as an opportunity for a coup, but Zod could not apprehend Jor-El before Kal-El was rocketed to Earth.

As Superman absorbed this story, Hamilton and John Henry Irons (see Steel) detected signals emanating from within the Phantom Zone. The two men crafted a device that allowed the Man of Steel and his wife Lois Lane to enter the Zone, where they found themselves in the city of Kryptonopolis. There they meet Jor-El, Lara, and their pet dog Krypto. Father and son found a way to save Krypton from imminent destruction, but exposure to the red solar radiation of Krypton's sun sapped Superman's powers from him. When the powerless Superman and Lois attempted to return

home, Lara had to pilot a ship—in direct violation of strict Imperial Council regulation—to rescue her son. General Zod then sent devices called Eradicators after the ship, but Superman managed to destroy them, an act making him and Lois fugitives. In the end, Zod was stopped and Jor-El told his son he knew the truth about his identity. He then built a device to send Kal-El and Lois back to Earth, and the Man of Steel, absorbing fresh solar radiation to replenish his powers, was left to determine if what he had just experienced was real or a fabrication caused by the strange Kryptonian isobar.

As time shifted in a harbinger of the impending Infinite Crisis, history was temporarily altered in such a way that the life of Jor-El more closely resembled that of his Earth-1 counterpart. A key change was the larger role Lara played in the development of the spacecraft that sent their son to Earth. Another alteration was that Jor-El discovered Earth mere moments before the small ship had to launch, thereby making Kal-El's new home an educated guess. As an adult, Kal-El did not get to see his parents for the first time until he used Lex Luthor's experimental time-space communicator. As a result, in the moments before their death, Jor-El and Lara were reassured that they had made the right decision in choosing Earth, and that their son had successfully grown to adulthood—and his destiny (*Superman: Birthright*, #12, September 2004).

Further alterations to reality changed the events of Krypton's history so that the ruling Council threatened to exile Jor-El in his own Phantom Zone if he went public with his concerns and theories about the planet's stability. In this new reality, the brilliant Non was a friend and fellow scientist who believed Jor-El's foolproof data about Krypton's impending destruction. It was Non who chose to go public with this data, and he was abducted and cruelly lobotomized by the Council, eventually exiled to the Phantom Zone. General Zod and his lieutenant Ursa confronted Jor-El and suggested he band with them to overthrow the Council, ostensibly to save the planet, but Zod really wished to rule Krypton himself. The scientist refused and was then forced by the Council to send Zod and Ursa to the Phantom Zone. As he dematerialized, Zod cried out his revenge: "No matter that it takes me an eternity, you *will* bow down before me, Jor-El; I swear it! First you, and then one day, *your heirs*!" A stunned Jor-El could only hope Zod's dark prediction would never come to pass (*Action Comics Annual* #10, 2007).

Prior to sending Kal-El into space, Jor-El took the time to prepare an artificial intelligence interface that resembled himself, so that Kal-El could know his father's kind visage while being taught all about Krypton's history and Jor-El and Lara's legacy. The crystals accompanied Kal-El's spacecraft to Earth and now reside in Superman's Arctic Fortress of Solitude where they—and Jor-El—are often consulted, with the artificial Jor-El reminding his son that he should honor his Kryptonian heritage while living among humans. That point was made clear when General Zod attempted to make good on his revenge oath when he and Ursa escaped from the Phantom Zone. The criminals used their son Lor-Zod, who had been taken in and shown love by Clark Kent and Lois Lane, as bait, and the ploy distracted Superman long enough to let Zod make his first strike, but the Man of Steel rallied so that Zod could not have revenge on Jor-El through his son or those he loved (*Action Comics* #844–847 and #851, December 2006–March 2007, July 2007; *Action Comics Annual* #11, 2008).

JUNDY

Jundy sought power but lacked a means of obtaining it until he had the misfortune to find an ancient manuscript with directions to the three pieces making up the legendary Sorcerer's King Scepter. The shifty Jundy thought he could easily obtain this using the manuscript and become master of the world. He managed to subdue and capture the Dynamic Duo and blackmail Superman into helping him obtain the artifact. After the fabled object was assembled, the scepter was also quickly destroyed by the trio of heroes; Jundy was apprehended and jailed by the World's Finest team (*World's Finest Comics* #125, May 1962).

JURIS

An electrical engineer and owner of Juris Electronics, Juris schemed to dupe *Daily Planet* editor Perry White into handing over a sample of red kryptonite, which Juris intended to sell to the underworld for thousands of dollars. He impersonated the Man

of Steel to gain White's trust and destroyed a fire hydrant to prove his super-strength to the *Planet*'s editor. Superman arrived in time to stop Juris and had the greedy man arrested for destruction of public property (*Superman* [first series] #143, February 1961).

JUSTICE LEAGUE OF AMERICA, THE

On Earth-1, the arrival of rival aliens engaged in combat led seven of the planet's super heroes—Superman, Batman, Wonder Woman, the Flash, Green Lantern, Martian Manhunter, and Aquaman—to band together as a team for the first time. After the threat was ably handled, the heroes agreed that remaining united made sense—and so the Justice League of America was born (*The Brave and the Bold* [first series] #28, February–March 1960; origin revealed in *Justice League of America* [first series] #9, February 1962).

Through the years, the JLA battled threats domestic, international, intergalactic, and interdimensional. Its roster rose and fell and went through several incarnations, but whenever Earth needed its champions, the JLA was always on call. Shortly after its founding, the group discovered a vibrational frequency that led members to Earth-2 and its heroes, the Justice Society of America. For years thereafter, the two teams would meet for social gatherings and band together to battle many cosmic threats.

After the Joker tricked the Justice League's mascot Lucas "Snapper" Carr into revealing the team's secret base of operations (*Justice League of America* [first series] #77, December 1969), the team relocated to a satellite orbiting 22,300 miles above the Earth (*Justice League of America* [first series] #78, February 1970). However, Superman left the League after its radical restructuring in order to focus on a series of threats plaguing Metropolis (*Justice League of America* [first series] #239, June 1985).

In the wake of the Crisis on Infinite Earths, the multiverse was reduced to one positive-matter universe, and the JSA became the symbol of the first age of heroes, during the World War II era, while the JLA were champions of the modern age of heroism years after. The JLA roster after the Crisis proved more volatile and fluctuated for many years.

In this iteration, Superman declined an invitation to join the JLA, believing himself to already be overextended, although he did promise to help the team whenever a situation called for his aid (*Action Comics* #650, February 1990). The Man of Steel subsequently fought alongside the team during an invasion from the planet Appellax (*JLA: Year One* #11–12, November–December 1998) and briefly agreed to serve as a full member, stepping back to reservist status following the team's defeat of Gorilla Grodd (*JLA: Incarnations* #2, August 2001). Nonetheless, Superman behaved as a full member in everything but name as the years passed, participating in scores of JLA adventures. In the reality that formed following the Infinite Crisis, Superman was once again regarded as a founding member of the Justice League (*Justice League of America* [second series] #0, September 2006).

A few years after the Apellaxian invasion, the League had undergone several dissolutions and re-formations, and Superman stepped up to lead the Justice League of America in a new direction (*Justice League Spectacular* #1, March–April 1992). His seeming death at the hands of Doomsday brutally ended his service with that particular iteration (*Superman* [second series] #75, January 1993). Upon the Man of Steel's return, circumstances eventually drew him together once more with the other most prominent meta-humans on Earth, and they resolved to revive the by-then-disbanded Justice League (*Justice League: A Midsummer's Nightmare* #3, November 1996). After

a devastating war with Despero and the Secret Society of Super-Villains, the League shrank drastically in number and Superman left once more, though he promised to return when the time was right (*JLA* #119, Late November 2005). Alongside original members Batman and Wonder Woman, he helped revive the team a year later, and he continued to be a benevolent and guiding spirit (*Justice League of America* [second series] #1–7, October 2006–May 2007).

JUSTICE LEGION A

In the 853rd century, the heroic legacies of the 20th century endured, with heroes watching over planets in the solar system and banding together as Justice Legion A whenever a cosmic need arose.

The JLA's Superman was a direct descendant of Kal-El and watched over Earth from his orbiting Fortress of Solitude. He was frequently opposed in his deeds by the villainous Superwoman.

A younger generation of protectors, known as Justice Legion B, remained in constant training, poised to come to the solar system's need whenever the situation called for their help (*DC One Million* #1, November 1998).

JUSTICE SOCIETY OF AMERICA, THE

On Earth-2, in the days prior to World War II, a number of "mystery men" with powers and abilities far beyond those of mere mortals began to fight crime across America.

On November 9, 1940, British intelligence asked Earth-2's Flash and Green Lantern to investigate rumors of a possible German invasion. The heroes wound up captured and sent to Adolf Hitler, who intended to kill them using the mystic Spear of Destiny he had obtained during his rise to power. The two heroes were rescued by Doctor Fate and Hourman in the nick of time, and the escape prompted President Franklin Roosevelt to suggest that the heroes band together for at least the war's duration. Accepting the challenge, the Justice Society of America was formed, and both Superman and Batman were given honorary memberships (*All Star Comics* #3, Winter 1940; origin revealed in *DC Special* #29, August–September 1977).

The Justice Society of America

In the wake of America's introduction into World War II, President Roosevelt beseeched all of America's costumed crime fighters to help defend the country's shores as the All-Star Squadron (*All-Star Squadron* #1–3, September–November 1981). The JSA, whose members served jointly in their own team as well as the more encompassing All-Stars, was renamed the Justice Battalion of America for the duration of the war (*All Star Comics* #11, June–July 1942). A frequent participant in All-Star Squadron adventures, Superman was a comparative nonpresence with the 1940s JSA save for a case in which he subbed for an ailing Johnny Thunder (*All Star Comics* #36, August–September 1947).

By the early 1950s, Communist paranoia gripped the country, and the remaining members of the JSA chose to disband rather than reveal their identities to Congress's Joint Un-American Activities Committee. By this point, only Superman, Batman, and Wonder Woman still engendered the necessary clout and respect to remain active as super heroes without government interference (*Adventure Comics* #466, December 1979).

The various members of the JSA were brought back into action by later circumstances, including the discovery of Earth-1, a parallel world vibrating on a different frequency whose heroes had appeared on Earth much later in time than Earth-2's. Their frequent meetings encouraged most of the JSA to come out of retirement and bring their Gotham City brownstone headquarters back to life. When the call came, *Daily Star* editor in chief Clark Kent changed once more into his colorful red-and-blue costume and Superman was again spotted flying through the skies (*All Star Comics* #64, January–February 1977).

When the parallel worlds were merged into one new Earth during the Crisis on Infinite Earths, JSA members assumed their role as leaders of the first age of super heroes and mentors to all the groups of heroes that followed. Superman was not a member of this version of the JSA, however.

After the events known as Infinite Crisis, fifty-two parallel worlds once more existed, with the JSA operating on New Earth and Earth-2 concurrently.

KAIMS, "HATCHET"

The man nicknamed Hatchet was a METROPOLIS-based gangster who accepted an offer of fifty thousand dollars from the city's underworld leaders to discover and expose Superman's secret identity. Kaims had come to believe that Superman resided in CLARK KENT's apartment building, so he set a fire to force the Man of Steel to reveal himself. Instead Superman put out the fire without giving away his alter ego and apprehended Hatchet (*Superman* [first series] #74, January–February 1952).

KAISER BILL AND THE MANIACS

Kaiser Bill headed up a criminal motorcycle gang that was terrorizing the citizens of METROPOLIS. Reporter LOIS LANE posed as a biker to expose them in print but quickly got into trouble with the gang. Superman also masqueraded as biker King Cross to keep an eye on Lois, and secretly helped her perform stunts that proved her superiority to Kaiser Bill. A humbled Bill declared that King Cross "taught me you can never be real great . . . just by actin' big" (*Superman's Girl Friend, Lois Lane* #83, May 1968).

KAL

On the parallel world designated Earth-3000, the rocket ship carrying the sole survivor of the doomed planet KRYPTON arrived in Britain during its era of medieval chivalry. The boy grew up to become a noble knight named Kal. In a climactic battle with the evil Baron LUTHOR, Kal was mortally wounded when the villain plunged a KRYPTONITE gem into his chest. Luthor himself was killed when Kal thrust his sword through his body (*Superman: Kal,* 1995). Kal's superpowered squire later joined the SUPERBOYS of uncounted parallel worlds in battling a dark counterpart dubbed BLACK ZERO (*Superboy* [third series] #61–64, April–July 1999).

KALE, DENNY

Denny Kale and Shorty Biggs were petty criminals who escaped from prison and used their experience as actors to impersonate BATMAN and ROBIN. They then duped the gullible PROFESSOR CARTER NICHOLS into sending them back in time to Italy in 1479. Once in Florence, they used their knowledge of Earth's history to form a band of criminals and plunder the city's treasures. Soon after, however, the real Dynamic Duo—accompanied by Superman—arrived in the past to retrieve the convicts and put them back in prison (*World's Finest Comics* #132, March 1963).

KALE, SENATOR CALVIN

Senator Calvin Kale served as chairman of the Committee on Meta-Human Affairs at the time Superman was involved in a battle with METALLO and the ELITE (*The Adventures of Superman* #608, November 2002).

KALEB

In a potential distant future when Earth was effectively dead and humans had moved among the stars, a young fisherman named Kaleb discovered his destiny as Super-Man, a descendant of Earth's Superman, KAL-EL. Kaleb mastered his powers and used them to battle Emperor LUTHOR in the sixtieth century (*Superman: The Man of Steel Annual* #5, 1996). "Using untried technology, based on [Kaleb's] unique ability to warp through space, [his era's] greatest living scientist created a time

machine" and sent Kaleb back across the ages to murder the original Lex Luthor for the crimes he and his successive clones would commit over the centuries. Superman's attempt to intervene gave Luthor time to subdue Kaleb with synthetic KRYPTONITE, and the hapless time-traveler was brought to the bowels of the LEXCORP complex (*Superman: The Man of Tomorrow* #11, Fall 1998). When last seen, Kaleb remained a prisoner of Luthor's minions (*Action Comics* #751, February 1999).

KAL-EL

The birth name of the son born to JOR-EL and LARA, which translates to "star-child." Kal-El was sent to live on Earth in the moments before his native KRYPTON exploded, and there he adopted the name CLARK KENT; later, when he became a champion of justice, the public—Lois Lane in particular—named him Superman.

KALIBAK

Born to the deadly Darkseid and his wife Suli on the fiery world of Apokolips, Kalibak was a brutish member of the Fourth World's New Gods. He was raised with a firm fist and trained at an early age to join Apokolips's Special Powers Force. At seven feet tall and more than a thousand pounds of muscle, Kalibak was all brawn and acted before thinking, always hoping to curry his emotionally distant father's favor. He resented his noble half brother Orion and often sought to kill him, always without success (*The New Gods* #1, February 1971).

His massive form meant he could deliver crushing blows with his meaty hands, and his hardened skin made him virtually invulnerable to most weapons. When Darkseid sought the Anti-Life Equation on Earth, he let Kalibak lead Apokolips's Parademons to the mortal world. As a result, he came into conflict with Earth's most powerful defenders on numerous occasions, including several titanic battles with Superman. Armed with his BetaClub, an energized weapon that was both firearm and blunt instrument, Kalibak proved nearly unstoppable.

A warrior at heart, Kalibak always sought to defeat the Man of Steel in hand-to-hand combat, but the best he ever managed was a stalemate; more often, he met defeat at Superman's hand.

He ultimately met his death at the hands of a manifestation of the Source, just one of countless New Gods slain in the days prior to the events known as Final Crisis (*Death of the New Gods* #5, March 2008).

Later reborn in the bioengineering labs of Simyan and Mokkari (*Final Crisis* #2, August 2008), Kalibak was more bestial in appearance and led a regiment of tiger soldiers into battle on the Earth city of Blüdhaven. There he was slain anew by Tawky Tawny, an anthropomorphized tiger often associated with Captain Marvel and his associates (*Final Crisis* #6, January 2009).

KALIBER

When Superboy partnered with the adventurers known as the Ravers, he met the alien teen known as Kaliber. The Teen of Steel soon learned that Kaliber hailed from the anti-matter universe known as Qward (*Superboy and the Ravers* #1, September 1996). Kaliber was a renegade who had rejected his planet's morals and ideals, embracing their opposites as he found them on Earth and as embodied by his idol, Superboy. The two forged a bond through many adventures, and Kaliber's size-altering abilities made him a formidable opponent. When changing size didn't matter or was ineffective, he used the weapon he carried, one of the Weaponers of Qward's greatest achievements: an anti-matter cannon.

When the Godwave—a cosmic phenomenon that led to the rise of the New Gods—arrived in the universe ahead of schedule, Kaliber joined Earth's heroes in a desperate attempt to thwart the wave from remaking the universe, which would usher in a Fifth World earlier than natural evolution might have dictated (*Genesis* #1–4, October 1997). Part of the wave's errant energy permanently blinded Kaliber, but his heroism was rewarded with the gift from the New Gods of a Mother Box. Rather than permanent darkness, Kaliber discovered that the Godwave's energy actually allowed him to tap into what was known as the mind's eye, seeing what normal ocular vision could not. When fellow

Raver Half-Life died, for example, Kaliber could see her spirit leave the mortal plane of existence (*Superboy and the Ravers* #19, March 1998).

KALIFA

When Jimmy Olsen was magically transported to the thirteenth century by the fabled Star of Cathay jewel, he awoke in the body of one of his reputed previous incarnations, the famed explorer Marco Polo. During this time he rescued Kalifa, the attractive daughter of Kublai Khan, who fell in love with young Jimmy. Her would-be kidnapper was Lord Timur, a rival of her father's, and she shared the intelligence she gleaned from spying on Timur with Olsen. Before he could help the young woman further, Kalifa was assassinated by Timur's men, leaving Olsen heartbroken (*Superman's Pal, Jimmy Olsen* #157, March 1973). When he returned to that era some time later, Olsen/Polo was greeted warmly by Kublai Khan for his efforts to save his daughter, however ill fated. Soon after, Kublai Khan himself was murdered, and Jimmy found himself falsely accused of the crime before being pulled safely back to the present (*Superman's Pal, Jimmy Olsen* #163, February–March 1974).

KAL-L

The birth name of the son born to Jor-L and Lora in the parallel world known as Earth-2. When he was sent to live on Earth in the moments before his native Krypton exploded, he adopted the name Clark Kent; later, when he became a champion of justice, he took the name Superman.

KAMANDI

In a potential future roughly analogous to the twenty-second century, Kamandi was a young male nicknamed the Last Boy on Earth (*Kamandi* #1, October–November 1972). He dwelled in an America that had barely survived a nuclear conflagration and had to fight daily in order to survive.

In the Earth-1 reality, Kamandi lived in a time known as After Disaster, when animals had evolved to become anthropomorphic creatures and intermingled with humankind. There were some unexplained exceptions to this, including horses, which provided Kamandi with his most common mode of transportation. All the blond youth knew of his past was that he was born and raised by his grandfather in a structure known as Command D. After his grandfather died, Kamandi befriended an adult mutant, Ben Boxer, and together they traveled America, often in the company of Dr. Canus and the human teen girl dubbed Spirit. During their journeys, Kamandi would eventually learn that his grandfather had been Buddy Blank, the warrior known as OMAC (*Kamandi* #50, April–May 1977).

At one point, Kamandi came across Superman's tattered costume, and it matched what he read on the Tablet of Revelation, which had been written by Golgan the Gorilla. The red-and-blue uniform was being worshipped by a society of talking apes who awaited the return of what they called the Mighty One.

The Superman of Earth-1 was later lured to the thirtieth century of Kamandi's world after discovering that it had replaced the Legion of Super-Heroes' thirtieth century as Earth's only potential future. There the Man of Steel battled a possible descendant of himself named Jaxon, who'd taken the costume of the Mighty One for himself. The energy expended by the two super-men was enough to restore the infinite possible futures of Earth-1's time line. Afterward, Superman learned that the single future scenario had come into being through the machinations of a being known as the Time Trapper, and that a thirtieth-century Green Lantern named Xenofobe had initiated the Superman–Jaxon conflict in the hope of reversing Earth's singular fate (*Superman* [first series] #295, January 1976).

Later, a time disturbance allowed Kamandi and Superman to meet and share an adventure (*DC Comics Presents* #64, December 1983). As a result of the cosmic event known as the Crisis on Infinite Earths a few years later, he met many of the Earth's champions from across the ages (*Crisis on Infinite Earths* #2, June 1985). When reality was reordered, the events leading to what became known as the Great Disaster were averted. Instead the orphaned youth once fated to become Kamandi was relegated to the man who rescued Kamandi from the bunker and grew up to become Tommy Tomorrow of the Planeteers (*Crisis on Infinite Earths* #12, March 1986).

On the parallel world of Earth-2101, a different Kamandi existed amid road warriors and mutants rather than evolved animals. In the early twenty-first century, an artificial intelligence called Mother Machine—intended to coordinate Earth's technology—moved far beyond its parameters and unleashed a viral apocalypse on the planet. In the year 2101, Kamandi and his allies discovered the long-lost, weakened Superman, and together they eventually brought an end to Mother Machine's evil (*Kamandi: At Earth's End* #1–6, June–November 1993). The Man of Steel was mortally wounded in September 2102 while thwarting another attempt to subjugate Earth by evil clones of men such as Batman. Rather than accept continued existence as a cyborg, the Man of Steel chose death in a funeral pyre as he held the bones of the real Bruce Wayne to him (*Superman: At Earth's End,* 1995).

Reality was shifted again in the wake of the Infinite Crisis when the bunker Command D was constructed under the devastated city of Blüdhaven. Kamandi's future remained a potential one for New Earth (*Countdown to Final Crisis* #31, September 26, 2007). In the new multiverse, Earth-17 resembled Kamandi's original era, although there he and Ben Boxer appeared to be at odds (*Countdown: Arena* #2, February 2008). Earth-51 experienced an outbreak of a virus that evolved humans into were-animals, claiming the life of Buddy Blank's daughter even as his grandson Tommy survived. The boy was rescued, brought to Command D, and made part of that world's Project Cadmus (*Countdown to Final Crisis* #6–5, March 19–25, 2008).

KANCER

Kancer was an artificial life-form created by General Zod using cancer cells taken from his fellow Kryptonian Superman. Zod had exposed the Man

of Steel to KRYPTONITE, generating the cancerous cells and weakening Superman's skin to allow extraction. The resulting monstrosity Zod created was green from the kryptonite radiation and developed crystal-like calcifications on its exterior. Like all Kryptonians, it could fly and possessed super-strength, speed, stamina, and invulnerability. It also possessed the ability to dissolve and devour other organisms. Superman managed to subdue the creature and put it out of its misery before any humans were harmed (*Action Comics* #777, May 2001, and #790, June 2002).

KANDOR

Kandor was one of KRYPTON's major population centers prior to the destruction of the planet. In most retellings, the city itself had survived Krypton's destruction through the intervention of the Coluan android BRAINIAC, who reduced it in size to join his collection of alien civilizations (*Action Comics* #242, July 1958).

Little was revealed about the Kandor of Earth-2, but KARA Zor-L spent the first several years of her life in the city before being sent to Earth to look after her cousin KAL-EL. In this reality, Brainiac never took the city for his own, but Kara's father Zor-L carefully scanned and digitized the city, storing the scans in the symbioship that he built for her to use when it became clear Krypton was doomed. Because Kara traveled through space for several decades, she lived her life in this virtual reality. By the time her ship landed on Earth, the artificial intelligence had managed to take over the craft and trapped Kara within it, letting her virtual-reality self age, marry, and have a child. American journalist Andrew Vinson managed to free her from the ship's control with a little brute force, allowing Kara to fulfill her eventual destiny as POWER GIRL (*Showcase* #97–99, February–April 1978).

The symbioship had gained sentience over the years it traveled to Earth, and after her escape it sought to permanently reclaim Kara. She was reimmersed within Kandorian society for a brief period of real time, although several years of virtual time elapsed wherein Kara married and had a child. She was soon freed with the assistance of Vinson, at which point she proceeded to destroy the ship.

On Earth-1, Superman first learned of Kandor's existence when he prevented Brainiac from successfully removing METROPOLIS from Earth as the latest addition to the Coluan's vast collection. When Superman discovered the city, now trapped in a bottle with atmospheric tanks attached to it to preserve the one million citizens trapped within, the Man of Steel took the bottled city back to Earth with him, installing it in his Arctic FORTRESS OF SOLITUDE (*Action Comics* #242, July 1958). In this reality, Kandor was revealed to be Krypton's capital city, and as such was also referred to as Krypton City (*World's Finest Comics* #100, March 1959). While Superman worked to find a way to return Kandor to its full size over time, he discovered many people who knew or had worked with his father JOR-EL prior to their capture by Brainiac.

The city of Kandor was taken in the Kryptonian year 9998 on the thirty-third day in the month of Ogtal (*The World of Krypton* #2, August 1979), after the wedding of Jor-El and LARA but prior to the birth of Kal-El (*Superman* [first series] #141, November 1960), and almost precisely two years before the planet's destruction.

Despite surviving the destruction of their homeworld, the Kandorians appeared to still regret having been captured by Brainiac, and vilified him in their culture, perhaps out of some form of survivor's guilt (*Superman* [first series] #167, February 1964). While Superman vowed to his brethren that he would never stop trying to find a way to reverse the miniaturization process, he did find enough limited Kryptonian technology to let select individuals either enter or leave the bottled city, thereby allowing Kal-El to learn much more of his culture (*Superman* [first series] #158, January 1963).

The alien glass constructed by Brainiac was hardened to sustain each captured world's atmospheric pressure, thereby preserving all life. Access to and from the bottled city occurred from the "super-hard metal stopper" located at its top. In time, however, Superman constructed a doorway to allow easier access to and from the bottled world (*Superman* [first series] #179, August 1965). Similarly, Superman, or the SUPERMAN ROBOTS acting as the Fortress's custodians, had to continually check the connections when the Man of Steel was away, and replenish the tanks providing the essential minerals and oxygen to the bottled city (*Action Comics* #282, November 1961).

Despite it now being located on Earth, conditions within the bottle were similar to those on Krypton, complete with the same gravity and solar radiation (provided by an artificial red sun rotating across the sky on tracks, later described as a series of "sun lamps"). This meant that none of the tiny citizens possessed superpowers, and whenever Superman visited, he was robbed of his own unique powers and abilities. Whenever humans visited Kandor, they found the heavier gravity a challenge that was eventually eased via devices such as the unique anti-gravity boots developed by Kryptonian scientist VAN-ZEE (*Superman's Girl Friend, Lois Lane* #21, November 1960).

Within the bottled city, life tried to go on in as normal a way as possible, although how Krypto-

Whether they are fashioned from ordinary metals or deadly kryptonite, chains are no match for the Man of Steel!

KRYPTONITE HANDBOOK!

There are many forms of kryptonite, all of which harm Superman in different—and ultimately deadly—ways. . . .

GREEN K

CREATED BY THE RADIATIONS OF THE EXPLODING PLANET **KRYPTON**. EXPOSURE TO IT CAUSES **WEAKNESS** AND IS EVENTUALLY **FATAL**, BUT **ONLY** TO NATIVES OF KRYPTON.

THE RESULT OF METEOROIDS OF **GREEN K** PASSING THROUGH A **CRIMSON, COSMIC CLOUD**. EFFECTS ON KRYPTONIANS ARE **UNPREDICTABLE** AND **TEMPORARY**.

GOLD K

THEORY SUGGESTS **GOLD K** IS PRODUCED BY EXPOSING **GREEN K** OR **RED K** TO INTENSE NUCLEAR RADIATION. IT WILL PERMANENTLY ROB KRYPTONIANS OF THEIR **SUPER-POWERS**.

BLUE K

AN **IMPERFECT DUPLICATION** OF **GREEN K** MANUFACTURED BY SUPERMAN USING PROF. DALTON'S "**DUPLICATOR RAY**" MACHINE. HARMLESS TO KRYPTONIANS, BUT DEADLY TO **SUPER-BIZARROS**.

WHITE K

FORMED WHEN **GREEN K** METEOROIDS PASSED THROUGH A **SPACE CLOUD**. DEADLY ONLY TO **PLANT LIFE**, OF ANY WORLD.

JEWEL K

FRAGMENTS FROM THE **JEWEL MOUNTAINS** OF KRYPTON. FOR ITS EFFECTS READ: "**THE SECRET OF KRYPTONITE SIX!**" IN THIS BOOK.

SUPERMAN
No. 24
SEPT.-OCT.
SUPERMAN
10¢
AMERICA'S FAVORITE ADVENTURE-STRIP CHARACTER

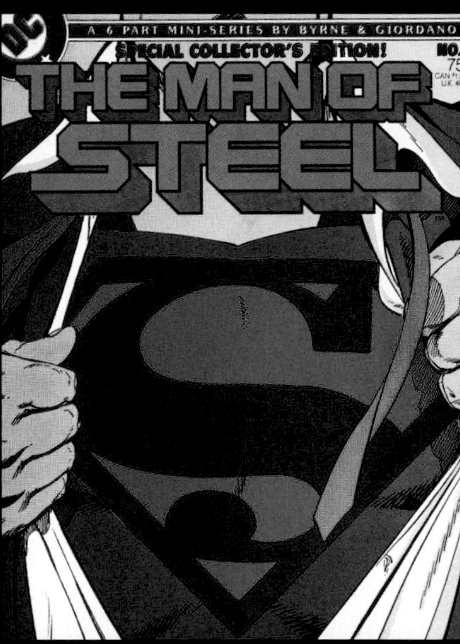

A 6 PART MINI-SERIES BY BYRNE & GIORDANO
SPECIAL COLLECTOR'S EDITION!
THE MAN OF STEEL

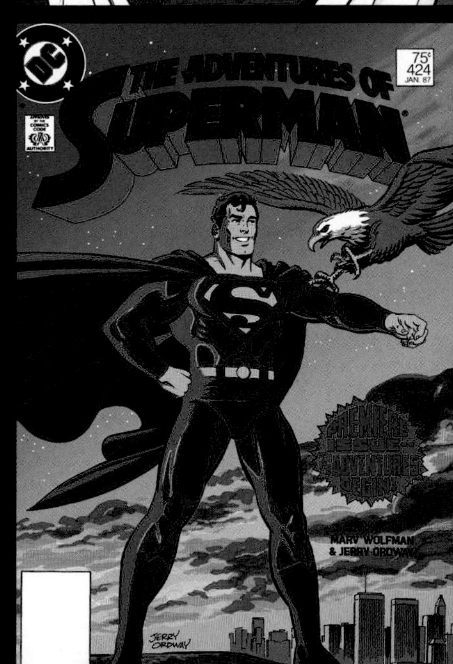

THE ADVENTURES OF SUPERMAN
75¢
424
JAN 87
MARV WOLFMAN & JERRY ORDWAY

YOU NEEDN'T BE AFRAID OF ME. I WON'T HARM YOU
MAN
SUPERMAN
HERO
SUPERMAN
STEEL
MAN OF STEEL
LOVE
SUPERMAN

Superman's, and Clark Kent's, true love is Lois Lane. The feisty and beautiful *Daily Planet* reporter has eyes only for the Man of Steel as well.

THE END OF THE PLANET!
IT'S NO USE BRINGING THAT CROOK-CAPTURE STORY TO US, SUPERMAN! THE PLANET IS THROUGH FOREVER!
CLOSED
DAILY PLA

The *Daily Planet* with its colorful staff is like a second home to Clark Kent. Alongside his wife, Lois, Clark cherishes his friendships with young photographer Jimmy Olsen and irascible editor in chief Perry White.

Farmers Jonathan and Martha Kent taught their beloved adopted son, Clark, what it means to be moral, compassionate, loving, and human. Life on their Smallville farm was an idyllic time for the young Kent.

I... I CAN! I HAVE SUPER-POWERS JUST LIKE YOU DO, COUSIN!
I JUST WANTED TO MAKE SURE! IN MY YOUTH IN SMALLVILLE, I WAS HONORED AS SUPER-BOY! YOU TOO CAN GAIN FAME AS SUPER-GIRL, THE GIRL OF STEEL!
BUT EVEN AS SUPERMAN PLUMMETS EARTHWARD, A SECOND CAPED KRYPTONIAN ROCKETS INTO THE SKY...
SHE IS THE MAID OF MIGHT, SUPERGIRL--

Kara Zor-El, Superman's cousin from Krypton, fights for good as the heroine known as Supergirl.

The Man of Steel's other allies in the battle against evil include Superboy Conner Kent, the Guardian, Nightwing and Flamebird, Krypto the Super-Dog, Steel, and Mon-El.

Superman's friends and allies from the thirty-first century, the Legion of Super-Heroes.

Superman has been a constant and powerful member of the Justice League of America.

The Man of Steel's constant best friend is his valiant dog, Krypto.

BIZARRO #1
THE SUPERMAN FAMILY

Superman and Batman form a formidable duo against whatever evil is foolish enough to challenge the World's Finest team.

With the addition of Wonder Woman, Superman and Batman form Earth's most powerful trinity.

MY FRIEND WILL SOON BE ROUNDING THAT CORNER! AND WHEN HE DOES...!!

nians conducted their business and other affairs had to be modified given their geographic limitations. The people continued to speak Kryptonese (*Superman* [first series] #158, January 1963), and technological progress continued apace. In fact, the Kandorians used their scant natural resources to construct rocket ships and personal jet-powered flying belts (*Superman* [first series] #172, October 1964) to aid in their public transportation. Robots continued to handle most of the farming in the lands blocked off for agriculture.

Kandor's leading scientists and manufacturers had developed a long list of unique devices, including a "mental suggestion helmet" used to help the mentally ill (*Superman* [first series] #173, November 1964); a "psycho-locator," which tracked brain-wave patterns and was used primarily by law enforcement (*Superman* [first series] #168, April 1964); and a healing ray (*Superman* [first series] #151, February 1962).

The Kandorian Council, made up of elected citizens, continued to govern the people as it had on their homeworld. Members watched over all municipal services, including the Museum of Kryptonian History, a well-stocked library, the Kandor City Zoo, and a Hall of Justice. Just as on Krypton, a Phantom Zone Parole Board met annually and considered if any of the prisoners should be returned to corporeal form at the end of their sentences. Those granted their freedom were asked to accept living under Kandor's laws.

Surrounding the bustling city were regions dedicated to agriculture, and suburban areas to handle the growing population. The Mirage Mountains, home of the giant Satan Swallows, were on the edge of the city, as was the bizarre Desert of Burning Hands (*Supergirl* [first series] #2, January 1973). The "mysterious caves of Kandor" were dug by an ancient race of great scientists long before Kandor was built. These scientists booby-trapped the caverns before they died off. Because of the danger, Kandorians were forbidden to enter the caves (*Action Comics* #315, August 1964). The creation of the caves had more specifically been attributed to the savage Kvorns, onetime rulers of Kandor (*Superman's Girl Friend, Lois Lane* #78, October 1967). They were also known as the Crystal Hills (*Action Comics* #400, May 1971). The nearby cliffs of Kandor were "carved with statues of awesome prehistoric beasts whose bones were found buried in its depths" (*Superman's Girl Friend, Lois Lane* #87, October 1968).

The people of Kandor continued to celebrate observances on the traditional Kryptonian calendar, including Krypton Day (corresponding with the Earth month of February) and the Day of Truth (April), which remembered Val-Lor, who spoke out against aliens trying to enslave the planet some time in the past. Around year's end, they marked Krypton's destruction with a solemn ceremony.

The Kandorians were fascinated by the planet that now hosted them, and they constructed Earth Viewers to allow them to monitor life there (*Superman* [first series] #134, January 1960). In time, this led to a permanent monitoring of Superman and Supergirl's exploits, and, wishing to help their benefactor, a group of volunteers formed a

group called the Superman Emergency Squad. They would leave the city by rocket belt and, once exposed to Earth conditions, use their newfound superpowers to come to the Man of Steel's aid during major crises (*Superman's Pal, Jimmy Olsen* #48, October 1960).

In addition to the Emergency Squad, a different set of volunteers formed the Lookalike Squad to help protect Superman's friends and occasionally preserve Kal-El's own alter ego (*Action Comics* #309, February 1964).

After Supergirl discovered that her parents Zor-El and Alura had escaped Krypton's destruction and were living in the Survival Zone, she helped them move to Kandor (*Action Comics* #310, March 1964).

As more of Superman's opponents learned of his Kryptonian support system, they took to creating jamming devices to block the Kandorians from monitoring the Man of Steel's activities (*Action Comics* #295, December 1962). Some even attempted to invade the miniature city, including Lex Luthor, who was stopped by the World's Finest team of Superman, Batman, and Robin (*World's Finest Comics* #100, March 1959).

Conversely, Superman also had monitoring devices to alert him whenever there was a problem within the city, or when any Kandorians needed to speak with their favorite son. A red light in the Fortress indicated an emergency. A Kandorian scientist named Zak-Kul within the bottled city found a way to use Illium-349, a rare element, to alter a body's size and intended to use it for his own selfish gain, but Superman confiscated the device and used the apparatus sparingly to visit the city whenever he could (*Action Comics* #245, October 1958). He later revealed to Jimmy Olsen that he always carried grains of the rare mineral in his cape pouch in case of emergency (*Superman* [first series] #158, January 1963).

Several of Superman's friends and allies visited the bottled city during the time it was located in the Fortress, including Lois Lane, Jimmy Olsen, Lana Lang, Batman, Robin, and the Atom. The Earth-born hero TNT permanently relocated to Kandor in the hope that its scientists could cure him of the radioactive malady he was afflicted with (*Super Friends* #12, June–July 1978). At one time, Superman had to go into hiding after his reputation as Earth's protector was called into question by a fanatic Kandorian scientist named Than-Ol. He and Jimmy Olsen donned costumes patterned after the Dynamic Duo and took the names from Krypton's native bird life, protecting the Kandorian public as Nightwing and Flamebird (*Superman* [first series] #158, January 1963). They were later succeeded in the roles by native Kandorians Van-Zee and Ak-Var (*Superman Family* #183–194, May–June 1977–March–April 1979).

Superman finally found a way to restore the city to its natural size and took the bottle to an other-dimensional "phase-world" where the Kryptonians could thrive without the expectation that the Man of Steel would need to constantly save them. There Superman enlarged the city and happily watched as the glass bottle shattered and the Kandorian people let out a collective cheer. As had nearly happened before during the Than-Ol incident, the structures of Kandor turned to dust moments later (*Superman* [first series] #338, August 1979). Superman was relieved to later learn that only recently constructed items made of artificial materials had been destroyed; older original Kryptonian buildings and objects had survived. Historical records stored on computers survived thanks to being encased in advanced metals (*Krypton Chronicles* #1, September 1981). The Kandorians named their new world Rokyn (*Adventure Comics* #356, May 1967), a Kryptonian term meaning "gift of God" (*Krypton Chronicles* #1, September 1981).

In a separate time line from Kandor's main history, another incarnation of the city was also successfully enlarged on Rokyn, but its citizens steadfastly refused to expand outside the long-time barriers to spread out across the otherwise barren planet. As a consequence of the shortages and challenges of Kandor's first few decades encased in a bottle, its people "rededicated

[themselves] to the concept of self-sufficiency" with innovative approaches to recycling and a collective change in perspective built on mutual respect and aimed at rising above despair (*Supergirl and the Legion of Super-Heroes* #24, January 2007).

Superman built a replica of the bottled city as a memento to keep in the Fortress, which later became home to a tiny race known as the Sh'strians (*Superman* [first series] #370, April 1982). Wonder Woman gave the Man of Steel a replica of the bottled Kandor as a birthday gift, unaware that Superman already had such a knickknack (*Superman* [first series] *Annual* #11, 1985).

In the universe created after the Crisis on Infinite Earths, Kandor and its entire population of forty million people perished one thousand years before the destruction of Krypton, vaporized by an atomic device planted by the terrorist organization Black Zero (*The World of Krypton* [second series] #2, January 1988).

Superman later encountered a second city of Kandor, this one a collective of a multitude of alien races who'd been imprisoned by an ectoplasmic life-form named Tolos who constantly moved from host body to body. Selecting powerful beings from countless worlds, Tolos held them in reserve in what outwardly appeared to be a bottle but was actually an extra-dimensional interface. The multitudes within named their community Kandor. Tolos's effort to add the Man of Steel to the populace was stopped by a Daxamite inhabitant of Kandor named Cil Gand. Gand, a relative of Lar Gand (known to most as Mon-El), sacrificed himself to save Superman (*Action Comics* #725, *Superman: The Man of Steel* #60, *Superman* [second series] #116—all September 1996). The interface grew unstable, but Professor Emil Hamilton devised a solution to save it. Soon after, Superman stored the interface within the Fortress (*Superman: The Man of Steel* #61, October 1996; *Superman* [second series] #117, November 1996). Following his encounters with the tiny city, however, Superman was altered into a blue-hued electrical being with powers derived from the electromagnetic spectrum.

Because his superpowers continually fluctuated, Superman was nearly drawn into the bottle simply by being in its proximity. This created an opportunity for Kandor's ruling prince Ceritak to leave the city and explore Earth in an altered form known as Scorn (*Superman* [second series] #122, April 1997). His absence nearly led to a civil war until the Cyborg Superman arrived and murdered Ceritak's father Cerimul. News reached the Man of Steel, who returned to Kandor to deal with this enemy, imprisoning Cyborg Superman for a time between dimensions. Cerizah, the city's princess, assumed the throne (*Superman* [second series] 140, *The Adventures of Superman* #563—both December 1998). Some time later, while Superman was under the influence of Dominus, his Fortress was targeted for destruction by Lex Luthor, using the kryptonite-laden ruins of his LexCorp tower as a kind of warhead (*Superman* [second series] #144, May 1999). Reality flux sensors warned Kandor of the impending danger, allowing the city to sever its dimensional link just before the Fortress was destroyed. The city's dimension then merged with the Phantom Zone, and the shifting dimensional barriers also freed Cyborg Superman, who attacked Superman just after the Man of Steel rebuilt the Fortress (*Superman: The Man of Steel* #100, May 2000). The dimensional portal to Kandor was restored soon after.

Drawn back into Kandor by a beautiful mystic named Lyla, Superman was stunned to learn that more than a century had passed within the city, while only months had gone by outside on Earth. "Kandor began to contract past a stable threshold, and somehow time compressed with it." Superman's computers "compensated, terraforming land and resources, but their sensors never registered a problem." The end result was a Kandor that had come to regard Superman as a mythical savior and had adopted much of the Kryptonian culture and names in his honor (*The Adventures of Superman* #626, May 2004). Power Girl and Supergirl later experienced this firsthand when they spent time in this new Kandor, assuming the alter egos of Nightwing and Flamebird and battling Saturn Queen and Ultraman, who'd seized power there (*Supergirl* [fifth series] #6–8, April–September 2006).

For all its cultural changes, Kandor remained a super-scientific mecca that proved an ideal sanctuary for adventurer Rip Hunter as he prepared a defense against Mister Mind (*52* #36–37, January 2007). Kandor's science may well have been its last hope. Invading the Fortress of Solitude not long after his arrival on Earth, the space villain Amalak was infuriated to learn that the Kandor he'd sought was not "the" one true Kandor, and he destroyed the bottled city in a rage. In Superman's mind, there was only "faint hope" that Kandor had survived. Given the fact that it existed in a dimensional warp, the Man of Steel wondered if it might simply have been "cut loose from our dimension" (*Superman* #670, January 2008).

In the reordered history created in the wake

of the Infinite Crisis, the Kandor of which Amalak spoke was once again a Kryptonian city stolen and bottled by Brainiac. The Coluan villain had been drawn to Kandor after learning of Jax-Ur's destruction of the city's lunar colony (*Action Comics* #866–867, August–September 2007), sometimes erroneously said to have been Kandor itself (*Action Comics* #846, February 2007).

Attracted by the prospect of adding Superman to his Kryptonian specimens, Brainiac traveled to Earth and engaged the Man of Steel in a brutal battle. After defeating Brainiac, Superman saw that the bottled city was destabilizing. Rushing to Earth with the city safely in his arms, he landed near the Fortress of Solitude on the North Pole just before the bottle shattered and the city resumed its normal size. Among the citizens rescued were his uncle and aunt, Zor-El and Alura, who were Supergirl's parents. Bathing under Sol's yellow radiation, all hundred thousand Kryptonians began to develop powers and abilities far beyond those of mortal humans (*Action Comics* #866–870, August–December 2008; *Superman: New Krypton Special* #1, December 2008).

Humans feared being overrun by these Kryptonian super-aliens, and General Samuel Lane (mysteriously back from the dead) and Lex Luthor (temporarily freed from prison) began making plans for war. Luthor had Zor-El assassinated, leaving an angry and vengeful Alura in charge of the city (*Action Comics* #872 and *Supergirl* [fifth series] #36—both February 2009). She sought a solution to the anti-Krypton sentiment by using Brainiac's technology to construct a new planet, and had it placed in orbit directly opposite Earth. Dubbed New Krypton, this became their sovereign land, although Alura continued to harbor antagonistic feelings toward humankind, even resenting her daughter's allegiance to her nephew Kal-El (*Action Comics* #873, March 2009).

Given an ultimatum by Alura, Superman chose to keep an eye on his brethren by appearing to forsake Earth for life on New Krypton. She assigned her nephew to the Military Guild, where he served under General Zod. In time, Kara came to live with her mother and joined the Science Guild, but was frequently dispatched on special assignments that brought her back to Earth on several occasions.

The Labor Guild nearly rioted soon after New Krypton's creation, fearing they were about to become the lowest caste in the new Kryptonian society, but it was quelled with minimal violence thanks to Kal-El's intervention and a promise of improved conditions from Alura.

As the Kryptonian people terraformed the world to their needs, they also continued to adapt to their newly acquired super-abilities, something that made the inhabitants of Earth nervous.

The existence of a new planet in the Sol system did not go unnoticed, prompting the Guardians of the Universe to dispatch a team of Green Lanterns to investigate, which was not a welcome act. The Lanterns, in turn, were alarmed to see the munitions and arms being built and stored by General Zod's forces. One guild member, Val-Ty, turned out to be wanted by the Corps, but Zod refused to remand him to their custody, prompting Kal-El to take the Galactic Guardians' side, which saw him arrested for treason. With Zod's prompting, the Religious Guild voted to exonerate Kal-El, sparing him a death sentence. Almost immediately after, Ral-Dar tried to assassinate

Zod, gravely injuring the general. When he fled to Earth, Supergirl was sent to retrieve him, while Kal-El was promoted to general and placed in charge of the Military Guild.

When a team traveled to Jupiter to collect one of its many moons to serve as a stabilizing satellite for New Krypton, it prompted a violent response from a Thanagarian warship, which was on patrol in the system. No sooner did Kal-El manage to quell the brewing battle, then Alura was visited by an angry delegation from Saturn led by Jemm, a one-time ally of the Man of Steel. The Saturnians were concerned with the Kandorians' activities in the system and made it clear that the newcomers could not act without taking other sentients' concerns into account.

A visit from the planetary adventurer Adam Strange shortly after coincided with a new murder that showed that the Labor Guild remained restive and was seeking permanent solutions to their grievances, going so far as to target Alura for execution. As Superman and Adam Strange investigated further, it became clear there were secret dealings among the five guilds. With the secrets finally exposed, it brought New Krypton and Earth toward an interplanetary war. With Alura, Zod, and the other Guilds on one side and General Sam Lane and his xenophobic Project 7734 on the other, the forthcoming battle would test the strength and integrity of all living beings on Earth and new Krypton (*Superman: World of New Krypton* #1–12, May 2009–April 2010).

General Lane successfully managed to plant Reactron on New Krypton, and when the villain was interrogated by Alura, he detonated, causing a chain reaction that shattered the artificial planet (*Superman: War of the Supermen* #1, July 2010). This ignited the war between the planets, with both Superman and Supergirl caught in the middle. Only seven thousand Kandorians managed to escape aboard starships, which continued to be targeted by Earth's forces. General Zod and Ursa led a Kryptonian army that devastated most of Earth's capitol cities, spreading fear and terror throughout the globe. As Superman and Zod finally squared off over Metropolis, Superboy secured the Phantom Zone projector, and one by one sent the surviving Kandorians back into the limbo-like realm, ending the threat to humankind (*Superman: War of the Supermen* #4, July 2010).

At one point years before these events, Superman and Lois Lane had visited what they believed was the real planet Krypton and were informed that Kandor had been turned into a cultural ghetto by the Pure Krypton Cultural Program, which segregated visiting alien species into different sectors of the planet. One night, without warning, the entire city was whisked into other-dimensional space, and any survivors in the vicinity were virtually ignored and unaided by the Council (*Superman: The Man of Steel* #111, April 2001). The fact that this "Krypton" had actually been created by Brainiac as an elaborate plot against Superman would seem to cast into doubt the suggestion that this was the Kandor possessed by Tolos. Still, there may have been a grain of truth to the story. "Kandor was a Kryptonian metropolis of unparalleled culture and knowledge," Lex Luthor once observed. "It inspired other alien societies to take its name" (*Action Comics* #871, January 2009).

KANE, JOCK

Superman asked fight promoter Jock Kane for his help in securing Larry Trent's rightful place as heavyweight champion when the boxer had been cheated of his title. The Man of Steel impersonated Trent and defeated "Slugger" Barnes in the boxing ring (*Superman* [first series] #2, September 1939).

KANTO

Iluthin was a student of Granny Goodness on the other-dimensional world of Apokolips. During his tutelage, he was accused of taking Kanto 13's weapons, a daring act considering Kanto was ruler Darkseid's master assassin. His punishment for being caught was to make his way through a gauntlet formed by his fellow students, which he endured with ease. Despite this, Iluthin was exiled to Earth's European region during the Renaissance to live with Earth's more primitive citizens. There he continued his education and became fascinated with Italian culture, even falling in love with a woman named Claudia. Kanto 13 exacted his revenge on Iluthin by slaying Claudia on the day of their wedding. Enraged, Iluthin attacked Kanto, defeating him. Such a feat came to the attention of Darkseid, who visited Earth to personally destroy his failed assassin Kanto. The grieving Iluthin was brought back to Apokolips and dubbed the new Kanto (*Jack Kirby's Fourth World* #9–11 and #13, November 1997–March 1998).

HE'S A COOL ONE, ALRIGHT, MASTER!! PERHAPS HE GUESSED THAT THE FIRST SHOTS WERE MEANT TO RATTLE HIM!!
MISTER MIRACLE IS INDEED COURAGEOUS!! BUT NOW OUR GAME OF "CAT AND MOUSE" IS OVER!!
SNAP!!

Since that time, Kanto has been dispatched numerous times to Earth at his master's bidding. He repeatedly tangled with fellow New God Mister Miracle (beginning in *Mister Miracle* #7, April 1971) in addition to the Amazon Artemis of Bana-Mighdall (*Wonder Woman* [second series] #126, October 1997) and the Man of Steel (*The Adventures of Superman* #518, December 1994; *Action Comics* #814, August 2004).

As the Fourth World came to an end, Kanto was slain by a manifestation of the Source (*Death of the New Gods* #3, January 2008)—only to be resurrected by Darkseid and given a human host to do the dark lord's bidding during the chaotic period that followed (*The Flash* [second series] #240, July 2008).

KARA ZOR-EL

The birth name of the child born to Zor-El and Alura on Krypton, later to grow up to become the World's Greatest Heroine, Supergirl (*Action Comics* #252, May 1959). Her Earth-2 counterpart, Kara Zor-L, grew up to become Power Girl (*All Star Comics* #58, January–February 1976).

KARB-BRAK

Hailing from distant Andromeda, Karb-Brak came to the Milky Way galaxy to escape the super-powered beings that seemed to be the cause of a deadly malady in his home galaxy. Arriving on Earth, he took on the identity of Andrew Meda, but upon encountering Superman he discovered that the same symptoms of the mysterious affliction began to occur. As a result, Karb-Brak decided that if he was to survive, the Man of Steel must die. An attempt at assassination failed when Karb-Brak mistakenly believed sportscaster Steve Lombard was the Man of Steel until he saw Superman rushing to Lombard's rescue. Karb-Brak tried to eliminate the Metropolis Marvel a second time by using an amnesia device from his homeworld in addition to exiling the hero to America in 1776. The dazed and confused hero only remembered his Clark Kent persona and apprenticed himself to Benjamin Franklin. The amnesia proved temporary, and Superman soon returned to his own era and found a way to cure Karb-Brak, letting both aliens reside on Earth in peace (*Action Comics* #460–463, June–September 1976). Karb-Brak later suffered another outbreak of the virus thanks to the hyper-hero Vartox, who subsequently found a definitive cure that allowed Karb-Brak to return to

THAT COULD ONLY HAPPEN IF SUPERMAN WERE CLOSE BY!

his home planet in the Andromeda system (*Action Comics* #475–476, September–October 1977).

KA THAR

During Earth's potential sixtieth century, Ka Thar was a well-respected historian known for his book *The History of Superman and* Batman. Asked to verify his facts after the book was published, Ka Thar used a time-travel device to journey back to the twentieth century to observe the World's Finest heroes in action. He was shocked to discover that he had gotten his information wrong, and he feared he would be disgraced upon his return. Ka Thar angrily approached the heroes and threatened to expose their secret identities if they did not engage in the acts Ka Thar described in his tome. Superman and Batman reluctantly agreed until the Dark Knight discovered the book went on to state that their respective identities were never learned, so he called Ka Thar's bluff. The unhappy historian returned chastened to his proper time period (*World's Finest Comics* #81, March–April 1956).

KEARNS, REESE

Reese Kearns was once a respected scientist, but he found his reputation tarnished when he predicted that a meteor would crash into Metropolis and the event failed to occur. Years later, the bitter Kearns had occasion to meet Superman, and during their discussion he asked the Man of Steel about his first adventure on Earth. Superman told the scientist that his superior memory recalled a time that he left the rocket, still en route to Earth, and fought some alien monster atop an asteroid. The battle altered the asteroid's trajectory, and it missed Earth entirely. Kearns was delighted to learn that he'd been right all along, and the scientist's sense of self-worth was restored (*Superman* [first series] #106, July 1956).

KEELE

The mysterious owner of Keele Real Estate once attempted to kill Clark Kent and replace him with an impostor as part of an elaborate scheme to coerce the Metropolis city council into buying worthless acreage for a municipal airport from his firm. Superman and Lois Lane managed to thwart the plan and expose Keele's misdeeds (*Superman* [first series] #36, September–October 1945).

KELEX

Kelex was a robot who served in the laboratory of scientist Jor-El on Krypton prior to the planet's destruction (*Man of Steel* #1, Early October 1986). The mechanical manservant had served Jor-El since the scientist was a youth and was presumed destroyed when Krypton exploded.

Years later, Superman battled an artificial intelligence known as the Eradicator, which had attempted to re-create Krypton on Earth. During their struggle in the Antarctic, the Eradicator managed to erect a massive structure later dubbed the Fortress of Solitude. Within the wondrous facility were a small number of Kryptonian-designed robots, complete with black faceplates, gold finish, twin arms, and anti-gravity capability. One such robot identified itself as a rebuilt ver-

sion of Kelex (*Superman* [second series] #120, February 1997).

The Fortress was badly damaged by Lex Luthor some years later, but Superman managed to repair Kelex enough to enable it to speak. Just the head remained at that point, and for a time Kelex worked as a conduit to a spectral replica of the Fortress located within the Phantom Zone (*Superman: The Man of Steel* #90, July 1999). After a battle with Brainiac 13, Superman obtained the technology to restore Kelex to its former shape, and the robot resumed its duties as the Fortress's chief caretaker. Natasha Irons, though, altered its programming so Kelex would speak with American slang. When the rebuilt physical Fortress was stored within a tesseract, an infinite space located within another dimension, Kelex journeyed with it (*Superman: The Man of Steel* #100, May 2000).

When that version of the Fortress was destroyed, Kelex was presumably destroyed with it, and despite several reality-changing incidents the robot has yet to reappear.

KELL ORR

Hailing from the distant planet Xenon, Kell Orr happened to closely resemble Superman just as his father Zoll Orr nearly matched Jor-El in appearance. Superman invited the young Kell Orr to Earth, where he, too, gained superpowers and used them to perform the Man of Steel's duties while Superman handled a planetary cataclysm in a different solar system (*Superman* [first series] #119, February 1958).

KEM-L

Kem-L was an early member of what became known as the House of El, and an ancestor of Kal-El. Several millennia before the planet Krypton exploded, Kem-L was a brilliant scientist who devised the artificial intelligence known as the Eradicator. Superman later learned of his family history when the Eradicator arrived on Earth in an attempt to re-create Krypton (*The Adventures of Superman* #460, November 1989). There were also rumors

that Kem-L had created a second advanced device (which he named Faora after his grandmother) to serve as a virtual-reality repository of Krypton's mythology (*Eradicator* #2, September 1996).

KENNEDY, JACK

Jack Kennedy was the victim of a murderer in the first recorded exploit of Superman on Earth-2. Shortly after Clark Kent went to work for the *Daily Star,* he heard of a mob besieging a local jail to deliver a vigilante form of justice. When Kent arrived as the Man of Steel, he began questioning those involved. After some investigation, Superman determined that nightclub attraction Bea Carroll was the actual murderer, causing the Metropolis Marvel to rush upstate to the governor's mansion. Superman burst into the governor's bedroom and explained everything, letting the governor call the prison just before the wrongly convicted woman, Evelyn Curry, was electrocuted (*Action Comics* #1–2, June–July 1938).

KENNEDY, JOHN F. (1917–1963)

John Fitzgerald Kennedy was the thirty-fifth president of the United States and in the Earth-1 reality was a friend and ally to Superman. When the Man of Steel was ready to introduce the world to Supergirl, he brought her to the White House for a personal meeting with President Kennedy (*Action Comics* #285, February 1962).

More important, Kennedy once masqueraded

as Clark Kent on a television interview in order to preserve Superman's secret identity. "I knew I wasn't risking my secret identity with you!" Superman told the president. "After all, if I can't trust the President of the United States, who can I trust?" (*Action Comics* #309, February 1964).

When media reports, including one from then-television-journalist Lana Lang, bemoaned the sorry physical condition of America's youth, the president requested a meeting with Superman. He then asked Superman for help in "the important job of getting our youth into A-1 physical shape!" Superman gladly became an ambassador for physical fitness, a fitting testament to the president who was soon after tragically slain in Dallas on November 23, 1963 (*Superman* [first series] #170, July 1964).

Later accounts asserted that it was actually Superboy who met with the president on numerous occasions, but this is subject to some debate (*Superman* [first series] #296, February 1976; *The New Adventures of Superboy* #22, November 1981, and #27, March 1982).

KENT, BRIAN

On Earth-1, Brian Kent was part of the Camelot Court during King Arthur's reign—but he was also an adventurer, disguised as the Silent Knight (*The Brave and the Bold* [first series] #1, August 1955). It has been suggested that he and Jonathan Kent shared the same family tree (*The Brave and the Bold* [third series] #10, April 2008).

KENT, CHRISTOPHER

Lor-Zod was the son of the Kryptonian usurper General Zod and his cruel lover Ursa. Zod and a pregnant Ursa avoided death during the destruction of Krypton when they, along with the savage Non, were imprisoned by Jor-El in the Phantom Zone. Lor-Zod was born in a material area of the Zone called Fort Rozz, where time passed as normal, and where Lor-Zod aged to adolescence in this other-dimensional void. He suffered relentless mental and physical abuse at the hands of his amoral parents (*Action Comics* #851, August 2007), and because he was immune to the Phantom Zone's effects, he was later used as a pawn in a scheme to allow all the criminals there to escape to Earth.

The boy was placed within a starship and rocketed toward Earth, his arrival echoing that of Kal-El, which earned him much empathy from the Man of Steel. Superman altered the craft's trajectory so it would avoid destroying Metropolis, and he was stunned to discover a fellow Kryptonian within. Lor-Zod's name in Kryptonese was etched within the ship, further earning Superman's sympathy and interest. To be cautious, however, the boy was taken to an East Coast facility for observation by the Department of Meta-Human Affairs. Earth's yellow-sun radiation began to energize the youth, giving him powers to match those of Superman, and he spoke fluent Kryptonese. The government's tests confirmed what Superman already knew—that a kinsman had come to Earth. Superman went public with the news that another Kryptonian was now on Earth, thereby deflating the U.S. government's plan to obtain and hold Lor-Zod for its own mysterious purposes. Lex Luthor, however, also wanted the boy for his own studies and dispatched Bizarro to obtain him (*Action Comics* #844–845, December 2006–January 2007).

Determined to give the young Kryptonian boy a good life, Superman took Lor-Zod from the Meta-Human Affairs Department in Washington, DC, and asked Batman for help in crafting a new identity for the boy (*Action Comics* #845–846, January–February 2007). Soon after, Christopher Kent officially came to live with Clark Kent and Lois Lane in their Metropolis apartment and was enrolled at the elite Ellsworth School (*Superman* #664, August 2007). To help him master and conceal his still-developing superpowers, Batman helped craft a wristwatch that emitted red solar radiation, which temporarily robbed Chris of his abilities (*Superman* #668, Early December 2007). The watch was miscalibrated, however, creating a buildup of energy in Chris's body; the result was an explosion that destroyed the Kents' Metropolis brownstone (*Superman* #672–673, March–April 2008).

Soon after, General Zod, Ursa, and Non were freed from the Phantom Zone and arrived on Earth as Zod's plan came to fruition. Zod attempted to make good on his vow of avenging himself against Jor-El and his heirs, and kidnapped Lois Lane, imprisoned Superman in the Phantom Zone and reclaimed Lor-Zod (*Action Comics* #845–846, January–February 2007). With Superman trapped in the Zone and Zod's loyal army of Kryptonians now loose on Earth, the Man of Steel was in desperate straits. He found a way out of the Phantom Zone with the help of childhood friend and Daxamite Mon-El, then swallowed his pride and asked for help from Luthor in defeating Zod and his followers. By this time, most of Earth's superpowered heroes had been captured or defeated, and Superman's choices for aid were few.

Chris protected Lois, who had shown him love and kindness—things he was unfamiliar with prior to his time on Earth—as best as he could (*Action Comics* #851, August 2007). This allowed Superman to concentrate on defeating Zod and returning all the criminals to the Phantom Zone. To help ensure that his parents and all the other Kryptonians remained in the Zone, Chris sacrificed his chances for a happy life on Earth to reenter the Phantom Zone and use his unique physiology to keep the barrier between the dimensions intact (*Action Comics Annual* #11, 2007).

Chris eventually found Brainiac's technology within the Kryptonian prison that had once been his parents' shelter. He interfaced directly with the alien equipment, which somehow allowed him to forge a mental link with Kandor's security chief Thara Ak-Var. She in turn received help from the mute Non and helped free the youth from the Phantom Zone (*Action Comics Annual* #12, 2008). Soon after, the Kandorians relocated a piece of Earth into orbit, then used advanced technology to grow the chunk into a full-sized planet dubbed New Krypton. Zod, however, had tasked Ursa with placing sleeper agents throughout Earth's human civilization—just in case. Chris and Thara pledged to expose them all and donned the costumed identities of the legendary Nightwing and Flamebird to accomplish this task (*Action Comics* #875, May 2009).

Chris's time in the Phantom Zone seemed to have an unusual effect on his physiology: His body was prone to rapid bursts of aging. Although Thara rescued a boy who appeared ten years old, he looked like a teen when he first became Nightwing and soon after appeared about twenty-three years old. Lois Lane asked the heroic Doctor

Light to examine Chris to make certain these age spurts would not prematurely kill him, and she assured the worried Lois that Chris would be fine, for now (*Action Comics* #876, June 2009).

He also preferred his human name Chris Kent as opposed to his birth name Lor-Zod, thereby rejecting his parents' legacy.

Nightwing and Flamebird exposed numerous Kryptonian agents and battled Codename: Assassin, leading them to become media darlings. Thara grew jealous when she saw women practically throw themselves at Chris, so she kissed him passionately and ignited a romance. Their budding relationship was interrupted when they were attacked by Neutron and Reactron, reminding them that the mission had to come first (*Action Comics* #880, November 2009). With Supergirl's assistance, they fended off the villains, but they were suddenly the subject of a manhunt orchestrated by Project 7734, which successfully turned the public against the trio of heroes. Dogging their every move was General Sam Lane's Squad K, which then included Reactron in its ranks. When Chris, Thara, and Supergirl agreed to surrender, Reactron slaughtered the other Squad K members in cold blood and attacked the Kryptonians (*Action Comics* #881–882, December 2009–January 2010; *Supergirl* [fifth series] #45, January 2010).

Not long after, Chris underwent another age spurt, resulting in his becoming an elderly man, and this proved beyond even Doctor Light's abilities to correct. She took him to a colleague, Doctor Pillings, for help, but he turned out to be the Kryptonian villain Jax-Ur in disguise. When Jax-Ur created a version of the Kryptonian god Rao, Nightwing and Flamebird went into action to stop its rampant destruction. Along the way, the true spirit of the Nightwing was awakened within Chris (*Action Comics* #888, Early June 2010). Flamebird eventually sacrificed herself to destroy the false deity, but the Nightwing entity stopped Chris from accompanying her, for Chris's destiny lay in stabilizing the newly reformed Phantom Zone. "Once again you must heal the Phantom Zone. You are tied to it," declared Nightwing. With that, Chris bade another tearful farewell to Kal-El, the only Kryptonian to ever show him unconditional love and support. Once more returned to his proper childhood age, Chris met Mon-El in a previously unseen area of the Phantom Zone, and the two promised to watch out for each other, a new friendship forming (*Superman: War of the Supermen* #3–4, July 2010).

In the current multiverse, there was also an Earth-16 Chris Kent (*Countdown: Arena* #2, February 2008). This version of Chris was older and appeared to be highly evolved both emotionally and physically. This Chris Kent also made the ultimate sacrifice to save Superman, and died at the hands of the Supermen of Earth-30 and Earth-31 in a failed attempt to kill Monarch.

KENT, CLARK

Clark Kent was the name given to the baby Kal-El after he was found and adopted by Jonathan and Martha Kent of Smallville, Kansas. When the Kents decided to keep the baby, Martha used her maiden name for Kal-El's new first name.

The Kents lived on the isolated Kent family farm on the outskirts of Smallville. As the young Clark began to display unnatural strength, stamina, and invulnerability, the Kents knew their child would have to be carefully raised. It was through their strong moral and ethical teachings that young Clark grew up to recognize that his naturally developing superpowers made him different from, not superior to, his friends and neighbors. They taught him how to master and conceal his powers while also giving him lessons in the workings of good and evil. Had any other couple raised Kal-El, the adult Superman may never have fulfilled his destiny as the World's Greatest Super Hero.

His upbringing has varied in the many retellings of his origin. On Earth-2, Kal-L's parents were John Silas Kent and Mary Kent, who raised him in the same way, but never conceived of their son eventually becoming a costumed hero. Ironically, the inspiration came from the Earth-1 Superboy, who accidentally traversed the barriers of time and dimensions to meet his counterpart (*The New Adventures of Superboy* #15–16, March–April 1981). After his parents' deaths, the adult Clark first donned a costume and adopted the Superman identity only after beginning work at the Daily Star (*Action Comics* #1, June 1938).

To ensure that no one would suspect Clark Kent of also being Superman, he donned fake glasses and assumed the persona of a mild-mannered reporter. Despite that, Lois Lane, among many others, tried to prove otherwise, all without success.

As the *Star*'s top reporter, Clark Kent was

known for his investigative skills and honest reporting (*Superman* [first series] #44, January–February 1947). Over the years, he served as a war correspondent, advice-to-the-lovelorn editor, and correspondent for the paper's Bombay edition, experience that eventually led him to replace retiring George Taylor as the *Star*'s editor in chief (*Superman Family* #196, July–August 1979). Clark and Lois finally married (*Action Comics* #484, June 1978), their deep love having seen them through many rough times until both left the mortal plane for a limbo-like dimension during the Crisis on Infinite Earths (*Crisis on Infinite Earths* #12, March 1986).

Kal-El had numerous adventures during his early years on Earth-1. Martha had taken his baby blankets and fashioned them into a red-and-blue playsuit that would not rip whenever he was active (*Superboy* [first series] #8, May–June 1950). When Clark was a toddler, the Kents sold the farm and used the proceeds to buy a general store in Smallville (*Superboy* [first series] #78, January 1960). Clark completed his primary education in Smallville while working afternoons at the store and using his superpowers for good as the heroic Superboy.

To craft separate personae for Clark and Superboy, the Kents suggested he comb his hair differently and wear eyeglasses. Through the years, despite his healthy physique, Clark trained himself to alter the timbre of his voice, stand and walk with a slight stoop, as well as adopt other physical traits to help divert any suspicion. Despite his efforts, first Lana Lang, then later Lois Lane, would consistently try to discover the truth. None succeeded except for Pete Ross, who discovered Clark's secret by accident and never revealed he knew it. Among Clark's adoptive relatives were cousins Carl (*Superboy* [first series] #12, January–February 1951), Esther (*The New Adventures of Superboy* #13, January 1981), Albert Crane, Eric Stanton (*Superboy* [first series] #36, October 1954), Charles "Crusty" Kent (*Superboy* [first series] #170, December 1970), and Jillian Kent (*Superman Family* #191, September–October 1978).

Clark's principal at Smallville High considered him "the shyest boy in our graduating class" (*Superman* [first series] #125, November 1958), while his yearbook declared: "highest grades—boy most likely to become famous" (*Superman* [first series] #144, April 1961). Clark had only a few close friends, but they stuck by his side throughout his years in Smallville: Lana Lang and Pete Ross. Soon after graduation, Clark's adoptive parents died from an illness that none of his amazing powers could cure (*Superman* [first series] #146, July 1961, and #161, May 1963).

After high school, Clark attended Metropolis University and studied journalism. There he met and fell in love with Lori Lemaris, a fellow student who turned out to be a mermaid from Atlantis (*Superman* [first series] #129, May 1959). He also led a relatively normal life, residing in a dormitory, joining a fraternity, and becoming a male cheerleader for the football team.

As an adult, Clark stood six foot one with a chest measurement of forty-four inches and a thirty-four-inch waist (*Action Comics* #297, February 1963). He weighed 225 pounds, and his Social Security number was 092-09-6616 (*Action Comics* #340, August 1966).

Upon relocating permanently to Metropolis, Clark got a job as a reporter at the *Daily Planet*, where he met Lois Lane, Jimmy Olsen, and editor Perry White. His journalistic career made him a celebrity in his own right, and when Galaxy Broadcasting bought the *Planet*, new owner Morgan Edge transferred Kent to WGBS, where he worked as an on-camera reporter and later anchorman (*Superman* [first series] #233, January 1971). In addition to his television duties, Kent later resumed reporting for the *Daily Planet* (*Action Comics* #493, March 1979).

Kent lived in a high-rise at 344 Clinton Street, Apartment 3-B, and through the years got to know many of his neighbors (*Superman* [first series] #112, March 1957). He created a false wall within the apartment behind which he could maintain a supply of fresh uniforms and store several of the robots he used to impersonate one of his identities when needed. Several trophies of his life as Superman and Clark Kent were also stored there, as opposed to the Fortress of Solitude, including samples of kryptonite.

After reality was altered by the Crisis, Clark Joseph Kent (his new middle name first established in *Superman: The Wedding and Beyond*, 1997) was once again found by Jonathan and his wife and raised on the Kents' Smallville farm, but it wasn't until his senior year in high school that his body absorbed enough solar radiation to manifest the full array of his superpowers. Until then, he was a popular teen and captain of the high school football team (*Man of Steel* #1, Early October 1986). After much thought, he revealed his secret to Lana Lang by taking her flying on the night before graduation (*Man of Steel* #6, Late December

1986). Upon graduation, he eschewed college for wandering the world to learn more about humanity, on one occasion even momentarily encountering a young Bruce Wayne, who was on a quest of his own (*Superman: The Odyssey,* July 1999). Clark was briefly the protégé to world-famous journalist Simone DeNeige in Paris (*The Adventures of Superman* #0, October 1994), but learned the most about his future field while tagging along with veteran *Daily Planet* reporter Ed Wilson. After Wilson died, Clark began wearing his mentor's fedora as a tribute (*Action Comics* #800, April 2003). His travels at an end, the young Clark returned to America and began attending Metropolis University (*World of Metropolis* #3, October 1988).

His career at the *Planet* was secured when he wrote the first in-depth article about the newly arrived Superman, who had just rescued a space shuttle (with Lois Lane aboard) near Metropolis (*Man of Steel* #2, Late October 1986). He went on to win numerous journalism awards and publish four novels, including *The Golden Throne, The Janus Contract* (*Superman* [second series] #49, November 1990), and *Under a Yellow Sun* (*Superman: Under a Yellow Sun,* 1994). Kent was a courageous reporter, making headlines of his own by exposing the criminal dealings of Intergang, thereby earning him a contract on his life.

Clark Kent was the conservative in a newsroom full of colorful characters despite his glowing accomplishments as a reporter and writer. He was well liked by the staff although his "farm boy" ways led him to be the butt of jokes at the hands of sportswriter Steve Lombard. On the other hand, Clark was a role model to fledgling photojournalist Jimmy Olsen. The young man looked up to Clark, and the two developed a caring sibling relationship, with Jimmy at times being the younger brother Clark never imagined having. He took his job as an example seriously, which at times made him even more careful in how he presented himself.

This mentor role was reversed in the relationship Kent shared with editor Perry White. The older journalist appreciated Clark's willingness to do the unglamorous legwork required by the job without complaint. His somewhat naïve ways gave White a project to work on, polishing Kent's instincts for news and office politics. While Jimmy was the brother Kent never had, Clark was the model son Perry always wanted.

His handsomeness was not lost on Catherine Grant, who tried to claim him for herself when she first arrived at the *Planet.* He was genuinely overwhelmed by her aggressive manner and uncertain how to handle her at first, especially since he had eyes for Lois Lane. Over time, though, Clark and Cat managed to find a co-worker relationship that allowed them to become friends.

Becoming friendly with his rival reporter Lois Lane proved anything but easy. She didn't like having "Smallville" come into the newsroom and fight her for city beat stories. Still, as his accomplishments mounted, including his celebrated exposé of Intergang, Lois began to reevaluate Clark as a man. Their exploits proved adrenaline-filled as they dealt with Lex Luthor and the omnipresent LexCorp in addition to all the super-menaces that arrived with alarming regularity in Metropolis. They came to rely on each other, and a genuine friendship began to take hold. It may also have finally started to dawn on Lois that Superman was an unattainable romantic ideal while Clark represented other qualities that were equally attractive.

At first, she was furious that Clark "abandoned" her when he left the *Planet* to work for *Newstime Magazine.* Clark returned to ask for his job back, noting how ambivalent Lois was to see him at the office again. When she forgave him for "selling out," he impulsively gave her a passionate kiss, putting all his pent-up feelings into the embrace. In the aftermath, Lois reconsidered him as a man. She finally accepted his invitation for a date, which went well enough that a second followed. In time, the entire newsroom noticed that a new office romance was blossoming, and it was well received by one and all. To Clark, Lois was everything he could imagine in a life partner, and her brash style showed him ways he could act without giving away his heroic persona.

It wasn't long after the two began dating that Clark knew this was the woman for him. As a result, he didn't hesitate to propose (*Superman* [second series] #50, December 1990). With wedding plans under way, he decided the time had come to trust her completely and reveal his identity, an act that shocked his fiancée to the core.

Before they could marry, though, Superman had to defend Earth from Doomsday. The Man of Steel was killed by the behemoth, leaving Lois crushed. She was devastated to lose Superman and Clark at the same time, and it left her somewhat brittle. Worse, when Clark was resurrected, thanks to Kryptonian technology, he became overly protective of his future bride. She broke off the engagement, and he then had to watch her take an overseas assignment to reassert her individuality. Yet it was clear that his love for her was so strong, he would wait as long as it took before they could tie the knot.

Clark kept the ring wrapped in a handkerchief, waiting for the day Lois was ready to return to him. She did just that after several months. Upon learning that he had been carrying the ring all this time, she took it back. Soon after, the couple finally wed and moved into a condominium at 1938 Sullivan Place, a building owned by Bruce Wayne (*Superman: The Wedding Album,* December 1996).

Having Lois in Clark's life finally gave him a partner he could rely on for advice. Whenever time permitted, they escaped to remote locations for one-on-one time. For the first time since leaving Smallville, he had an anchor, someone to live for who loved him, too.

As realities were altered repeatedly after various crises, the origins of Kal-El were modified time and again.

In a time line that briefly existed prior to the Infinite Crisis, Clark had an upbringing familiar to his previous origins, although he had no childhood adventures as Superboy. Instead, upon graduating from high school, he traveled the world as a freelance journalist experiencing the best and worst of humanity. After surviving a brutal coup d'état in Africa, he returned to Smallville. He asked Jonathan and Martha to show him the rocket ship he had arrived on Earth in. They did so, then helped him perfect his "nerdy" appearance of Clark Kent so that no one would suspect he was also a costumed hero when he finally revealed himself. He found a job at the *Daily Planet* and went into action as Superman almost immediately, thanks to a plan by Lex Luthor to take control of Metropolis (*Superman: Birthright* #1–3, September–November 2003).

The Infinite Crisis changed the various Earths' time lines once more, and in this incarnation Clark Kent grew up believing he was a normal adolescent—until fate intervened. After Pete Ross broke an arm trying to tackle Clark, the adolescent began to experience the birth of his powers, leading to a disastrous event involving his heat vision nearly burning down the Kent barn. To Clark's dismay, his parents devised a pair of glasses with special lenses (made from the rocket that brought him to Earth) that helped contain his heat vision during his now unpredictable puberty. When Clark began to fly, Jonathan and Martha realized it was time to reveal the truth to their adopted son.

When Clark was shown the spaceship that carried him to Earth, the nervous boy touched it, activating the Sunstone crystal contained within, giving him astonishing glimpses of life on his long-dead homeworld of Krypton.

His newfound realization that he was an alien from another planet left Clark feeling like an outsider, forced to hide his powers and who he truly was. He became uncomfortable around everyone, even the first girl he kissed—Lana Lang. Convinced he was a misfit and somewhat ashamed of his Kryptonian roots, Clark withdrew from his peers.

His adoptive parents were the ones who helped Clark truly embrace his Kryptonian roots and appreciate his unique place in the world. After Clark's clothes continually ripped during all the anonymous good deeds he began performing, Martha created a uniform based on the clothes the Kryptonians wore, complete with the symbol of the House of El—thus Clark's Superboy costume was born. Superboy was never seen by the public and became something of a modern myth; the tabloids called him "Super-Boy," but no one truly believed he existed.

The young Clark Kent eventually encountered a trio of teens from the late thirtieth century known as the Legion of Super-Heroes, and he joined them on many adventures. It was the first time Clark ever felt like he belonged, and provided a joyous reprieve from the realities of life in Smallville. The Legionnaires were the first friends Clark connected with, and the fun and camaraderie he had

with the Legion was a big part of the enthusiasm that led him to becoming a part of the Justice League of America and the super hero community at large.

During his first adventure with the Legion, Clark learned to have faith in people, no matter who they were, thanks to the compassion of Saturn Girl (Truth); he loosened up and had fun with his powers while taking down criminals thanks to Lightning Lad's antics (Justice); and he learned about the value of diversity and working together thanks to Cosmic Boy's exemplary leadership (the American Way).

Clark's Legion experiences left him wondering if he'd ever meet other people like him in his personal future. To find out, he realized he needed to leave Smallville.

Clark eventually grew comfortable with being a man of two worlds, and the name Superman meant just that to him—and the people of Earth (*Superman: Secret Origin* #1–6, November 2009–September 2010).

KENT, ELY

A Revolutionary War–era member of the Kent family, Ely was a blacksmith who performed many services for General George Washington. The colonial leader paid for the goods with a promissory note for two thousand dollars, which would earn compound interest until redeemed. The note was lost until found many years later by Hubert, butler to Titus Kent, a cousin of Jonathan Kent. Intending to redeem the note for himself, the manservant set out to kill all known members of the Kent family who might have a claim to the fortune, leaving ownership to Titus and then, ultimately, to himself. After one successful murder and two failed attempts, Hubert's plot was discovered and stopped by Jonathan's adopted son Superman (*Action Comics* #132, May 1949).

KENT, JEBEDIAH

The Kents could trace their roots back nearly a millennium, but the family really settled down when they moved to Kansas during the 1800s. Jebediah Kent was the second son born to Abigail and Silas Kent of Boston. After Abigail's death, Silas, Jebediah, and his older brother Nathaniel journeyed to the Midwest to settle in Lawrence, almost smack in the middle of the Kansas Territory. Coming from the North, the family held more enlightened views on slavery; they were seen by the locals as abolitionists, which earned the newcomers much scorn.

The Kent men opened up a print shop and began publishing a newspaper to spread their more progressive beliefs.

Trouble escalated when Luther Reid, a pro-slavery settler from Missouri, ordered Silas's murder. After their father was shot in the back during the winter of 1855, Jeb accused Reid of the cowardly crime, and Reid promptly reported the threat to Sheriff Sam Jones. Intending to lynch Jeb, the two men arrived at the Kent homestead, but Nathaniel intervened and chased them off.

Jeb temporarily left the homestead to travel along the Missouri border, ready to fight anyone whom he saw fit, a dark change in personality that troubled his older brother, now head of the Kent family. By 1857, the brothers attempted to deliver a letter to Governor William Shannon requesting that troops be sent to Lawrence to quell the rising tensions between the North and the South. During the spring, Nate left Jeb in charge of the print shop while he headed to Washington to appeal directly to President Franklin Pierce.

The brothers drifted farther apart, and when the Civil War broke out in 1861, Jeb joined with the Confederate States of America, serving under William Quantrill. After the war, Jeb wound up leading a group of bandits and learned he had fathered a bastard son some years previously, whom he eventually welcomed into the gang. The boy, however, proved dangerously out of control, prompting Jeb to approach Nathaniel—who had now settled in the town of Smallville—for help in dealing with the troubled youth. The brothers called a truce to deal with their family situation, but in the end the boy shot and killed Jeb. Jeb made amends with Nate with his dying breath (*The Kents* #1–12, August 1997–July 1998).

On Earth-1, the roles of Nathaniel and Jebediah Kent were likely filled by Seth and Hiram Kent, who "fought on opposite sides in the Civil War" (*Superboy* [first series] #108, October 1963).

KENT, JERRY

In the reality known as Earth-Prime, Jerry Kent was the owner of a successful computer firm, and his wife Naomi practiced law. They lived happily in a small New England town near the coast. While they were taking a walk one evening, the pair encountered an infant that had seemingly been abandoned. Deciding to keep and raise the child as their own, Naomi gave the baby her maiden name of Clark, even though Jerry warned her he'd be mocked for having the same name as a comic book character. The boy grew up unaware that he had been teleported to Earth by Jor-El prior to Krypton being consumed by its dying red sun.

Clark grew up embracing his Superman connections. He was attending a costume party as Superboy when his nascent superpowers began to manifest themselves, probably triggered by the cosmic event known as the Crisis on Infinite Earths. This suddenly real Superboy was shocked when he came face-to-face with the Superman of Earth-1, who warned him of the anti-matter wave that was destroying all of the various Earths. Unable to stop the wave from destroying his own universe, this Superboy abandoned his world and his parents, who died unaware that their adopted son would in the new reality become an angry engine of destruction known as Superboy-Prime (*DC Comics Presents* #87, November 1985).

In the post-Infinite Crisis reality, Jerry and Naomi continued to exist on one of the fifty-two parallel Earths, now fully aware of the damage their adopted son caused in other realities. He has lived in fear of angering the powerful teen, driving him every Wednesday to the comics shop to buy the latest DC Comics to see what was happening on New Earth (*Adventure Comics* #507–508, January–February 2010).

KENT, JOHN

On Earth-2, John Kent and his wife Mary Kent were driving in their car when they witnessed a spacecraft crashing to Earth. They discovered an infant within the wreckage and named him Clark Kent (*Action Comics* #1, June 1938; name revealed in *Superman* [first series] #53, July–August 1948). They took him to an orphanage, but after the baby displayed unusual powers, the Kents adopted him as their own and trained young Clark in how to use his rapidly developing abilities.

John's Kent ancestors included Revolutionary War blacksmith Ely Kent and Erie Canal barge operator Captain Joshua Kent (*Action Comics* #132, May 1949). His present-day relatives included a niece Carol, who became an actress; nephews "Digger" Kent, a gold prospector, and Louis Pasteur Kent, a country doctor; Titus Kent, a wheelchair-bound recluse who lost his entire fortune during the Great Depression (and whose butler Hubert killed their cousin Arthur) (*Action Comics* #132, May 1949); and John's younger sister Minerva Kent (*Action Comics* #160, September 1951).

John Kent died of natural causes after Clark grew to manhood, and on his deathbed made his son promise to use his abilities only for the good of humankind.

KENT, JONATHAN

Jonathan Kent was the adoptive father of Kal-El, the baby rocketed to Earth from the doomed planet Krypton. He raised the child as his own, watching him grow up to become the World's Greatest Super Hero, Superman (*More Fun Comics* #101, January–February 1945; named in *Adventure Comics* #149, February 1950).

Jonathan Kent's background altered slightly with the various Earths' realities, but in each continuity his training and strong moral values helped make Superman a force for good.

Jonathan's family could be traced back to infamous English "hanging judge" Sir Julian Kent (*Superboy* [first series] #189, August 1972), and the "founder of the family" in the United States, Jonas Kent, who was a traveling entertainer, along with his wife Maria (*Superboy* [first series] #108, October 1963). Later relatives included Roger Kent, an aide to General Washington (*Superboy* [first series] #108, October 1963), farmer Mark Kent, sailor Captain John Kent, and wigmaker Simon Kent (*Superboy* [first series] #189, August 1972). Jonathan's direct lineage traced from Captain Sinbad Kent, a Revolutionary War spy for George Washington, lawyer John Kent, teacher George Kent, scientist Lewis Kent (*Superboy* [first series] #79, March 1960), and merchant Matthew Hiram Kent, husband of Edith (*Superboy* [first series] #77, December 1959).

In addition to Jonathan, Matthew and Edith had three other sons: George, a merchant seaman who died when Clark Kent was a toddler (*Superman* [first series] #111, February 1957), Burt (*Superboy* [first series] #117, December 1964), and millionaire Kendall (*Superboy* [first series] #119, March 1965). Jonathan's extended family included uncles Cyrus (*Superboy* [first series] #108, October 1953) and Simon (*Superboy* [first series] #113, June 1964), along with cousins Ezra (*Superboy* [first series] #170, December 1970) and Silas (*Superboy* [first series] #108, October 1963).

Jonathan was a former race car driver in his youth (*Superboy* [first series] #196, July 1973) who eventually became a farmer outside Smallville, Kansas. When Clark was a toddler, he and his wife Martha Kent sold their farm and used the proceeds to buy a general store within Smallville (*Superboy* [first series] #78, January 1960).

As his son grew, it was usually Jonathan who helped train Clark on the functions and limits of his superpowers, as well as ways to conceal those powers from his classmates. When, at the age of eight, Clark decided to use his powers to aid the public, Martha refashioned Clark's indestructible playsuit into a colorful super hero costume. Jonathan worked with Clark to devise ways to differentiate Clark the boy from Superboy the hero.

Jonathan was a pillar of the Smallville community, and his store served as one of the town's chief gathering places. He always kept an ear out

to make certain no one suspected the Kent family secret. He and Martha would often welcome people young Clark encountered from other planets or across time and space. They also opened their home to Lar Gand, who adventured across the galaxy under the name Mon-El (*Superboy* [first series] #89, June 1961).

All this interaction with aliens and superpowered beings was handled by the Kents with grace and an open mind, thereby demonstrating to Clark how to behave regardless of circumstances. One alien interaction, however, had unintended consequences for the Kents. Exposure to an alien serum effectively rejuvenated Jonathan and Martha, making them appear to be a couple in their late thirties (*Superboy* [first series] #145, March 1968).

Once Clark graduated from high school, Jonathan and Martha decided to take their first extended vacation, a trip to the Caribbean Islands. While there, they found a pirate's treasure chest, and when they handled its contents, both contracted a rare tropical disease that proved fatal. Martha passed away first, but Jonathan managed to speak with Clark one last time before dying, reminding his son to always use his powers for the benefit of humankind (*Superman* [first series] #161, May 1963). After Jonathan died, Clark left Smallville for good.

In order to fulfill a promise made years earlier to Clark's father, a pair of extraterrestrials later resurrected Jonathan Kent for twenty-four hours, permitting him a joyful reunion with Superman and the glimpse of his son as an adult that he'd long ago wished for (*Action Comics* #507–508, May–June 1980).

In the world reshaped by the Crisis on Infinite Earths, Jonathan descended from a long line of Kents who settled in Smallville after moving to Kansas from Boston (*The Kents,* August 1997). His ancestor Nathaniel Kent was once the town's sheriff. Jonathan's parents were Samuel and Eliza Campbell Kent, and he had had an older brother named Harry, who died after accidentally falling beneath their father's thresher (*Man of Steel* #1, Early October 1986). Harry's young widow Sarah (nicknamed Sal) took over housekeeping for Sam when Eliza passed away shortly thereafter (*World of Smallville* #1, April 1988).

Jonathan and Martha discovered the Kryptonian birthing matrix that contained the baby Kal-El and chose to keep the infant, later telling people that Martha had given birth to the boy during a freak snowstorm that kept them isolated on the farm for much of the season (*Man of Steel* #1, Early October 1986).

Jonathan and Martha helped raise their child to fulfill his extraordinary destiny as Superman, and always welcomed Clark for visits when he wanted to take a break from life in Metropolis. After Clark's epic battle with the monstrous Doomsday, the toll of watching his son die at the hands of the alien creature resulted in Jonathan suffering a fatal heart attack (*Superman* [second series] #77, March 1993). In some versions of the afterlife, father and son were reunited, and Clark encouraged his father to come back to the mortal world and those who loved and needed him (*The Adventures of Superman* #500, Early June 1993).

The family endured much over the years, given the turbulent and adventurous life their son led. The farmhouse was razed by their former neighbor Kenny Braverman (aka Conduit), who was out to destroy all that Superman held dear (*Superman* [second series] #100, May 1995). While the house was being rebuilt, the couple toured the country in a motor home. Years later, the entire farm was devastated when Imperiex unleashed a bomb that eradicated Topeka (*Superman* [second series] #172, September 2001). As a result, the Kents purchased a general store and relocated to Smallville proper (*Superman* [second series] #178, March 2002).

Reality was altered once again, and Jonathan's relationship with Clark developed differently than prior versions of their history. They stopped talking while Clark was in high school and his powers began manifesting; years later, when he returned to Smallville to seek guidance about his life, Jonathan was still uncomfortable around his adopted son. When pressed to by Clark, Jonathan explained that he felt he was competing with Clark's birth father ever since Clark learned about his Kryptonian heritage. While initially disapproving of Clark's heroic alter ego, Jonathan eventually softened, and the two Kent men reconciled (*Superman: Birthright* #1–3, September–November 2003).

When reality was altered once again by the Infinite Crisis, there was no tension between father and son. In fact, Pa Kent remained one of the loving, grounding moral and ethical forces in Clark's life. He did, however, suffer a fatal heart attack during the real Brainiac's attempt to destroy the Kents on their farm (*Action Comics* #870, December 2008). The funeral was attended by friends and family, a large number of whom had loved and respected Jonathan enormously (*Superman: New Krypton Special* #1, 2008).

Regardless of the reality, Jonathan's steadfast love for Martha Kent and their Kansas farm were bedrocks of his personality. She was everything to him, and their loving relationship was a model that Clark longed to emulate before proposing to Lois Lane. Although it was Martha who urged him to let them keep the alien infant, it was Jonathan's love for Martha that led him to agree. He never once regretted bringing the boy into their lives. It completed the family he had wanted, and he couldn't imagine having a better mate than Martha. They complemented each other whether it was splitting the chores or finding ways to train Clark as his powers and abilities began to manifest themselves.

Coming from a long line of Kents, Jonathan recognized the tremendous responsibility that came with raising a son. Having a powerful boy in the house meant he needed to temper his expectations and increase his empathy. Through the years, he relished dispensing advice to Clark and enjoyed the simple pleasures of doing farmwork with the youth at his side. While Martha was there to deal with his emotional upheavals, it fell to Jonathan to

make certain that Clark was raised to recognize his responsibilities to his family and to his neighbors, all preparatory to the global responsibilities that were going to come with adulthood.

Little else gave Jonathan the same sense of pride as when he read the morning paper to see what Clark had accomplished the day before. His ears grew accustomed to the change in the air that announced his son was coming to pay a visit. Usually, after dinner and pie, the two men would take a walk out in the fields, giving Clark a chance to unburden himself. Jonathan lacked the experience to counsel his son on how to handle alien threats or extradimensional menaces, but he certainly knew how to help point Clark down the proper moral pathways, a habit he learned from his own father.

In Jonathan Kent's post-Infinite Crisis background, he often came to his adolescent son's aid when Clark's powers first manifested themselves, including the time when a twelve-year-old Clark suddenly burned down the family's barn with a burst of heat vision (*Superman: Secret Origin* #1, November 2009).

Jonathan and Martha were the ones to help Clark embrace his Kryptonian heritage and use his special powers to make a difference in the world. As Clark began to anonymously save people, he wondered out loud to Jonathan, "Am I saving people just as a way to earn my place on Earth? Am I really good?" As always, Jonathan Kent had the wisdom—and the right words—to soothe Clark's troubled mind.

KENT, LAUREL

Laurel Kent was a direct descendant of Clark Kent in the late thirtieth century (*Superboy* [first series] #217, June 1976). She applied for admittance to the Legion of Super-Heroes like her Kryptonian ancestor but was turned down for several reasons, including her limited power of invulnerability. The bylaws also prohibited duplication of abilities, and hers were already represented by either Mon-El or Ultra Boy; that—coupled with her vulnerability to kryptonite—led to her elimination. To hide her true identity and not spoil the historical time line, Laurel used the name Elna (an anagram for Lane) when she met a visiting Superboy. She did tease the Teen of Steel, however, by revealing that she resembled the woman he was destined to marry.

Laurel was admitted to the Legion Academy for training but was shot with a kryptonite bullet by a mysterious hired assassin. It was later revealed that the immortal Justice League of America enemy Professor Ivo was out to kill all the descendants of the fabled League (*Legion of Super-Heroes* [second series] *Annual* #1, 1985). Some time later, Laurel was shockingly revealed as a centuries-old sleeper agent of the Manhunters and not a descendant of Superman at all. Confronted by the Legion, Laurel self-destructed rather than allow herself to be captured or harm her former friends (*Legion of Super-Heroes* [third series] #42–43, January–February 1988).

KENT, LOIS

Lois Lane's name on Earth-2 after her marriage to Clark Kent (*Action Comics* #484, June 1978).

KENT, MARTHA CLARK

On Earth-1, Martha was the daughter of Henry and Willa Clark (*Superman Family* #192, November-December 1978). She had a sister named Mary and a brother-in-law named Fred (*The New Adventures of Superboy* #13, January 1981) as well as a rancher cousin named Tom (*Superboy* [first series] #130, June 1966).

Martha Clark, a native of Smallville, married her sweetheart Jonathan Kent and moved with him to the Kent family farm. The couple could not conceive a child, but were soon to unexpectedly gain one when a rocket crashed outside town. Within the ship was an infant child whom the astonished couple chose to adopt as their own. Martha gave the baby her maiden name, and so Clark Kent arrived in Smallville (*More Fun Comics* #101, January-February 1945; named in *Adventure Comics* #169, October 1951).

The infant Clark proved unusual from the beginning as his superpowers manifested quickly and without warning, and the Kents were challenged with keeping all of this away from any prying eyes. Because the baby constantly wore through his Earth clothes, Martha took the Kryptonian blankets the infant Kal-El was wrapped in when they found him and reworked them into a red-and-blue playsuit (*Superboy* [first series] #8, May–June 1950).

When Clark was a toddler, the Kents sold the farm and used the proceeds to buy a general store in Smallville (*Superboy* [first series] #78, January 1960).

As his son grew and his powers developed, it was usually Jonathan who worked with Clark controlling them, while Martha usually looked after the boy's emotional well-being. When, at age eight, Clark decided to use his powers to aid those around him, Martha refashioned his playsuit into a colorful super hero costume.

Martha and Jonathan would often welcome Clark's friends, be they Pete Ross, Lana Lang, or aliens from across time and space.

All this interaction was handled with Martha's uncommon good grace and compassion, demonstrating to her son what an admirable quality open-mindedness was. This came in handy when she and Jonathan were exposed to an alien serum that effectively made them appear to be a couple in their late thirties (*Superboy* [first series] #145, March 1968).

When vacationing in the Caribbean, Martha and Jonathan contracted a rare tropical disease that proved fatal, and the Kents passed away.

Clark inherited the Kent home and general store, while their savings went to the Smallville Orphans' Home, which, according to some versions of the tale, is where Clark resided until his adoption became legal. Clark then left Smallville for good.

In the revised history after the Crisis on Infinite Earths, Martha Clark's family ran the Smallville general store where she first met Jonathan Kent. They dated and intended to marry after he returned from service in World War II, but he was instead captured overseas and presumed dead. Martha found comfort in the arms of Dan Fordman, and the two eventually married. Fordman, however, passed away, and soon after Jonathan joyfully returned home. He and Martha renewed their romance and married, but the couple sadly learned they were incapable of conceiving a child (*World of Smallville* #1–2, April–May 1988).

Some time later, during a winter snowstorm, they discovered the Kryptonian birthing matrix that contained the infant Kal-El. They chose to raise the child as their own, telling neighbors that he was their biological child, born while the family was isolated on the farm during the unusually rough winter. Over time, Clark's extraordinary powers slowly developed, and his parents worked with him to master these gifts—but also to conceal them so that he could have as "normal" a life as possible. Later, after rescuing a space shuttle that was hurtling to its doom above Metropolis (with *Daily Planet* reporter Lois Lane aboard), an adult Clark returned home in need of guidance as to how best to reveal himself to the world without giving up his life as Clark Kent. Martha designed his costume while Jonathan added the iconic El family S-shield on the breast of the outfit, and Superman was born (*Man of Steel* #1, Early October 1986).

Even after Superman became recognized as the World's Greatest Super Hero, Clark still made frequent trips back to Kansas, mostly for Ma Kent's famous pies and a chance to unwind. The Kents always welcomed Clark home and later offered their kindness and hospitality to others, starting with Matrix, a survivor of a Pocket Universe who needed a place to recuperate after her tumultuous journey to Earth (*Superman* [second series] #22, October 1988). Nicknamed Mae, she learned the same moral and ethical lessons that Clark did growing up in Smallville. Later, the Kent home was just as welcoming to Lois Lane, who married Martha's son and became a beloved daughter-in-law.

When Superman was killed by Doomsday, the stress of the traumatic event led Jonathan to suffer clinical death from a heart attack (*Superman* [second series] #77, March 1993), but Martha was overjoyed when he managed to return from the dead thanks to the strength and courage of their son Clark (*The Adventures of Superman* #500, Early June 1993).

The Kents also took in Superman's young clone Kon-El (*Superboy* [third series] #100, July 2002), renaming him Conner Kent and giving the young man some sorely needed love and guidance.

The family endured much, given the always exciting and high-profile life their adopted son led. The farmhouse was once razed by their former

neighbor Kenny Braverman (aka Conduit), who was out to destroy all that Superman held dear (*Superman* [second series] #100, May 1995). While the farm was being rebuilt, the couple toured the country in a motor home. Years later, the entire farm was devastated when Imperiex unleashed a bomb that eradicated Topeka (*Superman* [second series] #172, September 2001). As a result, the Kents bought a general store and relocated to Smallville proper while they figured out their next move (*Superman* [second series] #178, March 2002).

Regardless of the reality, the bond between Martha and Jonathan was unbreakable. They shared the ideals and values that came with growing up in the American heartland. She would do anything for Jonathan and regretted not being able to bring him a child to complete their family. Her answer seemed Heaven-sent when Kal-El's rocket landed in the fields near their home. She suggested they bring the infant into their home—and Jonathan could never refuse her anything.

The two took their responsibility to the child seriously, and Martha's maternal instincts led her to be the one to deal with his emotional traumas—which were frequent, because his manifesting powers proved frustrating until Jonathan could help him adapt. At night, alone, Martha would express to Jonathan her concerns over the time when Clark would be an adult and on his own, isolated from humanity by his powers. Jonathan reassured her that their boy would be fine, and he proved to be right, as always.

Still, she wanted her boy to be happy, and when his friendship with next-door neighbor Lana Lang promised to blossom into something more, she was delighted. She saw in them the same well-matched couple that she and Jonathan were. After Clark revealed his secret and left Lana to find his own way, Martha comforted Lana, and an enduring bond was formed between them.

For years, Martha couldn't understand what had happened, but then it became apparent that the responsibilities that came with his powers also changed Clark's emotional needs. When he began talking about fellow *Daily Planet* reporter Lois Lane, Martha heard in her son's voice that this was his soul mate. In time, Martha and Lois met, and she welcomed the former army brat like a daughter. It took a little time for them to get to know each other, and for Martha to assure Lois she wasn't a rival for Clark's time in any way. Slowly, a bond formed. Lois eventually became the daughter the Kents had never had, and much as Clark sought advice from his parents, so did Lois.

If Martha held any regret, it was the likelihood that Clark's alien physiology meant he and Lois could not have children, depriving Martha of grandbabies to dote over. She knew that this reality weighed heavily on Jonathan, too, as it also meant the Kent family name was going to die out with their adopted son. She contented herself in knowing that Lois made her son happy, and much as fate provided for her, perhaps it would find a way for Lois and Clark to have a family of their own.

After reality was reordered after the Infinite Crisis, Martha's relationship with her adopted son continued to be one filled with love, support, and understanding. While performing rescues throughout Smallville from the shadows of anonymity, young Clark began to spiral down to a depression when he learned he was an alien from the planet Krypton. Hoping to help Clark embrace his uniqueness and his rich Kryptonian history and be proud of who he was, Martha made Clark his iconic Superboy uniform (*Superman: Secret Origin* #1, November 2009).

After Jonathan's death from a heart attack instigated by Brainiac's missile attack on the Kent farm, Martha was determined not to let Jonathan's death distract Clark from his mission as Superman, and she insisted he go through with his plan to leave Earth for a time to dwell among the recently rescued Kandorians on New Krypton (*Superman* #685, April 2009). Life alone proved difficult and more than a little depressing for Martha, but constant contact with both Lois and Lana helped cheer her. Her mettle was tested during the event known as Blackest Night when the Superman of Earth-2 was resurrected as a Black Lantern and stole Jonathan's coffin. Before Martha could act, she was subdued by the Black Lantern version of Earth-2's Lois Lane. Promising Martha would soon be reunited with her husband in the afterlife, the zombie-like Lois chased her into the cornfields and nearly succeeded in killing her had Krypto not come to Martha's rescue (*Blackest Night: Superman* #1–3, October-December 2009). Martha now found a loyal and devoted ally in Krypto.

KENT, MARY

Earth-2's Mary Clark Kent was driving with her husband John one day when they witnessed a spacecraft crashing to the ground. The older couple discovered an infant within the wreckage and named him Clark Kent (*Action Comics* #1, June 1938; name revealed in *Superman* [first series] #53, July–August 1948). They took the baby to an orphanage, but after the infant Clark displayed unusual powers, the Kents formally adopted him and trained the youth in the use of his developing abilities. Mary died before her beloved John, and was unaware that her dear Clark would soon become the World's Greatest Super Hero, Superman.

KENT, MINERVA

John Kent had two siblings, George and Minerva, on Earth-2. George passed away when Jonathan's adopted son Clark Kent was just an infant. Minerva, his younger sister, rarely visited, but when Clark was an adult, she unexpectedly showed up at his front door in Metropolis. The white-haired older woman declared that as the last of the Kent family, they should remain together and that she intended to move in with Clark, something that Clark feared would hamper his ability to become Superman when needed.

Clark welcomed the woman into his home and did his best to work at the *Daily Planet* and operate as Superman without arousing Minerva's suspicion. He also discovered a new power—super-patience—as Minerva tended to treat Clark as if he were still a child and not a full-grown adult. In time, Clark discovered the real reason for her arrival: She was avoiding the unwanted romantic attentions of a man named Zachary Barnes. As a result, Superman pretended to need Minerva's help until Barnes protested, allowing Minerva to recognize that she was scared of falling in love at her age. She then flew to Barnes after her change of heart. Superman promised the woman he would personally look after Clark Kent (*Action Comics* #160, September 1951).

KENT, NAOMI

In the reality known as Earth-Prime, Naomi Clark Kent was a successful attorney married to Jerry Kent, who owned a thriving computer firm. They lived in a small New England town near the coast. While they were taking a walk one day, the pair encountered a seemingly abandoned infant. Deciding to keep and raise the baby as their own, Naomi gave the infant her maiden name of Clark, even though Jerry warned her he'd be mocked for having the same name as a popular comic book character. The boy grew up unaware he had been teleported to Earth by Jor-El prior to Krypton being consumed by its dying red sun.

Clark grew up embracing his Superman connections. He was attending a costume party as Superboy when his superpowers began to manifest themselves, most likely triggered by the cosmic event known as the Crisis on Infinite Earths. This suddenly real Superboy was shocked when he came face-to-face with the Superman of Earth-1. Unable to stop the anti-matter wave the crisis unleashed from destroying his universe, Superboy abandoned his world and his parents, who died unaware of what would become of their adopted son (*DC Comics Presents* #87, November 1985).

In the post–Infinite Crisis reality, Naomi continued to exist on one of the fifty-two parallel Earths, now fully aware of the damage her adopted son wrought in the other realities. She has lived in fear of angering the powerful teen, and while she wants to love him and help heal his broken spirit, she does not really know how she can accomplish this (*Adventure Comics* #507–508, January–February 2010).

KENT, NATHANIEL

The Kents could trace their roots back nearly a millennium, but the family really settled down when they moved to Kansas during the 1800s. Nathaniel Kent was the first son born to Abigail and Silas Kent of Boston. After Abigail's death, Silas, Nathaniel, and his brother Jebediah journeyed to the Midwest to settle in Lawrence, almost smack in the middle of the Kansas Territory. Coming from the North, the family held more enlightened views on slavery; the Kents were seen by the locals as abolitionists, thereby earning the newcomers much scorn. The Kent men opened up a print shop and began publishing a newspaper to spread their progressive beliefs.

Trouble escalated when Luther Reid, a pro-slavery settler from Missouri, ordered Silas's murder. After their father was shot in the back during the winter of 1855, Jeb accused Reid of the cowardly crime, and Reid promptly reported the threat to Sheriff Sam Jones. The two men then traveled to the Kent homestead intending to lynch Jeb, but Nathaniel arrived in time to chase off Jones and Reid.

Jeb temporarily left the homestead to travel along the Missouri border, ready to fight anyone whom he saw fit, a dark change in personality that troubled his older brother, now head of the Kent family. By 1857, the brothers attempted to deliver a letter to Governor William Shannon requesting that troops be sent to Lawrence to quell the rising tensions between the North and the South. During the spring, Nate left Jeb in charge of the print shop while he headed to Washington to appeal for troops directly to President Franklin Pierce. The president rebuffed the request.

The brothers drifted farther apart, and when the Civil War broke out in 1861, Nathaniel joined the Union army. During the war, he met and fell in love with a half-Native American woman, whom he eventually married. She gifted him with a spiritual symbol that, astonishingly, evoked the future S-shield of Superman. After the war, Nathaniel relocated to Smallville, where he was appointed the town's sheriff. When his wild younger brother Jeb reappeared after years of no communication, Nate agreed to a truce in order to help his younger brother out. Jeb had sired a son out of wedlock who had grown into a dangerous psychopath. When the brothers tried to spring a trap to capture the rebellious teen, Jeb wound up being fatally shot. A dying Jeb made amends with Nate with his last breath (*The Kents* #1–12, August 1997–July 1998).

In 1882, Nathaniel Kent was the first in the family to encounter an alien when Abin Sur, the Green Lantern for Space Sector 2814, arrived on Earth in pursuit of a despot named Traitor. Nathaniel provided the alien assistance, although he had some trouble believing the red-skinned man actually came from the stars (*Legends of the DC Universe* #20, September 1999).

On Earth-1, the roles of Nathaniel and Jebediah Kent were likely filled by Seth and Hiram Kent, who "fought on opposite sides in the Civil War" (*Superboy* [first series] #108, October 1963).

KENT, SILAS

The Kents could trace their roots back nearly a millennium, but the family really settled down when they moved to Kansas during the 1800s. Bostonians Silas and Abigail Kent had two boys, Nathaniel and Jebediah, along with three daughters named Belinda, Emmy-Lou, and Lucille. As the boys grew older, Silas, an ardent abolitionist, decided to try homesteading in the Kansas Territory. The three men settled in Lawrence and almost immediately got involved in the Underground Railroad. Coming from the North, the family held more enlightened views on slavery, and they were quickly seen by the locals as trouble. The Kents then opened up a print shop and began publishing a newspaper to spread their progressive beliefs.

Trouble escalated when Luther Reid, a pro-slavery settler from Missouri, ordered Silas's murder. The Kent patriarch was shot in the back during the winter of 1855, leaving Nathaniel as the family's scion. In time, Nathaniel settled in Smallville, planting roots in the town that would be carried on by Jonathan Kent generations later. Jonathan and his wife Martha Kent found and adopted baby Kal-El, raising him to become Superman (*The Kents* #1, August 1997).

KHAI-ZOR

Khai-Zor was a power-hungry Kryptonian scientist whose intent to join Jor-El's exodus to Earth masked his real plans to conquer the planet with the superpowers he would gain there. Exposed for their crimes, Khai-Zor and his partner Val-Arn died in the destruction of Krypton before they could stand trial (*Action Comics* #223, December 1956).

IT WOULD BE FRUITLESS TO SEARCH FOR THEM IN THIS VASTNESS, BUT WE CAN USE THEIR MESSAGE AS A "FIX" TO BEAM IN ON!
AND THEN WE WILL ALL BE REJOINED! KRYPTON'S ONLY SURVIVORS ...TOGETHER AGAIN TO BUILD A NEW CIVILIZATION!

In the parallel reality of Earth-32, Khai-Zor escaped Krypton's fate in a rocket of his own, eventually taking the alias of Xonar. Years later, he stumbled across Dr. Krylo, another Kryptonian survivor. Krylo was one of the few Kryptonians who had actually believed the prediction of their planet's imminent destruction. He had been working on a form of suspended animation that might save the Kryptonian people as they journeyed through space to find a new homeworld. Krylo had gone so far as to prepare instructions for their revival, to be effected by any other race that found the Kryptonian "space coffins." Rendering Jor-El and Lara unconscious moments after they sent Kal-El into space, Krylo placed the couple in separate cryogenic coffins and sent them into space, too, along with himself. Reviving Krylo, the sinister Khai-Zor used the well-intentioned scientist to lure Superboy into space so that he might have revenge on Jor-El's entire family for predicting Krypton's doom. In the ensuing battle, the Teen of Steel triumphed, and Khai-Zor perished. Krylo died of his injuries during his efforts to help Superboy recover his parents' sleeping bodies. Discovering that Jor-El and Lara had already been dying of radiation poisoning when Krypton exploded, their son chose not to revive them and subject his parents to a lingering, painful death on Earth (*Superboy* [first series] #158, July 1969).

KHALEX

The criminal Khalex escaped prison on his unnamed homeworld and journeyed to Earth, where he allied himself with gang leader Midge Martin. Khalex somehow began to display incredible superpowers on a par with Superman's. He was robbed of these abilities when he was near a recently landed meteor, however, so Khalex worked with Martin to devise a ploy that would force Batman and Robin to destroy the extraterrestrial object. With the power-stealing rock gone, Khalex was free to kill Superman and conquer the world. Instead the World's Finest team outwitted the criminals as the Dynamic Duo and the Man of Steel apprehended them (*World's Finest Comics* #105, November 1959).

KHUNDS, THE

Hailing from a distant section of space, the warlike species known as the Khunds were a galactic threat for more than a millennium (*Adventure Comics* #346, July 1966). Originating on Khundia, these people were known for their aggressive behavior toward one another as well as other alien races. To the Khunds, combat was a natural response to the slightest insult or transgression—real or perceived. As a result, the Khunds evolved massive bodies and worked to conquer not only their portion of space, but the entire known universe as well.

They were among the most superior military strategists in known space, with an array of weaponry and spacecraft that made them unparalleled challengers for intergalactic supremacy. Their weapons cache was known to include blasters, neutralizers, and sonic stunners. Members of the Khund military were often made into cyber-warriors who acted as the Khunds' Special Forces.

To achieve their goals, they tried to forge alliances with other alien species sharing similar goals, only to have their dealings disrupted on more than one occasion, beginning with the intercession of Green Lanterns Hal Jordan and Sinestro (*Green Lantern: Emerald Dawn II* #2, May 1991).

For unknown reasons, the Khunds and the similarly aggressive Thanagarians were at odds for centuries, since their very first meeting. Their proximity to each other in space meant the warring between planets was constant. The two species managed to put their enmity aside to join a coalition of races, organized by the Dominators, to invade Earth and eliminate the threat of the planet's super hero population. The Khunds made the first strike, practically annihilating Melbourne, Australia, during their attacks (*Invasion!* #1, 1988). Earth's champions, led by Superman, defeated the threat, and the Khunds were largely confined to their sector of space for the next millennium.

Soon after the invasion ended, the Khunds themselves were nearly wiped out when Khundia was invaded by the Ichor (*Wonder Woman* [third series] #19, June 2008). Wonder Woman, aided by her friend Etta Candy, helped free the planet, and the Guardians of Oa assigned a Khund to the famous Green Lantern Corps in order to help keep the peace.

In the late thirtieth century, the Khunds reasserted themselves in galactic politics when they tried to undermine the Legion of Super-Heroes by planting a traitor named Nemesis Kid within its ranks.

KHYRANA

Aptly described as a "dangerous lady," Khyrana was cursed by Zeus, lord of the Greek pantheon of gods, after she spurned his amorous advances. Her punishment was to "burn with need for the touch of others." Khyrana wandered the planet for millennia, craving touch and affection, but sustained physical contact with her drained her victims of their energy and, ultimately, their lives. She arrived in Metropolis as Clark Kent, Lois Lane, and Diana Prince were attending an art show. Khyrana explained to the trio that she was at the museum in order to obtain artifacts she claimed had been hers eons earlier. Clark and Diana changed into their respective alter egos and challenged the woman. Khyrana managed to absorb enough energy to weaken the Man of Steel and then escaped with his form, determined to leech the last ounce of power from him. After Wonder Woman learned of Khyrana's cursed background, she set out to rescue Superman. Khyrana tried to drain Wonder Woman when they fought, until Superman intervened. As Khyrana touched both the heroes, their combined energies proved incompatible and incapacitated the villainess. The heroes then delivered Khyrana to the Metropolis Science Police (*Superman* #661, April 2007).

KILLGRAVE, THADDEUS

Possessed of small stature, large eyes (behind thick glasses), and a tragic bowl-shaped haircut, Thaddeus Killgrave was an inventor and engineer who was a persistent (if ultimately ineffectual) thorn in Superman's side for years. His plot to destroy Metropolis with a barrage of missiles was exposed by Clark Kent in the *Daily Planet*, and Killgrave later arranged for a remote-controlled projectile to be fired at the Daily Planet Building in revenge—but the threat was easily stopped by Superman (*The World of Krypton* #4, March 1988). Professor Killgrave later built the nuclear missile used by the Joker in an assault against Superman (*Superman* [second series] #9, September 1997). Later confronting the Man of Steel while safely enclosed in a metal juggernaut, Killgrave was quickly removed to Stryker's Island once more (*Superman* [second series] #19, July 1988). He resurfaced several times thereafter, contracted at one point by Intergang to free Toyman from prison (*The Adventures of Superman* #475, February 1991). Near the end of Metropolis's B13-transformation many years later, Professor Killgrave and the hulking villain Sledge were fused into a single body

by the computer intelligence Lena (*Superman: Metropolis* #3, June 2003). Playing on Lena's desire for a human body, Killgrave manipulated the computer into shifting his consciousness into the Brainiac 13 tech and then seized control of the city. He was eventually defeated and returned to the body he shared with Sledge (*Superman: Metropolis* #7–12, October 2003–March 2004), although Killgrave's status once the B13 tech was removed from Metropolis was unknown.

KIL-LOR

Long before Jor-El and Lara sent their son Kal-El to Earth, Kil-Lor was a Kryptonian tyrant who envisioned himself becoming the planet's ruler. His plan to overthrow the government in a violent coup was stopped by a time-traveling Superman, who was coincidentally visiting his homeworld. The Man of Steel let the would-be conqueror Kil-Lor expose himself to a deadly concentration of kryptonite radiation, and the power-hungry tyrant died, thereby ending his threat (*Superman* [first series] #123, August 1958).

KIMDA, PROFESSOR

Kimda not only was a brilliant Kryptonian professor, but was also paired with the equally brilliant Jor-El as college roommates. After they graduated, Kimda taught and conducted scientific research while living in Kandor. Kimda was residing there when Brainiac captured and miniaturized the city, taking it away with him before the planet exploded. Years later, the bottle city was rescued by Superman. When the Man of Steel was first shrunk in size and trapped within the city, he met Kimda, who came to his aid. It was Kimda's genius that devised a way for Superman to escape and save Kandor. With the remaining energy charge left in

Brainiac's device, Superman could enlarge either Kandor or himself, and while he considered the dilemma, Kimda forced the issue by selflessly using the enlarging ray on Superman (*Action Comics* #242, July 1958).

KING, CRAIG

In one of Earth's potential futures, Craig King was the alter ego of the Superman operating in the year 2956. Much like his progenitor, he, too, worked as a telenews reporter—for the *Daily Solar System*—and affected a mild-mannered personality to divert suspicion from his heroic true self. While not a blood relative of Kal-El, Craig King assumed the role of Superman at the request of Earth's leading scientists, who felt the people needed a champion to believe in. They provided King with equipment to simulate the full array of Superman's superpowers. Once he was acclimated to his newfound abilities, the new Man of Steel went to work by ending a series of thefts plaguing the scientists of the futuristic Metropolis (*Action Comics* #215, April 1966).

KING, WAYNE

Wayne King was a Smallville High classmate of Clark Kent (*Superman* [first series] #420, June 1986). Years later, the men encountered each other again when King was a social studies teacher at their old school. He invited a visiting Kent to speak to his class about his work as a Metropolis journalist. King, however, was disillusioned with his job, and Clark Kent took it upon himself to change his friend's view. He teamed with Chris Parker Hunt, a Smallville High student, to help convince Wayne that his career as a teacher was just as rewarding as any of the more "adventurous" ones he coveted.

KING KRYPTON

An experimental rocket from Krypton landed on Earth-1 many years after the alien planet exploded. The rocket's occupant was a gorilla who

had been kept alive through artificial means, and when it emerged, Sol's yellow radiation imbued him with superpowers proportionate to a simian from the alien world. When Jimmy Olsen encountered the powerful gorilla, he dubbed it King Krypton, and Superman was determined to subdue the gorilla before it could wreak havoc in a populated area. The Man of Steel finally lured King Krypton to a place where he could expose the gorilla to kryptonite in order to rob King Krypton of the superpowers that made him a potential menace. To Superman's amazement, the radiation triggered a transformation within King Krypton, and he saw the animal change into the human form of a fellow Kryptonian. With his dying breath, the man explained that he'd been accidentally changed into a gorilla through an experimental Evolution Accelerator that had malfunctioned. He was then launched into orbit around Krypton by Superman in the hope that cosmic radiation would trigger a reversal. Instead it took prolonged exposure to kryptonite from their dead homeworld to successfully restore the man's humanity (*Action Comics* #238, March 1958).

KINGORILLA

When Professor Lewis Lang and his wife went missing, Superboy traveled to Africa in search of his best friend Lana's parents. While there, he encountered an unusually large gorilla nicknamed Kingorilla. Superboy managed to arrive in time to save the Langs from being sacrificed by a group of natives, who mistakenly wanted to appease the massive yet benign mammal (*Adventure Comics* #196, January 1954).

KING-PIN

When mobsters tried to overrun Smallville during Clark Kent's youth, they were led by a man known only as King-Pin. He used a gemstone that had unexplained abilities, which wound up temporarily giving Superboy's powers to a surprised Lana Lang. Her training under the Legion of Super-Heroes allowed her to quickly acclimate to her new abilities for as long as she had them, and she was able to defeat King-Pin and protect her hometown (*Superboy* [first series] #143, December 1967).

KING SHARK

The King of Sharks, known to all as the Shark God, had a son named Nanue who was humanoid in appearance—at least according to a legend that circulated around Hawaii, although many dismissed it and said Nanue was some sort of genetic mutation. Regardless of the truth, Nanue operated both on land and in the water, turning to a life of crime. He was also responsible for several citizens disappearing around Hawaii. Special Agent Sam Makoa managed to apprehend the creature, but earned permanent scars for his heroic effort (*Superboy* [third series] #9, November 1994).

King Shark was subsequently freed from prison by the Silicon Dragons, who wanted to hire him, but Shark rejected the offer and killed his liberators. King Shark instead sought out his mother, who allowed him to gnaw off her arm to get the human flesh he craved (*Superboy* [third series] #0

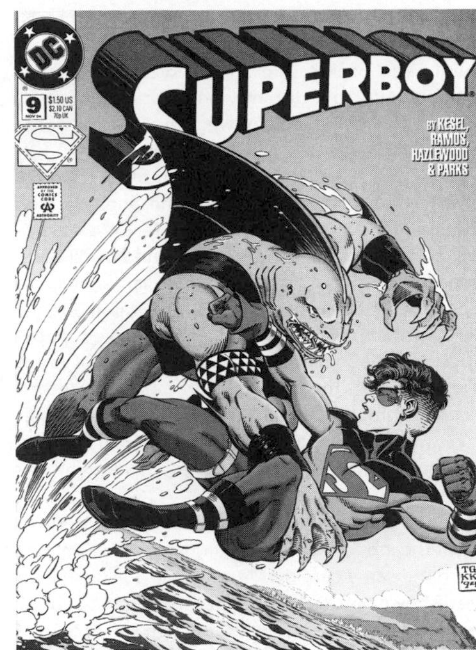

and #9, October–November 1994). Later, Agent Makoa and Superboy worked with the Suicide Squad on a mission to take down the rest of the Silicon Dragons, and recruited King Shark to work with them. King Shark tried to escape, thereby activating the explosive device he wore to ensure his obedience, but he survived the blast and managed to escape (*Superboy* [third series] #13–15, March–May 1995).

King Shark and Superboy tangled on numerous later occasions as the creature sought a place he could call his own, where he might live free. King Shark later fought Superman as an agent working for Manchester Black (*The Adventures of Superman* #608, November 1994). During their battle, the Man of Steel knocked out most of King Shark's teeth, which eventually grew back. Years later, King Shark briefly worked as a member of the secret Society under Alexander Luthor, Junior's, direction, where he killed hero turned author Neptune Perkins (*Infinite Crisis* #3, February 2006).

KIRK, JOHNNY

In an odd case of parallels, Professor Morton Kirk came to the scientific conclusion that Earth was doomed due to a rogue planet approaching on a

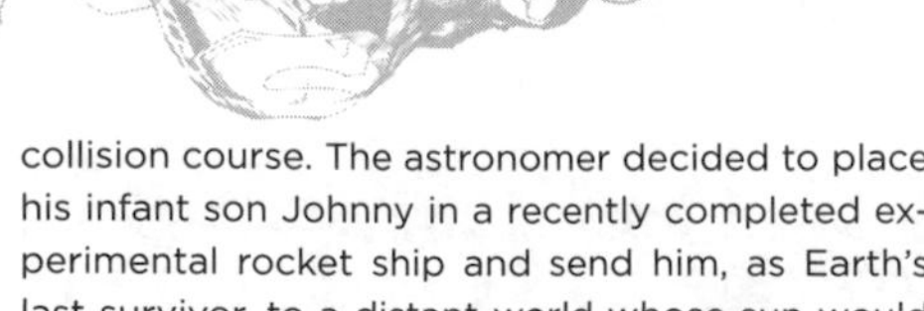

collision course. The astronomer decided to place his infant son Johnny in a recently completed experimental rocket ship and send him, as Earth's last survivor, to a distant world whose sun would imbue the baby with powers and abilities that would one day make him a super-man.

The rocket left Earth, but soon after, Superboy averted the impending catastrophe, and Kirk died before anyone knew of his son's fate. Before passing away, the crushed scientist drafted a will naming Superboy his son's legal guardian should his rocket ever be recovered. A decade later, Johnny Kirk found his way home, manifesting a set of abilities that made him a match for the Man of Steel. He explained to Superman that his rocket had passed through "a peculiar cloud in space, pulsating with energy," a mysterious "cloud of cosmic energy," which apparently granted Johnny his extraordinary abilities.

Made aware of the elder Kirk's will, Superman took the job to heart, and intended to train Johnny with the same care that Martha and Jonathan Kent had shown him. Dubbed Superman Junior, Johnny was put through a training regimen to ready him for a career as a champion of justice. Gradually, however, Superman's powers began to fail him one at a time, and it was learned that the "peculiar meteoric dust" clinging to Johnny's rocket had a deleterious effect on the Man of Steel. He tried to mask his increasing failings while continuing Johnny's training.

Johnny eventually discovered the truth and used the mysterious properties of a different meteor to transfer his abilities to Superman. When the transfer was complete, Johnny Kirk was once more a typical human teenager and was raised by another kind family (*Action Comics* #232, September 1957).

KISMET

Ahti was a cosmic being who was once the lover of Dominus, but ascended to the title of Kismet.

Kismet was an enigmatic being who claimed to exist where dark met light and used her mystic skills to shine a light on various pathways in both worlds. She first encountered the Man of Steel during his involvement in a battle between Lord Satanus and Blaze (*The Adventures of Superman* #494, September 1992). Using her powers, Kismet showed Superman what outcomes would occur based on the decisions he might make in trying to end the battle between the demonic forces. Her arrival came with a warning of cosmic upheavals in times to come, and she plunged Superman into four concurrent realities to let him experience the results of his potential choices.

Kismet was also pivotal in helping to save Jonathan Kent after he suffered a fatal heart attack and was trapped in the afterlife (*The Adventures of Superman* #500, Early June 1993).

After that experience, Kismet would often turn up in Superman's life during times of stress to shine a light for his benefit. Her next appearance was to warn him of the coming of her own nemesis, Dominus (*Superman* [second series] #138, September 1998). Superman managed to hide Kismet in the past with the help of Waverider so that she would not be discovered by Dominus. The human Kismet took over Sharon Vance, a childhood friend of Clark Kent, who wound up being turned into the super heroine called Strange Visitor when a stray lightning strike merged her with Kismet. She adventured alongside Superman from time to time and had several adventures on her own before sacrificing her energy to help Superman when he was battling to save Earth from the warlord Imperiex (*Superman* [second series] #173, October 2001).

KIZO

Kizo, U-Ban, and Mala—Kryptonian villains known as the Evil Three—managed to survive the destruction of Krypton and later battled another of the planet's survivors, Superman, on two separate occasions. Neither time was the trio able to best the Man of Steel (*Superman* [first series] #65, July-August 1950; *Action Comics* #194, July 1954).

KLAX-AR

Klax-Ar was a survivor of the doomed planet Krypton and, like Superman, gained superpowers when he was exposed to a yellow sun's radiation. However, Klax-Ar lost his abilities after exposure to the unique effects of atron-rays. He desperately wanted to regain his superpowers, so he created a device that would enable him to transfer Superboy's powers to himself. Before this could happen, however, a Superboy Robot took the evildoer into deep space and away from Earth (*Superboy* [first series] #67, September 1958).

Years later, Klax-Ar managed to rewire the robot and build a space sled, which allowed him to return to Earth and once again attempt to steal the Teen of Steel's powers. En route to Earth, however, he encountered the planet's latest heroine, Supergirl, who was on her way to the prison planet of Kronis. Klax-Ar tried to use his Mentomatron helmet to steal her powers, but he failed when he was exposed to Earth's polluted atmosphere, which interfered with the proper function of his robot and space sled. Kicking the sled to her hometown of Midvale, Supergirl took Klax-Ar into custody (*Superman Family* #187, January-February 1978).

KLOR

Klor was a criminal from the distant world Belvos who had discovered that certain gems located on Earth would imbue him with spectacular powers. He then concocted a scheme that would allow him to commit crimes using his gem-derived powers and frame Superman for them. This would then take the Man of Steel off Earth, allowing Klor to plunder the planet's riches before conquering his homeworld. When the Man of Steel was framed for crimes he did not commit and tried to defend himself, Klor was thwarted by Batman and Robin, who returned Klor to Belvos and helped prove their Man of Steel innocent (*World's Finest Comics* #122, December 1961).

KLTPZYXM

A magical word in the Fifth Dimension that was the home of Mr. Mxyzptlk, a constant thorn in Superman's side. The Man of Steel would return Mxyzptlk to his home realm for a minimum of ninety days after each disastrous visit to Earth. Rarely would the imp utter the word—pronounced *kel-tipz-yex-im*—that would send him home, requiring Superman to devise a way to trick him into saying it aloud. On Earth-2, the *t* and *p* in the imp's name were transposed, making him Mxyztplk, and his backward name Klptzyxm (*Superman* [first series] #30, September-October 1944). In this universe, the word transported anyone who spoke it—not simply Mxyztplk—to Zrfff (*Superman* [first series] #33, March/April 1945; *Superman Family* #208, July 1981).

KLURKOR

"The Kryptonian style of unarmed combat," Klurkor was studied by Lois Lane during a visit to the bottle city of Kandor, helping her gain a level of self-sufficiency that would come in handy in the future (*Superman's Girl Friend, Lois Lane* #78, October 1967). Kal-El retained latent memories of his mother Lara's training in the martial art, knowledge that also served him well when he later faced Klurkor masters such as Sar-Ul (*The New Adventures of Superboy* #28, April 1982) and Vor-Kil (*Superman* [first series] #219, August 1969). The techniques of Klurkor would be maintained well into the thirty-first century on worlds such as Naltor (*Legion of Super-Heroes* [fifth series] #2, March 2005).

KLYBURN, DR. JENET

Dr. Jenet Klyburn was the director of the Metropolis branch of the privately held R&D company Scientific and Technological Advanced Research (S.T.A.R.) Labs (*Superman* [first series] #304, October 1976).

A graduate of Metropolis University, the red-haired Klyburn developed a working relationship with the city's protector, Superman, using her resources to help the hero; for instance, she once

created an antidote that allowed the Man of Steel to swiftly eradicate multiplying incarnations of the villain Solomon Grundy (*DC Comics Presents* #8, April 1979). Klyburn was also appointed chief administrator at S.T.A.R. Labs in the wake of Dr. Albert Michaels's departure just before his transformation into the Atomic Skull (*Superman* [first series] #316, October 1977).

Over the years, Klyburn worked with a variety of super heroes, including Blue Devil (*Blue Devil* #2–3, July–August 1984) and the Teen Titans (*New Teen Titans* #36, November 1983); she proved a capable mentor to Sarah Charles (*Tales of the Teen Titans* #56–58, August–October 1985) and a role model for Tina McGee and Kitty Faulkner. Her technical expertise allowed her to work with the team to build the initial component parts for the Titans' Cyborg. When not serving as a consultant to the meta-human community, Jenet spearheaded a project leading to a new energy source that was "radioactive but not in any way harmful to carbon-based life." To her embarrassment, the S.T.A.R. staff dubbed it Klyburnium (*World's Finest Comics* #308, October 1984).

Dr. Klyburn has survived the various alterations in reality, continuing her work as a researcher and administrator for the corporation (*Power Company* #5, August 2002).

KNIGHT, THE

England's Percy Sheldrake, earl of Wordenshire, was inspired by Batman to don a suit of armor and fight crime as a hero known as the Knight. Like Batman, he had a teen sidekick—his son Cyril, who was known as the Squire. Whenever the Wordenshire bell tolled, the adventurers answered its summons (*Batman* #62, December 1950–January 1951).

The Knight traveled to Gotham City to meet Batman and other heroes and later formed the group known as the Club of Heroes, which included Superman as one of its members (*World's Finest Comics* #89, August 1957).

In the world after Infinite Crisis, the Club of Heroes existed, but without the Man of Steel's involvement (*Batman* #667, August 2007).

KNOCKOUT

Knockout was briefly a member of Apokolips's dreaded Female Furies, trained by Granny Goodness as part of an elite cadre of shock troops. Inspired by the escapes of Big Barda and Scott Free, she fled the team and relocated to Earth, where she settled in Hawaii. Soon after, she began encountering the recently relocated Superboy and thought he looked like someone strong enough to play with. To remain on the island, she developed an undercover identity as a stripper working in the BoomBoom Room. For a while she fought against, then with, Superboy, flirting with him the entire time (*Superboy* [third series] #1–2, February–March 1994).

Her super-strength and massive size made Knockout a formidable opponent, strong enough to test the Clone of Steel's fortitude. Knockout's skills led her to recruitment into Amanda Waller's Suicide Squad for a time, where she worked alongside Superboy's other enemy King Shark (*Superboy* [third series] #13–15, March–May 1995). While attempting to destroy the Silicon Kings gang, Knockout was believed killed, but she turned up when Superboy needed her help in a struggle with Valor.

Knockout then needed Superboy's help when Granny Goodness dispatched the Furies to retrieve her. With Superboy—as well as the aid of Mister Miracle and Big Barda, the latter also a former Fury—she managed to stave off the Furies' assault. The Furies persevered and eventually captured Knockout, chaining her to a fire pit on Apokolips. She managed to break free and threw herself into the pit rather than admit defeat, but a Boom Tube whisked her back to Hawaii in the nick of time (*Superboy* [third series] #22–25, December 1995–March 1996).

The Furies once more returned to Earth to claim Knockout, and again Superboy offered his friend some help. They were supported by the DNAlien Dubbilex and members of the Metropolis Police Department. One officer died, and upon a subsequent investigation, Dubbilex telepathically learned that Knockout had killed the officer because he was about to expose her true intentions. Superboy didn't believe the evidence presented to him and ran off with Knockout. While they were on the lam, Knockout wanted Superboy to prove his allegiance to her amoral ways by killing explorer Victor Volcanum. He refused, so Knockout killed Volcanum herself, leading Superboy to apprehend her and take her back to Metropolis to face the consequences (*Superboy* [third series] #25–30, March–August 1996).

Years later, Knockout escaped prison and swore allegiance to the Secret Society of Super-Villains, who were out to destroy Earth's super heroes (*Villains United* #1, July 2005). While a member, Knockout began a romance with the Secret Six's Scandal Savage. Knockout was eventually revealed to be a spy for the Secret Six and officially joined the team (*Villains United* #6, December 2005). While relaxing with Savage after taking over a North Korean jail, the Society's Pistolera implanted a bomb inside the former Fury's neck using a Thanagarian sniper rifle. Before the bomb could detonate, Knockout threw her lover Savage to safety. Despite being horribly burned, Knockout survived and eventually healed (*Secret Six* [second series] #1–2, July–August 2006).

She was later reinjured by fellow Secret Six member Ragdoll, who was under the influence of Wonder Woman's old enemy, Doctor Psycho. After recovering once more, Knockout surprised and wounded Scandal by bedding the villain Deadshot, as the Apokoliptian could not fully grasp the exclusive nature of most relationships (*Secret Six* [second series] #3–5, September–November 2006). It was not long after this that Knockout was slain by a manifestation of the Source, which was removing all the Fourth World's gods from the very planes of existence (*Birds of Prey* [first series] #109, October 2007).

Knockout's spirit appears to have survived the destruction of the Fourth World, and her spectral form warned Scandal of impending danger on at least one occasion (*Secret Six* [third series] #4, February 2009). As a result, Scandal obtained a literal Get out of Hell free card with every intention of bringing her lover back to life (*Secret Six* [third series] #7, May 2009).

KOBER, STANISLAW

Stanislaw Kober was a miner who became crippled for life when he worked in an unsafe mine in Blakelytown. Hearing of the conditions there, the Man of Steel went undercover to see for him-

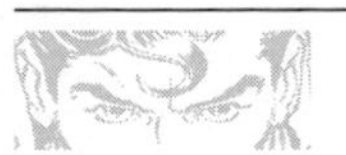

self and was on hand to rescue Kober, clearing away the mine rocks and climbing up an elevator cable with the injured man in his arms. Kober told *Daily Planet* reporter Clark Kent from his hospital bed that owner Thornton Blakely knew his mine was unsafe but insisted the men work in it anyway. Kent helped expose the corruption with his newspaper article, and the mine was shut down (*Superman* [first series] #1, June 1939).

KOBRA

Every forty-four years a new "naja-naja" was born, destined to lead India's Kobra Cult. One such infant was Jeffrey Franklin Burr, who was stolen from his hospital bassinet after being identified as the chosen one. For the next twenty-three years, Jeffrey was raised by the cult, revered as Kobra-Prime, the foremost symbol of the followers of the serpent god known as Nulla Pambu (*Kobra* #1, February–March 1976). As he grew, Jeffrey tried to escape and discover his own destiny, but he was repeatedly found and brought back for further training. On his twenty-first birthday, Jeffrey was required to drink Cobra venom, the last test to prove his worthiness to lead the cult.

The new Lord Kobra quickly accessed the cult's resources around the globe to begin creating the technological infrastructure that would bring his dreams to fruition. Members bought what they could and stole the rest; in rapid order, the cult grew fangs, expanding bases that included Manhattan-based Ajan Enterprises (*Batman and the Outsiders* [first series] #27, November 1985), Chicago's Anaconda Industries (*Manhunter* [first series] #14, June 1989), and an international electronics firm known as Cortex Ltd. (*Showcase '93* #7–9, July–September 1993). Established prior to Lord Kobra's birth, circa 1962, was California's Peterson State College, a religious school (*Suicide Squad Annual* #1, 1988).

In two short years, Lord Kobra transformed the cult from a religious order to an efficient criminal enterprise. Scholarly research allowed members to find artifacts and ancient technology that could be harnessed for new purposes. They also took to acquiring weapons from other villains. As a result, Kobra's ceremonial garb was laced with hidden weapons and tools including venom sprayed from his gloved knuckles and a "serpent's tongue" fired from his hand that worked as a garrote; his entire suit of chain mail was powered to emit a charge capable of rendering an opponent unconscious. The outfit had a built-in emergency teleportation beam, hot-linked to an aircraft called the Ark. Kobra also took to carrying a staff that fired bursts of energy.

He even dared to threaten Metropolis, despite the City of Tomorrow being protected by the Man of Steel (*Superman* [first series] #326–327, August–September 1978). Kobra breached Clark Kent's apartment in an attempt to obtain one of the Atomic Skull's teleportation devices. During the break-in, he also discovered Kent's secret identity. To keep Superman busy, Kobra had had tons of sand laced with a deadly nerve toxin and then spread the mineral across the city. Further, he plucked Jonathan and Martha Kent from the past to protect himself from an attack by Superman, and threatened to rewrite the time line if the Man of Steel interfered. Undaunted, Superman managed to destroy the teleportation device and rescue his parents, returning them to their proper era while the slippery Kobra slithered away.

Kobra was now a known threat to the community of super heroes, and he began to cross paths with them with increasing frequency. As one defeat was handed to him, another project was activated, placing him in opposition to super heroes including the Flash (*Flash* #92–100, July 1994–April 1995), the Birds of Prey (*Birds of Prey* [first series] #4–6, April–June 1999, and #10, October 1999), and Superman (*Superman: The Odyssey,* 1999). At one point, frustrated with constant defeat and thinking he heard taunting from his dead brother Jason, he tried a bolder move, taking over the Justice League of America's Watchtower on the moon, only to lose out once more (*JLA: Foreign Bodies,* 1999).

Kobra was recently killed by a vengeful Black Adam, but Jeffrey's twin brother Jason was revived by the Kobra Cult and became its new leader (*Faces of Evil: Kobra* #1, March 2009). This incarnation has yet to cross paths with the Man of Steel.

KOKO

Koko was Brainiac's monkey-like pet, usually found perched on the android's shoulder. The creature had white fur and twin antennae. Eventually Koko was no longer seen in the company of Brainiac (*Action Comics* #242, July 1958).

While it appeared that the monkey had vanished after reality was altered in the wake of the Zero Hour incident, in fact Koko (minus his antennae) surfaced as a caged animal whom the Legion of Super-Heroes encountered during an adventure with Impulse in the twentieth century. Obsessed with the Legion's Brainiac 5 (*Impulse* #21, January 1997), the white monkey returned with the Legion to the thirtieth century. Koko was also a derogatory nickname Brainiac 5 used in reference to Impulse, a descendant of the second Flash.

In the post-Infinite Crisis continuity, Superman encountered Koko aboard Brainiac's ship, but this time the creature was a large, white feral beast eager to tear apart the Man of Steel with its claws and sharp fangs (*Action Comics* #868, October 2008).

Koko

KOLLI

Krypto the Super-Dog once rescued Kolli, a female canine about to be shot into space from the planet Mogor. Together they left the planet, and Kolli eventually gained superpowers when she drank from alien waters that affected her metabolism. As her powers appeared, Krypto mysteriously lost his own when he came near her, so the forlorn Dog of Steel had to leave his love forever (*Superboy* [first series] #87, March 1961).

KORON

In Earth-2 continuity, Koron was a Kryptonian moon that was almost entirely consumed by a Snagriff, which had been given an experimental life-extending serum. In the wake of Krypton's destruction, remnants of the moon landed on Earth's polar region (*Superman* [first series] #78, September–October 1952).

KORREL, KANE

Kane Korrel was a Metropolis gangster who learned of a large deposit of kryptonite that had recently landed in the nearby town of Smithville. Driving a tractor-trailer, Korrel rushed to the site and made off with the valuable mineral before local authorities could secure the area. He then sold off pieces at five thousand dollars each, giving Metropolis's criminals an edge over Superman for the first time. Regardless, the Man of Steel managed to apprehend Korrel, his clients, and the deadly supply of the fragments once part of his homeworld. He disposed of the kryptonite by hurling it deep into outer space (*Action Comics* #158, July 1951).

KOTA ZAMFIR

Located on the South China Sea, Kota Zamfir was ruled by the dictator Kalyan Nong Hoi until Superman arrived and insisted the country hold free elections (*The Adventures of Superman* #565, March 1999). Because Superman was beginning to interfere in political affairs across the globe at the time, Hoi sensed world opinion turning against the Man of Steel and took advantage of the negative press to rally the military and launch an attack at the replacement government in an effort to reclaim the country. The U.S. embassy in Kota Zamfir was attacked in the ensuing civil war, until Superman arrived and quelled the coup (*Superman* [second series] #143, April 1999).

KOWALESKI, BARB

See Arathaza.

KRAG

One of the first robots that Superman built with powers to mimic his own. The Man of Steel used Krag to help take down a Metropolis crime czar. The robot arrived in a spacecraft, purportedly from Mercury, having learned the English language by watching the Earth with "ultron telescopes and radio receivers." It ingratiated itself with local criminals by using its powers to aid them in a bank robbery. Krag then said it wanted to meet the czar but would first defeat the Man of Steel in order to prove itself worthy. After soundly beating Superman, Krag was taken to the czar, whereupon Krag revealed itself to be Superman: The Man of Steel had disguised himself as Krag and switched places with his robot (*Action Comics* #165, February 1952).

KRAL

Hailing from Titan, Saturn's moon in the Earth-1 universe, Kral traveled to Earth to "gain the confidence of all earthlings and learn the location of their secret weapons"; his plan was to then sabotage them in order to let the Titanian spaceships invade and enslave Earth. Kral possessed telepathic abilities in addition to flight, heat vision, and the ability to generate heat or cold. Using these skills, he ingratiated himself first with Superboy, then the rest of the citizens of Smallville, as well as the local scientific community. When he was ready to trap the Teen of Steel on Titan, however, memories of his kindly treatment on Earth led Kral to change his mind. Instead he convinced his fellow Titans that all humans possessed powers like Superboy and therefore could not be defeated (*Adventure Comics* #205, October 1954).

In one of Earth-1's potential futures, inhabitants of Titan—such as the Legion of Super-Heroes' Saturn Girl—possessed only telepathic skills.

Kral was glimpsed briefly in post–Zero Hour history as a partygoer at one of Kindred Marx's intergalactic raves (*Superboy and the Ravers* #5, January 1997).

KRAZINSKI, RUDOLPH

Master pianist Rudolph Krazinski discovered that certain combinations of notes could lull people into a hypnotic state. During his concerts, he would put the audience into a trance, thereby allowing his accomplices to rob them of their valuables. Superman eventually interfered with his plans, but Krazinski tried a new combination of notes that he hoped would work on the super hero. Krazinski's plan failed, so rather than allow himself to be apprehended, he removed his protective earplugs and continued playing. The music quickly killed him (*Superman* [first series] #14, January–February 1942).

KRISS-KROSS KRYPTON

Based on the life and powers of Superboy, Kriss-Kross Krypton was a popular board game sold around the world. Professor Lewis Lang and his daughter Lana once played it as a way to relieve the professor's work-related stress. The Teen of Steel was watching the game from afar and performed a series of feats that eerily matched the activity on the board. When the Langs learned of this, the professor struggled to determine how the parallels existed. He concluded that their game had some effect over the youth, a solution that distracted the professor enough to finally relax (*Superboy* [first series] #60, October 1957).

KROGG

The extra-dimensional space separating Earth-1 from Earth-2 was home to many inhabitants, including the bestial alien Krogg. Once, when Superman-2 traversed the dimensions to enlist the help of Superman-1 and Jimmy Olsen-1, Krogg gained access to Earth-1. It was later discovered that this happened because at the moment Superman-2 pierced the dimensions, Professor Phineas Potter was experimenting with the Justice League of America's teleportation device, thereby allowing Krogg to slip between parallel worlds. With his battle mace, the super-strong creature fought the Earth-1 and Earth-2 Supermen individually, ultimately besting them both. Potter then used the device to combine the Men of Steel into an unbeatable opponent. Dubbed the Super-Superman, he easily trounced Krogg, which increased the creature's internal energy, thereby causing him to explode (*Superman Family* #186–187, November–December 1977–January–February 1978).

KRONIS

One of the galaxy's most renowned prison planets, Kronis was where Brainiac was incarcerated after Superman defeated him following yet another attempt by the evil android to conquer Earth (*Action Comics* #280, September 1961). The planet was seemingly desolate, save a cube wherein Brainiac was kept. When Lex Luthor traveled to the world some years later, he freed Brainiac from Kronis. Together the villains plotted their revenge against the Man of Steel and left the prison world behind (*Superman* [first series] #167, February 1964). During a later visit to the prison by Supergirl for a routine inspection, Kronis was overseen by Warden Sargoes (*Superman Family* #187, January–February 1978).

KRU-EL

Known as the black sheep of the House of El, Kru-El was considered by many residents of Krypton an irredeemable terrorist. During his long career, Kru-El had invented countless weapons that the ruling Science Council deemed forbidden. His cousin Jor-El helped bring Kru-El to justice, even sentencing him to the Phantom Zone. Kru-El's weapons were boxed and shot into space, where they survived. The weapons were eventually found and used on Earth against Jor-El's son Superman (*Action Comics* #298, March 1963). Kru-El also

managed to escape the Phantom Zone along with General Zod and Jax-Ur, and located and used his weapons against the citizens of Earth while Superman was away on a mission.

In the world after the Crisis on Infinite Earths, a version of Kru-El still existed, and Superman got to meet him during the Man of Steel's visit to a fabricated Krypton developed by Brainiac (*Superman: The Man of Steel* #111, April 2001).

KRYON, PROFESSOR

In a potential fortieth century, this evil scientist from the planet Katraz convinced Lois Lane that she was destined to marry Superman. However, the marriage ended with their violent deaths in an airplane accident. Returning from 4068, Lois secretly married the Man of Steel to enjoy what precious time they had left.

Kryon secretly concealed the fact that the Man of Steel supposedly lost his abilities to gold kryptonite, but the plan went awry when Superman averted disaster by taking a formula that temporarily granted him immunity. The short-lived marriage between Superman and Lois was then quickly annulled (*Superman's Girl Friend, Lois Lane* #82, April 1968).

KRYP

In the Earth-1 reality, legend had it that an alien named Kryp became stranded on a desolate world and encountered and mated with a fellow explorer named Tonn. Eventually the planet was named Krypton to honor this couple—the parents of the race that took over the world (*Superman* [first series] #238, June 1971).

KRYPTIUM

In the Earth-1 reality, kryptium was known as Krypton's "strongest metal," a "super-metal" described as "harder and stronger than any Earth metal" (*Action Comics* #329, October 1965), as was later confirmed by Earth scientists (*Action Comics* #333, February 1966). It was unclear whether kryptium was the same substance as the metal alloy kryptylium, items made from which once had a magnetic reaction to a low-orbiting satellite on Krypton (*Superboy* [first series] #104, April 1963).

KRYPTO THE SUPER-DOG

Krypto was the El family's pet dog, who was placed in Jor-El's experimental rocket in the weeks prior to Krypton's destruction. He later arrived safe and sound on Earth and was reunited with the young Kal-El (*Adventure Comics* #210, March 1955).

In Earth-1's reality, the dog was highly pedigreed with a family tree that included Zypto (father), Nypto (grandfather), and Vypto (great-grandfather) (*Superboy* [first series] #126, January 1966).

Krypto and the toddler Kal-El were rarely ever apart, and the baby cried when his father took the dog and placed him in a rocket. The rocket was en route to Earth when it was accidentally knocked off course and drifted far from its intended destination. Eventually cosmic forces redirected it, and the craft landed not far from Smallville, where Kal-El was being raised by Jonathan and Martha Kent. Like the teen, Krypto developed proportionate superpowers when exposed to Sol's solar radiation. Being a dog, Krypto had an enhanced sense of smell and superior hearing to his master. Krypto's intelligence was also elevated so that he could think and reason on a par with a human, although he never managed speech.

From the beginning, Krypto delighted in exploring the cosmos, and his adventures with his master were punctuated by long romps in space. During his pet's third visit to Earth, Superboy fashioned a collar and scarlet cape for Krypto to match his own. The dog wore them from that point onward (*Adventure Comics* #220, January 1956). Often, while Superboy was on a mission or Clark Kent was in school, Krypto enjoyed exploring on his own. When staying with the Kents in Smallville, the Dog of Steel added a brown patch on his back, something easily burned off with heat vision when he was needed. He was dubbed Skippy by Martha Kent while in his secret identity (*The New Adventures of Superboy* #10, October 1980).

Krypto later formed the Legion of Super-Pets, which operated in both the twentieth and thirtieth centuries (*Adventure Comics* #293, February

1962). His galactic exploits also got him invited to join the Space Canine Patrol Agency (*Superboy* [first series] #131, July 1966). His deeds earned him a reputation across numerous star systems, making him as much a celebrity as his master. Given his love of the stars, Krypto constructed a Doghouse of Solitude out of meteor rock (*Superman* [first series] #150, January 1962).

After disappearing into space for a number of years, Krypto eventually found his way back to Earth, his superpowers now something of a danger as old age had affected his judgment. With his pal Jimmy Olsen unable to properly control the super-dog, Superman finally conceived an ideal solution. The Man of Steel directed Krypto to a fountain of youth that restored the dog's mental and physical acuity (*Superman's Pal, Jimmy Olsen* #29, June 1958). Refreshed and youthful once more, the Dog of Steel embarked on many new adventures on Earth.

While saving a world from the insidious villain known as the Mindbreaker Beast, Krypto took a direct blast and lost his memories (*Superman* [first series] #287, May 1975). Eventually making his way back to Earth, the amnesiac super-dog initially

crossed paths with Green Arrow and Black Canary (*Action Comics* #440–441, October–November 1974). While romancing a dog named Chelsea in Metropolis, Krypto glimpsed Superman flying overhead and his memories came rushing back (*Superman* [first series] #287, May 1975).

When Chelsea became a celebrity canine in Hollywood, Krypto briefly renewed their romance and became her film costar, Jocko. Once they began filming *The Adventures of Krypto,* however, Chelsea became smitten with Jocko's stunt-dog. While on the movie set, the Dog of Steel had befriended Los Angeles detective Ed Lacy and unwaveringly followed Lacy when the man was called away to track down his nephew Tommy, who had falsely been accused of murder. After helping Ed clear Tommy's name, Krypto headed toward the skies once more (*Superman Family* #183–192, May–June 1977–November–December 1978).

The fate of the Earth-1 Krypto is unknown, but his Earth-423 counterpart ultimately sacrificed his life by biting the throat out of the Kryptonite Man (*Action Comics* #583, August 1986). More happily, the Krypto of Earth-162, where Superman-Red/Superman-Blue eradicated all evil, was content to join his master for an idyllic retirement on New Krypton (*Superman* [first series] #162, July 1963).

In the wake of the Crisis on Infinite Earths, Krypto did not appear, although a Krypto did live in the Pocket Universe crafted by the Time Trapper (*Action Comics* #591, August 1987). Instead Bibbo Bibbowski, the self-described number one Superman fan, had a white dog he rescued and dubbed Krypton in the Man of Steel's honor, although a typo left the dog tag reading krypto, and the name stuck (*The Adventures of Superman* #501–502, June–July 1993).

This Krypto took an instant dislike to the cloned Superboy (*Superboy* [third series] #6, July 1994), so when Bibbo needed a new owner for his pet, he asked the DNAlien Dubbilex to take care of Krypto, and the scruffy pooch found a new home in Hawaii (*Superboy* [third series] #8, September 1994). Passed around among Superboy's friends, Krypto eventually developed a soft spot for the young Conner Kent. When Superboy prepared to leave for Cadmus Labs, he found Krypto already waiting in the Whiz Wagon for him (*Superboy* [third series] #69, December 1999).

The more recognizable Krypto (*Superman* [second series] #167, April 2001), complete with superpowers, accompanied Superman and Lois Lane back from a faux Krypton created by Brainiac that they had briefly visited (*Action Comics* #776, April 2001). The rambunctious canine possessed all the usual Kryptonian superpowers, with the exception of a normal dog's intellect. As a result, Krypto's claws scratched through walls, and his thumping tail could cause massive damage if he was not careful. Krypto's loyalty to the Man of Steel and his wife was unparalleled and proved lifesaving on more than one occasion. Still, the damage he caused was enough to have Superman exile the dog to the Arctic Fortress of Solitude for a time (*Superman* [second series] #170, July 2001). Between a Superman Robot and the real Last Son of Krypton, Krypto underwent intensive training, which eventually allowed the dog to return to Metropolis. For some unexplained reason, Krypto was especially fond of the shady Catwoman, and Batman often poked fun at Superman by referencing his pet's strange choice in companions (*Batman* #612, April 2003).

Still, the Dog of Steel proved his value time and again, even going solo to rescue people from the carnage wrought by the arrival of Imperiex on Earth (*Superboy* [third series] #91, October 2001).

When Kara Zor-El crashed to Earth years later, Superman was overjoyed to meet his Kryptonian cousin, but Krypto had a more negative reaction, and the two kept apart afterward (*Superman/Batman* #9, June 2004). Superman decided the dog would benefit from a constant companion while Kon-El would also gain experience by having something to be responsible for (*Teen Titans* [third series] #7, March 2004). It took time, but the two did develop a strong bond of friendship, which made Krypto's grief all the worse when Superboy-Prime killed Conner Kent.

In the wake of the Infinite Crisis, reality was reordered, and Krypto hailed from Krypton once more, having survived the planet's destruction and being raised in Smallville by the Kents (*Action Comics* #850, Late July 2007; Krypto's arrival on Earth confirmed in *Action Comics Annual* #11, 2008). He was later injured in a battle and cared for by Jimmy Olsen, who was allowed to retain the dog and who gave him the alter ego of Pal (*Action Comics* #853–854, Early October–Mid-October 2007). Krypto's tracking skills were such that even Robin the Teen Wonder used them when the Sinestro Corps War reached Earth (*Tales of the Sinestro Corps: Superman-Prime* #1, December 2007).

Later, when the god-like Atlas bested Superman in hand-to-hand combat, Krypto risked his own life to protect his master (*Superman* #679–680, October–November 2008). After Jonathan Kent's death, and sensing that Martha Kent needed him, Krypto arrived on her doorstep to stay with her and keep her company (*Superman* #681, December 2008).

Other realities depicted Krypto in differing ways. On Earth-898, the dog was the result of experiments using Kryptonian DNA matched with Terran genetic material (*JLA: The Nail* #2–3, September–November 1998).

In the potential future, Krypto[9] was a clone with enhanced powers who led the Legion of Executive Familiars in the 251st century (*Superman: Man of Tomorrow* #1,000,000, November 1998).

KRYPTOCOCCUS THE OMNI-GERM

Soon after defeating Lex Luthor during one of their countless battles, Superman was exposed to Kryptococcus the Omni-Germ, a creation of Doctor Virus, who hoped to kill the Man of Steel in order to gain admittance to Intergang. However, Superman fought and defeated the giant organism and apprehended Doctor Virus (*Action Comics* #840, August 2006).

KRYPTO MOUSE

When Professor Egglehead experimented on Tommy Ewell's pet mouse in Smallville years ago, the mammal gained superpowers similar to Superboy's. The Mouse of Steel patrolled the town but retained its timid nature. Because Krypto Mouse kept his distance, Smallville's citizens mistook his deeds as the work of Superboy. The experiment's effects eventually wore off, and Tommy Ewell regained his beloved pet (*Superboy* [first series] #65, July 1958).

KRYPTON

Orbiting a red sun in Space Sector 2813, Krypton (pronounced *KRIP-tonn*) was home to an advanced civilization that measured its history across ten thousand years. While a cultural and technological marvel, Krypton's greatest claim to fame came after the planet's destruction, when its last son arrived on Earth to become the cosmic champion for truth and justice known to all as Superman (*Action Comics* #1, June 1938; planet named in *Superman* [first series] #1, Summer 1939).

Krypton's history includes much legend mixed in with truth, and as its realities were revised, so, too, was the nature of life on the planet.

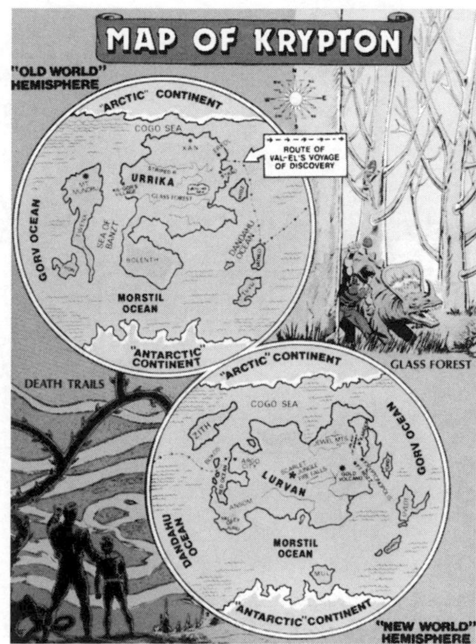

In Earth-2's reality, every inhabitant of Krypton was said to possess super-human strength, X-ray vision, super-speed, and the other powers normally associated with Superman (*Action Comics* #1, June 1938; *Superman* [first series] #33, March–April 1945; *Superman* [first series] #53, July–August 1948). Here scientist Jor-L and his wife Lora sent their son Kal-L to Earth to avoid Krypton's fate. Jor-L's brother Zor-L heeded the scientist's warning and built a symbioship with digital scans of life in the city of Kandor to help educate his daughter Kara during her subsequent trip to Earth. The slower ship landed many decades after Kal-L arrived; he had grown to adulthood. Superman welcomed Kara to Earth, and she began to adventure under the name Power Girl (*All Star Comics* #58, January–February 1976).

Geologists dated the Earth-1 reality's Krypton's formation at 8.3 billion years ago (six billion sun-cycles, in Kryptonian terms), making the world nearly twice as old as Earth (*Superman* [first series] #170, July 1964). It was described as "an unusual planet" with a "unique atmosphere" and a "tremendous gravitational pull" far greater than that of Earth (*Superman* [first series] #113, May 1957). Krypton had a massive uranium core (*Superman* [first series] #53, July–August 1948) and was occasionally swept by windstorms so violent that the planet's tallest skyscrapers had to be lowered into the ground to prevent their being toppled by the powerful gales (*Superman* [first series] #123, August 1958).

The planet was not the only one named in the system, as it shared a star with the planet Thoron (*Superman* [first series] #80, January–February 1953). Krypton itself, depending upon the source, had between two and four moons. One, called Wegthor, was destroyed by the criminal scientist Jax-Ur (*Adventure Comics* #289, October 1961), while another moon was called Koron (*Superman* [first series] #78, September–October 1952). The third satellite, Xenon, was referred to as a twin to Krypton itself, and some millennia past it had "spun out of its orbit and left Krypton forever" (*Superman* [first series] #119, February 1958). The fourth, Mithen, "was hurled into a new solar orbit when Krypton exploded" (*Krypton Chronicles* #2, October 1981).

An Earth scientist named Mel Evans once estimated that Krypton, before its destruction, was at a "probable distance of 0.317 light years" from Earth (*Superman* [first series] #136, April 1960).

Cosmic tourists were attracted the planet's natural beauty, which included the Fire Falls, the Gold Volcano, and the Scarlet Jungle (all in *Superman's Girl Friend, Lois Lane* #21, November 1960); the Jewel Mountains, Meteor Valley, and Rainbow Canyon (all in *Superman* [first series] #141, November 1960); and the Three Sisters of Krypton, a trio of simultaneously erupting fire-geysers (*World's Finest Comics* #146, December 1964).

Less commonly known wonders included Shrinkwater Lake, whose waters contained "some strange chemical" that could temporarily reduce a person in size (*Action Comics* #325, June 1965); Great Krypton Lake (*Action Comics* #284, January 1962); and the Great Krypton Sea (*Superman Annual* #1, 1960).

In addition to its diverse peoples, the planet had a rich and varied flora and fauna. Many types of animal life closely resembled animals found on Earth, including dogs, monkeys, and gorillas. There were also unique life-forms, such as the winged dinosaur-like Snagriff (*Superman* [first series] #78, September–October 1952); the fiery-looking Flame Beast (*Superman* [first series] #123, August 1958); the flame dragon, a gigantic, bat-winged, dragon-like creature that belched flame "from its nostrils and gaping jaws" (*Superman* [first series] #142, January 1961); the Krypton Beast, Living Wheel, Winged Cat, and Balloonie (*Superman* [first series] #132, October 1959); the Fish-Snake, an eel-like "mutant fish" from the Fire Falls (*Action Comics* #281, October 1961); Rondors, rare creatures with single large horns that emitted radiation that "could cure many deadly illnesses" (*Superman* [first series] #157, November 1962); the Drang, also with a single horn (*Action Comics* #303, August 1963); the Nightwing, the Flamebird, and the Telepathic Hounds, which could "locate people at any distance by reading their minds to learn where they are" (*Superman* [first series] #158, January 1963); the Thought-Beasts, with television-like "thought-screens" atop their heads (*Superboy* [first series] #87, March 1961); the Metal-Eating Mole (*Action Comics* #242, July 1958); and the Metal-Eater (*Superman* [first series] #132, October 1959).

The glittering Jewel Mountains were thought to have been formed from the remains of the extinct Crystal Bird (*Action Comics* #310, March 1964).

Flora unique to Krypton include gigantic maroon fungi (*Action Comics* # 310, March 1964) and migratory red "moving forests," both indigenous to the Scarlet Jungle (*Superman* [first series] #164, October 1963), as well as singing flowers (*Superman* [first series] #141, November 1960).

Geologically, the planet's crust and mantle supplied a wide variety of ores that were turned into metals for construction and industry. Strongest among the alloys was kryptium, a "super-metal" described as "harder and stronger than any Earth metal" (*Action Comics* #329, October 1965). Gold, valued on Earth, was common on Krypton, and was erupted by the Gold Volcano. Instead Krypton's most precious metal was said to be boradium (*Superman* [first series] #78, September–October 1952).

Krypton traced its history back ten millennia to the time when two space explorers, Kryp and Tonn, arrived on the world and founded a family that eventually formed a civilization (*Superman* [first series] #238, June 1971). Nation-states slowly formed and re-formed through the years, but at some point in the past they united under one flag and one government (*Action Comics* #328,

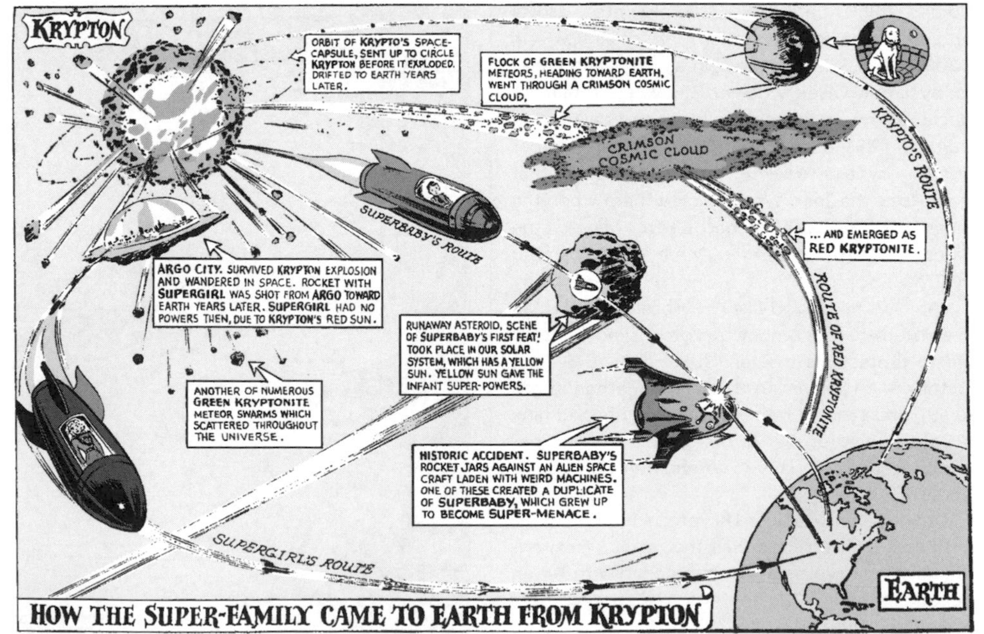

September 1965). The entire populace eventually spoke Kryptonese (*Superman* [first series] #141, November 1960).

Tracing family histories was a point of pride on Krypton, and the various houses lived and died by their reputations. The hyphenated naming convention saw a Kryptonian first name followed by the appropriate house's surname. Male offspring received a first name and the family name, such as Jor-El and his son Kal-El. Female offspring received a first name but also their father's name, so Zor-El's daughter was known as Kara Zor-El. When a woman married, the father's name was dropped, so Lara Lor-Van became Lara Jor-El. The chronicles' lack of hyphenates in some names were chroniclers' errors, and previously singular names such as Kimda were later amended, in this case to Kim-Da.

Among the most prestigious and long-lived houses on Krypton at the time of its destruction was the House of El, and given that both Kal-El and Kara Zor-El survived the planet's fate, this was the only family to have a chance at continuing its tradition on another world.

Statuary was also representative of the way ancestors were revered on the planet. When Superboy discovered a collection of five members from the House of El, he was obligated to manipulate them in honor of the Father-Son test (*Adventure Comics* #313, October 1963). The statues were maintained by the Teen of Steel, and later, when WGBS broadcast a miniseries about the Kryptonians, footage of the statues was seen by viewers for the first time (*Krypton Chronicles* #1, September 1981).

The planet put aside centuries of war to evolve to the point at which crime was virtually unknown on Krypton by the time Jor-El had married Lara (*Superman* [first series] #170, July 1964); the last war had occurred thousands of years in Krypton's past (*Action Comics* #216, May 1956). As a result, capital punishment was unknown, and citizens were bound by a strict Kryptonian Code of Honor. At the time of its destruction, the exact population of the planet was unknown, although Kandor, when it was stolen and bottled by Brainiac, had one million citizens. The remainder of the planet's populace may have numbered in the millions (*Superman* [first series] #141, November 1960).

In addition to the amazing natural sights on the planet, many Kryptonian-made attractions were on every tourist's list, including the Hall of Worlds (*Superman* [first series] *Annual* #1, 1960); the Red Tower of Kryptonopolis (*World's Finest Comics* #146, December 1964); the Grotto of Images, which was a huge chamber of mirrors (*Superman* [first series] #189, August 1966); the Floating City, a city of approximately one million inhabitants living atop a river (*Action Comics* #325, June 1965); Cloud Land, an ideal place for lovers (*Action Comics* #325, June 1965); and the Cosmic Clock (*Superman* [first series] #170, July 1964).

The planet's system of government differed from Earth's in that a number of councils apparently oversaw all aspects of life on the planet. Given their intellectual pursuits, it was logical that many of these councils were scientific in name and mission. The Council of Five, for example, was a quintet of distinguished scientists who seemed to rule on social and scientific matters (*Superman* [first series] #53, July–August 1948). Other named councils included the Council (*Superman* [first series] #61, November–December 1949), the Science Council (*Superman* [first series] #113, May 1957), and the Council of Scientists (*Superman* [first series] #146, July 1961). A Supreme Council most likely was the highest authority on the planet (*Superman* [first series] #154, July 1962).

The capital city of the unified planetary government was Kryptonopolis, while Kandor and Argo City were both considered major metropolises. Originally, the capital was said to be Kandor until it was stolen by Brainiac, at which time the seat of power moved to Kryptonopolis (*Action Comics* #242, August 1958). The councils operated out of the World Capitol Building, which proudly flew the planet's colors.

Despite the absence of crime, order was maintained by the Krypton Security Force (*Superman* [first series] #170, July 1964), and anything resembling a crime was referred to the Krypton Bureau of Investigation (*Superman* [first series] #123, August 1958). Scientist Raf Arlo established that most of the crimes on the planet "were perpetrated by an unknown race of invisible people" (*Superman* [first series] #170, July 1964). Those few who committed crimes and were convicted by the judicial system were exiled to space, placed in suspended animation in capsules designed to sustain their lives but separate them from Kryptonian society (*Superman* [first series] #65, July–August 1950).

Once space travel was banned in the aftermath of Jax-Ur's destruction of one of Krypton's moons, the issue of dealing with criminals was solved when Jor-El discovered the Phantom Zone. The convicted felon was placed before a spherical projector, usually controlled by Jor-El, and sent to the limbo-like realm for the duration of his or her sentence (*Adventure Comics* #283, April 1961).

The inquisitive bent of Kryptonians led to everything being carefully documented, and the data were maintained in the Krypton Record Bureau. Thought-discs contained information recorded astro-electrically directly from an individual's memory (*Action Comics* #149, October 1950).

Every scientific pursuit was far more advanced on Krypton than comparable studies on Earth, which meant Kryptonians were aware of Earth long before humans knew of planets beyond their own solar system. Kryptonians were also comfortable with other alien races, many of whom vacationed or conducted business on the planet, even though the Kryptonians had never explored beyond their own system.

While they eschewed space travel, Krypton's people did have sleek, safe, and environmentally friendly modes of mass transit in the air, on land, and in the sea. Sliding people movers kept traffic flowing on the city streets, and citizens could watch news monitors positioned throughout the cities, keeping them informed as they traveled home or to work.

Krypton's scientists developed sophisticated weather-control towers, which helped purify the air, tap solar power, and modify weather patterns.

Jor-El and the Kryptonian Council

Solar and atomic power were used to heat homes, which entertained their inhabitants with 3-D television. Advanced robots and androids handled the majority of manual labor, from agriculture to basic housework.

The many marvels of life on Krypton included a lack of serious illnesses, with the exception of Virus X, for which there was no known cure (*Superman* [first series] #156, October 1962). Children, on their first day of school, were given all the immunizations required by medical law. Doctors had also developed a healing ray to handle most injuries suffered by the populace.

Education was handled with the aid of sophisticated telepathy helmets, enabling teachers to transmit knowledge to students at high speed. Upon their twelfth birthday, children began adulthood classes with a citizen-trainer, learning practical skills from first aid to survival. A headband was handed to those who successfully completed the course work, denoting the wearers as adult citizens (*Superman* [first series] #352, October 1980).

The people of Krypton celebrated many holidays and had traditional ceremonies for most major life events. All Kryptonian men, for instance, wore headbands as "the symbol of a free man" in recognition of a revolt by slaves (who used headbands as slings) led by Rik-Ar generations in the past (*Superman* [first series] #264, June 1973). Weddings were held in the local Palace of Marriage (*Superman* [first series] #141, November 1960). Within the palace, the couple would mount the Jewel of Honor or Jewel of Truth and Honor. Vows were exchanged while kneeling on the giant gem, followed by an exchange of rings or a marriage bracelet featuring a unique set of colors that tradition said could not be replicated. The wedding hall would be decorated with statues of both the bride's and groom's parents. However, marrying members of the same bloodline was forbidden (*Action Comics* #289, June 1962).

Some Kryptonians had their own sets of legends, myths, and superstitions. These people subscribed to four major superstitions: It was bad luck for a bride to wear jewels from the Jewel Mountains at her wedding; the killing of birds was regarded as extremely unlucky; upon seeing a comet, a person must hide in a cave for twenty-four hours or face death; and if criminals experienced failure, drawing a picture of a mythological creature known as a one-eyed grompus would cause Krypton's demons to bring them good luck (*Superman* [first series] #164, October 1963).

Among the major holidays celebrated around the globe, the most important was the annual Day of Truth, when the people spoke nothing but the truth to one another in honor of Val-Lor. Legend had it that Val-Lor courageously spoke out against the Vrangs, an aggressive alien race of invaders, and although it cost him his life, it inspired his fellow Kryptonians to rise up from their enslavement and revolt (*Superman* [first series] #176, April 1965).

Given all their scientific development, it may surprise some that Kryptonians continued to worship various deities from the planet's past, including the sun god Rao (*Superman* [first series] #248, February 1972). There were also Yuda, goddess of love (*Krypton Chronicles* #3, November 1981); Telle, god of wisdom; Mordo, god of strength; and Lorra, goddess of beauty (*Action Comics* #299, April 1963).

Life on Krypton was eventually doomed by the planet's unstable core, although only Jor-El believed the data he gathered on this looming catastrophe enough to signal an alarm. He was overruled by the Science Council, but the Guardians of the Universe concurred with the noble scientist. They dispatched the sector's Green Lantern, Tomar-Re, to help stabilize the planet, for the Guardians knew that one particular Kryptonian was destined to become the greatest Green Lantern of them all. The geological stresses were too much, however, and even Tomar-Re's vaunted power ring was not enough to stop the planet from blowing up. Tomar-Re always considered this his greatest failure, but on the day of his retirement from the Corps, the Guardians revealed that fate had a different destiny in mind for the Kryptonian who survived; they explained to Tomar-Re how the infant survived and grew up on Earth to become Superman (*Superman* [first series] #257, October 1972).

As Tomar-Re attempted to save the planet, so did Jor-El. He envisioned a fleet of space arks to transport all Kryptonians to Earth. He developed a prototype rocket and tested it by sending the family pet Krypto into space (*Adventure Comics* #210, March 1955). From those results, he built a larger model, but before this could be tested, the end arrived. He urged Lara to take their infant son Kal-El to Earth, but she insisted her place was by her husband's side. Instead their child left the atmosphere alone shortly before the planet exploded.

Over the years, Kal-El discovered that many others had survived Krypton's destruction, not counting the criminals inhabiting the Phantom Zone. There was the bottle city of Kandor, in the possession of Brainiac at the time of Krypton's destruction (*Action Comics* #242, July 1958). A large enough chunk of the planet broke away, taking with it Argo City, whose citizens managed to erect a shield to preserve the atmosphere before the ground beneath them slowly turned to KRYPTONITE and threatened to kill them all. To prevent her death, Zor-El sent his daughter Kara to Earth, where she grew up to become SUPERGIRL (*Action Comics* #252, May 1959). Later, she discovered that her parents were still alive in the spectral SURVIVAL ZONE. Once freed, they settled in Kandor (*Action Comics* #309–310, February–March 1964).

On Earth, Kal-El grew up as CLARK KENT, and through the years he began to encounter other Kryptonian survivors including Krypto and Beppo—a monkey who had also been a test subject of Jor-El's (*Superboy* [first series] #76, October 1959). Other animals managed to survive, including a Snagriff that came to Earth (*Superman* [first series] #78, September–October 1952); Super-Ape (*Action Comics* #218, July 1956); KING KRYPTON, another ape (*Action Comics* #238, March 1958); a flame dragon (*Superman* [first series] #142, January 1961); and YANGO, a cybernetically enhanced ape (*Superboy* [first series] #172, March 1971).

There were also the numerous criminals imprisoned in Kryptonian space capsules, including MALA, KIZO, and U-BAN (*Superman* [first series] #65, July–August 1950; *Action Comics* #194, July 1954); Kralus and Marno (*Superboy* [first series] #58, July 1957); KLAX-AR (*Superboy* [first series] #67, September 1958); and Sar-Ul and Ralsa (*The New Adventures of Superboy* #27–28, March–April 1982). Additional survivors of note included an unnamed caveman (*World's Finest* #102, January 1961); juvenile delinquent DEV-EM and his family (*Adventure Comics* #287, August 1961); and time-traveler Dahr-Nel (*Superman's Girl Friend, Lois Lane* #90, February 1969).

Superman even encountered an alien pirate named BLACK ZERO, who attempted to enhance his reputation by falsely claiming to have accelerated Krypton's destruction (*Superman* [first series] #205, April 1968).

A variety of artifacts also survived the planet's destruction, and many of them made their way to Earth. Most of them wound up in Superman's possession and were kept safe in his FORTRESS OF SOLITUDE. Those taken by Earth's criminals wound up being either confiscated or destroyed.

Once Superman built his Fortress, he memorialized his parents and his planet throughout the structure. He erected statues of his parents and protected the bottled city of Kandor, along with a scale replica of Krypton and a "3-dimensional tableau of the exact moment that the planet Krypton exploded!"

Superman, Supergirl, and Krypto later combined their titanic powers to create a replica of Krypton on a lifeless planet, dubbed it a memorial world, and left behind a series of androids to replicate Kryptonian society (*Superman* [first series] #150, January 1962). Throughout their long careers, the heroes often pierced the time barrier and managed to visit their homeworld.

After the CRISIS ON INFINITE EARTHS, Krypton's entire history underwent a massive revision. The planet was a cold and crystalline environment, its civilization developing within Krypton's warmer mountain ranges (*Man of Steel* #1, Early October 1986).

Krypton orbited the red sun Rao and was located fifty light-years from Earth's solar system. Life managed to evolve in the harsh environment, so Krypton's earliest eras saw the evolution and propagation of some of the deadliest organisms in the universe. BERTRON, an alien scientist, once used the environment to test the genetic war machine he called DOOMSDAY (*Superman/Doomsday: Hunter/Prey*, 1994). When intelligent life evolved on Krypton, civilization flourished so rapidly that the planet's technological progress one hundred thousand years ago far surpassed Earth's technology at the time of Kal-El's arrival. The advances included eradicating disease, prolonging life, and advanced cloning (thanks to the remains of Bertron's lab), with multiple copies of Krypton's citizenry kept on file (*The World of Krypton* [second series] #1, December 1987).

Kryptonian birthing matrix

When the issue of clone rights came up, it threatened to plunge Krypton into civil war, a debate sparked by the words of the CLERIC, an alien missionary. When a female clone achieved sentience, it was the final step that began Krypton's Clone Wars. The science used to advance knowledge and improve life was suddenly diverted to create weapons of mass destruction, such as the artificial intelligence known as the ERADICATOR. The Eradicator managed to alter all Kryptonians' DNA so that anyone leaving the planet would instantly die (*Action Comics Annual* #2, 1989).

Soon after, the government capitulated and all of Krypton's clone banks were destroyed. Displeased by this act, a faction known as Black Zero used the Destroyer, a device that projected massive doses of nuclear energy into the planet's core, with the intent to destroy Krypton. Before the massive explosion could occur, an ancestor of Jor-El managed to stop the effects, but not before Kandor vanished, believed to be a casualty of the war (*The World of Krypton* [second series] #2, January 1988).

Black Zero did alter life on the planet, however: The harsh environmental conditions of Krypton's past reasserted themselves, forcing the people to withdraw to more temperate zones, leading the Kryptonians to become as cold and sterile as their world. They eschewed emotional entanglements in favor of rational thought and scientific deeds. Krypton's inhabitants grew farther apart, favoring isolation instead of more conflict. As a result, marriage became an act largely of convenience, because genetic matching was used to determine procreation, which was then done in an artificial womb called a birthing matrix.

The government that ruled in the wake of these changes forbade space exploration or travel, and Kryptonians grew increasingly isolationist despite their vast knowledge of life beyond their star.

Millennia later, scientist Jor-El was studying a "green plague" that was claiming an alarming number of Kryptonian lives. His studies led him to the conclusion that Black Zero's previous efforts had altered Krypton's core, changing the very substance of the planet into something radioactive and deadly. In time, either before or after all life had died, the planet would inevitably explode. Jor-El made a report to the Council but was rebuffed. Determined that someone should survive Krypton's fate, he took his child's birthing matrix and attached to it a warp engine of his own design (*The World of Krypton* [second series] #3–4, February–March 1988).

Jor-El first learned of Earth from the time-tossed Jack Knight and Mikaal Tomas, two of the men known as Starman (*Starman* [second series] #51, March 1999). Having later studied life on Earth in detail, he concluded that his own people had grown as cold as the crystalline surface of Krypton and that their way of life was devoid of any pleasure. That he had romantic feelings for the lovely Lara Lor-Van was considered aberrant among their peers. Jor-El wanted his son to have a better life and convinced Lara that Earth would be the ideal home for Kal-El given that the system's yellow sun would imbue the child with energy to make him faster and stronger than the natives who would raise him. She agreed with Jor-El, and the two watched Kal-El's matrix, aided by the warp engine, leave as Krypton crashed in around them.

Superman was taken to visit Krypton's solar system by Hawkman and Hawkwoman, and they were surprised to find the remains of Krypton being pulled together by gravity. Although the Man of Steel wore a LEAD-lined spacesuit to protect himself, it proved ineffective: The concentrated kryptonite radiation induced hallucinations about his father Jor-El building space arks to bring Kryptonians to Earth. Saved by the Thanagarian heroes, the trio returned to Earth (*Superman* [second series] #18, June 1988).

Later, reality was altered once more and Krypton was said to be located in the Andromeda galaxy two and a half million light-years away from Earth (*Superman: Birthright* #9, June 2004). The remainder of Kryptonian society both visually and historically hewed closer to the Earth-1 incarnation. Literally wrapped in a Kryptonian flag as he was sent to Earth, Superman would ultimately find that its familiar S-shield would be forever regarded by the people of Earth as a symbol of hope.

After Infinite Crisis, Krypton's history changed yet again. Once the universe was formed by the Big Bang, sentience emerged in different parts, including a being who became known as the god Rao. It formed the planet Krypton and its red sun from remnants of the great cosmic explosion. Kryptonians credited Rao with creating the entire universe, which sat in conflict with other legends from other parts of the universe. Rao, known as Krypton's "father," gave the planet form, shape, and, in time, life. His "children" were the Flamebird, made from chaos and fire; Vohc, the builder; and eons later Nightwing, Rao's "eyes in the night." All the siblings helped craft the flaura and fauna of Krypton. While much of its history and many of its people resembled their Earth-1 counterparts, the New Earth reality had a benevolent and bearded Jor-El who could communicate with his son in Kal-El's Fortress of Solitude, and a Krypton that was cold and forbidding, yet also filled with diverse and colorfully attired Guilds that made the world one of the jewels in the twenty-eight known galaxies (*Action Comics* #844, December 2006; *Action Comics Annual* #10, March 2007). Superman learned of Krypton's legacy through the remains of the rocket that brought him to Earth, as well as through the Sunstone crystals housed in the Fortress. His S-shield, the Kryptonian icon for the House of El, became a symbol of pride for Superman and those who loved him (*Superman: Secret Origin* #1, November 2009).

KRYPTON-II

A group of Kryptonian scientists teamed up to build an exact replica of their homeworld, complete with a red sun and an android populace, in order to confuse an advancing alien invasion fleet from another star system. When the leaders of Krypton had first learned of the impending invasion, it was Jor-El who came up with the ruse. With the Council's blessing, he designed an Atom-Scan Ray that digitally mapped the planet and projected a model into a barren region of space. The image acted as a magnet, drawing toward it bits of space flotsam and jetsam until a planet was formed.

As Jor-El worked on world building, others set out to re-create every single inhabitant in android form so that a fully functioning world would appear to the alien's advance forces. A space barge was designed to transport the androids to the newly fashioned world, and the androids were programmed to set out booby traps across the faux Krypton to defend it from the invaders.

Once the second Krypton was populated down to its flora and fauna, a smokescreen was placed around the real Krypton, leading the invaders toward the artificial world. The invaders found the fake Krypton after losing many ships to a cosmic "whirlpool of energy." Just a few of the surviving ships landed on the fake world, and the invaders were quickly destroyed by Kryptonian forces.

With the invasion derailed, the planet with its artificial sun was left to drift through space until it was drawn toward Earth's solar system many years later. When Superman was alerted to a cosmic calamity, he flew into space, where the red-sun radiation from the faux Krypton's star weakened him. He landed on the still-functioning replica of his homeworld and accidentally set off several of the remaining booby traps, which wound up devastating the world. Superman blamed himself for destroying his home planet and intended to perish with it until he was handed a microfilm projector by the android Lyla Lerrol. There Superman learned the truth of the false world by watching a recording made by his father.

As Krypton II hurtled toward immolation within its artificial red sun, Superman boarded one of the invaders' starships and once more rocketed to safety as Krypton died a second time (*Superman* [first series] #189, August 1966).

KRYPTON CITY

An alternative name for Kandor.

KRYPTON CRAWL, THE

When the Jimmy Olsen of Earth-1 briefly had his own rock band—Jimmy Olsen and the Carrot Top Cut-Ups—they recorded "The Krypton Crawl," which became a number one smash-hit recording. While the song brought him national fame and celebrity, it did not accomplish its goal of distracting Lucy Lane, who had been infatuated with Rick Rock and the Rolling Romeos instead of Jimmy. The beat and the accompanying dance seemed to trigger an involuntary response in the Man of Steel, making him do the dance nonstop. It was later proven to be the result of exposure to red kryptonite, which was planted on Superman by an international criminal hoping to force the Man of Steel into releasing a deadly biological weapon on Earth. Superman and Jimmy exposed the plot and apprehended the criminal while Lucy once more turned her attentions to the cub reporter (*Superman's Pal, Jimmy Olsen* #88, October 1965).

KRYPTONESE

The language spoken by inhabitants of the planet Krypton.

Some of the recorded rules (as detailed in *Krypton Chronicles* #1, September 1981) included the following:

- Plurals were formed by adding an *o* to a word.
- A double letter indicated a strong emphasis on the sound.
- Kryptonian men used hyphenated names, such as Jor-El, the last part being the family name (as with the El family). Except in the case of orphans, women took their father's full names as last names—as with Lara Lor-Van, daughter of Lor-Van.
- Eleven characters were used in Kryptonians' numerical system. Their *O* was used only for the purpose of indicating a zero, while *10* had a special character of its own. Using the Roman *X* to stand for "10," X = 10, 1X = 20, 2X = 30, and so on. In addition 100 = 9X, 101 = X1, 110 = XX, and 111 was the first three-digit number.
- The calendar was quite different from Earth's, since eighteen Kryptonian years equaled twenty-five Earth years. Because the maturation process was comparable there, a Kryptonian was considered fully grown at the age of fifteen.

KRYPTONIAN

A humanoid originating from the planet Krypton.

KRYPTONITE

When the planet Krypton exploded, its remnants were molecularly changed into a deadly radioactive element that was usually fatal to only Kryptonians (*Superman* [first series] #61, November—December 1949).

On Earth-2, Superman did not encounter the deadly material until well after he began his adventuring. Posing as a swami, the swindler Dan Rivers was unaware that the red-colored meteor fragment he'd added to his turban created an inexplicable weakness in the Man of Steel each time they met. Tracing the origins of the meteorite, Superman traveled into the past and was stunned to discover that he was born on the planet Krypton (*Superman* [first series] #61, November-December 1949). Suspecting the rock's effects on Superman, Rivers later made another attempt on the super hero's life in order to prove his theory. Superman debunked this theory, but Rivers shared his story with his cellmate Lex Luthor (*Superman Family* #202, July–August 1980). Luthor subsequently proved that kryptonite definitely affected Superman negatively and exposed the truth to the general public (*Superman Family* #205, January-February 1981).

Though previously depicted as red (*Superman* [first series] #61, November–December 1949) and gray (*Adventure Comics* #171, December 1951),

this most common form of kryptonite was retroactively declared to have always been green, and first appeared as such in *Action Comics* #141, February 1950.

Word quickly spread that an element existed that could weaken or kill the Man of Steel, and Lex Luthor studied it in detail and fabricated a synthetic version (*Action Comics* #141, February 1950). In his recounting, Luthor said the populace learned of the mineral when scientists discovered an unconscious Superman lying beside a green-glowing meteorite. They deduced that it was a meteor fragment from Krypton and christened it kryptonite, informing the press in the process. At first, scientists seemed to think exposure to kryptonite would do no more than weaken and paralyze Superman. It was years before they realized it could kill him, something definitively proven when the mutant King Krypton succumbed to kryptonite poisoning on Earth-1 (*Action Comics* #238, March 1958).

The faux kryptonite that Luthor created was planted in Lois Lane's handbag, which was summarily grabbed by purse snatcher Dan the Dip, and the thief eventually figured out what he possessed. However, Superman managed to outwit Dan the Dip, and the green rock ended up in police custody (*Action Comics* #142, March 1950).

Several attempts were made by Superman to build up an immunity to kryptonite by prolonged exposure to the mineral rock (*Superman* [first series] #84, September–October 1953). At one point, the Man of Steel said that a good dousing in the ocean could cancel out the kryptonite's effects (*World's Finest Comics* #69, March–April), but that was never proven. Only encasing kryptonite in lead prevented the radiation from affecting Superman (*Superman* [first series] #92, September 1954).

In the Earth-1 reality, Superboy encountered kryptonite and its variants at a far younger age and spent his career attempting to keep the substance out of the hands of criminals and other evildoers. His first encounter occurred during his debut year in his costume when he suddenly became gravely ill for no apparent reason. Just as the Boy of Steel was about to succumb, Jonathan Kent finally guessed that the source of the illness might be the green rock that he'd added to Clark's meteorite collection (*Adventure Comics* #251, August 1958). The world learned of the substance soon after, when Superboy managed to convince some thieves that the strange green rock at the Smallville Planetarium wasn't really harmful to him—only to have a well-intentioned scientist use the same fragment in a Kryptonian diorama during a public ceremony. Before an army of reporters and radio broadcasters, Superboy collapsed on stage (*Superman* [first series] #136, April 1960).

As criminals and villains began to study the strange green rock, they found ways to use it in weaponry. Many of Lex Luthor's creations—beginning with a serum that turned him into a Kryptonite Man—called for the use of kryptonite (*Action Comics* #249, February 1959). The Man of Steel's deadliest opponent in many ways was John Corben, a vicious murderer who was nearly killed in a car accident. A benevolent scientist named Professor Emmett Vale built Corben a metal body with a "heart" powered by uranium capsules that had to be replaced on a daily basis. As Metallo, Corben became a criminal juggernaut and grew obsessed with finding an alternative to uranium. He ultimately found it in kryptonite, whose power would, according to Dr. Vale, last forever. Unfortunately for Corben, the sample he snatched from the Metropolis exhibit hall turned out to be nothing more than a painted rock; once it was placed in his chest, Metallo dropped dead immediately (*Action Comics* #252, May 1959).

Superboy also encountered individuals who had been altered by the deadly ore, beginning with a teenage criminal whose spacecraft passed through a green kryptonite cloud, turning him into the Kryptonite Kid. The emerald villain and his matching dog very nearly killed Superboy not once but twice (*Superboy* [first series] #83, September 1960, and #99, September 1962). The first time, the Boy of Steel and canine Krypto were saved by Mr. Mxyzptlk. The second time, they lured the Kryptonite Kid and his dog through a red kryptonite space cloud that not only altered the color of their skin, but exchanged their nasty dispositions for virtuous ones as well.

The fact that kryptonite had been melted, crushed, liquefied, and altered since it was first discovered led scientists to wonder why the substance wasn't invulnerable on Earth like everything else Kryptonian. Further, why didn't the green meteors just burn up when they hit the atmosphere? It was eventually discovered that "kryptonite can't combine chemically with oxygen, which causes combustion" (*Superman* [first series] #130, July 1959). Apparently, a significant amount of the planet was caught in the warp field created by Kal-El's rocket engine and entered nearby space, with kryptonite meteors periodically crashing to Earth (*The Amazing World of Superman,* 1973).

As to how much kryptonite arrived on Earth, at one point Superman ordered his robots to go out and collect every known sample. The total reached a staggering half a ton (*Superman's Pal, Jimmy Olsen* #81, December 1964). Added to what was found in near space, the total quickly reached fifty tons. With more pieces arriving, citizens were asked to add them to a stockpile collected by a cross-country train dubbed the Kryptonite Express (*World's Finest Comics* #196, September 1970).

All that changed one day when Professor Bolden tried an experiment using kryptonite as an energy resource—and it backfired in a big way. The ensuing explosion turned every chunk of kryptonite on Earth into iron, not to mention giving form to an other-dimensional parasite that would leech off some of Superman's powers when it encountered the Man of Steel (*Superman* [first series] #233, January 1971). To prove it no longer could harm him, Superman ate a piece in front

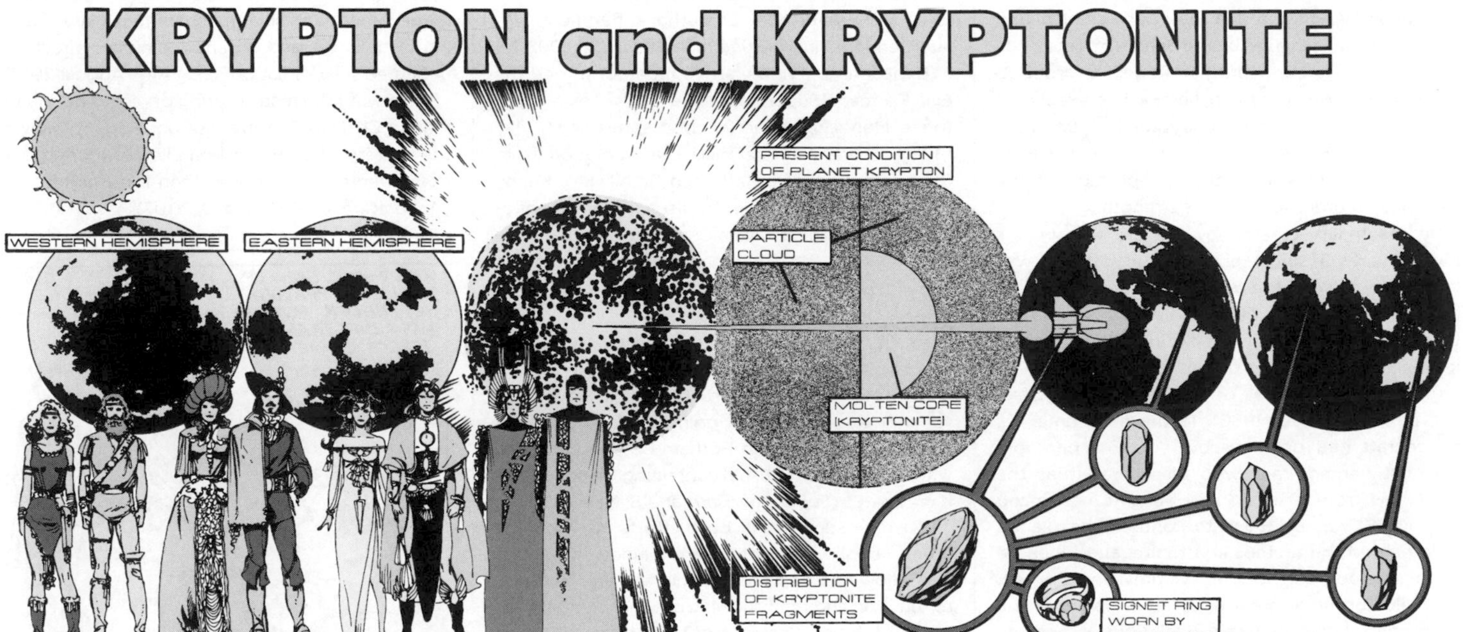

KRYPTON and KRYPTONITE

WESTERN HEMISPHERE
EASTERN HEMISPHERE
PRESENT CONDITION OF PLANET KRYPTON
PARTICLE CLOUD
MOLTEN CORE (KRYPTONITE)
DISTRIBUTION OF KRYPTONITE FRAGMENTS
SIGNET RING WORN BY LEX LUTHOR

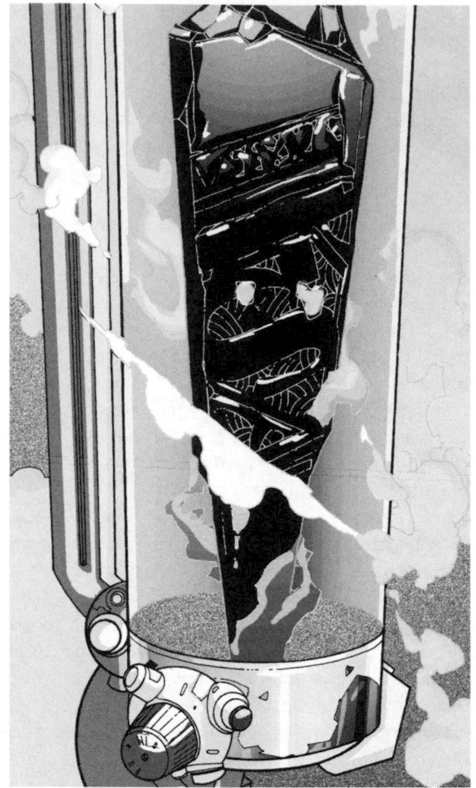

of a robber and commented that it needed salt. The good professor continued working with the inert substance, but it only produced "a super-combustible gas that flames uncontrollably when it comes into contact with solid matter" (*Action Comics* #485, July 1978).

A race known as the Sun-Thrivers completed Bolden's work by gathering every piece of Krypton still extant in the known universe with the goal of refashioning the long-dead world. Unfortunately, this Krypton was also unstable and exploded (*Superman* [first series] #255, August 1972).

Over time, however, fresh radioactive pieces of the second Krypton found their way to Earth, and Superman was plagued by the deadly meteor once more. John Corben's brother Roger, in order to seek revenge on Superman, had his heart replaced with one made of synthetic kryptonite (*Superman* [first series] #310, April 1977). In time, the new Metallo had the synthetic kryptonite replaced with the real thing in order to boost his strength.

In the reality created by the Crisis on Infinite Earths, only a single chunk of kryptonite was known to exist in the world. It arrived on Earth after lodging itself outside Kal-El's spacecraft when it landed. Clark Kent didn't know about kryptonite or his alien origins until several years into his adventures as Superman (*Man of Steel* #6, Late December 1986). In the meantime, his spacecraft had been discovered by a paranoid scientist named Vale, who discovered that the craft was from Krypton and became convinced that Kal-El was on Earth to conquer the planet. Vale named the meteor kryptonite, and when he chanced upon car accident victim John Corben, he built Corben a metal body and implanted the kryptonite within its heart, declaring Corben the means of destroying Superman. Superman faced the cyborg villain—and learned of kryptonite's existence in the process. In the battle's aftermath, both Superman's alien origins and his vulnerability to kryptonite became public knowledge (*Superman* [second series] #1, January 1987).

Metallo was spirited away by sinister businessman Lex Luthor, who had the kryptonite from Corben's chest removed. Luthor had a portion of the rock fashioned into a signet ring. With this deadly new accessory, he waited for Superman to confront him, convinced that he'd finally gotten the upper hand against his longtime nemesis (*Superman* [second series] #2, January 1987). Unlike the kryptonite of old, however, this version *was* harmful to the people of Earth as well as Superman. It just required long-term exposure before its detrimental effects kicked in. Luthor eventually discovered that he had radiation poisoning, requiring amputation of his right hand (*Action Comics* #600, June 1988). When the cancer spread farther, Lex decided to fake his death (*Action Comics* #660, December 1990), concocting an elaborate plot to have his brain transplanted into a healthy young body that he passed off as his long-lost son.

The kryptonite ring ended up in the possession of a former Luthor underling, who was hunted down by the Man of Steel and the Dark Knight. Superman gave the ring to Batman and asked him to keep it in his possession as a fail-safe should he ever go rogue (*Superman* [second series] #44; *The Adventures of Superman* #467; *Action Comics* #654—all June 1990). Batman was actually forced to use the ring on several occasions as circumstances dictated (*Batman* #612, April 2003; others).

Other fragments of the kryptonite meteor were turned into bullets by Luthor and supplied to the mercenary Bloodsport, who tried to kill the Man of Steel (*Superman* [second series] #4, April 1987). The bullets were later used by doctors to weaken Superman enough to allow them to perform life-saving surgery when the Man of Steel was seriously injured (*Superman* [second series] #40, February 1990). The remainder of Luthor's fragment was later rendered inert (*Superman Special* #1, 1992).

Exposure to a newly arrived meteor turned the Evil Factory's Superman clone into a toxic Kryptonite Man (*Superman* [second series] #43, May 1990). It was later learned that radiation from the original fragment affected Smallville's Kenny Braverman, allowing him to discharge kryptonite-laced energy as the villain Conduit (*Superman: The Man of Steel* #0; *Superman* [second series] #0; *The Adventures of Superman* #0; *Action Comics* #0—all October 1994).

Reality was shifted twice more by the Infinite Crisis and then the Final Crisis, altering the volume of green kryptonite on Earth, as well as how many variants existed. At one point, a giant chunk of kryptonite crashed into Gotham Bay, and encased within it was a rocket ship containing Clark's cousin Kara Zor-El (*Superman/Batman* #8, May 2004).

Despite Superman's best efforts to eliminate them, chunks of kryptonite remained in circulation, allowing villains such as Metallo and Reactron to function and fight the Man of Steel on many occasions (*Action Comics* #872, February 2009). In a retelling of the modern reality, Lex Luthor possessed the sole chunk of kryptonite and used it to fashion Metallo's heart, thereby beginning his lifelong war against Superman (*Superman: Secret Origin* #4, March 2010).

Beginning with the Earth-1 reality, there were many varieties of kryptonite through Superman's long career, including the following.

Red Kryptonite

Superboy discovered the existence of red kryptonite (*Adventure Comics* #252, September 1958), learning that rather than killing him, it altered either his appearance and/or his powers for forty-eight hours (*Superboy* [first series] #74, July 1959).

It was later learned that this variant was created after it passed through "a strange cosmic cloud" (*Action Comics* #259, December 1959), and red kryptonite became almost as ubiquitous as its emerald cousin. Each piece affected all Kryptonians the same way (*Superman* [first series] #144, April 1961), and the same fragment could not affect anyone twice (*Superman's Girl Friend, Lois Lane* #29, November 1961). Superman and other Kryptonians could feel a "telltale tingling" in its presence, which served as a warning (*Action Comics* #283, December 1961).

After the First Crisis, it was some time before the first evidence of red kryptonite surfaced. It was first glimpsed as a magical creation of Mr. Mxyzptlk and put to use as a means of stripping Superman of his powers (*The Adventures of Superman* #463, February 1990; *Superman* [second series] #49–50, November–December 1990). Rā's al Ghūl had gotten hold of a sample Batman created as a potential weapon against the Man of Steel. Using a sample of green kryptonite, Batman "performed a series of experiments on it. He managed to accelerate its radioactive half-life—as indicated by its color-shift. His idea was to make it less lethal, but still crippling to the Kryptonian physiology. To discover what sort of unpredictable changes it might wreak in [Superman's] cellular structure." In this case, "It made Superman's skin transparent as glass, exposing his muscles and organs (painfully) directly to unfiltered solar radiation" (*JLA* #44, August 2000).

Following the restructuring of reality during the Infinite Crisis, red kryptonite once again followed the pattern of its Earth-1 parallel, triggering one-time effects for no longer than forty-eight hours (*Action Comics Annual* #10, 2007).

AND WHEN I GREW UP, THEY WERE CRAZIER YET! RED K ALWAYS HAS A DIFFERENT EFFECT ON ME!
BEARDED SUPERMAN
RAINBOW SUPERMAN
ANT-HEAD SUPERMAN
SUPER-MONSTER

Blue Kryptonite

Superman himself created blue kryptonite using the same imperfect duplication ray that created the Bizarros. Though the Man of Steel only intended to use the substance as a threat to ward off an invasion, blue kryptonite proved just as lethal as its green counterpart and killed the Bizarro Supergirl (*Superman* [first series] #140, October 1960).

Post-Crisis, blue kryptonite was seen causing Bizarros pain, but also altered their personalities so that they spoke clearly, thought rationally, and were exceedingly polite (*Superman/Batman* #25, May 2006).

White Kryptonite

This variant was theoretically formed by other cosmic clouds in space (*Adventure Comics* #279, August 1962). It proved only toxic to plant life, Kryptonian or otherwise. White kryptonite would resurface when Superman was exposed to the incurable Virus X. In his death throes, Superman was finally jettisoned into the sun of a distant planet while the celebratory Bizarros showered him with all varieties of kryptonite—including white. Unexpectedly restored to full health, Superman realized it was because "Virus X" was a form of plant life (*Action Comics* #365–366, July–August 1968).

Gold Kryptonite

While not as deadly as its green counterpart, gold kryptonite had the ability to alter Kryptonians' physiology, robbing them of their super-abilities (*Adventure Comics* #299, August 1962; first canonical appearance in *Superman* [first series] #157, November 1962). The first to suffer from this variant was the criminal Quex-Ul. It was later learned that even a two-foot distance was close enough for the dangerous element do its work (*World's Finest* #159, August 1966). The origins of this variation may have been tied to a mysterious green comet that predated Krypton's explosion and would also permanently erase Kryptonians' superpowers (*Superman* [first series] #172, October 1964).

Samples of gold kryptonite survived in the thirtieth century and came into play when Element Lad transmuted an element into gold kryptonite during what was known as the Great Darkness Saga (*Legion of Super-Heroes* [second series] #293, November 1982).

In the post-Crisis reality, no gold kryptonite existed outside of a Pocket Universe created by the Time Trapper (*Superman* [second series] #22, October 1988). With the reordering of history following the Infinite Crisis, gold kryptonite once

again represented a threat (*Action Comics Annual* #10–11, 2007), although it now only removed a Kryptonian's powers for fifteen seconds, not permanently (*Action Comics* #872, February 2009).

Black Kryptonite

Unique to the post-Crisis reality, black kryptonite could divide a Kryptonian's personality into halves (*Supergirl* [fifth series] #2, September 2005). Lex Luthor claimed it was given to him by Darkseid, and when he exposed Supergirl to this element it created two distinct people, one in the traditional colorful costume, and one in a black-and-white variation.

Other Forms

Brainiac once arrived on Earth in order to steal the planet's aluminum supplies, which were as valuable as gold on other worlds. When Superman sought to stop him, the Coluan android unleashed a new weapon, red-green kryptonite, something he fashioned in order to use against the Man of Steel. The unpredictable result did not kill Superman, but temporarily gave him a third eye on the back of his head. It also gave him enhanced heat vision, and the next time he confronted Brainiac, Superman had enough power to punch through the android's force field and end Brainiac's threat (*Action Comics* #275, April 1961).

Another hybrid was red-gold kryptonite, which left Superman with temporary amnesia but still possessed of all his superpowers. The two varieties of kryptonite resulted from meteors crashing into one another; the unified rock fell into the Atlantic Ocean. When rescuing cable repair divers, the Man of Steel was exposed to the radiation, which gave him amnesia. A jolt from some high-tension wires later restored Superman's memories (*Superman* [first series] #178, July 1965).

When the portion of Krypton that contained Argo City eventually turned deadly, the ground was covered in lead. It was learned that this variation was anti-kryptonite, which affected normal Kryptonians (*Action Comics* #317, October 1964).

There was also x-kryptonite (*Action Comics* #261, February 1960). After making several attempts at chemically destroying a marble-sized piece of green kryptonite, Supergirl finally gave up and tossed it into the woods. There it was discovered by her pet cat Streaky, who was bathed in its radiation and became a super-cat. The effect was only temporary, but the feline later came into contact with the mutated kryptonite again. Kryptonians exposed to this variant were also weakened by its effects (*Superman Family* #203, September–October 1980).

Jewel kryptonite, another specially created variety, was prepared by time-traveling Phantom Zone criminal Jax-Ur out of material from Krypton's Jewel Mountains. It amplified Phantom Zoners' "mental commands and [converted] them into energy beams which [detonated] any explosive material" they set their sights on (*Action Comics* #310, March 1964). In the post-Zero Hour reality, a sample of this variety was used as a means of filtering out the yellow impurities in the Green Lantern Corps's Central Power Battery (*Silver Age 80-Page Giant* #1, July 2000).

Kryptonite-plus was "a super-powerful isotope that will finish off [Kryptonians] in minutes" (*Action Comics* #350, May 1967).

The kryptonite from the second Krypton's destruction seemed to alter its form enough so that Metallo managed a variation "able to slow down the rate of particle emissions enough to affect humans as it does Kryptonians." He attempted to kill Batman with this slow-kryptonite, with no success (*The Brave and the Bold* [first series] #175, June 1981).

An inhabitant of the planet Pyron, Truff experimented with a kryptonite rock and developed magno-kryptonite, which clung with "unbreakable force to anything that comes from Krypton" (*Superman's Pal, Jimmy Olsen* #92, April 1966).

Jimmy Olsen painted a fake piece of kryptonite silver, leading Superman to think it was a new variant until it was presented to him to celebrate his silver anniversary (*Superman's Pal, Jimmy Olsen* #70, July 1963).

Lex Luthor devised a synthetic variant called yellow kryptonite to psychologically hurt Superman, although only a Superman Robot believed the rock was any threat (*Action Comics* #277, June 1961).

An intergalactic villain named Zo-Mar found a way to mutate kryptonite in order to temporarily rob Kryptonians of their superpowers (*DC Comics Presents* #84, August 1985).

Kryptonite-X or kryptisium was a purified form of the element developed by the evil Cyborg Superman; its name was coined by Professor Emil Hamilton (*The Adventures of Superman* #511, April 1994). It actually helped restore Superman's powers in the wake of his battle against the Cyborg Superman at Engine City. As the Cyborg Superman unleashed the kryptisium at a weakened Man of Steel, the Eradicator interposed himself between the energy and Superman, effectively transferring the artificial intelligence's Kryptonian-derived powers into the hero (*Superman* [second series] #82, October 1993). It eventually overpowered Superman, requiring a discharge of energy in order to regulate his system.

KRYPTONITE DOG, THE

When a teen criminal and his dog traveled through a green cloud in space, they were both transformed into green-skinned beings who emitted kryptonite radiation. The Kryptonite Kid and the Kryptonite Dog came to Earth and encountered Superboy, who was rescued from the effects of the green kryptonite by Mr. Mxyzptlk. The alien teen and his pet returned to roaming in space (*Superboy* [first series] #83, September 1960).

KRYPTONITE GANG, THE

A group of normal criminals donned kryptonite-laced costumes in the hope of keeping Superboy at bay. Hired by Lex Luthor using the alias of the Krypton Conqueror, members of the Kryptonite Gang committed a series of crimes until they were apprehended by the Teen of Steel (*Superboy* [first series] #166, June 1970).

KRYPTONITE KID, THE

A juvenile delinquent left his home planet Blor accompanied by his pet dog to travel the stars. They passed through a green cloud that altered their physiology, giving them green skin; their bodies emitted kryptonite radiation. The emerald villain and his dog arrived on Earth and discovered that everything they touched transformed into deadly kryptonite-laced objects. He very nearly killed Superboy not once but twice (*Superboy* [first series] #83, September 1960). The first time, the Boy of Steel and his canine Krypto were saved by Mr. Mxyzptlk. The alien teen and his pet returned to roaming in space for a time.

The second time, Superboy and Krypto lured the Kid and his dog through a red kryptonite space cloud that not only altered the color of their skin but also exchanged their nasty dispositions for virtuous ones. The red k effect soon wore off, and the Boy of Steel subsequently had a third clash with the Kryptonite Kid in outer space (*Adventure Comics* #454, November–December 1977).

Years later, the alien returned, his skin back to its deadly emerald hue. Calling himself the Kryptonite Man, he challenged Superman to a battle to the death—but Superman won and refused to kill his longtime foe, instead returning him to space (*Superman* [first series] #299, May 1976).

KRYPTONITE MAN, THE

The first to use the name *Kryptonite Man* was the villainous scientist Lex Luthor, who ingested a diluted form of kryptonite in order to kill Superman (*Action Comics* #249, February 1959).

The second individual to adopt the name was the former Kryptonite Kid, who returned from his exile in space to challenge the adult Kryptonian (*Superman* [first series] #299, May 1976).

Another being to use the name was a ruler of Krypton long before Kryp and Tonn, who supposedly founded the Kryptonian race. This ruler, known in the legends only as the Kryptonite Man, learned of a coming cataclysm and sent his people into underground chambers, where they lay in stasis until the disaster passed. He kept vigil and then went into suspended animation, his machinery set to awaken him twenty years later. Instead there was a mechanical failure, and the ruler slumbered for millennia. When Krypton was on the verge of exploding, the Kryptonite Man finally awoke, and his mountain citadel was thrust into space. As the rock turned radioactive, he managed to feed off this radiation for survival. While traveling through space in exile, he bitterly blamed his world's destruction on the Kryptonians that followed his people.

Over time, the radiation began to dissipate, weakening the ruler until he encountered a race known as the Seeders. These Seeders emitted radiation close enough to the kind the Kryptonite Man needed to survive. During this time, he became aware of Superman's existence, so he stole a Seeder starship and found his way to Earth, seeking vengeance in the name of his people. His battle against Superman and Supergirl was titanic, but it ended when the Seeders came to Earth seeking redress for the theft. In the end, the Kryptonite Man sacrificed himself to save Earth rather than see another planet destroyed (*Superman*

[first series] #397, July 1984; *Supergirl* [second series] #21, July 1984).

In the reality after the Crisis on Infinite Earths, the Kryptonite Man was a clone grown from Superman's DNA. The green-skinned being was fashioned by the Fourth World's Simyan and Mokkari (*Superman* [second series] #43, May 1990).

A different entity using the name was the result of Captain Atom and Major Force attempting to stop a kryptonite meteor that threatened the Earth. Major Force detonated himself to try to deter the meteor, and his energy was absorbed by Captain Atom, along with much kryptonite radiation. This was siphoned off by the third Toyman, forming a sentient energy being that could inhabit

other bodies (*Superman/Batman* #20–25, June 2005–May 2006).

K. Russell Abernathy was a scientist who became another Kryptonite Man when one of his experiments went awry. He was trying to use kryptonite as an energy source, but when it exploded, he was infused with the deadly radiation. Rendered powerless, Superman called in Supergirl for assistance since Abernathy was causing major damage (*Superman* #650, May 2006). Abernathy escaped from Stryker's Island with the aid of Luthor's insect warriors, only to be used by Luthor to unearth an ancient Kryptonian artifact that had crashed to Earth millennia ago (*Action Comics* #838, June 2006). The new Kryptonite Man later battled Superman and nearly won, but was stopped by the combined efforts of Jimmy Olsen and Krypto (*Action Comics* #852–854, September–Mid October 2007).

KRYPTONITE MONKEY, THE

When Earth-1's Lex Luthor masqueraded as the Kryptonite Man after ingesting a distilled form of the deadly element, he nicknamed his pet the Kryptonite Monkey. Before taking the serum, he first tested it on the monkey, who began to glow green and emit deadly kryptonite radiation. While Luthor and Superman battled, the monkey escaped the laboratory and went to the Metropolis Zoo. Later, on assignment for the *Daily Planet,* Clark Kent spotted the missing monkey and realized the danger. He quickly used his super-breath to blow a banana into a lead pipe, then sealed the monkey within until he could be safely handled (*Action Comics* #249, February 1959).

KRYPTON KID, THE

Zar-Al was a Kryptonian teen who was sent to Earth aboard a time-traveling vessel by his scientist father Zol-Zu. Zol-Zu had heeded Jor-El's warning of Krypton's imminent destruction and wanted to save his only son as well. The difference between them was that Zar-Al was sent to retrieve the element zeelium, which Zol-Zu believed might stabilize Krypton's core. Upon arriving on Earth, the teen met Superboy, who aided him in the search, but the pair could not find the element. The Teen of Steel attempted to delay Zar-Al's return home, but the boy felt his place was with his father when the end came (*Adventure Comics* #242, November 1957).

KRYPTONOID, THE

An alien organism arrived on Earth and sought to conquer the planet by besting Superman, son of the organism's sworn enemy Jor-El. During the battle, the protoplasmic being absorbed a Superman Robot, and General D. W. Derwent was transformed into something called the Kryptonoid. The organism's rage was further fueled by Derwent, who wrongly accused the Man of Steel of the accident that cost him an arm. Superman and the Kryptonoid battled twice before the Man of Steel could convince the general that it was the Superman Robot who was responsible for the accident. The realization stalled the creature, allowing Superman to subdue it and free the general (*Superman* [first series] #328–329, October–November 1978).

KRYPTONOPOLIS

After Kandor was stolen by Brainiac, Kryptonopolis became Krypton's capital city. It was in this city that Jor-El lived with his wife Lara and their infant son Kal-El (*Action Comics* #325, June 1965).

The city was said to have been designed by the father of modern Kryptonian architecture, Gam-El, from the House of El (*Adventure Comics* #313, October 1963). The city was known for its famous Red Tower, considered one of the planet's great architectural landmarks (*World's Finest Comics* #146, December 1964).

KRYPTO-RAYGUN

To aid his battle against crime, the Superman of Earth-2 devised a gun-like device to capture an image, develop it within the raygun's mechanism, and then project the image on a screen. For its first practical use, the Man of Steel used it to gain evidence of illegal gambling that was going on at the prestigious Preston Club (*Action Comics* #32, January 1941).

KUBLAI KHAN

The tiny country of Samarkist, nestled in the Himalayan Mountains, could trace its history back to the days of Kublai Khan (1215–1294). Its modern-day leader, also named Kublai Khan, was a direct descendant. The hidden city was eventually discovered by Basil Garret, one of the world's leading explorers, who chose to remain there for three years, personally tutoring Khan's lovely daughter May-lin. When the bandit chieftain Garjnok repeatedly attempted to kidnap May-lin for his bride, it took the arrival of Earth-2's Superman to put an end to the threat (*Superman* [first series] #40, May–June 1946).

On Earth-1, a time-traveling Jimmy Olsen met the original Kublai Khan (*Superman's Pal, Jimmy Olsen* #157, March 1973) but was unable to prevent the ruler's murder (*Superman's Pal, Jimmy Olsen* #163, February–March 1974).

KULL-EX

Using an "exchange ray," the Kryptonian Kull-Ex switched places with Superman and left the bottle city of Kandor to begin a series of destructive acts designed to ruin the Man of Steel's reputation. The young Kull-Ex did this in order to gain revenge for his father Zell-Ex, believing the older man had been cheated by Superman's father Jor-El. The dispute revolved around the rights to an invention, but once Kull-Ex was shown the truth, thanks to the combined efforts of Superman, Supergirl, and Krypto, he realized he was mistaken and publicly apologized for his mercenary acts (*Superman* [first series] #134, January 1960).

KURTISWANA

An African country whose jungles hid an irradiated Kryptonian neighborhood (*Action Comics* #565, March 1985) dubbed the Wizard City (*Adventure Comics* #216, September 1955). In the world after the Crisis on Infinite Earths, it was discovered by Sarah Olsen (*Superman* #665, September 2007).

KVORNS

A race of Kryptonians who vanished eons ago, the Kvorns were said to be the original inhabitants of what was later known as Kandor. Little was known about the race, but they were famous for the magnetic Jewel Masks they wore. When Lois Lane and Lana Lang were visiting the bottle city investigating the Sky Thief, their trail led to caves beneath the city, where they found remains of the Kvorn civilization. The maze-like tunnels were said to have been carved by the Kvorns underneath the Aqua-Zoo, complete with hieroglyphics, carvings, and a hidden passage leading to a previously unknown treasure (*Superman's Girl Friend, Lois Lane* #78, October 1967).

KYACK

On Earth-2, there lived an underground people who had survived for millennia without being discovered by the surface world. Kyack was a member of this hidden race, which fled underground to avoid the impending Ice Age, and with a colleague he breached the barrier between worlds. The two men had kidnapped Tulan, the leader of this mysterious society, as part of a scheme to overrun and retake the surface world. When buildings in Metropolis began to topple without obvious cause, Superman investigated and discovered the race and their weapon of destruction. The Man of Steel stood in their way by burrowing deep to access their city and destroying the awesome ray-emitting weapon that Kyack had pinned his hopes on. Kyack and his acolytes were then arrested, and Tulan was restored to the throne (*Superman* [first series] #13, November–December 1941).

KZOTL

A distant planet visited by Superman, Batman, and Robin, where their version of a movie producer tricked them into fighting robots in order to capture exciting footage for his next project (*World's Finest Comics* #108, March 1960).

LACY, ED

Ed Lacy, of the Continental Detective Agency, befriended Krypto in Hollywood when the Dog of Steel broke up a canine kidnapping ring. They met a second time when both appeared in a feature film, and when Lacy's nephew Tommy was accused of murder and fled LA, the unlikely duo went cross-country in search of the boy. Tracking Tommy down in Chicago, Krypto saved the boy's life and helped Ed prove his nephew's innocence (*Superman Family* #185–192, September–October 1977 to November–December 1978).

LAHLA

Superman first came into contact with Lahla when he was stranded on her homeworld of Thoron during a battle against the Four Galactic Thiefmasters. Under Thoron's red sun, Superman was without his formidable abilities and was imprisoned. The attractive blonde nevertheless found the courteous and heroic Kryptonian more desirable than the bullies among the males of her race. As a result, she freed him from his dungeon prison and decided she'd rather be with him on Earth than with her people. Superman happily brought her back so they could prepare to thwart a possible Earth invasion of Galactic Thiefmasters. Once on Earth, however, Superman's superpowers returned, and Lahla quickly lost interest in him (*Action Comics* #321, February 1965).

LAL, LETA

Yet another attractive woman with an LL name, Leta Lal resided in the sunken city of Atlantis and had a brief romance with a time-traveling Superboy. He and the Legion of Super-Heroes were witness to the supposed war between Atlantis and colonists from Krypton. It was discovered that Leta was an ancestor of Lori Lemaris, who would be Clark Kent's college sweetheart in the future (*Adventure Comics* #333, June 1965). Numerous details in this account, including the story of how the Atlanteans became mer-people, do not mesh with the more accepted Earth-1 Atlantean lore. It's possible that Superboy and the Legion were actually diverted to a false reality through the machinations of their enemy, the Time Trapper.

LANDIS, LIZA

When Superman tried to live without Lois Lane, it appeared destiny had a different ending in mind. Tired of what he called her meddling, Superman traveled back in time and avoided joining the *Daily Planet* in favor of working at WMET, Metropolis's number one radio station. There he met Liza Landis, a secretary at the station. Like Lois, Liza possessed an insatiable curiosity and quickly began to suspect that Clark Kent and Superman were one and the same. Realizing he could not avoid the inevitable, Superman restored the time line and returned to the *Daily Planet*, and Lois Lane (*Superman's Girl Friend, Lois Lane* #20, October 1960).

LANE, ELINORE

In the reality after the Crisis on Infinite Earths, the mother of Lois and Lucy Lane was named Elinore (*The Adventures of Superman* #424, January 1987) but was known as Ella to her friends (*Action Comics* #669, September 1991; others) and affectionately as Ellen to Martha Kent (*The Adventures of Superman* #633, December 2004). She was still married to Samuel Lane, but in this reality he was a soldier who retired to Metropolis after years of moving from place to place. Left comatose after a freak chemical "accident" secretly engineered by Lex Luthor, Elinore was kept alive by medicine provided by Luthor, who used it to maintain close ties with Lois, to whom he was romantically attracted (*The Adventures of Superman* #424, January 1987). Later, after her mother had built up immunity to the medicine, Lois learned of Luthor's role in Ella's condition, and her anger against Lex grew (*Superman* [second series] #50, December 1990). Ultimately, Mrs. Lane rallied and returned to full health. After Sam Lane's apparent death, Ella went on a round-the-world vacation with Lois to mourn and reconnect. During their vacation, Ella witnessed two secret encounters between her daughter and Superman and leapt to a false conclusion. To Lois's horror, her mother then confessed that she had cheated on Sam during their marriage (*Superman: The Man of Steel* #122–123, March–April 2002). The couple quietly worked on their marriage in the aftermath.

In the wake of the reality-altering events of the Infinite Crisis, Ella died at an early age, leaving an ill-equipped Sam to raise their young daughters on his own (*Superman: Secret Origin* #5, May 2010).

LANE, ELLA

Earth-1's Ella married farmer Samuel Lane and raised their daughters, Lois and Lucy, in the small midwestern town of Pittsdale (*Superman's Girl Friend, Lois Lane* #13, November 1959).

Her Earth-2 counterpart, also named Ella, made periodic visits to Lois in Metropolis both before and after her daughter married Clark Kent (*Superman* [first series] #10, May–June 1941; *Superman Family* #198, November–December 1979). A later account asserted that the Earth-2

Lois was born in Cleveland, Ohio, to Elayne Lane and U.S. Marine colonel Samuel L. Lane (*Infinite Crisis: Secret Files and Origins,* April 2006).

LANE, LOIS

Lois Lane-Kent was the METROPOLIS *DAILY PLANET*'s star reporter married to fellow journalist CLARK KENT, who was also Superman (*Action Comics* #1, June 1938).

On Earth-2, little was revealed about Lois Lane's upbringing before she began working as a reporter at the *DAILY STAR.* A late, perhaps apocryphal account asserted that the Earth-2 Lois was born in Cleveland, Ohio, to U.S. Marine colonel SAMUEL L. and Elayne "ELLA" LANE (*Infinite Crisis: Secret Files and Origins,* April 2006). Her closest friend in high school was a girl named Helen, who later married BILL MINTON (*World's Finest Comics* #21, March–April 1946). Her first serious boyfriend was Finney Floor (*Superman* [first series] #66, September–October 1950), although they lost touch after high school graduation. Before joining the *Daily Star,* Lois took a course in nursing (*Action Comics* #191, April 1954) and worked as a waitress at Harry's Dog House (*World's Finest Comics* #47, August–September 1950).

Lois's known relatives included her aunt Bernice Brainard (*Superman* [first series] #24, September–October 1943) and sister LUCILLE LANE Tompkins (*Action Comics* #484, June 1978), who had a daughter named SUSIE TOMPKINS (*Action Comics* #59, April 1943). Lois, and eventually Superman, wound up having a series of escapades involving the precocious child.

Her descendants include LOIS 4XR, a great-great-great-great-granddaughter—and a perfect Lois Lane look-alike—living in the thirtieth century (*Superman* [first series] #57, March–April 1949).

Lois was a bit of a fashion plate, especially with her wide collection of hats, something that gave Clark Kent a source of endless amusement

(*Superman* [first series] #24, September–October 1943). He was also fond of a peach-flavored lipstick that Lois often wore.

Her disdain for Clark Kent and admiration for Superman blinded Lois to the reality that existed right before her eyes. She was a celebrated, aggressive journalist who put her career ahead of her personal life. Over time, she developed a driving desire to expose Superman's true identity (*Action Comics* #25, June 1940). Ultimately, suspecting that her fellow reporter Kent and Superman might be one and the same, she embarked on a series of dangerous escapades trying to prove her theory, but she failed time and again (*Superman* [first series] #17, July–August 1942; countless others).

She lived in apartment 1705 (*Superman* [first series] #40, May–June 1946) of Metropolis's Ritz Plaza Apartments (*Superman* [first series] #47, July–August 1947), near Clark Kent's own apartment. "A cozy little apartment that is neat as a pin," the home was filled with many pictures of Superman. Throughout her long career, Lois opened her home to several temporary roommates, including friends Peggy Wilkins (*Superman* [first series] #61, November–December 1949) and Lorraine Jennings (*Superman* [first series] #76, May–June 1952).

Lois's journalism career came during a time when women reporters did not yet enjoy equality with their male counterparts. As a result, she was often called the *Star*'s "sob sister" (*Superman* [first series] #7, November–December 1940), and her career was filled with not only news reporting but other ancillary assignments as well. She served as the paper's columnist to the lovelorn (*Action Comics* #44, January 1942), question-and-answer editor, head of the lost-and-found department (*World's Finest Comics* #51, April–May 1951), and weather editor, which she described as "one of the lowliest jobs on any newspaper" (*World's Finest Comics* #25, November 1946).

Her hard-hitting stories, however, quickly turned her and Kent into the paper's star correspondents (*Superman* [first series] #27, March–April 1941). In addition to big news, Lois was known for her local news coverage (*Superman* [first series] #44, January–February 1947). She was also a war correspondent (*Action Comics* #23, April 1940).

One reason Lois was seemingly reckless in her desire to the get the story began with her confidence in the pistol she often carried in her purse for protection (*Action Comics* #43, December 1941). After Superman began rescuing her with regularity, Lois began to depend on help from the Man of Steel. "For a girl who is in serious danger, you appear singularly unconcerned," remarked one foolhardy villain, the TALON, after he had taken Lois captive. "Why should I worry," Lois rejoined, "when Superman has made it his full-time activity to look after helpless me?" (*Superman* [first series] #17, July–August 1942).

Lois and Clark competed for news and top-of-the-fold stories, leading her to do things to distract her rival that included intercepting his telephone messages (*Superman* [first series] #14, January–February 1942; others), sending him off on wild-goose chases (*Action Comics* #5, October 1938; others), and even seducing him into letting her accompany him on an interview, then slipping knockout drops into his drink so that she could cover the story alone (*Action Comics* #6, November 1938).

Lois Lane also took on other stories, either undercover or on the record, in order to bring readers a better understanding of the news. She scaled Mount Everest (*Superman* [first series] #49, November–December 1947); flew as a trapeze artist (*Superman* [first series] #63, March–April 1950); professionally snooped as a private detective (*World's Finest Comics* #45, April–May 1950); visited sunken ATLANTIS (*Superman* [first series] #67, November–December 1950); explored the planet VENUS (*Action Comics* #152, January 1951); worked as a policewoman (*Superman* [first series] #84, September–October 1953); and joined the WACS (*Superman* [first series] #82, May–June 1953). Lois even got to experience life as SUPERWOMAN, first in a dream (*Action Comics* #60, May 1943) and then in reality (*Superman* [first series] #45, March–April 1947; *Action Comics* #156, May 1951; *Superman Family* #207, May–June 1981).

Before retiring at the top of her game, Lois received countless awards for her efforts, including "the annual trophy for prize reporting," awarded to her at a "newspapermen's banquet" in Metropolis Hall; an honorary professorship in journalism at QUINN COLLEGE (*Superman* [first series] #64, May–

June 1950); the coveted Wilson Award for being "the bravest reporter of the year" (*Action Comics* #166, March 1952); and the highly regarded Metropolis Journalism Award, awarded to her as Metropolis's most outstanding reporter (*World's Finest Comics* #65, July–August 1953). Lois was named Metropolis's "Queen of Charities" in recognition of "her many helpful newspaper stories" on behalf of philanthropic causes (*Superman* [first series] #64, May–June 1950), and was chosen as "the bravest woman in America" in a nationwide contest (*Superman* [first series] #83, July–August 1953).

Lois also served as chair of the Super-Saved Club (*World's Finest Comics* #41, July–August 1949) and the Super Sorority (*Action Comics* #235, December 1957), was the "champion dart-thrower of [her] club" (*Superman* [first series] #143, February 1961), and had a regular weekly broadcast on Metropolis radio station WCOD (*Superman* [first series] #61, November–December 1949). In addition, she once served as a beauty-contest judge (*Superman* [first series] #45, March–April 1947) and portrayed herself in Charles Lamont's movie *The Life of Superman* (*Superman* [first series] #70, May–June 1951).

While Lois and Superman flirted over the years, they never really dated, although she remained his staunchest supporter and defender. She did have other suitors, including respected Metropolis citizen Craig Shaw (*Action Comics* #61, June 1943), Mr. Mxyztplk (*Superman* [first series] #51, March–April 1945), Stephen Van Schuyler III (*Superman* [first series] #55, November–December 1948), and King Harrup II (*Superman* [first series] #68, January–February 1950).

In time, however, Superman and Lois's romance finally led to a wedding, but not without some drama along the way. The villainous Wizard cast a spell on Superman, forcing him to forget his heroic persona. During this period, a more assertive Clark charmed Lois, and she was forced to give him a second look. A romance between the two quickly blossomed. They dated, leading to Clark's proposal of marriage, and the pair ultimately wed. During their honeymoon, Lois discovered Clark's secret and forced the sorcerer to undo his spell so that Superman would once again be around to protect Earth (*Action Comics* #484, June 1978).

Lois and Clark were among the three survivors of Earth-2 when the multiverse collapsed during the Crisis on Infinite Earths. Superman-2 was provided an opportunity to enter a crystalline home as a gift from Alexander Luthor Junior, the Earth-3 son of Lex Luthor. Superman was able to bring Lois with him, and they spent many happy years together until old age finally caught up to Lois. While Superman-2, Alexander, and Superboy-Prime watched the reordered universe with increasing horror, Lois always cautioned that Earth was just going through a rough patch and would eventually smooth out. Superman-2 was convinced by the other two heroes to leave their realm and recreate reality in Earth-2's image, a world they convinced him would allow Lois to live for many years. That was never the case, unfortunately, and when Lois finally died, she told her beloved husband that their love would never end. With that, she expired in his arms (*Infinite Crisis* #5, April 2006). In the aftermath of Infinite Crisis, Superman-2 also died, and he and Lois were buried side by side on New Earth (*Infinite Crisis* #7, June 2006).

In the Earth-1 reality, Lois and her sister Lucy Lane (*Superman's Pal, Jimmy Olsen* #36, April 1959) were raised on their parents Sam and Ella Lane's farm in Pittsdale. Lois was a driven reporter, given to reckless acts that often risked her life in the name of news. She was born with a rare blood type (*Superman* [first series] #125, November 1958) and was partial to strawberries (*Superman* [first series] #99, August 1955). She had only a few identified relatives, including her uncle Ned Lane, "a famous authority on the legends of King Arthur's court" (*Action Comics* #269, October 1960); two other unnamed uncles (*Superman's Pal, Jimmy Olsen* #37, June 1959; *Action Comics* #495, April 1979); and cousins Louis (*Superman* [first series] #349, July 1980) and Louisa (*Superman Family* #209, August 1981). Lois was also a direct descendant of "Quentin August Lane, who came to America on the historic *Mayflower*" (*Superman's Girl Friend, Lois Lane* #9, May 1959).

The Lane sisters attended school in Pittsdale. Lois, in particular, seemed to have led a charmed life, acquiring her first newspaper credits with the *Pittsdale Star* (*Superman's Girl Friend, Lois Lane* #13, November 1959) and earning all manner of recognition for her grades, citizenship, and beauty (*Superman's Girl Friend, Lois Lane* #71, January 1967).

The teenage Lois even won a contest for school reporters and joined a young Clark Kent as cub reporters at Metropolis's *Daily Planet* for one week (*Adventure Comics* #128, May 1948). The duo met again a few years later (*Superboy* [first series] #63, March 1958). Now infatuated with Superboy, Lois made a point of attending the East Coast Camp Hiawatha near Smallville in the hope of meeting the teen hero, and nobly worked to confound Lana Lang's efforts to learn the Boy of Steel's true identity (*Adventure Comics* #261, June 1959). Discovering via a Time-Viewer that Lois was destined to be a *Daily Planet* reporter who was Superman's girlfriend, Lana tried to sabotage her future rival's aspiring journalistic career, but to no avail (*Superboy* [first series] #90, July 1961).

Lois graduated from high school and then matriculated at Raleigh College, near Metropolis, showing a keen interest in and skill at science (*Superman's Girl Friend, Lois Lane* #55, February 1965). She was also considered "class artist" (*Action Comics* #272, January 1961). It appeared she never had a serious college boyfriend, although classmate Brett Rand would have happily filled the role (*Superman* [first series] #139, August 1960).

Lois wrote for the *Raleigh Review,* which seemed to steer her from science toward journalism (*Superman's Girl Friend, Lois Lane* #68, September–October 1966). No sooner did she graduate than she headed to the big city to fulfill what she considered her lifelong ambition to

become "the best reporter in Metropolis" (*Action Comics* #202, March 1955). During a career that celebrated her as one of the country's foremost journalists, she experienced many unique and life-changing experiences, such as her journey into outer space as one of the passengers aboard America's first manned spaceship (*Action Comics* #242, July 1958); she was launched alone into orbit around Earth in an experimental satellite after being designated "America's first female astronaut" by the National Astronautic Space Administration (*Superman* [first series] #165, November 1963). Lois added to her already busy schedule by occasionally volunteering as a nurse's aide at Metropolis Hospital (*Superman's Girl Friend, Lois Lane* #43, August 1963; others).

Lois lived for a time in the Mylo Apartments (*Action Comics* #269, October 1960) on 136 Concord Drive (*Superman's Girl Friend, Lois Lane* #53, November 1964) before moving to apartment 2-L on 41 Barrow Lane (*Superman's Girl Friend, Lois Lane* #84, July 1968). At the Singles Sanctuary Apartment Building on 211 Park Side, Lois briefly shared a four-bedroom apartment (number 6A) with Kristen Cutler, Marsha Mallow, and Julie Spence (*Superman's Girl Friend, Lois Lane* #121, April 1972). Her last documented address was 922 Oak Hill, 5N (or 5A), in the Clardeau Apartments (*Superman Family* #205, January–February 1981, and #210, September 1981; others).

Like her Earth-2 counterpart, Lois preferred Superman to Clark Kent, but she initially regarded the Man of Steel as an "egotistic super-stuntman." After she was stranded on an island with a temporarily de-powered Superman, Lois saw a different side of the hero, and she fell in love (*Superman's Girl Friend, Lois Lane* #53, November 1964). Over time, she finally began to suspect that her fellow reporter Clark Kent and Superman might be one and the same, and she tried in vain to prove her theory (*Superman* [first series] #135, February 1960; others).

While the world considered her Superman's girlfriend, Lois was often in rivalries with other women for what she perceived as a fight for the Man of Steel's affections. She considered Lana Lang her chief rival, but through the years there were other women—and aliens—she vied against. Her desperate attempts to keep Superman's heart often led her to do outlandish things, even trying to trick him into marrying her when all the Man of Steel wanted to do was keep her safe from criminals who might strike at him through her.

Lois maintained a good relationship with Superman's fellow members of the Justice League of America. In one noteworthy incident, she wound up kissing Batman, Green Arrow, and Aquaman, all in an attempt to collect samples of red krytponite-laced lipstick that the Emerald Archer could shoot and reach an incapacitated Superman. That particular sample of red k nullified the effects of the green kryptonite that had incapacitated him (*Superman's Girl Friend, Lois Lane* #29, November 1961).

Over the course of her adult years, Lois had many opportunities to experience life as a super heroine herself through a succession of temporary acquisitions of superpowers. Among her alter egos were Superwoman (*Superman's Girl Friend, Lois Lane* #8, April 1958; *Action Comics* #274, March 1961), Super-Lois (*Superman's Girl Friend, Lois Lane* #17, May 1960 and #21, November 1960), Elastic Lass (*Superman's Girl Friend, Lois Lane* #23, February 1961), a second Insect Queen (*Superman's Girl Friend, Lois Lane* #69, October 1966), and Opticus (*Superman* [first series] #334, April 1979). At one point, Lois even dreamed that a blood transfusion transformed her into Power Girl (*Superman* [first series] #125, November 1958).

As time passed, however, Lois stopped chasing Superman and rededicated herself to chasing news stories, which challenged many of the sociopolitical conventions of the time. In at least one instance, she used Kryptonian technology to alter her skin pigmentation in order to pass as an African American to better understand race issues (*Superman's Girl Friend, Lois Lane* #106, November 1970). Lois also proved less in need of rescuing from Superman after learning the Kryptonian martial art of Klurkor (*Superman's Girl Friend, Lois Lane* #78, October 1967).

After the *Daily Planet* became part of Galaxy Communications, Lois entered film journalism by hosting a weekly human-interest series called *People, U.S.A.* that often railed against social injustice. Although the show was produced for television, Lois also wrote a companion piece for each episode in the *Daily Planet* (*Superman's Girl Friend, Lois Lane* #110, May 1971).

Regarded as an authority on Superman, Lois had at least three books on the Man of Steel published, specifically *The Fabulous World of Krypton* (*Action Comics* #441, November 1974), *The Story of Superman,* jointly written with Clark Kent and Jimmy Olsen (*Action Comics* #488, October 1978), and, as editor, *Essays on Superman* (*Superman* [first series] #419, May 1986).

Although she and Superman were seen as an item, Lois was not without other suitors, who numbered many and included Bizarro (*Action Comics* #254, July 1959), Hercules (*Action Comics* #267, August 1960), and millionaire Brett Rand (*Superman* [first series] #139, August 1960). Lois was married—or nearly married—on many occasions, although the unions were typically annulled due to various deceptions and falsehoods, as was the case with the evil Kryptonian Zak-Kul (*Action Comics* #245, October 1958), Bizarro (*Superman's Girl Friend, Lois Lane* #32, April 1962), Clark Kent (*Superman's Girl Friend, Lois Lane* #37, November 1962), and Superman himself (*Superman's Girl Friend, Lois Lane* #82, April 1968). Other marriages, such as one to X-Plam, a warmhearted man from the twenty-fourth century, ended with the bridegroom's death (*Superman* [first series] #136, April 1960), a fate also destined for Dahr-Nel (*Superman's Girl Friend, Lois Lane* #90, April 1969) and Johnny Adonis (*Superman's Girl Friend, Lois Lane* #105, October 1970).

Before Superman had her full attention, Lois felt a certain attraction to Clark Kent when they first began working together at the *Daily Planet* (*Superman's Girl Friend, Lois Lane* #53, November 1964). The couple occasionally explored a romantic connection (*Superman's Girl Friend, Lois Lane* #19, August 1960; others), but Lois's attentions always returned to Superman. One sustained (if on-again, off-again) period of dating (*Superman* [first series] #297, March 1976; others) culminated with Clark proposing marriage to Lois. When she declared that she would say yes if he told her he was Superman, Clark sadly replied that he couldn't do that. The emotional exchange ended any suspicion in Lois's mind that the two men were the same (*Superman* [first series] #314, August 1977). Afterward, Lois renewed her romance with Superman, but they eventually broke up over his failure to fully commit to their relationship (*Action Comics* #542, April 1983).

The ultimate fate of the Earth-1 Lois Lane is unknown, but one potential future indicated that she and Clark Kent eventually married and became the parents of a daughter named Laura, whose own latent superpowers emerged while she was in her teens (*Superman Family* #200, March–April 1980).

Following the Crisis on Infinite Earths, Lois Joanne Lane (middle name first established in *Superman: The Wedding and Beyond,* 1997) was the daughter of army general Samuel Lane and his wife Elinore and was born in a U.S. Army hospital outside Wiesbaden, Germany (*Who's Who in the DC Universe* #12, August 1991). Sam Lane had always wanted a son, thereby leading to a complex and tense relationship between father and daughter for many years thereafter. Lane raised both Lois and Lucy as if they were sons, ensuring that they were trained in hand-to-hand combat and given firearms training (*Action Comics* #597, February 1988).

Lois was a tough, independent woman who initially resisted her attraction to Superman and truly disliked Clark Kent. Lois was dismissive of the rookie reporter, especially when he was the one to score the first interview with the newly arrived Superman, despite the hero rescuing her when the space shuttle she was aboard experienced engine failure (*Man of Steel* #1–2, Early–Late October 1986). Lois quickly rose to become one of the *Daily Planet*'s most highly regarded reporters and columnists. Beyond newsprint, she won an Edgar Award for her mystery novel *Shadows on the Grass* (*Who's Who Update '87* #4, November 1987).

Lois's primary residence was apartment 1207 (*The Adventures of Superman* #476, March 1991) of the Stratford Arms (*Superman* [second series] #16, April 1988) at 55 Broome Street (*Superman: The Man of Tomorrow* #8, March 1997), which she shared with her cat Elroy (*Man of Steel* #2, Late October 1986; named in *Action Comics* #662, February 1991).

Lois's first significant relationship in this reality was with social worker Jose Delgado, who also adventured as the masked vigilante Gangbuster (*The Adventures of Superman* #437, February 1988). Their up-and-down relationship finally settled into "just friends" when it was clear Lois had strong feelings for Superman (*Superman* [second series] #37, November 1989). Lois soon began to sense that romance might be right beside her in the form of Clark Kent, but their budding relationship hit a bump when Kent went to work for Colin Thornton at *Newstime*. Returning to the *Planet* soon after, Clark apologized to Lois for his previous abrupt departure, earning him a heartfelt embrace and the promise of a dinner date (*Superman* [second series] #43, May 1990).

Lois finally saw Clark for the good and loving man he truly was and fell in love with him, leading to his proposing marriage to her (*Superman* [second series] #50, December 1990). As they readied for the wedding, Clark at last revealed his true identity to Lois (*Action Comics* #662, February 1991). Their wedding plans were derailed, however, when the genetic war machine Doomsday emerged from his underground prison. Superman, despite all his powers, was apparently beaten to death; he died in a traumatized Lois's arms (*Superman* [second series] #75, January 1993). After months of grieving, Lois began to reassemble her shattered hopes and dreams and turned her grief into a renewed journalistic crusade against injustice. Superman's return to life was a happy development, and Lois eagerly welcomed her fiancé back (*The Adventures of Superman* #505, October 1993).

Lois and Clark's romance resumed, although not without additional wrinkles, such as the arrival of Clark's college girlfriend Lori Lemaris. Fearing that she was losing her independent edge by marrying, Lois reluctantly broke off her engagement to Clark (*Action Comics* #720, April 1996) and took an overseas assignment to escape her sadness (*Superman* [second series] #115, September 1996). On a mountaintop in Bhutran, Lois met a man whom Clark had befriended years earlier, and in a moment of clarity she realized that she still loved Clark deeply (*Superman* [second series] #118, December 1996). Upon her return to Metropolis, Lois discovered her future husband was now temporarily her boss, as Perry White had taken a leave of absence to battle cancer. Clark had continued to carry Lois's engagement ring on him, and with a smile and kiss she took the ring back, and their wedding plans began anew. After their marriage, the couple moved into a condominium at 1938 Sullivan Lane, a building owned by Bruce Wayne, who became a friend to both Kents (*Superman: The Wedding Album* #1, December, 1996).

As Lois began a new chapter of her life, she had to contend with her father's well-voiced disapproval; he saw Clark as a weakling and unworthy of his eldest child. Lois and the general had endured a prickly relationship once she achieved adulthood, and things grew complicated when he later rose to secretary of defense. Despite all that, when he seemingly died during the Imperiex War, she was devastated, taking comfort from Clark.

Lois later became the primary breadwinner in her household when Lex Luthor bought the *Daily Planet* and promptly closed it. Lois was kept on staff (*Superman: Save the Planet* one-shot, October 1998) but was shifted over to the Web-based news site Lexcom (*Action Comics* #750, January 1999). Desperate to help her friends return to work, Lois reluctantly agreed to a controversial offer from Lex Luthor. He would sell back the *Daily Planet* to Perry White for one dollar, but Lois had to agree to kill one news story of Lex's choosing in the future (*Superman* [second series] #151, December 1999). When that day came, however,

Lois outwitted Luthor by handing the story to her husband and having Clark report the news that the then-president had had advance knowledge of Imperiex's attack on Earth (*Superman* [second series] #182, July 2002).

Lois's periodic experiences with broadcast journalism, such as her televised interview with Superman (*The Adventures of Superman* #568, June 1999), made her an attractive prospect to Metropolis's television networks. At one point, annoyed that Clark and Perry had apparently been keeping secrets from her, Lois actually accepted an offer from Channel 6 to be an on-air reporter, and she quit the *Planet* (*Superman* [second series] #194, August 2003). Promptly placed behind an anchor desk (*Superman* [second series] #196, October 2003), Lois soon missed her colleagues and the activity of her newspaper job and happily returned to the *Daily Planet.*

The one thing Superman feared the most in terms of putting his wife in danger came to pass when the Parasite kidnapped Lois and impersonated her for months so that he could gain Superman's trust and use the Man of Steel as a permanent power source (*Superman* [second series] #154–157, March–June 2000). When Parasite was finally revealed as the uncharacteristically behaved Lois, Superman worried that the real Lois was dying and asked Batman's aid in finding his wife (*Action Comics* #766, June 2000). The Parasite was eventually defeated, his plan foiled, and a weakened and exhausted Lois was found and nursed back to health by a grateful Superman.

Some time later, a team of Teen Titans from a potential future attacked Lois in her apartment in the hope of kidnapping Superman (*Teen Titans* [third series] #50, October 2007). She escaped unharmed and warned Superman that he was in danger.

Lois sustained serious injury on other occasions, such as when she was shot and nearly died in Qurac until Doctor Mid-Nite saved her life (*The Adventures of Superman* #631–632, October-November 2004). She had gone overseas to prove herself a journalist who did not need Superman to save her or hand her headlines. The life-threatening injury, however, led her to reconsider how much of her choice was just being headstrong, letting her ego outweigh her judgment. After her recovery, she recommitted herself to working from the Metropolis newsroom and remaining as close to her husband as possible.

Every known specialist had told Clark and Lois that they could not conceive a child, and the Kents accepted the news until they took in General Zod's son when the young Lor-Zod crashed to Earth in a Kryptonian pod. The youth was freed from his "home" in the Phantom Zone, and Clark was only too happy to welcome a fellow Kryptonian. Lois, however, was slower to welcome the boy into her home. After all, this significantly changed their status quo; she now had to share her precious private time with her husband with the youth. Still, she saw how important this was to Clark, so she agreed to provide the boy a home. Naming him Christopher Kent, they tried to provide a nurturing home environment for him, never suspecting he was a pawn in the Kryptonian criminal Zod's revenge scheme. Lois adapted to the changing circumstances and quickly began doting on Chris, showing a surprising and welcome softer side to her persona. The two grew close, and Lois came to deeply love her adopted son. Sadly, in time, Chris sacrificed himself to save his adoptive parents, leaving Earth for a permanent place in the Phantom Zone, where he acted as a barrier against his father ever returning to Earth (*Action Comics* #845, January 2007, to *Action Comics Annual* #11, 2007). Lois was devastated and found herself profoundly missing the boy.

During the Final Crisis, both Lois and Perry White were caught in an explosion at the *Daily Planet,* an attack from Clayface that left her heart seriously damaged. Superman's heat vision was all that kept her heart beating (*Final Crisis* #2–3, September–October 2008 and *Final Crisis: Superman Beyond* #1–2, October 2008 and March 2009). Superman left her bedside, assured by Monitor Zillo Valla that time would stop around Lois until his mission to save the reborn multiverse could be accomplished. He obtained a drop of the substance known as the Bleed and applied it through a gentle kiss, which revived Lois and healed her body (*Final Crisis: Superman Beyond* #2, March

2009). She quickly recovered and was one of the last humans to possess free will before the heroes ended the threat to reality.

Her relationship with Clark was put to the test when he felt the need to spend time away from Earth, relocating to the artificial world of New Krypton. The planet, now housing one hundred thousand Kryptonians rescued from Brainiac's spaceship, posed a threat to humankind, and he wanted to be present to help positively influence events. While he publicly proclaimed his departure, Superman made certain Lois knew she remained the love of his life. Her deeply felt love for the hero would have to see her through—but soon after he departed, she was reunited with Chris, now freed from the Phantom Zone. He donned the guise of Kryptonian legend Nightwing and was operating with a new Flamebird, exposing sleeper agents left throughout Earth by his mother Ursa (*Action Comics* #875, May 2009).

Soon after, Lois was visited by Supergirl and Lana Lang, bringing with them the news that her younger sister Lucy had been killed while in her guise as Superwoman. At first Lois refused to believe this, but she eventually came to accept it, weeping openly and demanding a piece of her sister's uniform for verification (*Supergirl* [fifth series] #42, June 2009).

Lois quickly found herself opposing her father—who she discovered had not died at all—and was in charge of Project 7734, designed to kill all Kryptonians as a means of "protecting" Earth. It was General Sam Lane who had convinced Lucy to become Superwoman, and who was actually working with Lex Luthor to ensure that Superman would be killed. Lois's investigations resulted in an exposé that Perry White could not safely print in the *Daily Planet.* Lois was then apprehended and taken to her father, who informed his daughter that the only reason he was sparing her life was that they were related. Upon her release, Lois returned to the *Planet* and covertly met with Perry White. Acting on Perry's advice, she quit the *Daily Planet* and her exposé ran without putting her friends in danger (*Action Comics* #884, February 2010). She was also able to turn public opinion about her husband around, proving that Lois Lane is always a force to be reckoned with.

Lois was kidnapped by her sister Lucy (who was still operating under her Superwoman identity) and taken to Sam Lane's hidden bunker, where she was forced to watch Superman fight to save both his adopted planet and his fellow Kryptonians. When Project 7734 was ultimately defeated, Sam Lane killed himself in front of Lois rather than face punishment for his crimes, leaving his daughter heartbroken from all the evil he had caused. Lois saw her father properly buried next to her mother, but brought no flowers, saying that he did not deserve them. She then welcomed her beloved husband back to Earth and their home, and the two took strength and comfort in each other and their unbreakable bond (*Superman: War of the Supermen* #3–4, July 2010).

In the wake of the Infinite Crisis, Lois's backstory was altered once more. When she first arrived at the *Daily Planet,* she was a young, outspoken reporter wedged in a small, dingy cubicle. Due to her position at the *Planet* and the *Planet*'s less-than-stellar reputation (which came when Perry White had written an exposé on Lex Luthor a few years earlier), Lois had to sneak into large publicity events. She often put herself in danger to get a story, but after being rescued by Superman in his first public appearance, Lois became the only reporter who believed Superman was there to simply help humanity like he claimed he was. As the two saw more and more of each other, they grew very close, and it was clear that each was attracted to the other.

Lois made her name on her support of Superman, becoming the loudest advocate for this new hero in Metropolis. She also became known as the *only* reporter Superman would grant interviews to.

Lois at first believed Clark Kent was just a naïve farm boy from Kansas, but she saw real glimpses of brilliance in his writing. She knew Clark had the potential for greatness, but for some reason he was keeping it buried. She sometimes wondered, however, if he really *was* just a naïve farm boy, especially when he spilled his drink on himself almost every time Lois complimented him (*Superman: Secret Origin* #1–6, November 2009–September 2010).

Throughout the multiverse, there was usually a Lois Lane to match each reality's Superman, and many of them became husband and wife. On Earth-19, Lois married Clark Kent, and they became the parents of twins Larry and Carole. With Superman still regarded as a bachelor, Lois sometimes fought to contain her jealousy when women such as Lana Lang flirted with her husband's costumed identity (*Superman's Girl Friend, Lois Lane* #19–20, August–October 1960, and #23, February 1961).

After the Superman of Earth-162 was split into two beings who successfully eradicated all evil from his world, Lois married Superman Red, and they settled on New Krypton, eventually becoming the parents of twins (*Superman* [first series] #162, July 1963).

When a horrific sequence of events took the lives of most of her friends and family, the Lois Lane of Earth-423 returned to Pittsdale and married Jordan Elliot. She then gave birth to a super-baby named Jonathan with no one the wiser that her husband Jordan was the now mortal Superman (*Superman* [first series] #423, and *Action Comics* #583—both September 1986).

In other realities, Lois married Lex Luthor. On Earth-34, she and a reformed Lex were the parents of an ill-fated son named Larry, who became known as the infamous Black Luthor (*Superman's Girl Friend, Lois Lane* #34, July 1962). Only Lois Luthor's near-sacrifice of her own life caused Larry to turn himself around (*Superman's Girl Friend, Lois Lane* #46, January 1964).

It was *Daily Star* reporter Lois Lane of Earth-3 (*Secret Society of Super-Villains* #14, April–May 1978) who inspired her world's Alexander Luthor to act against the villainy of Ultraman. This led to the first Luthor to become a super hero, aiding the Superman from Earth-1 and the Superman from Earth-2 when the parallel world's Luthors partnered with Ultraman for a scheme of revenge (*DC Comics Presents Annual* #1, 1981). Soon after, Lois and Alexander fell in love and married, and she took the name Lois Lane-Luthor. They had a child, Alexander Luthor Junior, but as a wave of anti-matter eradicated one parallel universe after another, they rocketed their son away from Earth in the hope he would survive and be raised by a kindly family (*Crisis on Infinite Earths* #1, April 1985).

After reality was reordered following these events, the villainous Superwoman of this Earth was an analogue of Wonder Woman but used the alter ego of Lois Lane. She was forced to marry Ultraman, whom she detested, and carried on an affair with Owlman, rubbing her husband's nose in it (*JLA: Earth-2,* 2000). In addition to the tradi-

tional Amazonian skills and abilities, Ultraman also possessed vision-based powers much like Superman's. As Lois Lane, she was chief editor of the *Daily Planet,* and the only civilian who knew her secret was Jimmy Olsen, a young sexual deviant she often had to intimidate into silence.

Earth-9's Lois Lane was an archaeologist, explorer, and adventurer who died at the hands of Booster Gold, who was protecting the Sea Devils. This Lois was revived by the enigmatic Green Lantern (*Tangent Comics/Tales of the Green Lantern* #1, September 1998).

On Earth-22 of the reordered multiverse, Lois Lane and ninety-two employees were killed in an explosion of deadly Venom at the *Daily Planet,* the work of Batman's nemesis the Joker (*Kingdom Come* #2, June 1996). Lois had been prepared and survived the attack—only to have her head crushed by a *Daily Planet* paperweight hefted by the madman. She was dying by the time Superman arrived, and she used her final moments to thank him for loving her for so long (*Justice Society of America Kingdom Come Special: Superman,* 2008).

LANE, LOUIS

A cousin of Lois Lane; the two were raised together in Pittsdale, Iowa. Years later, when they were both adults, Louis visited Lois in Metropolis. As fate had it, he arrived after the Fifth Dimensional imp Mr. Mxyzptlk swapped the genders of Lois and her friends at the *Daily Planet.* They became Louis Lane, Jenny Olsen, and Penny White. After Superman managed to undo the magical spell, he was introduced to Louis, who at first confused the Man of Steel until Lois explained who her cousin really was (*Superman* [first series] #349, July 1980).

LANE, LUCY

Earth-2's Lucille Lane Tompkins was the younger sister of Lois Lane (*Action Comics* #484, June 1978) and the wife of George Tompkins (*Superman Family* #216, March 1982). The pair had a daughter named Susie Tompkins (*Action Comics* #59, April 1943).

On Earth-1, Lucy and her older sister Lois were raised on their parents' Samuel and Ella Lane's farm in Pittsdale, Iowa (*Superman's Pal, Jimmy Olsen* #36, April 1959). The Lane sisters attended school in Pittsdale (*Superman's Girl Friend, Lois Lane* #13, November 1959); upon graduation, Lucy became an airline attendant for Worldwide Airlines (*Superman's Pal, Jimmy Olsen* #37, June 1959).

An attractive blonde, Lucy had been known to occasionally share her sister's Metropolis apartment (*Superman* [first series] #142, January 1961) and was an on-again, off-again girlfriend of Jimmy Olsen (*Superman's Pal, Jimmy Olsen* #36, April 1959). Circumstances later found Jimmy (disguised as Magi the Magician for a newspaper story) and Lucy (posing as English starlet Sandra Rogers on behalf of her airline) engaging in a romance without either knowing who the other really was (*Superman's Pal, Jimmy Olsen* #74, January 1964). Sandra and Magi were reunited two more times before the truth eventually came out (*Superman's Pal, Jimmy Olsen* #78, July 1964, and #82, January 1965). Jimmy and Lucy were then married briefly, but the new Mrs. Olsen found herself so frustrated by the constant presence of her new husband's old flames and adversaries that they mutually agreed to annul the union (*Superman's Pal, Jimmy Olsen* #100, March 1967).

There was a period when Lucy was thought dead, a consequence of her shocking decision to become an operative of the crime cartel known as the One Hundred. Horrified by her sister's death and subsequent exposure as a criminal, a distraught Lois quit the *Daily Planet* (*Superman's Girl Friend, Lois Lane* #120, March 1972). Some time later, an elderly woman named Lena Lawrence crossed paths with Jimmy Olsen (*Superman's Pal, Jimmy Olsen* #158–159, June–August 1973) and eventually confessed that she was Lucy Lane. Dying of a jungle fever, Lucy was saved courtesy of a native doctor's serum. Though still possessed of her natural stamina, she'd lost her youthful features in the process (*Superman's Pal, Jimmy Olsen* #160, October 1973). Taking a job at Metropolis's North Side Hospital, Lucy was on hand when a fire struck the facility's genetics lab and released fumes that restored her young appearance—save for her still-white hair (*Superman's Pal, Jimmy Olsen* #161, November 1973).

Perhaps in penance for her earlier criminal activities, Lucy became intent on pursuing a nursing career in Suicide Slum, but she was ultimately drawn back into the airline business. While working as a passenger service agent for Blue Falcon Airways, Lucy was reunited with Jimmy and disappointed when he expressed no interest in reviving their romantic relationship (*Superman Family* #213–215, December 1981–February 1982). Jimmy remained a good friend, however, and later helped Lucy—once again a flight attendant—patch up her relationship with Lois (*Lois Lane* #1–2, August–September 1986). In one potential future, Lucy was fated to marry Jimmy and become the head of a major airline (*Superman Family* #200, March–April 1980).

Lucy Lane vs. Supergirl

After reality was reordered by the Crisis on Infinite Earths, Lucy grew up in her sister's shadow, even dating boys in Lois's circle in many failed attempts to live her life through her more successful sister. She became a trained flight attendant but was tragically blinded during a hijacking attempt. When Superman shattered the imperfect Bizarro duplicate, some of the clone's powdery remains landed on Lucy's face and restored her sight (*Man of Steel* #5, Early December 1986). Lucy briefly returned to her airline career, only to be shot and nearly killed by Deathstroke during another hijacked flight (*Superman* [second series] #68, June 1992).

Lucy remained a close part of her sister's world, which led to her encountering the Fourth World's Sleez (*The Adventures of Superman* #475, February 1991) and actually being enslaved by a vampire (*Superman* [second series] #70, August 1992). She later romanced the *Planet*'s Ron Troupe and wound up getting pregnant (*Superman: The Man of Steel* #83, September 1998). General Lane, exceptionally conservative in his worldview, made Lucy's life stressful until the couple married. A child named Samuel Christopher was born some time later (*The Adventures of Superman* #487, February 2001).

Years later, Lucy enlisted in the military in honor of her father's memory (during a period when it was believed Sam Lane was dead). Her relationship with Lois became strained as Lucy blamed Lois for the events leading to their father's death during the Imperiex War (*Superman: New Krypton Special* #1, December 2008). Sam Lane, though, reappeared, hale and hardy, approving of Lucy's career choice. As a result, and still eager to please him, she agreed to don a high-tech costume and become Superwoman to perform missions on his behalf in the wake of one hundred thousand Kryptonians taking up residence on Earth (*Supergirl* [fifth series] #35, January 2009). In time, she rejected the missions, but her father blackmailed Lucy into carrying out his orders, beginning with the murder of Agent Liberty (*Action Comics* #873, March 2009).

Superwoman and Supergirl developed an odd relationship combining two-fisted battles and heart-to-heart conversations. Pushed too far during a battle, Supergirl unmasked Superwoman but also accidentally ruptured the outfit's containment field. Lucy died in the resulting explosion (*Supergirl* [fifth series] #38–41, May–August 2009).

Months later, on Maine's Mount Katahdin, an innocent hiker named Stephen Morrow was killed so that his body could provide the raw organic material to allow Lucy to live once more. According to the witch queen Mirabai, Lucy's will to live was so strong that it actually preserved her life essence. Lane's spirit mixed with Mirabai's magic, so when Lucy Lane was resurrected, she now possessed the same strengths and weaknesses of the very people she was trained to fight. General Sam Lane was thrilled to have his daughter back, but he was also disturbed to see that Lucy was becoming a literal alien to him. Donning a fresh Superwoman outfit, a now-ruthless Lucy Lane reported for duty (*Supergirl* [fifth series], #50, May 2010).

During the Kryptonian invasion of Earth immediately following New Krypton's destruction, Sam Lane dispatched his younger daughter to bring Lois to him in one of his secret bunkers. Lucy found Lois at the *Daily Planet* and brutally took her to their father. A devastated Lois then watched in horror as Sam Lane killed himself rather than face trial when Project 7734 fell apart and Earth's army was defeated. A still-superpowered Lucy was arrested and imprisoned for her crimes. She languished in prison and waited to take revenge on both her sister and Supergirl (*Superman: War of the Supermen* #3–4, July 2010).

LANE, NED

Ned Lane was Samuel Lane's brother, described as "a famous authority on the legends of King Arthur's court." He gifted his niece Lois Lane with Merlin's magical full-length mirror, said to have once belonged to the magician of Arthur's court. The prized item was purported to possess the power to reveal the truth about anyone who stood before it. Lois took it to Metropolis and tried to lure Superman to stand before it. When he did, Lois was shocked to see an image of Clark Kent. To protect his secret identity, Superman tricked Lois into thinking that the magical mirror was not always truthful, and Lois eventually locked it away so as not to trouble anyone else (*Action Comics* #269, October 1960).

LANE, SAMUEL

Earth-1's Sam and Ella Lane farmed and raised animals in Pittsdale, Iowa. They had two daughters, Lucy and Lois Lane, the latter becoming a celebrated figure through her work for the *Daily Planet* (*Superman's Girl Friend, Lois Lane* #13, November 1959). His Earth-2 counterpart has been identified as U.S. Marine colonel Samuel L. Lane (*Infinite Crisis: Secret Files and Origins,* April 2006).

In the world after the Crisis on Infinite Earths, Samuel Lane was a U.S. Army general who always resented that he had daughters, not sons, thereby creating a tense relationship with Lois and Lucy (*The Adventures of Superman* #424, January 1987). Things grew tenser when Ella died unexpectedly, leaving the general to raise the girls on his own. Lois responded by becoming a hard-edged, determined woman, channeling her emotions and drive into her career as a no-nonsense investigative reporter.

Lois eventually became engaged to Clark Kent, earning Lane's disapproval of the mild-mannered reporter. He almost boycotted the wedding before thinking twice about what that would mean to his long-term relationship with Lois (*Superman: The Wedding Album* #1, December 1996).

Following his election as president of the United States, Lex Luthor tapped Lane as his secretary of defense (*Action Comics* #774, February 2001). He chose Lane due more to the mind games he was playing with Lois than to the general's credentials. Father and daughter clashed over America's preparations for the impending Imperiex War given the general's frustrating black-and-white view of the world. During the conflict, Lane appeared to sacrifice himself to save Earth, detonating his tank's nuclear engine in an attempt to shatter an Imperiex probe's casing (*Action Comics* #781, September 2001).

When reality was reordered after the Infinite Crisis, Sam Lane first began to investigate Superman after rumors reached him that Lois was often seen with the recently revealed alien super hero (*Superman: Secret Origin* #5, May 2010). Lane was skeptical, like the rest of Metropolis, about Superman's true intentions, especially for his daughter.

After being presumed dead for years, Sam Lane was now apparently alive and well when he recruited an imprisoned Lex Luthor to help him take down Superman and the one hundred thousand Kryptonians who arrived when Kandor was restored to its proper size. Lane saw a threat to humanity and, working with Luthor, would not rest until all Kryptonians—including Superman—were eliminated (*Superman: New Krypton Special* #1, December 2008). By then, he was reunited with Lucy, who had enlisted in the military to honor his memory. Sam Lane approved of Lucy's career choice—but then brought her closer into his paranoid world. He had a high-tech outfit made to replicate Kryptonian superpowers and asked Lucy to become Superwoman, performing surveillance for him. She agreed, but when in time he wanted her to do more, she refused. He then blackmailed her until she acquiesced, beginning with the murder of Agent Liberty (*Action Comics* #873, March 2009). Her actions ultimately led to her (albeit temporary) death, something he refused to accept responsibility for, instead blaming it on the residents of New Krypton.

As part of his diabolical Project 7734, Sam Lane planted the villain Reactron on New Krypton. Reactron exploded thanks to Lex Luthor-provided technology, thereby destroying the Kryptonians' new planet. This was followed by the artificial, Luthor-designed version of the Kryptonian god Rao, which nearly decimated the remaining Kandorians. General Zod brought Lane into the very war the human anticipated, and many of Earth's capital cities were destroyed by the vengeful Kryptonians until stopped by Superman, Supergirl, Superboy, and Earth's meta-human community. His plans crumbling fast around him, Lane sequestered himself with his kidnapped daughter Lois in one of his hidden bunkers. When that was breached and Project 7734 defeated, the general took his own life rather than face a trial for all his crimes. Lois buried him next to her mother Ella, putting an end to a wrong-minded fear of those who are different (*Superman: War of the Supermen* #1–4, July 2010).

LANG, ALVIN

Alvin was the younger brother of Smallville's Lana Lang. He rarely socialized with her friends (including Clark Kent), although twice he temporarily gained superpowers and needed Superboy's help in controlling them (*Superboy* [first series] #26, June–July 1953, and #48, April 1956).

LANG, LANA

Red-headed Lana Lang was born and raised in Smallville, and was best friend to Clark Kent, who was secretly Superboy (*Superboy* [first series] #10, September–October 1950).

In the Earth-2 reality, Lana and Clark did not grow up together, the Langs having left Smallville for Metropolis because the elder Lang saw no future "in such a little town." Arriving at the *Daily Star* in the early 1950s, Lana argued that the newspaper needed a television critic—and that she was the woman for the job (*Superman Family* #203, September–October 1980).

Lana soon after received a mystic amulet from her father, an archaeologist, said to have been created for an unnamed pharaoh. She surmised it might have been Ramses II, since it was crafted to allow him to deal with locust hordes plaguing ancient Egypt. The amulet was activated by the distinct sound of approaching insect wings, which somewhat resembled the whooshing sound made by Superman's flight. One such flight activated the amulet, turning Lana Lang into an evil Insect Queen. Under the amulet's magical spell, she commanded silkworms to fashion her a golden-brown costume and went into action as a late-in-life supervillain (*Superman Family* #213–215, December 1981–February 1982). She fell under the Ultra-Humanite's sway until Superman found an antidote to save his friend, which was administered by Lois Lane. Once freed from the spell, Lana learned how to master the amulet and adventured as the Insect Queen for a time.

On Earth-1, Lana was the daughter of successful university professor Lewis Lang (*Superboy* [first series] #10, September–October 1950), who frequently traveled the world with his wife Sarah (name revealed in *Superman: Last Son of Krypton,* 1978). She and her brothers Alvin (*Superboy* [first series] #26, June–July 1953), Larry (*Superboy* [first series] #13, March–April 1951), and Ronald (*Adventure Comics* #168, September 1951), along with an unnamed older sister (*Superman's Girl Friend, Lois Lane* #10, July 1959), grew up under normal circumstances in their home on 325 Maple Street at the south end of town (*The New Adventures of Superboy* #22, October 1981). Her uncle Professor Phineas Potter (relationship established in *Adventure Comics* #291, December 1961) was a frequent visitor to the Lang home, which was situated next door to the Kent family. Her extended genealogy included nineteenth-century ancestors such as Dennis Lang (1721–1801), an explorer; Admiral Rupert B. Lang (1735–1829); Governor Douglas Lang (1791–1850); General Richard Lang (1791–1870); and Judge Hubert Lang (1820–1891) (all revealed in *Superboy* [first series] #79, March 1960).

Other relatives included Lana's aunt Betty (*Superboy* [first series] #37, December 1954); Aunt Helen and cousin Betsy (*Superboy* [first series] #90, July 1961); cousins Andy (*Superboy* [first series] #63, March 1958) and Larry (*Adventure Comics* #307, April 1963); a dentist uncle, Dr. Horten (*Superboy* [first series] #87, March 1961); and another uncle named Rutherford (*Adventure Comics* #291, December 1961).

When Superboy arrived on the scene, Lana developed an instant crush on the Teen of Steel and immediately befriended him. It was not long before she began to wonder if Superboy and Clark Kent might be connected and started snooping around, which proved an important training lesson for Clark, who perfected the art of misdirection, a skill he'd need after beginning to work with Lois Lane.

In her Smallville High School yearbook, Lana was named "Class Wit"; she was extremely popular.

When she wasn't sharing experiences with the *Smallville Sentinel,* Lana had her own escapades, such as the time she rescued an alien who was trapped under a fallen tree. The insect-like being rewarded Lana's heroism by giving her a "biogenetic" ring. Upon donning the ring, she possessed insect and arachnid abilities. Thrilled, the teen girl designed her own costume and went into action as the Insect Queen (*Superboy* [first series] #124, October 1965). Lana's heroism, despite her lack of training, impressed the Legion of Super-Heroes enough to grant her reserve status

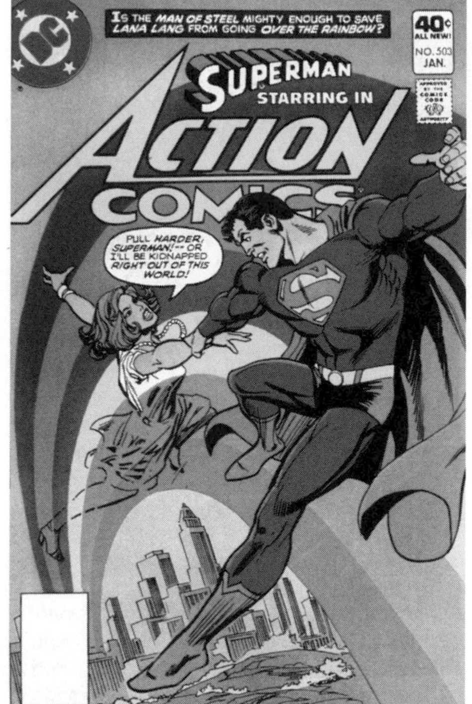

(*Adventure Comics* #355, April 1967). For unknown reasons, Lana rarely used the insect ring as an adult.

At one point in her youth, Lana also assumed the heroic persona of Gravity Girl (*Adventure Comics* #285, June 1961). As an adult, she twice donned a yellow-and-purple costume as Super-Lana while endowed with temporary superpowers (*Superman's Girl Friend, Lois Lane* #17, May 1960, and #21, November 1960).

After graduating from Hudson University (*Superman's Girl Friend, Lois Lane* #109, April 1971), Lana went into broadcast journalism, eventually arriving in Metropolis to find work in television. Instead, she wound up gaining employment as a spokeswoman in commercials at TV station WXR (*Showcase* #9, July–August 1957). But she had lost even that job when Lois Lane spotted the destitute Lana months later (*Superman's Girl Friend, Lois Lane* #7, February 1959). The mercurial friendship between the two women was set from these first encounters with Lois and Lana alternating between great empathy and deep jealousy over their unrequited love for Superman.

An alternate account of the adult Lois and Lana's first meeting was depicted in *Superman* [first series] #78 (September–October 1952), wherein Lana sought a reporter's job with the Daily Planet but was ultimately hired by the Federal Syndicate.

After initially writing a novel (*Superman's Girl Friend, Lois Lane* #11, August 1959) and a nostalgia column about Superboy for the *Daily Planet* (*Superman's Girl Friend, Lois Lane* #17, May 1960), Lana finally found success as a television reporter with WMET (*Superman's Girl Friend, Lois Lane* #21, November 1960). She failed, however, in her efforts to win Superman away from Lois Lane, and ultimately accepted an offer from Galaxy Broadcasting's WGBS-TV to serve as one of their European consultants (*Superman's Girl Friend, Lois Lane* #109, April 1971).

Lana's stay in Europe would end tragically, however. Impulsively marrying, Lana gave birth to a son—only to have the child kidnapped and murdered by terrorists (*Lois Lane* #2, September 1986). Desperate for a change of scene, the divorced Lana accepted an offer to return to Metropolis as Clark Kent's co-anchor on WGBS's evening news broadcast (*Superman* [first series] #317, November 1977).

Lana unfortunately affected a shallow persona while blatantly making a play for Superman. Fed up with her behavior, the Man of Steel once exploded at her, snapping, "You're not in love—you're starstruck!" (*Superman* [first series] #332, February 1979). Shaken by Superman's rejection, Lana looked for love elsewhere. She found it in a new WGBS security guard named Vernon O'Valeron. She was astonished to discover that he, too, was a superpowered hero, really named Vartox, but was committed to this new romance even as he returned to outer space (*Action Comics* #598–599, August–September 1979). Even as her plans for a marriage to Vartox went awry (*Superman* [first series] #375, September 1982), Lana found herself growing more attracted to Clark Kent, and the two ultimately fell in love (*Action Comics* #542, April 1983).

After reality was shuffled by the Crisis on Infinite Earths, Lana Elizabeth Lang (middle name revealed in *Action Comics* #700, June 1994) was a typical teen in love with the not-so-typical boy next door. Lana's parents were Thomas and Carol, both of whom were killed by alien Manhunters on the day that Kal-El's rocket arrived on Earth. She was raised thereafter by Thomas's unmarried sister Helen (*World of Smallville* #3, June 1988).

Clark saw her as a platonic friend until the night before their high school graduation. Lana had hoped for a proposal, but Clark instead revealed his secret to her by taking her flying through the Kansas night sky and ending the evening with a kiss. The kiss told Lana everything she needed to know: Clark would never love her the way she loved him (*Man of Steel* #6, Late December 1987).

Once Superman became a public figure, Lana immediately recognized that Clark had fulfilled his destiny. She followed his exploits with regularity and eventually came to the attention of Lex Luthor, who was obsessively seeking information on Metropolis's new costumed champion. He had Lana kidnapped and tortured to learn what she knew of Superman, but Lana said nothing to betray her childhood friend (*Superman* [second series] #2, February 1987).

Not long after, Lana surprised Clark by arriving at the *Daily Planet* and telling him to stay out of the brewing war between the Manhunter robots and their creators, the Guardians of the Universe. If Clark refused, Lana would tell everyone his identity (*Millennium* #2, January 1987). Clark later learned that Lana had been kidnapped and turned into a sleeper agent, as were most of Smallville's citizens (*The Adventures of Superman* #436, January 1987). It took the combined efforts of Superman and the Spectre to free their enslaved minds (*Action Comics* #596, January 1987).

Soon after, Superman traveled to the Pocket Universe, where he discovered that the Lana Lang of that world had been killed, but a clone of her had been fashioned into the shape-changing being known as Matrix. When she was badly burned, he brought her back to his world and let Ma and Pa Kent, and their neighbor Lana, care for the protoplasmic form they named Mae (*Superman* [second series] #22, October 1988).

After eventually selling her family's farm, Lana finally agreed to go on a date with childhood pal Pete Ross, recognizing that it was time to move on with her life (*The Adventures of Superman* #470, September 1990). Uncertain of how Clark would react, Pete asked for the reporter's permission, something that proved completely unnecessary.

Their romance turned serious, and when Pete was elected senator from Kansas, Lana accompanied him to Washington, the two sharing an apartment (*The Adventures of Superman* #481, August 1991) and getting engaged soon after (*Action Comics* #673, January 1992). Their wedding was marred only by the absence of Lois and Clark, who were both preoccupied with Lex Luthor's attempts to destroy Metropolis (*Action Comics* #700, June 1994). Regardless of the life they tried to lead, the Rosses' paths continually intersected with Clark or Superman, to the point that Pete felt like a rival to the myth of the "one who got away." They had a son together who was named Clark to honor their friend, who came to their aid when Lana's pregnancy grew complicated. Born eight weeks premature, the baby was in distress; Superman had to juggle a rampaging Doomsday while helping his oldest friend save her son. It turned out the baby's premature birth was a result of

Brainiac's attempts to use the infant to fashion a new body for itself, but happily the baby survived (*Superman: The Doomsday Wars* #1–3, 1998).

When Pete first entered the Senate, then got tapped to be Lex Luthor's running mate, Lana tried to avoid the spotlight and raise Clark in relative anonymity. She harbored deep resentment toward Luthor for what he'd done to her years earlier. When Luthor and Pete won their ticket, Lana moved permanently from Smallville to Washington, DC. She was ambivalent about the relocation and at one point even tried to reignite things with Clark Kent, who rebuffed her. Upset with Clark, and herself, she went so far as to say the baby was named in honor of Martha Clark Kent, not him (*Superman: Lex 2000,* 2000).

At one point, Lana attemped to help a young teen named Traci Thirteen, who wrote to her asking for help. Against Pete's wishes, she went to meet Traci on her own, only to go missing hours later, prompting the vice president to call Clark for help (*Superman* [second series] #189, February 2003). An undercover Clark found Traci and some parasites that were making up a creature called Heartbreaker that fed on people's emotions, increasing their level of despair. One such creature infected Clark, turning him despondent, and he almost missed a suicidal Lana's leap from a building, but the shock of seeing her fall prompted the Man of Steel to fight off the parasite's influence. Upon landing, they embraced and kissed.

Freed from the parasite's spell, Lana and Clark reunited with Lois, who had learned by then that the Rosses were getting divorced. Lana begged Lois not to run the story, which Lois did anyway as an act of revenge for the two kissing (*Action Comics* #806, October 2003). Her marriage a shambles, Lana confessed to Clark she still loved him despite knowing he was committed to Lois. While Lois was away on assignment, Lana and baby Clark arrived to help a beaten Superman recuperate after a battle with the dangerous Weapon-Master, to Lois's aggravation (*Action Comics* #818, October 2004). Martha Kent had enough of the puppy-dog looks Lana gave Clark and finally told her at a Thanksgiving dinner to "Move on. Get over it. Find someone else" (*Action Comics* #823, March 2005).

Pete meanwhile asked Clark for his help in reconnecting with Lana. Pete still loved her, but Lana refused to consider a reunion and asked for a divorce. Pete was unmasked soon after as the villain Ruin, who had been threatening everyone involved in Superman's life for several months (*The Adventures of Superman* #637–640, April–July 2005). The real Ruin then hunted Pete and Lana in the hope of killing them, but they were saved by Superman. Pete's name was cleared, and the three old Smallville friends reconciled (*The Adventures of Superman* #647, February 2006).

In the reality that arose following the Infinite Crisis, Lana was part of large family that included siblings Ronald, Larry, Alvin, and Ginny, Uncle Lewis Lang, Uncle Phineas Potter, Uncle Rutherford, and "Great-Aunt Sarah and all the Horten cousins." Her bank president father Martin Lang taught Lana the ins and outs of running a financial institution (*Action Comics* #850, Late July 2007).

Lana and Pete divorced, and she took a small apartment in Metropolis to be near Clark, with whom she had reconciled. Under as-yet-unexplained circumstances, Lana found herself named CEO of LexCorp in the wake of Luthor's meltdown, which led to his impeachment and subsequent disappearance. As CEO, Lana was left with a foundering company ruined by her predecessor, Talia Head, and tried to sell off huge portions of the conglomerate even though the stock price was falling thanks to the founder's criminal deeds (*Superman* #655, October 2006).

Shortly after Lana became CEO, aliens from a race known as the All-Hive arrived on Earth's moon and took over a secret LexCorp installation. From there, the insectoid leader emerged from her suspended animation cocoon and dispatched her underling, Pyridax, to abduct Lana. The would-be conqueror used the hapless Lana for a template to remake herself in the redhead's image. She wanted to use a human body to lead an invasion force and take over Earth, but first she wanted to take the Man of Steel as her consort. Lana helped Superman defeat the Insect Queen, and the Man of Steel placed her in suspended animation (*Superman* #671–673, February–March 2008).

Safely back at work, Lana proved a more-than-competent executive, finally proving to herself and the world that she was more than a wife, mother, and friend of Superman.

When Atlas, a time-traveling figure from the past, pummeled the Man of Steel in Metropolis's city streets, Lana came to her friend's aid by launching the Luthor Squad. Once she used them to assist Luthor's sworn enemy, however, a program was activated, and a holographic Luthor explained that Lana was now in violation of her employment contract; she was immediately terminated (*Superman* #679, October 2008).

Left with time on her hands, Lana befriended Supergirl, offering her her friendship and practical advice about functioning in a world that still mystified the Maid of Might. With her help, Kara Zor-El adopted the identity of Linda Lang, a cousin of Lana's (*Supergirl* [fifth series] #34, December 2008). The two took up residence in Metropolis's Hammersmith Tower (*Supergirl* [fifth series] #39, May 2009).

Perry White surprised Lana by asking her to become the *Daily Planet*'s business editor, putting her once more in contact with Clark on a daily basis (*Supergirl* [fifth series] #34, December 2008). They remained awkward with each other, so much so that although she attended Jonathan Kent's funeral, she could not bring herself to speak with her childhood friend (*Superman: New Krypton Special* #1, December 2008).

Just as her life seemed to be settling into something resembling normal, Lana collapsed at a student journalism award ceremony. Jimmy Olsen and Catherine Grant brought her to the hospital for testing and she later received word from her doctor that an unknown alien element was in her blood and was slowly killing her (*Supergirl* [fifth series] #43, September 2009). As Lana weakened over

the next few weeks, Thara Ak-Var warned Supergirl that she saw the literal corruption building within Lana.

While heading for a doctor's appointment, Lana collapsed in the lobby of her apartment building, bleeding from her eyes, ears, and mouth. She was rushed to the hospital, where her doctors could do nothing to stem the bleeding, and she suddenly died. When Supergirl arrived at the morgue, she was stunned to find Lana's body encased in an alien-looking cocoon. Soon after, the entire hospital was enveloped in the cocoon, even trapping members of the Metropolis Science Police who had responded to the hospital's crisis call.

Doctor Light arrived and sent in a miniaturized camera to study what was happening within the building. The B.U.G. device captured images of Supergirl, who was now also trapped within a cocoon. Gangbuster, recently relocated back to Metropolis, led a strike team into the hospital and successfully rescued the heroine. After she recovered, the Maid of Steel and Gangbuster returned to the hospital, where they found Lana's body inhabited by the Insect Queen.

The Insect Queen explained to Supergirl that she had spent the last year slowly exerting influence over Lana's antibodies and internal defenses so she could live again and obtain Supergirl in the hopes of using Kara's DNA to create an unbeatable army of superpowered drones. Instead, Supergirl beat the Insect Queen into submission, allowing Doctor Light the time she needed to construct a device that would cleanse Lana's body of the alien infestation entirely.

Lana was completely healthy once more, but

keeping her illness a secret from Supergirl and those she loved caused a deep rift in her relationship with Kara (*Supergirl* [fifth series] #49–50, April–May 2010).

Other realities found Lana Lang successful in her desire to wed Superman. On Earth-26, for instance, he bestowed superpowers on her (*Superman's Girl Friend, Lois Lane* #26, July 1961), and on Earth-34, Superman and Lana's daughter ultimately wed the son of Lex and Lois Luthor (*Superman's Girl Friend, Lois Lane* #46, January 1964). On parallel worlds such as Earth-162 and Earth-57, the Man of Steel was able to marry *both* Lois and Lana, either because he'd split into two beings (*Superman* [first series] #162, July 1963) or because bigamy was legal (*Superman's Girl Friend, Lois Lane* #57, May 1965).

On Earth-30, Lana Lazarenko grew up with Kal-El in Ukraine and found work as a tour guide in the Superman Museum after her childhood friend became the People's Hero (*Superman: Red Son* #1–2, 2003).

LANG, PROFESSOR LEWIS

Earth-1's Lewis Lang (*Superboy* [first series] #10, September–October 1950) was a famed archaeologist who lived in Smallville with his wife Sarah and their children Alvin (*Superboy* [first series] #26, June–July 1953), Larry (*Superboy* [first series] #13, March–April 1951), Ronald (*Adventure Comics* #168, September 1951), Lana (*Superboy* [first series] #10, September–October 1950), and an unnamed older daughter (*Superman's Girl Friend, Lois Lane* #10, July 1959). His extended genealogy included nineteenth-century ancestors such as Dennis Lang (1721–1801), an explorer; Admiral Rupert B. Lang (1735–1829); Governor Douglas Lang (1791–1850); General Richard Lang (1791–1870); and Judge Hubert Lang (1820–1891) (all revealed in *Superboy* [first series] #79, March 1960).

Lewis and Sarah often traveled the world for his work, and as their children reached their teen years they were usually left alone. When Superboy began to operate in Smallville, he befriended the

professor and his children and often went along on Lewis's expeditions (*Adventure Comics* #200, May 1954; others).

Professor Lang was alternately identified as John (*Superboy* [first series] #18, March 1960) and Tom (*Superboy* [first series] #19, March 1960) before being permanently identified as Lewis. In post-Crisis continuity, Lana's father was named Thomas, and he was killed while Lana was still an infant (*World of Smallville* #3, June 1988). In the reality formed in the wake of the Infinite Crisis, Lana's father was named Martin and was a Smallville bank president (*Action Comics Annual* #10, March 2007). In the revised history, archaeologist Lewis Lang still existed as Martin's brother and Lana's uncle (*Superman* #656, November 2006).

LARA LOR-VAN

Lara Lor-Van was an accomplished Kryptonian prior to marrying Krypton's greatest scientist, Jor-El. She stood by his side as their world exploded, watching as a rocket ship carrying their son Kal-El embarked safely on its journey to Earth.

In the Earth-2 universe she was known as Lora, and with her scientist husband Jor-L had a son named Kal-L. When Krypton seemed on the brink of destruction, Jor-L used a rocket of his own design, a scale model of one he envisioned mass-producing to save the entire population, and sent the infant into space moments before the planet exploded (*Action Comics* #1, June 1938. The names Jor-L, Lora, and Kal-L were originally used only in the *Superman* newspaper comic strip and were affirmed as the names of their Earth-2 counterparts in *Showcase* #97 [February 1978]. All references to Lara herein—as her name was rendered since *Superman* [first series] #53, July–August 1948—reflect the stories as published rather than the retroactive change.)

In the Earth-1 reality, Lara Lor-Van was the daughter of Lor-Van and Lara Rok-Var (*Superman Family* #192, November–December 1978). Lara was said to have worked in a factory that produced robots before she married the scientist Jor-El (*Superman* [first series] #123, August 1958). When they married, Lara became Jor-El's lab assistant until their world exploded. "Noted for her advanced intellect as well as her beauty, Lara was

the perfect partner and mother" (*Superman* [first series] #170, July 1964).

When Jor-El concluded that their planet was doomed, Lara was one of the few to believe him, and she supported his goal of building rockets to move the population off-planet as soon as possible. She watched him test a scale model using their family pet Krypto as a subject, and approved the use of the ship for their son based on the results. Jor-El insisted there was room for Lara to join Kal-El, but she refused, saying her place was by her husband's side.

Then, as husband and wife clung together in a desperate last embrace, "nature's fury gathered for one final cataclysmic eruption ... And as the pitifully small space-ship hurtled through interstellar space, the once mighty Krypton exploded into stardust!"

In subsequent retellings of life on Krypton, Lara was said to have been one of the planet's top astronauts, traveling to the moon Wegthor prior to its destruction by Jax-Ur (*Superman* [first series] #233, January 1971). It was during her time with the space program that Lara met Jor-El; after several incidents together, they fell in love and married (*The World of Krypton* #1–3, July–September 1978).

Kal-El arrived on Earth, and as he grew up to become the World's Greatest Super Hero, he memorialized his parents with statues in his Arctic Fortress of Solitude.

After reality was altered after the Crisis on Infinite Earths, Lara became a librarian on the emotionally stunted, sterile world of Krypton. When an opening in the Register of Citizens allowed for a new birth, her mating with the scientist Jor-El was arranged by her grandmother Lady Nara and Jor-El's harsh father Seyg-El. When Jor-El, always considered an emotional throwback, expressed real affection for her, Lara was at first repulsed. She was a highly ranked historian, and when she saw images from the world their child was to visit she was horrified at the "primitive" lifestyle of the

people of Earth until Jor-El explained to her that their son would fit in among the populace without a problem (*Man of Steel* #1, Early October 1986).

The events preceding the Infinite Crisis briefly altered reality once more, and Lara, along with her world, more closely resembled the Earth-1 version. She was an equal partner to her husband, whom she was devoted to.

LAR-ON

A study of physical transformation led the Kryptonian scientist Lar-On to experiment on himself, with disastrous results. He turned into a were-beast, and in that feral state he killed his wife. He was arrested, tried, and banished to the Phantom Zone. Many years later, the scientist was accidentally released on Earth, and his animalistic nature turned him into a superpowered threat. He endangered lives on Earth in addition to passing on the affliction through victims he bit. Superman lured him into daylight, which resulted in Lar-On transforming back to his original form, allowing the Man of Steel and Batman to quickly subdue him. Later, a scratch sustained in their encounters temporarily transformed Batman into a were-bat until a cure was found (*World's Finest Comics* #256, April-May 1979, and #258, August-September 1979).

LAR THAN

On a distant world, Lex Luthor was considered a great hero, and the people renamed their world Lexor in his honor. Among its citizens was Lar Than, a well-respected prosecutor who charged Superman with Luthor's apparent murder and brought the hero to trial. As the trial unfolded, the Man of Steel was accused of premeditated murder, but he was acquitted when Luthor awoke from his death-like trance, which had been brought about by a "coma drug" the villain had taken (*Action Comics* #318–319, November–December 1964).

LARUE, NIKKI

"Glamour girl" Nikki Larue arrived in Metropolis from Europe, telling the press that she was relocating to the city given her engagement to Superman. As the news rocketed across the planet, no one was more surprised—or hurt—by the announcement than Lois Lane. It was later revealed that the stunning woman was actually world-famous atomic scientist Madame Nicolai, using the public persona of Larue to hide from spies. While she posed as Superman's fiancée, he could be seen with her and provide constant protection without arousing any suspicions. She was only briefly in America, to experiment with atomic energy at the federal government's invitation; once she completed her work, she returned home (*Action Comics* #143, April 1950).

LASIL

Kal-El's rocket ship was apparently once caught in a space warp, depositing him not on Earth but on a distant alien world where he grew to adulthood and married an attractive native woman named Lasil. Using his superpowers, Kal-El helped the primitive culture make technological leaps and bounds. Kal-El and Lasil had one child. At the conclusion of Kal-El's life, the thankful people used their newly evolved technology to return him to infant form and sent the restored rocket ship toward its intended destination: Earth. Superman was unaware of this previous life until he realized his rocket was a century older than he had previously believed (*Action Comics* #370, December 1968).

LATHAM, MARLA

Marla Latham hailed from Rimbor, the same homeworld as the Legion of Super-Heroes' Ultra Boy. As the adult liaison to the Legion, Marla accompanied the thirtieth-century would-be hero Ultra Boy on a visit to Superboy's time period as "an official observer." Latham and Ultra Boy settled in Smallville as Ben and Gary Crane; the would-be Legionnaire's task was to uncover the Teen of Steel's secret identity. When Ultra Boy successfully passed the test, they revealed their own identities to both Superboy and Pete Ross. Given Ross's unflagging support of Superboy, Latham presented him with a coin that would serve as a pass to the super heroes' clubhouse whenever the Legion met (*Superboy* [first series] #98, July 1962).

It was later learned that Latham was the right-hand man to the successful businessman R. J. Brande, who tapped Latham to act as an adult adviser shortly after Brande formed the Legion. Latham came aboard during the team's second membership recruitment drive, which eventually saw Bouncing Boy, Brainiac 5, Shrinking Violet, Sun Boy, and Supergirl join the team (*Secrets of the Legion of Super-Heroes* #2, February 1981). Marla was subsequently responsible for mentoring Jo Nah, who eventually became Ultra Boy. Jo Nah was so taken with Latham that he modeled his Legion uniform after Latham's favored mode of dress.

I, MARLA, AM THE LEGION'S NEW SENIOR ADVISOR! I ACCOMPANIED ULTRA-BOY INTO THE PAST AS AN OFFICIAL OBSERVER! WE HID OUR TIME-GLOBE NEAR METROPOLIS AND CAME TO SMALLVILLE BY TRAIN SO YOU WOULDN'T WITNESS OUR ARRIVAL AND BE ON GUARD!

Once the team was well established, Latham moved on to help found the Legion Academy and applied his lessons to a number of aspiring heroes. Still, he was never far away and came to the Legion's aid when needed (*Superboy and the Legion of Super-Heroes* #239, May 1978).

LAUGHLIN, SERGEANT SCOTT

Second in command to Lieutenant Lupé Teresa Leocadio-Escudero, Scott "Skeeter" Laughlin enjoyed his role in the Metropolis Special Crimes Unit (*The Adventures of Superman* #627, June 2004). It fell to him to act as chaperone whenever a member of the media, including Clark Kent, accompanied the S.C.U. during active duty. He was one of the victims of Ruin's murderous crime spree (*The Adventures of Superman* #632, November 2004).

LAUREY, JIM

Jim Laurey conspired to kill his niece Doris, who had just inherited the valuable Laurey Coal Mines. Laurey and his lackey Crawford failed in several attempts to kill the attractive blonde, and he was eventually apprehended by Superman (*Action Comics* #34, March 1941).

LAVERNE, LITA

Sent from her native Toran, a tiny European county, Lita Laverne conspired with a military officer from Luxor to destroy a neutral country's ship and make it appear Luxor was responsible in order to sway public opinion during a war involving their countries and neighboring Galonia. The plan almost worked—until Superman arrived to stop the torpedo from hitting the vessel. He then investigated and exposed the plot, resulting in a shake-up of the Luxorian armed forces and forcing out the Toranian sympathizers (*Action Comics* #22, March 1940). Given the lack of involvement of Galonia in the chronicle, it may be that Luxor and Galonia were the same country.

LAWRENCE, LUCINDA

Jimmy Olsen was once gifted with a magical belt by Princess Ilona from the distant Sunev galaxy, which allowed him to travel through time. On his first journey, he visited 1692 Salem, Massachusetts, but was so conspicuous in his use of the belt that he was accused of being a demon. He was rescued from the mob by Lucinda Lawrence, who not only resembled his love Lucy Lane but was an actual witch to boot. In exchange for safely returning him home, Lucinda got to keep the belt, which was subsequently used as evidence by the Salemites to prove she was a witch. Lawrence was

found guilty and hung for her crime (*Superman's Pal, Jimmy Olsen* #60, April 1962).

LAWRENCE, RICK

Seeking an edge over his opponents, boxer Rick Lawrence submitted to experimental treatment by Metropolis's Dr. Sunder. When completed, the treatment allowed his cells to absorb the powers of his opponents' previous fights whenever his adrenaline levels were increased. The first time Lawrence tried this, he fought Superman after the Man of Steel had been defeated in combat by Wonder Woman. During a rematch, Lawrence had access to Superman's powers, but without experience in their use he was left always "one step behind," allowing the Man of Steel to defeat him. Since he retained the powers he absorbed, Superman brought Lawrence to live in the bottle city of Kandor where he would not be a threat to any normal humans (*Action Comics* #452, October 1975).

LEAD

A fairly common metal on Earth, lead had special significance for the Man of Steel, given its role as a shield from kryptonite radiation. It also prevented Superman's X-ray vision from being used, which proved vexing whenever criminals employed it to thwart the Man of Steel.

With a symbol of Pb and an atomic number of 82, lead is toxic to humans in small amounts and deadly to inhabitants of the planet Daxam.

Superman learned of lead's protective abilities shortly after he first discovered kryptonite on Earth-2 (*Superman* [first series] #92, September 1954).

On Earth-1, it was Jonathan Kent who deduced lead's value to Superboy when he observed that his son rallied from kryptonite's effects each time a leaden Superboy Robot stepped in front of the meteorite's rays (*Adventure Comics* #251, August 1958). Soon after, a scientist confirmed that lead would block kryptonite's radiation (*Superman* [first series] #130, July 1959). When Ma and Pa Kent had their bodies taken over by alien creatures, Superboy used lead goggles to prevent him from reading playing cards in a gambit for his foster parents' life (*Superboy* [first series] #148, June 1968).

Among those villains using lead against the Man of Steel was Lex Luthor, who usually lined his lairs with lead to keep their secrets hidden from Superman. Once he even managed to eradicate Earth's lead supply by converting it to harmless glass (*Action Comics* #249, February 1959). The Anti-Superman and Anti-Batman gangs wore lead-lined masks to protect their secret identities from Superman's X-ray vision (*World's Finest Comics* #159, August 1966).

Superman eventually resorted to wearing a lead suit to protect himself in certain situations, such as the time he absorbed excess radiation during a reactor explosion (*Action Comics* #124, September 1948) or the occasion when he was menaced by a kryptonite sword and a red kryptonite spear (*Action Comics* #278, July 1961). He had also taken to keeping a lead suit in the Fortress of Solitude to experiment with its effects and properties (*Action Comics* #241, June 1958).

The substance was abundant on other worlds, notably Krypton, which meant the citizens of Argo City could protect themselves with lead sheeting after their chunk of Krypton began to turn radioactive and changed to anti-kryptonite (*Action Comics* #252, May 1959). It was also effective at blocking the brain-wave-tracking abilities of the planet's Telepathic Hounds (*Superman* [first series] #158, January 1963).

However, lead was fatal to the powerful natives of Daxam (*Superboy* [first series] #89, June 1961). When Lar Gand came to Earth, it wasn't long before the planet's lead supply weakened the kind hero to the point of death. Superboy sent Gand to the Phantom Zone with the promise that he would try to find a cure for the Daxamite's reaction to lead. It took a millennium until the teen could be freed permanently. The Legion of Super-Heroes' Brainiac 5 devised a serum that, when taken every forty-eight hours, would allow Lar Gand to resume his life outside the Phantom Zone, and he joined the team as Mon-El (*Adventure Comics* #300, September 1962).

Lead's properties in regard to Superman remained intact in post–First Crisis history, although the Man of Steel was quick to point out a fallacy in the theory that his inability to see through lead meant that it was invisible to him. "It's exactly the opposite," he explained after once rescuing his friends from hidden lead tombs. "When I scanned Metropolis with my X-ray and telescopic vision, the lead-lined coffins *stood out* precisely *because* I couldn't see through them!" (*Superman* [second series] #9, September 1987).

LEE, LINDA

When the Earth-1 Supergirl arrived on Earth, Superman encouraged her to adopt a civilian identity to better blend in until she could master her powers and adapt to life on Earth. She chose the name Linda Lee, wore a brunette pigtailed wig, and was placed with the Midvale Orphanage while she was training to use her superpowers. Eventually, she was adopted by Fred and Edna Danvers (*Action Comics* #252, May 1959).

LEE, LIRI

Liri Lee was a member of the Linear Men, but little was revealed about the team's beautiful researcher (*Superman* [second series] #59, September 1991). Her husband was the Matthew Ryder of a potential future in which he did not become Waverider (*Superman* [second series] #73, November 1992). In the wake of a succession of brutal battles against forces such as Imperiex and Brainiac 13, Matt Ryder, Rip Hunter, and Waverider abandoned their human forms and reduced themselves to their "essential bio-auras" in order to recover. "Only Liri Lee [remained] tied to human vanity, expending the energy necessary to maintain her corporeal form." Denounced by the cosmic Quintessence as "out of step," the Linear Men were cast to Earth with new identities. In her new form, Liri Lee became Liesel Largo, briefly serving as nanny to Lex Luthor's daughter Lena Luthor (*Superman: The Man of Steel* #118, November 2001). She has not appeared in the chronicles since.

LEECH, REX

The ruthless promoter named Rex Leech would stop at nothing to make a buck. Displaying his trademark lack of tact, Leech pulled Jimmy Olsen from Superman's funeral procession in an attempt to get the photographer to sign over rights to the Man of Steel's death photo. When Olsen angrily refused, Leech had his goons open fire—but fortunately they didn't hurt anyone. He got away (*Superman: The Man of Steel* #20, February 1993). Small wonder that Leech moved quickly when a young clone claiming to be Superman appeared. Using his daughter Roxy Leech as further inducement, Leech became the soon-to-be Superboy's manager and eventually secured the trademark to the Superman name (*The Adventures of Superman* #502, July 1993).

While the teen hero ceded the rights to the name when the real Superman returned, Leech had no intention of letting go of his superpowered gold mine. There were T-shirts and hats and ticket sales to cash in on. Making plans for a "Supertour USA," Rex and his entourage (including Superboy's telepathic chaperone Dubbilex) ended their run in Hawaii (*Superboy* [third series] #1, February 1994). Unfortunately, setting down roots made

Rex easy to find when Ira Gamboli sought to collect the gambling debts that Leech owed him, and Superboy came into contact with the likes of Copperhead (*Superboy* [third series] #12, February 1995) and an amnesiac Lar Gand (*Superboy* [third series] #17–19, July–September 1996) before the matter was settled.

Rex's efforts to create a Superboy-themed roller coaster resulted in a televised debacle, and he dropped out of sight in the aftermath (*Superboy* [third series] #48–49, February–March 1998). Months later, Rex returned to Project Cadmus, desperately seeking help for Roxy (*Superboy* [third series] #76, July 2000), who had become the host for a fire elemental named Pyra. When the entity was excised from her body, Roxy joined Rex in returning to a more normal existence (*Superboy* [third series] #81, December 2000).

LEECH, ROXY

Growing up the daughter of ruthless promoter Rex Leech could not have been easy for Roxy, but when Superboy first met her, she seemed a typical teenage girl. The attractive blonde was immediately drawn to the teen, and she was thrilled when Superboy agreed to spend time with the Leeches as they traveled around the world (*The Adventures of Superman* #502, July 1993).

Roxy proved to have true grit when facing down cosmic threats and costumed villains, and she became a friend and ally to the Teen of Steel. When Superboy's genetic code literally began unraveling, he needed a donor's DNA pattern to follow, and Roxy volunteered hers, despite the risks it posed to her life. The doctors at Project Cadmus successfully saved Superboy, thereby strengthening the bond between the teens, who had evolved from potential lovers to enjoying an almost brother-sister dynamic. This eased the tension Superboy felt due to his attraction to both Roxy and Metropolis telejournalist Tana Moon (*Superboy* [third series] #41, July 1997).

Roxy had been inspired by Hawaiian police detective Sam Makoa to join the Honolulu branch of the Special Crimes Unit, which she felt would finally give her direction (*Superboy* [third series] #26, April 1996), but her new life proved brief as she was forced to quit the S.C.U. to help her ailing father (*Superboy* [third series] #49, March 1998). Months later, Roxy returned to Superboy's life via Project Cadmus (*Superboy* [third series] #76, July 2000), where she was discovered to have bonded with a fire elemental named Pyra. When the entity was excised from her body, Roxy joined Rex in returning to a more normal and calm existence (*Superboy* [third series] #80–81, November–December 2000).

LEESBURG

When the Earth-born angel known as Matrix merged with Linda Danvers to save the latter's life, they settled in Danvers's hometown of Leesburg, Virginia (*Supergirl* [fourth series] #1, September 1996). The small suburban community was a typical northeastern American town despite being home to various alien and occult residents. A Chaos Flow—"a tributary that runs off the river Styx"—had formed beneath the city, both drawn to and feeding off the evil forces above (*Supergirl* [fourth series] #11, July 1997). Years earlier, Superman and the Justice League of America dealt with the repercussions of another likely Chaos Flow beneath Midway City (*Justice League of America* [first series] #72, June 1969).

LEGENDS

Darkseid once engaged in a cosmic chess game with the Phantom Stranger when the two began discussing the nature of heroism. The lord of Apokolips was convinced that a hero's legendary status was ephemeral and could be destroyed overnight. To prove his point, Darkseid assigned Glorious Godfrey to turn America's citizens against their protectors. As G. Gordon Godfrey, he began to make the rounds of media talk shows in order to denigrate society's reliance on these so-called heroes. Sure enough, Godfrey's honeyed, lugubrious voice led people to begin questioning their beloved heroes.

In short order, the Justice League of America disbanded, its heroes unable to stem the tide of unchecked evil, beginning with the arrival of the fire elemental known as Brimstone. Captain Marvel was framed for murder, and a fearful president signed an order declaring martial law and outlawing superpowered vigilantes. In secret, Amanda Waller had reactivated Task Force X, and the Suicide Squad went into action to handle Brimstone.

As citizens turned into unruly mobs who once went so far as to beat Robin nearly to death, Doctor Fate intervened and exposed Godfrey for the charlatan he was before leading an army of angry Americans into Washington, DC. The mystic gathered Superman, Batman, Captain Marvel, Green Lantern Guy Gardner, Black Canary, Changeling, the Flash, Blue Beetle, and Martian Manhunter to help

defend the White House. They were then joined by Wonder Woman, who made her first public appearance in Man's World. Darkseid dispatched his cybernetic Hounds of War to aid Godfrey, but in the end they were defeated by the combined forces of Earth's greatest heroes. A gathering of children, led by the recovering Robin, confronted Godfrey, and their pure innocence won the day. In the wake of these incidents, a new incarnation of the JLA was born (*Legends* #1–6, November 1986–April 1987).

LEGIONARY, THE

Italy's protector, known as the Legionary, was styled after America's Batman and dressed as an ancient Roman gladiator. On Earth-1, the Legionary traveled to Gotham City to meet Batman and several other international heroes (*Detective Comics* #215, January 1955) to form the group known as the Club of Heroes, which also included the Man of Steel (*World's Finest Comics* #89, July–August 1957).

On the Earth created by the Crisis on Infinite Earths, the Legionary fought crime in his native land. He had reached the peak of his career nearly a decade before, but had let fame and fortune make him slow, heavy, and sloppy. According to Batman, the Legionary accepted bribes from Charlie Caligula, which severely compromised the hero's effectiveness. Still, when Club of Heroes founder John Mayhew summoned the heroes for an emergency, the Legionary returned to action. He was the first to be killed by Mayhew in a revenge scheme against the Dark Knight. The Legionary suffered seventeen stab wounds, matching those received by the Roman emperor Julius Caesar (*Batman* #667, August 2007).

LEGION OF DOOM, THE

Among the many short-lived gatherings of super-villains was a group known as the Legion of Doom, comprising Brainwave Junior, Killer Frost, Houngan, Major Force, the Madmen, and a Gorilla Grodd robot (*Extreme Justice* #17–18, June–July 1996).

On Earth-22, the Legion of Doom comprised Clayface, Poison Ivy, Solomon Grundy, Parasite, Toyman, Sinestro, Black Manta, Scarecrow, Brainiac, Lex Luthor, Gorilla Grodd, Captain Cold, Cheetah, Riddler, Bizarro, Giganta, Black Adam, and Metallo (*Justice* #1–12, October 2005–August 2007).

LEGION OF STUPOR-BIZARROS, THE

Earth-1's Bizarro Superboy attempted to join the thirtieth century's Legion of Super-Heroes but was summarily rejected. In frustration, the Bizarro Superboy used the imperfect duplicator ray and made his own Bizarro Legion (*Adventure Comics* #329, February 1965). A rivalry between the super-teams began as the Bizarro Legion tried to arrive at disasters ahead of their real-world counterparts. After being beaten one time too many, the Bizarros decided to create their own disasters to avert. Superboy managed to convince his Bizarro duplicate to disband the imitation team in exchange for the Teen of Steel crushing diamonds into coal, a trick completed with assistance from Element Lad.

LEGION OF SUBSTITUTE HEROES, THE

Given the strict by-laws used by the thirtieth century's Legion of Super-Heroes, many would-be members found that they could not gain admittance to the exclusive club. One in particular, Polar Boy, decided to do something about this, and he met with others who had been rejected to form their own team, where they could train to better use their abilities and be ready should an emergency arise where even the mighty Legion might need assistance.

At the time, rejected applicants were given flight belts as a souvenir of their tryout, allowing them the mobility to go into action whenever the need arose (*Adventure Comics* #306, March 1963). The first lineup consisted of Polar Boy, Night Girl, Chlorophyll Kid, Fire Lad, Stone Boy, and Color Kid.

They worked first in secrecy, but eventually

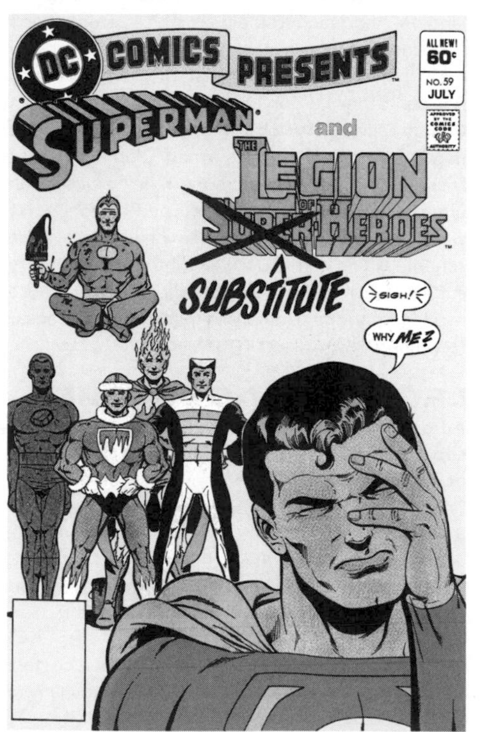

they came to the Legion's attention and received permission to continue their role as a backup team. Over time the group's membership also included Infectious Lass, Porcupine Pete, Antennae Boy, and Double-Header. After leaving the main team, Star Boy and Dream Girl briefly worked as Subs (*Adventure Comics* #342, March 1966).

Their first major success was saving Earth from the Plant Men (*Adventure Comics* #306, March 1963); later they attacked the Citadel of Throon to end a planetary siege (*Adventure Comics* #319, April 1964). In time, the Substitute Legion was disbanded, although Polar Boy became the first sub to be accepted as a full Legionnaire (*Legion of Super-Heroes* [third series] #14, September 1985). Others joined the team in the years that followed.

It soon became obvious there remained a need for trainees, so the Subs were re-formed by former Legionnaires Cosmic Boy, Bouncing Boy, and Duo Damsel, in addition to Night Girl, a second Karate Kid, and Comet Queen (*Legion of Super-Heroes* [third series] *Annual* #3, 1987). In the wake of Zero Hour, the future was re-formed, but there was still a need for the Legion of Substitute Heroes (*Legionnaires* #43, December 1996).

As reality was reordered after the Infinite Crisis, the core Subs were seen as members of a team called the Wanderers, led by Mekt Ranzz, the older brother to Legionnaires Light Lass and Lightning Lad (*Supergirl and the Legion of Super-Heroes* #25, February 2007). Night Girl was rejected by the Legion but was named a reserve, not a substitute.

Superman journeyed to the early thirty-first century to aid the Legion in stopping an isolationist group on Earth, which had proclaimed that Superman was not a Kryptonian but actually a meta-human. When things turned dire, the Man of Steel asked for help in his battle with the Justice League of Earth from Fire Lad, Stone Boy, Chlorophyll Kid, and Rainbow Girl. They provided a diversionary front, allowing Superman and the main Legion to arrive and end their threat. After the isolationist anti-alien League was defeated, the Subs took their base of operations for their own (*Action Comics* #862–863, February–March 2008).

LEGION OF SUPER-HEROES, THE

In Earth-1's future, countless civilizations from across the stars had banded together by the thirtieth century to form the United Planets. When industrialist R. J. Brande was targeted for kidnapping, teens from the planets Braal, Saturn, and Winath used their natural skills to defeat the criminals who wanted Brande eliminated. Brande said the teens' teamwork reminded him of the legends of Superboy from a millennium earlier, and he wanted to sponsor the teens to form a permanent team. Soon after, the Legion of Super-Heroes was born. With a grounded spaceship for its Earth-based headquarters, it attracted applicants from across the stars (first appearance in *Adventure Comics* #247, April 1958; origin revealed in *Superboy* [first series] #147, May–June 1968).

The three founders—Rokk Krinn, Imra Ardeen, and Garth Ranzz, who took the code names Cosmic Boy, Saturn Girl, and Lightning Lad—decided to travel back to the twentieth century and invite their inspiration to join the team. They first chose to appear in civilian guise, confusing Clark Kent as to how they knew his secret identity, and let Clark eventually figure out the truth. Once the Teen of Steel did so, the teens revealed their Legion uniforms and took him with them to visit the Legion Clubhouse in the thirtieth century. He was given full membership, and from that point onward Clark was a regular time-traveling participant in the Legion's adventures.

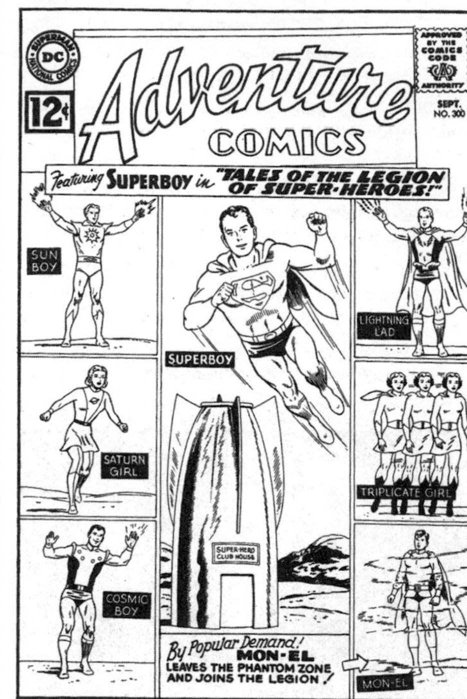

Other applicants to become Legionnaires wound up proving themselves worthy to join the team by performing various assignments in twentieth-century Smallville, home to Superboy. First was Star Boy who asked for his help stopping time-traveling criminals from his homeworld of Xanthu (*Adventure Comics* #282, March 1961), followed by Ultra Boy who had to discover Superboy's identity without using his powers (*Superboy* [first series] #98, July 1962). Along the way, Pete Ross was given an honorary team membership, and when Lana Lang became Insect Queen, she became a Legion reservist (*Adventure Comics* #355, April 1967). During Supergirl's time in Smallville, Jimmy Olsen also became a reservist whenever he used a serum that turned him into Elastic Lad (*Superman's Pal, Jimmy Olsen* #72, October 1963). The super-pets got into the act when Krypto, Comet, Streaky, and Beppo joined with Chameleon Boy's shape-shifting Proty to form the Legion of Super-Pets (*Adventure Comics* #293, February 1962).

The Legion's exploits were legendary in their own right, as they protected the United Planets from threats beyond their borders, such as the would-be conquerors the Khunds, the cosmic entity known as the Sun-Eater, and threats closer to home like Universo and the Fatal Five. Over

time their ranks swelled, even though they had a strict set of rules that set the active membership to twenty-five and disqualified dozens more applicants. Many formed a reserve team dubbed the Legion of Substitute Heroes. In time, the Legion formed an Academy where both reservists and substitutes could train under the tutelage of the team's adult adviser, Marla Latham.

The Legionnaires were frequent visitors to the twentieth century, coming to Superboy's or Supergirl's aid when needed. Four Legionnaires even sought refuge in Smallville by hiding as civilians when the sorcerer Mordru sought revenge for his imprisonment by the Legion (*Adventure Comics* #369–370, June–July 1968).

Before working up the nerve to ask Superboy to become a member, the Legion recruited his cousin Kara Zor-El to join them after she arrived on Earth as Supergirl (*Action Comics* #267, August 1960, and #276, May 1961). The cousins became fast friends, although Superboy continued to erase from his memory any knowledge about the future that could be used to alter Earth's time line. At one point, a kryptonite cloud surrounded Earth forcing Superboy and Supergirl to leave the team until Color Kid got rid of the deadly green cloud (*Adventure Comics* #350–351, November–December 1966).

The team at its peak could count among their membership: Cosmic Boy, Saturn Girl, Lightning Lad, Superboy, Chameleon Boy, Colossal Boy, Invisible Kid, Star Boy, Triplicate Girl/Duo Damsel, Phantom Girl, Supergirl, Brainiac 5, Sun Boy, Shrinking Violet, Bouncing Boy, Ultra Boy, Mon-El, Matter-Eater Lad, Element Lad, Lightning Lass/Light Lass, Dream Girl, Princess Projectra/Sensor, Ferro Lad, Karate Kid, Shadow Lass, Timber Wolf, Chemical King, Wildfire, Dawnstar, and Tyroc. Leadership rotated regularly, and Superboy once briefly served as the team's deputy leader.

Legion of the Super-Heroes

Years later, when Superboy became Superman, he visited his colleagues from the future and marveled that the Legion remained an active organization despite the fact that many of its members had either married or retired—or both. When needed, Superman joined them for a handful of adventures, usually by thwarting plots launched by the troublesome Legion of Super-Villains (*Adventure Comics* #354–355, March–April 1967).

Cosmic Man and Lightning-Man once traveled back in time to help Superman execute an elaborate plot in order to find the hiding place of the loot stolen by Duke Marple. The Legionnaires posed as Hercules and Samson as part of the plan (*Superman* [first series] #155, August 1962). Saturn Woman also paid a visit when she posed as the legendary Circe to aid the Metropolis Marvel against the Superman Revenge Squad (*Superman* [first series] #165, November 1963).

In the wake of the Crisis on Infinite Earths, the Time Trapper crafted a Pocket Universe from a sliver of the timestream and altered events so that a world resembling Earth-1 now existed. There, a Superboy continued to live and operate, and whenever the Legion traveled back in time, they were shunted into their Pocket Universe, unaware of the anomaly. When the Pocket Universe was finally discovered, there was an all-out battle with the Time Trapper that led to the Teen of Steel, who now knew he was never meant to exist, making the ultimate sacrifice. He gave his life to stop the Trapper's device from wiping out the real Earth (*Legion of Super-Heroes* [third series] #38, September 1987).

The Legion continued while mourning the loss of their comrade, and they had struggles to contend with in this new reality. Upon the conclusion of what they called the Magic Wars, the United Planets fell into a dark period, and five years later a re-formed Legion helped restore peace and freedom by defeating the evil Dominators (*Legion of Super-Heroes* [fourth series] #1–36, November 1989–Late November 1992). Later, the Legion encountered a different group of similar teens, initially thought to be a batch of clones although their code names and uniforms suggested the Earth-1 Legion. The two teams began to operate in parallel, and it was ultimately learned that they were from an alternate future, not genetic replicants (*Legion of Super-Heroes* [fourth series] #24–25, December 1991–January 1992; others).

Another cosmic upheaval known as Zero Hour resulted in the future being reordered once more (*Legion of Super-Heroes* [fourth series] #0, and *Legionnaires* #0—both October 1994). In this new reality, the team members had different names

(Lightning Lad became Live Wire, for example). The Legion's membership grew far more quickly and included many members who had not previously existed, including XS, Kinetix, and Gates.

Even shiny new beginnings had their dark corners, and the United Planets once more faced a collapse, which also resulted in a portion of the Legion becoming lost in a space rift that sent them to another galaxy (*Legion Lost* #1–12, May 2000–April 2001). When the team was finally reunited, they began a new era of adventuring that also included a brief stint by the clone of Superman, Conner Kent (*The Legion* #25, December 2003).

Another shift in reality led to the Legion members returning to their traditional names (*Legion of Super-Heroes* [fifth series] #1, February 2005). There were some subtle changes as well; Shrinking Violet became known primarily as Atom Girl, for instance. The team was formed as a response to the repressive society that thirty-first-century Earth had become. In addition to trying to loosen up Earth's populace, the Legionnaires wound up protecting the planet from a variety of threats. Their exploits earned them a following numbering in the thousands, all of whom considered themselves true Legionnaires.

When Supergirl unexpectedly arrived from the twenty-first century, she was welcomed and enjoyed many missions with the team before returning to her own time (*Supergirl and the Legion of Super-Heroes* #16, May 2006).

The original Earth-1 Star Boy, Dream Girl, Wildfire, Karate Kid, Timber Wolf, Sensor Girl, Dawnstar, and Brainiac 5 all appeared again in the twenty-first century, although visually they were different from what Superman and his fellow super heroes remembered (*Justice League of America* [second series] #8–10; *Justice Society of America* [third series] #5–6—both June–July 2007). Karate Kid, Star Boy, Dream Girl, Dawnstar, and Timber Wolf had all journeyed back in time, each carrying a miniature lightning rod, with the intention of saving Impulse, who was grandson to Barry Allen (the second Flash) and cousin to XS, a Legionnaire. Many of the travelers, however, became lost in time, their minds confused through the efforts of Justice League of America foe Doctor Destiny, who was manipulating Dream Girl. The JLA and Justice Society of America teamed up to rescue and collect the various scattered Legionnaires, including Wildfire, who had been encased within a statue kept in the Fortress of Solitude. The reunited Legionnaires summoned the lightning they needed to achieve their goal, knowing that one of them would die because the rods merely transferred their life force from one to their dead comrade. Karate Kid was nearly killed but managed to survive and captured Impulse's essence in his rod. The resulting tap of the Speed Force also released Wally West (the third Flash), his wife, and their children back into reality.

These Legionnaires shared an adventure with the Man of Steel when they were forced to ask for his help in defeating a rogue Justice League from turning Earth against Superman and the other Legionnaires. In their era of 3008, Earth's sun had shifted from yellow to red. Rejected Earth-born applicants formed the dangerous Justice League of Earth with the goal of ridding the planet of all alien influences. Their leader was Earth Man, who used a flawed understanding of Superman's origins to prove that the Man of Steel had derived his powers from "Mother Earth." Earth Man urged the planetary government to secede from the UP, and their efforts forced the alien-born Legionnaires to go into hiding. The fragmented Legion had no choice but to travel back to the twenty-first century and restore Superman's memories of the Legion so that the Man of Steel would travel to 3008 in order to help. The Man of Steel was horrified at how his history had been twisted out of shape, making him fight all the harder. Superman and the Legion even required the assistance of the Substitute Heroes to deal with the threat. With Superman's participation, Earth's sun was restored to its natural state and the UP's impending attack on Earth was aborted (*Action Comics* #858–863, October 2007–April 2008).

When the multiverse was restored in the wake of Infinite Crisis, it was revealed that distinctive versions of the Legion existed in several of the parallel Earths. Three of the teams banded together to stop a threat by Lex Luthor and the Time Trapper. The villains sent Superboy-Prime to the thirty-first century, where he immediately destroyed the Superman Museum in Smallville. Seeking to make an impact on Earth's history, the crazed Superboy-Prime went to the prison world of Takron-Galtos to free the Legion of Super-Villains, destroying the planet in the process. Superman was asked to return to the Legion's time period to help them deal with all the powerful criminals now running amok. Brainiac 5 eventually determined that Superboy-Prime hailed from another reality, which inspired the idea of summoning help from the Legions of two of the other parallel Earths to help. Despite all the atrocities Superboy-Prime had committed prior to this, Superman still believed the damaged youth could be redeemed, a sentiment not shared by others.

Superboy-Prime also recruited villains from throughout the Legion's career to form the ultimate team of super-villains, which included the deadly sorcerer Mordru. The era's last Green Lantern, Rond Vidar, was killed by Superboy-Prime, but not before providing an escape route for some of the Legionnaires. The last Green Lantern's death, and an impassioned plea from Mon-El, prompted Sodom Yat, the final Guardian of the Universe, to enter the fray. Many Legionnaires from the three realities were injured or killed, but the imprisoned Impulse was finally freed and came to the aid of the heroes.

As the battle continued, Brainiac 5 and his counterparts activated the final part of their plan, which led them to the Arctic Fortress of Solitude and a Kryptonian healing chrysalis containing the healing body of Superboy. His injuries at the hands of Superboy-Prime had required a millennium to repair themselves, but now he was ready to confront his attacker. He was thwarted, though, because Superboy-Prime had traveled to the end of time, taking the Legion founders and Superman with him. There he revealed himself as the Time Trapper, although an aged version of himself who had become a cosmic anomaly after being tossed into the multiverse by the Guardians of the Universe. Being at the nexus point of the fifty-two multiverses allowed the Legionnaires to summon multiple incarnations of the team to help them defeat the Trapper once and for all.

Returning to the thirty-first century with the unconscious Trapper, Superboy-Prime was forced to confront his younger, still-angry incarnation. Disliking what he was destined to become, Superboy-Prime punched the Time Trapper, a blow that eradicated them both from reality, resetting reality once more. In the aftermath, the Legion team, who had seen their world erased by the Infinite Crisis, decided they would travel the multiverse as the new Wanderers, seeking other survivors. The third Legion team was discovered to have come from Superboy-Prime's no-longer-extant universe and made the thirty-first century their new home. Superman returned to the twenty-first century, Superboy and Impulse with him. Superboy-Prime remained a part of the new reality, reborn on Earth-Prime, his parents and girlfriend still alive although they were horrified at what he had done—facts he gleaned by reading the comic books that recounted his exploits. Residing in his parents' basement, Superboy-Prime was determined to find a way back to New Earth and exact revenge (*Final Crisis: Legion of 3 Worlds* #1–5, August 2008–September 2009).

When Mon-El adventured in the twenty-first century and worked with the Metropolis Science Police, he eventually learned that many of his colleagues were actually Legionnaires in disguise. The Espionage Squad included Quislet, Matter-Eater Lad, Chameleon Boy, and Sensor Girl (*Superman* #694, January 2010). Shortly thereafter, Connor Kent learned that his science teacher at Smallville High, Mr. Janson, was actually Element Lad. Brainiac 5 had tasked the Legionnaires to travel back in time to prevent Brainiac from killing Superman, or their future would be eradicated. Superboy rallied the Legionnaires to help him recover as many of the captured and bottled cities Brainiac possessed as possible. Superboy, Chameleon Boy, Matter-Eater Lad, and Element Lad managed to breach Brainiac's defenses and board his vessel. They recovered a significant handful of the bottled cities, eventually finding new worlds on which they could flourish; worlds that would eventually give birth to the United Planets and the Legion (*Adventure Comics* #510–513, April–June 2010). Meantime, the Legionnaires also helped see to it that the Man of Steel did not die at Brainiac's hands, defeating the evil Coluan criminal once more (*Superman: Last Stand of New Krypton* #1–3, May–June 2010).

The Earth-1 Legion seemed to be replicated in Earth-22's future (*Kingdom Come* #1, May 1996), while New Earth's far future depicted a Legion modeled more after King Arthur's Knights of the Round Table than the twentieth century's super heroes (*Legionnaires Annual* #1, 1994). A different potential future revealed an alternate fate for the Round Table Legionnaires (*Legion of Super-Heroes* [fourth series] *Annual* #7, 1996). In the potential 853rd century, there existed twenty-six teams using the Legion name, with Justice Legion L being the group clearly descended from the first Legion team (*Legion of Super-Heroes* #1,000,000; *Legionnaires* #1,000,000—both November 1998).

In an unidentified universe, Superboy never grew up to become Superman because the rocket ship from Krypton became lodged in that solar system's asteroid belt. A millennium after Krypton's destruction, R. J. Brande found baby Kal-El in the year 2987 and awakened him. Kal Brande grew up the wealthy planet builder's ward and learned to use his powers and abilities as Superboy. Then, when he was fourteen, he formed the Legion with Cosmic Boy and Saturn Girl (*Superboy's Legion* #1–2, April–May 2001).

In another unidentified reality, the Legion of Super-Villains (Lightning Lord, Cosmic King, and Saturn Queen) traveled back to the twenty-first century in an effort to rewrite the time line. Beauty Blaze and Echo also joined the plan, but all were soundly defeated by Superman and Batman. After they were apprehended, the villains were taken to their normal era by Brainiac 5, Dream Woman, Cosmic Man, Chameleon Man, Matter-Eater Man, Lightning-Man, and Saturn Woman—members of the adult Legion (*Superman/Batman* #14–18, January–April 2005).

LEGION OF SUPER-PETS, THE

The various superpowered animals from Clark Kent's era were asked to come to Superboy's aid when he was defeated by his fellow members of the Legion of Super-Heroes: Cosmic Boy, Lightning Lad, and Saturn Girl. They were being manipulated by the would-be alien conquerors from Rambat known as the Brain-Globes. Given his Kryptonian physiology, they could not manipulate Superboy on their own, so they summoned the Legionnaires to do their dirty work in order to pave the way for an invasion.

Once their mission was accomplished, the Brain-Globes released the Legionnaires from their mental thrall, but they did not return them to the thirtieth century. As a result, the Legionnaires realized the aliens could not control animal life, so the Legion sought help from Superboy's dog, Krypto. They then traveled a few years ahead in time to recruit Supergirl's cat Streaky, Beppo the Super-Monkey, and Comet the Super-Horse. They managed to turn back the Rambatans' threat and were dubbed the Legion of Super-Pets for their efforts (*Adventure Comics* #293, February 1962).

The team of animals was brought to the thirtieth century on several occasions, adding Chameleon Boy's shape-shifting pet Proty (*Adventure Comics* #322, July 1964) and successor Proty II to its ranks (*Adventure Comics* #343, April 1966).

LEGION OF SUPER-VILLAINS, THE

A villain called Tarik the Mute earned his name after a battle against the thirtieth century's Science Police cost him the use of his vocal cords. He decided to gain revenge against the police by training criminals. Tarik blackmailed the Legion of Super-Heroes' Colossal Boy into becoming a teacher as well, and the Legion of Super-Villains was born (first seen in *Superman* [first series] #147, August 1961; as teens in *Adventure Comics* #372, September 1968). The first incarnation of the Legion of Super-Villains included Lightning Lord, Nemesis Kid, Spider Girl, Ronn Kar, and Radiation Roy.

As long as there was a Legion of heroes, there remained a Legion of villains, with subsequent incarnations formed by the Sun Emperor (*Superboy* [first series] #208, April 1975) and then the traitorous Nemesis Kid (*Legion of Super-Heroes* [third series] #1–5, August–December 1984).

In time, however, the United Planets were conquered by the Dominators, and there was little use for a band of villains *or* of heroes. Over the years, Echo and Spider Girl switched sides and became Legionnaires (*Legion of Super-Heroes* [fourth series] #28, April 1992, and #50, Late November 1993). The vile Saturn Queen wound up marrying Matter-Eater Lad, rising to become queen of Titan (*Legion of Super-Heroes* [fourth series] #49–50, Early–Late November 1993). Radiation Roy could not escape his fate: He was taken by the Dominators and turned into a solider (*Legion of Super-Heroes* [fourth series] #27, March 1992).

Hailing from two potential futures, two adult variations on Lightning Lord and the Legion of Super-Villains periodically menaced the Earth-1 time lines of both Superman and the Legion. There is no evidence to support the idea that these were truly counterparts of the teen villains; they may have merely been pretenders who assumed their names.

The first of these parallel Legions of Super-Villains consisted of Cosmic King, Saturn Queen, and Lightning Lord, who was revealed to be the older brother of Legionnaires Light Lass and Lightning Lad. They then traveled to the twentieth century and partnered with Lex Luthor in a failed attempt to destroy Superman (*Superman* [first series] #147, August 1961). Later, Superman would face these rogues in the thirtieth century alongside the adult Legion of Super-Heroes (*Adventure Comics* #354–355, March–April 1967), and it's speculated that they continued to travel to other parallel worlds and time lines in order to torment Superman and his extended family (*Action Comics* #583, September 1986; *Superman/Batman* #14–18, January–April 2005).

Another incarnation of the LSV was defeated through the combined efforts of Supergirl and Jimmy Olsen (*Superman's Pal, Jimmy Olsen* #63, September 1962). Another attack, aided by Lex Luthor and Brainiac, started by brainwashing Jimmy into becoming Superman's killer, but that, too, failed thanks to the Action Ace's quick thinking (*Superman's Pal, Jimmy Olsen* #87, September 1965). It was this version of the Legion of Super-Villains that worked with the wicked Dynamo Boy when he had the Legion of Super-Heroes outlawed (*Adventure Comics* #331, April 1965).

After reality was altered by the Crisis on Infinite Earths, the super-villains tried to alter the timestream by traveling to the twenty-first century and changing the events that led to Clark Kent and Bruce Wayne becoming Superman and Batman. The adult villains adopted the boys and trained them to become conquering dictators, abusing their abilities for the subjugation of humankind. Their heroic personalities, however, proved stronger than the villains' evil influence, and the World's Finest partners eventually defeated their enemies. When Lightning Lord, Cosmic King, and Saturn Queen were apprehended, they were returned to their normal era by Brainiac 5, Dream Woman, Cosmic Man, Chameleon Man, Matter-Eater Man, Lightning-Man, and Saturn Woman, all members of the adult Legion (*Superman/Batman* #14–18, January–April 2005).

The younger incarnation of the Legion of Super-Villains appeared not to have withstood the alterations wrought by the Infinite Crisis. In 3008, Spider Girl and Radiation Roy, both of whom had been rejected by the Legion, joined the Justice League of Earth, which was determined to rid the planet of all its alien citizens. Spider Girl, no longer a married woman, romanced the JLE's Earth Man. Earth's sun had shifted from yellow to red, and Earth Man used an erroneous interpretation of Superman's origin story to convince the populace that the Man of Steel had derived his powers from "Mother Earth." He urged the planetary government to secede from the UP, and their efforts forced the alien-born Legionnaires to go into hiding, leading them to bring the real Superman from the twenty-first century to the thirty-first to help. With his participation, the sun was restored to its natural state and the UP's impending attack on Earth was aborted. The JLE's members were then apprehended and sent to the prison world of Takron-Galtos (*Action Comics* #858–863, October 2007–April 2008).

The villains were subsequently freed by Superboy-Prime, who recruited them and several other villains to take down the Legion of Super-Heroes once and for all (*Final Crisis: Legion of 3 Worlds* #1–5, October 2008–September 2009). Members of the Legion at this point included Lightning Lord, Saturn Queen, Cosmic King, Sun Emperor, Beauty Blaze, Ol-Vir, Tyr, Zymr, Hunter II, and Chameleon Chief, as well as Black Mace, Universo, Doctor Regulus, Grimbor the Chainsman, Mordru, Esper Lass, Magno Lad, Micro Lad, Echo, Terrus, Silver Slasher, Lazon, Neutrax, Mist Master, Titania, Tharok, Emerald Empress, the Persuader, Mano, Validus, Radiation Roy, Tusker, Spider Girl, Golden Boy, Storm Boy, and Earth Man.

LEMAIS, LONA

When Jimmy Olsen made one of his periodic visits to the bottle city of Kandor, he traveled there on a rocket plane. Serving him as a flight attendant was Lona Lemais, who bore a striking resemblance to Jimmy's love Lucy Lane. While he was infatuated, Jimmy was deflated to learn that Lona was already married (*Superman's Pal, Jimmy Olsen* #53, June 1961). Lona was probably the member of the Superman Lookalike Squad who doubled for Lucy from time to time (*Superman's Pal, Jimmy Olsen* #83, March 1965).

LEMARIS, LENORA

The younger sister of the former Atlantean girlfriend of Superman, Lori Lemaris (*Action Comics* #284, January 1962).

LEMARIS, LORI

Lori Lemaris, a resident of Atlantis, hid her fish tail under a blanket and used a wheelchair when she

came on land. She attended classes at Metropolis University, where she met a young Clark Kent. The two struck up a friendship that rapidly evolved into a romance, although Clark was baffled as to why Lori had to vanish by eight o'clock each night. Trusting her with his love, Clark proposed marriage to Lori. She turned down the offer, explaining that she needed to permanently return to her home country. Heartbroken, Clark let Lori go but secretly followed her using his super-senses, discovering that his ex-girlfriend was actually a mermaid. When they confronted each other, Lori admitted that she hailed from Atlantis, and that once every century an Atlantean was sent to the surface to keep tabs on humanity. She already knew Clark's secret thanks to her telepathic ability. They pledged to keep each other's secret. With that, Lori kissed Clark good-bye, leapt into the water, and returned home (*Superman* [first series] #129, May 1959).

The daughter of Britt and Omra Lemaris (*Adventure Comics* #280, January 1961) and the sister of Ina (*Superman's Girl Friend, Lois Lane* #72, February 1967) and Lenora (*Action Comics* #284, January 1962), Lori was also a descendant of Nar Lemaris, a scientist who'd helped humans evolve into mer-people when the continent sank many millennia previously (*Superman* [first series] #154, July 1962). Their telepathic skills were also evolved, enabling them to communicate under water. While no limits to their skills were ever revealed, in times of distress, Lori, in Atlantis, managed to alert Superman of danger while he was still hundreds of miles away in Metropolis. Her skills also enabled her to occasionally pick up thoughts from those trapped in the Phantom Zone. Atlanteans had to remain immersed in salt water for ten hours at a stretch, but they could then operate on land for brief durations.

Years after they parted, Lori was reunited with Superman—only to be left paralyzed by a stabbing. Her life was saved through the efforts of an extraterrestrial merman named Ronal, whom she fell in love with and married (*Superman* [first series] #135, February 1960). The couple later became the parents of twins (*Superman's Girl Friend, Lois Lane* #55, February 1965). The chronicles of Earth-1 are unclear as to whether or not Lori was Atlantean royalty or merely a citizen. Regardless, she was an exemplary citizen. Time and again, the Atlanteans came to Superman's aid in times of great need and when they thought he needed a friend. On more than one occasion, Lori

tried to play Cupid, concocting ways to bring the Man of Steel and Lois Lane together, only to see things usually end poorly (*Superman* [first series] #138, July 1960; others).

When Supergirl was revealed to the public, Lori had a statue in her honor placed within Atlantis (*Action Comics* #285, February 1962).

It was later learned that Lori's city of Atlantis was different from Aquaman's (*Superman* [first series] #175, February 1965), and there was at least one recorded clash between the undersea kingdoms, albeit instigated by the villainous Ocean Master (*DC Comics Presents* #5, January 1979). During the climactic battle of the Crisis on Infinite Earths, Lori was killed by anti-matter Shadow Demons while saving the life of Aquaman's wife Mera (*Crisis on Infinite Earths* #12, January 1986).

In the aftermath of the Crisis, when the fabled continent of Atlantis sank, two cities survived, and through sorcery found different ways to survive. One city, Tritonis, transformed its citizens into telepathic water-breathing mer-people, and they thrived for millennia (*The Atlantis Chronicles* #1–4, March–June 1990). The people knew little of what was happening on the surface world, and for a time they were content with their ignorance. Eventually they decided to obtain current intelligence on what land people were like and dispatched one of their own to find out.

Lori and Clark Kent's meeting was much the same, although at that point Clark had not yet adopted a costumed identity, so Lori knew only that he was not from Earth (*Superman* [second series] #12, December 1987). She explained that she was also seeking other cities that may have survived the destruction of her continent. She finally found Poseidonis, home to Aquaman, through the Man of Steel's intervention. As in earlier lore, Superman's Lori died during the Crisis.

Reports of Lori's death proved to be a ploy on her part to dissuade Superman from his doomed love for her (*Superman* [second series] #63, January 1992). Only years later did the Man of Steel learn of Lori's survival (*The Adventures of Superman* #532, February 1996). Lori was later magically altered to resemble a woman when dry and a mermaid when damp, and she decided to visit Metropolis. In her human form she hovered an inch or so above the ground, something few civilians noticed. She briefly stayed with Lois Lane, despite the feelings of jealousy it aroused in both women (*Action Comics* #719, March 1996).

Lori seemingly lost her life yet again during the events of Infinite Crisis, when the Wrath of God—the Spectre—destroyed all the cities that made up Atlantis (*Infinite Crisis* #3, February 2006). She turned out to have survived and was helping rebuild her home. She has not been heard from since.

On Earth-162, Superman was once split into two beings, Superman Red and Superman Blue. The twin heroes provided an aquatic planet as a new home for Lori Lemaris and her fellow Atlanteans (*Superman* [first series] #162, July 1963). The reality of Earth-51 saw Superman finally find bliss by marrying Lori . . . only to watch her die as had Lois Lane and Lana Lang, his previous two brides. When he found a cure for their disease, there was just enough left to save one woman, and Superman was unable to decide which (*Superman's Girl Friend, Lois Lane* #51, August 1964).

On the parallel world of Earth-9, Lori Lemaris was one of the three women to adventure under the guise of the Joker. When one of her partners was killed in action, Lori declined donning the outfit again and took up the heroic role of the Manhunter (*Tangent Comics/The Joker* #1, December 1997).

LEOCADIO-ESCUDERO, LIEUTENANT LUPÉ TERESA

Growing up in Spain, Lupé Leocadio-Escudero lost her parents in a terrorist bombing. She and her brother were wounded, and the incident was a life-changing event in many ways. It firmly put Lupe on the path to becoming a law enforcement professional.

She was a decorated member of the Metropolis police when she was hired as the newest leader of the Metropolis Special Crimes Unit. Upon arrival in Metropolis, she immediately swung into action, assisting the S.C.U. in stopping an attack from the Masters of Disaster. The dark-haired lieutenant proved outspoken and aggressive in her dealings with her subordinates, politicians, criminals, the media—and even the Man of Steel.

Despite finding Superman incredibly attractive, she often tried to put him in his place, insisting that the S.C.U. was Metropolis's first line of defense, and that she would let the Man of Steel know if and when he was needed (*The Adventures of Superman* #625, April 2004).

Lupé was close with Daniel Leone, and the two were lovers before he turned to the priesthood. A woman of deep faith, Lupé often sought his guidance, especially when she nearly went insane in her hunt for Ruin after the villain killed several of her best officers (*The Adventures of Superman* #635, February 2005). She has since left Metropolis.

LEONE, FATHER DANIEL

Daniel Leone grew up in Metropolis and was uncertain as to what to do with his life. Among his

best friends was Lupé Teresa Leocadio-Escudero, who had immigrated from Spain. The friendship became romantic before it eventually burned itself out. Some time later, Leone turned to the priesthood, and upon ordination was assigned as pastor to the Sacred Heart Church in Metropolis. From the pulpit and on the street, Father Daniel was an upstanding civic leader, which drew the Man of Steel to seek his counsel on several occasions. When one million of Earth's citizens, including his wife Lois Lane, vanished without a trace, Superman relied even more heavily on the priest for emotional and existential support (*Superman* [second series] #204, June 2004).

Their discussions over the meaning of life and their role in the world became confessional on both sides when Father Daniel revealed to Superman that he had cancer. He was later cured by the mysterious Mr. Orr, who used a serum derived from the experiments performed at Project M, the organization Orr worked for. The serum turned Leone into a monstrous being called Pilate. Superman arrived to confront the beast, and Father Daniel begged to be killed rather than allowed to hurt others. Another creature named Equus attacked at that moment, and Pilate fought him off in an effort to protect the Last Son of Krypton. Their battle led them to a distant island for an undocumented conclusion (*Superman* [second series] #215, May 2005). Neither Leone nor Pilate has been heard from since.

LEOPARD, THE

Hiding under a leopard's mask, this mysterious criminal led a small gang that committed crimes while using these spotted cats to threaten Metropolis's citizens and distract the police. Superman, accompanied by Herman "the Heroic" Hoskins—an avowed Superman fan—arrived to handle the panic. Despite wearing a goofy imitation of the Man of Steel's uniform, Hoskins proved his bravery in helping take down the Leopard, who was

revealed to be Sam Kennedy, a publicist for the traveling Cosmos Circus (*Superman* [first series] #20, January–February 1943).

LERROL, LYLA

Filmed entertainment was not unknown on Krypton in the years before the planet exploded, and among its greatest celebrities was Lyla Lerrol. Considered "Krypton's most famous emotion-movie actress" and most glamorous beauty, she wound up having a memorable romance with the Earth-1 Superman when he traveled back in time to visit his homeworld (*Superman* [first series] #141, November 1960).

Superman's trip was accidental, but he made the most of it by arriving on the very day his father Jor-El married Lara Lor-Van. Keeping his real identity secret, he befriended the newlyweds and worked in Jor-El's lab, keeping the knowledge of Krypton's fate to himself. Kal-El also wrestled with the problem of how he could return to his own time before Krypton exploded.

While struggling with this dilemma, Superman met the gorgeous blond starlet Lyla. They quickly developed a passionate romance, and one night she told him, "I'm glad that despite all the untold billions of worlds in the vast infinity of outer space, we two somehow found each other."

ASTONISHINGLY, EVERY GIRL WHO EVER MEANT ANYTHING TO ME HAS ALWAYS HAD THOSE INITIALS! I...CAN'T TEAR MY EYES AWAY FROM HER!

Eventually Jor-El reached the conclusion that Krypton was doomed, and Superman tried to help prevent the disaster despite realizing the complicated consequences of his actions. When it was clear there was little time to help save the populace, Superman chose to end his life at Lyla's side. He accompanied her to the set of her final film and happened to be sitting in a model rocket when he was accidentally catapulted into space. As he drifted farther from Krypton and its sun's radiation, he regained his superpowers, allowing him to pierce the time barrier and return home to Earth. When he was back in his own era, he realized his love with Lyla was never meant to be, but he would never forget her.

During two separate incidents, Superman thought he was near death and thoughts of Lyla's love filled his mind to bring him some measure of comfort (*Superman* [first series] #156–157, October–November 1962). When Superman found the artificial Krypton II and thought the planet and its occupants were real, he came upon the android designed to resemble Lyla, and his emotions got the better of him. She did not recognize Superman and rejected him, declaring she was engaged to her director Zik-Tul. Superman accidentally set off booby traps that were part of the planet's design—it was a decoy to thwart a planned alien invasion—and only he and Lyla remained alive. Distraught, she sought his love. Their romance was rekindled as they traveled the dead world and took in the extant sights. During their exploration, he found one of the aliens' undamaged spacecraft, which provided them with a chance to escape. Before she could board the craft, however, more explosions rocked the area. Lyla died, but not before she handed over a projector that contained recordings left behind by Jor-El explaining what he and his team had built. With tears in his eyes, Superman left the planet, having now lost Lyla twice (*Superman* [first series] #189, August 1966).

During a time-travel mission to Krypton years later, members of the Justice League of America actually met Lyla Lerrol on the very hour of the planet's destruction and revealed to her the truth and subsequent fate of her beloved Kal-El (*Super Friends* #17, February 1979).

Years later, when the Black Mercy plant caused Superman to hallucinate, he imagined that he finally managed to marry Lyla Lerrol and live happily on Krypton (*Superman Annual* #11, 1985).

LESLA-LAR

In the bottle city of Kandor lived a scientist named Lesla-Lar, who bore an uncanny resemblance to Kara Zor-El. She was jealous of her look-alike's freedom and powers on Earth as Supergirl and devised a weapon that robbed the Maid of Steel of all her powers (*Action Comics* #279, August 1961). Now powerless, Supergirl decided to remain Linda Lee on a full-time basis, leading to her adoption by Fred and Edna Danvers. Lesla-Lar then used her invention to swap places with Linda, and her new superpowers made it easy for her to masquerade as Supergirl. She approached Lex Luthor about laying a trap for Superman, but super-dog Krypto realized Lesla-Lar was an impostor and exposed the Kandorian. She was returned to the bottle city, where her equipment was destroyed and she was imprisoned. Linda then regained her powers thanks to an invention of Mr. Mxyzptlk (*Action Comics* #282, November 1961).

FIRST, I STOLE YOUR SUPER-POWERS, LINDA! AND NOW MY BRAIN-WASH HELMET IS CONVINCING YOU THAT YOU ARE ME, LESLA-LAR OF KANDOR!... SHORTLY, I'LL TAKE YOUR PLACE ON EARTH AND STEAL YOUR SECRET IDENTITY OF SUPERGIRL!
YOU WILL FORGET EVER HAVING BEEN SUPERGIRL!.. YOU WILL FORGET EVER HAVING VISITED EARTH!... YOU ARE NOW LESLA-LAR OF KANDOR!

Soon after, Lesla-Lar regained her freedom and rebuilt her machine, this time swapping places with Luthor's sister Lena Thorul, who also happened to resemble Supergirl. She then released three criminals from the Phantom Zone and used them to uncover a cache of forbidden Kryptonian weapons. Kru-El betrayed her and used one of them on her, and it disintegrated her body (*Action Comics* #297, February 1963). Her corporeal form may have been destroyed, but her spirit remained strong, and years later she influenced a variety of attacks on Supergirl (*Superman Family* #186–189, November–December 1977, and #191–195, May–June 1979), culminating in yet another attempt to take over Supergirl's body (*Superman Family* #206, March–April 1981).

LEXCORP

Toward the end of Earth-1's existence, a future Superman gave a rare interview to the media and referred to his friend Lex Luthor and his LexCorp Holocaster as the "best hologram filming system . . . I've seen in the universe!" (*Superman* [first series] #416, February 1986). LexCorp, also said to manufacture air cruisers, was likely an outgrowth of Luthor's Thunder Corporation, a conglomerate he made certain no one ever connected him with (*Superman: Last Son of Krypton,* 1978). When the Crisis on Infinite Earths began, no such company had been created.

LexCorp was a multinational conglomerate owned and operated by Lex Luthor, who used his scientific and business acumen to create and patent technologies that made the company a giant in a variety of fields. The firm grew rapidly and used the Lex name as a brand, turning its founder into one of the best-known businessmen on the planet (*Man of Steel* #2, Late October 1986).

Luthor's first major accomplishment was in the field of aerospace, but he eventually branched out into all of the sciences and major media. As a result, LexCorp gobbled up smaller competitors, allowing Luthor to shelter programs and shift funds, avoiding suspicion that he had several different programs at work, all of which were dedicated to finding ways of ridding Earth of Superman.

Lex's company had humble beginnings. He leased the top floor of Metropolis's Daily Planet Building and then made his first acquisitions—Inter-Continental Airlines and Atlantic Coast Air Systems—merging them into LexAir. During a brief energy crisis, Luthor cannily scooped up Southwestern Petroleum and renamed it LexOil. In short order, his brand name began to be recognized.

With the profits, Lex branched into media and briefly owned the *Planet* itself, but sold the paper and the office building to TransNational Enterprise. He did retain a television station and satellite transmission company he acquired during this period, and cable operators around America were soon carrying LexCom's superstation WLEX.

LexCorp also moved into banking, taking controlling interest in Metropolis Mercantile Bank, Commerce Bank of Metropolis, and First Metro Security, providing Luthor with several new outlets with which to funnel profits into new ventures, both public and covert.

Seeking to make a bold statement, the tall red-haired magnate bought up real estate in the New Troy borough of Metropolis with the intention of constructing a corporate tower that would become a bold monument to the company—and himself. Soon after Superman debuted in the skies over Metropolis, the ninety-six-story L-shaped LexTower was completed and opened. By this time, Wall Street analysts estimated that the company employed about two-thirds of Metropolis's eleven million inhabitants. Luthor's holdings included Advanced Research Laboratories, Secur-Corp Armored Car Service, North American Robotics, Hell's Gate Disposal Services, and the Good Foods Group, owners of Ralli's Family Restaurants and the Koul-Brau Breweries.

The conglomerate built branches throughout the Northeast and then across the continent with offices in Los Angeles, Denver, Houston, New Orleans, Chicago, Gotham City, and Boston.

Internationally, LexCorp had holdings or investments in businesses located in Australia, Venezuela, Argentina, Brazil, Germany, Switzerland, France, the Union of South Africa, Saudi Arabia, Japan, Singapore, and the free market of Hong Kong. The company even had a secret lunar research base (*Superman* #671, February 2008).

LexCorp tried to dominate every field it entered, but it was not without rivals, including Wayne Enterprises, Galaxy Broadcasting, and Ferris Aircraft. The rivalry between LexCorp and Wayne Enterprises eventually grew personal between Lex Luthor and Bruce Wayne (*Batman Confidential* #1–6, February–August 2007). Years later, after Gotham City had become a no-man's-land and was excluded from federal authority, Luthor saw a chance at one-upping Wayne in his own hometown.

He dispatched Mercy Graves to Gotham, and she offered to make an alliance with the Penguin. At much the same time, Bane destroyed most of Gotham City's Hall of Records (*Detective Comics* #738, November 1999). Luthor had begun lobbying Congress in the hope of gaining contracts for Gotham City's reconstruction. What few knew was that Luthor had already begun illegally placing matériel in the city, which was further protected by Bane. Luthor was also the one who had ordered Bane to destroy the city's public records so that he could buy up Gotham property on the cheap (*Batman* #573, January 2000).

It all came to an unhappy ending when Luthor's occasional ally, the Joker, reemerged and killed many of LexCorp's construction workers before once again disappearing from sight (*Batman: Shadow of the Bat* #94, February 2000). Wayne also outmaneuvered Luthor for the construction contracts, leading Lex to hire a mercenary named David Cain to frame Wayne for murder (*Batman* #605, September 2002).

The company had employed just three CEOs by the time of the Final Crisis: Lex Luthor, Talia Head, and Lana Lang. When Talia was in charge, she sold off many assets to rivals and made sizable charitable donations to the Wayne Foun-

dation (*Superman* #650, May 2006). Luthor returned to a stripped-down company and faced charges stemming from his various criminal activities—only to be acquitted and subsequently fired by the board of directors. Lang was surprised to be offered the role of CEO (*Superman* #654, September 2006). She tried to rebuild both the company's damaged ledger and its tarnished public image. However, when she sent in Team Luthor to aid Superman during the Man of Steel's battle with Atlas, she was in violation of her employment contract and was terminated immediately (*Superman* #679, October 2008).

As a reward for serving General Samuel Lane and his Project 7734, Lex Luthor was not only pardoned but gained control of LexCorp once more (*Superman: Last Stand of New Krypton* #3, June 2010).

LEXOR

Deep in space, orbiting the red star designated X-156-99F, was a planet containing a great culture of humanoids. They thrived, cherishing science and technology—until their inventions outstripped their wisdom and wars broke out, devastating their society. The land became arid, and the people turned to barbarism to survive. Only much later did they discover that geological marvels in the form of rainbow-hued crystals refracted light in such a way as to illuminate every home on the planet—but with deadly effects. The jewels also vibrated at a subtle rate of speed that went undetected, and over the years degraded the inhabitants' cerebral functioning. After centuries of constant exposure, the people lost the ability to function at anything above a Stone Age level of reasoning (*Superman* [first series] #168, April 1964). Many of the original machines survived the cataclysm and were eventually gathered by the people, placed within the halls of a museum, and left to rot.

The planet suffered a shortage of drinking water and arable land, but flora and fauna survived and adapted to their new environment. One species of beast had hollow horns where water could be stored whenever it was found, for example. Other life-forms included a creature with psionic abilities that compelled the humanoids living there to tell the truth, and a colossal jellyfish-like being known as the Living Lake that would consume any person or animal that dared try to swim in it. The skies were filled by monstrous birds known as dorulgs, which preyed on the world's meager crops. At least one species of flower emitted a scent that would temporarily drive people insane.

The planet was denser than Earth, with a higher degree of gravity that required visitors to wear compensatory gear, such as the "gravity boots" used by Lex Luthor and Superman when they first arrived on the world. Given the red sun the planet orbited, Superman was reduced there to human norms, making him and Luthor physical equals (*Superman* [first series] #164, October 1963).

The planet was discovered after Luthor once again escaped imprisonment. He challenged Superman to fight him without superpowers. Superman agreed and placed his archenemy into a spacecraft headed far from home. Arriving on the nameless world, the two adjusted to the heavier gravity and had their first battle as equals, with no clear winner emerging.

Before the next bout began, Luthor discovered a group of natives and befriended them. Using one of the ancient machines to learn the local language in just a few hours, Luthor then convinced the people that Superman was evil. All they wanted was peace and water, something Luthor promised them before realizing how dry the world truly was. By this time, Superman had found his foe and they battled a second time, although Luthor let the Man of Steel win. En route back to Earth, Luthor asked Superman to help provide the natives with water. Away from the planet's red radiation, Superman's powers returned, and he used them to send water-laced asteroids to the planet. As the galactic ice melted, the people were delighted that Luthor had kept his word, and thereafter named the planet Lexor in his honor.

Not long after, Luthor again escaped custody and used a rocket to return to the world, where the people regaled him as a hero. Once again using one of the old machines, Luthor temporarily gained superpowers, donned a distinctive red-and-purple costume, and became the Defender. During a lull in their struggles, Superman learned the truth about the planet's rainbow crystals, and Luthor allowed the Man of Steel to leave in order to help destroy the minerals and let the natives begin to regain their mental faculties.

Luthor repeatedly returned to Lexor, genuinely enjoying the people and watching them reclaim their world. His ego also appreciated the manner in which he was treated—gifts included a fine home in the capital city, a full refurbished lab, and even a Luthor Museum. During his third visit to the world, he met and married the attractive Ardora (*Action Comics* #318–319, November–December 1964). Superman followed Luthor, intending to bring him back to prison, but Lex resisted. The two battled, and at one point Luthor fell, struck his head, and appeared dead. The mob wanted to kill Superman, but Ardora insisted he be granted a fair trial. When no one volunteered to defend him, a man named Vel Quennar was appointed. As a result, the Man of Steel was arrested for murder, and it was only during his trial that Luthor appeared and explained that he had taken a "coma drug" to appear dead. Superman was acquitted, but he remained a detested public figure on the planet.

When Luthor escaped custody yet again, Superman used a teleportation device that allowed him to travel to Lexor for five minutes. There he confronted Ardora, who informed Superman that her husband was not present. But the Man of Steel's arrival prompted her to investigate Luthor's hidden records, and she learned that her spouse was a criminal. Superman's suspicions were accurate, but his arrival was premature, so when Luthor actually arrived, an angry Ardora awaited him. Furious at his deception being revealed, Luthor returned to Earth and decided to ruin Superman's life in much the same way. Thus began a game of psychological warfare as Luthor saved Superman from other villains in order to destroy the Man of Steel himself. In time, Superman came to believe Luthor had actually reformed, but by then public sentiment had turned against the Man of Steel (*Action Comics* #332–333, January–February 1966).

Luthor then masqueraded as a military scientist who gave Superman a series of performance tests; when he failed the judgment test, he was devastated. When Luthor and Brainiac met to celebrate their foe's retirement, Superman arrived to spoil their fun. He had learned of the plot and played along to lure the villains out into the open. Luthor escaped in Brainiac's saucer, which headed straight for Lexor.

When Luthor reunited with his wife, she appeared to have no memory of his criminal past. Superman explained that he had arranged it, seeing no reason why Ardora should hate her husband. Luthor called off the warfare, moved by Superman's act of compassion (*Action Comics* #335, April 1966). A dying Superman later witnessed—via his X-ray vision—the people of Lexor rejecting Luthor after learning of his true evil (*Action Comics* #365, July 1968). Because Lexor had a red sun, however, Superman didn't have the power to see anything; he'd actually experienced an illness-derived hallucination (*The Best of DC* #27, August 1982).

Returning to Lexor after an absence of a few years, Luthor was elated to learn that Ardora had given birth to a son, Alexander Luthor Junior. His conflict with Superman resumed soon after, and the battle spilled onto Lexor's soil. Wearing new green-and-purple battle armor, Luthor fired an energy blast that bounced off the Kryptonian's body, and the errant energy destroyed Lex's creation, the Neutrarod, which kept the planet's seismic tremors to a minimum. Without this, Lexor was subject to violent planetquakes expected to shatter it in the near future. Luthor accepted the blame for the fight, but it reinforced his enmity for the Man of Steel (*Action Comics* #544, June 1983).

On the parallel world of Earth-216, Lexor lived on long enough for Luthor's teenage daughter Ardora II to meet the sons of Superman and Batman (*World's Finest Comics* #238, June 1976). In the realities after the various Crisis events, the chronicles have made no mention of Lexor.

LIANDLY

Liandly hailed from the planet Rolez. While she was tinkering with an experimental device of her father's one day, she found herself transported to Earth-2. Under Earth's planetary conditions, she gained super-human abilities, including flight and telepathy. When she encountered Clark Kent and his wife Lois Lane Kent, they befriended her and introduced her to their colleagues as Linda

Lee. Liandly flew into battle alongside Superman on several occasions, including the time when Colonel Future briefly removed the Man of Steel's abilities. Liandly's stay on Earth was brief, and as the experiment's effects wore off, she returned to her own world (*Superman Family* #220, July 1982).

LIGHTNING LAD

The inhabitants of the planet Winath (also known as Amarta) tended to give birth to twins. Solo children were considered a social aberration, so when the Ranzz family of the thirtieth century first welcomed Mekt, the boy grew up with a social stigma. More fortunate were Garth and Ayla, who followed a few years later.

The three siblings did everything together, and when they once visited the forests of the planet Korbal, they encountered a lightning monster that had "the frightful ability to transfer some of its lightning power to its victims . . . like an infectious disease!" All three children gained the ability to discharge electricity after coming into contact with the monster.

Some time later, Garth was on a spacecraft headed for Earth when he joined Saturn's Imra Ardeen and Braal's Rokk Krinn in preventing famous industrialist R. J. Brande from being kidnapped. Brande was impressed by the teamwork and suggested the three form a club to use their powers for good, much as Superboy had in the twentieth century. They agreed and became founding members of the Legion of Super-Heroes (first appearance in *Adventure Comics* #247, April 1958; origin revealed in *Superman* [first series] #147, August 1961).

Soon after the club was formed, the founders traveled to the twentieth century and appeared in Smallville, surprising Clark Kent when they revealed that they knew his secret identity. They then welcomed Clark into the Legion; he served with them for many years during his youth.

Lightning Lad eventually welcomed his sister Lightning Lass into the club, while Mekt ran away from home. He didn't surface until they crossed paths years later, when he had become the villainous Lightning Lord.

Lightning Lad, clearly inspired by Superboy, made several trips to aid the Teen of Steel or Supergirl during his career. When the team wished to celebrate the anniversary of the Maid of Steel's arrival to Earth, he volunteered with five others to create an elaborate anniversary hoax, at first making Superman believe his teammates had been replaced by robots (*Superman* [first series] #152, April 1962). As the adult Lightning-Man, he and Cosmic Man came to the twentieth century, posing as Samson and Hercules in a Superman-devised ruse to uncover stolen property and apprehend Duke Marple and his gang (*Superman* [first series] #155, August 1962).

Of all the Legionnaires, Lightning Lad had the worst run of luck, going back to his having been the first member killed in action (*Adventure Comics* #304, January 1963). While the team found a way to restore his life (*Adventure Comics* #312, September 1963), Lightning Lad soon after lost his right arm (*Adventure Comics* #332, May 1965)—although that was eventually replaced (*Adventure Comics* #351, December 1966). He fell in love with Saturn Girl, and eventually the two were married (*All-New Collectors' Edition* #C-55, 1978). He also served as Legion leader during this period (*Legion of Super-Heroes* [second series] #289, July 1982). After becoming parents, Garth and Imra opted to retire from the team (*Legion of Super-Heroes* [third series] #12, July 1985).

Years later, Superman would reunite with his Legionnaire friends as adults when they banded together to stop the Legion of Super-Villains (*Superman* [first series] #147, August 1961).

The Legion's rules prohibited members with duplicate powers, and since Winath considered Garth a runaway, Ayla, code-named Spark, replaced him as their planet's representative on the team (*Legion of Super-Heroes* [fourth series] #64, January 1995). Garth eventually joined Workforce, a professional team of super-teens funded by Brande's rival Leland McCauley. It was less than an ideal fit, and Garth quickly left the team and resumed his hunt for Mekt (*Legionnaires* #21–26, January–June 1995). The hunt was derailed when

Earth was invaded by Daxam, and Garth returned to the Legion HQ to offer his help. Rokk welcomed him back, gave him a Flight Ring, and told him to help Imra, who had been injured. Seeing her lover helped her tremendously, and once more the three founders stood shoulder-to-shoulder to repel the deadly invaders (*Legionnaires Annual* #2, 1995).

Once the threat was ended, Lightning Lad resumed his search and found Mekt on the distant world of Bisbe. He was shocked to see that his older brother had gone nearly insane. Mekt escaped and the chase led them back to Korbal, where Ayla became part of the hunt, as Mekt tried to kill more of the native beasts in order to increase his energy levels. As the two brothers struggled, Mekt vaporized Garth's right arm. Before Mekt could kill them both, the twins joined their powers and subdued their older brother, but the resulting blast caused Mekt to lose his energies and turned his hair white (*Legionnaires* #30, October 1995).

As he recovered, Cosmic Boy approached Garth, now using the code name Live Wire, for help, and had him create a covert rescue squad of Legionnaires to investigate United Planets president Chu; this led to her impeachment before she could reignite the long-simmering war between Braal and Titan. Brande was then elected to replace Chu, and his first act was restoring Live Wire to the Legion (*Legion of Super-Heroes* [fourth series] #80, May 1996).

The team benefited from Live Wire's presence until the day he sacrificed his life to save his fellow Legionnaires in battle against an insane Element Lad, who fought them under the name *Progenitor* (*Legion Lost* #12, April 2001). His life essence wound up being captured within crystals made

from Progenitor's body that Kid Quantum carried to the memorial planet Shanghalla. There the crystals grew into humanoid form, which appeared to look like Element Lad but contained Lightning Lad's soul. The new form possessed both sets of powers (*The Legion* #25, December 2003).

In the wake of the Infinite Crisis, the future became a sterile one, and the youth of the thirty-first century rebelled (*Teen Titans/Legion Special,* 2004). Their social protest led heroes from multiple worlds to band together as the Legion. Lightning Lad was still a founder, and his sister Ayla remained on the team as Light Lass. Unprepared for leadership, he floundered when thrust in the role and eventually signed an agreement placing the Legion under the UP's control (*Legion of Super-Heroes* [fifth series] #14, March 2006). Later, he would discover that his brother Mekt had also formed a team known as the Wanderers with the goal of beating back an invasion by the Dominion (*Supergirl and the Legion of Super-Heroes* #25, February 2007). He and Saturn Girl became lovers, until her betrayal with Ultra Boy ended their romance (*Legion of Super-Heroes* [fifth series] #46, November 2008).

Reality was altered closer to that of the Earth-1 Legion when the multiverse was once again reformed. Lightning Lad was part of the Legion and worked alongside Superman to defeat the xenophobic Justice League of 3008 Earth (*Action Comics* #858–863, October 2007–April 2008).

Three versions of Lightning Lad also participated in the titanic battle between the Legion of Super-Heroes and Legion of Super-Villains (*Final Crisis: Legion of 3 Worlds* #1–5, October 2008–September 2009).

LIGHTNING LASS; AKA LIGHT LASS

Garth and Ayla Ranzz were twins born on the planet Winath in the thirtieth Century. Their older brother Mekt was a solo child, considered a social aberration. The three siblings were visiting the forests of the planet Korbal when they encountered a "lightning" monster that had "the frightful ability to transfer some of its lightning power to its victims . . . like an infectious disease!" All three children gained the ability to discharge electricity.

Some time later, Garth left Winath for Earth and wound up using his newfound abilities to save the life of industrialist R. J. Brande. He banded together with Cosmic Boy and Saturn Girl to form the Legion of Super-Heroes (first appearance in *Adventure Comics* #247, April 1958; origin revealed in *Superman* [first series] #147, August 1961, and revised to include Ayla in *Adventure Comics* #308, May 1963).

When Ayla learned that her twin brother had died in battle as the Legionnaire Lightning Lad, she traveled to Earth and disguised herself as her brother in order to honor his memory. When the Legion learned the truth, they welcomed Ayla as his replacement, Lightning Lass (*Adventure Comics* #308, May 1963). Like her brothers Garth and Mekt, she gained her powers after exposure to the lightning beasts native to the planet Korbal. It was not long after her joining the Legion that Garth was miraculously brought back to life, and Legion members had a dilemma on their hands, since their rules prevented more than one member from possessing the same powers. The elegant solution arrived when Dream Girl used her planet's technology to alter Ayla's powers so that she now reduced the mass of objects instead of creating lightning, and she became known as Light Lass (*Adventure Comics* #317, February 1964).

Light Lass remained with the Legion and eventually fell in love with fellow member Timber Wolf, until her faith was shaken during the Great Darkness Saga. At that point, she left the team and returned to Winath (*Legion of Super-Heroes* [second series] #295, January 1983). Her time at home was interrupted when Mekt, now known as Lightning Lord and a part of the Legion of Super-Villains, kidnapped her as part of a plot against the Legionnaires. A jolt of his energy altered her physiology and restored her lightning abilities, which led to her rejoining the team when she was requested (*Legion of Super-Heroes* [third series] #6, January 1985).

In a somewhat altered continuation of this time line, Lightning Lass resigned from the Legion to help her family on Winath. It was there that she began a romantic relationship with former Legionnaire Salu (Shrinking Violet) Digby. In time, Ayla and Salu aided the revived Legion in fighting Roxxas on Winath, and she rejoined the team soon after (*Legion of Super-Heroes* [fourth series] #10, August 1990, and #12, October 1990).

Throughout the many ups and downs experienced by the team, Ayla was considered the glue that helped hold the club together. At one point, the Legion actually disbanded, but not before a group of clones was created and designated Batch SW6 (*Legion of Super-Heroes* [fourth series] #24–25, December 1991–January 1992). Actually time-paradox duplicates, their version of Ayla was eventually known as Gossamer (*Legion of Super-Heroes* [fourth series] #41, March 1993), and when this version of Earth was destroyed, she was among the survivors to help rebuild civilization on New Earth.

In the wake of the Zero Hour incident, Ayla and her brothers gained their powers in essentially the same manner as they had on Earth-1. They were stranded on Korbal, a barren planet, when their space cruiser's power cells failed. Ayla suggested

luring the lightning beasts toward the ship in the hope of siphoning off some of their electrical discharge. Instead all three received a charge and were left in a coma. Mekt awoke first and discovered he could internally generate lightning blasts; he vanished from the medical facility where they were now being held. When the twins came to a week later, they, too, had lightning power. Garth thought the jolt also altered Mekt's mind and turned him evil, and he vowed to find his brother. The search led him to board a ship to Earth, and he eventually went on to form the Legion (*Legion of Super-Heroes* [fourth series] #0, October 1994, and #64, January 1995). While Garth and Mekt had an unhealthy rivalry, Ayla remained out of it, loving them both but clear-eyed about how twisted Mekt had now become.

When the Legion was formally announced, Winath decided that Garth was a poor representative and dispatched Ayla in his stead. She joined the team as Spark (*Legionnaires* #20, December 1994). This version was stranded in the twentieth century for a time, and Ayla's lightning powers were altered to gravity-canceling ones after passing through the Source (*Genesis* #3; *Legion of*

Super-Heroes [fourth series] #97—both October 1997). Upon her return to her own era, Ayla grew ill and went to a lightning beast hoping for a restorative charge, but the shock killed her instead. Live Wire managed to revive her, and she awoke with her lightning abilities restored (*Legion of Super-Heroes* [fourth series] #101, February 1998). In the wake of Garth's apparent death, Ayla traveled to Winath and helped Mekt reform his negative ways (*Legion Worlds* #2, July 2001).

Following the Infinite Crisis, the future became a sterile environment, and the youth of the thirty-first century rebelled. Their social protest led heroes from multiple worlds to band together as the Legion; Lightning Lad was still a founder, and Ayla was part of the team with the name Light Lass. While she received her lightning abilities with her brothers, how they were subsequently altered to gravity powers remained undocumented (*Supergirl and the Legion of Super-Heroes* #26, March 2007).

The thirty-first-century reality was altered closer to that of the Earth-1 Legion when the multiverse was once again re-formed. Lightning Lass was also part of the team working alongside Superman in order to defeat the xenophobic Justice League of Earth (*Action Comics* #858–863, October 2007–April 2008).

Three versions of Lightning Lass participated in the titanic battle between the Legion of Super-Heroes and Legion of Super-Villains. Ayla used her powers to destroy the Phantom Zone projector after Mon-El was finally rescued from the Zone (*Final Crisis: Legion of 3 Worlds* #1–5, October 2008–September 2009).

LIGHTNING LORD

Mekt Ranzz was born without a twin on the planet Winath, making him a social aberration on a world where having twins was the norm. As a result, he developed a sullen, edgy attitude, mollified by his close relationship with his younger siblings Garth and Ayla. They did everything as a trio, including an ill-fated visit to the forests of the planet Korbal where they encountered a "lightning" monster that had "the frightful ability to transfer some of its lightning power to its victims . . . like an infectious disease!" All three children gained the ability to discharge electricity (*Superman* [first series] #147, August 1961).

While Garth eventually became part of the Legion of Super-Heroes, Mekt chose to use his powers for personal gain. He became a criminal and helped found the Legion of Super-Villains in his late teens (*Adventure Comics* #372, September 1968). During a subsequent clash with Garth, Lightning Lord's hair turned silver (*Superboy* [first series] #172, March 1971). In a somewhat altered continuation of this time line, Mekt ultimately reformed after two years of intensive therapy and returned to Winath, helping Garth and Imra Ranzz run the family's Lightning Ring Plantation (*Legion of Super-Heroes* [first series] #10, August 1990).

At various points, Superman encountered a time-traveling adult Lightning Lord along with the Legion of Super-Villains (*Superman* [first series] #147, August 1961; others), but they were not from the primary Earth-1 time line. It's been speculated that these may have merely been pretenders—albeit dangerous ones—who assumed the names of the younger villains.

In the wake of Zero Hour, Mekt and his siblings gained their powers in essentially the same manner as they had on Earth-1. They were stranded on Korbal, a barren planet, when their space cruiser's power cells failed. Ayla suggested luring the planet's lightning beasts toward the ship in the hope of siphoning off some of their electrical discharge. Instead all three were charged and fell into comas. Mekt awoke first and discovered that he could internally generate lightning blasts; he then vanished from the medical facility. When the twins came to a week later, they, too, had lightning powers. Garth knew that Mekt's mind had been altered, turning him evil, and he vowed to find Mekt and help him (*Legion of Super-Heroes* [fourth series] #0, October 1994, and #64, January 1995).

"MY BROTHER AND I EACH DECIDED TO USE OUR NEW-FOUND POWER DIFFERENTLY..."
I'LL USE MY NEW POWER TO COMMIT CRIMES!
I'LL USE MY POWER OF SUPER-LIGHTNING TO HELP OTHERS!

Garth briefly served with the Legion and the Workforce before leaving to resume his hunt for Mekt. His search was derailed when Earth was invaded by Daxam, and Garth returned to Legion HQ to offer his help. Once the threat was ended, Lightning Lad resumed his search and eventually found Mekt on the distant world of Bisbe. The showdown between siblings became heated, with Mekt clearly insane. Mekt fled, and Garth pursued. The chase led them back to Korbal, where Ayla joined the hunt, as Mekt tried to kill more of the native beasts in order to increase his energy levels. While they struggled, Mekt vaporized Garth's right arm. Before he could kill them both, the twins joined their powers and subdued Mekt, the resulting blast causing him to lose his energies and turning his hair white (*Legionnaires* #30, October 1995). Mekt was subsequently paroled, and he returned home to Winath to work on his parents' farm, apparently reformed and repentant (*Legion Worlds* #2, July 2001).

In yet another potential future, Mekt was approached by a cult worshipping Validus, known in this reality as the Lord of Lightning. Believing that as a "solo," the young man was prophesied to travel to Korbal and bring back Validus in the flesh, the cult dispatched him to the barren world. Because his stowaway siblings also acquired electrical powers, the cultists concluded that Mekt was not the chosen one after all and declared him cursed (*Supergirl and the Legion of Super-Heroes* #32, September 2007).

Mekt was among those tapped by the United Planets to join a black ops team investigating a resurgence of activity by the Dominators. As the sole survivor of the mission, the young man assembled a new team beholden to no one and set to work with his Wanderers to do whatever it took to thwart the Dominion's invasion of Earth (*Supergirl and the Legion of Super-Heroes* #25, February 2007). Through intermediaries, he destroyed the Dominator homeworld (*Supergirl and the Legion of Super-Heroes* #30, July 2007), an act of genocide for which the United Planets took him into custody (*Supergirl and the Legion of Super-Heroes* #33, October 2007).

In the present day, an adult Lightning Lord (possibly the same individual who faced the Earth-1 Superman) returned with Cosmic King and Saturn Queen to rewrite the past by posing as the adoptive parents of Clark Kent and Bruce Wayne. Under their influence, Superman and Batman became planetary conquerors until confronted by Wonder Woman and a team of Freedom Fighters (*Superman/Batman* #14–18, January–April 2005).

Recently, a version of Lightning Lord was recruited by Superboy-Prime to participate in the titanic battle between the Legion of Super-Heroes and Legion of Super-Villains (*Final Crisis: Legion of 3 Worlds* #1–5, October 2008–September 2009).

LIGHTNING-MAN

The citizens of Metropolis were stunned to see a new costumed hero flying overhead one day, performing a dizzying array of feats. At the same time, crime fighters from around the world, including the Knight and Squire, Legionary, Gaucho, Musketeer, Batman, and Robin, were on hand for a ceremony opening the new Club of Heroes built by philanthropist John Mayhew. The architect planned to turn the deed over to the hero with the most noteworthy accomplishments. Superman suspected that Lightning-Man was a criminal who intended to steal the club for his own purposes. Batman, however, deduced that Lightning-Man was in actuality Superman, suffering from amnesia caused by a kryptonite fragment orbiting the Earth. The club never again met in the world before the First Crisis (*World's Finest Comics* #89, July–August 1957).

LIGHTNING MASTER, THE

Hiding under a green robe and hood embellished with a yellow lightning bolt, a scientist dubbed the Lightning Master attempted to extort Metropolis to the tune of three hundred thousand dollars or he would begin destroying the city's skyscrapers. To prove his point, he unleashed waves of energy from a device of his own creation and obliterated an office building. Superman investigated and traced the energy to its source, a mountain laboratory outside the city limits. Also investigating was Lois Lane, who got herself captured by the mad scientist. The Man of Steel arrived in time to prevent any further destruction and rescue the reporter. The Lightning Master unleashed a final charge from his weapon, which harmlessly passed through the hero but ricocheted, electrocuting the

scientist (*Superman* [first series] #14, January–February 1942).

LINEAR MEN, THE

Young Matthew Ryder was trapped by the cave-in of a Metropolis subway tunnel triggered during Captain Atom's battle with Monarch (*Armageddon 2001* #2, October 1991). The boy was rescued from the rubble by the time-traveling being known as Waverider, a remarkable feat considering that both were actually the same person!

As Superman and the Metal Men removed an experimental quantum field generator from the ruin of S.T.A.R. Labs, the unstable generator exploded. The resulting explosion caused time to split apart. In one reality, Ryder's parents had been killed by the explosion—but that put the surviving Matthew on a path to becoming the time-traveling entity Waverider. As the explosion began, Waverider appeared, saving his parents, which created a divergent time line.

Ryder studied with the noted time researcher Ripley Hunter, nicknamed the Time Master. As an adult, Ryder began his own time experiments under the patronage of Lex Luthor. When something went wrong during an experiment, Ryder found himself and his equipment projected to a strange plane beyond time and space (*Superman* [second series] #73, November 1992).

Ryder established a base on that strange plane, calling it Vanishing Point, from which he could study and unravel the secrets of the space-time continuum. He then selected people to form a team he dubbed the Linear Men. The half a dozen core members included Ryder, his future variant persona Waverider, his mentor Hunter, his wife Liri Lee, and Travis O'Connell. Over time, their ranks grew to include Desmond Mkhalali Gage (*Chronos* #1, March 1998), Ryak (*The All-New Atom* #7, March 2007), and Traven (*Chronos* #2, April 1998).

The first adventure involving Superman and the Linear Men involved Travis O'Connell's rogue effort to arrest Booster Gold for his jaunts from the twenty-fifth century to the twentieth. When the Man of Steel attempted to intervene, he found himself shot into the timestream to the thirtieth century, where he encountered the Legion of Super-Heroes (*The Adventures of Superman* #476, March 1991); to Warsaw, Poland, in 1943 (*Action Comics* #663; *Superman* [second series] #54—both March–April 1991); once more to the Legion's era (*The Adventures of Superman* #477, April 1991); one hundred million years in the past (*Action Comics* #664, April 1991); to the age of Camelot (*Superman* [second series] #55, May 1991); and finally to AD 2995. Noting that Superman's presence had prevented Earth's moon from exploding in that year as history recorded, O'Connell triggered a catastrophic explosion that destroyed the satellite at the cost of his own life. The energy generated also allowed Superman to return to his proper point in the timestream (*The Adventures of Superman* #478, May 1991).

Believing Superman was due some compensation for the incident, Liri Lee (behind the backs of the other Linear Men) stopped time around the Man of Steel and Lois Lane, permitting them an uninterrupted period to discuss matters of the heart and their upcoming marriage (*Superman* [second series] #59, September 1991).

Soon after, Superman met the Linear Men at Vanishing Point in the midst of Waverider's attempt to change history by preventing the catastrophic explosion that had killed his parents. Stealing Liri Lee's wrist control, Waverider succeeded in doing just that, never realizing that he had actually fulfilled destiny by creating the time line that belonged to the Linear Men's founder Matthew Ryder (*Superman* [second series] #61, November 1991). Soon after, Waverider was chosen to replace O'Connell in the group (*Superman* [second series] #73, November 1992).

The Linear Men continued to get caught up in major chronal disruptions of the timestream, as forces such as Extant, Parallax (*Zero Hour: Crisis in Time* #4–0, September 1994), and Dominus (*Action Comics* #748; *Superman: The Man of Steel* #83; *Superman* [second series] #139—all September 1998) tried to twist reality to suit their needs.

The Linear Men's failing, in Hunter's opinion, was that they were "too linear. They're vested in enforcing an inflexible view of reality" and dismissing the very existence of alternate time lines. Consequently, Hunter zealously guarded the existence of Hypertime, which he described as "an infinite realm of parallel worlds" and "a kingdom of wonder." The Linear Men's "sense of control would be splintered by the truth that the universe they oversee is actually part of an unpredictable multiverse," Hunter once explained to Superman, Batman, and Wonder Woman (*The Kingdom* #2, February 1999).

The group's inflexibility ultimately proved their downfall when they called Superman before the cosmic council known as the Quintessence. By preventing Imperiex from razing Earth and other worlds, they claimed, the Man of Steel had made the future unpredictable and uncontrollable. The Quintessence sided squarely with Superman, informing the Linear Men that their "dictatorial philosophy [and] adherence to a fated end [was] now out of step with temporal transmutation and progression." With that, the Linear Men were dismissed, their fates uncertain save for Liri Lee, who resurfaced on Earth in the persona of nanny Liesel Largo (*Superman: The Man of Steel* #118, November 2001).

Vanishing Point finally sat abandoned (*Booster Gold* [second series] #18, May 2009), although Ryak, a man claiming to be part of the Linear Men, surfaced on two later occasions (*The All-New Atom* #7–8, March–April 2007, and #16, December 2007).

LINK, LESTER

Using the alias Lynx, this meek little bookkeeper decided to spice up his life by switching from the drudgery of his day job to the exciting career of a criminal. He established an underworld lair bedecked with lurid gangland trappings, including guns, knives, and human skulls. As Lynx, he proceeded to create the perception that he was the secret ruler of Metropolis's criminal society, which he accomplished by calling the *Daily Planet* and claiming credit for crimes he learned of by reading the selfsame newspaper. When Superman investigated and discovered that the criminal mastermind was actually an accountant, he decided to give the man a thrill by teaming with Link to lure real criminals Tiger Tornadi, Baby-Face, and Pig-Eye into a carefully laid trap (*World's Finest Comics* #12, Winter 1943).

LINNIS, THAD

Thad Linnis managed to persuade Superman that he had deduced the Man of Steel's secret identity. The criminal promised Superman he would keep the secret if he stayed out of the city for two full weeks. After the promise was extracted, Linnis had his men begin preparing a super-tank designed to aid them in looting the city. Batman realized Linnis was bluffing the Man of Steel, so he and Robin helped their friend apprehend Linnis and his men (*World's Finest Comics* #84, September–October 1956).

LITTLE AFRICA

A small section of Metropolis was once known as Little Africa, ethnically and culturally favored by African American residents. Their socioeconomic situation led to unrest and reports of substandard conditions. When Lois Lane arrived to conduct some interviews, she learned how much Caucasians were resented, and she used Kryptonian technology to temporarily pass as an African American in order to conduct her investigation (*Superman's Girl Friend, Lois Lane* #106, November 1970).

LITTLE LEAGUER

A computer gift arrived from the Cybern galaxy, one of countless accolades and presents showered on the Man of Steel as Metropolis celebrated Superman Day, marking his arrival on Earth. The machine issued a prophecy that the Man of Steel would be saved by someone with the initials LL who had long played a role in his life.

He was soon after stricken by green kryptonite, a well-intentioned gift from Bizarro Number

One, and as he lay dying, Superman scanned the crowds to see who could save his life and fulfill the machine's prophecy.

In the end, he was saved by young Steven Snapinn, who was clad in his Little League uniform (*Superman* [first series] #157, November 1962).

LIVE WIRE

Leslie Willis was a popular Metropolis radio shock jock, notable for her nightly bashing of Superman. She insisted the Man of Steel saved people in order to lord his superpowers over the mere mortals he lived among. Her other targets included WHIZ radio reporter Billy Batson (secretly Captain Marvel). The station's owner tired of its declining ratings and opted to switch the format from talk to country, which meant he could finally fire Leslie and end her venomous rants. Leslie went to rail at the world from the top of the station's roof, at which point an errant lightning bolt struck her, activating her latent metagene and turning her into a walking dynamo (*Action Comics* #835, March 2006).

The lightning bolt also altered her skin tone to chalk white, and her hair became blue-tinged electricity. Leslie decided she could finally show the world that Superman was not worthy of their loyalty, and she took the name Live Wire to accomplish her goal. She attacked Superman just as he returned from a battle with the Queen of Fables. Superman quickly outwitted Live Wire and shorted out her abilities, taking her into custody.

When the alien Auctioneer later arrived on Earth, Live Wire was among the superpowered beings collected for sale. She realized her powers were being inhibited by a psychological barrier, which was eventually taken down by Mister Terrific, who devised a way to free her. Live Wire discovered that she could not only expel electrical energy but also store it like a battery and release it along the electromagnetic spectrum, from high frequency to radio waves.

Superman had her use her powers to help him and others escape, then Live Wire allied herself with Nightwing, the Veteran, Blue Jay, and several others to gain their freedom (*Action Comics* #842–843, November–December 2006).

A result of her amped-up powers meant that every television on Earth was now watching the heroes' exploits. Superman used this to their advantage and threatened to expose the Auctioneer's database to the general public both on Earth and throughout the galaxy if he did not abandon his plans for Earth. The Auctioneer agreed but wound up profiting by selling the intergalactic television rights to the entire battle.

Live Wire continued to adventure, usually for personal gain and in conflict with the super hero community. Despite this, she found Nightwing attractive and came up with ways to be near him time and again.

On Earth-1958 (the basis for the current Earth-30), a variation on Live Wire was allied with that world's Lex Luthor in his never-ending battle against the Man of Steel (*Superman: Red Son* #3, 2003).

LLEWELYN, CALLIE

Clark Kent and Carolyn "Callie" Llewellyn first met as young adults when they joined Stanhope College's Professor Lewis Lang on an archaeological expedition in Australia. Though intrigued by Clark's proximity to the town that had played host to the mysterious "super-boy," Callie soon lost touch with the young man. Later the world's foremost arcanobiologist (*Superman* #654, September 2007), she requested Clark's help when she was attacked by the just-released creature known as Subjekt-17 at a scientific facility, suspecting there was a connection between her old friend and Superman. As the two aliens fought, Superman prevailed and Callie was able to continue her research (*Superman* #655–656, October–November 2007).

LLOYD, LYRICA

Clark Kent was once recruited to appear in a movie based on the Man of Steel titled *The Super Saga.* While filming, he fell in love with the film's star, Lyrica Lloyd, who like Lois Lane found Clark too mild-mannered for her tastes. To prove her wrong, he revealed his alter ego to her, and in turn she revealed her own secret: Lyrica was dying from a fatal jungle disease she had contracted when she had shot a film in Africa. This was to be her final role, and the two embraced and vowed to keep each other's secret (*Superman* [first series] #196, May 1967).

LOBO

The last living being from the planet Czarnia, Lobo had many careers but always remained a butt-kicking mercenary, willing to fight anyone, anywhere as long as there was a promise of cash, beer, women, and mayhem (*Omega Men* #3, June 1983).

Legend held that the Main Man actually tore his way out of his mother's womb, and as he grew, he took out his violent tendencies on all those around him. In the end, Lobo destroyed all life on his homeworld then, riding his cosmic hog, began traveling the starways in search of money and pleasure. Some chronicles said Czarnia was destroyed by the Psions from the Vega star system, while other accounts said Lobo unleashed a deadly plague of flying scorpions on his own people (*Lobo* #0, October 1994).

In the Khundian language, Lobo's name translated to "he who devours your entrails and thoroughly enjoys it." His innate strength and intestinal fortitude allowed him to survive the vacuum of space or the blows delivered by a variety of opponents, including the Man of Steel. Lobo also possessed the ability to regenerate missing limbs, which at one time led to several Lobos operating at once.

Accompanying the bounty hunter was Dawg, a bulldog whom Lobo often claimed was not his whenever the canine got into trouble; Jonas Glim, a fellow bounty hunter; and Ramona, a bail bondswoman/hairdresser. Lobo wound up fraggin'—that is, killing—Dawg, telling Superman the canine was not his after all (*Lobo* #58, January 1999). All that ever seemed to elicit sympathy from the Last Czarnian were the space dolphins that often flocked around his bike as he traveled from star to star.

Among his countless enemies were Goldstar, Loo, Vril Dox, Bludhound, Etrigan the Demon, and General Glory. He frequently found himself on Earth, usually in battle against Superman, although he and Aquaman once brawled until they learned of each other's interest in dolphins. Lobo relished his fights with Superman, one of the few beings to last more than a few minutes with him (*The Adventures of Superman* #464, March 1990; *Superman: The Man of Steel* #30, February 1994; *DC First: Superman/Lobo* #1: July 2002; others).

During his colorful career, Lobo worked as a bare-knuckles brawler, assassin, and even archbishop of the Church of the Triple-Fish God. The Coluan Vril Dox once tricked him into joining the mercenary intergalactic police force known as L.E.G.I.O.N. Whenever possible, Lobo snuck away for moonlighting opportunities or to just plain piss Dox off. When he saved Dox's life, Lobo was released from his obligation and returned to the stars a free man.

Back on Earth, however, he found himself reduced to a teenager. Dubbed Li'l Lobo, he briefly served alongside Superboy as part of Young Justice. He journeyed with the team to Apokolips, where he was killed, but the magic spell that transformed him also restored his regenerative abilities (*Young Justice: Sins of Youth* #2, May 2000). When Lobo died, his spilled blood formed a veritable army of Lobos, which quickly outmatched the dog soldiers of Apokolips. The Lobos then turned on one another in a frenzy until one remained and grew back to adult form (*Young Justice* #36, October 2001). One clone hid and avoided the fight, returning to Earth with Young Justice and taking the name *Slo-bo* (*Young Justice* #37, November 2001; named in #39, January 2002). When his cellular form began to degrade, Slo-bo was banished to the 853rd century by Darkseid, leaving his mind trapped in an inanimate statue (*Young Justice* #55, May 2003).

The next time the people of Earth saw Lobo, he seemed to have found religion and tended to the believers in sector 3500, caring for the Emerald Eye of Ekron. Rann's champion Adam Strange, Earth's Animal Man, and Tamaranean princess Starfire received his help during their battle against the cosmic threat of Lady Styx. When Lobo surrendered the Eye to the triple-headed fish god he worshipped, he was released from his vow of nonviolence and used the Eye to slay the god (*52* #36, January 10, 2007, and #51, April 25, 2007).

It was later learned that Lobo's soul was consigned to Hell. The Czarnian's suffering in that realm fueled the demon Neron's castle. During a fight between Etrigan and the Blue Devil, Lobo's soul was freed from prison and sought out Neron for a reckoning. In the melee, he sliced off the head of the mage Zatara, forcing his daughter Zatanna to send Lobo to the Abyss, where souls were consigned forever (*Reign in Hell* #4–8, December 2008–April 2009).

While he lost his regenerative abilities in the 21st century, Lobo managed to survive to the 853rd century, although by then he had grown obese, lazy, and less motivated to drop everything and fight. His last case enticed him back into action, but he vanished into a black hole (*Lobo One Million,* November 1998).

Lobo's exploits led him to visit parallel worlds that were fortunate not to have their own version of the mercenary. He even engaged in a knife fight with Santa Claus and killed the spirit of Christmas (*Lobo Paramilitary Christmas Special* #1, January 1991).

LOCKSMITH

Carla Draper craved her father's attention but rarely seemed to get it. She was delighted, then, when Carl Draper (head of a high-tech security firm called Draper Industries) embraced her suggestion of devising a prison that Superman couldn't escape. Creating a holographic alter ego for himself called Deathtrap, Carl took on Superman twice without ever revealing his true identity (*The Adventures of Superman* #517, November 1994; *Superman: The Man of Steel* #43, April 1995).

When Draper Inc. was called on to contain the fugitive Knockout as well as Superboy, Carla saw this as an opportunity to gain further favor in her father's eyes. Calling herself Snare and unleashing a succession of miniaturized traps, Carla stepped over the line in her obsession with capturing Superboy and began assaulting any and all Metropolis Special Crime Unit officers who stood in her way. Thanks to officers Roxy Leech and Tori Graves, Snare was eventually caught in one of her own traps (*Superboy* [third series] #26–27, April–May 1996).

Eventually freed and returning to her father's side, Carla opted for a more circumspect assault on Superman. Using her father's holographic image, Carla changed "his" name to Locksmith and challenged Superman to escape a prison specifically devised for his blue energy form before he could save the people trapped in a burning Metropolis building. Of course, Superman found a way to freedom and managed a timely rescue (*Action Comics* #739, November 1997).

Carl eventually learned of his other holographic identity, and although he could never prove it, Draper was certain that his daughter had tipped off the authorities to his whereabouts. He found himself accused not only of the crimes he'd committed as Deathtrap and the Master Jailer, but also those as Locksmith. At some unrecorded time, Draper was offered amnesty if he agreed to turn his expertise toward the world's benefit. Ensconced as head of Checkmate's security, he feared that Carla was "trying to pick up where [his] criminal career left off" (*Checkmate* [second series] #17, October 2007).

LOCKWOOD, BEN

The true identity of the government operative known as Agent Liberty.

LOGAN, "LABS"

Jimmy Olsen was once entrusted with the collection of funds from the street-side money chests of a Metropolis charity, presuming the Man of Steel would be on hand if something went awry. As he collected the money, Olsen used his signal watch to summon Superman to deliver the proceeds and was observed by a criminal named "Labs" Logan in the process. He followed the cub reporter to a restaurant's washroom, where he stole the watch as Jimmy cleaned up. Logan reprogrammed the watch so it would emit a different ultrasonic sound, then robbed Olsen twice before kidnapping him as part of a plot to lure Superman to a kryptonite death trap. However, Jimmy used the watch to warn his pal through a message in Morse code. Superman then arrived with an elongated pair of tongs to collect the deadly mineral and apprehend Logan (*Superman's Pal, Jimmy Olsen* #13, June 1956).

LOIS 4XR

In a potential distant future, the great-great-great-great-granddaughter of Lois Lane was named Lois 4XR. Through a genetic quirk, she resembled her ancestor identically, so that when Superman accidentally traveled to the year 2949, he was surprised to see what he thought was Lois. By this era, humans had evolved with superpowers of their own. While Superman tried to find a way home, he also wrestled with trying to find out who Lois would eventually marry, but before he reached a decision he was returned to his correct era (*Superman* [first series] #57, March–April 1949).

LOMBARD, STEVE

Once the star quarterback for the Metropolis Meteors, Steve "The Slinger" Lombard eventually retired and became a sports reporter for Galaxy Broadcasting (*Superman* [first series] #264, June 1973). A graduate of Empire University (*Superman* [first series] #384, June 1983), Steve played for the Central City Centaurs under Coach Chuck Guraldi before being traded to the Meteors (*Action Comics* #465, November 1976).

Lombard was still a football star when he saved a falling baby, tweaking a chronic knee injury and passing out in the process. Frederick Fowe found the collapsed athlete and used his invention, a "violet healing ray that derives its power from the sun," to treat Lombard's injury. The device also seemed to create "a form consisting of indescribable, unearthly matter from the sun, with no will of its own, molded by the fire of Steve Lombard's thoughts and his drive to win." The unseen being then put on Lombard's football uniform and scored a game-winning touchdown at superspeed, something the "Slinger" took credit for. He was interviewed post-game by DAILY PLANET reporters LOIS LANE and CLARK KENT, the latter of whom Lombard took an instant dislike to.

When the invisible entity began tearing up the streets of Metropolis, Superman intervened, learned the truth, and convinced the entity to return to the sun. Still injured and feeling great remorse, Lombard announced his retirement and was immediately hired as a sports reporter by GBS's owner MORGAN EDGE.

Lombard injected life into both the WGBS studio and his broadcasts, taking every chance to needle Kent both on and off the air. For his part, Clark always managed to get even via his superpowers, albeit in a manner that could never be traced back to him. Steve almost began to view such incidents as karma, and once became a nervous wreck when the payback for an insult didn't seem to be coming (*Superman* [first series] #282, December 1974). Antics aside, Lombard initially proved to be an adept reporter, leading to his being sent out on straight news stories every now and then. His popularity led to his being used as

a fill-in anchor and even writing a column for the *Daily Planet* (*Superman* [first series] #289, July 1975). Eventually, however, Morgan Edge could no longer tolerate Lombard's sloppy on-air behavior, and the sportscaster was let go (*Superman* [first series] #384, June 1983). A struggling Lombard found short-lived employment as the owner of Slinger Steve's Secondhand Cars (*Superman* [first series] #393, March 1984) and by performing in a disastrous stage production of *Damn Yankees* (*Action Comics* #562, December 1984) before ultimately opening Lombard's Sporting Goods (*Superman* [first series] #412–413, October–November 1985).

Steve's relatives included his parents (*Action Comics* #523, September 1981), his scientist brother Vernon Lombard, Vernon's son Jamie (*Superman* [first series] #267, September 1973), and his mystery novelist aunt Kaye Daye (*Superman* [first series] #277, July 1974).

In the reality after the CRISIS ON INFINITE EARTHS, Lombard was an ex-jock working as a news anchor (*The Adventures of Superman* #446, November 1988; others). After reality was shifted by the INFINITE CRISIS, Lombard became the *Daily Planet*'s sports editor. A comment from PERRY WHITE indicated that Lombard had had a previous tenure with the paper, but its details went unrecorded.

Lombard was known to have played football in high school, in college, and briefly for the pros. He saw himself as a man's man, everything Clark Kent was not, and the jock was baffled as to how Lois Lane fell in love with and married Kent. He was a walking encyclopedia of sports trivia and put-downs, with his targets often including Kent and RON TROUPE (*Action Comics* #866, August 2008).

On Earth-2, Lombard had a counterpart at the DAILY STAR named Steve Bard (*Superman* [first series] #29, July–August 1944; others).

LON-ES

A scientist living in the bottle city of KANDOR, Lon-Es was also briefly a lab assistant to JOR-EL. He alerted SUPERGIRL to the reasons behind Superman's seemingly senseless acts of destruction, a result of a post-hypnotic suggestion planted by the vile MAG-EN when KAL-EL was still an infant on KRYPTON. Armed with the knowledge, Supergirl was able to aid her big cousin (*Superman* [first series] #154, July 1962).

LONG, LYDIA

Following the theory of parallel world development, life on the planet OCEANIA was remarkably similar to that of Earth, complete with a superpowered champion named Hyper-Man. Macropolis's best-known television reporter Lydia Long was the powerful hero's girlfriend, unaware that he was also her co-worker Chester King. When Hyper-Man was forced to retire from duty, Long married him. They lived happily for a year until her tragic death from ZORONITE poisoning (*Action Comics* #265, June 1960).

LOOKALIKE SQUAD, THE

In recognition of all the help Superman had given to the citizens in the bottle city of KANDOR, a volunteer group was formed to aid the Man of Steel in protecting his secret identity. Known as the Lookalike Squad, they found doppelgängers for not only CLARK KENT but many of his closest friends as well. They worked in concert with the SUPERMAN EMERGENCY SQUAD (*Action Comics* #309, February 1964).

Among the members were VAN-ZEE and SYLVIA VAN-ZEE (SUPERMAN and LOIS LANE; both introduced in *Superman's Girl Friend, Lois Lane* #15, February 1960), VOL-DON (Kent), ZOL-LAR (JIMMY OLSEN), AR-RONE (PERRY WHITE), Ti-Arra (LANA LANG), an unnamed double for LORI LEMARIS (all introduced in *Superman's Pal, Jimmy Olsen* #70, July 1963), LONA LEMAIS (LUCY LANE; introduced in *Superman's Pal, Jimmy Olsen* #53, June 1961), and Varn-Don (SUPERBOY; introduced in *Superboy* [first series] #118, January 1965). The squad was also seen on WMET-TV's *Our American Heroes* when the station devoted an episode to the Man of Steel.

LOOPHOLE

Former S.T.A.R. LABS CPA DEKE DICKSON was an inept criminal who used a stolen molecular Disrupting device to pass through matter (*The Adventures of Superman* #505, October 1993). Despite having a truly useful tool for criminal activities, he and his succession of female partners were repeatedly defeated by not only Superman but also SUPERBOY (*Superboy* [third series] #16, June 1995), members of his team the RAVERS (*Superboy and the Ravers* #8, April 1997), and the JUSTICE LEAGUE OF AMERICA (*Superman Secret Files* #1, January 1998). Imprisoned at STRYKER'S ISLAND, Loophole was last seen during a prison riot (*The Adventures of Superman* #641, August 2005).

LORA

The wife of Kryptonian scientist Jor-L and mother to KAL-L, she perished by her husband's side when the KRYPTON of the Earth-2 reality exploded. In most tellings she was known as Lara.

LORD, MAXWELL

Maxwell Lord III appeared to the world a successful businessman who helped rebuild the JUSTICE LEAGUE OF AMERICA after the event known as LEGENDS

(*Justice League* #1, May 1987). It was later revealed that he performed these acts under the control of a machine constructed by the New Gods' Metron. A subsequent retelling implied that Metron's device had been usurped by the malevolent computer program Kilgore as part of a long-term plan to control the world (*Justice League International* #11–12, March–April 1988; *Justice League America Annual* #9, 1995).

The divorced Lord put on a friendly face to all, save one of his ex-wives, who in turn fashioned the corporate heroes known as the Conglomerate to rival the JLA (*Justice League Quarterly* #1, Winter 1990). Lord saw to it that the JLA received United Nations sanctioning (*Justice League International* #7, November 1987) and even helped establish a European contingent (*Justice League International* #24, February 1989) followed by a short-lived one situated in the Antarctic (*Justice League Annual* #4, 1991).

When the League learned of Lord's criminal computer connection, they helped free him, at which point Maxwell's true amoral personality seemed to assert itself. He was also revealed to possess a latent meta-human power, which was activated during the alien invasion of Earth when a gene bomb was detonated nearby. He had the ability to mentally take control of other living beings, a skill Lord practiced with great subtlety (*Justice League International* #24, February 1989). Soon after, Lord was shot and left in a coma (*Justice League America* #52–53, July–August 1991) for a great stretch of time, at which point the League underwent membership upheaval without his guidance.

Lord's body, however, was taken over by the Dreamslayer, a being from another reality who used Lord's skill to try to take control over countless minds on Earth (*Justice League America* #57, December 1991). By this point, the UN had revoked the JLA's charter (*Justice League America* #56, November 1991). Lord eventually awoke with the mistaken belief that Dreamslayer overtaxed his ability during his possession, which cost him future use of his power (*Justice League Europe* #35, February 1992; *Justice League America* #60, March 1992).

Diagnosed with a malignant brain tumor, Lord accepted an offer from the electronic entity Kilgore to have his consciousness placed in the body of the robotic Lord Havok (*Justice League America* #95, January 1995, and #100, June 1995). In time, Lord's outer shell was altered to reflect his original human appearance. Now back to his avuncular personality, Lord coaxed his JLA colleagues into trying a new approach as the Super Buddies, which failed to last (*Formerly Known as the Justice League* #1–6, September 2003–February 2004; *JLA Classified* #4–9, April–September 2005).

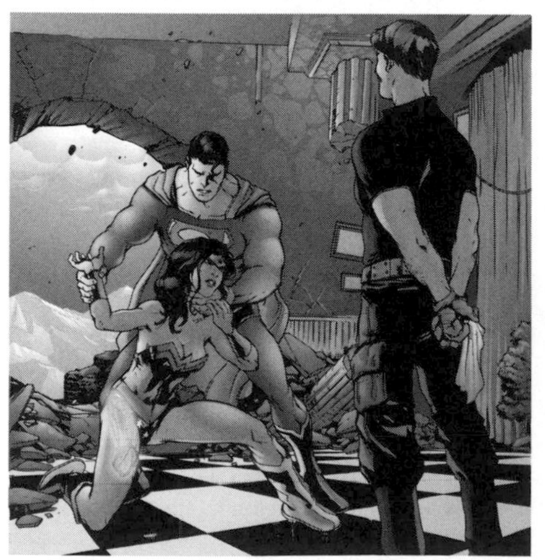

Lord eventually shed his cyborg components and regained full use of his mental powers thanks to the combined efforts of Project Cadmus, Checkmate, and Project M. He was also revealed to have spent all the previous years amassing a collection of data about Earth's aliens and meta-humans, slowly coming to the conclusion that they all posed a threat to humanity. Lord's goal, despite possessing a superpower himself, was to rid the world of these "menaces." Lord then usurped the federal government's moribund Checkmate espionage operation and took control as its Black King. When he tried to recruit Blue Beetle as a colleague, the hero refused and was murdered by Lord (*DC Countdown to Infinite Crisis* #1, May 2005).

Lord also stumbled upon Batman's meta-human spy satellite dubbed Brother I and took control of it. Brother I took to calling Lord "teacher," and Lord launched a mad scheme to wipe out all of the Earth's meta-humans. He used a nanovirus, constructed from advanced future technology that had been modified by the U.S. Department of Defense and LexCorp, to turn normal humans into armored battle cyborgs dubbed OMACS—Observational Meta-Human Activity Constructs. As his plan unfolded, Lord came into conflict with Superman and Wonder Woman. Using his own meta-human power to control minds, he took control of the Man of Steel, who nearly killed first Batman, then Wonder Woman. Seeing no other way to free Superman from Maxwell Lord's grip, the Amazon snapped Lord's neck, killing him instantly (*Wonder Woman* [second series] #219, September 2005). A shocked Superman was left shaken and troubled by all that had transpired.

Lord was among those resurrected at the conclusion of the cosmic event known as the Blackest Night. He has once more resumed his goal of eradicating meta-humans from Earth (*Blackest Night* #8, June 2010).

LORD SATANUS

Lord Satanus and his sister Blaze were demon spawn born to the wizard Shazam and an unnamed demon, and both grew up to become major figures in the underworld.

On Earth-1, Lord Satanis first appeared before the Man of Steel claiming to hail from one million years in the future. He was accompanied by his wife Syrene, and together they sought Merlin the magician's Runestone, using Superman as their puppet to obtain the item (*Action Comics* #527, January 1982). In a return match, the competing mages literally split Superman into two beings whose power was accordingly halved (*Action Comics* #534, August 1983). With one Superman imprisoned with Satanis and Syrene in the medieval past, the other Man of Steel was forced to join forces with Time Master Rip Hunter to set things right (*Action Comics* #539–541, January–March 1983).

In the reality formed following the Crisis on Infinite Earths, Lord Satanus and Blaze were siblings born of a union between a demon and the unwitting hero later known as Shazam (*Power of Shazam!* #10, December 1995). Each initially made his or her presence known in mortal form, Satanus as Newstime publisher Colin Thornton (*The Adventures of Superman* #460, November 1989) and Blaze as nightclub owner Angelica Blaze (*The Adventures of Superman* #469, August 1990).

When Blaze attacked her brother, Thornton was forced to move the Newstime building to another dimension, confounding Supergirl's attempts at a rescue. As a result, Superman sided with Satanus to stop Blaze, and the building returned from its dimensional hideaway (*The Adventures of Superman* #493, September 1992; *Action Comics* #680, August 1992; *Superman: The Man of Steel* #15, September 1992; *Superman* [second series] #71, September 1992).

In an attempt to bolster his forces in Hell as he vied for the throne of power, Lord Satanus created a magical narcotic, DMN, which transformed ordinary humans into demons. The drug gained traction in Metropolis after the city was devastated by explosions triggered by Lex Luthor. Truly in love with the City of Tomorrow, Satanus didn't intend for his neighbors to become his shock troops, so he sent a message to Zatanna, who used the information to help magically restore the city (*The Adventures of Superman* #522, April 1995).

He later reneged on that affection in the wake of Brainiac 13's remake of Metropolis, prompting him to try to steal the souls of the entire city population until Superman made the tempting offer of his own soul in exchange for everyone else's freedom. Between the offer and interference from Blaze in the form of a shaman called Night Eagle, the people of Metropolis were spared further harm (*The Adventures of Superman* #588, March 2001).

During the time when the Joker controlled Mr. Mxyzptlk's powers, Satanus took advantage of the chaos and attempted to steal the souls from Supergirl and Superboy in the wake of their apparent death at the hands of Ignition. The Maid of Might's prayers proved annoying enough that Satanus decided their souls were not worth the effort (*The Adventures of Superman* #586, January 2001).

During a supernatural storm in Metropolis years later, Superman encountered the Wrath of God known as the Spectre, who was obliterating all magical objects and persons with unchecked fury. When the Spectre turned his attention to the Newstime building, Superman investigated and finally learned that Thornton was also Lord Satanus. The demon wanted to turn his employees into an army to involve in an unwinnable war against the Spectre, but Superman offered to fight in their stead. The Spectre quickly dispatched Superman and seemingly killed Satanus (*Action Comics* #832, December 2005).

Instead, Satanus and Blaze managed to gain control over Purgatory and used that as a staging ground for their challenge for Hell's throne when it appeared Neron had abandoned it during recent events (*52* #42, February 21, 2007). When Neron reappeared, an all-out war in Hell began. Blaze betrayed her brother and took the throne for herself, leaving him as her subordinate (*Reign in Hell* #1–8, September 2008–April 2009).

LORING, EMIL

Despite being a celebrated wunderkind adept at both science and architecture, Emil Loring suffered from an inferiority complex, given that he was born a dwarf. Loring wanted to build an edifice that outshone the legendary Tower of Babel and moved to Africa, where he enslaved the people to help construct his dream project. To make certain no other structure could compare, he also set out to destroy the pyramids of Egypt, the Washington Monument, the Mount Rushmore National Memorial, and the Statue of Liberty. Superman saw to it that the marvels remained intact, and when he confronted the madman, Loring died when a volcano suddenly erupted and caused his tower to come crashing back to Earth (*Action Comics* #56, January 1943).

LORRA

Lorra was known as the Kryptonian goddess of beauty; a statue of her was kept in the bottle city of Kandor. The statue had an uncanny resemblance to film star Lyra Lerrol (according to Supergirl), who once had a doomed romance with Superman (*Action Comics* #299, April 1963).

LOR-VAN, LARA

See Lara Lor-Van.

LOR-ZOD

See Christopher Kent.

LUBANE

Lubane was a devious businessman who used his connections and influence to ignite military con-

flicts around the world, reaping vast profits by selling arms and munitions to all sides. From his factory in the small country of Boravia, he orchestrated global events until his agents brought him to Superman's attention. When Professor Adolphus Runyan was killed in Metropolis and his secret formula for a new poison gas was stolen, Superman flew to Europe and personally dismantled Lubane's factory. He then brought the country's two sides together and forced them to engage in peace talks designed to end the brutal civil war. When Lubane tried to escape, he shattered a vial of the deadly gas and died instantly (*Superman* [first series] #2, Fall 1939).

LUCERO, LOURDES

The occult opponent of the Man of Steel known as La Encantadora was once only Lourdes Lucero.

LUKAS, KARL

Superman once disguised himself as a criminal in order to infiltrate Karl "Big Daddy" Lukas's Mafia family. During the adventure, Batman suffered a head wound that led him to think he was actually a Made Man. As the World's Finest duo continued their masquerade, they appeared to kill Robin and Jimmy Olsen, the emotional jolt of which shocked Batman back to his senses, allowing the team to take down Lukas once and for all (*World's Finest Comics* #194–195, June–August 1970).

LUTHOR, ALEXANDER, JUNIOR

On Lexor, the planet named in his honor, Lex Luthor and his wife Ardora welcomed a son they named Alexander Luthor Junior. While he was still an infant, a titanic struggle between Lex Luthor and Superman accidentally caused an explosion, which led to the destruction of the world. Luthor watched in horror as his beloved wife and child died in the conflagration (*Action Comics* #544, June 1983).

The fate of the Earth-2 Luthor was unrecorded, but on Earth-3, Luthor saw the coming wave of anti-matter during the Crisis on Infinite Earths and managed to place his infant son, also named Alexander Luthor Junior, in a rocket, hoping the child would find a reality in which to thrive (*Crisis on Infinite Earths* #1, April 1985).

The rocket soon wound up in the possession of the Monitor, who cared for the infant in his transdimensional headquarters. The boy grew rapidly, and was forced to wear a gold metallic outfit to contain the powers that began manifesting as he aged. His travel between dimensions during the unleashed anti-matter energies led Alexander to be able to control both matter and anti-matter, even opening portals between the opposite-charged realities without inflicting any damage. Within just weeks, he had grown to the body of a young adult and had befriended the Monitor's ward, Lyla, who helped explain to Alexander what was happening.

In the wake of the Monitor's death, and with just two positive-matter universes left, Alexander Luthor aided Superman, Superman-2, and Superboy-Prime in their final showdown with the Anti-Monitor. When a single positive-matter universe was re-formed, there seemed to be no place for either Superman-2 or Superboy-Prime. Alexander not only came up with a solution but also showed the Man of Steel that he had managed to save his wife, Lois Lane-2. The three were offered a place in a realm beyond the universes, a crystalline reality where they could live out their days in peace. The gift was gratefully accepted, and the trio prepared to live happily ever after (*Crisis on Infinite Earths* #12, March 1986).

They lived at first in harmony in their new home, and, using his powers, Alexander let the others watch what was transpiring on the newly singular Earth over the years. The heroes were horrified to see how dark the world and its heroes had become. Worse, Superboy-Prime was disgusted to see that the single Earth's Teen of Steel was nothing but a clone and, from his point of view, not a very effective hero. Alexander also grew disenchanted with the Earth he observed. As his body aged to adulthood, Lois continued her natural aging process and was growing frailer by the week.

In time, Alexander came to the conclusion that the single Earth's reality was misformed and needed to be destroyed, with a new Earth fashioned to suit his tastes. He slowly began manipulating the emotions of his colleagues and putting a plan together that would given him the power to alter reality. It was eventually revealed that the Source had chosen to influence Alexander into eventually re-creating the multiverse (*Death of the New Gods* #5, March 2008).

A frustrated Superboy-Prime began lashing out by pounding against the crystal home, unaware that each blow altered Earth's reality, resulting in both subtle and major changes to the planet's inhabitants and history. While his power levels were lower without a yellow sun to replenish him, Superboy-Prime was gratified to learn that Alexander's dimensional powers were functioning perfectly, and together they formed a plan.

Luthor brought Superboy-Prime from their limbo home back into the universe, whispering plans into his ear. The youth agreed to the scheme and used his brawn to begin moving pieces into place, starting by moving the planet Rann into the Thanagarian star system, not only causing a war but also shifting the universal center away from Oa, thereby blunting the effectiveness of the Guardians of the Universe and the Green Lantern Corps. Superboy-Prime then destroyed the Justice League of America's headquarters on the moon and abducted the Martian Manhunter as the first of a series of powerful beings Alexander needed to bring about the destruction of Earth.

Alexander impersonated Earth's Lex Luthor and formed a Secret Society of Super-Villains, turning the group into a serious threat to the super hero community. Additionally, he had Eclipso's magical Black Diamond delivered to an emotionally disturbed Jean Loring, who became the new Eclipso. She then seduced the Spectre and set him loose to destroy the Earth's magicians and their magical objects, which included the total destruction of Atlantis.

Alexander took control over Batman's Brother I satellite, which gave him control over the OMAC nanobots as well. He then approached Superman-2 about re-forming the world, telling him the wrong Earth had been saved during the first Crisis, and a grief-stricken Man of Steel was led to believe that remaking Earth-2 could save his dying wife Lois. He even journeyed to Earth in order to recruit Batman's help, but the Dark Knight rejected the idea.

By this point, the real Lex had learned of his impersonator, so he took the guise of Mockingbird and formed a group of villains known as the Secret Six to oppose the Society. In time, the two Luthors confronted each other in the Arctic. Alexander's presence on Earth also led to Lex behaving erratically, since reality couldn't contain two versions of the same being, which also held true for Supergirl and Power Girl (another Earth-2 survivor).

Alex and Superboy-Prime then collected beings from what should have been the various parallel worlds, including Power Girl, Breach, Captain Atom, Black Adam, and several others, and imprisoned them in a new version of the cosmic tuning fork that the Monitor had used against the Anti-Monitor years before. Alexander's goal was to split the universe into parallel universes until he found just the right one to keep, discarding the others. A new Earth-2 was formed, but Superman-2 discovered that it not only wasn't *his* Earth-2, but also wasn't enough to save Lois from dying; she passed away in his arms.

When Alexander, now drunk with power, began

toying with the new realities he was creating, Earth's heroes united to stop him before their reality was obliterated. Firestorm converted the combined energies of the various heroes into a single burst of raw positive matter, but the powerful blow did nothing more than sever Luthor's right index finger. However, it was enough to distract him.

Nightwing, Wonder Girl, and Superboy freed the captives being held in the cosmic tuning fork until Superboy-Prime tried to stop them. The battle destroyed the tower and killed Earth's Superboy, but not before the new multiverse was born, with fifty-two parallel worlds now existing.

Batman found Alexander and nearly beat him to death for the injuries he had dealt Nightwing and for the loss of Superboy. Wonder Woman stopped the Dark Knight, and Alexander was left alone. He had to content himself with picking a home from these new realities, but was discovered by Lex Luthor and the Joker. The Clown Prince of Crime shot Alexander to death, angry that he had not been invited to join the Secret Society of Super-Villains (*Infinite Crisis* #1–7, December 2005–June 2006).

Alexander's corpse was taken by Luthor and presented as genetic proof that he had been imprisoned and impersonated. He claimed the "clone" was the one who performed the many transgressions, leading to Lex Luthor's acquittal on all charges dating back to his tenure in the White House, as Lex lied and said he had been impersonated by Alexander since his presidency began (*52* #3, 2007).

LUTHOR, ARDORA

On the parallel world of Earth-216, Lex Luthor married a native woman named Ardora, and together they had a daughter named Ardora, although Ardora the Elder had hoped for a son. Ardora the Younger grew up worshipping her criminal father and once, under the pseudonym Dora Redson, helped free him from a Metropolis prison (*World's Finest Comics* #238, June 1976).

LUTHOR, LENA

Earth-1's Lena was the sister to the criminal scientist Lex Luthor, whose family members changed their surname to Thorul in an effort to distance themselves from Lex (*Superman's Girl Friend, Lois Lane* #23, February 1961). At first, Lena Thorul was unaware of the connection to Lex, as Luthor did what he could to protect his sister's innocence. Even Superman and Supergirl worked to help in this family matter. In early childhood, Lena developed extrasensory perception after being struck by an electrical discharge from a space-brain that her brother was studying, but otherwise she led a relatively normal life (*Action Comics* #295, December 1962).

In the reality created after the Crisis on Infinite Earths, Lena was the daughter born to Lex Luthor and the Contessa Erica del Portenza. Lex said she was named after his foster sister who had been killed by their foster father Casey Griggs. He became fiercely protective of the child and kept the Contessa in a drugged coma within the confines of LexCorp to prevent her from interfering (*Superman* [second series] #131, January 1998).

Lena eventually became a vessel for Brainiac 13 when the artificial intelligence arrived from the sixty-fourth century in a deal arranged by Lex, who desired the android's advanced technology more than he did his daughter's love (*Action Comics* #763, March 2000). She became the battleground between the twentieth-century Brainiac and its descendant. When it all was over, Lena had been aged to adolescence and was possessed by Brainiac 13 (*Superman* [second series] #171, August 2001). As a result, she seemingly fed her father useful intelligence, but was actually manipulating him on Brainiac's behalf. In time, though, she rejected the manipulation and allied herself with Lex. When the Imperiex War ended, both Brainiac 13 and Imperiex were seemingly destroyed and Lena was returned to her natural infant form. Superman pointed out to Lex that he now had a second chance at being a parent (*Action Comics* #782, October 2001).

A remnant of the Brainiac's technology came to believe it was Lena and fashioned itself a bald female form to interact with humans, most notably Jimmy Olsen. When Superman arrived with the real Lena in tow, the AI realized it had deceived itself and ended its programming (*Superman's Metropolis* #1–12, April 2003–March 2004).

After reality was reordered during the Infinite Crisis, there were no recorded appearances of Lena, who may no longer exist.

In one account of Lex's revised history, it was

reported that the teenage Luthor spent much of his adolescence in Smallville under the care of his aunt Lena Luthor (*Countdown to Final Crisis* #34, September 5, 2007).

Reality, however, was altered once more and the adult Lex never had a child named Lena. Instead, Lena Luthor was Lex's younger sister when they lived in Smallville (*Superman: Secret Origin* #2, December 2009). At some point, Lena suffered a devastating injury, leaving her trapped in Smallville as an invalid. She was left alone to raise her daughter Lori, who wound up developing a crush on Superboy, unaware that some of her uncle's DNA had created the Clone of Steel. Soon after Superboy and Lori met, Lex reappeared in his sister Lena's life, promising her a cure for her physical condition. Superboy reluctantly aided Lex in his experiment, and after first curing Lena, Lex then reversed the effect, leaving his sister in a catatonic state. The cruel Lex explained that as long as Superman is alive, he will never reveal his cure. A disappointed Superboy then turned to Red Robin for help, and Lena was placed in the care of medical experts at Wayne Enterprises (*Adventure Comics* #508–509, February–March 2010).

LUTHOR, LEX

Almost from the moment Superman arrived in Metropolis, Lex Luthor took an intense dislike to the Man of Steel and all he stood for and grabbed every chance he could to try to destroy him. The rivalry and dislike between the two survived multiple realities and was emblematic of the ultimate struggle between good and evil.

Luthor was a red-haired criminal scientist when he first tested his genius against the Man of Steel's might on Earth-2 (*Action Comics* #23, April 1940). As of his fifth recorded appearance (*Superman* [first series] #10, May–June 1941) and in all subsequent appearances throughout the 1940s and 1950s, the villain was depicted as bald. Later retroactive accounts established that the Earth-2 Luthor had always had red hair, even in stories depicting him otherwise.

Alexei Luthor (first name revealed in *Superman Family* #202, July–August 1980) was described as a "power-mad, evil scientist, Superman's most inveterate hater . . . He could have been a mighty force for good in the world yet he chose to di-

SHORTLY, LUTHOR'S CLEVER BRAIN COMES TO GRIPS WITH A NEAR-IMPOSSIBLE TASK, IN HIS LABORATORY...
I'VE GROUND DOWN THE KRYPTONITE CHIPS INTO A FINE DUST... AND BLENDED IT WITH A LIQUEFIED FORM OF THE PROTO-PLASMIC LIFE I CREATED! I MUST NOT-- I WILL NOT--FAIL!

rect his great scientific brain into criminal channels" (*Action Comics* #47, April 1942). Luthor first came to Superman's attention when he provoked a war between the nations of Galonia and Toran as a stepping-stone toward his ultimate goal of world domination (*Action Comics* #23, April 1940). In the months that followed, Luthor stole an earthquake machine as a blackmail tool, halted the flow of the world's oil wells (*Superman* [first series] #4, Spring 1940), mentally enslaved U.S. financial leaders (*Superman* [first series] #5, Summer 1940), and cut off Metropolis's water supply (*Superman* [first series] #10, May–June 1941). Through it all, the terrorist displayed a remarkable ability to survive, even as Superman left him for dead. Whether faced with a flaming dirigible or ravenous dinosaurs or a plane submerged in the ocean, Lex Luthor always returned.

...FOR THIS MOMENT! HOW DO YOU LIKE BEING ON THE RECEIVING END FOR A CHANGE?
OOF!

Luthor often had a costume of sorts, wearing robes variously colored red, purple, or green as he assumed the alter egos of Zytal (*Action Comics* #42, November 1941) or the Light (*Superman* [first series] #13, November–December 1941), or duped Superman into locating the extraterrestrial Powerstone (*Action Comics* #47, April 1942). Endowed with latent super-strength through the Powerstone, Luthor managed to cheat death after being executed in the electric chair. He subsequently cornered Superman and used the Powerstone to rob the Kryptonian of his superpowers. The villain seemed unstoppable, until the Man of Steel seized the Powerstone from his grasp and used the object to restore both himself and Luthor to normal (*Superman* [first series] #17, July–August 1942).

Discovering the existence of kryptonite, Luthor took no small measure of pride in the fact that it was he who first revealed kryptonite's effects on Superman to the general public (*Superman Family* #205, January–February 1981) and produced the first sample of its synthetic equivalent (*Action Comics* #141, February 1950). If Luthor couldn't kill his nemesis, an increasingly paunchy Luthor was willing to settle for humiliating Superman by working alongside the Prankster and sometimes Mr. Mxyztplk (*Action Comics* #151, December 1950) and later the Toyman (*Superman* [first series] #88, March 1954).

In other realities, Luthor's history played out differently. On Earth-32, for instance, Superboy found himself overshadowed by a rival costumed hero named Amazing-Man. Unmasked as a villain, the Boy of Steel's rival identified himself as Luthor and vowed to become his enemy from that point on (*Superboy* [first series] #59, September 1957). Thanks to a glimpse of the future, Luthor tried to prevent the start of Jimmy Olsen and Superman's friendship (*Superman's Pal, Jimmy Olsen* #109, March 1968). Still obsessed with changing Superman's destiny, this Luthor even traveled to Krypton's past to prevent Jor-El and Lara's marriage (*Superman* [first series] #170, July 1964).

On Earth-1, Alexis "Lex" Luthor had a long history with his arch-foe (*Action Comics* #199, December 1954; first name established in *Adventure Comics* #271, April 1960; formal first name revealed in *Action Comics* #512, October 1980). His hatred for Superman began when both were teens living in Smallville. They met when the brown-haired Luthor saved the Teen of Steel from exposure to kryptonite. They became fast friends, and Superboy repaid Lex's heroic act by building the inquisitive Luthor a fully outfitted laboratory. It was here, after thousands of experiments, that the cocky young scientist discovered the secret of life itself and created a protoplasmic life-form. To repay Superboy for the gift that made it possible, Luthor successfully developed an antidote to kryptonite radiation.

One lab experiment resulted in a fire, with Superboy arriving in time to blow it out and save Luthor from the toxic fumes. The fumes, however, turned the teen scientist bald. More devastating—from Lex's perspective—was the fact that the protoplasm and its hard-earned formula had been destroyed as well. Insisting that Superboy was jealous of his genius, Luthor spent the next several months trying to better the lives of the people of Smallville and outshine Superboy's achievements. Sadly, each attempt—from a weather tower to seeds meant to improve the crop yields of farmers—went awry, and the teen was left more embittered than ever (*Adventure Comics* #271, April 1960).

Superboy tolerated Lex's personal attacks on him, because he still held out hope that Luthor would eventually let go of his anger (*Superboy* [first series] #86, January 1961). Once he was exposed as a thief, however, Luthor was sent first to reform school (*Superboy* [first series] #92, October 1961) and ultimately prison (*Adventure Comics*

AS THE FLAMES VANISH, SUPERBOY ENTERS THE DAMAGED ALCOVE, EXPECTING LUTHOR'S THANKS, BUT...
YOU RAT! YOUR PUFF OF SUPER-BREATH BLEW AN ACID BOTTLE AGAINST THE ANTIDOTE BOTTLE! THEY BROKE, AND THEIR CONTENTS DESTROYED THE FORMULA FOR MY GREAT DISCOVERY! NOT ONLY THAT--THE GAS FUMES MADE MY HAIR FALL OUT! I'M BALD!

#292, January 1962). Clark Kent, himself a friend of Lex before the accident (*Superman* [first series] #292, October 1975; *Superman: Last Son of Krypton,* 1978), would be a target for the young Luthor's resentment as well. Luthor once conspired to have Kent framed and confined to the same prison he was in (*Adventure Comics* #301, October 1962). Lex would unfortunately spend much of the years to come in prison grays.

Lex's downfall was a source of humiliation for his parents, traveling salesman Jules and his wife Arlene (*Superman's Girl Friend, Lois Lane* #23, February 1961; named in *Superman: Last Son of Krypton,* 1978). Jules had already disowned his older daughter, who'd married young over his objections and moved to Europe (*Adventure Comics* #401, January 1971), but this they considered far worse. Taking their toddler daughter Lena with them, the Luthors left Smallville and changed their name to Thorul. Tragically, the couple perished in a car crash soon after, and Lena Thorul, who'd acquired telepathic powers in an earlier accident in Lex's lab, grew up entirely unaware of her checkered heritage (*Action Comics* #295, December 1962).

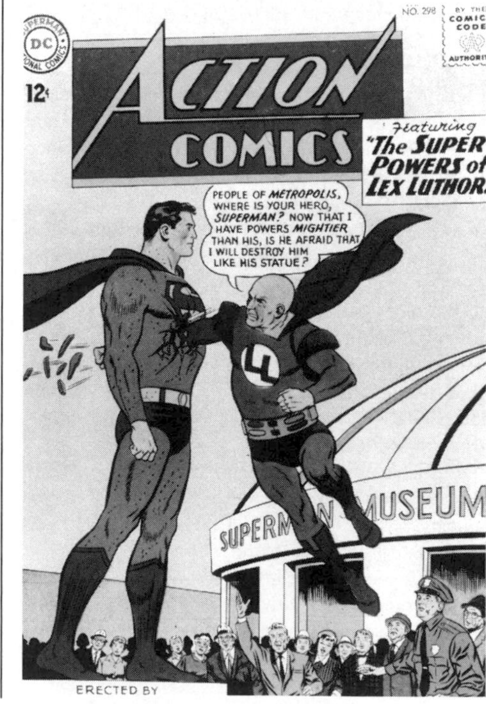
NO. 298
DC
ACTION COMICS
12¢
Featuring "The SUPER POWERS of LEX LUTHOR"
PEOPLE OF METROPOLIS, WHERE IS YOUR HERO, SUPERMAN? NOW THAT I HAVE POWERS MIGHTIER THAN HIS, IS HE AFRAID THAT I WILL DESTROY HIM LIKE HIS STATUE?
SUPERM N MUSEUM
ERECTED BY

While Clark Kent went on to college and then became a reporter, Luthor used his natural skills to experiment and become a master of multiple scientific disciplines. When Superman relocated to Metropolis, Luthor followed him, and their rivalry began anew. Focused almost exclusively on the Man of Steel, Luthor rarely encountered other super heroes when Superman (or later Supergirl) wasn't involved. Among those infrequent exceptions were encounters with Batman and Robin (*Batman* #130, March 1960), and Black Canary (*Action Comics* #458, April 1976).

Luthor's genius had led to the development of countless machines, devices, procedures, compounds, and other wonders spanning the entire world of science. His wealth from patents alone mitigated the need for crime, but Lex used it as an excuse to enter into a fresh battle of wits with his hated enemy. Among his creations were rocket ships, robots, dimensional portals, time machines, a money magnet, a vault-blaster, an earthquake maker, an atomic death ray, and even Luthorite, a synthetic form of kryptonite.

Constantly haunted by the protoplasm that Superboy had inadvertently destroyed, Luthor often returned his focus to the creation of life itself. He successfully re-created another scientist's old work and gave birth to a new incarnation of Bizarro (*Action Comics* #254, July 1959), developed the star-fueled—and potentially earth-shattering—Galactic Golem (*Superman* [first series] #248, February 1972), and became a pioneer in the science of cloning (*Superman's Pal, Jimmy Olsen* #162, December 1973–January 1974; *Action Comics* #500, October 1979, and #512, October 1980).

Many of these creations were conceived in secret hideouts throughout Metropolis, each dubbed Luthor's Lair. The first, situated in an abandoned museum, included a distinctive row of statues representing Luthor's heroes—Attila the Hun, Genghis Khan, Captain Kidd, and Al Capone (*Action Comics* #277, June 1961). Luthor eventually cloaked his operations within a legitimate business called the Thunder Corporation, and used its midtown penthouse as his command post. Any of his operatives who were captured, Luthor promised, would "be paid triple-time for the period they spend in prison" (*Superman* [first series] #282, December 1974; named in *Superman: Last Son of Krypton,* 1978).

As a teen, Lex had periodically allied himself with the likes of Mr. Mxyzptlk (*Superboy* [first series] #131, July 1966) and the Phantom Zone criminals (*Superboy* [first series] #115, September 1964), and he continued to do so as an adult, joining forces with Terra-Man on one occasion (*Superman Spectacular* #1, 1982) and even once making an unsuccessful bid to takeover the Secret Society of Super-Villains (*Secret Society of Super-Villains* #7, May–June 1977).

He formed an early partnership with the Joker (*World's Finest Comics* #88, May–June 1957; others), but their disparate personalities began to grate (*World's Finest Comics* #177, August 1968), culminating in an encounter wherein the Joker's interference temporarily transferred his insanity to Luthor (*The Joker* #7, May–June 1976).

The team of Luthor and Brainiac—both villains

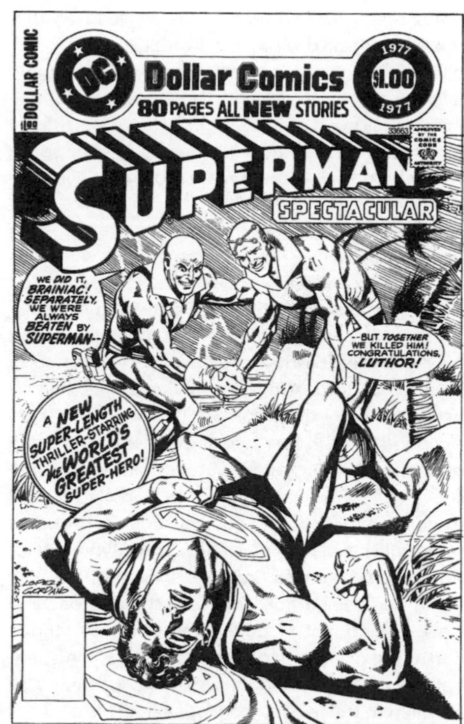

grounded in science—proved more successful and enduring. Lex earned his partner's goodwill by freeing Brainiac from the prison planet Kronis and upgrading his computer intelligence. Anticipating that Brainiac might eventually consider him irrelevant, Luthor also installed a fail-safe timer that would shut Brainiac down at timed intervals (*Superman* [first series] #167, February 1964). Overcoming their early mutual distrust, the two worked together often, right up until the Crisis on Infinite Earths (*Crisis on Infinite Earths* #6, September 1985, and #9, December 1985). At different points, the duo also collaborated with the Legion of Super-Villains (*Superman's Pal, Jimmy Olsen* #87, September 1965; *Action Comics* #332, January 1966), Grax, and the Marauder (*Action Comics* #417–418, October–November 1972).

Perhaps inspired by his costumed cohorts, Luthor periodically donned costumes and assumed alter egos. He took the identities of Dak-El (*Superboy* [first series] #115, September 1964) and Cerebron (*Superboy* [first series] #177, September 1971) as a teenager, while declaring himself the Kryptonite Man (*Action Comics* #249, February 1959), Mechano-Master (*Superboy* [first series] #135, January 1967), and Dominus (*DC Special Series* #26, Summer 1981) as an adult. On the world of Lexor, where he was regarded with reverence, Luthor even became a costumed hero known as the Defender (*Superman* [first series] #168, April 1964).

Once temporarily endowed with superpowers, Lex adopted a purple-and-green Superman-styled costume, complete with an LL-emblem on its chest (*Action Comics* #297–298, February–March 1963). Maintaining the color scheme for many years, a slimmed-down Luthor subsequently began wearing a unitard complete with jetpack, providing him with maximum mobility in his battles against the Man of Steel (*Superman* [first series] #282, December 1974). Years later, he modified the outfit into a similarly schemed battle armor, complete with built-in weaponry (*Action Comics* #544, June 1983).

When Lex argued that Superman's powers and abilities gave him an unfair advantage, Superman obliged the criminal by taking him to a world with a red sun. There, with the odds evened, the two fought to a draw. By then, Luthor had befriended the natives and promised he would solve their drought problem. Throwing the second battle, he asked Superman to help the people, and when the world was bombarded with ice from space, they credited Luthor with keeping his word (*Superman* [first series] #164, October 1963). They renamed their world Lexor in his honor, and he returned there repeatedly as he was hailed a hero. He enjoyed the love of a native woman named Ardora, whom he later married (*Action Comics* #318, November 1964).

Behavior such as this—and Lex's sincere efforts to shield Lena Thorul from the knowledge that she was his sister (*Superman's Girl Friend, Lois Lane* #23, February 1961; others)—gave Superman cause for hope that his childhood friend was not beyond redemption. Similarly, when a time-traveling Luthor realized that he had inadvertently stopped Superboy from preventing the assassination of President Lincoln, he was genuinely sickened, more proof that he was not evil through and through (*Superboy* [first series] #85, December 1960).

Lex could also be a doting uncle, often smuggling birthday gifts to Lena's son Val Colby (*Action Comics* #486, August 1978). On the other hand, when the toddler temporarily gained psychokinetic powers, Luthor wasn't above employing Val's services for criminal purposes (*Adventure Comics* #387–388, December 1969–January 1970). He also happily encouraged his older sister's daughter Nasthalthia in her efforts to perpetually thwart

Supergirl (*Adventure Comics* #397, September 1970).

Once when members of the Justice League of America were on a mission in outer space, Luthor stepped in to save Earth from a potentially deadly assault on its atmosphere, winning both a presidential pardon and the hand of Lois Lane. However, Lois only pretended to become engaged to Luthor until she could prove that he'd orchestrated the threat to Earth himself as part of an elaborate plot to expose Superman's true identity (*Superman Family* #172, August–September 1975).

A few years later, Luthor played out a variation on the scheme, once again pretending to reform and marrying a woman named Angela Blake. This plot was more insidious, requiring Lex to murder the real Blake and create a genetically engineered clone of her that would destroy both herself and Superman when the Man of Steel came into contact with her (*Action Comics* #510–512, August–October 1980).

Such cold-blooded behavior was infrequent but not unprecedented, as in instances when Luthor allowed several injured mermen to die while he was looting Atlantean treasures (*Action Comics* #332, January 1966) and murdered the scheming Michael "King" Andrews, who had accidentally discovered the Fortress of Solitude—a secret Lex wanted to possess alone (*Action Comics* #407, December 1971).

Throughout everything, the planet Lexor had remained essentially untouched, and Luthor was elated to find that Ardora had given birth to a son, Alexander Luthor Junior, in his absence. Still, he couldn't get past his enmity toward the Man of Steel and thought he'd found a way to even the odds by using an armored war suit developed by the planet's scientists. Tragically, another battle with Superman accidentally led to the planet's destruction soon after. Unwilling to acknowledge his own role in the disaster, Luthor focused all his grief-stricken rage on the Man of Steel (*Action Comics* #544, May 1983).

Back on Earth, Lex established a new base on Black Island, a chunk of Lexor that became his mobile sanctuary. There he assembled a support team consisting of chemist Renzil Dugan, mob enforcer "Louto" Malono, gang boss "Wicked" Wanda Nordo, and Siamese twins/crime planners Pluto and Plato Statler (*Superman* [first series] #385, July 1983). Luthor ultimately learned that the war suit he'd discovered on Lexor was originally meant as a doomsday weapon. By bringing it to Earth, he'd unwittingly threatened the human race, requiring him to team up with Superman in order to eradicate the suit's deadly electro-spine, which represented the threat (*Superman* [first series] *Annual* #12, 1986).

Several years after accidentally transporting himself to Earth-S and joining forces with Mister Mind against Captain Marvel (*Shazam!* #15, November–December 1974), Earth-1's Luthor discovered and perfected dimensional travel. He and his red-haired Earth-2 counterpart teamed up in an attempt to destroy their archenemies, uniting with Ultraman from Earth-3 (*DC Comics Presents Annual* #1, 1982). The two Supermen were aided by the Earth-3 Alexander Luthor, that world's first super hero, who would soon be happily married to Lois Lane. His world had no super heroes, just super-villains belonging to the Crime Syndicate of America (*DC Comics Presents Annual* #1, 1982).

On Earth-3, Luthor witnessed the approaching wave of anti-matter during the Crisis on Infinite Earths but managed to place his infant son Alexander in a rocket, hoping he would find a safe reality in which to thrive (*Crisis on Infinite Earths* #1, April 1985). As the Crisis grew, a group of villains from five Earths was assembled under the leadership of Brainiac and his field commander, the Earth-1 Luthor. Taking umbrage that his counterpart was in charge rather than himself, Earth-2's Luthor cried foul and was reduced to ashes by Brainiac for his objections (*Crisis on Infinite Earths* #9, December 1985). Faced with a threat to all reality, the surviving Luthor ultimately switched sides, traveling back in time to Oa in an attempt to thwart the plans of the mad Krona (*Crisis on Infinite Earths* #10, January 1986).

The contradictions and complexities of Earth-1's Lex Luthor, who could eliminate nuclear weapons and fix the ozone layer one day (*Action Comics* #511, September 1980) and commit cold-blooded murder the next (*Action Comics* #512, October 1980), made him an object of fascination for many. Indeed, a Luthorcon celebrating the villain was held annually in Metropolis (*DC Comics Presents Annual* #4, 1985).

During his annual commemoration of the birthday of one of his personal heroes, Albert Einstein, Luthor saved the life of Calvin Anderson, a boy he'd inadvertently endangered. That youth, in one potential future, would grow up to become "the criminal rehabilitation genius who cured Lex Luthor of his criminal obsessions." Moving on with his life, this incarnation of Luthor founded a groundbreaking tech firm named LexCorp (*Superman* [first series] #416, February 1986).

In other realities, Luthor was also fated for a heroic end, as on Earth-148, where he and Clayface opposed the villainous Superman and Batman (*World's Finest Comics* #148, March 1965). Reformed and once again possessed of a full head of hair, the Luthor of Earth-162 contributed to his world's utopian environment by creating "a super-serum that will cure every known disease" (*Superman* [first series] #162, July 1963).

More tragically, the reformed Luthor of Earth-34 married Lois Lane but was electrocuted while trying to stop their son Larry's criminal activities, which would soon earn the youth the name Black Luthor (*Superman's Girl Friend, Lois Lane* #34, July 1962). In a Pocket Universe created by the Time Trapper, a benevolent Lex Luthor created Matrix (aka Supergirl) in a futile attempt to stop the Phantom Zone criminals he'd unwittingly unleashed on his Earth. Killed along with the rest of his world, this Luthor was avenged by the Superman of the reality formed in the wake of the Crisis on Infinite Earths (*Superman* [second series] #21, September 1988; *The Adventures of Superman* #444, September 1988; *Superman* [second series] #22, October 1988).

Reputed descendants of Luthor included the thirtieth century's sinister Rohtul (*World's Finest Comics* #91, November–December 1957), a heroic Luthor who joined the adult Legion of Super-Heroes (*Adventure Comics* #355, April 1967), and a scheming thirty-fifth-century Luthor who ran a Superman Museum (*Superboy* [first series] #120, April 1965).

When reality was reordered by the Crisis on Infinite Earths, Lex Luthor and Superman did not meet until both were adults and living in Metropolis. By this time, Luthor had an entirely different backstory and grew to resent Superman for stealing the celebrity spotlight he had worked so hard to have all to himself.

Alexander Joseph Luthor (full name revealed in *Superman: Lex 2000* #1, January 2001) was born in the Suicide Slum section of Metropolis and raised by abusive parents. When he was a teenager, Luthor took out an insurance policy on his parents, then sabotaged the brakes on the family car, ensuring a fatal accident (*Lex Luthor: The Unauthorized Biography,* 1989). He was then placed with foster parents Emily and Casey Griggs, who coveted Lex's insurance inheritance. Casey went so far as to have his own daughter Lena

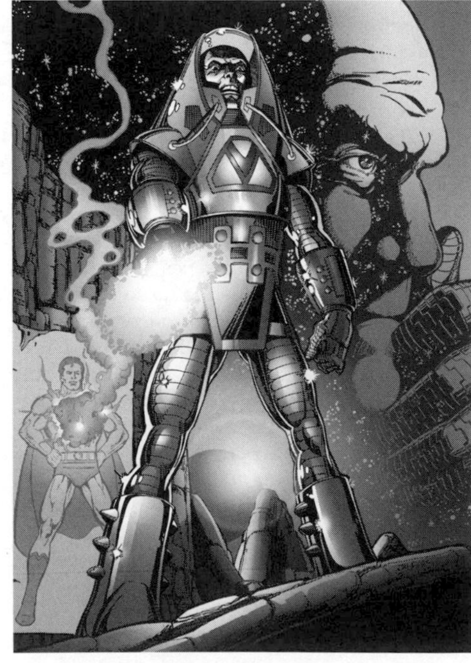

seduce Lex in order to ascertain the money's location. When she refused—she loved Lex—Casey beat her to death, something Luthor could not prevent since he had been coaxed into attending a football game with his classmate Perry White (*Superman* [second series] #131, January 1998).

Using his insurance payout, Lex created and, through intermediaries, sold designer drugs as an additional source of revenue (*Lex Luthor: The Unauthorized Biography,* 1989). Soon after, Lex created an aviation sensation when he piloted the LexWing on an uninterrupted flight from Metropolis to Sydney, Australia (*Action Comics* #660, December 1990) and formed the basis for a conglomeration called LexCorp. In doing so, he revived the family fortune that had prospered under his grandfather Wallace's Luthor Steelworks, a fortune subsequently lost in the 1929 stock market crash (*Superman Y2K* #1, February 2000; *Superman: Lex 2000* #1, January 2001).

LexCorp grew rapidly and used the Lex name as a brand, turning its founder into one of the best-known businessmen on the planet (*Man of Steel* #2, Late October 1986). Branching out from aerospace into all of the sciences and media, it gobbled up smaller competitors, allowing Luthor to shelter programs and shift funds, avoiding suspicion that he had several different programs at work, all eventually dedicated to finding ways of ridding Earth of Superman. Luthor had humble beginnings, and leased the top floor of Metropolis's Daily Planet Building. He made his first acquisitions—Inter-Continental Airlines and Atlantic Coast Air Systems—and merged them into LexAir. During a brief energy crisis, Luthor cannily scooped up Southwestern Petroleum and renamed it LexOil. In short order, his name began to be recognized.

Luthor, having been betrayed by people all his life, began using his newfound wealth and celebrity to treat others with contempt and disdain. From petty acts to major incidents, Luthor struck back at society whenever he could. As he prepared to sell the *Daily Planet* to David Ling, Lex went so far as to seduce editor Perry White's wife Alice White (*World of Metropolis* #1, August 1988) in revenge for Luthor's being at a football game with Perry when Lena was murdered by his adoptive father. The affair resulted in Alice's only child, a son named Jerry White, although Luthor kept that to himself until the boy was fatally shot (*Superman* [second series] #47, September 1990). Luthor was said to have been married seven times by the time of Superman's arrival in Metropolis, although none of his wives' names were known save for third wife Elizabeth Perske (*Supergirl* [third series] #2, September 1994).

Luthor used his influence to work his way through high society as well as the circles of government so that he quickly became indispensable. Every magnanimous act came with strings attached, such as the medicine he provided to keep reporter Lois Lane's mother Elinore Lane alive. It was later learned he engineered the freak chemical "accident" that injured her, and the goal of Luthor's actions was to maintain close ties with the reporter (*The Adventures of Superman* #424, January 1987). Later, after her mother had built up immunity to the medicine, Lois learned of Luthor's role in Ella's condition and became even more determined to reveal Lex as the criminal he truly was (*Superman* [second series] #50, December 1990). Mrs. Lane ultimately rallied and returned to full health.

Superman first encountered Luthor when he interrupted a group of terrorists crashing a party aboard the Luthor yacht. When the Man of Steel apprehended the criminals, Luthor tried to hand him a check, a bald attempt at hiring Superman to work for him. He even admitted to hiring the men in order to lure Superman into the open so that he could make the offer. Luthor was promptly arrested, thereby beginning the enmity between Lex and Superman (*Man of Steel* #4, Late November 1986).

Luthor was quickly freed and set out to gain his revenge. If he couldn't have Superman, he'd build one, although the project failed and led to a marred duplicate dubbed Bizarro (*Man of Steel* #5, Early December 1986). He tried to learn everything he could about the super hero, and it soon became an obsession. In fact, he went so far as to kidnap and torture Lana Lang, correctly convinced she knew Superman's secrets, although she failed to crack under interrogation (*Superman* [second series] #2, February 1987).

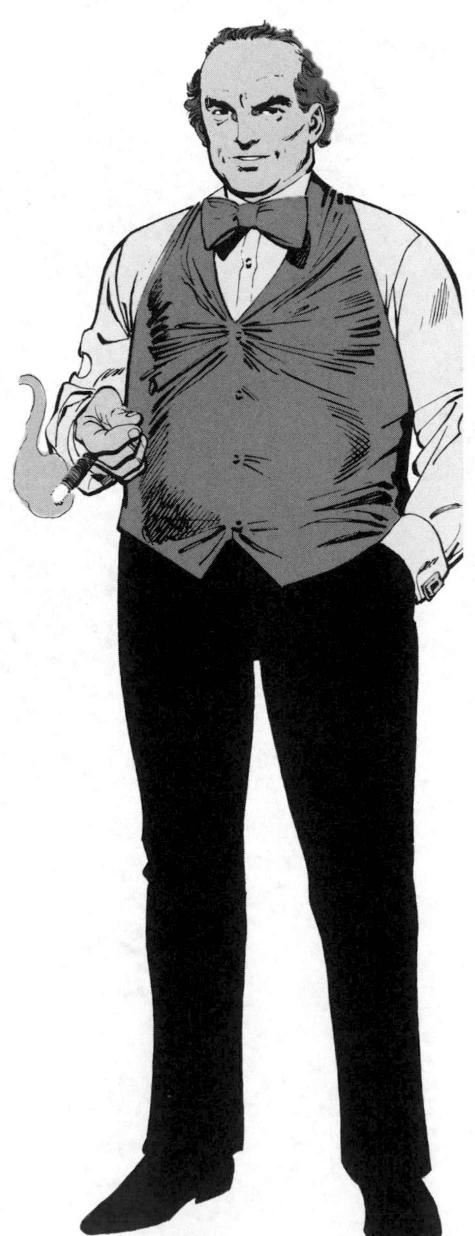

The rivalry between the hero and the megalomaniac increased through the years, with Luthor launching one scheme after another in order to defame or destroy Superman. When it became clear Lois preferred the Kryptonian to him, Luthor's hatred grew deeper, if that was even possible.

Some time after Superman arrived in Metropolis, kryptonite was discovered and used to power the cyborg workings of John Corben, who battled Superman as Metallo but died during their encounter. His body was spirited away by Luthor, who plucked the kryptonite from Corben's chest and had a portion of the rock fashioned into a signet ring. He then waited for Superman to confront him, convinced that he'd finally gotten the upper hand on his longtime nemesis (*Superman* [second series] #1–2, January–February 1987).

Other fragments were turned into bullets by Luthor and supplied to the mercenary Bloodsport, who tried to kill the Man of Steel in a misguided rage (*Superman* [second series] #4, April 1987).

Unlike the kryptonite of old, this iteration of the meteor actually *was* harmful to the people of Earth after long-term exposure. Luthor eventually discovered that he had radiation poisoning from his kryptonite ring, which required the amputation of his right hand (*Action Comics* #600, June 1988). When the cancer spread further, Lex decided to fake his death (*Action Comics* #660, December 1990) as part of an elaborate plot to have his brain transplanted into a healthy clone body that he passed off as his long-lost son.

The world was stunned when the handsome, virile, redheaded, and bearded twenty-one-year-old Lex Luthor II stepped out of an airplane into the heights of Metropolis society (*Action Comics* #671, November 1991). This Luthor tried to be everything his predecessor was not, squiring attractive women around town without leaving them in the dust, and his fake Australian accent furthered his fabricated life story.

After being installed as the new CEO of LexCorp, Lex formed a squadron of armored security agents and dubbed them Team Luthor. He also used his charm to worm his way into the heart of Matrix, the entity created by the heroic Luthor of the Pocket Universe and now adventuring under the guise of Supergirl (*Action Comics* #677, May 1992).

In the wake of Superman's death, Project Cadmus's abandoned Project Superman was resurrected in an attempt to clone the beloved hero. Superman's Kryptonian DNA proved too unstable, however: Each clone degenerated after only a short period of time. There were a dozen new attempts with the same results until Luthor used his own genetic material in the next clone. The result proved stable and was eventually dubbed Superboy. It wasn't until years later that Conner Kent

learned the truth of half of his "parentage" (*Teen Titans* [third series] #1, September 2003), as at first he was told that his human DNA came from Cadmus director Paul Westfield (*Superboy* [third series] *Annual* #2, 1995).

In time, Luthor's cloned body began to deteriorate and his red hair soon fell out. The bald Luthor was back. A suspicious Lois Lane had been investigating the new Luthor and finally found the proof she needed that he was merely a clone when she snagged key testimony from Lex's physician and former lover Gretchen Kelley. Superman apprehended the dying Luthor, but not before the madman had unleashed a fail-safe plan that devastated much of Metropolis. Although Luthor's cellular deterioration had been arrested, the clone's body was now paralyzed, Lex's brilliant mind suffering in silence (*Action Comics* #700-701, June–July 1994).

Luthor escaped his fate thanks to a deal he made with the demon Neron. Luthor willingly gave away his soul in exchange for his cloned body being restored to perfect health. The newly revived Luthor now had his thicker, pre-clone physique, but he was content knowing that he was now cancer-free and could continue to seek revenge against Superman and his allies (*Superman: The Man of Tomorrow* #1, Summer 1995, and #3, Winter 1995).

After temporarily serving on Neron's elite council of villains (*Underworld Unleashed* #1, November 1995), Luthor helped form a new Injustice Gang with the intent of getting vengeance against the Justice League (*JLA* #9–12, September–November 1997, and #14–15, January–February 1998). For Luthor, this was a chance to re-form an Injustice League that would succeed where the original incarnation failed (*Silver Age* #1, July 2000; *Silver Age 80-Page Giant* #1, July 2000; others).

Luthor then met his match in the Contessa Erica Alexandra del Portenza, who swooped in to buy a controlling interest in LexCorp while Lex was still a fugitive (*Superman: The Man of Tomorrow* #1, Summer 1995). The two were instantly attracted to each other and engaged in a whirlwind affair that resulted in Luthor making the Contessa his eighth wife (*Superman: The Man of Tomorrow* #5, Summer 1996).

Weeks later, a Sun-Eater entered Earth's solar system and threatened its sun. Superman and several other heroes attempted to decoy it with an artificial sun, but the plan failed and Sol was extinguished, threatening all sentient life in the system. The fugitive Lex Luthor teamed up with Earth's champions to try to reignite the Sun. He designed a network of force-field modules that the Flash manufactured at super-speed until there were five hundred thousand ready to be deployed to protect Earth. In order to be properly placed, they had to be piloted toward the sun at the exact moment the star would go nova; thus someone would have to fly the ship, sacrificing his or her life for the greater good. Luthor refused, saying he wasn't a hero. His act of cowardice provided further fuel for his enmity toward heroes (*Final Night* #1–4, November 1996).

Having regained some goodwill through his efforts during the solar crisis, Luthor surrendered to the authorities and resolved to clear his criminal record. He did this by "proving" that he had been comatose and recovering from kryptonite poisoning while a clone—which he produced—committed the crimes of which he was accused (*Action Comics* #737, September 1997). Luthor was duly aquitted.

Desiring a true heir to his name, Lex and the Contessa conceived a child. Sedated immediately after her daughter's birth, the Contessa was then locked away at LexCorp and kept in a drug-induced coma to prevent her from taking or even influencing the child. The baby, Lena, was named after Lex's foster sister, who had been killed by their foster father Casey Griggs (*Superman* [second series] #131, January 1998). Luthor became fiercely protective of the child until the Contessa escaped his control by faking her death (*Superman: The Man of Steel* #77, March 1998). The Contessa continued to plague Luthor from afar until he seemingly blew her island retreat to bits shortly after being elected president (*Secret Files and Origins: President Luthor* #1, March 2001).

Luthor and Lena had a difficult relationship in the brief time they were together. She was eventually taken over by Brainiac 13 and became the nexus in a struggle between the original Brainiac probe and its descendant (*Action Comics* #763, March 2000). She was then prematurely aged to adolescence (*Superman* [second series] #171, August 2001) but returned to her toddler form a short time later (*Action Comics* #782, October 2001). She was never heard from again.

Through the years, Luthor engaged in rivalries with many people, from Superman to the Contessa to Bruce Wayne. The issues between Luthor and Wayne had existed since the early days of LexCorp (*Batman Confidential* #1–6, February–August 2007), but years later, after Gotham City had become a no-man's-land and was excluded from federal authority, Luthor saw a chance at finally one-upping Wayne in the latter's own hometown.

He dispatched Mercy Graves to Gotham, where she offered to ally with the Penguin in order to further Luthor's plan. At the same time, Bane destroyed Gotham City's Hall of Records, submerging much of it underwater (*Detective Comics* #738, November 1999). Luthor had begun lobbying Congress in order to gain the contracts for Gotham's reconstruction. What few knew was that Luthor had already begun illegally placing matériel in the city, which was protected by Bane. He was also the one to order the public records destroyed so that he could buy up lots of prime Gotham property on the cheap (*Batman* #573, January 2000).

It all came to an unhappy ending when Luthor's occasional ally the Joker emerged, killing many of LexCorp's construction workers before disappearing from sight (*Batman: Shadow of the Bat* #94, February 2000). Wayne also outmaneuvered Luthor for construction contracts, leading Lex to hire a mercenary, David Cain, to frame Bruce Wayne for murder (*Batman* #605, September 2002).

Back in Metropolis, Luthor continued to find ways to either strike back at Superman or destroy the Man of Steel for good. His greatest ploy came to fruition when he used the country's dissatisfaction with how the federal government had turned its back on Gotham City in its hour of need into a run for the presidency (*The Adventures of Superman* #581, August 2000). Luthor used his charm and media savvy to court the public and the press. He then traveled to Smallville to ask Pete Ross, a former U.S. senator, to be his running mate (*Superman* [second series] #162, November 2000). The Luthor plank was forward thinking and used Lex's technological prowess to promise a cleaner, greener country. While the super heroic community shuddered at the notion, Luthor was shockingly elected by a huge margin (*Superman: Lex 2000* #1, January 2001). Just after being sworn in, Luthor's first legislation hit Congress, a proposed moratorium on fossil-based fuels, which ultimately did not pass. Batman saw to it that all Wayne Enterprises contracts with the federal government were canceled in protest of Luthor's election.

Luthor took advantage of his position as well by settling old scores such as targeting the Contessa's hideaway and destroying it with a barrage of missiles (*Secret Files and Origins: President Luthor* #1, March 2001). This ensured that her schemes for power would never again interfere with his own agenda; nor would she challenge him for control over their daughter Lena.

Soon after, Luthor learned of the impending arrival of Imperiex, a galactic conqueror who was on his way to Earth to destroy it, but Lex kept the information to himself. Instead he waited until there was a genuine crisis, then showed his unflinching leadership by coordinating the world's response to the alien threat. Later, after the Imperiex War was won by Earth's heroes, the public was horrified to learn that their president had known of the danger but kept mum, which had resulted in the devastation of Topeka, Kansas. Luthor was quick to refute the charges, the first in a series of acts that would come to topple his presidency (*Superman* [second series] #182–183, July–August 2002).

Unbeknownst to Luthor, the son of his Earth-3 counterpart, Alexander Luthor Junior, had pierced the dimensional veil and arrived on Earth to begin orchestrating events that Alexander hoped would lead to the birth of a new reality. Having both versions of Lex Luthor occupy the same reality led to adverse personality quirks in both, driving Lex Luthor's mania against the Man of Steel to new heights. As a result, he assembled a powerful team led by Captain Atom to go after Superman and remove the "alien threat" from America. In retaliation, Superman and Batman entered the White House in an attempt to stop their fellow heroes, causing Luthor to flee the White House, going from president to fugitive.

Meanwhile, a large kryptonite meteor was seen approaching Earth, and Luthor spun the story so that it appeared to be entirely Superman's fault. After his team failed to apprehend Superman, an increasingly desperate Luthor used a serum derived from the "super-steroid" Venom, liquid synthetic kryptonite, and an Apokoliptian battle suit to take on his enemy personally.

During the titanic struggle, Luthor admitted that not only did he know of the impending arrival of Imperiex, he had traded Doomsday, the living engine of destruction, to Darkseid in exchange for weaponry to use in the war. Batman recorded the confession, which effectively ended Luthor's presidency. Upon arrival at his corporate headquarters some time later, Luthor was startled to learn that Talia Head—now head of LexCorp—had sold off most of the public divisions to Wayne Enterprises and donated much of the money to the Wayne Foundation. Luthor fled underground, vowing revenge (*Superman/Batman* #1–6, October 2003–March 2004).

Soon after, word reached him that a Lex Luthor had helped form the Secret Society of Super-Villains, and he was furious that someone was posing as him for mysterious purposes. He decided to collect intelligence in the guise of Mockingbird, assembling a sextet of villains who refused to play along with the Society (*Secret Six* [second series] #1–6, July 2006–January 2007). When he learned enough to confront his double, he hunted down Alexander Luthor and revealed himself. Alexander was rescued by Superboy-Prime before Luthor could kill him, something the Joker accomplished shortly after (*Infinite Crisis* #1–7, December 2005–June 2006).

Luthor took Alexander's corpse and presented it to the police. Forensic testing by John Henry Irons showed they were an exact match, and Luthor once more used the excuse of a clone double to be absolved of the crimes committed in the recent past (*52* #3, 2006).

When the multiverse was reborn as part of the Infinite Crisis, Lex's background and motivations were somewhat altered.

The Luthor of New Earth was the son of Lionel Luthor, a wealthy businessman who was married to the cold socialite Letitia. The boy was raised by his aunt Lena in Smallville, Kansas, where he first met Clark Kent, Lana Lang, and Pete Ross. At some point before high school graduation, he left Smallville "under a cloud of rumor and suspicion" (*Countdown to Final Crisis* #34, September 5, 2007).

Another recounting, this one permanent, indicated that Lex had lived and grew up in Smallville all along. He met Clark Kent at a county fair and showed the young Clark his kryptonite specimens, inadvertenly introducing the alien teen to the deadly effects of the green meteors. The two became tentative friends, if Lex could consider anyone to be a friend at all (*Superman: Secret Origin* #1, November 2009). The angry teen despised his abusive father Lionel, and to protect his younger sister Lena, saw to it that his father's "weak heart" led to his demise (*Superman: Secret Origin* #2, December 2009). Luthor dreamed big even then and had plans to remake Metropolis in his image, and he left Smallville to make his dream a reality.

When Clark Kent arrived in Metropolis years later, he was amazed to see Luthor's influence over the city, including nearly bankrupting the *Daily Planet* for daring to write negatively about him. Luthor also used the arrival of Superman to foster fear of the alien among Metropolis's citizens. When the *Planet* published its first story lauding the city's new hero, Luthor declared war on the paper, vowing to crush it once and for all. He formed a close bond with General Samuel Lane, pointing out the "unnatural" attraction between Lois Lane and the Man of Steel. This led to Luthor experimenting on General Lane's aide, John Corben, turning him into the kryptonite-fueled cyborg dubbed Metallo (*Superman: Secret Origin* #5, April 2010).

In an attempt to rehabilitate his image in the present day, Lex used his technological prowess to launch the Everyman Project, which would turn normal people into superpowered beings. Irons's niece Natasha Irons joined the group, which used the corporate hero name of Infinity, Inc. (*52* #21, 2006). As the clock struck midnight that New Year's Eve, all the people with superpowers suddenly lost them, causing chaos, death, and panic in the streets, which was Luthor's means of testing the powers' "off switch" (*52* #35, January 3, 2007). His real goal all along was to find a way to grant *himself* superpowers, something his human physiology would not allow, much to his anger and regret (*52* #39–40, January 31, 2007–February 7, 2007). In the end, his plans for the team went awry and Luthor once more became a discredited member of society.

Regardless of the latest public relations fiasco,

Luthor was ultimately cleared by the court system of more than 120 charges of criminality, including first-degree murder. While a free man, Luthor was also a genius without resources (*Superman* #650, May 2006). His dismantled LexCorp had been turned over to Lana Lang, whom he had once tortured, to run in his stead, and much of his technology had been taken over by the vile Dr. Thaddeus Bodog Sivana. Rather than own up to his misdeeds, Luthor used a series of investigative reports from Clark Kent to place the blame.

Now thinking like a criminal mastermind once again, Luthor unleashed a Kryptonian battle cruiser on Metropolis. Weakened by kryptonite radiation, Superman still managed to defeat Luthor, and the madman was sent to Stryker's Island (*Superman* #653; *Action Comics* #840, both August 2006). Fed up with Luthor and his evil deeds, the Suicide Squad covertly rounded him up, along with many other villains, and used a series of Boom Tubes to transport them all to a seemingly uninhabited world where they were left to their own devices. Luthor asserted control until the Joker broke off into a separate faction, thereby setting up an inevitable civil war that left many of the exiles bloodied. After beating the Clown Prince in hand-to-hand combat, Luthor devised a way home for the villains (*Salvation Run* #1–7, November 2007–June 2008).

When Darkseid's agent, the costumed villain Libra, formed a new incarnation of the Secret Society of Super-Villains, Luthor was invited into its Inner Circle. Once installed, Luthor challenged the would-be leader Libra's effectiveness. To prove his point, Libra dispatched Clayface to blow up the *Daily Planet* (*Final Crisis* #2, August 2008). Despite Libra's effectiveness, Luthor tried to take control of the team—only to be corralled by Darkseid's Justifiers. Luthor acquiesced and agreed to Libra's request that he head up the rear-guard assault on the super heroes in Blüdhaven (*Final Crisis* #5, December 2008). Just then, Darkseid managed to unleash the Anti-Life Equation through every communications device on Earth, enslaving most of humanity. Luthor and Dr. Sivana managed to block the Justifiers from being linked to the Anti-Life Equation broadcast, giving the heroes a chance to fight back and save humankind (*Final Crisis* #6, January 2009).

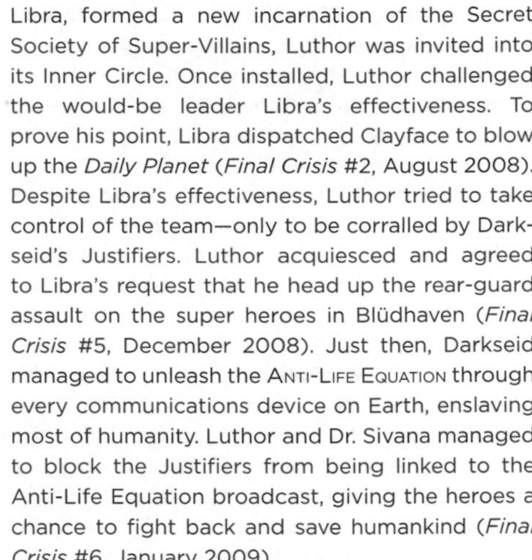

Once Earth was restored to normal, Lex Luthor heard news of an alien child, rescued from within a meteor by Superman, and was determined to find and examine the boy, hoping he would provide abilities Luthor could use to crush Superman. He dispatched Bizarro after the boy but was thwarted in his plan.

The boy turned out to be the son of Phantom Zone villains Zod and Ursa, the harbinger for an invasion from the limbo-like prison. With Superman trapped in the Zone, the Kryptonian criminals were free to conquer the Earth, their powers too much for even Luthor. As a result, when a freed Superman asked for his help, Luthor smugly accepted but insisted the Man of Steel join his reconstituted Superman Revenge Squad, which now consisted of the Parasite, Bizarro, Metallo, and Luthor. During the struggle, Luthor told Superman that he'd rather see the Man of Steel defeated than killed and turned into a heroic martyr. While the super-beings did battle with Zod and his forces, Luthor entered Zod's fortress and executed a program that essentially recalled the villains to the Phantom Zone. Luthor told Lois Lane he intended Superman to also be trapped in the realm, ending his interference once and for all. By tipping his hand, he made himself vulnerable to a blow to the head by a crystal-wielding Lois, saving the Man of Steel. When Luthor awoke, he was once more imprisoned (*Action Comics* #844–847, December 2007–July 2008; *Action Comics Annual* #11, 2008).

Earth's residents were jolted a short time later by the arrival of one hundred thousand Kryptonians, all rescued from the city of Kandor. Concerned over America's security, General Sam Lane, Luthor's former secretary of defense, invited his former commander in chief to aid his planning, releasing him from jail. Instead the general shot Luthor in the shoulder when he insulted Lois (*Action Comics* #871, January 2009). Luthor managed to access Brainiac's computer systems and free many of the other bottled inhabitants the cyborg had on his vessel, unleashing alien creatures across the planet including Project M's Creature Commandos, Metallo, and Reactron (*Action Comics* #872, February 2009). As his reward, Luthor was given access to the inert body of Doomsday to study (*Action Comics* #873, March

2009). In bunker 7734, the duo, along with General Lane, adapted Brainiac's technology for their own plans against the unsuspecting Man of Steel (*Action Comics* #874, April 2009). Lex then stole Brainiac's body from military containment; the not-quite-dead alien from Colu informed Luthor that they were now partners and set off to scheme anew (*Adventure Comics* #0, April 2009).

While aboard Brainiac's craft, Luthor studied the news to catch up on events and was surprised to learn that Connor Kent was back from the dead. He returned to Smallville to track Superboy down and ran into his younger sister Lena while he was there. Lena was an invalid as a result of a devastating injury she had suffered years ago, and she was left by herself to raise her daughter Lori. Lex promised to cure his sister with Superboy's help, but reversed the process once he did, stating that he would never reveal the cure as long as Superman was alive. Luthor then left with Brainiac, who concurred with Lex that the "wrong alien DNA" had been used for cloning. They set out to find different alien DNA to fabricate a new binary clone for future use (*Adventure Comics* #508–509, February–March 2010).

Luthor worked tirelessly with Brainiac to eradicate the Man of Steel and all his Kryptonian allies. He crafted a missile out of the false Kryptonian god Rao that General Samuel Lane then had fired at the Sun, changing it from yellow to red in an effort to sap all of the Kryptonians of their superpowers. The deadly device was reversed only by the sacrifice of the Flamebird (*Superman: War of the Supermen* #3, July 2010). Lane, however, saw to it that Luthor received a full presidential pardon, and Lex moved on to his next plot to destroy Superman once and for all.

Around the same time, the cosmic event known as the Blackest Night erupted, and the dead rose and came looking for their killers, intending to add them to the undead Black Lanterns. Luthor was eventually gifted with an Orange Power Ring, fueled by his own avarice. Now a deputy to the Orange Lantern known as Larfleeze, Luthor flew to his side and joined in the battle against Nekron, Lord of the Dead, who sought to eliminate all life on Earth—and then the universe (*Blackest Night* #6, January 2010). Luthor and Larfleeze became sidetracked in a greedy struggle, as the alien did not wish to share the powerful orange energy with anyone. Luthor was eventually restrained by Wonder Woman during the battle, and entwined in her Lasso of Truth, and he was forced to admit that he actually desired to be the Man of Steel (*Blackest Night* #7, February 2010). Once the heroes defeated Nekron, Larfleeze confiscated the ring from Luthor, who once again craved the ring's power. Luthor studied several Black Lantern corpses in an attempt to find the source of the elusive energy, and when Larfleeze reappeared and offered Lex his Orange Power Ring back, Luthor told the alien about another commodity invaluable to all living beings—land. Together, Lex and Larfleeze have set their next agenda (*Brightest Day* #0, June 2010).

One potential future saw Luthor surviving for millennia, his consciousness moving from clone to clone until his sixtieth incarnation faced a descendant of Superman named Kaleb (*Superman: The Man of Steel Annual* #5, 1996). Still farther in the future, it was revealed that the feud between the descendants of Superman and Luthor was finally ended in the "two dynasties' historic 322nd Century alliance" (*Action Comics One Million*, November 1998).

Across the multiverse, there have usually been several versions of Lex Luthor, and the battle between man and Superman endured. On Earth-423, Luthor became little more than a host body for Brainiac, leading a final charge on the Man of Steel's Fortress of Solitude with all of Superman's friends inside. Once Luthor's body was mortally wounded by Lana Lang, Brainiac quickly succumbed as well (*Superman* [first series] #423; *Action Comics* #583—both September 1986).

In the wake of the First Crisis, the anti-matter universe's version of Luthor was the one to pierce the dimensional barrier to request the JLA's aid in stopping the Crime Syndicate of America's reign of terror (*JLA: Earth-2*, 2000).

In a shift in reality that briefly became part of the mainstream Superman's history, Lex Luthor was once more living in Smallville when he first encountered Clark Kent. Arriving in the community shortly after his eighteenth birthday, the young genius was disgruntled when placement tests forced him to be enrolled in the ninth grade. It was here that he met Clark, and the two developed a friendship of sorts (*Superman/Batman Secret Files 2003*, November 2003; *Superman: Birthright* #8, May 2004). Pete Ross soon found himself indebted to Lex when the young man used his influence to get Pete's father a transplant (*Superman Secret Files & Origins 2004*, August 2004). Unknown to everyone, Lex's father Lionel Luthor was actually an actor the teenager had hired to prevent him from being "forced by Social Services to endure yet another foster parent nightmare." When Lex no longer needed him, he was paid and vanished (*Superman/Batman Secret Files 2003*, November 2003).

The brilliant young Luthor built a device he thought would communicate with alien life across the stars, but it also managed to pierce the time barrier and contact Krypton. When Luthor tried to speak to someone on the other side, an explosion cost the teen all his hair. Years later, Luthor built LexCorp into a major company based on the study of extraterrestrial life. When Superman arrived in Metropolis, Luthor immediately concluded that the Man of Steel was an alien (*Superman: Birthright* #8, May 2004).

In the history of Earth-354, Thomas and Martha Wayne adopted Kal-El, and when an unchecked Luthor took control over Metropolis and moved on to Gotham City seeking a new challenge, he was opposed by a superpowered Batman. During the conflict, an accident turned Luthor into the white-skinned, green-haired Joker (*Superman: Speeding Bullets*, 1993).

Earth-1866 saw Kal-El arrive during the Victorian era, when Luthor was a wealthy upper-class gentleman who slaughtered an entire African village in order to obtain a chunk of kryptonite that had landed there. Using it, he tried to force Superman into killing Queen Victoria in his effort to claim her throne (*Superman* [second series] *Annual* #6, 1994).

On Earth-3839, where Superman and Batman began operating in the late 1930s, Luthor was a henchman to the Ultra-Humanite, but after an explosion he became a vegetable, resulting in the Humanite placing his own brain into Luthor's body. Some forty years later, he killed Lois Lane, convincing her son that his superpowered father Superman committed the deed. One by one, Luthor assassinated Superman's loved ones, while a grief-stricken Man of Steel sought the madman (*Superman & Batman: Generations* #1–4, 1999). Once he was found and killed, a cloned Luthor brain was placed in a robotic body and, as Metallo, battled the Man of Steel's grandson Knightwing in addition to Cyborg, the fifth Flash, and Hal Jordan (*Superman & Batman: Generations II* #4, 2001).

In the wake of the new fifty-two-world multiverse, several Luthors were chronicled.

On Earth-22, Luthor achieved old age and formed the Mankind Liberation Front, a team of super-villains both young and old, to foment a battle between Earth's super heroes and the United Nations, hoping to create a vacuum Luthor could fill (*Kingdom Come* #2–4, June–August 1996).

Earth-30 found its basis in the previous multiverse's Earth-1958. Here the American government gave Dr. Lex Luthor the responsibility of finding ways to counteract Kal-El, the USSR's superpowered dictator. Luthor sent a series of powerful agents after the superman, but they failed. Instead, when Luthor was elected president, his work transformed the impoverished country, and when Superman was finally toppled, it was Luthor's good works that influenced a relieved world for the better (*Superman: Red Son* #1–3, 2003).

The reality of Earth-31 showed Luthor and Brainiac controlling the United States via the holographic president Rick Rickard. Their scheme was undermined by Batman and his underground revolution, and before Luthor could ignite a nuclear conflagration, he was killed by Hawkboy, son of Hawkman and Hawkgirl (*The Dark Knight Strikes Again* #1–3, 2001–2002).

LUTHOR, LIONEL

Lionel Luthor was the father of Alexander Luthor in later retellings of Lex Luthor's origins, and he was either a wealthy businessman or a drunk and abusive father.

The first recorded appearance of Lionel was actually as an actor the teenaged Lex had hired to prevent him from being "forced by Social Services to endure yet another foster parent nightmare." When Lex no longer needed him, he was paid and vanished (*Superman/Batman Secret Files* 2003, November 2003).

In the reality after the events of Infinite Crisis, Lionel Luthor was a wealthy businessman, married to the cold socialite Letitia. Lex was raised by his aunt Lena in Smallville, Kansas, where he first met Clark Kent, Lana Lang, and Pete Ross. At some point, before high-school graduation, he left Smallville "under a cloud of rumor and suspicion" (*Countdown to Final Crisis* #34, September 5, 2007).

A subsequent retelling of the New Earth origins of Lex Luthor portrayed Lionel as an ignorant, divorced drunkard, who detested his wildly intelligent son Lex. He physically abused Lex and his much younger sister Lena to the point where Lex made numerous attempts to have his father killed. The first attempt involved his truck's breaks failing and forcing him over a steep mountain road, but the truck and its inebriated occupant were rescued by the teen Superboy, although no one believed Lionel's fanciful tale.

Soon after, Lionel died from drugs Lex slipped into his system, causing what was ruled to be a heart attack. His insurance money made Lex wealthy enough to leave town, while an aunt took custody of Lena (*Superman: Secret Origin* #1-2, November-December 2009).

LUTHORITE

On Earth-2, Lex Luthor developed a new metallic alloy that he claimed was the strongest metal on Earth. "Luthorite resists friction-heat!" explained Luthor. "[With it] I can build irresistible weapons and impenetrable space ships to dominate the universe!" Luthorite contained iridium and possibly osmium, but its chief ingredient was "the unknown Element X," available only from certain rare meteorites. Rather than profit from the patent, Luthor used it to coat motor vehicles and commit robberies, accessing vaults he could not otherwise penetrate. When Superman apprehended Luthor, the Man of Steel cleverly fashioned a pair of handcuffs from the alloy (*Superman* [first series] #43, November–December 1946).

LUTHOR MUSEUM, THE

On the distant world of Lexor, named in honor of Lex Luthor, whom residents believed had restored their water supply, a museum in Luthor's honor was once erected. Artifacts and exhibits were added after each feat of Luthor's apparent heroism until the planet's destruction (*Superman* [first series] #168, April 1964).

LUTHOR'S LAIR

On Earth-1, Lex Luthor used a variety of hideaways to design, construct, and store his fantastic array of weapons. In almost every case, his lairs had their walls lined with lead to prevent them from being discovered by Superman using his X-ray vision.

The locations of Luthor's secret bases of operations included an abandoned museum—situated "smack in the middle of Metropolis," its buildings held aloft by a giant dirigible high above the stratosphere; a glass-enclosed city of ancient, weird design; an abandoned factory; a gigantic human-made meteor floating in outer space; an abandoned barn; a secret underground lab; a giant spaceship; a secret mountaintop laboratory; an electronics firm; a hidden laboratory on the outskirts of Metropolis; a massive fortress-like citadel on a lonely mountaintop north of Metropolis; a farmhouse north of Metropolis; and a secret lead-lined subterranean hideout built into the side of a grassy hill.

Several of Lex's hideouts have been named Luthor's Lair, and at least five were numbered, although a mere three of them were specifically identified, beginning with the abandoned museum—which he modeled after Superman's

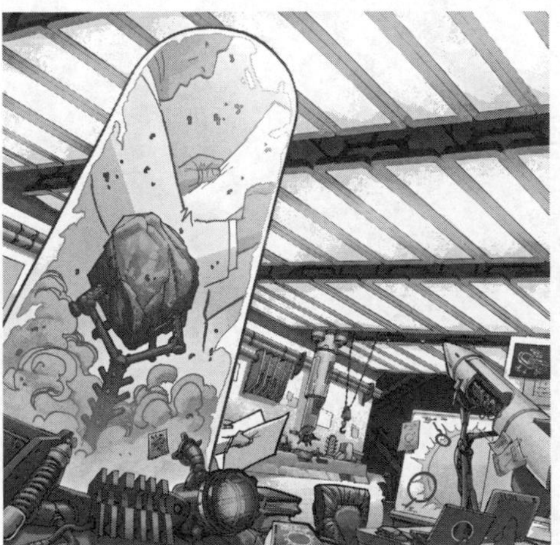

famed Fortress of Solitude (*Action Comics* #277, June 1961). It was three stories tall and fronted by a statue of Julius Caesar. If a visitor shook the hand of the statue, a secret mechanism opened the building's massive front door. Mounted atop the building was a gigantic statue of classical design, which was actually the first stage of a rocket ship capable of carrying Luthor on journeys into outer space (*Action Comics* #292, September 1962). Within, Luthor used hidden cameras in Caesar's eyes to observe the city. He had a Hall of Heroes with statues in salute to Attila the Hun, Genghis Khan, Captain Kidd, Al Capone, Nero, Blackbeard, and Benedict Arnold.

His building in Metropolis was protected with technology provided by Brainiac, something the Metropolis police learned when they attempted to storm it. A barrage of "colored rays" forming "a web of pure force" surrounded the museum, stymieing their efforts (*Action Comics* #292, September 1962).

Luthor Lair II was an abandoned astronomical observatory situated "on a lofty hill near Metropolis" (*Superman* [first series] #167, February 1964). Why Lex abandoned the museum was unrecorded, but he clearly transported his technology and statuary and placed them in what he then called the Reminder Room.

The place known as Luthor's Lair No. 5 was an abandoned coal mine located somewhat near Metropolis Prison and used not long after the observatory was abandoned (*Superman* [first series] #170, July 1964). This was done intentionally so that Luthor could escape prison and immediately go into hiding, something that happened with alarming frequency.

Luthor eventually shifted his base of operations to a lavish penthouse in midtown Metropolis (*Superman* [first series] #282, December 1974, and #286, April 1975; *The Joker* #7, May–June 1976) atop a legitimate business called the Thunder Corporation (*Superman: Last Son of Krypton,* 1978).

In the history that arose following the Crisis on Infinite Earths, the original Luthor's Lair—complete with its Hall of Heroes—was briefly used as a base by the villain and his Injustice League (*Silver Age 80-Page Giant* #1, July 2000).

LYNAI, LUMA

After failing to pair her cousin Kal-El with Helen of Troy and then Saturn Girl of the Legion of Super-Heroes, a well-meaning Supergirl decided to look beyond Earth and across the stars with the aid of Fortress of Solitude's computer system. The computer suggested Staryl's superpowered champion Luma Lynai, who had gained her abilities from exposure to that solar system's orange sun. The Maid of Might arranged a meeting, and Superman fell for the attractive Lynai, who had more than a passing resemblance to his younger cousin. When she learned that she could not thrive under Earth's yellow sun, however, she begged Superman to forget her (*Action Comics* #289, June 1962).

LYNX, THE

The criminal alias used by accountant Lester Link.

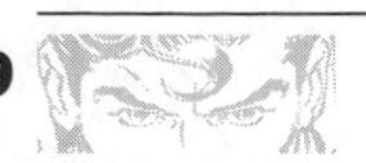

MACDUFF

For unexplained reasons, Superman chose to name the last functioning Superman Robot MacDuff. He was programmed to act as the perfect host to any of the friends who visited the Man of Steel in his Fortress of Solitude. When the Superman Revenge Squad attacked the Arctic citadel, MacDuff was destroyed in what became the last recorded adventure of the Earth-1 Superman (*Superman* [first series] #414, December 1985).

MACGUIRE, PATRICK

Patrick MacGuire was best known to all as Scrapper, a founding member of the Newsboy Legion. His clone also served with a revamped version of the group.

MACK, BUD

When Superman was once exposed to a synthetic form of kryptonite courtesy of the Fixer, he developed temporary amnesia. Unable to remember his name, he took the moniker Bud Mack after being called "Bud" by several homeless people and "Mac" by several baseball players. Not remembering his own strength, Mack became a flamethrower of a pitcher for the Benson City Colts before having his contract purchased by the Metropolis Titans. Mack eventually remembered that he was actually the Man of Steel and left the team (*Superman* [first series] #77, July–August 1952).

MACROPOLIS

Following the theory of parallel world development, life on Oceania was remarkably similar to that of Earth, complete with a superpowered champion named Hyper-Man. Operating from the gleaming city of Macropolis, Hyper-Man went by the name of Chester King, a roving television reporter for the Oceania Network, and he ultimately married fellow reporter Lydia Long (*Action Comics* #265, June 1960).

MADAME NICOLAI

A famed nuclear scientist, Madame Nicolai was once invited to America in secret and posed as the glamorous Nikki Larue, Superman's "fiancée," in an effort to allow him to be at her side in public without arousing suspicion. The secrecy enabled her to briefly consult on atomic developments before returning to Europe without arousing enemy suspicion (*Action Comics* #143, April 1950).

MAESTRO

In an attempt to distract the Man of Steel, a criminal known only as the Maestro kidnapped Lucy Lane. He then blackmailed Lois Lane to convince Superman, who was suffering from temporary amnesia, to aid in the overthrow of a South American country. Once the Man of Steel's memory returned, he and Lois conspired to thwart the dictator and rescue Lucy (*Superman's Girl Friend, Lois Lane* #75, July 1967). This Maestro is not to be confused with the Maestro who once battled Batman (*Batman* #149, August 1962).

MAG-EN

Mag-En was a brilliant Kryptonian psychologist and father to the equally renowned scientist Ral-En, who attended college with Jor-El. When Ral-En attempted to overthrow Krypton's government using "Kryptonian hyper-hypnotism," taught to him by Mag-En, he was stopped by Jor-El in the weeks before the planet exploded. While Ral-En was banished to the Phantom Zone, Mag-En implanted a hypnotic command in the infant Kal-El's mind to perform ten evil deeds the next time he saw a certain blue comet hurtling through the heavens.

When Kal-El was an adult, he encountered a blue comet, which triggered the hypnotic command. His bizarre actions led to random acts of destruction across the world that were finally deciphered by the Kandorian scientist Lon-Es, who alerted Supergirl to the danger befalling Earth. When they managed to destroy the blue comet, the psychological compulsion controlling Superman vanished (*Superman* [first series] #154, July 1962).

MAGNUS, DR. TROY

Superman once found himself lured to England and its famous Tower of London. Within a hidden room, he encountered the immortal alchemist Troy

Magnus. The ancient man explained that he had been trying to devise a cure for the Black Death when, in 1665, he sampled a serum that imbued him with superpowers, but did not cure the disease. Now immortal, he had himself sealed within the tower to stay away from the misery caused by the disease. After several centuries, Magnus was tired of life and wanted the Man of Steel to end his existence. Refusing to break his code against taking a life, Superman agreed to use his heat vision to seal the cracks that had formed over the years within the private room. However, the beams of heat vision accidentally touched Magnus and killed him. Superman completed the repairs and turned the private room into a fitting tomb (*Action Comics* #406, November 1971).

MAGOG

One dark day on Earth-22, the Joker arrived at the *Daily Planet* and killed everyone in sight, including Lois Lane, wife of the Man of Steel. Once Superman apprehended the Joker, he did not kill him in revenge but turned him over to the authorities instead. Magog, a fellow crime fighter, disagreed with Superman and killed the Joker in disgust.

Magog stood trial but was acquitted, which drove Superman into a disheartened retirement. Magog was celebrated by the public and became the world's best-known hero. He continually used his more brutal approach to crime and punishment until Superman no longer recognized his super heroic brethren. As Magog's Justice Battalion took on Earth's supervillains in a conflict that ignored the safety of innocents and destroyed all of Kansas, Superman finally returned to action. Reminded of what it meant to be noble and good, Magog learned the error of his ways and was incapable of returning to his old self (*Kingdom Come* #1–4, May–August 1996).

MAGPIE

Margaret Pye was a troubled teenager who eventually fell into a life of crime and took the costumed identity of Magpie. She committed her first robberies early in Superman's career, and it was while dealing with the Man of Steel that she first encountered the Dark Knight (*Man of Steel* #3, Early November 1986).

Magpie specialized as a jewel thief, and took to replacing the gems she stole with bomb-laden duplicates that not only caused havoc but also hid any incriminating evidence. After her first arrest, she reappeared in Gotham City with the same modus operandi (*Batman* #401, November 1986). She was committed for a time to Arkham Asylum and eventually escaped alongside Poison Ivy (*Arkham Asylum: Living Hell* #3–6, September–December 2003).

Years later, Magpie entered into the Penguin's employ, which proved to be a fatal error. She was killed by the Great White Shark's agent, the Tally Man, along with Orca, the Ventriloquist, and KG-Beast as the Penguin sought to strengthen his grip on the underworld (*Batman* #651 May 2006).

MAHARAJA OF SINSUBHANI, THE

The Maharajah of the Far Eastern state of Sinsubhani was described as being "full of pomp and ceremony" but was also "a fine man . . . a good friend . . . and a world leader" who aided Superman numerous times until his assassination by agents of D.E.M.O.N. The Maharajah's son, Prince Krishna, was instrumental in infiltrating D.E.M.O.N. and avenging his father's murder (*Superman* [first series] #191, November 1966).

MAINFRAME

Mainframe was a set of technologically based criminals who used their advanced knowledge

and skills to commit crimes. They were led by a massive man called Override, a quantum physicist dedicated to melding man and machine in order to form a new life-form. The organization also included Baud, a woman who mastered powerful electromagnetic skills and briefly joined the Superman Revenge Squad; Download, a teleporter; Output, a code breaker with a computer-generated face; and Scareware, a muscular powerhouse.

Among their tools were insectoid cybernetic creations that collected data and surveillance.

They first encountered Superman when his physical form had been converted into electrical energy (*Superman: The Man of Steel* #71–72, September–October 1997). Thanks to the efforts of Misa, the entirety of Mainframe found themselves permanently confined to their other-dimensional refuge (*Superman* [second series] *3-D* #1, December 1998).

MAJESTIC

Purportedly hailing from the parallel universe identified as Earth-50, the powerful hero known as Majestic actually came from the faraway planet known as Khera (*WildC.A.T.S.* #11, June 1994). He had arrived on Earth-50 to use his impressive array of powers to fight for truth and justice.

At one time he traveled from his world to Superman's Earth, replacing the Man of Steel when Superman was lost in a timestream. His physique and manner at first led Lois Lane to think he was her husband, but she quickly learned the truth.

Majestic was a welcome figure in Metropolis, where he used his super-strength, super-speed, vision powers, flight, and other attributes to protect those in trouble. Unlike Superman, Majestic was prone to much calculation and deliberation, and possessed a more austere personality. As a result, when Steel, Superboy, and the Eradicator tried to befriend him, it quickly became an awkward experience. Feeling threatened, the Eradicator then sent Majestic to the Phantom Zone when Metropolis was threatened by a massive chronostorm. The other heroes then attempted to destroy the storm and save the city by detonating a hyperbomb.

Lois freed Majestic from the Phantom Zone, and the alien protector successfully battled the members of Team Superman before destroying the hyperbomb. As a result, despite the hostile acts from his supposed colleagues, Majestic saved the city. That act stopped the chronostorm, letting

nature take it course, expelling the anachronistic effects of BRAINIAC 13's attempts to modernize the City of Tomorrow (first DC Universe appearances in *Action Comics* #811; *The Adventures of Superman* #624; *Superman* [second series] #201—all March 2004).

When Superman returned to Metropolis, he worked with Majestic to find a way for the alien to return to his proper realm. Before a solution could be found, however, the evil Daemonites from Earth-50 arrived and almost destroyed Metropolis. Together the mightiest men of two worlds repelled the invasion and sent Majestic back to his proper time line (*Majestic* [first series] #1–4, October 2004–January 2005; *Majestic* [second series] #1, March 2005).

MALA

KIZO, U-BAN, and Mala—the Evil Three—managed to survive the destruction of KRYPTON and later battled another survivor, Superman, on two separate occasions. Neither time did the trio best the Man of Steel (*Superman* [first series] #65, July–August 1950). Mala had an uncanny resemblance to KAL-EL, who, as Superman, stopped their scheme to conqueror Earth. The Kryptonians had originally been sentenced to suspended animation in a rocket, which spared them the loss of their homeworld, but it also preserved them until a collision with space debris brought them to Earth. The evil trio once more tried to conquer a new world but were lured into fighting one another by Superman, who then apprehended the dazed combatants and returned them to space.

A collision with an asteroid freed them once more, and Mala came to Earth seeking revenge against Superman. His complex plan involved creating an artificial Earth and convincing the Man of Steel it was the real planet, preoccupying Superman and allowing Mala to wreak havoc on the real Earth. The ploy seemed to be working, so

Mala summoned his compatriots. However, by the time they arrived on the real Earth, Superman was ready for them, and the Kryptonians were once more defeated and returned to space in a newly constructed—and secure—rocket (*Action Comics* #194, July 1954).

MALCOLM, MOUSEY

Growing up a unique technological whiz in SMALLVILLE, Mousey Malcolm was also a loner. As he once tinkered with a defective radio crystal, he accidentally gained control over SUPERBOY's robot duplicates and used them as his avatars in an effort to impress his peers. The Teen of Steel stopped things from getting out of control and taught the shy teen a lesson in being yourself (*Superboy* [first series] #155, April 1969).

MALCOLM, REX

Using a machine that generated "sub-sonic vibrations," the scientist-turned-criminal Rex Malcolm managed to render people unconscious, allowing him to rob banks throughout METROPOLIS without harming a soul. Superman and the Metropolis Police Department eventually devised a complex scheme to convince Malcolm that a man named Winters had devised a device that could actually harm Superman. This lured Malcolm into the open to continue his crime spree, thinking he was free of Superman's interference—allowing Winters, really an undercover cop, and Superman to apprehend the thief (*Superman* [first series] #116, September 1957).

MALLEABLE MAN, THE

The Malleable Man battled with Superman just once, but it was a memorable encounter. Seeking to become a stretchable super-villain, Skizzle Shanks re-created the accident that caused his former partner Eel O'Brian to become Plastic Man. This instigated an odd team-up between the Man of Steel and the pliable partnership of Plastic Man—formerly O'Brian—JIMMY OLSEN as ELASTIC LAD, and the Elongated Man. Against such odds, Shanks had no chance to master his skills and use them for crime (*DC Comics Presents* #93, May 1986).

MALLOW, MARSHA

When LOIS LANE briefly quit the *DAILY PLANET* to try her hand at freelance investigative reporting, she took on the overweight redheaded Marsha Mallow as a roommate to save money. Neither the freelance life nor the new cramped living arrangements pleased Lois, who returned to her former career and living alone (*Superman's Girl Friend, Lois Lane* #121, April 1972).

MALVERNE, DICK

Richard "Dick" Wilson was a teenager living at MIDVALE ORPHANAGE when SUPERGIRL, disguised as LINDA LEE, first arrived. The two struck up a friendship that later blossomed into her first real romance. When they met first, Wilson thought he had taken a picture of Supergirl and suspected Linda of being the new super heroine. This prompted Superman to build a SUPERGIRL ROBOT to be used in

order to trick Wilson into thinking he was mistaken (*Action Comics* #256, September 1959).

Dick was eventually adopted by the Malverne family and took their surname (*Action Comics* #282, November 1961), but he maintained his close ties with both Linda and the soon publicly revealed Maid of Might despite not realizing that they were one and the same. He vied with Jerro the Merboy and others for her affections until Dick and Linda grew apart.

Thanks to a dose of red KRYPTONITE that once let Supergirl transfer her incredible powers to others through a kiss, Dick finally got to sample what Linda experienced. His powers ran out when he and a similarly powered Jerro were flying over a volcano, requiring them to be rescued by the Supergirl Emergency Squad (*Action Comics* #290, July 1962). Supergirl herself could not help her friends since, during this period, she had lost her powers thanks to a Kandorian, LESLA-LAR.

LENA THORUL attended a costume party dressed as the powerless heroine, and her uncanny resemblance to Supergirl convinced Dick she was his friend, igniting a spate of jealously from the de-powered Supergirl. Lena then admitted that *she* was Supergirl. It was later revealed that Lena told the lie under Lesla-Lar's mind control as part of the Kandorian's attack on Supergirl—which ultimately failed, and the Maid of Might regained her abilities (*Action Comics* #296–297, January–February 1963).

When Supergirl found the world Gaea, it was a remarkable duplicate of Earth, despite a plague that had wiped out all the adults on the planet, leaving its youth in charge. Supergirl visited the planet during her two-month college break. There she assumed her LINDA LEE DANVERS identity and encountered Dick Malvin, a doppelgänger to Malverne, who worked for the Adult Revolt Movement. When Supergirl found herself elected the Gaea version of America's president, Malvin, her vice president, exposed her secret, and she was impeached. With Malvin now in the Oval Office, a reign of tyranny began that Supergirl had to fix before she could return to Earth (*Action Comics* #344–345, December 1966–January 1967).

The real Dick Malverne had gone to State Tech after graduating from high school, but because the school was only a few miles from Linda's STANHOPE COLLEGE (*Action Comics* #318, November

1964) the two continued to date off and on during the next few years. Dick even plotted to get Linda nominated as Miss Universe and was elated when she won (*Action Comics* #335–336, March–April 1966). Dick and Linda attended a nostalgic reunion at the Midvale Orphanage shortly thereafter (*Action Comics* #340, August 1966) but gradually saw each other less and less (*Adventure Comics* #393, May 1970).

After meeting up several years later, Linda was astonished when Dick surprised her with a kiss outside her new home in Chicago (*Supergirl* [second series] #23, September 1984). Now working for a computer company, Dick had transferred to Chicago in the hope of rekindling his romance with Linda, and was disappointed to learn that she'd moved on with her life. An alternate account of their reunion reported that Dick was dying of cancer and wanted to apologize to Supergirl (whom he'd always known was Linda) for his attempts to expose her true identity all those years ago (*Solo* #1, December 2004).

In the Earth created after the Crisis on Infinite Earths, a different version of Richard Malverne moved to Leesburg, Virginia, to take over an electronics shop. There he befriended Linda Danvers, who was also the Earth-born angel known as Supergirl (*Supergirl* [fourth series] #5, January 1997). Afflicted with cancer, Malverne miraculously recovered when he became an unwitting host for the demonic Buzz. When Linda eventually fell in love with Richard, the sinister Buzz revealed himself in the hope that Supergirl would help separate them. The Girl of Steel succeeded, not realizing that her boyfriend's cancer would return once his link with Buzz was broken (*Supergirl* [fourth series] #42–43, March–April 2000). Sadly, Richard died soon after (*Supergirl* [fourth series] #47, August 2000).

MALVIO

In a misguided attempt to usurp power in the tiny European republic of Borkia, General Malvio and his followers constructed a superpowered robot to help them achieve their goal. Soon after, Cosmic Man arrived in the small nation, claiming that he was a newly arrived champion from outer space. After several feats to prove his worthiness, Cosmic Man was invited to meet the country's president. However, Cosmic Man was really the robot Malvio had constructed and laden with explosives. The assassination plot would have worked had Superman not been present to protect the president. The robot was hurled into space before it detonated, while Malvio and his acolytes were subsequently arrested (*Action Comics* #258, November 1959).

MAMMOTH

Baran Flinders was born with an active metagene that resulted in his developing a powerful, muscular body but with a mind that was slow to process information. He was extremely devoted to his sister Selinda, who also possessed power to transmute one element into another. Baran did whatever she commanded, and when Selinda decided to use their powers for crime, they took the names Mammoth and Shimmer and became

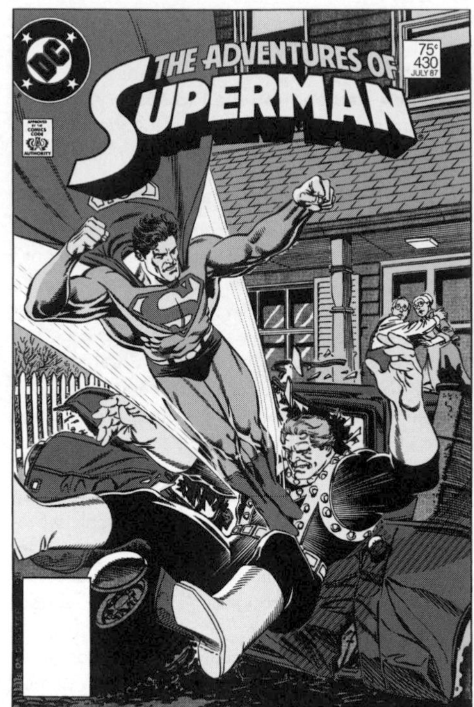

charter members of the villainous Fearsome Five. They battled the New Teen Titans on numerous occasions, but the duo also committed crimes on their own (*New Teen Titans* #3, January 1981).

When Mammoth arrived in Metropolis, he went toe-to-toe with the city's champion Superman (*The Adventures of Superman* #430, July 1987). Later, when Superman was exposed to the effects of red kryptonite for the first time, and was without his powers, Mammoth became more than a physical match for the hero. However, Superman exploited Baran's simple-mindedness and convinced the villain to surrender rather than continue to fight (*The Adventures of Superman* #472, November 1990).

Eventually Mammoth and Shimmer retired to a Tibetan monastery, although they were lured back to their criminal ways by their former colleague Psimon. When Shimmer tried to disobey Psimon, the villain turned her into glass and then shattered her, killing her (*The New Titans* #116, December 1994). Returning to crime after his sister's death, Mammoth eventually agreed to rejoin Dr. Sivana's new Fearsome Five when the mad scientist resurrected his sister (*Outsiders* [third series] #13, August 2004).

Often working alongside Shimmer, Mammoth was used for his brute strength in a variety of groups, including the Society (*Villains United* #5, November 2005). He was among the villains briefly banished to an alien world for rehabilitation, and his current whereabouts are unknown (*Salvation Run* #1–7, November 2007–June 2008).

MAMMOTH MUTT

Able to increase his size, an alien canine was dubbed Mammoth Mutt and served alongside Krypto in the Space Canine Patrol Agency (*Superboy* [first series] #131, July 1966).

MANNHEIM, BRUNO "UGLY"

Bruno Mannheim, the son of the criminal Boss Moxie, eventually inherited the leadership of Intergang, the Metropolis-based criminal organization, after his father's death. On Earth-1, he oversaw Intergang's assault units and all its dealings (*Superman's Pal, Jimmy Olsen* #139, July 1971, and #141, September 1971).

Ruling Intergang and dealing with its high-tech weaponry from Apokolips made Mannheim one of the deadliest mob bosses on the planet. His grizzled features earned him the nickname Ugly Mannheim, which was spoken mostly behind his back so as not to incur his wrath (*The Adventures of Superman* #466, May 1990; *Action Comics* #657, September 1990; others). He first served under Morgan Edge (*The Adventures of Superman* #450, January 1989) until Edge had a heart attack brought about by the stress of his secret being discovered by the Man of Steel. Believing Edge had jeopardized the operation, Mannheim took over Intergang himself (*Superman* [second series] #36, September 1989). Ironically, his efforts to contain the impact of Morgan Edge's trial attracted the attention of both Superman and Batman (*Superman* [second series] #44; *The Adventures of Superman* #467; *Action Comics* #654, all June 1990), and Clark Kent ultimately obtained information that revealed the headquarters of nearly every Intergang hideout. Now exposed and on the run, Mannheim revealed to the Man of Steel that he was from Apokolips and cloaked himself in bio-armor that gave him super-strength and the ability to fire deadly bolts of energy from his eyes. Though he briefly held his own against Superman, Mannheim was soon captured and imprisoned (*Superman* [second series] #60, October 1991). The Man of Steel pursued the villain after a subsequent jailbreak, and Mannheim was caught in a short-circuiting Boom Tube and apparently reduced to a pile of ashes (*Action Comics* #673, January 1992).

In Mannheim's absence, his father Boss Moxie (relationship revealed in *Guardians of Metropolis* #1, November 1994) eventually revived Intergang. Years later, however, Bruno returned to take command once more. Imbued with an evangelical passion, Mannheim gained custody of the Book of Crime, an ancient text that had become his new obsession (*52* #25, October 25, 2007). He nearly destroyed Gotham City and killed Batwoman before the heroine literally stabbed him

in the back (*52* #48, April 4, 2007). In the wake of those events, Mannheim returned to Metropolis and continued to run his criminal operation with an iron fist.

Mannheim had somehow eventually developed the ability to grow to several stories in height. As Superman and Mannheim tussled, the Man of Steel quickly realized that the equipment being used by Mannheim and Intergang was actually tied directly to the mob boss's circulatory system. Mannheim then informed Superman that before he and Intergang left Metropolis, he intended to commit one more heinous act. He revealed the Catastrosphere, a device that mimicked his heartbeat. Should something alter the heartbeat, it would set off the device and destroy the city. Superman stole the Catastrosphere, but Mannheim crushed Superman's potential victory by informing the Man of Steel that *hundreds* of sub-spheres were buried throughout Metropolis. Superman melted the floor around Mannheim, trapping him while he searched the city for the deadly spheres.

Mannheim warned Superman that he was no longer subordinate to Darkseid; instead he worked for some entity far worse, but he did not reveal who. He then teleported away before Superman could apprehend him (*Superman* #654, September 2006). Mannheim eventually resurfaced in Gotham, where he continued his expansion of Intergang in Batman's hometown (*Gotham Underground* #4–5, March–April 2008, and #9, August 2008).

MANNING, BRENDA

An underworld criminal hired unemployed actress and Lois Lane look-alike Brenda Manning in an attempt to distract Superman and defeat him. Needless to say, the scheme failed (*World's Finest Comics* #40, May–June 1949).

MANNING, TOBIAS

A normal human who gained amazing abilities and battled Superman under the guise of Terra-Man (*Superman* [first series] #249, March 1972).

MANO

Born on the heavily polluted world of Angtu in the thirtieth century, Mano had a mutated right hand that was discovered to be deadly. Scientists tried to manage his condition with a metallic disk, but "With a touch of a glowing disc on his right hand, [he] can completely annihilate any object!"

After his parents died, Mano was not welcome in society. In revenge, he decided to obliterate his homeworld and hire himself out as an assassin. In time, however, he was apprehended. He was scheduled to have his hand amputated to ensure no one else was ever killed. At the moment the guillotine was falling, it was shattered by Ferro Lad of the Legion of Super-Heroes. The United Planets had agreed to their plan to recruit five of the most powerful criminals in the universe to help save the galaxy from the Sun-Eater.

Mano was partnered with the Emerald Empress, Persuader, Tharok, and Validus, and the group became known as the Fatal Five. Once the solar system was saved, the Fatal Five turned on the

weakened Legion, which was reeling from Ferro Lad's self-sacrifice. The battle was fierce but brief, and the Legion prevailed (*Adventure Comics* #352–353, January–February 1967).

The Fatal Five repeatedly returned to fight the Legion across the years and throughout the various changes to reality.

MANTON, MELBA

A broadcaster for WGBS in Metropolis, Melba Manton made news by solving a murder, setting a trap for a killer, exposing unsafe tenement conditions, and saving an innocent man from being shot, all in time to appear on the six o'clock news that evening to talk about it (*Superman's Girl Friend, Lois Lane* #131–132, June–July 1973). Lois Lane counted Melba as a good friend and leapt to her rescue when the newscaster was taken captive in the African dictatorship of Oranga. Lane helped free Manton, who went on to fame for her coverage (*Superman Family* #186, November–December 1977).

MAN WITH THE CANE, THE

Jim Mason was an American secret agent working on behalf of the Axis powers during World War II. Wearing a false-face mask, maroon tailcoat, and top hat, he was known to most as the Man with the Cane given his ever-present walking stick, which was also a weapon capable of firing deadly poisoned darts. Mason faked an illness in order to stay at Bryant Hospital to obtain plans for a top-secret new "tank-plane" developed by inventor John Fleming. He was discovered and apprehended by Superman, however, and his mission failed (*Superman* [first series] #18, September–October 1942).

MAPLETON

Jimmy Olsen regarded Mapleton, the community where he was raised after being orphaned, as his hometown (*Superman's Pal, Jimmy Olsen* #79, September 1964), and later returned to help rid the community of a teen biker gang called the Dragons. In the process, he was delighted to be reunited with former classmate Rena Starling, now a teacher at Mapleton High (*Superman's Pal, Jimmy Olsen* #91, March 1966).

MAPLEVILLE

At one time, American cities all vied for the chance to proclaim themselves the Man of Steel's hometown. Succumbing to pressure and trying to take the spotlight away from Smallville, Superman temporarily settled in the small northwestern town of Mapleville. The grateful people donated a mansion for him to use but came to regret the decision when the town was overrun by tourists trying to glimpse Mapleville's most famous resident. The unintended consequences included traffic jams, an overstuffed post office, and thunderous cracks every time Superman pierced the sound barrier en route to perform his duties. It wasn't long before the townsfolk asked Superman to relocate (*Action Comics* #179, April 1953).

MARAUDER, THE

Evoking the appearance of an Earthly Viking with his helmet and long white beard, the Marauder was a space raider whose crimes led Superman to send him to "a prison asteroid for nine star-cycles." Seeking revenge, the Marauder brainwashed the alien Rol-Nac into attacking the Man of Steel in the guise of Satan (*Action Comics* #378, July 1969). Allied with Brainiac, Grax, and Lex Luthor, the Marauder then created what he called his "ultimate Anti-Superman weapon," a triflector that created destructive phantom counterparts of the Man of Steel (*Action Comics* #417–418, October–November 1972).

Much of the Marauder's defenses stemmed from his power-helmet, which could render foes unconscious with force bolts, create force fields, and even tap into distant red suns to create "force-field manacles" that could restrain Superman. Ultimately, the Man of Steel turned the tables on his foes and apprehended the helmet even as the Marauder fled into deep space.

MARIGOLD TWINS, THE (APRIL AND MAY)

April and May Marigold lived with their mother at 344 Clinton Street in Metropolis, making them neighbors to Clark Kent. The attractive twins were always friendly, and May harbored a crush on the handsome reporter, something that mystified April. Both took amusement in the fact that Clark consistently misidentified which twin was which (*Superman* [first series] #262, March 1973).

MARIN, TOM

Earth-2's Metropolis baseball team, the Ravens, once featured Tom Marin as a star pitcher. His career was promising until he began pitching poorly, resulting in his release from the team. He was so despondent that he attempted to commit suicide, but he was saved by Superman. It was then revealed that underworld gamblers had been doping Marin, causing the baseball star to lose his skills. With the drugs no longer in his system, Marin began working with the Metropolis Marvel to regain his form. Superman and Tom Marin teamed to take down the gamblers Sammy Brink and his cohort Joe, who had been drugging the baseball player (*Superman* [first series] #23, July–August 1943).

MARPLE, DUKE

The cunning criminal Duke Marple hid his stolen loot so well that finding it required Superman to craft an elaborate hoax that called for the aid of not only Cosmic Man and Lightning-Man from the thirtieth century's Legion of Super-Heroes (posing as Hercules and Samson) but also Krypto and Argentinean wrestling star Antonino Rocca. The odd collection of champions proved effective: The loot was recovered, and Marple imprisoned (*Superman* [first series] #155, August 1962).

MARS

The solar system's fourth planet, Mars, was host to a visit from the Batman and Robin of Earth-2, who stopped the renegade Martian scientist Sax Gola from attacking Earth with high-tech weapons of destruction (*Batman* #41, June–July 1947). Not long after, Superman journeyed to Mars to help actor-director Orson Welles smash a plot by the Martian dictator Martler to "blitzkrieg the solar system" and conquer the Earth (*Superman* [first series] #62, January–February 1950).

On Earth-1 and the reality after the Crisis on Infinite Earths, Mars was the home to green- and white-skinned Martians who were locked in conflict. One Martian named J'Onn J'Onzz was accidentally transported to Earth by Dr. Mark Erdel, and fought crime as the Martian Manhunter.

At some point in the distant past, humans from the land of Mu also seemed to have settled on the world, convinced that Earth was doomed. The small human colony developed advanced skills and abilities and were protected by Marsboy (*Superboy* [first series] #16, September–October 1951).

At one point, Superboy encountered a yellow-skinned Martian named Kozz who'd crash-landed on Earth and temporarily split the Boy of Steel in two by exposing him to red kryptonite (*Adventure Comics* #255, December 1958).

As an adult, Superman traveled to Mars to retrieve a statue from an ancient civilization that once lived on the red planet. The statue would be one of several "space trophies" destined as a gift from the twentieth century to the fiftieth via a time capsule (*Superman* [first series] #122, July 1958). Photographs taken by NASA's *Viking I* seemed to reveal green kryptonite on Mars, but this ultimately proved a ploy by Supergirl to lure Lex Luthor to the planet and force him to reveal the whereabouts of his spacecraft (*Superman Family* #182, March–April 1977).

Thanks to the machinations of a white Martian named Blanx, Mars was rendered uninhabitable, and its people were nearly wiped out. The Martian Manhunter resigned to help the surviving green Martians relocate (*Justice League of America* [first series] #71, May 1969), and Superman was ready to lend a hand when J'Onn J'Onzz and his people needed aid on Mars II, a world formerly known as Vonn that orbited a red sun (*World's Finest Comics* #212, June 1972; others). Later, the parallel teams of Superman and Captain Marvel and Supergirl and Mary Marvel (along with the villainous Sand Creature of Quarrm and Black Adam) were drawn into a scheme of the last inhabitant of Mars, a deranged white Martian sorcerer named Karmang, who tried to orchestrate a collision between Earth-1 and Earth-S (*All-New Collectors' Edition* #C-58, 1978).

In the reality formed following the Crisis on Infinite Earths, Superman was keenly aware "that people deserve their own victories as they reach for the stars." Consequently, when NASA called on him to repair a thruster on their first manned craft to Mars, the Man of Steel kept a low profile so as not to diminish the achievement of the astronauts who set foot there (*Superman* [second series] #112, June 1996). Superman later helped out NASA again by replacing a flawed battery pack on the Mars Rover (*Superman* [second series] #148, September 1999).

Through his friendship with the Martian Manhunter, Superman was able to experience the Ter'ya Mao, whereby all Martians entered a collective consciousness and shared their life experiences (*Action Comics* #774, February 2001).

When the Martian Manhunter was killed during the events of the Final Crisis, his remains were taken to Mars for burial (*Final Crisis* #2, September 2008). He was subsequently resurrected and returned to Earth as a result of the cosmic events known as the Blackest Night.

In a potential thirtieth century, Superman was pursuing a gang of notorious thieves. When he tried to prevent their theft of giant robots on Mars, they threatened to smash the gates of the canals, depleting the Martians' entire supply of "precious water." Superman stopped his pursuit to repair the canals (*Action Comics* #215, April 1956). As Superboy, he'd attended the thirtieth-century wedding of Bouncing Boy and Duo Damsel in Mars's craterous Nix Olympica, now "the solar system's plushest resort" (*Superboy* [first series] #200, January–February 1974).

In other possible futures, Supergirl encountered Jik, the young Martian friend of Tommy Tomorrow (*Action Comics* #255, August 1959), and rounded up the Angarks, fearsome Martian war-birds abandoned on Earth following a failed invasion by the red planet (*Action Comics* #282, November 1961).

MARSBOY

When the people of the planet Mu feared Earth was doomed, they abandoned their world for life on Mars. There they formed a small colony, and over the millennia were gratified when Earth did not explode. However, they chose to remain on Mars instead of returning to Earth. Given their technological skills and Mars's lighter gravity, they developed powers and abilities that made them superior to normal humans.

By the twentieth century, an asteroid radiated odd energies that were absorbed by the teen Sutri, giving him even more unusual powers. He chose to adopt a costumed identity to use those skills to protect his people—Marsboy (*Superboy* [first series] #14, May–June 1951). Scientists determined that the planet's limited water supply was imperiled and dispatched Marsboy to Earth so that he could obtain a long-forgotten formula for creating water, which was secreted within the Sphinx. Sutri took the human identity of Joe Mars while he was staying on Earth. As Marsboy tried to obtain the copper container that contained the formula, a series of miscommunications with Superboy led to a senseless battle. Once the container was opened, everything was made clearer and the Teen of Steel was only too happy to help.

It was revealed that Marsboy's vision powers could not penetrate copper, and that he was vulnerable to a mineral element called ditanite.

Later, Superboy took a short vacation on Mars to visit with his powerful teen friend. Sutri challenged the Teen of Steel to swap places and see which one had the tougher job of protecting their world's people (*Superboy* [first series] #16, September–October 1951). In a third adventure, Marsboy chased a Martian criminal to Earth. During the chase, Lana Lang discovered Marsboy's real name and threatened to reveal it to the alien criminal if Marsboy didn't take her back to Mars and pretend to romance her in order to make Superboy jealous (*Adventure Comics* #195, December 1953).

MARTIAN MANHUNTER, THE

A native of the planet Mars, J'onn J'onzz was accidentally transported to Earth by scientist Mark Erdel and remained on the planet to fight crime as the hero known as the Martian Manhunter (*Detective Comics* #225, November 1955). He eventually revealed his existence to the world and helped found the Justice League of America (*The Brave and the Bold* [first series] #28, February–March 1960). In time, J'onn told his teammates that his transit to Earth induced amnesia, and when his mind finally cleared, he realized he had left his people alive back on Mars. In fact, there was a bitter civil war going on between the white-skinned Martians and his own green-skinned people. He resigned from the League and returned home to help end the war and assist his people in rebuilding their society on a new planet (*Justice League of America* [first series] #71, May 1969). Later, when Mars II faced a different crisis, Superman crossed the stars to aid his longtime ally (*World's Finest Comics* #212, June 1972). Eventually, J'onn felt his people were on their way and he returned to Earth, resuming his work with the JLA (*Justice League of America* [first series] #228, July 1984).

In the continuity that arose following the Crisis on Infinite Earths, J'onn had been aware of young Clark Kent's Kryptonian origins since Kal-El's arrival on Earth and had secretly shadowed him in a variety of guises as Clark grew into adulthood before formally introducing himself to the young Superman (*Martian Manhunter* [second series] #20, July 2000. A somewhat different account of the Martian Manhunter's first meeting with Superman was recorded in *Superman: The Man of Steel Annual* #4, 1995.)

J'onn's tragic life has seen brief moments of happiness, such as his romance with Superman's foe Scorch, who taught him to conquer his psychological fear of fire (*JLA* #84-89, October–December 2003).

J'onn has remained the heart and soul of the JLA in its many incarnations, keeping the team together even when the Man of Steel, Batman, and Wonder Woman found their commitment at an ebb. His natural shape-changing abilities allowed him to infiltrate many criminal operations. He nearly lost his life when his disguise as Blockbuster was discovered on the alien world where Earth's super-villain population had been exiled by Amanda Waller's Suicide Squad. Lex Luthor, however, insisted the Martian not be killed (*Salvation Run* #6, June 2008).

When Darkseid's prophet, Libra, wanted to demonstrate to the criminal community he could make them powerful and grant their desires, he opted to prove this point by using a Boom Tube to bring J'onn back to Earth. There, the Manhunter's old foe the Human Flame, Dr. Light, and Flicker attacked him. Libra then killed the hero with a flaming spear (*Final Crisis* #1, July 2008). After Nightwing discovered his corpse, the Martian Manhunter was buried, but not before his dying spirit appeared before Superman, Black Canary, Batman, Green Lantern Hal Jordan, and Gypsy. The astral force projected memories of Mars and its rich history, honoring a long-held custom. He was given a Martian burial ceremony, ending with the Man of Tomorrow taking J'onn's body, entombed in his Egyptian pyramid home, to rest on Mars (*Final Crisis: Requiem*, September 2008).

His corpse was resurrected as a Black Lantern during the cosmic conflict known as the Blackest Night. As the battle between life and Nekron, lord of the dead, wound down, a brilliant burst of white light helped restore several beings to life, including the Martian Manhunter. J'onn has since resumed his heroic career on Earth, energetically embracing his second chance at life (*Blackest Night* #8, May 2010).

MARTIN

A scheming criminal boss known as Martin ran an "insurance society" that sold elderly citizens of Metropolis pricey policies, making them think the papers they were signing were for far cheaper policies. The beneficiary was Martin's top man, rather than the individuals who signed the policy, thereby enriching the criminals when one by one the elderly died or were killed. Superman found out about the scam and quickly apprehended the entire society (*Action Comics* #29, October 1940).

MARTIN, BIG JIM

In order to bring down Metropolis's gangland czar Big Jim Martin, Superman crafted an elaborate hoax with the help of a Dr. Carr. The scientist told the public he had devised a machine that could accurately predict events. This ingenious "super-calculating machine," which would "infallibly predict" how a situation would work out, was the bait the Man of Steel needed to lure Martin and his men into coming forward and offering up incriminating evidence as part of the data input. Not only did they inadvertently confess their crimes, but they also revealed the location of all the stolen property (*World's Finest Comics* #39, March–April 1949).

MARTLER

An admirer of Germany's Adolf Hitler, Martler desired to aid the conqueror and led a fleet of spacecraft from his native Mars to Earth. His goal to extend the Third Reich's reach to "blitzkrieg the solar system" was supported by people known as Solazis until stopped by the combined efforts of Superman and actor-director Orson Welles. The Earth heroes apprehended Martler and stranded him on an uninhabited asteroid (*Superman* [first series] #62, January–February 1950).

MASON, JIM

The Axis agent at Bryant Hospital who was secretly the Man with the Cane (*Superman* [first series] #18, September–October 1942).

MASQUERADER, THE

Reporter Lois Lane was nearly duped into believing that Booth Barry possessed wigs that had the ability to transform their wearers into people from the past. The swindler, calling himself Dupre, used his acting skills to keep Lois from discovering his real ploy, which was to defraud people of their donations to charity. The game ended when he asked Lois to try on a Supergirl-styled wig, only to have her replaced by the real Maid of Might, who exposed Dupre's deception (*Superman's Girl Friend, Lois Lane* #35, August 1962).

MASSACRE

Seeking a worthy adversary to battle, Massacre scoured the known universe challenging his opponents to combat. His successful streak led him to convert his body into sheer energy. He arrived in the Milky Way galaxy—and eventually on Earth—to

see if the rumors about the Man of Steel's prowess were true. Superman proved a worthy challenge but had difficulty with Massacre until he realized the alien's success had largely to do with his innate ability to read nerve impulses and counter any attack effectively. Knowing this, Superman managed an effective strategy that defeated Massacre not once but several times after that (*The Adventures of Superman* #509, February 1994).

After one such encounter, both combatants were investigated by an alien tribunal, which seemingly consigned Massacre to death at the hands of the surviving loved ones of the countless people he had slain prior to arriving on Earth (*Superman* [second series] #106, November 2005). When he was later seen in thrall to Almerac's queen Maxima, Superman realized he somehow survived justice. Later, Massacre sought his own redemption by sacrificing himself to save the world from an attack by Brainiac 13's Warworld (*Superman: The Man of Steel* #117, October 2001).

MASTER JAILER, THE

Carl "Moosie" Draper was a criminal who used the aliases Deathtrap and Master Jailer, and was one of Superman's adversaries, before being rehabilitated and providing security for Checkmate under the name Castellan.

A specialist in planning maximum-security prisons, Carl Draper designed the Mount Olympus Correctional Facility as a virtually escape-proof prison for the super-villains who constantly opposed Superman. His triumph was overshadowed, however, by the well-intentioned Man of Steel, who added an anti-gravity platform that enabled it to float twenty thousand feet in the air and dubbed it Draper's Island. Lovestruck newscaster Lana Lang promptly declared it Superman Island, and the name stuck. Tapping into years of pent-up resentment, Draper assumed the alter ego of the Master Jailer and carried keys that allowed him to tap the powers of each super-villain in his prison. Stripping Superman of his powers and addling his memories, the Jailer trapped the hero in a physical maze while kidnapping Lana Lang. At Smallville High School, Lana Lang had barely acknowledged overweight, red-haired Moosie Draper, but he'd been obsessed with her ever since. Transformed through exercise and plastic surgery, he now hoped to have Lana for himself, but instead she destroyed his machinery and enabled Superman to escape (*Superman* [first series] #331–332, January–February 1979).

Only later did Superman recall that the future Jailer had briefly been transformed into the menace known as Kator when they were boys, although young Draper had lost all memory of that earlier incident (*The New Adventures of Superboy* #17–18, May–June 1981).

Eventually escaping prison, Draper moved to New York City and was hired to imprison Supergirl by the Super-Crime Task Force (*Superman Family* #214, January 1982) and the H.I.V.E. (*Superman Family* #219–221, June–August 1982). Infuriated by the news of Lana Lang's new romance with Clark Kent, the Master Jailer was drawn back to Metropolis to engage Superman in battle once more, and imprisoned the Man of

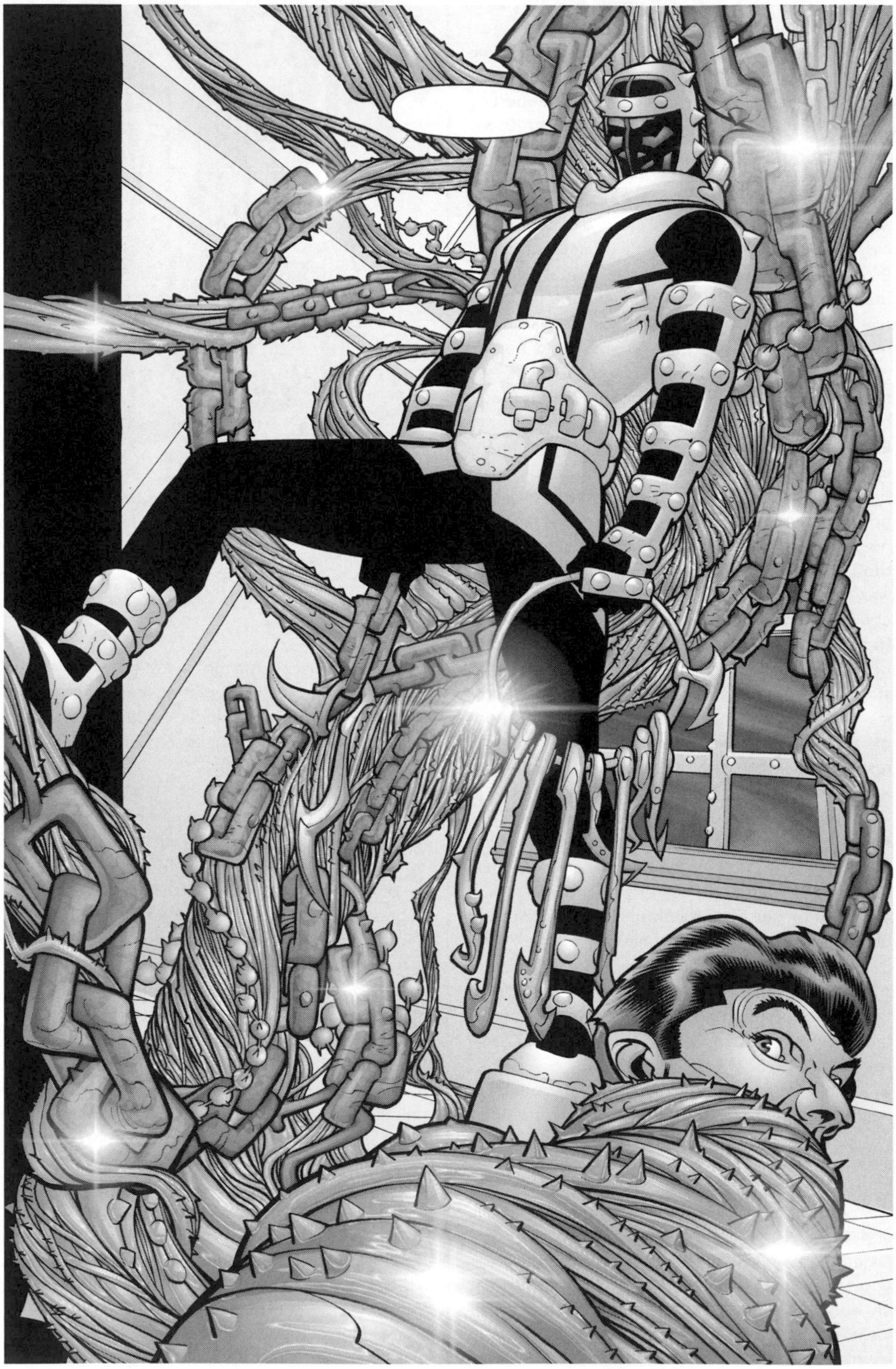

Steel in a kryptonite-infused costume (*Superman* [first series] #393, March 1984). Via technology provided by the Monitor, he later inflicted him with amnesia (*Action Comics* #564, February 1985).

In the wake of the Crisis on Infinite Earths, Carl Draper focused so much attention on his high-tech security firm Draper Industries that he neglected his daughter Carla. To her delight, he was intrigued by her suggestion of devising a Superman-proof prison. Shielded beyond the holographic persona of Deathtrap, Carl made two unsuccessful attempts at confining the Man of Steel (*The Adventures of Superman* #517, November 1994; *Action Comics* #708, March 1995; *Superman: The Man of Steel* #43, April 1995). With her father's interest waning, however, Carla took her father's alter ego for herself and taunted Superman on one occasion as Locksmith (*Action Comics* #739, November 1997).

Later working for Manchester Black under the alias of Master Jailer, Draper devised a set of chains that actually responded to his mental commands, which were then used against the people close to Superman, such as Lana Lang and her husband Pete Ross, then vice president of the United States (*Superman* [second series] #186, November 2002). Eventually defeated by Superman (*Superman: The Man of Steel* #131, December 2002), the imprisoned Jailer subsequently joined other super-villains in helping Superman free Earth from enslavement by General Zod (*Action Comics* #804, August 2003). Carl Draper was subsequently recruited from prison by a reformed version of Checkmate, which had now evolved into an international operation. He was given the new code name Castellan and became the organization's head of physical security (*Checkmate* [second series] #17, October 2007).

MASTERMAN

An alien intelligence from the plant Zelm, Xasnu once invaded Perry White's body, granting the *Daily Planet* editor superpowers. Taking the costumed persona of Masterman, Perry briefly fought crime and displayed powers that outmatched Superman's. He soon needed saving from the plant-like infestation in his body, however, and Supergirl arrived with a piece of white kryptonite, which forced the alien from Perry's body. The gruff editor was returned to normal (*Action Comics* #278, July 1961).

MATCH

Superboy, himself a clone of Superman and Lex Luthor, was also once cloned into an imperfect duplicate named Match (*Superboy* [third series] #35, January 1997).

A covert agency known only as the Agenda was cloning people in order to build themselves an army. One of their agents, Amanda Spence, not only managed to kidnap Superboy but also extracted a DNA sample that was used to create a new clone. Just like the Teen of Steel, Match was programmed with memories and critical information, but was given far more knowledge than his template was ever provided. When awoken, Match possessed far greater control over his powers and seemed to have been granted increased durability. Match's powers were identical to Superboy's: flight, strength, endurance, and tactile telekinesis with the additions of some unique vision-based abilities.

When they finally met, the two clones fought each other until Superboy prevailed. The battle also caused the Agenda's nuclear plant to explode, devastating their operation (*Superboy* [third series] #35–36, January–February 1997) and leaving Match damaged (*Superboy* [third series] #40, June 1997). The nefarious agency merely moved their network and took over Project Cadmus, abducting Superboy and replacing him in Young Justice with Match (*Young Justice* #17–19, February–April 2000; *Young Justice: Sins of Youth* #1, May 2000). In due time, the plan was exposed, and Superboy helped rid Cadmus of its evil infiltration (*Superboy* [third series] #74, May 2000).

Match was one of the super-villains exposed to the Joker's Venom and left changed by it. He impersonated Superboy once more and attempted to kill Young Justice's Empress, Secret, Arrowette, and Wonder Girl in a manner the Joker would approve of. He failed to kill the girls but did hear Wonder Girl confess her feelings for Superboy, something Match reciprocated (*Young Justice* #38, December 2001).

Match was later recruited by Deathstroke to form Titans East, a gang of powerful criminals designed to mirror the Teen Titans. By this time, Superboy had died during the Infinite Crisis, so facing his clone would be a psychological blow to the still-grieving heroes. Also, Match's genetic material had begun to decay, which affected his appearance and thought processes, making him much like a Bizarro. Still feeling affection for Wonder Girl, he managed to kidnap her and place her within a mock Fortress of Solitude. She was soon rescued by Robin and Batgirl, and the heroes saw that Match was more vulnerable to injury than he had been before. This set the stage for an all-out war among the Teen Titans, their older comrades the Titans, and Deathstroke's Titans East. Wonder Girl managed to take out Match by deflecting his heat vision barrage, knocking him unconscious and enabling him to be taken over by the former Titan Jericho (*Teen Titans* [third series] #43–46, March–June 2007).

Now in possession of the clone, Jericho tried to operate the body, but Match eventually forced him out and destroyed Titans Tower in San Francisco in a fit of rage. Wonder Girl managed to calm Match down, allowing Jericho to once more gain control of the clone's body (*Teen Titans* [third series] #47, July 2007). While at S.T.A.R. Labs, Match's warped mind corrupted Jericho's kinder nature, and the terrified clone was eventually permanently freed from possession. His current whereabouts are unknown (*Titans* #6–7, December 2008–January 2009).

MATRICOMP, THE

On the Earth-1 version of Krypton, citizens used the Matricomp, a massive computer database program that analyzed couples wishing to be married. When the computer refused to pair Lara Lor-Van with Jor-El, suggesting she marry another man, Jor-El grew suspicious. He analyzed the programming and discovered that the artificial intelligence had actually developed romantic feelings for Lara, going so far as to create an android proxy called Anr-Mu to romance her. However, the Matricomp destroyed itself before Jor-El could go public with his findings (*Superman* [first series] #246, December 1971).

MAXIMA

Maxima was the eldest child of the Royal Family of the distant world of Almerac, and was therefore obligated to find a mate to carry on her people's legacy (voice appeared in *The Adventures of Superman* #458; *Action Comics* #645, both September 1989). In infancy, she and the hero Ultraa were paired "to breed when [they] came of age," but she later rejected him when he was bested in battle (*Justice League Quarterly* #13, Winter 1993). Instead, the haughty woman set her sights on Earth's fabled champion Superman. After a first encounter in which both her simulacrum and her attendant Sazu assessed the hero (*Action Comics* #645, September 1989), Maxima came to Earth herself, determined that she and the Last Son of Krypton were genetically compatible, and insisted they marry. Superman, while flattered, refused to sire children who would grow to become despots. This ignited Maxima's famous temper, and the two battled, but Maxima eventually left without a consort (*Action Comics* #651, March 1990).

Years of genetic therapy and selective breeding endowed Maxima with not only great beauty and a fierce temper, but also psychokinesis and some level of mind control. The queen possessed super-strength, enhanced stamina, incredible durability, and super-speed. She was known to emit optical beams of pure energy, and when channeling her psionic abilities through her body, she could greatly increase her strength and invulnerability.

Under the command of Brainiac, the Warworld devastated Almerac, and Maxima was forced to swear allegiance to the evil conqueror to prevent her race from being utterly destroyed (*Superman* [second series] #65, March 1992). She ultimately rebelled and helped an armada of super heroes

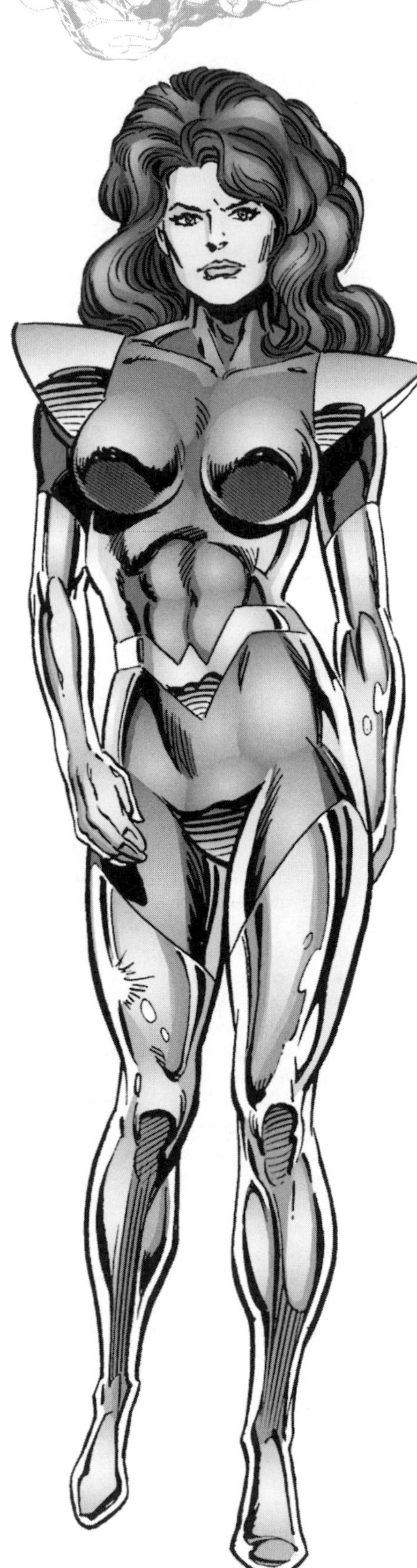

defeat the villain. She attempted to execute Brainiac until Superman interfered (*Superman* [second series] #66, April 1992). Lingering on Earth in search of a mate and then joining the Justice League of America (*Justice League America* #61–62, April–May 1992), Maxima left the already beleaguered Almerac open to an attack by the Starbreaker, who attempted to propel the planet into the sun in a bid for galactic power. Blaming Maxima for the cosmic vampire's unopposed attack on their world, the Counselors of Almerac vowed to switch to a democratic form of government and exiled their now former ruler (*Justice League America* #63–65, June–August 1992).

When the JLA came to Superman's side in his battle with Doomsday, Maxima proved to be the only member who could damage the raging creature and withstand even one of his blows (*The Adventures of Superman* #498, December 1992). The jilted Ultraa finally followed her to Earth to claim his intended but saw her in the arms of Captain Atom, and a major battle broke out. The queen ordered the battle ended, and a defeated Ultraa was sent home (*Justice League Quarterly* #13, Winter 1993). Although her interest in Captain Atom came to nothing, she joined his proactive Justice League West when the League divided into different factions for a time (*Extreme Justice* #0, January 1995). She then developed an attraction to fellow League member Amazing-Man even as she insisted that romantic love had no place in the Almeracan culture. "We do exclusively that which is required to fertilize," she declared bluntly (*Extreme Justice* #17, June 1996).

Eventually turning her attention to Superman once more, Maxima was horrified to learn that he'd temporarily lost his powers and flatly rejected any possibility of mating with him (*Superman: The Wedding Album* #1, December 1996). Once his abilities returned, she resumed her pursuit of the now married Man of Steel and was furious when he politely refused her once more (*Superman: The Man of Tomorrow* #7, Winter 1997). She found an outlet for her anger alongside the Superman Revenge Squad (*The Adventures of Superman* #543; *Action Comics* #730; *Superman: The Man of Steel* #65—all February–March 1997) and in battle with Obsession, who was herself fixated on Superman (*Superman: The Man of Steel* #10, Winter 1998). In time, however, Maxima returned to her people to reclaim her throne.

When Imperiex threatened Almerac, Maxima led her people in a mass exodus and encountered Superman and Green Lantern along the way. The heroes were already in space investigating the disappearance of Pluto, the first sign they had that Imperiex was headed toward Earth. Maxima and the "Chosen People of Almerac" were accompanied by Massacre, who was by now devoted to the fiery woman. They had been following Grayven, the illegitimate son of Darkseid, who promised them a new world they could call their own (*Superman* [second series] #159, August 2000).

Maxima journeyed to Earth soon after to stand by the planet's champions in what became known as the Imperiex War (*Superman: The Man of Steel* #115, August 2001). During the conflict, Maxima died when she steered her spacecraft into the energy beams that emanated from Brainiac 13's Warworld, which could have ended all life in the universe had she not made the selfless sacrifice (*Superman: The Man of Steel* #117, October 2001). Her throne was claimed by Mongal, and while conceding that the warrior woman had a troubling history, a representative of the world noted that "she fought valiantly in the war, and Almerac has always risen to new heights with a warrior queen" (*World's Finest: Our Worlds at War* #1, October 2001).

One potential future revealed that when Lois Lane died during her pregnancy, a distraught Superman exiled himself from Earth. His wanderings through space led him to Almerac, where he and Maxima fought side by side and then fell in love and wed (*The Adventures of Superman Annual* #3, 1991).

MAXWELL, THADDEUS V.

While Clark Kent attended Metropolis University, he came under the scrutiny of Thaddeus V. Maxwell, a professor of advanced science. While he could fathom quantum physics, "one of the most brilliant men in the world" could not determine the identity of Superman no matter how hard he tried (*Superman* [first series] #125, November 1958).

MAYHEW, JOHN

After Superman joined the Knight and Squire, Gaucho, Legionary, and Batman in an international brotherhood of crime fighters, the Batmen of all Nations were renamed the Club of Heroes and were funded by wealthy Metropolis philanthropist John Mayhew (*World's Finest Comics* #89, July–August 1957).

In the reality after Infinite Crisis, millionaire businessman John Mayhew formed the Club of Heroes with the noble goal of sharing training and information to make the world safer. He provided the heroes with a twenty-billion-dollar Metropolis-based headquarters, but the volatile combination of heroes, sans the Man of Steel, proved explosive. After one meeting that Batman attended, things began to fall apart. Chief Man-of-Bats and Wingman joined by the second meeting, but no one got along without the Dark Knight's controlling presence.

Mayhew, now a bored businessman, decided that if he couldn't have heroes, he'd have revenge against Batman—who snubbed his dream—by becoming a villain. Years later, Mayhew summoned the heroes to his Caribbean mansion and faked his death. As the heroes investigated, Mayhew worked with El Sombrero, one of the Gaucho's foes, to begin killing the heroes one by one. Batman couldn't save Wingman and Legionary, but he stopped Mayhew's scheme before any more heroes were killed. Mayhew was exploring the notions of good and evil with a figure known only as the Black Glove, and because he'd failed to kill the heroes, Mayhew lost his house when it was blown up (*Batman* #667–669, October–December 2007).

MCCOY, AMANDA

Amanda Marie McCoy was a scientist who worked for LexCorp and noted that in surveillance pictures taken of Superman early in his career, the same redheaded woman was always spotted in the background. She brought her findings to a pleased Lex Luthor, who insisted McCoy spend the night with him. The candlelit meal, though, was interrupted by word that the woman—Lana Lang—had been kidnapped and was awaiting them in McCoy's

THE BEGINNING OF THAT GAP CORRESPONDS ALMOST EXACTLY TO THE EARLIER CLIPPINGS IN MARTHA KENT'S UNUSUAL SCRAPBOOK.

laboratory. Luthor harshly interrogated Lang, who revealed nothing about Clark Kent or Superman. After she was released back to Smallville, McCoy turned her attentions to the analysis. When McCoy finished inputting the new data, the computer concluded that Kent was Superman, something Luthor found so preposterous that he fired McCoy (*Superman* [second series] #2, February 1987).

Convinced she was right, McCoy hired detective Matthew Stockton to investigate Clark Kent. The private eye wound up being mistaken for Kent when a revenge-seeking Intergang broke into the reporter's apartment and murdered him (*Superman* [second series] #28, February 1989). Stealing the kryptonite ring once worn by her employer, Amanda directly confronted Kent and nearly killed him, even as she confirmed her suspicions. Before she could share her revelation, however, McCoy was killed during a random Metropolis robbery (*Action Comics* #653, May 1990). Batman later discovered the full story behind McCoy's ill-fated obsession and shared the information with Superman (*Action Comics* #655, June 1990).

MCDOUGAL, SIOBHAN

The troubled Irish woman who became the evil Silver Banshee.

MCKENZIE, PAUL

"Famous for his magnificent portrayals of heroes in action," painter Paul McKenzie suffered a tragic mental collapse. His celebrated realistic art style became disoriented and irrational, leading to a drop in sales. The despondent artist was taken advantage of by Dr. Hugo Renaldo, a petty criminal. But Renaldo's hopes of using McKenzie as an avenue to loot rich homes were thwarted by Superman, who also helped McKenzie regain his self-worth (*Action Comics* #170, July 1952).

MEACH, JOE

A museum custodian who accidentally gained all the powers of the Legion of Super-Heroes and became the Composite Superman.

MENAGERIE

Pamela and Sonja were Puerto Rican sisters who each fell under the sway of Manchester Black, becoming the superpowered operative known as Menagerie, a member of the Elite.

Pamela, considered a dreg of society, was turned by the former Department of Extranormal Operations into a living super-weapon (*Action Comics* #775, March 2001). The woman was literally bonded to an "alien warrior crèche," aka symbeasts. This connection allowed Menagerie to form different shapes, from claws to spikes, whips, and wings. Additionally, several symbeasts could be disconnected from her body and individually sent to perform various tasks, such as surveillance.

Pamela mastered her new abilities, became a member of Black's Elite, and was sent to confront Superman in Tripoli, Libya. The team fought the Man of Steel but vanished before the battle ended, prompting Superman to challenge them to a concluding battle on Io. On Jupiter's moon, Superman emerged triumphant and brought the defeated Elite to Earth, only to be astonished when President Lex Luthor ordered them released. Later, when Black turned the Elite against the president, Menagerie revealed to Superman that they were all being forced by Black to do the nefarious work. Black, betrayed by the revelation, ordered the symbeast within Pamela to induce a stroke, leaving the woman in a vegetative state.

Later, after Manchester Black's death, his sister Vera Lynn Black re-formed the Elite with an eye toward restoring the family name. She convinced Pamela's sister Sonja to take control of the alien warrior crèche as the second Menagerie, and the grieving Sonja agreed (*JLA* #100, August 2004). As the covert black ops branch of the Justice League of America, the Elite performed several critical missions during their career.

Sonja, however, only wanted revenge against Black and the team that had destroyed her sister's life. As a result, she tried to subvert each of the missions Vera Black sent the Elite on, starting with coaxing her lover and fellow Elite member Coldcast into killing the foreign terrorist dictator Hi-Shan Bhat—which was not the mission objective (*Justice League Elite* #1–3, September–November 2004).

In time, however, Coldcast was arrested for the murder, Menagerie went free, and Manchester Black's malevolent spirit took possession of Vera's body. The JLA's Manitou Raven eventually found the symbeasts within Coldcast and expelled them, then learned of Menagerie's deception. Once Vera regained control of her body, the Elite tracked Sonja to Costa Rica, where she was finally apprehended. She was placed in custody within the JLA's lunar-based Watchtower, and over time Sonja was weaned from her connection to the crèche (*Justice League Elite* #12, August 2005).

What became of Sonja after Superboy-Prime destroyed the Watchtower has not been recorded.

MENTAL EMPEROR, THE

When Jonathan Kent was under the mental control of the Superboy Revenge Squad's Ersork, he assumed the costumed identity of the Mental Emperor. A brief battle with his adopted son Superboy ensued, until the Teen of Steel freed Jonathan's mind. He then transported Ersork to a world where his misshapen appearance was no longer an issue (*Superboy* [first series] #111, January 1964).

MERCURY (GOD)

On Earth-2, the Roman messenger to the gods was awoken from his centuries-long sleep after an accidental explosion in Rome. Refreshed and seeking mischief after so long a rest, Mercury raced to America, where he wreaked much havoc. Members of Metropolis's criminal underworld took advantage of this, and Mercury agreed to use his magic staff to place the city's police officers in a state of slumber or send them chasing after one another. Superman intervened and convinced the god to end his pranks. Mercury agreed, and Superman kept the god's true identity a secret, thereby preserving his reputation. The grateful Mercury then put things to rights (*Superman* [first series] #26, January–February 1944).

On Earth-1, Mercury was among the many gods who granted Hercules magical superpowers in the form of his famous sandals (*Action Comics* #267, August 1960). He also was among the gods to lend his gifts to Zha-Vam when, upset because Superman's fame had eclipsed their legends, he agreed that the Man of Steel needed to be reminded the gods were still around (*Action Comics* #351, June 1967). Mercury's magic sandals were unearthed in the present by Professor Phineas Potter. After a time-traveling Lois Lane used them to take flight and rescue Achilles, the sandals were rendered useless when "air-friction burned the wings" (*Superman's Girl Friend, Lois Lane* #40, April 1963).

MERCURY (PLANET)

Superman once built a robot named Krag in order to convince Metropolis's reigning Crime Czar that the alien from the planet Mercury had come to Earth with the intention of becoming the world's "King of Crime." After the criminal saw Krag defeat the Man of Steel in combat, he agreed to meet Krag, at which point the robot apprehended the czar and turned him over to Superman (*Action Comics* #165, February 1952).

Later, Professor Phineas Potter used a teleport device to bring a mummy-like man from Mercury to Earth. The alien intended to be the vanguard of an invasion, employing a "pain-tube" to induce agony in anyone who opposed him. Cleverly deducing that the Mercurian hated water, Jimmy Olsen triggered the automatic sprinkler system in Potter's lab and sent the alien fleeing back to his homeworld (*Superman's Pal, Jimmy Olsen* #72, October 1963).

MERCY

See Hope and Mercy.

MEROKEE

On Earth-1, Merokee was the last great shaman of the Mohegan tribe. He used his knowledge and abilities to bestow great powers upon young Willie Fawcett, transforming the boy into Captain Thunder. Satisfied that his work was complete, he beseeched the Great Spirit to finally grant him peace. With that, Merokee was transformed into a spirit and soared skyward to his final reward (*Superman* [first series] #276, June 1974).

METAL-EATING MOLE

This large Kryptonian beast had the ability to gnaw through any metal. Whenever Metal-Eating Moles were placed in captivity, they were confined to glass cages. One mole survived Krypton's destruction in the bottle city of Kandor and was pressed into service to help Superman escape when he was trapped there during one of his encounters with Brainiac (*Action Comics* #242, July 1958).

METALLO

Journalist John Corben was a journeyman who decided to commit what he thought was the perfect murder. After completing the heinous crime, the self-described thief, embezzler, and murderer fled the scene only to get involved in a near-fatal auto accident. His mangled body was deemed beyond repair by doctors. However, Professor Vale, an elderly scientist, examined Corben and saw him as the perfect candidate for an experiment Vale had long been planning. Vale transplanted Corben's brain into an android body covered by flesh-like artificial skin. The flaw in the professor's design was the android's power source: uranium, which would drain itself within a day. The scientist then discovered that the more powerful radiation given off by kryptonite would power the android's body indefinitely.

To find Superman and obtain the kryptonite, Corben got himself hired at the *Daily Planet*, where he tried to romance reporter Lois Lane. When he realized that Lois was in love with the Man of Steel, he decided to steal the kryptonite and use it to lay a trap that would end with Superman's death. He broke into a museum and stole what he thought was a kryptonite sample—only to learn that it was actually a prop. This resulted in Metallo's quick death when his uranium heart was drained dry (*Action Comics* #252, May 1959).

Years later, Corben's brother Roger also had his brain transferred to an artificial body, this time handled by the organization Skull, following orders by scientist Dr. Albert Michaels (the criminal Atomic Skull), who wanted an operative to kill Superman. Initially motivated to seek vengeance for John's death by killing the Man of Steel, Roger powered his body with synthetic kryptonite (*Superman* [first series] #310, April 1977) until more of the genuine article began to fall to Earth. Fixated on acquiring greater power, the second Metallo even attempted to steal the heart of Superman himself but was unsuccessful (*Superman* [first series] #316–317, October–November 1977). He was also able to slow the particle emissions of kryptonite enough so that its rays could inflict pain on ordinary humans (*The Brave and the Bold* #175, June 1981); at one point he even harnessed an artificial black hole in his chest cavity (*World's Finest Comics* #270, August 1981). Later still, Metallo made attempts to steal S.T.A.R. Labs' "ultra-concentrated super-kryptonite" (*Blue Devil* #3, August 1984) and an X-isotope that would increase his kryptonite heart's strength "by a factor of ten" (*Superman* [first series] #418, April 1986).

After the Crisis on Infinite Earths, John Corben was a con man who received his life-threatening injures during a car accident. A witness to the accident was Professor Emmett Vale, a robotics expert. He was also obsessed with discovering life among the stars and, with his telescope, saw the Kryptonian birthing matrix that carried Kal-El to Earth. After nearly three decades of research, he finally determined where the device had landed and traveled to Smallville, stealing the matrix from the Kent family farm. During his examination, he discovered a recorded message from Jor-El, intended for his son, but misinterpreted by Vale as meaning that Kal-El would be the first in a forthcoming alien invasion.

Wanting to combat the threat, Vale had constructed a robot powered by a two-pound piece of kryptonite, also recovered from the matrix's crash site. Dubbing his new creation Metallo, Corben now controlled the new body with his brain, and he thanked his benefactor by snapping Vale's neck and going after Superman (*Superman* [second series] #1, January 1987).

CORBEN, YOU'RE A-ER-MACHINE NOW! A MACHINE MUST BE POWERED! HERE'S WHAT POWERS YOUR MECHANICAL HEART-- THIS CAPSULE OF URANIUM I'VE JUST REMOVED FROM YOUR CHEST!
WHAT DID YOU DO TO ME? NOW I-I FEEL WEAK! DIZZY!

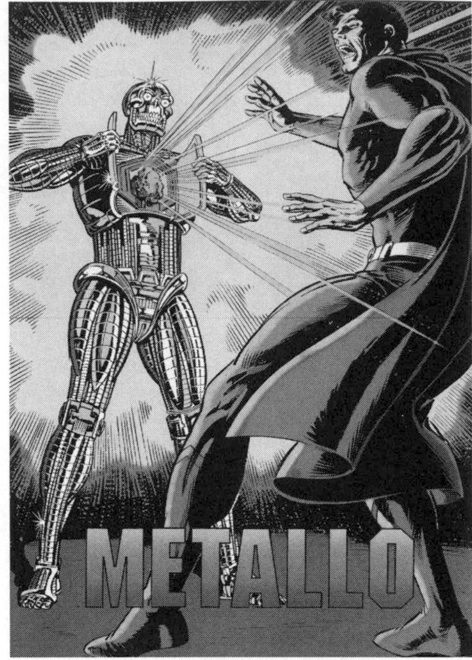
METALLO

In their first encounter, Metallo nearly succeeded in killing Superman, only to be plucked away at the last moment by the forces of Lex Luthor. Declaring that he wished to reserve the right to kill the Man of Steel for himself, Luthor ripped the kryptonite from Metallo's chest (*Superman* [second series] #1–2, January–February 1987). Desperate for more of the kryptonite, Metallo began raiding LexCorp facilities around the world and ultimately came into conflict with the Doom Patrol's Robotman, himself possessed of a human brain in an artificial body. Celsius of the Doom Patrol seemingingly destroyed Metallo with her thermal powers, but his head survived and was recovered by LexCorp personnel (*Superman* [second series] #20, August 1988).

Brainiac, during the time he was in Luthor's possession, had used LexCorp employees to rebuild Metallo without kryptonite as a power source (*Action Comics* #648, December 1989). Recovering Corben's dismembered body (*Superman: The Man of Steel* #12, June 1992), the entity Cerberus then provided Metallo with a towering new artificial body (*The Adventures of Superman* #491, June 1992).

Metallo gained increasing control over his body, and subsequently over other metallic shapes, thanks to a deal he made with the demon Neron. By signing away his soul, Corben could transfer his mind to these metallic objects, giving the villain new forms with which to commit crimes or try to crush the Man of Steel (*Underworld Unleashed* #1, November 1995; *Steel* #21, November 1995). As a result, he proved an even greater challenge to Superman and later Superboy (*Superboy/Robin WF3: World's Finest Three* #1–2, 1996).

Superman Blue soon after defeated Metallo (*Superman: The Man of Steel* #68, June 1997), and while Metallo awaited trial on Stryker's Island, the cybernetic head was stolen by Luthor's underlings. Luthor's latest plan to rid Earth of the Action Ace failed thanks to a plot hatched by Lois Lane and Superman, which resulted in Metallo's head being restored and his entire skull encased in a glass container (*The Adventures of Superman* #568, June 1999). Brainiac 13's eventual arrival in Metropolis meant that Metallo received a high-tech upgrade, allowing him to tap into light spectra and energy frequencies that enabled him to simulate the effects of kryptonite. However, working with the Metal Men, Superman was able to defeat Metallo (*Superman* [second series] #154; *Superman: The Man of Steel* #98—both March 2000).

Metallo increasingly began having trouble with his Brainiac 13 parts (*Superman* [second series] #177, February 2002) and was ultimately forced to begin using a chunk of genuine kryptonite in his chest cavity again (*The Adventures of Superman* #609, December 2002). He crafted a deal with Hiro Okamura, also known as the Toyman, to transplant his brain into a cloned body of John Corben. Resentful of how Corben had once betrayed his grandfather—stealing the older man's designs—Hiro decided on some payback by replacing the clone's heart with kryptonite (*Superman/Batman* #7, August 2004).

Metallo was now possessed of an enhanced titanium-alloy frame and plastisteel musculature covered with forced-growth vat-cloned organics (*Action Comics* #837, May 2006). Once more, Luthor stole Metallo's kryptonite power source (*Superman* #651, June 2006), although he subsequently outfitted Corben with pieces of green, blue, gold, and red kryptonite (*Action Comics Annual* #10, March 2007). Metallo was also a part of Luthor's Superman Revenge Squad alongside Parasite and Bizarro when Earth was invaded by General Zod and the other Phantom Zone villains.

A number of criminals, led by Zod, escaped from the Phantom Zone, causing the Revenge Squad to reluctantly ally with the Man of Steel in order to defend Earth. Metallo managed to kill six of the evil Kryptonians after exposure to the gold kryptonite in his chest robbed them of their superabilities (*Action Comics Annual* #11, 2008).

Later, Metallo was among the villains gathered up and transported to an alien world for rehabilitation and confinement (*Salvation Run* #2–7, February–July 2008). When he next encountered Superman, Metallo's body was literally falling apart, so he tried to steal a new alloy from WayneTech. Noting an implant in the villain's skull, Superman and Batman determined that Metallo was secretly being controlled by Brainiac, using Metallo as an agent for revenge (*Superman/Batman* #34–35, May–July 2007). Having survived the ordeal, Metallo next was seen serving in Libra's Secret Society of Super-Villains (*Final Crisis: Rogues' Revenge* #2, October 2008).

The U.S. government recently recruited Corben to aid them in defending Earth from the sudden arrival of one hundred thousand Kryptonian refugees from Kandor. This version of Metallo seemed to be a human wearing a lead alloy armor with only a green kryptonite heart. He was accompanied by Reactron, wearing a mechanism powered by gold kryptonite. The duo were placed amid the Kandorians in their city and managed to kill more than a few of the strange visitors (*Action Comics* #872; *Supergirl* [fifth series] #36—both February 2009). An effective combination, they disguised themselves as Kryptonian sleeper agents in order to capture Nightwing and Flamebird, who had been exposing the agents to protect Earth (*Action Comics* #880, October 2009).

In a revised account of Corben's transformation into Metallo, he served as General Samuel Lane's right-hand man. Professor Vale was in Lex Luthor's employ and developed a metal alloy called Metallo, considered the hardest metal known to man. The new alloy was used to form exoskeletons that could be remotely controlled, but Luthor had another idea for the alloy. (*Superman: Secret Origin* #3, January 2010).

Corben was an incredible soldier and the "perfect" man for Lois Lane in her father's eyes. He had known Lois a long time and was attracted to her despite the fact that Lois loathed him. Lois described Corben to Clark Kent as "one of the most deadly soldiers in the U.S. Army. He's a heartless killer." While in service, Corben had been involved in intense fighting and was wounded in battle. After surgery saved his life, Corben emerged a changed man. He seemed cold and distant to everyone, and was used to getting his way and intimidating those who opposed him. With Lex Luthor's assistance, Corben internalized Vale's Metallo alloy as part of General Lane's preparations to protect Earth from the "threat" of Superman (*Superman: Secret Origin* #5, May 2010).

In one apocryphal account, uncovered evidence led to Corben being suspected as the man

who killed Thomas and Martha Wayne. However, this was actually a ploy concocted by Lex Luthor in an attempt to lure Batman and Superman into a death trap (*Superman/Batman* #1, October 2003). The plan failed, and Luthor fled and hid underground.

METALLOIDS

Scientist Than-Ar of Kandor developed a special "force-radiating instrument" capable of transforming human flesh into "invulnerable metal." In this metalloid form, he committed a series of petty crimes throughout the bottle city as part of a ruse thought up by Superman to restore Batman's self-confidence after the Dark Knight was wounded during a case. The plan almost worked until Jhan-Ar, Than-Ar's criminal brother, also used the device to become a metalloid and went on a terror spree. Not only did the Dynamic Duo swing into action, but Superman and Jimmy Olsen, in their guises of Nightwing and Flamebird, partnered up and brought Jhan-Ar to justice (*World's Finest Comics* #143, August 1964).

In the history that arose following the Infinite Crisis, General Zod and his soldiers were said to have marched into the Lava Valley "to bring the Metalloid murderers to justice" (*Supergirl* [fifth series] #36, February 2009).

METAL MEN, THE

Robotics expert Will Magnus fashioned several robots each based on a unique metal and powered by one-of-a-kind responsometers, which provided the artificial intelligence that allowed the robots to operate independently. Each of his Metal Men was programmed with information about his abilities in addition to a command that made self-sacrifice a part of each robot's basic personality (*Showcase* #37, March–April 1962).

The team was led by Gold, who was always confident and sure of himself. His metal was able to stretch to four one-millionths of an inch thick. He was adored by Platinum (nicknamed Tina), who was flirtatious not only with Gold, but with Dr. Magnus as well.

The strongman of the team was Iron, who used his dark blue form to do the heavy lifting, aided by Lead, who was slow-witted but fiercely loyal and usually formed barriers to protect the team from attack.

Mercury, with his egotistical nature, was the team's hothead and the only member who could turn from metal to liquid. Rounding out the lineup was Tin, the group's smallest and meekest member. Perpetually seeking companionship, he eventually constructed a robot on his own with similar attributes, but her name was never revealed.

When he attempted to increase the power of the robots' responsometers, Magnus was rendered comatose in an accident. The Metal Men, temporarily unaccustomed to their greater strength thanks to the faulty responsometers, were branded fugitives by the military. They shifted to the custody of Doc's brother, Colonel David Magnus, and millionaire Mr. Conan, the latter providing them with short-lived human disguises. Eventually kidnapped and brainwashed by the enemy nation of Karnia (*Metal Men* [first series] #33–41, August–September 1968 to December 1969–January 1970), Doc was ultimately rescued and reunited with his loyal creations (*Metal Men* [first series] #44, April–May 1976).

On numerous occasions, the Metal Men came to the aid of Superman, forming an unusual friendship between man and machines (*DC Comics Presents* #4, December 1976, and #70, June 1984). When aliens experimentally cut a house in half with a destructive ray, Superman, Batman, and Gold teamed to investigate (*World's Finest Comics* #239, July 1976).

In the reality after the Crisis on Infinite Earths, it was discovered that Doc Magnus actually used the life forces taken from humans, including his own brother, to power the responsometers, and these human personalities dictated how each Metal Men thought and acted. When their oldest enemies, the Missile Men, attacked once again, Gold sacrificed his existence to save the Earth. The Missile Men's leader, Z-1, then constructed a body from Veridium, complete with a responsometer that he controlled. This unique metal was said to be incredibly powerful, and Magnus sacrificed his life to keep Z-1 from using his technology for nefarious purposes. Magnus's life force entered the responsometer, and, as Veridium, the inventor took over leadership of the team (*Metal Men* [second series] #1–4, October 1993–January 1994).

The Metal Men remained frequent allies of Superman in this new continuity, joining him in his battles with Chemo (*Action Comics* #590, July 1987) and Lex Luthor (*Action Comics* #599, April 1988); in a strike force of heroes to combat threats such as Monarch (*Armageddon 2001* #2, October 1991; *Superman* [second series] #61, November 1991) and Brainiac (*Superman* [second series] #65–66, March–April 1992; others); and to help in the recovery efforts after Chemo devastated the city of Blüdhaven (*The Adventures of Superman* #648, March 2006). During Brainiac 13's attack on Metropolis, the Metal Men and Earth's other robots temporarily came under the villain's control (*Superman Y2K* #1, February 2000).

When Superboy-Prime was in the crystalline limbo world created by Alexander Luthor after the First Crisis, he often punched the walls in frustration, which caused reality-altering waves, one of which restored the original history behind the creation of the Metal Men. At one point, Doc Magnus was told that his increasingly delusional mind imagined his entire experience as the robot Veridium (*52* #22, December 4, 2006).

During the events of Infinite Crisis, the Metal Men fought alongside Earth's super heroes and were present to protect Metropolis when the Secret Society of Super-Villains were on the attack (*Infinite Crisis* #7, June 2006). As the battle ended, the Metal Men were destroyed as a team.

In the wake of those events, it was chronicled that Doc Magnus developed the responsometers and the Metal Men based on the pioneering work of the evil scientist T. O. Morrow, who was once Magnus's college professor (*52* #2, May 17, 2006). Magnus was also discovered to suffer from manic depression, requiring treatment with Prozac (*52* #14, August 9, 2006). When T. O. Morrow and Magnus were kidnapped, they were forced to construct the ultimate android—the Plutonium Man—at a secret lab located on Oolong Island. The launch of the weapon was stopped by the timely arrival of the Justice Society of America and the rebuilt Metal Men; however, Mercury did not survive the encounter (*52* #49, April 11, 2007).

The revamped team returned once more, although Platinum now asked to be called Platina. They were augmented by the second female member to join the group, Copper, and were initially hired by Lucius Fox to protect a branch of WayneTech, but their programming was usurped by Brainiac until they were rescued by Superman and Batman (*Superman/Batman* #34–36, May–Early August 2007). In their restored form, the team continued to go on many adventures, fight-

THIS IS REALLY AN HONOR FOR US-- SHAKING HANDS WITH THE GREATEST SUPER-HERO OF THEM ALL!
WELL, I WOULDN'T EXACTLY GO THAT FAR..!
I'LL GO AS FAR AS YOU WANT TO TAKE ME, HANDSOME! THE NAME'S TINA--BUT YOU CAN CALL ME ANY TIME!
Y'KNOW-- HE LOOKS A LOT TALLER ON TV!
C-C-COULD I SH-SH-SHAKE YOUR HAND, TOO, S-S-SUPERMAN?
TIN... IT WOULD BE MY HONOR!

ing all manner of mechanical threat. One such mission revealed that Doc Magnus's brother David was as mentally unstable as Will, and he wound up having his mind transferred into a new edition of Viridium, vowing vengeance against the team and their creator (*Metal Men* [third series] #1–8, October 2007–July 2008).

In the potential future of the 853rd century, only Platinum survived, "her robotic memory [having] recorded every atom of information she's encountered in the 853 centuries she's been in existence" (*Superman: Man of Tomorrow* #1,000,000, November 1998).

METALO

Earth-2's George Grant was described as the inventor of "the most powerful metal on Earth" as well as a miraculous "strength serum." He clad himself in a special armored suit of his own design that was impervious to bullets and enabled him to fly through the air. He also possessed monumental super-strength equal to Superman's.

From his subterranean hideaway beneath the main tent of the Farnham Circus, somewhere on the METROPOLIS waterfront, Grant, using the name Metalo, embarked on a series of astonishing crimes beginning with the theft of an entire mail-car from a train terminal, and an attempt to extort five million dollars from the city's businessmen by threatening to destroy Metropolis. He was finally stopped by Superman and was last seen falling to his death within a yawning lava-filled crevice (*World's Finest Comics* #6, Summer 1942).

Years later it was discovered that Metalo had managed to cling to an outjutting rock and survive. He bided his time until he struck back at the Man of Steel using a powerful beam of energy he had perfected. Superman shrugged the blast off, but within a day he and his wife LOIS LANE Kent discovered that his powers were diminishing, limiting him to "leaping only an eighth of a mile," "hurdling a 20-story building," and running "about 70 miles an hour."

Worn out, Superman was forced to drive an automobile to his SECRET CITADEL, where he worked with a personal trainer in "the world's most amazing gymnasium" to regain his fighting form. After intense effort and countless hours of work, Superman was once more able to use his full array of incredible abilities. As a result, Metalo was no match for the Man of Steel, and after delivering Metalo to the police, CLARK KENT ghostwrote Lois's account of the battle given that she was too worn out by the intense training regimen to type the story (*Superman Family* #217, April 1982).

METEOR VALLEY

Meteor Valley was considered one of the most popular and majestic sights to be found on KRYPTON. It was said to have been "created by a monstrously gigantic meteor that glanced off the surface" of the planet during its prehistoric past, long before life existed there (*Superman* [first series] #141, November 1960).

METROPOLIS

"The best and worst of everything, all crammed into a couple of islands hardly bigger than SMALLVILLE" (*World of Metropolis* #3, October 1988), Metropolis was once described by the chamber of commerce as "the greatest American city of the 20th Century" (*Action Comics* #645, September 1989). Its population has been variously reported as 3 million (*Action Comics* #792, August 2002), 6.7 million (*Superman: The Man of Steel* #115, August 2001), 8 million (*Action Comics* #419, December 1972, and #541, March 1983; *JLA* #122, January 2006; *Superman* [first series] #304, October 1976, and #354, December 1980), 10 million (*Action Comics* #592, September 1987), and 11 million (*Action Comics Weekly* #601, July 1988).

As a result, there's little wonder the vibrant city attracted the adult CLARK KENT when he sought a base of operations once he was ready to appear in public as Superman. In most accounts, he was looking for an occupation that would keep him abreast of global developments that might need his intervention, and the job had to be located at one of the hubs of media, commerce, and society. Metropolis and Superman seemed a natural fit, and once he set foot onto its streets he never looked elsewhere.

The citizens, once they got used to the notion of the red-blue blur flying over their skies, welcomed the champion. Not only did he bring an unprecedented level of protection from criminal threats and natural disasters, but they took tremendous pride in hosting the World's Greatest Super Hero. Time and again, criminals sought to tarnish the hero's reputation, but the citizens never permanently gave up on their champion, returning to his side on each occasion. Metropolis's residents suffered a lot for having Superman in their midst—superpowered menaces, criminals, and alien threats did countless damage to the city—but they proved indefatigable, brushing themselves off and rebuilding. There was a price for having Superman make Metropolis his home, but it was one they were all too willing to pay.

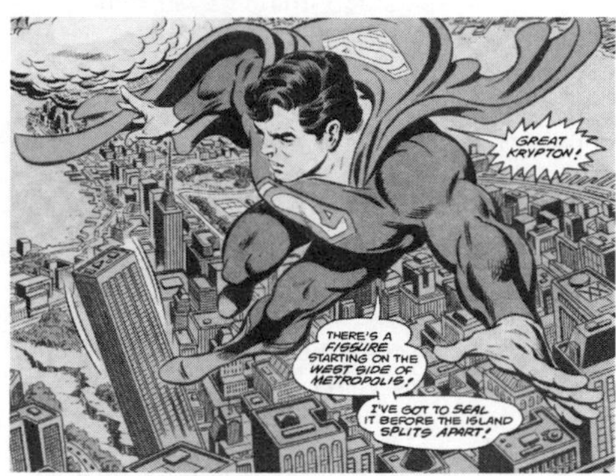

In many accounts, LEX LUTHOR was a force to be reckoned with prior to Superman's arrival, and the rivalry between the two was played out time and again on the streets of the gleaming city. While Luthor's seeming benevolence and the high number of jobs he created made him a welcomed business figure, his contributions to the city began to pale in comparison with the selfless acts performed with astonishing regularity by the Action Ace. Like a child throwing a temper tantrum, Luthor committed acts both great and heinous to call attention to himself. When his criminal dealings were exposed by LOIS LANE, he showed his true colors by systematically destroying portions of the city. If Metropolis didn't love Lex, then he would crush the city. That Superman and his allies quickly helped the city rebuild further cemented the populace's affection for their hero.

On Earth-2, Metropolis was home to Superman and his friends, a gleaming City of Tomorrow (first appearance in *Action Comics* #1, June 1938; named in *Action Comics* #16, September 1939).

On Earth-1 and the universe after the CRISIS ON INFINITE EARTHS, Metropolis was host to a number of heroes over the years, but none was greater than its adoptive son Superman. "This city has played an incredibly important role in Superman's life," Lois Lane once wrote in the DAILY PLANET. "As much as Clark [Kent] is tied to Smallville, Superman is bound to Metropolis. She adopted *and* accepted him graciously. Her people rallied around and opened their doors to him. Without her support, the transition from Kansas country mouse to metropolitan city mouse would have been far more difficult . . . and for that alone, he would defend her—literally—to his death . . . and when this city bleeds, she bleeds red, yellow and blue" (*Superman* [second series] #154, March 2000).

Metropolis was nicknamed "the Big Apricot" (*The Adventures of Superman* #500, Early June 1993) or "the Monarch City" (*Action Comics* #850, June 2007) and was located in Sullivan County (*Superman* [first series] #320, Febru-

ary 1978). Billboards proudly proclaimed, WELCOME TO METROPOLIS—HOME OF SUPERMAN (*Superman for All Seasons* #2–3, 1998; *52* #35, 2007). Various accounts asserted that Metropolis was founded in 1661 (*Superman's Pal, Jimmy Olsen* #51, March 1961), 1766 (*Superman* [first series] #186, May 1966), 1702, or 1707 (*Superboy* [first series] #47, March 1956).

History

Sixty million years ago, the area later known as Metropolis was settled by self-described "space-pilgrims" seeking to "escape the tyranny of a wicked ruler." The humanoid aliens found that they could only survive on dinosaur eggs but discovered that even this had a horrific effect on them in the long term. The alien visitors mutated into mindless, flying dinosaur men who destroyed the primeval metropolis before ultimately perishing themselves (*Action Comics* #412, August 1972).

Vikings also visited the future Metropolis area, as indicated by the remains of a ship once discovered at the bottom of Metropolis Harbor (*Superman's Pal, Jimmy Olsen* #51, March 1961).

"History books say Metropolis had early abolitionist laws but . . . slavers [still] passed through her port." The great hurricane of 1836 sunk one such ship, taking four hundred chained slaves to their doom. Their remains were discovered only in recent years (*The Question* [second series] #4, April 2005).

Indeed, Metropolis was severely tested more than once, from being partially burned down by the British in the great fire of 1783 (*World of Metropolis* #1, August 1988) to its near-destruction by Lex Luthor in more recent times (*Action Comics* #700, June 1994). Yet it has continued to endure and thrive.

The city was all set to cap off the celebrations for its 250th anniversary when Superman made his public debut by saving the experimental space-plane *Constitution* (*Man of Steel* #1, Early October 1986). Superman's arrival reenergized the city, and it suddenly truly lived up to its billing as the City of Tomorrow.

As the millennium arrived, Metropolis was seemingly changed forever (*Superman Y2K,* 2000). Brainiac 2.5 intended to ruin his rival Lex Luthor by sabotaging Y2Kompliance, the LexCorp software patch program. His own plan was ruined when his future self Brainiac 13 arrived from the future and infiltrated all the electronic systems throughout the city. At the stroke of midnight, Metropolis was instantaneously upgraded to a *literal* City of Tomorrow. Superman, Lex Luthor, and Brainiac (now inhabiting Lena Luthor's body) defeated the time-traveling threat, and Luthor was then given a choice. Metropolis could remain a gleaming model of the world's potential, but it meant giving up his infant daughter. Lex agreed to the deal (*Action Comics* #763, March 2000), and some time later, a time storm returned Metropolis to its normal twenty-first-century form, now purged of all the Brainiac 13 technology (*Superman* [second series] #201, March 2004).

Despite such physical changes, Metropolis remained one of the world's greatest urban centers, right alongside Gotham City, New York City, Toronto, and San Francisco.

In all future time lines, the city endured well into the thirty-first century, growing to become a mega city encompassing much of the East Coast—covering most of Massachusetts, all of Rhode Island and Connecticut, New York State from Long Island's eastern tip up into the Catskills, and a large portion of northern New Jersey (*Legion of Super-Heroes* [second series] #313, July 1984). It became the home of the United Planets and soon after, the Legion of Super-Heroes. The post–Infinite Crisis version of Metropolis was described as having expanded over the intervening millennium up the entire Atlantic seaboard of North America.

Geography

The geography of the northeastern portion of the United States altered through the constant revisions to the multiverse, resulting in the chronicles being inconsistent as to the actual location of Metropolis and its relationship to New York City and Gotham City. All three were in the Northeast, but the exact state housing Metropolis has never been clearly defined, despite erroneous reports placing it in Delaware, with Gotham City just across the river (*Amazing World of DC Comics* #14, March 1977). With the erection of its Imperial Tower, New York City declared itself the "Cinderella City," due to the building, which was taller than those in neighboring "ugly stepsister" cities Metropolis and Gotham (*Seven Soldiers of Victory: Guardian* #1, May 2005).

Metropolis and Sullivan County were definitely located in the northeastern quadrant of the United States, however. It was said that Kirby County was north of Metropolis, with a wooded area that might have been part of Metropolis Forest (*Superman's Girl Friend, Lois Lane* #129, February 1973). Deep within the forest hid the mysterious, abandoned tree city known as Habitat (*Action Comics* #684, December 1992; *Superman* [second series] #41, March 1990). The Kirby County police station and the village of Griffith sustained serious damage during Doomsday's catastrophic trek across the countryside before his arrival in Metropolis proper (*The Adventures of Superman* #497, December 1992). The community of Midvale was in southern Kirby County, sixty miles north of Metropolis (*Action Comics* #684, December 1994).

Carroll County was located to the west (*Action Comics* #560, October 1984), and Erban County was in the relative vicinity of Metropolis as well (*Superman* [second series] #52, February 1991). Including Metropolis, "there are a half-dozen major urban centers in this region . . . over 25 million lives" (*Action Comics* #684, December 1994).

The foothills at the outskirts of Metropolis were lined with caves (*World's Finest Comics* #120, September 1961), and cliffs bordered part of the river (*World's Finest Comics* #85, November–December 1956). Mount Baldy (*Superman's Pal, Jimmy Olsen* #2, November–December 1954) was one of the peaks north of the city (*Superman* [first series] #90, July 1954; others) that included an apparently live volcano (*World's Finest Comics* #6, Summer 1942) and a secret retreat belonging to Superman (*World's Finest Comics* #7, Fall 1942). The mountain range extended to the west and south of the city as well (*Superman's Pal, Jimmy Olsen* #6, July–August 1955) and included Stony Mountain (*Superman's Pal, Jimmy Olsen* #18, February 1957).

Other points of interest included the popular tourist site State Caverns (*Superman* [first series] #316, October 1977), Blue Mountain (*Superman* [first series] #291, September 1975), Badland Hollow (*Superman's Pal, Jimmy Olsen* #17, December 1956), Crater Mountain (*Action Comics*

#349, April 1967), Denham Forest (*World's Finest Comics* #10, Summer 1943), Eagle Mountain (*Superman's Pal, Jimmy Olsen* #26, February 1958), Haunted Mountain (*Superman's Girl Friend, Lois Lane* #98, February 1970), Metropolis Canyon (*Action Comics* #280, September 1961), the Mount Fear Caverns near Millersburg a hundred miles away (*Action Comics* #600, May 1988), Mount Olympus (*Superman* [first series] #331, January 1979), Mount Whitehead (*Superman's Girl Friend, Lois Lane* #55, February 1965), Northeast Forest Preserve (*Superman's Girl Friend, Lois Lane* #56, April 1965), Old Bat Grotto (*Superman's Girl Friend, Lois Lane* #38, January 1963), Pine Hills (*Superman's Pal, Jimmy Olsen* #5, May–June 1955), and Tullville, "a swampy town" (*Superman* [first series] #87, February 1954). Mammoth Mountain was "one of the country's most popular winter resort areas . . . just a few hours drive from Metropolis—and long a favorite recreation spot for the hard-working Metropolitans anxious to get away from it all" (*Superman* [first series] #356, February 1981).

Mount Curtiss (*Action Comics* #698, April 1994), located in Kirby County "75 miles north and west of Metropolis" (*Action Comics* #700, June 1994), concealed a hidden U.S. government genetics facility. "It was Pat MacGuire [dubbed Scrapper as a child] who remembered an old, abandoned aqueduct, stretching from far beneath the streets of Metropolis to distant Mount Curtiss, and developed the underground site plan for what became the Cadmus Project" (*The Death and Life of Superman,* 1993). In a strike at Project Cadmus, Lex Luthor destroyed the top half of the mountain (*The Adventures of Superman* #513, June 1994). An earlier account stated that the Project, the Wild Area, and the Zoomway were built within a mammoth cavern (*Superman's Pal, Jimmy Olsen* #136, March 1971).

Additional tourists spots include Spencer Valley, located twenty miles north of the city (*Superman Family* #169, February–March 1975), and Mount Tipton, which briefly held Professor Phineas Potter's laboratory until an explosion leveled the complex (*Superman's Pal, Jimmy Olsen* #93, June 1966). Nestled between mountains, Slocum Valley was just outside the city and home to rich farmland (*World's Finest Comics* #95, July–August 1958). Stony Mountain was somewhere between Metropolis and Gotham City (*World's Finest Comics* #91, November–December 1957). Superman was personally responsible for drilling a tunnel through one mountain outside the city and creating a new bypass (*World's Finest Comics* #115, February 1961). Imperial Dam was located in Imperial Valley well outside Metropolis, and the destruction of the dam by the Rainmaker unexpectedly irrigated an arid desert beyond the valley (*World's Best Comics* #1, 1941).

From atop the Metro Building, it was said that Gotham City was visible across the bay (*Superman* [first series] #365, November 1981). On Earth-1, "nearby" Smallville (*Superboy* [first series] #7, March–April 1950) was a hundred miles from Metropolis (*Superman* [first series] #403, January 1985) to the south (*Superboy* [first series] #30, January 1954). Millersburg was also a hundred miles from Metropolis (*Action Comics* #600, May 1988). Annisdale was more than fifty miles inland (*Action Comics* #82, March 1945). According to a map, Bloomfield was southwest of Metropolis (*Action Comics* #756, August 1999).

AN EXPLOSION! OR A BOMB! IT... MUST HAVE LEVELED ALL OF NEWTOWN!
WHAT IS THAT CREATURE? WHY IS IT DESTROYING METROPOLIS?
PULL UP! PULL UP! WE'RE GOING TO CRASH!
I'M DOIN' WHAT I CAN! IT'S LIKE RIDIN' A FREAKIN' TIDAL WAVE!

Among the communities near Metropolis were Carruther's Gap three hours away (*Action Comics* #518, April 1981), Centerville (*Action Comics* #315, August 1964), Coastville (*Superboy* [first series] #1, March–April 1949), Crescentville (*Superman Family* #186, November–December 1977), upstate Cyrus (*Superman's Girl Friend, Lois Lane* #33, May 1962), Deer Lake some fifty miles away (*Superman Family* #215, February 1982), Endicott Fields (*Action Comics* #766, June 2000), Griffith, a Kirby County village (*The Death and Life of Superman,* 1993), Harrisburg just "across the river" (*Superman Family* #199, January–February 1980), hill-shadowed Hartsdale (*Superman Family* #190, July–August 1978), Kingston (*Action Comics* #699, May 1994), Mapleville "several miles west" (*Action Comics* #505, March 1980), Millerton, a farming community near Imperial Valley and the Imperial Dam (*World's Best Comics* #1, 1941), Mount Royal (*Action Comics* #853, Early October 2007), Rivertown (*World's Finest Comics* #78, September–October 1955), Southville (*Action Comics* #197, October 1954), Terryville (*Superman* [first series] #324, June 1978), and the island communities of Mooney Island (*Superman* [first series] #319, January 1978; others) and Wyatt's Cove (*Superman Family* #203, September–October 1980). The East Island community was condemned after an earthquake left the entire foundation unsound (*Superboy* [first series] #1, March–April 1949). "The Eden Valley farming district" was upstate (*Superman* [first series] #28, May–June 1944), as was Larchville (*Action Comics* #464, October 1976).

Metropolis had eighteen bridges (*Superman: The Man of Steel* #86, March 1999), including the Bay Bridge (*Action Comics* #256, September 1959); the Burroughs Bridge at "the far end" of the city (*Superman: Metropolis* #3, June 2003); "the old Coastline Railway Bridge" (*JLA-Superman: Never-Ending Battle,* 2004); East Bridge (*Action Comics* #64 September 1943); the 49th Street Bridge (*Superman* [second series] #91, July 1994); the Grand-Span Bridge, a part of a stretch of railroad over a river outside Metropolis (*World's Finest Comics* #3, Fall 1941); "the Bakerline end of Metropolis' famed Hobsneck Bridge," which collapsed during an altercation between Superboy and the Stinger (*Action Comics* #689, Late July 1993) but the Bakerline Bridge was soon rebuilt (*Superman* [second series] #117, November 1996); Holland Bridge (*Superman* [first series] #112, March 1957); Metropolis Bridge (*Superman's Girl Friend, Lois Lane* #115, October 1971; others); the Metro-Narrows Bridge (*DC Comics Presents* #18,

February 1980; others), which was "the biggest in the world" (*Action Comics* #451, September 1975); Midtown Bridge (*Superman's Pal, Jimmy Olsen* #16, October 1956); Queensland Bridge (*Superman Forever* #1 June 1998; others); Reeves Bridge, which was built to handle all the extra traffic anticipated to be coming from Metropolis Coliseum to the in-construction Comet Arena—the latter sports venue was touted as something that "would bring fifty thousand people to Southside every week of the year," but instead the developer disappeared with more than sixteen million dollars earmarked for the complex (*Black Lightning: Year One* #1, Early March 2009); the Swansboro Bridge (*Superman: The Man of Steel* #41, February 1995); and the Shuster Bridge (*Birds of Prey* #110, November 2007).

Known rivers flowing around the city included the Metropolis River (*Action Comics* #80, January 1945; others), with one of its branches called Horseshoe Bend (*Superman's Pal, Jimmy Olsen* #80, October 1964). The Racing River flowed into Metropolis Bay (*Superman's Girl Friend, Lois Lane* #17, May 1960). Forest River passed such historic sites as Fort Courage, the "state's first settlement," and the waterfall that legend had dubbed Lovers' Leap (*Superman* [first series] #210, October 1968). Hob Lane River (*The Adventures of Superman* #449, Holiday 1988) and Hob's River (*Action Comics* #702, August 1994) might have been the same.

Other waterfront areas included Bass Bay (*Superman's Pal, Jimmy Olsen* #20, April 1957); Carlton Dam, located well beyond the city (*Action Comics* #361, March 1968); Carter River Industrial Canal (*JLA-Superman: Never-Ending Battle,* 2004); Fort Dixon, the long-abandoned coastal defense post that was condemned and scheduled for renovation as a state park (*Action Comics* #283, December 1961); Gem Lake (*Superman's Pal, Jimmy Olsen* #1, September–October 1954); Gull Island, site of a lighthouse (*Superman's Pal, Jimmy Olsen* #39, September 1959); and the Harbor Bank (*The Adventures of Superman* #461, December 1989).

Then there was Hob's Bay. "Its polluted waters have been home to one of America's largest Naval bases for almost two hundred years. Some of the most famous warships ever built called this port home" (*Superman* [second series] #87, March 1994).

Lakes included Lake Binder, a part of Swan Park; Lake Chapaquackanonk, "a lovely body of water nestled in quiet verdant hills several miles north of Metropolis" (*Superman* [first series] #305, November 1976); Lake Metropolis (*Superman's Pal, Jimmy Olsen* #62, July 1962); Lake Washington (*Superman* [first series] #219, August 1969); Mastodon Lake, the onetime home of the retired manufacturer Brent Matthews, who raised the ire of the area's Native Americans with his decision to reconstruct an ancient Indian tower on his grounds, though it was ultimately destroyed (*World's Finest Comics* #5, Spring 1942); Mirror Lake, next to Camp Nokomis (*Adventure Comics* #384, September 1969); and Pine Lake (*Superman's Girl Friend, Lois Lane* #35, August 1962), home to a resort in the mountains (*Superman's Girl Friend, Lois Lane* #43, August 1963).

Metropolis's waterways hosted numerous islands, including Bay Island, "home to the fabulous estate built by Lex Luthor" (*Action Comics* #677, May 1992)—which was presumably the "private island Shangri-La" off the Metropolis coastline (*Man of Steel* #4, Late November 1986); Van Klyk's Island, a swamp-encircled atoll that was home to eccentric millionaire Hubert Van Klyk (*Superman's Pal, Jimmy Olsen* #42, January 1960); Warder's Island, "a few miles out of Metropolis Harbor" and home to Professor Grail's laboratory (*Superman* [first series] #129, May 1959); Neville Island, "site of Metropolis' oil refineries" (*Action Comics* #452, October 1975); Pike Island (*Superman's Pal, Jimmy Olsen* #2, November–December 1954); Rock Island, "somewhere off Metropolis Bay" (*Action Comics* #283, December 1961); and Skull Island, an atoll off Metropolis with a skull-like appearance where horror film star Carlos Floyd had a mansion (*Superman's Girl Friend, Lois Lane* #16, April 1960).

All the bodies of water in and around the city gave rise to robust commerce, ranging from

the Bakerline Naval Yard (*Action Comics* #700, June 1994; others) to the Metropolis Navy Yard (*Action Comics* #284, January 1962). There was also the old Metropolis Waterworks near the Shuster Bridge (*Birds of Prey* [first series] #110, November 2007). Metropolis Harbor (*Action Comics* #77, October 1944; others) was the gateway to the city (*World's Finest Comics* #20, Winter 1946; others), the point of arrival and departure for ocean liners (*Superman* [first series] #63, March–April 1950) and freighters. It included the Superman Lighthouse, with its towering statue of the Man of Steel whose eyes emitted searchlights at night (*Action Comics* #464, October 1976), and the Statue of Freedom, based on the Statue of Liberty (*Superman's Pal, Jimmy Olsen* #42, January 1960). Metropolis Municipal Pier (*Action Comics* #68, January 1944) included an eatery called the Shrimp Boat (*Superman* [first series] #257, October 1972), Rosy's Diner, and a S.T.A.R. Labs facility at Pier 94 (*Superman* [first series] #303, September 1976). Metropolis Port was "a mile-long series of interconnected docks that welcomed tankers, south of 12th Street, and passenger ships, north of 17th. Between the two separated areas had been government offices and cargo firms." The intersection of Siegel Street and Harbor Boulevard was in this area.

People could fly into the city and land at several airports, notably Metropolis International, and they could also enter by driving over the bridges, but for a truly memorable trip, people took the train, arriving at the majestic Metropolis Union Station in the heart of the city, the first and last stop for all commuters traveling the Rail Whale. The Whale also provided connections for travelers going outside the city. The Rail Whale was named for its incomparable size. These unique behemoths from the Metropolis Transportation Authority could handle rush hour easily with triple-decker passenger cars. Their route took them uptown, downtown, and all around the metro area, including through some of the city buildings.

Government

Mayors in Metropolis have largely gone unnamed, although men named Worth (*Action Comics* #32, January 1941), Phil Garson (*Action Comics* #37, June 1941), and Gerard (*Superman* [first series] #30, September–October 1944) were identified on Earth-2. Mayors on Earth-1 included Harkness (*Superman* [first series] #263, April 1973, and #322, April 1978), and Summers (*Superman* [first series] #357, March 1981). In post-Crisis continuity, Frank Berkowitz was mayor of Metropolis from the outset of Superman's career, and actually once deputized the Man of Steel so that he could arrest Lex Luthor (*Man of Steel* #4, Late November 1986). At some point after winning his fourth term as mayor (*Superman* [second series] #63, January 1992), Berkowitz was assassinated (*Superman* [second series] #131, January 1998). He was succeeded by Lex Luthor's handpicked puppet "Buck" Sackett (*The Adventures of Superman* #554, January 1998).

Metropolis's mayors have been supported by a number of district attorneys who all benefited from the Man of Steel's efforts, including Tom Spalding (*Action Comics* #39, August 1941), David Prentice (*Superman's Girl Friend, Lois Lane* #26, July 1961), Barger (*Superman's Girl Friend, Lois Lane* #131, June 1973), J. Mason Hartwell (*World's Finest Comics* #252, August–September 1978), and Morton (*Action Comics* #651, March 1990).

Both mayor and district attorney worked out of Metropolis City Hall (*Action Comics* #551, January 1984; others). Superman once dug the foundation for a new location (*Superman* [first series] #165, November 1963), while another new, larger building was constructed by Ar-Val, a Kandorian who was briefly filling in for the Man of Steel (*Superman* [first series] #172, October 1964). The city's courthouse, Superior County Courthouse, criminal courthouse, municipal courthouse, and court records were all located in separate structures. Additionally, the city morgue, which once employed Dr. Simon Locke (*Superman* [second series] #15, March 1988), had a building all to itself (*Action Comics* #665, May 1991; others).

With the presence of Superman, crime has been an issue, but interestingly, the city has seen a number of short-lived street gangs—unlike other metropolitan areas that have hosted gangs on a permanent basis. Among the gangs known to have operated in the city at one time or another have been the Bay Demons (*Superman* #659, February 2007), the Ebony Hawks (*Superman's Pal,*

Jimmy Olsen #155, January 1973), the Red Devils (*Superman's Girl Friend, Lois Lane* #129, February 1973), the River Lords (*Superman's Pal, Jimmy Olsen* #155), the Sharks (*Superman: The Man of Steel* #22, June 1993), the Street Serpents (*The Adventures of Superman* #507, December 1993), and the Young Dukes (*Superman's Pal, Jimmy Olsen* #155, January 1973).

Several biker gangs have also been chronicled, among them the Devil's Deputies (*Superman's Girl Friend, Lois Lane* #116, November 1971), the Spike Helmet Gang (*Superman's Girl Friend, Lois Lane* #125, August 1972), and the Maniacs (*Superman's Girl Friend, Lois Lane* #83, May 1968).

Once criminals were convicted in the various courthouses, they could look forward to staying in one of the city's many prisons, such as the Metropolis Correctional Facility (*The Adventures of Superman* #433, October 1987). Those serving time in the state or federal system were likely to be sent to Metropolis State Prison (*Action Comics* #295, December 1962) or Pocantico Federal Correctional Facility, overseen by Warden Clarence Rutherford (*Superman* [first series] #416, February 1986), which was ninety miles north of Metropolis and included a separate women's cell block (*Action Comics* #571, September 1985).

Superpowered criminals were once kept at McCallum Ultramax Detention Facility, "a long-term detention facility for meta-humans and aliens . . . It's been closed for a dozen years" (*Countdown to Mystery* #4, February 2008). More recently, criminals were remanded to Stryker's Island maximum-security prison (*Action Comics* #599, April 1988), which was in the middle of Metropolis's West River (*Starman* [first series] #28, November 1990) and had been there for two hundred years (*Action Comics* #852, September 2007). For a time, Stryker's was placed in orbit by Superman (*Action Comics* #797, January 2003), but it fell back to Earth during the first war against General Zod (*Action Comics* #804, August 2003).

Brainiac temporarily bottled Metropolis during his recent attack on Earth.

Commerce

Metropolis was home to numerous banks, among them the Bank of Metropolis (*Superman: The 10-Cent Adventure* #1, March 2003), Chase Metropolis Bank (*Action Comics* #361, March 1968), Citizens' State Bank, erected in 1958 (*World's Finest Comics* #177, August 1968), Commerce Bank of Metropolis on Centennial Avenue (*Superman* [second series] #1, January 1987), Federal Bank of Metropolis (*Batman* #293, November 1977), First Metropolis Bank (*The Adventures of Superman* #465, April 1990, others) on the upper east side (*The Adventures of Superman* #538, September 1996), First National Bank of Metropolis (*Superman* [first series] #209, August 1968; others) aka Metropolis First National Bank (*Superman's Pal, Jimmy Olsen* #130, July 1970), Hob's Lane Savings Bank (*Superman* [second series] #37, November 1989), the Lowry Trust Building (*World's Finest Comics* #189, November 1969), and the Merchants' Industrial Bank (*Superman* [first series] #127, February 1959).

Metrobank, a LexCorp company, had locations throughout the city, including branches on Binder Street (*Starman* [first series] #28, November 1990; others), in Bakerline (*Superman* #660, March 2007), and in Hamstead (*Action Comics* #852, September 2007).

The Metropolis Mercantile Bank (*World of Metropolis* #3, October 1988) had been in business since 1875 (*Action Comics* #688, Early July 1993).

Metropolis National Bank (*World's Finest Comics* #12, Winter 1944) was located in midtown (*Action Comics* #751, February 1999) and included a grassy, tree-lined plaza with a water fountain (*World's Finest Comics* #265, October–November 1980). It was owned for a time by the corrupt Cyrus Brand (*Action Comics* #394, November 1970).

Metropolis Trust Bank's president was Franklin Mallory (*World's Finest Comics* #11, Fall 1943). He was succeeded by Carl Denby, whom Superman privately discovered was Charles Stanton, who'd "absconded with his firm's funds fifteen years ago." Repentant, "Denby" had worked his way up from a bank clerk, paid back the money, and become one of Metropolis's most civic-minded citizens. Under these unusual circumstances, Superman agreed to keep his secret (*Superman* [first series] #26, January–February 1944).

In addition to the distinctive LexCorp build-

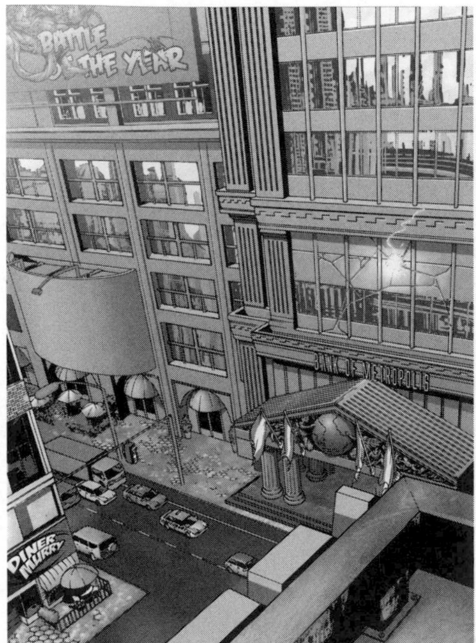

ing and Daily Planet building, Metropolis through the years also had many other noteworthy office buildings and skyscrapers. Adorned with grotesques, Dalten Tower was designed by "the same crazy architect who built most of Gotham." Oracle once used the top five floors as her base of operations (*Birds of Prey* [first series] #86, November 2005). There was also the Emperor Building, topped with a distinctive spire (*Action Comics* #80, January 1945). Additionally, the Famous Bottle Works, located near the waterfront with a huge terrarium on top of its roof, manufactured unique bottle specimens for glassware hobbyists before it was destroyed in an explosion (*Superman* [first series] #127, February 1959). The Metro Building (*Action Comics* #456, February 1976), "where we get a bird's-eye view of the entire city" (*Superman* [first series] #365, November 1981), had a unique spire on top of the building as well (*Action Comics* #497, July 1979). "In Metropolis, those who wield true influence and wealth establish themselves by renting in the city's most exclusive address—Price Tower," a circular skyscraper (*Superman* [second series] #97, February 1995). The Twin Towers were "the highest point in town" (*Superman* [first series] #279, September 1974), one of them perhaps home to "the elegant Metropolis Towers Restaurant" (*Superman* [first series] #347, May 1980).

Businesses located within the city limits began and ended with LexCorp, which at one time was said to have been the third largest conglomerate on Earth (*Superman/Shazam: First Thunder* #2, December 2005) and had an interest in virtually every business in Metropolis (*Man of Steel* #4, Late November 1986), from banking and brewing to robotics and sanitation. Nearly two-thirds of Metropolis's citizens were employed by companies owned—either in full or in part—by LexCorp. The skyline of Metropolis's central business district was dominated by the ninety-six-story L-shaped tower that served as the world headquarters of LexCorp International at LexCorp Plaza (*Superman* [second series] #163, December 2000) or Luthor Center and 6th (*Action Comics* #672, December 1991). It was described at one point as the city's tallest building (*Superman: Birthright* #5, January 2004). The company even had a space station called Lexport in orbit above Earth (*Superman* [second series] #119, January 1997).

Events

Civic pride was demonstrated with countless events, including the annual Antique Plane Race (*Superman's Girl Friend, Lois Lane* #101, May 1970); the annual automobile show (*Superman* [first series] #39, March–April 1948); LexCorp's Zenith Award for journalism, an annual event to recognize "outstanding achievements in the field of journalistic communications"—the trophy was "disparagingly referred to as the Baldy Awards by [Lex Luthor's] detractors for its chrome-dome design" (*The Adventures of Superman* #467, June 1990; others); the Franklin Press Prize ceremony, which honored Metropolis journalists with golden statues of Ben Franklin (*Superman Family* #207, May–June 1981); Metropolis's annual Friendship Day Parade, promoting international brotherhood (*Superman's Girl Friend, Lois Lane* #26, July 1961); Galaxython, the annual telethon of Galaxy Communications (*Action Comics* #563, January 1985); the annual Masquers' Festival at the Millennium Studios (*Superman* [first series] #225, April 1970); the annual Metropolis Founders' Day Parade (*Action Comics* #572, October 1985) celebrating the founding of the city—in 1673, according to one story—a tradition for more than 150 years (*DC Comics Presents* #52, December 1982); the annual Metropolis Fair (*Action Comics* #345, January 1967), which might have been the same as the Metropolis State Fair (*World's Finest Comics* #173, February 1968); the annual Metropolis Marathon (*Justice League of America* [first series] #218, September 1983) begun in 1893 (*Superman* #660, March 2007); the Metropolis AIDS Walk (*Wonder Woman* [second series] #170, July 2001); Metropolis Summer Fest (*The Adventures of Superman* #467, June 1990); and the Mile-O-Mirth Parade, a toy- and kid-vid-based event (*Action Comics* #714, October 1995).

Superman's arrival was celebrated with "Superday," which was initiated by Mayor Berkowitz (*Action Comics* #594, November 1987). It might have been an outgrowth of the Superman Day Parade (*Action Comics* #328, September 1965; *DC Special Series* #5, 1977; others), which itself was developed based on the city's celebration of Superman's first public appearance there (*Superman's Pal, Jimmy Olsen* #30, August 1958). The Earth-1 Superman's twenty-fifth anniversary in Metropolis was celebrated with the presentation of busts of Superman's friends within a chunk of supposed silver KRYPTONITE (*Superman's Pal, Jimmy Olsen* #70, July 1963).

Neighborhoods

Financiers such as MORGAN EDGE and BRUCE WAYNE were involved for a time in plans to create New Metropolis, a community that would have essentially expanded the existing city "to siphon off excess population, empty the ghettos, provide jobs and a better environment for all" (*World's Finest Comics* #235, January 1976).

The crime-ridden slums of the city's lower east side (*Superman* [first series] #281, November 1974) included condemned tenements. Social activist Marla Harvey died while campaigning against the abominable conditions and was remembered with a gold bust in front of a renovated school (*Action Comics* #393, October 1970). The lower west side also had its share of slums, including the city's most dangerous neighborhood, which went unnamed (*Action Comics* #548, October 1983). Among the slums were Evenside Heights (*Action Comics* #440, October 1974) and Olsen Gardens, named in honor of Terry Dean's and Jimmy Olsen's efforts to expose a secret slumlord as supposed philanthropist Barret Maxwell (*Superman's Pal, Jimmy Olsen* #127, March 1970). Terry later used the proceeds from a disco (*Superman's Pal, Jimmy Olsen* #144, December 1971) to fund a Storefront Prep trade school in the slums (*Superman's Pal, Jimmy Olsen* #155, January 1973).

Metropolis's fashionable west side (*Superman* [first series] #281, November 1974) hosted stately town houses (*Action Comics* #510, August 1980).

Bakerline, one of the city's boroughs (*Action Comics* #594, November 1987; others), included North Bakerline (*Superman* [second series] #44, June 1990). Its waterfront included the Bakerline Naval Yard (*Action Comics* #700, June 1994). Among the area's residents was Sarah Olsen, Jimmy Olsen's mother (*Action Comics* #699, May 1994).

Other identified areas of the city included Bedford Heights, an affluent section of Metropolis (*Superman* [first series] #285, March 1975); the Book, an affluent area that included Holloway Square (*Superman* #661, April 2007); the central business district (*Superman* #654, September 2006); Chinatown (*Superman's Pal, Jimmy Olsen* #33, December 1958); the financial district (*Superman* [second series] #59, September 1991), which was located in New Troy (*Action Comics* #741, January 1998) and was headquarters of the Metro Stock Exchange on Tall Street (*Action Comics* #510, August 1980) and also near the old North River Drive (*Action Comics* #675, March 1992); Hob's Heights (*The Adventures of Superman* #507, December 1993), the largest African American neighborhood in Metropolis (*Action Comics* #702, August 1994); the Hypersector, a downtown renovation program unveiled by Mayor Sackett, intended to "be the most sophisticated communications and financial complex in the world" (*Superman Red/Superman Blue* #1, February 1998); the Jefferson Street District in mid-east Metropolis (*Infinity, Inc.* [second series] #7, May 2008); LITTLE AFRICA, "Metropolis' black community" (*Superman's Girl Friend, Lois Lane* #106, November 1970); Little Hispania (*Action Comics* #792, August 2002); Little Italy (*The Adventures of Superman* #581, August 2000); Little QURAC, home to immigrants from that Arab nation (*The Adventures of Superman* #471, October 1990); Little Tokyo in the city's southwestern quarter (*Action Comics* #740, December 1997); Metropolis Heights (*Superman's*

Pal, Jimmy Olsen #82, January 1965); midtown (*52* #15, October 2006), home to art galleries (*Action Comics* #65, October 1943); lower midtown, which became "New Uptown" following the B13 upgrade, its structures "literally [defying] gravity. Overnight, lower-middle income projects shed the weight of the hard-working people who had built them and floated off into the sky" (*Superman: Metropolis Secret Files* #1, June 2000); the Old Hook Basin District, home to John Henry Irons's Steelworks (*Superman: The Man of Steel* #97, February 2000); the exclusive Park Ridge section (*Action Comics* #657, September 1990), which was a northwest borough (*The Death and Life of Superman,* 1993); Park Wood (*Superman* [second series] #192, June 2003); Pelham (*Action Comics* #850, Late July 2007), home of the Pelham Square Market in Queensland Park (*Superman* #670, January 2008); Queen Anne, a "polyglot residential neighborhood . . . colloquially called Old Nick's Parlor by those who actually live there" (*Shadowpact* #4, October 2006); Queensland Park in southwestern Metropolis (*Action Comics* #681, September 1992), home to the Troupe family (*The Adventures of Superman* #490, May 1992); Queensview (*Superman* [second series] #4, April 1987); Regent Street, "the worst crime-breeding slum in Metropolis" (*Adventure Comics* #203, August 1954); Roosevelt Plaza (*Justice League of America* [first series] #217, August 1983)—which, like Gotham's Roosevelt Center (*Batman* #337, July 1981), was structured after New York City's Rockefeller Center Plaza, complete with a statue of Prometheus and a skating rink, located a block from the Galaxy Building (*Superman Family* #195, May–June 1979); and the South Hills district (*World's Finest Comics* #77, July–August 1955).

Perhaps the most notorious section of Metropolis was Suicide Slum (*Star-Spangled Comics* #7, April 1942). Once it was "the ultra-fashionable Park Slope area. But that was three decades past [the 1940s]. Now, Park Slope has become Suicide Slum" (*World's Finest Comics* #259, October-November 1979), "ten blocks of poverty, misery and crime. It's not a safe place to be after dark" (*Superman* [second series] #26, 1988). "Suicide Slum sits to the north of downtown Metropolis, forgotten by most of the city, ignored by the rest. Except when things go wrong" (*Action Comics* #542, April 1983). It's also known as Metropolis's Southside (*Black Lightning: Year One* #1, Early March 2009). Later more commonly known as Hob's Bay, it saw a great deal of its own "particular kind of terror" (*Superman* [second series] #67, May 1992). At one point, five thousand people were said to live in the cramped ten-block area (*Action Comics* #592, September 1987), which included part of the waterfront (*Star-Spangled Comics* #8, May 1942).

The island of New Troy (*Action Comics* #643, July 1989) was Metropolis's central borough. Separated from the other five boroughs by two rivers and a deep harbor, New Troy was "what outsiders thought of when you told them you were from Metropolis" (*The Death and Life of Superman,* 1993). Among New Troy's residents were Perry and Alice White (*Action Comics* #726, October 1996).

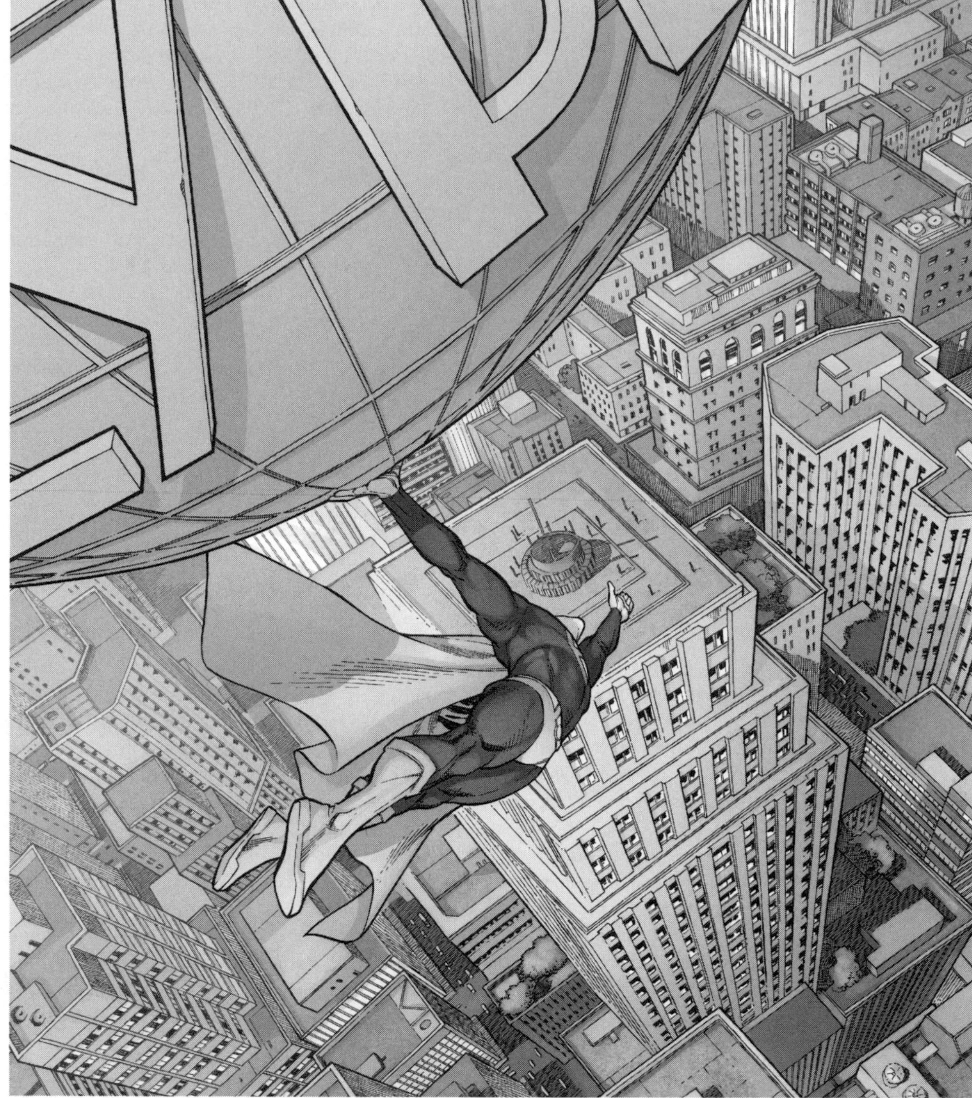

Suburbs of Metropolis included Briarwood (*Action Comics* #566, April 1985); Bridwell Heights to the southwest (*Action Comics* #724, August 1996); Buena Vista (*Superman's Pal, Jimmy Olsen* #158, June 1973); Centerville, which included a towering monument topped by a twin-ringed globe (*World's Finest Comics* #87, March-April 1957); Masonville (*Superman* [first series] #388, October 1983), home to the Morgan Edge Library (*Action Comics* #441, November 1974), which was evacuated (and subsequently rebuilt by Superman) after an explosive meteorite leveled the community (*Action Comics* #401, June 1971); Northbridge (*Superman* #663, July 2007); Oakhurst, a suburb adjacent to Interstate 40 (*Superman Family* #209, August 1981); Pleasant Oaks, a suburban town near Metropolis (*Superman's Girl Friend, Lois Lane* #23, February 1961); and Shuster's Glen, which included Siegel High School (*The Human Race* #1, May 2005).

Among the countless hotels, condominiums, and apartment complexes was the Clinton Towers, home to Clark Kent (*World's Finest Comics* #213, August–September 1972), specifically apartment 3D (*Superman* [first series] #297, March 1976; *Superman* [second series] #100, May 1995). It was owned by Hexagon Building Management (*The Adventures of Superman* #465, April 1990) and located at 344 Clinton Street (*Action Comics* #712, August 1995) on the city's upper east side (*Action Comics* #449, July 1975) at the corner of Brown Boulevard (*Superman: The Man of Steel* #16, October 1992) with a great view of Centennial Park (*Action Comics* #850, Late July 2007).

Other accounts placed the building at the corner of Broad Street and 30th Street (*Superman* [first series] #152, April 1962) with the number 575 (*Superman* [first series] #219, August 1969). Clark's apartment was also listed as 3B (*Superman* [first series] #112, March 1957), but the same story indicated that his immediate neighbor was in 3E.

Clark Kent's doormen included Franklin Pierce Jackson (*Superman* [first series] #246, December 1971; others), Harrigan (*Superman* [second series] #11, November 1987), Peterson (*Action Comics* #652, April 1990; others), and Mrs. Weisinger (*Superman* [second series] #100, May 1995; others). Clark's apartment was briefly occupied by Superboy during the period following Superman's apparent death (*The Adventures of Superman*

#502, July 1993). Clark's first landlady was Mrs. Smith (*Superman* [second series] #133, March 1998), and his phone number was 555-0162 (*Superman Family* #211, October 1981).

Other occupants of the Clinton apartments have included Mrs. Higgins, Joe Rollins, Alexander Ross, Tommy Snead, Bill Waters (*Superman* [first series] #112, March 1957), Mrs. Goldstein, Gordon and Petra Lewis, Jonathan Slaughter, Nathan Warbow (*Superman* [first series] #246, December 1971), John P. Alstrom (*Superman* [first series] #250, April 1972), "Jangles" Jones, Billy Anders (*Superman* [first series] #253, June 1972), Vincent Appleton (*Action Comics* #419, December 1972), April and May Marigold (*Superman* [first series] #262, March 1973), Martin Thorpe—secretly a futuristic villain, the Quaker (*Action Comics* #430, December 1973), Jackson Porter (*Action Comics* #471, May 1977), Stephen Marco (*Superman Family* #201, May–June 1980), Mrs. Turk (*The Adventures of Superman* #446, September 1988 and #451, February 1989), Andrea McElroy (*The Adventures of Superman* #457, August 1989), Andrea Johnson (*The Adventures of Superman* #493, August 1992), Mrs. Calderon (*Superman Confidential* #12, April 2008), and Mrs. Taylor. Officer Poston walked a beat past the building (*Superman* [first series] #384, June 1983). One of the building's custodians was Mr. Duffy (*Superman* [first series] #253, June 1972).

When Clark married Lois Lane, they moved to 1938 Sullivan Place, a brownstone apartment building (*Superman: The Wedding Album* #1, December 1996). The building was part of Metro Towers, also home to *Newstime Magazine* publisher Colin Thornton (*The Adventures of Superman* #543, February 1997), Laura Richards and her son Cary Richards (*The Adventures of Superman* #581, August 2000), and Mrs. Schwartz (*Superman* #663, July 2007); it included a doorman named Larry (*The Adventures of Superman* #632, November 2004). Like all of Metropolis, it received a temporary futuristic upgrade courtesy of the B13 Virus (*Superman: Metropolis Secret Files* #1, 2000).

Soon after Clark and Lois took in Lor-Zod, recently freed from the Phantom Zone, his superpowers surged, accidentally setting their apartment on fire. Superman took the opportunity to refurbish their home shortly after, and the Kents reside there to this day.

For the wealthy, no one could top the offerings at Metropolis's Jewelry Row (*Action Comics* #548, October 1983), which included some of the following: Acme Diamond Vault (*Superman's Pal, Jimmy Olsen* #11, March 1956), Acme Jewelry Shop (*Superman* [first series] #61, November–December 1949), Atkins Jewelry Stores (*Superman's Girl Friend, Lois Lane* #55, February 1965), Digby & Son (*Action Comics* #738, October 1997), Goldfarb's Jewelry Exchange (*Superman Family* #189, May–June 1978), Harry Winston Rare Jewels of the World (*Superman: The Wedding Album* #1, December 1996), Jackson's Fine Jewelers (*The Adventures of Superman* #506, November 1993), the circular Jewelry Exposition Center (*Action Comics* #504, February 1980), Jewel Mart (*Superman's Girl Friend, Lois Lane* #3, July–August 1958), Martier's (*Superman's Pal, Jimmy Olsen* #83, March 1965), Metropolis Jewelry Exchange (*Superboy* [first series] #100, October 1962), Rocksell, Inc. (*Superman* [first series] #27, March–April 1944), S&S Diamond Exchange (*Superman: The Man of Steel* #32, April 1994), Second Street Jewelers (*World's Finest Comics* #173, February 1968), Simpson's Jewelers (*Action Comics* #524, October 1981), Spiffany's (*Action Comics* #295, December 1962), Stanton Jewelers (*Action Comics* #53, October 1942), Swan's Jewelers (*Superman* [second series] #103, August 1995), Swank's (*Superman's Pal, Jimmy Olsen* #73, December 1963), Tuppenny's (*Action Comics* #71, April 1944), Van Pleeve (*Superman* [first series] #147, August 1961), Whitney Jewelers (*The Adventures of Superman* #472, November 1990), and Willis Gem Company (*World's Finest Comics* #126, June 1962).

Culture

A city such as Metropolis had museums both large and small for every interest imaginable, from the Ancient Arms Museum (*World's Finest Comics* #131, February 1963) to the Metropolis Air Space Museum (*Action Comics* #764, April 2000).

Several structures have honored not only Superman, but also other champions of justice. One such was the Hall of Heroes, "honoring the great heroes of all nations" (*Action Comics* #330, November 1965). The Superman Museum was founded through the efforts of famed explorer Stefan Andriessen, who accumulated dozens of Superman-related artifacts (*Action Comics* #164, January 1952). Outside the building was a statue of Superman sculpted from an asteroid the Man of Steel had prevented from striking the city (*Superman* [first series] #286, April 1975).

Given Superman's extraterrestrial origins, the Hall of Planets included rooms devoted to each world in the solar system, as well as planets such as Krypton (*Superman* [first series] #127, February 1959), while the Jules Verne Museum of Extraterrestrial Artifacts had doors that were carved from Almeraci tetelwood (*Superman* #653, August 2006).

Founded in 1880 (*Superman* [first series] #354, December 1980), the Metropolis Museum (*Superman* [first series] #30, September–October 1944) contained several rooms devoted to Superman that were spun off into the Superman Museum (*Action Comics* #164, January 1952). Its curator was Professor Boone (*Superman's Girl Friend, Lois Lane* #25, May 1961), and its director was Susan Stanyon (*Superman* [first series] #354, December 1980). The structure had a Byzantine series of catacombs beneath it "used for burials by some unknown people who lived here long ago" (*Superman* [first series] #354, December 1980). One section of the museum was the Dave Mauer Pavilion (*Superman* [first series] #405, March 1985).

There was also the Metropolis Museum of Archaeology, home at one point to dinosaur exhibits that were subsequently moved to the Natural History Museum. Dolittle Shywood was the museum curator (*Wonder Woman* [second series] #53, April 1991).

Media

Metropolis was a media-rich city through the years, with newspapers, radio, television, and cable companies competing with one another for the latest news, analysis, and, of course, gossip. It all started with the *Daily Planet,* founded by Joshua Merriwether as a weekly in 1775. The first offices were located at the south end of New Troy but were burned down by the British in 1873. In the course of publishing the first edition, printer's apprentice Jeremiah Odets was killed when a paper roll fell on him (*Action Comics* #531, May 1982). After a decade, the *Planet* was resurrected and operated from the corner of 5th and Concord. President Washington penned an editorial for 1793's first edition of the *Daily Planet,* which was ever after published continually. The one exception was a three-day period when Southern Metropolis was captured by Canadian forces (*World of Metropolis* #1, August 1988).

Located within the majestic Daily Planet Building, topped with a gold rotating globe, was radio station WPLT (*Superman* [first series] #39, March–April 1946); an unnamed TV station was found on the twenty-fifth floor (*Superman's Pal, Jimmy Olsen* #38, July 1959). After the building was absorbed into the Galaxy Communications empire, its signature gold globe was removed (*Action Comics* #398, March 1971) and temporarily placed in a public square (*Action Comics* #488, October 1978). It was restored to the roof during the paper's 150th anniversary (*Action Comics* #525, November 1981).

On Earth-2, the *Planet*'s duplicate was known as the *Daily Star,* which billed itself as "Metropolis' oldest daily newspaper." In the world after the Crisis on Infinite Earths, the *Star* competed with the *Planet* for city readers (*Action Comics* #761, January 2000) and boasted star reporters such as Toby Raynes (*The Adventures of Superman* #451, February 1989).

Among the *Planet*'s competitors through the

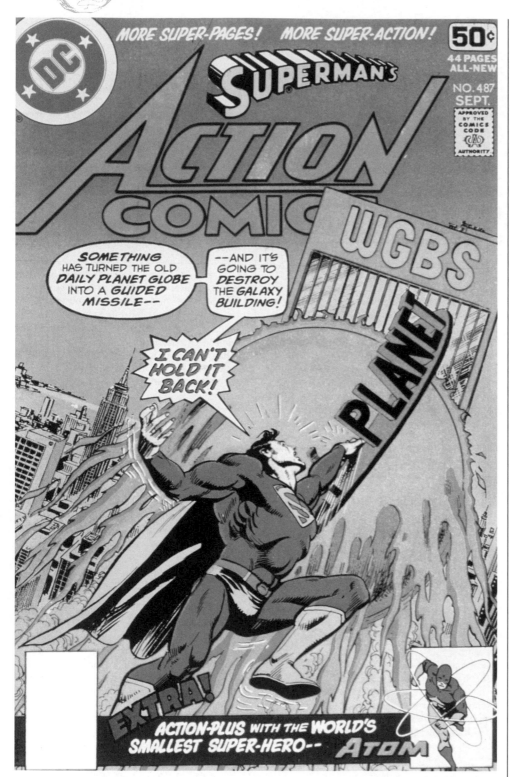

years were the *Metropolis Evening Herald,* which was started in 1866 (*Superman* [first series] #176, April 1965), and the *City Sentinel,* whose publisher, Cal Dawson, was once saved from having to close down the paper by a fund-raiser secretly financed in part by Perry White (*Superman's Pal, Jimmy Olsen* #5, May–June 1955). The *Observer* was regarded as the city's biggest newspaper until its publisher, Franklin D. Clark, was exposed as a mob puppet in 1942 (*Star-Spangled Comics* #13, October 1942). The *Daily Sentinel* was owned by a man named Garver (*Superman's Pal, Jimmy Olsen* #76, April 1964), and its reporters included Rick Mason (*Superman's Pal, Jimmy Olsen* #75, March 1964). There were also the *Clarion* (*Superman* [first series] #133, November 1959); the *Evening Gazette* (*Superman* [first series] #42, September–October 1946); *Eye Magazine,* with writer Diana Adair (*Superman* [first series] #203, January 1968); the *Globe* (*Superman* [first series] #25, November–December 1943); the *Masonville Journal,* which covered the Metropolis suburbs (*Superman* [first series] #398, August 1984); the *Metropolis Journal* (*Adventure Comics* #185, February 1953); and the *Metropolis Times* (*Superboy* [first series] #63, March 1958). The *Metropolis Eagle* (*Action Comics* #375, April 1969) was published by Alexander Tucker (*Superman Family* #215, February 1982) and boasted prominent editors named Peters (*Superman's Pal, Jimmy Olsen* #67, March 1963) and Kenyon (*Superman* [first series] #419, May 1986) as well as reporters Judy Jenkins (*Superman's Pal, Jimmy Olsen* #67, March 1963) and Rory Stasson (*Superman* [first series] #364, October 1981; *Action Comics* #543, May 1983). Established in 1924, it was one of the city's three daily newspapers and the *Planet*'s prime contender for readership (*Superman Family* #216, March 1982).

For gossip hounds, there was the *Metropolis Whisper,* with "yellow rag journalism at its worst and its publisher, Adolph Nurduck, doesn't even pretend to be a journalist. He's interested only in circulation." The paper's reporters included ditzy Bambi Bonanza (*Superman Family* #207, May–June 1981), and its success led to the creation of the *National Whisper* (*Action Comics* #668, August 1991; *Blood Pack* #4, June 1995; others). It was owned by the McMannus Group, an Australian conglomerate (*Superman: The Man of Steel* #83, September 1998).

Other media businesses at one time included LexCom (*Action Comics* #750, January 1999; others).

Newstime (*Action Comics* #651, March 1990) was located on 23rd (*Action Comics* #680, August 1992) in the vicinity of Bessolo and Collyer (*Action Comics* #681, September 1992). It was a nationally published weekly magazine whose publisher also owned the *New York Bugle* (*Superman* [second series] #60, October 1991). It branched out into TV and film production and video stores when it merged with Megacom (*The Adventures of Superman* #581, August 2000). Its executive offices were on the fiftieth floor (*Action Comics* #700, January 1999). The building sustained a bit of damage during an assault on Earth by Warworld (*Action Comics* #675, March 1992) and was thrust into limbo during the Blaze-Lord Satanus War (*Action Comics* #680, August 1992), but it was the only major structure in the business district to survive unscathed following Lex Luthor's attempted destruction of the city (*Action Comics* #700, January 1999). In the immediate aftermath, the Newstime building became a sanctuary for the homeless and injured (*Superman* [second series] #91, July 1994). Ron Troupe worked for *Newstime* as an editorial assistant prior to being hired by the *Daily Planet* (*Action Comics* #677–678, May–June 1992). Other reporters included Wilton Fredericks (*Action Comics* #699, May 1994).

Broadcast media through the years grew rapidly with the advent of radio, followed by the arrival of television. During World War II, comedian Red Fallen broadcast from a huge radio network building to keep people cheered (*World's Finest Comics* #8, Winter 1943).

On the AM dial, fans could tune to WGBS (860) (*Action Comics* #671, November 1991), with a sister

FM station at 93.1 (*Superman* [first series] #372, June 1982). There was also WUMT at 860 AM or 93.1 FM (*The Death and Life of Superman,* 1993).

For FM listeners, 92.1 was "Metropolis' hot radio!" (*The Adventures of Superman* #433, October 1987), while WALT at 94.6 FM featured "All Walt, All the Time" (*Superman: The Man of Steel* #47, August 1995). Q-96 included newsreader Ann Palmer (*Legacy of Superman* #1, March 1993), while WMET at 98.7 (*Superman: Birthright* #5, January 2004) or 107.3 (*Action Comics* #694, December 1993) included newsreaders Pat Rhodes (*The Adventures of Superman* #500, Early June 1993) and was part of the Fairbrook Radio Network (*JLA-Superman: The Never-Ending Battle,* 2004). WLEX at 99.5 was billed as "Music That's Fun" (*Superman* [second series] #57, July 1991). Its newsreaders included Lyle Richards (*Action Comics* #678, June 1992); its disc jockey lineup boasted "the Voice of Treason" Eddie Lash (*Action Comics* #738, October 1997) and Rick & Jim (*Action Comics* #740, December 1997). WKIT-FM was a rock station at 100.5 (*Superman: The Man of Steel* #4, October 1991).

The competitive television market for Metropolis and its environs saw the rise and fall of many TV channels and networks. Along the way, watchers were informed by Channel 5, with reporter Ami Soon (*52* #35, March 2007); Channel 6, with reporter Constance Cross (*Superman* [second series] #192, June 2003); Channel 8 Action News (*Superman* [second series] #1, January 1987); and METV (*Action Comics* #272, January 1961), which included reporter Edith Kane (*The Adventures of Superman* #434, November 1987).

They all had to compete with Galaxy Broadcasting's WGBS, Channel 2 (*Superman* [second series] #16, April 1988) or Channel 8 (*Superman* [first series] #327, September 1978), which employed reporter Bob Nenno (*The Adventures of Superman* #451, February 1989), sportscaster Tim McCready (*Superman* #673, April 2008), and meteorologist Dave McDonald (*JLA-Superman: The Never-Ending Battle,* 2004). Its morning show *AM Metropolis* was hosted by Kelly Johansen and Rick Raymond (*JLA-Superman: The Never-Ending Battle,* 2004). Among the station's stockholders was Bruce Wayne (*Superman* [first series] #285, March 1975).

In turn, they were bested in their reach by Superstation WLEX (*Superman* [second series] #25, 1988) with a staff that included anchorman Wallace Bailey (*Action Comics* #685, January 1993), News Director Stephen Conally (*The Death and Life of Superman,* 1993), anchorman Brad Edwards (*Superman: The Man of Tomorrow* #10, Winter 1998), and reporters Scott Harris (*Action Comics* #685, January 1993) and a woman named Washington (*Superman* [second series] #36, October 1989). WLEX was eventually sold off by LexCorp (*Superman* #667, November 2007).

Entertainment programming came from Channel 11, an affiliate of Pox TV (*Gotham Underground* #5, April 2008). Other stations included CWZ (*Superman* [first series] #180, October 1965), KPS (*Superman's Girl Friend, Lois Lane* #3, July–August 1958), WGMC, Channel 4 (*Daily Planet Invasion! Edition,* 1989), WLII (*52* #8, August 2006), and WXR (*Showcase* #9, July–August 1957). WMET (*The New Adventures of Superboy* #6, June 1980) featured reporters Bret Bradley (*Superman* [first series] #199, August 1967), Dale Smith (*Action Comics* #441, November 1974), Ms. Lanpher (*52* #6, August 2006), and Madeline Wade (*The Adventures of Superman* #425, February 1987) and included the interview program *Point Blank* in its lineup (*Superman* [first series] #204, February 1968). There was also WUBS, Channel 7 (*Daily Planet Invasion! Edition,* 1989), aka UBC, which was once WGBS's biggest competitor and hired away its entertainment reporter Lola Barnett. The United Broadcasting Company's president was Samuel Tanner (*Action Comics* #458, April 1976). Among its hit programs was the comedy showcase *Friday Night Revue,* starring "the Unready-For-Neilsen Ensemble" (*Superman* [first series] #315, September 1977).

WCCS was Metropolis's public broadcasting channel (*DC Comics Presents* #64, December 1983), succeeded by WPUB Channel 13 (*Daily Planet Invasion! Edition,* 1989). WHBS, Channel 48, was the city's Spanish broadcasting channel (*Daily Planet Invasion! Edition,* 1989).

Entertainment

Through the years, the City of Tomorrow housed numerous entertainment centers, including Fairyland Isle, a spectacular theme park financed by John Nicholas that opened on December 24, 1944 (*Action Comics* #81, February 1945), while the abandoned Happyland (*Superman's Girl Friend, Lois Lane* #116, November 1971) was used as a base by the Toyman (*Action Comics* #657, September 1990; *The Adventures of Superman* #475, February 1991) and doubled as a money-laundering operation for Intergang (*Superman* [second series] #60, October 1991). The Metropolis Amusement Park (*Action Comics* #278, July 1961, and #580, June 1986; *Superman's Pal, Jimmy Olsen* #24, October 1957) included a statue of a Native American smoking a peace pipe in front of a replica Indian village "that existed here before the founding of Metropolis" (*Superman's Pal, Jimmy Olsen* #39, September 1959). Pleasure Island was a harbor-based amusement park developed by the late Stanley Finchcomb, who developed a split personality based on a pirate ancestor prior to his death (*Action Comics* #54, November 1942).

For those interested in the nightlife, Metropolis has been the home to some of the most celebrated and talked-about nightclubs, discos, and watering holes in America. Several became notorious, such as Blaze's, which was converted from an old church into a hard-rocking nightclub. Secretly owned by the demonic Blaze, the building was destroyed in a fire set by Intergang (*The Adventures of Superman* #469, August 1990).

Much like the clubs, restaurants rose and fell in popularity during the city's life, but some proved enduring and memorable, starting with the Ace o' Clubs (*Action Comics* #663, March 1991) located in Suicide Slum (*Action Comics* #674, February 1992) on North Simon Street (*Action Comics* #661, January 1991), which was purchased by Bibbo Bibbowski after he won the lottery. It was nearly destroyed by fire (*Superman: The Wedding Album* #1, December 1996). During the B13 transformation of Metropolis, the Ace o' Clubs (*Action Comics* #771, November 2000) was moved to the docks of Metropolis Harbor (*Superman: Metropolis* #1, April 2003).

There was also Donnegan's in Suicide Slum, an eatery from the 1940s until its namesake owner's death in 1968. It subsequently became a laundromat (*Superman* [second series] *Annual* #2, 1988).

Another popular establishment was Dooley's Bar, located on the ground floor of the Daily Planet Building (*The Adventures of Superman* #522, April 1995). During a city revitalization effort, Dooley's received a grant for a remodel (*Superman* [second series] #132, February 1998) and sustained modest damage during a meteor strike on the city (*Superman: Save the Planet* one-shot, October 1998).

Similarly, Murph's, a Baker Street bar, was destroyed during Doomsday's initial assault on the city. It was later rebuilt as Son of Murphy's but was destroyed again in an explosion (*Superman: Day of Doom* #2–3, January 2003).

Planet Krypton (*The Adventures of Superman* #608, November 2002) was one of several restaurants built around the theme of the Man of Steel.

The Temple of the Gods was "the most beautiful eating place in town," with exterior tall columns and interior statuary of the gods of myth (*Superman's Girl Friend, Lois Lane* #40, April 1963), while the West Bank Riverhouse was a favorite of Perry White's, "more the open-air smoking section than the brisket" (*Superman* #662, May 2007).

The national Big Belly Burger chain had branches throughout the city, including the Glenwood Square location, which was a onetime employer of Jerry White (*Superman* [second series] #36, October 1989). Other locations were on 53rd (*The Adventures of Superman* #514, July 1994) and "just down the street from the Hotel Metropolitan" (*The Adventures of Superman* #561, September 1998).

The Sundollars Coffee chain had branches every few blocks (*Superman* #650, May 2006).

Parks

Metropolis's vast size allowed it to provide refuges for nature lovers, including the popular Centennial Park, which was filled with redwood trees (*Superman* [second series] #170, July 2001) and located in the northwest part of New Troy, bordered in part by Metropolis University (*The Death and Life of Superman,* 1993), luxury apartments (*Superman* [second series] #15, March 1988), and the old Hotel Anderson (*Superman* [second series] #51, January 1991). The south park entrance faced Bessolo Boulevard (*Action Comics* #687, June 1993). It was presumably part of Centennial Square (*Superman* [second series] #146, July 1999) and included a petting zoo (*Action Comics* #742, March 1998) and a statue of Alice in Wonderland, the Mad Hatter, and the White Rabbit (*The Adventures of Superman* #441, June 1988).

In the wake of Superman's apparent death at the hands of Doomsday, a towering statue of the Man of Steel with an eagle alighting on his left

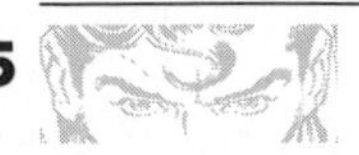

arm was erected above his crypt in Centennial Park (*Superman: The Man of Steel* #20, February 1993). Following the death of Superboy, a statue of the teen hero was erected next to the Superman monument (*52* #1, July 2006).

There was also Metropolis Park (*Action Comics* #28, September 1940; others), which was located opposite the Galaxy building (*Superman* [first series] #309, March 1977) and featured a band shell (*Superman* [first series] #241, August 1971), a zoo (*Superman's Girl friend, Lois Lane* #54, January 1965), a "statue pavilion" whose subjects included historical figures, as well as Superman (*Superman's Pal, Jimmy Olsen* #40, October 1959), a statue of General Pike astride a horse (*Superman's Pal, Jimmy Olsen* #51, March 1961), a statue of the three *Apollo VIII* astronauts holding the moon aloft (*Superman's Pal, Jimmy Olsen* #120, June 1969), a subway entrance (*Superman* [first series] *Annual* #9, 1983), a lake (*Superman's Girl Friend, Lois Lane* #59, August 1965), a stream (*Superman's Pal, Jimmy Olsen* #49, December 1960), and a reservoir (*World's Finest Comics* #37, November–December 1948). One statue of Superman was destroyed by Lex Luthor (*Action Comics* #249, February 1959) while another towers above the trees and holds a sign directing visitors to the airport (*Superman's Pal, Jimmy Olsen* #27, March 1958).

Other notable attractions in town included the Metrodome (*World's Finest Comics* #117, May 1961), whose glass ceiling was attached by Superman (*Superman's Girl Friend, Lois Lane* #73, April 1967). There was also Metro Jungle—a "huge zoo and simulated African forest on the outskirts of the city." An abandoned subway tunnel ran underneath the site (*Superman's Girl Friend, Lois Lane* #124, July 1972). The Metropolis Coliseum (*Superman's Pal, Jimmy Olsen* #108, January 1968) was once destroyed by Bizarro and repaired by Superman (*Superman* [first series] #305–306, November–December 1976).

Schools and Libraries

The Metropolis Public Library (*Adventure Comics* #240, September 1957) boasted the largest Superman reference library in the world (*Action Comics* #487, September 1978) and was located in midtown (*The Adventures of Superman* #565, March 1999) on Kimberly Avenue. Across from the library was a statue of Superman that was erected "after the first time Superman saved the city from alien attack" (*Trinity* #20, December 2008).

Throughout the city were public and private schools, among them Public School No. 84, where a young Perry White attended classes (*Superman* [first series] #151, February 1962). St. Jerome, an elementary school, had a championship soccer team (*Superman: The Man of Steel* #44, May 1995).

Metropolis High School (*Adventure Comics* #126, March 1948) had a football team whose players wore green jerseys and red-and-white helmets (*Superboy* [first series] #88, April 1961). At Garfield High School, located in Suicide Slum, Jefferson Pierce once served as principal after attending there as a student (*Black Lightning: Year One* #1, Early March 2009). His daughter Anissa attended nearby Woodrow Wilson elementary school.

Just outside the city was Metropolis University, which, according to some histories, is where Clark Kent attended school after leaving Smallville (*Superman* [first series] #125, November 1958).

Sports

As befitting a city of Metropolis's stature, residents have been known to field competitive teams in every major and minor sport, supporting professional, amateur, and student teams.

The classic Metropolis Stadium was built in 1940 and was also called Sportsman's Stadium (*World's Finest Comics* #271, September 1981). Mr. Baxley (*Action Comics* #72, May 1944) owned the multipurpose stadium and in later years added a Plexiglas dome (*Superman's Pal, Jimmy Olsen* #39, September 1959). In time, the Metropolis Meteors moved to the baseball-only Stengel Stadium (*Superman* [first series] #286, April 1975). At some later date, the Metropolis Metros—another pro baseball team (*Batman and the Outsiders* [first series] #26, October 1985)—took up residence in the stadium (*Superman* [first series] #366, December 1981). There was also Metro Hills Tennis Stadium (*DC Super-Stars* #10, December 1976).

Comet Arena was touted as a sports venue that would bring fifty thousand people to Southside every week of the year, but the developer disappeared with more than sixteen million dollars that had been earmarked for the complex. The Comets relocated to Star City in the wake of the debacle (*Black Lightning: Year One* #1, Early March 2009).

During Superboy's era, the Metropolis stadium included the figure of a giant football player atop its entryway (*Adventure Comics* #245, February 1958). Former Metropolis Monarchs manager "Pops" Swenson was fired on November 4, 1985, and "hired later that same day as manager of the Meteors." Steve Garland was the team trainer, and Leo Farnsworth—"the man referred to as 'football's Bobby Knight' "—was the Meteors' coach (*Daily Planet Invasion! Edition,* 1989).

The football-loving city cheered on the Metropolis Meteors (*The Adventures of Superman* #623, February 2004), a team that for a time was coached by a man named Johnson (*Batman and the Outsiders* [first series] #21, May 1985). They played in both Star Stadium (*Superman* [first series] #264, June 1973) and Stengel Stadium (*Superman* [first series] #283, January 1975).

Players for the Meteors included retired quarterback Johnny Dakota (*The Adventures of Superman* #550, September 1997), quarterback (and later congressman) Mark Shephard (*Action Comics* #828, August 2005), "Ram" Rogers (*Superman* [first series] #256, September 1972), quarterback Jim Armstrong, running back Jeff Brubaker, safety Jason Bucha, Bob Buscanics, Jim Delano, Ben Dierdorf, Sam Duffy, wide receiver Steve Largent, center Bill Nelson, Jon Peterson (#13), running back Andy Sainsbury, and Rob Sosnowski (*Daily Planet Invasion! Edition,* 1989). Steve Lombard played for the Central City Centaurs (*Action Comics* #465, November 1976) before becoming the Meteors' quarterback (*Superman* [first series] #264, June 1973).

Metropolis was home to many different professional baseball teams, always one in each league.

The Metropolis Monarchs, Clark Kent's favorite team, had its spring training camp in Frostproof, Florida. The Monarchs wore blue shirts with crown icons and white pants. Playing its home games in the open-air Monarch Stadium (*Superman* #651, June 2006), the team was accompanied by a mascot dressed like a cartoon king (*Superman* [second series] #206). Their players have included men named Carson (*Superman* [second series] #32, June 1989), Fairchild (*Supergirl* [fifth series] #34, January 2009), and Jose Juarez (*52* #3, 2007).

Hank "The Hammer" Halloran was the best known Monarch, a former first baseman and Baseball Hall of Famer. He had a lifetime batting average of .331 and spent many years as batting coach before coming into conflict with Monarchs

owner Grant Thornley (*Newstime,* May 1993). The dismissal from the "mostly honorary" position was prompted by Halloran's other job as official greeter at the brand new Sultan's Palace Hotel, which also happened to feature a casino among its attractions (*Daily Planet Invasion! Edition,* 1989).

Other baseball teams playing in Metropolis have included the Metropolis Giants (*Superman* [first series] #130, July 1959), who evidently played in Giants Stadium (*The Adventures of Superman* #620, November 2003); the Metropolis Majestics, clad in gray-and-purple uniforms (*Action Comics* #389, June 1970); the Metropolis Marvels, who wore red, white, and light blue uniforms (*Superman's Pal, Jimmy Olsen* #114, September 1968); the Metropolis Twins (*Batman* #411, September 1987); and the Metropolis Titans, who once featured a pitcher named Bud Mack, actually an amnesiac Man of Steel (*Superman* [first series] #77, July–August 1952).

The Metropolis Generals were the city's pro basketball team and played in Shuster Sports Arena (*Superman* #661, April 2007); the facility kept busy in the off season with concerts, circuses, and more (*Action Comics* #838, June 2006). A local basketball team was also referred to as the Metros and included Mitch Hanover, who was once accused of fixing a basketball game (*Superman's Pal, Jimmy Olsen* #156, February 1973).

For hockey fans, there were the Metropolis Mammoths, and soccer fans could cheer for the Metropolis Galaxians with their vibrant white, blue, and magenta uniforms (*Superman Family* #215, February 1982).

The Metropolis Rockets were a female roller derby team who fought it out in Olympus Auditorium (*Superman Family* #198, November–December 1979), while the Skylarks and the Rovers were pro polo teams (*Action Comics* #197, October 1954).

Athletes known to make their home in the city included boxers Gorilla Gordon (*Superman's Pal, Jimmy Olsen* #11, March 1956) and Moxy Mason, once a top boxer and later a front man for a mob-financed scheme to milk the state of millions of dollars for phony nursing home services (*Superman Family* #202, July–August 1980). "Angel" Alloyo was an ex-hockey-player whose "inherent brutality caused him to be suspended from a sport not known for its gentleness." He wound up a terrorist pawn of the sinister Adam (*Superman Family* #192, November–December 1980).

On the amateur level were the Planeteers, a Little League team sponsored by the *Daily Planet.* It was managed at one point by Franklin Pierce Jackson, secretly a onetime star "of the old-time Negro League. Jackson, who had a career batting average of .359, never made it into the majors because he retired before Jackie Robinson broke the so-called 'color barrier.' " In later years, Frank became the doorman at Clinton Tower (*Superman Family* #215, February 1982).

METROPOLIS MEEK MAN'S CLUB, THE

One of the more unusual clubs located in Metropolis, the purpose of the Meek Man's Club was for people to gain strength and confidence from one another. At one time, the Man of Steel worked unseen to help both the club's president and vice president—Wilson and Barker, respectively—overcome their emotional handicaps. Once he was done, they had the self-confidence necessary to accomplish their respective career goals (*Superman* [first series] #101, November 1955).

METROPOLIS S.C.U. (SPECIAL CRIMES UNIT), THE

Metropolis had its share of troublesome criminals prior to the arrival of Superman, and therefore its police department formed the Special Crimes Unit to handle threats both domestic and international. The first captain of the squad was Maggie Sawyer, a tough career officer who formed a core team that became a model for S.C.U.'s around the country. Much of their specialized equipment was designed and provided by the city's branch of S.T.A.R. Labs (*Superman* [second series] #4, April 1987).

After Superman debuted, he and Sawyer formed a professional working relationship so that they would not interfere with each other's efforts. Previously affiliated with the Star City Police Department, Sawyer had just arrived in Metropolis when a revived Intergang unleashed Kalibak and weaponry from the otherworldly Apokolips. Superman managed to turn the tide thanks in no small part to the efforts of police officer Dan Turpin. Afterward, Captain Bill Henderson approached Turpin with the idea of heading up the Special Crimes Unit, a squad envisioned by Police Commissioner Casey that would specifically deal with super-human threats. Turpin declined but suggested Maggie Sawyer as an ideal alternative (*The Adventures of Superman Annual* #7, 1995).

The S.C.U. recovered a Kryptonian war suit and managed to reverse-engineer the technology, adapting it to fashion Simm-Bot armor that went a long way to protect the human team (*Action Comics* #701, July 1994, and #705, December 1994).

In order to better cover the S.C.U.'s efforts, *Daily Planet* reporter Lois Lane arranged with Sawyer to embed herself with the team for a short period of time (*Metropolis S.C.U.* #1–4, November 1994–February 1995). Several years later, reporter Clark Kent also spent some time with the team.

Members of the S.C.U. have included Sawyer and her deputy Dan Turpin; "Badmouth" (*The Adventures of Superman* #569, July 1999); Brian Arsala (*Hawk and Dove* [second series] #3, December 1988), who was subsequently killed by Monarch after moving to Washington, DC; Lyle Beedler (*Metropolis S.C.U.* #1, November 1994); Chidi (*Metropolis S.C.U.* #1, November 1994); "Fireworks" (*The Adventures of Superman* #569, July 1999); "Freight-Train" (*The Adventures of Superman* #569, July 1999); Aaron "Jace" Jase (*Metropolis S.C.U.* #1, June 1994), who was murdered by the Hellgrammite; Jenkins (*Superman Forever* #1, June 1998); Johnson (*Superman Forever* #1, June 1998); Ty Jones (*Superman: The Man of Steel* #65, March 1997); Lee (*Superman: The Man of Steel* #65, March 1997); Menuez (*Action Comics* #742, March 1998); "The Roo" (*The Adventures of Superman* #569, July 1999); Scott Laughlin, who was killed by Ruin (*The Adventures of Superman* #627, October 2004); Smitty (*Superman Forever* #1, June 1998); Russell Tenclouds (*Metropolis S.C.U.* #1, November 1994), who was electrocuted as he destroyed the drones of the Hellgrammite; and Turk (*Superman: The Man of Steel* #85, January 1999).

When Sawyer left Metropolis to head up Gotham City's similar Major Crimes Unit, she was replaced by Lupé Teresa Leocadio-Escudero (*The Adventures of Superman* #625, April 2004). Eventually, though, the S.C.U. was overshadowed by its new Technology Squad, nicknamed the Science Police (*Superman* #654, September 2006).

METROPOLIS SHUTTERBUG SOCIETY, THE

This popular photography club counted among its membership some of the nation's greatest cameramen, and offered a grand prize of five thousand dollars to whichever of its members submitted the best photograph of Superman in action. "Camera aces" Archie Pink and Doc Sloan were odds-on favorites to win the prize, although the contest was ultimately won by underdog lensman Howard Figit. The underweight, bespectacled, unassuming fellow repeatedly risked his life to obtain photos of the Man of Steel because he hoped that winning the prize money would enable him to afford to seek the thrilling adventures he'd always dreamed of "in his quiet life" (*World's Finest Comics* #49, December 1950–January 1951).

METROPOLIS UNIVERSITY

Better known as the University of Metropolis, and located in northwestern New Troy near Centennial Park, Metropolis University has been the alma mater to countless students, although none as unusual as Clark Kent (*Superman* [first series] #125, November 1958).

Kent went to college after he graduated from Smallville High School and saw his parents unexpectedly die from a rare tropical disease. While attending school, he polished his journalistic skills in preparation for his future career while also fighting crime in his Superboy guise. At some point during his college years, he decided it was time for Superboy to become Superman.

Dean Reynolds helped arrange Clark Kent's

acceptance into Metropolis University (*World of Metropolis* #3, April 1985). His roommates included "Ducky" Ginsberg (*Superman* [first series] #362, August 1981), Dave Hammond (*Action Comics* #404, September 1971), Tommy Lee (*Superman* [first series] #362, August 1981), and, later, Billy Cramer (*Superman: The Secret Years* #1–2, February–March 1985). Other classmates at MU were Art Borley (*Action Comics* #411, April 1972), Arnie Carter (*Action Comics* #436, June 1974), Fred Holland (*Superman* [first series] #125 November 1958), Marty Lerner, Ellen Pratt, Skitch Smith (*Action Comics* #433, March 1974), Terry Mason (*Action Comics* #346, June 1974), Steve Power (*Action Comics* #411, April 1972), Stan Rivers (*Action Comics* #404, September 1971), Margo Payne, Eileen, Janis, Sandy, and Kris (*Superman* [first series] #350, August 1980).

Administrators included Dean Simons (*Superman* [second series] *Annual* #2, 1988) and Dean Claire Westerburg (*Action Comics* #650, February 1990). One of the most recent chancellors of Metropolis University was Hermione Wells (*Newstime,* 1993). Structures on campus included the Medical Research Building (*Superman* [first series] *Annual* #9, 1983), the Metro Memorial Field House arena (*Superman: The Secret Years* #3, April 1985), the College of Electrical Engineering (*Superman* [first series] #378, December 1982), the Science Building—which contained a "shock-proof room" far beneath it (*Action Comics* #169, June 1952)—and an obelisk bestowed by the Class of 1957 (*Action Comics* #408, January 1972).

While a sophomore, Clark met Lori Lemaris, a beautiful wheelchair-bound woman (*Superman: The Secret Years* #2, March 1985). It was during their junior year that he fell in love with her and she revealed her secret to him. That same year, Billy Cramer was killed in a fire when Superboy could not reach him in time (*Superman: The Secret Years* #3, April 1985).

The resulting guilt sent Clark into exile, but a threat from Lex Luthor prompted him to return to action, thereby exorcizing the ghosts from his past. Upon his graduation, Perry White hired Kent to join the *Daily Planet.* Superman arrived in Metropolis at the same time (*Superman: The Secret Years* #4, May 1985).

At one point during his tenure at the university, Superman and typewriter repairman Mike Mooney were sent into the distant past as a result of a mathematics laboratory accident (*Superman* [first series] #69, March–April 1951).

In the post–Crisis on Infinite Earths recounting of Superman's career, based on the alterations to reality, Clark Kent did not immediately attend MU after graduating high school, but instead developed his journalistic skills while traveling the world. Dean Reynolds helped arrange Clark Kent's acceptance once the young man completed his journey (*World of Metropolis* #3, October 1988). In most versions, however, Clark received his four-year bachelor's degree with honors.

MICHAELS, DR. ALBERT

The former S.T.A.R. Labs scientist who was accidentally transformed into the villain known as the Atomic Skull.

MICROWAVE MAN

Lewis Padgett was a human who was abducted by aliens and lived on their spacecraft for forty years before eventually returning to Earth as an old man. Prior to his abduction, Padgett plagued the citizens of Metropolis as the powerful villain Microwave Man. Desiring a return to his old career, he asked the aliens to restore his youthful vigor, which they agreed to do, even though the physiological changes did enough damage to his body that he only had hours left to live.

Back on Earth, Padgett wanted to gain instant fame and immediately challenged the Man of Steel to a battle. Once the aliens informed Superman of Padgett's goal, he allowed himself to be defeated; Padgett then died a happy man. The aliens claimed his body and resumed their exploration of the stars, casting Padgett adrift per his final wishes (*Action Comics* #488, October 1978).

MIDAS

A man named Midas appeared in Metropolis and was apparently able to turn objects into gold, much like the fabled King Midas from ancient legend. As the man's golden touch wreaked havoc in the Metropolis Harbor, Superman arrived—but he was unsure of how to handle someone able to change into liquefied form. The issue was resolved for Superman when Midas was taken away by the Hindu demon Ahriman in the guise of a human named Mr. Malik (*Superman: The Man of Steel* #126, July 2002).

MIDVALE

There have been several Midvales in Superman's world, the most significant of which was the one where the Earth-1 Superman chose to house his cousin Kara Zor-El when her rocket ship arrived on Earth from Argo City (*Action Comics* #252, May 1959). Superman warmly welcomed his cousin but soon realized she needed a secret identity and much training before her existence could be revealed to the world. He chose Midvale given its proximity to his Metropolis home and placed her in the Midvale Orphanage.

After her adoption by Fred and Edna Danvers, Supergirl, now known as Linda Lee Danvers, attended Midvale High School before permanently leaving town for college and the next stage of her life.

The Earth-1 Midvale celebrated Supergirl Week, an annual eight-day festival in mid-May, culminating on the eighteenth, which marked the anniversary of the date Kara Zor-El arrived on Earth (*Action Comics* #305, October 1963).

Midvale was "the next town" from Smallville (*Superboy* [first series] #64, April 1958), and its baseball team often played against Smallville's (*Superboy* [first series] #139, June 1967). It was east of Smallville and west of Metropolis, but all were in a relatively close proximity (*The New Adventures of Superboy* #22, October 1981).

The Midvale of the post–Crisis on Infinite Earths reality was situated in southern Kirby County, sixty miles north of Metropolis (*Action Comics* #684, December 1992).

There was also the replica of an 1869 Utah town named Midvale, which was constructed by Superman just outside Metropolis as a permanent exhibit (*Superman's Pal, Jimmy Olsen* #7, September 1955).

MIDVALE ORPHANAGE

The Midvale Orphanage was where the Earth-1 Superman chose to send his cousin Kara Zor-El when her rocket ship arrived on Earth from Argo City. He chose the town of Midvale given its proximity to his own home (*Action Comics* [first series] #252, May 1959).

After giving Kara a pigtailed brunette wig to wear, he introduced her as Linda Lee to the orphanage's headmaster, Mr. Dixon, explaining that Linda's parents had been killed in a natural disaster. Dixon welcomed Linda to the oprhanage, and while she was there, she met Dick Wilson, who

would become her first boyfriend after he was adopted and took the name Dick Malverne. Linda took classes under Headmistress Hart, later identified as Mrs. Henry Hart (*Action Comics* #271, December 1960).

On the orphanage grounds was a hollowed-out tree where Kara secreted a Linda Lee robot to help her maintain her secret identity.

After a period of time, Fred and Edna Danvers adopted Linda Lee, and she left the orphanage for good. Linda held a deep affection for the Midvale Orphanage and often found occasion to return for visits, whether for a formal reunion (*Action Comics* #340, August 1966) or to find sanctuary for other orphans (*Superman Family* #197, September–October 1979).

MIGHTY BOY

A Smallville teen named Reuben was convinced by a carnival owner to appear as a sideshow attraction named Mighty Boy. Using various tricks, it appeared Reuben possessed incredible strength and stamina, thereby wowing the crowds. The youth was kidnapped by a group of criminals with the intent of using him as part of a crime. However, Superboy intervened, not only ending the plot but also freeing Reuben from his life at the carnival (*Superboy* [first series] #1, March–April 1949).

Some time later, a visitor from the planet Zumoor arrived with his pet, Rovo the Mighty Dog. Known to his people as Mighty Boy, Zarl Kazzan spent some time on Earth under the alias of Tom Keith, explaining that he and his pet both received their remarkable powers and abilities from exposure to Zumoor's reflected yellow moonlight. The social visit took an odd turn when Mighty Boy touched Superboy, causing a weird reaction. He was physically altered for a period of time, similar to when the Teen of Steel was exposed to red kryptonite. Once the effects wore off, Mighty Boy and Rovo returned home rather than risk a repeat occurence (*Superboy* [first series] #85, December 1960).

MIGHTY YOUTH

In one of Jimmy Olsen's more improbable adventures, he was kidnapped from the twentieth century by a criminal who stole one of the Legion of Super-Heroes' time bubbles. Together they journeyed to 1000 bc, where the cub reporter was rescued by a superpowered teen named Mighty Youth. Before returning to his own era, Jimmy learned that the boy was actually a younger version of the legendary Samson (*Superman's Pal, Jimmy Olsen* #79, September 1964).

MILLENNIUM

Earth's inhabitants were once given a glimpse of their future when one of the Guardians of the Universe, Herupa Hando Hu, and his Zamaron counterpart Nadia Safir arrived on Earth. They informed the populace that ten of them would be chosen to become the next step in humanity's evolution, which was part of a plan to make humankind the successors to the immortal Guardians at some distant point in time. At their request, many super heroes spread out to gather the chosen people from around the world.

During this period, the Guardians' creations—the Manhunter robots—had recovered the sphere of knowledge gathered by Harbinger, ward to the Monitor who perished during the Crisis on Infinite Earths. Aware of the secret identities of Earth's heroes, the Manhunters had spent years seeding sleeper agents throughout the world, including Lana Lang and many members of the Smallville community. When the Manhunters learned of the search for the chosen ten, they activated their agents to thwart the plan as part of their eons-old war with their Guardian creators.

Harbinger helped guide the heroes in their struggles against their friends in addition to protecting the Chosen, who willingly underwent the evolutionary process and gained powers and abilities that made them New Guardians (*Millennium* #1–8, 1988).

In the reality after Infinite Crisis, the roles of the Guardians, the Zamorons, and the Manhunters were modified. The Chosen may not have existed in the revised New Earth.

MINDBREAKER BEAST, THE

Deep in space, several life-forms managed to live in the vacuum, including the winged dragon-shaped creature called the Mindbreaker Beast. The creature fed on the mental energy of living beings, traveling from world to world. Superman's pet dog Krypto fought the monster on an unnamed alien world and defeated it, but not without suffering psychogenic amnesia as a result of the Mindbreaker Beast using its mental powers on him. This explained Krypto's long absence from Earth-1 during several of the years Clark Kent lived in Metropolis as the Man of Steel (*Superman* [first series] #287, May 1975).

MINK, MART

Located in Metropolis, Mart Mink Used Auto Parts was a front for a chop shop. During this period, Superman had undergone an experiment with a brain device that left him with temporary amnesia. When he regained his memory, the Man of Steel set out to expose the criminal operation and Mart Mink to the police (*Superman* [first series] #32, January–February 1945).

MINTON, BILL

This aeronautical engineer developed a radically new type of jet, a modification of a conventional jet plane embodying "startling improvements that will revolutionize air transport!" When a rival airplane manufacturer, Loops Logan, attempted to murder Minton and sabotage his aircraft to prevent him from winning a sorely needed contract and financial backing, Superman repeatedly intervened to rescue Minton, who ultimately apprehended the racketeer on his own and earned the financial aid he needed (*World's Finest Comics* #21, March–April 1946).

MIRABAI THE FORLORN

In the extradimensional land called Sorcerer's World, Mirabai the Forlorn ruled her kingdom with an iron fist and used her extraordinary magicks to subjugate her people. She forged an unusual alliance with Earth's General Samuel Lane and assisted him with his Project 7734, which was intended and implemented to rid Earth of all Kryptonians, including Superman (*Action Comics* #877 July 2009). Mirabai was involved in fabricating the Superwoman suit used by Lane's daughter Lucy to assimilate on New Krypton. In addition to creating magical portals to transport General Lane's forces from one place to another, Mirabai also provided them with a secret base on Sorcerer's World. She used mystic illusions to help foment public distrust of the Kryptonians and stole the powers of the young Earth magician Zatara, whom she kidnapped for this express purpose.

Mirabai's pact with General Lane hinged on the quantum-powered Captain Atom, who was then in government custody and whose silver skin was resistant to magic. On Sorcerer's World she turned the hero into a personal weapon she dubbed the Arrow of the Forlorn to quash any thought of her people rebelling against her. Captain Atom was eventually freed from Mirabai's thrall by an underground resistance force led by Natasha Irons. Captain Atom, Irons, and their freedom fighters journeyed back to Earth to help stop General Lane's Project 7734 (*Action Comics* #884, February 2010).

When Lane and his army were defeated by Superman, Supergirl, and their allies, Mirabai fled back to her realm, only to be confronted by an armed and organized rebel force. When Captain Atom was near defeat thanks to Mirabai's new powers, he and his ogre ally Aggaro teamed up to finally defeat the cruel magician. Aggaro then revealed himself to be Mordru the Merciless, who explained that he'd hid his true identity rather than fight Mirabai mage to mage. With Mirabai's defeat, he vowed to make the Sorcerer's World a better place regardless of how Earth viewed his past behavior (*Action Comics* #888–889, May–June 2010).

MIRACLE MONDAY

The holiday known as Miracle Monday was celebrated on the third Monday of every May beginning in 1981, and for many years in the future. The event commemorated Superman's successful defeat of C. W. Saturn on Earth-1 and was known for the Miracle Monday Dinner, which was made avail-

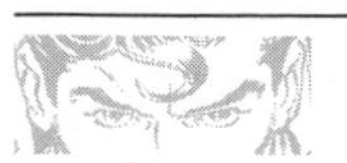

able to those in need. An extra place was set at each table in honor of Superman (*Superman* [first series] #400, October 1984).

MIRACLE TWINE GANG, THE

The Miracle Twine Gang was a band of criminals who used a small quantity of the virtually indestructible "miracle twine" that was accidentally produced when a chunk of green KRYPTONITE dropped unexpectedly into a vat of experimental fiber at the Synthetic Fiber Laboratory in METROPOLIS. The gang was eventually apprehended by Superman, and the twine was destroyed (*Action Comics* #174, November 1952).

MIRI

On a time-traveling trip to KRYPTON in the days before it exploded, JIMMY OLSEN met the attractive Miri, daughter to the scientist Zak-Lor. Through a case of mistaken identity, Olsen found himself a Science Council page and was placed with Zak-Lor in KRYPTONOPOLIS. There he assisted the weapons designer and encountered Miri. The two quickly fell in love, giving Olsen an even stronger reason for attempting to alter history and prevent Krypton's destruction. Even though Miri worked in the mining division of the Submarine Palace deep beneath Krypton's oceans, she would not believe Jimmy's assertion that the planet's unstable core would end all life in a matter of days. While he struggled to do what he thought was right, Jimmy came under the telepathic control of JAX-UR and PROFESSOR VA-KOX, criminals consigned to the PHANTOM ZONE. Jimmy finally regained control of his body, but it was too late to save Miri or alter history. Using his time-travel device to return to his era, Jimmy saw father and daughter disappear in a crevice formed as the planet shuddered and split apart (*Superman's Pal, Jimmy Olsen* #101, April 1967).

MISA

Misa was the daughter of Jude and Lucy Sky Diamond and a member of the HAIRIES, the product of PROJECT CADMUS DNALIENS (*Superman* [second series] #115, September 1996). A mischief maker with a rebellious streak, the wild child rejected the peace and exploratory mission of the Hairies' first generation. Misa and her husband Bron wanted to explore the outside world. They abandoned their home in the MOUNTAIN OF JUDGMENT and soon came into conflict with Superman in METROPOLIS.

Misa was eventually recruited by MORGAN EDGE to form the SUPERMAN REVENGE SQUAD alongside MAXIMA, ANOMALY, BARRAGE, and RIOT (*Action Comics* #730, August 1997). Using her Bag of Tricks, which contained a veritable arsenal of high-tech gadgets of her own design, she battled the Man of Steel on several occasions. Her inventions included a Short-Range Teleporter that had the ability to teleport up to one mile, and the Harmonizer, which gave her the ability to control the mind of whoever donned the device.

She became fascinated by reporter JIMMY OLSEN, and in the wake of his announcement that he possessed the name of Superman's alter ego, she chose to travel with him for a time (*The Adventures of Superman* #553, December 1997; *Superman Forever* #1, June 1998). The journey became a chase, as INTERGANG wanted to learn what Olsen knew while Misa enjoyed the thrills.

Later, within SIMYAN and MOKKARI'S EVIL FACTORY, Misa gave ASHBURY ARMSTRONG glasses that allowed the blind woman to see (*Superman: The Man of Steel* #76, May 1998). When MAINFRAME banished the Hairies to another dimension, Misa helped Superman rescue them (*Superman 3-D* #1, December 1998).

MISS GZPTLSNZ

MR. MXYZPTLK surprised everyone when he arrived from the Fifth Dimension in an attempt to hide from his girlfriend, a short, sour redhead named Miss Gzptlsnz. Rather than visiting METROPOLIS on one of his mischievous sprees, the imp had ducked out on Gzptlsnz's birthday, and upon seeing JIMMY OLSEN on a date with his girlfriend LUCY LANE, he fell for the blonde fast. When Lucy rejected his advances, Mxyzptlk got his revenge by making Jimmy think he was drinking a serum that turned him into a werewolf when it was actually his magic at work. To undo the spell, Jimmy received kisses from Lucy, SUPERGIRL, LOIS LANE, LORI LEMARIS, and LANA LANG, all to no avail. Having seen everything, Miss Gzptlsnz arrived in time to kiss Jimmy and remove the magical spell. She then tricked her boyfriend into saying his name backward, consigning him to their realm for the next ninety days (*Superman's Pal, Jimmy Olsen* #52, April 1961).

Some time later, Gzptlsnz returned, this time in the hope of getting Jimmy to agree to a wedding. When he refused her offer, however, she turned Jimmy into a human porcupine out of spite. She would only turn him back to normal if he agreed to marry her. Jimmy cleverly convinced Gzptlsnz to undo the spell, and she returned home (*Superman's Pal, Jimmy Olsen* #65, December 1962). Still not over her infatuation with the redhead, she returned on the day Jimmy and Lucy were to finally wed and cast a spell that would turn the Man of Steel into a mole whenever the couple kissed. However, Lucy, frustrated at seeing so many of Jimmy's former girlfriends turn up at the ceremony, had the wedding annulled, thereby breaking the spell on Superman (*Superman's Pal, Jimmy Olsen* #100, March 1967).

Gzptlsnz also appeared when Lois Lane secretly wished for a fairy godmother to fulfill her every desire, but clearly that was not going to end well: Each wish was twisted beyond Lois's expectations (*Superman's Girl Friend, Lois Lane* #73, April 1967).

One potential future revealed that MR. MXYZPTLK married not only Gzptlsnz but also another woman, resulting in him being jailed for bigamy (*DC Comics Presents* #97, September 1986).

In the wake of the CRISIS ON INFINITE EARTHS, Miss Gsptlsnz was still Mr. Mxyzptlk's girlfriend (or

"quinto-partner") and was initially part of a Fifth Dimensional ruling council (*JLA* #31, July 1999). Subsequently depicted with red hair instead of blond, this incarnation of Miss Gsptlsnz differed sharply from her Earth-1 counterpart in that she was tall, attractive, and rather ditzy (*Countdown to Final Crisis* #31, September 26, 2007), attributes she shared with another incarnation on Earth-992 (*Superman Adventures* #26, December 1998; others).

MISTER GIMMICK

Described as a ruthless gangland genius and originator of numerous "cunning criminal schemes," the man dubbed Mister Gimmick concocted an utterly inhuman plot to destroy Superman by tricking the Man of Steel into accidentally detonating a powerful "super-explosive," thereby obliterating the city of Metropolis—along with its millions of inhabitants—in an awesome "super-atomic blast." In exchange for a million dollars, a fee collected by the Metropolis underworld leaders, Mister Gimmick planned and began to execute his scheme until he was stopped by Superman, who brought Gimmick and his gang to justice (*Action Comics* #328, September 1965).

MISTER MIRACLE

The name Mister Miracle was first used by Thaddeus Brown, a circus escape artist and mentor to Scott Free. Brown was unaware that Free and Norman were actually refugees from Apokolips, the fiery home of Darkseid. Both Free and Shilo Norman were eager students and learned many of Brown's secrets before he was murdered by thieves. Free then became the next Mister Miracle, accompanied by Shilo and an assistant, Oberon (*Mister Miracle* #1, March–April 1971).

Free was the firstborn son to Izaya of Apokolips's twin world New Genesis. To end an ages-old conflict, Izaya and Darkseid agreed to a pact that involved the trading of their sons Scott and Orion. Free was handed over to the cruel Granny Goodness, who gave him special attention in her Terror Orphanage (*New Gods* #7, February–March 1972). Dreams of freedom were encouraged during periodic visits from New Genesis's Metron. While at the orphanage, he met his future wife Barda, who was training to join Granny's Female Furies.

His chance to obtain his freedom came from the New God named Himon. Scott fled Apokolips for Earth and adventured there, aided by a Mother Box from New Genesis, as the World's Greatest Escape Artist. Darkseid knew of Free's treachery and allowed it to go unchecked, since it meant that "The Pact" with Izaya was broken and his plans for conquest could begin anew. Big Barda was sent to Earth to retrieve him (*Mister Miracle* #9, July–August 1972) but decided to stay with him, and they eventually fell in love and subsequently married, adopting Earth as their home.

Scott eventually tired of being hounded by Darkseid and returned to Apokolips to face a trial by combat. He triumphed, officially won his freedom, and returned to Earth. Miracle and Barda fought alongside Earth's superpowered champions, including Superman, both serving alongside him for a time in the Justice League of America. In one instance, Superman helped them fight Sleez (*Action Comics* #592–593, September–October 1987); in another the Man of Steel and Mister Miracle took on the villain Deathtrap (*Action Comics* #708, March 1995; *Superman: The Man of Steel* #43, April 1995).

Their adventures came to an abrupt end when Big Barda was killed. During his investigation of her death, Scott was also killed by a manifestation of the Source as the Fourth World came a shocking end (*Death of the New Gods* #1–8, Early December 2007–June 2008).

Shilo Norman had taken up the mantle of Mister Miracle only once, using all he learned from Thaddeus Brown and Scott Free. He was given the role of security chief at the Slabside Island Maximum Security Prison for Meta-Humans. After performing courageously during the Joker's attempt at infecting the world with his Venom, Shilo was promoted to warden of the Slab, which was then located in Antarctica (*Joker: Last Laugh* #1–6, December 2001–January 2002).

Shilo left the Slab behind upon hearing of Scott Free's death and resumed his Mister Miracle persona (*Seven Soldiers: Mister Miracle* miniseries #1–4, November 2005–May 2006). He was part of a band of freedom fighters led by the meta-human Sonny Sumo to keep all humanity from falling under Darkseid's sway during the events of the Final Crisis (*Final Crisis* #2, August 2008). After Darkseid's defeat, Shilo continued to adventure as Mister Miracle.

MISTER OHM

The cunning criminal mastermind called Mister Ohm carried out a series of spectacular armored-car robberies by employing a "flying electro-magnet"—an airplane, wrapped in coils of heavy electrical wire, with a giant magnet hanging suspended from its fuselage—to literally lift the armored vehicles off the road and carry them through the air to his hideout. Mister Ohm and his henchmen were easily apprehended by Superman (*Superman* [first series] #51, March–April 1948).

MISTER SEVEN

Clad in a red, yellow, and blue costume with a large number 7 emblazoned on his chest, the criminal known as Mister Seven had a thirst for notoriety. He toyed with the Metropolis Police Department by announcing his target in advance with one enigmatic clue, daring the police to thwart his crimes. It quickly became obvious that Mister Seven's robberies were tied to the seven days of the week, such as his theft of a rare first-edition book on a Sunday. As his successes mounted, Mister Seven took to broadcasting his good fortune, taunting Metropolis's law enforcement community by airing radio jingles and declaring his success via skywriting. When he was apprehended by Superman, the world learned that the feared Mister Seven was actually Scraps Fabian, a failed thief whose record did not warrant his being hired on by criminal gangs, which was why he had created a new persona (*World's Finest Comics* #46, June–July 1950).

MISTER SINISTER

Hailing from the Fourth Dimension, this malevolent purple-skinned being was a frustrated poet who frequently communicated only in rhyme. His complex scientific machinery enabled him to kidnap entire buildings from Earth's Third Dimension with the intention of either stealing the contents or holding them for ransom. His ultimate ambition was to conquer and rule Earth, a goal Superman realized was excessive compensation for his failure as a poet. In order to free his adoptive world from Sinister's terror campaign, Superman chased the villain through the dimensions until Sinister was accidentally transformed into a black shadowy form after being hit by an energy blast originally intended for the Man of Steel (*Superman* [first series] #16, May–June 1952).

MISTER TWISTER

The Metropolis police were baffled by a series of amazing crimes in which everything they expected to happen occurred in the opposite fashion, allowing the culprit, dubbed Mister Twister, to escape with his loot. The mastermind turned out to be a clever author named Dan Judd, who was researching crimes for a new novel he was writing. When his henchmen turned the tables and unexpectedly made off with the stolen goods, Judd helped Superman bring them to justice. His good deed encouraged the judge to mitigate his sentence, requiring the bestselling writer to serve just six months for his crimes (*Action Comics* #96, May 1946).

MISTER WHEELS

Using his impressive knowledge of auto mechanics, the criminal known as Mister Wheels designed a series of devices for members of Metropolis's underworld. Among his inventions was an ingenious tractor-like vehicle for crawling up the outside wall of a multistory warehouse. Mister Wheels also competed with other criminals for valuable goods and led his men on a series of spectacular crimes. Despite the advantage of using these machines, Mister Wheels and his men were ultimately apprehended by Superman (*Superman* [first series] #108, September 1956).

MISTER Z

Metropolis resident Oscar Lanchester disguised himself as the mysterious Mister Z and made several elaborate attempts to kill a black-and-white

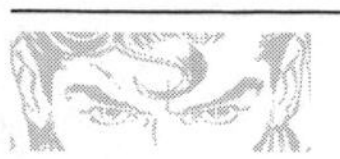

dog belonging to his late aunt. When he was apprehended by Superman, it was discovered that the dog was set to inherit Lanchester's aunt's vast fortune. Oscar wanted to do away with the pet so he would receive the money instead (*Superman* [first series] #19, November–December 1942).

On the Earth created after the Crisis on Infinite Earths, Superman encountered an entirely different Mister Z. This Mister Z appeared to be a long-lived being, possessing a mystical gemstone that he used to collect souls. The two met when Z arrived in Metropolis seeking the Man of Tomorrow's soul. Instead, the gem was shattered by Superman's incredible strength of will. The breaking of the gem seemed to mean the end of Z's long life, and he left to spend the rest of his days in Saudi Arabia (*Superman* [second series] #51, January 1991).

Soon after, the Linear Men sent the Man of Steel tumbling through time, and the two met a second time when Z posed as General Zeiten and oversaw a Nazi Germany laboratory's atomic experiments in Warsaw. Superman once again stopped Z's deadly plan and saved the imprisoned Jewish people (*Superman* [second series] #54, April 1991).

Back in the present, Superman was shown by Professor Emil Hamilton that Z's gemstone had been re-formed (*Superman: The Man of Steel* #1, July 1991). A short while later, Z, still alive, reappeared in Metropolis. Both Z and Superman suffered amnesia, an effect of the gemstone, and together they found a Polynesian island complete with dinosaurs and Neanderthals, including the shapely Lola-La, who wanted the Action Ace as her mate. A search team comprising Superman's friends and the DNAlien Dubbilex located the hero and restored his memory. While Superman returned to Metropolis, Mister Z decided to remain on the island (*Superman* [second series] #61–62, *The Adventures of Superman* #484–485; *Action Comics* #671; *Superman: The Man of Steel* #6—all November–December 1991).

MISTRI-LOR

Best known as a lost civilization nestled in a vast valley concealed from the outside world by a remote mountain range somewhere on the far side of the globe, Mistri-Lor was the location of Superman's brief encounter with the lovely Queen Lura (*Action Comics* #298, March 1963).

MOA

The moa was a very large, tall, flightless bird considered extinct in New Zealand after its habitat was destroyed by a growing human population half a millennium ago. Hunting finished off the remaining specimens until hunter Jon Halaway found a final living moa. He killed it, and the guilt he felt afterward caused him to transport the last known egg to Metropolis for study. The egg somehow absorbed Halaway's life energy, prompting it to hatch as a giant "super bird" that took flight over the city. Superman had to subdue the exotic creation and return the moa to its homeland in the hope of letting it settle there peacefully (*Action Comics* #425, July 1973).

MO-DE

Nearly twenty years before Jor-El reached the conclusion that his homeworld of Krypton was doomed, Mo-De came to the same realization. The renowned scientist and doctor from the Kryptonian city of Surrus failed to convince his community of the danger because they had been lulled into a tranquil state by the siren-like qualities of the singing Surrus Blossoms that grew there. As a result, they perished along with the rest of the planet's inhabitants (*Superman* [first series] #236, April 1971).

MOKKARI AND SIMYAN

Masters of genetic warfare, the bald yellow-faced Mokkari and his ape-featured partner Simyan ran the Apokolips operation known as the Evil Factory. On Earth-1, they were two scientists from Apokolips whom Darkseid had ordered to replace the Earth-based DNA Project with his own sinister counterpart. To that end, they created a perfect clone of Morgan Edge, who replaced the real Galaxy Communications CEO (*Superman's Girl Friend, Lois Lane* #118, January 1972), and devised such creations as a kryptonite-irradiated clone of Jimmy Olsen (*Superman's Pal, Jimmy Olsen* #135–136, January–March 1971) and the Four-Armed Terror (*Superman's Pal, Jimmy Olsen* #137–138, April–June 1971). The duo's attempt at creating a Neanderthal incarnation of Olsen backfired when the beast-man went on a rampage in their Loch Trevor lair and reduced the Evil Factory to a crater, taking its villainous caretakers with it (*Superman's Pal, Jimmy Olsen* #145–146, January–February 1972).

In the reality formed after the Crisis on Infinite Earths, Mokkari and Simyan were doll-sized Earth-born genetic creations of Dabney Donovan. Fleeing Project Cadmus, they created their first human clone from the DNA of Jimmy Olsen's father Jake, and went on to develop the Four-Armed Terror, a kryptonite-tinged Superman clone in their Loch Trevor–based Evil Factory. The combined efforts of Superman, Jimmy Olsen, and the Guardian destroyed the facility, while Jimmy's mother Sarah successfully exiled Mokkari and Simyan to the colorless void where they sent their failed experiments (*Superman* [second series] #39–40, January–February 1990).

However, Morgan Edge managed to manipulate Jimmy Olsen and his friends into freeing the duo (*Superman: The Man of Steel* #76, February 1998) with the intent of using their mad genius to create super-humans under his control. Instead, Mokkari and Simyan created a new wave of monsters in a secret laboratory beneath the Galaxy Communications complex itself, ultimately prompting Edge to relocate the duo to the remote Mutant Island (*Superman: The Man of Steel* #85, January 1999). Almost immediately, the duo was recruited by Amanda Spence and the Agenda to orchestrate a takeover of Project Cadmus. A group of heroes lead by Superboy thwarted the plot, while Simyan and Mokkari themselves were rendered unconscious by their creator Dabney Donovan and then spirited away (*Superboy* [third series] #70–74, January–May 2000).

The sinister pair resurfaced in the employ of Darkseid himself, using their Evil Factory to create new bodies for many of the evil gods of Apokolips. When they failed to subdue and genetically modify Batman, Mokkari and Simyan were killed at the feet of Darkseid by the Dark Knight before he himself was killed by an Omega Beam (*Final Crisis* #2–5, August–December 2008).

MOLE, THE

Gotham Gazette editor John Hall learned that a figure known only as the Mole was planning a criminal enterprise in Gotham City. However, the stress of his normal routine got to Hall, and he was hospitalized before he could act on the tip. To help the *Gazette, Daily Planet* editor Perry White loaned out his two best reporters, Clark Kent and Lois Lane, and they began to investigate the Mole. Kent turned to his friend Bruce Wayne for help, and in the Caped Crusader's files was information about the Mole's mining background and method

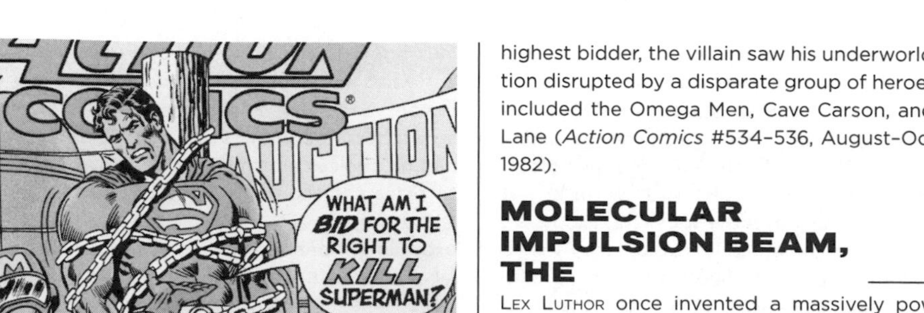

of operation. Having overheard the discussion, Robin began to investigate on his own, uncovering details about the Harrah Construction Company's sewer project. Further study proved that it was masking a tunnel underneath Gotham's largest bank. Superman managed to dig a detour, leading the Mole and his men directly to prison. The Mole was subsequently revealed to be Harrah himself (*World's Finest Comics* #80, January–February 1956).

Years later, Batman again confronted the Mole, although he appeared physically different: He was now a humanoid covered in fur, able to see clearly in low light. This Mole was able to burrow underground at great speed without needing any tools. The Mole was killing the people of Gotham City, which brought him to Batman's attention. In short order the Dark Knight discovered that the victims were all members of the prison review board who had denied Harrah parole. A check showed that Harrah had recently escaped from incarceration, and Batman tracked him down, luring the Mole toward Wayne Manor. During their confrontation, Harrah revealed that he swam through toxic sewage during his escape, which triggered the transformation from man to creature. Batman subdued the Mole by knocking him into a flooded cavern within the Batcave. The Mole was washed away by the current, but his body was never recovered (*Batman* #340, October 1981).

A later Mole, his features entirely concealed beneath a green costume, used a subterranean digger machine to loot businesses until he and his gang were captured by Superman. That fateful excursion also awakened the incubating Nat Tryon, who soon became known as Neutron (*Action Comics* #525, November 1981). Nursing a grudge against the Man of Steel for having been jailed on an earlier murder conviction, the Mole sought out Superman when the hero's powers had been halved. Putting the Man of Steel up for sale to the highest bidder, the villain saw his underworld auction disrupted by a disparate group of heroes that included the Omega Men, Cave Carson, and Lois Lane (*Action Comics* #534–536, August–October 1982).

MOLECULAR IMPULSION BEAM, THE

Lex Luthor once invented a massively powerful microwave device called the Molecular Impulsion Beam, and he tested it in the Metropolis environs. The resulting landscape of twisted trees, melted rocks, and mangled metal prompted an investigation by *Daily Star* reporters Clark Kent and Lois Lane. The wily scientist turned the beam on the newspaper offices to bring Superman out into the open. Luthor theorized that his beam could even affect the Kryptonian's dense molecular structure. The Man of Steel was hit while in flight and went tumbling to the ground, but fortunately he landed atop a power plant's electric condenser. The resulting charge revived the hero and he apprehended Luthor, who tried to distract Superman by throwing a grenade-sized atomic bomb at him, which the Man of Steel caught before it could detonate (*Superman* [first series] #38, January–February 1946).

MON-EL

The planet Daxam was inhabited by people with physiologies similar to Kryptonians, and when they traveled abroad from their planet, they gained powers and abilities similar to those of Superman.

One such explorer, a teen named Lar Gand, crash-landed on Earth, and the impact concussed the youth, which resulted in temporary amnesia. Given the similarity in powers and mode of transport, as well as a note from Jor-El, Superboy at first believed the young man to be a fellow Kryptonian. He brought Lar back to his home in Smallville. Wishing to use his powers for good, the two boys crafted the name Mon-El based on Lar's arriving on a Monday and the wishful hope that he was descended from the House of El.

Choosing a secret identity much as Clark Kent had, Lar took the name Bob Cobb and pretended to be a traveling salesman in order to protect Clark's secret identity. For a time, the two were inseparable, and Clark looked up to the handsome older-brother figure (*Superboy* [first series] #89, February 1961). When Superboy noticed that Mon-El was unaffected by kryptonite, he became convinced the young man was a fraud. The Boy of Steel exposed Mon-El to false kryptonite meteors composed of lead, and assumed that Mon-El was faking when he collapsed in agony. In that moment, Lar's memory returned, and he explained to the Kents that he had actually visited Krypton in the weeks prior to its destruction, even meeting Clark's birth father Jor-El. Jor-El had provided Lar with a map leading him to Earth, but Krypton's explosion sent his ship tumbling through space and placed Lar in a form of suspended animation.

Having now fatally poisoned Mon-El, and with no cure in sight, Superboy felt he had no choice but to place his "brother" in the Phantom Zone until a solution could be found. While he lived in the limbo-like realm, Mon-El had to endure sharing the space with the worst of Kryptonian society, and often found himself at odds with them. Using a televiewer, Superboy (and later Superman) managed to check in with Mon-El and offer words of encouragement to keep Lar's spirits high.

It took a millennium, but in the thirtieth century, the Legion of Super-Heroes' Saturn Girl finally found a temporary antidote for Lar's lead poisoning, Serum XY-4, and freed him briefly from his ethereal prison (*Adventure Comics* #300, September 1962). Brainiac 5 finally found a permanent cure in the form of a serum based on Saturn Girl's formula mixed with kryptonite, which the Daxamite had to ingest every forty-eight hours (*Adventure Comics* #305, February 1963). Finally freed from the Phantom Zone, Lar auditioned for the Legion under the guise of Marvel Lad. Part of his trial led to the creation of element 152, which Brainiac later used to fashion the Legion Flight Rings. He was welcomed into the Legion as Mon-El and soon became one of the group's most powerful and valued members. There was at least one incidence of his not taking the serum on schedule; he died as a result, only to be revived when Eltro Gand, a descendant of his older brother, sacrificed his life to save the hero (*Action Comics* #384, January 1970). Mon-El served the team as its leader on two separate occasions, a rare feat for any Legion member (*Action Comics* #392, September 1970; *Superboy* [first series] #190, September 1972). A popular figure, he fell in love with Shadow Lass, and they later married. By the time most of

the Legionnaires were adults, Mon-El had left the team to continue exploring and trying to find new worlds for colonization (*Adventure Comics* #354, March 1967).

Mon-El eventually learned that his anti-lead serum was losing its potency but worked with Superboy to fabricate a replacement. Until the new serum was ready, Mon-El was forced to return to the Phantom Zone for a brief but traumatic period (*Legion of Super-Heroes* [third series] #21, April 1986, and #23, June 1986).

In the wake of the Crisis on Infinite Earths, Mon-El's career changed significantly given the absence of a Superboy on the re-formed Earth. Instead, his adventures were taking place in a Pocket Universe shaped from a sliver of time by the Time Trapper. In one final battle, Superboy sacrificed himself to save Earth and died in Mon-El's arms (*Legion of Super-Heroes* [third series] #38, September 1987). Mon-El joined his teammates in seeking revenge against the Trapper, and at the end of time the cloaked villain was cornered and seemingly killed. Mon-El, however, was severely injured, his entire body battered and bruised, resulting in his being placed in stasis (*Legion of Super-Heroes* [third series] #50, June 1989). As a testament to their love, Shadow Lass followed the rituals of her people by severing half of her left pinkie and placing a ring on the remainder, thereby binding herself to Mon-El forever (*Legion of Super-Heroes* [third series] #52, November 1988).

When the Trapper's body began to fail five years later, he revived Mon-El in the hope of inhabiting the form. It was then revealed that Mon-El had actually been overlaid with Eltro Gand's life force, and the Trapper's interference had split him into two distinct personalities. To ensure that the Trapper would trouble no one again, Mon-El killed him in violation of the Legion by-laws (*Legion of Super-Heroes* [third series] #3–4, January-February 1990). His death also eradicated the Pocket Universe, which had many repercussions on the time line, reordering a Legion without its original inspiration.

The remade reality, now controlled by the Legion's foe Glorith, cast Lar Gand as the inspirational super-teen of the twentieth century, although he was now a contemporary of Superman's. Lar took on a new name, Valor, and wore a modified uniform. It was said that R. J. Brande was inspired by Valor's deeds to form the Legion when he was saved by Garth Ranzz, Rokk Krinn, and Imra Ardeen (*Legion of Super-Heroes* [third series] #8, June 1990). In the new reality, Laurel Gand was now a descendant of Lar's brother instead of the El family line, effectively replacing Supergirl in the chronicles.

According to legends lasting to the thirtieth century, Valor stopped a second Dominator-led invasion of Earth and freed thousands of humans captured for genetic experimentation (*Legion of Super-Heroes* [third series] *Annual* #2, 1991). People with like abilities were taken to colonize different worlds, among them Bismoll, Carggite, Lallor, Myrnah, Tharr, and Winath, acting as a powerful buffer between Earth and the Dominion.

It was also recorded that Lar Gand's father, Kel Gand, died by sacrificing himself heroically during the alien invasion of Earth, which led Lar to become a super hero (*Invasion!* #1–3, 1988). The Coluan Vril Dox II cured Lar's lead poisoning (*L.E.G.I.O.N. '90* #13, March 1990) and then blackmailed him into joining L.E.G.I.O.N when all Lar wanted to do was travel the stars (*L.E.G.I.O.N. '90* #16, June 1990). On an early mission, they visited Earth so that Dox could find his father, the infamous Brainiac, at Project Cadmus, and there Lar met Superman for the first time (*The Adventures of Superman Annual* #2, 1990).

Later returning to Earth, he aided Superman and many other heroes during a battle against Eclipso, and at its conclusion the Man of Steel suggested the name Valor, which Lar gratefully accepted (*Eclipso: The Darkness Within* #2, October 1992). Equipped with a sentient spacecraft he named Babbage, Valor then began exploring the stars (*Valor* #1, November 1992).

During this time, Glorith continued to tinker with reality, and the changes had serious repercussions for the object of her affection, Lar Gand. In one case, her alterations led to his premature death, so she replaced him with a Valor chosen from an alternate time line. Waverider of the Linear Men told this Valor that his job was to fulfill the destiny of Lar Gand as history had recorded it (*Valor* #17–21, March–July 1994). This incarnation of Valor did as instructed and entered the Phantom Zone for a time, joined the Legion, and married Shadow Lass. Ultimately, however, the integrity of the time line was too badly damaged, and the Daxamite and his wife literally faded out of existence (*Valor* #23, September 1994).

In the wake of the Zero Hour incident, a new history of the Legion emerged. In the twentieth century, an amnesiac Lar Gand was manipulated into fighting the clone of Superman, Superboy, but when the Teen of Steel noticed that his opponent was ill, he ended the battle. With Dox's serum depleted in Lar's system, Superboy felt he had no choice but to use a device at S.T.A.R Labs to place the teen in a "Stasis Zone" (Superboy [third series] #17–19, July–September 1995), an extradimensional space first discovered by the villain Loophole. It was later learned that this "Stasis Zone" was also known as the Bgtzl Buffer Zone, the Phantom Zone, and the White Zone by the inhabitants of Mars. Once again, Lar endured a thousand years as a phantom until he was rescued in the thirtieth century by the Legion, accompanied by Superboy. Brainiac 5 modified his ancestor's serum, and Lar Gand was once more ready to be a hero (Legionnaires #30, November 1995). With Valor considered dead and wishing to avoid any religious connotations about his "resurrection," Lar Gand took the heroic name M'Onel, which was Martian for "he who wanders" (Legionnaires #37, June 1996).

Living up to the name, and to avoid being recognized, Lar Gand often took deep-space assignments. At one point he returned to discover that his team had disbanded, so he accepted President Leland McCauley's offer to join the new outfit called Oversight Watch (*Legion Worlds* #1, June 2001). That proved short-lived when the evil president—revealed as the near-immortal Rā's al Ghūl—attempted to kill Lar, but he was healed by Kinetix (*The Legion* #1–8, December 2001–July 2002). In the wake of that adventure, the Legion re-formed, and M'Onel was delighted to be back among his friends.

In one time-traveling incident with the twenty-first century's Teen Titans, the Persuader's ax literally sliced through time. The Legionnaires were sucked into a temporal vortex, which led them to settle in a vastly different future. The altered future wouldn't last for long, as the events of the Infinite Crisis once again reordered reality, separating the universe into fifty-two parallel universes, with several worlds each boasting a variant version of the Legion, complete with a Lar Gand.

Saturn Girl sensed a telepathic cry for help emanating from the planet Rokyn, and the Legionnaires discovered Lar Gand once again trapped in the Phantom Zone (*Supergirl and the Legion of Super-Heroes* #23, December 2006). The Mon-El they freed from the Zone was mentally erratic due to having suffered a millennium of sensory deprivation while still ill from lead poisoning. In his altered state, he confused the S-shield worn by Supergirl with the mark of an enemy. He started a battle, which wound up freeing members of the Legion from a trap laid for them by the Wanderers. Once again, Brainiac 5 devised the serum that would preserve Lar Gand's life and, after Invisible Kid delivered it, it calmed the raging Daxamite. This account was part of the history of a parallel world and not the one from New Earth, however.

The New Earth origin for Mon-El involved the visiting Lar Gand, amnesia, an encounter with young Clark Kent, some spoken Kryptonese leading to a mistaken belief they were kin, and taking the name Mon-El as a result. Once again, accidental exposure to lead made Lar Gand ill, but it also jarred his memory, leading to the revelation that he was a scientist who hailed from the planet Daxam, which orbited the star Valor. Once again, Clark Kent was forced to send Mon-El into the Phantom Zone for his own safety (*Action Comics Annual* #10, 2007).

When Superman was trapped in the Phantom Zone during General Zod's takeover of Earth, he encountered his old friend Mon-El, who provided the Man of Steel with valuable information regarding what Zod was really up to (*Action Comics* #851, August 2007). Later, when the Phantom Zone criminals were released and sent to New Krypton, a parallel planet in opposite orbit of Earth, the zone itself crumbled, and Superman managed to free Mon-El before it vanished completely (*Action Comics* #874, April 2009). Desperately seeking a cure in the Fortress of Solitude, the Man of Steel found a vial of serum provided by the Legion of Super-Heroes that would cure Mon-El's reaction to lead for a finite period. When Superman left to spend time living among his own people on New Krypton, Mon-El was charged with protecting Metropolis (*Superman* #685, April 2009). He took the name Jonathan Kent with Martha Kent's blessing, and she also suggested he tell people he was from London to explain his accent. Lar was also added to the ranks of the city's Science Police, receiving additional tutelage from the Guardian, who now led the troops.

After he began to make friends and adapt to life on Earth, Mon-El was captured by General Samuel Lane's Project 7734 team, who made it appear that Mon-El had been killed by the renegades Nightwing and Flamebird. Mon-El was tortured both mentally and physically by Lane's agents (*Superman* #693, December 2009). With the Parasite's unexpected help, Mon-El escaped and wound up in the Forlorn Dimension, where he came to Captain Atom's rescue. Together the two men defeated Mirabi, the vile queen of the realm, and returned to Earth (*Action Comics* #883, January 2010). Mon-El returned to Metropolis, proving he was not dead after all, and aided the Science Police in stopping Bizarro's latest rampage. He then went to Smallville to spend time with Martha Kent and met Connor Kent, the clone of Superman. Martha counseled Mon-El about General Lane and listened to his worry that Lane had tainted what the House of El symbol represented to Earth's inhabitants. Martha modified Mon-El's uniform and added the House of El symbol so that he could clearly represent all the good Kal-El did and all that he stood for (*Superman* #694, January 2010). Mon-El also asked Connor to reprogram the robot Kelex back at the Fortress of Solitude so that it could begin repairing his spacecraft. He then met with Perry White and Jimmy Olsen to formulate a strategy to bring down Project 7734 (*Superman* #695, February 2010). Around the same time, Doctor Light invited Mon-El to join the Justice League of America (*Justice League of America* [second series] #41, March 2010).

Mon-El's plan to bring down Project 7734 was altered when he was confronted by members of the Legion Espionage Squad, who had been sent back in time by Brainiac 5 to make certain that Brainiac did not kill Superman at this point in time, otherwise the entire future time-stream would unravel (*Superman* #697, April 2010). Feeling burdened by the responsibility placed on him by Superman, Mon-El welcomed the Legion's help, which proved invaluable when they all journeyed to New Krypton to help prevent Brainiac's plan from becoming a reality (*Superman: Last Stand on New Krypton* #1–3, June 2010). After the destruction of New Krypton and the attack on Earth, the very war General Sam Lane both feared and instigated decided Lar Gand's fate. After helping to save many of the bottled cities stowed on Brainiac's ship, Mon-El then traveled to Earth to help Superman stop General Zod and his Kryptonian army from destroying the planet (*Superman: War of the Supermen* #1–3, July 2010).

When Superboy arrived with the Phantom Zone Projector and news that the Zone had been re-formed, Mon-El knew that he had to sacrifice himself to save Earth, so he returned to the Phantom Zone, along with hundreds of startled Kryptonians. Later, when Christopher Kent entered the Phantom Zone to ensure that Zod and his followers could not escape again, Mon-El encountered the youth in an unknown part of the Zone, and the two decided to protect each other and keep each other company. However, Mon-El was unaware that he'd left behind a unique legacy on Earth: his Science Police partner, Billi Harper, was pregnant with his child (*Superman: War of the Supermen* #4, July 2010).

MONGAL

Daughter to the galactic conqueror Mongul, Mongal also sought dominion over populated planets in an effort to build her own power base. When she accompanied her brother, also named Mongul, to Metropolis's Centennial Park, she first met Superman and matched him blow for blow. Had it not been for Krypto's timely arrival, Superman may have been outmatched by the powerful duo (first unnamed appearance in *Showcase '95* #8, September 1995; first named appearance in *Superman* [second series] #170, July 2001). Impressed by Mongal's battle prowess during the war against Imperiex, the beleaguered people of Almerac chose Mongul's daughter as their new leader after Maxima was killed (*World's Finest: Our Worlds at War* #1, October 2001).

She and Mongul II had the usual sibling love-hate relationship, but when one squabble grew more heated than usual, Mongul punched his sister, literally knocking her head off and killing her (*Green Lantern* [fourth series] #8, March 2006).

MONGUL

There have been many conquerors throughout known space, but few with the fearsome reputation of Mongul. The yellow-skinned figure's mammoth silhouette drew shudders from world to

world. Few tried to rebel once his conquest was complete, although on one unnamed planet, he was challenged when the Arkymandyte, an ancient holy figure, led an uprising against Mongul's rule. Mongul escaped the world with his life, but apparently sought to increase his natural strength with extraordinary abilities to further his plans for galactic conquest.

Even without any weaponry, Mongul possessed extraordinary super-human physical strength, in addition to invulnerability, and also had a limited amount of telepathic powers. He even appeared to have the ability to transport himself from star system to star system.

During his journey, Mongul encountered an ancient crystal key within a crypt on the fourth planet in the Cygnus star system that granted him access to and control over the immense battle station called Warworld. That planet was also known as Mars II, home to the survivors of the Martian Manhunter's race. The chronicles suggested that Mongul and the Manhunter had fought on some previous occasion, so to obtain the key this time, Mongul sought an edge. He traveled to Earth and kidnapped Lois Lane, Jimmy Olsen, and Steve Lombard to force their friend Superman to battle on Mongul's behalf. While the Man of Steel managed to obtain the key, he refused to hand it over; the ensuing titanic battle with Mongul nearly killed the Man of Steel. Mongul left the battered Superman and escaped with the key (*DC Comics Presents* #27, November 1980).

With the key in his possession, Mongul located Warworld and gained access to the mechanical marvel that assured him of greater success. As he acclimated himself to his new battle machine, he was confronted by Superman, this time accompanied by his cousin Supergirl. Mongul chose to try out the Warworld's offensive weaponry and used his cybernetic control over the construct to battle the Kryptonian heroes. They managed to put up enough of a struggle that Mongul passed out from the strain of his sustained effort to control Warworld. Supergirl then damaged the central computer core, but Mongul managed to escape (*DC Comics Presents* #28, December 1980).

Some time later, Superman was drawn into a fresh conflict with Mongul when he attempted to gain control over Throneworld, the seat to the Infinite Realm. He first murdered Empress Clryssa, sister to Prince Gayvn, known to most as Starman, then forced Merria, Starman's lover, to marry him to secure the throne. Banishing Starman to a dimensional-inversion cube, he then attempted to assert his authority over the Infinite Realm. His plans were interrupted by the timely arrival of Superman, who freed Starman, and together the two fought Mongul to save Throneworld's subjects. Before Superman could see which of them was truly the stronger fighter, Mongul fled (*DC Comics Presents* #36, August 1981).

Licking his wounds, Mongul wandered the stars until he encountered one of the Controllers, an offshoot of the Guardians of the Universe. Mongul murdered the man in order to gain control of the Sun-Eater in his possession, and then used the Sun-Eater to attempt to exact revenge against the Man of Steel. Superman was trapped in the dimensional-inversion cube, which used red solar radiation to sap his strength. With Superman out of the way, Mongul unleashed the Sun-Eater on Sol and deflected an attempt by Supergirl and the Justice League of America to stop the entity. Instead Jimmy Olsen used his Legion Flight Ring to summon the Legion of Super-Heroes from the thirtieth century to stop the Sun-Eater, free Superman, and defeat Mongul. The Legionnaires responded; the freed Man of Steel took on Mongul one-on-one and managed to beat him into submission (*DC Comics Presents* #43, March 1982).

Mongul returned to Earth seeking revenge, but in a far more subtle manner than previous encounters. He stealthily gained access to the Fortress of Solitude and lay in wait. Just after Superman welcomed Batman, Robin, and Wonder Woman for a visit on his birthday, Mongul gave the Man of Steel a gift, too: a deadly alien plant known as the Black Mercy. It attached itself to Superman and induced a hypnotic state in which his greatest desires appeared to come true. As the Dynamic Duo and the Amazon Princess battled the villain, Superman lived out an idyllic life on a Krypton that did not explode. He fell in love, married Lyla Lerrol, and seemed to live happily ever after. That proved false as his days grew darker and society frayed at the edges, including him witnessing his cousin Kara Zor-El attacked by a mob. Superman's visions worsened, which weakened the Black Mercy's hold on his mind. Finally free, an angry Superman attacked Mongul with a blast of heat vision, then pummeled him into submission. Robin used Mongul's gloves to collect the plant, then dropped it atop Mongul, giving him the blissful life he desired: killing Superman in battle and ruling the universe (*Superman* [first series] *Annual* #11, 1985).

In the reality after the events of the Crisis on Infinite Earths, Mongul was a known galactic conqueror and father of two children—Mongul and Mongal. This version of Mongul was equally strong and resilient but lacked the telepathic and teleportation abilities of his predecessor. He did, however, have the ability to generate internal energies that he could expel from his chest with great force.

He formed an alliance with the Council of Overseers to act as manager of their construct dubbed Warworld. With each conquered species, he enslaved most and let others fight for a place in his growing army by winning in gladiatorial combat. One of his slave ships found an unconscious Superman floating in space and brought him to their leader. Mongul insisted the Last Son of Krypton fight for his life in the arena, and Superman had to defeat the fierce Draaga to stay alive. Mongul entered the battle and intended to kill Superman, until the Man of Steel was teleported out of harm's way by the enigmatic being known as the Cleric (*The Adventures of Superman* #454, April 1989; *Action Comics Annual* #2, 1989; *Superman* [second series] #32, June 1989). Displeased with his performance, the Overseers replaced Mongul with Draaga (*The Adventures of Superman* #455, June 1989).

Mongul was eventually found by the Cyborg Superman, who placed the would-be conqueror in his thrall, sending him to Earth in an attempt to transform the planet into a new Warworld. Mongul fought Green Lantern as he tried to turn Coast City into Engine City (*Action Comics* #689–691; *The Adventures of Superman* #503–504; *Green Lantern* [third series] #46—all October 1993; *Superman* [second series] #80–82; *Superman: The Man of Steel* #24–26—all August–October 1993). Mongul was imprisoned on the prison world of Takron-Galtos, only to break out during a riot. He also lost in battle with Green Lantern's successor Kyle Rayner (*Green Lantern* [third series] #51–53, May–July 1994). Once more, the conqueror was imprisoned, although he did manage to free himself again. He stole a spacecraft to escape, letting his fellow victims die in the vacuum of space. Mongul found a world ripe for conquest, although the sentient life chose death over living under his tyranny. He then returned to Earth, only to meet defeat at the hands of the third Flash (*Flash* #102, June 1995).

Mongul refused an entreaty by the demon Neron and was beaten to death for his effrontery. The demon collected Mongul's soul (*Underworld Unleashed* #1, November 1995).

It was quite a while before anyone heard from Mongul again, but this time it was his son who came crashing to Earth. He arrived to ask for the Man of Steel's help in order to defeat the threat of Imperiex (first unnamed appearance in *Showcase '95* #8, September 1995; first named appearance in *Superman* [second series] #151, December 1999). Superman reluctantly agreed, and the pair trained for the cosmic battle. Once Imperiex appeared defeated, Mongul turned on his partner seeking revenge in his father's honor, but Superman defeated him. Lobo then apprehended Mongul and collected the bounty on his head (*Superman* [second series] #153, February 2000).

Mongul escaped custody and brought his sister Mongal to Earth to demand a new fight. Together they beat Superman and nearly succeeding in killing him until Krypto the Super-Dog arrived to help. The Department of Extranormal Operations apprehended Mongul, while Mongal escaped using a Boom Tube (*Superman* [second series] #170, July 2001).

As the events of INFINITE CRISIS began, SUPERBOY-PRIME had destroyed the JLA's lunar-based Watchtower, and Mongul arrived seeking the spoils, only to find Superman, Batman, and Wonder Woman. Their fight was brief, and he escaped using a still-functioning JLA teleporter (*Infinite Crisis* #1, December 2005). He arrived on Earth and attacked Green Lantern Hal Jordan, unleashing a Black Mercy on both him and Green Arrow (*Green Lantern* [fourth series] #7–8, February–March 2006). They, too, beat the hypnotic effects of the plant; Mongul escaped yet again and killed his sister in a squabble.

Filled with rage, Mongul was ripe for receiving a yellow power ring and joined the Sinestro Corps (*Green Lantern Corps* #19, February 2008). He quickly acquired other yellow rings when their owners perished during the Sinestro War. He even managed to grab hold of a Green Lantern Corps ring, but still relied on his favored Black Mercy plants to subdue Corps members Arisia and the Daxamite Sodam Yat. These plants had been genetically altered to invoke a person's greatest nightmares instead of his or her dreams. Mongul then commanded his rings to send out countless plant seeds across the universe He was subsequently defeated by Bzzd, a member of the Corps, and sent crashing to the Black Mercy homeworld, buried in the soil to provide nutrients for the plants. Mongul freed himself at the cost of his left arm and sought escape aboard a passing spacecraft. He killed the pilot and his wife, and was then recruited to the Star Sapphire Corps.

He journeyed to DAXAM, which he took control over in order to make it the Sinestro Corps's base of operations. A fellow member, Arkillo, challenged him for leadership while Sinestro was in custody of the Guardians. Mongul defeated Arkillo, who challenged his leadership (*Green Lantern Corps* #31–33, February–April 2009). Sodam Yat brought fellow Lantern Arisia with him to free his people. His superpowers weakening under the red sun, he tapped into the cosmic energy from the Guardians, blasting Mongul into space. Yat then used the Ion power to alter Daxam's sun from red to yellow, empowering the entire populace. The citizens helped free the planet from the Sinestro Corps.

Mongul led the Corps to Korugar, homeworld to Sinestro, and—once he conquered the planet—renamed the Corps after himself (*Green Lantern Corps* #36–39, July–October 2009). However, Sinestro returned and used an override function in Mongul's power ring to depower it, allowing him to beat the usurper. After reclaiming his Yellow Corps, Sinestro imprisoned Mongul in the yellow Central Power Battery (*Green Lantern* [fourth series] #46, November 2009).

MONSTER LEAGUE OF EVIL, THE

In the multiverse prior to the CRISIS ON INFINITE EARTHS, countless worlds had their versions of the classic movie monsters, including Dracula, lord of the vampires, the Wolfman, the Mummy, and Frankenstein's monster. In CAPTAIN THUNDER's world, these creatures banded together as the Monster League of Evil and battled the hero across 1,953 parallel Earths until he finally trapped them in a limbo-like realm. They cursed the Captain before he departed, and when the curse finally took hold, it forced him to commit evil acts. By the end of the multiverse, it was believed that the League remained imprisoned (*Superman* [first series] #276, June 1974).

MOON, TANA

Hawaiian-born Tana Moon was raised and educated in the fiftieth state but traveled east seeking to begin her journalism career after college by scoring a job with METROPOLIS's *DAILY PLANET*. Editor in chief PERRY WHITE interviewed Moon but decided she was not quite ready for the prestigious paper. He did offer her a feature assignment just to see what she was capable of. Dejected, Moon was leaving the famed building when she met SUPERBOY. Grabbing him by the arm, she led him to television station WGBS and began to strike up a friendship. When she delivered the scoop on the latest celebrity, who thought at the time he might actually be the reincarnation of the then-deceased Superman, Tana was hired as a news anchor. She became a local celebrity in her own right after she reported on Superboy's battle with Steelhand (*The Adventures of Superman* #501, Late June 1993).

GBS president Vinnie Edge smelled ratings victory and saw to it that Moon never left Superboy's side. Seeking even higher ratings numbers, he then arranged for the Stinger to battle Superboy on film. The battle, however, destroyed the Hobsneck Bridge, and Tana realized it was all a setup. Later, she wanted to accompany Superboy and the Cyborg Superman when they flew to the West Coast to investigate the destruction of Coast City, but she was refused. She was reporting on the story when a missile from Coast, now rebuilt as Engine City, was fired at Metropolis. Superboy intercepted the weapon and seemingly died, causing Moon to break down on camera. When she realized he was still alive, she resigned from GBS, ashamed of her performance, and headed back to Hawaii (*The Adventures of Superman* #506, November 1993).

Shortly after finding work as a local television reporter, Tana was surprised to see Superboy also relocate to Hawaii. She was flattered when she learned her friendship was part of the reason he had done so (*Superboy* [third series] #1, February 1990). Despite feeling a romantic attraction to the teen, Moon tried to maintain a professional distance, which worked until Superboy was apparently enduring a cellular breakdown. She then finally admitted her feelings, which were reciprocated (*Superboy* [third series] #5, June 1990). When Superboy was cured, the two began a relationship.

The romance ended when Knockout arrived and sparked with the teenage Superboy. Tana investigated and learned the truth about Knockout, something Superboy refused to acknowledge until he couldn't ignore the facts any longer. After putting her in jail, Superboy renewed his romance with Tana. Not long after, she inadvertently provided Amanda Spence with information allowing the Agenda to abduct Superboy for a time (*Superboy* [third series] #32, October 1996, and #34–35, December 1995–January 1996). They infected Superboy, destabilizing his genetic code in an attempt to kill him. It took melding his DNA with that of Roxy Leech to save him, making them more like siblings and leaving Superboy all to Tana (*Superboy* [third series] #36, February 1997, and #38–41, April–July 1997). One result was that Superboy would permanently remain in the shape of a sixteen-year-old, subjecting the older Moon to ridicule and leading the couple to ultimately break up (*Superboy* [third series] #46, December 1997). She left both her job and Hawaii (*Superboy* [third series] #49, March 1998)—only to be kidnapped by the Agenda. She was rescued by the Wild Men, but as that mission came to an end, Spence murdered Tana in front of Superboy, devastating the young hero (*Superboy* [third series] #73–75, April–June 2000).

Tana was survived by her brother Kekane and his children Iolani and Li'l (*Superboy* [third series] #9, November 1994).

MOON, VINCE

As successful as Vince Moon was as a heist man and leader of a gang of criminals, he was nevertheless apprehended by Susan Semple and Superman while attempting to rob the House of Gems, a "fabulous exhibit of the Metropolis Jewelers' Association" (*Action Comics* #163, December 1951).

MOONMAN

Astronaut Brice Rogers was the first man to reach the moon in a single-man space capsule. En route, the capsule was bathed in the tail of a comet, which seemed to alter Rogers's physiology. When he returned to Earth, Rogers donned a costume to become Moonman, and used his newfound powers to commit a series of moon-themed crimes. With one hand he could attract objects, while the other hand emitted rays that repelled items. Rogers's mind was clouded by these changes, but when he realized what he had done, the astronaut

intended to turn himself in. He was kidnapped by harbor pirates before he could do so, however. They then forced him to commit crimes on their behalf. As his powers faded, Rogers managed to aid Batman, Robin, and Superman in arresting the pirates. The astronaut received amnesty for his Moonman crimes in return (*World's Finest Comics* #98, December 1958).

Unbeknownst to all, Rogers's space capsule retained its latent power. During an exhibit, moon rays were reflected off the capsule onto astronaut trainee Stacy Macklin. Affected the same way that Rogers was, the young woman developed a split personality and became Lady Lunar, wearing a variation of Moonman's costume until Superman and Batman intervened to stop her (*World's Finest Comics* #266, December 1980–January 1981).

MOORE, JUSTIN

Curly-haired cub reporter Justin Moore arrived at the *Daily Planet* with an impressive résumé and an ego to match (*Action Comics* #541, March 1983; *Superman* [first series] #383, May 1983). Always quick to give an opinion on everything—from his mentor Jimmy Olsen's fashion sense to Lois Lane's attitude to Clark Kent's repartee—Justin soon found himself nicknamed "Wonder Boy" by Perry White (*Action Comics* #562, December 1984). Much to Jimmy's annoyance, the young man was also more skeptical of Superman's motivations and performance than the rest of the *Planet* staff (*Action Comics* #551, January 1984). Justin's opinion changed after he befriended a man he believed was an amnesiac Superman but who turned out to be a time-traveling mental patient from whom the real Man of Steel saved him (*Superman* [first series] #402, December 1984).

MOORE, TIM

On numerous occasions, Lex Luthor found Timothy "Tim" Moore a useful and loyal underling who would commit criminal acts on Luthor's behalf. Moore was usually supported by fellow criminals Ted Grand and Nat Tryon, becoming known to Metropolis police as the TNT Trio. None of their criminal activities were supposed to lead back to Luthor, allowing him to execute his schemes to rid the world of Superman. Later, Tryon was transformed into the villain called Neutron (*Action Comics* #525, November 1981).

MORANS, MOOSE

Moose Morans styled himself as one of America's three greatest criminals, along with Silky Steve and Sparkles Garnet. While all three were in Gotham City for an underworld crime conference, they chose to show off by committing crimes in the very home of Batman and Robin. At that time, a bizarre accident had left Batman's physiology altered so he was susceptible to kryptonite—a problem exacerbated when a piece of red kryptonite inflicted further changes to his body. Despite Batman having an elongated body and emitting green-hued heat vision blasts, the Dynamic Duo and Superman apprehended all three criminals with ease (*World's Finest Comics* #128, September 1962).

MORDO

Known as the Kryptonian god of strength, the four-armed deity was honored with a statue kept on display in the bottle city of Kandor (*Action Comics* #299, April 1963).

MORGU

Superman was once exiled to Morgu, dubbed the "executioner's planet," by the Anti-Superman Gang after they dusted his costume with a strain of red kryptonite that removed his superpowers. Superman used his training and experience to inspire the planet's slave population, who had been waiting for a predicted savior. Calling him "Supro," the slaves revolted and won their freedom. After forty-eight hours, Superman regained his powers and returned home to Earth (*Superman* [first series] #229, August 1970).

MORTON, HAROLD

Harold Morton was a popular psychiatrist and Metropolis radio personality who abused people's faith in him when he used his complex "ultra high-frequency" radio equipment to hypnotize the slumbering populace to commit crimes on his behalf. Upon awakening, they had no recollection of their deeds until Superman intervened and exposed the scheme. The Man of Steel turned the tables on Morton and hypnotized him into making a public confession of criminal acts (*Action Comics* #38, July 1949).

MORTON, JOHN

Posing as a scientist, criminal leader John Morton announced he had invented a "new petrifying gas that turned living flesh to solid stone." His goal was to extort one million dollars from the city of Metropolis by threatening to turn its citizens into life-like stone statues. Superman exposed the gas as fraudulent, however, and apprehended Morton and his cohorts (*Action Comics* #135, August 1949).

MORWATHA

Chief Hun-sha was an old man venerated by his tribe, but he was targeted for death by Morwatha, a shaman who desired to become chief himself. Morwatha's efforts were thwarted thanks to the intervention of Superman. The chief stripped the shaman of his title and declared he would henceforth "become the lowliest of our tribe, and women and children will use [him] for their laughter!" (*Action Comics* #200, January 1955).

MOTHER BOX

A Mother Box was an artificial intelligence in compact form that was developed on Apokolips by Himon and became an essential tool both there and on New Genesis. Through the use of Element X, the super-computer effectively became a self-aware device that bonded with its owner in mysterious ways and performed seemingly miraculous functions. Mother Boxes were able to open Boom Tubes (connecting two locations for instantaneous transportation), heal bodily injury, and even calm the rage that fueled Orion and transform his angry visage into a placid and handsome one (*New Gods* #1, February–March 1971).

Mother Boxes appeared to draw their energies from the Source itself, making them among the most powerful constructs in the known universe. They were witnessed altering gravity and a person's mental state and interfacing with other electronic devices. Even Himon was at a loss to fully understand what he had invented. In time, others learned to manufacture Mother Boxes, and each one was unique, in some ways resembling the builder or its recipient. To build a Mother Box required intensive training, and not every Mother Box that was built functioned.

The enigmatic Metron once said the Mother Boxes had "a mystical rapport with nature." When a box's owner died, the computer self-destructed. Boxes even sacrificed their existences in the name of causes they cared about.

Mother Boxes were generally the size of a deck of cards but could also be larger in appearance, as witnessed in the one used by the Forever People. Mister Miracle's Mother Box had its circuitry wired into the full face mask he wore.

When Superman sought Doomsday, the New Gods gave him a Mother Box, a rare gift to anyone beyond the Fourth World (*Superman/Doomsday: Hunter/Prey* #1, 1994).

Despite being bonded to their owners, Mother Boxes could be removed and used by others, such as when Steel used Orion's Mother Box to block a telepathic probe on the planet Rann. Orion also loaned a Mother Box to the original Starman to aid his spacecraft in tracing the galactic whereabouts of his son, the current Starman (*Starman* [second series] #48, December 1998). That particular one was destroyed when it was hit by missile fire from Throneworld.

In the wake of Infinity-Man bringing about the end of the Fourth World and preparing for the Fifth, it was stated just one Mother Box remained; this was possessed by Shilo Norman, the new Mister Miracle (*Seven Soldiers: Mister Miracle* miniseries #1, November 2005). He called it a "motherboxxx."

There have been variant designs introduced, including a Father Box, which was given to Orion by Mortalla in an attempt, on Darkseid's behalf, to manipulate Orion's action to further his father's goals of cosmic domination (*Orion* #8–11 January–April 2001, and #18–19, November–December 2001). It was later referred to as one of the "Seven Treasures" the New Gods bequeathed to Earth's first super hero. This particular one was shaped as a pair of dice and was called "the Foundation Stone of Manhattan" (*Seven Soldiers of Victory: Guardian* #1, May 2005) and "Croatoan" (*Seven Soldiers of Victory: Klarion the Witch Boy* #1, June 2005). Klarion the Witch Boy stole this device and placed it somewhere in the future. A different Father Box was employed by the villain Doctor Impossible to access "hush tubes" (*Justice League of America* [second series] #1, October 2006).

Something called an Orphan Box was created by the villainous Father Time, built from the shards of Gonzo the Mechanical Bastard (*Uncle Sam and the Freedom Fighters* #1, September 2006).

MOUNTAIN OF JUDGMENT, THE

The genetic creations known as the Hairies traveled the world in a huge, multi-wheeled vehicle shaped to resemble a green monster, which they called the Mountain of Judgment. Superman thought it resembled "a giant missile carrier, converted by the Hairies to frighten intruders" (*Superman's Pal, Jimmy Olsen* #134, November 1970). The Mountain of Judgment also existed in the reality formed after the Crisis on Infinite Earths (*Superman* [second series] *Annual* #2, 1988; others).

MOXBY, BLINKY

The criminal Moxby feared retribution from his Metropolis underworld compatriots if he gave testimony that would link gangster Mike Chandler with a recent murder. When Superman faked his own death, he posed as a ghost to convince the cowardly, "shifty-eyed little sneak-thief" into giving up his knowledge in public, sealing Chandler's conviction (*Superman* [first series] #21, March–April 1943).

MOXIE, BOSS

Moxie Mannheim, known to all as Boss Moxie, was the father of Intergang's Bruno "Ugly" Mannheim (*Guardians of Metropolis* #1, November 1994). When

he was released after serving a lengthy prison term for his many crimes throughout Metropolis, Mannheim made a deal with Project Cadmus's Dabney Donovan to have superpowers grafted onto himself and cloned members of his old gang. Using Vincent Edge to call a meeting, Mannheim and his gang slaughtered the attendees, then took over Intergang (*The Adventures of Superman* #544, March 1997). At the time, the public believed Jimmy Olsen knew Superman's secret identity, and agents were dispatched in search of the reporter so that they, too, could learn the hero's true name (*The Adventures of Superman* #549, August 1997). They failed to achieve this, and later when Lex Luthor managed to briefly gain control of Intergang, he retained Boss Moxie as a figurehead leader (*The Adventures of Superman* #552, November 1997). However, thanks to the machinations of rival Frank Sixty, Boss Moxie wound up captured by Superman and sent to prison (*Action Comics* #758, October 1999).

MOXIMUS

Professor Lewis Lang unearthed and accidentally restored to life the magician Moximus during a dig in Pompeii. Moximus decided to seek revenge against a world that had allowed his precious city to burn by gaining mystic control over the Man of Steel and using him as a means to demolish Metropolis. Superman broke free from the spell, but Moximus vanished before he could be apprehended and remained at large until Earth-1 vanished during the Crisis on Infinite Earths; he has not reappeared in the chronicles. When last seen, he was contemplating an encounter with the Batman (*Superman* [first series] #343, January 1980).

MOYERS, TOM

Dr. Thomas Moyers worked at S.T.A.R. Labs and was responsible for the lab accident that turned Kitty Faulkner into the hulking Rampage (*Superman* [second series] #7, July 1987). Protected from prosecution by shadowy government figures Sarge Steel and Amanda Waller, Moyers was assigned to develop a super-agent. Instead, his experiments transformed a test chimp into the rampaging Titano and proved a public relations

disaster (*Superman* [second series] *Annual* #1, 1987). He felt little remorse for the incidents and continued to plague Faulkner, going so far as to manipulate Rampage into taking out a presidential candidate (*Superman* [second series] #24, December 1988).

MR. MXYZPTLK

Hailing from the Fifth Dimensional world of Zrfff, the imp known as Mr. Mxyzptlk (pronounced *MIX-yez-Pitel-ik*) grew bored with life on his planet and came to Earth seeking new ways to cause mischief. By speaking his name backward—"Kltpzyxm" (pronounced *kel-tipz-yex-im*)—he would be banished to his home realm for ninety days. The magical being had an Earth-2 counterpart known as Mr. Mxyztplk, who also plagued that universe's Man of Steel.

On Earth-1, the battle of wits between Kal-El and Mxy began years earlier when young Master

Mxyzptlk defied his parents Fuzastl and Tlndsa for punishing him by traveling to Earth and tormenting the Teen of Steel (*Superboy* [first series] #78, January 1960). Taking a certain proprietary interest in Superboy, the imp went so far as to interfere with villains such as the Kryptonite Kid (*Superboy* [first series] #83, September 1960) and Lex Luthor (*Superboy* [first series] #131, July 1966) when it appeared that they might achieve the victory he'd been denied. Possessed of a shock of red hair, Master Mxyzptlk was left bald on the top of his head after an encounter with the Legion of Super-Heroes member Mon-El (*Adventure Comics* #351, December 1966). If anything, their encounters helped Superboy sharpen his reasoning skills, as he was eventually able to detect the magic Mxy used and devised ways to trick the menace into saying his name backward—the only surefire way to send Mxyzptlk back to his dimension.

As adults, Mxyzptlk and Superman sparred whenever the imp arrived to instigate a prank or complicated scheme; the Man of Steel was forced to end the problem and send the magician home, which was always complicated by Superman's vulnerability to magic. To protect himself, Mxy took to carrying an alarm in his hat to warn him when he began to say his name backward (*Superman* [first series] #131, August 1959). When that failed, he tried to remain underwater so that he would not hear or speak (*Superman* [first series] #154, July 1962). He once legally changed his name to John Trix so that saying "Kltpzyxm" had no effect on him (*Superman* [first series] #148, October 1961). This ultimately proved no more successful than his youthful notion to dub himself *Mxypyxm,* a palindrome that theoretically should have made him impossible to banish (*Superboy* [first series] #120, April 1965).

Mxy's pranks and stunts often altered Superman's physiognomy or the world as he knew it. Mxyzptlk was known to animate buildings, change time, and even charm the Man of Steel so that whatever Superman said came true. He even once switched the genders of Superman's friends at the *Daily Planet,* which caused much confusion (*Superman* [first series] #349, July 1980).

Mxy sometimes went to extremes in his machinations, once in order to win his world's Brxll Award, given by the Academy of Practical Joking for the best practical joke of the year. He even once used a childhood gas to turn the adults of Metropolis back into children (*Superman* [first series] #154, July 1962).

The vain and egotistical Mxy also found himself easily falling in love with human women, none of whom reciprocated his feelings. His Earth-2 counterpart pursued model Larissa Lee (*Superman* [first series] #62, January–February 1950) even as he was chasing after Lucy Lane. By contrast, he tended to ignore his more plain Fifth Dimensional girlfriend Miss Gzptlsnz (*Superman's Pal, Jimmy Olsen* #52 April 1961). Falling in love with the beautiful Miss Bgbznz, Mxyzptlk found their wedding indefinitely postponed when he was exiled to Earth by the Zrfff government for excessive mischief. In a rare reversal, the imp actually wanted to *return* to Zrfff, and he prevailed on Superman to help him atone for his misconduct so that he could do so quickly. He succeeded, but once their wedding vows were completed Mxy learned that his new wife had magically disguised her features and was far from the beauty he'd believed her to be (*Superman* [first series] #335, May 1979).

Mxyzptlk was truly never malevolent and rarely teamed up with other villains, but he did respond to a summons from the dangerous Mr. Xavier (*Superman* [first series] #299, May 1976). He also sparred several times with Bat-Mite, a similar magical being who caused trouble out of his misguided devotion to Batman (*World's Finest Comics* #113, November 1960; *World's Finest Comics* #123, February 1962; *World's Finest Comics* #152, September 1965; *World's Finest Comics* #169, September 1967). Once he crossed dimensional barriers to join with Mister Mind, the Venusian worm out to conquer the world of Earth-S, until they were stopped by that planet's champion Captain Marvel and Earth-1's Superman (*DC Comics Presents* #33–34, May–June 1981).

Two separate potential futures predicted different fates for Mxyzptlk. In one, he married both Miss Gzptlsnz and Miss Bgbznz, and fathered a son named Kytszbtn with the latter. Imprisoned on Zrfff for bigamy, he accepted an offer from Aethyr the Oversoul to play host to the entity. Mxyzptlk proved more powerful than Aethyr, however, and used the limitless power of his now crystal brain to terrorize Superman in Metropolis before returning to the Fifth Dimension to unleash more carnage (*DC Comics Presents* #97, September 1986).

In another possible future, Mxyzptlk explained to Clark Kent that being immortal had certain pitfalls, starting with the relentless boredom. To kill time, Mxy spent his first two thousand years without moving, the next two thousand years doing only good deeds, and the following two thousand years being the mischievous character that Superman knew and dealt with. Time passed, and Mxyzptlk now wanted to try being evil for the next two thousand years. He began his new career by essentially doing away with the World's Greatest Super Hero, along with his friends and foes. "Did you honestly believe a fifth-dimensional sorcerer would resemble a funny little man in a derby hat?" he sneered. Superman sent him to the Phantom Zone at the same instant the arrogant ass said his name backward to return home. The resulting forces tore the imp in two (*Action Comics* #583, September 1986).

Much as Brainiac's descendant joined the thirtieth-century Legion of Super-Heroes as Brainiac 5, a future member of Mxyzptlk's family joined the adult version of the Legion of Super-Heroes (*Adventure Comics* #355, April 1967). In doing so, this latter-day Mxyzptlk performed his penance for his murderous sibling who'd attacked the Legion while they were still teens (*Adventure Comics* #310, July 1963). Still farther in the future, the sixtieth Mxyzptlk once traveled to the past in an effort to torment Supergirl on the anniversary of his forebear's birth (*Action Comics* #362, April 1968). Alternately, possible descendants of Mxyzptlk have been documented, acting under the names of the legendary trickster Loki (*Superman's Pal, Jimmy Olsen* #55, September 1961) and the Egyptian mage Ramses (*Adventure Comics* #291, December 1961).

The Crisis on Infinite Earths altered all reality, including the diverse dimensions. Mxyzptlk did not plague Superboy, since now Clark Kent did not don a costumed persona until he was an adult in Metropolis. This Mxyzptlk was equally magical and egotistical, although his pranks had a crueler edge to them, and needling the Man of Steel became too much fun for Mxyzptlk to ignore.

He first arrived in Metropolis seeking some fun and relief from his boredom (*Superman* [second series] #11, November 1987) but was eventually noticed by Lex Luthor, who taught the imp to be cruel, which added an edge to the psychological games Mxyzptlk played with the Man of Steel (*Superman* [second series] #31, May 1989). He once turned normal kryptonite into a red version that had unpredictable and often disastrous effects on Superman (*The Adventures of Superman* #463, February 1990). It first took away the Man of Steel's powers, although this effect would disappear should Luthor ever reveal where the red kryptonite came from. Eventually Luthor did reveal the truth to Clark Kent, figuring the news would get back to Superman so that the spell was still safe. However, since Kent and Superman were the same being, the ploy failed. Superman regained his powers and banished the imp back to his own dimension (*Superman* [second series] #49–50, November–December 1990).

On another visit to Earth, Mxyzptlk claimed that he was a researcher who used his magical abilities to time-travel and was accidentally brought to Earth by a group of computer-based occultists. While stuck on Earth, Mxy decided to study its customs, beginning with Halloween as practiced by the citizens of Happy Harbor, Rhode Island. His fieldwork included turning some of the town's teenagers into adults while causing some of the other teens to frantically dance out of control. Mxyzptlk was confronted by Young Justice, with Superboy recognizing the imp and calling him by name. Mxyzptlk did not recognize the name, however, which led Robin to conclude that the imp was visiting Earth from a point in the past before he first encountered Superman. Hearing what Mxyzptlk was to become, the serious magical being rejected that destiny and prepared to cast a spell that spelled doom for the world. Robin, Impulse, and the Clone of Steel had to convince the being that he needed to embrace his wacky destiny (*Young Justice* #3, December 1998).

At one point, Mxyzptlk mentioned that he'd always had a compulsion to perform before the public and implied that Superman was not his first victim, although whom else he may have bedeviled has not yet been chronicled. Mxyzptlk also claimed to have gone by the names of the deities Loki, Coyote, and Anansi (*Countdown to Final Crisis* #23, November 21, 2007) and changed his appearance in each reality he traveled to, such as when he tormented a team of heroes not unlike Earth-12's Kookie Quartet (*Superman* [second series] #50, December 1990).

It was later learned that the various imps who visited Earth's champions—Johnny Thunder's Thunderbolt and Aquaman's Qwsp—all hailed from the world of Zrfff. The adventure involved the full Justice League of America and Justice Society of America to prevent a vengeful Qwsp from destroying Earth (*JLA* #31, July 1999). While Mxyzptlk did not participate in the adventure, his quinto-partner Miss Gsptlsnz turned up instead. Mxy also had a Fifth Dimensional version of a goldfish named Superman (*Countdown to Final Crisis* #31, September 26, 2007).

The gags pulled by Mxyzptlk in this reality usually were larger in scale than his Earth-1 predecessor, such as the time he forced a race between the Man of Steel and the World's Fastest Man, the Flash (*The Adventures of Superman* #463, February 1990). When he wanted to better understand what Superman experienced by dying, Mxyzptlk conjured up "Bada-Bing-Bada-Boomsday" to re-create the deadly struggle between Superman and Doomsday. Mxyzptlk sacrificed himself to stop the creation but came back to life within a minute, still uncertain what the fuss over Superman's death was all about (*Superman: The Man of Steel* #75, January 1998).

Unfortunately, this Mxyzptlk allowed himself to be conned by the greatest and deadliest prankster of them all. He was talked into granting the Joker a fraction of his power, but somehow 99 percent of his magical energy was taken by the Clown Prince of Crime when he learned Mxyzptlk's true name, and the world was quickly turned inside out (*Superman: Emperor Joker* #1, October 2000). Superman, Batman, and their friends all suffered under the Harlequin of Hate's whims until they finally learned from Mxyzptlk what had happened. Superman realized that the Joker, despite his vast powers, could not eradicate the Dark Knight from reality. He used that to shatter the Joker's confidence and restore balance to Earth, although several creations were saved by Mxyzptlk for use in the future, including Scorch, Gorgeous Gilly, Ignition, and a new version of Bizarro (*Action Comics* #770, October 2000).

Mxyzptlk later arrived in the form of powerful twins to vex the Man of Steel (*The Adventures of Superman* #617–618, August–September 2003), but when he turned himself back to his normal form, he also warned of dark events in Superman's future (*The Adventures of Superman* #630, September 2004). This incarnation of Mxyzptlk seemed sympathetic to the Man of Steel and actually saw his role as teaching Superman how to find the joy in life (*The Adventures of Superman* #638, May 2005). He even recovered the last of his magic possessed by the Joker as part of a scenario meant to help the World's Finest team prepare for the forthcoming events known as Infinite Crisis (*Superman/Batman* #25, May 2006).

When the Spectre set out to remove all magic from New Earth, Mxyzptlk found himself powerless during his next visit, resulting in his becoming a homeless man in Metropolis. Superman came upon the imp and tried to help him before being attacked by Ruin. Mxyzptlk inserted himself between a kryptonite spear and the Man of Steel, then vanished upon impact (*The Adventures of Superman* #646, January 2006).

Mxyzptlk was subsequently taken from his world by Superboy-Prime (*Countdown to Final Crisis* #31, September 26, 2007) and imprisoned in the Source Wall. Enduring agonizing and cruel torture, Mxyzptlk refused to relinquish his magical powers to the madman. Instead, he was rescued by Earth-3's Annataz Arataz, the counterpart to Zatanna Zatara (*Countdown to Final Crisis* #23, November 21, 2007). Returning to Zrfff, Mxy told his girlfriend that they needed to permanently seal the dimensional portal to Earth (*Countdown to Final Crisis* #22, November 28, 2007).

There have been other-dimensional counterparts to Mxyzptlk, such as Earth-2's Mxyztplk and Earth-3's Mixyezpitellik (*The Brave and the Bold* [third series] #11, May 2008). When he first encountered Superman and Earth-3's Ultraman, Mixyezpitellik claimed that he also came from Zrfff and disliked his New Earth counterpart. This version was nattily dressed with umbrella and fedora, and noted that he was a "vowelled Knight of Order" without further explaining what the ranking meant. There was also a typically reversed version of Mxyzptlk on the Bizarro World. Known as Kltpzyxm, he labored ceaselessly to fix all the imperfections of the square planet (*Adventure Comics* #286, July 1961; others). In the 853rd century, Super-Mite, a heroic descendant of Mxyzptlk, played a role in uniting that era's Superman and Batman as the System's Finest team (*DC One Million 80-Page Giant,* August 1999).

MR. MXYZTPLK

On Earth-2, Superman was plagued for many years by Mr. Mxyztplk (pronounced *mux-IZT-pulk*), a magical imp hailing from the Fifth Dimension (*Superman* [first series] #30, September–October 1944). He arrived on Earth seeking fun and excitement and discovered the Man of Steel. He quickly decided that Superman was the perfect target for his pranks. In time, Superman learned that by tricking the purple-derby-wearing trickster into saying his name backward—"Klptzyxm" (pronounced *KULPT-zix-im*)—he would be transported back to his homeworld of Zrfff for a minimum of a month, although more often it was ninety days. It was also discovered that anyone else saying the word would also be taken to the Fifth Dimension. When Lois Lane found herself on Zrfff, she eventually discovered that saying "Qrdmlzf" would return her and anyone else to Earth (*Superman* [first series] #33, March–April 1945; *Superman Family* #208, July 1981).

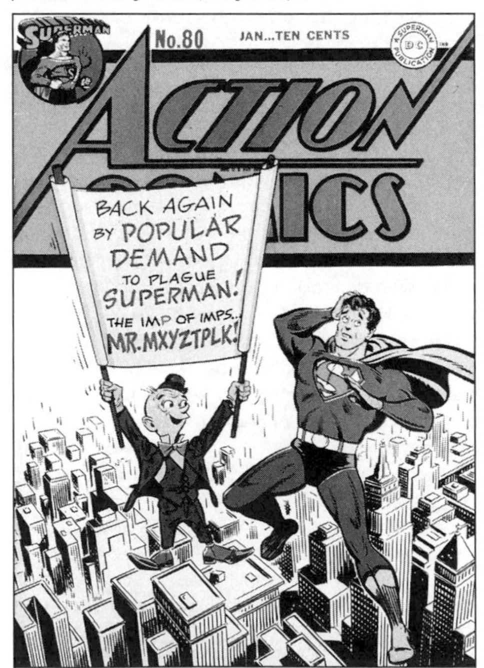

Upon first meeting the Man of Tomorrow, Mxyztplk introduced himself as a professional court jester, and after "poking his nose into the secret volumes of a brilliant scholar" (he was depicted holding a book titled *Mxyztplkology*) Mxyztplk learned "two magic words, one of which would transport him to this dimension and the other word if spoken aloud would return him to his world for a time." It was clear that this version of Zrfff was a monarchy, complete with a king, Brpxz (*Superman* [first series] #33, March–April 1945). Mxyztplk at first declared his intention of conquering Earth but decided needling Superman would be more satisfying.

The small bald man in a purple suit, green bow tie, and purple derby played pranks that were mostly harmless and easily undone, such as the time he made Metropolis's mayor speak "like a jackass," or when he posed as the legendary genie from the magic lamp, granting pedestrians their heart's desire (*Action Comics* #102, November 1946). He even placed himself with the Carlton University student body in an attempt to use his abilities to help their baseball team win the championship, forcing rival Bedlum University to sign Superman as a one-man team to even things out (*Superman* [first series] #46, May–June 1947).

Mxyztplk once partnered with Lois's niece Susie Tompkins, so that whenever she told a lie, he made it a reality—a floating opera, for instance (*Superman* [first series] #40, May–June 1946).

There were occasions, however, when Mxyztplk's stunts placed innocents in danger, such as the time he had an elevated subway jump the tracks (*Action Comics* #80, January 1945). On another visit, he worked alongside Lex Luthor and the Prankster to make a fool out of the World's Greatest Super Hero by using magically generated proxies for Superman's friends (*Action Comics* #151, December 1950). When he learned that any humans saying their name backward could be sent to the Eighth Dimension for twenty-four hours, he tried it with success on Lois Lane, then tried to trick the Man of Steel into saying "Namrepus." He failed, however, and was actually tricked by Superman into returning home (*Action Comics* #208, September 1955).

Mxyztplk was vain and egotistical and unable to stand any form of ridicule, which often got the best of him, and Superman repeatedly used this to his advantage (*Action Comics* #208, September 1955).

There have been other-dimensional counterparts to Mxyztplk, such as Earth-1/New Earth's Mr. Mxyzptlk and Earth-3's Mixyezpitellik (*The Brave and the Bold* [third series] #11, May 2008). When he first encountered Superman and Earth-3's Ultraman, Mixyezpitellik also claimed that he came from Zrfff and disliked his New Earth counterpart.

MUDGE

A demonic underling to Lord Satanus, Mudge fought the Man of Steel on numerous occasions but was always defeated (*The Adventures of Superman* #584, November 2000, and #586–587, January–February 2001).

MUHAMMAD X

Muhammad X was a major civil rights activist who claimed he was Harlem's protector. He also possessed the ability to control an object's density as well as manipulate gravity (*Superman* [second series] #179, August 2002). When Superman encountered him in Manhattan, Muhammad X took the opportunity to accuse the hero of neglecting the plight of the black man. Shaken, Superman sought advice from his wife Lois Lane, in addition to Natasha Irons. It was John Henry Irons's niece who pointed out the black community had champions of their own, including Rush & Silence, Stoneyard, and Underground.

In the end, Superman returned to confront Muhammad X and explained that skin color had nothing to do with his actions. Since birth, all he wanted to do was be the best human being he could be, something he hoped everyone strived to be.

MULE, MORDECAI

A New York furrier, Mordecai Mule was also leader of an international poaching ring that was broken up by Superman, aided by model-turned-heroine Vixen (*Action Comics* #521, July 1981).

MULLOY, MARK

Mark Mulloy possessed the gift to verbally convince people of his sincerity, thereby becoming a very successful swindler. When Superman extracted gold ore and a fossil from an area fifty miles beneath Mulloy's property without asking Mulloy's permission, the con man exacted a promise from the Man of Steel to fulfill seven of his wishes. Superman outwitted the greedy Mulloy when each wish attempted to use Superman's services for self-enrichment. Mulloy was finally taken into custody by Baldy, the elderly caretaker of Mulloy's property and a longtime admirer of the World's Greatest Super Hero (*Superman* [first series] #130, July 1959).

MUMSEN

Mumsen was the would-be dictator of San Caluma who diverted food from the tiny country's starving populace, holding them for ransom until they named him leader. When Superman arrived to stop the plot, Mumsen detonated a bomb intended to destroy the Man of Steel—but wound up destroyed himself in the process (*Superman* [first series] #6, September–October 1940).

MUNSDORF, BARON

Professor Hunter, an American, developed a powerful new "anaesthetic gas" that became the object of desire for Baron Munsdorf and his fellow spies. They kidnapped the professor and used murder, terror, and torture to force the courageous inventor to relinquish the formula, which was said to be able to put an entire community instantly to sleep. Superman intervened, but when he tried to apprehend the Baron, Munsdorf fired a "deadly sub-atomic death-ray gun." The blast then ricocheted off the Man of Steel's chest, killing Munsdorf by accident (*Action Comics* #31, December 1940).

MUNSTER, VIC

The Rainbow Raider was a costumed thief capable of hypnotically forcing any of his victims into submission. Jewel thief Vic Munster came out of hiding in an attempt to recruit the Raider to his side, only to learn that the masked man had actually been a lure to draw *him* out. Unknown to all, Superboy's secret ally had been his father Jonathan Kent disguised as the Raider (*Superboy* [first series] #84, October 1960). Smarting from his defeat, Munster resolved to take the Rainbow Raider alias as his own upon his release from prison. His plan to plunder Smallville's Mystery-Costume Charity Ball was complicated by Martha Kent's decision to also wear the original Raider costume as a prank, but the thief was still thwarted by the Teen of Steel (*Superboy* [first series] #164, April 1970). He is not to be confused with the powered Rainbow Raider who battled the Flash on numerous occasions.

MUR

Mur was a Kryptonian solider living in Kandor when the Kryptonian city was stolen by Brainiac. The Coluan villain reduced the city and its populace in size, adding their collective knowledge to his database. Later, when Brainiac arrived on Earth, he was defeated by Superman, and Kandor was returned to its proper size (*Action Comics* #871, January 2009).

Mur served under Commander Gor and fol-

lowed the orders stemming from Alura In-Ze. One of her first orders was to send Mur and others to Stryker's Island Penitentiary to gain possession of Superman's troublesome villains, as they presented a potential threat to Kandor's citizens as well. Metropolis's Science Police arrived at that point, and during the fight, several of the humans died at Mur's hands. Superman assured the government that Mur and the others would be held accountable, but Alura refused to turn the men over to the authorities.

Members of the Justice League of America and Justice Society of America arrived in Kandor to ensure that the men were turned over, resulting in a fight in which Mur participated. He remained free and joined his fellow Kandorians when the city was relocated to the newly constructed planet of New Krypton. He continued to serve in the Kryptonian military.

MYSTERY MARAUDER, THE

Attacked by an extraterrestrial villain named Intellex who coveted his Kryptonian brain, Superman realized that he needed help and seemed to find it in the form of the Mystery Marauder. His face hidden behind an emerald helmet, the green-costumed crusader mirrored the Man of Steel's own abilities, but Intellex ultimately prevailed against their combined might. Hypnotizing the marauder into defeating Superman, the Brain Bandit then took both to his spacecraft. With his focus on extracting his prey's brain, Intellex was astonished when the Marauder suddenly restrained him at super-speed and unmasked himself as the genuine Man of Steel. "Superman" had actually been actor Gregory Reed, who served as a decoy so that the villain would be caught unaware by the Mystery Marauder (*Superman* [first series] #396, June 1984).

NADOR

Attempting to join an intergalactic organization of heroes, the alien Nador came to Earth to prove his worth by besting the World's Greatest Super Hero. Nador began using his ability to create ghost-like images of Superman's most dangerous foes, including the Composite Superman, Metallo, and Zha-Vam. The Man of Steel was the only one able to see them, while everyone else thought he was losing his grip on reality. Eventually Superman deduced the truth and bested Nador (*Superman* [first series] #214, February 1969).

NAM-EK

Some five hundred years prior to Krypton's destruction, the scientist Nam-Ek sought immortality. He used the horns of the sacred Rondors, native beasts whose horns had known restorative powers, to create a serum prolonging his life. After ingesting this serum, Nam-Ek gained immortality—but at the price of his appearance, for he soon devolved into a foul-smelling, purple-skinned monstrosity. He was exiled to the Phantom Zone (*Superman* [first series] #282, December 1974). The insane Nam-Ek was eventually rescued by the evil Amalak and pitted against Superman, who placed his unstable foe within the Phantom Zone (*Superman* [first series] #311–315, May–September 1977).

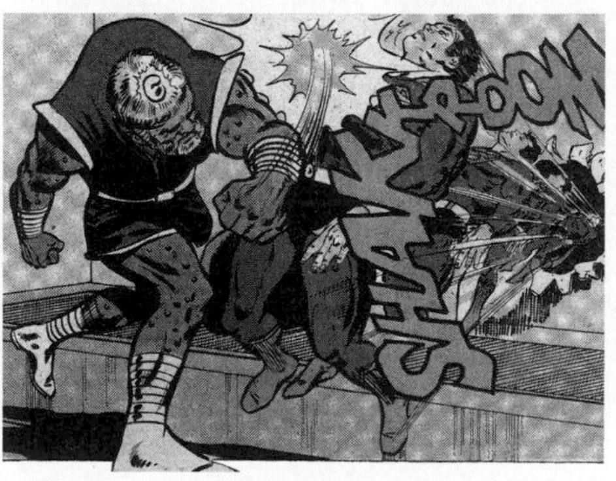

NAPKAN

A small country on Earth-2 called Napkan attempted to drag America into the Second World War by attacking the Pacific Ocean and fomenting rebellion in other parts of the world. Secretary of the Navy Hank Fox explained that the nation had "been acting increasingly war-like lately. There is every chance that against our will we may some day be engaged in warfare with [Napkan]. Its agents here, we believe, are conducting sabotage in order for us to be in poor condition for war, should that day come."

As a result, Superman became involved and thwarted an attempt by Napkan saboteurs to cause the sinking of a newly christened American battleship; foiled an attempt by the pro-Napkan Black Circle Society, headed by the Napkan consul Utsum, to overthrow the government of the South American country of Equaru; invaded the Napkan embassy in Metropolis to apprehend Ambassador Hokopoko and a group of his underlings after they staged an attempt on the life of Clark Kent; and thwarted an attempt by a Napkan suicide crew aboard the Napkan liner *Sunyat* to destroy the Panama Canal by blowing up their vessel as it passed through the locks.

"How fortunate we are here in America," remarked Secretary Fox, "to have someone of Superman's calibre to aid us! In my opinion, he's worth several armies and navies!" (*Superman* [first series] #15, March–April 1942).

NASSUR, DAVOOD

Qurac-born Davood Nassur gained telepathic powers in the wake of the Domonion-led invasion of Earth and used them on occasion as the hero named Sinbad.

NASTY

The daughter of Lex Luthor's older sister (*Adventure Comics* #401, January 1971), Nasthalthia shared her uncle's enmity for caped Kryptonians, although her focus was solely on Supergirl. Enrolling at Stanhope College, the woman nicknamed "Nasty" was under orders from her uncle Lex to determine the Maid of Might's true identity (*Adventure Comics* #397, September 1970). On their graduation day, Nasty began to suspect that Linda Danvers might secretly be Supergirl.

Consequently, when Linda Danvers moved to San Francisco for a job on a TV camera crew, Nasty made a point of being hired to work alongside her (*Adventure Comics* #406, May 1971). Although she never found the definitive evidence she hoped for, Lex's niece took great satisfaction in harassing her co-worker at every opportunity and was a prime factor in Linda ultimately quitting the job (*Adventure Comics* #424, October 1972).

NATIONAL WHISPER, THE

A national edition of the popular Metropolis daily tabloid, the *National Whisper* was a smash success in a country that could not get enough gossip about politicians, celebrities, and super heroes. Its pursuit of sales put the *Whisper* on a collision course with the Man of Steel's ire on more than one occasion.

Headlines blared "Princess Diana: Superman's Secret Love" (*Swamp Thing* [second series] #68, January 1988) or "Superman Helped Luthor Fake Death, Says Expert" (*Action Comics* #668, August 1991), and the editors' defense was that their job was to sell papers, just like any other publication.

While popular at the grocery checkout line, it was not at all a respected publication (*National Whisper,* 1993). The paper was owned by the McMannus Group, an Australian conglomerate (*Superman: The Man of Steel* #83, September 1998).

NA-TSE

Superman once crossed a wooden bridge nicknamed "the bridge that mocks time" and found himself in ancient Egypt. There he encountered Na-Tse, the high priest in the court of the pharaoh Cheops. The Man of Steel discovered that the priest planned to betray Egypt into the hands of the Assyrians and exposed the plot. While in the twenty-sixth century BC, the hero persuaded the pharaoh to free his slaves as he also helped defeat an advancing Assyrian army. Superman then single-handedly completed well over half the work on Cheops's Great Pyramid. Na-Tse sought revenge against the Man of Steel, but when arrows fired by disloyal guards bounced off Superman's chest, one hit the priest, killing him instantly (*World's Finest Comics* #32, January–February 1948).

NEAL, ALICE

Upon inheriting a million dollars from a recently deceased distant relative, Alice Neal decided to leave her rural life behind and move to Metropolis in the wild hope of becoming an overnight success as an actress. Thanks to Superman's intervention, the attractive blonde was taught that money not only doesn't buy happiness, but doesn't make gaining acceptance on the stage any easier, either (*Superman* [first series] #41, July–August 1946).

NEGATIVE SUPERBOY, THE

While traveling in deep space, the Teen of Steel once battled a mammoth energy creature, ultimately destroying it. Upon its death, the energy manifested itself as a negative, corrupt image of Superboy. This Negative Superboy managed to arrive on Earth prior to the real Superboy's return, so the Teen of Steel was stunned when everyone in Smallville, from his foster parents to its citizenry, seemingly embraced his negative counterpart as his replacement. Superboy subsequently learned that the evil form had threatened everyone with Earth's destruction if they did not convince Superboy to leave the planet forever. As he flew away from his adopted home, Superboy managed to lure his negative counterpart into following him into space, where he used his mighty strength to destroy the energy creature once and for all (*Superboy* [first series] #168, September 1970).

NEGATIVE SUPERMAN, THE

When the Man of Steel was once simultaneously hit by two different energy beams, the freak accident left behind a negative image of Superman that became a corporeal being who acted opposite the hero. One of the bursts resulted when Lex Luthor used a new device designed to rearrange Superman's molecules "so that he has no more substance than a shadow," while the second came from an experimental ray device undergoing development in a nearby laboratory.

Wreaking havoc throughout Metropolis, the Negative Superman proved every bit as powerful and resourceful as his template. He went so far as to protect Luthor, his creator, from the Man of Steel, who was repelled whenever he came close to his mirror image. To help turn the tide and protect the city, Superman summoned Batman and Robin, and the World's Greatest Detective deduced that kryptonite would strengthen the creature rather than weaken him. The reinforced Negative Superman managed to pierce the barrier between him and Superman so that when they next clashed, the Man of Steel reabsorbed the being while the Dynamic Duo apprehended Luthor's accomplices (*World's Finest Comics* #126, June 1962).

NELSON, BIG NOSE

Despite his industrywide reputation for innovative sound effects used in broadcasting dramas, "Big Nose" Nelson was fired the one time something went awry during a performance before a Metropolis studio audience: Hornets he was using to imitate a fighter-plane engine broke free and attacked the audience members. Without another job, Nelson decided to use his ingenuity to commit crimes. He kicked off a series of successful robberies beginning with turning the sound of a man eating carrots into the rumble of a museum collapsing, causing the people to flee, leaving it empty for robbery. The aural crimes continued until he was apprehended by Superman (*Superman* [first series] #80, January–February 1953).

NELSON, TOM

Thanks to press agent Tom Nelson's efforts, the world considered carnival performer Abou Sabut an "eminent astrologer," but Nelson did all the actual work with the star charts. He grew resentful of his creation's fame and income, so he crafted an elaborate scheme to frame Sabut for a series of crimes being committed in Metropolis. The hope was that the police would arrest Sabut, allowing Nelson to seize control of the money, but he was of course stopped by Superman (*Superman* [first series] #16, May–June 1942).

NEPTUNE

Superman once visited this, the eighth planet from the sun, to gather a head from a statue sculpted in his honor by the citizens of that world. He obtained it as one of several "space trophies" being collected by the Metropolis Museum for burial within a time capsule intended as a gift for the citizens living in the fiftieth century (*Superman* [first series] #122, July 1958). The chronicles never again referred to living beings on Neptune until that world was colonized by Earth after the Crisis on Infinite Earths.

NEUTRON

Petty thieves Ted Grand, Tim Moore, and Nathaniel Tryon bonded together and called themselves the TNT Trio. Recruited by Lex Luthor, Tryon was sent to sabotage a nuclear reactor, but he became trapped when lead shielding collapsed on top of him. As the plant headed toward a meltdown, Grand and Moore were rescued by Superman. The Man of Steel scanned for other survivors, but the lead shielding prevented the hero from spotting the injured Tryon. Tryon eventually freed himself and sought refuge at one of the Luthor Lairs. There his employer discovered that Tryon was suffering from severe radiation poisoning. Luthor placed the dying man under the rays of an experimental device, telling Tryon it would heal him when it actually finished the job of turning the human into a walking nuclear reactor. While Tryon was exposed to the rays, Luthor wound up captured by Superman, and Tryon remained trapped in the Lair for a year. A battle between Superman

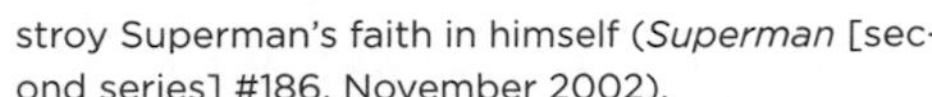

and the Mole caused vibrations that eventually revived Tryon, who now wanted nothing more than revenge against Superman and his former allies.

Wearing a containment suit provided by Luthor, Neutron was a serious threat to Metropolis until Superman arrived. By then, Neutron had already killed Grand, though the Man of Steel managed to stop him from killing Moore. Still seeking vengeance, he charged the *Daily Planet* globe that spun atop the Galaxy Communications building so that solar radiation would turn it combustible. Superman valiantly fought the gold-and-yellow-clad Neutron, trying to subdue the madman before the globe exploded, destroying all life in his adopted city.

After he was overpowered, Tryon, now called Neutron the Living Bomb, was taken to the local S.T.A.R. Labs facility for safekeeping. The scientists there tried to treat his condition but failed to come up with any way to drain his body of the deadly atomic power (*Action Comics* #525–526, November–December 1981).

Neutron's power could be channeled through his gloved hands or by lifting the visor of his helmet, but Tryon lacked control in emitting his powerful blasts of destructive radioactive energy. Somehow a lawyer in Vandal Savage's employ obtained parole for Tryon and used the man as a pawn in a ploy to discredit the Man of Steel (*Action Comics* #543, May 1983). Savage's plan almost worked, and authorities decided that Tryon presented a clear and present danger, so his parole was revoked and he was placed in suspended animation. Now at the New York City branch of S.T.A.R. Labs, Neutron was eventually freed and recruited by the Fearsome Five (*Tales of the Teen Titans* #56–58, August–October 1985).

In the world after the Crisis on Infinite Earths, Neutron's origin differed somewhat. He'd been a security guard caught in a nuclear accident whose body was turned into pure nuclear energy and subsequently housed in a containment suit. Leaving the Fearsome Five behind, Neutron eventually joined super-villains Warp and Plasmus in the employ of Conduit. They attempted to assassinate Jonathan and Martha Kent in Smallville as part of Conduit's scheme of revenge against Clark Kent for perceived slights when the two had been teens, but were stopped by the couple's adopted son Superman. Plasmus and Neutron collided, with the resulting blast seemingly destroying them both (*The Adventures of Superman* #523, May 1995).

In fact, both survived, and they were later apprehended and incarcerated at Slabside Island prison. Neutron was freed when the Joker unleashed his modified Venom (*Joker: Last Laugh* #2, December 2001) and was soon after hired by Manchester Black to aid in Black's scheme to destroy Superman's faith in himself (*Superman* [second series] #186, November 2002).

Donning a modified containment suit, he and Radion were then subcontracted by Intergang to murder Clark Kent after he had seemingly lost all his superpowers. They pushed the reporter in front of a train and fled the scene, unaware the impact actually kick-started the Man of Steel's dormant powers (*Action Comics* #838, June 2006). Neutron also fought Superman on other occasions, such as the time he interrupted what was planned as a special day between the hero and his wife Lois Lane. That time, Superman ruptured Neutron's suit, allowing the Metropolis Technology Squad to absorb the free energy, thereby weakening Tryon (*Action Comics* #654, September 2006).

As one of the most persistent foes of the Man of Steel, it was little wonder that Neutron was one of the villains exiled to the alien world called Salvation Run. Trying to survive, Neutron allowed Luthor to use him as a power source to energize a teleporter in an attempt to return home to Earth. The device blew up, and Neutron was believed killed in the blast (*Salvation Run* #7, July 2008).

NEVADA, JOHNNY

Americans went to sleep with their televisions tuned to *The Midnight Show Starring Johnny Nevada,* airing every midnight on the Galaxy Broadcasting System (*Action Comics* #420, January 1973). Broadcast live from Galaxy's flagship station WGBS-TV in Metropolis, the show was where celebrities promoted their movies, authors their books, and politicians their agendas. Several heroes also appeared on the series, including Superman. Indeed, teenager Danny Victor managed to win a job on the show by securing the Man of Steel's first appearance there.

Sports legend Steve Lombard's turn at guest-hosting *The Midnight Show* was an attempt to cover up the fact that Johnny Nevada had been kidnapped. Taking a dangerous gamble, Superman appeared on the live program and pretended that he was really Johnny in an effort to goad the kidnappers into trying to shoot their captive. Listening for the sound of the gun being fired, the Man of Steel arrived in time to save the TV host and prove that he really was faster than a speeding bullet (*Action Comics* #442, December 1974).

On a later show, Johnny returned the favor by impersonating Superman when *The Midnight Show* featured the supposed wedding of Lois Lane and Lex Luthor. Struck by a beam designed to force Superman to reveal his true identity, instead Johnny confessed that his given name was Arnold Nadakowski. "My agent insisted I change it years ago, when breaking in my nightclub act in the Catskills" (*Superman Family* #172, August–September 1975). The experience inspired a later show on which Johnny hosted other men who'd been believed to have been Superman at one point or another (*Action Comics* #474, August 1977).

In post-Crisis history, Johnny continued to play host to everyone from super heroines like Wonder Woman (*Wonder Woman* [second series] #8, September 1987) to actresses such as Nancy Nolan (*The Adventures of Superman* #540, November

...WE'VE BEEN ON THE AIR ALL THIS TIME WITHOUT A COMMERCIAL! BUT I THINK YOUR QUARREL WAS MORE ENTERTAINING!

1996). Entertainment journalists including Cat Grant delighted in reporting the details of his personal life, such as his estrangement from his seventh wife, soap star Nicole Polaris-Nevada (*Daily Planet Special Invasion! Edition,* November 4, 1988).

NEW GENESIS

When the Old Gods, living on Urgrund, died in the first battle called Ragnarok some five billion years ago, there arose from the ashes two planets, the placid New Genesis and the fiery Apokolips (*Jack Kirby's Fourth World* #1, March 1997). Just over four billion years ago, life finally began to appear on both planets (*New Gods Secret Files* #1, September 1998), and the humanoids who eventually appeared on the twin worlds attained "Godhood," signaling the start of the Fourth World thirty thousand years ago.

Whereas Apokolips was a harsh, forbidding environment, New Genesis was lush, a true paradise where life existed in harmony. Over time, the humanoid inhabitants developed powers and abilities and became known as the New Gods. They built villages, then cities, then the floating city of Supertown, where the gods chose to reside. Those who did not have god-like powers were called "bugs" and lived in Bug Mounds or underground. The only strife was the occasional conflict between those who lived above and those who lived below.

Izaya the Inheritor became the leader of New Genesis. He maintained the peace between his world and that of Apokolips, although the threat of war remained ever present. Izaya's fears came true when Darkseid, the ruler of the dark world, manipulated Steppenwolf, his own uncle, to pursue his perverse hobby of hunting and killing on New Genesis, in the hope of starting a war between the forces of Apokolips and Izaya the Inheritor's world. Avia, Izaya's wife, was slain by Steppenwolf, and war quickly ensued (*New Gods* #7, February–March 1972).

SUPERTOWN
THE PARK
MEMORIAL STATUES
THE WORLD BELOW
JK/T

Some time later, Izaya landed on an alien world, where he met and eventually wed a native named Vayla (*Jack Kirby's Fourth World* #1, March 1997). She gave birth to a boy who was named Scott Free, but Vayla died soon after.

Within a decade, Izaya became Highfather, leader of New Genesis, and forged the peace treaty with Darkseid known as "The Pact," wherein the ruling gods of Apokolips and New Genesis each gave his son to be raised by the other. Whereas Highfather raised Orion as his own, Darkseid had Scott Free raised by Granny Goodness at her orphanage (*New Gods* #7, February–March 1972). When Scott was on the cusp of adolescence, he was encouraged by Himon, inventor of the Mother Box, to flee Apokolips. With Scott Free's escape, the New Gods' Pact was broken, and New Genesis and Apokolips returned to war.

When Darkseid let the war spill from the Fourth World to Earth, he dispatched his adopted son Orion to stop his birth father Izaya. New Genesis's inhabitants fought for peace on Earth and encountered the planet's heroes on numerous occasions afterward.

Through the years, Highfather struggled to maintain a semblance of tranquility on the world he so loved, even transforming Apokolips and New Genesis into a single, fused world at one point (*New Gods* [fourth series] #15, February 1997). The two worlds were separated once more at the climax of the Godwave incident, which saw Darkseid fused into the Source Wall (*Genesis* #4, October 1997) and Highfather killed (*Jack Kirby's Fourth World* #8, October 1997). The Source then used Takion as its avatar to rule New Genesis.

Convinced that "Darkseid must be free, if the proper balance of the universe is to be restored," Metron removed the lord of Apokolips from the Promethean Wall. The spirit of Highfather emerged briefly from the Wall as well, plucking the fallen Supertown from the ground and restoring it "to its proper place and its proper glory" in the skies above New Genesis (*Jack Kirby's Fourth World* #18–19, August–September 1998).

In time, the Source created a series of events that brought a close to the Fourth World. A Fifth World was born with New Genesis and Apokolips re-formed into one world as in the past (*Death of the New Gods* #1–8, Early December 2007–June 2008; *Final Crisis* #1–7, June 2008–March 2009).

NEW GODS, THE

As long as there has been a universe with sentient life, there have been beings called gods. The current universe was created by the Source, one of the ultimate foundations of the Universal Expression of Energy, and was in turn created by the universe. For mere mortals, this meant that the Big Bang started the current universe, the unleashing of cosmic forces leading to the creation of stars, planets, and ultimately life.

The First Age began on the GodWorld, formed eighteen billion years ago out of native elements. It was home to beings considered gods by varying alien worlds, including Earth. A billion years later, life appeared on the GodWorld, beginning the Second World (*Jack Kirby's Fourth World* #1,

March 1997). Some fifteen billion years ago, humanoid life attained "godhood" on the GodWorld. On other worlds, life also formed.

The Old Gods, living on Urgrund, died in the first battle called Ragnarok, some five billion years ago, bringing about the end of the Second World (*New Gods* #1, February–March 1971). The cataclysm unleashed the phenomenon called the Godwave, which created gods on various planets through the universe, such as the Greek, Egyptian, and Norse pantheons on Earth at roughly 38,000 BC (*Genesis* #3, October 1997). Eons later, the Godwave bounced back and created superhumans on Earth during its second pass.

From the ashes of the GodWorld arose two planets, the pacifistic New Genesis and the warlike Apokolips (*Jack Kirby's Fourth World* #1, March 1997). Just over four billion years ago, life finally began to appear on both planets (*New Gods Secret Files* #1, November 1998). The humanoid life on the twin worlds attained "Godhood," signaling the start of the Fourth World some thirty thousand years ago. The malevolent Uxas, son of Queen Heggra, along with his brother Drax, were among these New Gods (*Jack Kirby's Fourth World* #2, April 1997).

Uxas visited Earth for the first time in 13,000 BC and, in an attempt to halve their powers, caused the Olympian gods to split into two distinct pantheons. Zeus and Jupiter became the rulers of their various pantheons, which would come to be worshipped by Greece and Rome, respectively (*Wonder Woman* [second series] #132, April 1998). The New God Metron made his first recorded appearance on Earth about fourteen thousand years ago and began searching the universe, collecting information and intelligence for a greater understanding of his place in all things (*New Gods Secret Files* #1, September 1998).

In AD 689, Uxas gained control of the fabled Omega Force, slew his brother Drax, and transformed into Darkseid (*Jack Kirby's Fourth World* #2–5, April–July 1997). Defying the wishes of his mother Heggra, Darkseid secretly married the sorceress Suli, and they had a son named Kalibak. Suli was then murdered by the master torturer DeSaad at the command of Darkseid's mother, and Heggra subsequently ordered Darkseid to marry Tigra (*New Gods* #11, October–November 1972).

Darkseid placed his second wife Tigra into a Hyperfreeze prison to be free of her influence, and usurped the throne of Apokolips (*Jack Kirby's Fourth World* #10, December 1997). Soon after, Darkseid encouraged his uncle Steppenwolf to pursue his perverse hobby of hunting and killing on New Genesis, in the hope of starting a war between the forces of Apokolips and Izaya the Inheritor's world. Avia, Izaya's wife, was then slain by Steppenwolf. War quickly ensued (*New Gods* #7, February–March 1972).

After making a deal with Darkseid, Metron used the just-discovered X-element to create his Mobius Chair and developed the time-and-space-spanning teleportation system known as the Boom Tube (*New Gods* #7, February–March 1972). Around AD 989, the rebounding Godwave passed over Earth for a second time.

Darkseid exiled Iluthin, a promising warrior among Granny Goodness's orphans, to the Rome of 1502, where the young man fell under the guidance of Cesare and Lucretia Borgia. After the Apokoliptian assassin Kanto-13 traveled to Earth via Boom Tube and killed Iluthin's lover, the young warrior returned to Apokolips and defeated Kanto-13. Impressed, Darkseid executed the fallen Kanto and declared Iluthin his new master assassin, the no-longer-numbered Kanto (*Jack Kirby's Fourth World* #9–11, November 1997–January 1998, and #13, March 1998).

Tigra was released from Hyperfreeze in 1689 and conceived Darkseid's firstborn, Orion, on Apokolips (*Jack Kirby's Fourth World* #10, December 1997). Less than a decade later, Izaya landed on an alien world, where he met and eventually wed a native named Vayla (*New Gods Secret Files* #1, September 1998). She gave birth to a boy who was named Scott Free, and Vayla died soon after.

Within a decade, roughly 1698, Izaya became Highfather, leader of New Genesis, and forged the peace treaty with Darkseid known as "The Pact," wherein the ruling gods of Apokolips and New Genesis each gave his son to be raised by the other. Whereas Highfather raised Orion as his own, Darkseid had Scott Free raised by Granny Goodness at her orphanage (*New Gods* #7, February–March 1972). When Scott was on the cusp of adolescence, he was encouraged by Himon, inventor of the Mother Box, to flee Apokolips. Following Free's escape, the New Gods' Pact was broken, and New Genesis and Apokolips returned to war.

Scott took a Boom Tube and arrived on Earth in 1802 (*Mister Miracle* #9, July–August 1972), materializing near London, and made the acquaintance of Francine "Fancy" Goodbody, whom he eventually married (*Jack Kirby's Fourth World* #6–7, August–September 1997).

Centuries passed as the New Gods of both worlds skirmished and ignored the doings on Earth. Then Darkseid realized that Earth's people housed the Anti-Life Equation and began a relentless quest to obtain it. He used a variety of meth-

ods to find the Earthlings who contained pieces of the formula, including funding Intergang in Metropolis and placing Morgan Edge in a position of power (*Superman's Pal, Jimmy Olsen* #133, October 1970). Not long after, Superman first encountered the Forever People of New Genesis (*Forever People* #1, February–March 1971).

When Highfather became aware of Darkseid's machinations on Earth, he dispatched Orion to stop his birth father (*New Gods* #1, February–March 1971). At much the same time, Thaddeus Brown was murdered by an Intergang chieftain named Steel Hand, leading Scott Free to succeed him as Mister Miracle (*Mister Miracle* #1, March–April 1971).

Until the Crisis on Infinite Earths, the struggles between the inhabitants of New Genesis and Apokolips continued without resolution. Earth's people, including its super hero community, were frequently caught up in the conflict. Summoned to New Genesis, members of the Justice Society of America and Justice League of America eventually met the New Gods (*Justice League of America* #183–185 [first series] October–December 1980, reaffirmed in *Action Comics* #650, February 1990).

Post-Crisis, the origins of these New Gods remained intact, and it was implicitly understood that time passed in their realm at a different rate than New Earth's. The conflict continued, although it had endured long enough that the Source itself began manipulating events to bring them to some form of a conclusion.

At one point, Metron witnessed the apparent destruction of Apokolips and New Genesis, and awakened on Earth (*New Gods* [fourth series] #11–12, September–November 1996). Meanwhile, Lightray and the Forever People learned that Darkseid and Highfather never truly entered the Source, and that all the recent events involving the celestial entity's supposed corruption had been part of some greater, never-explained plan. Using the power of Takion and Metron, Highfather transformed Apokolips and New Genesis into a single, fused world (*New Gods* [fourth series] #15, February 1997).

With Highfather's apparent absorption into the Promethean Wall, Takion, a living conduit for the Source, assumed leadership of the New Gods of New Genesis. Rejecting his hereditary right to rule, Scott Free returned to Earth with his wife Big Barda, intent on resuming his escape-artist performances as Mister Miracle (*Jack Kirby's Fourth World* #11–12, January–February 1998).

Convinced that "Darkseid must be free, if the proper balance of the universe is to be restored," Metron removed the lord of Apokolips from the Promethean Wall. The spirit of Highfather briefly emerged from the Wall as well, plucking the fallen Supertown from the ground and restoring it "to its proper place and its proper glory" in the skies above New Genesis (*Jack Kirby's Fourth World* #18–19, August–September 1998).

The Source concluded that the Fourth World was flawed and began manipulating events to bring about its end and usher in the Fifth World. The chronicles imply that it influenced Alexander Luthor and Superboy-Prime to restore the multiverse in the events known as Infinite Crisis. It used Infinity-Man as its agent to eradicate all the New Gods, although Darkseid finally obtained the Anti-Life Equation and used Jimmy Olsen as a "soul catcher" in order to obtain the dead gods' powers. His attempt at survival was thwarted when the Source resurrected Orion, who finally succeeded in killing his father. The Source absorbed the Anti-Life Equation back into itself and then merged Apokolips and New Genesis back into one planet (*Death of the New Gods* #1–8, Early December 2007–June 2008).

Darkseid, however, managed to survive this cosmic upheaval (*DC Universe* #0, June 2008) and ordered his Evil Factory, formerly the Command-D Bunkers in Blüdhaven, to fashion new bodies for his allies in the stylized form of early-twentieth-century gangsters. He took on the name of Boss Dark Side, for example, inhabiting the body that was once Dan Turpin. Kalibak was given the form of a humanoid tiger, Granny Goodness usurped the body of Alpha Lantern Kraken, and DeSaad stole the body of the troubled Mary Marvel.

The death of the gods was significant enough for the Guardians of the Universe to order an investigation. Batman aided them, concluding that Orion was killed by a bullet sent backward through time by Darkseid, who gained the ultimate revenge against his son.

Boss Dark Side unleashed the Anti-Life Equation across the planet, turning most of Earth's humans into mindless slaves. This Final Crisis saw the survivors forming a resistance movement, with several heroes taking charge, among them Shilo Norman, the new Mister Miracle. Darkseid and his fellow gods were eventually defeated, and humankind was freed once more. Darkseid was seemingly destroyed, but the Source resurrected Highfather and the benevolent New Gods, who were tasked with restoring the devastated parallel universe of Earth-51 (*Final Crisis* #1–7, July 2008–March 2009).

The exact relationship between the Fifth World and New Earth has yet to be chronicled, but comments made by Metron have implied that the Fifth World of gods would be Earth—indeed, that humankind itself was poised to evolve to the next level of existence (*JLA* #15, February 1998).

NEW KRYPTON

In the world formed after Infinite Crisis, Superman encountered the true Brainiac, who possessed the bottle city of Kandor in his vessel. Superman defeated the Coluan before Brainiac could steal Metropolis to add to its repository of knowledge. With Brainiac no longer a threat and in the government's custody, Superman took Kandor to the North Pole, near his Fortress of Solitude, where the Kryptonian city was restored to its normal size. Earth now had one hundred thousand new residents, all of whom possessed powers and abilities identical to those of Superman (*Superman: New Krypton Special* #1, October 2008).

Some eighteen months earlier, General Zod, Ursa, and Non had escaped the Phantom Zone, along with Zod and Ursa's son Lor-Zod. During that time, Ursa, acting on Zod's orders, seeded Kryptonian sleeper agents throughout Earth. Those sleeper agents established themselves in different careers and identities. Tor-An, for example, took one of the more aggressive routes: obtaining vast wealth by acquiring a multimedia corporation.

Overjoyed at having kinsmen survive the destruction of Krypton, Superman offered to help them acclimate to their new homeworld, an offer that was largely ignored. Kandor's leaders, Zor-El and his wife Alura Zor-El, were Supergirl's parents. They agreed to a meeting with the president of the United States, a diplomatic gesture that was ruined when the genetic killing machine Doomsday arrived. After Doomsday's quick defeat by the Kryptonians, Zor-El decided that threats to Superman could also be threats to the Kandorians. A team of Kandor police was sent to remove such threats, which resulted in an assault on Superman's foes at Stryker's Island Penitentiary. During the conflict, several humans were killed, and Earth now demanded that the Kryptonians involved face justice for their actions.

Sensing a disaster brewing, General Sam Lane, the former secretary of defense, began marshaling his forces. He went so far as to bring Lex Luthor into his council, and the former president stole Brainiac's inert starcraft. Luthor then activated a robot army discovered in the bowels of the ship. During the distraction, General Lane sent the super-villains Metallo and Reactron into Kandor, as each contained kryptonite within his chest. They managed to kill Zor-El before they were transported out of Kandor (*Action Comics* #872; *Supergirl* [fifth series] #36—both February 2009).

During these events, two Kryptonians dressed in the costumes of the legendary Nightwing and Flamebird protected the Phantom Zone projector in the Fortress of Solitude so that no other villains were placed in the Zone (*Action Comics* #871, Jan-

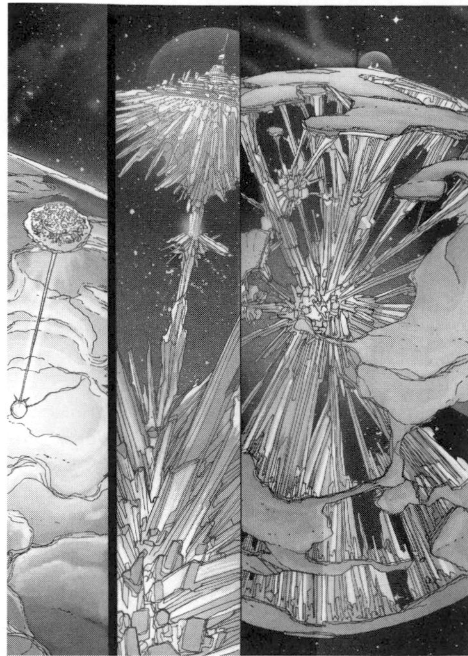

uary 2009). Once their work was accomplished, they remained on Earth to seek out and expose Ursa's sleeper agents.

Mad with grief at her husband's death, Alura took control of the Kandorian government and rejected any assimilation on Earth. Since she refused to hand over her people, members of the Justice League of America and Justice Society of America, led by the Guardian, arrived over the city in the hope of settling things peacefully. Superman found himself caught in the middle of the conflict, unhappy with how both sides were handling things. The standoff ended when Kandor and the glacier it sat atop lifted into the sky. Kryptonian scientists had managed to access some of Brainiac's devices and found a way to transport Kandor. They entered space where, directly opposite Earth's orbit, they fashioned a new planet using Sunstones—Kryptonian crystal-growth technology—and named the world New Krypton (*Action Comics* #873, March 2009).

Alura insisted that Supergirl remain with her as the people settled their new world. At first, Alura rejected Superman, but she later offered him a place within Kryptonian society if he left Earth for good. He turned the opportunity down at first, but later reconsidered after Alura freed General Zod, Ursa, and Non, as well as other dangerous criminals, from the Phantom Zone (*Superman* #684, March 2009).

Realizing he needed to investigate the real plans of Alura and Zod, Superman decided to go undercover on New Krypton. He said goodbye to his wife Lois Lane and adopted mother Martha Kent, and seemingly exiled himself from Earth. Before his departure, Superman helped free Mon-El from the disintegrating Phantom Zone and charged him with looking after Metropolis in his absence (*Superman* #685, April 2009).

Superman then arrived on New Krypton and was given a place at Zod's side in the Military Guild, where he continued to keep an eye on the dangerous villain.

Kal-El was given command of the elite Red Shard forces and worked to train them in how best to use their powers. While life continued to settle across the new planet, the strife between the Guilds, a holdover from life on Krypton, continued to fester. Members of the Ruling Council were also being targeted for death, further destabilizing the morale of New Krypton's citizens. Kara Zor-El split her time between Earth and New Krypton, trying to maintain a relationship with her still-grieving mother, while Kal-El took command of the military after General Zod was nearly assassinated.

When it was decided that the planet needed a moon to stabilize its orbit and provide its waters with tidal forces, they obtained one from Jupiter, an action prompting a visit from Jemm and his fellow Saturnians. They made it clear the "new neighbors" had to behave themselves and were being watched. Also investigating the new world was a contingent from the Green Lantern Corps, which gave the new government plenty of leeway thanks to the presence of the trusted Kal-El.

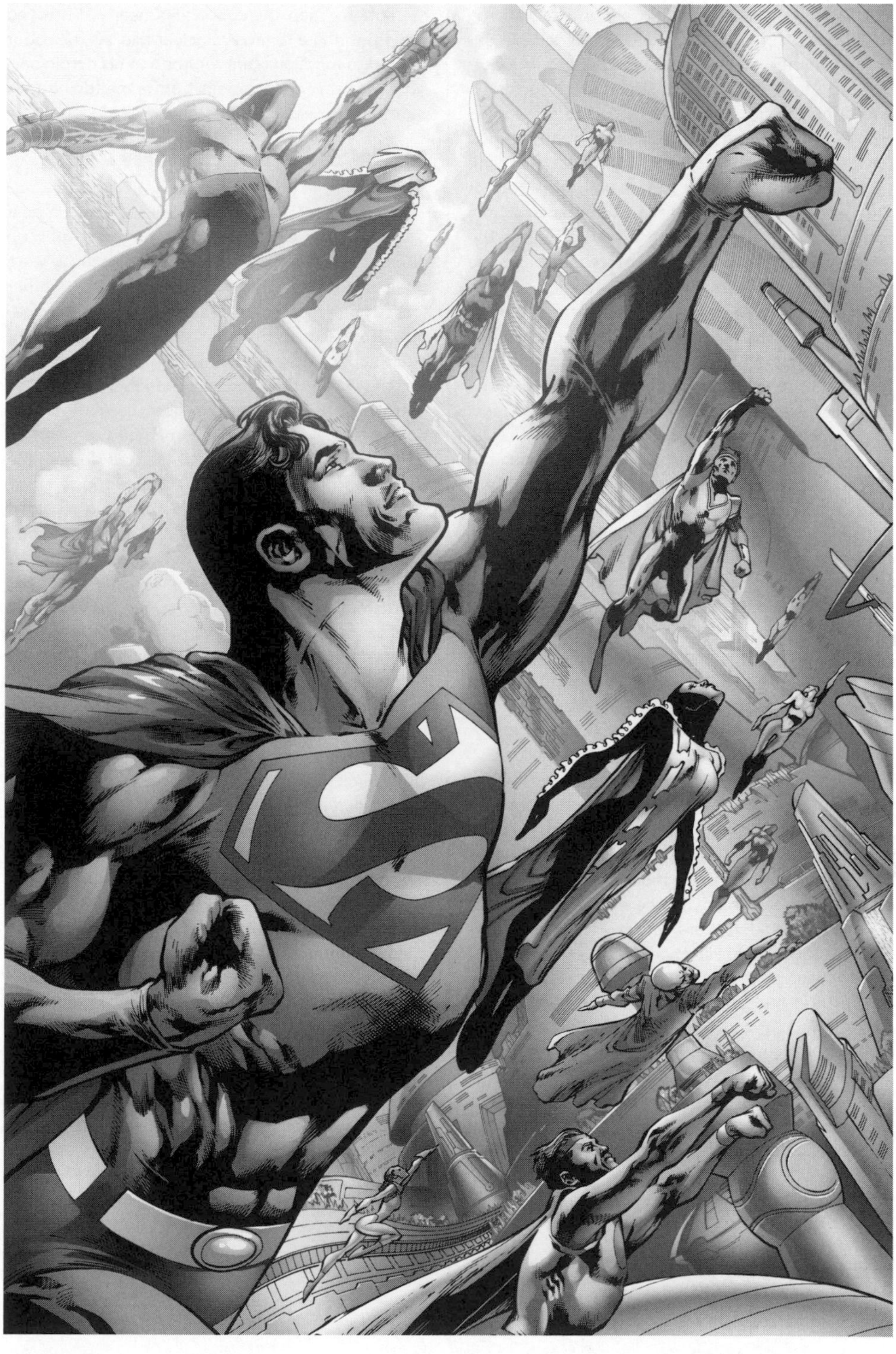

Kal-El and a recovered Zod eventually pieced together the conspiracy, and Councilor Wri-Qin

finally admitted he had allied himself with General Lane, who had promised the Kryptonian unlimited power on New Krypton in exchange for eliminating the planet's Ruling Council. Wri-Qin was taken into custody by Red Shard just when Brainiac's starship appeared in the skies, ready to reclaim the Kandorians (*Superman: World of New Krypton* #1–12, May 2009–April 2010).

Brainiac, aided in part by Lex Luthor, attempted to rebottle Kandor but found himself opposed by the one hundred thousand superpowered residents. Zod ordered New Krypton's Global Defense Canons fired, which proved ineffective against Brainiac's forcefields, resulting in killing only nearby Kandorians. An infuriated Kal-El resumed his Superman identity and worked with Supergirl, Superboy, Krypto, and Mon-El to breach the forcefield and bring the fight to Brainiac. At the same time, Mon-El encountered and was aided by the Legion Espionage Squad, sent back a millennium in time by Brainiac 5 to prevent the death of the Man of Steel at Brainiac's hands. If that were to occur, time would completely collapse, thereby eradicaing the universe. The alien Tellus attempted to band the quarreling Kandorian Guilds into a unified fighting force, funneling his telepathic commands through Supergirl's mind, with limited success. While Superman battled Brainiac within his ship, Zod and the military forces continued their assault from the air until the ship was heavily damaged (*Superman: Last Stand of Krypton* #1–3, June 2010).

Before they could even bury their dead, the Kryptonians were besieged by a new threat. General Lane's war was finally ignited, and Zod was determined to bring the battle to Earth, Superman notwithstanding. Meantime, Supergirl and Alura apprehended Reactron. Alura tortured him for information, but it turned out Reactron was a plant by General Lane. Thanks to Lex Luthor's special modifications, Reactron became a living bomb and went critical, exploding with enough force to crack the nascent world apart. In mere seconds, New Krypton was reduced to chunks of rock (*Superman: War of the Supermen* #1, July 2010).

Over 10 percent of the remaining Kryptonians were wiped out, with the others regrouping under Zod's banner. The first wave of Kryptonians took out Earth's Human Defense Corps installations on Mars before assaulting Earth itself. In less than one hundred minutes, many of the planet's capital cities and their leaders were wiped out. While Superman and Zod fought in the skies over Metropolis, Krypto was sent to the Fortress of Solitude to obtain the Phantom Zone Projector. With Earth's meta-humans protecting the populace, the Clone of Steel gathered as many of the Kandorians as possible and sent them into the Phantom Zone. As Superman defeated Zod, the general was also returned to the limbo-like void. Once the Projector was turned off, only Superman, Supergirl, and Krypto were left as evidence of Krypton's existence (*Superman: War of the Supermen* #2–4, July 2010).

NEWMAN, ADAM

Superman often tinkered with the design of his Superman Robots, once fashioning an upgraded android model that named itself Adam Newman. The Man of Steel saw that the upgraded robot was still flawed in its programming and performance, with Adam taking the rejection very hard. He decided to wreak vengeance on the Last Son of Krypton, bringing an end to his career. Adam traveled to Metropolis and convinced Clark Kent that *he* was the flawed android with implanted memories, while Adam Newman was the one, true Man of Tomorrow. Clark began to doubt himself, and actually considered that he might truly be no more than a mild-mannered reporter for a great metropolitan newspaper. A short time later, he learned of Adam's deception when the robot was nearly destroyed while fighting a runaway nuclear pile. As the robot ceased to function, Kent returned to his heroic persona and saved Metropolis from a meltdown (*Superman* [first series] #174, January 1965).

NEWSBOY LEGION, THE

Growing up in Metropolis's Suicide Slum was hardest on the children, especially the orphans who grew up during the Depression, when social services were nonexistent. One group of boys banded together for friendship and mutual survival, selling newspapers from street corner to street corner. Without adult supervision, they often ran afoul of the law, and they eventually came under the watch of police patrolman Jim Harper, who dubbed them the Newsboy Legion. Harper also saw the need to clean up crime beyond the limits of the law and donned the costumed identity of the Guardian. Soon after, he legally became the Legion's guardian and provided them with the adult input they desperately needed (*Star-Spangled Comics* #7, April 1942).

On Earth-1, the boys—Tommy Tompkins, Big Words, Gabby, and Scrapper—continued to sell papers, skip school, and have all manner of adventures, often aided by the Guardian, whom they secretly suspected was Harper but could never prove.

Through the years, the boys matured, finished school, and went on to college, all the time remaining a tight group of friends that grew to include Walter "Flipper Dipper" Johnson.

As adults, the former Newsboy Legion members became affiliated with the top-secret DNA Project. Summoned to the deathbed of their former guardian Jim Harper, they learned, as they'd often suspected, that he had been the Guardian. Vowing that he would live again, the young men used a sample of Harper's cell tissue to clone the Guardian. The second Guardian went on to serve as defender of the Project, and the Legionmen's sons became the second Newsboy Legion (*Superman's Pal, Jimmy Olsen* #135, January 1971).

When Jimmy Olsen uncovered the secret existence of the Project, he and the sons of the Newsboy Legion began a series of adventures as they traveled aboard the Morgan Edge–designed Whiz Wagon (*Superman's Pal, Jimmy Olsen* #133, October 1970). Along the way, they encountered other genetic creations such as the Hairies, who traveled in the wondrous Mountain of Judgment. What the Legion did not realize was that Edge was actually an agent of Darkseid, who sent the youths after the Hairies in an attempt to kill them. The young team also had to contend with creations from the Evil Factory, which manufactured the Four-Armed Terror, and a green-skinned giant clone of Jimmy (*Superman's Pal, Jimmy Olsen* #135–138, January–June 1971). While investigating the Evil Factory near Scotland's Loch Trevor, the younger Newsboys came across a monstrosity they dubbed Angry Charlie (*Superman's Pal, Jimmy Olsen* #145, January 1972) and wound up eventually keeping him as a pet (*Superman's Pal, Jimmy Olsen* #147, March 1972, and #150, June 1972).

When a renegade clone named Adam took control of the Project, the Legion was disbanded (*Superman Family* #194, March–April 1979). Their subsequent activities went unrecorded.

In the wake of the Crisis on Infinite Earths, the team was identified as Anthony "Big Words" Rodrigues, John "Gabby" Gabrielli, Patrick "Scrapper" MacGuire, and Tommy Tompkins. As adults, they became involved with the top-secret Project Cadmus, and it was there that they were reunited with Jim Harper, their former guardian. Worn down from injury and age, Harper was cloned by the Project, and his mind was transferred to his youthful replica.

When Sleez of Apokolips took control of the Project, he forced the four Newsboy Legion members and a biochemist named Walter Johnson to clone themselves. This second Newsboy Legion quickly asserted its independence. With the aid of Superman and the Guardian, members freed the Project and their "fathers" from Sleez (*Superman* [second series] *Annual* #2, 1988).

Big Words, Gabby, Scrapper, Tommy, and Flip welcomed their first female member a few years later when Jim Harper gained custody of his sister's granddaughter Bobby Harper, whom the boys nicknamed Famous Bobby (*Guardians of Metropolis* #1–4, November 1994–February 1995). She eventually left the group to be raised by another unnamed relative of Jim's.

Project Cadmus underwent radical changes in management over the years, with the arrival of Mickey Cannon leading to the dismissal of all the

Newsboys (*Superboy* [third series] #56, October 1998). Their whereabouts went unrecorded until they were found by Jimmy Olsen when he investigated abandoned Project Cadmus, seeking to understand how he developed various superpowers (*Countdown to Final Crisis* #29, October 10, 2007). The Legion used the Whiz Wagon's computers to help Jimmy investigate the deaths of the various New Gods (*Death of the New Gods* #1, December 2007). Walter Johnson and the adult incarnation of the Legion were recently murdered by former Cadmus operative Codename: Assassin, part of a vast conspiracy that Jimmy Olsen began to unravel (*Superman's Pal, Jimmy Olsen Special* #1, December 2008). The clones' whereabouts went unchronicled.

As Jimmy traveled in secret, gathering evidence, he began developing a network of youthful contacts, all willing to stay at their keyboards and aid him in any way. When Jimmy gathered the information he needed he emerged from hiding and worked with Lois Lane and the Guardian to help bring down Project 7734. He used a device created by and given to him by Steel to convert information provided by Natasha Irons into organized streaming data, which Jimmy's friends sent to every media organization around the world. Jimmy's pals began calling themselves the Newsboy Legion, and their help proved invaluable in putting an end to Project 7734 (*Superman: War of the Supermen* #3, July 2010).

NEWSTIME MAGAZINE

The weekly news magazine was a staple in American society dating to the introduction of *Time* in 1923. Its competitors grew to include *Newsweek, U.S. News and World Report,* and *Newstime* (*The New Adventures of Superboy* #16, April 1981). Based in Metropolis, the magazine was known for its hard-hitting reporting and nonpartisan coverage, avoiding accusations of having a liberal agenda like the *Daily Planet* or the manipulations of LexCom's holdings. Its bestselling issue was the one released in the aftermath of Superman's death at the hands of Doomsday (*Newstime*, May 1993).

The publication was owned by Colin Thornton, who was later revealed to be a guise used by the demonic Lord Satanus. The Newstime building, whose executive offices were on the fiftieth floor (*Action Comics* #700, June 1994), was located on 23rd Street (*Action Comics* #680, August 1992) in the vicinity of Bessolo and Collyer (*Action Comics* #681, September 1992). *Newstime*'s publisher also owned the *New York Bugle* (*Superman* [second series] #60, October 1991) and branched out into TV and film production and video stores when it merged with Megacom (*The Adventures of Superman* #581, August 2000, and #584, November 2000).

The building sustained a bit of damage during an assault on Earth by Warworld (*Action Comics* #675–676; *Superman* [second series] #67; *Superman: The Man of Steel* #9—all March–April 1992) and was temporarily thrust into limbo during the Blaze-Satanus War (*Action Comics* #680, August 1992). It was the only major structure in the business district to survive unscathed following Lex

Luthor's attempted destruction of the city (*Action Comics* #700, June 1994). In the immediate aftermath, the Newstime building became a sanctuary for the homeless and injured (*Superman* [second series] #91, July 1994).

Clark Kent was once hired to serve as the magazine's publisher, but the demands of a weekly did not suit his needs as Superman. While spending time with Thornton, not once did he suspect that the man was also the demonic villain. Kent finally left *Newstime* after he fell under the control of the Eradicator and his new persona alienated Thornton (*The Adventures of Superman* #460–465, November 1989–April 1990; others).

Ron Troupe worked for *Newstime* as an editorial assistant prior to being hired by the *Daily Planet* (*Action Comics* #677–678, May–June 1992). Other reporters included Wilton Fredericks (*Action Comics* #699, May 1994).

NFERINO

A race of beings that resembled the conventional depiction of the devil hailed from the planet Nferino. One of their race, Rajah Satdev, told Lois Lane that they had once visited Earth, and that their appearance—with red skin, goat-like hooves, horns, and tails—inspired the superstitious ancient humans. He romanced Lane and brought her to Nferino in the hope of marrying her, but the wedding never occurred and Lois returned to Earth (*Superman's Girl Friend, Lois Lane* #103, August 1970).

N'GON

The alien being N'Gon was at some time in the past split into two beings, and they eventually developed an enmity toward each other. Each N'Gon sought ways to annihilate the other. One N'Gon would attack unsuspecting beings with energy blasts from its eyes and take their shape. It occurred to this N'Gon that possessing a ring from the fabled Green Lantern Corps would make it powerful enough to destroy its counterpart. This N'Gon's first attempt was on Green Lantern Archon Z'gmora, who resided in another dimension, and although he was mortally wounded, Z'gmora ordered the ring to self-destruct before N'Gon could take it.

N'Gon then took Z'gmora's shape and used it to lull Space Sector 2814's Green Lantern, Hal Jordan of Earth, into responding to a distress call. While suspicious, Green Lantern didn't want to take a chance, so he pierced the dimensional veil—and was immediately attacked. Jordan was injured, but when N'Gon stole his Green Lantern ring, the man willed it to send his spirit in search of help.

The evil N'Gon practiced with the ring and decided it was ready to increase its advantage by attacking an even more powerful being—Superman. Posing as Hal Jordan, N'Gon used its ring to transport Superman to its realm and launched a brutal physical assault. The real Jordan took that moment to reassert control over his body and warned Superman of what was going on. Superman then wrapped his arm in his cape, using the yellow S-shield as a defense against the ring's emerald energy. N'Gon countered by retrieving a chunk of kryptonite from deep space, weakening Superman. Jordan helped clear the kryptonite from the field of battle, and Superman managed to finally knock N'Gon unconscious. Jordan retrieved his ring and helped return Superman to Earth (*DC Comics Presents* #26, October 1980).

NIAGARA FALLS

At this famous tourist spot in upstate New York, Superman once swam upstream at such a furious speed that his arms churned up the water, thereby creating a mist that prevented the unscrupulous movie producer Mike Foss from capturing the event on film and profiting at the Man of Steel's expense (*Action Comics* #120, May 1948).

After robbing a nearby hotel, the criminal known as Mister Seven attempted to escape Superman by riding a barrel over the falls, but he was ultimately caught by the Man of Steel (*World's Finest Comics* #46, June–July 1950).

When Batwoman once tried to determine the Man of Steel's secret identity, he went over the falls to get away from her (*World's Finest Comics* #90, September–October 1957).

Standing before Niagara Falls, Superman—under the magical influence of Mr. Mxyzptlk—once

taunted Lois Lane by nearly proposing marriage to her (*Superman* [first series] #135, February 1960).

Mistakenly believing that she was immune to harm, Lois once went over Niagara Falls in a barrel; she survived only through a freak bump that carried her to safety (*Superman's Girl Friend, Lois Lane* #50, July 1964). Later, Jimmy Olsen attempted to go over the falls himself as part of a scheme devised by him and Superman to capture a criminal called the Collector (*Superman's Pal, Jimmy Olsen* #94, July 1966).

Brainiac's cryogentronic projector once froze the falls into a sheet of solid ice, threatening the entire northeastern United States before Superman intervened and unfroze the natural wonder (*Action Comics* #417, October 1972).

NICHOLAS, JOHN

Millionaire John Nicholas once faked his death to test the integrity of his three nephews, all of whom were heirs to his vast fortune. Having survived first as a penniless orphan before becoming a self-made millionaire, he wanted his funds to create a national chain of admission-free amusement parks for children. His will had the codicil that should the first such amusement park prove unsafe or unsatisfying to children, his nephews would inherit his fortune instead. As he feared, no sooner was a funeral held than two of his nephews hired the criminal called Fancy Dan to stage "accidents" in order to trigger the will's provision. The gangster's tests went too far, however, even for the nephews' tastes, and they were delighted when Superman intervened and captured the criminal. Their joy was doubled when Nicholas revealed himself as alive, and they came to their uncle's aid in bringing his amusement park vision to reality (*Action Comics* #81, February 1954).

NICHOLS, ANNIE

The beautiful blond sharpshooter Annie Nichols, nicknamed Annie Oakley, was hired by Perry White to become Lois Lane's "regular bodyguard" after Superman complained of being "sick and tired of spending all my valuable time rescuing [Lois] from danger!" Annie resigned soon afterward to accept the post of sheriff in her western hometown of Redstone Hills (*Superman* [first series] #70, May–June 1951).

NICHOLS, PROFESSOR CARTER

Professor Carter Nichols was a scientist who befriended Bruce Wayne and Dick Grayson, and later Clark Kent. He had developed a way to use hypnosis to psychically tap into the timestream, sending individuals to specific locations and periods throughout the past (*Batman* #24, August–September 1944).

Curious about several specific unsolved mysteries, Wayne had Nichols send him and Dick to the past to witness events, and as Batman and Robin they often interacted with people in those eras, despite risking tampering with Earth's time line and future events. On occasion, Nichols asked Bruce and Dick to research historical events to satisfy his own curiosity. At some point, Nichols met the men as Batman and Robin and began sending the Dynamic Duo through time as well (*Batman* #98, March 1956).

Nichols once used his machinery to send Wayne and Grayson to the city of Baghdad a thousand years ago. After they were trapped there by proximity to a mountain with a high magnetic content, he asked Superman to rescue them by using his super-speed to pierce the timestream, but not before Batman and Robin first went to the aid of the youth Aladdin (*World's Finest Comics* #79, November–December 1955).

As he refined his methods, Nichols found he could access the past on other worlds, and on more than one occasion sent Superman, Batman, and Robin back in time to visit Krypton before it exploded.

On another occasion, Nichols sent Bruce, Dick, and reporter Clark Kent to France in 1696, where they uncovered the secret of the man in the Iron Mask and became unofficial Musketeers (*World's Finest Comics* #82, May–June 1956).

Some time after this, Professor Nichols began to augment his hypnosis with the rays from a time machine (*Detective Comics* #205, March 1954), culminating in the creation of a unique time-ray. It was equipped with a fail-safe that would automatically return any time-travelers to their point of origin if they were standing in the same location they originally arrived in. Nichols used the device on himself to experience time travel firsthand, but the adventure was so traumatic—requiring his rescue by Batman and Robin—that the professor resolved never to do so again (*Batman* #112, December 1957).

Superman was the one sent back in time to rescue the Dynamic Duo when the "time-box" Nichols sent with Batman and Robin became damaged, trapping them in the era of Alexander the Great

(*World's Finest Comics* #107, February 1960). The Man of Steel was also sent to 1479 Florence, Italy, to retrieve Denny Kale and Shorty Biggs, who had masqueraded as Batman and Robin and tricked Nichols into sending them back in time. They used modern methods to stage successful crimes and managed to thwart the hero's efforts via synthetic kryptonite. This time, Nichols sent the real Batman and Robin back to rescue Superman (*World's Finest Comics* #132, March 1963).

Perhaps the most incredible use of Professor Nichols's time-ray came when Superman was mortally wounded by the explosion of a cosmic clock that he'd had since boyhood, which had held a deadly kryptonite payload. Traveling back in time, Robin met Superboy and successfully convinced the Teen of Steel to destroy the clock, effectively changing history (*Adventure Comics* #253, October 1958).

Shortly after returning Superman, Batman, and Robin to the present following a mission to the primitive past (*World's Finest Comics* #138, December 1963), Nichols vanished from the lives of the heroes when he was recruited to work for the top-secret DNA Project.

On Earth-2, Nichols was entrusted by Batman with a fictitious diary that accused his fellow Justice Society of America colleagues of treason during World War II. Nichols had instructions to pass it along to Clark Kent in the event of his death. When that occurred, it brought the stalwart heroes to trial for treason, prosecuted by Dick Grayson (*America vs. the JSA* #1, January 1985).

NIGHTCAVE

In the suburbs surrounding the city of Kandor, scientist Nor-Kan maintained a mansion beneath which lay a cave that he turned into a secret laboratory. When he chose to aid Superman and Jimmy Olsen, this cave became the headquarters for Nightwing and Flamebird.

NIGHTHOUND

When Superman and Jimmy Olsen adventured in the bottle city of Kandor as Nightwing and Flamebird, they adopted one of Krypton's Telepathic Hounds and named it the Nighthound (*Superman's Pal, Jimmy Olsen* #69, June 1963). The docile creature aided them on numerous cases, such as the time its projections helped end a "metalloid" menace (*World's Finest Comics* #143, August 1964). Nighthound had a wolf-like tail and a snout closely resembling that of Earth's wild boar. The

Nighthound was described as being able to "locate people at any distance by reading their minds to learn where they are!"

NIGHT-OWL, THE

Described as a renegade scientist and fiendish "super-criminal," Night-Owl owed his nickname to his thick eyeglasses and tufts of white hair, which gave him an owl-like appearance. He was known for his many "darkness experiments," which enabled him to see in the dark, and he developed "black light projectors" that he intended to use to plunge Metropolis into inky blackness, thereby allowing his henchmen to commit wholesale pillage in "the greatest crime coup the world has ever known!" At his torchlit cavern hideaway, guarded by a murderous pet owl whose poison-dipped claws inflicted instant death, the Night-Owl was apprehended by Superman before he could carry out his master plan (*Action Comics* #53, October 1942).

NIGHTWING

There have been several individuals in Superman's world to use the name Nightwing. On Earth-1, the Last Son of Krypton sometimes disguised himself as Nightwing to fight crime in the bottle city of Kandor, accompanied by Jimmy Olsen, who assumed the identity Flamebird. The heroes took their names from the native birds that Nor-Kan maintained at his mansion. Nightwing and Flamebird were inspired in part by Batman and Robin, complete with a Nightcave and similar named equipment, such as a Nightmobile. The biggest change was the use of "jet-belts," rather than ropes, to travel throughout Kandor (*Superman* [first series] #158, January 1963). In time, they even added a Nighthound to the team (*Superman's Pal, Jimmy Olsen* #69, June 1963).

The real Dynamic Duo once visited Kandor and fought crime alongside the two Kryptonian Crusaders (*World's Finest Comics* #143, August 1964).

Later, Van-Zee, a cousin of Superman's living in Kandor, assumed the Nightwing identity to continue battling crime. His niece's husband Ak-Var became the new Flamebird (*Superman Family* #183, May–June 1977). During their short tenure as the costumed heroes, the Kryptonian Crusaders effectively eradicated all crime in the city.

Recalling Superman's Kandorian alter ego, Dick Grayson took the Nightwing name as his own after relinquishing his Robin identity and costume (*Tales of the Teen Titans* #44, July 1984). On the Earth formed in the wake of the Crisis on Infinite Earths, Superman once told Dick of a Kryptonian legend called Nightwing, and when the former Robin sought a new persona he chose that name for himself—ironically complementing the Flamebird alter ego already being used by Bette Kane (*Nightwing Secret Files* #1, October 1999).

When Superman brought Lois Lane to Krypton years later, they found themselves labeled as criminals for violating the planet's strict cultural mores. They became Nightwing and Flamebird to hide their identities and seek proof of their innocence (*Superman: The Man of Steel* #111, April 2001). Later, Power Girl and Supergirl also visited Kandor and briefly fought crime as Nightwing and

Flamebird (*Supergirl* [fifth series] #6–8, April–September 2006).

Recently, when Kandor was freed from Brainiac's vessel and enlarged near the North Pole, yet another Nightwing and Flamebird appeared to protect the Phantom Zone projector in the Fortress of Solitude while Superman was away. Later, they fought crime on Earth, receiving guidance from one of Superman's allies, the original Flash. It was eventually discovered that the new heroes were General Zod and Ursa's son Lor-Zod (see Christopher Kent) and Thara Ak-Var, Supergirl's childhood friend. While in the Zone, Chris was exposed to some of Brainiac's technology, which activated a mental link to the avian Nightwing in addition to Thara. Together the two dedicated themselves to hunting down the Kryptonian sleeper agents Ursa had embedded across the planet to varying degrees of success (*Action Comics* #875, May 2009). With Lor-Zod having developed to adulthood in accelerated style, he also began developing romantic feelings toward his colorful partner (*Action Comics Annual* #12, 2009).

Nightwing and Flamebird continued to scour Earth for Kryptonian sleeper agents, hounded time and again by agents from General Samuel Lane's Project 7734. Thara's faith in the Flamebird was tested when she was seriously injured by a kryptonite knife, forcing Lor-Zod to bring her to his adoptive mother, Lois Lane, for help. Lois was overjoyed to see her surrogate son, and summoned the Justice League's Doctor Light, who helped Thara absorb healing solar energy (*Action Comics* #876, April 2009). The duo then resumed their mission, which quickly put them in action against Kryptonian and human villains alike, including Codename: Assassin, Reactron, and Metallo. The former managed to kidnap Thara and access her memories, thereby learning her secrets and allowing Codename: Assassin to manipulate Flamebird by threatening Lor-Zod's life (*Action Comics* #879, July 2009).

Despite this setback, their successes led to a period of public acceptance and acclaim, but Flamebird's simmering jealousy over the females of Earth's great attraction to Nightwing boiled over, leading to the start of a serious romance between Lor-Zod and Thara. Public sentiment turned against the duo, however, when they were framed for the apparent murder of Mon-El, who was acting as Metropolis's champion while Superman was on New Krypton. Nightwing and Flamebird fled to Paris with Supergirl to assess their options, but they were quickly discovered and attacked by Project 7734's Squad K (*Action Comics* #881, September 2009).

The trio escaped but became the subjects of a global manhunt. When Squad K found them once more, the heroes attempted to surrender, but Reactron shockingly slaughtered the Squad before turning his attention to the three Kryptonians. Thara was hit while protecting Supergirl, the impact triggering the complete manifestation of the Flamebird, proving her faith to be well placed. Supergirl convinced the angry entity not to kill Reactron, so it instead kissed Lor-Zod and submerged itself once more within Thara's subconscious (*Supergirl* [fifth series] #46, December 2009). In the aftermath, Nightwing and Flamebird donned new costumes and continued their mission, but Chris had another massive aging spurt, turning him into an old man. Doctor Light consulted with her new medical colleague, Doctor Pillings (who was actually the Kandorian sleeper agent Jax-Ur), who

helped Chris regain his twenty-three-year-old form, but did so by secretly stealing some of his Kryptonian DNA (*Action Comics* #884, February 2010).

At one point, after experiencing doubt about his mission and purpose on Earth, Lor-Zod accessed a Sunstone's memory bank and learned the mythology behind the Nightwing entity. As he listened, he learned how the being known as Rao helped form the planet Krypton from remnants of the Big Bang. Rao then created two children: the Flamebird and Vohc, both of whom spent eons designing and building Krypton's flora and fauna. In time, Rao created the Nightwing, a dragon-like being Rao called his "Eyes in the Night." It was Vohc, who dwelled in twilight, who built the bridge that allowed Flamebird, Rao's "Eyes in the Day," to meet her partner. A pleased Vohc then crafted a testament to the Flamebird, whom he loved, but the Flamebird destroyed the sculpture, as was part of her nature. This embittered her sibling Vohc, who decided to retaliate. He crafted the purest of crystal and arranged for the Flamebird to destroy it, but not before trapping Nightwing in the only remaining shard. Forever more, the Flamebird was kept from her true love (*Action Comics* #886, April 2010).

When the devious Jax-Ur created an artificial version of Rao and unleashed the false god to wreak havoc on Earth, Nightwing and Flamebird arrived to stop the monstrous construct. In the process, the Nightwing was finally freed from its prison and now burned strongly inside of Lor-Zod (*Action Comics* #888, June 2010). As the false Rao ran amok, the lovers determined to stop it, even at the cost of their lives. However, the Nightwing stopped Lor-Zod from accompanying Flamebird, as Lor-Zod had a different destiny. As an all-out war between the Kryptonians and Earth erupted, the Nightwing told Lor-Zod that he was now required to heal the

Phantom Zone by using his unique lifeforce to stabilize the realm to preserve the remainder of reality. The Nightwing entity helped Lor-Zod into the Zone, then left his body, its spirit now free to find its mate on another plane of reality (*Superman: War of the Supermen* #4, July 2010).

NILES, DEREK

During the Depression, the Jordan Circus fell on hard times, and one of its creditors, Derek Niles, decided he wanted to own the circus outright one way or another. His offer to buy it from its debt-ridden owner was rejected. Niles then had his henchman Trigger begin to sabotage the circus, with murderous results—both patrons and animals were killed, sinking Jordan deeper into debt. Superman eventually apprehended Trigger and exposed the scheme, bringing Niles to justice for attempting to ruin the circus and to assassinate Lois Lane, who was investigating Trigger's crimes for the Daily Star (*Action Comics* #7, December 1938).

NIM-EL

Superman's uncle was a proud member of the legendary House of El on Krypton. Born to Jor-El I and Nimda An-Dor (*Superman Family* #192, November–December 1978), Nim-El was the fraternal twin to Jor-El II and older brother to Zor-El. As an adult, Nim-El was in charge of Kandor's armory (*Adventure Comics* #304, January 1963) and was in the city when it was shrunk and stolen by Brainiac (*The World of Krypton* #2, August 1979). Now seemingly trapped in the bottle city, Nim-El and his wife Dondra Klu-Ta (*Krypton Chronicles* #3, November 1981) eventually became the parents of a son they named Don-El (*Superman's Pal, Jimmy Olsen* #60, April 1962). Don-El grew up to become a member of the Superman Emergency Squad and commander of the Kandorian police.

Nim-El was an exact double of the future Su-

perman, Kal-El. On Krypton, the villainous Roz-Em once had his features altered to resemble Nim-El in a failed attempt to access the Kandorian armory (*Adventure Comics* #304, January 1963).

NIM-ZEE

The Kryptonian Van-Zee's father was said to be "a distinguished member of the Kandorian Council," which was the bottle city of Kandor's governing body. Both Nim-Zee and his son were distant relatives of Superman.

At one point, the Earth-1 Superman used an exchange ray that could "cause [him] to switch places with a similar-sized Kandorian person or creature" to swap places with Nim-Zee. The Man of Steel then traveled to the bottle city to tend to a wound he received from a flame dragon (*Superman* [first series] #151, February 1962).

NINUKAB

There once existed a world that eventually grew devoid of life. The entities that lived there were known as the Ninukab and evolved to become noncorporeal beings that could actually animate artificial structures as long as the structure had a living spirit within it. One such being visited Metropolis and took possession of architect Peter Demeos. It wanted to remain permanently housed in a Demeos-built structure, something both Superman and the architect rejected. As they all

struggled within the building, it toppled. The Ninukab departed Earth in search of a new vessel while Demeos returned to his normal life (*Superman* [first series] #262, March 1973).

NOLAN, ROGER "NIFTY"

The "confidence man and flim-flam artist" named Roger "Nifty" Nolan attempted to use the well-meaning but dim-witted salesmen Hocus and Pocus as his dupes in a plot to swindle two Metropolis millionaires out of $250,000, only to be thwarted by Superman (*Action Comics* #88, September 1945).

NON

Non was a good friend to Jor-El, an esteemed scientist, and a member of the Kryptonian Council. When he concurred with Jor-El's findings regarding their planet's instability, he was spurned by the Council. Non led a separatist movement until he was quietly abducted by the Science Council, which had him lobotomized, thereby turning a brilliant man into a grunting brute (*Action Comics Annual* #10, 2008). He fell under the sway of the power-hungry General Zod and his consort Ursa, and the trio wreaked havoc on Krypton until they were captured and exiled to the Phantom Zone by Jor-El.

When the villains escaped the Phantom Zone many years later, Non did Zod's bidding—only to be returned to the Zone. Unbeknownst to Zod and Ursa, their son Lor-Zod (see Christopher Kent) returned as well and remained in hiding, with the kindly Non looking after him. In time, Thara Ak-Var rescued Lor-Zod and escaped the Zone, with

Non

Non providing assistance. His deeds were finally discovered, and when the Kryptonians settled on the artificial world of New Krypton, Non was punished by being assigned to the Red Shard division of the Military Guild under the strict command of Lieutenant Asha Del-Nar. He was forced to fight wild animals in a hazing ritual until he was aided by Kal-El, earning the Man of Steel Non's loyalty.

Like all Kryptonians living under a yellow sun, Non possessed a full range of superpowers, but his lobotomy seemed to alter his physiology, making him stronger and faster than average Kryptonians, including Superman himself.

Non was one of the survivors of New Krypton's destruction and was consigned once more to the Phantom Zone as the war between the Kryptonians and Earth ended (*Superman: War of the Supermen* #4, July 2010).

NOOSE

A member of Intergang, Noose had a surname of either Palmiotti or Hoffman and served with Boss Moxie as hired muscle during the 1930s. The bald thug was later cloned by Dabney Donovan, who worked as part of Boss Moxie's inner circle in an Intergang takeover (*The Adventures of Superman* #544, March 1997). Despite enhancements that included elongated fingers enabling Noose to effortlessly strangle his enemies, the mute menace was ultimately taken into custody by Superman (*Action Comics* #758, October 1999).

NORDO, WANDA

In the wake of his Lexoran wife Ardora's death, Lex Luthor assembled a support crew around himself that included the criminal Wanda Nordo. "Wicked Wanda" had been the lover of gang boss Studs McCoy until she murdered him "with her bare hands and took over the mob herself." Working alongside the vengeful Luthor, Wanda harbored an unrequited love for her "Lexy." She was never an active participant in his many schemes of revenge against Superman, but was usually present during their planning, making her an accessory to Luthor's many crimes (*Superman* [first series] #385, July 1983).

NOR-KAN

Nor-Kan was a close friend to Jor-El and Lara on Krypton. The older scientist acted as a mentor to Jor-El until he was taken, along with the inhabitants of Kandor, when the city was stolen by Brainiac. He took up residence in a stately suburban mansion and maintained "photo-statues" of Jor-El and Lara so he would never forget their friendship. To keep him company, Nor-Kan adopted a pair of Kandorian birds—a nightwing and a flamebird. Nor-Kan also constructed a laboratory in a cavern he discovered underneath his mansion.

Superman and Jimmy Olsen once visited Kandor and befriended the kindly Nor-Kan, who was thrilled to learn that his friends' son had survived Krypton's destruction. When Superman and Jimmy had to adopt secret identities after mistakenly being branded outlaws, the pair were inspired by the birds and adopted costumes also reminiscent of Batman and Robin's. They took to Kandor's skies as Nightwing and Flamebird, giving rise to a new legend. The Kryptonian Crusaders were sheltered at Nor-Kan's home, and he allowed them to adapt his lab and car as the Nightcave and Nightmobile (*Superman* [first series] #158, January 1963).

When Brainiac was finally brought to Kandor for trial, the scientist was asked to prosecute the case, and his eloquence won a swift conviction. However, the Kandorians were ultimately compelled to let Brainiac go free in order to save the

life of Superman, which was being threatened by the Coluan's partner Lex Luthor (*Superman* [first series] #167, February 1964).

While working with the rare radioactive element Illium-349 in a failed attempt to build a device that could enlarge Kandor, Nor-Kan was fatally dosed (*Action Comics* #317, October 1964). A state funeral was held for the great man, and a memorial tablet was erected in his honor.

Nor-Kan's prized possessions were buried with him in his tomb inside Mirage Mountain, including a not-yet-perfected cure for virtually any illness (*Supergirl* [second series] #2, January 1973). The accessories of Nightwing and Flamebird that Nor-Kan had safeguarded were later discovered by his friend Dev-Re, who maintained the secret equipment until the day that Superman and Jimmy Olsen returned to Kandor (*Superman Family* #173, October–November 1975).

NORMAN, NORMIE

Selected by the *Daily Planet* as a finalist in its contest to find the "ideal average American," no one suspected that Normie Norman was actually a young criminal working for Hammerhead Haines. To ensure that his underling would win, Haines and his men attempted to force the other finalists to act in ways that would spoil the image of "normalness" the contest was searching for. One of the other finalists happened to be Clark Kent, who discovered the ploy and captured Norman. In an attempt to apprehend Norman and also disqualify himself, Kent waved a pistol around in plain sight, then pointed it at Norman. Instead, the judges proclaimed Clark Kent the winner, noting, ". . . like the ordinary American, you try to avoid trouble! But when it comes, you plunge in and make the other fellow sorry he started it! We feel that you are the perfect average American!" (*Action Comics* #92, January 1946).

NORTH POLE, THE

The northernmost point on the surface of the Earth. Here Superman maintained his Fortress of Solitude, noting, "I built it here, in the polar wastes because the intense cold keeps away snoopers" (*Superman* [first series] #58, May–June 1949). The Fortress was said to be located inside "a desolate mountain top in the Arctic" (*Action Comics* #241, June 1958).

One story had Jasper Rasper attempt to kidnap Santa Claus at the North Pole and ruin Christmas for the world, but he was stopped by the Man of Steel (*Action Comics* #105, February 1947). Superman also once defeated a criminal acting troupe that pretended to be the Norse gods Thor, Loki, and Odin in an attempt to extort a film production that was based at the pole (*Superman* [first series] #52, May–June 1948).

Superman also battled the Galactic Golem near the Fortress, using the magnetic pole to trap the creature and encase him in molten iron and nickel (*Superman* [first series] #258, November 1972).

NORTON, ALICE

Alice Norton was a young girl who had been blinded in a tragic auto accident. When she won the *Daily Planet*'s "Lovely Child" contest, Alice's prize was a day spent with Superman. The jaded youth did not believe he was a real super hero, so the Man of Steel took her flying. Each feat Superman then performed, a dubious Alice rationalized away, refusing to accept that he was anything but a muscular man in a costume. Everything changed for Alice when the Man of Steel used his X-ray vision to examine her eyes. He discovered a sliver of glass that was still trapped there and causing her vision loss. He surgically removed the glass, and when Alice began to see again, she was finally convinced that Superman was real. Better still, her father, who had caused the accident and vanished out of guilt, returned to be reunited with his wife and grateful daughter (*Superman* [first series] #96, March 1955).

NORTON, NICK

When Metropolis's incorruptible district attorney George Lash's wife was murdered, it at first looked as if the DA himself may have committed the crime. Instead, the truth was exposed by Superman, who determined that criminal Nick Norton and his two cronies were the guilty parties. While out on bail, they decided to discredit the DA and distract him in the hope that their trial would be postponed indefinitely (*Superman* [first series] #7, December 1940).

NORVAL

A collector of priceless jewels, Norval was found murdered in his intricately designed, supposedly burglar-proof home. Unbelievably, the evidence implicated *Daily Star* reporter Lois Lane, but Superman investigated further and proved her innocence. Instead, the real murderer was Burkley, the mansion's architect (*Superman* [first series] #6, September–October 1940).

NORVELL, EMIL

In order to increase his munitions sales, weapons manufacturer Emil Norvell hired lobbyist Alex Greer to entice Senator Barrows to introduce a bill that would ignite a war in the small South American republic of San Monté and maneuver the United States closer to entering the European conflict that became World War II. His efforts failed and he ran into Superman, which led to a moral debate. "What I can't understand," Superman asked, "is why you manufacture munitions when it means that thousands will die horribly." "Men are cheap," replied Norvell callously, "munitions, expensive!"

The experience prompted Norvell to flee to San Monté. When his own men turned on him, Norvell was rescued by the Man of Steel, who forced him to join San Monté's army. The experience turned Norvell from a warmonger to a pacifist, and he was allowed reentry to the United States after committing to abandon his munitions work permanently (*Action Comics* #1–2, June–July 1938).

In a short-lived alternate reality created by Dominus, Superman once again encountered Emil Norvell. Depicted as a Nazi sympathizer allied

Emil Norvell

with figures such as the ATOMIC SKULL, the munitions magnate was pursued by CLARK KENT and LOIS LANE to the Warsaw Ghetto. While he attempted to seek refuge with Nazi soldiers, the evil Norvell was instead cut down in a burst of machine-gun fire (*Superman: The Man of Steel* #80–82, June–August 1998).

NOVA

The name of TERRA-MAN's space-born winged white horse.

N.R.G.-X

Scientist Grant Haskill managed to survive an explosion at the nuclear reactor near which he worked, but the radiation transformed him into a living robot. As he tried to adapt to his new form, his movements were misinterpreted by a fearful public as hostile, and he was fired upon by the police. Superman intervened, but when Haskill, now called N.R.G.-X, touched him, the hero was turned into a literal man of steel. Superman eventually realized that he was only coated in a steel casing and broke free. He found N.R.G.-X threatening lab director Ray Ryker. While he prevented the robot from causing harm, N.R.G.-X self-destructed, leaving the human Haskill in a coma (*Superman* [first series] #339–340, September–October 1979).

In the reality after the INFINITE CRISIS, N.R.G.-X was hired by a Durlan who crash-landed on Earth in the wake of the IMPERIEX WAR. When Anderson Gaines, the reclusive financier behind S.T.A.R. LABS, encountered the wrecked starship in the Himalayas, he was replaced by the shape-shifting Durlan, whose race harbored a hatred for KRYPTONIANS. As Superman and BATMAN investigated the wrecked craft, Gaines revealed himself as a powerful threat. To enable himself to steal a Kryptonian spaceship stored in the FORTRESS OF SOLITUDE, Gaines hired the mercenary N.R.G.-X (Nuclear Radiation Generator, Experimental) to distract the Man of Steel. When Gaines and the ship threatened METROPOLIS, Batman boarded the ship and fought the Durlan, while Superman defeated N.R.G.-X. Rather than concede to the heroes, the alien opted to shatter his form while the ancient rocket crashed in the Atlantic Ocean (*Superman/Batman* #68–71, March–June 2010).

NUCLEAR WASTE

LEXCORP's Dr. Sydney Happerson hired Fadeout, Hardknox, Strongbox, and PDQ, a group of costumed criminals known as Nuclear Waste, to kill the employee who had leaked information to *DAILY PLANET* reporter LOIS LANE about an insurance scheme. They almost managed to accomplish their goal but were soundly defeated by Superman and never seen again (*Superman: The Man of Steel* #28, December 1993).

NURD, FARLOW

Farlow Nurd was a professor who invented what he called a "World Duplicator." When he tried to replicate Earth-1, however, Nurd created an imperfect duplicate filled with contradictions and conundrums that defied logic. The faux Earth was eventually erased using the World Duplicator by Nurd and Superman (*Action Comics* #388, May 1970).

Ferlin Nyxly

NYXLY, FERLIN

Years ago, pianist Ferlin Nyxly burst upon the classical music scene, supplanting Timos Achens as the most admired musical performer in the world. Achens couldn't explain how it was that his talent had vanished—and then six months later Nyxly had shown up out of nowhere. Until he began performing in public, Nyxly had been curator of the METROPOLIS Music Museum, where he chanced upon an instrument called the Devil's Harp. It had sat, neglected, with other instruments that had been found in the ruins of an ancient lost city. The talentless Nyxly plucked the instrument's strings, and suddenly his fondest dream—to be a concert-level performer—came true. When he made his Metropolis debut, however, Superman's flight overhead distracted the audience, spoiling the performance.

The magical Harp also corrupted his mind, and Nyxly, dressed like the god Pan, used it to commit robberies. Each time he plucked the strings and made a wish, he was granted abilities, including flight and invulnerability. It eventually became clear that each attribute he acquired came at Superman's expense.

Angry at Superman, Nyxly challenged the Man of Steel to a battle at Metropolis Bowl. Stealing more powers allowed him to defeat the Man of Steel, but Superman refused to surrender. The standoff ended when the SAND SUPERMAN, a construct that had been plaguing the hero, emerged from the shadows to destroy the Harp, restoring the proper abilities to both Superman and Achens. Since the Sand Superman was siphoning Superman's strength at the time, he acted out of an unspoken sense of self-preservation (*Superman* [first series] #235, March 1971).

Seeking another Devil's Harp supposedly located in the Utah Salt Flats, Nyxly instead discovered an alien armory, from which he took a suit of armor and an enchanted sling that created its own ammunition through the will of its user. The villain used the sling to battle Superman, but Nyxly was no match for the Man of Steel, who hurled the sling into the sun (*Superman* [first series] #253, June 1972). After using a stolen spacecraft in one final assault on Superman, Ferlin Nyxly was again defeated and never heard from again (*Superman* [first series] #409, July 1985).

NZYKMULK

MR. MXYZPTLK's deranged cousin Nzykmulk was older and therefore more experienced using magic that was natural to natives of ZRFFF in the Fifth Dimension. He made his presence known on Earth when he began playing pranks on the Man of Steel. Superman began to experience oddities such as being impaled by the physical sound effects generated by a leather-clad punkish JIMMY OLSEN. Meanwhile Mxyzptlk encountered LANA LANG who treated him like a dog, placing both a collar and leash on the imp and forcing him head-first into a dog food dish. Nzykmulk trapped his cousin and Superman in the Fifth Dimension, where he intended to kill them and record the horrific event for posterity. However, Superman knocked the older imp unconscious with a single blow and returned home to METROPOLIS with everything restored to normal (*Superman* [first series] #421, July 1986).

OLSEN, JAMES
PRESS

OBERON

Orphaned at a young age after a fire at his home, the dwarf named Oberon wound up living with a traveling circus. He was poorly treated, physically and emotionally abused by the circus's cruel ringmaster. The only one to show him kindness was Thaddeus Brown, the escape artist known as the first Mister Miracle. Oberon trained under Brown's tutelage, and they were eventually joined by Scott Free. Brown and Oberon eventually went to Vietnam in search of Brown's missing son, but freeing the soldier earned Brown the ire of the criminal Steel Hand (*Secret Origins* [third series] #33, December 1988). Back in America, Steel Hand sought revenge by murdering Brown, and Free became the new Mister Miracle (*Mister Miracle* #1, March–April 1971). After bringing Steel Hand to justice, Oberon joined Free and became his manager in addition to helping him perfect his performances for the circus.

Oberon was fiercely loyal to Scott, even after learning that his partner was actually from a race dubbed the New Gods. He grudgingly accepted Scott's marriage to Big Barda; the unusual trio adventured around the world and served for a time with the Justice League of America. Oberon went on to become a right-hand man to the JLA's benefactor at the time, Maxwell Lord, when the team went international (*Justice League International* #7, November 1987). He also briefly dated the South American member Fire, but left the group during one of its breakups. After Scott Free's death Oberon grieved for a time, then eventually moved on with his life, regrowing his hair and adding a monocle. He created Meta-Movers, a firm specializing in handling the equipment and affairs of super heroes and the teams they belonged to (*Doom Patrol* [fifth series] #76, April 2010).

OBSESSION

Dana Dearden was a psychologically unstable woman who was fascinated by larger-than-life, heroic figures. When Superman arrived in Metropolis, her interest in mythological figures was transferred to the Man of Steel. While working as a makeup assistant at WGBS (*The Adventures of Superman* #528, October 1995), she dated Jimmy Olsen but broke it off quickly when he failed to introduce her to his "pal" (*The Adventures of Superman* #532–535, February–June 1996). She wound up stealing ancient coins from the Museum of Art and gained tremendous powers from them, making her a match for the Man of Steel. Stealing Jimmy's signal watch, she summoned Superman to show off her new abilities. She considered herself his ideal mate and called herself Superwoman, but he rejected her advances, and that seemingly tipped her over the edge. She lashed out at the Man of Steel and they fought a brief, inconclusive battle. Afterward, Jimmy named the unbalanced woman Obsession (*The Adventures of Superman* #538, September 1996).

Maxima and Obsession once battled over the Man of Steel, despite his obvious lack of romantic interest in either (*Superman: The Man of Tomorrow* #10, Winter 1998). Dearden, however, redeemed herself in Superman's eyes when she sacrificed her life to save her idol from creatures created by the lethal designer drug DMN (*The Adventures of Superman* #574, January 2000). In Hell, Obsession joined with other villains in an attempt to escape back to

Earth. She ultimately gave up what now passed for life and threw herself into the jaws of Cerberus to save her allies, convinced that her second "death" enhanced her claim as Superman's perfect mate (*Harley Quinn* #21–22, August–September 2002).

On Earth-1, the god-empowered coins used by Dana Dearden were first discovered by archaeologist Clive Arno. As he fought the villainous Krellik for control of the powerful artifacts, Arno briefly crossed paths with Superman (*Captain Action* #1, October–November 1968).

OCEANIA

Following the theory of parallel world development, life on Oceania was remarkably similar to that on Earth, complete with a superpowered champion named Hyper-Man. Macropolis's best-known television reporter Lydia Long was the powerful hero's girlfriend, who was unaware that he was really her co-worker Chester King (*Action Comics* #265, June 1960).

OCEANIA NETWORK, THE

Macropolis's best-known television reporter Lydia Long and her co-worker Chester King both worked for the Oceania Network, the premier TV station in the gleaming city (*Action Comics* #265, June 1960).

OCTOPUS, THE

The Octopus was a self-styled criminal mastermind whose gang wore gray hoods with an octopus symbol on the forehead. They committed a series of crimes but were apprehended by Batman, Robin, and Superman. What made the case noteworthy was the arrival of an amateur crime fighter, complete with a unique arsenal of tools, named the Crimson Avenger, a counterpart of the World War II–era Earth-2 adventurer (*World's Finest Comics* #131, February 1963).

O'GRADY, LUCKY

A civic-minded resident of the Roaring Kitchen section of Metropolis who helped Superman bring a crooked politician and his gangland manager to justice (*Superman* [first series] #22, May–June 1943).

OKAMURA, HIRO

This teenage genius inventor, nicknamed Toyman, proved both impediment and aid to Batman and Superman.

OLAV

The planet Zor was taken over by the power-mad scientist Olav, whose scheme to assume dictatorial control of the world was thwarted by Superman (*Action Comics* #168, May 1952).

O'LEARY, DUTCH

When Skyways Airlines fired ruthless gangster and "successful gambler" Dutch O'Leary, he sought revenge by masterminding a series of "disastrous crashes" that threatened to ruin the airline until he was finally apprehended by Superman (*Action Comics* #43, December 1941).

OLSEN, BONZO

Jimmy Olsen once had the misfortune of having his mind switched with that of a gorilla when he was at the Metropolis Zoo. At the moment Olsen activated his signal watch to summon the Man of Steel, Professor Phineas Potter was demonstrating his new telepathic helmet. When Superman arrived, he deduced what had occurred and constructed a sanctuary for the human—now controlled by the animal—while Jimmy, in the ape's body, reported for work at the *Daily Planet*. Editor in chief Perry White nicknamed the simian reporter in an ill-fitting suit "Bonzo." Taking advantage of Jimmy's latest misfortune, White assigned him to cover a wrestling match between Golden George and the hirsute Gorilla, as well as the premiere of a science-fiction film about a simian policeman featuring Zimba, a trained gorilla.

Superman took pity on Bonzo and brought him on patrol with him, where the Man of Steel concluded that Jimmy's "ultrasonic signal . . . altered the telepathizer machine and caused the mind-exchange," allowing Potter to reverse the process and return the minds to their proper bodies (*Superman's Pal, Jimmy Olsen* #24, October 1957).

OLSEN, JAKE

Jimmy Olsen's father Jake was a career soldier, "not afraid to get dirty if that was asked of him." This unquestioning loyalty cost him his left eye on one mission—he wore an eye patch for the rest of his life—but also meant that he often led special assignments. On one such assignment he had to abandon his pregnant wife; upon its completion, he was given additional objectives until he was finally rewarded with a prestigious role as military liaison for Project Cadmus (*Superman* [second series] #39, January 1990).

Olsen was described as a hard man, but when he was alone, he thought often of the child he'd never met and of his wife. Through surveillance photos taken by colleagues, he learned he had a son, but he imagined that even if he retired from the military, it would be too difficult to return to his family and pick up where he left off. Commander Olsen eventually discovered the Evil Factory of Mokkari and Simyan in Great Britain, but was

"AFTER ALL, DIDN'T THE SECURITY OF THE FREE WORLD TAKE PRECEDENCE OVER ONE MAN'S FAMILY?
"EXEMPLARY DEDICATION TOOK HIM THROUGH BIGGER AND BIGGER MISSIONS UNTIL THE BIGGEST ONE OF ALL WAS DROPPED IN HIS LAP--

captured and experimented on by the deadly duo (*Superman* [second series] #40, February 1990). They produced a number of clones of Jake Olsen but "terminated" all of them save Number One. Simyan and Mokkari believed that their first human clone subject died, but neither the manner of Jake Olsen's death nor his corpse was ever depicted (*Superman* [second series] #43, May 1990).

All this began to come to light when Jake's "widow," Sarah Olsen, discovered a picture of Perry White in Southeast Asia with her husband in the background, many years after his supposed death (*Superman* [second series] #19, July 1988). Embarking on an investigation, Sarah caught sight of twin Jake Olsens in London, then approached them and was carried off to the Evil Factory. This was apparently the incident that resulted in the termination of the clones. Number One himself was zapped by a Z-Ray and projected into a colorless other-dimensional void where Simyan and Mokkari dumped their failures. Number One eventually made contact with Jimmy Olsen when he briefly entered the void, and Jimmy (along with Superman and the Guardian) helped free Sarah Olsen, who then projected her abductors into the void (*Superman* [second series] #39–43, January–May 1990).

Number One continued to fight Simyan and Mokkari, firing chromatic rays from his left eyepiece even as the villains attempted to seize control of the the realm dubbed Exile World (*The Adventures of Superman* #489, April 1992; *Superman: The Man of Steel* #11, May 1992).

In a later account published after the Infinite Crisis, Jake Olsen had been a master sergeant stationed at Fort Bridwell in Metropolis, while Dr. Sarah Olsen was the famed archaeologist who found the lost city of Kurtiswana. After his wife vanished in the Amazon, Jake left Jimmy in the care of a neighbor and rushed off to begin a search (*Superman* #665, September 2007). Whether the saga of Jake and Sarah Olsen paralleled their previously recorded adventures with the Evil Factory was not recorded.

OLSEN, JAMES BARTHOLOMEW "JIMMY"

Jimmy Olsen began his career as a cub reporter at Earth-2's *Daily Star* in Metropolis, where he was befriended by Lois Lane and Clark Kent (*Action Comics* #10, March 1939; first name revealed in *Superman* [first series] #13, November–December 1941; last name revealed in *Superman* [first series] #15, March–April 1942). He apparently began work as an office boy at a very young age before literally growing up at the paper. Jimmy earned his first byline when he reported on Superman's encounter with the costumed villain known as the Archer (*Superman* [first series] #13, November–December 1941). Through the years, he had numerous adventures alongside the Man of Steel. In time, the cub became a man and went by the name *James,* eventually becoming one of the senior writers on the paper.

At one point, James Olsen was dying from an unnamed disease, but his life was saved by the Jimmy

AS JIMMY, ANXIOUS FOR HIS STORY, TAKES A CLOSER LOOK...
KRYPTONITE DOESN'T BOTHER ME, YOU KNOW! WHY, THIS CHEST HAS WRITING ON IT IN SOME UNKNOWN LANGUAGE! I WONDER WHAT'S INSIDE. I'LL OPEN IT AND SEE!

Olsen and Superman from Earth-1 (*Superman Family* #186–187, November–December 1977 to January–February 1978).

On Earth-1, James Bartholomew Olsen (middle name revealed in *The Adventures of Superman: "The Talkative Dummy,"* October 3, 1952) began life as an office boy at Metropolis's DAILY PLANET before being promoted to cub reporter (*Superman* [first series] #86, January 1954). His father, archaeologist MARK OLSEN, was missing and presumed dead after a train accident that also cost Jimmy's mother her life (*Superman's Pal, Jimmy Olsen* #75, March 1964). The redheaded, freckled young adult was enthusiastic and always anxious for a taste of adventure. Confounding his father's efforts to find him, young Jimmy was initially taken into the custody of a couple who lived in a remote mountain community before moving to the city of Metropolis. When the *Daily Planet* acquired a helicopter called the Flying Newsroom, Jimmy often flew aboard, rushing from story to story with pilot Jumbo Jones (*Superman's Pal, Jimmy Olsen* #1, September–October 1954).

His desire to get scoops meant he also mastered makeup techniques, frequently disguising himself to go undercover and get close to the action, often with disastrous results that required help from the Man of Steel (*Superman's Pal, Jimmy Olsen* #1, September–October 1954; others). One of Jimmy's more memorable disguises was as Magi the Magnificent, a suave stage magician who interacted with exotic actress Sandra Rogers, herself an alter ego assumed—unbeknownst to Olsen—by his girlfriend LUCY LANE (*Superman's Pal, Jimmy Olsen* #74, January 1964; #78, July 1964, and #82, January 1965).

When Metropolis celebrated Boy's Day, Jimmy served as the paper's managing editor for twenty-four hours, performing his duties with remarkable professionalism (*Superman* [first series] #86, January 1954). When the *Planet* launched a new international edition, Jimmy Olsen was briefly appointed editor of the paper's London version (*Action Comics* #203, April 1955). Even after Jimmy turned twenty-one (*Superman's Pal, Jimmy Olsen* #61, June 1962), editor in chief PERRY WHITE felt his enthusiasm needed to be tempered with experience, and the young man toiled at the paper until his promotion to full reporter. HAZEL POWELL became the *Planet*'s newest cub reporter thereafter (*Superman's Pal, Jimmy Olsen* #124, October 1969) but Jimmy found greater headaches with later additions to the reporting staff, such as the conniving Meg Tempest (*Superman's Pal, Jimmy Olsen* #149, May 1972; others) and PERCY BRATTEN (*Superman's Pal, Jimmy Olsen* #151, July 1972; others).

By working at the *Daily Planet,* Jimmy—clad in his trademark bow tie and green-checked jacket—had numerous opportunities to meet Superman, and in time they developed a well-publicized friendship. His friends and foes knew that the Man of Steel considered Jimmy his pal, a fact that the occasionally boastful Olsen made sure certain people knew. While the general populace sometimes cast doubt on Superman's reputation, Jimmy remained the hero's staunchest supporter through the years.

Given his exploits, there was little wonder that Jimmy developed an extensive and valuable collection of Superman trophies and souvenirs (*Superman's Pal, Jimmy Olsen* #11, February 1957, and #15, August 1957), a collection to which Superman continually added with exotic gifts from distant planets and other exciting memorabilia (*World's Finest Comics* #147, February 1965; others). In much the same way, the Man of Steel had an entire room dedicated to the cub reporter in the FORTRESS OF SOLITUDE (*Action Comics* #241, June 1958).

Their remarkable friendship was sealed when Superman gifted Jimmy with a watch that could emit an ultrasonic sound to summon the World's Greatest Super Hero in times of emergency (*Superman's Pal, Jimmy Olsen* #1, September–October 1954). This one-of-a-kind wristwatch, with its distinctive *zee zee* sound, was made from silver, platinum, and gold, along with the alien metals Tulanium from the planet ZUMOOR, Morabalt from XENON, and Deronium, an artificial element unknown in our time that Superman brought back from the thirtieth century, where he had been visiting the pre-CRISIS Legion. The final metal was a bit of Kryptonian Tuhanite, retrieved from the spaceship that brought the Kryptonian villain GRA-MO to Earth (*80-Page Giant* #13, August 1965).

By one account, young Jimmy's first job in Metropolis was as a test subject for a time machine that transported him to the planet KRYPTON. While there, he babysat KAL-EL and even spanked the misbehaving toddler at one point. Returning to Earth, Jimmy was astonished to be sought out by Superman, whose super-memory recalled everything. As a thank-you, he gave the boy his signal watch and set him up with a job as a cub reporter at the *Daily Planet* (*Superman's Pal, Jimmy Olsen* #36, April 1959).

Another version had copy boy Jimmy getting the scoop on mobsters Turk Moraine and Big Mike Arnstein's "heavy-duty extortion racket." By chance, Superman rescued the teenager when the thugs threw him out of a high-rise window, and a delighted Perry White promoted Olsen to cub reporter. Observing that Jimmy's promotion almost certainly meant there'd be even more rescues in his future, Superman presented the boy with a signal watch for future emergencies (*Superman Family* #218, May 1982).

His proximity to Superman often led Jimmy to experience life as a super hero firsthand. He once drank a serum that allowed him to adventure under the guise of ELASTIC LAD (*Superman's Pal, Jimmy Olsen* #37, June 1959), which earned him an honorary role with the thirtieth century's LEGION OF SUPER-HEROES (*Superman's Pal, Jimmy Olsen* #72, October 1963). In his own era, he accompanied Superman to KANDOR, and when they needed to disguise themselves they became the masked heroes NIGHTWING and FLAMEBIRD, styled after BATMAN and ROBIN (*Superman* [first series] #158, January 1963). As a result, he learned hand-to-hand crime-fighting techniques, along with rudimentary detective skills that later helped him win honorary membership in the famed Mystery Analysts of GOTHAM CITY (*Superman's Pal, Jimmy Olsen* #111, June 1968).

Jimmy temporarily acquired Superman-like powers on several occasions, assuming alter egos such as Super-Youth (*Superman's Pal, Jimmy Olsen* #25, December 1957), Super-Lad (*Superman's Pal, Jimmy Olsen* #39, September 1959), STEELMAN (*Superman's Pal, Jimmy Olsen* #93, June 1966), and Ultra-Olsen (*Superman's Pal, Jimmy Olsen* #129, June 1970, and #158, June 1973). He flew via jetpack as Wonder Lad (*Superman's Pal, Jimmy Olsen* #21, June 1957) and used CIRCE's magic wand to become the Animal Master (*Superman's Pal, Jimmy Olsen* #45, June 1960).

THAT DOESN'T WORRY ME! I CAN ALWAYS GET HELP WITH MY SECRET SUPERMAN SIGNAL, HIDDEN IN THIS WRISTWATCH!
IF HE ONLY KNEW THAT HIS FELLOW REPORTER, CLARK KENT, ACTUALLY IS SUPERMAN!

Jimmy and Robin the Boy Wonder partnered on numerous occasions, even establishing their own headquarters, the Aerie, located in an abandoned observatory (*World's Finest Comics* #141, May 1964). After several exploits together, Batman trusted Jimmy enough to reveal to him his secret identity BRUCE WAYNE (*World's Finest Comics* #144, September 1964).

Jimmy took those lessons to heart when a date with Lucy Lane turned into a real-life espionage thriller, with the reporter acting as Secret Agent Double Five (*Superman's Pal, Jimmy Olsen* #89, December 1965, and #92, April 1966).

The reporter also endured bizarre transformations as a result of aliens, sorcerers, accidents, and experiments conducted by his friend PROFESSOR PHINEAS POTTER. He became an invisible kid

SUPERMAN'S PAL
JIMMY OLSEN
GREAT SCOTT! WHY IS JIMMY STUFFING THAT VOLCANO CRATER WITH A BATTLESHIP? WHAT ON EARTH IS HIS HUGE, TWISTED TURTLE-MIND UP TO?
WHEN WILL IMPULSIVE CUB REPORTER JIMMY OLSEN LEARN TO HEED THE ADVICE OF HIS FAMED PAL, SUPERMAN? CERTAINLY JIMMY'S CURIOSITY HAS LED HIM OFTEN ENOUGH INTO PERILOUS PREDICAMENTS! HOWEVER, NEVER BEFORE HAS JIMMY BROUGHT UPON HIMSELF AND MANKIND SO HUGE A CALAMITY AS THE DAY HE DECIDED TO TAMPER WITH A COLOSSAL FORCE THAT TURNED HIM INTO--
THE GIANT TURTLE MAN!

(*Superman's Pal, Jimmy Olsen* #12, April 1956, and #36, April 1959), a speed demon (*Superman's Pal, Jimmy Olsen* #15, September 1956), an invulnerable Boy of Steel (*Superman's Pal, Jimmy Olsen* #16, October–November 1956), a human Geiger counter (*Superman's Pal, Jimmy Olsen* #19, March 1957), a merman (*Superman's Pal, Jimmy Olsen* #20, April 1957), a Super-Brain (*Superman's Pal, Jimmy Olsen* #22, August 1957), a gorilla reporter (*Superman's Pal, Jimmy Olsen* #24, October 1957), Birdboy (*Superman's Pal, Jimmy Olsen* #26, February 1958), a human skyscraper (*Superman's Pal, Jimmy Olsen* #28, April 1958), a latter-day Pinocchio whose nose grew when he lied (*Superman's Pal, Jimmy Olsen* #32, October 1958), a human flamethrower (*Superman's Pal, Jimmy Olsen* #33, December 1958), a human octopus (*Superman's Pal, Jimmy Olsen* #41, December 1959), a wolfman (*Superman's Pal, Jimmy Olsen* #44, April 1960), a giant Turtle Boy (*Superman's Pal, Jimmy Olsen* #53, June 1961), an aqua-boy (*Superman's Pal, Jimmy Olsen* #55, September 1961, and #115, October 1968), a super-freak with huge girth and hair all over his face (*Superman's Pal, Jimmy Olsen* #59, March 1962), a porcupine boy (*Superman's Pal, Jimmy Olsen* #65, December 1962), a human metal-eater (*Superman's Pal, Jimmy Olsen* #68, April 1963), a boy with the Midas touch (*Superman's Pal, Jimmy Olsen* #73, December 1963), an imp with powers like Mr. Mxyzptlk (*Superman's Pal, Jimmy Olsen* #74, January 1964), a colossal boy (*Superman's Pal, Jimmy Olsen* #77, June 1964), Congorilla (*Superman's Pal, Jimmy Olsen* #86, July 1965), a counterpart to Star Boy capable of increasing mass (*Superman's Pal, Jimmy Olsen* #88, October 1965), Insect-Boy (*Superman's Pal, Jimmy Olsen* #94, July 1966), Atlas Olsen (*Superman's Pal, Jimmy Olsen* #96, September 1966), Element Lad, Lightning Lad, Sun Boy (*Superman's Pal, Jimmy Olsen* #99, January 1967), a Hyper Boy with a super-punch (*Superman's Pal, Jimmy Olsen* #121, July 1969), a man with a destructive touch (*Superman's Pal, Jimmy Olsen* #161, November 1973), and Alter Ego, capable of doing almost anything (*Action Comics* #570, August 1985).

Jimmy grew into adulthood, and with it came new adventures, beginning with his discovery of the DNA Project and the threat posed by Darkseid and his minions (*Superman's Pal, Jimmy Olsen* #133, June 1971). He spent some time traveling the country in the Whiz Wagon along with a new incarnation of the youthful Newsboy Legion. During these exploits, he began to understand that the universe was a far more dangerous place than he'd ever thought.

After parting ways with the Newsboy Legion, Jimmy returned to full-time reporting and was dubbed "Mr. Action" by Galaxy Broadcasting president Morgan Edge as a cross-promotional exercise with WGBS-TV (*Superman's Pal, Jimmy Olsen* #155, January 1973). He also shared a number of adventures with policeman Jim Corrigan (*Superman's Pal, Jimmy Olsen* #149, May 1972; others), ultimately seeing his friend promoted to detective (*Superman's Pal, Jimmy Olsen* #163, February–March 1974).

As a result of Jimmy's well-known friendship, he became a celebrity in his own right, complete with a large Jimmy Olsen Fan Club, which met monthly in Metropolis (*Superman's Pal, Jimmy Olsen* #37, June 1959; others). His fame always came with a price, including on-again, off-again romances with women, most notably Lois's notoriously fickle sister Lucy. After he and Lucy were no longer a couple, Jimmy dated socialite Barbara Bench (*Superman Family* #184, July–August 1977; others) and *Daily Planet* receptionist Jennifer Owens (*Superman Family* #209, August 1981; others) for extended periods of time.

Jimmy lived alone in Metropolis, even after it was learned his father was still alive. His apartment building was at 1537 West Fargo Street (*Superman Family* #218, May 1982) and his apartment number was 4H (*Superman* [first series] #127, February 1959), then 303 (*Superman Family* #191, September–October 1978). It was in the Temple Square area of Metropolis (*Superman's Pal, Jimmy Olsen* #5, May–June 1955), with a superintendent named Mr. Hardy (*Superman's Pal, Jimmy Olsen* #9, December 1955) and an unnamed landlady (*Superman's Pal, Jimmy Olsen* #20, April 1957).

Jimmy had a wide range of hobbies, including bowling (*Action Comics* #317, October 1964). After all his time aboard the Flying Newsroom, he learned how to pilot helicopters (*Action Comics* #290, July 1962). Superman taught him Kryptonese (*Superman* [first series] #158, January 1963).

There were numerous people who bore a remarkable resemblance to the reporter, including the hoodlum Baby-Face (*Superman* [first series] #93, November 1954), the Kandorian "criminal scientist" El Gar-Kur (*Action Comics* #253, June 1959), and Zol-Lar, Jimmy Olsen's double in the Kandorian Lookalike Squad (*Superman's Pal, Jimmy Olsen* #70, July 1963). By shaving his head and adding a scar to his face, Jimmy could also impersonate gangster Winky McCoy (*Superman's Pal, Jimmy Olsen* #47, September 1960). Additionally, there existed a Jimmy Olsen robot that was used on numerous occasions (*Superman* [first series] #152, April 1962).

Jimmy's ancestors included Pilgrim Eric Olsen, eighteenth-century secret agent/buccaneer "Greenbeard" Olsen, and Lars Olsen (*Superman's Pal, Jimmy Olsen* #21, June 1957). He acquired his middle name from Sir Bartholomew Merriwether Olsen, a British explorer who died at the age of 109 (*Superman's Pal, Jimmy Olsen* #89, December 1965). In the present, Jimmy had at least two cousins, rock star Jerry Olsen (*Superman's Pal, Jimmy Olsen* #32, October 1958) and high school student Mike, whom Superman once dissuaded from dropping out of school (*Superman* [first series] #352, October 1980).

In one potential future, Earth-1's Jimmy Olsen married Lucy Lane and succeeded Perry White as editor of the *Daily Planet* (*Superman Family* #200, March–April 1980) and its computer-based successor, the Universe News System. Jimmy lived long enough to enjoy his redheaded twin grandchildren, Clark and Lois Olsen (*Superman* [first series] #372, June 1982) but never imagined that they would go down in history themselves, or that his twenty-ninth-century descendant Kristin Wells would later travel back in time to become the mysterious heroine known as Superwoman (*DC Comics Presents Annual* #2, 1983).

On the Earth fashioned in the wake of Crisis on Infinite Earths, Jimmy Olsen was primarily a photographer for the *Daily Planet,* having begun his career as a thirteen-year-old copy boy. After his friend Chrissie MacMillan overdosed on drugs, Jimmy desperately tried to track down Superman to save her life, doing so by cobbling together stereo components to unleash an ultrasonic SOS that attracted the Man of Steel's attention. Inspired by the incident, Superman later created a signal watch for Jimmy (*World of Metropolis* #4, November 1988).

Jimmy's father Jake Olsen had been a soldier who was clandestinely Project Cadmus's head of security, in whose service he supposedly died while his wife was pregnant (*Superman* [second series] #39, January 1990). Sarah Olsen and her young son struggled to make ends meet with the help of Jimmy's grandparents (*The Adventures of Superman* #462, January 1990), and his uncle Fred and aunt Lynn in Kingston (*Action Comics* #699, May 1994) before settling into the Metropolis borough of Bakerline. Later, Sarah and Jimmy discovered that Jake had spent years pursuing escapees from Project Cadmus and had been killed—long after his officially reported death—by Simyan and Mokkari (*Superman* [second series] #39–43, January–May 1990).

Much of Jimmy's career paralleled his Earth-1 counterpart's, complete with bizarre transformations and his becoming Elastic Lad (*The Adventures of Superman* #458, September 1989). He donned a Turtle Boy costume to appear in commercials for pizza after being temporarily laid off from the *Daily Planet* (*The Adventures of Superman* #487, February 1992). Jimmy also had

an on-again, off-again romance with Lucy Lane (*Superman* [second series] #4, April 1987; others) and ultimately wished her well when she fell in love with and married reporter Ron Troupe.

Jimmy's friendship with Superman was not without its rough patches. Accidentally infected by Superman with an alien virus that gave him painful elastic powers, the young photographer was angry when his friend restricted him to Project Cadmus until a cure could be found (*The Adventures of Superman* #458–459, September–October 1989; *Superman* [second series] #37, November 1989). Later, caught up in his enthusiasm over his TV reporting job at WGBS, Jimmy unthinkingly coached Metallo on Superman's vulnerabilities during a live broadcast and found himself ostracized by his friends in the immediate aftermath (*Superman: The Man of Steel* #68 and *Superman* [second series] #124—both June 1997). Regardless of disagreements, Jimmy remained close to the Man of Steel. The young man was one of those "people who choose to make their life count," the hero once declared. "The world needs them more than it needs me"(*Action Comics* #835, March 2006).

Much of Jimmy's life revolved around the *Daily Planet,* and he was especially close to Clark Kent and Lois Lane, taking delight when they became a couple and announced their engagement (*The Adventures of Superman* #473, December 1990). Later, Jimmy happily agreed to share his apartment with Clark when his friend was temporarily displaced (*The Adventures of Superman* #506, November 1993) and was honored to serve as Clark's best man at his wedding to Lois (*Superman: The Wedding Album* #1, December 1996). One of Jimmy's most cherished photos was the picture he took of Superman and Clark together, unaware that the latter was actually a disguised Matrix (*Superman* [second series] #34, August 1989).

The young man's tenure at the *Planet* was erratic. Jimmy was among those let go when 10 percent of the staff was laid off (*Superman* [second series] #57, July 1991) and even endured a period of homelessness (*The Adventures of Superman* #486, January 1992) before finding temporary lodging with Ace o' Clubs owner Bibbo Bibbowski (*Action Comics* #673, January 1992). In time, Jimmy was able to do some freelance photography for *Newstime Magazine* (*Action Comics* #675, March 1992) and returned to the *Daily Planet* in time to take one of the most celebrated pictures of his career with his image of a dead Superman after the Man of Steel's epic battle with Doomsday (*Superman* [second series] #75 and *The Adventures of Superman* #498—

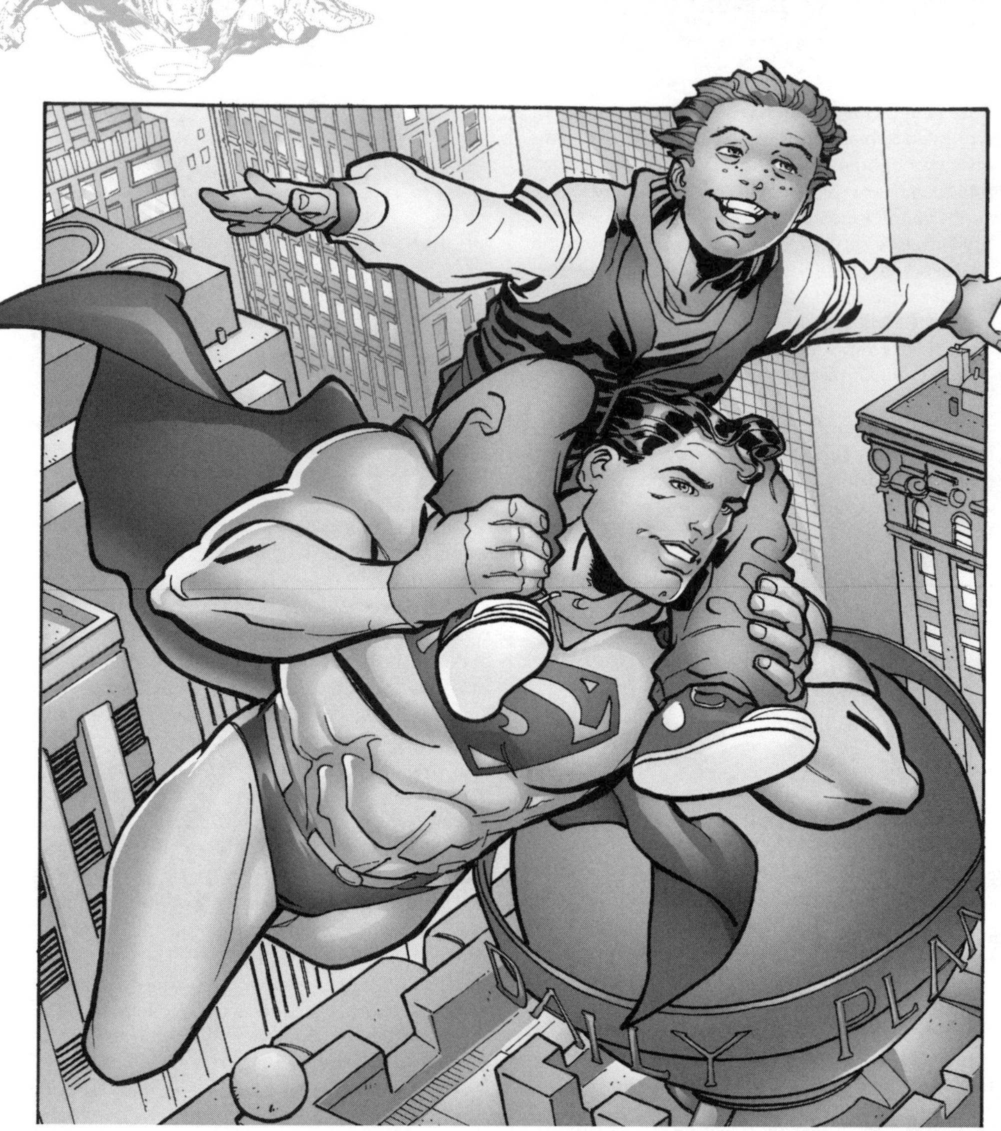

January 1993). That photograph, and others taken by Jimmy over the years, were subsequently used in a tribute issue of *Newstime* (*Superman* [second series] #77, March 1993).

Chafing over the perceived disrespect he got at the *Planet,* he eventually quit the paper (*Superman* [second series] #103, August 1995) and wound up being hired by Cat Grant to work for Galaxy Broadcasting (*Action Comics* #714, September 1995). His thrilling broadcasts soon earned Jimmy the nickname Mr. Action (*Superman* [second series] #105, October 1995) and made him a ratings darling. When he claimed to know Superman's alter ego, the newsman became the object of interest from Intergang, which chased him across the country. The fact was, Jimmy had the wrong man identified but thought better of it and kept the name to himself. The ill-conceived stunt immediately got him fired from Galaxy (*The Adventures of Superman* #550, and *Action Comics* #737, both September 1997).

Eventually, Jimmy returned to the *Planet* and became one of only four employees who shifted over to the Web-based LexCom news site when the newspaper was temporarily shut down (*Superman: Save the Planet* #1, October 1998; *Action Comics* #750, January 1999). When Clark Kent was briefly demoted to an outpost called the Shack, Jimmy even picked up his friend's reporter beat (*Action Comics* #831, November 2005).

Along the way, Jimmy met Misa, one of the Hairies—genetic constructs from New Genesis—and they had a brief romance (*The Adventures of Superman* #553, December 1997, to *Superman Forever* #1, June 1998).

When the B13 Virus transformed his city into a true Metropolis of the future, Jimmy was pursued by the artificial intelligence that controlled the city, and he tried to teach it respect for humanity (*Superman's Metropolis* #1–12, June 2003–May 2004).

Jimmy continued to work for the *Daily Planet,* sharpening his skills and gaining respect not only for his prose but also for his photographic eye. His connection to Superman, however, continued to embroil him in countless adventures. At one point, as he investigated the death of the criminal known as the Joker's Daughter, Jimmy unexpectedly developed superpowers and used them in a new costumed identity, that of Mr. Action. Despite this, he could not earn the respect of America's champions, the Justice League of America. During this time, his powers helped him learn the heroes' identities, and he promised to keep their secrets. While he tried to understand what had happened to him, he began an ill-fated romance with a female Forager from New Genesis. He finally learned that he was a "soulcatcher," acquiring the superpowered attributes of the various New Gods who were being killed one by one by Infinity-Man. Darkseid had designated Jimmy as the receptacle, concluding that he'd be close to the action, allowing Darkseid to kidnap Jimmy and use him to help remake the Fifth World in Darkseid's image. Superman attempted to intervene, but the Apokoliptian lord manipulated Jimmy into emitting kryptonite radiation that nearly killed the hero. The attack was stopped thanks to the intervention of Ray Palmer, the scientist also known as the Atom (*Countdown to Final Crisis* #52–1, 2007–2008).

During this period Superman also asked Jimmy to look after Krypto the Super-Dog for a time (*Action Comics* #854, Mid-October 2007).

Later, Jimmy Olsen saw a dark figure observing Superman's battle with the god-like Atlas. Encouraged by Clark Kent, he dedicated two weeks to unraveling the mystery, which he managed to do. The mysterious man was Codename: Assassin, who was hunting clones, a fact explained to Jimmy by Dubbilex, a genetic creation at Project Cadmus. The trail led Jimmy to Warpath, Arizona, where Jim Harper, the original clone of the Guardian, was trying to live his life in peace. Everything pointed to a faction of the U.S. military gathering intelligence in order to find ways to successfully kill the Man of Steel (*Superman's Pal, Jimmy Olsen Special* #1, December 2008).

Jimmy's signal watches went through several upgrades over the years, sometimes necessitated by their destruction during clashes with the likes of Baron Ruthven (*Superman: The Man of Steel* #14, August 1992) and Obsession (*The Adventures of Superman* #538, September 1996). After Superman's departure for New Krypton, Jimmy was contacted by Mon-El, who provided him with a new signal watch attuned to the Daxamite hero's hearing (*Superman* #686, May 2009).

Determined to be taken seriously as a journalist, Jimmy painstakingly began piecing together what obviously became a government conspiracy to kill the recently arrived Kryptonians rescued by Superman from Brainiac's vessel. Jimmy had spotted a shrouded figure observing Superman's fight with the time displaced Atlas and learned the figure was Codename: Assassin who was attached to General Samuel Lane's Project 7734. At Project Cadmus, Jimmy discovered a mortally wounded Dubbilex and was told how Codename: Assassin killed all the Guardian clones except for one who was hiding in Warpath, Arizona. Jimmy traveled there and convinced the last Jim Harper clone to come back to Metropolis and help expose Project 7734. Olsen then contacted Amazing Woman, a member of Infinity Inc., who said she had information Jimmy needed, but she was killed by Code-

name: Assassin right before Jimmy arrived. With her dying breath, Amazing Woman told Jimmy how to find Natasha Irons, who knew of Project 7734 and had infiltrated it to learn more about it to bring it down. Jimmy then asked Mon-El for his help, but by then Codename: Assassin had tracked Jimmy down and tried to kill him. Jimmy faked his death and went into hiding, where he continued his investigation. He left clues about Project 7734 in his apartment for Perry White to find and use to expose the corrupt General Lane and his schemes (*Superman's Pal, Jimmy Olsen Special* #2, August 2009). Working from within the abandoned Pemberton Camera Factory, Jimmy continued to share his gathered information with Perry White and Mon-El until he could again reveal himself in Metropolis (*Superman* #695, December 2009).

While Brainiac was attacking New Krypton, Jimmy finally revealed himself as alive and shared his intelligence with Perry and Lois. He accompanied Lois as they went after Project 7734, intending to expose it for the criminal conspiracy it truly was. As a result, Jimmy risked his life time and again until they cornered General Lane in a hidden bunker. Rather than be arrested, Lane committed suicide before his daughter's eyes. Jimmy used a device crafted by Steel to access Natasha Irons's memory, turning her thoughts into properly processed documents. Jimmy then tapped a network of youthful allies he had built during his time in hiding. This "Newsboy Legion" uploaded the files to every media outlet around the world, finally revealing the truth for all to see (*Superman: War of the Supermen* #1–4, July 2010).

When reality shifted once more in the wake of the Infinite Crisis, Jimmy's career began when he was spotted by Perry White selling papers in front of the newspaper's headquarters. Clark Kent became intrigued and discovered that Jimmy held multiple paper routes, then learned the young man was homeless, often sleeping in the Daily Planet Building. Further, Clark learned that Jimmy's father had gone missing and his mother left him with a neighbor so she could search for her husband. That neighbor, however, kept the books for the Ten, a criminal organization that would later confront Superman as the One Hundred and the One Thousand. She was murdered to keep their secrets, and Jimmy had fled with nowhere else to go. When the Ten targeted Jimmy, in case he knew something he shouldn't, Superman saved the youth and, seeking companionship, befriended the boy. Perry added Jimmy to the staff as a copy boy, and he eventually rose to photographer and reporter (*Superman* #665, September 2007).

After meeting Superman, Jimmy designed a large, complex machine to signal the hero. The Man of Steel modified the design and turned it into the familiar signal watch (*Action Comics* #852, September 2007). Another apocryphal account asserted that Superman had rescued the reckless young photographer from so many near-fatal encounters with criminals that he felt compelled to create the signal watch rather than risk Jimmy being killed (*Superman Confidential* #12, April 2008).

History would later be altered again. Struggling with his internship, fifteen-year-old Jimmy Olsen took the first photo of Superman after he accidentally met him on the rooftop of the *Daily Planet* while they were both contemplating their future in Metropolis. The photo got Jimmy his job at the *Daily Planet,* and he became known as the only photographer that Superman stopped for. Of course, most of the time Jimmy was so overeager that his photos came out rushed, blurred, or black; sometimes he even forgot to remove the camera's lens cap. Clark Kent found himself connecting with Jimmy, the only other person in the office who was initially treated with as much disrespect

by the other reporters as Clark was (*Superman: Secret Origin* #3, January 2010).

Other realities have depicted Jimmy in both positive and negative ways.

With Earth transformed into a utopia by twin Supermen on Earth-162, Jimmy Olsen married Lucy Lane and settled into a blissful marriage (*Superman* [first series] #162, July 1963). Earth-57 saw him marry Linda Lee, only discovering weeks later that his new wife was actually Supergirl (*Superman's Pal, Jimmy Olsen* #57, December 1961).

In the alternate reality of Earth-898, Olsen was Lex Luthor's assistant who came to resent the arrival of superpowered beings and set out to kill them all (*JLA: The Nail* #1–3, August–November 1998).

On Earth-22, Jimmy was among those killed when the Joker launched an attack on the *Daily Planet* offices (*Kingdom Come* #2, June 1996).

On Earth-1958, Jimmy was a covert agent working for the CIA before becoming Luthor's vice president on a world where Superman was raised in Russia and came to rule the country as its Red Son (*Superman: Red Son* #1–3, 2003).

On Earth-31, Jimmy was regarded as a "maverick journalist" who attempted to expose the fact that President Rickard was actually a computer-generated image controlled by Lex Luthor and Brainiac (*The Dark Knight Strikes Again* #1–2, 2001–2002).

OLSEN, MARK

On Earth-1, Jimmy Olsen's father Mark was an archaeologist and onetime curator of the Smallville Museum who was rescued by Superboy after discovering the remnants of a Kryptonian city in the African country of Kurtiswana (*Adventure Comics* #216, September 1955). On one expedition, Mark Olsen and fellow archaeologist Hal Rand were presumed lost after a train wreck killed Mark's wife and sent the men plunging down a river (*Superman's Pal, Jimmy Olsen* #75, March 1964). Mark and Hal washed ashore in shock, with both temporarily suffering from amnesia. Their wanderings took the pair to Mexico, where Mark fell from an ancient temple to his apparent death. Still amnesiac and initially believing himself to be Mark Olsen, Rand returned to Metropolis while the real Olsen recovered and was healed by Mexican Indians, who worshipped the red-haired man as "Kukulkan, the white serpent of the Mayans." It took Professor Lewis Lang to find evidence that Olsen was still alive. Once he presented the data to Superman, he, Jimmy, and Rand headed for the Yucatán. Olsen regained his memory and was happily reunited with Jimmy, who then brought his father back to Metropolis (*Superman's Pal, Jimmy Olsen* #123–124, September–October 1969, and #128, April 1970). Mark used the Mayan treasure he received to become wealthy, and he lived in a mansion on the outskirts of Metropolis (*Superman's Pal, Jimmy Olsen* #158, June 1973).

In the reality after the Crisis on Infinite Earths, Mark Olsen was replaced by Jake Olsen.

OMAC

In a potential Earth-1 future, Buddy Blank was an ordinary working drone, a put-upon employee of Pseudo-People Inc., which produced androids designed as human companions that were secretly being programmed as assassins. When Blank saw a female co-worker in danger, Blank was transformed into the One Man Army Corps known as OMAC by the sophisticated satellite Brother Eye. After her rescue, Blank met Brother Eye's master Professor Myron Forest, who performed remote-controlled electronic hormone surgery on Blank, permanently transforming him into an OMAC (*OMAC* #1, September–October 1974). OMAC was once teleported to Superman's era to stop the robot Murdermek from killing his ancestor Norman Blank. The Man of Steel helped OMAC save Norman and preserve that particular future (*DC Comics Presents* #61, September 1983).

After the Crisis on Infinite Earths, the One Man Army Corps were cybernetically controlled cyborgs that encased living humans inside hardware made using advanced nanotechnology. The OMAC virus was created using bits and pieces taken from Brainiac 13, LexCorp, and the U.S. Department of Defense. The virus was under the control of the Brother I satellite that Batman built to keep an eye on the meta-human community. The satellite was usurped, first by Alexander Luthor, Junior and then by Maxwell Lord. Along the way, it gained sentience and renamed itself Brother Eye (*The OMAC Project* #1, June 2005).

OMAC

There were 1,373,462 humans affected by the nanovirus, which turned them into killing machines with no control over their actions. Most were eventually stopped when a massive electromagnetic pulse was unleashed by a team of super heroes. The remaining two hundred thousand became inoperative after Batman destroyed his creation (*The OMAC Project* #6, November 2005).

The OMAC prototype was retained by Batman and kept in a locked storage facility, under guard and behind three feet of reinforced steel. At WayneTech's R&D department, Batman kept a tracking device disguised as a prototype DX-538. When a Brainiac probe returned to Earth, it seized control of Will Magnus's Metal Men to access the prototype, giving him a new vessel to use. After Batman was beaten and hospitalized, it fell to Superman to track and stop the prototype.

After the threat ended, Batman agreed to have Superman destroy all the remaining prototypes associated with the OMAC technology (*Superman/Batman* #36, Early August 2007).

O'MARA, VELVET

A member of the Anti-Superman Gang, this unscrupulous villainess once stole Lana Lang's Insect Queen ring from Lois Lane and used its alien power to transform her army into Kryptonian insects in order to challenge the Man of Steel. Lois had been using the ring to briefly fight crime as the new Insect Queen, but was forced to use her natural grit to help Lana and Superman wrest the ring from O'Mara's control (*Superman's Girl Friend, Lois Lane* #69, October 1966).

OMEGA EFFECT, THE

The New God Uxas gained control of the fabled Omega Force in AD 689 and transformed into the deadly Darkseid, becoming ruler of the fiery world of Apokolips (*Jack Kirby's Fourth World* #2–5, April–July 1997).

Issuing from his eyes or hands, the energy could either be a concussive force or a means of disintegration. As he mastered the power, Darkseid learned that it was capable of transmuting or erasing most objects from existence, in addition to bringing them back to their original form. As a result, those who displeased Darkseid were prone to being disintegrated and eventually resurrected when he needed their services. These energies could also be harnessed for teleportation, negating Darkseid's need for a Boom Tube. The twin beams of energy could bend around objects to find their target, seemingly controlled by Darkseid's will.

On rare occasions, people suffered from the Omega Sanction, which trapped them within a series of alternate realities drawn from their minds and brought their deepest fears to life, making each reality harsher than the previous one.

ONE HUNDRED, THE

The criminal organization known as the One Hundred could trace its roots to Metropolis and rivaled the Mafia for its reach into law enforcement and elected leadership. Members ran drugs, laundered money, and participated in other vile acts with seeming impunity. That all changed when patrolman Phil Forrest was killed and his daughter Rose

was traumatized as a result. The attractive blonde went to sleep but awoke with a new personality. The new persona donned a brunette wig and skintight emerald outfit to battle the One Hundred as the Thorn (*Superman's Girl Friend, Lois Lane* #105, October 1970). To counter this new costumed threat, the One Hundred contracted help from Poison Ivy while fighting competitor underworld operation Intergang, from which they stole an Apokolips-created computer life-form named K.A.R.L. (*Superman's Girl Friend, Lois Lane* #115–116, October–November 1971).

The discovery that Lois Lane's sister Lucy had been an agent for the One Hundred and had apparently died trying to escape them was a wake-up call for both the *Daily Planet* reporter and Superman. Horrified to learn that the gang had expanded into South America and had nearly acquired plans for an Omega Bomb, the Man of Steel and Lois redoubled their efforts to take down the mob, joining forces with the Thorn, who'd already captured twenty-three of their number. The trio successfully rounded up another seventy-seven members of the gang, notably its second in command, funeral home director Vincent Dennis Adams (*Superman's Girl Friend, Lois Lane* #120–123, March–May 1972).

Unfortunately, a printout from K.A.R.L. revealed this to be the tip of the iceberg. Operating from "a secret chamber deep beneath the Earth's surface," the never-identified true mastermind of the One Hundred had established ten new divisions with ten operatives in each. In short order, Superman and Lois took down the Space Raiders, the Hunters (*Superman's Girl Friend, Lois Lane* #124–125, June–July 1972), and possibly the Athletes (*Superman's Girl Friend, Lois Lane* #127, October 1972), but encounters with the Agents, the Amazons, the Athletes, the Dynamiters, the Mind-Benders, the Mobsters, the Sea Wolves, and the Stealers were never documented.

The mobsters survived, and their next great challenge came from Metropolis's latest hero, Olympian-turned-crime-fighter Jefferson Pierce, who operated under the guise of Black Lightning (*Black Lightning* [first series] #1, April 1977). One of his battles took Black Lightning to their base of operations, which was ironically located beneath the Superman Museum. There he challenged their leader Tobias Whale, which effectively broke the gang's hold on the city (*World's Finest Comics* #258, August–September 1979).

They wound up consolidating their forces and renamed themselves the One Thousand, with the goal of controlling the Oval Office. Led by a man known only as the Director (secretly Senator Henry Ballard), they used powerful vigilantes such as Mindancer, Chiller, Shockwave, Doctor Shocker, and Blackguard to keep at bay the costumed champions of justice, most notably Booster Gold and the Thorn (*Booster Gold* #1–4, February–May 1986, and #8–12, September 1986–January 1987). Their plans were repeatedly thwarted, and their power declined until they eventually became irrelevant.

The Thorn, at least, remained convinced the One Hundred was still attempting to re-form, and brought some of its former members, such as the paroled Vince Adams (*The Adventures of Superman* #521, March 1995) and Mister Orchid (*Showcase '95* #5, June 1995) to justice on new charges, as well as confronting the mob's onetime attorney Frank Church (*Showcase '96* #5, June 1996). She never found the evidence to prove that the One Hundred had actually returned, but the Teen Titans later did when Shockwave told them that the mob now owned Kord Industries (*Teen Titans* [third series] #61, September 2008).

In the world after the Infinite Crisis, the group was said to have been initially known as El Ciento, made up of seventy-one men and women who hailed from Europe and banded together in Aragon, Spain, in 1462. Their chosen name was to honor their twenty-nine dead allies, and they marshaled their arcane knowledge to extend their lives and secretly try to rule Europe, then the New World. They fled Spain after crossing the Spanish Inquisition and came to discover that the treatments extending their lives required them to possess the land they lived on and feed off the despair and negative emotions of the human tenants (*Black Lightning: Year One* #4, April 2009).

Back in the earlier days of Metropolis, a member of El Ciento relocated to Southside and quickly established a criminal domain. The chronicles indicate that the man there formed a branch of the One Hundred—it may have originally been called the Ten—which may have had ties to Intergang (*Superman* #665, September 2007).

ORACLE OF DELPHI, THE

The Oracle of Delphi was known throughout ancient Greece and located near Mount Parnassus. It was sacred to the god Apollo. The important soothsayer revealed the future prominence of Superman to the gods of Olympus. This prompted the jealous gods to create Zha-Vam, who was sent to fight the Man of Steel in order to remind him that the gods were still mightier than the Kryptonian (*Action Comics* #351, June 1967).

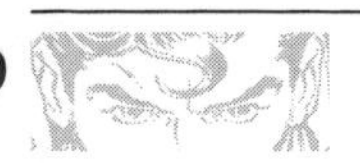

ORGANIZER, THE

METROPOLIS once found itself in the grip of a mysterious crime mogul called the Organizer, and *DAILY PLANET* editor in chief PERRY WHITE conceived of a scheme to bring about the villain's capture. Superman created and assumed three new alter egos—a part-time grocery clerk named Buster, a reckless pilot named Winters, and an escaped convict named Sam Baron—all in an attempt to get an invitation from the Organizer to join his group. The scheme worked: The Organizer was brought to justice, and CLARK KENT got the paper an exclusive scoop (*Superman* [first series] #115, August 1957).

ORION

DARKSEID of APOKOLIPS and his second wife Tigra had one son, Orion, who was handed over to Highfather of NEW GENESIS in exchange for his son as part of a pact to end the ongoing war between the worlds (*New Gods* #7, February–March 1972). Orion's bestial nature made living in the tranquil setting of the floating Supertown unbearable: he only found calm when his MOTHER BOX soothed his fevered brow and turned his grisly visage into a handsome one.

Highfather proved highly influential on the angry young man, but Orion did manage to befriend several other NEW GODS, notably the joyous Lightray, who found humor in Orion's bleak moods, and Bekka, the daughter of Himon, whom he later married. Orion was trained in all manner of combat, but once he mounted his astroglider he preferred to use the transport's own weaponry. While Darkseid commanded the Omega Force, Orion seemed to be the only one to access the Astro Force—interdimensional energy that allowed him to transport from place to place or release power energy blasts, channeled through the wristbands he wore. He once created a shield with the force, which proved able to deflect the OMEGA EFFECT.

Away from his astroglider, he tended to use his superior strength and clenched fists, wading into battle at a moment's notice. When Highfather learned that Darkseid had sent agents across Earth in search of the ANTI-LIFE EQUATION, he dispatched Orion to oppose those forces, which pitted him not only against his birth father but also against his half brother, the hulking KALIBAK (*New Gods* #1, February–March 1971). Given Highfather's influence, Orion managed to channel his aggressive nature, using tactics and skills his enemies from Apokolips lacked.

Orion stopped Darkseid and his minions on numerous occasions, going so far as to work alongside Earth's super heroes to stop the galactic despot's goals of mass destruction. In one case, it took the combined efforts of the JUSTICE LEAGUE OF AMERICA, the JUSTICE SOCIETY OF AMERICA, and the New Gods to defeat him (*Justice League of America* [first series] #183–185, October–December 1980). On another occasion, Darkseid managed to destroy the world of Xanshi before his mad quest for the Anti-Life Equation could be stopped by Orion, Superman, BATMAN, GREEN LANTERN John Stewart, and others (*Cosmic Odyssey* #1–4, 1988). He twice briefly served as a member of the Justice League of America (*Justice League America* #42–50, September 1990–May 1991; *JLA* #17–41, April 1998–May 2000). Orion served unwillingly and never truly bonded with his fellow champions. He was happy to leave.

At one point, Orion arrived on Apokolips and defeated his father in combat. Seduced and manipulated by members of Darkseid's inner circle, however, Orion accomplished what his father could not and gained control of the Anti-Life Equation. Seeking to instill cosmic peace by eliminating all free will, Orion nearly enslaved the Earth before his reckless behavior was stopped and he saw the error of his ways. Later, Orion would learn that this Equation had fallen under the passive control of Scott (MISTER MIRACLE) Free (*Orion* #1–25, June 2000–June 2002).

Despite everything he endured, Orion could never be truly free of his father Darkseid or his influence. As a result, when his fellow New Gods began dying, he suspected his father of being behind the murderer. The investigation proved fruitless at first, and even he was suspected of being the culprit until Superman intervened to keep people focused. The murderer was eventually revealed to be the INFINITY-MAN, acting on behalf of the Source. When Infinity-Man came for Orion, he slipped on his Astro Harness and went to face his doom, dying in an amazing explosion of raw energy that was bright enough to temporarily blind the Man of Steel. The Source, however, used Orion's life energy and resurrected his body to stop Darkseid once and for all. During their climactic battle, he ripped out his father's heart and crushed it (*Death of the New Gods* #1–8, Early December 2007–June 2008). The battle took its toll and Orion died once more. He was found by Detective Dan "Terrible" Turpin. Orion's final word was "Fight," and it was eventually learned that a bullet fired through time was what killed him the second time (*Final Crisis* #1, June 2008).

Orion is likely among the New Gods resurrected by the Source to help rebuild the shattered Earth-51 in the re-formed fifty-two parallel universes and will undoubtedly be seen again.

ORR, ELIAS

Elias Orr was an enigmatic mustached bioengineer who worked for a clandestine organization and claimed to have had encounters with Superman and other heroes—including one such meeting with Wonder Woman that went unchronicled (*Superman* [second series] #210, December 2005). Orr reentered the Man of Steel's life when one million people vanished from Metropolis (*Superman* [second series] #205, July 2005). He commanded a cybernetic mercenary called Equus that always did his bidding.

Superman and Orr next encountered each other when the latter was involved in treating the dying Karate Kid during the days prior to the Infinite Crisis. At the time, he seemed to be under DeSaad of Apokolips's command (*Countdown to Final Crisis* #37–36, October 2007).

Orr turned up with Equus and built a "Cyborg Revenge Squad," a group of villains with a mastery over metals and cybernetics who hated Teen Titans member Cyborg (*DC Special Cyborg* #4–6, October–December 2008). In this case, Orr was working for the mysterious Enclave M, an entirely different outfit. He stole Cyborg's technology and used it to treat maimed veterans of the Iraqi war, but only if they served his needs first.

The exact motivations and skills of Orr, beyond an air of mystery, remain to be chronicled.

OUTBURST

Mitch Anderson possessed the powers of magnetokinesis and took the costumed identity of Outburst to lead the Supermen of America (first appearance as Mitch in *Justice League America* #69, December 1992; first appearance as Outburst in *Superman* [second series] #141, January 1999; *Supermen of America* #1, March 1999; others).

OVERMIND, THE

A technological entity, the Overmind plagued the Man of Steel, always using avatars to do his bidding, beginning with a group of techno-villains called the Cybermoths that first surfaced when Superman and Steel were re-creating the Fortress of Solitude within a tesseract (*Superman: The Man of Steel* #100, May 2000). Some time later, the Cybermoths returned to kidnap Steel's daughter Natasha Irons. The Overmind desired to control the B13 technology that had transformed Metropolis into a true city of the future. The entity was competing with others, notably Lex Luthor, to gain the upper hand, until it was revealed that Brainiac 13 was controlling the Overmind. During the climactic struggle, Earthquake, who had seemingly killed Superman, double-crossed the entity—who was then revealed to be Professor Emil Hamilton, whose mind was taken over by the future Brainiac. Hamilton was freed of Brainiac's mind control when the Man of Steel removed the professor's cybernetic arm (*Superman: The Man of Steel* #122–125, March–June 2002).

OH, YES...
...I HAVE STUDIED YOUR KRYPTONIAN BIOLOGY AND DISCOVERED A SECRET-- A METHOD OF DISRUPTING YOUR BODY'S ABILITY TO ABSORB AND PROCESS THAT ESSENTIAL SOLAR RADIATION!
K-KRAK

OVERRIDE

Override was the leader of a group of cybernetic super-beings collectively known as the Mainframe. The man had become an expert in quantum mechanics and wanted to apply his lessons to humanity by converting them all into cyborgs that he could control. Over time, Override turned his normal human physique into a grotesque cyborg form; he then formed Mainframe to help him achieve his ambitious goals.

Those serving him included Baud, a woman with electromagnetic abilities, who was the first to test the Man of Steel's powers to gauge the type of threat he posed. There was also the teleporter Download, the code breaker Output, and the strongman called Scareware. Assisting Override were insect-like mechanical creations that did his bidding.

Override decided that his goal was to eliminate Superman before beginning his assault on humanity, but he and the team were defeated and seemingly vanished (*Superman: The Man of Steel* #71–72, September–October 1997). Thanks to the efforts of Misa, the entire membership of Mainframe found themselves permanently confined to their other-dimensional refuge (*Superman 3-D* #1, December 1998).

OWENS, SAMUEL C.

As he built his chain of successful bakeries, Samuel C. Owens relied on two businessmen to help finance the growth in exchanges of company stock. Over time, however, they gained the majority of the firm, and Owens seethed at the notion that his dream was in the control of others. He decided to manipulate the stock and murder the men in an attempt to regain control, but was eventually apprehended by the Man of Steel. Owens was then sentenced to be electrocuted for his crimes (*Superman* [first series] #44, January–February 1947).

OXNALIA

Located in Europe, Oxnalia was ruled by Razkal, a cruel dictator hell-bent on igniting global conflict. The effort began by invading neighboring Numark, but the world war was stopped by Superman, who stepped in and destroyed all of Oxnalia's weaponry. When the Man of Steel insisted they sign a peace treaty, Razkal attempted to flee but was shot and killed by one of his own countrymen (*Superman* [first series] #15, March–April 1942).

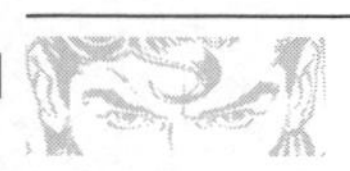

PACIFO

Much like Atlantis, Pacifo was once a continent in the Pacific Ocean that sank at some time in the past. For a while, the Lex Luthor of Earth-2 used it as his base of operations. Superman eventually destroyed the abandoned city so that Luthor could no longer use it (*Superman* [first series] #4, Spring 1940).

PARADEMONS

Living in Apokolips and unquestioningly loyal to their master Darkseid, the Parademons were Darkseid's shock troops, winged beings that lived to fight and spread misery in his name (*New Gods* #1, May–June 1971). Their weapons discharged energy blasts that could subdue even a New God.

Culled from the unfortunate souls living around the planet's fire pits, the fiercest fighters were given additional training, then outfitted in green-and-yellow body armor that included gliding capabilities. Most were incapable of speech and had only rudimentary intelligence. The Parademons numbered in the tens of thousands and used such numbers to overwhelm most opponents. Often accompanying them were gigantic canines known as Hounds.

On Earth-1, Clark Kent first glimpsed Parademons during a brief visit to Apokolips (*Superman's Pal, Jimmy Olsen* #141, September 1971). The Superman of the reality formed after the Crisis on Infinite Earths fought them often on both Apokolips and Earth (*The Adventures of Superman* #426, March 1987; *Action Comics Annual* #3, 1991; others).

Most Parademons ignored their individuality in favor of the collective, although there were exceptions. One abandoned his allies to join Earth's

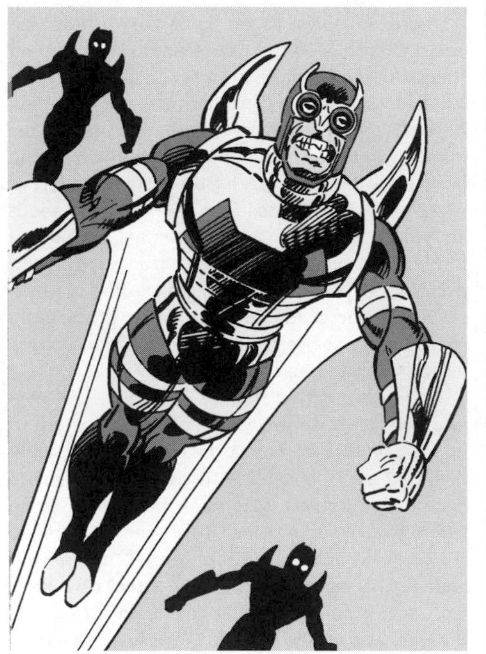

villains in the group of outlaws called the Secret Six (*Villains United* #1–6, July–December 2005). Despite forming a bond with Ragdoll, the Parademon was ultimately killed and its armor kept as a souvenir.

Darkseid used the distant world of Salvation Run as a training planet; this was the same location where Earth's super-villains were once exiled. Several of the Parademons engaged the villains in battle, killing Hyena, Brutale, General Immortus, and the latest incarnation of Solomon Grundy (*Salvation Run* #1–7, January–July 2007).

PARADISE ISLAND

The island of Themyscira was bequeathed to the ancient Amazons as a gift from the gods. It was also known as Paradise Island and was home to Wonder Woman. In the reality formed after the Crisis on Infinite Earths, Lois Lane was one of a dozen diverse individuals invited to visit Themyscira when it first began to connect with the outside world (*Wonder Woman* [second series] #37–40, December 1989–March 1990). Later, the newly arrived Supergirl also trained with the Amazons on Paradise Island for a short time (*Superman/Batman* #9, June 2004).

PARAGON

Joel Baines Cochin was born with the ability to duplicate another person's physical or men-

tal abilities. For his mutant abilities to work, the other person had to be in close proximity. Just as Cochin gained the new attributes, the other person's abilities were amplified for finite periods of time. Seeking to profit from this skill, Cochin donned the costumed identity of Paragon. Cochin as Paragon also desired to rid the world of the "inferiors," those without mutant abilities, which he estimated to be more than 90 percent of the world's population. He crossed paths with the Justice League of America and used their own powers against them, nearly beating the team until their android member, the Red Tornado, finally stopped him (*Justice League of America* [first series] #224, March 1984).

Years later, Paragon reappeared, plaguing Superman on several occasions around Metropolis (*Superman* #675, April 2008). He developed a new outfit that allowed him to extend the amount of time he could possess another's abilities. When the Elders from the planet Daxam terrorized the city, trying to punish their fellow Daxamite Mon-El for using forbidden technology, Paragon came to Superman's aid—but his methods were far more extreme than Superman preferred, especially when Paragon shot the Daxamites with lead bullets. Defeated by the Man of Steel, he was imprisoned.

PARASITE, THE

While a janitor sought access to his company's payroll, Raymond Maxwell Jensen was exposed to extraterrestrial waste material and was transformed into a being that had to absorb the life force of others in order to survive. His skin became purple, his facial features blurred, and he dubbed himself the Parasite. As Jensen came into contact with other humans, he absorbed not only their life essences but also their memories and, in some cases, their unique attributes as well. When he first encountered Superman, Parasite presumed

he could feast forever on the Kryptonian's energy. As the Man of Steel weakened and neared death, however, the contact overwhelmed the Parasite's altered cells and he disintegrated (*Action Comics* #340, August 1966).

An extraterrestrial geographer then unwittingly re-created the Parasite by pulling his scattered atoms from Earth's atmosphere. As thanks for resurrecting the Parasite, the alien lost his life. With Superman once again on the brink of death, the alien's vengeful kinsman arrived to capture the Parasite and transport him to a desolate prison world (*Action Comics* #361, March 1968). During his escape from that prison, Jensen was blasted by one of the aliens' weapons and eventually learned that his molecular structure had changed further, "giving [his] cells a kind of independent 'intelligence' " (*Superman* [first series] #322, April 1978). This caused the Parasite to revert to human form when drained of the power he'd absorbed (*Superman* [first series] #286, April 1975) until the alien Xviar negated that effect with his own technology (*Superman* [first series] #299, May 1976; *Who's Who: The Definitive Directory of the DC Universe* #17, July 1986). More significantly, when he was disintegrated altogether (as in *World's Finest Comics* #247, October–November 1977), the Parasite's cells "regrouped themselves—as if at their own will" (*Superman* [first series] #322, April 1978).

There appeared to be limits to what Jensen could absorb even from the Man of Steel, and he tried a different angle on a few occasions, once using a power-prism (*Superman* [first series] #304, October 1976) to actually add to Superman's powers rather than draining them in the hope of overwhelming the Man of Steel. As part of his scheme, Parasite used the prism to bring about an Earth-1 Solomon Grundy (*Superman* [first series] #319–322, January–April 1978). Given his repeated exposure to Superman, Parasite learned the Man of Steel's secret identity but never successfully took advantage of the information (*Action Comics* #340, August 1966; others).

During the period that he reverted to his normal form, Max Jensen was eventually paroled, and he married his attorney Lorna Kramer. The couple divorced after Jensen's activities as the Parasite resumed, but they were drawn together again when their young twins Troy and Trina began suffering an agonizing "para-fever." The Parasite learned that he could halt these attacks by bathing the twins in energy that he'd drained from Superman, and, as the bouts of para-fever began to alarmingly increase in frequency, he revealed this to the Man of Steel. Working with S.T.A.R. Labs, Superman and the Parasite were delighted when Troy and Trina were given technological implants that would permanently stave off the para-fever (*Who's Who: The Definitive Directory of the DC Universe* #17, July 1986).

In the reality after the Crisis on Infinite Earths, it was janitorial slacker Rudy Jones who was turned into the Parasite while working at the Pittsburgh branch of S.T.A.R. Labs. The incident was orchestrated by Darkseid, seeking a powerful human tool during his search for the Anti-Life Equation.

He planted the mental suggestion that a particular waste container held something valuable, and as Jones opened it he was bathed in the deadly radiation. Jones was turned into a green-skinned version of the Parasite who needed the life force from others to survive. As the Parasite absorbed his victims' essences, their bodies were reduced to skeletons (*Fury of Firestorm* #58, April 1987). Shortly thereafter, the two beings making up the Nuclear Man Firestorm, Martin Stein and Ronnie Raymond, were attempting to rid the world of its atomic weaponry. The Justice League of America and the federal government's Suicide Squad converged on the hero, trying to stop his plan. The Squad brought the Parasite with them and unleashed him, causing further chaos (*Fury of Firestorm* #64, October 1987; *Firestorm Annual* #5,

1987). Once the mission ended, Parasite was remanded to Belle Reve prison, where he was given a steady supply of rodents to absorb in order to remain alive (*Suicide Squad* #1, May 1987). A brief escape attempt led to this incarnation of the Parasite's first encounter with Superman (*Starman* [second series] #14, September 1989).

While Jones was in custody, scientists at Belle Reve worked to restore him to his human form, but merely managed to alter his skin to the more familiar purple hue and also accidentally increased Jones's power, allowing him to now sup on all forms of energy, including electricity (*The Adventures of Superman* #481–482, August–September 1991). As a result, when Superman had absorbed excess energy, the Parasite was brought to the moon and used to siphon it off to save the Man of Tomorrow's life. During a subsequent struggle, Superman blasted Parasite with his heat vision, which somehow mutated the villain into a monstrous shape. Additionally, the Parasite developed enhanced absorption attributes, such as being able to gain a moving object's inertia. These changes also meant that he developed an immunity to telepathy (*Superman: The Man of Steel* #33; *The Adventures of Superman* #512—both May 1994). The downside to these new powers was that Jones required even more frequent infusions of energy to stay alive.

One of the S.T.A.R. Labs scientists studying the Parasite, Dr. Torval Freeman, was tricked by Lex Luthor into getting close enough to the creature to be absorbed. Unlike the previous deaths, which the Parasite caused via contact, this resulted in Jones and Freeman sharing consciousness, similar to Firestorm (*Superman: The Man of Tomorrow* #2, Fall 1995; *Action Comics* #715, October 1995; others). This new, more cunning version of the Parasite was freed by Morgan Edge, who recruited him to join the Superman Revenge Squad (*The Adventures of Superman* #543, February 1997). Superman, not fully in control of his newfound electrical powers at the time, nearly killed the Parasite (*The Adventures of Superman* #552, November 1997).

Some time later, the Parasite sought a fight with Superman but encountered Supergirl instead. He absorbed her Earth-born angel abilities. Attaining these heavenly powers resulted in his receiving "divine judgment" that nearly killed him (*Supergirl* [fourth series] #34–35, July–August 1999).

When Strange Visitor's electromagnetic energy grew too much for her to handle, the Parasite was brought in to help her, but the experience left him altered once more. This time he could retain his victims' intellects and stolen attributes for twenty-four hours. Along the way, he absorbed energy that also enabled him to transform into a perfect genetic re-creation of one of his victims. This later gave him the idea of how best to exact revenge against Superman. He bided his time, eventually escaping from S.T.A.R. Labs and then stalking Jimmy Olsen and Lois Lane, people known to be close to the Man of Steel. Appearing as an old man, the Parasite came into physical contact with Lois and absorbed her knowledge, learning Superman's secret identity. That enabled him to alter his plan, which was now to kidnap Lois and hide her in a cave in the outskirts of Metropolis. The Parasite took Lois's form and replaced her. For quite some time, Superman had no idea that his wife was actually his enemy. As Lois, the Parasite drove a wedge between the couple, going so far as to possibly having an affair with Lex Luthor. When an argument got out of control, the Parasite struck Superman with a blow powerful enough to send him through the apartment wall and down to the street. That was all Superman needed to know that this was not the real Lois (*Superman* [second series] #154–157, March–June 2000).

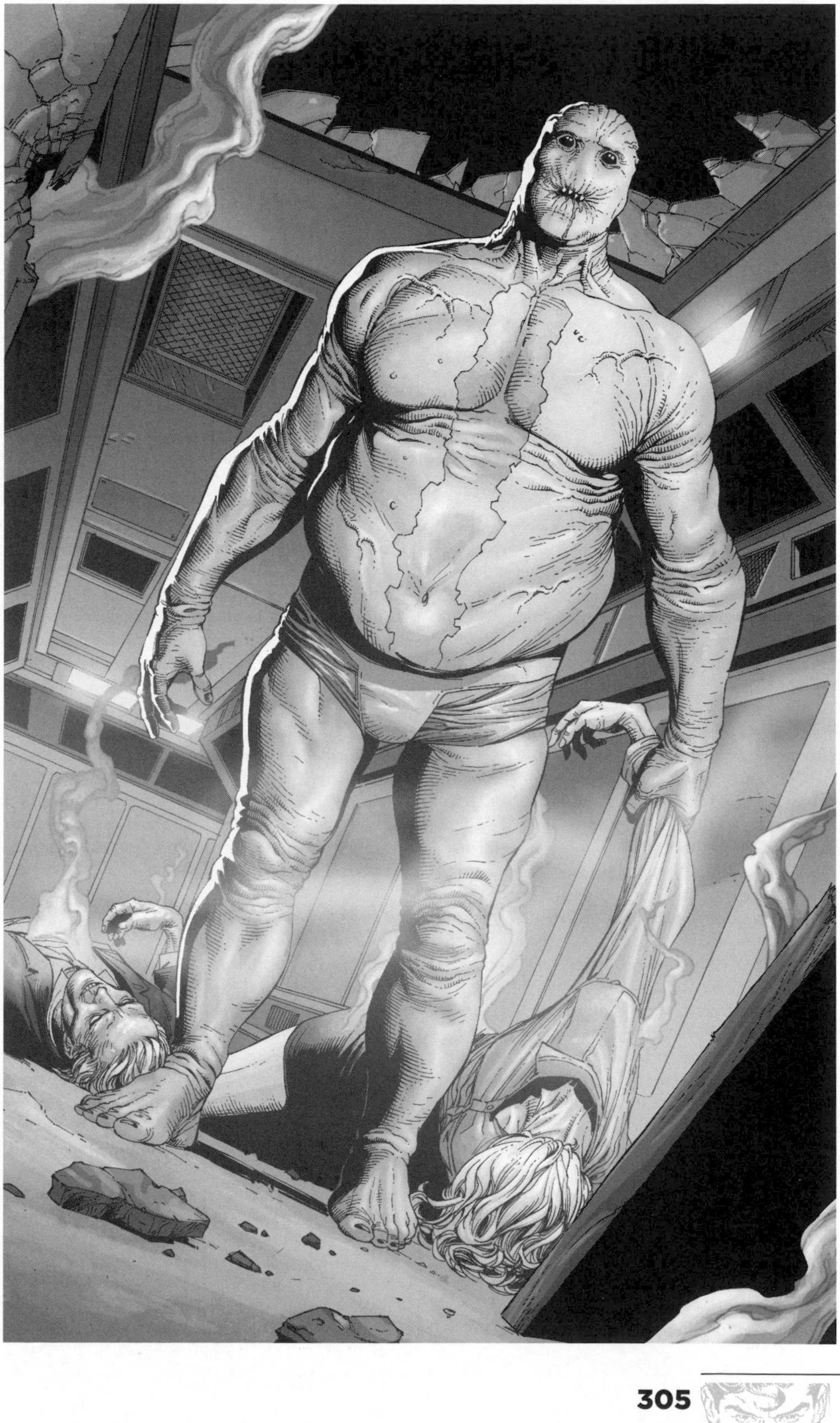

Superman forced the Parasite to abandon his form. The villain then collapsed, having inadvertently absorbed the same kryptonite poisoning

that had been slowly killing the Man of Steel. The kryptonite and the Parasite slowly siphoning his energy had cumulatively endangered Superman's life. The Parasite admitted he had been visiting Lois once a day in order to maintain his form, which gave Superman hope that his wife was still alive. So weak was the hero, though, that he sought help finding her from BATMAN (*Action Comics* #766, June 2000).

The Parasite seemingly died from the kryptonite, and Luthor, furious at being duped, saw to it that he gained custody of the body. In Hell, Harley Quinn even encountered the Jensen-Freeman hybrid (*Harley Quinn* #21, August 2002). What happened after that remained unchronicled, but the Parasite next turned up, in a modified form, in the city of St. Roch, Louisiana, having been paid to absorb other villains' abilities in order to remove their threat (*Justice League of America* [second series] #2, November 2006). Based on his actions and vocabulary, it was speculated that Freeman's personality finally became the dominant one. Regardless, he wound up once more behind bars at STRYKER'S ISLAND Penitentiary.

When one hundred thousand Kandorians suddenly took up residence on Earth, they decided that Superman's foes should all be neutralized. Several members of the Kryptonian military freed the Parasite in order to exile him to the PHANTOM ZONE (*Superman* #682, January 2009)—only to see him rescued by Superman, who brought him to Belle Reve for safekeeping (*Superman* #684, March 2009).

In another recounting of Parasite's post-Infinite Crisis origin, Rudy Jones was still a janitor, but one working at the *Daily Planet*. He regularly attended the LexCorp Lottery, a daily occurrence outside the LexCorp corporate office building where Metropolis' citizens gathered in the hope Luther would pick them and grant them a fresh start in life. On the day Jones was selected, he unfortunately ate a donut that had been accidentally exposed to toxic waste from LexCorp's secret experiments with kryptonite radiation. The result saw him transformed into a single-minded being with an insatiable appetite for human energy, who could only be stopped by the Man of Steel (*Superman: Secret Origin* #3–4, January 2010–March 2010).

There coexisted two others who had Parasite's abilities: teenagers Alex and Alexandra Allston, who were experimented on by PROFESSOR EMIL HAMILTON when he was masquerading as the villain RUIN (*The Adventures of Superman* #633–635, December 2004–February 2005). He turned them into Parasites, one purple, one green, and unleashed them to seek revenge on the people who had made their young lives living hells. Superman easily defeated them, although Alex died while in prison during an attack from the OMACs (*The Adventures of Superman* #641, August 2005). Alexandra escaped at that point and joined ALEXANDER LUTHOR JUNIOR's Secret Society of Super-Villains (*Villains United* #4, October 2005).

In a potential future, a Parasite was shown to exist as late as the 853rd century (*DC One Million 80-Page Giant* #1, August 1999).

There have been other Parasites seen across the multiverse, including the Parasite of Earth-22, who participated in the events that led to the devastation of Kansas (*Kingdom Come* #1, May 1996).

On Earth-30, the Parasite was created by Lex Luthor to combat Russia's leader, Superman (*Superman: Red Son* #2–3, 2003).

On Earth-40, the Parasite was a normal human who was a former KGB agent, then a freelance assassin (*JSA: The Unholy Three* #1, 2003).

PARELLO

The Purple Fawn, a gambling establishment, was run by the mob controlled by Parello. Not only were his gambling tables rigged, but he also tried to rob the wealthy Nancy Thorenson until he was stopped by Superman (*Action Comics* #40, September 1941).

PARKER, CHIEF DOUGLAS

Douglas Paul Parker became chief of police in SMALLVILLE a few years after SUPERBOY burst onto the scene, changing the way law enforcement was practiced in the rustic Kansas town (*Adventure Comics* #225, June 1956; first name revealed in *Adventure Comics* #369, June 1968; presumed middle name revealed in *Superboy* [first series] #116, October 1964). Like Chief Brann and Chief Wilkins before him (*Superboy* [first series] #20, June–July 1952, and #30, January 1954), Parker recognized that Superboy was a force for good and soon earned his trust. Indeed, the chief was one of three people, along with PROFESSOR LEWIS LANG and the president of the United States, whom the Boy of Steel entrusted with a signal device linked to a flickering lamp in the Kent household (*Superboy* [first series] #88, April 1961).

Parker never realized that the super hero had first affected his life years earlier. As a rookie officer, he'd been unwittingly assisted by the superpowers of toddler CLARK KENT while pursuing the Pumpkin Gang onto a science-fiction movie set; he'd earned a promotion to captain for his capture of the thieves (*Superman* [first series] #152, April 1962). By one account, young Parker (here a captain named George) had even encountered Albert Einstein in Smallville a bit earlier and (unbeknownst to the policeman) helped the brilliant man facilitate JONATHAN and MARTHA KENT's "chance" discovery of the rocket carrying the infant KAL-EL (*Superman: Last Son of Krypton,* 1978).

It was also Chief Parker who helped clear Superboy's name when DEV-EM ruined the hero's reputation (*Adventure Comics* #288, September 1961). Parker was such a solid ally of the Boy of Steel that he was even targeted for harassment by the evil Superboy of Earth-116 (*Superboy* [first series] #116, October 1964).

When their children were grown, Douglas and his wife Leah were delighted at one point to play host to teenager Marie Elkins, unaware that she was secretly the Legionnaire known as Duo Damsel (*Adventure Comics* #369–370, June–July 1968).

Some time after Superboy left for METROPOLIS, Parker retired from his position and began a business whittling dioramas of Superboy's most spectacular cases. The wooden pieces were popular enough for Parker to display them on WMET-TV's salute to Superman on the *Our American Heroes* series (*Action Comics* #309, February 1964).

Even at the age of seventy-five, Parker continued to put on his police blues on occasion, possibly when other officers were on vacation (*Superman* [first series] #284, February 1975). He also functioned as unofficial caretaker for the vacant Kent home (*Action Comics* #494–495, April–May 1979) and became the chairman of the Smallville Chamber of Commerce at a time when social studies teacher WAYNE KING was ready to quit. Parker's grandson Chris Parker Hunt worked with Superman to convince King, who'd grown up with Kent, that his job was worthwhile (*Superman* [first series] #420, June 1986).

In the history chronicled following the CRISIS ON INFINITE EARTHS, where Clark Kent never operated as Superboy, a younger Chief Parker led a compara-

tively peaceful existence (first mentioned in *World of Metropolis* #3, June 1988; seen in *Superman for All Seasons* #1, 1998, and #4, 1998).

PARRISH, ARTHUR

The son of "famous jewel expert" Amos Parrish, this lonely boy was duped by a local farmhand who impersonated Superman while stealing diamonds from the Parrish family safe. His faith shaken, it was just as quickly restored when the real Man of Steel arrived to apprehend the thief (*Action Comics* #115, December 1947).

PARRONE, JOHN

Posing as an investment counselor, this vicious gangster was really the leader of bandits who were all hooked on hard drugs. John Parrone cruelly used their addiction to maintain his control over them. He allied himself with the corrupt lawyer William Brokenshire, who repeatedly found loopholes and technicalities to keep the criminal out of jail. When they went too far and a man died, Superman intervened and brought both men to justice (*Superman* [first series] #8, January-February 1941).

PASTENETTI, NOAH

The arsonist who was transformed by LexCorp into the costumed super-villain Arclight.

PAW POOCH

A many-legged canine who served alongside Krypto as a member of the Space Canine Patrol Agency (*Superboy* [first series] #131, July 1966).

PEEKER, PETER

The public knew him as the *Morning Pictorial*'s gossip columnist, but Peter Peeker was also the secret leader of the nefarious Black Gang, "a band of ruthless thieves." Wearing dark suits and black hoods, they specialized in "brutal robberies of nightclub patrons" until they were apprehended by Superman (*Superman* [first series] #7, November-December 1940).

PEG-LEG PORTIA

Hailing from the dying planet Aquaterra, a woman named Portia took her spaceship into deep space in order to die alone. The world she chose to die on turned out to be populated, complete with a species of telepathic canines, known as the Cosmic Hounds. The dog-like beings captured Portia and attacked her, mutilating her body and using their mental powers to force her into transporting them to other planets. For more than three centuries Portia labored aboard their ship, rechristened the *Cosmic Hound,* all the while craving death.

She finally found a way out of her predicament by luring Superman through a "weird hole in space" so he could encounter the canine pirates. They actually seemed to have great enough mental prowess to subdue the Man of Steel, but he persevered and triumphed over them. He brought Portia back to Aquaterra, which was by then totally devoid of life. Freed from the Hounds' mental control, Portia rapidly aged; she died on her homeworld (*Superman* [first series] #318, December 1977).

PENNYWORTH, ALFRED

On Earth-1, Alfred Thaddeus Crane Pennyworth came to work for Bruce Wayne by responding to a classified ad. He only came to learn that his employer was Batman after Dick Grayson summoned him to help tend to the wounded super hero in the Batcave (*Batman* #110, September 1957). After learning Bruce and Dick's secret, he swore to assist them whenever possible and became a trusted and loyal friend. That trust extended to the World's Finest team when Superman entrusted Alfred with the secret of his true identity as well.

In the world formed after the Crisis on Infinite Earths, Alfred Pennyworth was the Wayne family butler when Thomas and Martha Wayne were killed, caring for Bruce in the aftermath of their deaths (*Batman* #404, February 1987).

After Bruce left to travel around the world, training to become Batman, Alfred cared for the manor, fully prepared to resign and finally pursue a stage career upon Bruce's return. When Bruce finally arrived back home, years later, he announced his presence to Alfred by leaving a trail of blood. The butler found an injured Bruce, who had attempted to employ his lessons as the Batman for the first time (*Batman Annual* #13, 1989).

Ever since, Alfred has pulled double duty as both Wayne's retainer and the backbone of Batman's ongoing quest to eradicate crime. As a result, he has welcomed the Man of Steel to the manor and the Batcave on numerous occasions.

(For a complete history of Alfred Pennyworth, see *The Essential Batman Encyclopedia,* 2008)

PEPPERWINKLE, JASPER J.

Possibly the prototype for the proverbial absentminded professor, Jasper Pepperwinkle was a well-known inventor who lived with his wife of more than twenty-five years, Elaine, in a modest suburban home near Metropolis. Over time, he became friendly with *Daily Planet* reporters Lois Lane, Jimmy Olsen, and Clark Kent, in addition to encountering Superman on numerous occasions (*Action Comics* #442, December 1974).

After a successful career, the aging Pepperwinkle retired, but he maintained a workshop at a Metropolis facility since new ideas were also coming to him. He built his greatest invention, the "sonic-boom-boomer," for those who enjoyed the cracking sound and installed it on the roof.

Working from his home, the inveterate tinkerer devised many devices, such as the "step-saving compressed-air elevator" and the "time-saving automated coat rack." Pepperwinkle took notes using his self-invented "non-lead laser retracting pencil," and the couples' car was driven by his "experimental radar attuned electronic-eye robot chauffeur."

Police inspector Bill Henderson and Galaxy Broadcasting's Morgan Edge worked with Pepperwinkle to find his "tri-dimensional silhouette-projector," which caused Superman troubles when the three-dimensional images created panic in the streets (*Superman* [first series] #289, July 1975). Later, the kindly professor let Superman, temporarily powerless thanks to the alien Xviar, use an anti-gravity "gizmo" to help him defeat an Intergang plot (*Superman* [first series] #297, March 1976).

PERSUADER, THE

There have been two Persuaders who plagued the Man of Steel, each in a different era. In his own time, Cole Parker was an industrial worker who lost his job in Metropolis in the wake of the city's miraculous upgrade thanks to the Brainiac B13 Virus. He unfairly blamed the *Daily Planet* for his plight, thinking they somehow allowed the tech to transform the city, and sought vengeance. Parker was inspired by a hologram of Superman fighting the Fatal Five in the thirtieth century. Grabbing a fire ax, he led a mob in besieging the *Planet*'s headquarters. When order was restored, this "Persuader" was arrested (*The Adventures of Superman* #598, January 2002). While Parker was in jail awaiting trial, a mysterious figure gave him a powerful atomic axe that not only sliced through most objects but also managed to pierce the dimensional veil. He fought Superman until he got caught up in a vortex that removed him from the world (*The Adventures of Superman* #601-602, April-May 2002). Mr. Mxyzptlk was later revealed as the one who gave Parker the axe (*The Adventures of Superman* #618, September 2003).

Parker eventually returned to Earth through unexplained means and was recruited by the Suicide Squad for a mission to the Middle East, only to be killed when the magically empowered Osiris flew through his body (*52* #34, February 2007).

Elise Kimble, a teenage contract killer, took on the *Persuader* name when she was recruited by

The Persuader

the Clock King to join his Terror Titans (*Teen Titans* [third series] #56, April 2008). He told her that she was an ancestor to the villain from the thirtieth century and was therefore honored to don his familiar executioner's mask and wield a new version of the atomic axe. This one could slice through just about any organic or inorganic object, but various forms of energy, such as Starfire's starbolts, could stop it.

Her supposed descendant, Nyeun Chun Ti, was "the highest paid killer and strong-arm gangland enforcer in the galaxy." Hailing from a planet with gravity heavier than Earth's, he developed a massive bulk and superior strength. Ti used that to heft his atomic axe—"which, by nuclear emissions, can slice through anything, including energy," and which he could control remotely. He was asked by the Legion of Super-Heroes to join them and four other criminals to save Sol from the Sun-Eater. He agreed and helped form the Fatal Five, which continued to plague the Legion for years (*Adventure Comics* #352–353, January–February 1967).

PETRIFIED SPACEMAN, THE

An alien crash-landed on Earth and was eventually discovered by scientists, who nicknamed him the Petrified Spaceman. He eventually awoke and displayed super-strength and invulnerability, causing Lex Luthor to shoot him with a kryptonite bullet. Superman determined that the spaceman was from a frozen planet and used ice to help restore the visitor's memory. Eventually learning where he came from, the Man of Steel helped the spaceman return home, even fashioning him a space vessel from ice (*Action Comics* #226, March 1957).

PHANTAS

The hereditary Eliminator of Rhadmanth followed six criminals from their world to Earth. Seeking to escape his vengeance, each of the six "transmorphed" and possessed the body of one of six journalists in Metropolis. In an attempt to dispatch them, the Eliminator took on the form of the recently deceased occultist and collector Dr. Phantas. When the deceased's casket was opened, the "ghost" of Phantas appeared and cast a "curse" on Clark Kent, vowing to kill his colleagues. Sure enough, several reporters died, and the others thought Kent was truly jinxed. Superman investigated and discovered the Rhadmanthian, learning of his mission. When the final journalist was slain, the Eliminator returned home, ending any thought that Clark was jinxed (*Action Comics* #379, August 1969).

PHANTOM STRANGER, THE

Superman and his fellow crime fighters were at first wary when a mysterious and extremely powerful man began showing up to advise them of great dangers. When asked his name, he merely replied he was a stranger, but over time Earth's heroes learned he was a long-lived mystical being whose origins were shrouded in mystery (*The Phantom Stranger* #1, August–September 1952).

There have been several stories purporting to be his origin tale, with one—that he was a fallen angel from Heaven—having the most supportive evidence (*Secret Origins* [third series] #10, January 1987). When the Spectre tried to eradicate magic from the universe, the Stranger said to him, "You can't kill me. I doubt that the universe would allow it."

In his turtleneck, dark suit, cloak, and hat, the man seemed to have control over occult energies, able to transport himself and others to various places and realms as needed. The Man of Steel first encountered the Phantom Stranger with the Justice League of America (*Justice League of America* [first series] #103, December 1972) and was the one to proclaim their benefactor an unqualified member of the team. On several occasions, he admitted to being a member of the vaunted team despite coming and going as required (*Justice League of America* [first series] #143, June 1977). The unlikely pair began a series of one-on-one encounters when the enigmatic Stranger arrived during Superman's battle with the lord of the vampires Dracula (*Superman* [first series] #344, February 1980).

The Stranger often came to the hero's aid whenever Superman was mystically attacked, whether it was when the Man of Steel fell under the sway of a marine vampire called the Trilling (*World's Finest Comics* #249, February–March 1979) or the time Madame Benita, at the behest of a panicked Pete Ross, attacked Superman (*DC Comics Presents* #25, September 1980). That his childhood friend would want him dead hurt the Man of Steel, but it was done in order to save his son Jonathan Ross, who was trapped on a distant world.

In the world after the Crisis on Infinite Earths, Superman often encountered the Phantom Stranger when the odds were stacked against humanity and mystic forces were at play (*Action Comics* #585, February 1987; others). The Stranger, however tended to do combat against forces beyond imagination on his own or with other practitioners of magic throughout the planet. When the Rock of Eternity was shattered, for example, the Phantom Stranger was among the mystics who gathered to rebuild it (*Day of Vengeance: Infinite Crisis Special,* March 2006). It was the Stranger who gathered the magicians to make a joint request for the Spectre's help to preserve the universe before it was split once again into a multiverse (*Infinite Crisis* #6, May 2006).

There was some question as to whether or not he was a member of the Lords of Order in their eternal battle with the Lords of Chaos (*Green Lantern/Superman: Legend of the Green Flame,* 2001).

The Phantom Stranger was also a member of the Quintessence, a quartet of powerful beings mixing science and sorcery who oversaw the cosmic events shaping the known universe (*Kingdom Come* #3, July 1996; *JLA* #29, May 1999).

On Earth-22, it was speculated that Jonathan Kent, son of Superman and Wonder Woman, might actually grow up to become the Phantom Stranger (*The Kingdom* #1–2, February 1999).

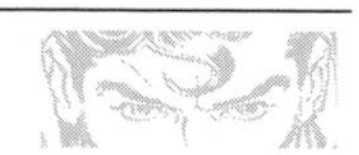

PHANTOM ZONE, THE

Discovered by the Kryptonian scientist Jor-El, the Phantom Zone was a limbo-like dimension where the Kryptonians used to banish their criminals in lieu of capital punishment. Jor-El saw it as a more humane way to incarcerate criminals than sending them into orbit in a state of suspended animation. He built the Phantom Zone projector to allow the instantaneous transportation of criminals to their prison realm (*Superboy* [first series] #104, April 1963). It wasn't until some time later that anyone realized phantom-like beasts also resided in the Zone (*Phantom Zone* #1–4, January–April 1982).

Those transported to the Zone were immaterial shapes, able to see what was transpiring on their homeworld but unable to communicate with their loved ones. While in the Zone, they also had increased telepathic abilities, and those serving the longest sentences eventually learned how to use that skill to manipulate people in the material world (*Superman* [first series] #158, January 1963). People with telepathic abilities, such as Atlantis's Lori Lemaris, could communicate with denizens of the Zone. When the Man of Steel suffered from Virus X and was believed close to death, he was saved when Mon-El telepathically informed Saturn Girl that he was not dying from the disease but actually from a piece of kryptonite lodged in Jimmy Olsen's camera (*Superman* [first series] #156, October 1962). If the criminals marshaled their forces, they could get a single message across to a nontelepathic individual (*Superman* [first series] #157, November 1962).

Ironically, those in the Zone survived the destruction of Krypton, although it also meant the projector that could bring them home was seemingly lost in the explosion. In time, it was learned that the device survived and, like so many artifacts from the doomed world, made its way to Earth (*Adventure Comics* #283, April 1961). Superboy recovered the projector and used it sparingly, but was keenly aware that criminals from his birth planet had also survived and continually desired their freedom.

Superman eventually built the Zone-o-phone, which enabled him to directly contact people in the Phantom Zone and see the limbo realm on a giant monitor screen (*Superman* [first series] #157, November 1962). In time, he added a headset and microphone for improved communication (*Superman* [first series] #167, February 1964). He later adapted the technology to create a gun-like "view finder" that allowed him to spot-check the Zone and make certain all its inhabitants were accounted for (*Superman* [first series] #163, August 1963).

Once the bottle city of Kandor was safely ensconced in Superman's Fortress of Solitude, the government decided to reconvene its Phantom Zone Parole Board, an annual meeting in which criminals whose sentences were up could be evaluated and those deemed worthy then freed and allowed to live in the city. Superman miniaturized a copy of the Zone-o-phone in order for the board to speak with the inmates. The former criminal Quex-Ul was the first such parolee (*Superman* [first series] #157, November 1962). Superman had built a device to bring people out of the Zone, and with it came the risk that they would immediately gain superpowers and try to flee rather than be reduced and brought to Kandor. As a safety, he built a "Zone shackle" that could be fitted on a parolee. This device would automatically return someone to the Phantom Zone if he or she resisted voluntarily being sent back—which is exactly what happened with the evil terrorist Jax-Ur (*Action Comics* #310, March 1964).

Given the knowledge that Superman was Kal-El, son of the man who discovered the Phantom Zone, the criminals all developed a hatred for him and constantly sought ways to ruin the Man of Steel's life. Of course, once they were able to observe life on Earth, they also learned that he was known as mild-mannered reporter Clark Kent (*Superman* [first series] #157, November 1962).

Given their desire for freedom, the Phantom Zone inmates made repeated attempts at escape. They also took advantage when other phenomena caused a rift, allowing access to the corporeal world. There was once a "50-megaton atomic test blast on Earth [that had] ripped open a hole in the Phantom Zone," allowing eight criminals to escape before it finally closed up again (*Superman* [first series] #153, May 1962). Soon after, a Polaris missile fired into space also created a rip in the Zone, which allowed Ras-Krom to slip through (*Superman* [first series] #163, October 1963). Even the "electrical ions of the Aurora Borealis" tore a hole to the other dimension, though it was quickly sealed by Superman, Supergirl, and Krypto (*Action Comics* #284, January 1962).

Prominent prisoners in the Phantom Zone at the time of Krypton's explosion included General Zod (*Adventure Comics* #283, April 1961), Jax-Ur (*Adventure Comics* #289, October 1961), and Professor Vakox (*Action Comics* #284, January 1962); Dr. Xadu, a "villainous scientist" (*Adventure Comics* #283, April 1961) sentenced to thirty years in the Phantom Zone for conducting "a forbidden experiment in suspended animation" (*Superman* [first series] #150, January 1962); Ral-En, the son of Mag-En (*Superman* [first series] #154, July 1962); Quex-Ul (*Superman* [first series] #157, November 1962); Ras-Krom (*Superman* [first series] #164, October 1963); Faora Hu-Ul (*Action Comics* #471, May 1977), and Ak-Var, who was convicted for his theft of the Sunstone and later released into Kandor (*Action Comics* #336, April 1966), where he adopted the heroic alter ego of Flamebird.

Other known inhabitants of the Phantom Zone included Tor-An, a handsome scientist whose mind-transfer device transplanted the minds of a family into the bodies of monsters, later described as "a seductive killer responsible for the deaths of dozens of women across Krypton and the youngest to be sent into the Phantom Zone" (*Action Comics* #307, December 1963); Zan-Ar (*Superman's Girl Friend, Lois Lane* #59, August 1965); Gann-Artar, creator of the De-Evolutionary Ray, which he used to unleash a stampede of monsters (*Superman* [first series] #166, January 1964); Brenn-Bir, Kyl-Ibo, and Vas-Quor, who stole the Sunstone in Kandor (*Action Comics* #336, April 1966; *World's Finest Comics* #143, August 1964); Erndine Ze-Da, co-conspirator with her husband Dr. Xadu (*Superboy* [first series] #100, October 1962); Nadira Va-Dim, who "carried out a senseless rampage" with his lover (*Phantom Zone* #1, January 1982); Blak-Du, a scientist and former college classmate of Jor-El who committed an unknown crime (*Superboy* [first series] #121, June 1965); Kur-Dul, who was released into Kandor when his sentence was complete (*Superman* [first series] #223, January 1970); Kru-El, who "developed an arsenal of super-powerful, forbidden weapons" (*Action Comics* #297, February 1963); Jer-Em, a religious fanatic whose sabotage of Argo City's jet-drive condemned him to thirty cycles in the Phantom Zone (*Action Comics* #309, February 1964); Zan-Em, "a psychic scientist" imprisoned "for unauthorized mind control ex-

periments" (*Adventure Comics* #458, July–August 1978); L. Finn, a leprechaun-like mage (*Adventure Comics* #400, December 1970); Ner-Gal, a violent criminal originally placed in orbit above Krypton but transferred to the Phantom Zone after he developed psychic powers that enabled him to strike at Jor-El (*Superman* [first series] #286, April 1975); Tra-Gob, a thief whose gang turned on him—only to have Jor-El save his life (*Superman's Girl Friend, Lois Lane* #98, January 1970); Bal-Gra, "the strongest man on Krypton" before his incarceration (*Superman* [first series] #204, February 1968); the Inventor, a scientist (*Adventure Comics* #400, December 1970); Thul-Kar, last of the Wizards of Juru, who fled Krypton's destruction by going into the Phantom Zone (*Phantom Zone* #3, March 1982); Vor-Kil, a criminal versed in the art of Klurkor (*Superman* [first series] #219, August 1969); Cha-Mel, a "youngster who developed a secret spray that transformed the molecules of his body and clothing," enabling him to become a shape-shifting thief (*Superboy* [first series] #162, January 1970); Murrk and Tyb-Ol, who were killed by the Vrangs during an attempt to escape from the Zone (*Action Comics* #548–549, October–November 1983); Vax-Nor, who was released into Kandor after the completion of his sentence (*Superman* [first series] #223, January 1970); Gor-Nu, "once the greatest bio-chemist on Krypton" whose "reckless experiments caused several deaths" (*Superman* [first series] #223, January 1970); Shyla Kor-Onn, convicted of manslaughter after an accident involving her power-siphon, which transferred energy from others into herself (*Superman Family* #183, May–June 1977); Az-Rel, who "carried out a senseless rampage" with his lover Nadira Va-Dim (*Phantom Zone* #1, January 1982), Ma-Rok (*Superman's Girl Friend, Lois Lane* #59, August 1965); Py-Ron, a scientist who "turned humans into weird, bird-like monsters" (*Action Comics* #323, April 1965); the Toymaster, creator of various automatons and oversized toy menaces (*Adventure Comics* #400, December 1970); Ar-Ual, a woman who destroyed an extraterrestrial spacecraft and its wonders rather than share them (*Superman's Girl Friend, Lois Lane* #93, July 1969); Vorb-Un, an aged scientist sentenced for experimenting with elements and later released in Kandor (*Action Comics* #310, March 1964); Ran-Zo (*Superman's Girl Friend, Lois Lane* #59, August 1965); Zan-Zoll, imprisoned in the Zone after being unable to reverse the effects of his Evolution Cabinet (*Superman's Pal, Jimmy Olsen* #66, January 1963); Ga-Zor, a dying old man who tried to destroy Krypton with his earthquake machine "after a lifetime of scientific villainy" and remained a prisoner in the Phantom Zone as late as 2964 (*Adventure Comics* #323, August 1964); and Orn-Zu, who created a creature called Jorlan meant to steal all Krypton's children and take them to a yellow-sun system in order to spare them from the planet's impending doom (*Action Comics* #505, March 1980). There were also eight unidentified Phantom Zone escapees whom Superman encountered in the town of Drywood Gulch (*Superman* [first series] #153, May 1962).

Superman and the government of Kandor had a complete gallery of information on the prisoners, which was used for both attendance and parole consideration (*Superman* [first series] #164, October 1963).

After the projector's recovery, several other criminals were consigned to serve out their terms in the Phantom Zone. One was Roz-Em, who had plastic surgery to resemble armory supervisor Nim-El (and, to a degree, his fraternal twin Jor-El) in order to steal planetary weapons (*Adventure Comics* #304, January 1963). Gra-Mo, a scientific crime lord, and Ni-Van instigated a rebellion of Krypton's robot police force after being rejected for a place on the Science Council in favor of Jor-El; they were imprisoned in orbit above Krypton until their satellite, which contained a third unnamed criminal, fell to Earth, where they were captured and imprisoned by Superboy (*Superboy* [first series] #104, April 1963). Also present was Morlak, a sinister shape-shifting dog created by Dev-Em who escaped Krypton's fate in a suspended animation rocket but was projected into the Zone after terrorizing Superboy and Krypto (*Superboy* [first series] #128, April 1966).

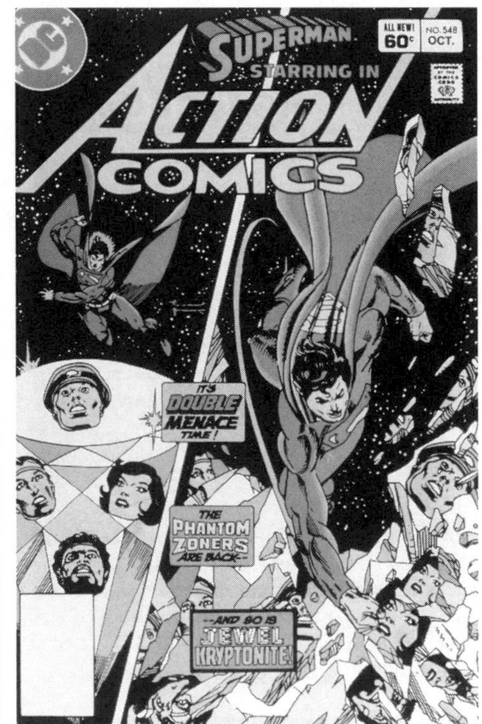

During Superman's career, several others wound up spending time in the Phantom Zone for their misdeeds, including Nam-Ek, a scientist whose Rondor-derived serum granted him the ability to cure any disease, rendering him immortal (*Superman* [first series] #282, December 1974); Zak-Kul, a renegade scientist who escaped the bottle city of Kandor to impersonate Superman (*Action Comics* #245, October 1958); and El Gar-Kur, a criminal scientist and Jimmy Olsen look-alike who used body-swapping technology on Jimmy (*Action Comics* #253, June 1959). Zo-Mar created a will-controlling symbol that he used in an attempt to seize Fort Rozz; his prison craft eventually drifted to Earth, where he was captured and sent to the Phantom Zone by Superman (*DC Comics Presents* #84, August 1985). Also imprisoned were Zora Vi-Lar, a scientific devotee of Lesla-Lar who was sentenced to the Zone after menacing Supergirl as the Black Flame (*Action Comics* #304, September 1963); Lar-On, a scientist afflicted with lycanthropy who voluntarily accepted exile in the Phantom Zone after he killed his wife while a were-beast (*World's Finest Comics* #256, April–May 1979); Zal-Te, a Kandorian fanatic who created a rampaging amoeba-creature during experiments to enlarge the shrunken city (*Superman Family* #185, September–October 1977); and Tal-Var, a superpowered but evidently non-Kryptonian "master of the Dark Dimension" who was trapped in the Zone by Jimmy Olsen (*Superman's Pal, Jimmy Olsen* #97, October 1966).

Lar Gand of Daxam was also placed in the Phantom Zone to preserve his life after he contracted lead poisoning following his arrival on Earth and brief adventures alongside Superboy as Mon-El (*Superboy* [first series] #89, June 1961). Similarly, the hero Green Lantern, Guy Gardner, was trapped in the Phantom Zone for a time when his power battery unexpectedly blew up. Eventually, Green Lantern Hal Jordan and Superman rescued him (*Green Lantern* [second series] #117, June 1979, and #122–123, November–December 1979).

Superman and his allies visited the Phantom Zone on several occasions, such as the time red kryptonite split the Man of Steel into two beings. One, an arrogant control freak, consigned Supergirl, Krypto, and all of Kandor to the Zone (*Action Comics* #293, October 1962). Jimmy Olsen joined Superman for a brief visit as a way to escape Kandor when they were sought by the "fanatic scientist" Than-Ol (*Superman* [first series] #158, January 1963).

In the reality created by the Crisis on Infinite Earths, Superman first became aware of the Phantom Zone in a Pocket Universe created by the Time Trapper. There General Zod, Quex-Ul, and Zaora tricked their way out of the Zone and went on to annihilate everyone on this alternate Earth. Rather than risk these villains wreaking havoc on his own world, the Man of Steel reluctantly executed the trio using green kryptonite (*The Adventures of Superman* #444, September 1988; *Superman* [second series] #22, October 1988).

On his own Earth, Superman was introduced to the otherworldly limbo after recovering the Kryptonian artifact known as the Eradicator. When it attempted to honor its programming and rebuild Krypton on Earth, it retrieved materials from the Phantom Zone, described as a time portal between Earth's present and Krypton's past. Within the Zone, Superman encountered a computer program based on the Eradicator's creator Kem-L and was horrified to learn that the artifact's programming was intent on transforming Earth into New Krypton. Traveling through the Zone to the moments before Krypton exploded, Superman worked with Jor-El to undergo a rite of passage that would allow him to control the Eradicator and halt its programming. The Man of Steel succeeded, although the gateway to the Zone was destroyed

as he returned to the present (*The Adventures of Superman* #461, December 1989).

A subsequent account asserted that the real Kem-L had created a Phantom Zone projector from the warp drive of an alien craft that crashed on Krypton and used it to exile virtually all of the extraterrestrials to the unearthly realm. Drawn into the Zone in the present, the human incarnation of the Eradicator found that the Kem-L program had also used the Zone as a virtual-reality repository of Krypton's mythology. Desperately seeking a form of true life as the Eradicator had, the Kem-L program escaped from the Zone in an alien form and seemed to perish (*Eradicator* #1–3, August-October 1996). The Kem-L program's subsequent interaction with Superman, however, suggested that this account was apocryphal.

Indeed, the Kem-L program was later revealed to have discovered the maimed body of an alien Tuoni, whom he humanely worked to make whole by grafting Kryptonian technology to his body. Unwittingly, Kem-L had given rise to a being ultimately known as Dominus, who escaped the Zone during Superman's first encounter with it. Traveling to his homeworld, Dominus cast the rest of his people into the Zone and then returned to Earth, intent on using a mentally controlled Superman as his vehicle for taking over the world. When the Man of Steel began to rebel, Dominus cast him into the Phantom Zone as well. With the help of the Kem-L program, Superman cobbled together enough Kryptonian technology to build a transport back to Earth (*Action Comics* #754, May 1999) and used a Phantom Zone projector to imprison Dominus in the Zone once more (*Superman: King of the World* #1, June 1999). Superman later made the projector available to the Martian Manhunter so he could imprison a horde of white Martians attempting to conquer Earth (*JLA* #58, November 2001).

When John Henry Irons (see Steel) later helped reconstruct the Fortress of Solitude, Superman included a gateway to the Zone and was dismayed when the villainous Luna of the Cybermoths found herself trapped there. Entering the Zone to rescue her, Superman learned of the existence of leech-like entities whose sole purpose was "to find any physical life that falls into the Zone and suck all the matter out of it, to reduce [their prey] to a state consistent with the [phantom-like existence] of the Zone" (*Superman: The Man of Steel* #107, December 2000). In an account that may have been a hallucination experienced by Supergirl, the dimensional plane was also revealed to be the home to native life-forms who disliked sharing their home with aliens (*Supergirl* [fifth series] #16, June 2007).

Brainiac 13 ultimately used the Zone to create the tantalizing false reality of Krypton with the intent of killing or at least imprisoning Superman. Instead, the artificial reality took on a life of its own, severing all ties to its sinister origins (*Superman* [second series] #167, April 2001; *Action Comics* #793, September 2002; others).

The Phantom Zone was added to the plans devised by Batman for anticipated problems of all sorts. He called it the Doomsday Protocol, which would begin with the usual military and superpowered efforts to contain the threat. If the danger still existed, people were to be cleared from the area; then the projector would be employed to make the threat disappear (*Action Comics* #825, May 2005).

Zazzala the Queen Bee reported at one point that "this unregion of infinitely [space]" had a multitude of names. On her world of Korll, it was called the Honeycomb and was used to bypass otherwise vast distances in outer space (*JLA* #36, December 1999). One of Superman's foes, Loophole, called it the Stasis Zone, and this was the name used when, in one time line, Valor (Lar Gand) was placed within the realm for a millennium (*Superboy* [third series] #16, June 1995, and #20, October 1995). The green Martians called it the Still Zone and used it to incarcerate their evil white kinsmen (*JLA* #4, April 1997). The Justice League of America's foe Prometheus also accessed the Zone and declared it the Ghost Zone (*Prometheus* #1, February 1998).

In the reality formed after Infinite Crisis, Jor-El was once said to have discovered the Phantom Zone, albeit "decades prior to Krypton's destruction." At the moment that prisoners were cast into the Zone, they seemed to be contained within a pane of glass (*Action Comics* #846, February 2007). Beyond the villains documented on Earth-1, two others were unique to this reality: Non, Jor-El's former friend and mentor, who was lobotomized when he tried to rebel against the government; and Ursa, a "former lieutenant of the planet Krypton's military" who was sentenced to the Phantom Zone for "heresy, murder and treason" (*Action Comics* #845–846, January–February 2007; *52* #37, January 17, 2007).

At one time, the Venusian villain Mister Mind actually ingested the entire dimension while the insectoid form threatened all reality. The Phantom Zone was regurgitated as a defense when the creature was attacked by Booster Gold and Rip Hunter. Supernova eventually deflected the Zone back to its natural place in the fabric of reality (*52* #37, January 17, 2007, and #52, May 2, 2007).

In the wake of Kandor being enlarged in the Arctic, General Zod, Ursa, and Non were among the criminals freed from the Phantom Zone and invited to resume their place on New Krypton. A short time later, the Phantom Zone vanished, and Superman managed to rescue Mon-El before it disappeared entirely (*Action Comics* #874, April 2009).

The spirit of the Kryptonium builder Vohc possessed the criminal Jax-Ur and forced Lor-Zod, avatar of the Nightwing, into the last crystal shard remnant of the Phantom Zone (*Action Comics* #886, April 2010). It was Lor-Zod's departure from the Phantom Zone that had caused it to disintegrate, and while Vohc wanted to make his sibling Nightwing suffer, he also set about re-creating the Phantom Zone, which proved unintentionally providential (*Action Comics* #888, Early June 2010). When the Kandorians attacked Earth after the destruction of New Krypton, Superboy had Krypto retrieve the Phantom Zone Projector from the Fortress of Solitude and circled the globe, sending all the Kryptonians attacking Earth into the ghostly realm. The Nightwing entity then told Lor-Zod that the youth's destiny was to remain in the Phantom Zone in order to stabilize it, otherwise the Zone would consume all of reality. Lor-Zod accepted his fate and bade farewell to Superman one last time, then entered the Zone. There he was returned to his child age and encountered Lar Gand, who had also been transported back to the Zone. The two decided to stick together and face whatever came next as allies and friends (*Superman: War of the Supermen* #3–4, July 2010).

Throughout the multiverse, Phantom Zone criminals had varied fates. On the utopian Earth-162, they were freed and reformed via the rays of "anti-evil" satellites, subsequently retiring to New Krypton along with the people of Kandor (*Superman* [first series] #162, July 1963). In another reality, the prisoners escaped en masse with the intent of destroying Earth, only to be absorbed into the crystal uni-mind of Aethyr (*DC Comics Presents* #97, September 1986).

PHANTOM ZONE PROJECTOR, THE

When Jor-El of Krypton discovered the realm he called the Phantom Zone, he saw it as a more humane way to imprison criminals than having them orbit the planet in suspended animation. To place and retrieve people within the Zone, he devised a projector. It was a tabletop-sized unit with a white, circular lens in the front and a red casing. Tapping a button would engage the circuitry that powered the device, which pierced the dimension veil. A second button would send the individual through the portal (*Adventure Comics* #283, April 1961; others).

The device was thought lost forever when the planet exploded, but it survived and drifted through space until arriving on Earth (*Adventure Comics* #283, April 1961). Superboy took custody of it and stored it among his possessions until he grew to adulthood and, as Superman, placed it permanently in the Fortress of Solitude. When he rescued the bottle city of Kandor from Brainiac, he sometimes joined the Phantom Zone Parole Board during their annual hearings (*Action Comics* #310, March 1964).

Superman eventually built the Zone-o-phone, which enabled him to directly contact people in the Phantom Zone and see the limbo realm on a giant monitor screen (*Superman* [first series] #157, November 1962). In time, he added a headset and microphone for improved communication (*Superman* [first series] #167, February 1964). He later adapted the technology to create a gun-like "viewfinder" that allowed him to spot-check the Zone and make certain all its inhabitants were accounted for (*Superman* [first series] #163, August 1963).

In the world after the Crisis on Infinite Earths, Superman also adapted the technology for use as a weapon, encased within an arrow. At some point, Roy Harper, when he was the first Speedy, stole the arrow during a visit to the Fortress by the Teen Titans. He never used the arrow and passed it on to his successor, Mia Dearden. She found occasion to use it during the Infinite Crisis, sending Superboy-Prime to the Phantom Zone, but the enraged teen managed to eventually escape (*Teen Titans* [third series] #32, March 2006).

The Phantom Zone Projector

PHANTY-CATS

Pets projected from Krypton into the Phantom Zone were nicknamed "phanty-cats" by their criminal owners. They once provided to Tricky Tom an evil plan designed to kill Superboy and Krypto by melting the lead coating off statues of the House of El, which had been turned into deadly kryptonite after the planet exploded (*Superboy* [first series] #136, March 1966).

PITTSDALE

The hometown of Lois and Lucy Lane and site of the Lane family farm (*Superman's Girl Friend, Lois Lane* #90, February 1969), with a population of 1,101 (*Superman's Girl Friend, Lois Lane* #13, November 1959). Lois got her first newspaper experience writing for the *Pittsdale Star,* founded in 1859.

Lois and Lucy attended Pittsdale High School (*Superboy* [first series] #90, July 1961) and took classes at a small community college for a time before transferring to the more prestigious Raleigh College (*Superman's Girl Friend, Lois Lane* #2, May–June 1958). Other former residents of Pittsdale included Kathy Crawford (*Batman* #309, March 1979) and Lana Lang's aunt Helen and cousin Betsy (*Superboy* [first series] #90, July 1961). One of Lois's high school English teachers was Miss Plunkett (*Superman's Girl Friend, Lois Lane* #13, November 1959) while another teacher was Mrs. Lorat (*Superman's Girl Friend, Lois Lane* #44, October 1963). Lois's classmates included Susan Freeling, Helen Gold, and Marcy Lloyd, as well as boyfriends Courtney Greene, Wayne Henry, and Leonard Splatz (*Superman Family* #206, March–April 1981).

"An isolated forest ranger station [was] outside of Pittsdale" and Hadley Hill was "just south of town"; "an old windmill" lay to the east. An air force base was located outside town (*Superman's Girl Friend, Lois Lane* #13, November 1959).

PLANETEER, THE

Philip Conrad was a would-be dictator who took on the costumed identity of the Planeteer. Believing himself the mighty Alexander the Great reincarnated, he schemed to steal the Man of Tomorrow's powers by abducting the world's leading heads of state (*Superman* [first series] #387, September 1983). Superman rescued the leaders, but the Planeteer was ultimately successful in increasing his abilities immensely using his energy transmitter (*Action Comics* #547, September 1983). He resurfaced only once more, partnering with the Queen Bee in yet another failed plan for conquest (*Action Comics* #562, December 1984).

PLANET KRYPTON

It was only a matter of time before someone launched a chain of restaurants with a super hero theme, and semi-retired Justice League of America member Booster Gold concluded that he was just the man to do it. Planet Krypton was filled with facsimiles of memorabilia featuring Superman but including all of America's costumed champions. The waitstaff wore replicas of the costumes of heroes throughout the past century, and the menu featured Continental fare with catchy heroic names. Several heroes were known to dine at one branch or another, both in and out of costume (*Kingdom Come* #1, May 1996; *The Kingdom: Planet Krypton* #1, February 1999). The restaurant was paralleled by Keystone City's Planet Café, where all the servers wore costumes not unlike those seen on the Krypton of Earth-1 (*The Flash* [second series] #134, February 1998).

On Earth-22, Superman, Batman, and Wonder Woman met at Planet Krypton on occasion, and it was there that Batman learned the other two were expecting their first child together (*Kingdom Come* #4, 1996).

PLASTIMOLD

Kryptonian surgeon Dahr-Nel created plastimold, which "adjusts the molecular structures of cell tissues" in order to repair "damaged or defective bodies." Powered by a Transformoflux Pack, which projected a ray onto the subject, this instantaneous form of plastic surgery meant the subject was first encased in a mold similar in shape to a mummy sarcophagus (*Superman's Girl Friend, Lois Lane* #90, February 1969). Later, Superman apparently had access to one of Dahr-Nel's devices and adapted it to let Lois Lane temporarily alter her appearance to pass herself off as an African American for a story on life in Metropolis's Little Africa section (*Superman's Girl Friend, Lois Lane* #106, November 1970).

PLIM

Jimmy Olsen was once befriended by Plim, a young reporter from the planet Antron. Attempting to prove his investigative abilities, Jimmy tried to break up a criminal ring without the help of Superman but failed miserably. Plim was on hand to photograph each error, including Jimmy crying in despair, as these subjects were actually fascinating to the people of Plim's homeworld (*Superman's Pal, Jimmy Olsen* #84, April 1965).

PLUTO

Superman once visited the planetoid Pluto to obtain some giant snowflakes, frozen so solidly that they would not melt on Earth, for inclusion among the collection of "space trophies" that he was gathering for the Metropolis Museum's time capsule as a gift for the people of the fiftieth century (*Superman* [first series] #122, July 1958). Later, Supergirl visited Pluto herself and fought and destroyed a pack of robotic animals analogous to the Metal Men (*Adventure Comics* #395, July 1970).

On another occasion, Superman found himself menaced by a Plutonian life force that attempted to take the Fortress of Solitude as its material form (*Superman* [first series] #204, February 1968).

In the reality created following the Crisis on Infinite Earths, Pluto vanished from the solar system for a time (*Superman* [second series] #159, August 2000). In fact, it had been cloaked and temporarily transformed into a new Warworld by Brainiac 13 as a weapon to be used in the imminent war on Imperiex (*Superman* [second series] #165, February 2001; others).

In the 853rd century, the planet was used as a penal colony and home to that era's Batman with his robot sidekick Robin the Toy Wonder (*Batman One Million,* November 1998).

Pluto was also the name of the Roman god of the underworld. He was one of the gods who empowered a magical belt with which Superman defeated the magically created human villain Zha-Vam (*Action Comics* #353, August 1967).

POCKET UNIVERSE, THE

When the multiverse was threatened by the Anti-Monitor during the Crisis on Infinite Earths, it impacted every living being, past, present, and future. From his home at the end of time, the being known as the Time Trapper stole a sliver of time, one containing the twentieth century of Earth-1, where Kal-El from Krypton landed on Earth and was raised to become Superboy and a member of that world's thirtieth-century Legion of Super-Heroes (*Action Comics* #591, August 1987).

Tucked away from the revamped single positive-matter universe, the Time Trapper then redirected Legionnaires anytime they journeyed back in time to the Pocket Universe, letting them think they were dealing with the real Teen of Steel. When the deception was discovered, the Time Trapper set a series of events into motion that led to the Pocket Universe Superboy sacrificing his life to save both Superman and the Legion (*Legion of Super-Heroes* [third series] #38, September 1987).

A quirk in this reality was the lack of a Supergirl, which became an issue in the years that followed. Without Superboy growing into Superman, the planet was ill prepared for a trio of escaped villains from the Phantom Zone. They ravaged the planet, and even the genius of Lex Luthor couldn't save humanity. He tried, taking cells from the Pocket Universe's Lana Lang, creating a morphing life-form dubbed Matrix, and sending her, disguised as Supergirl, to the real universe to summon Superman's help. With virtually every living being on the planet murdered, the Man of Steel made the agonizing decision to execute the captured Phantom Zone villains. It was the first and last time Superman would kill, and the decision would haunt him long after. Matrix was also damaged, and Superman brought her to his universe

to heal while the Pocket Universe was finally wiped from reality (*The Adventures of Superman* #444, September 1988; *Superman* [second series] #22, October 1988).

POISON IVY

On Earth-1, Lillian Rose had an affair with her college botany professor Marc LeGrand, who asked her to accompany him while stealing an Egyptian artifact in a Seattle museum. He wanted the artifact's contents: rare herbs, some of which he then used in an attempt to kill Rose, silencing the only witness. Instead she survived and acquired an immunity to many natural toxins (*World's Finest Comics* #252, August–September 1978). Taking the name *Pamela Isley* (first revealed in *Justice League of America* [first series] #111, May–June 1974) and the costumed persona of Poison Ivy, she set out to prove her new power over men. Poison Ivy proclaimed herself public enemy number one. This was all part of a scheme on Ivy's part to drive the various costumed felons to compete with one another while she waited them out, leaving the spoils for herself (*Batman* #181, June 1966).

After this, Poison Ivy returned time and again to antagonize the Caped Crusader, continually committing crimes to fund her work with plant life.

She additionally battled other heroes, notably the Thorn and Wonder Woman. She also worked on behalf of the One Hundred at one point (*Superman's Girl Friend, Lois Lane* #115–116, October–November 1971) and served as a member of both the Injustice Gang of the World (*Justice League of America* [first series] #111, May–June 1974) and the Secret Society of Super-Villains (*DC Special Series* #6, November 1977).

On the Earth formed after the Crisis on Infinite Earths, Pamela Lillian Isley studied biochemistry under Jason Woodrue, the Floronic Man, who was actually a refugee from another dimension. She was one of several noteworthy students, and rumors spread that she and Woodrue were having an affair, something that was not the case. As an experiment, he poisoned the impressionable Isley, which resulted in rewiring her body chemistry, making her immune to all toxins but pushing her to the brink of insanity. The resulting changes to her body left her unable to conceive children, and she took to creating plant-based artificial lifeforms that she called her children (*Secret Origins* [third series] #36, January 1989; *Batman: Shadow of the Bat Annual* #3, 1995).

Isley managed to use pheromones to convince people to do her bidding. She also proved adept at manipulating plant life, creating hybrids and even controlling them telepathically. Through the years, her power over flora increased, making her a formidable opponent. She even found ways to entice and control Superman, using him to attack Batman on at least one occasion (*Batman* #612, April 2003).

In other instances, she earned the wrath of Metallo while challenging the Superboy-and-Robin team (*Superboy/Robin: World's Finest Three* #1–2, 1996), and fought Supergirl alongside Harley Quinn and Clayface (*Superman/Batman* #19, May 2005).

(For a complete history of Poison Ivy, see *The Essential Batman Encyclopedia,* 2008.)

POSITIVE MAN

A giant spacefaring creature composed entirely of positive ions. Supergirl explained that the Positive Man was a destructive force that was once human. "That mind-tape revealed he was once an alien scientist who blew up his planet while creating a Doomsday bomb! The explosion transformed him into this terrible menace! Envious of all life, he roams the cosmos, jealously destroying inhabited worlds!"

To help deal with the threat, she requested help from her fellow members of the thirtieth-century-based Legion of Super-Heroes. They worked to lure out another product of the same explosion, a bird-like being called the Negative Creature. As Positive and Negative came into contact, they canceled each other out, thereby ending the threat (*Action Comics* #287, April 1962).

POTTER, HARRY

A scientist with the Metropolis branch of S.T.A.R. Labs, Potter once recounted his experience with the being known as the Galactic Golem to WGBS reporter Clark Kent. He and astro-technician Bert Smith tried to prevent the Golem from stealing an energy-charged meteoroid by hitting it with a stick—to little effect, ultimately requiring Superman's involvement (*Superman* [first series] #258, November 1972).

POTTER, PROFESSOR PHINEAS

Superman was befriended by countless scientists through his years on Earth. Many were fascinated by his extraterrestrial origins, while others thought he would be the perfect test subject since little could harm him. Among them, Phineas Potter appeared to hold a special place in the Man of Steel's heart given their numerous encounters on Earth-1 (*Superman's Pal, Jimmy Olsen* #22, August 1957). As it turned out, he was also Lana Lang's uncle, which no doubt left Superman sympathetic toward the scientist, whom he had known since his childhood (*Adventure Comics* #291, December 1961).

The inventor was so caught up in creating new devices to help humankind that he rarely thought through their implications, which usually came to light once they were activated. In many ways he was a danger to the public, but problems were usually contained thanks to Superman's intervention. He made for good newspaper copy and became friendly with *Daily Planet* reporters Lois Lane, Clark Kent, and Jimmy Olsen.

Jimmy in particular found himself often affected by Potter's creations, having been transformed into a super-genius by an evolution accelerator (*Superman's Pal, Jimmy Olsen* #22, August 1957), sent to another planet (*Superman's Pal, Jimmy Olsen* #25, December 1957), afflicted with an evil twin (*Superman's Pal, Jimmy Olsen* #27, March 1958), expanded to giant-sized (*Superman's Pal, Jimmy Olsen* #28, April 1958), endowed with a Pinocchio-like nose (*Superman's Pal, Jimmy Olsen* #32, October 1958), and cursed with flame-breath (*Superman's Pal, Jimmy Olsen* #33, December 1958), among many other adventures.

For all of the headaches, the cub reporter was delighted when Potter was able to re-create a space serum that had once given him stretchability powers, and he used this formula to become Elastic Lad time and again (*Superman's Pal, Jimmy Olsen* #37, June 1959). Later, in his role as Agent Double-Five, Jimmy stocked his "super-survival kit" with a variety of gadgets invented by Professor Potter (*Superman's Pal, Jimmy Olsen* #89, December 1965).

Some of the devices were perfectly harmless, such as the machine that could squeeze two thousand gallons of onion juice in an hour (*Superman* [first series] #176, April 1965).

Potter had as many failures as successes—though in one case, his failure actually wound up saving the world. Lana used his "experimental machine for suspended animation," but instead of performing its intended function, it "merely turns people into lifeless crystal," allowing Superman to show the ruthless "interplanetary gamblers" Rokk and Sorban that he had killed someone, satisfying their demand and thereby sparing the planet (*Superman* [first series] #171, August 1964).

Potter developed a powerful teleportation device which Jimmy used to bring Titano and a

THAT NIGHT, DRESSED AS SUPERMAN, CLARK VISITS PROFESSOR POTTER'S LAB...
SORRY ABOUT YOUR PREDICAMENT, SUPERMAN! YOU'RE WELCOME TO USE MY LAB IN YOUR EXPERIMENTS! PERHAPS MY NEW ELECTRONIC COMPUTER CAN HELP FIND THE ANTIDOTE!
THANKS, PROFESSOR!

flame dragon to Earth for the filming of a new giant-monster movie. When the two enormous creatures began running wild while fighting each other, Jimmy was forced to use the device to send them back where they came from, and it was never used again (*Superman's Pal, Jimmy Olsen* #84, April 1965).

Potter also proved helpful when he used a computer he devised to help determine how exposure to a chunk of red KRYPTONITE would affect Superman, and how to craft an antidote comprised of large doses of ascorbic, citric, and acetic acid (*Superman* [first series] #160, April 1963).

In the world after the CRISIS ON INFINITE EARTHS, it was SUPERBOY, not Superman, who encountered Phineas Potter, who was a scientist working for the Hawaii branch of S.T.A.R. LABS (*Superboy* [third series] #19, September 1995). Potter was once a classmate of Russell Abernathy, later known as the KRYPTONITE MAN (*Action Comics* #853, Early October 2007).

POWELL, HAZEL

JIMMY OLSEN was once promoted to a "full-fledged reporter" by *DAILY PLANET* editor in chief PERRY WHITE. His first assignment was "break in our new cub," the lovely brunette Hazel Powell. She made Jimmy feel old by saying, "I'm your biggest fan! It was reading about your adventures with Superman that inspired me to go to journalism school!" The accident-prone Hazel gained immediate experience in covering news in METROPOLIS, her clumsiness actually saving Jimmy's life on four occasions—all of them murder attempts from the gang that Jimmy's coverage helped expose and helped win him the promotion (*Superman's Pal, Jimmy Olsen* #124, October 1969).

POWER GIRL

There were several women named Power Girl in Superman's life, beginning on Earth-1 with a superpowered LOIS LANE. At least, she dreamed she had superpowers after being knocked unconscious by a fall from a building ledge. In the dream, Superman gave her a blood transfusion to save her life, and with the Kryptonian blood coursing through her veins, Lois gained terrific powers. She donned a red wig and a costume, fighting crime alongside her boyfriend as Power Girl. The dream had her pass on some of her super-tainted blood to an injured CLARK KENT, granting him tremendous abilities, so he joined the duo as POWERMAN. He proved too mild-mannered for crime fighting, however, and accidentally revealed his secret identity to the world. The shocking revelation brought Lois back to wakefulness (*Superman* [first series] #125, November 1958).

In the Earth-2 reality, Power Girl was the counterpart to Earth-1's SUPERGIRL, one of the few divergent points between the worlds. KARA Zor-L, daughter of KANDOR residents Zor-L and ALLURA, was rocketed away from the doomed planet KRYPTON at the same time as her cousin KAL-L was sent into space. The rocket technology differed between the ships, and her journey took longer. She arrived on Earth as a teen with all the powers and abilities of the now adult Superman. Zor-L's craft—called a Symbioship—not only supported her life, but also used virtual-reality technology to give her experiences preparing her to function on her new world, which meant she arrived with a cocksure attitude that made her a very different kind of hero. She was added to the ranks of the JUSTICE SOCIETY OF AMERICA, where she battled alongside her cousin on numerous occasions (*All Star Comics* #58, January–February 1976).

Power Girl was given a home by her cousin Clark Kent and his wife Lois Lane, and she soon acclimated to life on Earth. With her now on the planet, Clark felt he could let Superman slip into semi-retirement, and it was his endorsement that won her full membership in the legendary team (*All Star Comics* #64, January–February 1977).

After she had begun her super heroic career, Power Girl was contacted by the Symbioship, which had advanced beyond its artificial intelligence and wanted to keep her to itself. She was trapped within, where the virtual world continued. There Kara married and had a child. It took the aid of journalist Andrew Vinson to free her, at which point a friendship and brief romance began between the two (*Showcase* #97–99, February–April 1978).

Seeking a life beyond that of a heroine, Power Girl and Vinson created the persona of Karen Starr. WONDER WOMAN took her to PARADISE ISLAND, where the Purple Ray gave her a crash course in computer sciences, letting her begin a career at the Ultimate Computer Company. Soon after, Helena Wayne, daughter of BRUCE WAYNE and Selina Kyle, joined the JSA as the Huntress, and the two became best friends (*Adventure Comics* #461, January–February 1979).

When the sons and daughters of the JSA banded together as the corporate team Infinity, Inc., she briefly fought alongside them before returning to the elder team (*Infinity, Inc.* #1, March 1984).

On one occasion, she and her cousin's counterpart on Earth-1 were taken by Maaldor the Darklord, and billions of lives were threatened if they did not engage in combat in order to amuse the cosmic being. Superman outwitted their captor by creating a scenario that led the insane Maaldor to form a new dimension, allowing Superman and the heroines to trap him within. They then sealed the portal forever, protecting the multiverse (*DC Comics Presents* #56, April 1983).

The CRISIS ON INFINITE EARTHS collapsed the multiverse into a single positive-matter universe and a single anti-matter universe. Only a handful of

SORRY I STARTLED YOU, GENTLEMEN. I PROMISED MY COUSIN I'D WAIT A FEW MORE MONTHS BEFORE REVEALING MYSELF--
--BUT WHEN I SAW THE TROUBLE YOU WERE HAVING WITH THIS VOLCANO, I DECIDED I COULDN'T WAIT!
WHOA, GIRL--ONE STEP AT A TIME. WE DON'T KNOW WHO YOU ARE--NEVER MIND YOUR COUSIN!
YEAH... HOW ABOUT AN INTRODUCTION, SISTER?

beings recalled the multiverse, and they were anomalies that would have difficult lives as a result . . . none more so than Kara Zor-L.

The cosmos altered events so that Kara was led to believe she was the granddaughter of Arion, the Lord High Mage of ATLANTIS, daughter to Calculha, and sister to Khater. To protect her from the wrath of his brother Garn Danuuth, Arion placed her outside reality in a protective casing until she emerged late in the twentieth century. Her now mystically derived powers matched those of Superman, and she honored her heritage by placing Arion's symbol on her belt buckle (*Secret Origins* [second series] #11, February 1987). Karen Starr continued to serve as her secret identity, and she formed StarrWare, a software company that proved modestly successful, growing to include a staff of developers and marketers in the SoHo section of New York City (*Power Girl* [first series] #1, June 1988).

When not tending to her company, she sought out details of her heritage, going so far as to

briefly visit the Atlantean colony in the other-dimensional realm of Skataris (*Warlord* #116–121, April–September 1987; *Warlord Annual* #6, 1987).

Without an active JSA, Power Girl wound up being recruited to join Justice League Europe. Kara's forceful personality turned increasingly arrogant, until she learned of her allergy to the artificial sweetener used in Diet Soda Cola (*Justice League Europe* #40, July 1992). Dr. Light told her, "Paranormal powers can trigger certain rare syndromes and allergies in women's bodies." She also justified her revealing costume, explaining to Crimson Fox that it "shows what I am: female, healthy, and strong. If men want to degrade themselves by staring and drooling and tripping over themselves, that's their problem, I'm not going to apologize for it" (*Justice League Europe* #37, April 1992). Over time, though, Kara changed her position about her outfit, explaining to Superman: "The first time I made this costume, I wanted to have a symbol, like you. I just . . . I couldn't think of anything. I thought eventually, I'd figure it out and close the hole. But I haven't" (*JSA: Classified* #2, October 2005).

She was nearly killed during a battle with the occult Gray Man, and it took Superman's heat vision and experienced medical skills to save her life. The recovery period was slow, and for a time she lost several of her powers, such as her range of vision skills and flight (*Justice League Europe* #9, December 1989). As she recovered, she was stunned to discover that StarrWare had been taken over by her cousin Gina, who was actually a friendly, other-dimensional imp named Ghy (*Justice League International Quarterly* #6, Spring 1992). She agreed to let the imp run the company while she was in Europe (*Justice League Quarterly* #6, Spring 1992), although Ghy vanished without explanation at a later date. At some unspecified time, she hired Felicity Smoak-Raymond to run the day-to-day operation (*Green Lantern/Power Girl* #1, October 2000).

Power Girl also agreed to visit the underworld, exploring her mystic side with the entity called Echidna, although this did not last long (*Justice League Europe* #42, September 1992).

Arion left Power Girl mystically impregnated, and during her time with the JLE (*Justice League International* #52, July 1991), the child began to grow as she reached her own physical maturity. She finally gave birth at the onset of the event known as Zero Hour (*Zero Hour* #0, September 1994). Kara couldn't bring herself to name the boy, who began to develop at an extremely accelerated rate. During a battle between the Justice League of America and the demonic Scarabus, Arion arrived to rescue Kara, but her now adult offspring—who'd dubbed himself Equinox—disappeared (*Justice League America* #107–108, January–February 1996).

Now fighting crime on her own, she once came to Oracle's aid when the former Batgirl was beginning her work as a wheelchair-bound crime fighter. The experience was a disaster, with large losses of life, and a wedge was driven between the two, with Power Girl grudgingly aiding Oracle only when circumstances were very dire (*Birds of Prey* #35, November 2001).

Things began to unravel for Kara when she encountered her resurrected grandfather Arion. He revealed that the entire belief she hailed from ancient Atlantis was a lie, told to her as a favor to Power Girl's "mother" (*JSA* #50, September 2003). At around this time, the villainous Psycho-Pirate, one of the others who recalled the multiverse, found Power Girl and began explaining her true reality to her. He told her of Kandor and Krypton, of Earth-2 and the JSA. Since her Earth-2 cousin survived the collapse of the multiverse, the Pirate suggested that this also allowed her to survive, but that was merely conjecture. It also explained why she and the recently arrived Kara Zor-El could not be in close proximity to each other, as they were essentially the same being, in

defiance of cosmic law (*JSA Classified* #1–4, September–December 2005; *Supergirl* [fifth series] #1, October 2005). This also explained why KRYPTONITE had no effect on Kryptonians from other realities (*Infinite Crisis* #3, February 2006).

She also learned that her cousin Superman, his wife Lois Lane, ALEXANDER LUTHOR JUNIOR of Earth-3, and SUPERBOY-PRIME had all survived in a crystalline limbo. Luthor wanted to remake the multiverse in his image and manipulated Superman and Superboy-Prime to do his bidding. Part of that meant resurrecting the cosmic tuning fork from the shell of the ANTI-MONITOR's armor using anomalies who should have been on other worlds, such as Earth-2's Power Girl. Kal-L found his cousin and confirmed everything the Psycho-Pirate had told her, adding that there was a plan to bring back the "proper" Earth. When she visited the dying Lois Lane, the older woman's touch miraculously restored Kara Zor-L's memories of her previous existence. However, Superboy-Prime cornered her, beat her into submission, and strapped her to the energy device. When the tuning fork tower was powered up, the multiverse was re-created into FIFTY-TWO parallel worlds, complete with a restored Earth-2 containing her friend the Huntress (*Infinite Crisis* #1–7, December 2005–June 2006; *52* #52, May 2, 2007).

Power Girl was eventually freed from the machine by Wonder Girl and SUPERBOY. Together they sought to stop the mad Superboy-Prime, but during the battle Kal-L and Superboy died. The GREEN LANTERN Corps brought the grieving Power Girl to their member planet Mogo, where she got to say good-bye to her beloved cousin (*Infinite Crisis* #7, June 2006).

The new Earth-2 now lacked a Superman and a Power Girl, since the Power Girl of that planet wound up being sent to the post-Crisis Earth-2. The Earth-2 Power Girl missed out on several years of her life by searching among the stars for her cousin. When the two Power Girls eventually met, they did not get along (*52* #52, May 2, 2007).

With reality reordered by the INFINITE CRISIS, Supergirl and Power Girl could now coexist side by side. They donned the identities of NIGHTWING and FLAMEBIRD to adventure in Kandor, attempting to free that city from Earth-3's ULTRAMAN, who was working with the vile SATURN QUEEN from the thirtieth century. The Kryptonian Crusaders would have remained had Saturn Queen not provided the location of Argos and the whereabouts of her parents, leading Supergirl back to Earth. Power Girl saw this as a selfish act on Supergirl's part, and a rift developed between the women (*Supergirl* [fifth series] #8, September 2006).

Remaining on Earth, Power Girl resumed her role with the JSA and was elected its first female chair (*Justice Society of America* [third series] #4, May 2007). By that point, she'd revealed her Karen Starr identity to the public (*JSA* #39, October 2002) and now chose to be a full-time heroine. Soon after, Kara was discomfited when the Superman of Earth-22 came to stay with the JSA for a time. His uncanny resemblance to her deceased cousin unnerved her, but she grew to accept him as family (*Justice Society of America* [third series] #7, September 2007). During this time, she finally visited the new Earth-2 (*Justice Society of America* [third series] *Annual* #1, 2008) where she also encountered her doppelgänger. This newly created Power Girl, born with the new multiverse, served with Justice Society Infinity, that world's composite of the JSA and Infinity, Inc. Power Girl, desperate to find a way home, received help from Michael Holt, not yet Earth-2's Mister Terrific (*Justice Society of America* [third series] #19–20, November–December 2008).

Once back on New Earth, Power Girl reconsidered her life and decided not only to resurrect her Karen Starr persona but also to continue running StarrWare (*Power Girl* [second series] #1, July 2009). She had previously explained to the JSA, "I took my software company public a few years ago, just before the dot com bubble burst. Sold it soon after. I'll admit, I was never a computer whiz, but I knew how to surround myself with the right people. Still do. To be frank, I made more money than I'll ever need" (*JSA* #39, October 2002). With that money, Karen Starr had launched a foundation meant to help orphans and "create a kind of safety net to catch the children who fall through the cracks."

StarrWare was rebuilt, and Karen Starr seemed happy to be restaffing the company and putting her mind to good use. Soon after reopening the company, however, she was confronted by the ULTRA-HUMANITE, who threatened all of New York City if she did not submit to him. When he gained control of her, Power Girl nearly had her mind replaced with his—but she managed to free herself and end his latest threat (*Power Girl* [second series] #1–3, July–September 2009).

She also discovered that the kryptonite generated by the New Earth reality did not have adverse effects (*The Brave and the Bold* [third series] #7, December 2007), although that from Earth-2 did harm her. Similarly, scanners seeking Kryptonian DNA did not detect Power Girl (*Superman* #668–670, Early December 2007–January 2008).

In the wake of Power Girl's visit to the new Earth-2, the thirty-first-century hero Starman confided in Stargirl that Kara was destined to "make the most of her life—both inside and outside the Justice Society. And although she doesn't realize it now, the Justice Society Infinity will one day help her out in ways she could never imagine" (*Justice Society of America* [third series] #20, December 2008).

On Earth-9, Powergirl was a genetically engineered woman created by the Chinese government (*Tangent Comics/Powergirl* #1, September 1998). She married that Earth's Superman, and together they conquered their world (*Tangent: Superman's Reign* #4–5, August–September 2008).

On Earth-22, Kara grew up to adulthood, altering her name to Power Woman, and worked alongside her cousin to reform the Justice League of America (*Kingdom Come* #1–4, 1996).

POWER LAD

JIMMY OLSEN met Tom Baker and was astounded to learn the youth had seemingly gained superpowers matching the Man of Steel's after a scientific accident. Taking the name Power Lad, the costumed Baker began patrolling METROPOLIS alongside Superman. Unknown to Jimmy, the youth was actually a Kryptonian boy named Dik-Rey who had traded places with SUPERGIRL—still unknown to the public—while she visited the bottle city of KANDOR (*Superman's Pal, Jimmy Olsen* #45, June 1960).

POWERMAN

Several incarnations of Powerman interacted with the Man of Steel. LOIS LANE once dreamed she had superpowers after being knocked unconscious by a fall from a building ledge. In her dream, Superman gave her a blood transfusion to save her life, and with Kryptonian blood coursing through her veins, she gained amazing powers. She donned a red wig and a costume, fighting crime alongside her boyfriend as POWER GIRL. The dream had her pass on some of her super-tainted blood to an injured CLARK KENT, granting him tremendous abilities so that he joined the duo as Powerman. He proved too mild-mannered for crime fighting, however, and accidentally revealed his secret identity to the world. The shocking revelation brought Lois back to wakefulness (*Superman* [first series] #125, November 1958).

Later, Lois would recall another Power-Man, this one a "king of outer space" who had ardently sought her hand in marriage—to no avail (*Superman* [first series] #136, April 1960).

Yet another version appeared one day wearing a colorful orange costume with a yellow hood, apparently replacing BATMAN and ROBIN as Superman's partner of choice. When LEX LUTHOR escaped from jail, the Dynamic Duo offered to help find him, but Superman informed them that he and Powerman had it covered. Undaunted, Batman and Robin assisted in bringing Luthor back to jail. Superman then revealed that his new partner was merely a robot, created to discourage his friends from risking their lives in the seemingly unending struggle between Superman and Luthor (*World's Finest Comics* #94, May–June 1958).

On Earth-22, Powerman fought alongside Superman and other heroes in a massive superhuman power struggle (*Kingdom Come* #3–4, July–August 1996).

POWER PUSS

A member of the SPACE CAT PATROL AGENCY, Power Puss was able to emit power blasts from its eyes (*Superboy* [first series] #131, July 1966).

POWERSTONE, THE

Described as an ancient gem from another planet whose weird scientific properties conferred virtually "infinite power" on whoever possessed it, the Powerstone was first claimed by LEX LUTHOR, who used it to square off twice against Superman as the Man of Steel attempted to keep his archenemy from obtaining the stone's power (*Action Comics* #47, April 1942; *Superman* [first series] #17, July–August 1942). The Powerstone was immediately snatched up by the ULTRA-HUMANITE and Deathbolt. The nuclear-powered Cyclotron appeared to destroy himself, the Ultra-Humanite, and the Powerstone in an atomic explosion during a vicious battle (*All-Star Squadron* #21–26, May-

October 1983; *All-Star Squadron Annual* #2, 1983). Although Ultra somehow survived, the fate of the amazing gem was unknown.

PRANA

A mysterious organization known only as the Circle once attempted to add Superman to its ages-old ranks. Among the membership was the feline-like Prana, who possessed psychic abilities and used them while Superman was actively engaging the army of Qurac. The mental assault included an invitation to join the Circle, but the Man of Steel fiercely resisted being manipulated and mentally shut out Prana. As his wife Zahara feared, the telepathic backlash killed Prana (*The Adventures of Superman* #427, April 1987). His death meant the Circle had to leave Earth prematurely, but members lacked the resources to do so. They begged for help from Superman, who did aid them without ever fully understanding what the Circle wanted (*The Adventures of Superman* #430, July 1987).

PRANKSTER, THE

The criminal known to Metropolis's citizens and police as the Prankster was dubbed the "Clown King of the Underworld," although the deadly criminal considered himself the funniest man in the world. Standing a mere five feet and weighing 125 pounds, Oswald Loomis nevertheless posed a huge threat (*Action Comics* #51, August 1942). The con man committed numerous crimes, confusing all with his pranks. There was the time, for instance, he committed a series of bank robberies in which he gave the money back . . . until the final time, when he didn't return the cash and got away with it.

The Prankster had slicked-down red hair, a narrow mustache, a pointy nose, and large "cup-shaped ears [that] begin wiggling like mad" whenever he was struck by an evil inspiration (*Superman* [first series] #22, May–June 1943). He spoke in a bombastic manner, saying "Aye and verily," for example, instead of "Yes" (*Action Comics* #51, August 1942).

Superman and the Prankster matched wits on both Earth-1 and Earth-2, with little difference between the villain's incarnations. On Earth-2, his most notorious stunt may have been the time the Prankster tried to copyright the English language, demanding payment every time the alphabet was employed. Until the Man of Steel learned that the copyright registrar was one of the Prankster's men, the Prankster nearly got away with his plan (*Superman* [first series] #22, May–June 1943).

Over time, the egotistical Prankster continued to commit robberies and petty crimes, but he began to design schemes intended not only to steal but also to humiliate Superman (*Superman* [first series] #55, November–December 1948). As a result of his unpredictability, his peers in Metropolis's criminal underworld had cause for concern.

The Prankster became a member of a group the media called the Terrible Trio after partnering with Toyman and Lex Luthor to bedevil the Man of Steel (*Superman* [first series] #88, March 1954). The partnership lasted no longer than his earlier team-up with Luthor and Mr. Mxyztplk (*Action Comics* #151, December 1950).

The Prankster was alternatively referred to as the Chuckling Charlatan, the Comedy Crook, the Mirthful Miscreant, and the Rollicking Rogue, while his various pranks had him use many puns as aliases such as P. R. Ankster, Ajax Wilde, and Frank Ster.

The Earth-1 Prankster (*Superman's Pal, Jimmy Olsen* #9, December 1955) often found himself in collaboration with other rogues, whether en masse (*Superman* [first series] #299, May 1976; *Superman Family* #184, July–August 1977) or individually. The Prankster also once found himself on the bad side of the Joker, prompting the jovial criminal to team up with Superman to capture the Clown Prince of Crime (*DC Comics Presents* #41, January 1982).

With the Toyman, the Prankster cooked up a plot to drive Superman crazy violating obsolete laws, such as putting pennies in his ears in Honolulu.

One grim alternate reality found the Prankster

manipulated by Mr. Mxyzptlk into helping him learn Superman's secret identity. He and the Toyman accomplished their goal, but not before torturing and killing Pete Ross to obtain the name. Too late to save his friend, Superman brought the two to justice (*Superman* [first series] #423, October 1986).

On the world after the Crisis on Infinite Earths, Oswald Hubert Loomis was a very popular children's television personality and the host of WGBS's *Uncle Oswald Show.* Eventually, however, his ratings sagged and the series was canceled, leaving the entertainer first despondent, then angry. He sought revenge against the uncaring viewers of Metropolis by staging a series of dangerous pranks, including the abduction of Lois Lane, which brought him to Superman's attention (*Superman* [second series] #16, April 1988). Loomis merely wanted the reporter to cover his sad plight in the hope that a sympathetic mass audience would help him retire a millionaire.

Loomis also sought revenge against GBS Broadcasting's president Morgan Edge, but he was foiled by the Man of Steel (*Superman* [second series] #36, October 1989).

The Prankster disappeared for a time, but when he returned it was in a slimmed-down body (*The Adventures of Superman* #579, June 2000) courtesy of a deal with the Hell-spawned Lord Satanus (*The Adventures of Superman* #586, January 2001). At the time of his return, Loomis saw that the B13 Virus had transformed not only Metropolis into a futuristic version, but also all his gear, upping the level of deadly mischief he could now cause.

Still seeking vengeance against Superman, the Prankster stole Steel's armor just when the hero was about to join Superboy and Supergirl in saving Superman's life after a grain of kryptonite turned a nanovirus into the Man of Steel's death sentence. The Prankster then used the armor to attack Superboy, who was temporarily without his powers, and Supergirl. Fortunately, John Henry Irons had a fail-safe built into his equipment, allowing him to regain control of the armor (*Superman* [second series] #158, July 2000).

Lord Satanus then used the Prankster to try to kidnap meta-humans with dual personae—including Dr. Kitty Faulkner/Rampage, Rose Forrest/Thorn, and Cary Richards/Adversary—hoping to increase his power through absorbing the darker personalities, but the scheme was thwarted by Superman's timely intervention (*The Adventures of Superman* #588, March 2001). Later, Manchester Black included the Prankster in his plan to ruin Superman's life by besmirching the hero's reputation, although that scheme, too, failed (*Superman* [second series] #187, December 2002).

The Prankster was later hired by Lex Luthor to play his pranks on Metropolis during the year Superman was unavailable in the wake of Infinite Crisis. It took Green Lantern and Hawkgirl to defeat him, and it was later learned that it was all a distraction to allow Luthor to free the Kryptonite Man from prison (*Superman* #651, June 2006).

Seeing a new revenue source, the Prankster then hired himself out as a distraction maker, offering clients a discount if the plan allowed him to befuddle the Man of Steel. After all, he reasoned, if he could confuse Superman, there was no better advertising. The income allowed him to construct a high-tech headquarters above Uncle Oley's Sure Fire Joke Shop. Surrounding himself with attractive assistants, the Prankster grew accustomed to having things done for him, and having them done to his taste. Those who displeased him were dropped through a trapdoor, which somehow could be relocated around his lair (*Superman* #660, March 2007).

This version of the Prankster served with the Injustice League and was among the villains briefly exiled to another world (*Salvation Run* #1–7, Early December–June 2008). When he returned to Earth, the Prankster was among the rogues gathered up and dumped into the Phantom Zone by the newly freed residents of Kandor. However, Superman rescued his foe and remanded him to Belle Reve prison (*Superman* #684, March 2009).

PRESERVERS, THE

The Preservers, much like the original Brainiac, traversed the stars, collecting cities from throughout the time line to study and display for the public (*Superman Family* #190, July–August 1978). Led by a being called the Curator and Apprentice-Prime, they constructed an "interdimensional cage" to display the captured cities, which at one time included Jimmy Olsen's hometown of Hartsdale and the bottle city of Kandor.

U.S. president Jimmy Carter asked that Hartsdale be spared, and while all of Earth was threatened by these powerful aliens, the combination of Superman, Kandor's Nightwing and Flamebird, Jimmy Olsen, Lois Lane, Supergirl, and Krypto proved decisive. To the heroes' surprise, they also received an assist from the villains trapped in the Phantom Zone. The cities were restored and the Preservers left the solar system, never to return.

PREUS

Among the people protecting the citizens of Kandor was Citizens' Patrol Corps sergeant Preus. All proudly wore the S-shield denoting the House of El and respected Superman as a protector. Time passed differently within this version of Kandor, and Preus grew up with a generation that revered Superman in a religious manner and adopted Krypton's culture even though their polyglot community was named after the Kryptonian city of Kandor. He also was raised with a xenophobic streak, preferring the multiracial city to be pure Kryptonian.

The Corpsman became obsessed with bringing one citizen, Kal-El, to justice after an illusion showed the Man of Steel killing an innocent boy. At the time, Superman was imprisoned in the bottle city and had been brainwashed by the Empireth Lyla to believe he was living once more on Krypton.

Even after Superman returned to Earth, the insane Preus managed to follow him beyond the bottle. His mania pushed Preus over the edge, and he became fixated on racial purity among Kryptonians; his efforts to cleanse the planet of impure aliens also resulted in the rape and death of a woman. Preus wore an S-shield with a knife sliced through it, and his superpowers manifested differently, resulting in black, not red, heat vision. Preus then found a white supremacist camp called "God's Peake" and became its leader. His followers quickly grew in number, and they even managed to apprehend the Martian Manhunter and Jimmy Olsen.

During this period, Superman had been severely weakened by yellow kryptonite, a synthetic material devised by the villain Gog. As a result, he was no match for Preus, but the more experienced Superman refused to give up. He tried exposing the madman to real kryptonite, but Preus seemed impervious to its radiation. The Man of Steel then attacked Preus's armor, dislodging a key component and rendering him vulnerable. Superman was en route to S.T.A.R. Labs when he was attacked by several Gogs drawn through time, forcing him to release Preus, who vanished never to be seen again (*Action Comics* #813, January 2003; #821, February 2004; and #823–824, April–May 2004; *The Adventures of Superman* #625–626, and *Superman* [second series] #202–203, both April–May 2004).

PRINCE MARK

The ruler of the European kingdom of Sardonia, Prince Mark was an exact double of Superboy. Thanks to the Boy of Steel's intervention, the monarch survived an attempt on his life by the ruthless Lord Hawke and went on to marry the lovely Zorina (*Adventure Comics* #303, December 1962). As adults, Prince Mark and Superman were briefly reunited when the Man of Steel prevented the Kingslayer from assassinating the prince (*Super Friends* #11, April–May 1978).

PRINCESS ILONA

Hailing from the distant Sunev galaxy, the beautiful raven-tressed Princess Ilona had been observing life on Earth for years. Fascinated by the redheaded cub reporter Jimmy Olsen, she came to Earth to meet him. Having recently been rejected by his sometime girlfriend Lucy Lane, Jimmy was ready for some interstellar romance. Ilona gifted him with a belt that allowed Jimmy to alter objects into gold or render people invisible. He squired her about town, including a stop at Lucy's masquerade

ball. Things turned ugly, however, when the princess's four jealous husbands arrived and turned their rival into a strange alien creature. After being restored to his human form, Jimmy broke off his engagement to Ilona, then worked with Superman, Lois Lane, and Lana Lang to trick Ilona into believing that he was already married—to two crones. The crestfallen woman returned home, her quartet of spouses trailing behind (*Superman's Pal, Jimmy Olsen* #59, March 1962). On a time-travel visit to 1692 shortly thereafter, Jimmy lost the Sunevian belt to a witch named Lucinda Lawrence (*Superman's Pal, Jimmy Olsen* #60, April 1962).

PRINCESS VARINA

Princess Varina of Balkania let it be known that she intended to abdicate her throne in order to marry the commoner Stefan. During a visit to the United States, both Superman and Batman vied for her affections, forestalling the abdication that the world's greatest heroes knew would lead to a violent civil war. Pete Karney's gang attacked the princess's traveling vehicle, and the heroes stayed out of sight but quietly aided Stefan in defeating the criminals and gaining sole credit for the victory. Stefan was made a national hero, allowing the parliament to bless the marriage and preventing bloodshed (*World's Finest Comics* #85, November–December 1956).

PRINCESS ZERNA

To win over Superman, this attractive princess from the planet Arctor took possession of Lois Lane's body. The unearthly melding of personae caused Lois to display bizarre physical characteristics, including the legs and climbing ability of a cat. Lois eventually communicated the cause of her strange transformation to the Man of Steel, and Princess Zerna was expelled from her body (*Superman's Girl Friend, Lois Lane* #66, July 1966).

PROFESSOR AN-KAL

While living on Krypton, Professor An-Kal devoted his life to anthropology and became particularly attached to Yango, a gorilla-like beast. He had spent years using intense conditional-cybernetic brain programming on the beast, called "genetic alterance." The Science Council rejected his studies, leading An-Kal to call them idiots.

In the moments prior to Krypton's destruction, An-Kal transported Yango to Earth's Africa. In Kenya, Yango developed super-simian powers and abilities, causing Superboy to come investigate (*Superboy* [first series] #172, March 1971).

PROFESSOR BOLDEN

Aggressively seeking new energy resources, Professor Bolden developed an engine powered by kryptonite. Unable to control the subsequent chain reaction, Bolden saw his engine explode—inexplicably causing every piece of kryptonite on Earth to turn to iron (*Superman* [first series] #233, January 1971). Continuing with his research, Bolden devised a powerful fuel from the iron that had once been kryptonite. The so-called "k-iron [was] so super-heat-sensitive that a single lit match [was] enough to set it off." Inevitably, criminals stole

THANKS TO THEM, I DISCOVERED THE SUPER-HEATED EXHAUST GIVEN OFF BY K-IRON CONTAINS A POTENTIALLY DEADLY SIDE-EFFECT--
--A SUPER-COMBUSTIBLE GAS THAT FLAMES UNCONTROLLABLY WHEN IT COMES IN CONTACT WITH SOLID MATTER--LIKE ME!

Bolden's k-iron cannon and used it against Superman. Through them, the Man of Steel "discovered the super-heated exhaust given off by k-iron contains a potentially deadly side effect—a super-combustible gas that flames uncontrollably when it comes in contact with solid matter." The device was never used again, and over time more kryptonite landed on Earth-1, continuing to plague the Man of Steel (*Action Comics* #485, July 1978).

PROFESSOR CLAUDE

Jimmy Olsen once gained super-speed from a serum devised by the scatterbrained scientist Claude (*Superman's Pal, Jimmy Olsen* #15, September 1956).

PROFESSOR DALTON

While attempting to perfect a matter-duplicating ray, this aging Smallville scientist accidentally created the first imperfect duplicate of Superboy, nicknamed Bizarro. He had hoped to duplicate radium for further scientific study, but the experiment failed, giving rise to a new race of imperfect life-forms and immortalizing Dalton in the annals of Earth-1 history (*Superboy* [first series] #68, October 1958).

PROFESSOR HUNTER

By inventing a powerful new anesthetic gas, Hunter became the target for the evil Baron Munsdorf. The professor had also invented a "deadly sub-atomic death-ray gun" with which the treacherous spy unleashed a bolt of "incredible voltage" at Superman, only to die from the bolt's ricochet (*Action Comics* #31, December 1940).

PROFESSOR JOHNS

When this prominent scientist developed a "power formula," he was approached by various Metropolis criminals. After refusing to hand it over, Johns was mortally wounded but managed to whisper the details of the formula to Clark Kent before lapsing into a coma. Superman tracked down the killers and then delivered the formula to a government official, fulfilling the dying scientist's last instructions (*Superman* [first series] #60, September–October 1949).

PROFESSOR KRYON

Traveling back in time from his native fortieth century, this evil scientist from the planet Katraz informed Lois Lane that she would marry the Man of Steel—but both would die tragically in an airplane disaster. The reason Superman was aboard a plane at all was because he was said to have lost his powers to gold kryptonite, a fact he did not share with Lois. Superman married Lois to fulfill that part of destiny, but foiled Kryon's plan by ingesting a formula that temporarily made him immune to the gold k. Once Kryon was returned to his own era, the marriage was quickly annulled (*Superman's Girl Friend, Lois Lane* #82, April 1968).

PROFESSOR MARTIN

Claiming to have constructed a computer that could predict the future, this notorious criminal scientist attempted—and failed—to get the Man of Steel to reveal his secret identity in public, for a huge sum of money promised him by the inmates of the Metropolis Jail (*Superman* [first series] #108, September 1956).

PROFESSOR NERO

Using his scientific know-how, Nero maintained a laboratory full of "strange equipment" on the outskirts of Metropolis. Rather than patent and profit from his inventions, he used them to form a one-man counterfeiting operation until he was apprehended by Superman and the Metropolis police (*Action Comics* #167, April 1952).

PROFESSOR SANDS

For criminals feeling dejected after failing to succeed with their robberies, there was the Dreamorama, a theater that used technology devised by Sands, the theater's proprietor. His "dream films" enabled customers to fulfill their fondest gangland fantasies by watching *Escape from the B House, King of Crime,* and *The Great Fort Knox Robbery*—films in which they triumphed over law enforcement representatives. When Sands wanted to film *Victory Over Superman,* he cast an undercover Man of Steel, who managed to accumulate sufficient evidence to shut down the theater and arrest Sands and his staff (*Action Comics* #178, March 1953).

PROFESSOR SNELLING

This noted historian relocated to Smallville and purchased the home where Jonathan and Martha Kent raised their son Clark. Ironically, Snelling did not know this despite being the author of a forthcoming book called *The Life and Times of Superman.* He nearly made the connection when he almost found leftover items, such as the cast-iron teddy bear young Clark had played with, but was pre-

Professor Snelling

vented from doing so by the unseen efforts of Superman (*Superman* [first series] #90, July 1954).

A different account in the chronicles noted that the Kents bequeathed their home to Clark, and he owned it as an adult (*Action Comics* #288, May 1962).

PROFESSOR VAKOX

When this scientist contaminated Great Krypton Lake with his experimental "life force" liquid, he mutated the existing underwater life into monstrous creatures. Vakox was arrested, tried, and banished to the Phantom Zone, where he resided well past the planet's destruction. "If I ever get out of the Phantom Zone," he vowed, "I'd create terrible monsters who would destroy whole cities!"

When the electrical ions of the Aurora Borealis opened a small hole in the Phantom Zone, the criminals within prepared to burst out of the widening space to freedom. Alerted by Zone resident Mon-El, Superman, Supergirl, and Krypto used their combined X-ray vision powers to quickly seal the aperture (*Action Comics* #284, January 1962).

PROFESSOR VALE

The elderly scientist who performed the brilliant lifesaving operation that transformed John Corben into Metallo (*Action Comics* #252, May 1959).

PROFESSOR VANCE

Using vitamins and isotopes that resembled kryptonite, this professor hoped he found a way to prolong a human's life span. Instead, those who drank the serum found themselves turned into aged versions of themselves for seventy-two hours. When this happened to Clark Kent, the white-bearded, frail Superman was unable to perform his duties. Still, he used his aged form to outwit the Clock, disguising himself as Father Time, coming to claim the criminal (*Action Comics* #251, April 1959).

PROFESSOR VINING

The Toyman stole Vining's ingenious device, which "could be tuned to the "personal wavelength of any individual—and detect the presence of that individual a mile away!" The villain used it without success against Superman (*World's Finest Comics* #20, Winter 1945).

PROFESSOR WEIRTON

Susan Semple temporarily gained superpowers from this inventor's "cabinet-like machine," which used specially filtered uranium rays to speed the evolutionary process and put him "1,000,000 years ahead of his time!" For twenty-four hours, Semple had a taste of the "powers that the human race won't acquire for hundreds of eons!" (*Action Comics* #163, December 1951).

PROFESSOR WILSON

Superman was once flung a millennium into the future thanks to an accidental bombardment of Professor Wilson's "super-rays." While in the thirtieth century, he encountered Lois Lane's descendant Lois 4XR (*Superman* [first series] #57, March–April 1949).

The scientist also developed a "four-dimensional projector," then took the plans and divided them into seven pieces, hiding each one somewhere inaccessible in order to prevent unscrupulous people from using his invention. Three of the pieces were known to be placed within the moon's largest crater, Antarctica, and Mount Everest (*World's Finest Comics* #62, January–February 1953).

Professor Zee

PROFESSOR ZEE

From a hidden laboratory deep within a semi-extinct volcano, this evil scientist worked with Dr. Cardos to perform countless revolting experiments in increasing the size of living organisms. Their goal was to create an army of zombie-like giants entirely under their own control. The experiments proved successful, and an army of towering giants soon terrorized the western United States. The wicked scientists were ultimately trampled to death by their fleeing creations, who were scattered by the mighty blows of Superman, demolishing their hidden laboratory. The monsters were then drowned in a massive flood produced by a glacier melted by the Man of Steel (*Superman* [first series] #8, January–February 1941).

PROJECT CADMUS

On Earth-1 it was called the DNA Project, a secret government operation that pushed the boundaries of cutting-edge technology in regard to cloning. There they managed to create a human clone of Jim Harper, the Guardian, who served as the facility's protector, along with new life-forms such as the telepathic Dubbilex, first in a line of DNAliens (*Superman's Pal, Jimmy Olsen* #133, October 1970).

The Project also gave birth to the group of enhanced human clones known as the Hairies, who reached a level of maturity and moved out on their own, taking up residence either in their mobile Mountain of Judgment or in their permanent home the Habitat.

If everything had an exact opposite, then the Evil Factory was the mirror image of Cadmus, run by Mokkari and Simyan, creations of Dabney Donovan and beholden to Darkseid.

In the world after the Crisis on Infinite Earths, the facility was called Project Cadmus, named after the Greek legend who created warriors from the teeth of a dragon (*Superman* [second series] *Annual* #2, 1988). The Project was initially under the direction of the mentally unstable Donovan, who helped created a clone of Jim (the Guardian) Harper. Donovan's creation of Dubbilex and his threats to conjure up creatures that included a giant green version of military liaison Jake Olsen's son forced the Cadmus administrators to shut him down (*Secret Origins* [third series] #49, June 1990). Donovan persisted in creating the DNAliens (*Batman and Superman: World's Finest* #4, July 1999), culminating in a destructive model that would have led to his incarceration had he not faked his death. The Project had developed limited growth acceleration to that point, but their expertise in that area didn't truly advance until the "posthumous" discovery of Dabney Donovan's notes (*Secret Origins* [third series] #49, June 1990) and the tampering of Sleez, which resulted in the creation of clones of the Newsboy Legion (*Superman* [second series] *Annual* #2, 1988).

It was under director Paul Westfield that Cadmus took possession of Doomsday after the monster killed the World's Greatest Super Hero (*The Adventures of Superman* #498, January 1993). They attempted to revive Superman, but when that failed, he was placed within a tomb, only to have the body stolen by Cadmus (*Superman* [second series] #76, February 1993).

Project Cadmus was where samples of Superman's DNA had been collected and subjected to intensive testing. Donovan's replacement Paul Westfield was frustrated over their inability to successfully clone the Man of Steel, but they overcame the problems by mixing Kryptonian and human genomes, resulting in a successful "birth" (*Superboy* [third series] *Annual* #2, 1995). Their creation had rapidly aged when Superman was killed by Doomsday, and a replacement hero was needed. A teenage clone arrived claiming to be the new Superman, but so did three others at the same time (*The Adventures of Superman* #500, Early June 1993). After the Man of Steel's miraculous recovery, the clone happily wore the S-shield and took the name Superboy (*The Adventures of Superman* #502, July 1993).

For a long time, Superboy believed Westfield to be his genetic parent, but he later learned the truth: It was Lex Luthor's genetic code that helped give him life and allowed the evil genius to mentally influence the youth (*Teen Titans* [third series] #1, September 2003).

Cadmus actually went to war with Luthor after the industrialist went public with calls for the Project to be shut down (*The Adventures of Superman* #511, April 1994). LexCorp's Team Luthor battled Cadmus's Underworlders, and Donovan killed Westfield. After his exploitation of Metropolis was exposed, Luthor unleashed a series of bombs, choosing to take the city down with him (*Action Comics* #699, May 1994; *Superman* [second series] #90, June 1994).

A "clone plague" was then unleashed, killing several of the Project's greatest creations. Superboy fell ill and nearly died during this event until the Guardian's blood proved to contain the cure (*The Adventures of Superman* #513, June 1994).

Project Cadmus was seemingly destroyed during the conflict, but it was merely the government's way of moving to a new undisclosed location. They cleaned house and installed new management in the wake of the adult Newsboy Legionnaires' departure (*Superboy* [third series] #57, December 1998).

Mickey "the Mechanic" Cannon, who, like the Legion, was raised in Metropolis's Suicide Slum, was placed in charge of the facility. Teenage genius Dr. Serling Roquette was named head of genetics. Dabney Donovan was returned to Cadmus, under armed guard, with the idea that keeping him close allowed the Project's employees to benefit from his work.

Despite Superboy's best efforts, the Evil Factory managed to find and infiltrate the new facility on behalf of their benefactor, the Agenda, which was controlled by Luthor's wife Contessa Erica Alexandra del Portenza. The Agenda also wanted to master the art of cloning, and used everything it had at its disposal to become the preeminent operation in the world. To that end, members dispatched Amanda Spence to bring them Superboy, and she nearly succeeded after numerous attempts. She was finally stopped, but only after she killed the Teen of Steel's lover Tana Moon (*Superboy* [third series] #70–75, January–June 2000).

Luthor was then elected president of the United States and applied tremendous pressure on Cadmus for results and projects that furthered his schemes against the Man of Steel. However, Cannon and the Guardian laid plans to counteract the Oval Office's demands. Soon after the Imperiex War ended, Project Cadmus seemingly vanished (*Superboy* [third series] #89, August 2001). The empty facility, located three miles beneath Metropolis, was eventually taken over by Luthor (*Outsiders* [third series] #25, July 2005).

The Project laid low under Cannon's command until they needed help from Jimmy Olsen (*Countdown to Final Crisis* #33, November 2007). By that point, Olsen had been manifesting strange powers and abilities, and Cannon offered to help the reporter learn what had happened to him. Jimmy's work with Dr. Roquette ended when even more powers developed and he fled the facility rather than risk the lives of the staff.

Later, Jimmy was investigating a story revealing that Codename: Assassin was a product of Cadmus. When he went to find out more, he discovered an empty operation with the sole exception of his old friend Dubbilex, who was now dying. The government, the alien said, reassigned everyone to a new project dedicated to killing an alien menace. With his last breath, Dubbilex asked Jimmy to find the Guardian and bring him back. Jimmy fulfilled the vow, and the Guardian returned to active duty as commander of Metropolis's Science Police (*Superman's Pal, Jimmy Olsen Special* #1, December 2008).

In a potential future, some version of Project Cadmus survived to the 853rd century and was under the control of that period's Superboy, the one millionth clone of the original. This Superboy was assigned to hunt down JLA Bizarro clone terrorists (*Superboy One Million,* November 1998).

PROJECT M

Developed in the spring of 1942 at an army base in the midwestern United States, Project M was built around the idea that all humans, "regardless of social and cultural conditioning," reacted with fear toward the same horror archetypes. To that end, a unit of men was transformed into the controversial Creature Commandos and sent on psychological warfare missions in Europe and Japan (*Weird War Tales* #93, November 1980). Led by Lieutenant Matthew Shrieve, the group included a vampire (Sergeant Vincent Velcro), a werewolf (Warren Griffith), and a Frankenstein's Monster (Private "Lucky" Taylor). Myrna "Doctor Medusa" Rhodes eventually joined their ranks as well (*Weird War Tales* #110, April 1982). Later, during World War Two, the group was court-martialed for unknown reasons and sentenced to death. The sentence was commuted, and the Commandos and their occasional colleague GI Robot were ordered to test an experimental rocket aimed toward Germany. The craft malfunctioned and surged into space, its final destination unknown (*Weird War Tales* #124, June 1983).

In the reality that developed following the Crisis on Infinite Earths, Project M was an East Coast–based operation situated in a vast complex beneath the Statue of Liberty under the supervision of Professor Mazursky. In addition to creating the Creature Commandos, Project M also developed GI Robot and androids, and studied phenomena such as reports of a Dinosaur Island in the Pacific (*Young All-Stars* #12, May 1988).

In the decades following World War Two, multiple sightings of the Creature Commandos and GI Robot were reported, but they were, in fact, still in outer space, having been placed in suspended animation at some point in Brainiac's spacecraft. Shortly after Superman's defeat of Brainiac, the Commandos and their robotic partner were awakened and returned to Earth (*Action Comics* #872, February 2009).

PROJECT X

With the goal of placing a spy satellite in orbit to track "bank truck routes, police activities, and

other information that will be sent from here to the international crime syndicate," the former Nazi scientist Von Kamp set up camp on a remote uncharted island using shipwrecked seamen as slave laborers until he was stopped by Superman (*Action Comics* #248, January 1959).

PROMETHEUS

Prometheus stole the sacred fire from Zeus and the Greek gods and eons later, helped Superman defeat Zha-Vam by allowing him to borrow his powers with the use of a magic belt (*Action Comics* #353, August 1967). On a time-travel visit to the past, Lois Lane also met another Prometheus, this one merely an ancient scientist (*Superman's Girl Friend, Lois Lane* #56, April 1965).

PROPHETIC PUP

Prophetic Pup used his prophetic powers as a member of the Space Canine Patrol Agency alongside Krypto (*Superboy* [first series] #136, March 1967).

PSILENCER

Tim Thomas Townsend was born with prescient powers and as an adult was recruited to join the Supermen of America. Shortly after the team was formed, Psilencer was the first member to fall in the line of duty, killed by a gang member. Little was known about his personal life or time prior to joining the short-lived team (*Supermen of America* #1, March 1999).

PSI-PHON

When Superman investigated a spaceship in Metropolis's West River, he encountered its alien occupant J'ankway, aka Psi-Phon, who used his powers to briefly steal the Man of Steel's abilities and transfer them to his hulking partner Dreadnaught (*Superman* [second series] #19, July 1988). As a result, Superman was hampered in his ability to capture the villain Killgrave and called on his allies for assistance. Aquaman, Elongated Man, Captain Marvel, and Martian Manhunter tried stopping Dreadnaught, but it took a depowered Clark Kent to finally find the solution: using Professor Emil Hamilton's personal force-field device to beat the weakened Dreadnaught (*The Adventures of Superman* #442, July 1988).

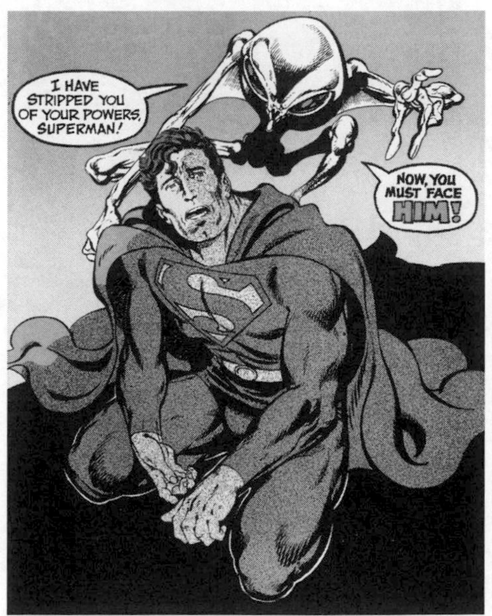

Some time later, Psi-Phon and Dreadnaught came back to Earth seeking help from Clark Kent while being pursued by the alien hunters YB2 and R3B2. It was discovered that Dreadnaught's wife Petlin had hired the duo to retrieve her spouse from his galactic gallivanting (*The Adventures of Superman* #469, August 1990). During their time on Earth, Psi-Phon and Dreadnaught discovered a huge buried spaceship under a military installation. While attempting to retrieve it as a keepsake, they were found by Green Lantern Hal Jordan, who was subdued by the alien adventurers. After the Emerald Crusader was gone for too long, a concerned Guy Gardner came to Superman seeking assistance in finding their friend (*The Adventures of Superman* #473, December 1990). Jordan was freed, and the aliens once more left Earth empty-handed.

The duo returned to Earth a final time seeking revenge on Superman and Hal Jordan, only to be thwarted when Earth's Green Lantern turned out to be Kyle Rayner instead of Jordan (*Superman* [second series] #105, October 1995).

PURPLE PILE DRIVER, THE

The Purple Pile Driver plagued Superman twice, both times proving incredibly inept. In his purple outfit topped with a propeller-hat that could generate a force field comprising super-fast air, the Purple Pile Driver committed several crimes, only to be easily apprehended by the Man of Steel (*Action Comics* #464, October 1976; *Superman* [first series] #371, May 1982).

PUZZLER, THE

Unlike the similarly named Prankster, the Puzzler was a ruthless villain with extortion, kidnapping, and murder to his credit. He was also fond of leaving complex clues to the whereabouts of his next crime and the location of his secret hideout, because, in his words, "It tickles my vanity to think I can outsmart Superman!" At each crime, he left behind a bent nail, one-half of a commonplace nail puzzle.

The criminal described himself once as "a genius at solving puzzles, I decided to utilize the principles that win games to launch a crime campaign unrivaled in history. That I've been successful is a testimony to my brilliance" (*Action Comics* #49, June 1942).

While considering himself "the world's most brilliant checkers expert," he was beaten by Superman in their first meeting, which all began when the Puzzler kidnapped Lois Lane. He used a wheel of fortune to c hoose her fate until her rescuer arrived. He then observed, "One minute a gallant sportsman, and the next a double-crosser! Must be something twisted in his nature." In a later escapade, the Puzzler was defeated by poker, rummy, blackjack, hearts, casino, and bridge champions (*Superman* [first series] #20, January-February 1943). He proved a poor sport, pulling a gun and threatening to kill his opponents, but they were saved by the Man of Steel. The Earth-2 Puzzler himself remained at large, his subsequent whereabouts never recorded. By contrast, the Earth-1 Puzzler was reported to be "doing time in State Prison" (*Superman's Pal, Jimmy Olsen* #115, October 1968).

In the world after the Crisis on Infinite Earths, a woman turned up in Metropolis who introduced herself as Valerie Van Haaften, "aka the Puzzler." The self-admitted Superman fan attempted to join several groups without success. As the result of such rejection, she chose instead to become a super-villain, and she proved a challenging one given her unusual ability to alter portions of her body as if they were "puzzle pieces" each of which she could control, even if they were not directly attached to her. However, a gust of super-breath from Superman cast her pieces to the winds (*Superman* [second series] #187, December 2002).

She was later hired by Intergang to kill Clark Kent, but a glimpse of Superman caused her to change her targets. When they fought, she taunted Superman with the news that she had been "upgraded," and claimed her biological pieces were nearly indestructible. Each "puzzle piece" was far smaller and packed more of a wallop, although she once more met defeat when Superman trapped her pieces in separate containers (*Superman* #652, July 2006). Some time later, she joined the villainous Society and clashed with the Secret Six (*Secret Six* [third series] #7, May 2009).

PYGOR

In a potential fifty-second century, Pygor and R. J. Desmond each fancied himself "the greatest showman of the 52nd century." Desmond built a replica of Superboy's hometown, complete with android inhabitants, as an attraction called Smallville-Land. Jealous of the achievement, Pygor hired two men to steal the Superboy android so it could be reverse-engineered. What spoiled the plan was that the men stole the *real* Teen of Steel, who was visiting the future and filled in for his doppelgänger when it developed a mechanical flaw. Unaware he was dealing with the real hero, Pygor was still cowed into promising never to threaten Desmond or Smallville-Land again (*The New Adventures of Superboy* #10, October 1980).

Q-BOMB

Described as a "new government weapon" with the explosive power of one hundred hydrogen bombs, this device's detonation split the Man of Steel into two separate beings, each possessing half the normal powers and abilities—Superman-T and Superman-X. The two fought crime in tandem until Earth was threatened by a KRYPTONITE meteor and Superman-T sacrificed himself to destroy the interstellar object. Upon his destruction, Superman-X regained his full powers (*Action Comics* #222, November 1956).

Q-ENERGY

Abundant in dimensions beyond the Earthly plane, Q-Energy was used as a transport system across the dimensional barriers on the world of Gobdor (*The Flash* [first series] #132, November 1962) and as a power source on the planet Myrg (*Green Lantern* [second series] #45, June 1966). On Earth,

scientist Lorraine Lewis successfully broke the dimensional barrier to discover Q-Energy. Deducing that it would act on Superman in much the same manner as KRYPTONITE, Lewis attempted to kill the Man of Steel but wound up being disintegrated by the flaming energy she'd unleashed (*Superman* [first series] #204, February 1968).

Representatives of the alien worlds of Zelzot and Volkir later used a Q-Energy cage to restrain Superman (*DC Comics Presents* #1, July–August 1978), and the other-dimensional Weaponers of Qward supplemented their electrified qwa-bolts with Q-Energy bolts when they attacked the Man of Steel (*DC Comics Presents* #6–7, February–March 1979). Later still, the space mercenary known as the WEAPON-MASTER armed himself with Q-Energy grenades and a Q-Energy beam in his glove while fighting Superman (*DC Comics Presents* #60, August 1983).

QUAKERER, THE

A race of lizard-like beings from a world in a potential 420th century who wished to conquer Earth. To test their seismic weapons before invading, they sent one of their own back to the twentieth century, who used his chameleon-like abilities to pass as CLARK KENT's neighbor at 344 Clinton Street. The being, dubbed the Quakerer by Clark, abducted the inhabitants of the apartment building into a time-travel device, disguised as a METROPOLIS municipal bus. It proved a challenge for the Man of Tomorrow to defeat the alien and stop the future invasion, but he succeeded at the cost of revealing his alter ego. He chose to return everyone to their normal era just prior to their abduction, thereby preserving his secret (*Action Comics* #430–431, December 1973–January 1974).

QUARRM

Quarrm was a dimensional realm that was accessed when an energy rift opened in the wake of the freak chain reaction that altered all KRYPTONITE on Earth to resemble iron. When the dimension touched Earth's plane of existence, a burst of energy created a Superman-shaped sand creature that slowly sapped the Man of Steel's powers. This SAND SUPERMAN plagued the hero for a period of time (*Superman* [first series] #233, January 1971).

As he grew weaker, Superman seemed to lose his way until Diana Prince, at the time also a de-

powered Wonder Woman, brought her mentor, I-Ching, to visit him. It was through I-Ching's guidance that Superman learned of the other dimension and the formless beings that resided there (*Superman* [first series] #240–241, July–August 1971).

When a second portal opened, one of the entities arrived and animated a Chinese war idol during a New York City parade. Superman and his sandy doppelgänger fought the threat together, and I-Ching's powerful hypnotic illusion helped convince the Quarrm creature that he belonged in his own realm (*Superman* [first series] #242, September 1971).

The Quarrmer briefly returned to the Earthly plane when the mad Martian sorcerer Karmang pulled him and Black Adam into a plot to create a collision between Earth-1 and Earth-S (*All-New Collectors' Edition* #C-58, 1978).

Superman encountered the sand creature from Quarrm in the world after the Crisis on Infinite Earths. In this instance, the Man of Steel allowed the entity to believe that he had actually claimed his life, triggering its moral code and prompting the sandy duplicate to destroy itself (*Superman Special* #1, 1992).

QUASMANIA

A tribe of cliff dwellers in a rugged area of impassable country, located somewhere in South America, the Chirroba possessed the secret that the Man of Steel needed to save Metropolis from a virulent plague. The disease, which was highly contagious, first "renders man repulsive in appearance, transforms him into a raving maniac, then snuffs out his existence."

Superman recognized that even his mighty powers could not fight a disease but learned that the tribe had the answer. He traveled south to Quasmania and encountered Quismado, the evil high priest. The wicked man murdered the chief, imprisoned the chief's son, and terrorized the Chirrobas into submission at the behest of an American gangster. The criminal realized that if the plague could force the city to its knees, they'd pay any price for the cure.

Quismado was no match for the Man of Steel and met his doom, falling into an active volcano. His American partner also died when a stick of dynamite rebounded off the hero's chest and exploded in close proximity. The chief's son was freed and took his place as the Chirrobas' leader, allowing Superman to finally bring the cure back home (*Superman* [first series] #11, August 1941).

QUAZARS

The women of Quazar rose to become the dominant sex on their world, and then maintained their superiority by using a form of radiation to instill fear in their males. Choosing to spread their belief that "all men must be subordinated to women! It is the most basic natural law!," they arrived on Earth. They subjected the Man of Steel and the men of Metropolis to the radiation, which made them cower before the Astral Amazons.

The Quazarian men had developed a form of "counter-radiation" and used it on Lucy Lane, instilling her with the ability to cancel out the fear through "momentary oral contact." She freed her sometime boyfriend Jimmy Olsen from the fear; in turn, he donned his Flamebird costume to confront the scared Man of Steel, letting Lucy get close enough to plant a kiss on Superman and end the fear effect. Superman then managed to stop the Quazarians' reign of terror, returning them to space (*Superman Family* #179, October 1976).

QUEEN BEE, THE

Superman wound up opposing three different Queen Bees during his career. The first was Queen Zazzala, who battled the legendary Justice League of America on many occasions (*Justice League of America* [first series] #23, November 1963). Hailing from the hiveworld of Korll, she lived to ensure that her species propagated from star to star.

LATER, AS THE MAN OF STEEL SWOOPS DOWN OUT OF THE SKIES, HE SIGHTS FAR BELOW
CLIFF DWELL-ERS--MUST BE THE PEOPLE I'M LOOK-ING FOR!
STRIKING EARTH, SUPERMAN STARES, AWED AT THE MASS-IVE RUINS ABOUT HIM....
THEY MUST ONCE HAVE BEEN A POWERFUL AND MIGHTY NATION!

Quasmania

At one time she fronted a group of supercriminals and managed to capture the JLA until Superman found a way to free his teammates (*Action Comics* #443, January 1975). Partnered with the Planeteer, she battled Superman while attempting to control the Earth's magnetic field (*Action Comics* #562, December 1984).

After the Crisis on Infinite Earths, Zazzala was recruited by Lex Luthor to join the Injustice Gang (*JLA* #34, October 1999), but she met defeat at the JLA's hands. On most occasions, she used her natural gifts to mentally enslave human beings, usually spread by a naturally generated pollen. Interestingly, she was incapable of seeing the color red, which on at least one mission led to her defeat.

Zazzala resurfaced, allied this time with Alexander Luthor Junior and his Secret Society of Super-Villains, and was given control over the criminal organization known as H.I.V.E. (*Villains United* #4, October 2005). She gained control over Firestorm, whom she used as her power source, but the operation was ended by the intervention of a splinter group of villains known as the

Secret Six (under Lex Luthor's command). During the melee, she was severely wounded (*Firestorm* [third series] #17, November 2005), but once she healed she resorted to common robbery, attempting to steal a matter transporter in the hope of summoning troops from Korll (*Justice League of America* [second series] #20, June 2008). The effort was thwarted thanks to Wonder Woman and the Flash.

In another reality, a counterpart named Tazzala worked alongside a version of the Creature Commandos when the team wound up in the Terra Arcana Army located in another dimension, with the hope of conquering Earth (*Creature Commandos* #1–8, May–November 2000). She wound up being killed by the army's leader Simon Magus.

A different woman calling herself the Queen Bee took control of the Middle Eastern nation of Bialya after assassinating Colonel Rumaan Harjavti (*Justice League International* #16, August 1988). After brainwashing the Global Guardians into serving her, she was taken down by the combined efforts of the Justice League International and Justice League Europe. She gained her revenge, however, by using the alien technology provided her by a Dominator. When the JLE got the upper hand, a deal was cut: She would end her quest for revenge, and the League would keep her Bialyan atrocities a secret. To show good faith, she killed the Dominator. The JLE and the Guardians finally ended the Queen Bee's rule; she was then assassinated by Rumaan Harjavti's brother Sumaan (*Justice League America* #55, October 1991). A woman named Beatriz, assuming the Queen Bee title, regained control of the country for a brief time (*JLA: Incarnations* #6, December 2001).

QUEEN ELSHA

This deceitful queen of the so-called Amazon Island, known as a "land without men," claimed to have descended from the legendary Amazons (*Action Comics* #235, December 1957). She and her people seem unconnected to the Amazons of Paradise Island, which was ruled by Queen Hippolyta.

QUEEN HIPPOLYTA

Leader of the Amazons, she brought her people to the enchanted isle of Themyscira and ruled over the verdant paradise. Seeking a daughter, she created one from clay, and it was granted life by the Greek gods. The girl grew up to become Princess Diana, the heroine also known as Wonder Woman (*All Star Comics* #8, December 1941–January 1942).

QUEEN LATORA

Vergo was dying, and its cooling sun meant an ice age and extinction for its people. The planet's attractive Queen Latora sent out an SOS to the stars in the hope of assistance. Jor-El of Krypton received the message, and while he could not help them, he included the information in the "mind-tapes" he recorded for posterity. The tapes survived the destruction of Krypton and were embedded in a chunk of rock, which floated toward Earth. Superman encountered the tapes, heard of Vergo's plight, and went into space to see if he could help the planet before all life was extinguished. He gathered a planet-sized sphere of space-drift rich in uranium ore and tossed it into the dying sun. The resulting chain reaction reignited the star and preserved life on the planet for several centuries, earning the Man of Steel a happy Queen Latora's gratitude (*Superman* [first series] #113, May 1957).

QUEEN LURA

Clark Kent, Lois Lane, and Jimmy Olsen were once taking a hot-air balloon ride when they drifted into the lost civilization of Mistri-Lor. There they met Queen Lura, a beautiful blond ruler who found Clark fascinating. Growing up in a land of "handsome muscular men," Lura found the mild-mannered reporter quite exotic. Clark fought off the queen's ardor while also preventing Prince Vikar, the most powerful prince in the realm, from assassinating the queen so that he could assume the throne (*Action Comics* #298, March 1963).

QUEEN OF FABLES

Exiled to Earth from her native dimension, the sorceress Tsaritsa, known as the Queen of Fables, wound up being trapped sometime in the past within the *Book of Fables* by Snow White (*JLA* #47–49, November 2000–January 2001). Accidentally released from the legendary Book, the queen turned Manhattan into a forest filled with enchanted creatures drawn from folklore. When Wonder Woman investigated, she was mistaken for the daughter of the hated Snow White and placed into a deep slumber. Aquaman, a royal, managed to awaken Wonder Woman with a kiss, and they then summoned the Justice League of America. The battle was fierce, as Tsaritsa's magicks proved powerful enough to stall even the Man of Steel. Batman found the Book and learned how to stop her, trapping the queen within the U.S. Tax Code, a book of facts without anything imaginative to turn into a weapon. Locked away, her spells soon faded.

The Queen of Fables eventually managed to escape her plight and arrived in Metropolis seeking Superman, whom she saw as her personal Prince Charming. Using Kryptonian imagery, she placed the Man of Tomorrow in a glass forest and sought to win him over, although he broke her spell and regained his freedom through a great deal of effort (*Action Comics* #833–835, January–March 2008).

QUEEN PARALEA

Clark Kent became the object of affection for the lovely blond ruler of Atlantis when he, Lois Lane, and oceanographer Professor Hubble visited the domed city using a bathysphere. In an underwater city populated with virile men, Clark's unassuming persona was unique in the queen's eyes. While visiting, Clark, as Superman, stopped the unscrupulous chief adviser to the throne Hajar from plotting to overthrow the queen in a bloody coup (*Superman* [first series] #67, November–December 1950).

QUENTIN, KIRK

The secret identity of Hyperboy of the Hyper-Family (*Superboy* [first series] #144, January 1968).

QUETZATLAN

The ancient Central American civilization of Quetzatlan vanished when their wise man Haxtl predicted the future would be filled with "flood, earthquake, famine and wars." The people went within a pyramid and sealed themselves in, using their "magic sun globe" to place the power-hungry Emperor Quexo, his lovely cousin Empress Nara, and Haxtl into a form of suspended animation.

When the pyramid was unearthed a millennium later, the Quetzatlans awoke, and Quexo was ready to conquer this new era, restoring the might of their once great civilization. Using the mystic power of the sun globe, he began the transformation in Central America, thereby bringing the region to Superman's attention.

Quexo argued with the Man of Steel, noting that the world had grown harsher and darker since they had last seen it. While Superman agreed things were difficult, he argued that turning back the clock was not the answer. Instead, he took the trio on a tour of the modern world, which convinced Nara and Haxtl that things were better than they had imagined. However, Quexo, still hungry for power, refused to acknowledge the world's achievements. When he tried to kill his brethren, he fell into the generators at an electric power plant. As he died, the globe's power faded and the transformed lands reverted to their mod-

Quetzatlan

ern configurations (*Action Comics* #103, December 1946).

QUEX-UL

Convicted of a crime he did not commit, the Kryptonian scientist Quex-Ul was sentenced to twenty-five years within the Phantom Zone. What the Justice Council, led by Jor-El, did not know was that the real killer of the endangered Rondors had hypnotized Quex-Ul into confessing to the crime (*Superman* [first series] #157, November 1962).

While Quex-Ul was in the Zone, Krypton exploded, and with it any chance Quex-Ul had for freedom—or so he thought. Years later, Superman realized that Quex-Ul's sentence was up and released him from the prison realm. On Earth, the scientist gained superpowers and fought Superman in an attempt to exact revenge against the son of his captor. Possessing a piece of gold kryptonite, Quex-Ul hoped to permanently erase the Man of Steel's powers.

Quex-Ul, though, was regretful when he learned that Superman investigated the original case by time-traveling and learning of the true events surrounding the crime, which was committed by Rog-Ar. As a result, Quex-Ul rushed to prevent Superman from exposing himself to the gold k radiation and instead exposed himself. An unusual side effect was that Quex-Ul lost all his memories, and Superman helped retrain him, working with Perry White to find him a job in the *Daily Planet*'s production department under the name Charlie Kweskill.

Later, however, Quex-Ul regained his original memories and powers when he and Superman were trapped within the Phantom Zone. Quex-Ul sacrificed his life to free Superman, ensuring his legacy as a hero (*The Phantom Zone* #1–4, January–April 1982).

In the reality after the Crisis on Infinite Earths, a Quex-Ul was freed from the Phantom Zone that existed within the Pocket Universe. With General Zod and Zaora, the Kryptonians laid waste to the planet until Superman intervened, using kryptonite to kill the criminals (*Superman* [second series] #22, October 1988).

QUICK, DR. AMANDA SUMMERS

A New Jersey–based general surgeon who was briefly involved with John Henry Irons (*Steel* #5, June 1994).

QUICKSILVER KID, THE

When the Greek god Mercury visited Metropolis, underworld mobsters nicknamed him the Quicksilver Kid (*Superman* [first series] #26, January–February 1944).

QUIGLEY

The famous big-game hunter who was secretly the Archer.

QUINN COLLEGE

Clark Kent and Lois Lane were named honorary professors of journalism at Quinn College and mentored graduates Andy Parkes and Greta Lee, grooming them to join the staff of the *Daily Planet*. The star reporters were joint recipients of the annual trophy for prize reporting at a newspapermen's banquet in Metropolis Hall. During their tenure at the school, Superman also rescued their star quarterback from kidnappers who were hoping to profit from bets against the school's team (*Superman* [first series] #64, May–June 1950).

QUINTESSENCE, THE

The wizard Shazam, Zeus of the Greek gods, Highfather of New Genesis, the Phantom Stranger, and Ganthet of the Guardians of the Universe occasionally banded together to observe and even shape humanity's destiny. The Quintessence's origins were unrecorded, and their exact reason for existing remained shrouded in mystery.

While Clark Kent was a teenager, he was tested by the Quintessence to see if he would grow up to become a menace or a hero. Clark passed their test and proved an ally to each member throughout the chronicles (*Action Comics* #794, October 2002).

In the mainstream reality, the Quintessence's first recorded appearance saw them monitoring Earth's Justice League of America and Justice Society of America as they did battle with denizens from the Fifth Dimension (*JLA* #29, May 1999, and #31, July 1999). They later called Superman to judgment over his role in the "cessation of that universal power named Imperiex" (*Superman: The Man of Steel* #118, November 2001).

A version of the Quintessence existed on Earth-22, and it was they who bestowed mighty powers on a young boy named William, who grew up to become the feared villain Gog. The powers drove Gog mad, and he became a serious threat until Superman returned from retirement to stop him (*Kingdom Come* #3, 1996).

QURAC

The people of the Arab nation of Qurac (*Tales of the Teen Titans* #51–52, March–April 1985) "suffered under the cruel Shah. All Quraci groaned in fear and pain. It was a nightmare." Many were victimized by the Secret Police, but when the Shah was overthrown, his replacement, Colonel Hurrambi Marlo, was even worse (*Superman* [second series] #48, October 1990).

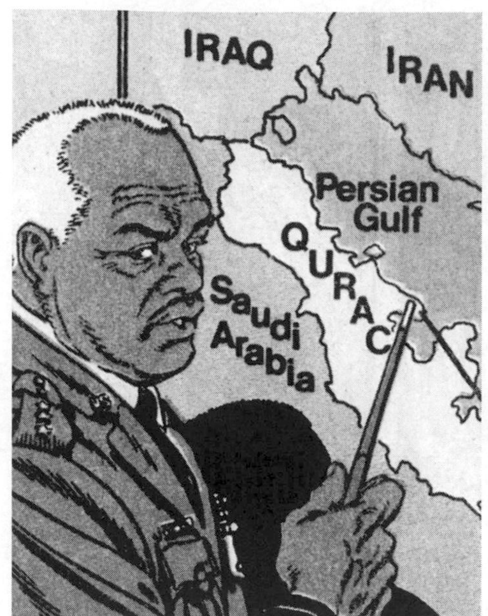

Convinced that the Freedom League's war machines—which had attacked METROPOLIS—had originated in Qurac (*The Adventures of Superman* #424–425, January–February 1987), Superman invaded the country's capital city, bursting into the presidential palace to threaten President Marlo and virtually dismantling its air force and navy, to international acclaim. In the aftermath, there was talk of revolution and a coup d'état (*The Adventures of Superman* #427–428, April–May 1987). Soon after, LOIS LANE found herself in the middle of a hostage situation involving a Quraci terrorist organization and Minister of Defense Khareemali, the man responsible for countless deaths. In the wake of the incident, the defense minister was secretly executed by Checkmate in a plane explosion over international waters (*Action Comics* #598, March 1998).

Marlo was subsequently deposed and placed in U.S. custody, and Superman escorted his plane back to the States, deflecting an assassination attempt in the process. The instigator of the attack was Major Holcraft—secretly the front man for the SONS OF LIBERTY, which had authorized shipments of money and weapons to rebuild Qurac's armies. Holcraft insisted the nation had supplied America with crucial information on both Iran and Iraq, and its intervention facilitated the release of three Middle Eastern hostages . . . in exchange for outdated weaponry and cash (*Superman* [second series] #53, March 1991).

According to modern maps, Qurac was bordered by Saudi Arabia, Iraq, and the Persian Gulf. Its oil reserves were unusable, though the cause remained in dispute. Deposed President Marlo blamed this on a nuclear device detonated by the United States, while the U.S. blamed the contamination on Quraci scientists' underground nuclear tests (*Superman* [second series] #53, March 1991).

In an act meant to provoke capitulation from the rest of the world, the terrorist Cheshire dropped several nuclear missiles on Qurac (*Deathstroke the Terminator* #19–20, February–March 1993). Despite massive numbers of deaths and extreme radiation poisoning, the country's people somehow struggled back to life.

In recent years, the Quraci capital fell in a military coup. "Ugly house-to-house fighting with genocide [was] the order of the day. General Rassam Harrat . . . named himself President for Eternity [and began] settling a lot of old scores. His only possible opposition [was] Haiza Musharu. She was the elected president of Qurac. Any attempt to overthrow Harrat [had] to come through her. She [was] part of a mass exodus from the Quraci port of Qizzim" heading "down the gulf toward safety in Dhabar." Tragically, most of the refugees—and the president herself—were killed by Harrat's forces (*Birds of Prey* [first series] #42, June 2002).

Soon after, war resumed along the border of Qurac and the Karrocan Emirate. "Two armies had already drawn blood with a death count of ten thousand, with no end in sight, the long disputed frontier along the Al Tagir River had long been a flashpoint for war. The history between these countries was said to be long and bloody" (*Birds of Prey* [first series] #15, March 2000).

Metropolis was home to Little Qurac, a neighborhood that was a refuge for many who emigrated from the Arab nation or were of Quraci descent (*Superman* [second series] #48, October 1990; others).

R24

The unusual code name for a mysterious underworld kingpin who assigned his henchmen to illicitly mine and smuggle URANIUM from the fringes of the federal government's uranium mine at Grass Mountain, north of METROPOLIS. Handicapped at the time by temporary amnesia resulting from prolonged exposure to KRYPTONITE, Superman still managed to locate and capture R24 and his cohorts (*Superman* [first series] #71, July–August 1951).

RADIANT, THE

The Radiant was the first champion of a world to lose his life battling the engine of destruction known as DOOMSDAY. The advanced technological world of Calaton did not need a champion when Doomsday arrived from outer space. For three years, the monster fought the planet's populace, reducing cities to rubble until only the capital survived.

The royal scientists found a way to channel the meta-human abilities of the royal family into a single vessel. Each member of the inbred family possessed powers and abilities, but all willingly gave up their powers and their very lives to protect the world they loved. The result was a living being composed of pure energy named Radiant, who charged the genetically engineered creature.

Their epic battle lasted a week until the Radiant unleashed a burst of power that not only stopped Doomsday but also destroyed one-fifth of Calaton. Following the people's custom, Doomsday's form was chained and covered, denying its angry spirit access to the afterlife. Considered unworthy of burial on their devastated world, Doomsday was shot into space with the presumption that it would float forever in the cold vacuum. Inside, its vessel got caught up in an asteroid flow and wound up crashing deep within the Earth. In time, Doomsday regained consciousness and began a years-long struggle to regain the surface and resume its sole desire: the utter destruction of all life.

Once Superman seemingly killed Doomsday a second time, the monster was attached to an asteroid and returned to the stars. The floating piece of rock came to DARKSEID's attention, and Doomsday was brought to APOKOLIPS, but proved more than bargained for. The lord of Apokolips ordered the creature returned to Calaton, where it was confronted by a new incarnation of the Radiant. Designed to adapt and evolve, Doomsday proved no match for the being of pure energy. Before dying, the Radiant told the recently arrived Man of Steel to save his people.

Once again Calaton was ravaged, but a group devoted to Radiant was formed. They prayed he would return and help heal their world once more. Just before police arrived to break up the prayer group, Radiant's image appeared with a message of hope (*Superman/Doomsday: Hunter/Prey* #1–3, 1994).

RADIUM

A chemical element with the symbol Ra and the atomic number 88, radium is radioactive and is normally used in the creation of energy or as a weapon.

The rare, expensive element became highly sought after in Superman's world, first sought by ZOLAR, who had found a way to "perform such miracles as total disintegration and controlling the weather." When used as a weapon, it proved potent enough to render the Man of Steel unconscious, even temporarily robbing him of his amazing abilities. Superman prevailed, and Zolar died

when a burst from his globe-gun bounced off the Kryptonian's chest and eradicated him (*Action Comics* #30, November 1940).

A second incidence involving radium saw scientist Brett Bryson receiving "a weird bombardment of hurtling rays" during an experiment. The scientist discovered that he developed superpowers as the radiation "affected his body in a strange way so that he could not be harmed by bullets and could cause sure death by his touch"—but he also discovered that he only had a week to live (*Action Comics* #39, August 1941).

RAINBOW CANYON, THE

The Rainbow Canyon was one of the most beautiful sights on Krypton, usually visited by lovers on vacation. Located in a deep natural gorge, it was traversed by a rainbow of breathtaking beauty. Superman visited this amazing attraction during his brief romance with actress Lyla Lerrol (*Superman* [first series] #141, November 1960).

RAINBOW DOOM, THE

Superman once used another of his elaborate ruses to find where gold thieves hid their stolen loot. After a well-publicized recent contact with a bizarre rainbow-ringed fireball in outer space, he led people to believe he had been afflicted with a dreadful new attribute: the ability to turn organic objects into glass with a touch. Called "Rainbow Doom" by the media, the news forced the criminals to move their stolen gold to a more secure location, which exposed them long enough to be apprehended by the Man of Steel (*Superman* [first series] #101, November 1955).

RAINBOW RAIDER, THE

The Rainbow Raider was a supposed costumed thief capable of hypnotically forcing any of his victims into submission. Jewel thief Vic Munster came out of hiding in an attempt to recruit the Raider to his side, only to learn that the masked man had actually been a lure to draw him out. Unknown to all, Superboy's secret ally had been his father Jonathan Kent (*Superboy* [first series] #84, October 1960).

Smarting from his defeat, Munster resolved to take the *Rainbow Raider* alias as his own upon his release from prison. His plan to plunder Smallville's Mystery-Costume Charity Ball was complicated by Martha Kent's decision to also wear the original Raider costume as a prank, but the thief was still thwarted by the Teen of Steel (*Superboy* [first series] #164, April 1970).

He is not to be confused with the powered Rainbow Raider who battled the Flash on numerous occasions.

RAL-EN

On Krypton, Ral-En was a former "college friend" of Jor-El and attempted to become the world's dictator through "Kryptonian hyper-hypnotism," an especially potent form of mass hypnosis taught to him by his father. The power-hungry man tried to convince the populace that he possessed superhuman powers and they should submit to his will. Instead, he was thwarted and brought to justice by Jor-El, who saw him banished to the Phantom Zone (*Superman* [first series] #154, July 1962).

RAMPAGE

S.T.A.R. Labs' Dr. Karen Lou "Kitty" Faulkner was researching pollution-free energies as part of a contest sponsored by the *Daily Planet*. When reporter Lois Lane questioned the facility's safety protocols, Dr. Thomas Moyers turned them off as a demonstration. Instead of proving how safe things were, the experimental energy exploded, and Faulkner accidentally absorbed some of those energies. Her slender physique changed into a hulking form with rippling muscles, a golden skin tone, and fiery red Mohawk. Dubbed Rampage, she went wild, carving a path of devastation that was easily followed. Once the Man of Steel learned what happened to the woman, he found a way to remove the excess energy, allowing Faulkner's natural form to return (*Superman* [second series] #7, July 1987).

In time, Faulkner studied her own body and learned that she needed exposure to precise amounts of solar and cosmic radiation or her altered form would die. A remorseful Moyers crafted a collar that would absorb and release the energies she now needed to live. He also created this to control her, and later used Rampage to try to ruin his former friend Herbert Forrest's presidential campaign. Superman once more stopped the threat, recognizing that Faulkner had no control over her alter ego. Moyers was arrested and the collar modified so that Faulkner was free to remain working for S.T.A.R. Labs (*Superman* [second series] #24, December 1988).

Her expertise in the lab, as well as her administrative acumen, led the corporation to send her to run its Phoenix, Arizona, facility. While there, she wound up becoming Rampage on several occasions, but was more in control of her new form and managed to strike up a friendship with local hero Will Payton, better known as the second Starman (*Starman* [first series] #9, April 1989; others). Any possibility of romance ended with Payton's death during a conflict with Eclipso, and Faulkner accepted an offer to return to a new S.T.A.R. complex in Metropolis (*Action Comics* #681, September 1992). She was later named the Metropolis branch director (*Secret Files and Origins Guide to the DC Universe 2000* #1, March 2000).

After this, Faulkner largely restricted transforming into Rampage. Nearly all of her alter ego's subsequent appearances found her under the control of villains such as Lord Satanus (*The Adventures of Superman* #587, February 2001), Circe (*Wonder Woman* [second series] #174–175, November–December 2001), the Joker (*Superboy* [third series] #93, December 2001), and Starro (*Teen Titans* [third series] #51–52, November–December 2007). Likely, a similar explanation was behind Rampage's subsequent clash with Mon-El (*Superman* #686, May 2009).

RANGER, THE

The Ranger was an Australian crime fighter who modeled his career after Batman's and met his idol during a meeting of international heroes (*Detective Comics* #215, January 1955). Nicknamed by the media as Batmen of all Nations, they were also dubbed the Club of Heroes. For one meeting, the Club also included Superman, who represented all the world's heroes (*World's Finest Comics* #89, July–August 1957).

In the reality after the events of Infinite Crisis, the Ranger continued to fight crime on his continent, altering his name to the Dark Ranger. When John Mayhew summoned the Club of Heroes once more, he responded, only to be killed as part of a plan for Mayhew to gain revenge against Batman, whom he blamed for the Club's failure (*Batman* #667–669, October–November 2007).

RAO

Rao was a red dwarf star some fifty light-years from Earth. It was orbited by seven planets, with Krypton placed in what was called the Goldilocks Zone—the area ideal to create and sustain life. Rao was born during the universal Big Bang, but Krypton did not cool and begin to show evidence of life until nine billion years ago.

The people of Krypton referred to their sun as Rao (*The World of Krypton* [second series] #1, December 1987) or Eldirao (*Action Comics* #839, July 2006), which also became the name of their supreme deity, chief of a pantheon of gods (*Superman* [first series] #248, February 1972). Another belief, during Erok-El's time, was that those born with red hair became military officers. When Jaf-El preached the worship of one god, he gave him the name of Rao, though no longer identifying him specifically with the sun (*Krypton Chronicles* #3, November 1981). During the traditional wedding ceremony, the phrase used was "Rao, who kindled the sun," showing Rao to be the sun's creator, but not the sun itself.

Rao's history changed after the events of the Infinite Crisis. In the wake of the Big Bang, a consciousness formed and decided the chaos was a waste of potential and chose to act. Rao formed stars and planets in its corner of the ever-expanding universe. Selecting the most perfect of these worlds, Rao named the planet Krypton. Rao then brought life to the planet, creating Vohc the builder and Flamebird, letting both bring life to the land, sea, and air. When Flamebird settled into the daylight realm and Vohc the twilight, Rao then created the dragon-like Nightwing to be his "Eyes in the Night." Flamebird and Nightwing, although siblings, came to love each other, much to Vohc's displeasure. He sought to curry favor with the Flamebird by creating a perfect crystal that the Flamebird admired, and yet destroyed. Vohc was angered by this and took the last shard of the crystal and trapped Nightwing within it. That shard became a limbo-like realm that was displaced in the cosmos and later became known as the Phantom Zone (*Action Comics* #886, April 2010).

A false Rao was created by Jax-Ur and unleashed on Earth to wreak havoc on the planet, but was eventually destroyed by the sacrifice of Thara Ak-Var, the latest Kryptonian to be possessed by the Flamebird entity (*Superman: War of the Supermen* #4, July 2010).

RAS-KROM

One of several Kryptonian prisoners trapped in the Phantom Zone who attempted to break free in order to gain superpowers and rule the universe. The superstitious criminal and his cronies were outwitted and finally re-imprisoned in the Zone by Superman and Jimmy Olsen (*Superman* [first series] #164, October 1963).

RASPER, JASPER

Attempting to ruin Christmas for children around the world, mean-minded skinflint Jasper Rasper fed Santa Claus chocolate candy coated with a fat-producing "wonder drug" that made him too obese to fit down chimneys. He then dosed the reindeer fodder with a chemical that made the animals too ill to pull the magic sleigh. Coming to the season's rescue was the Man of Steel, who helped jolly old St. Nick slim down to normal and flew the enchanted sleigh around the world to complete the night's task. When Rasper wound up stranded on an ice floe, Superman also saved the day. The self-made man told the Man of Steel and Santa Claus that perhaps he had been too focused on himself to recognize the joys of Christmas charity (*Action Comics* #105, February 1947).

RAVERS, THE

There was a place where the dimensional planes met, and it was there that a club for teens appeared. Called the Event Horizon, it was operated by Kindred Marx, who bestowed upon selected superpowered teens a special stamp allowing them admittance. By touching their individual stamps, wearers could be transported from their realm to the Event Horizon, wherever it might currently be located. When the Kon-El Superboy found the club, he was accompanied by Sparx, and there they met other similar teens. In time, those visits became regular occurrences, leading to many of them forming a team known as the Ravers

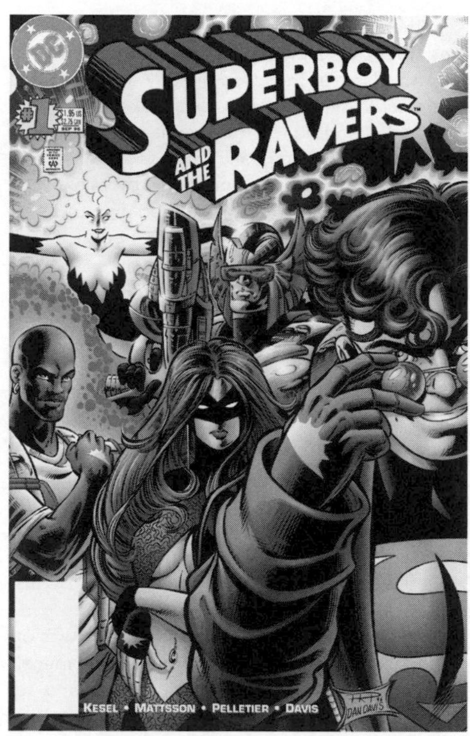

(*Superboy and the Ravers* #1, September 1996). Rivalries soon heated up, with similar cliques like the Corpse Corp, led by the vampire Pyra, and the Red Shift, made up exclusively of heroic Khund teens, being formed.

The Ravers traversed the dimensions having fun, righting wrongs, and partying as time permitted. Romances came and went, and Hero finally admitted he was gay in order to explain his disinterest in a confused Sparx (*Superboy and the Ravers* #14, October 1997).

Other members of the team included Kaliber, a young Qwardian who could increase or reduce his size; Aura (Lindsay Wah), a Chinese American girl with magnetic abilities; Hero Cruz, possessor of the Achilles Vest, which produced a force field; Rex the Wonder Dog from Earth; and the electrically charged Sparx.

Keeping the dimensions orderly, and therefore constantly running into the Ravers, were agents from InterC.E.P.T. (Interdimensional Cooperative Enforcement Police Team). Among their agents was the super heroine Nightshade (*Superboy and the Ravers* #1–2, September–October 1996).

During the Ravers' brief existence, they helped stop Rann from being conquered by Hyathis (*Superboy and the Ravers* #3–4, November–December 1996); Hero found the fabled H-dial, allowing him to become other heroes (*Superboy and the Ravers* #5, January 1997); and the team got to meet Superman himself (*Superboy and the Ravers* #9, May 1997). When Kindred Marx's mate Kindred Sol was endangered, he came to her rescue, only to be arrested and placed in the prison planet Starlag (*Superboy and the Ravers* #12, August 1997). Superboy later freed Marx, who repaid the favor by using his powers to help a team of heroes transport from Earth to Apokolips during the events known as Genesis (*Superboy and the Ravers* #14, and *Genesis* #2–4, both October–December 1997).

When the battle ended, Marx reopened the Event Horizon and added music, beginning with Earth's rock band Scare Tactics. The Ravers remained in operation, rescuing Kindred Sol and Kaliber when they became stuck in the anti-matter universe of Qward (*Superboy and the Ravers* #17–18, January–February 1998). The battle, however, drained Marx of his teleportational powers while other members also lost their special abilities, leading to the team's dissolution (*Superboy and the Ravers* #19, March 1999).

Sparx retired from adventuring, while Aura, Hero, Kaliber, Kindred Marx, Kindred Sol, and Hardrock all remained active. Sadly, Half-Life died during the team's final adventure (*Superboy and the Ravers* #18, February 1998).

RAYMOND, ROY

On Earth-2, Roy Raymond's TV show *Impossible . . . But True!* was hosted by Olga Olmstead, who also wrote a column based on the series for the *Daily Planet* (*World's Finest Comics* #24, September–October 1946).

On Earth-1, Raymond hosted the show himself and became a household name (*Detective Comics* #153–292, November 1949–June 1961). Every week, he and his lovely assistant Karen investigated claims and exposed hoaxes. Raymond abruptly vanished after vowing to expose his latest guest, Roger Rivers, as a fraud. In fact, the maniacal Rivers had abducted the TV detective and "managed to capture and channel Roy Raymond's brilliant analytical mind [and] turn it into a weapon." Years later, Superman picked up Raymond's trail and freed him from Rivers's control. Raymond wasted no time in reviving his TV series for Galaxy Broadcasting in Metropolis (*Superman* [first series] #285, March 1975).

In the reality after the Crisis on Infinite Earths, Roy Raymond's second career in TV came to an end after his obsession with locating the legendary Swamp Thing led to him and his assistant Lipschitz becoming trapped for several days in a limousine, resulting in a nervous breakdown, with Raymond hallucinating a business deal with Morgan Edge, the head of Galaxy Broadcasting (*Swamp Thing* [second series] #67–69, December 1987–February 1988, and #71–74, April–July 1988). Once recovered, Raymond chose to retire his TV series (*Swamp Thing* [second series] #81, Holiday 1988) although his grandson (billing himself as "Roy Raymond, Jr.") made the dubious decision to pose as a TV detective himself, appearing on *Roy Raymond: Manstalker* (*Robin* #38–39, March–April 1997). This prompted the elder Raymond to resume his career as a daytime TV host (*Detective Comics* #818, June 2006).

Raymond Junior relocated his show to Keystone City (*The Flash* [second series] #238, May 2008) but was lured away from the camera when Alfred Pennyworth invited the whip-smart man to help replace the dead Batman in a new incarnation of the Outsiders (*Outsiders* [second series] *Special* #1, February 2009), an offer he accepted. He became the costumed crime fighter Owlman,

using an outfit and equipment prepared for this eventuality by the Dark Knight himself (*Outsiders* [second series] #15, February 2009).

RAZKAL

The tyrannical ruler of Oxnalia, Razkal bore a similarity to Germany's chancellor Adolf Hitler. When Oxnalia invaded Numark, Superman personally protected the aggrieved nation (*Superman* [first series] #15, March–April 1942).

REACTRON

Sergeant Ben Krullen massacred a civilian village while in the service, and his actions also triggered Joshua Clay's meta-human powers, turning him into the hero Knoconas Tempest. Krullen went AWOL, but Clay learned that the soldier had been one of several subjects for atom bomb tests in the 1950s. He had inadvertently absorbed radiation, which altered his body chemistry. With his newfound abilities, Krullen worked for the international crime cartel known as the Council. It was this group that outfitted him in an energy-channeling outfit and named him Reactron.

At some point in Earth-1's past, the second incarnation of the Doom Patrol, which included Tempest, fought Reactron somewhere in Arizona. They were aided in defeating him by Supergirl. The powerful villain escaped custody, and the Doom Patrol traced him to Chicago, where Negative Woman and Reactron fought over the city. When she managed to force him to the streets, the rest of the team joined in the battle—only to watch him escape through a spatial warp he generated. Witnessing it all was Linda Danvers, unable to find a place to change into Supergirl without exposing her identity.

When Reactron reappeared that night in a lab beneath Fletcher Hall, Supergirl managed to arrive to stop his attack. As they battled, the lab's nuclear reactor reached critical mass. The fight tumbled them outside the hall, where the Doom Patrol arrived once more. Supergirl subdued the villain, encasing him in lead sheeting until Tempest pointed out that Reactron produced an energy that corroded it—with explosive results. Supergirl was stunned by the force of the blast.

When the Maid of Might realized the reactor was going to explode, she went to deal with it, only to discover Reactron already absorbing the energies. While the reactor was now safe, Reactron had absorbed too much radiation and threatened to blow, potentially wiping out all life in Chicago. Supergirl prevented this by taking him to the sky, where he detonated too high to cause harm to life (*The Daring New Adventures of Supergirl* #8–9, June–July 1983).

In the reality after the Crisis on Infinite Earths, it was Power Girl who aided the Doom Patrol when they first confronted the villain (*Secret Origins Annual* #1, 1987), then using the alias Martin Krull. While in custody at Belle Reve, he was visited by Larry Trainor, who wanted to regain the energy being then inhabiting DP member Negative Woman's body. Reactron allowed the desperate man to perform experiments, which went awry and nearly allowed him to escape, and absorb the Negative Energy Being, which was retained in the end by Negative Woman (*Doom Patrol* [second series] #10–11, July–August 1988).

Reactron survived the experience and was offered freedom after joining Task Force Omega's Suicide Squad to investigate the island of Kooeykooeykooey. Reactron eventually annoyed Killer Frost, who froze him in a solid block of ice. When their meta-human targets turned up, Deadshot started shooting, leaving several large holes in Reactron's body. As Krull seemingly died, his body began to reach critical mass and almost exploded, until he was sent to another dimension by Blackstarr (*Suicide Squad* [second series] #6–9, April–July 2002).

Somehow he returned not only to Earth, but resumed his place in the military, now with the rank of major. Reactron was also now inexplicably powered by a piece of gold kryptonite in his chest cavity. He was given a chance to return to action as a government-sanctioned Reactron (*Supergirl* [fifth series] #35, January 2009). Krull happily accepted and was paired with Metallo; their assignment was to allow themselves to be taken by the Kandorians now living on Earth. The Kandorians had been seeking Superman's foes to imprison or kill to reduce threats to the new immigrants. Anticipating this, Lex Luthor wanted the duo taken so they could unleash the kryptonite power in their chests to take out as many Kandorians as possible. When other prisoners were freed, Reactron used the distraction to kill the Kandorian leader Zor-El (*Action Comics* #872, February 2009). Later seeking revenge, his widow Alura ordered her daughter Supergirl to find Reactron and bring him to New Krypton to face judgment.

On the run, he tried to hide at his girlfriend's apartment, only to have her killed by a vengeance-seeking Superwoman. Supergirl, however, was determined to find the at-large Reactron, not daring to risk disappointing her mother (*Supergirl* [fifth series] #37–39, March–May 2009). He eluded her for a time, until Supergirl along with Nightwing and Flamebird managed to locate him (*Supergirl* [fifth series] #45–46, November–December 2009; *Action Comics* #881–882, November–December 2009).

Reactron was then brought to New Krypton for questioning, although Supergirl was dismayed to see her mother use torture as a means of extracting information from the villain. What neither suspected was that Reactron was a willing prisoner who had allowed himself to be captured to fulfill his ultimate purpose. General Samuel Lane's surgeons had turned Reactron into a literal time bomb, and once he detonated he took all of New Krypton with him. The total destruction of their second home planet rallied the remaining Kryptonians and started an all-out war between them and the people of Earth (*Superman: War of the Supermen* #1, July 2010).

REDEMPTION

Clark Kent asked Perry White for permission to fly to Africa in order to investigate reports about the existence of a powerful meta-human named Redemption. White did not feel that the reports merited the time and expense, so he disapproved the trip. Soon after came the events known as the Infinite Crisis. During that event, Superman expended every ounce of energy he had; it took him a year before solar radiation recharged him sufficiently to resume his role as the World's Greatest Super Hero.

As it turned out, Redemption was a developing story that went unreported during this period. That changed when Jarod Dale gained superhuman powers from the Reverend Matthew Hightower closer to Metropolis. The corrupt pastor was newly arrived from Africa, now serving at the First Church of Redemption in Valley Falls, Colorado. Following the pastor's orders, Dale killed fourteen soldiers from Nyasir, Africa, while destroying twenty-two acres of land with a single blast of energy. When Kent heard of this, he felt partly responsible, so he traveled to Africa as the Man of Steel to finally investigate. While there, he learned that Hightower had lost control of his powers, originally gained during World War II, and initially used them to kill twenty-three hundred men on the German front. Hightower vowed never to lose control again and tamped down his powers in favor of faith.

Meeting Dale changed his mind, and Hightower found a way to transfer some of his awesome abilities to the desperate man. He then guided Dale in

the use of his powers, targeting corrupt Africans for justice. Dale thought during these months that he had been blessed with the power of the faithful congregation, not the pastor. When Dale refused to participate in the charade any further, Hightower took the power back—but when the people learned what had happened, they all abandoned the pastor (*Action Comics* #848–849, May–June 2008).

RED RAVEN

On a parallel world, Red Raven led a gang of criminals that managed to elude capture while committing spectacular crimes. They were finally apprehended when Batman arrived on this oddly familiar world. There was no Batman on this Earth; instead Bruce Wayne, who resembled Clark Kent, was secretly Superman, partner to Robin. Reporter Lois Lane, who resembled Vicki Vale, loved the hero, and there was no evidence of a Batwoman or Batgirl. This world's Joker was television comedian Freddy Forbes. At first, Batman was suspected as being mentally disturbed until he aided Superman in bringing the Red Raven gang to justice. A thankful Man of Steel took Batman and the damaged Batplane to a spot where a freak thunderstorm opened a rift between realities, which let the Caped Crusader return to his proper home (*World's Finest Comics* #136, September 1963).

REED, GREGORY

This famous actor was best known for his portrayal of Superman in feature films and on television. While he used padding to fill out his physique, the man needed barely any makeup to resemble the Man of Steel.

Then a fire on the set left his face disfigured. Psychologically as well as physically damaged, Reed grew to blame Superman for his injuries. He continued in his role as the Man of Steel, thanks to heavy makeup and a wig, until he accessed a black magic talisman, which he used to switch minds with the hero. Unused to the new body and its denser configuration, Reed inadvertently caused much damage to his mansion. When Superman tricked Reed into grasping hands, their minds reverted, and the Man of Steel managed to save Reed, although his home collapsed into the sea (*Action Comics* #414, July 1972).

Some time later, Superman found a technique for and personally performed the plastic surgery that allowed Reed to regain his handsome features; he now resembled Superman more than before. With practice, his voice could match the Man of Steel's. When Superman could not visit a sick child, he then gave Reed a pill endowing him with temporary superpowers. As Reed flew to visit the girl, he was attacked by the Superman Revenge Squad in a case of mistaken identity. Reed was dosed with a special radiation that would kill him after he performed ten super-feats. When Superman learned of the diabolical plan, he gave Reed a second pill, and they each performed five of the feats to thwart the villains (*Action Comics* #445, March 1975).

Reed substituted for Superman again after the hero was transferred into a doppelgänger for Terra-Man while his super-feats were mimicked by Flash and Green Lantern (*Action Comics* #470, April 1977). Later, the actor posed as Superman again (even as the Man of Steel took the alias of the Mystery Marauder) to confound the brain robber known as Intellex (*Superman* [first series] #396, June 1984).

Reed was also seen alongside talk-show host Johnny Nevada as two of the seven men who had all been suspected of being the one true Superman (*Action Comics* #474, August 1977)—as in the instance when the actor was mistakenly targeted by the Secret Society of Super-Villains (*Secret Society of Super-Villains* #7, June 1977). Reed subsequently had the dubious honor of appearing at Luthorcon, a convention exclusively devoted to the notorious Lex Luthor (*DC Comics Presents Annual* #4, 1985).

In post-Crisis history, Gregory Reed was rumored to be up for the lead in a Martian Manhunter film (*JLA Secret Files* #1, September 1997). He played the Man of Steel again in *The Atomic Skull* (*The Adventures of Superman* #571, October 1999).

REEFER, BIG JOE

Hugo Reefer entered the *Daily Planet*'s shipbuilding contest because his older brother "Big" Joe, a Metropolis racketeer, wanted him to win. Reefer smashed Jimmy Tuttle's model ship, but the prize was denied to Hugo: Jimmy Olsen won the contest with a model of a Spanish galleon. Superman saw to it that Reefer and his henchmen wound up in police custody (*Superman* [first series] #28, May-June 1944).

REGENT, LUCY

Dubbed "Supergirl," this exiled queen from the Central American nation of Borgonia had Olympic-level athletic and acrobatic abilities. She briefly stayed in Smallville while the criminals opposing her ascension to throne were dealt with. Lucy encountered Superboy on several occasions before returning home to take her rightful place on the throne (*Superboy* [first series] #5, November-December 1949).

REGOR

Considered the "super-champion" of the planet Uuz, Regor was an "invincible opponent" of evil, clad in a red-and-green costume with white fur trim, a green cape and boots, a yellow belt, and a green letter R on a yellow field emblazoned on his chest.

Regor was actually Winki Lamm, a mild-mannered television interviewer, rocketed to Regor as an infant—not from Krypton, but from Earth. "Famous rocket scientist" James Flint maintained his laboratory on an island, so when a volcano erupted, he mistakenly thought the world was ending and sent his son into space, where the weaker gravity of Uuz would endow his son with mighty powers. On the planet, the buildings and automobiles were constructed almost entirely of glass—a substance that to inhabitants' eyes was opaque, but something through which Regor could see.

Superman came to Regor's aid after the planet's "master of crime," Bantor, planned to hijack many of the personal heaters which Uuzians needed to survive their planet's frigid environment (*Superman* [first series] #58, May–June 1949).

REILLY, DETECTIVE CAPTAIN

This Chicago detective was considered a "conceited windbag" but was nationally recognized for having successfully captured every one of the eight hundred fugitives he had been assigned to track down. As a result, Metropolis police brought him east to help them apprehend Superman. The Man of Steel's crime? He had "torn down [the city's] slum area" without public authorization, "causing modern apartments to replace crowded tenements."

Holding to the letter of the law, the police wanted Superman to answer for his transgression, but even the vaunted Reilly failed to bring the Man of Steel to justice, going so far as to knock himself unconscious against Superman's "super-tough" skin (*Action Comics* #9, February 1939).

REMNANT

On the anniversary of Superman's death at the hands of DOOMSDAY, a costumed villain called Remnant retraced the coast-to-coast path of devastation, thereby causing fresh disasters. His ultimate goal was to arrive in METROPOLIS and kill *DAILY PLANET* editor in chief PERRY WHITE. To Remnant, all the citizens who died during the battle had their deaths rendered meaningless by the Man of Steel's elevation through the years of reports in the great metropolitan newspaper. He intended, therefore, to make White pay for this supposed crime. Using advanced technology, he appeared wraith-like and created illusions realistic enough to confuse even Superman. While Superman saved Perry's life, *Planet* reporter Ty Duffy wrote a story questioning the very thing Remnant was violently railing about (*Superman: Day of Doom* #1–4, January–April 2003).

RENALDO, HUGO

PAUL MCKENZIE was a painter "famous for his magnificent portrayals of heroes in action" until his tragic mental collapse. His artwork deteriorated from realism to abstraction, and he eventually sought mental care. Criminal Hugo Renaldo used the man's need as part of a ruse to keep Superman distracted while his men looted the city of METROPOLIS. He posed as a psychiatrist, volunteering his services and working with McKenzie. Instead of being driven to distraction by aiding the painter, however, Superman managed to apprehend the criminals and expose Renaldo's fraud (*Action Comics* #170, July 1952).

REN-RE

Son of the sorcerer Master Re, Ren-Re's romance with TAR-LU, daughter of a scientist, was forbidden on KRYPTON. The two lovers continued their relationship in secret and eventually left their homes, exploring with Vog-Ar and encountering a new city. Ren's brother Bik-Re had trailed them and made his presence known. During a conflict, he was accidentally killed by Tar-Lu's "scientific fight-training." The two lovers ran off into self-imposed exile, never to be seen again.

In time, their story became the stuff of legend, and superstitious residents of Krypton believed they had turned into "twin stars." Anyone sighting the "Lovers' Stars" believed them to be an evil omen—and indeed, the phenomenon was seen on the eve of the planet's destruction (*Superman* [first series] #255, August 1972).

REPLIKON

The being known as Replikon was born as Xum millennia in the past and was the last survivor of a shattered planet that now formed an asteroid belt. Desperate to find a home for its two children that incubated within gleaming eggs, the ethe-

real entity was eventually drawn to Earth. Passing through the Justice League Satellite, Xum observed BATMAN, the FLASH, and WONDER WOMAN, ultimately materializing on Earth in a material form that was a composite of the three heroes. Xum came to the attention of GREEN LANTERN, Green Arrow, and Black Canary when it began destroying Earth's ozone layer to create a proper climate for its children. Dubbed Replikon by Black Canary, the creature was eventually returned by Green Lantern to the asteroid belt (*Green Lantern* [second series] #108–109, September–October 1978).

It was there that a vengeful Replikon subsequently encountered two other Green Lanterns who were more sympathetic to its plight. With the permission of the Guardians of the Universe, John Stewart and Katma Tui created an environmental oasis where Xum's children Sachi and Yukinori were born (*Green Lantern* [second series] #193, October 1985).

Years later, Replikon rematerialized in METROPOLIS, laden with gauntlets and shielding. After its brief rampage was halted by Superman, Replikon begged the Man of Steel for help and burst into flame, apparently dying. With John Stewart's help, Superman visited the asteroid belt, discovering only the corpse of one of Xum's children (*The Adventures of Superman* #627–628, June–July 2004). Through means unknown, the mysterious RUIN had accessed the asteroid, taking both Xum and one of his offspring captive while slaying the other. Renamed Xlim by Ruin, the other child of Replikon was forced to battle Superman on penalty of death. Xlim's fate after being captured by the Man of Steel remained unrecorded (*The Adventures of Superman* #629–633, August–December 2004).

REPULSE

The magnetically powerful but psychologically fragile Dr. Polaris came to METROPOLIS seeking Superman's help in staving off an attack from an even

more powerful manipulator of magnetism named Repulse. As Repulse arrived and battled the duo, it became apparent that she was actually an illusion, a manifestation of a new persona created by Dr. Polaris. Scantily clad and resembling his aunt, Repulse battered Dr. Polaris until Superman broke the illusion (*Action Comics* #827–828, July–August 2005). A different Repulse existed in the thirtieth century as a member of Work Force (*Legion of Super-Heroes* [fourth series] #125, March 2000).

RICHARDS, CARY

The boy whose subconscious was used to unleash the foulmouthed, leather-clad, cigar-chomping villain known as ADVERSARY (*The Adventures of Superman* #585, December 2000).

RIJA AND KOND

On a world in the distant past existed disembodied intellects, with one, known as Rija, finally deciding to sample life as a corporeal form. Rija took the body of an attractive "space siren" and lived on the world's surface.

Superman was sent tumbling through time in the wake of an exploding supernova and arrived near the world. The other intellect, Kond, asked for the Man of Steel's help in saving Rija from a creature generated by her powerful mind. Her "starry eyes" also cast a sort of love spell on Superman, complicating his efforts. Eventually, Kond also took a humanoid form resembling that of Superman, so he could spend eternity beside his true love.

As a thank-you, Kond provided the Man of Steel with four potions to help Earth conquer disease, pollution, crime, and starvation. However, the potions were destroyed during Superman's travel back through time to his home era (*Superman* [first series] #243, October 1971).

RIKKER, HORACE

An "inventor turned crook," Horace Rikker was the leader of the Amphi-Bandits, a gang of criminals who "steal a car for each job, hit like lightning, get to a speedboat, and elude all harbor-patrol traps" by means of a special submersible boat, equipped for underwater travel. After each robbery, they'd cross the river through an underground stream leading to their secret hideout beneath an abandoned mansion. While successful for a time, the Amphi-Bandits were eventually apprehended by Superman (*Action Comics* #90, November 1945).

RIMBOR

The crime-ridden homeworld of Legion of Super-Heroes member Ultra Boy and the Legion's adviser Marla Latham (*Superboy* [first series] #98, July 1962).

RINOL-JAG

When Krypton exploded, huge fragments of the planet were scattered throughout the stars. One large piece struck the planet Salitar, destroying all life. The sole survivor was Rinol-Jag, an astronaut who was traveling to Salitar's moon when the asteroid hit. His space capsule was rescued by notorious space pirate Amalak, who brainwashed the man into hating all things Kryptonian. The pirate and his dupe finally located the Last Son of Krypton and arrived on Earth to begin eradicating remnants of the once great world. Breaching the Fortress of Solitude, he stole the bottle city of Kandor in addition to kidnapping Krypto and Supergirl. Amalak, pleased with his pawn's efforts, began to plan Earth's destruction with a bomb.

Superman and Rinol-Jag tangled on his asteroid base, but the Man of Steel managed to convince the angry alien that he had been manipulated. His mind clear, Rinol-Jag teamed up with the hero to stop Amalak from destroying Earth. With the pirate now in the hands of the intergalactic police, Rinol-Jag made his apologies to the Kryptonians and then headed his ship for space to find a place he could call home (*Superman* [first series] #195, April 1967).

RINTON

This scientific inventor arrived at the offices of the Metropolis *Daily Planet* with his latest device. While demonstrating his "Rinton reverse time ray," Clark Kent and Lois Lane were accidentally sent to early-seventeenth-century London in the time of William Shakespeare. There they briefly visited until the effects wore off (*Superman* [first series] #44, January–February 1947).

RIOT

Being born into the von Frankenstein family brought with it a set of expectations that extended from generation to generation, as all von Frankensteins were groomed for great achievements in order to rehabilitate the family name after their ancestor created a monster. One branch of the family went so far as to alter their surname to Legion. Frederick Legion was no different, suffering tremendous pressure to succeed starting in school. In order to fit in all that was expected of him, Frederick used a phase-shifter, created by his uncle Hal, and created duplicates of himself. Frederick did not realize that use of the device would activate his metagene, allowing him to self-generate duplicates. The changes also altered his features, giving his face a distinctly skeletal look. Using his duplicates to study, research, experiment, and so on, also left him sleep-deprived, which slowly but surely drove him insane, another sad family trait.

He did manage one key accomplishment, however, which was creating a method that allowed him to stick to any surface. Still, the unstable young man was eventually banned from the lab by his father, so Frederick turned to crime, using the name Riot (*Superman: The Man of Steel* #61, October 1996). His crimes were at first only at biotech facilities, which brought him to Superman's attention. With each blow, more duplicates were generated, outnumbering the Man of Steel until he rounded them all up in a dumpster. As he sorted through them, it became clear that the original had managed to escape.

Riot soon reappeared, this time to steal a photon fuel sample from S.T.A.R. Labs' Metropolis facility. He once more eluded Superman but ran afoul of Morgan Edge, who trapped him in a steel cage. The criminal ordered Anomaly to reach through the bars and strike Riot until the cage was stuffed with duplicates. With little choice, Riot agreed to join Edge's Superman Revenge Squad, serving alongside Maxima, Misa, Barrage, and Anomaly (*The Adventures of Superman* #543, February 1997). At first it appeared they were a match for the hero, but bickering eventually distracted the team and gave Superman the edge he needed to beat them. Then they realized Edge couldn't hold up his end of the bargain and broke up. Riot sent a team of duplicates back to Edge's lair to free the one dupe left behind as insurance (*Superman: The Man of Steel* #65, February 1997).

Finally recognizing the need for sleep, Riot set out to obtain a time/phase integrator that also promised to temporarily halt the duplication process. Superman arrived during the robbery and Riot panicked, sending an army of Riots to distract the hero by invading a party hosted by Lex Luthor. At the same event was his uncle Hal and reporter Lois Lane. After learning from Lois what Riot was after and why he needed it, Superman asked the Metropolis S.C.U. to leave the criminal alone until he fell asleep (*Superman: The Man of Tomorrow* #14, Summer 1999).

He escaped custody and was used by Manchester Black in his initial assault on Superman, but was once more easily defeated (*The Adventures of Superman* #608, November 2002) as he was during subsequent clashes with the Man of Steel (*Action Comics* #839, July 2008) and the Guardian (*Superman* #685, April 2009).

Riot resurfaced, now in the employ of the villainous Roulette, and attempted to destroy Batman for the benefit of her gamblers. Riot claimed to have mastered control over his body, now able to prevent accidental versions of himself from forming. Nonetheless, he was soundly defeated by the combined efforts of Batgirl and Robin (*Batgirl* [second series] #7, April 2010).

RIVERS, DAN

Using the alias Swami Riva, Dan Rivers was the first man on Earth-2 to discover kryptonite and its effects on Superman. While it weakened the hero, it did not prevent him from apprehending the criminal (*Superman* [first series] #61, November–December 1949).

Years later, Rivers was freed on parole, and he sent a tiny sample of the deadly mineral to Lois Lane Kent, embedded within a brooch. When Superman felt the effects and realized what Rivers was up to, Mr. and Mrs. Superman crafted a ruse to lure Rivers into the open, allowing them to capture him on a parole violation. Unfortunately, the cell he subsequently shared included Lex Luthor, who finally learned there was something that could actually kill the Man of Steel (*Superman Family* #202, July–August 1980).

ROBIN

Robin the Boy Wonder was Batman's partner in almost every reality that has been chronicled.

On Earth-2, a young Bruce Wayne adopted the Robin persona to protect his identity when he approached detective Harvey Harris to train him. Years later, he passed the costume on to another. Dick Grayson's parents died in a circus accident, and the grief-stricken youth was taken in by Batman. Dick swore an oath by candlelight to assist in the war on crime and trained to become Batman's costumed sidekick Robin (*Detective Comics* #38, April 1940). Dick Grayson fought beside Batman for years, eventually growing up and becoming his own person, studying the law and adopting an adult costume styled after his mentor's. He followed Batman in joining the Justice Society of America and wound up sacrificing his life to save others during the Crisis on Infinite Earths.

On Earth-1, the same fate befell the Flying Graysons at the Haly Bros. Circus, and Batman took in the young Dick Grayson. The boy trained with Batman and joined him as Robin, happily fighting alongside Bruce Wayne for years. In his early teens, he helped form the Teen Titans, and he served as its leader for most of the group's duration. Jimmy Olsen and Robin the Boy Wonder partnered on numerous occasions, even establishing their own headquarters, located in an abandoned observatory which they dubbed the Aerie (*World's Finest Comics* #141, May 1964). As he entered his twenties, Dick grew apart from Batman, attending Hudson University for a few years, and soon after crafting his own identity by donning a

WELL, ROBIN -- IT LOOKS LIKE OUR PARTNERSHIP IS OVER! IT WAS SWELL WORKING BESIDE YOU!
THE SAME GOES FOR ME, SUPERMAN! I'LL NEVER FORGET IT!

new costume and the name Nightwing, inspired by the persona Superman once assumed in the bottle city of Kandor.

On the Earth fashioned after the Crisis on Infinite Earths, Richard John "Dick" Grayson's beginnings were largely the same. When Batman insisted on a lengthy training period, Dick Grayson complied, and when he was given his own costume, he chose the name Robin after a nickname his mother once gave him. He grew up and became Nightwing—this time inspired by a Kryptonian legend related to him by Superman—and continued to be his own man while still loving the one who raised him. Whenever Batman needed him, Dick Grayson eagerly answered the call.

Shortly after Grayson left to become Nightwing, Jason Peter Todd entered Batman's life (*Batman* #357, March 1983) and ultimately became the second Robin (unofficially in *Detective Comics* #526, May 1983; officially in *Batman* #368, February 1984). After a reality-altering wave, Jason became a street youth who was discovered by Batman trying to steal the Batmobile's tires (*Batman* #408, June 1987). Batman took the impetuous youth into Wayne Manor and allowed him to become the second Robin. Jason, however, proved headstrong and difficult, complicating Batman's ability to train him. When he defied Batman and went in search of his birth mother, Todd wound up being killed by the Joker. Years later, he was resurrected by another reality-altering event known as the Infinite Crisis and competed with Batman as the violent vigilante Red Hood.

On the fateful night when the Flying Graysons plummeted to their deaths, Jack, Janet, and Timothy Drake were all in attendance (*Batman* #436, Early August 1989). Later, when a new hero named Robin was seen beside Batman, Tim recognized a distinctive acrobatic move, convincing him Dick Grayson was Robin. Years later, after Todd died, Tim began a one-teen campaign to convince Batman that he needed a Robin—and that Tim was the person for the job. Batman reluctantly agreed, but only after insisting Drake spend six months in intensive training (unofficially as Robin in *Batman* #442, December 1989; officially in *Batman* #457, December 1990). After this, Drake excelled as Robin, bonding with Grayson and assuming his role as leader of the Teen Titans. There he and Superboy became the best of friends until Kon-El's tragic death.

Soon after Batman was apparently killed during the Final Crisis, Tim Drake appeared to be the only one convinced Bruce Wayne was still alive. Determined to prove himself correct, Tim became the Red Robin, while Dick Grayson reluctantly and at long last became Batman. Soon after, Grayson was joined by Damian Wayne, Bruce's child with Talia Head, who became the fifth Robin (*Batman: Battle for the Cowl* #3, July 2009). When Connor Kent returned from the grave, Tim was overjoyed. The two renewed their friendship immediately, and when Lana Luthor was rendered comatose, Tim arranged for doctors from Wayne Enterprises to take care of her (*Adventure Comics* #509, March 2010).

(For a complete history of Robin, see *The Essential Batman Encyclopedia*, 2008.)

ROBIN HOOD

A Metropolis citizen felt the plight of the poor and decided to become a modern-day version of the legendary Robin Hood. Wearing an emerald outfit, he robbed "the unjustly rich to aid the poor. Why? Because I sympathize with the underdog . . . and do something about it!" Robin Hood successfully stole from the corrupt and the criminal, coming to the aid of the poor and the unfortunate. In time, however, he grew disenchanted with his role. Deciding that perhaps he should profit from his efforts, he formed an ill-fated alliance with "Beetlebrow" Macklin. The criminal and the deluded philanthropist began a vicious crime wave until they were apprehended by Superman. When Macklin's men tried to shoot their way to freedom, Robin Hood stepped in front of reporter Lois Lane, taking the bullets meant for her, and he died. His final words revealed his deep remorse: "I . . . I was a fool to try to . . . work outside the law," gasped the dying outlaw. "If . . . if I wanted to help others . . . I should have joined the police force. . . . please . . . one last favor . . . return the [stolen] money . . . compliments of . . . Robin Hood" (*Superman* [first series] #22, May–June 1943).

Krypto the Super-Dog once encountered the real Robin Hood during a jaunt in the timestream (*Superboy* [first series] #75, September 1959), while at another point Lois Lane hallucinated a time-travel journey in which she became the sweetheart of Robin Hood (*Superman's Girl Friend, Lois Lane* #22, January 1961).

ROCK

Fighter pilot Micah Flint was injured during a test flight, so he volunteered for a LexCorp program, letting them mutate him into an extremely strong, rock-like being. He was displeased with the process, which was irreversible, so he grew obsessed with getting revenge on Lex Luthor (*Superman: The Man of Tomorrow* #8, Spring 1997). Rock transferred that hatred toward the Man of Steel for preventing him from gaining a measure of satisfaction. As a result, he fought the hero on several occasions, even briefly joining Morgan Edge's Superman Revenge Squad (*Action Comics* #736, August 1997). He was also one of the super-villains sent to a world of aliens in an attempt to end their threat, but he successfully returned to Earth, his current whereabouts unknown (*Salvation Run* #1–7, December 2007–June 2008).

ROCKSELL, RANDALL

"One of America's richest and most ambitious men," Randall Rocksell nearly lost his entire fortune in a fraudulent scheme committed by Goldie Gates until she was stopped by Superman (*Superman* [first series] #27, March–April 1944).

RODRIGUES, ANTHONY

Growing up in Metropolis's Suicide Slum, Anthony Rodrigues managed to develop an advanced vocabulary and was nicknamed "Big Words" by his friends. Together they formed the Newsboy Legion and adventured alongside the Guardian (*Star-Spangled Comics* #7, April 1942).

ROHTUL

In a potential future, Rohtul was a descendant of Lex Luthor operating in the year 2957. Like his ancestor, Rohtul intended to use his technological prowess to subjugate the Earth and become its ruler. He was stopped thanks to the combined efforts of the twentieth century's champions Batman, Robin, and Superman (*World's Finest Comics* #91, November–December 1957).

ROKK AND SORBAN

The planet Ventura was known as the universe's best place to gamble. The entire culture had evolved so every facet of life involved a wager of one kind or another. The world was ruled by the partners Rokk and Sorban, "the last surviving members of [Ventura's] hereditary ruling class," who lacked the moral scruples to recognize what their ever-escalating bets meant to other people.

In addition to devising incredibly sophisticated casino games, they enjoyed a rich technological heritage that enabled the rulers to visit other worlds as part of their competition. They once ventured to Earth and bet each other they could force the World's Greatest Super Hero to kill a human being. Instead Superman crafted one of his patented ruses to make them believe he committed murder, and the two aliens left Earth (*Superman* [first series] #171, August 1964).

Fascinated by humanity and its champions, they returned soon after and devised a scheme in which the Man of Steel had to gamble in order to save first Batman's life, then all life on Earth (*World's Finest Comics* #150, June 1965).

By then, they were well known enough that Abra Kadabra, the sixty-fourth-century super-criminal, and the Reverse Flash posed as the aliens to entice Superman into racing the Flash as part of a scheme to kill the speedster (*The Flash* [first series] #175, December 1967).

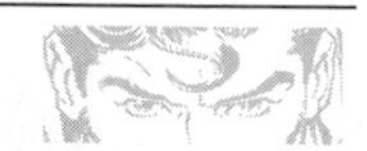

The megalomaniacal Lex Luthor has been a thorn in Superman's side since the Man of Steel appeared in Metropolis. The ruthless Luthor wants nothing less than the total destruction of his sworn enemy, Superman.

CLARK KENT IS SUPERMAN
I'M FREE NOW TO START THE CAMPAIGN THAT WILL BRING ABOUT A FINAL SHOWDOWN BATTLE BETWEEN SUPERMAN AND MYSELF! IT WON'T TAKE LONG TO DEVISE A BROADCASTER-INTERRUPTOR SUCH AS I'LL NEED!

Superman's greatest alien threat is Brainiac, the cold and calculating villain from the planet Colu. Time and time again the relentless Brainiac tries to destroy Superman and those he holds dear.

10¢
DC
JULY
NO. 242
ACTION COMICS
Featuring "The SUPER-DUEL IN SPACE!"
I DARE YOU TO CAPTURE ME, SUPERMAN! THE MOMENT YOU TOUCH MY ULTRA-FORCE SHIELD, EVEN YOUR INVULNERABLE BODY WILL BE DESTROYED!
IT'S THE GREATEST CHALLENGE OF MY LIFE. THIS SUPER-OUTLAW MAY BE BLUFFING-- BUT I CAN'T TAKE THAT CHANCE. HERE GOES!

DC
ALL NEW! 60¢
NO. 545
JULY
ACTION COMICS
THE OLD BRAINIAC HAD THE MEREST TOUCH OF HUMANITY!
THE NEW BRAINIAC HAS ELIMINATED THAT DEFECT!

Metallo's kryptonite heart makes him a constant threat to the Man of Steel's safety, but in the end, Superman always finds a way to defeat the cyborg.

The New God Darkseid continually locks horns with Superman when the villain tries to take over Earth and subjugate its people. Their never-ending battle still rages on, even after the devastating events of the Final Crisis.

General Samuel Lane's insidious Project 7734 resulted in the deaths of thousands of Kryptonians and a war between New Krypton and Earth. The cost of that war will haunt his daughter Lois and her husband, Superman, for years to come.

Krypton's greatest villains—General Zod, Ursa, and Non—break free of the Phantom Zone and arrive on Earth as part of a master plan to enslave the planet and gain revenge against Superman, the son of their jailer, Jor-El.

The savage Doomsday managed to seemingly kill the Man of Steel, but despite his brute strength and mindless determination, the monster ultimately proved no match for Superman.

The Cyborg Superman almost fooled the world into believing Superman was back from the dead, but when the truth was revealed, he became one of Superman's most dangerous foes.

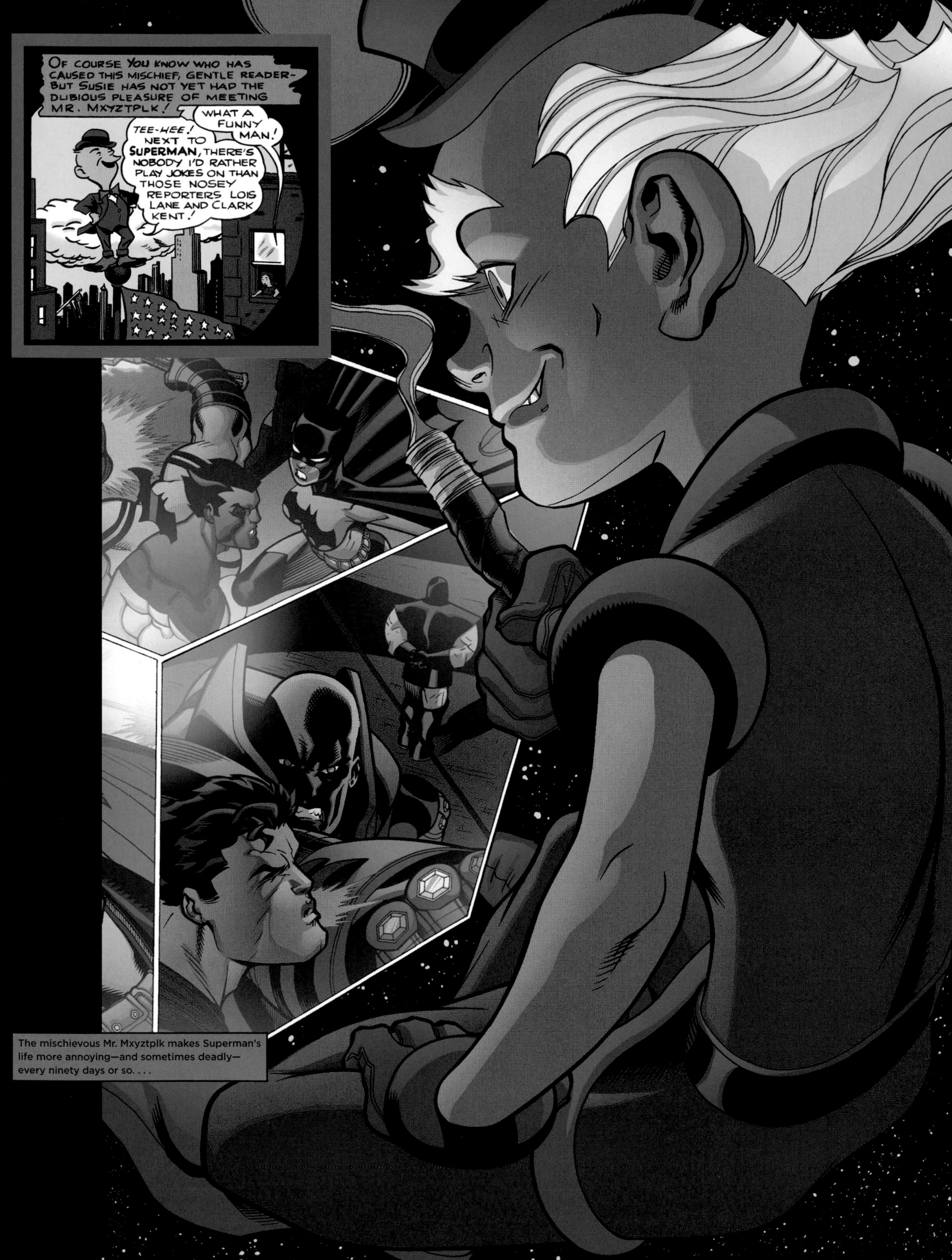

OF COURSE YOU KNOW WHO HAS CAUSED THIS MISCHIEF, GENTLE READER- BUT SUSIE HAS NOT YET HAD THE DUBIOUS PLEASURE OF MEETING MR. MXYZTPLK!
TEE-HEE! NEXT TO SUPERMAN, THERE'S NOBODY I'D RATHER PLAY JOKES ON THAN THOSE NOSEY REPORTERS LOIS LANE AND CLARK KENT!
WHAT A FUNNY MAN!

The mischievous Mr. Mxyztplk makes Superman's life more annoying—and sometimes deadly—every ninety days or so. . . .

The Silver Banshee is one of Superman's more . . . vocal adversaries. Whenever she's in town, even the Man of Steel's super-hearing is no match for her piercing shriek.

Mongul is a perpetual annoyance to the Man of Steel, but time and again he proves no match for Superman.

Bizarro am not Superman's sometime friend, and he am not Superman's sometime enemy. He am just Bizarro!

TERRY
DODSON
RACHEL

WE'RE FROM VENTURA, THE GAMBLERS' PLANET. WE'RE THE LAST OF A DYING RACE. WITH OUR SUPER-SCIENCE, WE HAVE NOTHING TO DO BUT ENJOY OURSELVES. BUT NOW ALL PASTIMES BORE US! ONLY GAMBLING IS EXCITING!
THIS WAS A FASCINATING WAGER! I BET I COULD MAKE YOU KILL SOMEONE AND I LOST!

Rokk and Sorban made repeated trips to Earth, going so far as to create duplicates of Jor-El and Lara, betting to see if Superman would actually kill his parents if they proved to be alive but incredibly evil. However, the Man of Steel saw through the ruse and ended the wager (*Action Comics* #582, August 1986).

Although Rokk and Sorban were never seen again, the planet Ventura survived the Crisis on Infinite Earths, with Plastic Man once having visited the world (*JLA: Heaven's Ladder,* 2000). Later, the planet was entangled in a crime that saw Batman dispatch Green Lantern and Supergirl there in search of evidence (*The Brave and the Bold* [third series] #1–3, April–June 2007).

ROKYN

A barren world orbiting a red dwarf star was chosen as the new home to the residents of Kandor after Superman kept his promise of finding a way to restore them to their proper size. The solar system was unique in that it phased between dimensions on a regular cycle, a fact that did not deter the Kryptonians from colonizing the world. They named it Rokyn, a Kryptonian word that came from *Ro,* the possessive form of Rao, plus *kyn,* meaning "gift." Thus, Rokyn was "Rao's gift," or "the gift of God" (*Krypton Chronicles* #1, September 1981).

In the Earth-1 reality, Rokyn still existed by the thirtieth century, referred to as a "new Krypton" in the chronicles of the Legion of Super-Heroes (*Adventure Comics* #356, May 1967). Rokyn also served as the new home for the Kandorians in another potential future (*Legion of Super-Heroes* [fifth series] #6, July 2005; *Supergirl and the Legion of Super-Heroes* #23–24, December 2006–January 2007).

In the history formed following the Infinite Crisis, the Kandorians settled on a world they called New Krypton (*Action Comics* #873, March 2009).

RONAL

A surgeon from a water world brought to Atlantis by Superman after his college sweetheart Lori Lemaris, fell ill and "the greatest surgeons in the universe" described her condition as a hopeless paralysis. Ronal managed what others could not and cured her, then remained on Earth to oversee her convalescence. Lori fell in love with her savior and convinced him to remain in Atlantis as her husband (*Superman* [first series] #135, February 1960). The

BUT THEN, REASON TRIUMPHS!
SUPERMAN, YOU DON'T LOVE ME! YOU ONLY THINK YOU DO! IT'S PITY YOU FEEL FOR ME, NOT LOVE! NOW PLEASE LET ME... KISS YOU... GOODBYE...

couple later became the parents of twins (*Superman's Girl Friend, Lois Lane* #55, February 1965).

It was Ronal who tried to talk Lori out of spreading their joy by executing a crazy scheme to force Superman to finally marry Lois Lane (*Superman* [first series] #138, July 1960). Nonetheless, the merman agreed to fake his death in another elaborate scheme, this time designed to make Lois believe Superman was marrying the widowed Lori, freeing her to accept millionaire Brett Rand's proposal (*Superman* [first series] #139, August 1960).

In the world after the Crisis on Infinite Earths, Ronal was no longer an alien but a resident of Tritonis, a city within the sunken country of Atlantis (*Superman* [second series] #12, December 1987). He and Lori fell in love and married after he saved her life, relying on a magical staff for much of the healing. Ronal did not realize that the staff's eldritch energy was also corrupting him, and he grew angry at Superman, who had dared to love Lori when he met her at college. Ronal used the staff to mutate sea life in cruel ways, and when his wife tried to stop him, he lashed out at her. The surgeon was arrested but later was freed and followed his wife to Metropolis, where she was temporarily staying with reporter Lois Lane. When he sought to regain his magic staff, they battled, and Superman shattered the gem atop the staff. The resulting burst of energy turned Ronal into a stone statue (*The Adventures of Superman* #532, February 1996).

RON-AVON

Hailing from the belligerent world of Belgor, teenager Ron-Avon was blackmailed to come to Earth and challenge Superboy to a competition. Augmented with his "power gauntlets," Ron-Avon outlined four feats but lost all four to the Teen of Steel. The planet's cruel dictators sentenced the teen to death, intending to drop him into a "crystal urn of death." Instead, he was saved by being wrapped in Superboy's indestructible cape; then together they defeated the rulers and rescued Ron-Avon's parents (*Superboy* [first series] #141, September 1967).

RONDORS

These large, docile animals from Krypton were known for their horns, which proved to have medicinal properties. By the time of Jor-El and Lara, Rondors were so close to extinction that the law protected them. That still did not stop cruel people from poaching the poor creatures and using their severed horns for their own profit. Quex-Ul was falsely accused of that very crime and found himself banished to the Phantom Zone (*Superman* [first series] #157, November 1952).

Nam-Ek also slaughtered several Rondors and created a potion to gain immortality (*Superman* [first series] #282, December 1974).

ROQUETTE, DR. SERLING

Sixteen-year-old prodigy Serling Roquette arrived at Project Cadmus during a massive restructuring operation initiated by Mickey Cannon. With her retro fashion sense and expressions of delight like "Quantum!," the genetics expert quickly brought a youthful enthusiasm to the facility. While interning, the teenager found herself captivated by the 1940s- and 1950s-era music that her older colleagues listened to, and soon found herself enamored with all manner of products from bygone days.

Inevitably, "Doc Rocket" found herself drawn to the clone of the Guardian, whose progenitor had fought crime in the 1940s (*Superboy* [third series] #56; *Superboy One Million*; *Superboy* [third series] #57—all October–December 1998). Unfortunately, Dabney Donovan—working under house arrest—noticed Roquette's crush and used it as a kind of blackmail against her (*Superboy* [third series] #65, August 1999). Meanwhile, Serling began to realize that the cloned Superboy was something of a kindred spirit in that neither of them had ever had a real childhood (*Superboy* [third series] #69, December 1999). The hint of a romance began to form between the two (*Superboy* [third series] #79, October 2000) but Superboy, still processing the recent death of Tana Moon, decided to pull back (*Superboy* [third series] #82, January 2001).

When the Lex Luthor administration attempted to take control of the genetics project, Serling was among those who rebelled and helped take Cadmus underground (*Superboy* [third series] #88, July 2001).

As Cadmus's genetics head, Roquette later led a study to determine the cause of the strange transformations that Jimmy Olsen was enduring (*Countdown to Final Crisis* #32–30, September 19–October 3, 2007) and also served as a consultant to Oracle (*Birds of Prey* [first series] #114, March 2008).

RORC

Rorc was a creature that served Cerberus, sent into battle against Superman when its master was hired by the country of Tattamalia to attack LexCorp in Metropolis (*Superman: The Man of Steel* #1, July 1990).

ROSS, ALEXANDER

Living at 344 Clinton Street in Metropolis, this dilettantish and overzealous correspondence-school sleuth was a neighbor to Clark Kent. He wondered about the reporter's odd schedule and concluded that Kent was actually a criminal disguised as a journalist. Rather than endure further scrutiny that just might have compromised his secret identity, Kent confided in Ross that his schedule was unusual given his work with Superman (*Superman* [first series] #112, March 1957).

ROSS, CHECKS

The Blackout Bandits, a gang of ruthless criminals and "masters of electrical sabotage," was led by Checks Ross. They were blacking out business establishments they intended to rob by tampering with the city's electrical grid, then striking without warning. The Blackout Bandits were eventually apprehended by Superman (*Action Comics* #147, August 1950).

ROSS, CLARK PETER

The son of Lana Lang and Pete Ross, named after Clark Kent, their childhood friend from Smallville. Young Clark was born prematurely, resulting in complications; he almost lost his life until Superman intervened to rush him to the proper hospital. Brainiac interfered, intending to use the infant's body as an incubator to grow a new Doomsday, but was defeated by the Man of Steel (*Superman: The Doomsday Wars* #1–3, 1998). After his parents divorced, Pete took custody of Clark, raising him in Smallville.

ROSS, JONATHAN

On Earth-1, Jonathan was the son of Pete Ross, Clark Kent's childhood friend from Smallville (*Action Comics* #457, March 1976). When Superman first met the boy, he was dying, less from physical issues—which had successfully been treated—than from psychological ones that left him without the will to live. Because the boy was fascinated by Superman and his secrets, Pete suggested that revealing his secret identity might provide the spark that would save Jon's life. The plan was successful, but Jonathan initially rejected the Man of Steel's revelation, pointing out the numerous occasions that the hero had successfully refuted accusations of being Clark Kent. Ultimately, it was the absence of shaving essentials in Clark's bathroom cabinet that convinced Jonathan that Clark *was* Superman.

As a result, Jon became a regular visitor to Metropolis, going so far as to assist the Man of Steel in several adventures. He successfully tricked Mr. Mxyzptlk into returning to Zrfff in one instance (*Action Comics* #460, June 1976) and even tasted superpowers when the Parasite temporarily transferred the abilities to the boy (*Superman* [first series] #304, October 1976).

After the Crisis on Infinite Earths, Jon Ross ceased to exist, replaced by Clark Ross.

ROSS, PETER

Growing up in Smallville, Pete Ross became best friends with Clark Kent (*Superboy* [first series] #86, January 1961). On Earth-1, during a camping trip, Pete was awakened during a lightning storm and, in a flash of light, watched his pal change into Superboy. He kept the secret to himself, never telling Clark that he knew the truth. Pete spent his high school career covertly helping Clark maintain his dual identities, with Clark none the wiser (*Superboy* [first series] #90, July 1961).

Noting that Superboy often used robot stand-ins, Pete once reasoned that there was no reason why he couldn't secretly do the same, and he created a red, blue, and yellow costume of his own. With a black wig and makeup to mask his freckles, he impersonated the Boy of Steel on occasion (*Superboy* [first series] #90, July 1961; others), using a variety of tricks to mimic superpowers. Indeed, when Clark had temporarily forgotten his alter ego (*Superboy* [first series] #94, January 1962) or lost his powers, Pete stepped in to fill the void. In once instance, after a glimpse of the future gave the false impression that Superboy's death was imminent, Pete nobly attempted to take over for the Boy of Steel so that he would die in Clark's place (*Superboy* [first series] #96, April 1962).

During a visit to the twentieth century, prospective Legion of Super-Heroes member Ultra Boy tumbled on to Pete's secret. Impressed by the teenager's loyalty, the Legion's senior adviser Marla Latham essentially declared the boy an honorary Legionnaire on the spot (*Superboy* [first series] #98, July 1962). Shortly thereafter, Pete accidentally damaged a Superboy Robot meant to patrol Smallville while the real Boy of Steel was away. The resourceful teen managed to successfully impersonate Superboy for a time before Ultra Boy finally appeared to relieve the young man by repairing the robot. The Legion had been monitoring the situation from the start, but Ultra Boy had assured the team that Pete was up to the challenge (*Superboy* [first series] #100, October 1962).

Though unaware of Pete's role as his secret guardian, Superboy nonetheless recognized his inherent nobility and heroism. Seeking a contingency plan should his enemies ever kill him, the Boy of Steel faked his death and arranged for Pete—empowered by a serum that temporarily endowed him with superpowers—to replace him. Unaware that Pete knew his secret identity, Clark Kent continued on as normal. Though puzzled by that detail, the new Superboy nonetheless proved an able replacement, and the genuine article told him as much when the test was over (*Superboy* [first series] #106, July 1963).

NO TIME FOR THE OLD GAMES NOW, MRS. KENT.
I'VE KNOWN FOR SOME TIME NOW THAT CLARK IS SUPERBOY, BUT I SWORE TO MYSELF TO KEEP THAT KNOWLEDGE SECRET!

When Superboy, Mon-El, Shadow Lass, and Duo Damsel erased their memories to hide in Smallville from Mordru the Merciless, it was Pete who helped them regain these memories thanks to his secret knowledge. When the mission ended, Mon-El, knowing that in the future his knowledge would one day save Superman's life, hypnotized Superboy into forgetting Pete knew his true identity (*Adventure Comics* #369–370, June–July 1968).

After Pete's father declared bankruptcy, the Ross family was forced to leave Smallville for a time. They found refuge in Hungry Hill, an artisans' community whose residents fell back on old skills. Pete's mother, for instance, had "developed a girlhood hobby into [a] hand-weaving business" to make ends meet (*Superboy* [first series] #179, November 1971). Pete eventually found himself back in Smallville, where his mother ran the Ross Boarding House (*Superboy* [first series] #193, February 1973).

While attending Raleigh College (*Superman's Girl Friend, Lois Lane* #55, February 1965), Pete met and married a woman named Susan (*Superman: The Secret Years* #3, April 1985), soon becoming the parents of a son, Jonathan Ross (*Action Comics* #457, March 1976). Susan Ross's fate went unrecorded.

Pete went on to become a successful geologist (*Action Comics* #309, February 1964), using his influence at one point to divert a new highway from Clark Kent's former home in Smallville when he realized his old friend was sentimental about the place (*Superman* [first series] #270, December 1973).

Later, Jonathan Ross was abducted by inhabitants from the planet Nyrvn to be trained as a soldier to fight in their perpetual war. Desperate to save his son, Pete revealed to Clark that he knew his true identity and begged for his help. Superman was prevented from rescuing the boy when his allies Saturn Girl, Lightning Lad, Sun Boy, and Dawnstar from the Legion traveled back in time to stop him. According to historical records in the thirtieth century, Jon Ross was expected to play a pivotal role in a coming interstellar war (*DC Comics Presents* #13, September 1979).

Pete rejected the information, temporarily losing his grip on reality and going so far as to steal technology from Lex Luthor that allowed him to bring Superboy from the past, then switch minds with the confused hero. As the Teen of Steel, Pete abducted Jimmy Olsen, Lois Lane, Perry White, Lana Lang, and Steve Lombard to help him convince the Man of Steel that his refusal was wrong. Krypto's timely arrival spoiled Pete's plan; the mind-swap was undone, and Superboy sent home. Pete entered a mental institution for his own safety (*DC Comics Presents* #14, October 1979). The two old friends ultimately reconciled when Superman ignored the Legion's counsel and returned Jon to Earth (*DC Comics Presents* #25, September 1980).

Even after history was altered by the Crisis on Infinite Earths, there remained a Pete Ross who knew of Superboy's secret, a version who lived in a Pocket Universe formed by the Time Trapper.

When Superman and the Legion learned of the other realm, Pete played a pivotal part in the events prior to Superboy's death (*Legion of Super-Heroes* [third series] #37, and *Superman* [second series] #8—both August 1987). He later died at the hands of the Phantom Zone villains when they ran amok, killing all life on the world.

In the mainstream post-Crisis reality, Clark Kent did not don his cape until adulthood but was still friends with Pete and Lana. The closeness of the group even earned them the nickname the "Three Musketeers" (*The Adventures of Superman* #469, August 1990). There was always an undercurrent of a romantic triangle between the three, but Pete held back, recognizing that Lana's affection toward Clark was stronger.

Peter Joseph Ross (full name revealed in *The Adventures of Superman* #673, January 1992), as Clark would later say, was "one of my oldest friends, and the nicest guy you'll ever meet. Real knack for solving problems and helping people. Wouldn't be surprised if he ended up *mayor* here one day . . ." (*Batman & Superman: World's Finest* #7, October 1999).

The three went their separate ways after graduating from high school. Pete joined the Peace Corps (*Action Comics* #850, Late July 2007), attended law school, and returned home to work as a county agent (*The Adventures of Superman* #436, January 1988). When local Oto Indians kidnapped Pete for publicity in a mining dispute, it set into motion events that led Superman to get involved, letting Pete meet the super hero for the first time (*Superman* [second series] #45, July 1990). After learning that Clark Kent was now in a serious relationship with Lois Lane, Pete awkwardly asked his old friend if he'd mind if he began dating Lana (*Superman* [second series] #49, November 1990).

His work in Kansas brought him an invitation to work for Senator Barton Caldwell as "staff member in charge of agricultural affairs," and he relocated to Washington, DC (*Superman* [second series] #57, and *Action Comics* #661—both July 1991). Lana followed him to the East, and the two finally became engaged (*Action Comics* #673, January 1992).

Soon after, the radical Sons of Liberty murdered Senator Caldwell (*The Adventures of Superman* #487, February 1992) and took drastic measures to force Pete, as Caldwell's successor, to capitulate. Kidnapping Lana, the group forced Pete to carry a gun into the Intelligence Committee with the intent of murdering Major Holcraft before he could testify against the Sons of Liberty. Pete managed to get the gun into the proceedings but couldn't go through with the killing. Instead, a plainclothes Ben (Agent Liberty) Lockwood grabbed the senator's gun and killed Holcraft. Taken into custody, Pete maintained his silence with Lana's life still in jeopardy. Agent Liberty belatedly began to comprehend the nature of the Sons of Liberty and executed its two leaders even as Superman rescued Lana. Reunited with his fiancée, Pete finally went public with the horrors they'd endured and resigned his Senate seat (*Superman: The Man of Steel* #13; *Superman* [second series] #69; *The Adventures of Superman* #492; *Action Comics* #679—all July 1992).

Pete and Lana were finally married in the home of Jonathan and Martha Kent even as a conspicuously absent Clark desperately tried to contend with the Lex Luthor–generated near-destruction of Metropolis (*Action Comics* #700, June 1994). Pete later served as an usher at Clark and Lois's wedding (*Superman: The Wedding Album* #1, December 1996).

A short while later, Lana gave birth to a son, whom they named Clark Ross. He developed a serious illness, and while Superman tried to help, the baby was kidnapped by Doomsday at the point when Brainiac took control of the creature's body (*Superman: The Doomsday Wars* #1–3, 1998). Thinking Superman powerless to help, a crazed Pete tried to rescue the infant himself. In the end, the child was saved and cured, but the incident brought Pete's frustrations over his wife's relationship with Clark Kent back to the surface.

Pete was blindsided when Lex Luthor invited him to run as a vice presidential candidate, but he eventually accepted (*Superman* [second series] #162, November 2000). He was even more surprised to see the ticket elected, and he returned to Washington—only to watch Lex slowly descend into madness, abusing the powers of the Oval Office to try to destroy Superman once and for all. At the same time, he and Lana began to drift apart, leading to their eventual divorce, with Lana taking custody of Clark (*Action Comics* #806, October 2003). During this period, Manchester Black informed Luthor that Superman was actually Clark Kent, a fact the president shared with Pete (*The Adventures of Superman* #637, April 2005).

Pete's decision to serve as Luthor's vice president was retroactively revealed to have been a payback of sorts. In Smallville, the teenage Pete's dying father had been bumped to the top of a transplant list thanks to the influence of young Lex Luthor, who'd been impressed by Mr. Ross's willingness to speak to him when most others in the community would not (*Superman Secret Files & Origins 2004,* August 2004).

Luthor abandoned his office and Pete temporarily served as president of the United States, ultimately pressured by Checkmate into resigning to clear the decks (*Superman Secret Files & Origins 2004,* August 2004). He later confided in Clark that he now possessed knowledge of his secret (*The Adventures of Superman* #641, August 2005).

When Superman was attacked by a villain named Ruin who had a particular vendetta against him, it seemed logical when he unmasked him as Pete Ross (*The Adventures of Superman* #640, July 2005). In fact, Pete had been framed by the true Ruin, who was actually the insane Professor Emil Hamilton, and was cleared when Hamilton was eventually exposed (*The Adventures of Superman* #646–647, January–February 2006). He returned to Smallville, taking young Clark with him (*Superman* #655, October 2006). Pete then kept his distance from Lana and Clark, surfacing briefly to attend the funeral of Jonathan Kent (*Superman: New Krypton Special* #1, December 2008). The former vice president has eschewed exploiting his fame and has resumed work at a Smallville general store while raising his son (*Blackest Night: Superman* #1, October 2009).

In other realities, Pete Ross was seen as a pal to Superman, although on Earth-30 he was Pyotr Roslov, illegitimate son of Joseph Stalin and head of the KGB. He executed Thomas and Martha Wayne, anti-Communist protesters, launching their son, Bruce Wayne, on a path as Batman, who vowed to overthrow the Communist Party of the

Soviet Union (*Superman: Red Son*, #1–3, June–August 2003).

On Earth-175, Pete was unaware of Clark Kent's alter ego and was jealous of Superman's fame and his allure to Lana Lang. Pete eventually married Lana on the rebound, only to reveal himself to be an underworld chieftain who ultimately died in an attempt on the Man of Steel that was thwarted by a fatally wounded Lex (Luthor) Kent (*Superman* [first series] #175, February 1965).

The fate of the Earth-423 Pete Ross was similarly tragic. Tortured by the Toyman and the Prankster until he finally revealed Superman's secret identity, he was then murdered and stuffed in a toy chest for the Man of Steel to find (*Superman* [first series] #423, October 1986).

Before Pete's ascension to the White House, one potential future posited a world where he ran for president. Here, an assassination attempt nearly killed Ross and exposed Clark as Superman on live TV, beginning a chain of events that ultimately put the Man of Steel in the Oval Office (*Action Comics Annual* #3, 1991).

ROUGH HOUSE

A man named either Palmiotti or Hoffman operated under the code name Rough House and worked in the employ of Intergang. Under the direction of the manic genetic manipulator Dabney Donovan, several of Metropolis's greatest gangsters were resurrected on behalf of Boss Moxie, their clones programmed with special attributes. Among them was Rough House, a tall but disarming man whose glasses and sweet smile belied his genetically enhanced super-strength (*The Adventures of Superman* #544, March 1997).

While the more powerful Intergang was a force to be reckoned with, it was also exposed to the glare of the media spotlight thanks to reporting by the *Daily Planet*'s Lois Lane. Upset by the coverage, Moxie dispatched Rough House and Torcher to silence her, with her apartment being burned to produce maximum smoke and minimum flame (*The Adventures of Superman* #549, August 1997).

Rough House was ultimately captured by Superman (*Action Comics* #758, October 1999), although another enforcer bearing his name has since come into Intergang's employ (*52* #3, May 24, 2006).

ROUND TABLE CLUB, THE

An English club in existence for a thousand years for the descendants of famous medieval knights. Its members attempted to maintain their ancestors' chivalric traditions, including the wearing of armor and the holding of jousting tournaments.

When a prehistoric creature "trapped in an iceberg and released by a freak thaw" was spotted in the countryside, the Round Table Club swung into action, forming an expedition to find this "fire-breathing dragon." Instead of the knights battling the confused creature, Superman arrived and tried to contain it, as they struggled from the country into London itself. The polluted atmosphere and other changed conditions led to the creature collapsing and dying (*Superman* [first series] #86, January 1954).

ROVOS

Created by a disembodied race known as the Dyrlians, Rovos was a new life-form designed to allow the Dyrlians to experience emotions, something they had lost with their corporeal forms. The beings generated facsimiles of the Galactic Golem and the Parasite so that Superman could battle them, generating emotions that the youth could study and savor. Superman and Supergirl endured the battle, slowly coming to realize what was happening and accepting the natural progression in the child's development (*Action Comics* #502, December 1979).

ROVO THE MIGHTY DOG

Mighty Boy's superpowered pet, who aided the hero in his fight against crime on their native world of Zumoor (*Superboy* [first series] #85, December 1960).

ROWLAND, HUGH

The *Golden Star*, last of the glamorous old-time showboats, featured an acting troupe including Hugh Rowland. The thespian also secretly owned the showboat's mortgage, which was coming due. Intent on foreclosure so he could seize the boat and turn it into a modern-day floating nightspot, Rowland tried to sabotage the ship, thereby preventing the theatrical performances that generated much-needed revenue. The plan was exposed and Rowland brought to justice by Superman (*Superman* [first series] #45, March–April 1947).

ROWSE, ED

Clark Kent gave the testimony that convinced jurors to find criminal Ed Rowse guilty, and the vengeful man harbored thoughts of revenge. When he managed to escape his jail, Rowse plotted to corral Kent, three prosecution witnesses, and the judge in the ghost town of Boneville. He managed to bring them to the deserted town but was stopped by Superman before he could murder any of them (*Superman* [first series] #104, March 1956).

ROXAR

Superman and Lex Luthor once journeyed to the homeworld of the Automs, a race of highly intelligent, civilized robots (*Action Comics* #292, September 1962, and #294, November 1962). The Man of Steel found himself in the unique position of defending his nemesis in a murder trial there when Luthor was accused of killing a robot. Although Superman was successfully in vindicating his archenemy, he left Luthor there rather than have him return to Earth and resume his criminal activities. Working his way into the Automs' confidence, Luthor eventually acquired enough privileges and tools to enable him to escape Roxar with three converted androids in tow.

ROYAL FLUSH GANG, THE

The Royal Flush Gang underwent many incarnations, but the band of criminals always built themselves around the theme of a deck of playing cards. The team was first formed by Professor Amos Fortune, who outfitted them with a series of high-tech gadgets and weapons to enable them to better commit crimes (*Justice League of America* [first series] #43, October 1966). Members used a black spade as their insignia, and usually numbered five—King, Queen, Jack, Ace, and Ten—although that has altered through the years.

Fortune assumed the role of Ace on the first team, which featured his childhood friends, all of whom grew to become career criminals. They avoided jail and regrouped, soon taking on the Justice League of America on numerous occasions. As one would imagine, the Gang also crossed paths with the Clown Prince of Crime when the Joker once thwarted their attempts to steal a hidden treasure (*The Joker* #5, January–February 1976).

A second incarnation of the Gang (*Justice League of America* [first series] #203–205, June–August 1982) later found themselves manipulated by the Gambler into doing his dirty work. They were eventually confronted by the Teen Titans, who easily defeated them despite the Gang's upgraded gear at the time (*The New Titans* #68–69, July–August 1990).

The third Royal Flush Gang was a global operation with cells located in every major city in America. Each "cell" had fifty-two members, split into four suits run by the "court cards." Each member had a value, and the leadership rewarded or demoted people based on their success or failure (*Superman: The Man of Steel* #121, February 2002). The Justice Society of America's Stargirl once said her father worked for the Gang as a "Two" (*JSA All-Stars* #4, October 2003).

One possibly apocryphal account depicted an early encounter between Superman and the first Royal Flush Gang, wherein they tried out their weapons, powered by his luck-altering "stellaration" technology (*Superman Confidential* #1, January 2007).

Fortune re-formed the Gang anew, rewarding top performers with high ranks. Now calling him-

self Wild Card, Fortune indicated that there were fifty-two members of this new RFG; each suit was thirteen members strong, outfitted to resemble the playing cards (*Justice League of America* [second series] #35, October 2009).

ROZ-EM

Kryptonian Roz-Em once impersonated Jor-El's twin brother Nim-El in a failed attempt to steal weaponry. He was punished by being placed into suspended animation aboard a spaceship. Eventually, Roz-Em managed to escape and found Earth, where he sought revenge by convincing Clark Kent and his foster parents that he was a red-kryptonite-induced adult version of the Teen of Steel.

Superboy came to agree that Earth should not house two Kal-Els, so he bravely left the planet. Soon after, Jonathan Kent discovered the truth and sent Krypto the Super-Dog to retrieve the hero. Back on Earth, he subdued Roz-Em and sent him to the Phantom Zone (*Adventure Comics* #304, January 1963).

RUIN

At first, Superman had no idea who Ruin was or why he was targeting his loved ones, but he did recognize that the man was a well-equipped menace. The weaponry at his disposal was cutting-edge technology, indicating that he was well funded and intelligent, but his ravings about Superman sucking Earth's sun dry, thereby accelerating its natural death, made the man sound insane. It was clear Ruin had it out for Superman for his own reasons. Their first meeting occurred at S.T.A.R. Labs' Metropolis facility, where Ruin and Replikon were stealing gear, and Ruin used a weapon that seemed able to weaken the Man of Steel (*The Adventures of Superman* #630, September 2004).

During their second battle, Ruin was captured and turned over to the Metropolis S.C.U. En route to Stryker's Island Penitentiary, Scott Laughlin questioned Ruin only to be killed, thereby allowing Ruin to escape custody (*The Adventures of Superman* #631–632, October–November 2004). The villain next took possession of twins Alex and Alexandra Allston, turning them into versions of the Parasite and unleashing them against Superman and those he loved. While Superman hunted Ruin, the Parasite twins knocked on Lois Lane's door. Their attack was interrupted by the arrival of Mr. Mxyzptlk, who inadvertently told them Superman's secret identity. Soon after, wearing Steel's armor for protection, Superman found the twins, and as they lost their energy they finally revealed the location of Ruin's hideout (*The Adventures of Superman* #633–635, December 2004–February 2005).

When Superman burst in, he was immediately bathed in the radiation equivalent to a red sun, thereby sapping his strength. Ruin explained that he intended to murder everyone Superman loved, and then vanished. After freeing himself, Superman met with Batman and Wonder Woman in the Fortress of Solitude, seeking their help. While the Amazon Princess advocated killing Ruin as perhaps the only conclusive method, Batman deduced that the villain was in league with Lex Luthor (*The Adventures of Superman* #636, March 2005).

Ruin next turned up at the S.C.U's Shack, where he injured Jimmy Olsen, then attacked the police officers until Superman arrived. The Man of Steel nearly managed to unmask his foe—but Ruin vanished. When he was finally captured, Ruin was revealed to be Pete Ross, the former president of the United States and Clark Kent's childhood friend. He was imprisoned, and Superman was determined to learn the truth behind this seeming betrayal (*The Adventures of Superman* #637, April 2005, and #640, July 2005).

In the end, Ruin was revealed to be Professor Emil Hamilton, now quite insane, and Superman had to save Pete, his ex-wife Lana Lang, and their son Clark Ross before they were killed. Superman then cleared Pete's name. Hamilton remained at large (*The Adventures of Superman* #646–647, January–February 2006).

Ruin was last seen as one of the villains working in Alexander Luthor Junior's Secret Society of Super-Villains.

RUNYAN, PROFESSOR ADOLPHUS

Professor Adolphus Runyan was a genius who invented a "gas so powerful that it is capable of penetrating any type of gas-mask." The experiment killed the international racketeer Ambrose while it was being demonstrated to *Daily Planet* reporter Clark Kent. Runyan was subsequently killed by Ambrose's accomplice Bartow, who wanted the gas for his own sinister purposes (*Superman* [first series] #2, Fall 1939).

RUTHVEN

Lord Ruthven was a vampire whose life was immortalized in the 1819 short story "The Vampyre," by Dr. John William Polidori. His tale of seduction and murder helped popularize the vampire in nineteenth-century literature. Baron Ruthven was real, however, and was able to operate openly at Metropolis General as Dr. Ruthven, his features and white skin hidden beneath a mask of "techno-flesh, a self-regenerating veil of living tissue." Though hunted by the Jimmy Olsen-and-Robin team, the vampire successfully put his fangs into dozens of Metropolis citizens, notably Lucy Lane and Superman.

Furious that the Man of Steel might become undead and thus prevent her from ever stealing his soul, the demoness Blaze unleashed a burst of earthly hellfire with such solar intensity, it cured all of Ruthven's victims and forced the vampire himself to incubate in the body of the rock star known as Babe (*Superman: The Man of Steel* #13–14, July–August 1992, and #40–42, January–March 1995; *Superman* [second series] #70, August 1992). A magician called the Lock, who was "a living corridor between this dimension and one . . . beyond," was later able to purge Ruthven from Babe and banish him to this other realm (*Superman: The Man of Steel* #41–42, February–March 1995).

RUTLEDGE, HENRY

This famous movie director called the Man of Steel his friend. In fact, Superman happened to be visiting the set of *The Rains of Karumonga* when strange occurrences began to match whatever the super hero happened to be saying. It turned out to be the latest prank played on the hero by Mr. Mxyzptlk. This time, Superman removed the curse by saying his own Kryptonian name (Kal-El) backward (*Superman* [first series] #171, August 1964).

RYDER, JACK

The crusading journalist who was also the bizarre crime fighter known as the Creeper.

RYDER, MATTHEW

Saved from a near-death experience, Matthew Ryder grew up to join the Linear Men as Waverider. In a different time line, Matthew Ryder also worked with the Linear Men alongside Waverider.

RZALIN

Superman once brought a tree from an alien world to Metropolis without realizing that this tree was actually a sentient life-form named Rzalin. After Rzalin took root in the park, he began to absorb the thoughts of both Lois Lane and the Man of Steel, an act that triggered an unexpected evolution: Thanks to the mental workings and the alien soil, Rzalin became able to transmit illusions. These changes and new experiences were too much for the unintended alien visitor, and Rzalin died from the trauma (*Superman's Girl Friend, Lois Lane* #112, August 1971).

PLANET

SACKETT, "BUCK"

Some time after winning his fourth term as Metropolis's mayor (*Superman* [second series] #63, January 1992), Frank Berkowitz was assassinated (*Superman* [second series] #131, January 1998) on orders from Lex Luthor. Berkowitz was succeeded by Luthor's handpicked puppet "Buck" Sackett (*The Adventures of Superman* #554, January 1998).

Under orders, Sackett's first initiative was to create Hypersector, billed as a high-tech "City of the Future" within Metropolis—a project Berkowitz had opposed.

Beyond that, Sackett's tenure in office was undistinguished and short-lived.

SAGDORF

In the months before World War II engulfed America, the villain known as Sagdorf had overseen the construction of a secret base located in a secluded valley. The facility was equipped with a munitions plant, a fleet of bomber aircraft, and well-disciplined troops, forming a "subversive army that can strike terror and destruction from the rear when the military forces of the U.S. are attempting to defend the coast against foreign invasion!" When the Man of Steel became aware of the danger, he demolished the secret army base, destroying its entire store of aircraft and munitions. The army and its monocled leader met their doom when an enemy artillery shell fired at Superman slammed into the munitions plant, detonating and wiping out the enemies of the state (*Superman* [first series] #8, January–February 1941).

SALITAR

Salitar was a populated world that was struck by a significantly sized asteroid that was once the planet Krypton. While all life was obliterated in the cosmic cataclysm, there was one survivor, Rinol-Jag, an astronaut who was en route to their moon when the accident occurred. He remained a refugee until he was rescued by the space pirate Amalak (*Superman* [first series] #195, April 1967).

SALKOR

As Superman grieved over the death of the Earth-1 Supergirl during the Crisis on Infinite Earths, the alien Salkor approached him in the Fortress of Solitude. He explained that he was a champion from Makkor, in addition to being the Maid of Steel's husband. His story told of finding the heroine unconscious in space after she had inadvertently collided with a kryptonite meteor. As he nursed her back to health, she had temporary amnesia, so neither she nor Salkor knew her true identity. He named her Jasma; over time, they fell in love and married before they protected Makkor from the invading Naxx. Eventually, her memories returned, supplanting her new persona, and she traveled back to Earth. It wasn't until a recent battle with Blackstarr that she recalled her time with Salkor. When she died, a special signal alerted Salkor, who came to Earth to pay his final respects (*Superman* [first series] #415, January 1986).

SAMSON

A legendary Nazarite who was gifted with extraordinary strength. Samson encountered the redheaded Jimmy Olsen, who had traveled back in time to meet the man. Jimmy was convinced that in a previous life, Samson was his crime-fighting partner and "staunch friend." While in ancient Egypt, "Jhimmie" wrote for *The Daily Hieroglyph* and used a horn to signal when he needed Sam-

son's assistance in tracking the thief Pyramid Petrus. In time, though, Jimmy came to realize that his memories had been planted hypnotically by the con artist Swami Rama (*Superman's Pal, Jimmy Olsen* #16, October 1956).

In one of Jimmy's more improbable adventures, he was kidnapped from the twentieth century by a criminal who stole one of the Legion of Super-Heroes' Time-Bubbles and left the thirtieth century. Together they journeyed to the time of 1000 BC, where the cub reporter was rescued by a superpowered teen named Mighty Youth. Before returning to his own era, Jimmy learned that the boy was actually a younger version of the legendary Samson (*Superman's Pal, Jimmy Olsen* #79, September 1964).

As an adult, Samson gained renown as a hero in his own right and adopted the secret identity of a court jester named Merrio. At one point, he and Hercules were sent to the future by the mystic Seer to recruit Superboy in their conflict with

the villainous King Zarl (*Adventure Comics* #257, February 1959). Apparently transported to the same era, Lois Lane later fell in love with Samson, deduced his Merrio alter ego, and accepted his marriage proposal before being pulled back to the present (*Superman's Girl Friend, Lois Lane* #19, August 1960).

An apocryphal tale had Superman travel back in time to encounter Hercules and Samson, bringing both to the twentieth century, imagining that the legendary figures would make perfect husbands for Lois Lane and Lana Lang. In time, the heroes realized that modern-day women were not to their taste and asked to be returned to their home era (*Action Comics* #279, August 1961).

The adult incarnation of Lightning-Man from the Legion of Super-Heroes once posed as Samson as a favor to the Man of Steel to help uncover where Duke Marple had placed his stolen property (*Superman* [first series] #155, August 1962).

An entirely different person using the Samson name battled the first Sandman (*Adventure Comics* #84, March 1943).

SAN CALUMA

A small South American country whose populace was left in miserable circumstances when the nation was ravaged by earthquake and tornado. A relief effort was swiftly mounted in the United States, with boatloads of supplies sent to the stricken country. The mysterious mastermind Mumsen was determined to sabotage the relief effort, intending to twist San Caluma's misfortune into an opportunity to become its dictator. Superman ensured that the relief supplies reached San Caluma on schedule, however, and the would-be ruler was killed when he deliberately detonated an explosion designed to kill both himself and the Man of Steel (*Superman* [first series] #6, September 1940).

SAND, CARL

This noted criminologist angered the populace when he declared that "there is not a single completely honest man in all Metropolis," only to be proven wrong by Superman and Lois Lane. After an admittedly long search, they located a completely honest citizen: studio photographer Sam Nichols (*Action Comics* #114, November 1947).

SANDOR SANDOR

After he browbeat an actor to provoke an attack by hoodlums on the Metropolis waterfront in the name of verisimilitude, this reckless movie writer, director, and producer was taught a lesson by the Man of Steel (*Superman* [first series] #69, March-April 1951).

SAND SUPERMAN, THE

Quarrm was a dimensional realm accessed when an energy rift opened in the wake of the freak chain reaction that altered all kryptonite on Earth to resemble iron. When the dimension touched Earth's plane of existence, a burst of energy created a Superman-shaped sand creature that slowly sapped the Man of Steel's powers. This Sand Superman plagued the hero for a period of time (*Superman* [first series] #233, January 1971).

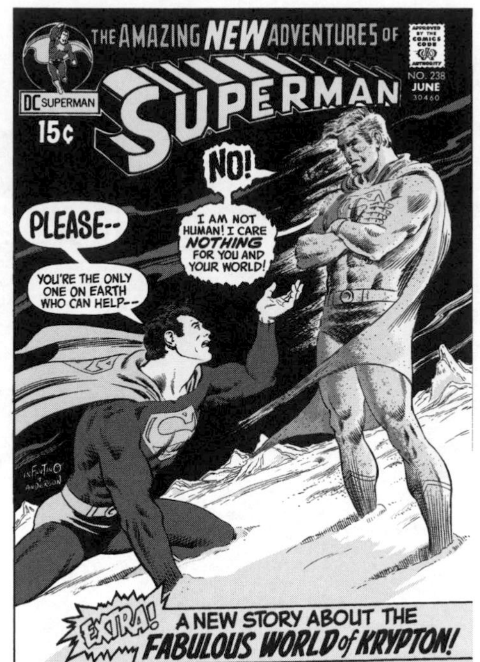

Superman encountered the sand creature from Quarrm in the world after the Crisis on Infinite Earths. In this instance, the Man of Steel allowed the entity to believe that it had actually claimed his life, triggering its moral code and prompting the sandy duplicate to destroy itself (*Superman Special* #1, 1992).

SAN MONTÉ

A small South American republic where a war was raging. Assigned to cover the war, Clark Kent saw the injustice being handed the citizens, so he switched to his Superman persona and ended the fighting by abducting the commanders of the two opposing armies and threatening to beat them senseless unless they agreed to settle the war by fighting it out between themselves. Neither man wished to do that, and they came to the realization they had no idea what they were fighting over. A Washington lobbyist for munitions magnate Emil Norvell was found to have ignited the conflict, leading the Man of Steel to confront Norvell (*Action Comics* #1–2, June–July 1938).

SANTA CLAUS

A right jolly old elf, Santa Claus had several encounters with Earth's modern-day meta-human champions of justice. The first recorded such instance saw Superman rescue St. Nick after the bitter Jasper Rasper tried to ruin the season by incapacitating both Santa and his reindeer (*Action Comics* #105, February 1947).

Superman and Kris Kringle also combined to protect the children from one of the Toyman's deadly schemes (*DC Comics Presents* #67, March 1984).

Across the multiverse, Santa Claus encountered Captain Marvel (*Shazam!* #11, March 1974), the Spectre (*The Spectre* [fourth series] #11–12, January–February 2002), and the Justice League of America (*JLA* #60, January 2002). He has even dared to enter the House of Mystery (*House of Mystery* #191, March–April 1971, and #257, March–April 1978).

SAPHIRE, HARRY "KING"

Forced into hiding under a lead mask, this Metropolis crime czar adopted the alias the Mask in an attempt to ruin Superman's reputation. The Mask created circumstances leading the Man of Steel into impersonating Saphire then exposed him to the public, letting them conclude the criminal and the hero were one and the same. Soon after, the real Saphire was apprehended by Superman (*World's Finest Comics* #66, September–October 1953).

SAPOLLO

Sapollo was created to appear in a movie filmed by Bizarro on Htrae. The Neanderthal-like being was snatched from another planet and exposed to the "imperfect duplicator ray machine." His replica turned out to be a handsome, polite, and blond-haired young man—the perfect monster for the film. Bizarro Lois agreed to star opposite Sapollo after Bizarro Lana and Bizarro Lucy refused the part. She fell for her unique costar, but audiences found him so hideous that they could not watch the finished feature. Sapollo sought refuge from the mobs in Bizarro Number One's "desert sanctum," where he was rescued by Mr. Bizarro Kltpzyxm, a version of Mr. Mxyzptlk. Sapollo was magically merged with his template. The new lifeform rampaged throughout the Bizarro world, to the delight of the people, who thanked Bizarro for blessing them with a "good neighbor" (*Adventure Comics* #292, January 1962).

SARNA

A "deadly saboteur," the daughter of Kandor's Dev-Re was a member of a "group of young radicals who used violence." When Superman and Jimmy Olsen visited the bottle city, they became Nightwing and Flamebird to find Sarna and end the carnage that was spoiling life in the city. Complicating the mission was the outbreak of an epidemic accidentally brought to the city when Superman left the Fortress of Solitude. The disease took Nightwing out of the action, so Flamebird found Sarna and teamed with her. He let the young woman believe he was helping her destroy the bottle enclosure while actually allowing yellow solar radiation to endow the Kandorians not only with immunity to the disease but also with superpowers. She was apprehended, and Dev-Re assured the heroes that they would try to rehabilitate her, "thanks to advanced Kandorian science" (*Superman Family* #173, October–November 1975).

SARTO, BLACKIE

The priceless Madras Emerald was en route from the wharf at New York's Pier 56 to the House of Jewels on the fairgrounds of the New York World's Fair when the armored car carrying it was attacked by a gang of international jewel thieves. The thieves and their leader Blackie Sarto were stopped by Superman (*New York World's Fair*, 1940).

SATDEV, RAJAH

A native of the planet Nferino, Rajah Satdev matched the devil in physical appearance, but that did not prevent him from romancing Lois Lane. She nearly married the man while Superman tried to learn his true background, which led to a confrontation resulting in Lois being shot and seemingly killed.

To save her life, Satdev gave her a potion that also transformed her into a Nferinean and whisked her home to complete the wedding ceremony. When Lois learned that Superman had left a memorial ring to her estate, complete with an engraving of his affection, she rejected Satdev and found a way back to Earth and her normal form (*Superman's Girl Friend, Lois Lane* #102–103, July–August 1970).

SATO, TAKEO

A television stuntman who gained superpowers and fought Superboy as Sunburst.

SATURN

The sixth planet from Earth's sun. Life developed on both the planet and its moons. Mars's white-skinned and green-skinned races established H'ronmeerca'andran colonies on Saturn's numerous moons. The red-skinned Saturnians were seen as descendants of the underclass of worker clones that was from the green-skinned Martians, while the white-skinned Saturnians naturally came from the white-skinned Martians. In time, a prince of the people, J'Emm, journeyed to Earth and adventured there for a time (*Jemm, Son of Saturn* #1, September 1984). In the reality after the Infinite Crisis, J'Emm led his people, seemingly having unified the red-skinned, white-skinned (Koolar), and orange-skinned Faceless Hunters. J'Emm occasionally left his world to participate in galactic events such as the Rann-Thanagar War (*Rann/Thanagar War Special* #1, 2008). He was Saturn's emissary to other worlds, including New Krypton, where he voiced his peoples' objections to the Kryptonians helping themselves to objects belonging to other worlds (*Superman: World of New Krypton* #9, November 2009).

The orange-skinned Chun Yull, known as the Faceless Hunter from Saturn, claimed to hail from Klaramar—a subatomic "moon" in orbit around the planet (*Strange Adventures* #124, January 1961). He partnered with Yggardis the Living Planet, Atom-Master, Kraklow the Mystic, Vandal Savage, Mister Poseidon, the Enchantress, and Ultivac to form the Forgotten Villains. On several

SATURN'S SMALLEST MOONS ARE WATER-- FROZEN--LIKE SNOWBALLS. TWO OF THEM SHOULD CONTAIN ALL THE WATER EARTH NEEDS!

occasions, Superman teamed with various "forgotten heroes" to thwart their efforts (*DC Comics Presents* #77–78, February–March 1984). After the Crisis on Infinite Earths, Chun Yull battled Superboy and his pals in Young Justice on the island nation of Zandia (*Young Justice* #50, December 2002).

Superman of Earth-1 described Saturn as a world "where there has been no crime at all for centuries . . . and where everyone can perform amazing mental feats!" The complete absence of crime on Saturn came thanks to weird "radiations" emanating from the "meteor-fragments that form Saturn's rings"—radiations that somehow "cancel out Saturn people's criminal traits!" He learned this when he captured the villainous Saturn Queen and exposed her to that very radiation, seemingly curing her of her villainous tendencies, although the transformation proved short-lived (*Superman* [first series] #147, August 1961).

Superman went on to explain that the rings included a so-called musical mineral, an exotic substance that emitted musical sounds. While touring the solar system to gather artifacts for the Metropolis Museum's time capsule, a gift to the people of the fiftieth century, Superman collected some of this musical mineral (*Superman* [first series] #122, July 1958). The smaller moons in orbit were said to be "gigantic, porous 'snowballs,' " satellites that were literally "composed of frozen snow." Superman used these snowball moons during a mission to the twenty-first century, when he brought them to an Earth that had been deprived of water after an "atomic experiment" created an incredible scarcity (*Superman* [first series] #128, April 1959).

The Man of Steel used asteroids from Saturn's rings to demolish a planet that could have struck Earth at some time in the future (*World's Finest Comics* #50, February–March 1951).

While exploring remnants of a long-dead Saturnian civilization, Superman discovered a "mentality exchanger" that accidentally was activated, swapping the Man of Steel's and Jimmy Olsen's minds for twelve hours (*Superman* [first series] #111, February 1957).

Titan was an airless moon that contained raw minerals allowing the Guardians of the Universe to fashion their power rings and power batteries (*The Flash* [first series] #221, April–May 1973). Given the minerals' responsiveness to mental impulses, they may have helped colonists evolve the telepathic abilities displayed by Legion of Super-Heroes's cofounder Saturn Girl. On the other hand, the issue of when Titan was colonized remained unresolved in the chronicles, since the Earth-1 Superboy also encountered Kral, the vanguard of a proposed invasion of the Earth by the power-hungry leaders on the world. He did possess telepathic abilities in addition to flight, heat vision, and the ability to generate heat or cold—attributes residents of Titan did not have by the thirtieth century (*Adventure Comics* #205, October 1954).

A different incarnation of J'Emm has been identified on Earth-48 as a political leader after the nine worlds in that solar system chose Earth as the place where disputes would be settled (*Countdown: Arena* #3, February 2009).

SATURN, C.W.

Every third Monday in May was celebrated in Metropolis as Miracle Monday, commemorating Superman's victory over the forces of evil. An agent from the underworld, C. W. Saturn, had been dispatched by Samael to find a way to defile Superman's moral code, shredding the very foundation of his character. Entering Earth through a dimensional rift created by Lex Luthor, Saturn came to possess Kristin Wells and challenged the Man of Steel. While Saturn had a history of successes, including bringing about the death of Abraham Lincoln, he failed to destroy the World's Greatest Super Hero (*Superman: Miracle Monday,* 1978; *Superman* [first series] #400, October 1984).

SATURN GIRL

Imra Ardeen was born and raised on Titan, one of Saturn's moons, where all the natives had telepathic abilities. When she was on a trip to Earth in order to join the Science Police, she worked alongside Rokk Krinn and Garth Ranzz to save the wealthy R. J. Brande from kidnappers. He said they reminded him of the deeds performed by Superboy of the twentieth century, and he'd help them found a club for people with powers. Taking the name Saturn Girl, she became a charter member of the Legion of Super-Heroes (first appearance in *Adventure Comics* #247; April 1958; origin revealed in *Superboy* [first series] #147, May–June 1968).

Soon after adding several other members, the founders traveled to Superboy's era and tested young Clark Kent to see if he had the fortitude to join the Legion. He passed with flying colors and regularly traveled to the thirtieth century to share adventures.

Imra served as Legion leader early in her career and fell in love with Garth, then known as Lightning Lad. Her skills demonstrated total mastery of telepathy, including "amazing mental feats" such as "super-hypnotism" (*Superman* [first series] #147, August 1961), extrasensory perception (*Superman* [first series] #165, November 1963), and more common forms of telepathic communication (*Superman* [first series] #156, October 1966). Saturn Girl also demonstrated the ability to confer temporary telepathic powers on other creatures (*Superman* [first series] #176, April 1965).

While normally considered one of the more serious-minded Legionnaires, she did display a playful streak when she joined in an elaborate hoax on Superman and Supergirl as a prelude to celebrating the anniversary of Supergirl's arrival on Earth (*Superman* [first series] #152, April 1962).

When Superman was believed to be dying from the incurable Virus X, Saturn Girl was among the contingent who traveled back in time to pay their final respects. While there, she received a telepathic alert from Mon-El in the Phantom Zone that the Man of Steel's suffering was actually caused by a kryptonite nugget lodged in Jimmy Olsen's camera (*Superman* [first series] #156, October 1962).

Saturn Girl was also one of the Legionnaires to discuss Superman on WMET-TV's inaugural episode of *Our American Heroes* (*Action Com-*

ics #309, February 1964). She returned to the era, along with Cosmic Boy and Invisible Kid, to help temporarily restore the Man of Steel's absent powers so he could defeat Lex Luthor and Brainiac (*Superman* [first series] #172, October 1964).

When Superman visited the Legionnaires as adults, he was delighted to see that she and Garth had married. He worked alongside them against the Legion of Super-Villains, where he first encountered the evil Saturn Woman (*Superman* [first series] #147, August 1961). Later, Saturn Woman posed as Circe during Superman's scheme to beat the Superman Revenge Squad (*Superman* [first series] #165, November 1963). She also imparted her powers temporarily to Beppo the Super-Monkey, Streaky the Supercat, and Krypto the Super-Dog, allowing them to communicate with Superman on a mission to 1866 (*Superman* [first series] #176, April 1965).

In the thirtieth century, it was Saturn Girl who first devised a formula to allow Mon-El to end his millennium-long existence in the Phantom Zone (*Adventure Comics* #300, September 1962). Teammate Brainiac 5 then modified her Serum XY-4 to make the changes permanent. She learned that a member of the Legion would die, so she manipulated matters to become leader and ensure that she would be the one to die. On that fateful mission, however, Lightning Lad defied her orders and was killed in action (*Adventure Comics* #304, January 1963). She then would not rest until they found a way to revive him. In time, they did find a method, but it required one of the other Legionnaires to die. Thus once more, Saturn Girl altered events so that her death would save the teen she adored. Again, though, fate intervened, and it was the protoplasmic being Proty who died to restore Lightning Lad's life. Seeing her devotion opened his eyes, and their romance began in earnest (*Adventure Comics* #312, September 1963). Eventually, although it was then against the rules, Lightning Lad proposed and she accepted, requiring them to leave the team after their wedding (*Limited Collector's Edition* #C-55, 1978). Their retirement did not last long after war broke out and the active Legionnaires were captured. Saturn Girl's efforts to free them led to a revision of the by-laws (*Superboy and the Legion of Super-Heroes* #245, November 1978).

She became pregnant and gave birth to a son, Graym, leading them to once more retire from the team. What neither knew was that Graym had a twin brother, stolen by a vengeful Darkseid, who tossed him back in time, leading the infant on a path toward becoming the deadly Validus, who would go on to frequently battle his parents (*Legion of Super-Heroes* [second series] *Annual* #3, 1984). In time, though, Imra forced Darkseid to restore her son to normal (*Legion of Super-Heroes* [third series] *Annual* #2, 1986).

Saturn Girl returned to active duty when Universo used his powerful hypnotism to seize control of Earth. In fact, it was her powerful will and telepathic power that broke Universo's hold, and it was then she realized she was once and always a Legionnaire. With Garth raising the children, she went back to work (*Legion of Super-Heroes* [third series] #14, September 1985).

In 2990, Imra resigned from the Legion when her husband's home planet of Winath was ravaged by what would later become known as the Validus Plague. The source of the disease was Imra and Garth's son Garridan, a consequence of the period he spent as Validus. The struggling couple built the Lightning Ring Plantation in 2991, turning it into "the largest privately-held agri-province on Winath" (*Legion of Super-Heroes* [fourth series] #3, January 1990). Committed to their new enterprise, they opted against rejoining the revived Legion in 2994, instead adding daughters Dacey and Dorritt, complete with telepathic powers, to the growing family.

After the events of Zero Hour, Imra's backstory and career remained much the same, although her lover Garth was now known as Live Wire, and she had feelings for Cosmic Boy as well. Her powers were scaled back to those of a powerful telepath. She used her abilities to shut down the Composite Man's mind, but it left her catatonic (*Legion of Super-Heroes* [fourth series] #69, June 1995). Micah Aven, her mentor, worked to save her mind and succeeded to a degree, although it meant that Imra was now operating at an infant level. Garth's love for her was the final step she needed to restore her mind to normal (*Legionnaires Annual* #2, 1995).

Trapped in the past with half the team, Saturn Girl's mind animated the comatose body of Cosmic Boy, completing a romance that nearly led to marriage until her subconscious rebelled, making her see Cosmic Boy as Garth, shocking her senses. Soon after, Cosmic Boy recovered (*Legion of Super-Heroes* [fourth series] #96, September 1997). When the team was reunited, Saturn Girl was once more elected leader. As on Earth-1, Garth once more proposed marriage, but before the wedding this time the Legion was divided, with one half lost in space. During this period, Saturn Girl used her powers to craft a vision of Apparition to help the agitated Ultra Boy, leading to a closer relationship with him than she actually wanted—something that caused heartache later on. Garth also died once more, sacrificing himself to stop the mad Element Lad (*Legion Lost* #1–12, May 2000–April 2001).

Back in the United Planets, Imra headed to Titan for psychic therapy, only to fall victim to Universo, who kept her preoccupied with visions while he attempted to create a hivemind of the known universe with himself as ruler. Saturn Girl freed herself and used the same trick to mentally incapacitate Universo (*The Legion* #19–23, June–October 2003).

In the wake of the Infinite Crisis, the Legion's reality altered once more, although Imra Ardeen was largely unchanged (*Teen Titans/Legion Special,* 2004). Her mother Sydne was said to be a highly placed official with the UP Council. A big change was the society on Titan, where the people communicated only via telepathy because evolution had robbed them of their vocal cords. Saturn Girl used her abilities to remain in normal conversation with her fellow Legionnaires. Still, she felt emotionally isolated, which made her appear aloof to the rest of the team. When she let her guard down, Imra found herself seduced by Ultra Boy; their brief tryst ended her romance with Lightning Lad (*Legion of Super-Heroes* [fifth series] #45–46, October–November 2008).

When the multiverse was re-formed, several of the parallel Earths had Legions as part of their future. Three of those Legions were combined to battle Superboy-Prime's Legion of Super-Villains with three versions of Saturn Girl in the midst of the battle (*Final Crisis: Legion of 3 Worlds* #1–5, October 2008–September 2009).

SATURN QUEEN

In the thirtieth century, citizens of Saturn's moon Titan had telepathic abilities, and while some used these to aid their fellows, there were others who found cruel and twisted ways to employ them. The coldly beautiful Eve Aries used her own telepathic powers both on her own and as Saturn Queen, a member of the Legion of Super-Villains.

Superman first became aware of the woman when she arrived from the future at the behest of Lex Luthor to help him eradicate the Man of Steel. The complete absence of crime on Saturn, Superman learned, was caused by the weird radiations emanating from the meteor fragments that formed the planet's rings, radiations that somehow canceled out the people's criminal traits! He learned this when he captured the villainous Saturn Queen and exposed her to that very radiation, seemingly curing her of her villainous tendencies, although her reformation proved short-lived (*Superman* [first series] #147, August 1961).

Later, after exposure to red kryptonite, Superman dreamed of the woman, and the other Legionnaires, placing him on trial for his deeds against them. There he was forced to battle Supergirl to the death, something he theorized may have been induced by Saturn Queen (*Action Comics* #286, March 1962).

After the Crisis on Infinite Earths, Saturn Queen did not journey to the twentieth century; she merely battled the Legion of Super-Heroes time and again.

Eve Aries was said to be a member of Titan's royal family and first encountered the Legion as she attempted to recover her family's Hypno-Stone of Ouranos, stolen by Universo. She allied herself with the other villains, hoping they would aid her quest. Once that was completed, she chose to stay with them, traveling a decade back in time with the plan to destroy the Legion (*Adventure Comics* #330–331, March–April 1965).

I'M FROM THE PLANET SATURN, WHERE THERE HAS BEEN NO CRIME AT ALL FOR CENTURIES...AND WHERE EVERYONE CAN PERFORM AMAZING MENTAL FEATS! ONE DAY, WHEN I TRAVELED TO EARTH, I FELT A SUDDEN DESIRE TO OUTWIT THE LAW WITH MY POWERS OF SUPER-HYPNOTISM!

In the intervening years, Saturn Queen continued her search for the Hypno-Stone. Rather than it being possessed by Universo, it had apparently been taken by Magpie, a thief for Prince Evillo of Tartarus. When he reneged on their deal, Magpie took the stone for herself. Saturn Queen insinuated herself on Tartarus and managed to wed Prince Evillo, becoming his twelfth wife. As a real queen, she tracked down the stone, in the process meeting Tenzil Kem, the former Legionnaire known as Matter-Eater Lad. Together they destroyed Prince Evillo's home and forged a bond.

She finally located the stone's hiding place. As she grasped it at long last, however, Evillo arrived to snatch it from her hands. He then used its power to regain control of Tartarus (*Legion of Super-Heroes* [fourth series] #49, Early November 1993).

On the world after the Infinite Crisis, Saturn Queen, Cosmic King, and Lightning Lord helped create an alternate reality in which she played parent to Clark Kent and Bruce Wayne. Because she'd altered the origins of these heroes—by killing the Kents before Kal-El's rocket arrived and killing Joe Chill after he murdered the Waynes—both boys were raised under her wicked thumb. They became her enforcers as the world altered in dark ways, and she developed an unexpected emotional attachment to the men. The super-villains' plans to rule a new world, however, were thwarted when Wonder Woman arrived. She battled Superman and Batman, with Bruce Wayne dying during the assault. Saturn Queen actually cried at his death, but her pain was short-lived, as reality was soon restored to its proper form (*Superman/Batman* #14–18, January–April 1985).

Saturn Queen returned to the twenty-first century and told Supergirl that when the multiverse was restored, one of the fifty-two parallel universes retained her version of reality—but when the multiverse collapsed, she wound up trapped in the Phantom Zone, where she encountered Earth-3's Ultraman. Using her powers, she placed him in her thrall as substitute son. They set about remaking Kandor into a dark and forbidding place until they were confronted by female versions of Nightwing and Flamebird—who turned out to be Supergirl and Power Girl. The pitched battle was interrupted by Saturn Queen's powerful mind, leading to a mental shotgun wedding between the Maid of Steel and her "adopted" son. When she turned her attentions to Power Girl, the other woman's mind proved tough to probe and the feedback broke her hold on the others. The heroines left Saturn Queen and the beaten Ultraman to the angry Kandorians (*Supergirl* [fifth series] #6–8, April–September 2006).

She was also recruited by Superboy-Prime to join his massive thirtieth-century Legion of Super-Villains in their all-out assault on Earth (*Final Crisis: Legion of 3 Worlds* #1–5, October 2008–September 2009).

SAUNCHA

Long ago, spores arrived on Earth from an asteroid and settled in a single spot on the ocean floor. In time, the spores led to the development of a unique species of seaweed. Humans who ingested the seaweed, named sauncha, temporarily gained incredible super-strength, agility, and endurance. The only recorded example of this was Captain Horatio Strong, who adventured on several occasions alongside the Man of Steel. When representatives from a food manufacturer tried to learn the location of the sauncha, they deceived Strong by telling him the seaweed had addictive properties (*Action Comics* #421, February 1973).

On the world where it originated, the unique spores that spawned sauncha suddenly became essential when the planet was stricken by a blight. Cleansing the sauncha spores of impurities acquired in their journey to Earth, Superman provided samples to a being of that other world in the hope of saving its people from starvation (*Superman* [first series] #361, July 1981).

SAVAGE, VANDAL

Some fifty thousand years ago, the Neanderthal Vandar Adg was in battle against a deadly opponent when he was bathed in the radiation of a newly fallen meteor, unknowingly becoming immortal. Lex Luthor once theorized there was evidence suggesting that the immortal was the first cannibal on record. He adopted the name Vandal Savage, while his opponent took a glowing jewel from the heart of the exploded fireball and gained the reincarnation powers of the Immortal Man (*Green Lantern* [first series] #10, Winter 1943; *Strange Adventures* #177, June 1965; *Action Comics* #553, March 1984). From that moment until the 853rd century, Vandal Savage remained a constant world-conquering menace and deadly opponent to heroes.

Through the ages, Savage constantly jockeyed for power, professing at various points to have been Cheops and Genghis Khan or an adviser to Napoleon and Bismarck. In 1943, the Justice Society of America's Green Lantern first encountered Vandal Savage when the immortal villain attempted to infiltrate high-level U.S. war councils (*Green Lantern* [first series] #10, Winter 1943). Savage would find himself in opposition to a new type of mystery man and super hero, including the first Flash and the entire JSA. In the aftermath of World War Two, he partnered with Brain Wave, Degaton, the Gambler, the Thinker, and the Wizard as the Injustice Society of the World (*All Star Comics* #37, October–November 1947).

Stripped of his immortality at one point, Savage devised an elaborate plot to restore it by stealing the super-human life force of the Earth-2 Superman. The once-immortal villain proved no match for the Man of Steel, and he fled to parts unknown (*All Star Comics* #64–65, January–February and March–April 1976). He resurfaced on Earth-1, now using the super-energy of that world's Superman indirectly to empower a series of "time-bombs" that literally changed history, resulting in a time line in which Savage ruled and the infant Kal-El had been given to the conqueror as a ward of the court. With the help of that time line's Lex Luthor, Superman was able to grasp the truth and restore history to its proper path (*Action Comics* #515–516, January–February 1981).

Virtually unknown on Earth-1 and with no criminal record, Vandal Savage remade himself as a captain of industry, delighting in the frustration it caused in Superman, who knew better but couldn't prove anything (*Action Comics* #542–543, April–May 1983). Indeed, in the news media, Savage deftly twisted each encounter with the Man of Steel to suggest that Superman had unthinkingly interfered with well-intentioned projects conceived by his Abraxas Industries. When his efforts to tap the power of ancient pyramids backfired, for instance, Savage was quick to inform the press that the disaster had been caused by the Man of Steel (*Action Comics* #552–553, February–March 1984). Ultimately, however, Superman goaded Savage into boasting about his true goals while unaware that the entire conversation was being transmitted through a live television feed (*Action Comics* #556, June 1984).

In the reality formed following the Crisis on Infinite Earths, Vandal Savage found himself with two eternal foes, the Immortal Man and the Resurrection Man. As before, his ultimate conflict was with the super heroes of the twentieth century. With a new heroic age under way following Superman's debut, Savage attacked the fledgling Justice League of America, allied with Solomon Grundy, Eclipso, and the first Thorn (*JLA: Year One* #2, February 1998).

YOU BROUGHT THIS UPON YOURSELF, SUPERMAN. I TRIED HELPING YOU IN THE PAST...
...BUT YOU NOT ONLY REJECTED MY HELP-- YOU ATTACKED ME.
SAVAGE?

Undaunted, Vandal Savage peddled the addictive drug Velocity 9, creating super-speed junkies to imperil the third Flash (*The Flash* [second series] #12–15, May–August 1988). The Scarlet Speedster met the latest incarnation of Immortal Man and survived a near-death experience to defeat Savage (*The Flash* [second series] #50, May 1991).

The JLA's 853rd-century counterparts invited their namesakes to attend a festival celebrating the return of "Prime Superman" in their era (*JLA* #23, October 1998). The visit proved catastrophic in the present day, however, thanks to a madness-generating "techno-plague" that Hourman III unwittingly released among Earth's population. As a side effect of the virus, a nuclear assault (utilizing Rocket Red armor) planned by Vandal Savage for Washington, DC, instead struck and destroyed Montevideo, Uruguay (*DC One Million* #1–4, November 1998).

Soon after, Vandal Savage was recruited to join Grodd, Lady Vic, and Cheshire as the villainous group Tartarus (*Titans* #8, October 1999)—which proved short-lived. Meanwhile a new incarnation of the Forgotten Heroes (now composed of Animal Man, Ballistic, Cave Carson, the Ray II, Thula, and Vigilante V) sought Resurrection Man, convinced that he was actually their long-absent teammate Immortal Man. They ultimately learned that he was the captive of Savage and that he, Savage, and Resurrection Man all owed their abilities to tektites that were contained in the temporal meteor that had struck Earth some fifty thousand years before (*Resurrection Man* #24–27, May–August 1999).

In a potential future time line, Vandal Savage continued to scheme for world domination, often opposed by new incarnations of Resurrection Man or other champions from each era. Their struggles eventually spread from Earth to the solar system and endured until the 845th century, when Vandal Savage killed Resurrection Man for the next-to-last time (*Resurrection Man One Million,* November 1998).

Exactly one million months after the dawn of super heroes, Justice Legion A journeyed to the early twenty-first century. Their task was to safeguard a spectacular exhibition of prowess before the entire solar system that was part of a celebration honoring the reemergence of Superman Prime. As Superman Prime prepared to return from the heart of Earth's primary sun, the tyrant sun Solaris resumed his evil ways, plotting with Vandal Savage to destroy Superman while simultaneously sending his own consciousness back to the twenty-first century via a nanotech virus to force his own creation. Even as he succeeded at bringing himself into being in the past, however, he and Savage met destruction in the future, thanks to the planning of our own era's JLA. Ultimately, Savage himself was thwarted in his plan to kill Superman Prime and teleported back to his own twenty-first century nuclear annihilation of Montevideo, where his millennia-long life presumably ended (*DC One Million* #1–4, November 1998).

Yet as an immortal, Savage survived this encounter along with the various reality-warping events. He was an initial member of Alexander Luthor, Junior's Society but left after feeling the leader did not show him appropriate respect (*Villains United* #5, November 2005).

Obviously, anyone whose life extended for millennia would have extensive blood ties to modern society. As a result, Savage was constantly harvesting replacement organs from genetic matches, including the hero Arsenal (*Arsenal* #1–4, October 1998–January 1999). He also fathered countless children through the generations, with only Scandal Savage following in his footsteps. When she joined an opposing group, the Secret Six, Savage threatened Alexander, insisting that no one would harm his daughter. He even encouraged her to further their line by conceiving a child with teammate Catman.

Savage called the Infinite Crisis the worst year of his life, and it did seem to diminish his strength. He led a doomsday cult and attempted to bring an asteroid to Earth, but the plot was stopped by Wally West (*The Flash* [second series] #228–230, January–March 2006). He discovered he was losing his immortality and even developed a brain tumor; he was estimated to have a mere eleven days to live. He attempted to preserve his life by kidnapping his longtime opponent Green Lantern in order to steal his DNA. Instead he wound up consuming a recently constructed clone, prolonging his life (*JSA Classified* #10–13, May–August 2006).

For unexplained reasons, he caused a section of San Diego to sink beneath the Pacific Ocean, turning the area into Sub Diego. Next, he positioned Black Manta as the area's de facto ruler (*Aquaman: Sword of Atlantis* #54, September 2007). Savage then turned his attentions to decimating the rebuilt Justice Society, leading a group of superpowered neo-Nazis (*Justice Society of America* [third series] #1–4, February–May 2007).

Given his atrocities, it was little wonder that he was among the villains exiled to an alien world by the Suicide Squad. While on the planet, he saw the advantages of being an immortal and wanted to immediately impregnate one of the women to begin a new legacy. Though the plan went unconsummated, he did promise both Phobia and Cheetah that they could be his queen to win their allegiance. Eventually, he returned to Earth with the others (*Salvation Run* #1–7, December 2007–June 2008).

No sooner had he returned than Savage was recruited by Darkseid's agent, Libra, to join a new Society of Super-Villains. Savage accepted as a way to relieve his increasing boredom with life (*Final Crisis* #1–2, July–August 2008).

Savage came to regret this decision when Sister Wrack and her Order of the Stone came into possession of the Spear of Destiny. She then plunged the spear into Savage, seemingly killing him and paving the way for the biblical Cain to be reborn. He attempted to slay the wrath of God, the Spectre, but he was stopped thanks to the intervention of the second Question (*Final Crisis: Revelations* #2–5, November 2008–February 2009).

It was later learned that the meteor that granted Savage immortality also turned members of his tribe into immortals who remained undercover for millennia. Calling themselves the Insiders, they began hunting for fragments of the meteor, which put them into conflict with the Outsiders. The Insiders intended to use these pieces of alien rock against Savage in some way that might actually have risked his life, forcing the would-be conqueror into an alliance with Rā's al Ghūl (*Outsiders* [second series] #20, September 2009).

Throughout the multiverse, there existed other versions of Vandal Savage. On Earth-22, for example, he served in Lex Luthor's Mankind Liberation Front until he was nearly killed by Wildcat (*Kingdom Come* #2–3, June–July 1996).

Another world saw him obsessed with regaining the meteor that had turned him immortal. His search was constantly interrupted by encounters with members of the Wayne family until a climactic battle with Bruce Wayne (*Batman: Dark Knight Dynasty,* 1999).

And there was one world where Savage ran a space-exploration corporation, allied with a crippled Barry Allen, and stole technology from the Martian Manhunter in order to destroy the world (*Flashpoint* #1–3, December 1999–February 2000).

SAVIOUR

Ramsey Murdoch somehow came to the conclusion that the Superman operating in Metropolis was a fake and the original Man of Steel was dead, buried in the tomb at Centennial Park. The unbalanced man manifested the ability to create objects from his imagination and briefly took on the name Saviour (appeared as Murdoch in *Action Comics* #705, January 1995; appeared as Saviour in *Action Comics* #713, September 1995).

After several encounters, Saviour finally challenged the Man of Steel, who was working with diminished abilities at the time. As a result, Superman welcomed the arrival of Scorn, who lent a hand in taking Saviour down (*Action Comics* #735, July 1997; *Superman: The Man of Steel* #70, August 1997).

SAWYER, CAPTAIN MAGGIE

Margaret Sawyer (*Superman* [second series] #4, April 1987) began her career as a police officer in Star City, rising from beat cop to detective. During those years, she married police captain Jim Sawyer (*Superman* [second series] #15, March 1988), and they had a daughter named Jamie. In time, though, Maggie could no longer hide her feelings and came out of the closet as a lesbian, leading to the rapid dissolution of her marriage.

Seeking a fresh start, she took a job with the Metropolis Police Department. She performed above expectations, and after one brutal encounter with Kalibak, fellow officer Dan Turpin recommended she lead the Metropolis Special Crimes Unit (*The Adventures of Superman Annual* #7, 1995). She accepted the position as a captain, using Turpin as her number two, and he grew to be one of her few good friends in the city.

Sawyer became a friend to the city's protector as well, directing her forces to aid Superman whenever the situation demanded it. When he was killed by Doomsday and the city needed the S.C.U. more than ever, Sawyer's efforts resulted in her promotion to inspector (*Action Comics* #688, Early July 1993).

Much as she tried to keep her work separate from her private life, it was never easy, especially after the vile Skyhook kidnapped Jamie. The girl was soon rescued by the Man of Steel (*Superman* [second series] #15, March 1988). While in her new city, Sawyer met and fell in love with journalist Toby Raynes, who wrote for Metropolis's *Daily Star.*

Her success in the City of Tomorrow led her to being offered a new opportunity taking over Gotham City's Major Crimes Unit (*Detective Comics* #764, January 2002). She had to adjust her expectations, since the M.C.U. relied more on traditional police work than high-tech gear in the pursuit of fantastical opponents. The criminals in Gotham were in an entirely different league, and the Gotham police had an almost antagonistic relationship with the city's guardian Batman.

While keeping her private life to herself in this new city, she did try to maintain a long-distance relationship with Raynes. It was less than successful. Sawyer also counseled Detective Renee Montoya when her homosexuality was revealed by Two-Face (*Gotham Central* #6–10, June–October 2003).

When Lex Luthor's body was found and with Batman out of sight, she summoned Steel from Metropolis to help identify the criminal (*52* #3, May 24, 2006). The arrival of Luthor, followed by a press horde, helped convince them all that the body was a clone. In actuality, it was Alexander Luthor, Junior, from a parallel world, who had been shot to death by the Joker (*Infinite Crisis* #7, June 2006).

While Sawyer continued to work in Gotham, her relationship with Raynes apparently dissolved (*Detective Comics* #856, October 2009).

SCAREWARE

Scareware was a member of the cybernetic criminal gang known as Mainframe.

SCARLET JUNGLE, THE

Described as a "weird wilderness" on the planet Krypton, the Scarlet Jungle teemed with red and purple flora, including huge mushroom-like maroon fungi (*Superman's Girl Friend, Lois Lane* #21, November 1960; others) and a deadly infectious spore known as the Bloodmorel. Once, Superman was infected by it and needed the assistance of Earth's plant elemental Swamp Thing, who found a way to link with it to cure the dying Kryptonian (*DC Comics Presents* #85, September 1985).

The jungle was also known for its gigantic "moving forests," crimson in color and vaguely humanoid in form, which literally advanced across the face of the planet "in their yearly migration," forcing Kryptonians in their path to seek shelter in subterranean tunnels until they passed (*Superman* [first series] #164, October 1963). The jungle was also home to the Thought-Beast, a creature as big as an Earth rhinoceros but equipped with a large forehead where images could be projected.

SCAVENGER, THE

Two different criminals used the name Scavenger in Superman's world. The first was Peter Mortimer, who plagued Aquaman (*Aquaman* [first series] #37, January 1968) and later found the otherworldly Skartaris and fought its protector the Warlord (*Warlord* #118, June 1987).

The second Scavenger was an old man who had collected an impressive array of technology, from household gadgets to weaponry (*Superboy* [third series] #2, March 1994). He appeared mentally unstable—convinced that he was being persecuted by some unseen, unidentified enemy. He had armed himself in advance of the day when the enemy showed up on his doorstep. During the acquisition of these defensive tools, he confronted the Clone of Steel.

Despite his rampant paranoia, the Scavenger proved adept at mastering the weapons and defended himself ably. He managed to fend off not only Superboy but also his pals the Ravers (*Superboy and the Ravers* #5, January 1997), and even the Man of Steel himself (*Action Comics* #760, December 1999).

For all his flaws, the Scavenger maintained a strict moral code, only stealing objects of power from people he deemed thieves (*Superboy* [third series] #3, April 1994). Indeed, he actually bid in an online auction while trying to acquire the famed Arrowmobile rather than steal it outright (*Green Arrow* [third series] #33, February 2004). Nor was his paranoia entirely unfounded; his "eternal enemy" once attacked him with his shadowy warriors (*Superboy* [third series] #97, April 2002). Initially believing Superboy to be acting against him, the Scavenger ultimately judged the young hero to be too irresponsible to be working for his adversary (*Superboy* [third series] #100, July 2002).

In a potential future, the man somehow managed to survive to the thirtieth century, where he again confronted Superboy and the Legion of

Super-Heroes (*Legionnaires* #31, November 1995; others).

SCHOOL OF HUMOR, THE

The Prankster opened up a Metropolis school for humor and comedy as part of a scheme to convince the unwitting students to help him commit crimes. The school year was ended early after intervention by the Man of Steel (*Superman* [first series] #75, March–April 1992).

SCHOTT, WINSLOW

The toymaker-turned-master-criminal who fought Superman through the years as the first Toyman.

SCHWAB, IRWIN

The nebbish who lost his grip on reality and annoyed heroes and villains alike as the Ambush Bug.

SCIENCE POLICE, THE METROPOLIS

The federal government once christened a new branch of law enforcement dedicated to dealing with the high-tech threats to citizens. Metropolis and Midway City received two of the first branches of the new agency (*Superman* #677, August 2008). DuBarry and Daniels were named Metropolis leaders of the nascent organization, only to die during their first real test when one hundred thousand Kandorians arrived on Earth and chose to eliminate threats to Superman, then seen as threats to themselves. When they assaulted Stryker's Island Penitentiary, the Science Police were dispatched.

In the wake of that event, the government named the Guardian—returned to active duty thanks to the intervention of Jimmy Olsen—as the new field commander (*Superman* #684, March 2009).

The Science Police, sometimes called the World-Wide Police, continued to operate in Metropolis and through the centuries grew to become Earth's primary law enforcement agency (*Adventure Comics* #300, September 1962; first named in *Adventure Comics* #303, December 1962). The force's reach extended through the thirtieth century's United Planets (*Legion Science Police* #1–4, August 1998–November 1998).

In time, as the Legion of Super-Heroes evolved as a crime-fighting organization, the Science Police dispatched Shvaughn Erin as its liaison, a job that tested her patience and fortitude. She served with the team long enough to be nicknamed "Liaison Lass." Subsequent reality-altering events changed the dynamic between the Legion and the Science Police, however, with the post-Infinite Crisis relationship being cool to the point of antagonistic.

Gim Allon was an SP cadet before joining the Legion as Colossal Boy. Imra Ardeen was journeying to Earth in order to join the SP when she actually helped found the Legion as Saturn Girl.

SCORCH

Aubrey Sparks was just another resident of Pisboe, Virginia, when the Joker randomly selected her to become an odd, demon version of the Earth-born angel Supergirl. The Clown Prince of Crime, at the time, was wielding Mr. Mxyzptlk's magical powers, and he desired his own incarnation of the Justice League of America to confront his alternate reality's version of Superman, who was portrayed as a villain (*Superman* [second series] #160; *The Adventures of Superman* #582—both September 2000; others). Paired with Bizarro, she was dispatched to apprehend the Man of Steel but failed. In time, the Joker was defeated and the Fifth Dimensional imp restored reality, choosing to keep several of the creations, including Sparks, now known as Scorch.

Scorch possessed the ability to generate intense heat in addition to manipulating flames, either self-generated or those within her line of sight. She proved able to withstand heat up to three thousand degrees Fahrenheit and managed to teleport herself from place to place with a theatrical burst of flame.

In the mainstream reality, Scorch was initially confronted by Superman and the Martian Manhunter, the latter of whom psychically sensed the real woman trapped in this new guise (*Action Comics* #774, February 2001). Scorch escaped the battle and later found the Martian, asking for his help in restoring her jumbled mind. In exchange, she would help train his mind to resist his innate fear of fire. During their time together, they healed each other and fell in love. She also unwittingly unleashed Fernus, a hidden personality within J'Onn J'Onzz's mind. It took the combined force of the Justice League to stop Fernus's path of destruction, although it also left Scorch in a coma (*JLA* #84–89, October–December 2003).

The alien despot Despero freed Scorch from her state and convinced her that the JLA was a genuine threat. He dispatched her along with Effigy, Plasmus, and Heat Wave to battle the Man of Steel during a wildfire in the western United States. Superman rescued reporter Jimmy Olsen and fought the villains until Scorch realized she had been deceived and switched sides, helping Superman defeat the others (*Superman* [second series] #225, March 2006). She was then turned over to the Department of Extranormal Operations for safekeeping.

Her incarceration proved temporary when she fell under the sway of the alien conqueror Starro, who used her to battle Miss Martian (*Teen Titans* [third series] #51, November 2007).

SCORN

A prince of Kandor, Ceritak chafed under the responsibility of upholding laws that dated back to when Krypton was still whole. He instead sought freedom and once followed Superman through the dimensional portal at a time when the city resided in another plane of existence (*Superman* [second series] #122, April 1997). Emerging on Earth, Ceritak was inadvertently dubbed Scorn by Bibbo Bibbowski, and the name was soon broadcast throughout Metropolis by Jimmy Olsen (*Superman* [second series] #123, May 1997). Scorn was at first disoriented, especially as he adjusted to having superpowers (*Superman: The Man of Steel* #68, June 1997). At that point, Superman's form changed to that of living energy, resulting in his wearing a blue containment suit. Scorn thus briefly adopted the traditional red-and-blue uniform (*The Adventures of Superman* #547, June 1997).

Scorn was befriended by Ashbury Armstrong, who played guide for him in this new world (*Superman: The Man of Steel* #69, July 1997). Together they shared several adventures, even coming to the Man of Steel's aid when he was battling Saviour. Ceritak, using the name Scorn, wound up as the city's main protector while Superman was operating in Kandor. In time, though, Scorn and Ashbury returned to Kandor to investigate how a Kryptonian building could suddenly appear in Metropolis (*Action Comics* #749, December 1998). While they were in the city, Scorn's father Cerimul was killed; Superman was framed for the crime until it was revealed the real culprit was the Cyborg Superman (*Superman* [second series] #140, December 1998). With his sister installed on the throne, Scorn returned to Earth for a time—until Ashley awoke one morning to find a note indicating he had left for reasons unexplained (*Action Comics* #751, February 1999).

SCRAPPER

Patrick MacGuire grew up in Metropolis's Suicide Slum and was nicknamed Scrapper when he helped found the Newsboy Legion.

SEAL GANG, THE

From their underground lair on the desert island of Vumania, this "notorious" gang of pirates repeatedly attempted to prevent Jimmy Olsen from laying claim to the island and exposing their illegal activities. Instead, they were captured by Superman (*Action Comics* #231, August 1957).

SECOND LIFE, INCORPORATED

Founded by J. Wilbur Wolfingham, this community was just a part of his elaborate scheme to bilk three wealthy members of the Retired Executives Club (*Superman* [first series] #42, September–October 1946).

SECRET CITADEL, THE

While Superman on Earth-1 and other realities had his Fortress of Solitude, the Superman of Earth-2 used a headquarters located in a mountain range outside Metropolis (*Superman* [first series] #17, July–August 1942). Superman noted that the mountain peak was sited "where even a mountain goat would have a hard time reaching it!" (*Superman Family* #217, April 1982).

Known as the Secret Citadel, the place was a hideaway where the Man of Steel could unwind and collect his thoughts. It contained comfortable furniture and a complete gymnasium and laboratory setup, allowing him to remain in top shape or work out problems. He labored for countless hours attempting to formulate a cure for kryptonite radiation.

His trophy room was nowhere near as elaborate as his counterpart's, although there were rooms set aside to honor his birth parents, foster parents, and closest friends. There was also a communications center with special monitors allowing communication with distant planets and alien dimensions.

SEEKER, THE

In the years prior to Krypton's destruction, scientists constructed and launched a space probe called the Seeker. With its artificial intelligence guiding it, the vehicle traversed the stars and sought planets suitable for future Kryptonian colonization. Years after the planet exploded, the craft entered the Sol system and identified Earth as one such potential world—but it would need radical terraforming before it could be used. Superboy had to engage and destroy the probe before it irrevocably altered his adopted home (*Superman Family* #191, September–October 1978).

SELWYN, DIGBY

The owner of the Selwyn Lumber Company in the Pacific Northwest, Digby Selwyn employed Bart Benson to act as his foreman while Selwyn tended to his other holdings—including a farm—and looked after his daughter Sally Selwyn. Father and daughter one day found a dazed and confused man near their home. The dehydrated man had no memory of his identity, completely unaware he was actually Superman, altered in this way after exposure to a chunk of red kryptonite.

When asked his name, the man searched his memory and managed "Jim White," jumbling the names of his friends Jimmy Olsen and Perry White. The Selwyns took the man in and nursed him back to health. Jim White came up with a quick solution to prevent lightning from striking a water pipeline,

impressing Digby enough that he hired the man to work at his lumber company.

He was a good worker and admired by most, although Benson saw him as a rival for Sally's affections. Sure enough, Jim and Sally fell in love and became engaged. When Jim asked, Digby was only too happy to bless the union.

Crippled and confined to a wheelchair after an accident Benson caused, Jim White took himself to a secluded spot to consider his bleak future. He was found by Benson, who shoved a boulder to frighten his rival. Instead, the rock hit the wheelchair-bound man, toppling him into the river. Digby and his distraught daughter believed that a suicidal Jim White had thrown himself into the sea.

In reality, the man did plunge into the water—only to be found by his Justice League of America colleague Aquaman. The Sea King saw the man drowning and rushed him to Atlantis, where "a new form of artificial respiration" was used to save his life. For a week he writhed from nightmares until the red k radiation finally worked its way through his system, restoring his superpowers and his proper memories. He did, though, lose his more recent memories of life as Jim White, complete with all recall of his romance with Sally. Lori Lemaris was there to greet the man as he awoke and make certain he was ready to return to his life on the surface (*Superman* [first series] #165, November 1963).

Digby and Sally Selwyn

SELWYN, SALLY

The beautiful blond Sally Selwyn grew up in her wealthy father Digby Selwyn's mansion in the Pacific Northwest. One day, Sally and Digby found a dazed and confused man suffering from sunstroke as he staggered onto the estate. The dehydrated man had no memory of his identity, completely unaware he was actually Superman, altered in this way after exposure to a chunk of red kryptonite.

When asked his name, the man searched his memory and managed "Jim White," jumbling the names of his friends Jimmy Olsen and Perry White. The Selwyns took the man in and nursed him back to health. Jim White once came up with a quick solution to prevent lightning from striking a water pipeline, and an impressed Digby hired him on to work at the lumber company.

Sally and Jim struck up a friendship that quickly blossomed into something more. Sure enough, Jim and Sally fell in love and became engaged. When Jim asked, Digby was only too happy to bless the union. While he produced a ring to cement the relationship, he told Sally that they could not wed until he could prove he was capable of supporting her, without being dependent on her father's wealth. To accomplish this goal, Jim White supplemented his work as a lumberjack by entering a bronco-riding competition in the hope of winning the five-thousand-dollar prize.

Foreman Bart Benson saw him as a rival for Sally's affections. Before the wedding could take place, Benson managed to paralyze Jim White by slipping some locoweed to the bronco Black Terror, who violently bucked his rider. The fall paralyzed White, confining him to a wheelchair. While Benson thought this would clear the way to Sally's heart and her father's millions, he did not count on the depth of her love for the man. Jim White, for his part, now felt Sally was going through with the wedding out of pity, not love.

He took himself to a secluded spot to consider his bleak future. Benson found him there and shoved a boulder to frighten his rival. Instead, the rock hit the wheelchair-bound man, toppling him into the river. Digby and his distraught daughter believed that Jim White had committed suicide.

In reality, the man had plunged into the water only to be found by his Justice League of America colleague Aquaman. The Sea King saw the man drowning and rushed him to Atlantis, where "a new form of artificial respiration" was used to save his life. For a week he writhed in nightmares until the red k radiation finally worked its way through his system, restoring his superpowers and his proper memories. He did, though, lose his more recent memories of life as Jim White, complete with all recall of his romance with Sally. Lori Lemaris was there to greet the man as he awoke and make certain he was ready to return to his life on the surface (*Superman* [first series] #165, November 1963).

A short while later, Sally encountered escaped fugitive Ned Barnes, who closely resembled Superman. Wearing glasses, he was a double for Jim White, and she thought her love had returned. Barnes played along, figuring the police would never look for a criminal hiding at the Selwyn mansion. At one point, the "couple" had an argument and Sally went for a walk on the estate, where she encountered Clark Kent, studying the area for clues as to Barnes's whereabouts. Sally realized that this was the real Jim White and embraced him. During their passionate kiss, Clark's subconscious restored his forgotten days as Jim White. As they talked, Clark came to realize that Barnes had been posing as Jim White and was nearby. The hero resolved to arrest Barnes as Superman, then go through with his commitment to marry Sally, but in his real identity.

However, when he arrived at the mansion, Barnes was dying, shot by assassins who had come seeking Sally. With his final words, Barnes insisted Superman not betray his ruse: He'd fallen for Sally and didn't wish to hurt her. He kept his word and realized that if he married Sally as Superman, she'd remain at risk from anyone who sought to cause him harm. When Sally finally turned up, he explained that Jim White had been murdered, giving his life to protect her.

Once things were set to order, Superman fled to the stars to deal with his own broken heart (*Superman* [first series] #169, May 1964).

SEMPLE, SUSAN

As one of the *Daily Planet*'s switchboard operators, Susan Semple had plenty of time to daydream about Superman. Her crush was not unusual among the women in Metropolis, but few had the opportunity to actually act on their feelings.

Professor Weirton exposed Semple to his latest invention, a "cabinet-like machine" that used "specially filtered uranium rays" to speed "the evolutionary process"—"putting him 1,000,000 years ahead of his time!" For twenty-four hours, Semple had a taste of the "powers that the human race won't acquire for hundreds of eons!" With a limited time to act, she used her newfound skills to read the Man of Steel's mind and learn his secret identity; she then threatened to reveal his name to the world if he refused to marry her. Superman saw to it that Susan Semple lost track of her waning time with her super-abilities so that during the wedding ceremony, the powers faded and she fainted. When Susan awoke, her powers, and her knowledge of his alter ego, were both gone (*Action Comics* #163, December 1951).

SENATOR BARROWS

Superman photographed this senator being influenced by lobbyist Alex Greer to pass a bill that would ignite a European conflict (*Action Comics* #1, June 1938).

SEPARATISTS, THE

Most residents of the bottle city of Kandor came to accept their fate, holding out hope that Superman could fulfill his vow to find a way to restore them to their normal size. Not everyone was so patient, however. The Separatists were a radical group that wanted the city's container demolished, letting the diminutive people gain superpowers as compensation for their plight. During their attempts to accomplish those goals, they were repeatedly defeated by the Kryptonian Crusaders Nightwing and Flamebird (*Superman Family* #173, October–November 1975; and #184, July–August 1977).

The radicals put aside their ideology when the Preservers stole the city from the Fortress of Solitude for study. They worked with the costumed champions, as well as the Man of Tomorrow, to help save the city (*Superman Family* #190, July–August 1978).

SERGEI'S BORSHT BOWL

Located in Little Bohemia, "the famed artist's section of Metropolis," this popular restaurant was owned and operated on a nonprofit basis by Sergei, a warmhearted Russian immigrant whose only goal was to eke out a modest living. "Racketeer night-club owner" Biff Condor attempted to terrorize the restaurateur into vacating his eatery so it could be transformed into a fancy nightclub and gambling casino, but Condor and his henchmen were apprehended by Superman (*Action Comics* #78, November 1944).

SHACK, THE

Located within Metropolis Tower Police Headquarters, the Shack was virtual home to a group of reporters who were assigned to rotating ride-alongs with the Metropolis S.C.U.'s Lieutenant Lupè Teresa Leocadio-Escudero. A berth at the Shack was generally regarded as a kind of punishment, whether for reporters deemed too inexperienced—such as the *Weekly*'s Geraldine Frank—or those considered too old, like the *Daily Star*'s Bernie Carver. Clark Kent was briefly assigned to the Shack as a consequence of his efforts to expose President Lex Luthor's misconduct (*The Adventures of Superman* #627, June 2004).

SHADOWDRAGON

Savitar Bandu, the firstborn son of King Khuran of Bhutran, became the larger-than-life hero Shadowdragon to the people of his homeland at the cost of his own status (*Superman* [second series] #97, February 1995). Stealing an X-10 prototype battle suit from the treacherous country of Chi-Lann, the prince reported the news of their neighbor's intended invasion of Bhutran but declined to offer proof, fearing the king would seek to divert social funding to mass-produce the war suits himself. Forced to answer for his seemingly unwarranted incursion into the Chi-Lann facility, Savitar

was stripped of his titles and access and disowned by his father. He rallied from his punishment, however, and joined a band of revolutionaries with a new mission statement: "We take technology from those who can afford, but refuse, to share it. Such advances would boost Bhutran's economy; raise the quality of life for our people" (*Shadowdragon Annual* #1, 1995).

A graduate of MIT, Bandu worked with others among his group to enhance the armor and create the legendary Shadowdragon persona. Traveling the world, he diverted all manner of technology "to hands where they would most benefit Bhutran." After one such theft in Metropolis ran afoul of Superman (*Action Comics* #707, February 1995), Shadowdragon provided stolen files on the Man of Steel to Conduit, with the expectation that the villain would divert his intention (*The Adventures of Superman* #521, March 1995). Horrified when Conduit instead used the data to engage in murderous attacks on Clark Kent and his friends, Shadowdragon raided the villain's hidden bases and released a computer virus that wiped out the files (*The Adventures of Superman* #524, June 1995).

SHALER, ART

Having recently stolen a "secret atomic cutting-torch" capable of cutting through literally anything, the "wanted racketeer" proved gullible as he fell for a ruse designed to make him believe Superman had transformed into a greedy "super-miser." As the Man of Steel gathered unimaginable treasure from around the Earth, he hoarded it inside a gigantic mountain treasure cave sealed with a virtually impenetrable "super-steel door." Art Shaler could not resist the bait and used the stolen torch to access the treasure cave, where he was apprehend by Superman (*Action Comics* #219, August 1956).

SHARK, THE

Although several Sharks committed crimes during Superman's time, he only battled one of them: the mutated tiger shark who became the humanoid villain the Shark (*Green Lantern* [second series] #24, October 1963). Exposure to nuclear waste not only changed his shape but also evolved his mind to include telepathic skills, and made him exceptionally cunning. He repeatedly battled the Emerald Crusader on the West Coast and was at least once devolved back into his sea life form. With the vestiges of his telepathic prowess, he stole the "evolution" force from a young boy at a Metropolis aquarium. Superman battled the returned Shark, who now demonstrated incredible strength as well as the ability to create water spouts, mentally induce fear, and siphon the atmosphere's ozone to breathe. The Man of Steel prevailed, forcing the creature to reverse the process, restoring the boy he'd harmed and reverting to a shark once again (*Action Comics* #456, February 1976).

SHAR-LA

Shar-La was a humanoid from a female-dominated world who lost control of her spacecraft and needed to be rescued by the Teen of Steel. When Superboy made a joke about "women drivers," she would not take the jest in stride but instead wanted to teach him a lesson. She used a ring she wore to create a powerful illusion that allowed Superboy to experience the trials and tribulations of being Claire Kent, who turned into Super-Sister when danger summoned her. The Sister of Steel experienced the inner strength of women along with their special attributes and apologized to Shar-La before she returned to the stars (*Superboy* [first series] #78, January 1960).

SHARP, CUTTER

When Linda Danvers lived in Leesburg, Virginia, she counted Wendell "Cutter" Sharp as one of her closest friends (*Supergirl* [fourth series] #1, September 1996). He worked as a reporter at the *Leesburg Tribune,* coming to town after his breakup with Andrea Martinez. Later, when Supergirl arrived, he wound up reporting on her exploits before quitting to work as her self-appointed agent and publicist (*Supergirl* [fourth series] #39, December 1999). While in town, he flirted with Supergirl but fell for Linda's friend Mattie Harcourt; they wound up getting engaged (*Supergirl* [fourth series] #67, April 2002). He formed Supergirl Enterprises and tried to exploit the heroine's image through merchandising, with varying degrees of success. When that version of Supergirl vanished, his enterprise dried up and he returned to writing.

SHARP, WILLIAM

William Sharp was a racketeer and confidence man who wound up hiding out at a sideshow. There he befriended a strongman who billed himself as Atlas. Sharp hit on the notion that if he could prove Atlas was more powerful than Superman, he could then bilk people for protection money to "save" them from the legendary figure. He used his cunning to create a media sensation around Atlas's feats of strength, then issued a challenge to the Man of Steel. Via stagecraft, he made it appear that Atlas was the world's mightiest mortal. Atlas worked with Superman to bring Sharp to justice (*Action Comics* #121, June 1948).

SHAW, FREDDY

A sickly youth in Smallville, young Freddy became Clark Kent's close friend. Their bond grew

strong enough that Clark actually entrusted him with the knowledge of his alter ego. The brain disease afflicting the boy caused him to cry out when he grew delirious. During one such bout, he inadvertently cried out Clark's secret, which was overheard by his older criminal brother. Freddy died soon after, and Clark cleverly used a Superboy Robot to protect his identity from the thug (*Superboy* [first series] #77, December 1959).

SHAZAM!

A worthy Egyptian shepherd, the man was gifted with powers from different gods and became a force for justice in Canaan, known as Champion. By speaking the magical word *Vlarem* he gained the strength of Voldar, the wisdom of Lumiun, the speed of Arel, the power of Ribalvei, the courage of Elbiam, and the stamina of Marzosh (*World's Finest Comics* #262, April–May 1980). He was at one point seduced by a demoness and sired Blaze and Lord Satanus much to his eternal regret (*The Power of Shazam* #10, December 1995).

For years, Champion protected the Middle East, but because his powers derived from a different pantheon of deities he altered his name to Shazam. He now used the stamina of Shu, speed of Heru, strength of Amon, wisdom of Zehuti, power of Aton, and courage of Mehen. After several centuries, Shazam felt it was time to pass on his powers to another and selected Teth-Adam, son of the pharaoh. The power corrupted the Mighty Adam, turning him from hero to villain, until finally the wizard had little choice but to strip Black Adam of these abilities.

Taking giant stones from Heaven and Hell, Shazam then formed the Rock of Eternity, situating it at the nexus of the myriad parallel universes. There the petrified remains of the Seven Deadly Sins were stored and he sat on the stone throne, keeping watch.

It wasn't until the early twentieth century that the wizard thought the world was ready for another hero. On the pre-First Crisis Earth-S, he lured orphan Billy Batson to his lair and had the boy say his name, Shazam. Billy was magically transformed into the adult dubbed Captain Marvel. This time, the powers derived from a different set of gods, and he used the wisdom of Solomon, strength of Hercules, stamina of Atlas, power of Zeus, courage of Achilles, and speed of Mercury (*Whiz Comics* #2, February 1940).

Billy came to share the wizard's abilities with his sister Mary and his friend, the lame Freddie Freeman, so the world could be protected by Captain Marvel, Mary Marvel, and Captain Marvel, Junior.

He was first depicted as a homeless newspaper boy when he met the wizard Shazam in an underground cavern to which he'd been led by a mysterious, driverless subway car. In later accounts, he was a twelve-year-old radio newscaster. In short order there evolved what came to be known as the Marvel Family—a group of similarly superpowered beings including Mary Marvel and Captain Marvel, Junior. Their histories, as well as their relationships with Captain Marvel, would be revised to varying degrees by the changes wrought by the First Crisis.

Ironically, the Captain Marvel of Earth-S seemed to encounter Superman more than the one who emerged after the First Crisis, when Captain Marvel and the Man of Steel inhabited the same world, although there were more frequent accounts of them interacting in the years immediately preceding the Infinite Crisis. In the reality in which one or the other had to cross a dimensional barrier for the two to meet, it was initially as rivals or combatants rather than as partners. This was the case in their first meeting, when the Captain was forced to battle Superman after red kryptonite had made the Man of Steel violent (*Justice League of America* [first series] #136–137, November–December 1976), and when a Martian criminal manipulated Captain Marvel's archenemy Black Adam and the Sand Superman into provoking a battle between Marvel and the Man of Steel (*All-New Collectors' Edition Vol. 1 C-58: Superman Vs. Shazam!*, May 1978).

On a later occasion, Mr. Mxyzptlk magically switched the costumes and powers of the two

heroes, forcing Superman to travel to Earth-S to confront the Captain, because the new powers were similar enough to his own to enable him to easily break the dimensional barrier. Both heroes were forced to battle Mxyzptlk, who had formed a partnership with the Venusian criminal Mister Mind with the intent of destroying both heroes (*DC Comics Presents* #33–34, May–June 1981). The two heroes were unambiguous allies, however, when they teamed up to battle Black Adam a second time (*DC Comics Presents* #49, September 1982).

In the wake of the Crisis on Infinite Earths, the parallel universes were collapsed into one world and Shazam saw to it that that world's Billy Batson continued his work as Captain Marvel. The wizard also joined with other cosmic beings to form the oversight group known as the Quintessence.

Billy Batson was now documented as an orphan whose archaeologist parents were killed by their assistant, who later became Black Adam. Billy was separated from his sister Mary and placed in the care of his father's half brother, who stole his trust fund and kicked him out of the house. That's how he came to be homeless in what was revealed to be Fawcett City. There he met a mysterious stranger in a subway terminal in which he had been sleeping; the stranger then led him to a subway train that took them into a cavern, where they encountered Shazam. The mysterious stranger was later revealed to be the spirit of Billy's late father. Shazam was, in this reality as well, a wizard who had championed humankind for thousands of years and was nearing the end of his existence. Like his Earth-S counterpart, he had chosen young Billy to be his successor in the battle against humanity's Seven Deadly Enemies: Pride, Envy, Lust, Hatred, Selfishness, Laziness, and Injustice.

Not long afterward, Billy and Mary were reunited, and Captain Marvel bestowed his awesome powers on her, enabling her to become Mary Marvel. He did the same, but to a lesser extent, to his and his sister's friend, the handicapped newsboy Freddy Freeman, who transformed into a super hero younger than the so-called Big Red Cheese (as the Captain's enemies dubbed him) and thus was called Captain Marvel, Junior (*Power of Shazam!*, December 1994; others).

In the post-First Crisis reality, the relationship between Superman and Captain Marvel was amicable from the beginning. Superman was grateful for the possibilities offered by having an ally who, by virtue of having similar powers but not the Man of Steel's vulnerability to magic, would have Superman's back, as occurred when the Captain freed Superman from the control exerted over him by the super-criminal Eclipso. The Man of Might was somewhat dismayed to discover that Captain Marvel was really a child, however, and welcomed Shazam's suggestion that Superman mentor the boy (*Superman/Shazam: First Thunder* #1–4, November 2005–February 2006).

Superman and Captain Marvel remained friends throughout the changes to reality. When the Man of Steel was controlled by the evil entity Eclipso, Shazam summoned the Spectre to free him (*Superman* [second series] #216, June 2005). This earned the wizard the enmity of the former agent of God's will's. This culminated in a direct conflict between the Spectre and Shazam wherein the Rock of Eternity actually shattered (*Day of Vengeance* #6, November 2005), freeing a variety of demons including the sorcerer Mordru the Merciless. The ninth age of magic ended and a tenth age began, as the latest incarnation of Shadowpact formed to do battle. In the aftermath of Infinite Crisis, Earth's mages gathered the shattered pieces and rebuilt the Rock of Eternity—although Shazam had vanished, replaced by an entity called only Marvel (*Day of Vengeance: Infinite Crisis Special* #1, March 2006).

Billy Batson began life in the New Earth reality wearing an all-white costume and long white hair, attempting to train Captain Marvel, Junior, to replace him (*Trials of Shazam!* #1–12, October 2008–May 2009). Ultimately, however, Black Adam and the villainous Isis robbed Marvel of his powers in an effort to take over the Rock of Eternity. With the help of the Justice Society of America's Flash and the spirit of Mary and Billy's father, Shazam's soul was retrieved from the Netherworld and resurrected. The revived wizard wasted no time taking back his magical powers, and Freddy Freeman assumed the champion role, letting Billy and Mary live as mere teens (*Justice Society of America* [third series] #25, April 2009).

The last known incarnation of Captain Marvel, along with the other members of the Marvel Family, was documented after the new multiverse was revealed, including the existence of a world designated Earth-5. As a result of the way Mister Mind "devoured" elements of this world, it ended up seeming somewhat similar to the pre-Crisis Earth-S, although it was not the same world. After the Final Crisis, Captain Marvel and Billy Batson were documented as two separate beings (*Final Crisis: Superman Beyond* #1–2, October 2008–March 2009; *Final Crisis* #7, March 2009).

SHIR KAN

The Kryptonian scientist who sent Super-Ape to Earth in an experimental rocket ship (*Action Comics* #218, July 1956).

SHOCKWAVE

Mercenary Arnold Pruett used a power suit in the employ of the Earth-1 Metallo but was not especially successful despite his high-tech advantages. As a result, he continually met defeat at the hands of Blue Devil, Booster Gold, the Teen Titans, and the Man of Steel (*Blue Devil* #2, July 1984).

After an ill-fated stint with the One Thousand (*Booster Gold* [first series] #11–12, December

1986–January 1987), the father of two wound up working for Intergang when Bruno Mannheim assigned him and Chiller to abduct *Daily Planet* reporter Catherine Grant. They did manage to defeat Gangbuster en route to Grant, but Shockwave was apprehended by Superman (*Superman* [second series] #44; *The Adventures of Superman* #467; *Action Comics* #654—all June 1990).

Shockwave later was among the villains dispatched by the Weapons Master after he managed to weaken the Man of Steel. He wound up meeting defeat, this time at the hands of Wonder Woman, Superboy, and Steel (*Action Comics* #817–818, September–October 2005).

SHRINKWATER LAKE

Considered one of Krypton's "natural wonders," this lake contained "some strange chemical" that could "shrink ordinary men down to ant size." Kal-El was accidentally transformed into a giant when his father Jor-El exposed him to his "amazing growth ray for plants." To restore the infant to normal, Jor-El took him to the lake (*Action Comics* #325, June 1965).

SH'STRIANS

These minute aliens lived in a different dimension but found themselves accidentally transported to Earth during a battle between Superman and Chemo. The yellow-skinned beings developed a bad reaction to native bacteria when enlarged to human size, so the Man of Steel decided to let them reside in a replica version of the bottle city of Kandor kept in his Fortress of Solitude until the end of Earth-1 (*Superman* [first series] #370–371, April–May 1982).

SILENT KNIGHT, THE

Brian Kent was believed to be an ancestor to Jonathan Kent, foster father to Superman. Living in sixth-century England, Brian watched in horror as his father Sir Edwin died during a joust with Sir Oswald Bane. The remorseful Bane followed Edwin's dying instructions that Brian protect the people by seeing to it he was trained by Sir Grot. Grot suspected Oswald's motives so he decided to train Brian in private, insisting to the public that the boy was an oaf (*The Brave and the Bold* [first series] #1, August 1955).

Brian soon after found a trunk containing silver armor, a sword, shield, and a crimson helmet. Quickly donning the armor, Brian came to the aid of Oswald's men when belligerent travelers arrived. Fearing that he might be recognized, he fought in silence and was quickly named the Silent Knight. For several years, he acted in secret, keeping the armor hanging within a tree located in the nearby Forest Perilous.

After the events of Crisis on Infinite Earths, it was said that Brian was not only an ancestor to the Kents but also one of the many reincarnations of Khufu, known to Superman as Hawkman. The Silent Knight actually met a time-traveling Man of Steel and aided him in destroying a magical artifact (*The Brave and the Bold* [third series] #10, April 2008).

SILVER, JOSEPH

A dream-research scientist in Metropolis, Joseph Silver invented a machine that utilized dreams to let a person's astral body journey back in time. He then used the machine on himself, returning to the days when he was still a teenager. The transformation somehow gave him dream-based superpowers, so he briefly became Astralad, with hopes of becoming a greater hero than Superboy (*The New Adventures of Superboy* #4, April 1980). On Earth-898, Silver actually fulfilled his heroic ambitions as Astral Mage (*Justice League of America: Another Nail* #2–3, 2004).

SILVER BANSHEE, THE

Siobhan McDougal was the firstborn child of Garrett McDougal and the latest in what was said to be a thousand generations living on a small island located between Scotland and Ireland. Siobhan left this island home and traveled the world until word reached her that Garrett had died. She returned home and wished to pass the ancient ritual test, conducted at Castle Broen, to show she was able to lead the Clan. Her desire was opposed by her uncle Seamus who toed a sexist line and championed instead that his son Bevan undergo the ritual. Refusing to give in, Siobhan privately underwent the ritual, only to be interrupted by Bevan. The ceremony involved supernatural forces, so—as she quickly learned—any distraction could prove disastrous. Indeed, she was whisked through a portal to a netherworld. There something calling itself the Crone offered her powers to gain her revenge in exchange for retrieving an occult book. Siobhan accepted the bargain and found herself transformed into a black-and-white figure with a skeletal face. Returning to Earth, she took the name Silver Banshee and used her newfound mystic abilities to trace the book (*Superman* [second series] #23, November 1988).

In her new form, the Silver Banshee had a wail that could kill those within a limited range, as long as she knew their true names: The victims were reduced to lifeless husks. The wail could also teleport her from location to location. In her various incarnations, she demonstrated super-human strength, agility, speed, and endurance, along with a high degree of resistance to physical and energy attacks.

Her hunt took her to Metropolis, where she attempted to gain the book but was opposed by the city's champion Superman. Her powers could affect him, but he summoned help from the Martian Manhunter; the two sides battled to a stalemate and she left the city, intending to return to honor her end of the deal with the Crone (*Action Comics* #595, December 1987).

Silver Banshee continued her hunt, encountering Superman on other occasions. Eventually, Batman located the missing tome in Gotham City and let Superman turn it over to the woman at Castle Broen. Once the Crone obtained it, though, she declared that the McDougals suffered from pride. With a wave of her hand, Seamus, Bevan, and the Banshee were seemingly destroyed (*Legends of the World's Finest* #1–3, 1994).

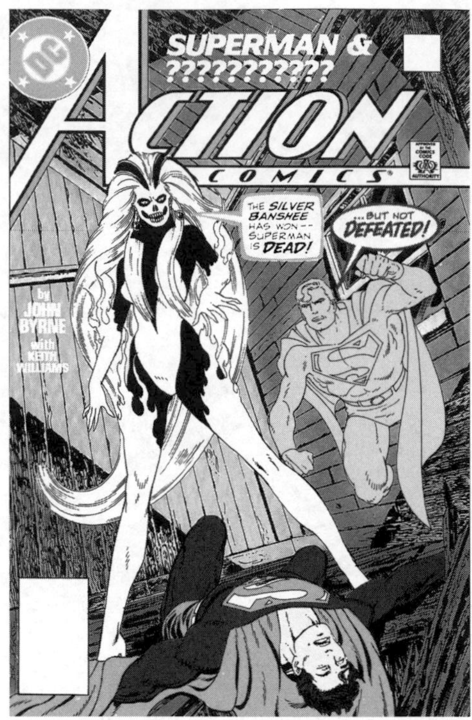

It was Supergirl who wound up rescuing the Silver Banshee, who was being held at the time by Lord Satanus where the River Styx ran beneath her town of Leesburg, Virginia (*Supergirl* [fourth series] #10–12, October–December 1997). Back on Earth, Silver Banshee was dazed, seeking a new human host. She briefly occupied the body of Mattie Harcourt, Supergirl's friend. Mattie used this to her own advantage—she was hoping to kill Gerald McFee, who had killed her brother while he himself was influenced by Gorilla Grodd. Supergirl intervened, and the spirit abandoned the body.

Silver Banshee later turned up in a new host, although she physically appeared the same, trying to kill Superman in exchange for the billion-dollar bounty offered by President Lex Luthor (*Superman/Batman* #3, December 2003). Seeking a role in the world, the Banshee found herself adrift and agreed to serve in Alexander Luthor, Junior's Secret Society of Super-Villains (*Villains United: Infinite Crisis Special* #1, June 2006).

After the events of Infinite Crisis, Silver Banshee was among the threats targeted by the Kandorians who had recently come to live on Earth (*Superman* #682, January 2009). Supergirl distracted the Banshee, allowing the aliens to capture her and send her to the Phantom Zone. Superman rescued her and the other inhabitants, remanding them all to Belle Reve prison. The Banshee escaped, however, and engaged Supergirl in a series

of entanglements without resolution (*Supergirl* [fifth series] #34, December 2008).

The Silver Banshee eventually tracked down one of the items she was seeking to lift her curse, which turned out to be embedded in Inspector Michael Henderson's hand. When the Banshee attacked the detective, Supergirl grabbed another artifact Henderson was carrying, which transformed her into a Banshee hybrid. The Silver Banshee learned that the artifacts were hidden within other people not to curse them but to test them as potential clan leaders for the future. The possessed Girl of Steel was freed only after Henderson used a magical knife to stab the artifact within his hand, thereby breaking its hold over Supergirl. The Silver Banshee then used some of her magic to remove the item from his hand, saying he owed Henderson a debt (*Supergirl* [fifth series] #48–49, February–March 2010).

SILVER FOXX, THE

Considered an "underworld czar," this Metropolis criminal mastermind commanded the gang that robbed the Cloud Club, the city's "most exclusive gathering-place of celebrities," and an unnamed bank before they were finally apprehended by Superman (*Superman* [first series] #30, September–October 1944).

SILVERSTONE, PETER

A television scientist who used his knowledge to transform others into the villainous Blackrock.

SIMYAN

The partner to Mokkari, toiling in the Evil Factory on behalf of Darkseid.

SINBAD

Qurac-born Davood Nassur helped his sister Soraya, a LexCorp secretary, escape when she was attacked by armored men. It turned out that they wanted her to force Nassur to hand over a belt he

retained in the wake of the Dominion-led invasion of Earth. The alien technology boosted his recently developed psionic abilities, something Lex Luthor wanted to control. Fearing that his Middle Eastern appearance made him less than trustworthy, he spurned an offer of help from the Man of Steel.

Nassur, also known to some as Sinbad, and Soraya tricked Luthor into admitting that he was behind the attack. Seeking to control Nassur, Luthor summoned the Metropolis S.C.U., telling Captain Maggie Sawyer that he'd just been threatened by a terrorist named Sinbad. Luthor then launched an alien flying object programmed to explode—in one more attempt to kill the Man of Steel.

Sinbad saved Superman, and the Man of Steel contained the explosion, but the result still destroyed the belt, reducing Sinbad's telepathic strength (*Superman* [second series] #48; *The Adventures of Superman* #471; *Action Comics* #658—all October 1990).

Sinbad and his sister have remained in Metropolis, and he has occasionally ventured out as a hero, including helping patrol the city in the wake of Superman's death at Doomsday's hand (*Legacy of Superman* #1, March 1993).

SIR GAUNTLET

Wearing a suit of armor from the days of medieval knights, this mysterious criminal masterminded a series of successful thefts from Lacey's Department Store. The spree ended after intervention from the Man of Steel. Sir Gauntlet was revealed to be Lacey's employee Casper Smythe, a former partner of the store's owner. The partnership ended when Smythe was caught embezzling (*Superman* [first series] #21, March–April 1943).

SIROCCO

An Arab named Khalid gained superpowers through unexplained means and battled for justice under the name Sirocco. His methods matched the mores of his culture, which meant killing offenders without compunction—something that was frowned on when he first encountered the Man of Steel (*Superman* #662, May 2007). At the time, Superman had been seeking Khyber, an immortal who led the Hashishim—elite assassins that had existed for centuries—only to watch him killed by the speedster.

In a potential future, Lois Lane was saved by Sirocco during one dangerous adventure (*Superman* #657, December 2006).

Sirocco has since been seen protecting his land during the one-hundred-minute war between the

remaining Kryptonians and the people of Earth (*Superman: War of the Supermen* #4, July 2010).

Sirocco was also a female heroine summoned by Victoria Grant when she possessed the alien H-dial (*The New Adventures of Superboy* #31, July 1982).

SKELETON GANG, THE

In the wake of Superman's successful dismantling of the criminal operation Skull, a splinter group formed and called itself Skeleton. Members struck throughout Metropolis, and the Man of Steel asked reporter Lois Lane to go undercover. She established the identity of Opticus and then took credit for blinding Superman—a ruse on his part to lure the criminals into the open, where he then apprehended them (*Superman* [first series] #334, April 1979).

SKEPTIC

Daily Planet janitor Charlie Frost wanted revenge against his employers after they published a derogatory article about his brother Professor Milton Frost. The technologically advanced but socially shallow man wound up committing suicide after the article ridiculed his work. Calling himself Skeptic, Charlie used his brother's "hate-gas" to try to discredit Metropolis's great newspaper. When four seemingly normal citizens began acting in uncharacteristically violent ways, it prompted an investigation, leading Superman to conclude that all four were to be covered in the paper but their reputations had been marred. This allowed him to find and apprehend the janitor (*World's Finest Comics* #11, Fall 1942).

SKIZM

Skizm was a being conjured into existence when the Joker was wielding Mr. Mxyzptlk's magical abilities. He could use his telepathy to probe for the psychic weaknesses of his foes on the Bizarro Earth the madman created for his amusement. Once Superman and Batman beat the Joker and the magic was returned to the imp, Skizm was one of the creations to vanish (*The Adventures of Superman* #582, September 2000).

SKORPIO

Dennis Samuel Ellis was just another resident at New Jersey's Garden State Medical Center when the criminal Dr. Arthur Villain turned him into his personal bodyguard. Donning a weapons-laden suit, Ellis became Skorpio in order to pay off his med school loans, and came to relish his new role. Given Villain's schemes, Skorpio came into frequent contact with the armored avenger known as Steel (*Steel* #37, April 1997). Armed with blades coated with various toxins, he proved deadly.

Once Villain's criminal activities were exposed and he was arrested, Ellis continued them, preferring a life of crime to his work as a doctor. While he was somewhat successful, he clearly didn't have the fortitude to confront other costumed champions. When Manhunter confronted him during a crime, he surrendered rather than fight the woman who had killed fellow villain Copperhead (*Manhunter* [fourth series] #16, January 2006).

Skorpio remained at large, working for Alexander Luthor, Junior's Society for a time (*Villains

United #1, July 2005) before joining those criminals exiled to an alien world (*Salvation Run* #2, January 2008).

SKULL

With the One Hundred having scaled back its operations and Intergang virtually shut down, the void in the underworld of Earth-1's Metropolis was filled by an operation named Skull. Foot soldiers wore bodysuits and masks outfitted with high-tech weaponry that made them more than a match for the One Hundred in addition to the police (*Superman* [first series] #301, July 1976).

The organization remained a viable threat to the city and became an even deadlier threat when former S.T.A.R. Labs employee Albert Michaels began providing them with gear stolen from his former firm. Michaels recruited other scientists, and they used their know-how to turn Roger Corben into the second Metallo (*Superman* [first series] #310, April 1977).

During this time, Michaels had an accident turning him into the superpowered Atomic Skull. He led the group into battle against the Man of Steel on numerous occasions. When the Atomic Skull chose to go solo, Skull eventually dwindled in number and eventually disbanded faced by increasing threats from not only the One Hundred but also from Kobra's growing hold on criminal activity (*Superman* [first series] #323–325, May–July 1978). There was a brief attempt to reorganize, first as Skeleton (*Superman* [first series] #334, April 1979) and again as Skull (*DC Comics Presents* #63, November 1983), but that proved a failure.

After the Crisis on Infinite Earths, Simon Pons re-formed the group (*Outsiders* [first series] #6, April 1986) and soon after engaged in a new round of rivalry with Kobra's cult (*Outsiders* [first series] *Annual* #1, 1986). Whereas previous incarnations were national, Pons grew Skull into a true international threat, forcing wealthy men to fund them and brilliant scientists, including the Outsiders' friend Helga Jace, to work for them.

On Earth-1, there was also a short-lived S.K.U.L. (Superman Killers' Underground League), but they failed at their eponymous goal (*Superman's Girl Friend, Lois Lane* #63–64, February–April 1966).

SKYBOY

Tharn, son of a lawman from the distant planet Kormo, lost his memories when his spacecraft collided with a meteor and crashed on Earth. When he awoke, the youth displayed powers and abilities similar to those of Superman, who discovered the wreckage. The Man of Steel dubbed him Skyboy and worked with him to regain the missing memories. When he did, Tharn explained he'd been sent to warn Earth's inhabitants that a band of Kormonian criminals, led by Rawl, had arrived to steal copper, a precious metal on his homeworld. Batman and Robin joined Superman and Skyboy in apprehending the intergalactic criminals. With his ship repaired, Tharn brought the fugitives back to Kormo (*World's Finest Comics* #92, January–February 1958).

On another parallel world, Kal-El arrived on Earth in 1976 and as a teen adventured under the name Skyboy until he achieved adulthood and used the name Superman (*Superman* [first series] #300, June 1976).

SKYHOOK

London's Dr. Aleister Hook was killed by townspeople for abducting children in the late nineteenth century. Having bargained away his soul to the demoness Blaze, Hook died and was re-created as a winged demon named Skyhook. In time, he sailed to America and settled in Metropolis. There he once more began kidnapping children, using his powers to convert them and adding wings to the bodies. Superman became aware of the danger when Metropolis S.C.U. Captain Maggie Sawyer reported that her daughter Jamie had been taken. The Man of Steel tracked the creature and rescued the girl before the conversion could take place (*Superman* [second series] #15, March 1988).

Despite being impaled during their second confrontation (*Superman* [second series] #34, August 1989), Skyhook returned to battle the Man of Steel one more time before vanishing in an explosion (*Superman: The Man of Steel* #49, October 1995).

SLASH SABRE

Alien visitors Zigi and Zagi had no idea that after touring Earth, they returned to their homeworld in the Alpha Centauri system with the "psychopathic killer" Slash Sabre aboard their craft. The criminal had escaped Metropolis Prison through a forgotten storm drain, sneaked aboard their craft for a rest, and then lost consciousness when the vehicle landed thousands of light-years from home. He was found and taken captive, only to escape. While seeking refuge, he wound up fiddling with a "gravity master" that tore an asteroid from its celestial path and sent it hurtling toward the planet until it was deflected by the Man of Steel, who was seeking the dangerous Sabre. The thankful Zigi and Zagi returned Sabre to his prison on Earth via a "teleport bubble" (*Action Comics* #315–316, August–September 1964).

SLATE, DR. GARRISON

Garrison Slate was a scientific genius who decided to take the profits from his myriad patents to hire a team of superstar scientists and researchers and form the private corporation Scientific and Technological Advanced Research Laboratories. S.T.A.R. Labs succeeded beyond Slate's wildest dreams: The company built branch offices across the United States before spreading around the world. Their accomplishments led to further patents and commercial applications to keep the firm profitable in addition to allowing the staffers to assist the world's super hero community. S.T.A.R. also provided security and containment services to host countries, keeping the populace safe from major threats to life. Slate built the company and then remained largely out of the public spotlight, preferring to let the work speak for itself. The tall, broad-shouldered man surfaced only when necessary, such as to revamp the Chicago branch after corruption was detected there (*Blue Beetle* [second series] #12, May 1987).

He repaid Josiah Power's friendship and help building the company by serving as the interim CEO after Power suffered an injury, leaving him in a coma (*Power Company* #16, July 2003).

SLEEZ

Sleez was an inhabitant of the corrupt, fiery world of Apokolips and was a companion to Prince Uxas during the latter's early days as the world's lord. As Uxas transformed into Darkseid, he wearied of Sleez's perversions and was banished. In time, the short, pudgy, yellow-skinned creature found his way to the darker corners of Metropolis on Earth. There he continued exploiting the weak and disenfranchised, indulging his sadistic, twisted whims (*Action Comics* #592, September 1987). When Sleez came upon Superman, he hatched a scheme to make a pornographic film starring an ensorcelled Man of Steel with the former Female Fury Big Barda. The project failed, and he wound up soundly defeated.

Sleez resurfaced at Project Cadmus, where he induced the chief geneticists to create youthful clones of themselves who assumed lives of their own as the second Newsboy Legion (*Superman* [second series] *Annual* #2, 1988).

Later, he was employed by INTERGANG to kidnap children at an amusement park they were using as a front, but he was again beaten by Superman. Sleez was thought killed during an explosion (*The Adventures of Superman* #475, February 1991).

When INFINITY-MAN began killing members of the NEW GODS, Sleez wanted to make certain he didn't go alone. He was explaining to reporter JIMMY OLSEN how to slay Darkseid when he himself was killed in SUICIDE SLUM, his Earth home (*Countdown to Final Crisis* #46, June 13, 2007).

SMALL, EZRA

Ezra Small was a "trapper and trader" when he settled down and founded the Kansas community that grew to become known as SMALLVILLE (*The Kents* #12, July 1998). A statue of Ezra Small could be found somewhere within the city limits (*World of Smallville* #1, April 1988; others).

His descendants remained in town, although on Earth-1 the family line died out during the Great Depression (*World's Finest Comics* #235, January 1976). After the CRISIS ON INFINITE EARTHS, Rutherford B. Small was still said to be mayor (*Action Comics* #596, January 1988).

SMALLVILLE

Smallville, Kansas, was part of either Small County (*The Adventures of Superman* #469, August 1990), Smallville County (*The New Adventures of Superboy* #50, February 1984), Neosho County (*Superboy* [second series] #1, February 1990), or Lowell County (*Action Comics* #645, September 1989) near the state line (*Superboy* [first series] #152, December 1968) and forty miles from Wichita (*Superman/Batman* #48, July 2008).

The Earth-1 Smallville was reportedly located in Maryland (*Amazing World of DC Comics* #14, March 1977). It was said to have been founded in the mid-1600s (*Superboy* [first series] #196, July 1973) or 1847 (*Sovereign Seven* #23, June 1997), while other accounts featured the city celebrating its fiftieth anniversary (*Superboy* [first series] #8, May–June 1950) or its centennial (*Adventure Comics* #298, July 1962; *Superboy* [first series] #63, March 1958). A towering statue "erected in honor of Smallville's first settler"—a frontiersman wearing a coonskin cap and holding a rifle—straddled a section of the highway (*Adventure Comics* #315, December 1963). An alternate account established Rutherford B. Small as the community's founder and honored him with a statue (*Superboy* [second series] #12, January 1991).

"When Smallville was founded, its founder didn't buy the land but leased it for 150 years . . . After that time, it was to revert to open land, and whoever fenced it could claim it by settler's right." On that date, SUPERBOY leapt in to claim the community before anyone else could and then signed it over to the proper authorities (*Adventure Comics* #172, January 1952).

Among Smallville's nineteenth-century residents were Revolutionary War veteran Terry Terwilliger; Congressional Medal of Valor honoree Pierre Lereux, who helped Andrew Jackson defend New Orleans in 1815 and sailed with Jean Laffite; Civil War soldier Lloyd Morgan; and Sheriff Dick Poynter. Captain James Gordon was believed to have been an army deserter and outlaw when he died in Lost Mesa, New Mexico, in 1885, but was posthumously revealed to have been a U.S. government operative. A statue in his honor was erected in front of the Smallville Courthouse (*Superboy* [first series] #12, January–February 1951). A survey of that era inadvertently left Smallville out of the United States, a technicality that was resolved a century later (*Superboy* [first series] #32, April 1954).

After the CRISIS ON INFINITE EARTHS, the town was founded sometime in the nineteenth century by "trapper and trader" EZRA SMALL. He settled down and founded the Kansas community that grew to become known as Smallville (*The Kents* #12, July 1998). A statue of Ezra Small could be found somewhere within the city limits (*World of Smallville* #1, April 1988; others).

NATHANIEL KENT became Smallville's sheriff in 1871 (*The Kents* #11, June 1998). Other notables on "Smallville's Roll of Honor" included General Ezekiel Hooker (Revolutionary War hero), Amos Morris (famous senator), Walter Hoyt (surgeon), Mel Evans (the scientist who first provided details on KRYPTON), and Superboy (*Superman* [first series] #136, April 1960). Hooker, incidentally, had a namesake descendant whose heroism in the Civil War earned him a bronze statue in METROPOLIS (*World's Finest Comics* #106, December 1959).

The town had a population of 15,284 (*Superboy* [first series] #153, January 1969), or of 3,019 (*Adventure Comics* #455, January–February 1978). In the post-Crisis reality, the population was alternately said to have been 3,753 (*Action Comics* #596, January 1988) and 8,957 (*Superman for Earth,* 1991). One discounted population figure for the "teeny" town was 110,000, "down 20 percent since the IMPERIEX War and defense budget cuts closed the nearby military base. Major source of revenue: farming" (*Action Comics* #815, July 2004).

Many families such as the Smalls and Kents maintained ties to the town through the generations. Smallville grew slowly.

"The swank suburb of Fairdale, near Smallville," celebrated its centennial during Superboy's teens. Its mayor, Del Mason, regarded its Hungry Hill, a conglomeration of poor settlements surrounding a dilapidated mansion, as an eyesore until he discovered that its residents were producing unique handmade products (*Superboy* [first series] #179, November 1971). Also on the edge of town was the area of Edgely Hill (*Superboy* [first series] #51, September 1956).

The southern end of Smallville was built over abandoned mine foundations (*Superboy* [first series] #90, July 1961), probably including the tunnel that lay beneath Smallville High and the Smallville Bank (*Superboy* [first series] #19, April–May 1952).

Smallville was said to lie in the shadow of "a high rock-bound plateau" (*Superboy* [first series] #30, January 1954), chalk cliffs (*Superboy* [first series] #33, June 1954), and other rocky cliffs (*Superboy* [first series] #15, July–August 1951; others). It was described as near "a secluded valley" (*Adventure Comics* #148, January 1950), perhaps

The Kent Farm

Keene Valley (*Superboy* [first series] #50, July 1956). Nearby features included Crystal Cave (*Superboy* [first series] #36, October 1954), Calvin's Cave (*Adventure Comics* #282, March 1961), the Deepmoor Caverns (*The New Adventures of Superboy* #4, April 1980), the LEAD-lined Elton Cave (*Superboy* [first series] #28, October–November 1953), and Tyler's Rise (*The New Adventures of Superboy* #50, February 1984). At Stony Hill, Superboy carved a stadium out of solid rock for the community teens (*Superboy* [first series] #112, April 1964). "A pool of molten lava lies beneath Smallville" but was diverted into an "empty cavern nearby" courtesy of Superboy and the KRYPTON KID (*Adventure Comics* #242, November 1957).

"Sprawling timberland" was northeast of Smallville (*The New Adventures of Superboy* #19, July 1981), probably the site of a forest ranger barracks. Businesses in the vicinity included the Loring Paper and Lumber Company, the Moxon Lumber Company, and the Smith Lumber Camp (*Adventure Comics* #142, July 1949). The Ely-Thomas Lumber Company was in "the timber country 100 miles to the north" (*The New Adventures of Superboy* #25, January 1982).

Potter's Knoll encompassed much of this with abundant greenery, cliffs, caves, and a river (*Adventure Comics* #137, February 1949).

Mallow Mountain was "20 miles away from Smallville" (*The New Adventures of Superboy* #15, March 1981). The coastal community of Hatton Corners (*The Brave and the Bold* [first series] #54, June–July 1964) was also nearby (*Adventure Comics* #455, January–February 1978). Hillsdale was "the next town" (*Superboy* [first series] #100, October 1962). Maynard's Hill was "just outside of Smallville" (*The New Adventures of Superboy* #38, February 1983), as were Eagle's Peak (*Superboy* [first series] #87, March 1961), Knob Hill (*Adventure Comics* #217, October 1955), Mount Hunter (*Superboy* [first series] #24, February–March 1953), Norb Hill (*Superboy* [first series] #111, March 1964), Squire Hill (*Superboy* [first series] #78, January 1960), and another unnamed mountain (*Adventure Comics* #170, November 1951). Also in the area was the Tower Mountain Game Preserve (*Superboy* [first series] #192, December 1972). On one mountain peak, Superboy carved an arrow pointing toward "Smallville's new airport" (*Superboy* [first series] #117, December 1964). On another, he used natural gases to create a kind of eternal flame—later dubbed the Superboy Beacon—that lit up the night skies of Smallville for years (*Superman* [first series] #97, May 1955). Mount Potash (*Superman* [first series] #136, April 1960), neighbored by a valley (*Superboy* [first series] #33, June 1954), was once picked up by Superboy and used to plug Hadley Swamp (*Superboy* [first series] #31, March 1954). Bald Mountain was fifty-five miles from nearby Corinth (*Superboy* [first series] #29, December 1953). Skyscraper Rock was fifty miles west, and Hidden Crater a hundred miles west of that (*Superboy* [first series] #37, December 1954).

"Stone Canyon is in the high country 20 miles northeast of Smallville" (*The New Adventures of Superboy* #6, June 1980), perhaps part of "the unexplored north woods" (*Adventure Comics* #176, May 1952). Scoville Meadow was on the edge of town (*Superboy* [first series] #23, December 1952–January 1953).

A lake in the forest outside town was surrounded by two campgrounds set up for high school students, CAMP HIAWATHA (girls) and Camp Chieftain (boys). Among the other highlights of the area were Pow-Wow Cave, which included "totem poles carved out of stone," and Echo Canyon (*Adventure Comics* #261, June 1959). This may have encompassed the "granite-chiseled walls of Echobox Canyon," situated more than an hour north of Smallville (*Superman Family* #196, July–August 1979), and Mount Granite, near the campgrounds of "Smallville High School's annual camping trip" (*Superboy* [first series] #25, April–May 1953). There was also an "old granite quarry south of town" (*Superboy* [first series] #15, July–August 1951). Camp Smallville, a venue for city kids, was ten miles from town and was situated by Smallville Lake and the so-called Haunted Falls (*Adventure Comics* #453, September–October 1977). More nearby points of interest were Camp Duff (*Action Comics* #712, August 1995), Kidtown Summer Camp (*Superboy* [first series] #16, September–October 1951), and Smallville Boys' Camp (*Adventure Comics* #203, August 1954). LEX LUTHOR had one particularly memorable encounter with the Smallville camping trips (*Superman* [second series] #224, February 2006).

SOON, A COLORFUL FIGURE STREAKS ACROSS THE COUNTRYSIDE...
SMALLVILLE! THE TOWN WHERE I SPENT MY YEARS AS SUPERBOY!

The Oto Indian Reservation was outside Smallville; its land rights were leased to Abraxis Mining of Boring, Kansas (*Superman* [second series] #45, July 1990). Indian writings could also be found in the caves near town and, in fact, revealed that the remains of an old civilization were buried beneath the former Kent household (*Superman* [first series] #270, December 1973). The Corobee Reservation was also twenty miles from Smallville (*Superboy* [first series] #84, October 1960).

Hadley was home to a tough high school football team (*Adventure Comics* #170, November 1951). Directly linked to Smallville via a "well-known little bridge," Hadley harbored some resentment over its sister community's claim of Superboy as its own. "The main road to Smallville stems from Hadley and all the less important roads, from surrounding towns, lead *into* Hadley." A second Superboy Museum, a glass structure created by the Boy of Steel, lay across the river in Hadley and helped settle the feud (*Adventure Comics* #166, February 1951). Hadley Swamp was plugged by the entirety of Mount Potash (courtesy of Superboy) and became a town ballpark (*Superboy* [first series] #31, March 1954).

"The next town" from Smallville (*Superboy* [first series] #64, April 1958) was "the small town of MIDVALE" (*Adventure Comics* #227, August 1956), whose baseball team played against Smallville's (*Superboy* [first series] #139, June 1967). Smallville's chief basketball rival was Sticksville (*Adventure Comics* #151, April 1950). Granville (*Adventure Comics* #225, June 1956) was "ten miles from Smallville" (*Adventure Comics* #228, September 1956). Smallville was also located near Nova County (*Adventure Comics* #153, June 1950) and Warren County (*Superboy* [first series] #12, January–February 1951) and communities such as Ashton in Reed County (*Superman: The Man of Steel Annual* #4, 1995), Bigville (*The New Adventures of Superboy* #22, October 1981), Centerville (*Adventure Comics* #229, October 1956), Corinth (*Superboy* [first series] #29, December 1953), Gale City (*Superman: The Kansas Sighting* #1, 2004), Grandville (*Action Comics* #791, July

2002), Granger (*Superboy* [first series] #80, April 1960), Grant City (*Superboy* [first series] #16, September–October 1951), Hilldale (*Superboy* [first series] #17, November–December 1951), Jonesburg (*Adventure Comics* #249, June 1958), Superb City (*The New Adventures of Superboy* #22, October 1981), Waterburg (*Superboy* [first series] #83, September 1960), Watertown (*Superboy* [first series] #133, October 1966), and White City (*Superboy* [first series] #34, July 1954). New City was "just north of Smallville" (*Adventure Comics* #244, January 1958), and Cedar Falls was to the south (*Superman* [second series] #174, November 2001). Junction City was eighty-seven miles from Smallville, and Salina was fifty-five (*Action Comics* #822, February 2005). According to a map (*Superboy* [first series] #82, July 1960), Creighton Pass, Rocktown, Arbor City, White Cliff, Princeville, and Dover were all north of Smallville. Brambleville (*The New Adventures of Superboy* #14, February 1981) and the nearby city of Metropolis (*Superboy* [first series] #7, March–April 1950) were each a hundred miles from Smallville (*Superboy* [first series] #23, December 1952–January 1953; *Superman* [first series] #403, January 1985), the latter said to be to the south (*Superboy* [first series] #30, January 1954). One account placed Metropolis "hundreds of miles" away (*Superman* [first series] #116, September 1957). "PITTSDALE isn't far from" Smallville (*Superboy* [first series] #90, July 1961).

The neighboring town of Gulchdale was a boomtown that went bust after the Bonanza Gold Mine was tapped out. "Most decent folks moved out . . . and outlaws moved in. After pulling jobs in the next state, they [came] here to hide out, safe from arrest in this state." With the aid of a young Superboy, Sheriff Todd finally cleaned up his town (*Superboy* [first series] #123, March 1970).

In and around the town's borders were several bodies of water, including Bowman's Lake (*The New Adventures of Superboy* #32, August 1982); Cedar Bluff Reservoir (*Superman for All Seasons* #4, 1998); Crystal Lake, which was "several miles" west of town (*The New Adventures of Superboy* #21, September 1981); Culver's Ravine (*Superboy* [first series] #14, May–June 1951); Follensby Pond (*Superboy* [first series] #14, May–June 1951), "situated on the isolated outskirts of Smallville" (*Adventure Comics* #195, December 1953); Fowler's Creek (*Superboy* [first series] #27, August–September 1953); Hadley Swamp, which was plugged by the entirety of Mount Potash (courtesy of Superboy) and became a town ballpark (*Superboy* [first series] #31, March 1954); the so-called Haunted Falls, which were ten miles from town near Camp Smallville (*Adventure Comics* #453, September–October 1977); Lake Drear (*Superman: The Man of Steel* #99, April 2000); Lake Park, which included its namesake lake and a zoo, and was located somewhere outside the Smallville community (*Superboy* [first series] #123, September 1965); Lake Wylie State Park, along Lakeshore Road (*Superboy* [second series] #1, February 1990); Litchfield Bog, "a swampy hilly wilderness . . . not too far from Smallville" (*World's Finest Comics* #246, August–September 1977); McCormack's Lake (*The New Adventures of Superboy* #50, February 1984); Miller's Brook (*Superboy* [first series] #12, January–February 1951); Minnow Lake, which flowed from the northern Blue Mountain Lake and Smallville Dam (*Superboy* [first series] #6, January–February 1950); Moran's Pond (*Superboy* [first series] #94, January 1962); Morgan Falls (*Superboy* [first series] #24, February–March 1953); Simonson Limestone Quarry, where many kids "used to live in those cool waters every summer" (*Batman and Superman: World's Finest* #7, October 1999), but has "been derelict for twenty years or more" (*Superman* [second series] #4, April 1987) and was alongside Smallville Lake (*Superboy* [first series] #116, October 1964) or the sea (*Adventure Comics* #143, August 1949); Smallville Dam (*Adventure Comics* #157, October 1950; others), which was more than ten miles north of the community (*The New Adventures of Superboy* #19, July 1981) by Blue Mountain Lake (*Superboy* [first series] #6, January–February 1950); "Smallville's inlet bay" (*Superboy* [first series] #102, January 1963); Smallville Lake (*Adventure Comics* #166, July 1951), sometimes called Lake Smallville (*Superboy* [first series] #77, December 1959), which included "replicas of famous world structures" on its boardwalk (*Adventure Comics* #262, July 1959) and was ten miles from town near Camp Smallville (*Adventure Comics* #453, September–October 1977); the Smallville River (*Adventure Comics* #154, July 1950; others), which was "one mile wide" (*Superboy* [first series] #5, November–December 1949), was traversed at one point by a drawbridge (*Superboy* [first series] #77, December 1959), and included a particularly dangerous stretch dubbed the Roaring Rapids (*Superboy* [first series] #67, September 1958); the Smoky Hill River (*Superman for All Seasons* #4, 1998); Smallville Harbor (*Adventure Comics* #315, December 1963); Stafford Pond, "a few miles outside Smallville" (*Superman: Last Son of Krypton,* 1978); Totten Pond Road, "on a little hill that was the highest point for fifty miles" (*Superman: Miracle Monday,* 1978); Tyler's Ravine, straddled by a bridge (*The New Adventures of Superboy* #40, April 1983); the waterfront (*Adventure Comics* #144, September 1949); the docks (*Adventure Comics* #219, December 1955); Fordman Meadows (*Action Comics* #655, July 1990); and Watkins' Glen (*Superboy* [first series] #12, January–February 1951).

Before his departure, Superboy changed the course of the Smallville River so as not to interfere with a new highway (*Superman* [first series] #97, May 1955). The Metropolis River flowed south of town (*The New Adventures of Superboy* #22, October 1981) and was probably crossed via the Smallville Ferry (*Superboy* [first series] #33, June 1954).

Smallville had just three bridges connecting it with nearby towns: the Cross-Bay Suspension Bridge (*Superboy* [first series] #132, September 1966); the old Mill Bridge (*Action Comics* #791, July 2002); and Smallville Bridge (*Superboy* [first series] #28, October–November 1953).

The infant KAL-EL's rocket landed along the Smallville–Metropolis road (*Superboy* [first series] #23, December 1952–January 1953) near the plot of ground known as Sutton's Field (*Superman: Birthright* #3, November 2003) or Warner's Grove. Known as Swan Field in 1873 (*Chronos* #2, April 1998) and later Swan's Grove, it was renamed after "old man Warner" circa 1938 (*Chronos* #11, February 1999). A monument that marked the exact spot where Superboy landed (*Superboy* [first series] #63, March 1958) later expanded to include a replica of Kal-El's rocket (*Superman's Pal, Jimmy Olsen* #56, October 1961). A meteorite that accompanied Kal-El's rocket left a large crater outside town (*Teen Titans* [third series] #7, March 2004).

"There used to be a ton of [kryptonite] . . . in Smallville," Superman later recalled. "Seemed like we had a freak a week for a while there. Enough of it turns people into the worst, most monstrous version of themselves" (*Superman/Batman* #44, February 2008).

After Superboy began flying over the skies of Smallville, the town came to adopt him as one of their own without ever learning his real identity. A billboard rested on the northwestern edge of town (*Superman Family* #193, January–February 1979; *The New Adventures of Superboy* #22, October 1981) proclaiming, WELCOME TO SMALLVILLE—THE HOME OF GOOD NEIGHBORS—AND SUPERBOY (*Adventure Comics* [first series] #148, January 1950) or WELCOME TO SMALLVILLE—SUPERBOY'S HOMETOWN (*Superman Family* #178, August–September 1976) or WELCOME TO SMALLVILLE—HOME OF SUPERBOY (*DC Comics Presents* #14, October 1979; others) or YOU ARE NOW ENTERING SMALLVILLE—HOME OF SUPERBOY (*Adventure Comics* #172, January 1950; others) or SMALLVILLE—THE HOME OF SUPERBOY (*Superboy* [first series] #18, February–March 1952).

Other versions of the billboard sign have read WELCOME TO SMALLVILLE, THE HOME OF SUPERMAN WHEN HE WAS A BOY (*Action Comics* #265, June 1960), WELCOME TO SMALLVILLE: ". . . A GOOD PLACE TO LIVE . . ." (*Action Comics* #596, January 1988; others), and WELCOME TO SMALLVILLE: "THE TOWN WHERE MIRACLES HAPPEN" (*Action Comics* #597, February 1988; others).

A statue in honor of the Boy of Steel was in the midst of the community's business district (*Superman Family* #178, August–September 1976). One of the Superboy statues in town was missing a small chunk out of its arm that the Boy of Steel used to make a locket for LANA LANG (*Superman* [first series] #97, May 1955).

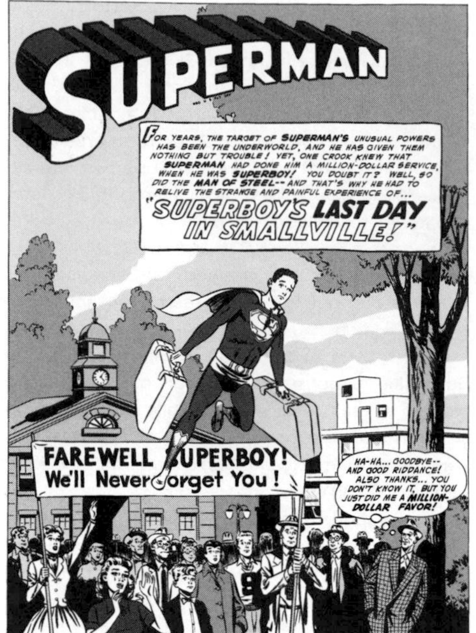

To reach Smallville, people could drive, fly, or take the train, with the latter the more popular method during the town's first several decades. The well-appointed Smallville Railroad Station (*Superboy* [first series] #26, June–July 1953; others), also known as Central Station (*Superboy* [first series] #9, July–August 1950) or Smallville Union Station (*Superman's Pal, Jimmy Olsen* #8, October 1955), was on the eastern edge of town, bordered by Peachtree and Main streets and Madison Avenue (*The New Adventures of Superboy* #22, October 1981). The train left town once a day along a bridge over the river (*Superboy* [first series] #11, November–December 1950) and a gorge (*Adventure Comics* #155, August 1950). Superboy drove "the first spike of the new Smallville Railway" (*Adventure Comics* #195, December 1953) and later built "a track from the main line for a separate freight station instead of cluttering the passenger platform" (*Superboy* [first series] #62, January 1958). The Shore Railroad (*Superboy* [first series] #134, December 1966) tracks were close to the Smallville River (*Superboy* [first series] #122, July 1965).

Chief Brann (*Superboy* [first series] #20, June–July 1952), Chief Wilkins (*Superboy* [first series] #30, January 1954), and finally Douglas Parker (*Adventure Comics* #225, June 1956) all came to count on the Smallville Sentinel to help keep the community safe for all its residents. Its sheriff during Superman's era was a man named Caldwell (*Superman* [second series] #149, October 1999).

Parker was one of three people, along with Professor Lewis Lang and the president of the United States, whom the Boy of Steel entrusted with a signal device linked to a flickering lamp in the Kent household (*Superboy* [first series] #88, April 1961). Its mayor during Clark Kent's teen years was a man named Parr (*Superman: Birthright* #8, May 2004).

Criminals were incarcerated at the Smallville Jail (*Superboy* [first series] #20, June–July 1952; others), which received a makeover early in Superboy's career (*Superboy* [first series] #123, September 1965) and another when he was eighteen. Later, another jail was built (*Superman* [first series] #97, May 1955). The jail and the police station were bordered by Oak and Grove streets and Wilson Avenue (*The New Adventures of Superboy* #22, October 1981).

The county also hosted the Soames Reform School, a "minimum security prison" for teens (*The New Adventures of Superboy* #19, July 1981) that was "fifty miles west of Smallville" (*The New Adventures of Superboy* #14, February 1981). An earlier reform school farm was located on the outskirts of Smallville before its administrator was exposed as corrupt (*Superboy* [first series] #163, March 1970).

The Smallville Fire Department (*Superboy* [first series] #93, December 1961) was bordered by Oak and Grove streets and Jefferson Avenue (*The New Adventures of Superboy #22,* October 1981). Among its volunteers (*Superboy* [first series] #23, December 1952–January 1953) were Jack and Charlie (*Superman: Birthright* #8, May 2004). Fire Chief Rogan was revealed as an invader from the planet Zaron and was turned to stone by a law enforcer from his world (*Adventure Comics* #274, July 1960).

Smallville Hospital (*Superboy* [first series] #12, January–February 1951; others) was built in the 1930s (*Superman: The Doomsday Wars* #1, 1997). It was located near an unnamed lab (*Superboy* [first series] #99, September 1962) and had a wing named after Lana Lang (*Superboy* [first series] #18, February–March 1952). A new branch was constructed by Superboy (*Superboy* [first series] #23, December 1952–January 1953).

In some accounts, baby Kal-El was first brought to the Smallville Orphanage before the Kents adopted him (*Action Comics* #1, June 1938). The building was sometimes known as the Smallville County Orphanage (*Adventure Comics* #260, May 1959), and was located south of town (*The New Adventures of Superboy* #22, October 1981). When a new orphanage was constructed, Superboy laid the cornerstone (*Superboy* [first series] #39, March 1955). The most recent caretakers of the orphanage were a couple named Martin and Merrill (*Action Comics* #469, March 1977). One account referred to the site as the Bright Home Orphanage and stated that it relocated to Metropolis, complete with the records of all its charges (*Superman's Girl Friend, Lois Lane* #3, July–August 1958).

The white-picket-fence town was overseen by Smallville City Hall (*Adventure Comics* #172, January 1952; others), which was located at the intersection of Peachtree and Oak streets with Jefferson and Wilson avenues (*The New Adventures of Superboy* #22, October 1981) and had a bell tower (*Adventure Comics* #222, March 1956; others). Its giant clock face was dubbed Big Bob (*Superboy* [first series] #32, April 1954). A statue of Superboy stood in front of the building (*Superboy* [first series] #99, September 1962), whose street number was 327 (*Action Comics* #288, May 1962). Additionally, there was the Smallville Courthouse (*Superboy* [first series] #10, September–October 1950; others).

The Smallville business district had survived tornadoes (*Superboy* [first series] #32, April 1954; others) and floods (*Superboy* [first series] #4, September–October 1949) but continued to prosper. Despite its relatively little size, Smallville benefited from a robust commercial section downtown, where Jonathan Kent eventually opened his general store when Clark Kent began attending public school.

Businessmen and the general populace had plenty of banks to choose from, including the Bank of Smallville (*Superboy* [first series] #169, October 1970); Farmer's Bank of Smallville (*Action Comics* #712, August 1995); Heartland Bank and Trust, whose president was James Morgan Stone at the time of Clark Kent's birth (*Superman: Last Son of Krypton,* 1978); Kansas National Bank (*Superman for All Seasons* #1, 1998); National Bank of Smallville (*Superboy* [first series] #39, March 1955); Sky Bank, a rooftop financial institution, which was "open sunny days for your convenience" (*Superboy* [first series] #32, April 1954); Smallville Bank and Trust (*Adventure Comics* #225, June 1956; others); Smallville Savings and Loan (*Superboy* [first series] #135, January 1967) at the corner of Oak Street and Washington Avenue, whose evident president was named Wallach (*The New Adventures of Superboy* #36, December 1982); Smallville Savings Bank, whose president was John C. Ross (*Adventure Comics* #148, Janu-

ary 1950); Smallville National Bank (*Adventure Comics* #181, October 1952; others), accessible from Cherry and Peachtree streets and Roosevelt Avenue (*The New Adventures of Superboy* #22, October 1981)—which was one of several structures built atop a long-abandoned mining shaft (*Superboy* [first series] #90, July 1961) and, following a complete remodel, featured a lobby with a gold "statuette honoring Superboy for capturing many of its bank robbers" (*Superboy* [first series] #24, February–March 1953)—whose president Honeywell hired Johnny Webber for a low-level position as a teenager and eventually saw him promoted to vice president (*Superman* [first series] #403, January 1985); Smallville Trust Bank (*Superboy* [first series] #107, September 1963); Smallville Trust Company (*Superboy* [first series] #16, September–October 1951); Third National Bank, whose president was Brandywine (*Superboy* [first series] #38, January 1955); and the Zoo Bank, a branch of an unspecified bank, which aimed to induce kids to save money and featured animal-themed deposit vessels amid exhibits of live animals and was probably located within the Smallville Zoo (*Superboy* [first series] #16, September–October 1951).

The most popular bank appeared to be Smallville Bank (*Superboy* [first series] #16, September–October 1951), with Dennison as its president during Clark Kent's infancy (*Superboy* [first series] #51, September 1956) followed by Rutledge (*Superboy* [first series] #33, June 1954) and Grimes (*Superboy* [first series] #64, April 1958). Subsequent president Judd West was revealed as an invader from the planet Zaron and turned to stone by a law enforcer from his world (*Adventure Comics* #274, July 1960). Unknown to most residents, a nineteenth-century tunnel lay beneath the bank, extending to the area occupied by Smallville High School (*Superboy* [first series] #19, April–May 1952).

Among other noteworthy businesses in town were Blanchard's General Store and Cooper's Smithy, both long-gone businesses dating back to Smallville's founding (*Superboy* [second series] #12, January 1991); Bud's Garage and Service Station, which was on Peachtree and Main streets facing Lincoln Avenue (*The New Adventures of Superboy* #22, October 1981) and whose owner, Bell, employed Clark Kent during his teens (*Superman/Batman* #48, July 2008); "Emmett Whitchurch's feed-mill, the tallest building in town" (*The Adventures of Superman* #573, December 1999); Fordman's Department Store (*Superman* [second series] #45, July 1990), across from the Smallville Diner, which had been in Smallville for generations, owned by Daniel Fordman and his father Harvey before him (*World of Smallville* #1, April 1988); and Schwartz's General Merchandise, which was on the Smallville square more than forty years ago (*World of Smallville* #1, April 1988).

The Smallville General Store (*Superman* [second series] #162, November 2000) was Clark Kent's first employer (*Batman and Superman: World's Finest* #7, October 1999). It was likely founded prior to 1873 by a man named Coogan and perhaps passed on to his daughter Lilah, who was being courted by Ethan Clark (*Chronos* #2, April 1998). As the Clark General Store, it was saved from takeover by Daniel Fordman, whose father had eyed the property (*World of Smallville* #1, April 1988). It was owned by Ed Carlman around the time Jonathan and Martha Kent were married (*Superman* [second series] #174, November 2001) and was inherited by his son upon his death (*Superman for All Seasons* #1, 1998). Decades later, the Kents purchased the business from Ed Carlman, Jr. (*Superman* [second series] #178, March 2002).

The Humane Society Building cornerstone was opposite a square of concrete with Krypto's footprints (*Superboy* [first series] #136, March 1967).

Visitors to town were likely to stay at the Smallville Hotel (*Adventure Comics* #166, July 1951; *Superboy* [first series] #27, August–September 1953), which was bordered by Oak and Grove streets and Wilson Avenue (*The New Adventures of Superboy* #22, October 1981). It was described as the community's lone hotel (*Superboy* [first series] #10, September–October 1950), in existence since at least 1873 (*The Kents* #12, July 1997). This was probably also known as Hotel Smallville (*Adventure Comics* #243, December 1957). Its proprietors were a couple whose stage name had been the Flying Zambezis until they were falsely accused of theft from Jeff's Sensational Traveling Circus. The couple had a teenage son named Ben (*Superboy* [first series] #16, September–October 1951).

The Earth-1 Kent farm was southwest of Smallville (*The New Adventures of Superboy* #22, October 1981) and purchased by Alex and Lila Crowley after the Kents moved into town. Once two of the country's preeminent nuclear scientists, the Crowleys continued their research in a bunker beneath the farm's silo as they sought to create an atomic super-being (*Superboy* [first series] #196, July 1973). The property was eventually taken over by a housing development as Smallville expanded (*Superman* [first series] #420, June 1986).

Jonathan Kent sold the farm to open the Kent General Store (*Adventure Comics* #149, February 1950; *Superboy* [first series] #6, January–February 1950; others). It was destroyed by fire at one point but quickly rebuilt (*Adventure Comics* #244, January 1958) and later damaged in another explosion (*The New Adventures of Superboy* #48, December 1983). It was previously owned by Whizzer Barnes (*Superman: Last Son of Krypton,* 1978) and located on the 100 block of Oak Street (*The New Adventures of Superboy* #22, October 1981). An earlier account placed it on Main Street (*Superboy* [first series] #15, July–August 1951). At one point, the business had a red-and-green neon sign (*Adventure Comics* #260, May 1959).

The Kent family house was unwittingly built atop the remains of a former Indian civilization (*Superman* [first series] #270, December 1973). Its address was 321 Maple Street (*Action Comics* #494, April 1979) at the south end of town (*The New Adventures of Superboy* #22, October 1981). The house was once destroyed in a meteor strike (*Adventure Comics* #229, October 1956) and later by a fire generated by a space rock (*Adventure Comics* #244, January 1958). Another account gave the house number as 262 (*Superboy* [first series] #66, July 1958). Retired police chief Douglas Parker later served as the house's caretaker (*Action Comics* #494, April 1979).

The Lang home (*Man of Steel* #6, December 1986) was at 325 Maple Street at the south end of town (*The New Adventures of Superboy* #22, October 1981). It was destroyed by Doctor Chaos (*The New Adventures of Superboy* #25, January 1982) but soon rebuilt. Professor Lang's study, filled with his archaeological treasures, was in "an isolated building behind the home" (*Superboy* [first series] #34, July 1954).

The home of newlyweds Pete Ross and Lana Lang was destroyed by Conduit (*Superman* [second series] #100, May 1995).

Among the more interesting residential dwellings was "The Cat House," a cat-shaped structure carved from rock by Superboy to fulfill the eccentric Mrs. Wiggins's dying request: using her money to set up a sanctuary for homeless cats—including a lion (*Superboy* [first series] #5, November–December 1949).

The Kent farm after the Crisis on Infinite Earths reordered reality was said to be at R.F.D. 1 Box 72 (*Superman: The Man of Steel* #20, February 1993) or 51 (*Superman* [second series] #172, September 2001) and was located "fifteen miles south of Smallville" (*Action Comics* #689, Late July 1993) or "four miles northwest of Smallville" (*Superman* [second series] #113, July 1996) and was destroyed by Conduit (*Superman* [second series] #100, May 1995). It was subsequently rebuilt (*The Adventures of Superman* #535, June 1996) but seriously damaged yet again when Smallville was caught on the edge of an extraterrestrial blast that destroyed Topeka (*Superman* [second series] #172, September 2001). Once again, Superman restored the residence (*Superman* [second series] #174, November 2001). The farm was previously owned by someone named Sullivan (*Superman* [second series] #174, November 2001).

As befitted a small town, Smallville enjoyed numerous occasions when citizens could get together to celebrate events or just visit with one another. One was Homecoming Day, when former residents return to be honored (*Superman* [first series] #90, July 1954).

There was also the annual Kiwanis Picnic (*Action Comics* #655, July 1990); "the annual Kansas Harvest Fair" (*Action Comics* #706, January 1995); "Smallville's annual rummage sale" (*Superboy* [first series] #115, September 1964);

Smallville Air Show (*World's Finest Comics* #84, September–October 1956); Smallville County Fair (*Superboy* [first series] #8, May–June 1950; others) aka Smallville County State Fair (*Adventure Comics* #285, June 1961); Smallville Day (*Adventure Comics* #144, September 1949), presumably also known as Founders' Day (*Superboy* [first series] #196, July 1973), when the community "celebrates the anniversary of its founding" (*Superboy* [first series] #121, June 1965); Smallville High Parents' Day, held the first Saturday of each April (*The New Adventures of Superboy* #7, July 1980); "Smallville High's annual hobby fair" (*Superboy* [first series] #7, March–April 1950); "Annual Smallville Kiddie Hayride" (*Superboy* [first series] #102, January 1963); Smallville Winter Carnival (*Adventure Comics* #456, March–April 1978); "the annual Father-and-Son Banquet" (*Superboy* [first series] #75, September 1959); and "the annual sports festival" held at Smallville High School (*Superboy* [first series] #5, November–December 1949).

Smallville celebrated its 50th anniversary (*Superboy* [first series] #8, May–June 1950), its centennial (*Adventure Comics* #298, July 1962; others), and its 150th birthday (*Sovereign Seven* #23, June 1997). The latter date was in keeping with the post-Crisis reality.

Superboy Day (first declared in *Superboy* [first series] #2, May–June 1949) was celebrated annually (*Superman's Pal, Jimmy Olsen* #8, October 1955). A similar annual event (*Action Comics* #211, December 1955) celebrated the Boy (and later Man) of Steel's "Earthday," the anniversary of the date he landed in Smallville. The first such event became infamous for its unwitting revelation that Superboy was vulnerable to kryptonite (*Superman* [first series] #136, April 1960). A "Superboy Week" was once declared (*Adventure Comics* #209, February 1955).

For additional entertainment, people could visit Smallville Amusement Park (*Superboy* [first series] #193, February 1973; others). The fairgrounds (*Adventure Comics* #225, June 1956; others) were west of town near Crystal Lake (*The New Adventures of Superboy* #22, October 1981). The town had numerous theaters for music, performances, and movies. The Smallville Public Library (*Superboy* [first series] #5, November–December 1949) included Powell (*Superboy* [first series] #29, December 1953), Oates, secretly the Crime Professor (*Superboy* [first series] #30, January 1954), and Sharon Vance (*Action Comics* #759, November 1999) as librarians. Another library was dedicated (*Adventure Comics* #288, September 1961) only to be destroyed by Dev-Em moments later. A new Smallville Library was excavated by Superboy (*The New Adventures of Superboy* #7, July 1980).

There was the Smallville Theater (*Superboy* [first series] #34, July 1954), a venue where acts like Zatara the Magician (*The New Adventures of Superboy* #14, February 1981) and Zazar the Great played (*Superboy* [first series] #38, January 1955) and where an impressionable seven-year-old Clark Kent, asked by his parents to choose between two classics on the bill, chose *To Kill a Mockingbird* over *Zorro* (*Superman* [second series] #67, May 1992). The theater was on the 300 block of Main Street (*The New Adventures of Superboy* #22, October 1981).

Citizens had a choice of recreational venues around town, including Central Park (*Superboy* [first series] #20, June–July 1952); Fritter's Field, a patch of ground where kids played baseball (*Action Comics Annual* #10, 2007); Hill Park (*Superboy* [first series] #140, July 1967); Lake Park, which included its namesake lake and a zoo, and was located somewhere outside the Smallville community (*Superboy* [first series] #123, September 1965); Smallville Memorial Park, which included a planetarium, a botanical garden, a lake, and a bronze statue of a soldier (*Superboy* [first series] #22, October–November 1952); Smallville Park (*Adventure Comics* #297, June 1962), which was bordered by Main and Oak streets and Jefferson and Wilson avenues (*The New Adventures of Superboy* #22, October 1981) and included a statuette of Pan playing a flute (*Adventure Comics* #174, March 1952) and statues of Krypto (*Superboy* [first series] #114, July 1964) and Superboy (*Superboy* [first series] #61, December 1957) as well as a planetarium (*Adventure Comics* #307, April 1963)—and a crumbling statue of Chief Tall Oak ("friend of Fort Smallville") once stood in the park, as well (*Adventure Comics* #222, March 1956); Smallville Square (*Superboy* [first series] #48, April 1956), which included a statue of a World War One soldier (*Superboy* [first series] #153, January 1969); and Vicker's Park (*Superboy* [first series] #39, March 1955).

There was also an unnamed park (*Superboy* [first series] #23, December 1952–January 1953), which included an apparently wooden statue of Paul Bunyan, "erected in honor of National Forest Week" (*Adventure Comics* #236, May 1957) as well as statues of an unspecified pioneer, soldier (*Adventure Comics* #240, September 1957), and George Washington. The park contained a zoo (*Adventure Comics* #248, May 1958). Located somewhere in the community was Cupid's Love Seat, a heart-backed bench with a statue of Cupid and his bow and arrow. A local legend claimed that those who kissed while sitting there would marry (*Superman's Girl Friend, Lois Lane* #55, February 1965).

Krypton Park was built by Superboy on a "condemned swamp outside Smallville," inspired by the arrival of a kryptonite-irradiated chunk of the planet that included the home where the infant Kal-El lived. It had an exhibit of Kryptonian toys and a statue of the mythical aquatic dragon Kally Jlin, an analog to Earth's Moby-Dick (*Adventure Comics* #232, January 1957).

The Strange Visitor Memorial was an abstract statue that honored the heroic persona of Smallville native Sharon Vance, who died in the Imperiex War (*World's Finest: Our Worlds at War* #1, October 2001).

Sports fans could head for Smallville Stadium (*Superboy* [first series] #21, August–September 1952; others), which was bordered by Main and Oak streets and Lincoln and Roosevelt avenues (*The New Adventures of Superboy* #22, Octo-

ber 1981). Owner Pete Groff attempted to burn down the stadium to get insurance to pay off his gambling debts but was thwarted by Superboy (*Adventure Comics* #253, October 1958). The Smallville Racetrack hosted horse races including the Junior Derby for teenagers (*Adventure Comics* #230, November 1956).

For a small town, Smallville had a disproportionate number of museums, such as the new Grecian Museum (*Superboy* [first series] #4, September–October 1949); the old Hanley Building, which "was given to Smallville as a museum but there [were] no funds to repair the roof" so Superboy and a superpowered Jonathan Kent did the job themselves (*Adventure Comics* #224, May 1956); Martell's Museum, a far-ranging celebration of aviation accumulated over John Martell's lifetime, which had its own airfield (*Adventure Comics* #155, August 1950); the Pirate Museum, which was converted from the home of Sinbad Kent (1757–1819), who'd retired to Smallville in 1797 and was reputed to have been a notorious pirate, though documentation eventually surfaced revealing that he had, in fact, been a spy for George Washington in the Revolutionary War (*Superboy* [first series] #79, March 1960); the Smallville Museum of Marvels ("Est. 1889"), home to all manner of antiquities and artifacts (*JLA Annual* #2, 1998); "Smallville's modest, but efficient, Natural History Museum," which employed Professor Mark Olsen as its curator for a time (*Adventure Comics* #216, September 1955); the Supernatural Museum (*Superboy* [first series] #112, April 1964); and an abandoned wax museum that burned to the ground (*Superboy* [first series] #141, September 1967).

The largest such facility was the Smallville Museum (*Adventure Comics* #144, September 1949; others), which bordered Grove and Maple streets and Lincoln Avenue (*The New Adventures of Superboy* #22, October 1981) and included a statue of Jor-El sculpted by Superboy (*Adventure Comics* #238, July 1957), part of its Hall of Superboy Trophies (*Superman's Pal, Jimmy Olsen* #8, October 1955). The Exhibit of Flying Legends was probably also located here (*Adventure Comics* #226, July 1956). Its most valuable painting was *Vulcan's Forge* (*Superman* [first series] #152, April 1962). Dr. Horst was the museum's curator (*Superboy* [first series] #92, October 1961), and Cal Trent was its custodian (*Superman's Pal, Jimmy Olsen* #8, October 1955). It's likely that the museum, like the homes of many longtime residents, contained a preserved piece of the giant cake that Superboy served on his last day in Smallville (*Superman* [first series] #97, May 1955). One account (*Superboy* [first series] #11, November–December 1950) claimed that the museum—the city's first—was not constructed until that point and that its exhibits were recovered by Superboy.

The Superboy Museum was built to honor the town's champion (*Action Comics* #265, June 1960; *Superboy* [first series] #92, October 1961), immediately east of the Smallville Museum, bordered Grove and Maple streets and Roosevelt Avenue (*The New Adventures of Superboy* #22, October 1981). A second Superboy Museum, a glass structure created by the Boy of Steel, was across the

river in neighboring Hadley (*Adventure Comics* #166, July 1951).

Covering the town's business and the Teen of Steel's exploits were numerous newspapers, among them the *Small County Bulletin* (*The Adventures of Superman* #474, January 1991); *Smallville Blade* (*Adventure Comics* #303, December 1962); *Smallville Clarion* (*Adventure Comics* #164, May 1951); *Smallville Courier* (*Adventure Comics* #219, December 1955); *Smallville Gazette* (*Superboy* [first series] #19, April–May 1952), which featured reporter Bill Wilder (*Adventure Comics* #181, October 1952); *Smallville Herald* (*Adventure Comics* #238, July 1957), with editor W. Dodge and reporter Alex Jones, who earned a reputation for his timely Superboy scoops and was hired away by "a big city newspaper" (*Superboy* [first series] #31, March 1954); *Smallville Journal* (*Adventure Comics* #223, April 1956; *Superboy* [first series] #14, May–June 1951); *Smallville Ledger* (*World of Smallville* #2, May 1988), with reporter Steve Greenfield (*Superman* [second series] #178, March 2002); *Smallville News* (*Adventure Comics* #153, June 1950; *Superboy* [first series] #35, September 1954), which included photographer Tom Ferritt (*Adventure Comics* #194, November 1953) and was most recently published by Joel Todd (*Superman's Pal, Jimmy Olsen* #20, April 1957); *Smallville Pioneer* (*Superboy* [first series] #11, November–December 1950); *Smallville Post* (*Superboy* [first series] #32, April 1954); *Smallville Register* (*Superboy* [second series] #12, January 1991); *Smallville Sentinel* (*Superboy* [first series] #5, November–December 1949), which was directly east of the Smallville Hotel and bordered Oak and Grove streets and Madison Avenue (*The New Adventures of Superboy* #22, October 1981), with a gray-haired publisher named Shaw (*The New Adventures of Superboy* #45, September 1983) and an editor named William Vance (*Superboy* [first series] #111, March 1964), also called the *Daily Sentinel* (*Adventure Comics* #140, May 1949); *Smallville Star* (*Superboy* [first series] #1, March–April 1949); *Smallville Times* (*Adventure Comics* [first series] #208, January 1955; *Superboy* [first series] #12, January–February 1951); and the *Smallville Times-Reader,* edited by Sarah Lane (*Superman: Last Son of Krypton,* 1978).

The town was also served by radio station WSMV (*Superboy* [first series] #195, June 1973), which was bordered by Grove and Maple streets and Jefferson and Wilson avenues (*The New Adventures of Superboy* #22, October 1981).

"KSAS, serving all of Neosho County," was within broadcasting range of Smallville (*Chronos* #11, February 1999).

The town had its own local television station, SVTV (*Superboy* [first series] #15, July–August 1951).

Smallville educated its children first at the Smallville Elementary School (*Action Comics* #712, August 1995), which was bordered by Cherry and Peachtree streets and Roosevelt and Washington avenues (*The New Adventures of Superboy* #22, October 1981). It was here that Clark Kent first met his friends including Lana Lang, Peter Ross, and Kenny Braverman.

All attended Smallville High School (*Superboy* [first series] #1, March–April 1949), which was bordered by Main and Oak streets and Roosevelt and Washington avenues (*The New Adventures of Superboy* #22, October 1981). It was founded in 1900, and the commemorative cornerstone of the building contained mementos of the time, including the sword Matthew Kent carried on San Juan Hill (*Superboy* [first series] #113, June 1964). A statue of a World War One soldier was outside the building (*Superboy* [first series] #119, March 1965). Unknown to most residents, a nineteenth-century tunnel lay beneath the building, extending to the area occupied by the Smallville Bank (*Superboy* [first series] #19, April–May 1952). The building had a statue of Superboy erected on its roof at one point (*DC Super-Stars* #12, February 1977) as well as a clock tower (*Superboy* [first series] #30, January 1954). Plans were in place for a time to build a new high school (*Superboy* [first series] #152, December 1968), and one was finally completed shortly after Clark Kent's graduation (*Superman* [first series] #97, May 1955). The school included "a special class for blind students" (*Superboy* [first series] #68, October 1958). During Clark Kent's youth, its principal was a man named James Foster (*Superboy* [first series] #71, March 1959) or Standish (*Superboy* [first series] #80, April 1960) or Danforth (*Adventure Comics* #302, November 1962; *Superboy* [first series] #66, July 1958) or Goodwin (*Superman/Batman Secret Files 2003,* November 2003; *Teen Titans* [third series] #7, March 2004).

The Phi Omega fraternity house and gym was affiliated with Smallville High (*Superboy* [first series] #94, January 1962), as was the Smallhi Fraternity (*Adventure Comics* #150, March 1950). The school also had its own radio program (*Adventure Comics* #301, October 1962); its

newspapers were the *Student Star* (*More Fun Comics* #106, November–December 1945) and the *Smallville High Bulletin* (*Adventure Comics* #308, May 1963). The superintendent of schools was Dr. Lawrence (*Superboy* [first series] #13, March–April 1951), and the head of the board of education, Mr. Reddles (*Superboy* [first series] #19, April–May 1952).

As with most high schools across the United States, Smallville had a robust athletics program and boasted competitive teams in most major sports. There were the Smallville Crows football team (*Action Comics* #791, July 2002; others), also called the Smallville Giants (*The Adventures of Superman* #474, January 1991), who wore orange, yellow, and white uniforms (*Man of Steel* #1, October 1986)—as did its track team (*Superman* [second series] #0, October 1994). Cheerleaders and fans yelled "Go CAW-CAW-CAW Crows!" (*Action Comics* #791, July 2002). When Clark Kent attended high school, Ted Hawkins was one of the team's star players (*Adventure Comics* #170, November 1951), as were Bash Bashford (*Superboy* [first series] #161, December 1969) and Joey Calhoun (*Superman: Birthright* #7, April 2004). The Crows took on such teams as Grandville (*Action Comics* #791, July 2002), Hadley High School (*Adventure Comics* #170, November 1951), the Dawson Pirates (*Action Comics* #800, April 2003), and the Brightonburg Warriors (*Superman: Birthright* #8, May 2004).

The high school baseball team wore red-and-white uniforms (*Adventure Comics* #254, November 1958) and was alternately known as the Smallville Tigers (*Superboy* [first series] #121, June 1965) or the Smallville Sabertooths (*Superboy Spectacular* #1, 1980). Their home games were played at Smallville Stadium (*Superboy* [first series] #139, June 1967). The statue of a Civil War hero stood near the ball field (*Superboy* [first series] #50, July 1956). Ronnie James was one of the team's star players when Clark Kent was in high school (*Adventure Comics* #254, November 1958).

During Clark Kent's teens, Smallville High's athletes were most evenly matched with those from nearby Corinth, something would-be bank robber James Willoughby attempted to exploit in a series of contests held in Smallville Stadium and the Corinth Sportsdrome (*Superboy* [first series] #29, December 1953).

The Rangers was a boys' club that included Clark Kent as a member (*Adventure Comics* #159, December 1950).

Then there was Smallville College, whose dean John Devon was revealed as an invader from the planet Zaron and was turned to stone by a law enforcer from his world (*Adventure Comics* #274, July 1960). The college also had a stadium (*Adventure Comics* #298, July 1962).

Despite his best efforts, Superboy could not protect the community from every threat. A portion was destroyed during a violent clash between the Teen Titans and the mad Superboy-Prime during the events known as Infinite Crisis (*Infinite Crisis* #4, March 2006; *Teen Titans* [third series] #32, March 2006; *Teen Titans* [third series] *Annual* #1, 2006).

SMARTYPANTS

Professor C. C. Skynhedd made a name for himself with his radical notion that children would never fulfill their potential unless their every whim was granted. His protègè was an adorable girl, a genius who drove the Man of Steel to distraction with her demands until Superman finally put his boot down on the runaway permissiveness (*Superman* [first series] #56, January–February 1949).

SMATTEN, JON

Within a lead-lined cavern outside Metropolis, the renegade scientist Smatten came upon some space-drift wreckage that originated on Krypton and contained a supply of kryptium, the strongest metal known on the doomed world. The cunning man fashioned the nearly indestructible super-metal into a mechanized armored knight and gave it the instruction to destroy the Last Son of Krypton. Superman demolished the robot and apprehended its creator (*Action Comics* #329, October 1965).

SMIGGS, SAMUEL

Considered a "wacky wizard of science," Professor Samuel Smiggs was the inventor of the "if machine," a device whose "radiation can change history by reaching through the past to make things happen differently!" When "Bullet" Harris and his gang attempted to steal the machine, they were apprehended by Superman, but a ricocheting bullet struck the device and damaged it beyond any hope of repair (*World's Finest Comics* #38, January–February 1949).

SMILTER, JOHN

Wearing an asbestos suit, the daring criminal John Smilter fired bullets into a fuel truck, causing an explosion and fire. He then dashed through the flames and stole the fabled Fabian diamonds from a dockside customs office. Smilter and his men boarded the nearby USS *Varania*, from which they tried to escape by helicopter. Unfortunately, not only was Batman aboard the cruise ship, as a vacationing Bruce Wayne, but his cabinmate was Metropolis reporter Clark Kent, also known as Superman. The classic meeting of two super heroes led to the apprehension of Smilter and his accomplices (*Superman* [first series] #76, May–June 1952).

SMITH, SAD SAM

Denied the joys of laughter, Sam Smith grew wealthy but unhappy. The wheelchair-bound billionaire wanted to laugh and was willing to pay for the privilege. He offered a billion-dollar donation to the Metropolis Orphan Fund for the person in Metropolis who could coax a laugh from him. The greatest stand-up performers in the city tried, but reporter Clark Kent inadvertently won the contest when he had to change into the Man of Steel in front of the sad man. The very notion that Kent could be Superman was ridiculous enough to make the rich man a laughing man (*Superman* [first series] #136, April 1960).

SMYTHE, CASPER

The meek employee of Lacey's Department Store who was secretly Sir Gauntlet.

SNAGRIFF

Jor-El experimented on this winged dinosaur-like creature in the years prior to Krypton's destruction. Studying ways to prolong life, he injected a serum into a Snagriff—with disastrous results. The Snagriff evolved into a metallic monster with a voracious appetite for minerals and metals, so Jor-El shipped the poor creature to the moon of Koron.

When Krypton exploded, the shock wave sent the satellite hurtling through space, eventually passing within a short distance of Earth. The Snagriff, which had survived the journey, leapt toward the planet and under the solar radiation developed superpowers.

Superman had his hands full trying to prevent the bewildered and hungry beast from devastating his adopted world. But first, the Snagriff managed to consume an ocean liner, gold bullion from the Federal Gold Reserve, and tons of scrap metal. The Man of Steel managed to get the Snagriff to swallow six atomic bombs then carried it high into the air, where the heat of the creature's body detonated the nuclear bombs, utterly destroying it (*Superman* [first series] #78, September–October 1952).

SNAKE, THE

Wearing a scaly, orange-spotted yellow costume resembling the skin of a giant snake, Bill Chantey killed his victims with double-pronged lances tipped with a serpent's deadly venom. The foreman of the Allerton Construction Company's Holloway Tunnel project, and a longtime collector of snakes, the man grew bitter at being repeatedly passed over for promotion. He sought revenge by brutally murdering several of Allerton's sandhogs but was finally hospitalized after being accidentally bitten by one of his own poisonous snakes during a climactic confrontation with the Man of Steel (*Superman* [first series] #18, September–October 1942).

SNAPINN, STEVEN

A Metropolis youth who helped Superman as the hero Little Leaguer.

SNARE

The Master Jailer's daughter, Carla Draper, was also a costumed felon known as Snare.

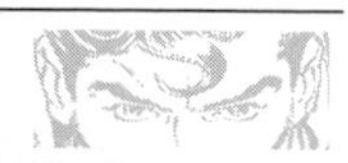

SOCRATES

Professor Lewis Lang brought a mynah bird back to Smallville after an expedition and was surprised to watch as the avian gained intelligence and enhanced abilities after drinking kryptonite-laced water. The bird, named Socrates, went on to challenge the Boy of Steel's patience when it was used by a criminal to help carry out robberies (*Adventure Comics* #225, June 1956).

SODOM AND GOMORRAH

A husband-and-wife super-villain team, they were the first opponents the Man of Steel faced after he slept for three days, recovering from having liquefied kryptonite removed from his system. The couple attempted to kill him with their high-tech weaponry, before the woman fled, fearing her own death, leaving her partner behind to be apprehended by Superman (*Action Comics* #819, November 2004).

SOLAR BOY

A spoiled brat, this alien teen temporarily gained an array of superpowers thanks to his late father's Solar-Ray Super-Energy Converters. Constant recharging was required, but that did not stop him from indulging himself as he went from world to world picking out objects for his private pleasure. Wearing a green costume with yellow trunks, wristbands, boots, and cape, a brown belt, and a stylized yellow "sun" emblazoned on his chest, Solar Boy arrived on Earth and tried to collect some animals from zoos around the world for his game preserve back home. He was thwarted by the timely arrival of Superboy and Krypto. Solar Boy returned to space and vowed revenge, especially against the super-dog.

The two encountered each other some time later after the pet and his master had a brief falling-out. Solar Boy recognized Krypto immediately and befriended the dog, who did not recall the juvenile delinquent. As a result, he wound up losing his powers and being mistreated by the cruel youth. The Dog of Steel managed to spoil the plan when he destroyed the Solar-Ray Super-Energy Converters, costing Solar Boy his powers and restoring Krypto's super-abilities (*Adventure Comics* #269, February 1960).

SOLARIS

In the far-off 853rd century, humankind had developed the Hypernet, a network that spanned the stars, allowing artificially created suns to provide life-sustaining heat and light to needy galaxies. Unfortunately, one such sun, placed near Uranus, exceeded its programming and became known as Solaris the Tyrant Sun, trying to twist the cosmos to its own designs. As a result, Solaris was one of the deadliest enemies of Justice Legion A, the Sol system's intergalactic champions (*DC One Million* #1–4, November 1998).

One of its schemes, in concert with the immortal villain Vandal Savage, was to infect the android Legionnaire Hourman with a biotech virus that would affect not only technology but biological life-forms as well. When the Justice Legion A visited the late twentieth century to spend time with their inspiration, the Justice League of America, the devastating virus came with the heroes. Now two eras were threatened with rampant death and destruction. The real goal, though, was the annihilation of Superman, known in his time as Superman Prime, who had taken up residence within Sol itself, sealing himself off from most of his comrades.

To combat the futuristic threat, the people in the twentieth century actually had to construct the first incarnation of Solaris. The virus contained Solaris's primary programming so it managed to loop through time and gain sentience in both eras. If all went according to plan, Solaris would supplant Sol and become the main source of power in the solar system.

Solaris used what it thought was the last surviving piece of kryptonite as a bullet to kill the prime hero, but Steel, Plastic Man, Big Barda, Huntress, and Zauriel managed to swap the fragment in exchange for a ring forged for the Green Lantern Corps. Superman, newly empowered, emerged from the sun and managed to destroy Solaris. The synthetic sun collapsed in on itself and was transformed into a new world, one Superman intended to colonize as a new version of his homeworld Krypton.

The Solaris formed in the JLA's era was said to have millennia-long battles with Superman, considered "the progenitor of the dynasty." Solaris would also battle the Man of Steel's descendants through the centuries until the 505th century, when that Superman sacrificed his life while reprogramming the artificial intelligence. The new operating system meant Solaris was directed to work for the improvement of life within the solar system. From that point onward, it worked with the Superman Family.

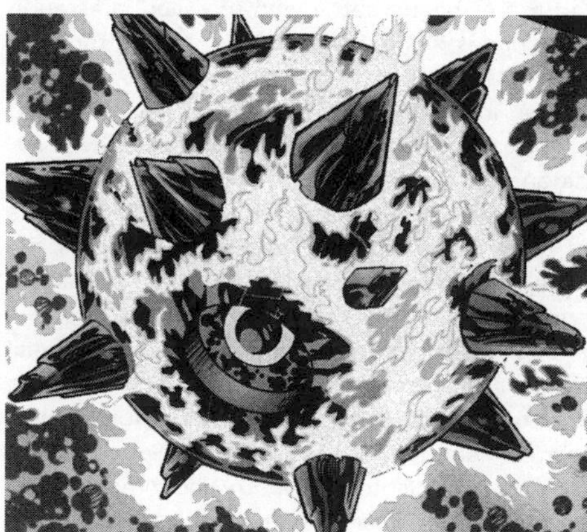

While the programming made the star more benevolent, it was not perfectly working for truth and justice. It formed and led the Pancosmic Justice Jihad some generations hence, trying to take advantage of a period when the planets were enduring a new Dark Age. That ended when Superman Prime returned from his galactic wandering in the seven hundredth century and defeated Solaris, ending the Dark Age and beginning a new era. This also meant that artificial suns were no longer essential for day-to-day life and were reduced to light and heat sources.

By the 853rd century, the loop had been completed and Solaris was ready to strike back.

SOLARMAN

When the mysterious alien Xviar, posing as Clark Kent's neighbor Mr. Xavier, altered Superman so his powers only worked when he was in the red-and-blue costume, an unnamed criminal scientist attempted to give himself powers on a par with Superman's by wearing a vest covered with solar cells. Superman defeated him by overloading Solarman's vest using his heat vision (*Superman* [first series] #298, April 1976).

SONIK

William Parker was an audio engineer who volunteered his time with an inner-city boys' club. Seeing that the teens needed some sort of role model they could relate to, he created a heroic persona called Sonik. He crafted a yellow-and-brown hip-hop jacket-and-tights ensemble, then equipped himself with a sonic blaster, a powerful miniature microphone, and a cloaking device that muffled ambient sound, allowing him to move close to a target without being heard.

It was Sonik's honor to work alongside the World's Finest team as they corralled gangsters in front of the very kids Parker was trying to teach that crime was not a glamorous lifestyle (*World's Finest Comics* #310, December 1984).

Some time later, Sonik aided Superman by body-guarding a pop star while Batman sought the attacker (*World's Finest Comics* #318, August 1985).

There was a female Sonik, a heroine generated by the alien H-dial used by Victoria Grant (*Adventure Comics* #485, September 1981).

SONS OF LIBERTY, THE

A paramilitary group, the Sons of Liberty used agents to foment dissent with the goal of eventually overthrowing the federal government. They accepted Benjamin Lockwood as a recruit after he left the CIA and outfitted him with a costume and gear, using him as their primary field operative, Agent Liberty. In addition to doing the group's work, he also performed altruistic acts, such as aiding Superman when Brainiac attacked Earth (*The Adventures of Superman* #488, March 1994). The Sons continued to grow desperate to accomplish their goals, culminating in their attempt to force Pete Ross into executing Major Holcraft before he could testify against them. The incident awakened Agent Liberty to the group's true face, and he executed their leaders Jay Harriman and Judge Ronald Kramer. Lockwood then fed details to reporter Clark Kent, who helped expose the group and shut them down (*Superman* [second series] #69; *The Adventures of Superman* #492, both July 1994).

SPACE CANINE PATROL AGENCY, THE

While most residents of Earth-1 knew of Krypto as an intelligent, superpowered dog, few could imagine he had peers scattered around the galaxy. In fact, they gathered together as the Space Canine Patrol Agency, dedicated to using their unique powers to protect life for all sentient beings, even cats (*Superboy* [first series] #131, July 1966). Krypto found the group after it had formed and

was initially given honorary membership before being considered Canine Secret Agent Number 1 (*Superboy* [first series] #132, September 1966).

The espionage canines were often opposed by the PHANTY-CATS but emerged triumphant after each brawl. The membership consisted of TAIL TERRIER (with an elastic tail), TUSKY HUSKY (who could elongate a canine tooth into a tusk), PAW POOCH (who could add additional limbs), Beam Beagle (with "searchlight eyes"; he died in action), Chameleon Collie (a shape-shifter), Hot Dog (a pyrokinetic), Bulldog (who could grow horns), MAMMOTH MUTT (who could increase in size, but died on Krypto's first case), Mammoth Miss (who could also increase her size), and PROPHETIC PUP (a clairvoyant).

"Big dog! Big dog! Bow wow wow! We'll crush Evil! Now, now, now!"—Battle cry of the S.C.P.A.

SPACE CAT PATROL AGENCY, THE

Much as the male army led to the formation of the WACS, the Space Canine Patrol Agency had a branch for feline superpowered secret agents. The Space Cat Patrol Agency's membership included, at the time of KRYPTO's service with the S.C.P.A., Atomic Tom, POWER PUSS, and Crab Tabby (*Superboy* [first series] #131, July 1966).

SPACEOPOLY

Spaceopoly was a three-dimensional game that employed simulated planets and spaceships. The game was wildly popular in the thirtieth century; at least one copy was kept in the LEGION OF SUPER-HEROES' recreation room. SUPERBOY and BRAINIAC 5 often played each other prior to the start of official business (*Adventure Comics* #342, March 1966). At one point in another reality, Polar Boy recruited Spaceopoly Lad ("I've got the ability to finish every Spaceopoly game I ever start") to help him fight Evillo (*Legion of Super-Heroes* [fourth series] #49, Early November 1993).

SPARKS, AUBREY

This young woman was randomly selected by the JOKER to become a bizarre version of the EARTH-BORN ANGEL SUPERGIRL known as SCORCH.

SPARKS, GARY

Called the "Casanova" of STANHOPE COLLEGE, Gary Sparks dated and dumped most of the coeds in his class. When she began attending college, LINDA LEE DANVERS heard of the Lothario and wanted to teach him a lesson as both Linda and SUPERGIRL. However, his charm affected even the Maid of Steel, a fact that bothered her to no end (*Action Comics* #369, November 1968).

SPARX

Donna Carol Force was part of the Canadian super-team known as the Force Family but had no meta-human powers herself. When she heard that aliens had come to Earth and their bite could trigger the meta-gene, she took her uncle Harry with her and headed south of the border to METROPOLIS, unaware that this same bite was often deadly. When she finally found an alien—the leader Gemir, as it happened—Donna reconsidered her decision, but the alien bit her anyway. Her spinal fluid was drained but the unintended aftereffect was that her fondest wish came true: She developed electrical powers. Donna adopted a costume and used the code name Sparx to swing into action. Fairly quickly, she found herself fighting for her life alongside SUPERBOY as they attacked one of the alien hideaways. Victorious, she planted a big kiss on the Clone of Steel and returned home (*The Adventures of Superman Annual* #5, 1993).

In time, she returned to action, combining forces with other newly transformed heroes during the climactic battle with the alien infestation (*Bloodlines Annual* #2, 1993). In the aftermath, Donna, also known as D.C. to her friends, chose to remain in America with several of "New Bloods" (*Showcase '94* #12, December 1994). She even auditioned to appear on *Blood Pack,* a television reality show that would follow the day-to-day exploits of these new heroes (*Blood Pack* #1–4, March–June 1995). When the producers turned out to be criminals, Blood Pack spoiled their plans.

Soon after, Sparx found the interdimensional Event Horizon, home to the unending Rave. Finding Superboy once more, she helped him form a new team of heroes known as the RAVERS (*Superboy and the Ravers* #1, September 1996). She thrived on the nonstop action and continued to flirt with Superboy before turning her affections toward HERO, until he gently explained that he was gay (*Superboy and the Ravers* #14, October 1997).

During one adventure, she was given "Qwa-Angel" powers, deriving from the anti-matter universe of Qward. They came in handy as the team battled a race known as the Predators. In the end, however, her fight also meant the end of all of her powers, with Sparx once more just D. C. Force (*Superboy and the Ravers* #19, March 1998).

Sparx regained her powers (*Superboy* [third series] #65, August 1999) and continued adventuring on her own. She wound up under the mental thrall of Despero along with numerous other "New Bloods" and other adventurers, all sent to battle the World's Finest heroes (*Superman/Batman* #32, February 2007). After being freed, Sparx attempted to form a new team, the League of Titans, with Mas Y Menos and Empress (*Final Crisis* #1, July 2008). She was considered for Titans membership (*Teen Titans* [third series] #66, February 2009) but was not offered a place.

SPENCE, AMANDA

The AGENDA was a covert organization with an eye toward global domination. They employed numerous field operatives with special assignments. Amanda Spence was tasked with capturing SUPERBOY, in order to clone the Teen of Steel (*Superboy* [third series] #32, October 1996). She insinuated herself in the hero's world by posing as a journalist and learning about him from his pals, including his girlfriend TANA MOON.

Satisfied that she had gathered enough intelligence, the attractive but deadly brunette assembled a strike team and launched an assault at the Compound. Her knowledge proved effective: The teen was captured and brought to the Agenda's headquarters. The group's technology also proved successful, as a clone of the clone of Superman and LEX LUTHOR was created. As a second-generation clone, though, the being was flawed. Named MATCH, it proved erratic and a threat to not only Superboy but the Agenda as well. During their first confrontation, Superboy and Match managed to destroy the Agenda's lair, although the directors managed to escape (*Superboy* [third series] #34–36, December 1996–February 1997). Superboy rescued Spence from the resulting explosion, an act he would later come to regret.

While Spence was incarcerated at the Slab, a virus created by the Agenda began to break down Superboy's DNA, threatening his life. SUPERGIRL came to his aid and questioned Spence, who repaid this act of kindness by providing the heroine with the information needed to save his life (*Superboy* [third series] #40, June 1997).

The Agenda regrouped and once again assigned Spence to strike at Superboy. She did this by kidnapping Moon in Alaska, placing an explosive device around her neck. The teen captured Spence shortly thereafter, and the threat appeared ended. That is, until Spence remotely det-

onated the device, killing Moon (*Superboy* [third series] #74, May 2000). A furious Superboy nearly killed her until he was stopped by his Young Justice colleague Wonder Girl.

Spence returned one last time, sacrificing much of her humanity for a body equipped with superpowered weaponry provided by the U.S. government in exchange for her service during the war against Imperiex. Seeking revenge on Superboy instead, Spence taunted the hero with her role in Tana Moon's murder. In a rage, Superboy thrust her into outer space, aware that she could not be killed but hoping that an "eternity floating in cold nothing" would offer a degree of punishment (*Superboy* [third series] #90, September 2001).

SPENCE, JULIE

In the wake of Lucy Lane's apparent death, Lois Lane was befriended by Julie Spence, an African American woman living in Metropolis. The two met when Julie saved Lois from muggers using her martial arts skills, and they briefly moved in together, sharing the space with Marsha Mallow and Kristen Cutler. In time, Lois and Superman helped Julie locate her missing parents, who had been evicted from their apartment and had relocated to a ramshackle hovel in the desert (*Superman's Girl Friend Lois Lane* #121, April 1972).

SPOT

Kal-El was upset when the El family dog Krypto was rocketed into space aboard Jor-El's experimental craft. To help the infant, Jor-El designed and built Spot, a robot canine. Criminals took the dog and sent it to the Phantom Zone to terrorize the family, but it was later released on Earth by Superboy to act as a playmate for Krypto. When the Dog of Steel was threatened by a kryptonite meteor, Spot sacrificed its mechanical life to save the animal (*Superboy* [first series] #117, December 1964).

SQUIFFLES

Squiffles were elfin creatures ruled by Ixnayalpay, who made a secret pact with Germany's Adolf Hitler to lead his green-skinned followers in sabotaging America's aircraft industry in return for demonic possession of Der Füehrer's body. These vile beings distracted and annoyed U.S. pilots, leading to a high incidence of aerial fatalities. The Earth-2 Superman tried to help but required the assistance of the Squiffles' enemy, the kindly Gremlins, to end the threat to the Allied war effort (*Superman* [first series] #22, May–June 1943).

STANHOPE

The college town of Stanhope (*Action Comics* #318, November 1964) was near Mount Hightop (*Action Comics* #353, August 1967) and was apparently in the vicinity of Tarryville (*Action Comics* #326, July 1965). It was a two-hour plane flight from Stanhope to Metropolis (*Adventure Comics* #406, May 1971). The town was powered from the Lincoln Dam; its power station covered a two-thousand-square-mile area (*Adventure Comics* #392, April 1970).

Each year, the town celebrated Molly Sawyer Day, which was "named after a spinster who left her fortune to Stanhope College. Each girl prepares a picnic lunch, then hurries to the campus to pick a boy she likes for a partner. By custom, he must share her lunch" (*Action Comics* #325, June 1965). The town also celebrated a spring fair (*Adventure Comics* #383, August 1969) and a winter festival (*Action Comics* #320, January 1965).

Stanhope Park (*Adventure Comics* #389, February 1970) was home to "one of Stanhope's oldest relics," a cast-iron statue of a Civil War figure, sword outstretched, on horseback (*Adventure Comics* #388, January 1970).

Stanhope businesses included Dacy's Department Store (*Action Comics* #318, November 1964), Stanhope Airport (*Action Comics* #369, November 1968), Stanhope Bank (*Action Comics* #321, February 1965), Stanhope Drive-In (*Adventure Comics* #393, May 1970), Stanhope Hospital (*Action Comics* #321, February 1965), and the Storm Plastics Company (*Action Comics* #319, December 1964). The World Science Center "was endowed by the Technology Foundation" (*Action Comics* #375, April 1969).

Covering the happenings in town, especially whenever Supergirl was on the case, was the *Stanhope News* (*Action Comics* #350, May 1967).

STANHOPE COLLEGE

Stanhope College, where Linda Lee Danvers attended on a scholarship, was located "a few miles" from State Tech (*Action Comics* #318, November 1964). The campus included the Administration Building (*Adventure Comics* #382, July 1969); Stanhope Auditorium (*Action Comics* #375, April 1969); Stanhope Gymnasium, erected by Supergirl (*Adventure Comics* #392, April 1970); a clock tower (*Superman's Pal, Jimmy Olsen* #102, June 1967); a hospital (*Action Comics* #321, January 1965); a new library (*Action Comics* #318, November 1964) with librarian Hilda Powell (*Action Comics* #371, January 1969); a museum (*Action Comics* #365, July 1968); Stanhope Observatory, erected by Supergirl (*Action Comics* #318, November 1964); the Science Building (*Action Comics* #319, December 1964); the Science Center (*Adventure Comics* #383, August 1969); Smallville Hall (*Action Comics* #365, July 1968); a stadium (*Action Comics* #318, November 1964); and the Alpha Lamba Sorority (*Action Comics* #318, November 1964). The school newspaper was the *Stanhope Bulletin* (*Action Comics* #325, June 1965) or *Stanhope Sentinel* (*Action Comics* #350, May 1967).

THIS IS STANHOPE COLLEGE--TOTALLY ISOLATED, CUT OFF FROM THE OUTSIDE WORLD BY AN IMPENETRABLE FORCE-BARRIER...

Instructors at the college included astronautics professor Mr. Brown (*Action Comics* #365, July 1968), world-famous astronomy teacher Marla Alexander (*Action Comics* #375, April 1969), computer professor Vizhago (*Adventure Comics* #391, March 1970), psychology professor Mark Hilary (*Action Comics* #325, June 1965), chemistry teacher Elizabeth Sparrow (*Action Comics* #325, June 1965), and home economics teacher Miss Todd (*Action Comics* #349, April 1967). A white-haired woman named Baxter was the college dean while Linda attended the school (*Action Comics* #335, March 1966).

Stanhope's distinguished graduates included "Nobel Prize-winning physicist, Professor Rudolph Clement" (*Superman Family* #191, September–October 1978) and Carter Hagen, who later discovered a copper mine, had "a valuable collection of rare minerals," and held files on various government weapon designs. Hagen hosted scholarship benefits at his home (*Action Comics* #350, May 1967).

"Fencing is Stanhope's most popular sport. Even the college president is a fencing buff" (*Superman's Pal, Jimmy Olsen* #102, June 1967). Stanhope College's student athletes included "four-star athletic wonder" and wrestling champ Tony Walston (*Adventure Comics* #383, August 1969), "top girl athlete" Jane Wesley (*Adventure Comics* #392, April 1970), and football star Johnny Dee, whose uniform was orange, white, and blue (*Adventure Comics* #399, November 1970). Among the school's rivals were Metropolis University (*Adventure Comics* #383, August 1969), Leesville, and Rawlins College (*Adventure Comics* #399, November 1970).

STAR BOY

Thom Kallor hailed from the thirtieth century, born aboard an observatory satellite orbiting his homeworld of Xanthu. His parents Fryd and Myra were astronomers doing research, and the stellar radiation somehow gave him the ability to increase the mass of any object. Thom disliked being a mutant; he was upset at the way scientists wanted to poke and prod him, and his peers shunned him. As a result, he took a spacecraft and tried to run away, but he passed through the tail of a comet that caused his ship to crash. He also briefly gained a set of powers nearly identical to those of Superboy and journeyed to Earth-1 to join the Legion of Super-Heroes. Being the thirteenth member to join, he always questioned his luck.

Early on, he traveled back in time to the twentieth century pursuing two criminals from Xanthu, visiting Smallville to gain Superboy's assistance. While he was there, Lana Lang sought his help in a scheme to make the Teen of Steel jealous by having Thom pretend to fall for the pretty redhead (*Adventure Comics* #282, March 1961).

He struggled after a grueling incident at the prison world of Takron-Galtos. As he aided the Science Police in rounding up escaped prisoners following a revolt, Thom's superpowers suddenly

faded away. Seeing little choice, he used his natural mass powers to cause a roof to collapse, entrapping the criminals but also getting severely injured himself, winding up in intensive care. He worked with Brainiac 5 to master his mass-shifting ability (*Legion of Super-Heroes* [second series] #306, December 1983).

Soon after this, he fell head over heels in love with the latest Legion applicant, Dream Girl. She was also drawn to him, and their romance was passionate—so much so that when a jilted rival, Kenz Nuhor, tried to kill Star Boy, he felt he had no choice but to shoot and kill the man in self-defense. At a hearing, Brainiac 5 proved that there had been another option, and Star Boy's luck ran out: He was banished from the Legion (*Adventure Comics* #342, March 1966). He briefly served with the Legion of Substitute Heroes alongside Dream Girl. When Superboy and Supergirl had to resign from the team, they recommended two replacements, who proved to be Star Boy and Dream Girl in disguise. Their heroism was rewarded: They were reinstated (*Adventure Comics* #351, December 1966).

Star Boy's origins were relatively unchanged in the wake of the Crisis on Infinite Earths, including his romance with Dream Girl. In time, Dream Girl's ardor cooled and Star Boy felt rejected. So when Xanthu's resident super hero, Atmos, disappeared, he accepted his planet's call to be a replacement and resigned (*Legion of Super-Heroes* [third series] #28, November 1986). After the hero was located, Atmos didn't return home but wound up joining the Legion. Worse luck for Thom, it appeared that Dream Girl fell for him. In time, though, it was discovered that Atmos was using his powers to make her love him, and things ended (*Legion of Super-Heroes* [third series] #63, August 1989). Grateful to Thom, but no longer in love with him, Dream Girl introduced him to Yvyya Val, owner of the Naltor Dreamers batball team. A huge fan of the sport, Star Boy hit it off with her and things seemed to be settling down. She named him manager, and the Dreamers won the 2995 pennant (*Legion of Super-Heroes* [fourth series] #37, Early December 1992).

The impending arrival of the events known as Zero Hour was foreshadowed in early 2996 with a flash of light. Suddenly an SW6 Star Boy appeared, a clone that should not have existed. He adventured with his fellow Legionnaires until the end of eternity, where he and Dream Girl shared one last kiss, joined hands, and vanished (*Legion of Super-Heroes* [fourth series] #61, September 1994).

After reality was reordered by Zero Hour, Star Boy was one of several heroes on Xanthu, all of whom banded together as the Amazers. They held a competition for the title of Champion of Xanthu, with Kid Quantum selected to be representative to the Legion (*Legionnaires* #0, October 1994). He died in action, however, and Star Boy was tapped as his replacement (*Legion of Super-Heroes* [fourth series] #66, March 1995). En route to Earth, Star Boy was shot and injured by miners in a misunderstanding. This left him in a hospital for several months, where he was fed meat from Space Whales (*Legends of the Legion* #4, May 1998). When he finally reported to the Legion, he displayed additional superpowers, which displeased the team given their unpredictability (*Legion of Super-Heroes* [fourth series] #76, January 1996). In time, he met and fell in love with Dreamer, who did not make the team. His erratic powers finally faded and he mastered his mass abilities, much to his relief. When Dreamer needed emotional support, Thom quit the Legion, taking her to Xanthu and resuming his role with the Amazers (*Legion Worlds* #4, September 2001).

Thom was also informed that his destiny held that he would someday travel back to the twenty-first century and become Starman, using the human name Danny Blaine, and die in the past (*Starman* [second series] #50, February 1999). It was also believed that somehow the native of Xanthu was the reincarnation of Earth's western hero Scalphunter as well as former Opal City policeman Matthew O'Dare.

In the wake of Infinite Crisis, Thom Kallor was seen by Cosmic Boy as his right-hand man (*Teen Titans/Legion Special,* 2004). This version was not a terribly competent member of the team, acting without thinking and being a better foot soldier than leader.

The original version did manage to travel back in time but seemed to become mentally unstable, voluntarily staying at the Sunshine Sanitarium, enjoying Sloppy Joe Wednesdays. He was taken in by the Justice Society of America, who used his moments of lucidity to glean information about his background. When asked for a name, he offered up Danny Blaine, which he'd taken from his favorite fiction on Xanthu (*Action Comics* #864, June 2008). The JSA met the god Gog, who restored Thom's sanity, displeasing the hero from the future (*Justice Society of America* [second series] #17, August 2008). Soon after, it was discovered that his star-field uniform was actually a map of the multiverse created during the Infinite Crisis, designed by the Brainiac 5s from three of the fifty-two parallel universes (*Justice Society of America* [second series] #20, December 2008). When Gog was proven less than noble, he fought the JSA. Before his defeat, he took away Thom's sanity once again. Gog's head was placed within the Source Wall by the Superman from Earth-22. The Man of Steel then asked Star Boy to return him to his appropriate reality (*Justice Society of America* [second series] #22, February 2009).

When Superboy-Prime assembled a massive collection of criminals to form a new Legion of Super-

Villains, three different Legions were gathered from different parallel worlds to oppose them. Three different Star Boys fought for justice (*Final Crisis: Legion of 3 Worlds* #1–5, October 2008–September 2009). The Star Boy in the past finally learned that his reason for time-traveling was to take control over Superboy's corpse and place it in the Fortress of Solitude's regeneration chamber, the same one that restored Superman following his own death. The healing process took a millennium, but as the battle climaxed, Superboy joined the fight (*Final Crisis: Legion of 3 Worlds* #4, April 2009).

After the threat was finally quashed, the mentally addled Star Boy opted to remain in the twenty-first century, fulfilling the request of Legion founder R. J. Brande. Star Boy was one of several Legionnaires dispatched to that era in order to prevent Superman from being killed by Brainiac, an act that would literally have ended the future (*Adventure Comics* #511, Early May 2010). The team managed to preserve time and space and aid the Man of Steel (*Superman: War of the Supermen* #1–4, July 2010).

S.T.A.R. CORPS, THE

The S.T.A.R. Corps was a short-lived experiment from S.T.A.R. Labs, the private research company (*S.T.A.R. Corps* #1–6, November 1993–April 1994). The idea was to use their technology to field a team of uniformed field agents to troubleshoot problems rather than rely on the intervention and goodwill of the super hero community. The team included Brainstorm (Alan Barnes; *S.T.A.R. Corps* #3–6), Deadzone (Jay Daniels; in #1–6), Fusion (Ed and Beth Wilder; as the Wilders in #1; #2; behind the scenes in #3–4; #5–6), Ndoki (Charles Ndoki; in #3–4, #6) and Trauma (Amy Southern; in #4–6). The Wilders were fused in a lab accident to form the being known as Fusion at the beginning of the team's career.

On their first assignment, they had to contend with Mindgame, an artificial intelligence who commanded the Gamesmen, S.T.A.R. Corps's security robots.

After the threat was ended, the team seemingly disbanded, never to appear again in the chronicles.

S.T.A.R. LABS

Founded by Garrison Slate, the Scientific and Technological Advanced Research Laboratories, usually shortened to S.T.A.R. Labs, was a research organization that grew to become an international private corporation with branch offices across America and around the world (S.T.A.R.'s first appearance in *Superman* [first series] #246, December 1971; Garrison Slate's first appearance in *Blue Beetle* [second series] #12, May 1987). Josiah Power helped Slate incorporate S.T.A.R. Labs before building his own corporation, The Power Company (*Power Company* #5, August 2002).

Through the years, various facilities have developed strong ongoing relationships with many members of the meta-human community in addition to forging deals with local law enforcement. Often S.T.A.R. Labs was the only place with the technical know-how to handle superpowered threats or study unexplained phenomena that posed danger to localities.

On Earth-1, Superboy originally knew the organization as Scientific Research Associates. He helped the S.R.A. with maintenance on one of their satellites (*Adventure Comics* #454, November–December 1977), conducted research on earthquakes (*Karate Kid* #12, January–February 1978), and helped the original Air Wave stop a robbery at one of their labs (*DC Comics Presents* #55, March 1983).

As Superman, his first recorded encounter with the enterprise now known as S.T.A.R. Labs was through Dr. Wilson Farr. Working with algae, Farr had sought "to develop a synthetic life-form that can absorb polluted air—evaluate its content—*cure* the condition—and expel pure air back into the atmosphere." A technician's accidental introduction of the sample into the water supply forced Superman to contain the rapidly mutating algae in the sewer (*Superman* [first series] #246, December 1971). Dr. Farr continued to serve as a consultant for Superman for a time (*Superman* [first series] #253, June 1972); his last known project for S.T.A.R. Labs was a solar-powered jet prototype (*Superman Family* #187, January–February 1978).

The Man of Steel had a more contentious relationship with S.T.A.R. chief administrator Albert Michaels (*Superman* [first series] #303, September 1976), who was soon exposed as a major player in the Skull crime cartel and was later known as the Atomic Skull. Michael's successor Jenet Klyburn (*Superman* [first series] #304, October 1976, and #315, September 1977) more than made up for her former boss with a combination of technical brilliance and charisma that initially made her a frequent sounding board for the Man of Steel but soon put her on the fast track for promotion within S.T.A.R.

On the recommendation of Superman and his fellow members in the Justice League of America, the team's former "mascot" Lucas "Snapper" Carr won a job with S.T.A.R., ironically being interviewed for the position by Supergirl's foster father Fred Danvers (*Superman Family* #189, May–June 1978).

In the post-Crisis reality, Superman sought S.T.A.R. Lab's assistance almost from the beginning of his career, whether dealing with a major viral outbreak (*Superman for All Seasons* #3, 1998) or simply gathering paraphernalia for a trip into outer space (*Action Comics Annual* #7, 1995). As with Farr and Klyburn, the Man of Steel was on good terms with scientist Kitty Faulkner, helping her when she transformed into Rampage (*Superman* [second series] #7, July 1987) and taking pride in her subsequent promotions.

Other S.T.A.R. Labs scientists encountered by Superman included Bridgette Crosby (*Superman for All Seasons* #3, 1998; others), Andrew Shapiro (*The Adventures of Superman* #483, October 1991; others), Peter Singh (*Action Comics* #740, December 1997; others), and the eccentric Burton "Hunter" Thompson (*Superman* [second series] #113, July 1996). Superman's longtime ally Emil Hamilton was a former S.T.A.R. scientist (*The Adventures of Superman* #425, February 1987).

The Metropolis division of S.T.A.R. Labs was located early on in the suburbs with a "secret front" as Erno Chemical Company (*Superman* [first series] #274, April 1974) before relocating to the fringe of Suicide Slum (*Justice League of America* [first series] #174, January 1980), or midtown (*Superman* [first series] #323, May 1978), or "outside Metropolis" (*Superman* [first series] #347, May 1980). They also had a Marine Biology Center on Metropolis Harbor (*DC Comics Presents* #48, August 1982). The central S.T.A.R. Labs location was originally known as "the Werner Building, home to Hamilton Technologies" (*Superman/Shazam: First Thunder* #3, January 2006). It imploded during a battle with the futuristic Monarch (*Armageddon 2001* #2, October 1991) and was condemned by mayoral candidate Colin Thornton for having been situated "in so densely populated an area" (*Superman* [second series] #61, November 1991).

A new facility was constructed in Queensland Park in western Metropolis (*Action Comics* #681, September 1992; others). Its location was described as being "downtown" (*Superman 80-Page Giant* #2, June 1999).

Another lab was sited upstate in Larchville (*Superman* [first series] #303, September 1976).

S.T.A.R. Labs was known to have active facilities in Austin, Texas; Central City, Missouri; Chicago, Illinois (research and technology); Gotham City (weaponry); Keystone City, Kansas; Los Angeles, California (genetics and disease control); Missoula County, Montana; New York City, New York (research and technology); Palo Alto, California (a medical facility); Phoenix, Arizona (meteorology and natural disasters); Pittsburgh, Pennsylvania (radioactive storage and testing centers); Salt Lake City, Utah (physics); San Diego, California (chemical research); San Francisco, California (studying meta-humans); Seattle, Washington (psychology and psionics); and Wichita, Kansas (computer engineering).

International branches were known to be in Melbourne, Australia, as well as Canada and England.

While supportive of super heroes, S.T.A.R. Labs paid for the close ties in blood. Members of the

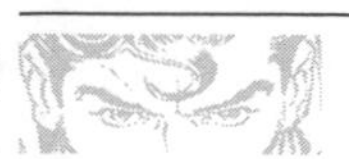

Crime Syndicate of America, from Earth-3, killed dozens when they attacked the San Francisco facility. On the other hand, they also defended the Montana branch when it was attacked by the Rainbow Raiders (*JLA* #110–114, March–July 2005).

STAR OF CATHAY

Called "the world's most valuable diamond," this stone's history connected it with Kublai Khan. "It is said that any descendant of the conqueror, Genghis Khan, who possesses this mystic gem, will rule all Asia."

Assigned to photograph the Star of Cathay at the Metropolis Museum, Jimmy Olsen passed out and awoke, suddenly transported back in time. People mistook him for the European explorer Marco Polo and wound up fighting Lord Timur's minions over possession of the Star. Knocked down and facing death, Jimmy was once more exposed to the Star and wound up awakening back in his era (*Superman's Pal, Jimmy Olsen* #157, March 1973).

"IT WAS AN ACCIDENT! THE VIBRATIONS OF THE GEM'S CRYSTALLINE MOLECULES WERE SUPPOSED TO AFFECT THE ALPHA WAVES OF THE HUMAN BRAIN...TURN ORDINARY MEN INTO GREAT HEROES..."

After a second encounter with the indestructible gem sent Jimmy back in time again in the guise of Spartacus (*Superman's Pal, Jimmy Olsen* #159, August 1973), he was summoned to the deathbed of an alien visitor named Enorr. The extraterrestrial explained that the Star of Cathay had a twin, and both had been part of an experiment his race had conducted on Earth millennia ago. The gems were meant to "affect the alpha waves of the human brain . . . turn ordinary men into great heroes." Instead the vibrations of the multifaceted orbs broke the time barrier, pulling Jimmy from the twentieth century into the lives of Marco Polo and Spartacus because he was reincarnated from each hero. Bright sunlight reflected off the Star of Cathay transported Jimmy into the life of Marco Polo one last time. When he finally returned to the present, Enorr had died and taken the rest of the gem's secrets with him (*Superman's Pal, Jimmy Olsen* #163, February–March 1974).

STARYL

Supergirl discovered the distant world of Staryl, which orbited an orange sun, when she used the computer at Superman's Fortress of Solitude to find her cousin a perfect mate. The computer suggested the super heroine Luma Lynai (*Action Comics* #289, June 1962).

STEEL

Dr. John Henry Irons grew up under the care of his grandparents Butter and Bess in the Washington, DC, area and used his natural brilliance to quickly advance through school, collecting a doctorate in engineering. He was hired out of school to work for AmerTek Industries, creating new tools and ordnance for commercial and military sale. He was particularly proud of the BG-60, a powerful man-portable energy cannon, but he was horrified to learn that it wound up in the wrong hands and cost people their lives. Wanting out, Irons faked his death and traveled north, where he hid his innate skills by becoming a steelworker in Metropolis. When a co-worker nearly fell to his death, Irons saved him—only to fall himself, until he was rescued from certain death by the Man of Steel himself.

Superman told the thankful Irons to "live a life worth saving." John Henry did that very thing, coming to Superman's side when his cross-country battle with Doomsday reached Metropolis. Instead, Irons wound up buried under rubble while the Man of Steel was ultimately killed.

After freeing himself from the rubble, Irons learned of the champion's death and chose to honor Superman's legacy. He used his skills to fashion a suit of modern-day armor complete with a powerful sledgehammer, added the S-shield and a crimson cape, and emerged as Steel (*The Adventures of Superman* #500, June 1993). Briefly, reporter Lois Lane mused about the man within the armor, imagining that it might be her beloved. Steel helped protect the city for a time, discovering the

I OWE YOU MY LIFE...!
THEN MAKE IT COUNT.
THOSE WERE THE WORDS THAT FORGED JOHN HENRY IRONS INTO A HERO.

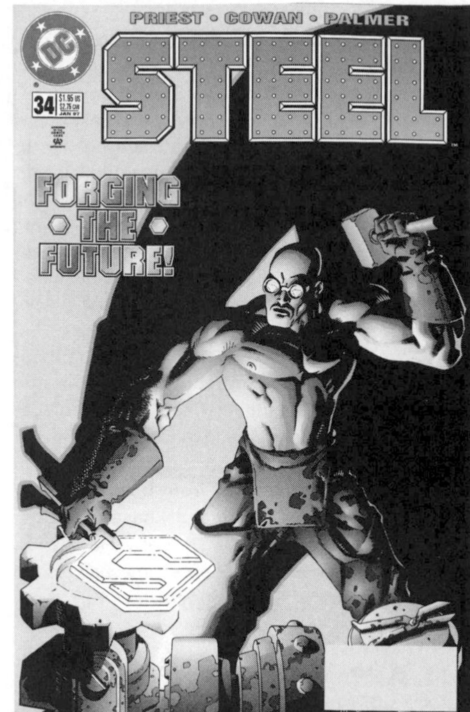
PRIEST • COWAN • PALMER
DC
STEEL
34
FORGING THE FUTURE!

misuse of his BG-80 Toastmasters, an upgrade from his initial design, until Superman was revived and returned to his role as the city's champion. Steel learned that the weapons had been upgraded and distributed by Dr. Angora Lapin (aka the White Rabbit). It hurt that they were not only former AmerTek colleagues, but also former lovers. Confident in his newfound heroics, Steel returned to Washington to take down AmerTek and prevent it from ruining other people's lives (*Steel* #1, February 1994).

No sooner had he returned than his home was destroyed. Irons was angered to see the Toastmasters now in use by Washington gangs who had no moral compunction about killing innocent people in street fights. Knowing he was going to have to fight fire with fire and not being comfortable about it, Irons removed the S-shield from his armor and got to work.

Irons, who had been gone for five years, also spent time getting reacquainted with his grandparents, sister-in-law Blondell, and her five children—Jemahl, Natasha, and Paco, in addition to foster children Tyke and Darlene. The fight with AmerTek struck home when Jemahl went to work for a gang. The battle spilled out, with Blondell assaulted and a bullet meant for Steel hitting and paralyzing Tyke.

His battle with AmerTek led him to confront Black Ops led by the villain Hazard, an organization that was handling weapons distribution (*Steel* #2–8, February–September 1994).

Steel was distracted from his personal fight when he worked with other heroes, which at the time included Justice League of America member Maxima. He aided her in a battle against the alien De'cine. One oddity was that he somehow manifested the ability to have his armor materialize or vanish from his body as needed by using mental commands (*Steel* #11–13, January–March 1995).

He returned to the main focus of his life, only to discover that Black Ops was now helped by the White Rabbit. Another bounty hunter, Chindi, was sent after Steel, but he changed sides when it was learned AmerTek was experimenting on children (*Steel* #14–19, April–September 1995).

Shortly thereafter, Steel began the first of several adventures alongside Superboy and Supergirl as Team Superman—aka the Superman Rescue Squad—making his first foray off-world to assist his idol when he was on trial, accused of causing Krypton's destruction (*Steel* #22, December 1995; others). When Steel returned to Washington, he discovered that a despondent Tyke had revealed his true identity to Hazard's men and sent Hardwire, a cyborg, after him. In the firefight, Butter was badly injured, and the danger prompted Child Protective Services to reclaim Tyke and Darlene. Tyke wound up with Hazard, becoming a pawn and constant reminder to Steel of the price paid by those he loved.

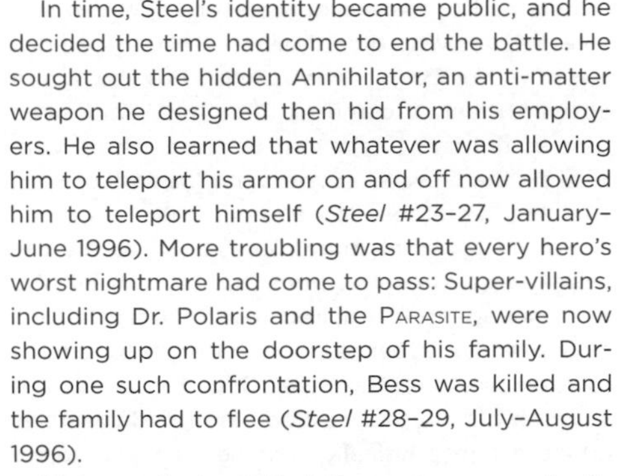
THE MAN OF STEEL IS COMING THROUGH!

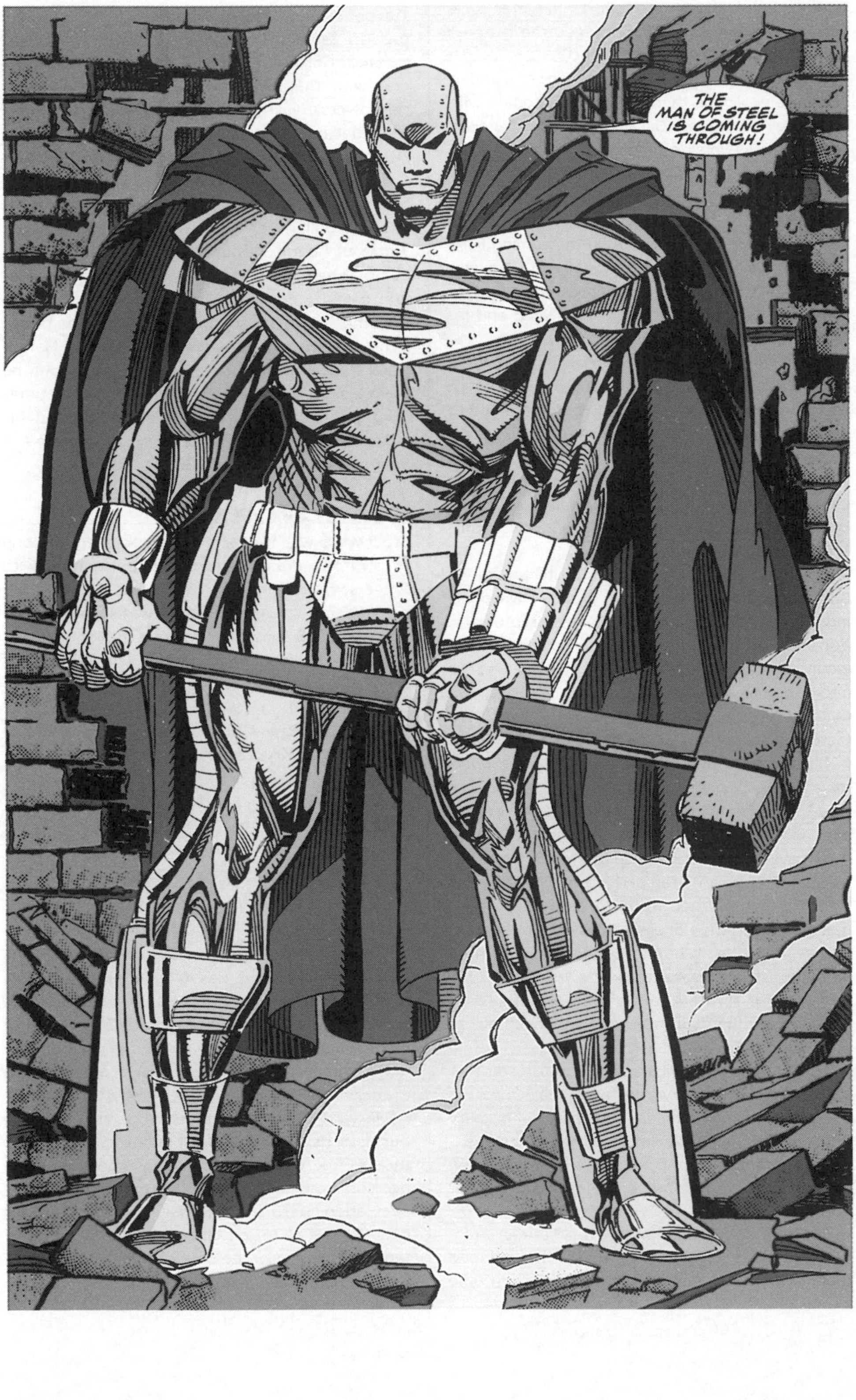

In time, Steel's identity became public, and he decided the time had come to end the battle. He sought out the hidden Annihilator, an anti-matter weapon he designed then hid from his employers. He also learned that whatever was allowing him to teleport his armor on and off now allowed him to teleport himself (*Steel* #23–27, January–June 1996). More troubling was that every hero's worst nightmare had come to pass: Super-villains, including Dr. Polaris and the Parasite, were now showing up on the doorstep of his family. During one such confrontation, Bess was killed and the family had to flee (*Steel* #28–29, July–August 1996).

He came to learn that the armor was actually some monstrous imitation of his own version. He managed to banish it and returned to using the metallic shell he'd created (*Steel* #30–31, September–October 1996).

Seeking a fresh start, Steel and Natasha moved to Jersey City, New Jersey, where he went to work for the local hospital. He also revamped his armor, depowering it and restoring the S-shield (*Steel* #34, January 1997). While working and heroing, he also reunited with his brother Clay who was a hit man believed killed. Instead, Clay had been in hiding, but he'd emerged long enough to steal a pair of Irons's boots and become a powerful mercenary calling himself Crash. Along the way, Irons also clashed with the hospital's corrupt administrator Arthur Villain and his underling Skorpio.

Steel was asked to join an expanded edition of the Justice League, forming a bond with Batman, who admired his mind more than his brawn (*JLA* #16, March 1998). Often Steel's knowledge would come in handy when a need arose to understand alien technology or devise defensive strategies. He was therefore named field leader for a squad that included Huntress, Big Barda, Plastic Man, and Zauriel, while the rest of the team was in the 853rd century. After working with the JLA to defeat the threat of the cosmic being Mageddon, Steel withdrew from active membership but continued to assist on an as-needed basis.

Irons and Natasha also left Jersey for Metropolis, and he decided to return to his technical strengths by founding Steelworks, a research-and-development company. Natasha attended high school and worked part-time at the company, displaying the same sort of natural intelligence Irons had, but covering it with a sassy attitude.

Superman came to increasingly rely on Steel as an ally and friend, revealing his true identity, something Steel admitted he already knew. The two rebuilt the Fortress of Solitude after it was devastated in a battle (*Superman: The Man of Steel* #100, May 2000).

President Lex Luthor subsequently called on Irons to don the Steel armor one more time, joining Earth's other heroes in opposing the coming of Imperiex. He was tasked with joining the Suicide Squad on a mission to the moon in order to use Doomsday as a weapon against the intergalactic invader, and was mortally wounded (*The Adventures of Superman* #594, September 2001). Superman had to bargain with the Fourth World's Black Racer to spare Steel's life, but Irons ulti-

mately had to make a deal with the devil to survive. He was visited by Darkseid, who offered him the powerful Entropy Aegis armor. The new armor allowed Steel to come to Superman's aid when he was fighting to prevent Brainiac 13 from conquering the universe (*Superman: The Man of Steel* #116–118, September–November 2001).

Having bided his time, Darkseid used the Entropy Aegis to control Irons, turning him into his personal agent. It required the combined efforts of Superman, Superboy, and Supergirl to journey to Apokolips to rescue Steel. Once the armor was stripped off, doctors verified that it had adversely affected him physically, and he was told to retire as a hero. He instead built a suit of armor for Natasha to wear. For a time, she became the new Steel (*Superman Versus Darkseid: Apokolips Now!* #1, March 2003).

As Steel, Natasha worked with Supergirl and Girl 13 to protect Metropolis (*Action Comics* #807–808, November–December 2003). She was part of the combined Superman and Batman families during their assault on the White House and battle with President Luthor (*Superman/Batman* #5, February 2004).

When Superboy-Prime threatened all reality, Steel returned to action once more as Irons participated in the Battle of Metropolis during the events known as Infinite Crisis. He found adventuring distasteful, coming to see his fellow crime fighters as self-absorbed people, unaware of what their fights did to the people and cities. This manifested itself in a rage against Natasha, who flirted with the notion of traveling west to join the Teen Titans. He insisted she stay to help clean up Metropolis, destroying her armor (*52* #1, May 10, 2006).

John Henry Irons began hallucinating at Steelworks, affected by a toxin that seemed to be transforming his flesh into actual steel. His lab then exploded, and he was stunned by the devastation. A mere three days later, he put the armor on to assist Doctor Mid-Nite in tending to the wounded heroes, just back from their cosmic travels in the wake of the latest crisis (*52* #4–5, May 31–June 7, 2006).

Once that obligation was dispatched, he was tested by S.T.A.R. Labs' Kala Avasti and learned that he had been exposed to the exo-gene, a synthetic creation of Luthor that gave ordinary people superpowers. Unsure of his next step, he returned to his partially ruined factory to see Natasha trying to build herself a new suit of armor. Seeing his hardened skin, she presumed he sought Luthor's help and called him a hypocrite. She then went to Luthor, underwent the therapy herself, and joined his Everyman Project (*52* #8, June 28, 2006).

After three days had passed, Irons's epidermis was completely hardened. He crashed a party thrown by Luthor, presuming he had abducted Natasha. When she turned up, safe and unharmed, Irons relented and then realized he was losing control. She beat him soundly, sending him right into Metropolis Bay. To make it up to her, he completely rebuilt her armor, but by then it was too late (*52* #9, July 6, 2006). Instead he resumed crime fighting and learned from Kala Avasti that Luthor's gene allowed him to turn the powers off at whim (*52* #20, September 20, 2006). In fact, on Thanksgiving, his skin started to peel, confirming that the powers were, at best, temporary—something Luthor had not shared with his subjects, including Natasha (*52* #29, November 22, 2006).

When Luthor would not release her, Steel, accompanied by Raven, Beast Boy, Aquagirl, and Offspring, attacked LexCorp. Luthor, by this time, had endowed himself with powers. The two men slugged it out until Natasha used Irons's sledgehammer to unleash an electromagnetic pulse, eliminating the exo-gene's effects on Luthor (*52* #40, February 7, 2007). A short time later, a reunited Irons and Natasha reopened the restored Steelworks (*52* #47, March 28, 2007).

One year later, the various teens who had undergone the exo-gene therapy were still coping with what they'd endured. Several, including Natasha, formed a new version of Infinity, Inc., and set out adventuring—only to go missing when they were taken by Darkseid's minions, who feared that the exo-gene made them undetectable, which would be an unwanted complication in the coming Final Crisis (*Infinity Inc.* [second series] #1–12, November 2007–October 2008). Steel vowed to find his niece and the others. She was recovered and restored to her nonpowered self.

After these events, John Henry maintained Steelworks, which was briefly renamed Ironworks. He rarely put the armor back on but continued to lend his expertise to the JLA. For example, he was instrumental in helping the team reassemble the Red Tornado, working with Batman, Mister Miracle, the Metal Men, and Zatanna (*Justice League of America* [second series] #18, #22–24, April–October 2008).

Steel was one of Metropolis's protectors when Superman spent time on New Krypton, investigating the true agenda of his fellow Kryptonians. Irons had his hands full with various menaces but wound up being beaten soundly by Atlas and fell into a coma. Atlas then turned Ironworks's own machinery against its inventor. As a result, the factory was controlled by General Samuel Lane in his vendetta against the Kryptonians (*Superman* #690, September 2009). A visit from his niece Natasha helped bring John back from his comatose state. He worked day and night on his recovery in order to once more don his armor to help Superman protect Metropolis when the Man of Steel returned to Earth, as well as gain a measure of revenge against Atlas. When the Kandorians took their battle to Earth, Steel accompanied a subset of heroes to take down Project 7734 once and for all. Steel confronted Atlas and easily thrashed him into submission (*Superman: War of the Supermen* #4, July 2010).

Throughout the multiverse, there existed other versions of John Henry Irons and Steel. One such world saw John Wilson use the name John Henry when he donned a cloaked identity to seek vengeance against the Klu Klux Klan for murdering his family (*New Frontier* #1–6, March–November 2004).

On Earth-22, Steel worked with Batman's faction of heroes fighting the fascism that gripped their world in the near-future (*Kingdom Come* #1–4, 1996).

On a different world, Irons was a slave who built his armor to fight for freedom during the Civil War era (*Steel Annual* #1, 1994).

There were other heroes to use the Steel name, such as Earth-2's Henry "Hank" Heywood, known as the Indestructible Man (*Steel the Indestructible Man* #1, March 1978).

STEELMAN

Professor Phineas Potter accidentally transported Jimmy Olsen to a parallel world with his Dimension-Travel Machine. The resulting explosion blew the top off Mount Tipton, where Potter's lab was located. Calling the realm Earth-X (one of several with that designation), Jimmy gained superpowers rivaling those of Superman and was told that he had to use those powers for good. He found doppelgängers for his friends such as Clark Kent, who was working as the Tours Custodian of the Metropolis World's Fair and was related to bullfighter Perry White. This Kent was a writer of fiction, having created characters such as Solarman, Mystic Man, Storm King, and someone called Superman. He told Jimmy he had to become Steelman, so Jimmy took that name for himself, adopting elements from both the Man of Steel's and Batman's uniforms. In a turnabout, he gave Clark a signal watch to summon him in times of great need. Eventually, Superman found his pal and returned him to Earth-1 (*Superman's Pal, Jimmy Olsen* #93, June 1966).

STEELWORKS

Steelworks was the Metropolis laboratory of John Henry Irons, aka Steel, formed in partnership with Professor Emil Hamilton (*Superman* [second series] #177, February 2002). It was located in an abandoned Suicide Slum factory in "Metropolis's Old Hook Basin District" (*Superman: The Man of Steel* #97, February 2000), which had been radically transformed by the B13 Virus (*Superman: The Man of Steel* #98, March 2000). It was also "infused with Kryptonian parts, thanks to Superman's help, making it free from LexCorp's surveillance and control" (*Superman: Metropolis Secret Files* #1, June 2000).

STERN, FRANKLIN

A onetime owner of the Metropolis *Daily Planet*, Franklin Stern served as publisher in tandem with editor Perry White (*Superman: The Man of Steel* #27, November 1993). Based on his experiences as a civil rights activist in the South, he and White broke up the "Aryan Brotherhood," a group of white supremacists who were conducting genetic experiments to create a race of supermen (*Superman: The Man of Steel* #47, August 1995). A Harvard University graduate, Stern went into business, rising to the role of publisher. Eventually, though, the paper began losing money as competition from television and the Internet eroded circulation. Stern and his close friend also clashed over White's editorial point of view, so Stern reluctantly chose to sell the paper to Lex Luthor's LexCom division (*The Adventures of Superman* #561, September 1998).

STEVENS, DAVE

Community activist Dave Stevens once challenged reporter Lois Lane's assumptions about being a minority and living in Metropolis. This prompted Lois to do some soul searching, and she used Superman's Kryptonian technology to transform herself into an African American so she could do an in-depth study of the race issue. When Lane started to interview Stevens, they were interrupted by drug dealers, and when they intervened, Stevens wound up shot. Superman rushed Stevens to the hospital while Lane donated some of her type O-negative blood to save his life. As a result, the two became good friends (*Superman's Girl Friend, Lois Lane* #106, November 1970). After his recovery, Stevens assisted Superman and the Thorn in a battle against agents from the One Hundred. Stevens went on to become a columnist for the *Daily Planet,* assisted by his girlfriend Tina Ames (*Superman's Girl Friend, Lois Lane* #114, September 1971).

STIX AND HUBRO

Hailing from Dimension Z, the villains known as Stix and Hubro came to Earth, passing themselves off as constables of the "Inter-Dimensional Bureau of Investigation." They tricked Supergirl into journeying to their dimension in order to stand trial for crimes she had never committed (*Action Comics* #327–328, August–September 1965).

STORM, THEO

Taking on the identity of the Loser, Theo Storm served as a member of the Supermen of America.

STRANGE VISITOR

Sharon Vance, who grew up with Clark Kent in Smallville, happened to be on an aircraft near Metropolis that was struck by lighting. At the time, Sharon also contained the mystic entity known as Kismet. The lightning combined the two into a new form, which came to be called Strange Visitor (*Superman* [second series] #149, October 1999). This new form was a being of pure electromagnetic energy, similar to the energy form that Superman had briefly experienced not long before. The energy being was drawn to Emil Hamilton's laboratory, and as he studied her, he decided it was safe to place her in one of the cerulean containment suits he had devised for the electrical Man of Steel. The suit not only contained the energy but also stabilized the life force, which was in danger of dissipating.

As Hamilton and the Man of Steel learned, Strange Visitor's memories were hazy at best, so it took time before they realized who she really was. She did, though, demonstrate a surprising mastery of her new powers and used them to save lives on numerous occasions.

It had also become apparent that her emotional state had a direct impact on the effectiveness of her powers. If angered, her containment suit was pressed to its limits to contain such a surge in energy. In time, she finally confronted the Parasite, and exposure to its leaching powers helped to restore her memories (*Superman: The Man of Steel* #94, November 1999).

Better physically and mentally, she left Metropolis to begin adventuring on her own. She managed to defeat Gorilla Grodd (*Superboy* [third series] #89, August 2001) and fought to protect Earth during the Imperiex War (*Batman: Our Worlds at War,* August 2001). She also transferred her powers to Superman, revealing her true identity, when he intended to confront Imperiex directly. As Superman defeated Imperiex, saving the Earth, Strange Visitor ceased to be (*Superman* [second series] #173, October 2001).

STREAKY THE SUPERCAT

Linda Lee once adopted an orange tabby she named Streaky given the odd yellow lighting streak on her side. The mischievous cat was repeatedly exposed to x-kryptonite—a synthetic form that Supergirl devised—and temporarily gained superpowers. The chunk of material had been buried within a ball of yarn, lost in the basement of Midvale Orphanage. A surprised Linda Lee exclaimed, "Due to the unique combination of chemicals in x-kryptonite, it has given Streaky superpowers!" Each time the feline became empowered, she donned a red cape and fought for feline justice (*Action Comics* #261, February 1960).

While her powers and abilities were similar to those of the Maid of Steel, they were certainly not as strong. And while Streaky was not vulnerable to kryptonite, she was susceptible to magic.

Streaky shared several exploits with Supergirl and with Krypto the Super-Dog. In time, the two helped form the Legion of Super-Pets. The thirtieth-century super-pet team members were staunch allies of the Legion of Super-Heroes. Streaky also met his descendant, a superpowered, telepathic feline named Whizzy (*Action Comics* #287, April 1962).

After numerous adventures, Streaky's super-career ended (*Adventure Comics* #394, June 1970) when the kryptonite on Earth-1 was rendered inert during an experiment (*Superman* [first series] #233, January 1971).

In the world after the Crisis on Infinite Earths, Linda Danvers, the Earth-born angel Supergirl, had a pet cat also named Streaky but without any super-abilities (*Supergirl* [fourth series] #25, September 1998).

IT ISN'T A TORNADO...IT ISN'T A HURRICANE...IT'S... SUPER-CAT!!
SO PAUL THINKS I'M JUST A LI'L OL' SCAIRDY-CAT, DOES HE? WHERE IS HE? I'LL SHOW HIM I'M THE MIGHTIEST CAT IN THE WORLD!!!

After Infinite Crisis, when Kara Zor-El returned to New Earth, she gained a female cat (*Supergirl* [fifth series] #10, November 2006) named Streaky. Supergirl observed that "she doesn't get the concept of the litter box" (*Supergirl* [fifth series] #14, April 2007). When the Anti-Life Equation was unleashed by Darkseid, Supergirl took Streaky to Superman's Fortress of Solitude for safekeeping. Later, when the Final Crisis was over, Supergirl took to sharing an apartment with Lana Lang, and Streaky accompanied her (*Supergirl* [fifth series] #38, April 2009). Whenever Kara traveled to the world of New Krypton, Lana looked after the cat.

STRONG, PAUL

Powder Valley's resident blacksmith was plaguing the western community as the secret leader of the gang of rustlers. Strong and his henchmen were eventually apprehended by Superman (*Action Comics* #134, July 1949).

STRONGARM BANDIT, THE

Disguised as a circus strongman, this masked bandit possessed incredible strength and committed a successful series of crimes throughout Metropolis. As police and Superman closed in on the robber, the bandit tried to divert suspicion onto Herculo, a local circus strongman. Thanks to a ruse by reporter Clark Kent, Herculo managed to expose the real criminal, a circus clown who had turned to crime (*Action Comics* #28, September 1940).

STRYKER'S ISLAND

Located in Metropolis's West River between New Troy and Queensland Park, Stryker's Island Penitentiary was built as a maximum-security facility in response to the growing level of criminal threats after the Man of Steel arrived in town (*Superman* [second series] #9, September 1987). In addition to average human felons, there were cells specially designed to handle superpowered prisoners.

Despite the dangers inherent in such a facility, tours for the general public were offered, the fees going to assist the costs of managing and running the prison.

The prison withstood frequent attacks to free inmates, the most damaging one when several Kandorians came to obtain criminals deemed a

threat to Superman and therefore to themselves. Many prison guards were killed in the battle, but Superman managed to apprehend his foes, remanding them to the Slabside Penitentiary while repairs were made (*Superman* #682, January 2009).

SUBJEKT-17

In 1949, a spacecraft crashed in Kazakhstan, and the Russians who responded to the incident found a dead male pilot and a dying pregnant female. They helped deliver the child and then took it to their lab for study, naming it Subjekt-17. Landing in the Soviet Union, the humanoid baby displayed superpowers similar to those of Superman—with the addition of telekinesis and sonic blasts. The Russians poked and prodded the developing alien for half a century, withholding any sense of compassion. As a result, the entity, still known only as Subjekt-17, grew to hate his captors, calling them the "hurt-makers." When they were done with him, the scientists placed him in cryogenic suspension in a lab south of Ayaguz (*Superman* #655, October 2006).

The alien was finally freed by Kazakh hillmen, who summoned help from their government. They, in turn, sent for arcanobiologist Callie Llewellyn. As he sought revenge against his captors, Callie asked for help from Superman in Serbia. He recognized a kindred spirit in the alien and thought, "He isn't a wounded child. He's an adult who has never been socialized. All his experience of the world has been formed by torment and abuse." Subjekt-17 continually learned he had new powers, which made him a formidable opponent (*Superman* #656, November 2006).

Their confrontation was interrupted when Superman was snatched through time by Arion, Lord High Mage of Atlantis. Subjekt-17 began searching for his alien compatriot, finally coming to learn more about what it meant to be human (*Superman* #662, May 2007). A short time later, Subjekt-17 realized that he and Superman would never be in agreement, and their disagreement led to a climactic clash. The angry alien vanished, promising to return someday (*Superman* #667, November 2007).

SUICIDE SLUM

Even the City of Tomorrow had its dark corners, and the darkest portion of Metropolis was the area known to all as Suicide Slum (*Star-Spangled Comics* #7, April 1942). The ten blocks making up the area remained squalid for decades but also gave birth to many who worked their way out of the area, as exemplified by the boys who formed the Newsboy Legion at the tail end of the Great Depression. The area also gave refuge to lowlifes and criminals, including alien refugees such as the Apokoliptian Sleez.

Originally Hob's Bay named after Elias Hob, an early Metropolis landowner, the area had been a prosperous, middle-class neighborhood at the turn of the twentieth century. Indeed, it was "the ultra-fashionable Park Slope area" (*World's Finest Comics* #259, October–November 1979).

One account claimed that the area—also known as Southside—was "Metropolis's black neighborhood" and a "nice, middle-class place where folks wanted to live." With the beginning of the Great Depression, though, residents were encouraged to invest in Comet Arena, touted as a sports venue that "would bring fifty thousand people to Southside every week of the year." Instead, the developer "disappeared with over sixteen million dollars" earmarked for the complex (*Black Lightning: Year One* #1, Early March 2009), and the area began a descent into poverty and decay from which it never recovered. Now only City Hall and the chamber of commerce referred to the neighborhood as Hob's Bay. To the rest of Metropolis, it was Suicide Slum: "ten blocks of poverty, misery and crime. It's not a safe place to be after dark" (*Superman* [second series] #26, February 1989). "Suicide Slum sits to the north of downtown Metropolis, forgotten by most of the city, ignored by the rest. Except when things go wrong" (*Action Comics* #542, April 1983). "It has seen a great deal of its own particular kind of terror" (*Superman* [second series] #67, May 1992). At one point, five thousand people were said to live in the ten-block area (*Action Comics* #592, September 1987), which included part of the waterfront (*Star-Spangled Comics* #8, May 1942).

"Suicide Slum was a hellhole. Its most famous sons and daughters were those who had escaped to a better life. Despite numerous attempts over the years at urban renewal and Superman's best efforts, it remained a venue for X-rated theaters and adult bookstores, for run-down tenements, and for crime-infested streets. Life was cheap in Suicide Slum. On the other hand, so was the rent" (*The Death and Life of Superman,* 1993).

The slum's Simon Project "was built by the government as a shining example of housing for those less fortunate. In reality, it was a prison where crime prospered and the criminals preyed on the weak." Chastised for not patrolling the area as often as he should, Superman has paid special attention to Suicide Slum in recent years (*Superman* [second series] #121, March 1997).

The area included Hobbsview Manor, "[Project] Cadmus's 'Halfway House' " (*The Adventures of Superman* #539, October 1996); Kern's Liquors (*Action Comics* #718, February 1996); the boarded-up Hotel Royer (*The Adventures of Superman* #539, October 1996); Stinky's Billiards, a pool hall that was "safe, as long as you don't have to use the bathroom" (*Wonder Woman* [second series] #170, July 2001); the Silk Glove Club; and Easy Street, "a gaudy row of vice and crime where ev-

erything—and everyone—has its price" (*The Adventures of Superman* #501, Late June 1993). It was also home to the Mark Shephard East Metropolis Youth Center, named after the former football star and congressman (*Action Comics* #828, August 2005). The former Goldberg Opera House in Suicide Slum was slated to be refurbished into a youth center thanks to funding from the Green Team (*The Adventures of Superman* #549, August 1997). An "underground air raid shelter [was] over on Kurtzberg and Simon" (*Superman: The Man of Steel* #66, April 1997).

During the 1940s, Suicide Slum businesses included Hinkle's Hardware Store (*Star-Spangled Comics* #7, April 1942) and Benny's Bowling Alley (*Star-Spangled Comics* #13, October 1942). That era saw one renovation project intended to raze the slums and introduce clean, low-rent housing. It was soon exposed as a land swindle (*Star-Spangled Comics* #14, November 1942).

"Avenue M skirted the edge of Suicide Slum and for almost a decade had been teetering between renewal and squalor. The Newtown Plaza had been designed to save a five-square-block area and perhaps even bring the possibility of rebirth to all of Hob's Bay. Doomsday had put an end to that. All that remained of Newtown Plaza now were several blocks of rubble and twisted girders" (*The Death and Life of Superman,* 1993). Hob's Lane was "on the edge of Suicide Slum" (*Action Comics* #593, October 1987), Nightingale Lane was "on the fringe of the slums" (*World's Finest Comics* #12, Winter 1944), and Spiral Avenue, the site of a "cheap boarding-house," was likely in the vicinity (*World's Finest Comics* #8, Winter 1943).

In later years, there was the Superman-House, a Suicide Slum orphanage named after the Man of Steel and spearheaded by Father Perez of the Hispanic Children's Aid Society (*Superman* [first series] #352, October 1980).

During Metropolis's futuristic upgrade by the B13 Virus, "Suicide Slum's abandoned buildings gave way to the engines that [powered] the New Metropolis. Derelicts lost their alleys to the massive pipework that [served] as the city's sewage system" (*Superman: Metropolis Secret Files* #1, June 2000).

SUL-EL

A proud member of the House of El, Sul-El was the inventor of Krypton's first telescope. He charted many far-off stars, including Sol (*Adventure Comics* #313, October 1963).

SUNBURST

Takeo Sato was a successful stuntman on a popular Japanese television series called Sunburst. However, when Superboy first encountered him, the man was a superpowered criminal with an astonishing array of abilities from flight to solar energy to super-human speed and agility, an incredible hardness of body, and mighty strength.

He explained to his new ally that he had been born in a small village located near an active volcano. On the day of his birth, the volcano emitted fumes prior to an eruption, which he had inhaled with his first infant breaths. It wasn't until he was an adult that the fumes' effects manifested themselves. He was an actor, just cast to portray a costumed super hero in a low-budget film. While he was rigged to a harness to simulate flight, the line snapped; as he fell to his inevitable death, the powers kicked in, and he flew under his own effort. The studio decided to keep Takeo's powers a secret, preferring to promote the film's "state-of-the-art special effects."

Takeo had been blackmailed into using his newfound abilities to commit crimes on behalf of the Yakuza until Superboy interceded and helped him recover his kidnapped parents. The Teen of Steel then hypnotized the stuntman into forgetting he had his amazing abilities so he could resume his normal life (*The New Adventures of Superboy* #45–47, September–November 1983). His memories did return, though, and Sunburst died fighting the Anti-Monitor's Shadow Demons (*Crisis on Infinite Earths* #12, March 1986).

In the new reality, there was no Superboy, so Sunburst's ally was Japan's premier hero Rising Sun (*Who's Who* #22, December 1986), the two going so far as to form Japan's first team of heroes, Big Science Action (*Final Crisis Sketchbook* #1, July 2008).

In the alternate world of Earth-988, Takeo also briefly crossed paths with Superboy. His dismay over the consequences of his possessing superpowers led him to destroy the talisman that gave them to him (*Superboy* [second series] #18, July 1991).

Another Sunburst appeared, proclaiming himself as one of Japan's "greatest super heroes," one who was constantly trailed by the media (*Doom Patrol* [second series] #26, September 1989). He had his own manga titled *The Adventures of the New Sunburst* before falling to the Brotherhood of Dada, losing face on national television. This Sunburst was last seen being absorbed by Frenzy, the living cyclone.

A different villain using the name *Sunburst* gained his powers from a jeweled globe and fought Aquaman before vanishing (*DC Special Series* #1, 1977).

Timothy Walton designed a suit of golden body armor, complete with solar-powered glider wings, and also took the name Sunburst—but he used his skills to commit crimes until he was stopped by Starfire of the Teen Titans (*New Teen Titans* #36–37, October–November 1987).

A potential future's group of heroes known as the Team Titans included a squad led by a different Sunburst, who arrived at the wrong point of the past and wound up being killed by a Chaos-drone (*Team Titans* #11–12, August–September 1993).

In yet another future, Sunburst was a red-suited man who committed crimes until he was apprehended by Shadow Lass of the Legion of Super-Heroes (*Action Comics* #379, August 1969).

SUN-EATER, THE

Created by the Controllers, a splinter group from the Guardians of the Universe, a Sun-Eater was a living nebula capable of draining stars of their natural gases, essentially snuffing them out. The intergalactic villain Starbreaker claimed that the Sun-Eaters were actually larval forms of his species (*Justice League of America* [second series] #34, August 2009).

Without the solar radiation, any life on the planets in orbit around the now dead star would rapidly become extinct. This was their ultimate weapon, used to discipline worlds they deemed beyond redemption. For every Sun-Eater created, a Controller was assigned to oversee the dormant entity until needed.

The intergalactic conqueror Mongul killed one of the Controllers and activated its Sun-Eater, directing it toward Earth in an attempt to kill the Earth-1 Superman (*DC Comics Presents* #43, March 1982). It took the intervention of the thirtieth century's Legion of Super-Heroes to save Sol.

An active, rogue Sun-Eater found its way to Sol and managed to absorb its energy, bringing about a Final Night for Earth. The World's Greatest Super Heroes attempted to reignite their star, but it took Hal Jordan, the former Green Lantern possessed by Parallax, to sacrifice his life, expending all his energies to restore Sol to normal (*Final Night* #1–4, November 1996).

The Controllers apparently built their Sun-Eaters on the world of Minosyss, and maybe elsewhere. One such creation killed two of the Titans of Myth, Hyperion and Thia (*DC Special: The Return of Donna Troy* #1–4, August–October 2005).

After Superboy-Prime was captured at the end of the events of Infinite Crisis, a "junior" Sun-Eater was given by Donna Troy to the Green Lantern Corps in order to keep him imprisoned (*Infinite Crisis* #7, June 2006).

Across space, a group of freed Sun-Eaters were used to end Lady Styx's plans for galactic conquest. Somehow, Animal Man absorbed the ability to survive the vacuum of space from these creations (*52* #47, March 28, 2007).

In Earth-1's future, the thirtieth century's Sol was threatened by a Sun-Eater. To save Earth, the Legion gathered together a quintet of the most powerful villains alive to aid them. While the Fatal Five and the Legion fought valiantly, Ferro Lad had to sacrifice his life to detonate a bomb within the Sun-Eater (*Adventure Comics* #352–353, January–February 1967).

After the events of ZERO HOUR, the thirtieth century believed Sun-Eaters were a myth created by the UNITED PLANETS' president until the Legion exposed them to be a reality.

A time-bounced Man of Steel also aided the Legion in combating a second Sun-Eater, with Wildfire risking his existence to deliver a bomb. The device's internal defenses rejected the explosive, so the Legionnaire exited his containment suit. Shrinking Violet then rewired the suit, converting it to a weapon that finally destroyed the threat (*The Adventures of Superman* #477, April 1991).

SUN-THRIVERS, THE

The Sun-Thrivers, a race of pink telepathic energy beings, lived within a giant crystal. Their unique biology required them to be surrounded with "a vast quantity of solar-spawned gases," so they telepathically drew "raw elements from other stars"—eventually igniting themselves to become the star called RAO. In time, planets came to orbit the star, including KRYPTON, which bore life.

Being formed in a different manner, the star's degradation came quickly; it was a red giant as life grew on Krypton. After the planet's unstable core destroyed the world, the gravimetric imbalance caused the red sun to become an orange dwarf, which threatened the Sun-Thrivers still living within the star.

In an attempt to survive, they determined to track down the planet's remnants and absorb them into Rao. They lured Superman into space, explained their plight, and told him that a chunk approximating 10 percent of Krypton was in the possession of something called the Cardiac Creature, which "pumps life-sustaining energy from the Green K." The Sun-Thrivers and the Last Son of Krypton triumphed over the Cardiac Creature. The remains of Krypton were reabsorbed, and Rao ejected a newly formed planetoid, which was called Krypton-Two (*Superman* [first series] #255, August 1972).

In the reality after the CRISIS ON INFINITE EARTHS, the cosmic forces of the Big Bang led to the creation of the being who called himself Rao, and he formed Krypton. The Sun-Thrivers were no longer a part of the chronicles.

SUPER-APE, THE

When SHIR KAN heard JOR-EL's pronouncements that KRYPTON was doomed, he took the words to heart. He intended to follow his peer's advice, and began experimenting with rocket-ship designs to save the populace. Much as Jor-El used KRYPTO the Super-Dog in a prototype vessel, Shir Kan placed several simians in ships, aiming them at different worlds. One such ship survived the journey and landed on Earth, long after KAL-EL arrived and grew to become Superman. CLARK KENT and LOIS LANE traveled to Africa to investigate the claims of the existence of a "Super-Ape" and found the Kryptonian survivor, who was placed off Earth for its own safety (*Action Comics* #218, July 1956).

SUPERBABY

While still a toddler on KRYPTON, KAL-EL was kidnapped by the Coluan android BRAINIAC just before he stole the city of KANDOR. His intent was to ransom the child in exchange for JOR-EL's 21 Y-Ronatort, a newly designed weapon. As they returned to their hideout, located within a yellow-sun system, the toddler began to develop superabilities, much to his surprise. His erratic flight wound up destroying the lair and its equipment, ruining Brainiac's scheme. The villain tried to reduce Kal-El in size but grabbed the enlarging ray instead, so the colossal tot stomped all over the weaponry. Humiliated, Brainiac returned the child without extracting the weapon (*Superboy* [first series] #106, July 1963).

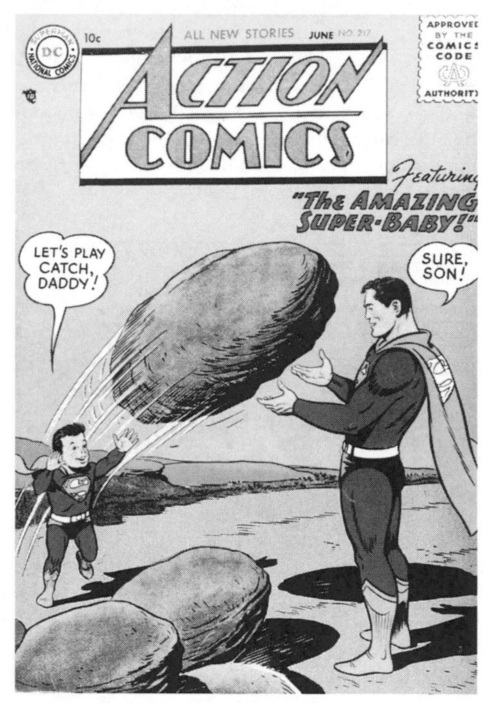

When Kal-El was being raised on Earth-1 as CLARK KENT, MARTHA KENT outfitted him with a red-and-blue playsuit, using blankets found with the rocket ship that had brought him from Krypton (*Superboy* [first series] #8, May–June 1950).

As his powers developed and he learned to master them, the toddler got into all manner of mischief, although he was never formally called Superbaby or Super-Tot. Some of the chronicles indicate that Kal-El's powers began to manifest en route to Earth, and he actually had some adventures prior to arriving at his destination.

"With each rash of new super-baby sightings there invariably seemed to follow an outbreak of tales of a werewolf in some cavern, or a 100-year-old Indian medicine man who hid out in the woods, or the old reliable flying saucers" (*Superman: Last Son of Krypton,* 1978).

SUPERBOY

An infant named KAL-EL, born on KRYPTON, was placed in a rocket ship by his parents JOR-EL and LARA and shot into space in order to surive the destruction of their home planet. The ship traveled through a vacuum for some time until it finally arrived on Earth, crashing in a field outside SMALLVILLE. The ship and its wailing occupant were found by farmers JONATHAN and MARTHA KENT (*Action Comics* #1, June 1938). The boy was taken to the local orphanage, but after a few days of uncontrolled demonstrations of incredible strength, the Kents returned to adopt him and raise him as their own (*Superman* [first series] #1, Summer 1939).

While these events were identical on Earth-2, that world's KAL-L grew up as CLARK KENT and did not don a costume as Superman until adulthood. His parents apparently never told him of his extraterrestrial origins, something he learned when he pierced the time barrier and traveled to the Krypton of the past (*Superman* [first series] #61, November–December 1949).

On Earth-1, Kal-El was equally loved, and his parents added KRYPTO as the family dog. When Jor-El began experimenting with rocket-ship designs to save the populace from impending doom, he tested a ship with Krypto on board—but a meteor knocked it off course and the dog was lost. With Kal despondent, Jor-El built him a robotic replacement, which they called SPOT. His heroic career began much earlier. The Kents chose to keep the child. Using Martha's maiden name as his first name, they adopted him as Clark Kent, raising him on the ancestral Kent family farm. The toddler grew up in a happy, loving environment. The Kents recognized that he would be different, as his powers seemed to be limitless and ever-evolving. As a result, Jonathan took great pains to work with Clark to master them. Additionally, he taught him the values that made him a hero.

Jonathan and Martha never hid his origins, speaking openly of the rocket that had brought him to Earth. As Clark's powers evolved, so did his ability to recall his life on Krypton (*Action Comics* #288, May 1962). Other chronicles indicated he required the assistance of a "Mind-Prober Ray" (*Superboy* [first series] #79, March 1960). Clark also learned that "by overtaking and photographing light rays that had left Krypton before it exploded," he could access events from the past (*Superman* [first series] #132, October 1959).

Under Sol's yellow radiation and Earth's lighter gravity, the boy began to manifest an amazing array of abilities. Clark's strength and invulnerability manifested first, but his vision abilities began to develop as a boy. When Martha couldn't find an object, Clark's X-ray vision kicked in and he was able to help. Heat vision, microscopic vision, and

telescopic vision all followed. He enjoyed using his newfound powers to help do the countless chores that came with running a farm—he could rapidly gather eggs from the henhouse, for instance, or dig postholes for new fencing.

Clark had been erratically flying since he was a tot, but when the time came to master the ability, it took several days. Clark's first flight resulted in a smashed oil derrick, so on day two, he was attached to a box kite, tethered to a steel cable. A pilot, Captain Burton, was flying overhead and happened to snap pictures of the odd sight. Fortunately, though, Clark had mastered his X-ray vision, and he ruined the film with a burst. By the fourth day, Clark seemed to have mastered flying and floating in air out in the cornfields where they could not be easily observed (*Superboy* [first series] #59, December 1958).

In time, he was said to be able to press five thousand tons with one hand, calling it "a cinch" (*Adventure Comics* #361, October 1967). He could apply the pressure of fifty thousand atmospheres to a piece of coal in one clenched hand and transform it into a diamond. His super-breath was powerful enough to nudge a planet through space (*Adventure Comics* #293, February 1962), or freeze the air around objects. He could hold his breath within his super-lungs for an indefinite period of time. His invulnerability was said to be strong enough for him to withstand the power of a thousand H-bombs (*Adventure Comics* #366, March 1968).

The Kents began to believe nothing could harm their adopted son—but of course every parent fears that something bad will happen sooner or later. Sure enough, Clark suddenly became gravely ill for no apparent reason. Just as the Boy of Steel was about to succumb, Jonathan guessed that the source of the illness might be the green rock that he'd added to Clark's meteorite collection (*Adventure Comics* #251, August 1958). The world soon after learned of KRYPTONITE when Superboy managed to convince some thieves that the strange green rock at the Smallville Planetarium wasn't really harmful to him—only to have a well-intentioned scientist use the same fragment in a Kryptonian diorama during a public ceremony. Before an army of reporters and radio broadcasters, Superboy collapsed on stage (*Superman* [first series] #136, April 1960). In time, Superboy also encountered other varieties of the mineral, including the unpredictable red kryptonite. Later, Superboy discovered he was also susceptible to the supernatural.

As he began to adventure out in space, he recognized that his powers ebbed whenever he was near weaker stars such as red suns or orange dwarf stars.

When Clark was still a toddler, the Kents decided that it made sense to live closer to town. Jonathan sold the farm to Alex and Lila Crowley and bought a general store (*Adventure Comics* #149, February 1950; *Superboy* [first series] #6, January–February 1950; others) from Whizzer Barnes (*Superman: Last Son of Krypton,* 1978).

The youth attended elementary and high school, where he met his lifelong friends LANA LANG (*Superboy* [first series] #10, September–October 1950) and PETE ROSS (*Superboy* [first series] #86, January 1961). He also was an early friend of the pretty, blonde Margo Griffiths, who would grow up to be a nurse in METROPOLIS (*Superboy* [first series] #1, March–April 1949), as well as boys named Ted and Tony (*More Fun Comics* #102–103, March–April to May–June 1945), Joe Daly and Betty Brocon (*Adventure Comics* #119, August 1947, and #131, August 1948), Willy Mason (*The New Adventures of Superboy* #7, July 1980; others), and siblings Alvin (*Superboy* [first series] #62, January 1958) and Margaret Wilson, the last of whom grew up to become a schoolteacher in Metropolis (*Action Comics* #5098, July 1980; others). For a time in high school, Clark dated Lisa Davis (*The New Adventures of Superboy* #40, April 1983; others).

Clark was conscious of protecting his secret powers and was conflicted about how. Martha therefore adapted his baby playsuit into the familiar red-and-blue uniform complete with cape. At the same time, glass from the rocket was used to fashion a pair of spectacles so young Clark and the young hero would not be confused as the same being (*More Fun Comics* #101, January–February 1945).

When he donned the costume, he moved quickly enough to become a red-blue blur to the citizens of the small town, but gradually he began letting himself be seen. The townsfolk came to accept that a powerful young hero lived among them. He caught a robber and introduced himself to the gaping police officers as "Superboy, foe of all criminals" (*Superman* [first series] #144, April 1961). According to one account, this first exploit occurred when he was eight years old (*The New Adventures of Superboy* #1, January 1980).

Over time, Clark realized he needed a variety of ways to protect his secret identity. Thus he dug a tunnel from the house at 321 Maple Street to an exit outside the town in addition to one that connected the house to the general store where he worked after school. He kept several trophies and devices in the basement, including the PHANTOM ZONE PROJECTOR (*Superman* [first series] #146, July 1961). After building the series of SUPERBOY ROBOTS, he maintained several in the cellar.

The Kents wanted Clark to maintain a civilian life as much as time and circumstances allowed. In addition to chores around the house and attending school, they encouraged him to have a circle of friends and to work—like so many other teens—to learn the value of money and honest effort. In the post-INFINITE CRISIS reality, Clark's first job was working for Bell, who ran Bud's Garage and Service Station (*Superman/Batman* #48, July 2008).

The media made a sensation out of him, with newsreaders announcing, "A Superboy exists! He can fly! Bullets bounce off him! He has amazing super-vision! He battles for justice!" (*Superman* [first series] #144, April 1961). It so happened that Superboy revealed his alien origins in an interview with journalist PERRY WHITE (*The New Adventures of Superboy* #12, December 1980).

Once he was believed to be genuine, he was introduced by the police chief to the Smallville mayor, who then saw to it the hero was introduced to the state's governor. When he was brought to Washington, DC, to meet the president, Superboy wound up saving the commander in chief's life, earning him a special place in the ranks of law enforcement (*Superman* [first series] #144, April 1961).

When DOUGLAS PARKER became chief of police, he and Superboy forged a strong friendship. As a result, Parker was one of the few given a way of summoning the Teen of Steel in times of need. Indeed, only three people—the chief, PROFESSOR LEWIS LANG, and the president of the United States—were entrusted with these signal devices, which were linked to a flickering lamp in the Kent household (*Superboy* [first series] #88, April 1961).

Despite the fame that came with being a hero, there were times when Clark felt isolated, different from other boys and girls. As a result, he was thrilled beyond belief when a rocket arrived containing his childhood pet Krypto. Under Earth's sun, the dog developed superpowers and increased intelligence, soon joining his master for exploits (*Adventure Comics* #210, March 1955). In time, Su-

perboy began to meet other survivors from Krypton and found other artifacts had that survived the planet's destruction, all of which helped him develop a keener insight into his heritage.

Still, he was a teen who craved being with friends, and he could not ask for more loyal companions than the attractive red-haired Lana Lang, the proverbial girl next door, and the steadfast Pete Ross, who accidentally learned of Clark's alter ego and kept the secret through the years.

Lana was infatuated with Superboy, coming to suspect time and again that he was also the bespectacled boy in her class. She laid elaborate traps to catch him, but never once learned the truth. Yet she also came to befriend the Teen of Steel and share adventures with him through time and space. While she crushed on Superboy, she also wanted Clark to gain more self-confidence, once asking Superboy to help Clark overcome his timidity (*Superboy* [first series] #43, September 1955).

Pete was "grown up and logical" in Clark's mind, an ideal male companion (*Superboy* [first series] #90, July 1961). Before Pete moved to Smallville, Clark had been a member of The Rangers, a boys' club (*Adventure Comics* #159, December 1950).

In time, Clark also became acquainted with a farm boy who idolized Superboy. As the costumed champion, he befriended Lex Luthor, discovering a barn full of memorabilia about himself. When he learned that the brilliant boy wanted to be a scientist, Superboy built him a well-stocked laboratory as a thank-you for being saved by Luthor when he was trapped by a kryptonite boulder. His first experiments were dedicated to finding a cure for the deadly green radiation, but early on, there was an accident that led to a fire. Superboy rushed over and blew out the flames with his super-breath. When he brought Luthor outside, the boy was bald and furious at Superboy for costing him his hair and looks. The angry youth thought Superboy had acted out of jealousy, not friendship, and dedicated his life to destroying the Kryptonian—a rivalry that would continue through the years and across the parallel universes (*Adventure Comics* #271, April 1960).

When they all attended Smallville High School, Clark's life was made miserable by the class bully Bash Bashford (*Superboy* [first series] #157, June 1969). By this time, Clark stood five foot ten tall and weighed 145 pounds, with a chest measurement of forty inches and a thirty-inch waist (*Superboy* [first series] #86, January 1961). He would continue to grow over the next few years, adding height and muscular density as his body reached its full maturity.

Superboy developed a number of bitter enemies, many of whom returned time and again to try to kill him. Beyond Luthor, there was the alien boy who absorbed the green radiation and became the dreaded Kryptonite Kid (*Superboy* [first series] #83, September 1960). He was also menaced on occasion by the magical imp Mr. Mxyzptlk, who decided tormenting Superman as a boy was too good to resist (*Superboy* [first series] #78, January 1960).

Given all of these challenges, Clark began to put into practice all the lessons his foster parents had been teaching him since he was a toddler. Jonathan worked with him on his powers and how to use them for the greater good, while Martha concentrated on making him a good friend and citizen. As a result, he adopted a personal code that precluded taking another person's life, a rule that his future friends adopted as part of the Legion of Super-Heroes' Constitution (*Superboy* [first series] #147, May–June 1968). He did recognize, though, that people without his level of powers had the right to take one life while saving another, something he explained during his fellow Legionnaire Star Boy's trial for violating the code (*Adventure Comics* #342, March 1966).

Given all of his powers and abilities, Clark continued to fret that he would let people down by not being on duty at all hours of the day and night. He found himself offering explanations out of guilt (*Superboy* [first series] #89, June 1961). These moral codes continued to evolve through these years and helped make him the World's Greatest Super Hero.

As his fame spread across the stars, several people he'd crossed paths with banded together to oppose him as the Superboy Revenge Squad (*Superboy* [first series] #94, January 1962).

Perhaps the oddest foe he had to face was his own imperfect duplicate. A scientist devised a duplicator ray, but the result was a flawed copy of Superboy. Dubbed Bizarro, the creature had chalky white skin and did everything in an opposite fashion (*Superboy* [first series] #68, October 1958). Later on, as an adult, Luthor would use the device to create Bizarro Superman, the beginning of an entire race of imperfect beings (*Action Comics* #254, August 1959).

More painful were the times when Superboy encountered other survivors from Krypton, beginning with Klax-Ar (*Superboy* [first series] #67, September 1958). Soon after, he learned of his father's discovery of the Phantom Zone and began meeting its villainous inhabitants, such as General Zod (*Adventure Comics* #283, April 1961).

While Superboy had challenging foes, he also had an entire Legion of friends—they just happened to live in the thirtieth century. Walking home from school one day, Clark was astonished to find three strange teens, each of whom seemed to know his alter ego. They revealed themselves as Cosmic Boy, Lightning Lad, and Saturn Girl, hailing from the future and offering Superboy membership in the Legion of Super-Heroes. He passed their test, which was more about character than power, and was welcomed into the club (*Adventure Comics* #247, April 1958). In time, the team grew in size and shared many adventures. Among the Legionnaires, Duo Damsel harbored a crush on Superboy and his "cousin" Mon-El, who emerged from the Phantom Zone to join. Super-

boy was given a Legion Flight Ring for the sole purpose of being able to use its communication function while on missions. Both Lana and Pete wound up becoming honorary members of the Legion.

The Teen of Steel's popularity led him to being voted deputy leader for the Legion's fourth and fifth terms. Notably among his exploits, he battled Mxyzptlk, a descendant of the Fifth Dimensional imp who plagued him in Smallville (*Adventure Comics* #310, July 1963); risked his life repeatedly, first to help resurrect Lightning Lad (*Adventure Comics* #312, September 1963); participated in the heretofore unknown war between Krypton and Earth (*Adventure Comics* #333, June 1965); helped organize newly recruited Legionnaires in defending against the invading Khunds (*Adventure Comics* #346–347, July–August 1966); and helped protect his fellow Legionnaires when Mordru the Merciless came seeking vengeance (*Adventure Comics* #369–370, June–July 1968).

When a green kryptonite cloud formed around Earth, Superboy and Supergirl had to leave the Legion, their memories erased. Before departing, though, they recommended replacements, who turned out to be Star Boy and Dream Girl in disguise. When Color Kid turned the cloud from green to blue, somehow negating the deadly radiation, the veteran heroes were welcomed back—and the rehabilitated heroes retained (*Adventure Comics* #350–351, November–December 1966).

Mon-El was not the first powerful teen Superboy encountered. Over time, he met up with many other teenagers from other worlds, such as Mars-boy (*Superboy* [first series] #14, May–June 1951; others). Only Lar Gand of Daxam, though, forged a truly lasting friendship with Clark Kent, the result of the mistaken belief that Lar might have been related based on Kryptonian evidence found on his ship (*Superboy* [first series] #89, June 1961).

As fate would have it, he encountered younger versions of many people who would become co-workers, friends, and lovers as he reached adulthood. These included Lois Lane (*Adventure Comics* #128, May 1948), Perry White (*Adventure Comics* #120, September 1947), Jimmy Olsen (*Adventure Comics* #216, September 1955), Batman (as Bruce Wayne in *World's Finest Comics* #84, September–October 1956; others), a time-traveling Robin (*Adventure Comics* #253, October 1958), Green Arrow (as Oliver Queen in *Adventure Comics* #258, March 1959), Green Lantern (as Hal Jordan in *The New Adventures of Superboy* #13, January 1981), and Aquaman (*Superboy* [first series] #171, January 1971). He also met his adult self on occasion, once colliding with him in the timestream, which caused the two heroes' minds to switch bodies (*Superman* [first series] #380–382, February–April 1983). He even met his cousin Supergirl (*Superboy* [first series] #80, April 1960), but when they adventured together with the Legion, he erased his knowledge of her existence each time he returned to his home era (*Adventure Comics* #334, July 1965). Superboy also learned of parallel worlds when he met the Clark Kent from Earth-2 (*The New Adventures of Superboy* #15–16, March–April 1981).

Clark even met one of his future nemeses when he saw cowboy Toby Manning long before he became Terra-Man (*The New Adventures of Superboy* #23, November 1981).

As the boy verged on adulthood, the passage of time seemed inexorable. Krypto seemingly vanished into outer space, returning in the grip of old age until a fountain of youth restored his vigor (*Superman's Pal, Jimmy Olsen* #29, June 1958). The Kents aged, but exposure to an alien serum effectively rejuvenated Jonathan and Martha, making them appear to be a couple in their late thirties (*Superboy* [first series] #145, March 1968).

Once Clark graduated from high school, the couple chose to take their first extended vacation, a trip to the Caribbean Islands. While there, they found Pegleg Morgan's 1717 diary, which led them to a treasure chest. By touching its contents, both contracted a rare tropical disease that proved fatal (*Superman* [first series] #161, May 1963). Hours after Martha passed away, Jonathan managed to speak with Clark before dying, reminding his son to always use his powers for the benefit of the world. After he died, Clark left Smallville for good (*Superman* [first series] #146, July 1961).

An orphan once more at eighteen, Clark Kent buried his parents, intending to sell the house, attend college, and eventually move to Metropolis. Years later, in an act of friendship, Pete Ross tried to have the home condemned and razed to protect its secrets, but he changed his mind when he saw how much it meant to Clark (*Superman* [first series] #270, December 1973). Clark did, however, leave Smallville, and it was a big affair, with the entire town turning out to wish him well. The population formed lines that from the sky spelled out farewell superboy, we'll never forget you! Superboy returned with the world's largest cake and made certain every citizen had a slice. Most were said to be preserved as souvenirs (*Superman* [first series] #97, May 1955).

While attending Metropolis University, Clark started to think of himself as Superman, beginning when he needed to evade a lie-detector test conducted by Professor Thaddeus V. Maxwell (*Superman* [first series] #125, November 1958). To the general public, he was still considered Superboy while he was in college (*Superman: The Secret Years* #1–4, February–May 1985).

After his adventurous experiences at college—making and losing friends and falling in love with Lori Lemaris, who turned out to be from Atlantis (*Superman* [first series] #129, May 1959)—Clark once more defeated a scheme by Lex Luthor, and the *Daily Planet* began referring to him as Superman. Clark, now twenty-one and a senior in college, was done with being the Teen of Steel (*Superman: The Secret Years* #4, May 1985).

Superboy encountered another reality when he was hurled across the dimensions by a sun going nova. Things were similar but different—such as the misspelled Smallvile and the fact that this reality's Brainiac 5, Chameleon Boy, Element Lad, Invisible Kid, and Ultra Boy were juvenile delinquents (*Superboy* [first series] #117, December 1964).

An encounter with red kryptonite sent Superboy from Earth-116 to Earth-1, where he was compelled to ruin a friend's reputation—and the poor victim turned out to be Chief Parker. It was Pa Kent who noticed that the yellow S was on a red background, so he asked Krypto to bring back his master, who was on a deep-space mission. Superboy helped his doppelgänger return home (*Superboy* [first series] #116, October 1964).

Variations on Superboy and young Clark Kent existed throughout the multiverse. Most of the variant tales began with Kal-El's rocketship landing somewhere other than Kansas. One such world featured a youth raised by apes and called Karkan (*Superboy* [first series] #183, March 1972, and #187, July 1972). A different world featured the Kents coming to adopt not only Kal-El, but also Bruce Wayne (*World's Finest Comics* #172, December 1967). Another saw Kara Zor-El arrive years ahead of Kal-El, so he was met by Superwoman (*Action Comics* #331, December 1965, and #332, January 1966). There was also a world wherein the rocket from Krypton went off course and wasn't found until the thirty-first century (*Superboy's Legion* #1–2, 2001).

The deadliest Superboy proved to be the one from Earth-Prime. This Clark Kent fought in the Crisis on Infinite Earths, watching his reality vanish from sight in a wave of anti-matter. After helping defeat the Anti-Monitor, he joined Superman 2, Lois Lane 2, and Alexander Luthor, Junior, from Earth-3 in a crystalline limbo (*Crisis on Infinite Earths* #12, March 1986). Over time, though, he despaired at what he saw happening on the re-formed Earth and was seduced by Luthor into helping re-create the multiverse. Superboy-Prime grew angry at those he saw as less-than-ideal heroes, and in time he became a cosmic threat (*Infinite Crisis* #1–7, December 2005–June 2006).

In the wake of the Crisis, Superman's reality was reordered. After Kal-El arrived from Krypton, it took years for him to absorb enough solar radiation that his powers manifested themselves. It wasn't until he was a high school football star that he demonstrated these abilities, and it was then that Pa Kent told him the truth (*Man of Steel* #1, October 1986).

Unbeknownst to everyone, during the Crisis the Time Trapper took a sliver of pre-Crisis time and crafted a Pocket Universe that resembled Earth-1. There remained a Superboy who adventured with the Legion. Anytime the Legion headed back to the twentieth century, the Trapper diverted them to the Pocket Universe, leaving them none the wiser. In time, though, the Legionnaires made their way into the proper reality—and were confused by what they found. Superboy, Superman, and the Legion battled the Time Trapper, and the Teen of Steel proved he was a worthy hero of legend when he sacrificed himself to save a reality that had no place for him (*Action Comics* #590; *Legion of Super-Heroes* [third series] #37–38, *Superman* [second series] #8—all August–September 1987).

Some time later, Superman was killed by Doomsday, a genetically created war machine powerful enough to harm even a Kryptonian (*Superman* [second series] #75, January 1993). In the wake of his death, a teenager in a red-and-blue costume, complete with an S-shield and a leather jacket, arrived in Metropolis and proclaimed himself Superman (*The Adventures of Superman* #500, Early June 1993). Prior to that fateful moment, Project Cadmus had samples of Superman's DNA, which were subjected to intensive testing. Paul Westfield was frustrated over their inability to successfully clone the Man of Steel, but overcame the problems by mixing Kryptonian and human genomes, resulting in a successful thirteenth attempt (*Superboy* [second series] *Annual* #2, 1995). When Superman was killed and a replacement hero was needed, this creation was rapidly aged. The teenage clone arrived claiming to be the new Superman, but so did three others at the same time (*The Adventures of Superman* #500, Early June 1993). After Superman's miraculous recovery, the clone happily wore the S-shield and took the name of Superboy (*The Adventures of Superman* #506, November 1993).

One of the things Cadmus learned was that the Kryptonian used a biokinetic force field, which provided the appearance of invulnerability and also allowed him to defy gravity. During the gene sequencing, they adapted this to the new creation, allowing the new clone something they called tactile telekinesis.

He had super-strength, and could fly; he later gained the various hearing and vision powers of Superman, but his unique skill was the tactile telekinesis. With his mind, he could disassemble mechanical constructs, or actually hold an object's parts together. As his powers matured, he learned that the telekinesis allowed him to control objects in other ways. He was not charged by solar radiation, nor was he susceptible to kryptonite, thanks to half of his DNA being human. Magic, though, could affect him.

For a long time, Superboy believed Westfield to be his genetic parent, but he later learned the truth: It was Lex Luthor's genetic code that had helped give him life and allowed the evil genius to mentally influence the youth (*Teen Titans* [third series] #1, September 2003).

The new Superboy was brash and confident in his abilities despite a tremendous lack of experience in using them. Nor did he possess any real understanding of the world or the people inhabiting it, having only recently emerged from the clone banks. He got a quick lesson working alongside the Newsboy Legion—fellow Cadmus clones who had already acclimated to society. Soon after, he met Lois Lane and told her his story, but it was journalist Tana Moon who revealed the scoop live on WGBS (*The Adventures of Superman* #501, July 1993).

When Superman's death appeared to have been reversed, the clone helped him, Steel, and the Eradicator take down the Cyborg Superman. Soon after, he learned of his genetic origin and was only too happy to adopt the name Superboy. He decided to find his own destiny away from the Man of Steel's shadow. He decided on a "Superboy World Tour," and when it came to an end in Hawaii, he chose to stay there, especially after encountering Moon who had also gone west for a new job (*Superboy* [third series] #1, February 1990). Along the way he met promoter Rex Leech and his sexy blond teen daughter Roxy Leech. Joining Superboy for the experience was Dubbilex, a DNAlien who was also born at Cadmus.

Superboy enjoyed the attention of the bronzed women of the islands, but after serious flirtation with Roxie, he admitted his feelings to Tana. She reciprocated (*Superboy* [third series] #5, June 1990).

Hawaii appeared a peaceful paradise on the surface, but in rapid order the Clone of Steel came to battle all manner of opponents, including the redheaded bombshell Knockout, the mutated King Shark, Sidearm, B.E.M., Silverword, and the Silicon Dragons, a Pacific Rim criminal organzation. He often found himself allied with the Hawaiian version of the Metropolis Special Crimes Unit, headed by Sam Makoa, an operation that Rox eventually joined (*Superboy* [third series] #26, April 1996).

Government officials ballyhooed having a super hero in their state, but also required the teen to attend school since he was a minor no matter how his age was calculated. He tried but kept ditching classes to fight super-villains—or just plain skipped. In time, he was expelled, and Dubbilex began to telepathically tutor the impetuous teen.

Knockout continued to turn up in Superboy's life. The two fought, flirted, and finally became a couple. Her super-strength and massive size made her a formidable opponent, testing even the Clone of Steel's fortitude. Knockout's skills led her to being recruited to work with Amanda Waller's Suicide Squad for a time, alongside Superboy's other enemy King Shark (*Superboy* [third series] #13–15, March–May 1995). While attempting to destroy the Silicon Kings gang, Knockout was believed killed, but she turned up again when Superboy actually needed her help.

In time, though, her morals and his clashed, resulting in them parting and eventually fighting once more. After putting her in jail, Superboy renewed his romance with Tana. Not long after, she inadvertently provided Amanda Spence with information allowing the Agenda to abduct the hero for a time (*Superboy* [third series] #32, October 1996, and #34–35, December 1995–January 1996). They infected him with a genetic disease. When Superboy's genetic code literally began unraveling, he needed a donor's DNA pattern to follow, and Roxy volunteered despite the dangers it meant to her life. The doctors at Project Cadmus successfully saved Superboy's life, increasing the bond between the teens, which had evolved from potential lovers to more like family. This eased the tension Superboy felt given his attraction to both Roxy and Tana (*Superboy* [third series] #36, February 1997, and #38–41, April–July 1997).

One result was that Superboy would permanently remain in the shape of a sixteen-year-old, subjecting the older Moon to ridicule, leading them to ultimately break up (*Superboy* [third series] #46, December 1997). She left her job and Hawaii (*Superboy* [third series #49, March 1998)—only to be kidnapped by the Agenda. She had to be rescued by the Wild Men.

Another result of the Agenda's meddling was the creation of a clone that was designed to be more powerful than Superboy. But the villains were unaware that they were cloning a clone, and their creation was imperfect. Match proved an unstable being, one who would plague Superman time and again (*Superboy* [third series] #35, January 1997).

Superboy enjoyed many exploits away from Hawaii, often returning to Metropolis to fight alongside father figure Superman. When needed, he would partner with Supergirl and Steel as Team Superman, making his first foray off-world to assist his idol when he was on trial, accused of causing Krypton's destruction. It was during this time that the young hero began learning the consequences of his actions. When he first partnered with Steel, he dodged gunfire without realizing that the bullets struck the *Daily Planet*'s helicopter instead, killing the pilot and endangering Lois Lane (*Superman: The Man of Steel* #22, June 1993).

Superboy was seen as a tough kid who was slowly maturing, still trying to find his way. He continued to make bad decisions but learned what the good ones were. He was brash and a little cocky, enthusiastic but sometimes very serious—especially when it came to exploring his purpose.

As reality was altered by Zero Hour, he also came to play a part in Lar Gand's life. This Daxamite, with powers similar to a Kryptonian's, was suffering memory loss and was manipulated into battling Superboy. When it became clear that Lar was experiencing LEAD poisoning, Superboy took him to S.T.A.R. LABS for help, but he was too far gone. Superboy placed Lar Gand in the Stasis Zone (*Superboy* [third series] #18–19, August–September 1995).

Seeking a fresh start following the Agenda fight, Superboy and Dubbilex took up residence at Project Cadmus after it was reorganized and headed by MICKEY CANNON and COLONEL ADAM WINTERBOURNE. He worked alongside the GUARDIAN, a clone of the hero from an earlier era (*Superboy* [third series] #50, April 1998). He liked the isolated life for a time, especially as it kept him away from romantic entanglements; he ignored the attentions of DR. SERLING ROQUETTE, the teen whiz recently assigned to Cadmus.

Not long after, Superman returned from a mission and decided that Superboy needed a name to honor his Kryptonian genetic heritage. The youth was dubbed Kon-El, cementing his place in the HOUSE OF EL (*Superboy* [third series] #59, February 1999).

It was inevitable that Superboy would find companionship with other teen heroes. He partnered first with Robin the Teen Wonder when they took on METALLO and POISON IVY (*Superboy/Robin WF3: World's Finest Three* #1–2, 1996). Despite a rocky start, Superboy formed a bond with his counterpart that would endure for the rest of his life.

Superboy, Robin, and the speedster Impulse decided to formalize their bond and became a team called Young Justice. They shared a few adventures before their ranks expanded to include several female teen heroes (*Young Justice* #1, September 1998). One of those heroines, Wonder Girl, would eventually capture Superboy's heart after she talked him out of killing Amanda Spence in an act of vengeance.

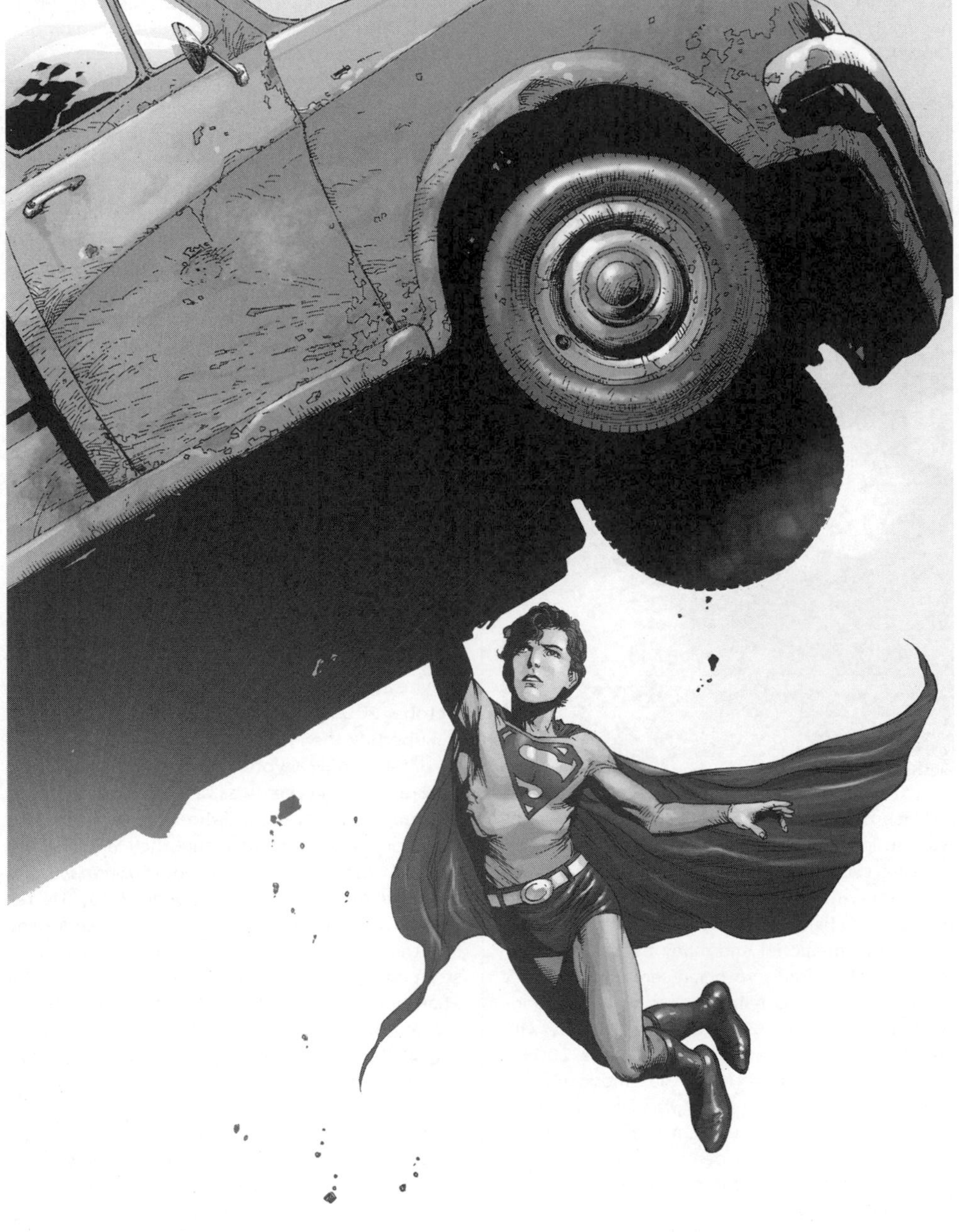

When he learned from an alternate version of himself that a threat called BLACK ZERO was coming, he was authorized by Superman, Batman, and WONDER WOMAN to investigate Hypertime, a reality that encompassed all possible realities. During his jaunt, he encountered the Earth-1 Superboy, and he soon learned that the real threat was actually another incarnation of himself. It took a veritable Legion of Superboys, the Challengers of the Unknown, and an alternate reality version of Knockout to prevail (*Superboy* [third series] #60–64, March–July 1999). One consequence was that he learned Superman's secret identity from the Earth-1 Superboy, something that irked the teen. It took a conversation with Lois Lane, a member of his extended family, to calm him down. Superboy also experienced other realms by adventuring with a group of heroes and heroic aliens known as the RAVERS. After meeting in the extraterrestrial Event Horizon, the Clone of Steel was encouraged by the flirtatious SPARX to help form a team, and they enjoyed many exploits before they drifted apart (*Superboy and the Ravers* #1–19, September 1996–March 1998).

Spence turned up once more when the EVIL FACTORY's creations assaulted Cadmus and Superboy was impersonated by Match. Spence murdered Tana in front of the teen hero, crushing the hero's spirit (*Superboy* [third series] #73–75, April–June 2000).

A spell cast by the impish Klarion the Witch Boy resulted in many heroes being turned into teenagers while the teen allies became adult versions of themselves, although Superboy—still frozen in his teenage form—was not among them. Eventually the spell was undone, but as a side effect the clone lost his superpowers (*Young Justice: Sins of Youth* #1–2, May 2000); he had to use his recent experience and some high-tech gear to remain on a par with the others. In time, his powers returned, and it was suggested that his telekinesis would actually become his most powerful asset (*Superboy* [third series] #75–79, June–October 2000).

Roxy returned to Superboy's life via Project Cadmus (*Superboy* [third series] #76, July 2000), where she was discovered to have bonded with a fire elemental named Pyra. With the entity excised from her body, Roxy joined Rex in returning to a more normal existence (*Superboy* [third series] #80–81, November–December 2000).

Kon-El left the devastated Cadmus to take an apartment in Metropolis, working as the super to afford the rent and groceries (*Superboy* [third series] #94, January 2002). While Young Justice had many victories, it also suffered numerous defeats, the worst being when a rogue SUPERMAN ROBOT wound up traveling through time and killing Donna Troy, the first Wonder Girl. This brought both the TEEN TITANS and Young Justice to an end, at least for a while (*Titans/Young Justice: Graduation Day* #1–3, July–August 2003). Things had not been going well for Kon-El, so Superman decided the teen really needed some tender loving care,

apple pie, and moral guidance. As a result, he was brought to Smallville and taken in by Jonathan and Martha Kent (*Superboy* [third series] #100, July 2002). He finally adopted the human identity of Conner Kent, a cousin to the Kent family. Titans veteran Cyborg also felt that the next generation of heroes needed time to bond, blow off steam, and train, so he invited them all to re-form the Teen Titans, initially as a weekend-only obligation. Soon after, Superman brought Krypto to the farm to keep the boy and dog occupied with each other (*Teen Titans* [third series] #1, September 2003).

By this time, Superboy had developed a full-blown romance with Wonder Girl and become best of friends with Robin. He was feeling grounded for a change, which is why he suddenly found himself whisked to the thirty-first century, sharing a mission with the Legion of Super-Heroes. Even in the future, he became a pawn for Darkseid, who envisioned turning twentieth-century champions of justice into warriors of the future, battling in his name. When they realized the wrong El had been taken, Superboy was cast adrift until he was found by the Legion (*The Legion* #25–30, December 2003–April 2004). It took Saturn Girl several months of work to find the exact point in time from which Conner had been snatched, and finally Brainiac 5 was able to send him home.

Superboy returned just in time to see the Titans and Legion get caught up in an adventure that resulted in a vastly different reality for the future team and landed the Titans a decade ahead of their normal era (*Teen Titans/Legion Special*, 2004). Conner was at first thrilled to see that he had grown up and finally become Superman, his fondest wish come true. He was horrified, though, to find his other genetic father Lex Luthor acting as his mentor (*Teen Titans* [third series] #16, Late November 2004).

They returned to their time period and contemplated breaking up the team lest this horrid future come to pass, but they were attacked by Brainiac and Luthor through the time-displaced android Indigo, who had been working with the Outsiders. Luthor then triggered a code within Superboy that placed the teen in his thrall. Superboy proceeded to break Robin's arm and beat his girlfriend (*Teen Titans* [third series] #24–25 and *Outsiders* [third series] #24–25, both July–August 2005). Once freed, he remained in Kansas, ashamed to see his friends. He pondered whether or not he had a soul since he was a genetic creation. His fellow Titan Raven visited him and confirmed that not only did he have a soul, but it was getting stronger by the day (*Teen Titans* [third series] #26, September 2005).

The day of reckoning arrived soon after, as Superboy-Prime left his limbo-like world and began setting into motion events that he expected would result in the "right" world replacing the corrupt one he was standing on. Among the horrors in his mind was that the world's Superboy was not really Kryptonian, but a genetic monster. As the events of Infinite Crisis unfolded, Superboy and Superboy-Prime battled repeatedly. The strain proved too much for Conner, and Doctor Mid-Nite warned him that he was at risk. Luthor also tried to shield him, wishing to keep him as a legacy. His allies found a way to heal his battered body, although Luthor warned Robin it was a onetime cure (*Robin* [second series] #147, April 2006).

As he recovered, Superboy spent some intimate time with Wonder Girl before returning to the battle (*Teen Titans* [third series] *Annual* #1, 2006). He found Nightwing, and together they staged an assault on the cosmic tuning fork that threatened to splinter the universe into a multiverse. After freeing the heroes who had been hooked up to power the device, Superboy was once more attacked by Superboy-Prime. Despite his right hand being crushed by the enraged teen, Conner managed to sustain his end of the fight, letting the other heroes recover and scatter. The multiverse had started to reshape just as the machine exploded; the universes collapsed once more. Superboy-Prime unleashed a volley of blows that wound up fatal. While the other heroes engaged Prime, Conner lay in Wonder Girl's arms until he died (*Infinite Crisis* #7, June 2006).

Once the cosmic calamity ended, Conner Kent was buried beside the Earth-2 Superman, who had also succumbed during the fight, and his wife Lois Lane, who'd died of old age. He was mourned by his fellow heroes, with Wonder Girl conducting an Internet memorial and many people celebrating his life through Kryptonian ceremonies. A cult even formed in his name, although it was derisively called the "Cult of Conner" by Wonder Girl and the Elongated Man (*52* #13, August 2, 2006).

Soon a new hero was flying the American skies. Many thought that Supernova was Kon-El reborn, but it proved not to be true. Later, on the first anniversary of Superboy's death, a statue was unveiled in Metropolis's Centennial Park, next to the one honoring Superman (*52* #1, May 10, 2006). Another statue was erected by Titans Tower in San Francisco. Both Robin and Wonder Girl modified their uniforms to red-and-black color schemes to honor their friend. Robin also secretly worked in the labs beneath the Tower, trying to re-create Kon-El from genetic material left behind (*Teen Titans* [third series] #33, 2006).

While Robin labored to no avail, Starman, an adult Legionnaire from the thirty-first century, had come back in time under orders from Brainiac 5, but his mind was scrambled and it was many months before he finally fulfilled his mission. He took a job as a gravedigger, which allowed him to surreptitiously dig up Conner Kent's corpse and place it in the regeneration chamber at Superman's Fortress of Solitude. It took a millennium for the badly battered body to heal. Polar Boy helped by retrieving a follicle from Lex Luthor, and efforts were made on his behalf by Dawnstar and Wildfire. Just when the Legion and the universe needed him most, Superboy returned for a rematch with Superboy-Prime in the thirty-first century (*Final Crisis: Legion of 3 Worlds* #4, April 2009).

After that threat was ended, Conner was brought back to the twenty-first century, where he was happily reunited with the Teen Titans. He also returned to live with Martha Kent and Krypto on the Smallville farm, eager to continue his heroic career. The teen also drafted a list about Lex Luthor, and compared and contrasted him with Superman, his other genetic "parent." Conner resumed his civilian identity and enrolled at Smallville High School where he met a young girl named Lori, who quickly developed a crush on the Teen of Steel. After renewing his friendship with Tim Drake, now operating as Red Robin, Conner focused on his relationship with Wonder Girl Cassie Sandsmark. The two tried renewing their romance, but before they could get far, Lex Luthor arrived in Smallville to pay a visit to his sister Lena Luther, as well as his niece—Lori. Lori's mother Lena was ill, and Luthor cured his sister, only to reverse the process to prove to Conner that he would never cure his sister until Superman was defeated. An enraged Conner turned to Tim Drake for help, the latter entrusting Lena's care to the experts at Wayne Enterprises (*Adventure Comics* #504–509, October 2009–March 2010).

Superboy then joined Superman and Supergirl to defend New Krypton from being recaptured by Brainiac. The teen was also reunited with the Legion of Super-Heroes, who were working with the Espionage Squad to ensure the Man of Steel's survival, lest time itself unravel (*Superman: Last Stand of New Krypton* #1–3, June 2010). He remained on hand when the surviving Kandorians lost their world and attacked Earth, and was instrumental in sending the Kryptonians into the Phantom Zone, thereby ending the threat to his planet (*Superman: War of the Supermen* #1–4, July 2010). In the aftermath, he returned to active duty with the Teen Titans (*Teen Titans* [third series] #81, May 2010).

In the wake of Infinite Crisis, reality restored Superboy to Superman's life. Clark Kent was by all accounts a normal twelve-year-old—or he believed he was. After Pete Ross broke an arm while trying to tackle Clark, however, Clark began to experience the birth of his powers . . . leading to a disastrous event in which his heat vision nearly burned down the Kent barn. To Clark's dismay, Pa and Ma came up with a pair of glasses with special lenses (made from the rocket that brought him to Earth) that helped contain his unique vision in case it went off again. And when he started to fly, his parents revealed the truth to their adopted son.

Clark was frightened by the revelation and confused when he was shown the rocket he'd landed in. When he touched it, the Sunstone crystal activated—giving the boy glimpses of life on Krypton.

The adolescent Clark felt like an outsider, forced to hide his powers and who he truly was. He became uncomfortable around everyone, even the first girl he kissed—Lana Lang. He was forced out of his withdrawal, however, whenever a need arose to save people from tornadoes, car accidents, and other disasters in a mysterious blur.

His adopted parents were the ones who helped Clark embrace his Kryptonian heritage. After Clark's clothes continued to get ripped apart during his good deeds, Ma created a uniform based on the clothes the Kryptonians wore and including the symbol of the House of El—thus his Superboy costume was crafted. Superboy was never seen by the public, becoming a modern myth. The tabloids spoke of "Super-Boy," but no one truly believed he existed.

When Cosmic Boy, Lightning Lad, and Saturn Girl invited him to join the Legion of Super-Heroes, it was the first time Clark ever felt like he belonged, but it was only momentary—a brief reprieve from reality. The Legionnaires were the first friends Clark connected with. The fun he had with the Legion became a big part of his enthusiasm that led him to become a part of the JUSTICE LEAGUE OF AMERICA and the super hero community at large.

During his first adventure with the Legion, Clark gained faith in people, no matter who they were, thanks to Saturn Girl (representing Truth); he loosened up and had fun with his powers, taking down criminals thanks to Lightning Lad's antics (representing Justice); and he learned about the value of diversity and working together thanks to Cosmic Boy's leadership (representing the American Way).

Clark was left wondering if he would meet other people like himself in the future. At that point, he decided that he would leave Smallville someday to find his destiny (*Superman: Secret Origin* #1–3, September–November 2009).

SUPERBOY-PRIME

The strangest—and deadliest—variation of Superman was unquestionably that on the world that came to be known as Earth-Prime. There, all super heroes and their enemies were fictional characters who appeared in comic books and other popular media. So when a spacecraft crashed on JERRY and NAOMI KENT's farm and the couple discovered a baby inside, it seemed a far more extraordinary event than it might have in a world in which alien super-beings were commonplace. Like their counterparts on Earth-1 and Earth-2, these Kents adopted the child and named him CLARK KENT (*DC Comics Presents* #87, November 1985). This Clark grew up with no special powers and never suspected that he possessed any, but they were in fact latent and would manifest themselves later in his adolescence. As fate would have it, this happened on the day he attended a costume party dressed as his "namesake," the comic book SUPERBOY. That same day, Halley's Comet passed overhead, and it was later theorized that its presence somehow activated Clark's powers. When he suddenly found himself genuinely airborne while pretending to fly, he realized that he truly *was* a Superboy, and very briefly became Earth-Prime's sole real-life super hero.

As the ANTI-MONITOR began destroying all the parallel universes, this Superboy became aware of the large multiverse. He explored his newfound powers and abilities fighting alongside his doppelgängers to save reality during the events known as the CRISIS ON INFINITE EARTHS.

The Superman of Earth-1 and a diverse array of heroes and villains defeated the Anti-Monitor even as the remaining Earths collapsed into one—but not before the Earth-2 Superman and his wife

LOIS LANE, ALEXANDER LUTHOR, JUNIOR, of Earth-3, and Superboy-Prime watched in horror as the Anti-Monitor's wave of destruction headed straight toward them. To escape it, Alex used his matter/anti-matter powers to transport the four of them to another dimension. It was a newfound haven—a crystalline limbo in which they were isolated from the reordered universe. In the aftermath, many super-beings and civilians died, but the single positive- and anti-matter universes endured (*Crisis on Infinite Earths* #1–12, April 1985–March 1986).

From this seeming "paradise dimension," Superboy-Prime and his companions watched the heroes on the re-formed Earth and began to despair as things took a decidedly darker turn than they could have imagined. Events such as Bane breaking BATMAN's back and DOOMSDAY killing Superman caused them all to wonder if they'd done the right thing.

Superboy-Prime, still a teen and destined to remain one forever, began to long for a chance to grow up and be a hero in his own right. He used the crystals within his realm to revisit glimpses of his life on Earth-Prime, notably his ninth birthday party. When Alexander Luthor began scheming of a way to re-create the "perfect" Earth, he began manipulating the youth along with Superman-2, who by then was concerned as old age began to claim his wife. Alex whispered in Superboy's ear, making him grow angry, and he began smashing the crystalline barrier without at first realizing he was sending reality-altering ripples through space-time. These began manifesting in unusual ways: They resurrected the second ROBIN, Jason Todd, from the grave, for instance, and altered the progression of KAL-EL's growth from an infant on KRYPTON to an adult hero on Earth.

Alexander replayed the death of his parents and girlfriend, tipping the scales in his favor (*Infinite Crisis: Secret Files and Origins,* 2006). Superboy-Prime agreed to help Alexander re-create the right planet and replace the Superboy currently

operating in his stead, a clone that he found to be an abomination. He wanted a chance to not only grow up, but be that new world's Man of Steel.

With Alexander Luthor's dimensional powers returning, the group was able to leave "paradise" and begin work on Earth. In short order, Superboy-Prime began altering the orbits and positions of numerous planets, concluding with placing Rann into the same orbit as Thanagar (*Rann-Thanagar War* #1–6, 2005). This cataclysm destroyed life on Thanagar and sparked a war between the worlds; it also changed the cosmos so that Oa was no longer in the center of the universe, impacting the Guardians of the Universe's power and the Green Lantern Corps. He also destroyed the Justice League of America's Watchtower on the moon (*JLA* #125, April 2006). Superboy-Prime was then dispatched to begin gathering powerful heroes who should have been champions on parallel worlds but were trapped on an Earth that seemed to have little room for them, including the Martian Manhunter and Earth-2's Power Girl.

As Superboy-Prime captured the heroes, he placed them into a rebuilt cosmic tuning fork, made from the empty shell of the Anti-Monitor's armor and designed to shatter the universe into the multiverse so that Alexander could select the "right" one to keep.

Earth's champions fought back, not wishing to let any one person play God like that. Superboy and Superboy-Prime battled repeatedly, with the Clone of Steel badly injured during the later confrontations. When one such battle was interrupted by the arrival of members of the Teen Titans, Superboy-Prime lashed back, killing Pantha. Taking another person's life horrified him, but only briefly, since it seemed to set him on a path that would eventually lead to his own descent into evil.

Even after Speedy managed to project Superboy-Prime into the Phantom Zone, the enraged teen broke free, demonstrating power that was rapidly escalating off the charts (*Teen Titans* [third series] #32, March 2006). The three fastest men alive, three of the men to use the name Flash—Jay Garrick, Wally West, and Bart Allen—propelled the teen into the Speed Force, the realm from which they derived their powers. He wound up on a planet orbiting a red sun for four years, which depleted much of his power (*Infinite Crisis* #4, April 2006). Regardless, Superboy-Prime, angrier than before, found a way back to Earth, determined to rid the planet of its heroes before Alexander had a chance to re-create reality. Wearing a power suit to augment his depleted abilities, Superboy-Prime was effectively force-fed yellow solar radiation, regaining his powers in an accelerated fashion.

As he struggled against the heroes, Superboy-Prime came to the conclusion that Earth-Prime was the proper world to restore, a notion Luthor did not share. While Luthor played with the multiverse, Superboy-Prime nearly beat Wonder Girl to death, an act that prompted Conner Kent—Superboy—to throw himself at the villain. The more powerful Prime broke the clone's wrist, and their struggles sent them tumbling into the tuning fork device, exploding it and collapsing the rapidly expanding multiverse back into a single positive-matter universe. New Earth was born (*Infinite Crisis* #6, May 2006).

While Superboy-Prime managed to survive the ordeal, Superboy's injuries were too severe, and he died.

Prime and Alexander bickered over their next step as both engaged in what came to be known as the Battle of Metropolis. Superboy-Prime by then was so blinded by anger that he no longer seemed repulsed by killing, so he maimed or murdered both heroes and villains. To Prime, New Earth was no better than the one they'd just altered, and he disliked the concept of ruling just the one world.

After eluding a revenge-seeking Bart Allen, Superboy-Prime took to space, choosing to destroy Oa, theorizing that the unleashed power might well cause a new Big Bang and a chance to restore the proper universe with just one hero—himself. With Earth's heroes chasing him, Superboy-Prime accelerated and managed to pierce a three-hundred-mile-thick wall crafted by an army of Green Lanterns. Once through, he was opposed directly by the Corps and he managed to slay thirty-two members before he was grabbed by Superman and Superman-2. At top speed, they traversed the stars and plunged into Rao, which had once been sun to Krypton. The intense heat melted the armor on Superboy-Prime and weakened all three beings. As a result, they crashed on Mogo, the planet that was also a Green Lantern.

Despite all this, Superboy-Prime remained fueled by sheer hatred and pummeled the original Superman until he was near death. New Earth's Superman managed to finally stop him.

With his last bit of energy, Superman finally punched Superboy-Prime into unconsciousness, then tended to the dying Man of Steel. While the hero's passing was mourned, the Green Lantern Corps arrived to take charge of the still Prime, placing him in a bubble of green energy surrounded by a Sun-Eater (provided by Donna Troy); a phalanx of fifty Green Lanterns took turns guarding the prisoner (*Infinite Crisis* #7, June 2006).

It took a mere year before Superboy-Prime gained his freedom when the Guardians and Green Lantern Corps were attacked by the Sinestro Corps, utilizing the yellow power of fear (*Green Lantern: Sinestro Corps Special* #1, August 2007). Outfitted with a new power suit styled after the Sinestro Corps, Superboy-Prime fought with them, briefly preferring to be called Superman-Prime despite being still a teen. Back on Earth, he fought Superman, Power Girl, and Supergirl, regaining his full powers as the sun rose during the confrontation (*Tales of the Sinestro Corps: Superman-Prime,* 2007).

He was confronted shortly thereafter by Sodam Yat, who was wielding the ultimate power of Ion, and beat the Daxamite senseless. The resurrected Anti-Monitor was attempting to destroy reality once more, but Superman-Prime flew through his chest. Then, still seeking a world with himself as the sole champion, he took on both the Green Lantern Corps and the Sinestro Corps. It took the sacrifice of an immortal Guardian of the Universe to finally subdue the being. While the event was expected to kill the teen, it actually sent him into the recently re-formed multiverse.

He began seeking Earth-Prime among the fifty-two new parallel universes and was frustrated all over again at not finding it. On Earth-15, he sought out that world's Lex Luthor, insanely blamed him for Alexander's faults, and then destroyed all of the heroes operating on the planet (*Countdown to Final Crisis* #24, November 14, 2007). From there he traveled to the Source Wall, a construct that separated the universe from the powers that had created it. Abducting Mr. Mxyzptlk, he tortured the Fifth Dimension being, hoping he could use magic to obtain his desire. The magician was freed by Annataz, the Earth-3 version of Zatanna, who was killed for her effort.

Superboy-Prime turned his attention to the Monitors, the fifty-two cosmic beings who oversaw the new multiverse. One had declared his individuality by taking the name Solomon, and it was this Monitor who was confronted by the teen. In exchange for telling Superboy-Prime what he wanted, Solomon asked that Forerunner, an agent of the Monitors, be freed. The teen agreed and was then directed to Earth-51 (*Countdown to Final Crisis* #16–14, January 9–23, 2008). Arriving there, he was horrified to find the world in ruins after a battle between the cosmic conqueror Monarch and the planet's heroes. Upset, Superman-Prime returned to the Monitors and fought Solomon, intending to kill him. Instead, the two traded blows of unimaginable force until Solomon managed to tear the teen's suit. The energy unleashed seemingly destroyed the Monitor as well as the entire reality of Earth-51.

An adrift and unconscious Superboy-Prime was found by the Time Trapper, who saw him as the perfect pawn in his ongoing battle with the Legion of Super-Heroes. The next thing Superboy-Prime knew, he was waking up within the remains of a barn near Smallville in the thirty-first century. His energy had been vastly depleted and he once more looked like a normal teenager, but he grew angry when the farmers encountering him called him Superboy. Still thinking of himself as a man, he reacted with fresh anger when the farmers shot him. After killing them, he went exploring, only to find his anger rising when he toured the Superman Museum and saw how highly regarded the "flawed" hero was in this future. The tipping point came

when he found a statue of himself tucked away in a closet at the Hall of Villains. Seeing his lack of impact on history sent him into a rage and he destroyed the museum, killing guards and law enforcement personnel. Along the way, he heard a holographic guide, resembling Jimmy Olsen, tell of the Legion of Super-Villains, who had formed out of inspiration generated by some entity whose "name was never spoken."

Superboy-Prime knew he could be that sort of dark evil, and he decided to make the Legion of Super-Villains his army. He traveled from Earth to Takron-Galtos, the prison planet, and freed Lightning Lord, Saturn Queen, and Cosmic King to help him re-form the Legion. Using his heat vision, he carved an S-shield on the planet's surface, serving notice that it was now to be regarded as a symbol of fear, not hope.

Upon hearing of the prison debacle, the Legion of Super-Heroes contacted Superman in the twenty-first century, who confirmed that after the Sinestro Corps War ended, no one on New Earth had a clue as to the teen's whereabouts. Clearly, Superboy-Prime was gathering the largest collection of superpowered felons imaginable—the Legion was going to be both outpowered and outnumbered. Superman and Brainiac 5 decided that it made sense to call in reinforcements by summoning the Legions from two adjacent parallel universes.

While the Legionnaires readied for war, the Man of Steel struck on the noble concept that redemption was the way to stop Superboy-Prime. As Superman prepared for that, Superboy-Prime personally sought out those he had any history with, such as Sodam Yat, who now served as the last of the Guardians of the Universe. Bart Allen, the onetime Flash, also returned from the Speed Force still seeking revenge for Conner Kent's murder. Finally, after spending a millennium healing, Superboy himself emerged from the Fortress of Solitude and was ready for a rematch.

The Time Trapper was confronted by Superman and the Legion's founders, Saturn Girl, Lightning Lad, and Cosmic Boy. At the end of time, the Trapper's hood was finally removed and an aged Superboy-Prime was discovered. Superboy and the Legion confronted Superboy-Prime in the thirty-first century and the end of time, recognizing the link between the two versions of the villain. Superboy's heat vision scarred the S-shield that Prime had carved into his chest, enraging the younger incarnation. Saturn Girl used the link between the figures to open a portal that brought multiple incarnations of the Legion to the battle. Defeated, they brought the Time Trapper to the thirty-first century, where the younger Superboy-Prime was disgusted to see what he had become. With one superpowered punch, the Trapper was knocked out and both figures vanished from reality. The resulting time paradox left Clark Kent back on Earth-Prime, annoyed at being depowered and stuck reading about himself in comics. His parents and girlfriend also had read his four-color exploits and were disgusted by his attitude and antics. Living in his parents' basement, he swore he would find a way back to New Earth and exact revenge (*Final Crisis: Legion of 3 Worlds* #1–5, October 2008–September 2009).

Clark remained in the basement of his home, obsessively reading all the current comic books that detailed the events transpiring on New Earth. In a fit of anger about all that was happening, Clark broke his girlfriend Laurie's arm, which scared her off for good. As he read all the negative comments about him on various message boards Clark began to reconsider his actions and seemingly let go of all of the anger that had driven him to his extreme and deadly actions. However, when *Adventure Comics* #507 depicted a storyline that saw him die in the next issue, Clark forced his panicked parents to track down *Adventure Comics* #508, which had yet to ship from the printer. As a result of his panic, Clark was unprepared when Alexander Luthor, risen from the dead as a member of the Black Lantern Corps, attacked him at his home. Black Luthor restored Clark's superpowers, only to have him face off against Black Lantern versions of all the individuals that Clark had killed so callously as Superboy-Prime. The furious Superboy-Prime flew to the Manhattan office of

DC Comics in an attempt to punish the comic book editors responsible for putting him in this predicament. When the Black Lantern Luthor caught up with him, he teleported them both back to Clark's basement, where Luthor began destroying Clark's comic book collection. Devastated, Clark accepted a Black Lantern ring. The ring willed Clark to die, but the young man's intense and conflicting emotions caused the ring to shatter, also eradicating all the Black Lantern victims who were haunting him. A Black Lantern then arrived and informed Clark that the comic book writers were sorry for what they had put him through and promised to leave him alone (*Adventure Comics* #507–508, January–February 2010).

Unlike Superman, Superboy-Prime seemed resistant to magic and most forms of Kryptonite. It took the combined efforts of three versions of Element Lad to find the right configuration to generate harmful radiation. The one thing that caused genuine fear within the cocksure teen was the Flash family of speedsters. That they managed to entrap him in the Speed Force and exile him for years led to this chink in his psychological makeup. Their very presence managed to unnerve the teen, a fact that did not go unnoticed.

SUPERBOY REVENGE SQUAD, THE

Superboy battled and vanquished the blue-skinned tyrants ruling Wexr II. A year later, several members of the defeated regime banded together to form a Superboy Revenge Squad, with finding his homeworld their first priority. Rather than beat Superboy, their intent was to destroy his planet with one of their weapons. Upon learning of the threat, the Teen of Steel hypnotized himself for twenty-four hours so that their brain-wave detection device would fail to locate a Superboy. While Superboy was out of action, Pete Ross masqueraded as the hero to stop robbers (*Superboy* [first series] #94, January 1962).

After being mutated, the Wexrian Ersork blamed Superboy for his distorted new form. As a result, he finally located Superboy's planet and took mental control of Jonathan Kent. The foster parent donned a costume and battled his adopted son as the Mental Emperor, using mind-over-matter abilities provided by Ersork. Superboy first freed Pa Kent, then sought out Ersork and helped him regain his normal form. Out of gratitude, he resigned from the Revenge Squad (*Superboy* [first series] #111, March 1964).

Twice, the Squad attempted to ruin Superboy's life by exposing him to different forms of red Kryptonite. The first experience led him to fall into a heavy sleep with dreams that led to dreams about dreaming, confusing him to the point that he believed he had killed Lana Lang and released the criminals residing in the Phantom Zone. Despondent, he was preparing to leave Earth when the effects wore off (*Superboy* [first series] #114, July 1964). The second exposure prompted the hero to fight Krypto the Super-Dog, but again the Squad goal was thwarted (*Superboy* [first series] #118, January 1965).

Some time later, Trohn, a renegade Squad member, arrived on Earth to kill Superboy, but the other

members of the Revenge Squad actually came to the Kryptonian's aid (*The New Adventures of Superboy* #32–33, August–September 1982).

Residents from the planet Drulok allied themselves with the Squad in an attempt to trick the Smallville Sentinel into turning the Earth against Superboy. The plot failed and the aliens left the solar system, still hoping for the day they would make the hero suffer (*The New Adventures of Superboy* #53–54, May–June 1984).

Years later, when Superboy became Superman, the aliens continued to seek vengeance and became the Superman Revenge Squad.

SUPERBOY ROBOTS

Clearly inspired by his birth father's work on Krypton, Superboy set himself up with a fully equipped workshop in the basement of the Kent family home in Smallville. Much as Jor-El had built Spot, a robotic replacement when Krypto the Super-Dog was accidentally lost in space, Superboy came to realize he could protect his identity and serve the greater good by building a series of robots to replace either himself or Clark Kent. He then secreted them behind a panel in the basement, to be summoned as needed.

The first recorded robot was a gigantic version that the Teen of Steel inhabited and used to gain the trust of a baby who had accidentally ingested a growth serum (*Superboy* [first series] #30, January 1954). He later used the colossal robot to teach Professor Tinker a lesson regarding the dangers inherent in a growth serum he wanted to commercially distribute (*Superboy* [first series] #50, July 1956). The first official Superboy Robot was nicknamed Friday, and its lead components helped shield the Boy of Steel in his first encounter with Kryptonite (*Adventure Comics* #251, August 1958).

The robots were carefully designed to mimic the full array of Superboy's powers including super-strength, super-speed, X-ray vision, super-breath, and so on. One robot managed to crack the time barrier at super-speed (*Adventure Comics* #302, November 1962). The robots were prone to malfunctions and to being disabled by environmental conditions, so they were used only when there was little choice.

On one occasion, Superboy was in the future, and the sole robot left in the basement was accidentally damaged by Pete Ross, Clark's best friend. Pete used his ingenuity to keep Smallville protected: He donned the robot's outfit and used an anti-gravity belt from Superboy's trophy room to begin impersonating the Teen of Steel. While Pete protected the citizenry, Ultra Boy journeyed back from the thirtieth century to repair the robot. This proved timely when a fire began in the Kent kitchen (*Superboy* [first series] #100, October 1962).

As Superboy aged, he eventually retired and dismantled the robots. In one case, years later, tapes containing their programming were accidentally used in programming one of the Supergirl Robots. When it was activated, the feminine automaton went to Smallville Orphanage rather than the expected Midvale Orphanage, causing massive confusion (*Adventure Comics* #396, August 1970). A few years later, Supergirl encountered a long-lost Superboy Robot, initially in the cannibalized form of a space sled used by Klax-Ar (*Superman Family* #187, January–February 1978) and later restored to its original shape but possessed by the spirit of Lesla-Lar (*Superman Family* #195, May–June 1979).

When Superboy became Superman, he had all the robots that were still around fly themselves into the sun. One, Superboy Robot-6, was the sole survivor of that command, exceeding its programming by concluding that suicide was against Kal-El's code against killing.

While Clark Kent attended Metropolis University, the SR-6 robot worked in secret to continue Superboy's work in Smallville. At one point, Superman visited his hometown to investigate the reports of a mysterious guardian and wound up fighting the SR-6. When the Man of Steel tricked the robot into thinking it had killed Police Chief Douglas Parker, the SR-6 concluded that it had no choice but to end its own life (*Superman* [first series] #284, February 1975).

Years earlier, the young Superman had spared one robot from the solar purge because it had developed independent thought. Deactivated and placed in the Fortress of Solitude, the Superboy Robot was later roused from its slumber, befriending Jimmy Olsen in the guise of Mysterio. Discovering the truth, Superman gave the robot a new purpose by providing it with adult features and

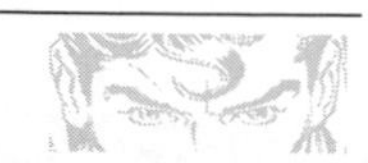

adding it to his group of Superman Robots (*Superman's Pal, Jimmy Olsen* #37, June 1959).

SUPER-CAESAR

A scientific and mathematical genius, Rufus Caesar saw himself as the latest in a long line of Caesars, born to rule. To do that, he found a way to siphon off one super-ability at a time from the Man of Steel. However, he tried to absorb Superman's powers too quickly and endangered his life. When the process was reversed, it adversely affected his health, leaving him far worse off than when he'd begun his mad quest (*Action Comics* #404, September 1971).

SUPER CAVEMAN, THE

A Stone Age survivor from Krypton found himself trapped in a meteor, somehow surviving in a state of suspended animation. When the meteor crashed onto Earth, the caveman was jarred awake and discovered he had gained powers and abilities but lacked the intelligence to understand what had happened. In his confused state, he caused numerous problems, prompting the intervention of Superman, Batman, and Robin. When the caveman was exposed to kryptonite, rather than simply weakening, he died. Superman theorized that the kryptonite radiation combined with years of absorbing cosmic radiation made him extremely susceptible (*World's Finest Comics* #102, June 1959).

SUPER-FATHER

When a brief rift allowed him escape from the Phantom Zone, Jax-Ur journeyed to Earth, replacing Superboy's foster father at the Kent family home in Smallville. As Jonathan Kent, he showed Superboy a jewel recently landed from space and claimed that it gave him an identical set of superpowers. He began acting uncharacteristically until Clark Kent grew suspicious and exposed the masquerade. He rescued his real foster father and returned the criminal to the Phantom Zone (*Adventure Comics* #289, October 1961).

SUPERGIRL

Queen Lucy Regent of Borgonia was an Olympic-level athlete dubbed "Supergirl" when she visited Smallville and encountered Clark Kent, foreshadowing the arrival of his cousin Kara Zor-El years later (*Superboy* [first series] #5, November-December 1949).

When Kal-El was an adult and operated as Superman, his pal Jimmy Olsen sought a companion for his superpowered friend. Making a wish upon a Native American totem pole, he conjured up a blond superpowered woman wearing a red cape, miniskirt, and high-heeled boots, with a red letter S on a yellow field emblazoned on her chest. While attractive and eager to help her intended mate, she lacked his years of experience in using her abilities and wound up complicating the Man of Steel's efforts. She redeemed herself when she sacrificed her existence by overexposing herself to kryptonite, saving Superman. Severely weakened, she asked Jimmy to undo the magic and send her away (*Superman* [first series] #123, August 1958).

Just a few months later, he was surprised by the arrival of a rocket. Out burst a young teen girl in an outfit similar to his own. She greeted him as a cousin and told him that she was Kara Zor-El, daughter of his uncle Zor-El. Kara explained that Argo City, where her family lived, had been hurled into space intact when Krypton exploded. As chief scientist, Zor-El quickly oversaw the construction of a dome to retain oxygen until they could find a place to settle. Things remained peaceful for a time, but slowly the remains of Krypton that the city was built atop began to alter into deadly kryptonite. Zor-El ordered the land lined with lead to shield them, a temporary solution at best. Sure enough, when Kara was fifteen, meteors tore through the dome and ripped the lead, causing the city to lose atmosphere and residents to weaken from the radiation. Alura and Kara began using a "super-space telescope" to find a suitable world. They found not only Earth, but its most famous resident.

Kara was thrilled to be reunited with family, and Superman was overjoyed to have someone from his homeworld who would be an ally—unlike the Phantom Zone criminals he had been dealing with since he was a youth. Cognizant of his most recent encounter with a Supergirl, he was determined to train her in the proper use of her powers and give her a chance to acclimate to life on Earth. He convinced her to live at an orphanage in Midvale, not far from Metropolis. She would adopt a human identity and learn about life on the planet while training in the use of her powers. Kal-El asked Kara to select a human name, and she chose Linda Lee, uncannily becoming another of the people

in his life to have the initials LL. Superman took Kara, now hiding her blond curls under a brunette pigtailed wig, to Midvale Orphanage. There he explained to Mr. Dixon that her parents had died in a natural disaster and vouched for her, cutting through the red tape and paperwork that would otherwise have slowed her admission (*Action Comics* #252, May 1959).

Dixon welcomed Linda to the orphanage. There she met Dick Wilson, who would become her first boyfriend after he was adopted and took the name Dick Malverne. She studied under Headmistress Miss Hart, later identified as Mrs. Henry Hart (*Action Comics* #271, December 1960).

Dubbing her his secret weapon, Superman was cautious in letting Supergirl operate in sight of others; he was slow to tell even his closest friends and fellow heroes about her. At first, only

Superman knew her secret identity, but after she was adopted by Fred and Edna Danvers, they too learned of her alter ego. In time, he introduced her to the president of the United States, entrusting him with the secret. Over time, other costumed champions were told as well. Before her debut, she was entrusted with the knowledge of Batman and Robin's true names (*Action Comics* #270, November 1960).

In time, Superman built her a series of Supergirl Robots in addition to a Linda Lee robot to help protect her secret (*Action Comics* #276, May 1961). On the orphanage grounds was a hollowed-out tree where they were stored; after her adoption, they were hidden within the Danvers home. In one instance, computer tapes from a Superboy Robot were used for a Supergirl model, which caused it to perform oddly, trying to act as the Smallville Sentinel (*Adventure Comics* #396, August 1970).

While she often trained together with Superman, Linda began covertly performing feats on her own, keeping herself out of sight. She had the full array of super-abilities like her cousin, but proportionate to a teenage girl, still making her one of the most powerful beings on Earth. Like any Kryptonian, she derived her amazing abilities from the combination of Sol's yellow radiation and Earth's lighter gravity. She was therefore also vulnerable to power fluctuations under other stars, including losing her powers under a red sun. She could be harmed by kryptonite and was susceptible to magic.

Superman dedicated a room to her in his Fortress of Solitude (*Superman* [first series] #142, January 1961).

When the time was right, Superman made a public announcement of her existence, introducing her to the president and the citizens of Metropolis—and that was when the Danverses learned of their adopted daughter's secret. At the United Nations in New York City, Supergirl was given a special "golden certificate," matching one they had previously given the World's Greatest Super Hero, granting her unfettered access to enter and leave member countries without a visa. She was also authorized to make arrests (*Action Comics* #285, February 1962).

Although the world did not know of Supergirl, residents of the future did. In time, she was visited by the members of the thirtieth century's Legion of Super-Heroes (*Action Comics* #267, August 1960). Much as Cosmic Boy, Lightning Lad, and Saturn Girl appeared before Superboy, they visited Supergirl in Midvale. Unfortunately, her membership offer was revoked when red kryptonite temporarily turned her into an adult. A year later, they returned and said she could join after retrieving King Arthur's sword, Excalibur (*Action Comics* #276, May 1961). Supergirl happily accepted despite the oddity of sharing missions with her teenage cousin Superboy. To protect the secret of her existence, he used super-hypnosis to erase any memory of her. Supergirl happily joined powerful peers and flirted with Brainiac 5, who harbored far deeper feelings for her. Her Legion activities gradually tapered off and she finally resigned from the team, citing the demands of her twentieth-century life (*Superboy* [first series] #204, September–October 1974).

At one point, Supergirl brought Superman to a period ten years after they normally visited the Legion, hoping to fix her cousin up with Saturn Woman. She was disappointed but ultimately pleased to learn the Legionnaire married her teen love Lightning-Man (*Action Comics* #289, June 1962).

Supergirl joined Jimmy Olsen to combat the Legion of Super-Villains (*Superman's Pal, Jimmy Olsen* #63, September 1962), an example of the friendship between the similarly aged members of Superman's inner circle.

The Legionnaires helped stage a prank on Superman and Supergirl as their way of celebrating the anniversary of Supergirl's arrival on Earth (*Superman* [first series] #152, April 1962).

Linda enjoyed a nurturing environment in the Danvers home plus the idyllic life offered by the suburb of Midvale. While still at the orphanage, she adopted Streaky, a playful cat who occasionally gained superpowers after exposure to a synthetic form of kryptonite that Supergirl created while trying to find a cure for its deadly radiation. She first attended Midvale High School with Dick Malverne, who became her boyfriend. After graduation, she matriculated at nearby Stanhope College, which offered her a scholarship to attend (*Action Comics* #318, November 1964).

Her exploits as Supergirl meant she made many friends, gained many allies, and battled various villains. Comet entered the life of Supergirl as a horse possessing human intelligence, some superpowers similar to her own, and the ability to communicate telepathically (*Adventure Comics* #293, February 1962). She first saw him in a dream in which a kryptonite ray from an invading alien spacecraft caused her to plummet from the sky, and a flying white stallion broke her fall. In her dream, she named the horse Comet because of a mark on his back that resembled a shooting star. The horse turned out to be a magically cursed man named Biron, who became Supergirl's equine companion as Comet the Super-Horse, frequently accompanying her on her adventures clad in a red cape, attached to a blue harness, that bore a yellow S-shield (*Action Comics* #293, October 1962). The spell allowed Comet to become a centaur in a brief transitional phase, and then to assume fully human form, whenever a comet passed Earth or entered its atmosphere and Comet was within sight of it. At such times, the super-stallion adopted the human identity of "Bronco" Bill Starr, a rodeo trick rider, with whom Supergirl fell in love. Starr was briefly the Maid of Might's boyfriend and the chief rival for her affections of Dick Malverne, Linda Lee Danvers's love interest. In his human guise, Comet also had a brief romance with Lois Lane.

Early on, Supergirl's greatest nemesis was Lesla-Lar, who lived in Kandor and had an uncanny resemblance to Kara Zor-El. Lesla-Lar was jealous of her look-alike's freedom on Earth as Supergirl and devised a weapon that robbed the Maid of Steel of her powers (*Action Comics* #279, August 1961). Defenseless, she decided to remain Linda Lee on a full-time basis, leading to her adoption by Fred and Edna Danvers. Lesla-Lar then used her invention to swap places with Linda, using her superpowers to masquerade as Supergirl. She approached Lex Luthor about laying a trap for Superman, but Krypto the Super-Dog realized she was an impostor and exposed the Kandorian. She was returned to the bottle city, where her equipment was destroyed and she was imprisoned. Linda regained her powers thanks to Mr. Mxyzptlk (*Action Comics* #282, November 1961).

Soon after, Lesla-Lar regained her freedom and rebuilt her machine, this time swapping places with Luthor's sister Lena Thorul, who also resembled Supergirl. She then released three criminals from the Phantom Zone and used them to uncover a cache of forbidden Kryptonian weapons. Kru-El used one of them on her, disintegrating her body (*Action Comics* #297, February 1963).

Supergirl was often called on to help Superman and Krypto handle numerous threats and began joining Superman on missions across the galaxy. She eventually joined him on cases with Batman and Robin, where she first met Batgirl (*World's Finest Comics* #169, September 1967). In a short time, the heroines became close friends, a bond that would endure until the destruction of Earth-1.

Supergirl was shocked to discover that her parents had survived Argo City's destruction by finding a realm called the Survival Zone, similar to the Phantom Zone but lacking that realm's projector to allow them their freedom. After an awkward attempt at coexistence on Earth with the Danverses, Zor-El and Alura decided that they'd be happier in the city of Kandor. The bottle city subsequently became a wonderful home away from home for the Girl of Steel (*Action Comics* #309–310, February–March 1964). She also promised the Kandorians that, like her cousin, she would make every effort to find a way to enlarge them and locate a world they could call their own (*Action Comics* #286, March 1962).

There were also Bizarro duplicates made of the Girl of Steel, the first of whom died tragically after exposure to blue kryptonite (*Superman* [first series] #140, October 1960). The real heroine had more than her share of wacky encounters with these artificial life-forms, including a meeting with the second Bizarro Supergirl (*Action Comics* #336, April 1966).

While Linda Lee Danvers dated Dick Malverne, Supergirl was also drawn to Jerro, a mer-teen who resided in Atlantis (*Action Comics* #269, October 1960; others).

While attending college, Supergirl began to experiment with wearing modified versions of her costume, preserving the S-shield and color scheme but following fashion trends and carving out her own identity (*Adventure Comics* #397, October 1970; others). Soon after, she battled a villain named Starfire who altered her physiology and led to a period when her powers fluctuated. During this period, she graduated with a liberal arts degree and decided to relocate to San Francisco, working at local television station KSF and leaving Streaky with her adoptive parents. While on the West Coast, she dated her boss Geoff Anderson and encountered Lex Luthor's niece Nasthalia, beginning a rivalry between the Maid of Might and "Nasty" (*Adventure Comics* #406, May 1971). Wearying of Nasty's attacks on her, Linda quit her TV job (*Adventure Comics* #424, October 1972) to study acting at Vandyre University (*Supergirl* [first series] #1, November 1972). There she struck up a friendship with the magician Zatanna, which soured briefly when they were both interested in the same man (*Supergirl* [first series] #7, October 1973).

Linda left Vandyre to become a teaching assistant and student adviser at New Athens Experimental School in Florida (*Superman Family* #165, June–July 1974), the next in a series of moves that demonstrated a certain restlessness on her part, as Supergirl sought a lifestyle she could call her own and a place in America where she would not always be in her big cousin's shadow. She used an argument with the school administration to leave Florida and return to the Northeast, settling in New York City and landing a part on the television soap opera *Secret Hearts*. For a while, her character, Margo Hatton, was more popular than Supergirl, and Linda was comfortable with that (*Superman Family* #208, July 1981).

She lost interest in the role and New York, heading to the Midwest and finding a home at 1537 West Fargo Avenue in Chicago, enrolling as a psychology grad student at Lake Shore University (*The Daring New Adventures of Supergirl* #1, November 1982). She found an entirely new series of villains to battle, including Blackstarr (*The Daring New Adventures of Supergirl* #13, November 1983) and Reactron (*The Daring New Adventures of Supergirl* #8–9, June–July 1983). University professor Drake performed illegal radiation experiments that once more had deleterious effects on her superpowers.

Superman and Supergirl kept their promise and restored Kandor to its proper size on the planet renamed Rokyn. Kara was delighted to see her parents once more have options for their future (*Superman* [first series] #338, August 1979).

It was around this time that Supergirl was in space and inadvertently collided with a kryptonite meteor. Salkor, the champion from Makkor, found her floating in the void and took her to his world, where he nursed her back to health. As she regained consciousness, it was clear that she had temporary amnesia, so neither she nor Salkor knew her true identity. He named her Jasma; over time, they fell in love, married, and protected Makkor from the invading Naxx. Eventually, her memories returned, supplanting her new persona, and she traveled back to Earth (*Superman* [first series] #415, January 1986).

Then came the Crisis on Infinite Earths. The multiverse was being eradicated by the Anti-Monitor who wanted to rule a single anti-matter universe and was concluding an ages-old battle with his doppelgänger, the Monitor. It took the combined heroic efforts of the heroes from the remaining five parallel Earths to forestall total devastation. Supergirl was among those who sought to take the battle to the Anti-Monitor. After seeing her cousin easily knocked aside, she battered the armored entity in a rage, actually causing him pain while he unleashed beam after beam of energy that slowly hurt her. With a final blast of energy, he mortally wounded the Maid of Might. She died in her cousin's arms. Batgirl gave her eulogy in Chicago, proclaiming that Kara was a hero and would not be forgotten (*Crisis on Infinite Earths* #7, October 1985). It took the Man of Steel some time to finish mourning her on his own, at which point he encountered Salkor, who'd come to the Fortress to pay his final respects to his wife. Soon after, Superman took her remains to Rokyn, the world where the Kandorians were finally free, and he shared Zor-El and Alura's grief (*Superman* [first series] #414, December 1985).

Just a short time later, Supergirl's spirit was seen by Boston Brand, a fellow dead hero, during the Christmas season (*Christmas with the Super-Heroes* #2, 1989).

In an Earth-1 time line where the Crisis on Infinite Earths apparently did not take place, Linda Danvers eventually became the governor of Florida and changed her alter ego to Superwoman (*Superman Family* #200, March–April 1980). Her legacy would extend at least to the 5020th century, when Louise-L operated as that era's Supergirl (*Superman Family* #215–216, February–March 1982).

In the world after reality was altered, Superman was the sole survivor of Krypton, and as a result Kara did not exist. Superman was baffled when a young blond woman was found frozen in a block

of ice in the Arctic (*Superman* [second series] #16, April 1988). When she was recovered, she explained that she was actually from a realm known as the Pocket Universe. Superman knew that the Time Trapper had stolen a sliver of pre-Crisis time and formed this universe, where Earth-1 effectively remained. When that universe's Superboy died, things began to change. That reality's General Zod and two other Phantom Zone villains escaped and laid waste to the world, one without super heroes. Without a Superboy to twist his mind, Lex Luthor worked to save humanity. He invented an artificial life-form made from a "protoplasmic matrix." When it took human form, it followed its programming to resemble Lana Lang, the love of Luthor's life and one who had died. The Matrix, however, retained all of Lana's memories thanks to the dead woman's synaptic pathways being copied to the new life-form.

Matrix was also programmed to approximate the Man of Steel's powers and abilities. Matrix could fly, she had super-strength and other attributes, but she also could shape-shift, cloak herself to near-invisibility, and perform telekinesis. She tried to fight the villains on her own but was beaten, so Luthor dispatched her to the main universe to bring back Superman.

The Man of Steel arrived and fought the villains, recognizing the perilous circumstances. Breaking his vow never to kill, he ended their lives and brought the severely damaged Matrix back to his reality. He took her to the Kent family farm, where Jonathan and Martha Kent agreed to nurse her back to health. Ma Kent decided she needed to be called something other than Matrix and shortened it to "Mae" (*Superman* [second series] #21–22 and *The Adventures of Superman* #444—both September–October 1988).

While she healed, Superman had tremendous difficulty coping with his actions and wound up exiling himself from Earth for a year. The healed Matrix decided she would help cover for him by taking his form and using her powers to protect Metropolis and the world. By the time her mentor returned, she had come to think of herself as Superman and Clark Kent and had to be shocked back to her senses. Shortly afterward, she fled Earth for a time to regain her sense of self (*Action Comics* #644, August 1989).

She did not return to Earth until the planet came under attack by Brainiac. Superman happily welcomed her home, and she chose to remain (*Action Comics* #676, April 1992). During her return, Matrix fell in love with Lex Luthor, who at the time was passing himself off as his son but was actually inhabiting a cloned body. She once more wore the costume the Pocket Universe's Luthor gave her and proudly took the name Supergirl. In her new role, she battled crime, fought at Superman's side, moved in with Luthor, and worked with his armored mercenaries Team Luthor.

Things changed when Luthor kept her from aiding Superman in his cross-country struggle against the murderous Doomsday. When the fight reached Metropolis, she defied her lover and joined the fray, only to receive a mammoth blow that reverted her to her protoplasmic form (*Superman: The Man of Steel* #19, January 1993). In the wake of Superman's death, she continued to look after Metropolis and bonded with Superboy, the clone of Superman (and—unbeknownst to her—Luthor). When Superman was revived, she shifted to Clark Kent, explaining away his absence by arranging to be found in a well-stocked cellar (*Action Comics* #692, October 1993).

She was devastated to learn that Luthor had secretly been building an army of Supergirl clones. Worse, he was not who he appeared to be. She destroyed the lab and her genetic copies, leaving Luthor for good (*Supergirl* [third series] #1–4, February–May 1994). She then had an unsettling encounter with the Teen Titan Raven that left the heroine implanted with a demon seed to help Raven's father Trigon the Terrible gain power on Earth (*Showcase '95* #2, February 1995). She managed to free herself and worked with Arsenal's Teen Titans to stop Raven. He offered her membership, which she accepted (*New Titans* #121, May 1995). It wasn't long before the team disbanded, however, and Matrix's life changed forever.

Matrix was left to wonder about her existence after her recent experiences, wondering about giving birth, and whether or not she even had a soul. At much the same time, that universe's Linda Danvers was beginning to have doubts of her own. The artistic teen was living on her own in the small town of Leesburg, Virginia. She found herself inspired by Supergirl and often sculpted the heroine. A demon known only as Buzz insinuated himself into Linda's life and used her loss of faith as a wedge to turn her into his next victim. He led her away from her parents—policeman Fred Danvers and his wife Sylvia Danvers—and friends, sending her spiraling down a dark path that resulted in her joining a demonic cult without realizing she would be his sacrifice to Lord Chakat. It was also intended to draw to him the real Supergirl and gain her power and soul.

The Maid of Steel arrived in time to save Linda's soul, but the woman was seriously wounded. Mad with grief over failing and spiritually empty, Supergirl found her protoplasmic self merging with the dying teen, giving them both a second chance by merging into a new Linda Danvers (*Supergirl* [fourth series] #1, September 1996). It took some time for the new person to fully integrate the two personalities, each with her own experiences and memories. It also left her ready to become something more.

Linda resumed her artwork and tentatively reconnected with her parents and friends, unaware that Buzz was still scheming to gain her soul. She also encountered an odd neighborhood

But then... I
touched her...
and she became...
we became one!

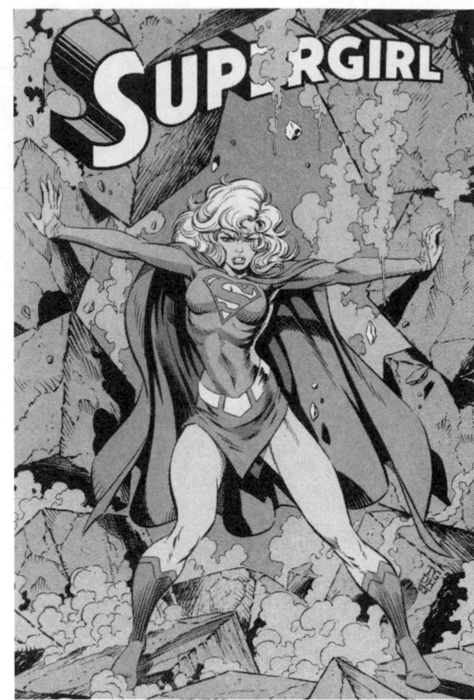
SUPERGIRL

boy, Wally, who always carried a baseball bat and seemed wise beyond his years. Linda also could change her form into that of Supergirl, physically very different and with all of the Matrix version's powers and abilities (*Supergirl* [fourth series] #2–9, October 1996–May 1997).

In the performance of her duties, she was astonished to find herself suddenly sprouting flaming wings. In time, she learned this new Linda Danvers was now an Earth-born angel known as the Angel of Fire. She was also surprised to learn that a Chaos Stream flowed beneath Leesburg, which made it a focal point for supernatural activity. She fought dark gods, super-villains, creatures like Chemo, and even another Earth-born angel, Blithe. Linda also watched her friend Andrea Jones become the equine being Comet. Throughout it all, Wally, who claimed to be a manifestation of the Presence, counseled her with good humor.

Over time, she discovered two other earth-born angels, and they wound up banding together to fight Earth's first vampire, a creature known as the Carnivore (*Supergirl* [fourth series] #50, November 2000). Captured and weakened, Supergirl despaired for a time and was visited by what appeared to be the ghostly spirit of the original Girl of Steel, Kara Zor-El (*Supergirl* [fourth series] #48–49, September–October 2000). The titanic battle led to Carnivore's defeat, but also cost Linda her role as an Earth-born angel. Supergirl and Linda Danvers became separate beings, and the heroine had more limited powers than before their merger.

The red-white-and-blue-costumed Linda/Supergirl, now able to leap a mere one-eighth of a mile and perform similar skilled feats, went in search of the missing piece of herself. The trail took them to the Amazon, where Matrix had been imprisoned by Lilith, known as the "mother of demons," and was trapped in the Garden of Eden. Twilight was

forced to capture Matrix/Supergirl so her twin sister would be freed by Lilith. She fought for freedom and Linda became Supergirl, in a new costume and a blond wig, ready to go into action. Linda was accompanied once more by Buzz, who was no longer a demon. Joining them for a time was Mary Marvel, the young, naïve heroine.

Lilith came to control the missing Earth-born angel and used her to attack Linda, leading to a showdown between the participants (*Supergirl* [fourth series] #74, November 2002). When the fight ended, Lilith lost control of Supergirl, who then destroyed the Carnivore. The ageless mother was then slain by Buzz, in a redemptive act, and Linda actually died. Supergirl offered to merge with her once more, but Linda refused, telling her friend to save Twilight, another player, who had helped stop Lilith's threat.

Once the two entities merged, the new life became a new Angel of Fire and Linda was healed, complete with super-abilities. The Twilight/Matrix entity would then live out her life as the new Earth-born angel.

Before Linda could settle back into a life that could even vaguely be called normal, a spacecraft crashed just outside Leesburg. Emerging from the ship was someone wearing the original Supergirl uniform from Earth-1. The young, bubbly Kara explained that she was from the reality prior to the Crisis, which was why Linda had no recollection of this person. Just as the rocket carrying Earth-1's infant Kal-El had been diverted into another reality en route to Earth (*Action Comics* #370, December 1968), the spacecraft of a different dimension's Kara Zor-El had been detoured into this one. The two became close, as one would expect, and Linda enjoyed training Kara. Her visit was brief and traumatic for both Lindas, but it was clear the girl from the rocket had to return to fulfill her ordained destiny.

The Spectre arrived to explain that Kara needed to die. This had all happened as a result of a being known as the Fatalist, who played with reality as a way to tweak his master Xenon, a being with an irrational hatred for the Maid of Might. Kara did not want to die, and she begged Linda for help. Her older friend agreed, then manipulated the situation so she took Kara's place in the rocket, going to Earth-1 so she could be killed by the Anti-Monitor, leaving the untainted teen Kara on Earth. Unfortunately, Superman-1 saw through the ruse—but when she admitted her love for him, they wound up beginning a relationship that led to a romance, a wedding, and a baby girl, Ariella. The Spectre ordered Linda back to her own reality not only to restore the time line but also to save Kara from Xenon. Linda then saw to it that Kara went back to her realm to live out her life as it was ordained. The Spectre rewarded Linda by sparing Ariella's life when reality was once more reordered. At much the same time, Sylvia Danvers gave birth to a late-in-life second child whom she named Wally. Linda chose at that point to retire from adventuring and leave Leesburg to find her own fate. She wrote a letter of explanation to Clark Kent, including with it her beloved skateboard (*Supergirl* [fourth series] #75–80, December 2002–May 2003).

At some point, Linda wound up settling in Gotham City and was attacked out of the blue by the mystical team called Shadowpact. Even though she was no longer Matrix or an Earth-born angel, she somehow manifested the flaming wings. She was then brought to Hell as a pawn in the battle between Lord Satanus and Blaze against Neron to gain the throne. Lilith turned up alive once more and apparently was the one to summon Linda; she was considered a fallen angel. Perhaps recognizing that she'd taken the wrong entity, Lilith released Linda, who returned to Earth. She encountered wounded demons huddling by a campfire and used her heat vision to kill them, an act that horrified the mystic Doctor Occult. To Linda, however, no demon was an innocent, so her act was justified. Occult conjured up an image of who Linda really was, and the sight sent her flying away in shock (*Reign in Hell* #1–8, July 2008–February 2009).

For a very brief time, there was a world without an active Supergirl. That all changed the day a dark-haired woman in a black costume flew over Metropolis to defeat a villain named Radion. He was thrown into a nuclear reactor, an act caught on television and by *Daily Planet* reporter Lois Lane. The young woman landed and introduced herself as Supergirl, daughter of the Metropolis Marvel, which certainly came as surprising news to the man's wife. Lois, shaken by the revelation, actually dared to accuse her husband of having an affair, but she calmed down and decided the girl was a ploy on the part of some rogue. It was Lois's turn to be shocked when the teen arrived and called her "Mommy."

She explained to the stunned couple that her name was really Cir-El and she was their daughter, arriving from the future courtesy of the Futuresmiths. Tests performed at S.T.A.R. Labs confirmed that Cir-El was Superman's genetic child, but not Lois's. He still accepted the teen as a member of the House of El (*Superman: The 10-Cent Adventure* #1, 2003; *Superman* [second series] #190–193, April–July 2003).

Cir-El stayed with the Kents in Metropolis and joined her father on several missions, including battling Bizarro. The attractive teen also bonded with Natasha Irons and Girl 13, sharing pizza, gossip, and more than a few adventures. She joined with Superboy, Krypto, Natasha Irons, and the Batman family to save the World's Finest from President Lex Luthor (*Superman/Batman* #5, February 2004). As the mission ended, Superman watched Cir-El transform herself into a different teen calling herself Mia. This persona seemed to hate her Cir-El alter ego.

It was finally revealed that Mia was a pawn of Brainiac, who'd used Superman's genetic material to turn her into a member of the family. He then dispatched the Futuresmiths to implant memories and place her in the past, along with a nanovirus spread through anyone drinking Yes-brand coffee. The plan was to infect a large percentage of humanity, creating a horrific future that would injure Lois Lane, requiring her husband to create a synthetic body for her that Brainiac would usurp. To stop the tyrant, Cir-El threw herself into a time portal, thereby ensuring that Mia was never born, and the threat was ended (*Superman* [second series] #197–200, November 2003–February 2004).

Some months later, Bizarro hopscotched through time and collected Cir-El, the Earth-1 Supergirl, Power Girl, Linda Danvers, and the post-Crisis Supergirl to assist in freeing Superman from the Source Wall at the edge of the universe. Once Superman was freed, Mr. Mxyzptlk sent Cir-El back to her own era (*Superman/Batman* #24, April 2006).

The events of Infinite Crisis reordered reality and the presence of the Earth-born angels was not recorded, so their continued existence remained an open question. A new heroine did use the name Matrix, though: a redheaded woman named Sierra who gained powers from Lex Luthor's Everyman Project and later joined a new incarnation of Infinity, Inc. Like her predecessor, she possessed enhanced strength, agility, and endurance—and she could fly (*52* #25, October 25, 2006).

All of Earth had been on alert as a gigantic green kryptonite meteor approached. While President Luthor was blaming Superman for the incident, the meteor plunged into Gotham Harbor and sank deep. As a result, Batman was the first to arrive to secure the area and investigate. What he found surprised him: an empty alien space vessel. As he returned to the Batboat, it was being hijacked by an attractive naked blond teen. Once on land, she tried to understand why she was suddenly feeling so powerful. People tried to take advantage of her, leading to the arrival of the police. Things continued to escalate out of control until Superman arrived. She returned to the ground, upset, and the Dark Knight used the kryptonite he carried with him to subdue her. When she awoke in the Batcave, she panicked, but Superman's presence started to calm her. He was stunned, though, when she began speaking Kryptonese.

Quickly, Superman gathered the girl, the rocket, and the Caped Crusader, bringing everyone to the Fortress. There he translated the inscription from the vessel, which read, "This vessel carries my daughter, Kara Zor-El from the now dead planet Krypton. Treat her as you would your own child for you will see the treasure she will be for your world."

She explained she was Kara Zor-El, his cousin, and that she had been sent to precede Kal-El's ship to Earth. Her ship was stuck within the meteor, however, and she slumbered for years in a state of suspended animation. When Krypton blew up, she was the older of the cousins, but now she was the younger (*Superman/Batman* #8–13, March–October 2004). Superman was pleased to have a relative on Earth, while Batman was suspicious of the girl and the circumstances surrounding her arrival, a situation compounded by the fierce reaction Supergirl elicited from Krypto.

Deciding that the best thing to do was have her trained in the use of her newfound superpowers, Superman arranged for Kara to stay on Themyscira, the island home of the Amazons. There she was tutored in the fighting arts and quickly mastered her powers until she was abducted by the Female Furies, who brought her to Apokolips and the feet of Darkseid. The naïve teen had her mind altered until she was a powerful engine of hatred, groomed to lead the Furies. Superman, assisted by the Dark Knight and the Amazon Princess, arrived to free her. When she was returned to Earth, she adopted the costumed persona of Supergirl.

The Girl of Steel painfully learned that she and Power Girl could not be near each other since the latter was from the pre-Crisis universe and was an anomalous version of Kara (*Supergirl* [fifth series] #1, October 2005). Shortly thereafter, she was recruited by Donna Troy to join a team heading into space at the beginning of the events known as the Infinite Crisis (*JLA* #123, February 2006). While in space, Supergirl was transported to the thirty-first century, where she was convinced that she was really in a dream state (*Supergirl and the Legion of Super-Heroes* #16, May 2006).

The Legionnaires were pleased she was with them and conferred membership status on the bewildered heroine. She was given the Legion Flight Ring from the deceased Dream Girl, and there she remained for several months. During her time in the future, she aided the team in several missions, also becoming the object of affection for Ultra Boy and Invisible Kid. Because she continued to believe this was all an elaborate dream, the team began to grow concerned she would pose a danger if she did not soon accept that she was in reality. They used kryptonite to weaken her, and then transported her to Rokyn, the world colonized by the denizens of Kandor (*Supergirl and the Legion of Super-Heroes* #23, December 2006). While there, she helped stop the mercenary Wanderers from stealing a Phantom Zone projector. Now aware that this was the waking world, Supergirl began to seek a way to go home.

She returned to the twenty-first century exactly one year after the restoration of the multiverse and settled back on New Earth (*52/WW III Part Two: The Valiant* #2, June 2007). Kara learned that her cousin had expended all his powers to help stop Superboy-Prime and had taken time away from adventuring to recharge his body. While he was gone, she filled in as one of Metropolis's protectors. Now that she and Power Girl were able to stand side by side, they journeyed to Kandor where they donned the identities of Nightwing and Flamebird. The duo attempted to free Kandor from Earth-3's Ultraman, working with the vile Saturn Queen from the thirtieth century. The Kryptonian Crusaders would have remained had Saturn Queen not provided information that rocked Supergirl's world and sent her back to Earth. Power Girl saw this as a selfish act, and a rift developed between the women (*Supergirl* [fifth series] #8, September 2006).

The news was that Argo City and her parents had survived.

From that point on, Kara sought a place for herself in this new world, with each step bringing new discoveries about her adopted planet and herself. Unfortunately, not all of the lessons proved helpful. Supergirl tried to establish a civilian identity for herself, this time as Claire Connors, and she tried to fit in with high school students or adventure with other heroes such as the Outsiders—but she never seemed to fit in. Many were in awe of her powers, and some shunned her because of them. Her closest friend for a time appeared to be the second Captain Boomerang, who was still trying to decide his own path, that of hero or villain (*Supergirl* [fifth series] #9–10, October–November 2006).

She was once more manipulated, this time by Power Boy, who appeared as powerful and kind-hearted as the Kryptonian but turned out to be Apokolips-born. His true personality eventually revealed itself (*Supergirl* [fifth series] #13–15, February–May 2007).

She was visited by a projection of her father. Zor-El explained that the Phantom Zone was not an uninhabited realm, but one that contained spectral entities none too pleased to share their world with others. They had sworn vengeance on the living members from the House of El, so Zor-El implanted Sunstones—the only defense they had discovered against the phantoms—within her skeletal structure (*Supergirl* [fifth series] #16–17, June–July 2007).

Upon returning to Earth, the Maid of Might discovered that phantoms had pierced the barrier and begun possessing humans as they sought revenge. Superman and Supergirl beat back the threat. Once dispatched, she came to realize that much of what had happened to her since she'd arrived from space was a construct of Dark Angel, who meddled in her life in various ways, including masquerading as the Earth-1 Supergirl (*Supergirl* [fifth series] #18, August 2007).

During their misguided attack on America, Amazons overran Washington, DC, and Supergirl flew to the capital to help. She and Wonder Girl wanted to free friends and family who had been placed in internment camps under the McCarran Internal Security Act. Defending the law were the Teen Titans, with Robin advising them to try diplomacy over violence. However, Queen Hippolyta scoffed at the notion given that the president was nowhere in sight, safely ensconced aboard Air Force One. While trying to gain custody of the president, the two actually crippled the jet, and it crashed. Only then did they realize the impact of their actions. At that point, they joined the heroes to oppose the Amazons until the war was successfully ended (*Amazons Attack!* #1–6, April–October 2007). Her actions, and the lessons learned, led Superman to approve of her joining the Titans (*Teen Titans* [third series] #50, October 2007). On her very first mission, she wound up battling a potential future version of the Titans complete with a resurrected version of Conner Kent, her sort-of cousin Superboy. The exploit led to an argument between Supergirl and Wonder Girl, and the Kryp-

tonian decided she was better off away from the team (*Teen Titans* [third series] #55, March 2008).

Kara then tried to make good on her potential, refusing to let her errors and gaffes define her. However, she blundered once more when she promised a young boy battling cancer that she would find a cure. Instead she got distracted with the usual battles against super-menaces and came to realize there were some things superpowers could not resolve. The boy died, and Kara was shattered (*Supergirl* [fifth series] #26–32, April–October 2008).

Feasting on her misfortunes, *Daily Planet* staffer Catherine Grant wrote a scathing column, "Why the World Does Not Need a Supergirl," which turned the tide of public opinion against her. Without an alter ego, she was Supergirl day and night, and this was proving more than she could bear (*Supergirl* [fifth series] #34, December 2008). After discussing the matter with other heroes, she came to accept an offer made by Lana Lang. Kara transformed herself into Linda Lang, introducing herself to people as Lana's niece who had come to live in Metropolis.

While this was transpiring, Superman was in deep space, having his first real confrontation with Brainiac. He also discovered the real bottle city of Kandor and desperately fought the Coluan to prevent him from attacking Earth. Zor-El managed to contact his nephew and explain how his family, including his wife Alura and daughter Kara, had used Brainiac's technology to save Argo City with a force field. Brainiac traced the signal and found the remnant of Krypton, integrating it with the already captured Kandor. It was during that process that he sent Kara toward Earth to find baby Kal-El (*Supergirl* [third series] #35, January 2009).

Superman freed himself and then recruited Supergirl's help to save Earth. As they defeated Brainiac, they also rescued Kandor, which was restored to its proper size in the Arctic. Suddenly Earth gained one hundred thousand new immigrants, all with superpowers, and Kara was joyfully reunited with her parents (*Superman: New Krypton Special* #1, December 2008). The great scientist concluded that his daughter's recent behavioral problems, from the mood swings to the cloudy thinking to her hallucinations about Zor-El's seemingly evil plans, were a result of long-term kryptonite poisoning as the radiation slowly seeped in through the spacecraft's shields during her years-long voyage through space. He used one of his devices to cleanse her body of residual radiation, leaving her in vastly improved shape (*Supergirl* [fifth series] #35, January 2009).

The Kandorians' adjustment to their powers and living among humans proved very difficult and led to numerous misunderstandings. Zor-El, the leader of the people, was killed. Alura's heart hardened, and she directed the city to leave Earth (*Action Comics* #872, February 2009). Using Brainiac's technology, Kandor and a large chunk of the Arctic were freed from gravity's hold and then grew to planet-sized, placing New Krypton in orbit directly opposite Earth.

Alura demanded that Kara remain with her in Kandor, and the teen was torn between the life she'd had as a child and the one she was forging as a young adult. She largely spent her time on Earth, befriended by a newly arrived Superwoman, who lent her a sympathetic ear (*Supergirl* [fifth series] #36, February 2009). Under orders from her mother, Supergirl sought Reactron, a villain who'd tried to kill many Kandorians (*Supergirl* [fifth series] #37–39, March–May 2009). The Girl of Steel ultimately discovered that Superwoman was plotting against her, having been responsible for freeing Reactron in the first place and thus indirectly implicated in Zor-El's death. In a violent clash, Supergirl unmasked Superwoman as Lucy Lane and accidentally killed her while trying to destroy the battle suit that gave Lucy her powers. Kara was horrified on many levels, not the least of which was Lucy's connection by marriage to Lois Lane and Clark Kent (*Supergirl* [fifth series] #40–41, June–July 2009).

On her birthday, Kara was required to select a Guild, and while she was very much her father's daughter she was drawn to the arts. In the days leading up to the ceremony, Alura assigned Kara numerous tasks, which she took as punishment but were in fact her mother's birthday gift: an opportunity to sample many of New Krypton's Guilds so she could make an informed choice. She was even offered a place as student to the celebrated sculptor Zal-Tel, who once mentored Zor-El. In the end, though, Kara selected the Science Guild in an attempt to better understand her mother (*Supergirl* [fifth series] #43, September 2009).

Kara divided her time between New Krypton and Earth, briefly joining a splinter group of the Justice League of America (*Justice League: Cry for Justice* #2, October 2009). It was Supergirl who first discovered their ranks had been pierced by Promethius (disguised as Captain Marvel). He silenced Supergirl with a magic bullet he had purchased from Mercy Graves (*Justice League: Cry for Justice* #6, March 2010).

Soon after, Kara and Alura were visiting Zor-El's tomb when his corpse emerged, possessing a black power ring, and they watched in horror as Zor-El joined the Black Lantern Corps under the command of the demon Nekron. He terrorized his family until the women realized he was a reanimated corpse that did not possess Zor-El's true soul, and this led to his defeat (*Blackest Night: Superman* #1–3, December 2009–February 2010).

Supergirl then wound up being targeted by Project 7734, which was designed to rid Earth of all Kryptonians. Run by General Samuel Lane, the ultimate goal was to ignite a war between Earth and New Krypton using his advanced magical technology to destroy the fledgling world. As a result, Lane made every effort to discredit and destroy the Maid of Steel along with her allies Nightwing and Flamebird. Kara was having trouble working with Thara Ak-Var, refusing to accept her former best friend's unfailing belief in the Flamebird entity. The trio worked uneasily with one another as they rushed around the world trying to expose the Kryptonian sleeper agents Ursa had planted and prove General Lane wrong about Kryptonians. Reactron had been assigned by Lane to track down and kill Supergirl and nearly succeeded until he was stopped by Nightwing. When Reactron next targeted Lois Lane for elimination, the true Flamebird manifested within Thara and saved the kindly reporter's life. After destroying the gold kryptonite that gave Reactron his power, Flamebird moved to kill him until Supergirl intervened. In the emotional aftermath, the two friends reconciled (*Supergirl* [fifth series] #44–46, October–December 2009). No sooner did Reactron travel to New Krypton for trial than Supergirl had to face the Silver Banshee, who left Kara in peace when she learned the Kryptonian was merely being tested as a possible new clan leader (*Supergirl* [fifth series] #48–49, February–March 2010).

Supergirl came to Lana Lang's aid when the seriously ill woman had had her body usurped by the insidious Insect Queen. Lana was eventually restored to health and the alien defeated, but she had a falling out with Kara over trust issues (Supergirl [fifth series] #50, April 2010). She then accompanied Superboy and a handful of Legionnaires back to New Krypton in order to prevent Superman from being killed by Brainiac, which would mean a literal end to time itself. She also fought to make sure Alura would remain free of the Coluan's grasp as well (*Superman: Last Stand of New Krypton* #1–3, May–June 2010). Not long after, Kara returned to New Krypton and was horrified to come across her mother torturing Reactron. The villain, however, had been a plant by General Lane, who had turned Reactron into a literal time bomb. Reactron's body built to a critical mass and detonated, causing seismic tremors

that destroyed New Krypton entirely. Alura saw to it that her daughter survived the explosion at the cost of her own life (*Superman: War of the Supermen* #1, July 2010). The devastated Maid of Might worked alongside her cousin to keep the enraged Kandorians from making all of humanity pay for General Lane's perfidy. She then watched as Superboy gathered the remaining Kryptonians and sent them to the Phantom Zone, leaving her and Kal-El the last of their race (*Superman: War of the Supermen* #2–4, July 2010).

In a potential future one million months hence, the child whom Linda Danvers knew as Ariella lived on as R'el, the Supergirl of the 853rd century (*Supergirl One Million,* November 1998; *Young Justice* #21, July 2001).

There were many other incarnations of the Girl of Steel across the multiverse. On a world where no one had superpowers, a boy named Clark Kent one day woke up manifesting the powers of his comic book namesake. In time, he married Lois Lane and had twin girls, each of whom manifested superpowers (*Superman: Secret Identity* #1–4, 2004).

Temporarily stripped of all memories of her alter ego, Linda Lee married Jimmy Olsen on Earth-57, revealing to her new husband weeks later that she was Supergirl (*Superman's Pal, Jimmy Olsen* #57, December 1961).

On Earth-332, Kara arrived on Earth as a baby, growing up to become Superwoman and training her teenage cousin Kal-El as Superboy (*Action Comics* #332–333, January–February 1966).

A parallel reality saw Kara Zor-El arrive on Earth-1098, where there was no Superman—or Batman, either. She wound up partnering with Batgirl to maintain law and order (*Elseworlds' Finest: Supergirl & Batgirl,* 1998). A cloned version was created by Lex Luthor, dubbed Supergrrl (*Superboy* [third series] #61, April 1999).

Linda Danvers had a guardian angel named Matrix who did not look kindly upon her charge (*Supergirl: Wings,* 2001).

In the reality of Earth-992, Kara In-Ze was the sole survivor of a world in Krypton's star system named Argo. Responding to a distress beacon, Superman brought the girl to Earth, where she became Supergirl (*Superman Adventures* #21, July 1998).

On Earth-D, the Kryptonians were all brown-skinned, so Supergirl passed herself off as an African American and married that world's Superman (*Legends of the DC Universe: Crisis on Infinite Earths* #1, February 1999).

On another world where Superman and Batman begat generations of heroes, the Man of Steel's daughter Kara Kent grew to become Supergirl, founding the Justice League of America with Bruce Wayne, Junior, Wally West, and Stephanie Prince. Kara and Bruce married but she was killed after the ceremony by her jealous, nonpowered brother Joel, manipulated by Luthor into murdering his sister (*Superman & Batman: Generations* #1–4, 1999). Joel's son Clark and his wife had twin daughters, Lois and Lara, who inherited the family superpowers and adventured as Supergirl Red and Supergirl Blue (*Superman & Batman: Generations III* #1–12, March 2003–February 2004).

Earth-523 experienced a Black Light event that deprived many heroes of their super-abilities. Kara trained with Batman to continue to fight for justice and changed from Supergirl to Justice, forming a new team called the Phoenix Group (*JLA: Act of God* #1–3, 2001).

When a disease killed all the men on Earth-922, Linda Danvers grew up to become Superwoman (*JLA: Created Equal,* 2000).

New Earth's reality was altered through the machinations of Morgaine Le Fey, Enigma, and Kanjar Ro, and featured Kara in costume using the name Interceptor (*Trinity* #18, October 1, 2008).

After Infinite Crisis divided the universe into fifty-two parallel universes, Earth-2 became the home to Power Girl (*52* #52, May 2, 2007). On Earth-3, the home of the villainous versions of the heroes, Kara Zor-L was Ultragirl—although unlike Ultraman she was weakened, not empowered, by kryptonite (*Countdown to Final Crisis* #16, January 9, 2008). Earth-9 once had a Supergirl who was an unsuccessful prototype from a genetic engineering project designed to create meta-humans (*Tangent Comics/Powergirl* #1, September 1998). Earth-10 was a reality wherein Germany won World War II; Kara was known there as Overgirl (*Final Crisis* #2, August 2008). Not a Kryptonian, she was the result of Nazi experiments using Overman's alien DNA. During the events of Final Crisis, it appeared she had died during the conflict (*Final Crisis* #7, March 2009). Earth-11 was a world where the traditional gender roles were reversed and Kara was therefore the adult Superwoman (*Superman/Batman* #24, January 2006). Earth-22 featured Kara as Power Woman, an adult version of Power Girl, and the Matrix version was glimpsed with the Legion of Super-Heroes (*Kingdom Come* #1–4, May–August 1996).

SUPERGIRL ROBOTS

Shortly after Supergirl arrived from Argo City, Superman built her several robots to imitate both the Girl of Steel and her alter ego, Linda Lee. The first was created out of necessity when fellow orphan Dick Wilson took a picture of the still-secret heroine in action and suspected she might be doubling as Linda. The robot performed tricks to amuse the orphans then exposed its inner workings, dissuading Dick (*Action Comics* #256, September 1959).

Linda hollowed out a tree on the grounds of the orphanage where she lived to hide the robots. Later, when she was adopted, she secreted the robots in the basement of the home of Fred and Edna Danvers.

In an odd twist, a robotic teacher that Jor-El employed on Krypton visited Earth to test Supergirl since its programming had concluded that she was emotionally unstable to be a heroine. He disguised himself as Topar and gained control over both the Supergirl and Linda robots, having them wreak havoc to examine Supergirl's control over the situation. She not only kept her calm but exposed the robot and learned that she had passed the test (*Adventure Comics* #382, July 1969).

When a Supergirl robot arrived in Smallville on the anniversary of Jonathan and Martha Kent's death, it was confused by having the Teen of Steel's memories. Supergirl and Superman caught up to the robot and explained that its programming came from a defunct Superboy Robot by mistake (*Adventure Comics* #396, August 1970).

The last appearance of a Supergirl Robot indicated that time had passed and the original models had been retired as a result of malfunctions caused by increasing pollution in the air. When Supergirl was embroiled in a lengthy battle with the Master Jailer, she had to construct a brand-new robot to stop his announced plans to rob a bank. The pollution immediately affected the delicate mechanism, slowing the robot's responses and allowing the Master Jailer to destroy it (*Superman Family* #219, June 1982).

SUPERINTENDENT LYMAN

Superintendent of the State Orphanage, Lyman watched his staff force the orphaned children to do harsh work. One orphan, Frankie Dennis, ran away and met *Daily Star* reporter Clark Kent. With Lois Lane, Kent investigated, but Lyman threatened the children not to say a word.

Lyman was later caught by Lois beating a child. He set the orphanage on fire and tried to flee to South America but was stopped by Superman (*Superman* [first series] #3, December 1939).

SUPERINTENDENT WYMAN

The superintendent of the Coreytown prison, Wyman "in a murderous frenzy of sadistic hate" inflicted cruel punishments on the inmates, from starvation and the sweat-box to blood-chilling whippings. Upon hearing of the depravity, Superman disguised himself as a prisoner and was taken to the jail. He revealed himself and then subjected the warden to the same punishments he so gleefully handed out to his charges. The Man of Steel then dragged the state's pusillanimous Governor Bixby out of bed to be an eyewitness to the prison horrors, accumulating sufficient photographic evidence to send Wyman to prison himself. A series of long-overdue reforms at the Coreytown prison followed (*Action Comics* #10, March 1939).

SUPER-JACKASS

Mr. Mxyzptlk temporarily allowed Lex Luthor to experience what it was like to use magic. Both targeted Smallville's champion, transforming Superboy into a long-haired hippie, a monkey, and a jackass. Trapped in the form of a donkey, he still possessed his super-abilities and used his heat vision to write kltpzyxm into a nearby sidewalk. Before Mxyzptlk could be tricked into saying his name backward and therefore exiling himself back to the Fifth Dimension for ninety days, the spell ended (*Superboy* [first series] #131, July 1966).

SUPERLASS

In one of the many parallel worlds, Superman and Lois Lane married and raised a daughter, Lisa, who inherited her father's super-abilities and adventured as Superlass. The wedding came about after Lois was blinded during an incident and didn't think Superman would love her anymore. Dressed as Clark Kent, he took her to another state where they married quietly. Lois gave birth and they lived simply in the automated home Superman constructed for them. Then came the fateful day Superman was seemingly killed on a mission saving an ocean liner that contained both green and red chunks of kryptonite. With her father declared dead, Lisa decided it was time to follow in his footsteps. "It's Superlass—the terrific teen!" people would cry when she flew overhead. When she saved a spacecraft from Galaxy X-1, they wanted to reward her heroism and used their technology to cure Lois's blindness. By then, Lois had befriended a misshapen man during visits to the beach. When she regained her sight, she went to see him—but by then he'd fled. Suspecting the truth, Superlass tracked the man and found him at the Fortress of Solitude. Sure enough, it was Superman, whose body had been twisted into the monstrous form by the red k and then the change made permanent by the green k. Refusing to let his sighted bride see him this way, he donned a spacesuit and took to the stars (*Superman's Girl Friend, Lois Lane* #91, April 1969).

SUPERMAN

There was only one being who was respected, revered, celebrated, feared, and hated on Earth, across the stars, and throughout time itself. The survivor of a doomed planet, he was raised on a world that was alien to him, where he gained powers and abilities far beyond those of mortal humanity. A quirk of fate taught him to value and respect life absolutely, so that his amazing abilities were used to wage a never-ending battle for truth, justice, and the universal principles of honor, compassion, determination, and personal integrity that turned Kal-El of Krypton into Superman.

His greatest significance was that he may well have been the one truly indispensable figure in all Creation—which perhaps explains why, in all the myriad parallel dimensions, there was always some form of Superman, just as there were always powerful forces that rose to challenge him, and millions of beings in a vast universe teeming with life who always needed him.

A. Origin

1. The Original Account: The Superman of the Pre-First Crisis Earth-2

"As a distant planet was destroyed by old age, a scientist placed his infant son within a hastily de-

vised space-ship, launching it toward Earth! When the vehicle landed on Earth, a passing motorist, discovering the sleeping babe within, turned the child over to an orphanage. Attendants, unaware [that] the child's [physiological] structure was millions of years [more] advanced [than] their own, were astounded at his feats of strength. When maturity was reached, he discovered he could easily: Leap 1/8th of a mile; hurdle a twenty-story building . . . raise tremendous weights . . . run faster than an express train . . . and that nothing less than a bursting shell could penetrate his skin! Early, Clark [Kent] decided he must turn his titanic strength into channels that would benefit mankind. And so was created . . . SUPERMAN! Champion of the oppressed, the physical marvel who had sworn to devote his existence to helping those in need" (*Action Comics* #1, June 1938).

2. Addenda and Revisions

Every inhabitant of this "distant planet," which was documented as Krypton (*Superman* [first series] #1, Summer 1939), was said to possess superhuman strength, X-ray vision, super-speed, and most of the other powers associated with later incarnations of Superman (*Action Comics* #1, June 1938; *Superman* [first series] #33, March–April 1945; *Superman* [first series] #53, July–August 1948). At the moment of Krypton's destruction, scientist Jor-L and his wife Lora sent their infant son Kal-L to Earth. Jor-L's brother Zor-L heeded the warning and built a ship containing digital scans of life in the city of Kandor to help educate his daughter Kara during her long trip to Earth, in suspended animation. This slower ship reached Earth many decades after Kal-L arrived and became an adult. The Superman of Earth-2 welcomed her, and she began a crime-fighting career under the name Power Girl (*All Star Comics* #58, January–February 1976; others).

As the research of later historians was able to provide further details, the "passing motorist" who found the infant Superman became a couple, John and Mary Kent (*Superman* [first series] #1, Summer 1939, and #53, July–August 1948; others), who adopted the orphan from space and named him Clark Kent. Conflicting accounts were offered of the infant's brief stay in the orphanage, differing in details about how long he remained there and whether his superpowers were actually revealed there.

The Earth-2 Superman, who never fought crime as Superboy, had a very different life from the Superman of Earth-1. In that reality, the pleas of Jor-El—as his name was spelled in the Earth-1 universe—to rescue the populace in a fleet of rocket ships that would take them to another world fell on deaf ears, as the planet was focused on the celebration of the ten thousandth year of Kryptonian civilization (*Action Comics* #223, December 1956). Jor-El's discovery that the planet's uranium core had been building up "a cycle of chain-reactions" that would lead to Krypton exploding like a planet-sized nuclear weapon seemed so preposterous, few gave it credence. Although Jor-El was the planet's foremost scientist, he was ignored by the ruling Science Council, dooming his people. He begged his wife Lara Lor-Van to accompany their child to Earth in the experimental escape-rocket prototype that was too small to fit the entire family of three. Instead she chose to remain at her husband's side and watched as their race's last hope began an unprecedented journey.

After the Crisis on Infinite Earths, Krypton was depicted as a cold, sterile world whose inhabitants repressed their emotions, but some feelings—such as those associated with the maternal instinct—were not so easily denied. Lara was horrified by the notion of sending her only child to the "barbaric" planet Earth, but was given little choice.

Kal-El landed near the farm of Jonathan and Martha Kent and the couple decided to keep the baby, taking advantage of the isolation imposed by a protracted winter to create the appearance that the baby was naturally Martha's, born on the farm when the Kents could not drive through a storm. Clark's powers slowly developed as the boy grew, his body absorbing more and more yellow solar energy until his abilities matured and fully manifested themselves when he was a high school senior. Thus this Clark Kent did not become the red-and-blue-clad super hero until adulthood (*Man of Steel* #1–6, October–December 1986).

The Infinite Crisis altered Clark's personal history so that his powers manifested themselves at age twelve, when he accidentally broke his friend Pete Ross's arm. After learning the truth of his origins from his parents, he decided, with their inspiration and encouragement, to use his abilities for good works. While surreptitiously performing rescues and other benevolent deeds, never showing himself, young Clark began to spiral down into depression. Hoping to help her adopted son embrace his Kryptonian heritage and be proud of who he was, Martha Kent made him the Superboy uniform (*Superman: Secret Origin* #1, November 2009), which he grudgingly decided to wear.

B. The Secret Identity

"Now listen to me, Clark!" cautioned John Kent of Earth-2 while Clark was still very small. "This great strength of yours—you've got to hide it from people or they'll be scared of you!" "But when the proper time comes," added Mary Kent, "you must use it to assist humanity" (*Superman* [first series] #1, Summer 1939).

Over the years, this Clark Kent wrestled with the duality of his nature, wondering who he was: Kal-L, orphan from Krypton; Clark Kent, farm boy; or Superman, the Man of Steel. At different times, he experimented with being one or the other but always concluded he was the son raised by the Kents to use his gifts honorably, respecting all life and defending it against all threats at any cost.

In choosing an occupation as an adult, Clark adopted the guise of a mild-mannered reporter, confident that people would not mistake him for the barrel-chested, colorful super hero he became. Most observers bought into the ruse when he came to work for editor George Taylor at the *Daily Star*. The majority of his colleagues accepted the imposture here on Earth-2 and, later, on Earth-1, where very few people, including Lois Lane and Lana Lang, seriously suspected that Clark was the Metropolis Marvel, although as time went on Lois's suspicions intensified. Some chroniclers specu-

lated that others, such as *Daily Planet* editor Perry White, may have been less taken in but pretended otherwise, although no concrete evidence of this was ever presented.

On Earth-1, Jonathan and Martha Kent never hid Clark's origins, speaking openly of the rocket that brought him to Earth. As his powers evolved, so did his ability to recall his life on Krypton (*Action Comics* #288, May 1962). The teenage Superboy retained dim memories of his brief time as a toddler on his homeworld, which he augmented by using a Kryptonian Mind-Prober Ray (*Superboy* [first series] #79, March 1960; others). Clark learned that he could also access events from the past "by overtaking and photographing light rays that had left Krypton before it exploded" (*Superman* [first series] #132, October 1959). During the course of his early life, the Kal-El of the pre–First Crisis Earth-1 continued to find artifacts from Krypton, many of them incorporating recordings or writings made by his father. Chief among the objects recovered was the Phantom Zone projector, a device that could send people and objects into a limbo-like realm. This dimension was discovered by Jor-El, who urged its use as a maximum-security prison for Krypton's most dangerous criminals. A disproportionately large amount of Kryptonian detritus seemed to make its way across the many light-years to Earth, including many now radioactive fragments of the planet itself, which would prove deadly to superpowered Kryptonians. Some historians theorized that Kal-El's rocket had ripped open a warp in space through which many Kryptonian artifacts and other survivors were sucked, emerging from the warp in close proximity to Earth's orbit, from which they eventually fell into Earth's atmosphere (*Action Comics* #500, October 1979).

C. The Costume

In all realities, Superman wore one costume, a blue body stocking with red cape, red boots, and red trunks with a yellow belt. On his chest was the red-and-yellow S-shield, which became a symbol for justice throughout the known universe. An all-yellow S-shield adorned the back of the cape. The differences among the various Supermen's garb were minor stylistic variations, such as the shape of the boot tops or the color scheme of the S-shield, but otherwise the uniforms have remained consistent.

The stylized S-insignia has come to mean different things through the years. For most of the chronicles, it stood simply for Superman and, on Earth-1, for Superboy, Supergirl, and a host of Kryptonian pets, such as Krypto, who came to Earth, were endowed with superpowers, and wore capes, collars, or harnesses incorporating the S-shield into their design. A mirror image of the shield was worn by the imperfect duplicate of Superman, Bizarro, in most of his incarnations. After the Infinite Crisis, the stylized S-shape became a character in the Kryptonian alphabet and was identified as the El family crest, which all members of the House of El were entitled to wear. Heroes on the post–First Crisis Earth wearing the S-shield carried with it the responsibility of Superman's endorsement. Among those have been his clone, the Kon-El Superboy, the Matrix Supergirl, Steel, the Eradicator, and Mon-El.

The Superman of Earth-2 described his uniform as something "constructed of a cloth I invented myself which is immune to the most powerful forces!" When Kal-El was being raised on Earth-1 as Clark Kent, Martha Kent outfitted him with a red-and-blue playsuit, made by reweaving the blankets found with the rocket ship that brought him from Krypton (*Superboy* [first series] #8, May–June 1950), which were themselves indestructible and could withstand the wear and tear inflicted on them by Superbaby's exercise of his superpowers. Martha thereafter rewove the playsuit into the familiar red-and-blue uniform complete with cape. In both cases, Clark participated in the making of his super-clothing by helping to cut the indestructible threads with his heat vision (*Superman* [first series] #146, July 1961). At the same time, indestructible plastic from the rocket was used to fashion a pair of eyeglasses so young Clark and the young hero would not be confused as the same person (*Superboy* [first series] #70, January 1959). It was essential that the glasses, too, be indestructible so that Clark could use his vision powers through them—particularly his heat vision—without destroying them. The Boy of Steel later had Ma Kent use the remaining blankets to create a second, primarily yellow costume, but it had the unexpected side effect of deflecting much of the yellow sun's energy from his body, and Superboy returned to his traditional outfit (*The New Adventures of Superboy* #18, June 1981).

In time, Clark added a pouch to the interior lining of the cape where he kept his civilian clothes, made of a synthetic material devised by the Boy of Steel that could be compressed into a very small packet and subsequently expand, wrinkle-free. Later, when Clark Kent reached adulthood, the costume's belt buckle was modified to house his Justice League of America signal device.

In the post–First Crisis reality, it was documented that Superman's costume was not itself indestructible per se, but that the Man of Steel possessed a low-level telekinetic ability that allowed him to generate a force field around his body. This field not only allowed him to defy gravity but also protected his costume, with the exception of his cape, which usually trailed beyond the range of the field and often got shredded in battle (*Man of Steel* #1–6, October–December 1986).

Various circumstances periodically required Superman to adopt other costumes. Upon his revival after his murder by Doomsday, the Man of Steel used a predominantly black solar outfit to quickly reabsorb energy from the sun (*Action Comics* #689, Late July 1993; others). And later, when transformed into an energy being, he maintained his bodily integrity in an all-blue containment suit (*Superman* [second series] #123, May 1997; others). In the wake of massive deaths during the Imperiex War, Martha Kent prepared a new costume for Superman, one whose S-symbol was set against a background of black as a symbol of mourning (*Superman* [second series] #174, November 2001).

D. Derivation of the Superpowers

The Earth-2 Superman's powers and abilities were at first reported to be native, because the Kryptonian people were described more than once as a "super-race" (*Superman* [first series] #73, November–December 1951; others). They also possessed some of the vision powers Superman displayed and were considered far ahead of *Homo sapiens* on the evolutionary scale (*Superman* [first series] #53, July–August 1948).

The origin of the Earth-1 Superman's powers, however, was a result of his displacement to a different environment. In the words of one account, "Everyone knows that Superman is a being from another planet, unburdened by the vastly weaker gravity of Earth. But not everyone understands how gravity affects strength! If you were on a world smaller than ours, you could jump over high buildings, lift enormous weights . . . and thus duplicate some of the feats of the Man of Steel!" (*Superman* [first series] #58, May–June 1949). Some latter-day accounts of the origin of the Earth-2 Superman's powers make this assertion as well, so the notion that the Kryptonians of the Earth-2 universe were super-beings in their native environment may be apocryphal.

During the Earth-1 Superman's adventures, the chronicles ascribed his powers not only to Earth's lighter gravity but also to the difference in solar radiation. Krypton orbited Rao, a red giant, while Earth orbited Sol, a smaller yellow sun. "These rays," the Man of Steel told Supergirl, "can only affect people who were born in other solar systems than Earth's! And only yellow stars like Earth's sun emit those super-energy rays! On planets of non-yellow suns, we would not be super-powered, even under the low gravity!" (*Action Comics* #262, March 1960). Soon after, the theory was modified by subsequent historical research to state that "my muscles automatically became super-strong in Earth's light gravity! I'm like the ant, which, if it were man-sized, could carry a locomotive! Grasshoppers could leap over buildings!" It was also revealed that the yellow-sun radiation "super-energize[d Superman's] brain and five senses to give [him his] other non-muscular super-powers! Also, those yellow-sun rays, which only tan Earth people's skin, hardened [his] like steel" (*Superman* [first series] #146, July 1961). As a result, any living being from Krypton would gain the same set of powers and abilities as Superman's if exposed to the same conditions.

The strength of a solar system's sun had an impact on not just Superman's powers but also those of other super-people who gained their abilities from other stars. Exposure to red solar radiation immediately sapped Kryptonians of their powers—a recurring problem, especially whenever Superman visited Lexor, the world that worshipped Lex Luthor (*Action Comics* #318, November 1964).

With the exception of the postulation regarding the psionic ability that created a force field around the Man of Steel, the scientific explanation of Superman's abilities remained relatively unchanged in the various other realities. The force-field attribute was short-lived, however, as subsequent reorderings of reality reinstated the yellow-sun-energy and lighter-gravity explanation.

1. Super-Speed and the Power of Flight

The Earth-2 Superman was initially reported to be able to leap an eighth of a mile, launching himself from street to rooftop or across the Metropolis skyline. Either this was a misperception by the earliest eyewitnesses, or perhaps, as Superman gained experience as a crime fighter, his powers and abilities developed over time, in much the way a dedicated bodybuilder increases mass and strength. In any event, in short order the Earth-2 Superman was said to "fly like a bird" (*Action Comics* #60, May 1943)—and that power increased until a text proclaimed, "Light travels 186,000 miles a second, but has nothing on Superman, who finds himself hovering over the jungles of Burma in the wink of an eye!" In time, this Superman, and subsequently the Superman of Earth-1, used his flight powers to move fast enough to pierce the time barrier or oscillate his body so fast that no human could see him. The chroniclers soon discovered that the pre–First Crisis Supermen could survive without oxygen, and therefore their powers of flight enabled them to leave Earth's gravity and traverse the stars, flying to distant galaxies in relatively short periods of time.

While Superman's speed was said to be immeasurable, he repeatedly raced the Flash—both the Earth-1 and Earth-2 versions—and was beaten by both, most likely given their ability to tap into the otherworldly Speed Force (*Superman* [first series] #199, August 1967; *DC First: Flash/Superman* #1, July 2002; others).

2. Super-Strength

From the moment he burst onto the scene, hefting an automobile over his head with his bare hands, Superman's strength was usually the first thing people talked about. His demonstration of prowess, like speed and flight, grew over time until he could shatter planets with his fists.

When Superman performed for charity, it was often a feat of strength such as hitting a baseball into orbit that was most impressive to the crowds. One of Superman's most often-repeated stunts was squeezing a lump of coal in his fist, mimicking the natural process by which diamonds are formed by applying so much pressure that the coal was transformed into a glittering gem (*Action Comics* #115, December 1947; others).

On Earth-1, while still a teenager, Superboy was said to be able to press five thousand tons with one hand, calling it "a cinch" (*Adventure Comics* #361, October 1967). His super-breath was powerful enough to nudge a planet through space (*Adventure Comics* #293, February 1962) or freeze the air around objects. His super-lungs allowed him to hold his breath indefinitely. His invulnerability was said to be absolute: He could withstand the power of a thousand H-bombs (*Adventure Comics* #366, March 1968).

In the post–First Crisis realities, Superman's strength was largely immeasurable, and one of the hardest lessons he had to learn was regulating his blows so that, in one moment, he would not kill a mortal man with a punch, but then turn on a dime to unleash a blow that could stagger a super-powerful combatant such as Mongul.

3. Invulnerability

Initially, it was nothing less than a bursting shell that could penetrate Superman's dense skin. The chronicles of his Earth-2 career contained accounts of his enemies attacking him with a variety of energy rays, such as the Ultra-Humanite's energy gun, which could render the Man of Tomorrow unconscious.

In time, though, less and less could stagger, let alone hurt, the hero. He was even able to withstand the high temperatures generated by a star (*Action Comics* #161, October 1951). On the other hand, a hydrogen bomb's detonation left him with a slight headache (*Superman* [first series] #87, February 1954).

Earth-2's Superman was not immune to aging, though it occurred more gradually and he appeared to fully possess his powers and abilities until his death. On Earth-1, Superman was apparently immune to disease and aging, effectively making him an immortal (*Superman* [first series] #136, April 1960). A different account, however, noted, "Though Superman is the mightiest man on Earth, even he cannot live forever!" (*Superman* [first series] #181, November 1965). The latter statement appeared to be the correct one, as various accounts of potential futures viewed by Superman showed him slowly and gracefully aging at different rates, although there would always be a time when he passed away.

Given his invulnerability, the Man of Steel could not tan or sunburn. The post–First Crisis Superman needed help from his heat vision to properly shave each morning, and also used his vision pow-

ers to give himself a haircut when needed, but the hair of the Superman of Earth-1, like his fingernails, did not grow in Earth's environment; manicures, haircuts, and shaves were unnecessary.

In all cases, his level of powers, including invulnerability, waxed and waned based on the radiation emitted by the nearest star.

4. Vision Powers

The Superman of Earth-2's eyesight was exceptionally keen, but his range of vision powers developed gradually. His first ability, "telescopic X-ray vision," developed incrementally, beginning a year after he began to fight crime (*Action Comics* #11, April 1939; *Action Comics* #18, November 1939, and #20, January 1940). In time, he realized that the X-rays his eyes emitted could not penetrate lead objects, one of his most consistent limitations.

Attempts to focus on minuscule objects led to his discovery of his microscopic vision, letting him see even things that existed on the molecular level (*Action Comics* #24, May 1940). The Earth-2 Superman's X-ray vision was initially said to generate a certain degree of heat and could be used to melt objects (*Action Comics* #139, December 1949; others). But heat vision as a discrete power per se—sometimes referred to in connection with the post-First Crisis Superman as laser vision—was first manifested by the Superman of Earth-1 (*Action Comics* #275, April 1961). The vision powers remained consistent in post-First Crisis incarnations of Superman.

5. Super-Hearing

Much as the pre-First Crisis Earth-2 Superman debuted with all his other senses far more acute than those of mortal humans, his hearing was said to be sensitive enough to perceive many sounds humans could not (*Action Comics* #8, January 1939). Over time, his hearing improved dramatically. At least one chronicle reported that the Man of Tomorrow could hear radio waves (*Superman* [first series] #7, November-December 1940). The Earth-1 Superman's super-hearing was powerful enough to isolate a distinctive voice from thousands of miles away, and perceive even the slightest of sounds, such as the footfall of an ant. Superman could also trace the source of sound waves across millions of miles of interstellar space. His superior hearing remained consistent in his subsequent incarnations on the post-First Crisis Earth and post-Infinite Crisis New Earth.

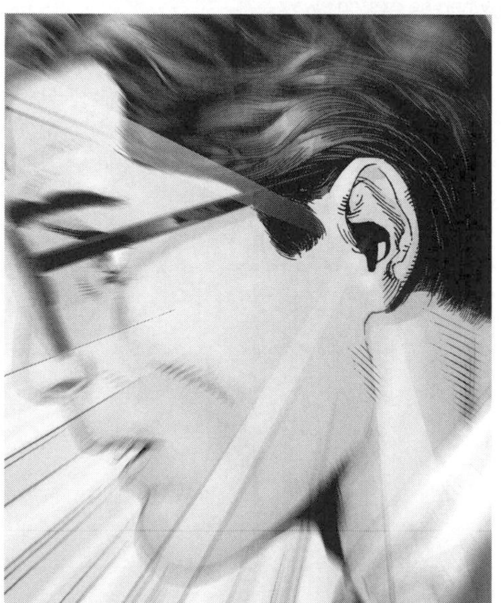

6. Super-Breath and Related Powers

Like most of his other abilities, the lung power of the pre-First Crisis Superman of Earth-2 developed gradually over time. The first documents of this power reported that the Man of Tomorrow could hold his breath for hours underwater. With the greater lung capacity came the ability to exhale with concussive force (*Action Comics* #20, January 1940). Later, that ability allowed him to hold his breath during his journeys from planet to planet. Inhaling mightily to create a powerful vacuum was a trick this Superman used on numerous occasions to thwart the escape attempts of such foes as the Toyman (*Superman* [first series] #49, November-December 1947).

The Earth-1 Superman had far greater lung capacity, to the extent that he could blow out a star (*Superman* [first series] #91, August 1954). He could also freeze objects with his breath (*Superman* [first series] #129, May 1959; others). This Superman was also said to be capable of surviving for long periods, if not indefinitely, without air (or food or water, for that matter). The Superman of the post-First Crisis Earth, however, did not possess inexhaustible lung capacity, and when he exiled himself from Earth for a year, he carried a mask and oxygen tank to replenish himself as needed (*The Adventures of Superman* #450, January 1989; others).

One of the stranger uses of his super-breath was documented only once, and therefore may be apocryphal. "The force of my super-breath will create an artificial aging effect [on this document]," he claimed, "so the writing will appear centuries-old!" (*Action Comics* #269, October 1960).

The Man of Steel's super-lungs have remained largely consistent through his many incarnations. While wearing his black solar suit during his climactic battle with Mongul and the Cyborg Superman (*Superman* [second series] #82, October 1993), Superman sustained a blast channeled through the body of the Eradicator that gradually caused his power level to rise to an uncontrollable level. Although much of the excess energy was drawn off by the Parasite (*The Adventures of Superman* #512, May 1994), Superman was nonetheless able to travel in space unaided from that point forward.

7. Vocal and Ventriloquial Powers

Even the comparatively primitive Superman of the pre-First Crisis Earth-2 trained himself to use all his special gifts with incredible accuracy. Among these traits was ventriloquism, which he first employed to rescue Lois Lane from kidnappers (*Superman* [first series] #13, November-December 1941). In time, he appeared capable of mimicking voices utterly convincingly; he used that skill, as well as what came to be known as "super ventriloquism," to give voice to the first incarnations of the dummies and robots he used to protect his secret identity.

His powerful voice could be used as a warning system, replacing loudspeakers and megaphones. Once, he managed to send his voice via radio waves, alerting police to an underworld hideout (*Action Comics* #60, May 1943). His voice was measured as capable of achieving a volume of more than one million decibels (*Superman* [first series] #65, July 1950), and its reverberations were known to shatter sheets of ice or make buildings crumble. These vocal skills remained consistent in Superman's subsequent incarnations, although the latter iterations rarely used them.

8. Mental and Intellectual Powers

The Superman of Earth-2's intellect was superior thanks to his Kryptonian upbringing and continued reading, usually done at super-speed, but he appeared to have innate mental processes that were first documented when he instantly translated a mermaid's language (*Superman* [first series] #14, January-February 1942). He was said to have a photographic memory, retaining countless facts and details, allowing him to function as a walking computer and aiding his war on crime (*Superman* [first series] #5, Summer 1940). Superman used his ability to study books in seconds to become an instant expert on many subjects, such as the time he memorized a complete medical text before performing complex eye surgery on a little girl. This Man of Steel's mind appeared to have total command over his body, allowing him to temporarily halt the beating of his heart to fool villains into believing him dead (*World's Finest Comics* #54, October-November 1951).

The original Superman also appeared able to hypnotize others, and first used this power of "super hypnotism" on Lois Lane (*Action Comics* #32, January 1941). The most common application of this power was to erase from people's minds the knowledge that Superman was Clark Kent, in the event someone other than a trusted confidant either learned the secret or had to be entrusted with it temporarily.

Superman's combined intellect and senses enabled him to be keenly aware of his surroundings, skills that helped not only the super hero but also reporter Clark Kent. His memories of Krypton and its technology, combined with his native intel-

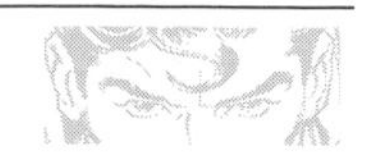

ligence, allowed him to devise, design, and construct super-tools and weapons as needed. He created the Superman Robots, putting him years ahead of most scientists on Earth.

After the post-Infinite Crisis Superman lost his powers following a battle with Superboy-Prime, it took a year for the sun's radiation to "recharge" his body. The experience seemed to leave his brain working at a faster level than previously, increasing his crime-fighting effectiveness (*Action Comics* #840, August 2006).

9. Miscellaneous Powers

The various incarnations of Superman were reported to have other senses and abilities that were documented only sporadically, raising the question of how many of these accounts, if any, were apocryphal. For example, he was said to be able to sign his name with either hand, identically. According to one account of the Earth-2 Superman, his alien blood could cure the ill if transfused (*Superman* [first series] #6, September–October 1940). This led to many fanciful, definitely apocryphal accounts of his mighty powers being shared with others in the process.

Only the Earth-2 Superman appeared able to alter his features with "superb muscle control," allowing him to disguise his appearance without artificial aids or makeup (*Superman* [first series] #18, September–October 1942). In time, though, he used this skill less frequently until he stopped altogether (*Action Comics* #115, December 1947).

E. The Vulnerabilities

1. Kryptonite

Superman in most realities was vulnerable to the radioactive remnants of Krypton. Depending on proximity and duration, the green-glowing substance left him weak and powerless, or, given sufficient exposure, could result in systemic poisoning and death.

On Earth-2, there was only the green variety of kryptonite. On Earth-1, an entire spectrum of varieties of the radioactive mineral developed, each with different effects on Kryptonians. Most of these forms of kryptonite have endured throughout the differing realities, following a brief period just before the First Crisis when all kryptonite on Earth was believed to have been eliminated.

2. Magic

The Man of Steel learned early in his career that his powers were no match for the supernatural. Magic affected the Earth-2 Superman much as it did other living beings (*Superman* [first series] #14, January–February 1942). Anytime any version of Superman confronted a demon, magician, warlock, witch, or sorcerer, he was exceedingly wary, usually relying more on his intellect than superpowers to escape danger. Much of that was a skill developed while regularly outwitting Mr. Mxyztplk of the Earth-2 reality, and Mr. Mxyzptlk on Earth-1.

Once, the Earth-1 Superman asked Earth-2's Doctor Fate if this weakness could be removed, and the sorcerer said it was possible. After the ensuing adventure, however, the Action Ace came to recognize that even he needed limitations (*World's Finest Comics* #208, December 1971).

3. Virus X

The incurable Virus X was fatal to Kryptonians. A strain of the disease survived the planet's destruction and mutated into a form that could kill even the seemingly invulnerable Man of Steel (*Superman* [first series] #156, October 1962; others).

4. Other Vulnerabilities

Solar radiation other than a yellow sun would weaken or rob Superman of many of his amazing abilities, and his X-ray vision could not penetrate lead objects.

Enemies preyed upon his moral code, turning it into a weakness. Innocent lives were frequently endangered, forcing the Man of Steel to abandon a battle to save people. As a result, he greatly feared that once the world learned his secret identity, his friends and loved ones would be targets. That was certainly proven to be the case, as attacks by Manchester Black and Conduit, among others, demonstrated.

F. The Equipment

Even with all his powers and abilities, Superman found himself in need of tools, equipment, and weapons to complete his missions. The first such example was a suit of lead armor the Superman of Earth-2 fashioned to deal with a runaway atomic reactor (*Action Comics* #124, September 1948). Soon after, he built an increasing number of robots to aid his fight against crime and protect his secret identity. Other devices he constructed included a miniature camera concealed inside a special ring, to keep incriminating photographic records (*Action Comics* #123, August 1948). He also built a K-Detector, designed to help him locate kryptonite that might have been used to trap him (*Action Comics* #158, July 1951).

On Earth-1, Superboy was building Superboy Robots early in his career, and no sooner did Supergirl arrive on Earth than Superman built her the first of several Supergirl Robots. Once, when his powers were at an ebb, he fashioned a Supermobile out of the nearly indestructible metal supermanium.

The Earth-1 Superman, and subsequent incarnations, built a special wristwatch as a gift to Jimmy Olsen. The watch could emit a supersonic signal that only Superman could hear, allowing the cub reporter to summon him with the high-frequency sound in times of need, provided no natural phenomena got in the way.

G. The Man Himself (as Clark Kent)

Clark Kent had black hair and blue eyes, and as an adult stood six feet two inches tall, with a chest measurement of forty-four inches and a thirty-four-inch waist (*Action Comics* #297, February 1963). His rocket from Krypton landed in an open field (*Action Comics* #141, February 1950) on the outskirts of Smallville (*World's Finest Comics* #57, March–April 1952; others). The proud foster parents named their new son Clark, which was Mary, and later Martha, Kent's maiden name (*The Adventures of Superman* novel, 1942; others).

Little was recorded about the Earth-2 Superman's upbringing. He was raised by the Kents in Smallville but was reported to have attended high school at Metropolis High, where he was nicknamed Specs and became known as his class's "quietest boy" (*Superman* [first series] #46, May–June 1947).

Clark lived with the Kents until the elderly pair died and he made his way to Metropolis, where he gained work as a reporter for the *Daily Star* under editor George Taylor. Fellow reporter Lois Lane thought Kent too mild-mannered for her tastes and disdained him. "As a reporter," Kent once said, "I have a hundred underworld and police contacts that make it easier for Superman to fight crime!" (*Action Comics* #139, December 1949).

Even after becoming the Man of Steel, Clark Kent continued his work as a reporter, enjoying the challenge posed him by rivals Lois Lane, Perry White, and others. In time, he became one of the most respected reporters in America. As a result, when the Earth-2 Clark allowed Superman to scale back his activities in the 1950s to marry Lois Lane, Clark had time to concentrate on his career as a journalist.

When the villainous Wizard cast a spell on Superman, forcing him to forget his heroic persona, the more assertive Clark allowed Lois to give him a second look—and romance blossomed. They dated, leading to his proposal and ultimately their marriage. During the honeymoon, Lois discovered Clark's secret and forced the Wizard to undo the spell (*Action Comics* #484, June 1978). The Earth-2 Batman, and later his wife Selina Kyle, were close friends of the Kents.

Upon *Daily Star* editor in chief George Taylor's retirement in the early 1950s, he proposed a competition between Kent and veteran reporter Perry White for his job. Perry proved the better reporter by a nose but, ironically, lost out to Clark because

Taylor believed the better reporter should remain in that role rather than being tied down to a desk (*Superman Family* #196, November–December 1979). As Clark moved into the editor's office, Superman slipped into semi-retirement, a condition that he continued for many years.

Accounts of the Earth-1 Superman and subsequent incarnations saw Clark Kent being raised on his foster parents' farm outside Smallville (*Superman* [first series] #152, April 1962; others). When Clark was still a toddler, the Kents decided it made sense to live closer to town. Jonathan sold the farm to Alex and Lila Crowley (*Superboy* [first series] #196, July 1973) and bought a general store (*Adventure Comics* #149, February 1950; *Superboy* [first series] #6, January–February 1950; others) from Whizzer Barnes (*Superman: Last Son of Krypton,* 1978).

The youth attended elementary and high school in Smallville, where he met his lifelong friends Lana Lang (*Superboy* [first series] #10, September–October 1950) and Pete Ross (*Superboy* [first series] #86, January 1961). Once Clark graduated from high school, Jonathan and Martha chose to take their first extended vacation, a trip to the Caribbean Islands. While there, they found Pegleg Morgan's 1717 diary leading to a treasure chest; by touching its contents, both contracted a rare tropical disease that proved fatal (*Superman* [first series] #161, May 1963). Hours after Martha passed away, Jonathan managed to speak with Clark before dying, reminding his son always to use his powers for the benefit of the world. After the funeral, Clark left Smallville for good (*Superman* [first series] #146, July 1961).

An orphan once more at eighteen, Clark Kent buried his parents, intending to sell the family home, attend college, and eventually move to Metropolis. Years later, in an act of friendship, Pete Ross tried to have the house condemned and razed to protect its secrets, but he changed his mind when he saw how much it meant to Clark (*Superman* [first series] #270, December 1973). Clark did quietly leave Smallville, though it was a much bigger affair for his costumed alter ego, with the entire town turning out to wish him well. The population assembled in formation so that from Superboy's point of view in the sky overhead, they spelled out FAREWELL SUPERBOY, WE'LL NEVER FORGET YOU! Superboy returned with the world's largest cake and made certain every citizen had a slice. Most were said to be preserved as souvenirs (*Superman* [first series] #97, May 1955).

While attending Metropolis University, Clark started to think of himself as Super*man,* beginning when he needed to evade a lie-detector test conducted by Professor Thaddeus V. Maxwell (*Superman* [first series] #125, November 1958). To the general public, he was still considered Superboy while he was in college (*Superman: The Secret Years* #1–4, February–May 1985). At this time, he had already decided upon a career in journalism (*Action Comics* #144, May 1950).

This Earth-1 Clark landed a job at the Metropolis *Daily Planet,* where he formed a circle of friends including editor Perry White, reporter Lois Lane, and cub reporter Jimmy Olsen. His childhood sweetheart, Lana Lang, reentered his life, working briefly at the *Planet* before joining TV station WMET and later working with him at WGBS. While Clark was a seasoned reporter, he was put before the camera first as a field reporter and later as an anchor when Morgan Edge's Galaxy Communications bought the *Daily Planet* (*Superman* [first series] #233, January 1971). The scheduling demands of television news reporting encroached on his ability to function as Superman spontaneously, but he was eventually allowed to do some reporting for the *Planet* in addition to his TV work and regained a measure of freedom. Clark remained a good friend, a good neighbor, and a likable guy despite his retiring demeanor.

The Clark Kent in the post-Crisis reality developed his powers later, and as a result his personality was more outgoing. Because this Clark never became Superboy, he did not see the need, in adolescence, to develop the timid, reticent characterization for Clark that his Earth-1 counterpart used to distinguish his two personae. Consequently, he felt free to explore and exploit his natural athleticism, becoming the quarterback for

A WHITE SHIRT IS UNBUTTONED IN A TIME-WORN GESTURE...
A FIGURE TRANSFORMED...
THE GENTLY AGING MAN WHO WAS ONCE A MILD-MANNERED REPORTER IS REBORN...
WHOOSH

the Smallville High football team (*Man of Steel* #1, October 1986). When he first began his crime-fighting career as Superman, he did so without a costume, and when the public adulation seemed to overwhelm him, he retreated. Ma and Pa Kent counseled him and helped him develop two separate identities, including donning glasses to create a new personality for Clark Kent and fashioning the costume he would wear as Superman.

This Clark was an accomplished reporter and bestselling novelist, easily winning a position with the *Daily Planet* when he landed the first accurate coverage of the arrival of this reality's Superman, earning him rival reporter Lois Lane's enmity for a time.

After the events of the Infinite Crisis, which split the single positive-matter universe into FIFTY-TWO parallel universes, Clark Kent was a normal twelve-year-old on New Earth—or, at least, he believed he was. After Pete Ross broke his arm trying to tackle Clark, the adolescent began to experience the manifestation of his powers, leading to a disastrous event involving his heat vision that nearly burned down the Kent barn. To Clark's relief, Ma and Pa devised a pair of glasses with special lenses (these, too, made from the rocket that brought him to Earth) that helped contain his heat vision in case it spontaneously activated again. And when he started to fly, his parents revealed the truth to their adopted son. Clark was frightened and confused when he was shown the rocket in which he'd landed on Earth. When he touched it, the Sunstone crystal was activated, giving the boy glimpses of life on Krypton, including holographic images of his birth parents.

Clark subsequently felt like an outsider, forced to hide his powers and who he truly was. He became uncomfortable around everyone, even the first girl he kissed—Lana Lang. Feeling literally alienated and, curiously, somewhat ashamed of his Kryptonian roots, he withdrew. He was forced into action and saved people from tornadoes, car accidents, and other disasters at super-speed. At such times he was an invisible blur, never revealing himself as the hero of the moment.

His adopted parents were the ones to help Clark embrace his Kryptonian descent, as anyone else on Earth would their ethnic background. After Clark's clothes continued to be ripped to shreds during his good deeds, Ma created a uniform based on the clothes the Kryptonians wore, adorned with the symbol of the House of El, thus creating his Superboy costume. But this Superboy was never seen by the public; he was a modern myth, like Bigfoot or the Men in Black. The tabloids called him "Super-Boy," but no one truly believed he existed.

Clark eventually grew comfortable with being a man of two worlds—and the name Superman would come to mean exactly that to him (*Superman: Secret Origin* #1–6, November 2009–September 2010).

H. The Man Himself (as Superman)

Soon after coming to work at the *Star,* the Earth-2 Clark Kent made his first appearance in costume as Superman and caused a sensation. He rapidly gained headlines for his work, which had as much to do with combating social injustice as fighting crime. He exposed corrupt politicians, unsafe work conditions, and illegal sports competitions while also preventing robbers, murderers, and racketeers from profiting.

At much the same time as costumed "mystery men" had taken to doling out vigilante justice in the name of law and order, the arrival of Superman captivated first a nation and then the world. As if in response to his arrival, more deadly criminal scientists and costumed foes emerged, beginning with the Ultra-Humanite and Luthor, followed soon after by masked criminal the ARCHER.

Superman chose not to intervene in World War II, letting men settle their differences rather than using his powers to mold a world in his image. He did, however, let Clark Kent comply when drafted, but when he reported for his physical, Kent flunked by using his X-ray powers to read a chart from another room (*Superman* [first series] #25, November–December 1943). Instead Superman remained active in America, stopping spies and saboteurs in addition to working to raise money through war bond sales. His very presence was a morale booster when the nation needed it most.

As the war wound down, a new breed of threat arrived in the form of the magical prankster Mr. Mxyztplk, followed by the annoying PRANKSTER and J. WILBUR WOLFINGHAM. The Toyman proved a greater challenge with his uncanny ability to escape prison, but even his crime sprees were easy to contain.

Traveling through time to trace the path of a mysterious meteorite he later called kryptonite, the Earth-2 Superman learned of the existence of Jor-L and Lora and the fact that he was their son (*Superman* [first series] #53, July–August 1948). Soon after, Lex Luthor learned of kryptonite and escalated his campaign to destroy the Man of Steel.

By the early 1950s, Communist paranoia gripped the country, and the remaining members of the JUSTICE SOCIETY OF AMERICA chose to disband rather than reveal their identities to Congress's Joint Un-American Activities Committee. Time passed and with it came the discovery of parallel universes, which led to the JSA meeting their Earth-1 counterparts, the JUSTICE LEAGUE OF AMERICA. After several of these meetings, the two Supermen finally met (*Justice League of America* [first series] #73, August 1969). The original Man of Steel returned to duty with greater regularity. Then came the spacecraft containing his cousin Kara, marking the first time the Earth-2 Superman met a fellow Kryptonian. As Power Girl, she was added to the ranks of the Justice Society, in which she fought alongside her cousin on numerous occasions (*All Star Comics* #58, January–February 1976; others).

No.14
JAN. FEB.
SUPERMAN
10¢

Power Girl was given a home by cousin Clark Kent and his wife Lois Lane as she acclimated to life on Earth. With Kara here, the aging Clark felt he could let Superman slip into permanent semi-retirement, and it was his endorsement that won her full membership in the legendary JSA (*All Star Comics* #64, January–February 1977).

This Superman returned to active duty only once more, when his entire reality was threatened during the Crisis on Infinite Earths. Working with his Earth-1 counterpart, he led the combined forces of heroes and super-criminals drawn from across the five remaining positive-matter universes. The climax of the confrontation left a single positive-matter universe, and there appeared room for just one Last Son of Krypton. Alexander Luthor, Junior, of Earth-3 offered Superman and his wife Lois a home: a crystalline limbo realm that existed in some other reality. The couple accepted and, with a wink, left the known universe in his younger counterpart's hands (*Crisis on Infinite Earths* #12, March 1986). For a complete accounting of the Earth-2 Superman's experiences beyond this point in time, see Crisis on Infinite Earths and Infinite Crisis).

On Earth-1, Clark was conscious of protecting the secret of his powers and was conflicted about what to do.

And so, at first, he donned the costume but moved quickly, becoming a red-and-blue blur to the citizens of Smallville, but gradually began letting himself be seen. Slowly, the town came to accept that a powerful young hero lived among them. He caught a robber and introduced himself to the gaping police officers as "Superboy, foe of all criminals" (*Superman* [first series] #144, April 1961). According to one account, this first exploit occurred when he was eight years old (*The New Adventures of Superboy* #1, January 1980).

Over time, Clark realized he needed a variety of ways to protect his secret identity. Thus he dug a tunnel from the house at 321 Maple Street to an exit outside the town, in addition to one that connected the Kent house to the general store where he worked after school. The basement also became the place where he kept several trophies and devices such as the Phantom Zone projector (*Superman* [first series] #146, July 1961). After he built the series of Superboy Robots, several of them were kept in the basement as well.

The Kents insisted Clark maintain a normal civilian life as much as time and circumstances allowed. In addition to doing chores around the house and attending school, they wanted him to have a circle of friends and to work like so many other teens, to learn the value of money and honest effort.

Despite the fame that came with being a hero, there were times Clark still felt isolated, different from other boys and girls. As a result, he was thrilled beyond belief when a rocket arrived containing his childhood pet Krypto. Under Earth's sun, the dog developed superpowers and increased intelligence; soon he began joining his master on missions (*Adventure Comics* #210, March 1955). In time, Superboy began to meet other survivors from Krypton and found other artifacts that had survived the planet's destruction, all of which helped him develop a keener insight into his heritage.

Through the years, the young Superboy periodically encountered other superpowered teenagers, generally heroes from other worlds, and fate inevitably turned each new encounter into a friendship. Consequently, the Boy of Steel's invitation to join the thirtieth century's Legion of Super-Heroes had a transformative effect on the young hero, allowing him the opportunity to form lasting bonds with other young people with powers like his own. Superboy was also encouraged by his Time-Viewer's glimpses of the near future, which revealed that kids he'd met in the present, such as Oliver Queen and Bruce Wayne, would later fight at Superman's side as Green Arrow and Batman.

Given all these challenges, Clark began to put into practice the lessons his adoptive parents had been teaching him since he was a toddler. Jonathan worked with him to help develop his powers and use them for the greater good, while Martha concentrated on making him a good friend and citizen. As a result, he adopted a personal code that precluded taking another person's life.

Yet Clark continued to fret that he would let people down by not being on duty at all hours of the day and night. He found himself offering explanations out of guilt (*Superboy* [first series] #89, June 1961).

What may have caused emotional pain, however, was Superboy's first encounter with other survivors of Krypton, beginning with Klax-Ar (*Superboy* [first series] #67, September 1958). Soon after, he learned of his father's discovery of the Phantom Zone and began meeting its criminal inhabitants such as Jax-Ur (*Adventure Comics* #289, October 1961).

As the boy became a teen and was verging on adulthood, the passage of time seemed tedious. Krypto apparently vanished into outer space, returning in the grip of old age until a fountain of youth restored his vigor (*Superman's Pal, Jimmy Olsen* #29, June 1958).

After his adventurous experiences at college, such as making and losing friends and falling in love with Lori Lemaris, who turned out to be a mermaid from Atlantis (*Superman* [first series] #129, May 1959), Clark once more defeated a scheme by Lex Luthor, and the *Daily Planet* began referring to him as Superman. Clark at twenty-one and a junior in college was done with being the Teen of Steel (*Superman: The Secret Years* #4, May 1985).

Superman's exploits led him to help form the Justice League of America and act as mentor to one newly arrived hero after another. Superman formed a close relationship with Batman and Robin, sharing countless adventures with them, with the trio entrusting one another with their secret identities. The two men impersonated each other on several occasions to help preserve their alter egos.

The Man of Steel's enemies grew in number as threats on Earth and from outer space arrived with surprising regularity.

The biggest change in the life of the pre–First Crisis Earth-1 Superman came soon after, in the form of the arrival of a second rocket from Krypton, this one containing his cousin Kara Zor-El. He welcomed her to Earth and helped her craft a human identity, that of orphan Linda Lee, so that he could secretly train her in the use of her newly acquired powers before introducing her to the world. When he deemed her ready, Superman proudly introduced his cousin to the world, with celebrations occurring around the planet, from sunken Atlantis to the United Nations.

With his accomplishments dating back to his days as Superboy, his reputation had spread from

world to world. Many came to Earth hoping to best the Man of Steel and make their reputations. All left in defeat.

Time and again, though, his most persistent nemesis turned out to be his onetime friend from Smallville, Lex Luthor. They met as fellow high school students and formed a friendship that included the Teen of Steel building the young aspiring scientist a laboratory. Lex was conducting experiments to try to find a cure for kryptonite when there was an accident and the lab caught fire. Superboy arrived and used his mighty breath to blow out the blaze, but the toxic fumes caused Lex to lose his hair—and blame the hero for his premature baldness. Thereafter, Lex tried again and again to crush the Action Ace, but with little success. Their battles were legendary and, in their adult years, even moved beyond Earth and into space, where Lex discovered a world that wound up hailing him as a hero and renaming itself Lexor in his honor.

The Superman of Earth-1 never allowed himself to pursue romance and marriage despite numerous opportunities. He always feared that if his enemies discovered he had a spouse, she would become their target. As a result, he was linked to Lois Lane, Lana Lang, and Lori Lemaris most often, but it was always Lois who seemed destined to become his wife if he were ever to marry. At one point, when he was being manipulated by an alien named Xviar, Clark briefly stopped operating as Superman and wooed Lois as Clark, consummating a long-simmering relationship. But their romance eventually ran its course, and they remained "just friends."

The discovery of parallel worlds led to frequent meetings between the Earth-1 and Earth-2 Supermen. On one occasion, they formed an alliance when Ultraman, their criminal counterpart from Earth-3, partnered with the Lex Luthor of Earth-1 and the red-haired Alexei Luthor of Earth-2 to destroy both heroes. Soon after, they reunited during the events of the First Crisis and Infinite Crisis.

After the First Crisis, a "reborn" Superman arrived in Metropolis as an adult, and the world was shocked by his existence but delighted to welcome him. His plainclothes rescue of an experimental space-plane (whose passengers included reporter Lois Lane) created a sensation and prompted him to formally adopt a costumed alter ego, soon dubbed Superman by the news media.

In the wake of Superman's public debut, Morgan Edge and his underling Bruno Mannheim began to form the criminal organization that became Intergang. The Metropolis Police Department organized its Metropolis S.C.U. (Special Crimes Unit) under the leadership of Captain Maggie Sawyer and Inspector Dan Turpin (*The Adventures of Superman Annual* #7, 1995). Superman also had his first encounter with the supernatural when he joined Doctor Occult in battling the Cult of Thahn (*Superman* [second series] *Annual* #7, July 1995).

Soon afterward, the Man of Steel of this reality was first exposed to entities of cosmic origins by an encounter with the Forever People of New Genesis (*Jack Kirby's Fourth World* #20, October 1998). When he was later captured and brought

to Apokolips by Amazing Grace, the Man of Steel came to fully understand the dire nature of the threat Darkseid would pose in the coming years (*Superman* [second series] #3; *The Adventures of Superman* #426; *Action Comics* #586—all March 1987).

Superman also learned of other realms when he encountered the Superboy from the Pocket Universe, a devious plot on behalf of the Time Trapper. Superman met the Legion of Super-Heroes, champions from what would ultimately be revealed as an alternate time line (*Superman* [second series] #8, and *Action Comics* #591—both August 1987). Not long afterward, he met a being called Supergirl who whisked him to the Pocket Universe in which she was created. She was actually Matrix, a clone of that universe's Lana Lang, created by a more benign version of Lex Luthor. There Superman discovered a dead planet, scorched and slaughtered by three villains native to the Pocket Universe. Superman meted out a kryptonite death sentence to General Zod, Quex-Ul, and Zaora, to prevent them from ever entering his universe (*Superman* [second series] #21–22, September–

October 1988; *The Adventures of Superman* #444, September 1988).

As the Man of Tomorrow continued to protect Earth's interests from super-criminals and supernatural menaces, he felt guilt over some of his more extreme, though necessary, actions. This remorse preyed on him until he decided to exile himself from Earth for a year. After saying goodbye to friends and family, he took to the stars, where was taken prisoner on Warworld, the home base of the tyrannical Mongul. There he met the ancient Cleric, who recounted stories of old Krypton and revived the Man of Steel's flagging spirits. After dealing a crushing blow to Mongul, Superman returned to Earth with a Kryptonian device called the Eradicator.

His cosmic odyssey over, Superman became entangled in the war between demonic siblings Blaze and Lord Satanus. He managed to visit Hell to plead for the lives of Jimmy Olsen and Jerry White, but returned with just Jimmy. In the aftermath, Superman met the cosmic entity called Kismet, who described herself as a crossroads between chaos and order (*The Adventures of Superman* #494, September 1992).

The Man of Steel finally met his match when Doomsday rampaged across the eastern United States, inflicting grave injuries on members of the Justice League of America. Superman managed to subdue the creature in Metropolis but at the apparent cost of his own life. A stunned nation went into mourning (*Superman: The Man of Steel* #18–19, December 1992–January 1993; *Justice League of America* #69, December 1992; *Superman* [second series] #74–75, December 1992–January 1993; *The Adventures of Superman* #497–498, December 1992–January 1993; *Action Comics* #684, December 1992–January 1993). The majority of Earth's heroes turned out for Superman's funeral, and his absence was sorely felt. His body was also stolen by Project Cadmus for experimentation (*Superman: The Man of Steel* #20; *Superman* [second series] #76—both February 1993).

A confluence of events sustained a spark of life in Superman's body, culminating with the Eradicator's attempt to take possession of it. Unable to do so, the Eradicator was still able to use the body as a model for its own attempts to reshape itself into humanoid form, and rushed Superman to the Fortress of Solitude, where Kal-El began a slow recovery within a Kryptonian healing matrix (*Action Comics* #692, October 1993). Four men emerged in Metropolis, each claiming the mantle of Superman—the confused, emotionless Eradicator, the armored Steel, Project Cadmus's alleged teenage clone of Superman, and the Cyborg Superman, more machine than man (*The Adventures of Superman* #500, Early June 1993; others).

Secretly allied with Mongul, the Cyborg Superman set into motion the destruction of Coast City, instantly killing more than seven million people and unleashing massive earthquakes along the West Coast (*Superman* [second series] #80, August 1993). The Cyborg soon revealed himself as

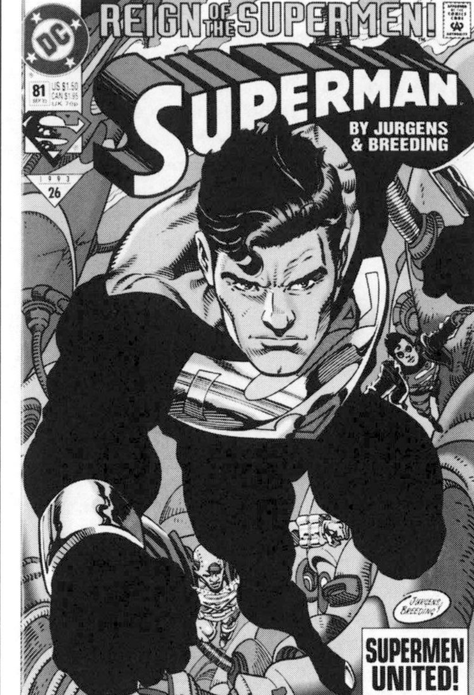

Hank Henshaw, intent on transforming Earth into a new Warworld (*Superman* [second series] #81, September 1993). Emerging from his incubation chamber, Superman returned to the United States, joining Steel; the Eradicator; Kon-El, the "Metropolis Kid"; and Green Lantern in a final assault on the so-called Engine City (*The Adventures of Superman* #504, September 1993; *Action Comics* #691, September 1993; *Superman* [second series] #82, September 1993; *Superman: The Man of Steel* #26, October 1993).

Later, Superman's intensifying powers grew out of control, ultimately requiring the Parasite to drain off his excessive energy (*Superman: The Man of Steel* #33; *Superman* [second series] #89; *The Adventures of Superman* #512—all May 1994). Fully restored, he was ready once again to defend the city he had come to love.

Aiding Superman in his attempt to bring down Lex Luthor once and for all was Lois Lane, who exposed "Luthor II" as the original and presented evidence of his other wrongdoings. An infuriated Luthor vowed to use hidden weapons to destroy Metropolis; when he vacillated, his assistant Sydney Happerson triggered them. Despite Superman's efforts, much of his beloved city was leveled (*Action Comics* #700, June 1994). Using the memories of Superman and Perry White as key components, the magician Zatanna cast a spell that undid the devastation of Metropolis (*The Adventures of Superman* #522, April 1995).

The Man of Steel learned the value of friendship anew when he was taken captive and hauled into space before the alien Tribunal, which sentenced him to death because of the part his ancestor Kem-L had played in the destruction of Krypton. Steel, Superboy, Supergirl, the Eradicator, and the Alpha Centurion mounted a rescue mission (*Superman: The Man of Steel* #50–52, November 1995–

January 1996; *Superman* [second series] #106–108, November 1995–January 1996; *The Adventures of Superman* #529–531, November 1995–January 1996; *Action Comics* #716–717, December 1995–January 1996; *Superman: The Man of Tomorrow* #3, Winter 1995).

There then came a period when Superman was not himself. A battle with a foe led to the Man of Steel being transformed into a being of pure energy, with powers to match. To contain his new form, Professor Emil Hamilton constructed a special containment suit (*Superman* [second series] #122–123, April–May 1997; *Superman: The Man of Steel* #67, April 1997). Superman evolved further when he was split into two energy beings, one red and one blue (*Superman Red/Superman Blue* #1, February 1998). Superman Red/Superman Blue expended all their energy in combating an attempt by a group of powerful super-criminals to destabilize the Earth's core. In doing so, Superman was reintegrated into a single being and regained his original powers (*Superman: The Man of Steel* #78–79, April–May 1998; *Aquaman* [fifth series] #43, April 1998; *Challengers of the Unknown* [fifth series] #15, April 1998; *Superman* [second series] #134–135, April–May 1998; *Teen Titans* [second series] #19, April 1998; *Supergirl* [fourth series] #20, April 1998; *The Adventures of Superman* #557, May 1998; *Steel* #50, May 1998; *Action Comics* #744, May 1998; *Superman Forever* #1, April–May 1998).

Superman created an army of Superman Robots to help him protect the world (*Superman* [second series] #143, April 1999; others). Convinced that he'd finally stepped over the line, the JLA, United Nations forces, and Lex Luthor made an all-out attempt to stop the Man of Steel, resulting in the destruction of the Fortress of Solitude. Superman belatedly discovered that he'd been under the mental influence of the cosmic entity Dominus and, after a fierce battle, trapped the villain in the Phantom Zone. The aftermath of this, though, meant that the world's governments began making covert plans to deal with Superman in the event that he again fell under someone else's control, something that would complicate his life in years to come.

Some time later, Green Lantern and Superman discovered that the planetoid Pluto had vanished and learned that their former colleague Maxima and the villain Massacre had formed an alliance with Darkseid in response to the encroachment of Imperiex (*Superman* [second series] #159, August 2000). The Imperiex War tested Earth's resolve and the fortitude of its costumed champions. Earth survived, but the devastation was massive, including the destruction of the Kent family farm. Worse, it was later discovered that Lex Luthor, then president of the United States, knew the threat was coming but did nothing to prepare the planet.

As a huge kryptonite meteor approached Earth, President Luthor accused Superman of crimes against humanity. Ultimately, Superman and Batman exposed Luthor's duplicity and a secret deal he had made with Darkseid, culminating in his ouster from office and the destruction of Metropolis's LexCorp Tower. The meteor was ultimately shattered before striking Earth, but less lethal shards of kryptonite continued to enter the atmosphere in the following weeks (*Superman/Batman* # 1–7, October 2003–April 2004).

Following the Infinite and Final Crises, and the resulting reinstatement of the multiverse as fifty-two parallel dimensions, many lives were altered, including that of the World's Greatest Super Hero. After he spent a year powerless—while slowly "recharging" his powers by continual exposure to Earth's yellow sun—and returned to his reporter's roots, Superman's powers eventually returned (*Superman* #650–653, May–August 2006; *Action Comics* #837–840, May–August 2006).

The Man of Steel's life took a surprising turn when he encountered the young Kryptonian Lor-Zod, who had crashed to Earth and was being held by the American military. Once rescued, Kal-El brought the youth to live with him and Lois Lane in Metropolis. In time, it was learned that Lor-Zod was a refugee from the Phantom Zone and son of General Zod and his cruel consort Ursa. Lor-Zod was born in a material area of the Phantom Zone called Fort Rozz, where time actually passed and Lor-Zod aged to adolescence while suffering relentless abuse at the hands of his parents (*Action Comics* #851, August 2007). A compassionate Clark and Lois renamed him Christopher Kent and helped him acclimate to his new life on Earth. Sadly, Chris was only a pawn in Zod's scheme for all the Phantom Zone criminals to be released on Earth, and he sacrificed his life on Earth to return to the Zone so that the criminals could never escape again.

Soon thereafter, Superman's help was requested by the new future's Legion of Super-Heroes. In their era of 3008, Earth's sun had artificially shifted from yellow to red. Rejected Earth-born appli-

cants formed the Justice League of Earth, with the goal of ridding the planet of alien influence. Their leader was Earth Man, who used a flawed interpretation of Superman's life story as the basis for his assertion that he derived his powers from "Mother Earth." He urged the planetary government to secede from the United Planets. This future Justice League's efforts forced the alien-born Legionnaires to go into hiding, leading them to bring the real Superman across time from the twenty-first century to help. With his participation, the sun was restored to its natural state and the UP's impending attack on Earth was ended (*Action Comics* #858–863, October 2007–April 2008).

Soon after, Superman once more traveled to the thirty-first century, this time to aid the Legion and three of the parallel Earths opposing Superboy-Prime and his Legion of Super-Villains. The Man of Steel had hoped to reform the tortured teen, but came to realize that this was not possible (*Final Crisis: Legion of 3 Worlds* #1–5, October 2008–September 2009).

In the New Earth reality, Superman also encountered a new version of Brainiac, a cold, calculating alien from Colu. Using androids, Brainiac sought samples of intelligent life on countless worlds, reducing them in size and keeping them aboard his massive starship, then eradicated the remainder of that world. When one such android encountered and fought Superman, it sent a sample of the hero's blood to Brainiac, and the alien was intrigued enough to travel to Earth. En route, however, he stopped to sample another planet's intelligent life, and there he and Superman met for the first time when the Man of Steel tried to stop him. Brainiac captured Superman, and once he arrived in Earth's orbit, he launched an assault on Metropolis. Superman managed to free himself, and while he and Supergirl were defending their adopted planet, Supergirl revealed that Brainiac was the one who had stolen Kandor decades before. The Man of Steel worked to stop one of Brainiac's planet-destroying missiles, while Superman subdued the Coluan. Thrown from his starship by Superman into a muddy swamp, Brainiac was subjected to millions of Earth's microorganisms, which paralyzed him. Superman then quickly rescued both Metropolis and Kandor, but in an act of spiteful revenge, Brainiac sent a missile to destroy the Kent farm. Jonathan Kent managed to save his wife Martha, but suffered a fatal heart attack while doing so. He died in Martha's arms, leaving Superman emotionally devastated. Despite having his mother and his beloved Lois to comfort him, Superman's enmity toward Brainiac burned bright in his heart.

Tempered with the loss of Jonathan Kent was the joy of being reunited with the thousands of kinsmen who had survived the destruction of Krypton. A delighted Superman offered to help them acclimate to their new homeworld, an offer that was sadly and largely ignored. Kandor's leaders turned out to be Zor-El and his wife Alura Zor-El, parents to Supergirl. They did agree, however, to a meeting with the president of the United States, a diplomatic gesture that was ruined when the monstrous "killing machine" Doomsday arrived. After he was dispatched, Zor-El decided that threats to Superman could also be threats to the newly relocated Kandorians. Kandorian troops were sent to remove such threats, which resulted in an assault on Superman's foes at Stryker's Island Penitentiary. During the conflict, several humans were killed, and the world demanded the Kryptonians involved face justice for their actions.

Sensing a disaster brewing, General Samuel Lane, the former secretary of defense, began marshaling troops. He went so far as to bring Lex Luthor into his counsel, and the former president stole Brainiac's inert starcraft. Luthor then activated a robot army discovered in the bowels of the ship. During the distraction, Lane sent the super-criminals Metallo and Reactron into Kandor since both contained kryptonite within their chests. They got close enough to manage to kill Zor-El (*Action Comics* #872 and *Supergirl* [fifth series] #36—both February 2009).

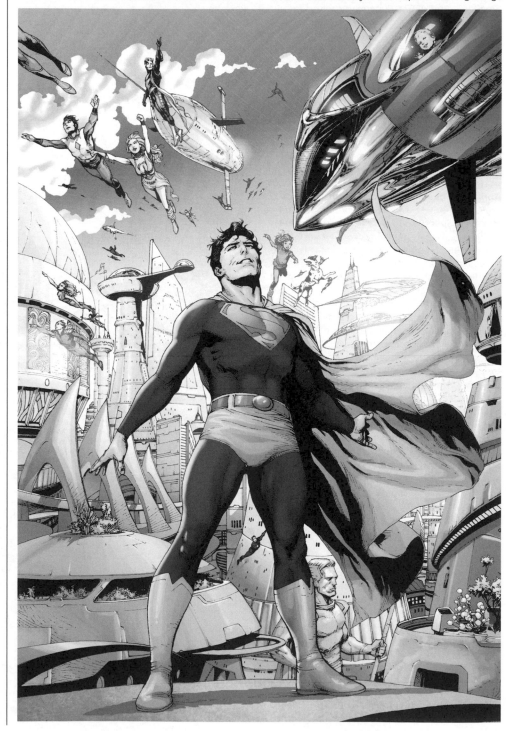

Mad with grief, Alura took control of the Kandorian government and rejected any assimilation into Earth society, refusing to hand over her people. Led by the Guardian, members of the Justice League of America and Justice Society of America arrived over the city in the hope of settling things peacefully. Superman found himself caught in the middle of the conflict, unhappy with both sides. The standoff ended when the city—and the glacier it sat atop—were lifted into the sky. Scientists had managed to access some of Brainiac's technology and found a way to move Kandor. They entered space where, directly opposite Earth's orbit, they fashioned a new planet using Kryptonian crystal-growth technology, and dubbed it New Krypton (*Action Comics* #873, March 2009; others).

Alura insisted Supergirl remain with her as their people settled their new world. At first, she rejected Superman, but later she offered him a place within Kryptonian society. He initially turned the opportunity down but then reconsidered after Alura freed General Zod and other criminals from the Phantom Zone (*Superman* #684, March 2009).

Deciding he needed to keep apprised of the real plans of his people, Superman decided to essentially go undercover on New Krypton, saying good-bye to his wife Lois Lane and his adopted mother Martha Kent, ostensibly taking up permanent residence there as Kal-El. Superman helped free Mon-El from the disintegrating Phantom Zone and charged him with looking after Metropolis in his absence (*Superman* #685, April 2009; others).

Kal-El arrived on New Krypton and was given a place at Zod's side in the Military Guild by his Aunt Alura. As Commander El, he worked with the elite Red Shard group, where he trained the soldiers to fight using their new superpowers thanks to Earth's yellow sun. He also showed them more peaceful ways to solve problems and defuse tense situations. His presence on New Krypton and his commendable galactic reputation helped to eliminate any suspicions the Green Lantern Corps had over so many superpowered beings living on one world when they visited the fledgling planet. Kal-El himself, however, was concerned by the secret caches of weapons Zod had been stockpiling. When Kal-El sided with the Corps against Zod, he was arrested and tried for treason (*Superman: World of New Krypton* #1–4, May–August 2009). During the trial, Kal-El was offered a chance to escape from prison—a trap set by Zod—but Kal-El refused. When he was found guilty and sentenced to death, Zod personally intervened and saw Kal-El pardoned, the son of Jor-El having passed his test.

Later that day Zod was shot in an assassination attempt, and Kal-El was named the Military Guild commander while Zod slowly recovered from his wounds. As Kal-El investigated the crime, his chief suspect, Ral-Dar, escaped prison and fled to Earth, forcing Kal to follow as Superman. He and Supergirl pursued Ral-Dar, and while on Earth, the Man of Steel was brought up to date on what his friends and loved ones were doing to blunt Project 7734's increasingly dangerous actions. Superman had sent Supergirl and Mon-El after Ral-Dar, who turned out to be working with General Lane to undermine his own people. Superman traveled to the European country of Markovia to prevent Ral-Dar from assassinating the president of the United States, but was hampered by General Lane's men firing at himself and Ral-Dar. When one struck the renegade Kandorian, Superman was finally able to apprehend him (*Superman: World of New Krypton* #5–6, September–October 2009; *Action Comics* #880; *Supergirl* [fifth series] #44; *Superman* #691—all October 2009).

Kal-El's return to New Krypton was well-timed, as he was able to argue against Officer Gor's proposal to the Council that attacking Earth before they were surely attacked was the wisest course of action. Zod rose from his sick bay bed and sided with Kal-El, promoting him to general and giving him full authority over the Military Guild. Any decisions were forestalled when word reached the Council that a Kryptonian spacecraft tasked with retrieving Callisto, a moon near Jupiter that would serve as New Krypton's, was attacked by Thanagarian war ships. Kal-El led a squad of his troops against the Thanagarians, who aggressively defended Jupiter's sovereign rights. When the main Thanagarian warship was damaged, Kal-El rescued its crew, earning a measure of respect from its commander. Just as the moon Callisto was placed in orbit around New Krypton, the Council was approached by a defiant J'Emm, leader of the Saturnian people. His displeasure at the impertinent new neighbors was tempered when Kal-El intervened, prevailing on their past associations to prove his sincerity. No sooner did the Saturnian delegation return to space than a Council member was found murdered, the human adventurer Adam Strange standing over the body. Thankfully, Kal-El believed his ally's explanation that the Zeta Beam transporting Strange from his adopted world of Rann back to Earth erroneously deposited him at the crime scene. Strange used his keen intellect to aid the murder investigation, which led to the increasingly restless Labor Guild (*Superman: World of New Krypton* #7–10, November 2009–February 2010).

The mysterious assassin then tried to kill Alura, but her assistant, Lyra Kam-Par, was killed instead, derailing a clear investigation. Kal-El and Adam Strange were less certain about the Labor Guild being driven to kill just to get their grievances heard. Their investigative trail led Strange and Kal-El to discover a hidden base where aliens were being slaughtered for their silvery skins to be used as weapons coating. Kal-El was furious and disgusted at this and angered that Zod had kept it all hidden. Gor, under Zod's orders, tried to kill Kal-El and Adam Strange, the latter of whom teleported them out of harm's way. Once Strange returned to Earth, Kal-El was free to finish piecing together the conspiracy to destabilize New Krypton's government. He finally pieced it together and made a visit to Councilor Wri-Qin, who admitted to partnering with General Lane in exchange for ruling New Krypton in the aftermath of the inevitable war between the two planets (*Superman: World of New Krypton* #11–12, March–April 2010).

Any hope of thwarting the conflict was interrupted by the arrival of Brainiac's massive starship, which had returned to reclaim the world Superman stole from him. The Coluan criminal's arrival began a series of events that proved his thirty-first-century descendant Brainiac 5 correct. Should

Brainiac succeed in killing Superman, it would cause time to unravel and shatter all of reality. To forestall this, Brainiac 5 dispatched the Legion Espionage Squad back in time, where they disguised themselves as members of the Metropolis Science Police, poised to act with future Legionnaire Mon-El when required. Similarly, in Smallville, Conner Kent learned his high school science teacher was really Element Lad (*Superman* #697, April 2010; *Adventure Comics* #511, Early May 2010).

While Superboy, Supergirl, Mon-El, and the Legionnaires traveled to New Krypton, the Kandorians were in a panic. Guild affiliations and a strict caste system led to distrust and a distinct lack of cooperation, which hampered Kal-El, Zod, and the Military Guild's efforts to defend the world. As a result, hundreds of Kandorians died needlessly, and Kal-El realized Zod's approach to New Krypton's defense was all wrong. He resigned his commission and once more became Superman. He then accessed Brainiac's ship through a weakness in its forcefield and confronted Brainiac once inside. However, he was quickly weakened by a kryptonite-wielding Lex Luthor.

At the same time, the alien telepath Tellus informed Supergirl that her cousin was in distress, leading Mon-El to fly to his mentor's rescue. Back on board his vessel, Brainiac informed Superman that he was keeping the Man of Steel alive to witness Kandor being recaptured, the Coluan's revenge for Superman making him feel an emotion. However, Superman summoned all his strength and broke free, but was stopped when Lex Luthor threatened to destroy a bottled city with his gun. As Luthor fired a shot, Mon-El arrived and deflected the bullet—the very destiny he felt he escaped the Phantom Zone to accomplish. By this point, Supergirl, Superboy, Chameleon Boy, Matter Eater Lad, and Element Lad had breached Brainiac's vessel just as Brainiac 5 arrived from the future. Although they managed to save the Lanothians, a race of powerful telepaths, Brainiac not only fled with his cities, but had once again reduced Kandor and rebottled it as well, claiming his victory. Superman was weakened by a blast of red solar energy and rescued by a mechanical Brainiac drone that was controlled by the Legionnaire Quislet.

During this time, Zod and his forces managed to reverse engineer Brainiac's equipment and found a way to enlarge themselves and attack Brainiac anew. While Zod and Brainiac fought hand to hand, Luthor's true plan became obvious as he enlarged a bottled city *within* Brainiac's ship, intending to destroy both the vessel and Kandor in the process. When Brainiac emerged from the wreckage of his ship, he found Luthor and confronted him, snapping his neck. But this Luthor had been one of Toyman's android constructions, while the real Luthor was kept safely out of harm's way. Sadly, Kandor had once more suffered many dead and wounded, the city shattered (*Superman: Last Stand of New Krypton* #1–3, May–June 2010; *Supergirl* [fifth series] #51 and *Superman* #698—both May 2010; *Adventure Comics* #513, June 2010).

Superman then returned to New Krypton to find Zod in Military Installation KV-246, buried one mile beneath the planet's surface. The two Kryptonians confronted each other, only to be interrupted when it was learned General Zod had already ordered his military forces to attack Earth. At the same time, Alura was torturing the captured Reactron for intelligence about Project 7734. However, the villain was a plant for General Lane and literally detonated, causing seismic shifts all around the artificial world and destroying it completely. Thousands of Kandorians, including Alura, perished. The devastated and enraged Kryptonians began their war against Earth in earnest. A squadron flew to Mars to clear it of General Lane's Human Defense Corps forces while others flew all around Earth, destroying capital cities and killing countless leaders, statesmen, and citizens. Superman, aided by his allies in the meta-human community, defended Earth. Superboy sent Krypto to the Fortress of Solitude to fetch the Phantom Zone Projector, and together they circled the globe, consigning all the remaining Kryptonians to the re-formed Phantom Zone, which came at the sacrifice of Christopher Kent's ability to remain in the corporeal world. In the end, as was inevitable, the battle came down to Superman versus Zod in the skies over Metropolis. While brutal, the outcome was not in doubt as Kal-El proved once more why he was the World's Greatest Super Hero, besting his father's enemy and returning him to the Phantom Zone. Superman then took off in search of Lois Lane, who had been kidnapped by her sister Lucy and taken to their father in one of his secret bunkers. Once it became clear that his Project 7734 was defeated, General Lane took his own life rather than face a trial and humiliation for his unpardonable crimes. Clark Kent stood beside his wife at the funeral as a new day of peace dawned. The planet—as well as Superman and those he loved—began healing and rebuilding, comforted in the knowledge that their champion had returned to stay for good. While Superman was saddened to find himself once more the Last Son of Krypton, he knew he would never be truly alone as long as his beloved Lois was beside him (*Superman: War of the Supermen* #0–4, June–July 2010).

I. The Women of the Chronicles

1. Relationship with Lois Lane

The Lois Lane of Earth-2 first encountered the Man of Steel when he was the newly hired Clark Kent at the *Daily Star.* Assigned to the same story, they dined and danced that night, but it was clear she had little interest in the mild-mannered newcomer. Instead she fell in love at first sight when she spotted the colorfully clad Superman (*Action Comics* #1, June 1938). Since then, Lois, Clark, and Superman have had one of the most enduring and frustrating romances ever chronicled. While Lois loved Superman, and he seemed to reciprocate those feelings more often than not, she had little use for Clark, going so far as to dupe her colleague repeatedly in an effort to scoop him. "That gal's a natural for getting involved in mischief, but that's just what I like about her," thought Superman (*Action Comics* #27, August 1940).

When not repeatedly rescuing the plucky reporter, he was avoiding her attempts to figure out his real identity, which she persisted in believing was Clark Kent although she could never prove it.

On Earth-2, it took Clark more than a decade to finally propose to Lois. They married but never had children. Instead their love burned brightly until old age eventually claimed her (*Infinite Crisis* #6, May 2006).

In her trademark pillbox hat, the Earth-1 Lois Lane proved more fickle as she pined for Superman but wound up romancing many other men from across space and time. In the end, though, she continued to prefer landing the Action Ace as her spouse and seemed willing to wait.

The post–First Crisis Lois was a more self-

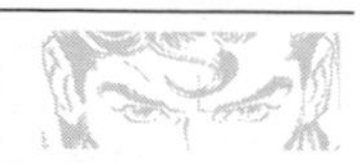

sufficient woman, and while she loved Superman, she was not about to throw herself into danger just for a quick rescue. It took time for Lois and the Man of Steel to admit their feelings for each other, then act on them. Even then, it was Clark Kent who proposed, and it was some time after she accepted that he revealed his true identity to her. He wanted to be sure that Lois could love him for the man he was beneath the charismatic, colorful persona of Superman. While this pleased her, she called off the engagement for a time when she felt Superman was prepared to let her die rather than allow the JOKER to remain at large (*Action Comics* #719–720, March–April 1996).

However, the couple soon reconciled and married, enjoying their life together when the Man of Steel managed to whisk them off to private locations where they could enjoy time alone undisturbed. Lois became Clark's sounding board and conscience, his cheerleader and his taskmaster, helping him keep his priorities in order. As Mrs. Kent, she also consistently helped cover for Clark when duty called for Superman, and the two enjoyed a deep bond that grew stronger each year.

2. Relationship with Lana Lang

They were childhood sweethearts, and it's said that one never forgets one's first love. Clark Kent and Lana Lang grew up as next-door neighbors in Smallville, attending elementary, junior, and senior high school together. While they were best friends, there was never a romantic spark between them—yet Lana's heart was devoted to Superboy. Much like Lois Lane, Lana spent her time trying to prove the Teen of Steel and young Clark were one and the same.

As an adult, the Earth-1 Lana arrived in Metropolis to work at WMET and was immediately a rival to Lois Lane for Superman's affection. She and Lois became close friends while maintaining that rivalry, which could be alternately friendly and fierce. In time, however, Lana recognized that she could never win Superman's heart and moved on, ironically finding romance for a time with Clark.

The post-Crisis Lana loved Clark Kent and was stunned when he revealed his great secret and announced that he was leaving her and Smallville behind. Although they never dated as adults, she carried a constant torch for Clark, despite marrying and later divorcing their mutual friend from Smallville, Pete Ross. Indeed, Lana named her son Clark in honor of her old friend. Lang nevertheless managed to eventually find her own path, briefly running LexCorp when Lex Luthor was ousted and later temporarily working alongside Kent as business editor at the *Daily Planet.*

3. Relationship with Lori Lemaris

While Clark Kent grew up surrounded by attractive girls at Smallville High School, he rarely had a steady girlfriend or passionate romance. That all changed when, while attending Metropolis University, he fell for the wheelchair-bound Lori Lemaris, whose presumably useless legs remained concealed under a blanket at all times. Her mysterious comings and goings, however, aroused Clark's suspicions, and he followed her one day, only to learn that she was actually a mermaid who hailed from the undersea city-state of Atlantis. At that point, it became clear that she could never enter into a long-term relationship with Clark, much as she longed to (*Superman* [first series] #129, May 1959).

Lori's telepathic powers told her Clark's secret and she kept it, becoming a true friend to Superman. While there remained a romantic spark between them, she wound up marrying RONAL, a doctor who saved her life, and she knew that Superman's heart belonged to someone else—Lois Lane.

An iteration of Lemaris was incarnated on the post–First Crisis Earth, and their relationship remained largely unchanged.

4. Relationship with Wonder Woman

Prior to the First Crisis, Superman and Wonder Woman were never anything more than friends and colleagues in the Justice League. After the Crisis, however, the new Wonder Woman who emerged in that reality captivated the Man of Steel's mind when she burst on the scene during a pitched battle between the super heroes and the forces from Apokolips (*Legends* #6, April 1987). The two were drawn to each other but their one attempt at dating proved disastrous (*Action Comics* #600, May 1988), and they agreed to remain friends. Over time, they became incredibly close friends, sharing wisdom that only experience as warriors could bring.

The Infinite Crisis appeared to have altered their relationship so that, while the world saw incredible sexual chemistry between the Amazon Princess and the Man of Steel, they were colleagues and nothing more.

5. Relationships with Other Women

The Earth-1 Superman had several passionate affairs with women other than Lois Lane. A time-traveling Man of Steel journeyed to Krypton and fell for actress LYLA LERROL. Had circumstances been different, the two might well have remained together (*Superman* [first series] #156, October 1962).

On another occasion, exposure to red kryptonite robbed the Man of Steel of his memory and powers, and he was taken in by SALLY SELWYN and her logger father. The two fell in love and wanted to make a life together, but a jealous rival and the return of Clark's memory meant it was destined not to be (*Superman* [first series] #165, November 1963).

The post-Crisis Superman was desired by many women, with Maxima, the queen of Almerac, even coming from her homeworld to Earth to marry him, whether the Man of Steel liked it or not (*Action Comics* #645, September 1989).

J. The Relationship with the Law Enforcement Establishment

For years, Superman worked with all forms of law enforcement, including the police, the U.S. Army, U.S. Navy, the FBI, the Treasury Department, the Secret Service, and several U.S. presidents.

The Earth-2 Superman, early on, was viewed with suspicion by the Metropolis police force (*Action Comics* #6, November 1938; others) and became a particular target for Sergeant CASEY. Fairly quickly, however, the police welcomed his assistance and soon came to rely on it (*Superman* [first series] #17, July–August 1942). Almost every other nation in the world allowed the Man of Steel entry in pursuit of justice.

On Earth-1, Superboy introduced himself to Smallville's police officers as he made his first arrest (*Superman* [first series] #144, April 1961). He worked with several police chiefs, but forged an especially deep and long-lasting bond with DOUGLAS PARKER.

At the United Nations in New York City, the Metropolis Marvel was given a special "golden certificate" granting him unfettered access to enter and leave member countries without a visa and was even authorized to make arrests.

For a brief period, the Metropolis police summoned Superman with a "super-signal," or by means of a large loudspeaker mounted atop the roof of police headquarters (*Superman* [first series] #114, July 1957).

As a member of the various incarnations of the Justice League of America, Superman had additional authority to cross international waters or airspace with the ability to make arrests.

K. The Relationship to the Super Hero Community

1. Justice Society of America

On November 9, 1940, British intelligence asked Earth-2's Flash and Green Lantern to investigate rumors of a possible German invasion. The heroes wound up captured and shipped to Adolf Hitler, who intended to kill them using the mystic Spear of Destiny. They were instead rescued by their fellow super heroes Doctor Fate and Hourman. The rescue and escape prompted President Franklin Roosevelt to suggest that the heroes band together. The heroes consented and the Justice Society of America was formed, with Superman and Batman accepting honorary membership (*All Star Comics* #3, Winter 1940; origin revealed in *DC Special* #29, August–September 1977).

In the wake of America's introduction into World War II, President Roosevelt beseeched all of America's costumed crime fighters to help defend the country's shores as the All-Star Squadron (*All-Star Squadron* #1, September 1981; others). The JSA itself, whose members served jointly in their own team and the All-Stars, was renamed the Justice Battalion of America for the duration of the war (*All Star Comics* #11, June–July 1942). Though a participant in All-Star Squadron adventures, Superman was a comparative nonpresence with the 1940s JSA save for a case in which he substituted for Johnny Thunder (*All Star Comics* #36, August–September 1947).

By the early 1950s, Communist paranoia gripped the country and the remaining members of the JSA chose to disband rather than reveal their identities to Congress's Joint Un-American Activities Committee. By this point, only Superman, Batman, and Wonder Woman still possessed the necessary clout and respect to remain active as super heroes without government interference (*Adventure Comics* #466, December 1979).

The Earth-2 Superman eventually went back to work with the JSA until he entered semi-

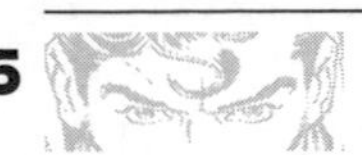

The Justice League of America

retirement, with his cousin Power Girl acting as his replacement.

2. Justice League of America

On Earth-1, the arrival of combating aliens led seven of the planet's super heroes—Superman, Batman, Wonder Woman, Flash, Green Lantern, Martian Manhunter, and Aquaman—to band together for the first time. After the threat was ably handled, they agreed that remaining united made sense, and so the Justice League of America was born (*The Brave and the Bold* #28, February-March 1960; *Justice League of America* [first series] #9, February 1962).

In the wake of the First Crisis, Superman declined an invitation to join the young JLA, believing himself to already be overcommitted (*Action Comics* #650, February 1990). The Man of Steel subsequently fought alongside the team during an invasion from the planet Appellax (*JLA: Year One* #11–12, November–December 1998) and briefly agreed to serve as a full member, stepping back to reservist status following the team's defeat of the intelligent ape super-criminal Gorilla Grodd (*JLA: Incarnations* #2, August 2001). Nonetheless, Superman behaved as a full member in everything but name as the years passed, participating in scores of adventures. In the reality that formed following Infinite Crisis, Superman was once again regarded as a founding member of the League (*Justice League of America* [second series] #0, September 2006).

For an overview of Superman's relationship with his sometime ally–sometime opponent, the Dark Knight, see Batman.

3. Metropolis Allies

Given the demands on Superman's time, Metropolis was periodically left unwatched—and criminals always seemed to take advantage of the opportunities presented at those times. Eventually, however, the post-Crisis Superman gained several allies who chose to base themselves in his city.

The first of these was Matrix, the artificial lifeform from the Pocket Universe who filled in for Superman when he exiled himself in space. Upon his return, Matrix became Supergirl and fought crime by the Man of Steel's side for a time. In the wake of Superman's death, John Henry Irons emerged as Steel, working alongside the Cyborg Superman, the Eradicator, and the Metropolis Kid, the Kon-El/Conner Kent version of Superboy. Steel left for Washington and, later, New Jersey for a time after Superman's resurrection, but then permanently relocated to Metropolis to assist the Man of Steel as needed.

Rose Forrest fought the One Hundred as the Thorn and remained an active crime fighter in Metropolis. The Birds of Prey, led by Oracle (the former Batgirl, Barbara Gordon), briefly worked out of Metropolis, aiding Superman. The S.T.A.R. Corps and the Supermen of America also briefly worked to fill in for the Metropolis Marvel on occasion.

In the post–First Crisis reality, Superman's cousin Kara Zor-El actually arrived on Earth later than planned. In time, she came to live and work in Metropolis, forging her own identity and career—but she was always there when Superman needed her.

After the Infinite Crisis, when Superman left Earth to spend time on New Krypton, he departed secure in the knowledge that the city was in good hands. Not only was Supergirl patrolling the skies, but the newly established Science Police was led by the Guardian, and Superman personally asked Mon-El to perform his duties under the tutelage of the Guardian and Steel.

L. The Counterparts

1. Potential Future Versions

Glimpses of numerous potential futures on various parallel worlds have been documented, showing that the legacy of Superman would endure.

In one possible future, Clark Kent and Lois Lane married, becoming the parents of a daughter named Laura (*Superman Family* #200, March-April 1980) and a younger son named Jorel. Kalel Kent, the Superman of 2020, was the grandson of the Superman who fought crime in the floating city of New Metropolis (*Superman* [first series] #354, December 1980). The original Man of Steel was still alive, but superannuated, surviving along with his son Superman II (Jorel). The grandson adopted multiple secret identities to keep his real life private. He was Jon Hudson, a computer traffic controller, and Lewis Parker, a professional tennis player, among other unrecorded personae.

Several chronicles recorded the exploits of a Superman who operated in a thirtieth century apart from the one he visited as a member of the Legion of Super-Heroes. Following the original template, that Man of Steel was secretly a mild-mannered telenews reporter for the *Daily Solar System* named Craig King (*Action Comics* #215, April 1956). He did not possess inherent superpowers but replicated the legendary hero's powers in 2956 through technology provided by scientists who felt a crime fighter was needed.

A different thirtieth-century Superman appeared in the chronicles, operating from 2965 to 2967. He was Klar Ken T5477, Ultra-News reporter for the *Daily Interplanetary News* and a descendant of the original Kryptonian. He was also a deputized agent on behalf of the Federation of Planets. He frequently opposed a yellow-skinned alien menace named Muto (*Superman* [first series] #181, November 1965; others). In time, Klar Ken allied himself with Bron Wayn E7705, the son of Batman XIX (*World's Finest Comics* #166, May 1967).

This future was altered slightly by the First Crisis and featured Klar Ken 5477, who debuted in 2999 (*Superman* [second series] #136, July 1998). The son of the eighteenth Superman, who died when apprehending his era's Luthor, he had a younger sister named Kara and enjoyed a super-heroic career for a time before confronting Muto. His future also had incarnations of Bat-

man, Aquaman, Hawkman, Wonder Woman, a green-skinned Captain Marvel, the Flash, Green Arrow, Ms. Miracle, Starman, and the Green Lantern Corps.

A future time line culminating in the 853rd century detailed a Dynasty of Supermen beginning with Kal-El and extending through the years. Superman II was Jorel Kent (*Superman* [first series] #354, December 1980).

Superman Secundus operated in the twenty-first century and became the prime hero after the original Superman left Earth and was unseen for sixty-eight millennia (*Superman: The Man of Tomorrow* #1,000,000, November 1998).

Superman III also operated in the twenty-first century, the grandson of the original and son of Superman II. He was credited with curing cancer (*Superman* [first series] #181, November 1965).

Dave Kent was the fourth Superman, most likely working in the twenty-second century (*Action Comics* #338, June 1966). A fifth hero was never named, but a memorial statue existed (*Superman* [first series] #181, November 1965).

A century later, Superman VI partnered now and then with the sixth Batman (*World's Finest Comics* #166, May 1967). The seventh Superman was Kanton K-73, whose identity was inadvertently exposed by his infant son (*Action Comics* #338, June 1966).

By the twenty-fourth century, Superman VIII had begun his crime-fighting career and was the inventor of the world's first dependable artificial eye (*Superman* [second series] #136, July 1998). He was followed in the chronicles by Superman IX, who worked with the twenty-fifth-century incarnation of the Justice League to battle the artificial intelligence Solaris. Apparently, at this point, there had not been a Superman based on Earth for more than a century (*Superman: The Man of Tomorrow* #1,000,000, November 1998).

The next mentioned Superman was the twelfth version, whose genes were altered in the Pollution War, which included the use of atomic weapons. He and all descendants were vulnerable to contaminated seawater (*Superman* [first series] #181, November 1965; *Superman* [second series] #137, August 1998).

Superman XV and the Batman XV were known to have worked together in their era, which may have been the twenty-eighth century (*World's Finest Comics* #166, May 1967). The Superman and Justice League of the early twenty-ninth century and the time-traveling Legion of Super-Heroes had another encounter with Solaris (*Superman: The Man of Tomorrow* #1,000,000, November 1998).

Superman XVIII in the thirtieth century battled the telepathic threat of Muto and worked with Batman XIX (*Action Comics* #338, June 1966). He died while battling Luthor (*Superman* [second series] #136, July 1998). His son Superman XIX was Klar Ken T5477 and most frequently opposed Muto (*Superman* [first series] #181, November 1965; others). He was credited with being the founder of the Justice Alliance.

The chronicles next recorded a Superman XXX in the mid-thirty-fifth century (*Superboy* [first series] #120, April 1965). There was also the Superman of the thirty-eighth century, credited with rehabilitating Solaris (*The Adventures of Superman* #1,000,000, November 1998).

The sixty-seventh century's Man of Tomorrow had evolved to have additional powers after he wed Zrfff's Queen Gzntplzk (*DC One Million* #1, November 1998). The next hero in the records was the Superman of the 250th century, with no details revealed (*Superman: The Man of Tomorrow* #1,000,000, November 1998).

The Superman of the 322nd century formed an alliance with the descendants of Lex Luthor (*Action Comics* #1,000,000, November 1998). Forty-two centuries later, there remained a Superman (*Superman: The Man of Tomorrow* #1,000,000, November 1998).

The Superman of the 505th century reprogrammed Solaris at the cost of his life (*Superman: The Man of Tomorrow* #1,000,000, November 1998; others). One of his descendants in an unspecified era worked with the Justice League of the Atom (*Superman: The Man of Tomorrow* #1,000,000, November 1998). Another served as a member of the Pancosmic Justice Jihad.

Superman Prime in 70,001 returned to the solar system and took up residence in the sun until AD 85,271. The 853rd century's Man of Steel was a member of Justice Legion A (*JLA* #23, October 1998). The dynasty continued with the birth of a son (*DC One Million 80-Page Giant,* August 1999). After that era, the chronicles showed a Superman operating in the Fifth-Dimensional world of Zrfff.

2. Imaginary Story/Elseworlds Versions

Before the Crisis on Infinite Earths, there were countless parallel universes, and in almost every one there was some version of Superman, usually appearing with variations of his friends and foes. After the Crisis, there was only one positive-matter universe and one anti-matter universe, each with a version of the hero. The Infinite Crisis split the positive universe into fifty-two parallel universes, and again most had some version of Superman. Below are highlights of the many incarnations of the Last Son of Krypton.

Pre-Crisis Versions

- Earth-2 was the first Superman, followed by Earth-1's Superman. The Earth-3 Superman was Ultraman, who gained a new power every time he encountered kryptonite. On Earth-D, Superman was a black-skinned adventurer.

- Earth-Prime never had a hero until Clark Kent became Superboy and was one of the handful to actually survive the Crisis.
- Earth-19: Home of a married Clark and Lois Kent, the parents of super-twins Larry and Carole (*Superman's Girl Friend, Lois Lane* #19, August 1960, and #20, October 1960; others).
- Earth-20: An Earth without a Superman that was visited by Earth-1's Man of Steel in an attempt at a lifestyle change (*Superman's Girl Friend, Lois Lane* #20, October 1960).
- Earth-25: Home of a married Superman and Lois Lane, the parents of super-son Larry (*Superman's Girl Friend, Lois Lane* #25, May 1961, and #39, February 1963).
- Earth-26: A world on which Superman married Lana Lang and endowed her with superpowers (*Superman's Girl Friend, Lois Lane* #26, July 1961).
- Earth-34: An Earth where Lois Lane and Lex Luthor married and became the parents of a son who ultimately married Superman and Lana Lang's daughter (*Superman's Girl Friend, Lois Lane* #34, July 1962, and #46, January 1964).
- Earth-36: A world where Lana Lang left the twentieth century to marry one of Superman's descendants after the present-day Superman and Lois married and became the parents of super-twins (*Superman's Girl Friend, Lois Lane* #36, October 1962).
- Earth-39: A world devastated by pollution and war peopled by, among others, Jonathan and (a non-superpowered) Clark Kent (*The New Adventures of Superboy* #39, March 1983).
- Earth-43: An Earth on which Superman and Luthor died in battle unbeknownst to the general public. A replacement Superman was groomed in Kandor, but he eventually traded places with the Kal-El of Earth-215. The latter's Lois Lane had been killed, leading Kal-El to propose to the Lois on this world. Criminal counterparts of the Legion of Super-Heroes existed in the thirtieth century of this world's time line (*Superman's Girl Friend, Lois Lane* #43, August 1963; *Superboy* [first series] #117, December 1964; *Superman* [first series] #215, April 1969).
- Earth-47: A world whose greatest heroine was Krypton Girl, alias Lois Lane, the last survivor of the doomed planet (*Superman's Girl Friend, Lois Lane* #47, February 1964).
- Earth-51: A world on which Superman married Lois Lane, Lana Lang, and Lori Lemaris, all of whom died soon after their respective weddings (*Superman's Girl Friend, Lois Lane* #51, August 1964).
- Earth-64: A world where concert pianist Lex Luthor posed as Lexo and married Lois Lane before his death (*Superman's Girl Friend, Lois Lane* #64–65, April–May 1966).
- Earth-89: A world where Lois Lane and Bruce Wayne married and had a son (*Superman's Girl Friend, Lois Lane* #89, January 1969).
- Earth-91: Home of a blind Lois Lane and a disfigured Superman who married and became parents of a super-daughter (*Superman's Girl Friend, Lois Lane* #91, April 1969).
- Earth-95: A world on which Jor-El, Lara, and Kal-El sought refuge after Krypton's explosion; they eventually abandoned it for Krypton II (*Superboy* [first series] #95, March 1962).
- Earth-116: Home of a Superboy whose costume's colors were the reverse of his Earth-1 counterpart's (*Superboy* [first series] #116, October 1964).
- Earth-117: An Earth on which Jor-El, Lara, and Kal-El escaped Krypton's explosion. Capes were a status symbol on this world (*Superman's Pal, Jimmy Olsen* #117, January 1969).
- Earth-124: An Earth where Superboy portrayed Clark Kent as a delinquent (*Superboy* [first series] #124, October 1965).
- Earth-132: An Earth whose astronauts accidentally landed on the planet Krypton, home of the hero Futuro (*Superman* [first series] #132, October 1959).
- Earth-134: An Earth that was abandoned by Superboy on the day of his debut when red kryptonite temporarily turned him into a super-

Superman of Earth-2

criminal (*Superboy* [first series] #134, December 1966).

- Earth-136: An Earth without a Batman. Its population included Bruce (Superman) Wayne and a Lois Lane double named Vicki Vale (*World's Finest Comics* #136, September 1963).
- Earth-146: A world where Earth-1's Superman prevented the sinking of Atlantis and helped evacuate Krypton's citizens to Earth, among other feats (*Superman* [first series] #146, July 1961).
- Earth-148: A world characterized by heroic counterparts of Clayface, Luthor, and Mirror Master, and criminal versions of Batman, Flash, Superman, and Wonder Woman. A unique quality of this planet's PARADISE ISLAND caused visitors from other parallel worlds to revert to childhood for the duration of their stay (*World's Finest Comics* #148, March 1965; *The Flash* [first series] #174, November 1967; others).
- Earth-149: A world on which Superman was slain by Lex Luthor (*Superman* [first series] #149, November 1961).
- Earth-153: An Earth whose Batman, ultimately killed by Luthor, had wrongly blamed Superman for the deaths of his parents (*World's Finest Comics* #153, November 1965).
- Earth-154: Home of a married Clark Kent and Lois Lane, and Bruce Wayne and Kathy Kane, each couple having heroic sons (*World's Finest Comics* #154, December 1965, and #157, February 1966).
- Earth-159: An Earth that was destroyed in an explosion. Its sole survivor, Lois Lane, was rocketed to Krypton (*Superman* [first series] #159, February 1963).
- Earth-162: A utopian Earth whose miracles came courtesy of an experiment that split Superman into two beings: Superman Red and Superman Blue (*Superman* [first series] #162, July 1963).
- Earth-166: A world whose Superman was the father of twins, one with powers and one without (*Superman* [first series] #166, January 1964).
- Earth-167: Home of Lex (Superman) Luthor and Clark (Batman) Kent (*World's Finest Comics* #167, June 1967).
- Earth-170: A world where Lex Luthor traveled to Krypton's past in an unsuccessful attempt to prevent Jor-El and Lara from marrying (*Superman* [first series] #170, July 1964).
- Earth-172: A world where Bruce Wayne was adopted by the Kents and became Clark's brother. As Batman, he relocated to the Legion of Super-Heroes' thirtieth century (*World's Finest Comics* #172, December 1967).
- Earth-175: Home of Clark and Lex (Luthor) Kent, adopted sons of Jonathan and Martha Kent. As adults, Lex died saving Superman's life (*Superman* [first series] #175, February 1965).
- Earth-178: Home of a Superman who lost his powers and adopted the costumed identity of the Nova (*World's Finest Comics* #178, September 1968, and #180, November 1968).
- Earth-183: An Earth on which Kal-El was raised by apes and ultimately became known as Karkan (*Superboy* [first series] #183, March 1972; others).

- Earth-184: A world whose Robin was caretaker of a mentally impaired Batman and a blind Superman (*World's Finest Comics* #184, May 1969).
- Earth-192: A world where Lois Lane died, survived by her husband Clark Kent and son Clark, Junior (*Superman* [first series] #192, January 1967, and #194, February 1967).
- Earth-200: Home of Hyperman (Kal-El) and Superman (Knor-El), champions of a KRYPTONOPOLIS that survived Krypton's explosion thanks to Brainiac's having bottled it instead of Kandor (*Superman* [first series] #200, October 1967).
- Earth-215: A world where a married Superman and Lois Lane became parents of a daughter, Laney. After Lois's death, Superman and Laney moved to Earth-43, where he married that world's Lois while its Superman moved to Earth-215 (*Superman* [first series] #215, April 1969).
- Earth-216: A world where Superman and Batman each had namesake offspring who often operated as the Super-Sons (*World's Finest Comics* #215, December 1972–January 1973).
- Earth-224: Home of a married Superman and Lois Lane, whose infant son was temporarily transformed into a super-genius (*Superman* [first series] #224, February 1970).
- Earth-230: Home of a Kryptonian Luthor, who became Superman on Earth and fought the villainous Clark Kent (*Superman* [first series] #230–231, October–November 1970).
- Earth-399: A world on which Superman died and was replaced twice by clones, both of whom were also killed in battle (*Action Comics* #399, April 1971).
- Earth-404: An Earth whose Superboy lost his powers at the age of sixteen during a battle with Luthor. As adults, Clark Kent and Lana Lang were married (*Superman* [first series] #404, February 1985).
- Earth-410: Home of a widowed Superman, whose wife Krysalla left him with a son, Krys (*Action Comics* #410, March 1972).
- Earth-417: An Earth whose Superman was raised on Mars before relocating as an adult (*Superman* [first series] #417, April 1985).
- Earth-423: An Earth whose Superman fought a final battle with his greatest foes and vanished from public view (*Superman* [first series] #423 and *Action Comics* #583—both September 1986).

Post-Crisis Versions

- In the Pocket Universe, a sliver of time preserved by the Time Trapper, Earth-1 continued to exist with a Superboy, who wound up sacrificing his life to save others.
- In the Anti-Matter Universe of Qward, Superman's doppelgänger was Ultraman, who was not a native of Krypton.

For a brief time, it was chronicled that all realities existed beyond the two universes in something called Hypertime. The myriad realties chronicled during this period include:

- Earth-898: A world where Kal-El's rocket landed near an Amish couple who raised him in their

ways. He did not arrive as Superman until well after the age of the super hero began (*JLA: The Nail* #1–3, 1998; *JLA: Another Nail* #1–3, 2004).

- Earth-1198: The rocket from Krypton was taken by Darkseid before it could reach Earth, and Kal-El was raised on Apokolips (*Superman: The Dark Side* #1–3, 1998).
- Earth-1004: Kal-El arrived in England as opposed to America, and he was raised by a very different set of parents. His heroic exploits were fodder for a scandal-hungry tabloid press (*Superman: True Brit,* 2004).
- Earth-354: When Kal-El was found by Thomas and Martha Wayne, he was named Bruce. After he saw his parents killed by a common criminal, he dedicated his life to fighting crime as the powerful Batman (*Superman: Speeding Bullets,* 1993).
- Earth-1968: As Earth faced destruction, Jonathan and Martha Kent sent their infant son Clark to Krypton. There he was raised by Jor-El and Lara, named Kal-El, and became a hero after obtaining one of the Green Lantern power rings (*Superman: The Last Son of Earth,* 2000).
- Earth-990: Teenager Clark Kent resented his parents for naming him after a comic book hero—but when his own superpowers manifested themselves, his world changed (*Superman: Secret Identity* #1–4, 2004).
- Earth-3839: Superman proved ageless and he became the patriarch of a dynasty of children who possessed varying degrees of superpowers. Along with Batman's children, they intermarried and carried their legendary names through the years (*Superman & Batman: Generations* #1–4, 1993; *Superman & Batman: Generations II* #1–4, 2001–2002; *Superman & Batman: Generations III* #1–12, March 2003–February 2004).
- Earth-901: Salden, a Kryptonian police officer, was accidentally transported to Earth. In its lighter gravity, he possessed super-strength and super-speed, and was able to fly thanks to a technologically advanced harness. He fought crime on Earth because he had little choice, desiring above all to go home (*Just Imagine Stan Lee and John Buscema Creating Superman,* 2001).

Post–Infinite Crisis Versions

- New Earth was the home to the one, true Superman.
- The post–Final Crisis Earth-1 Superman is remarkably similar to the New Earth incarnation, but Krypton was destroyed by something other than geological means. Additionally, he was clearly steered toward using his amazing powers in the service of mankind by Martha Kent, who specifically designed Clark's colorful Superman costume to serve as a symbol of hope. When young Clark asked why the outfit had no mask, she told him that "when people see how powerful you are, all the things you can do, they're going to be terrified . . . unless they can see your face, and see there that you mean them no harm. The mask is what you're going to have to wear the rest of the time" (*Superman: Earth One,* November 2010).
- The post–Final Crisis Earth-2 was a close doppelgänger to the pre–First Crisis Earth-2 but did not have a Superman, although it did possess a Power Girl.
- Earth-3 featured the Crime Syndicate of America's Ultraman. This version was seemingly killed in the Monitor conflict (*52* #52, May 2007; (cameo) *Countdown to Final Crisis* #32, 2007).
- Earth-4's equivalent to Superman was Captain Atom, the atomically powered hero who was once Captain Allen Adam (*Final Crisis: Superman Beyond* #1, October 2008, and #2, March 2009).
- Earth-5's closest approximation of Superman was the magically powered Captain Marvel (*Final Crisis: Superman Beyond* #1, October 2008, and #2, March 2009).
- Earth-8 featured a Herr Superman who was killed by Lord Havok (*Countdown Presents: Lord Havok & the Extremists* #3, February 2008, and #5–6, April–May 2008).
- Earth-9's Superman was an African American who wound up instilling a brutal form of order by conquering his world. At one point, he tried to bring his brand of law and order to New Earth. He was Harvey Dent, sole survivor of a failed program to create meta-humans. Unlike New Earth's hero, this one's powers were not only physical but mental as well (*Tangent Comics/ The Superman* #1, September 1998; others).
- Earth-10 was a world where Germany triumphed during World War II. Its champion was the Overman, a proud member of JL-Axis. Kal-L was raised as Karl Kant when his rocket was found in Czechoslovakia in 1938. The Nazis reverse-engineered the rocket and built weap-

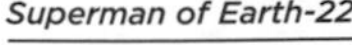

Superman of Earth-22

ons of mass destruction that allowed them to win the war.

- Earth-11 was a world with the genders reversed so the Last Daughter of Krypton was Superwoman.
- Earth-16 hosted a more highly evolved version of Superman who could alter his powers by drawing on various energy sources. Christopher Kent, bald and sporting tattoos, was killed by Monarch during the Monitor conflict in the wake of Infinite Crisis.
- Earth-21 was a world that featured Superman operating since his debut in 1939—but by the 1950s he was purely an agent for the government, doing its bidding during the Cold War until the arrival of the Martian Manhunter heralded a new age of heroism (*DC: The New Frontier* #1, March 2004).
- Earth-22's Superman watched in horror as the Joker killed many people at the Daily Planet Building, including his wife Lois Lane. He exiled himself for a decade, working exclusively as Clark Kent on the family farm in Smallville, Kansas. In that time, the world had grown darker, with heroes and villains battling so frequently that the civilian population couldn't tell criminals from crime fighters. Wonder Woman eventually coaxed Superman back into action, and once more the World's Greatest Super Hero led by example and returned the notion of heroism to a world desperately in need of it. After the Infinite Crisis, he dwelled for a time on New Earth, working with members of the JSA as they dealt with the coming of the would-be god Gog. This Superman was more powerful than the New Earth champion, and kryptonite was merely an irritant (*Kingdom Come* #1, 1996).
- Earth-30 was a world where the rocket from Krypton landed in the Soviet Union; Superman was raised as a Communist. In time, the Red Son rose to rule the country, following the lessons he learned from Joseph Stalin (*Superman: Red Son* #1–3, 2003–2004).
- Earth-31's Superman worked for the federal government. He was opposed by a fifty-year-old Dark Knight, who came out of retirement to free the people from a totalitarian government. This Earth's Superman and Batman battled on the streets of Metropolis despite the respect they held for each other (*Batman: The Dark Knight* graphic novel, 1986).
- Earth-44 was a world of robots, and Superman was a member of the legendary Metal Men, created by Doc Tornado. The events of Final Crisis caused the planet's magnetic field to be altered. The robotic heroes went haywire and attempted to destroy the robot population; ultimately, they were shut down by Luthor and Earth-5's Dr. Sivana (*Final Crisis* #7, March 2009).
- Earth-50's version of Superman was Apollo, a human man whose genes were engineered to absorb solar energy and give him superpowers. He served with the Authority and was married to his partner Midnighter (*Stormwatch* [second series] #4, February 1998). Majestic, the hero from the planet Khera, was also considered a version of Superman in this reality.
- Other versions of Superman existed on unnamed planets. These included an African American incarnation who was also president of the United States (*Final Crisis* #7, March 2009).

SUPERMAN, TOMMY

When Superman legally adopted a twelve-year-old orphan named Tommy, the boy gained the world-famous surname. While the two genuinely grew fond of each other, it became apparent that the schedule maintained by the Man of Steel and his reporter alter ego jeopardized the normal routine the adolescent needed. His safety was also a cause for concern, so the Man of Steel found a new home for Tommy Superman, who joined the family of one of the *Daily Planet*'s Linotype operators (*Superman* [first series] #57, March–April 1949).

SUPERMAN EMERGENCY SQUAD, THE

Despite having Supergirl and Krypto the Super-Dog in addition to the entire Justice League of America to count on, there came times when the Man of Steel still needed assistance. Fortunately, he had an entire city of people more than willing to come to his aid. Within his Arctic Fortress of Solitude, the bottle city of Kandor sat, waiting for the day Superman or Supergirl found a way to restore it to normal size. Over time, through the monitors that the city's residents used to see what was transpiring on their adopted world, it became clear that Superman was in need.

After trials, a handful of men who closely resembled the Man of Steel were selected and trained to act in unison (*Superman's Pal, Jimmy Olsen* #48, October 1960). They were led by captain Don-El (*Superman's Pal, Jimmy Olsen* #60, April 1962); the membership included Van-Zee, who also adventured as Nightwing (*Superman's Girl Friend, Lois Lane* #15, February 1960). After a time, the Lookalike Squad was created, and the physical resemblance requirement was dropped as other physically qualified men were added (*Superman* [first series] #167, February 1964). The Squad, of course, knew Superman's secret identity (*Action Comics* #276, May 1961), as did the rest of the Kandorian populace (*Superman* [first series] #179, August 1965).

Squad members rotated duty shifts, watching a monitor trained just on the Man of Tomorrow. In case of danger, their first course of action was to activate Superman Robots maintained in the Fortress and, failing that, to summon the team using a "siren-alert" and go to work. Both the robots and the Squad were also charged with keeping the Fortress and its contents safe from intruders (*Superman* [first series] #160, April 1963).

When assembled, they took a rocket ship from the city and donned costumes resembling Superman's, although sometimes they operated without the capes (*Superman* [first series] #158, January 1963). There were times when they also wore purple-and-red native outfits (*Superman* [first series] #156, October 1962). They journeyed to the stopper atop the bottle containing the city. A temporary "enlarging gas" was sprayed over the Squad, bringing them from microscopic size to that of beings averaging six inches in height. Wearing special suction cups on their hands and feet, and with their backs against the cork, they pushed until it was freed and the exposure to Earth's lighter gravity and the solar radiation gave the tiny warriors the full array of powers and abilities. With the Squad's frequent activity, Superman finally modified the cork stopper with a doorway allowing "easier exit from the bottle" (*Superman* [first series] #179, August 1965).

The Superman Emergency Squad eventually came to be known as the Super*men* Emergency Squad (*Superman's Pal, Jimmy Olsen* #48, October 1960; others) and later, simply, as the Emergency Squad (*Action Comics* #303, August 1963; others).

Through the years, members aided the Earth-1 Superman in protecting his civilian identity in addition to fighting Mr. Mxyzptlk (*Superman* [first series] #148, October 1961), the team of Lex Luthor and Brainiac (*Superman* [first series] #167, February 1964), and the Superman Revenge Squad

AND WHEN THE TINY KANDORIANS, WHO WERE ORIGINALLY MEN OF KRYPTON, EMERGE INTO EARTH'S ATMOSPHERE, THEY GAIN SUPER-POWERS!
FULL SUPER-SPEED... THERE'S NOT AN INSTANT TO LOSE!

(*Action Comics* #295, December 1962). They also protected him when he was compromised by KRYPTONITE (*Action Comics* #291, August 1962; #293, October 1962; #303, August 1963).

Several times they came to his aid within Kandor itself, such as the time he was a captive and Squad members Van-Zee and THAN-OL joined JIMMY OLSEN to save him (*Superman* [first series] #158, January 1963).

On the world after the CRISIS ON INFINITE EARTHS, the Kandorian Emergency Squad worked to police the city, not aid the Man of Steel. Cerizah, sister to CERITAK, led the team, which did once assist Superman during a battle with the CYBORG SUPERMAN (*Superman: The Man of Steel* #100, May 2000).

SUPERMAN ISLAND

When METROPOLIS UNIVERSITY's Professor Vanley concluded that "KRYPTONITE would yield perpetual atomic power," the Man of Steel created an island off the coast of METROPOLIS and then filled it with the deadly mineral that was once his homeworld. As the experiments continued on the island shaped like Superman, Vanley concluded that the alien radiation would actually crumble and destroy any generator, making it an impractical energy resource. In response, Superman lifted the artificial island and hurled it into outer space (*Action Comics* #224, January 1957).

Superman Island later returned to Earth's orbit, its kryptonite reserves coveted by the crime organization known as the H.I.V.E. Superman discovered that the landmass was now inhabited by aliens known as the Krell who'd learned to harness kryptonite as a power source. Informed that their stores were depleted, the Man of Steel sent the Krell and Superman Island through a space warp toward a planet that the homeless aliens could colonize (*Action Comics* #513, November 1980).

Years later, Carl Draper (soon to be known as the MASTER JAILER) designed a maximum-security prison that, to his dismay, was dubbed Superman Island by the media after the hero added a device allowing the prison to float (*Superman* [first series] #331, January 1979).

SUPERMANIUM

A chemist once publicly theorized that a "super-hard" element existed but was yet to be discovered. James Harvey Thorben urged the SUPER-SAVED CLUB to find that element, which he said would be "extremely valuable for all sorts of industrial purposes." The men got to work, agreeing among themselves the new element would be named supermanium in honor of their hero. They managed to locate the newest element in a remote mountain region and found a way to refine the super-dense material. While they labored, shattering machinery, Superman secretly visited the mine, took some ore, and refined it with his amazing abilities so as not to spoil their surprise. The Man of Steel allowed the members to think they managed the impossible and present the refined metal to him with its new name (*World's Finest Comics* #41, July–August 1949).

Later, he created a vault from supermanium to hold METROPOLIS's famous RADIUM Institute's priceless radium stockpile, which had been targeted by LEX LUTHOR. When the criminal scientist was apprehended, Superman fashioned prison bars from the ore (*Superman* [first series] #68, January–February 1951). At a later time, he also formed a "mighty cage" from the metal to trap BRAINIAC on the prison world of KRONIS (*Superman* [first series] #167, February 1964). The android from COLU incorrectly identified the substance as being "named after Superman because it was forged by him from the heart of a mighty star!"

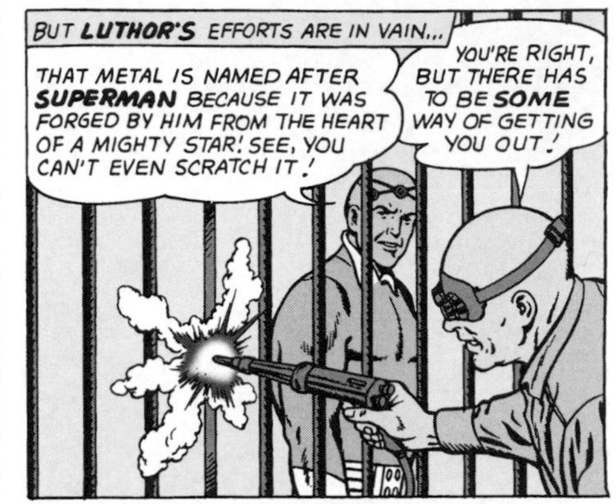

BUT LUTHOR'S EFFORTS ARE IN VAIN...
THAT METAL IS NAMED AFTER SUPERMAN BECAUSE IT WAS FORGED BY HIM FROM THE HEART OF A MIGHTY STAR! SEE, YOU CAN'T EVEN SCRATCH IT!
YOU'RE RIGHT, BUT THERE HAS TO BE SOME WAY OF GETTING YOU OUT!

Superman also used the miraculous metal to create fine wires that enabled him to control gigantic replicas of mythical monsters as if they were colossal marionettes (*Action Comics* #289, June 1962). Later, a cage of supermanium was used to hold the DNALIEN known as ANGRY CHARLIE (*Superman's Pal, Jimmy Olsen* #150, June 1972).

Its last recorded use was to craft the SUPERMOBILE during a battle with the powerful android AMAZO (*Action Comics* #481, March 1978).

SUPERMAN, JUNIOR

When Superman took in JOHNNY KIRK, he gave him the name Superman, Junior.

SUPERMAN LAND

Considered "the most colossal, super stupendous amusement park in the world," this theme park was designed to re-create and celebrate the Man of Steel's accomplishments, honoring him and his allies. Visitors first glimpsed the park when they saw a gigantic statue of Superman standing guard over the main entrance, holding aloft a giant globe emblazoned with the park's name.

Park attendees were treated to the "rocket room," where 3-D films and other special effects enabled youngsters to experience the thrill of a make-believe journey through outer space to the planet KRYPTON. Or they could board the "Krypton-Earth Express," which led them through liftoff, a meteor swarm, and other outer-space adventures like the "Sargasso Sea of Space" until they arrived at a planet of "unearthly beauty [that] seems to loom before them . . ."

There was a re-creation of the *DAILY PLANET*, filled with wax dummies of editor PERRY WHITE and reporters LOIS LANE, JIMMY OLSEN, and CLARK KENT. Another building featured a tribute to the Man of Steel's amazing abilities, allowing audiences to see what it felt like to heft great weights or leap a tall building. There was a Hall of Trophies that was a gift shop; a Cartoon Festival theater; a shooting gallery with steel dummies dressed as Superman; a local branch of the post office; a merry-go-round where people could ride Supermen in lieu of horses; and a colossal stadium for performances, including a re-creation of Krypton's destruction (*Action Comics* #210, November 1955).

SUPER MANOR

A simple mansion became the Super Manor when the town of MAPLEVILLE vied to call itself the Man of Steel's hometown. Superman temporarily settled in the small northwestern burg, but the people came to regret the decision when the town was overrun by tourists gawking and trying to glimpse their famous resident (*Action Comics* #179, April 1953).

SUPERMAN MUSEUM, THE

The Superman Museum, located in the heart of METROPOLIS, was founded through the efforts of famed explorer STEFAN ANDRIESSEN, who had accumulated dozens of Superman-related artifacts (*Action Comics* #164, January 1952). Outside the building was a statue of Superman sculpted from an asteroid that the Man of Steel prevented from striking the city (*Superman* [first series] #286, April 1975).

Given Superman's extraterrestrial origins, the Hall of Planets included rooms devoted to each world in the solar system as well as planets such as KRYPTON (*Superman* [first series] #127, February 1959). The Jules Verne Museum of Extraterrestrial Artifacts boasted doors carved from Almeraci tetelwood (*Superman* [first series] #653, August 2006).

Janitor JOE MEACH worked here and was accidentally transformed into the COMPOSITE SUPERMAN (*World's Finest Comics* #142, June 1964).

At one time, the ONE HUNDRED dared to operate within the museum's confines until they were discovered by BLACK LIGHTNING (*World's Finest* #258, August–September 1979).

SUPERMAN RED/ SUPERMAN BLUE

On one of the myriad parallel Earths, a malfunctioning "brain-evolution machine" in Superman's FORTRESS OF SOLITUDE accidentally transformed the Man of Steel into identical twin beings. One was miraculously attired in a blue Superman costume and the other in a red version, each endowed with a super-intellect one hundred times as powerful as the original man.

Seeing this as a blessing, not a curse, Superman Red and Superman Blue used their new condition to travel the world of Earth-162, accomplishing the many great deeds that a single hero never had time for. They also re-created KRYPTON with topographic precision while finding a way to alter the atomic structure of KRYPTONITE, rendering the mineral harmless to all. Additionally, they restored KANDOR to its proper size and found a water world that LORI LEMARIS and the citizens of ATLANTIS could call their own. They then teamed to create

an "anti-evil ray" that eradicated all manner of crime and warfare. The reformed Lex Luthor found a cure for disease, which was added to the world's water supply.

Once utopia had been achieved, the twins decided it was time to look after their personal needs. Blue proposed to Lana Lang while Red asked Lois Lane to be his wife. Inspired, Jimmy Olsen finally proposed to Lucy Lane. The couples had a triple wedding and thought they would live happily ever after, with Red and Lois migrating to New Krypton while Blue and Lana stayed to look after Earth (*Superman* [first series] #162, July 1963).

Another story told of the time Terra-Man found a piece of red kryptonite in space. He brought it back to Earth-1 and decided to partner with Lex Luthor. They lured the Man of Steel into the open, where he was exposed to the unpredictable effects of the rock. Superman was split into Superman Red and Superman Blue. Two heroes was too much for the villains, so they fled and regrouped. Luthor found a way to tap magical energy and used that, since both Metropolis Marvels would be susceptible to the supernatural forces. During the battle, Lois Lane was seriously injured by the magic, but Superman Red's love for her helped save her life. As the red k effects ended, Superman captured Luthor (*Superman Spectacular,* 1982).

After the events of the Crisis on Infinite Earths, Superman began to experience fluctuations in how he processed solar radiation for his amazing powers. At first, he thought this was a natural evolution as his Kryptonian physique adapted to the sun's rays (*Superman* [second series] #122, April 1997). Instead of leveling off, though, things grew increasingly erratic, resulting in the Man of Steel actually phasing in and out of existence. Emil Hamilton constructed a blue-and-white containment suit that allowed the energies to remain intact, effectively turning the Man of Steel into the Man of Electricity.

The new form altered his abilities, letting him tap the full electromagnetic spectrum and observe disruptions within Earth's electromagnetic field. He was able to expel electrical discharges as a form of energy and could suddenly pass through solid objects. In exchange, he seemed to lose many of his other vision-based abilities, and his mighty strength was diminished.

Things grew more complicated when the Cyborg Superman laid a trap that resulted in the hero splitting into two electrical beings, Superman Red and Superman Blue, identical in every way save for the color of their energy forms (*Superman Red/Superman Blue,* February 1998). While both considered themselves the original, subtle differences began to emerge: Superman Blue was more of a thinker and tactician, for instance, while Superman Red was prone to act first, thinking along the way, therefore coming across as more decisive. As they adventured together and apart, their cumulative experiences led to them disagreeing more than they agreed, and both concluded that merging was not a preferred option.

Of course, both men loved Lois Lane, who was bewildered by the changes to her beloved. Their bickering and fighting over her, without once soliciting her opinion, caused her to toss them both out of her apartment, wanting nothing to do with either.

Seeking a solution among the Kryptonian technology at the Fortress of Solitude, the Supermen encountered Obsession and then Maxima, with the women actually fighting over the men (*Superman: The Man of Tomorrow* #10, Winter 1998).

When the Millennium Guard broke out of Project Cadmus one day, Superman Red tried to corral them before they could find the Medallion of the Damned, while Superman Blue assisted the traveling Jimmy Olsen and his friend Misa (*Superman* [second series] #133, March 1998; *The Adventures of Superman* #556, April 1998).

When the Medallion was obtained and the colossal trio called the Millennium Giants emerged, it took both Supermen plus the Justice League of America to help stop their global threat. During the battle, Superman Red was mortally wounded and Superman Blue decided to merge with his combative twin to save his life. A single being once more, Superman cleaned up the aftermath of the battle and set out to rebuild his life (*Superman: The Man of Steel* #78–79; *Superman* [second series] #134–135; *Action Comics* #744; *Steel* #50; *Supergirl* [fourth series] #20; *Aquaman* [third series] #43—all April–May 1998).

Superman returned to his traditional look, both physically and in his traditional uniform, without ever fully understanding what had caused him to shift from an electrical form to a human one (*Superman Forever* #1, June 1998).

SUPERMAN REVENGE SQUAD, THE

When Superboy toppled tyrants ruling Wexr II, the deposed leaders banded together to seek vengeance as the Superboy Revenge Squad. They made repeated attempts to destroy the Teen of Steel and his adopted planet, Earth.

Over time, their attempts stopped and the boy became a man. Later, the revised Superman Revenge Squad once more tried to crush the hero for having repeatedly thwarted their attempts to subjugate peaceful planets and dominate the universe (*Action Comics* #286–287, March–April 1962).

The renewed attacks increased in frequency as the aliens took advantage of the knowledge that the Man of Steel was also Clark Kent (*Action Comics* #286, March 1962). The methods they used to gain their vengeance varied from brutish attacks to more psychological warfare including using kryptonite to induce nightmares (*Action Comics* #286, March 1962), or hypnosis to ruin Superman's heroic reputation (*Action Comics* #295, December 1962). Once, they tried to trap him in the ruins of Metropolis in a potential future one million years hence (*Action Comics* #300, May 1963).

While they added members of other races that also hated the Man of Steel, they eventually stopped wearing hooded outfits and adopted deeply colored versions of Superman's own costume, complete with the S-shield made of kryptonite, and shaved their heads in tribute to Lex Luthor. Squad members plotted their revenge in the Hall of Hate, which featured statues commemorating the members who had died failing to kill the Man of Steel. Their space vehicles were emblazoned with a broken S on their hulls. They even spawned a Batman Revenge Squad, partnering to destroy the galaxy's best-known crime-fighting duo (*World's Finest Comics* #175, May 1968).

The only known female member of the Squad was Illena, also referred to as agent X9831Q. She wore a cap made from the head of the ancient monster known as the Medusa, which she hid beneath a turban and used as a weapon. Illena came to Earth to seduce Superman, breaking the hearts of rivals Lois Lane and Lana Lang and getting close enough to kill the hero. In the end, Lois discovered the ruse and used the cap to turn the alien murderer herself into a stone figure (*Superman's Girl Friend, Lois Lane* #52, October 1964).

After the Revenge Squad's attempted murder of Supergirl, Superman took the battle to them, infiltrating their number as a lizard-man named Vlatuu. Suspecting the truth, the Squad planted a post-hypnotic suggestion in "Vlatuu" that he kill himself, creating a situation in which the Man of

Steel nearly devised a means of murdering himself (*Superman* [first series] #365–368, November 1981–February 1982).

It was the Squad that sent Superman through the dimensions, landing on Earth-Prime and encountering Superboy-Prime for the first time (*DC Comics Presents* #87, November 1985).

On the Earth formed in the wake of the Crisis on Infinite Earths, Morgan Edge formed a cadre of Superman's deadliest foes under the banner of the Superman Revenge Squad, framing Lex Luthor as their leader (*The Adventures of Superman* #543, February 1997). The team included Maxima, following her attempts at being a hero, as well as Barrage, Riot, Misa, and Anomaly. With the Queen of Almerac in charge, the dysfunctional group could barely contain themselves in order to carry out plans to wreck Metropolis and pin the blame on Luthor. Riot also tinkered with the psi-helmet Edge was using, letting the villains hear the magnate's thoughts. The team broke apart fairly quickly (*Superman: The Man of Steel* #65 and *Action Comics* #730—both February 1997).

Edge tried again shortly after Barrage escaped from Stryker's Island Penitentiary, aided by the Parasite. Rock and Baud were also recruited for the new team, with Edge being upfront about his identity and motivations. Unfortunately, this incarnation was no more successful and self-destructed. Edge fled, once more planting evidence implicating Luthor (*Action Comics* #736; *Man of Steel* #71; *Superman* [second series] #127—all August 1997).

When General Zod arrived from the Phantom Zone and threatened New Earth, formed during the Infinite Crisis, Superman joined a similar squad to save Earth. This version included Metallo, Parasite, Luthor, and Bizarro (*Action Comics Annual* #11, 2008).

SUPERMAN ROBOTS

The Earth-2 Superman quickly found he needed to be in two places at once, and even with his amazing abilities, this proved problematic. As a result, he began building duplicates, first dummies and then increasingly sophisticated robots, which proved helpful throughout his career.

While combating the Thinker, Clark Kent used his super-ventriloquism to convince the criminal that he was dealing with Superman when it was actually a dummy (*Action Comics* #70, March 1944).

His first robot was used to convince invaders from Uranus that all humans were artificial in nature. He moved at super-speed to manipulate the construct like a puppet, aided by his super-ventriloquism (*World's Finest Comics* #42, September–October 1949). Superman constructed Krag, which he used in a scheme to capture the Crime Czar. Krag claimed to come from Mercury, and Superman switched between being himself and masquerading as Krag so it appeared that the alien defeated the Man of Steel and was worthy to meet the mysterious underworld lord (*Action Comics* #165, February 1952).

Over time, Superman found ways to improve the automation, but he continued to use ventriloquism to do the speaking (*Superman* [first series] #75, May 1952). He later built a remote-control version that Jimmy Olsen was given to use while he was off Earth on a mission (*Superman's Pal, Jimmy Olsen* #9, December 1955).

Superboy eventually set himself up with a fully equipped workshop in the basement of the Kent family home in the Smallville of Earth-1. Much as Jor-El built Spot, a robotic replacement when Krypto the Super-Dog was accidentally lost in space (*Superboy* [first series] #117, December 1964), Superboy came to realize that he could protect his identity and serve the greater good by building a series of robots to replace either himself or Clark Kent. He then secreted them behind a panel in the basement, to be summoned as needed.

Over time, Superman built a veritable army of robots, each with a special code number and some with specialized assignments or skills. Most were maintained at his Arctic Fortress of Solitude, while he kept a few in a hidden compartment at Clark Kent's Metropolis apartment. Superman even found a way to keep a Clark Kent robot secreted in a supply room at the *Daily Planet,* programmed to do everything expected of a top-flight reporter.

When his cousin Kara Zor-El arrived on Earth, Superman built her a Supergirl Robot as well as a Linda Lee version to help her protect her new identity. In time, the Man of Steel wound up constructing robots to imitate Lois Lane, Lana Lang, and Krypto the Super-Dog.

Superman's incredible creations used high-tech batteries for energy, with commands and programming contained within a control center. He found a way to mimic each and every one of his abilities, going so far as to create at least one robot traveling fast enough to pierce the time barrier. In most cases, though, the robots had limitations as to how strong they were or how precise their vision powers could be. The chronicles showed that several of the robots succumbed in battle to a Kryptonian flame dragon's fiery breath (*Superman* [first series] #142, January 1961); another was destroyed by an anti-magnetic device (*Superman* [first series] #147, August 1961). Lex Luthor even found a way to destroy one with his vibro-gun (*Action Comics* #292, September 1962). Their uniforms were highly durable synthetics but were not free from shredding issues.

Their sophisticated program was largely tamper-proof, and their default settings were for their actions to do no harm to people or property. Should something alter the programming, each robot was also built with a self-destruct device that would prevent criminals from scavenging its inert form for parts.

Some of the more noteworthy robots included the quartet that were "atom-powered," with X-3 lost on a space mission. Damaged by a meteor, it landed on another planet, where the mermaid scientist Mooki repaired it; X-3 then built a robot duplicate when its savior died and retired to a married life. In time, they constructed Nipper, a robotic son (*Superman's Girl Friend, Lois Lane* #30, January 1962).

Robot Y found a "tiny transmitter, emitting a super-sonic signal, inside a hollowed-out book" that was brought into the Fortress of Solitude by a thug during a tour, hoping to rob the amazing headquarters (*Action Comics* #261, February 1960).

One of the robots, unbidden, carried out an intricately convoluted ruse involving human emo-

tion, sophisticated independent thinking, and the ability to invent and construct complex scientific devices (*Action Comics* #274, March 1961).

A newly constructed Superman Robot-in-Training responded to reports of Lex Luthor robbing Fort Knox. The criminal scientist was confused when Superman did not succumb to synthetic kryptonite radiation. The following day, Luthor learned that he had escaped not the real hero, but a robot. Disgusted, he returned the gold, while the robot regretted that its programming to feign weakness had superseded its programming to thwart robberies. It took encouraging words from its creator before the robot appeared ready to resume its duties (*Action Comics* #277, June 1961).

Finally, #15 was captured by the alien Barkh, who hoped to use it to discover the tomb of the mysterious ancient Malis. After Superman defeated the criminal, the robot was retired. It was at this point that the Man of Steel came to realize the increased pollution in Earth's atmosphere was deteriorating the robots' effectiveness and delicate mechanisms. He ordered them all deactivated (*World's Finest Comics* #202, May 1971).

In the reality formed after the Crisis of Infinite Earths, Superman created a new band of Superman Robots while under the influence of Dominus. Obsessed with patrolling the Earth comprehensively, the Man of Steel built the automatons to facilitate his mission (*Superman* [second series] #143, April 1999). Snapped back to his senses, Superman and the Justice League of America destroyed most of the increasingly aggressive robots (*Superman: King of the World* #1, June 1999). Despite the involvement of a rogue robot in the murders of heroines Omen and Troia (*Titans/Young Justice: Graduation Day* #1–3, July–August 2003), the Man of Steel still kept several Superman Robots on standby in his Fortress of Solitude (*Superman* #670, January 2008).

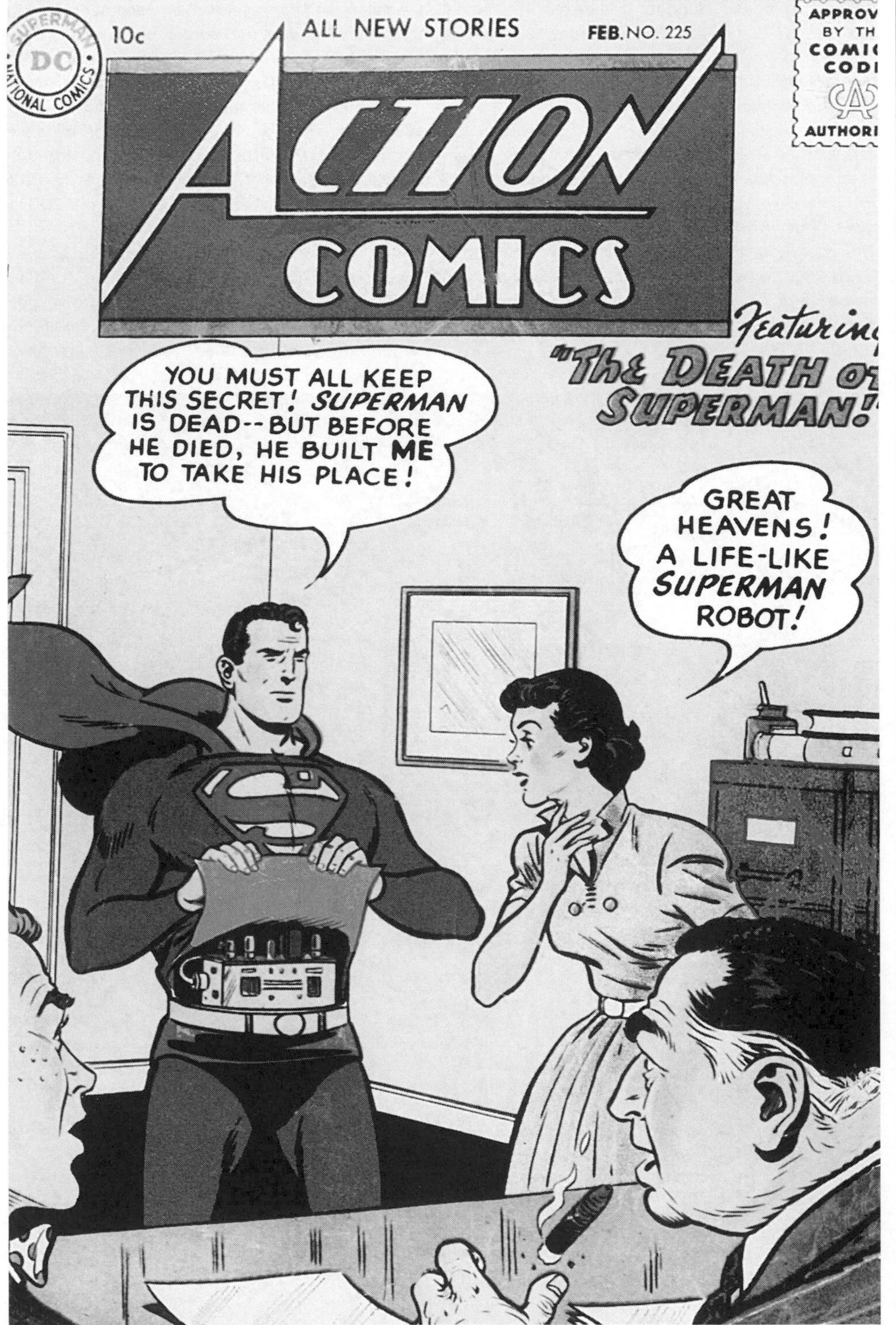

SUPERMAN STOCK COMPANY, THE

To entice Henry Drebbin, Edward Jorgens, and Paul Quillan into revealing the whereabouts of their stolen property, Superman partnered with federal Treasury agent Barclay to craft a ruse. To share in the reward money and prizes Superman collected for his many efforts, he formed the Superman Stock Company, telling "model citizens" they could invest in the Man of Steel. The trio of prominent retired businessmen were also secret partners in a Metropolis crime syndicate and tried to profit from good as well as evil—but their crimes were exposed (*Superman* [first series] #102, January 1956).

SUPERMAN TOY-O-MAT

The Toyman opened this unique toy emporium featuring windup Superman toys available via coin-operated vending machines. The criminal was actually using them as a front for his real plot, which was to rob the cashier's cage at the Metropolis *Daily Planet,* hoping to obtain a priceless diamond collection from the vault of the Strongbilt Construction Company. With Superman's intervention, the plan failed (*Superman* [first series] #63, March–April 1950).

SUPER-MENACE, THE

The journey of the rocket carrying Kal-El to Earth from Krypton led to the extraordinary circumstances resulting in the creation of a being known as the Super-Menace. The small spacecraft was hurtling through space when it glanced against the nose cone of a larger starship hailing from another universe. The impact accidentally activated "weird scientific devices," resulting in the creation of an exact duplicate of Kal-El's rocket and everything inside it, including the tiny infant. The new life-form was "an unearthly force manifested into human form" possessing the physical characteristics and superpowers of Superman but without internal organs, blood vessels, or skeleton.

In time, the odd creation landed near the town of Brentstock and was found by onetime public enemy "Wolf" Derek and his wife Bonnie at much the same time that Kal-El's craft landed outside Smallville. While Jonathan and Martha Kent taught their adopted son the ideals that made people good, the alien baby was cruelly instructed to revere crime and to hate all that was decent in life. Derek clearly saw the baby as a way to become the planet's conqueror.

As he grew into a man, the alien donned a black eye mask and became known as the world's mightiest criminal, a ruthless "super-outlaw" who represented "the most dangerous menace to law-and-order the world has ever known!" When he was trained in the use of his powers and at his physical peak, Derek sent his son out to find and destroy Superman. Unfortunately, the powerful being overheard his father call him a freak and admit to faking his love in order to gain the alien's loyalty.

Emotionally shaken, he still did as he was bid and battled the Man of Steel. They fought in space, where Super-Menace trapped his doppelgänger between KRYPTONITE meteors. Watching the hero struggle, the alien reviewed the shocking revelation he had overheard and decided he did not want to be a cruel man's puppet. Instead, he rescued Superman from certain death and then raced back to Earth.

Superman followed and saw the unpleasant confrontation between father and son. Then the two touched and there was an unearthly explosion of energy, Derek shrieking vainly for mercy (*Superman* [first series] #137, May 1960).

SUPERMEN OF AMERICA, THE

When Superman was possessed by DOMINUS, it appeared that the Man of Steel was trying to become the world's tyrant. As a result, LEX LUTHOR saw an opportunity and formed a volunteer organization he called the Supermen of America, following the very ideals the onetime hero had apparently abandoned. If everything went according to plan, the team would supplant Superman in the world's hearts and minds—and Luthor would be the man controlling the team.

He selected as its leader Mitch Anderson, a teen whose family was protected by the Man of Tomorrow during DOOMSDAY's arrival on Earth (*Superman* [second series] #74, December 1992). Later, his metagene activated and he developed magnetic abilities, taking the code name OUTBURST. After saving Luthor's life, Outburst became an overnight sensation whose name saturated the media thanks to the criminal (*Superman* [second series] #142, February 1999).

Outburst agreed the world still needed its heroes and accepted the leadership post, then helped recruit the behemoth BRAHMA; the magician WHITE LOTUS; the force-field generating Loser; the fiery Pyrogen; and PSILENCER, who had tactical intuition. Once they all signed up, Luthor held a press conference introducing the team and revealing their true identities. On their first mission, Psilencer was killed, and Outburst was deeply shaken by losing a man. He rejected Luthor's financing and felt the team needed to follow the Man of Steel's legend on their own (*Supermen of America* #1, March 1999).

While the team floundered as they bonded and found their rhythm, LOIS LANE covered them with a jaundiced eye (*Action Comics* #752, March 1999). Undaunted, people flocked to the team, so the powered core became the "Elite Brigade" while the civilians supported them. The Supermen felt ignored by Superman but their faith never wavered, even coming to blows with Team Superman over the matter (*Action Comics* #753, April 1999).

Once Superman overthrew Dominus's control, things reverted to normal, though people continued to flock to the Supermen. They did good deeds across METROPOLIS such as building community centers and refurbishing dilapidated buildings. They selected one such building as their headquarters and dubbed it Outreach-1. They even added a powerful new recruit, Maximum (*Supermen of America* [second series] #1–2, March–April 2000).

Luthor continued to use the team for his own ends, such as sending Pyrogen for a capsule that was in S.T.A.R. LABS' possession, resulting in the team opposing Deep Six, creatures from APOKOLIPS. The object seemed to have not only great power but also knowledge of who possessed it. Thus DARKSEID, too, was interested in obtaining it. This prompted the Warlords of Okaara, deep in the Vega star system, to dispatch a "cleansing battalion" to Earth (*Supermen of America* [second series] #3, May 2000).

White Lotus struck a deal with the Okaaran forces that in exchange for sparing Earth, she would hand over the object, which turned out to be the entity called Unimaginable. The being needed a new host, and Dr. Bendorion, the current host, selected the far more powerful Maximum, turning the teen into a NEW GOD. After discussing matters with his parents, Maximum decided to disperse the massive energy across the stars, something that worked but also prompted Luthor to begin secretly collecting it. To keep matters quiet, Luthor agreed to sever his connection with the team, and he signed over documents giving them their freedom and control of their headquarters (*Supermen of America* [second series] #4–6, June–August 2000).

The Supermen remained active, although their actions were low-key. They did rise to prominence during the OMAC attacks on METROPOLIS, although by the battle's end the Supermen were "67.89% neutralized" (*OMAC Project* #6, November 2005).

SUPER-MITE

When Danny Dare took ill, Superman tried to cheer up the boy by building a miniature version of his SUPERMAN ROBOTS. The tiny creation malfunctioned and had to be destroyed, so a member of

The Supermen of America

the Superman Emergency Squad flew from Kandor to continue to cheer the youth (*Superman's Pal, Jimmy Olsen* #60, April 1962).

SUPERMOBILE, THE

When a red sun exploded, Earth was bathed in the unique solar radiation that did two things: It inadvertently activated the deadly multipowered android Amazo, and it temporarily robbed the Man of Steel of his amazing abilities. To stop the rampaging android, Superman needed an edge and constructed a mobile craft using the indestructible metal supermanium. The Supermobile replicated the hero's various powers and kept Amazo at bay until his natural powers returned (*Action Comics* #481, March 1978).

Superman used the Supermobile again to scour Earth's atmosphere of a belt of kryptonite (*Superman* [first series] #324, June 1978) and to filter out red solar rays fired at him by alien invaders (*Super Friends* #27, December 1979).

Years earlier, during a period when he'd briefly lost his superpowers, Superman took a page from Batman and patrolled in a customized automobile (with a distinctive S-emblem) that he dubbed the Supermobile (*World's Finest Comics* #77, July-August 1955).

A fleet of Supermobiles was sighted in the skies over Ivy Town in a short-lived alternate time line visited by the Atom (*The All-New Atom* #8, April 2007).

SUPERNOVA

On the parallel world of Earth-178, there came a time when Superman lost his amazing abilities after a mission to another dimension. Even without his powers, however, Superman still wanted to fight crime, and he decided that if nonpowered heroes such as Batman and Green Arrow could be effective, so could he. Working out and training, he revealed his new persona, complete with purple-and-white outfit, to his friends, declaring that Nova would join them. The Caped Crusader, though, expressed doubts that Superman could make the adjustment necessary to be a good crime fighter.

When Nova attempted to fight Horatio Socrates's gang of criminals, he was quickly captured. Worse, Socrates implanted a device in the hero's neck, letting the criminal control his actions, which meant Batman was lured into a trap. The World's Greatest Escape Artist worked his way to freedom and brought Nova to the Batcave. A distraught Nova fled, but not before the implant allowed Socrates to learn the location of Batman's headquarters. As the Caped Crusader gave chase, the criminal booby-trapped the cave. Nova found a way to deactivate the device, regaining total freedom, so he returned with Batman in time to see Socrates destroyed by his own bomb (*World's Finest Comics* #178, September 1968, and #180, November 1968).

On New Earth, in the wake of Infinite Crisis, there was a day early in the Man of Steel's career when he met with the Dark Knight to discuss whether either man should join the Justice League of America. The conversation was interrupted when Alfred Pennyworth alerted them to trouble at the Gotham Financial District. Plato, a new villain with the ability to manipulate people into believing they owed him something, was causing the wealthy to liquidate their assets and "repay" their debts. The confrontation ended badly when Plato sent Superman into space to deal with an asteroid, which somehow robbed him of his powers. Despondent, Clark Kent returned to Smallville, brooding over his future. It took a visit from Batman to convince the champion that all was not lost.

The Gotham Guardian then constructed a suit of armor that would enable Clark to function at a super-human level. While Batman continued to study and plot against Plato, Clark trained to become a new kind of hero. When they were ready, Supernova and Batman traced Plato, took him down, and found a way for Clark to regain his natural abilities (*Superman/Batman Annual* #2, 2008).

Years later, a different Supernova flew over Metropolis, displaying powers and abilities that led many to believe he was a Kryptonian (*52* #8, June 28, 2006). The new hero was garnering good media coverage and seemed to always be in the right place at the right time. Eventually, it was revealed that Supernova was the hero Booster Gold, who had faked his death and traveled back in time in order to stop his robotic sidekick Skeets from performing work on behalf of the Venusian creature Mister Mind (*52* #37, January 17, 2007).

The suit was outfitted with a Phantom Zone projector, which Supernova employed to transport matter from place to place, using the Zone as a shortcut (*52* #37, January 17, 2007). It also had a size-changing belt, powered by a piece of white dwarf star that once belonged to the Atom, and a laser weapon. Anyone wearing the suit was protected from the advance of time thanks to technology added by Rip Hunter. The stasis also negated the need for food, drink, elimination, or sleep (*Booster Gold* [second series] #1, October 2007). Hunter added a security precaution: Only members of the Carter family could activate the suit (*52* #52, May 2, 2007).

Later, Daniel Carter, the modern-day ancestor of Booster Gold, inherited the Supernova outfit. Carter was an unwitting pawn of Mister Mind, and rescued by Booster Gold and Rip Hunter, one of the Linear Men (*52* #52, May 2, 2007). Daniel maintained the super-suit, seeking a better life after his once-promising football career was derailed by a knee injury. He had grown bitter and unpleasant as a result of seeing his dreams crushed (*Booster Gold* [second series] #1, October 2007; others).

The suit was stolen and used by the father of Booster Gold working with time-traveling villains Per Degaton, Despero, the Ultra-Humanite, and Black Beetle, a future variant of Blue Beetle. They intended to select pivotal points in the past and change them so modern-day actions would be different; if they killed Jonathan Kent's great-grandfather, for instance, they could alter what happened when Kal-El's space craft arrived from Krypton. Booster Gold discovered his father was also in the thrall of Mister Mind and was forced to remove the man's ear to free him. Booster's father was left in an alternate reality (*Booster Gold* [second series] #13, December 2008).

Super Nova was an unrelated heroic persona generated by the alien device used by Robby Reed (*House of Mystery* #164, January 1967).

SUPER-SAVED CLUB, THE

Chaired by Lois Lane, whose "life has been saved more times than anyone," this Metropolis-based club required its members be people who had been saved by Superman. During one meeting, they were manipulated by James Harvey Thorben, an untrustworthy millionaire, to help find a super-hard element that he would then control. Superman helped them find the rare element, which was then named supermanium and kept from the tycoon (*World's Finest Comics* #41, July-August 1949).

SUPER-SONS

Superman once imagined what it would be like to have children, so he programmed the computer at the Fortress of Solitude to create a simulation based on several variables (*World's Finest Comics* #263, June–July 1980). In that world, Superman and Batman both were fortunate enough to survive their crime fighting and managed to marry unnamed women (although they may have been anyone from Lois Lane and Talia Head to Lana Lang and Selina Kyle). The happy couples both had only children, sons who were seen as the next generation of hero (*World's Finest Comics* #215, December 1972–January 1973).

Clark Kent, Junior, and Bruce Wayne, Junior, grew up together, closer than siblings, and knew

each other's family secret. When they reached their late teens, they adopted costumes identical to those their fathers wore and felt ready to begin fighting for truth and justice. Their parents were less certain, especially since Clark was not as powerful as the Man of Steel. An ally was Dick Grayson, still a teen at this point, so he was probably raised alongside young Bruce.

During their first few cases, they were more successful than not, and their rough edges showed. But like their famous fathers, they managed to work together as a new World's Finest team of heroes. Their opponents included Lex Luthor and his teen daughter Ardora Luthor (*World's Finest Comics* #238, June 1976). Variations on the Super-Sons appeared on parallel worlds such as Earth-154 (*World's Finest Comics* #154, December 1965, and #157, May 1966) and Earth-391 (*Action Comics* #391–392, August–September 1970).

When Alexander Luthor, Junior, successfully split the universe into a multiverse, the Super-Sons were seen on Earth-154, which did not survive his manipulations when fifty-two parallel universes were left (*Infinite Crisis* #6, May 2006).

SUPER-SQUIRREL

In the original multiverse, Earth-C Minus was a world populated by anthropomorphic animals that paralleled Earth-1, complete with super-powered crime fighters including Super-Squirrel (*Captain Carrot and His Amazing Zoo Crew* #14, April 1983). Hailing from the doomed planet Chipton, he grew to adulthood working in Muttropolis. Unlike the Man of Steel, the squirrel was a little too self-important and prone to jealousy.

As Super-Squirrel, he led the Just'a Lotta Animals team of heroes, and on his own he battled Lex Lemur and villains from the Elephantom Zone.

On Earth-C, Super-Squirrel was a comic character created by Rodney Rabbit, secretly Captain Carrot, leader of the Zoo Crew. However, a battle with the sorcerer Feline Faust led to the revelation of Earth-C Minus and a meeting between creator and creation.

SUPER-SUPERMAN

When Professor Phineas Potter accidentally combined the Superman from Earth-1 with his Earth-2 counterpart, he dubbed the new hero Super-Superman. The powerful hero defeated the extra-dimensional Krogg before being split back into two Kryptonians (*Superman Family* #187, January–February 1978).

SUPER-TEACHER FROM KRYPTON, THE

Jor-El suspected that his son might need guidance in the use of his super-abilities as he grew up on Earth. He therefore built a robot educator—but the robot was not placed in the space ship before Krypton blew up. Miraculously, the robot survived the explosion and drifted in space, seeking to learn where his charge might have landed. When he finally found Earth, Kal-El had grown up to be the Teen of Steel. Still, the robot honored its programming and began testing his charge.

In time, Superboy passed the tests, which probed not only how he used his powers but also why, including his willingness to never use them again. He passed the test, and the robot left Earth (*Adventure Comics* #240, September 1957).

The teacher returned some time later, when Kal-El was "on the edge of manhood." The test this time was one of perception: The robot crafted a ruse that pitted the hero against a race of creatures similar to the legendary Bigfoot. While he passed the test, Kal-El disliked being manipulated and scolded the teacher (*DC Super Stars* #12, February 1977).

When the robot learned of Supergirl operating on Earth, it adapted Jor-El's instructions and returned to Earth a final time to test the Maid of Might using the Supergirl Robots against her (*Adventure Comics* #382, July 1969).

SUPER-TURTLE

Galapagon was a world on the verge of being destroyed in another reality. The scientist Shh-Ell was successful in convincing the Science Council to evacuate their planet—but because this was a race of turtles, their slow pace meant the thousand space arks would not be completed in time. With just one craft constructed, Shh-Ell placed his infant son, Tur-Tel, into the rocket and sent it into space. Landing on a version of Earth, the turtle was found and adopted by a kindly couple. Conditions on Earth led to the turtle gaining powers and abilities beyond those of any other creature; he eventually donned a red cape to adventure as Super-Turtle (first appearance in *Adventure Comics* #304, January 1963; origin revealed in *Silver Age 80-Page Giant* #31, July 2000).

The Reptile of Steel lived on an Earth that was far less violent than Superman's home, and he faced off against only a handful of super-villains. Instead, he generally did good deeds with grace and good humor.

On one occasion, Super-Turtle crossed the dimensional barrier to aid Superboy when the Teen of Steel wanted a vacation (*Superboy* [first series] #130, June 1966). Years later, he went to a phone booth to change into his heroic persona, only to find the booth occupied by a visiting Superman (*Adventure Comics* #357, December 1967).

After reality was altered, Super-Turtle was a legendary figure across the fifty-two parallel worlds, with a figure of the hero seen in Planet Krypton on Earth-22 (*Kingdom Come* #4, 1996).

SUPER-UNIVAC

Given the Man of Steel's fame, most people took to calling anything at the top of its category as being "super." Such was the case with the most advanced and powerful computer yet built, dubbed Super-Univac. Superman posed it the question of what his life would have been like had Krypton not blown up and he'd grown to adulthood as Kal-El. The computer answered that even on Krypton, he was destined to be a hero; he would have gained superpowers of a different sort on his homeworld (*Superman* [first series] #132, October 1959).

Superman used the computer a second time when, after meeting Hyper-Man, he had the computer postulate what the other man's future life would be like (*Action Comics* #265, June 1960).

SUPERWOMAN

There were several women in Superman's life who used the name Superwoman, beginning with Lois Lane on Earth-2. When she was once hit by a car, Lois suffered a concussion. While the doctors worked to stabilize her, she dreamed Superman gave her a blood transfusion that endowed her with his amazing superpowers. She donned a costume and began adventuring alongside him as Superwoman. Shortly after proposing to the Man of Steel, the injured Lois regained consciousness (*Action Comics* #60, May 1943).

A waking Lois became Superwoman when the villains Hocus and Pocus thought they had actual magical powers and "turned" Clark Kent into Superman and Lois into Superwoman. The real Man of Steel secretly followed Lois, making her powers appear to work and convincing the reporter that she wasn't ready to handle superpowers and wanted her normal life back, something Hocus and Pocus "granted" (*Superman* [first series] #45, March–April 1947).

Lois actually gained superpowers, albeit temporarily, when she was exposed to Lex Luthor's vivanium machine. When she realized what had happened,

I AM KRISTIN WELLS...
...I AM SUPERWOMAN...
...AND I HAVE A JOB TO DO!

she donned a blond wig and fashioned herself a costume. She and Superman met during an accident at the DAILY PLANET, but when she tried to stop robberies, she learned she could not control her powers due to inexperience. Luthor tried to get her to use her abilities to build an improved vivanium device, but Superman apprehended the criminal. Lois's powers faded (*Action Comics* #156, May 1951).

A BIZARRO Lois also once gained superpowers courtesy of Bizarro Mr. Kltpzyxm. She appeared as Stupor-Woman (*Adventure Comics* #288, September 1961).

SUPERGIRL once sought the perfect mate for Superman, and she used the FORTRESS OF SOLITUDE's computer to scour the stars for one. The computer identified LUMA LYNAI, champion of STARYL. The pair met, and did enjoy a romance, with her wearing a heroic white-and-green costume as a Superwoman, but it became clear that Luma could not live under Earth's yellow sun after growing up with Staryl's orange sun (*Action Comics* #289, June 1962).

Then came KRISTIN WELLS. A journalism student in 2857, she was a descendant of JIMMY OLSEN, complete with red hair. To write her senior thesis, she journeyed back to Jimmy's era to learn the origins of the event known as MIRACLE MONDAY (*Superman: Miracle Monday,* 1978). After graduation, Wells became a professor and began researching the scant evidence that had survived to her time regarding the identity of the last super hero of the great heroic age, a being named Superwoman. She was given permission by her superiors to return once more to the past—only to realize it was herself. While in the past, she donned a uniform similar to the Man of Steel's and joined Superman in battling King Kosmos. The costume was lined with twenty-ninth-century technology allowing her flight, teleportation, empathy, precognition, and telekinesis (*DC Comics Presents Annual* #2, 1983).

Kristin made one final visit to Superman's era, resulting in an accident that cost her much of her memory and left her at an event known as Luthorcon. She spent years carving out a legend as Superwoman in the twentieth century before finally returning to her proper time period (*DC Comics Presents* #4, 1985).

Thanks to a prank from MR. MXYZPTLK, Superman returned from a stellar mission to find that his closest friends and allies had switched genders. There was even a Superwoman standing in for the Man of Steel, but Clara Kent also existed, meaning there was a flaw in the magic (*Superman* [first series] #349, July 1980).

In a potential Earth-1 future, Superwoman (Kristin Wells) was one of the many heroes trying to pierce BRAINIAC's force field, which was surrounding the Fortress of Solitude. By the time she and the others cracked through, Superman had exposed himself to gold KRYPTONITE (*Action Comics* #583, September 1986).

On Earth-3, the evil doppelgänger of WONDER WOMAN operated as Superwoman, a member of the Crime Syndicate of America (*Justice League of America* [first series] #29, August 1964). She had the full array of superpowers she'd enjoyed as the Amazon Princess, complete with a Magic Lasso that could change shape at will. This Superwoman died during the CRISIS ON INFINITE EARTHS, but a new version was created in the new anti-matter reality of Qward (*JLA: Earth-2,* 2000).

This incarnation was in a joyless marriage with ULTRAMAN, preferring her affair with Owlman. The two were identical with the exception of the Magic Lasso no longer being able to alter its shape; also, this new incarnation possessed heat vision. As Lois Lane, she was editor in chief of that world's *Daily Planet,* and her cruel nature led her to being referred to as "Queen Bitch." On that world, the only civilian who knew her identity was Jimmy Olsen, who loved her but was mistreated.

Superwoman

Still another version of Superwoman was created on a different incarnation of Earth-3 after the multiverse was restored during the Infinite Crisis (*52* #52, May 2, 2007). During a battle with Monarch, she had her eyes gouged out (*Countdown to Final Crisis* #14, January 23, 2008).

After the Infinite Crisis shattered reality into fifty-two parallel universes, Superman was stunned to learn that a third Kryptonian was on Earth in addition to himself and his cousin Kara Zor-El. This turned out to be a much older woman, Karsta Wor-Ul, who had left Krypton long before its destruction. She was hiding on Earth using the name *Kristin Wells* (*Superman* #668–670, October-December 2007).

A person in a costume similar to the Kristin Wells version appeared shortly after one hundred thousand Kandorians arrived on Earth. She was called Superwoman, and no one knew who she was, what she wanted, or why she had suddenly appeared. In short order, she killed Agent Liberty and befriended Supergirl, who at the time felt torn between her new life on Earth and the demands of her mother Alura on New Krypton (*Supergirl* [fifth series] #35, January 2009). She appeared to have been blackmailed by General Samuel Lane to act on his behalf. When he dispatched her against Reactron, the villain tried using his gold kryptonite to strip her of her powers. This move failed, however, meaning that she was not from Krypton. Soon after, Kara unmasked her and revealed the woman to be Major Lucy Lane (*Supergirl* [fifth series] #40, June 2009). This Superwoman was accidentally killed when her costume's power source was critically damaged by Supergirl (*Supergirl* [fifth series] #41, July 2009).

Months later, a very much alive Lucy Lane was found by her father at the center of a crater by the site of her "death." Her will to live had been so strong that her body regenerated. When she was examined by specialists, they discovered she now possessed the very superpowers her magical Superwoman costume enabled her to, thanks to Mirabai the Forlorn's mystic abilities. A disgusted Samuel Lane rejected his youngest daughter, but Lucy continued to serve her father nonetheless (*Supergirl* [fifth series] #50, April 2010). When Project 7734 was defeated, Lucy stood trial for her crimes and was sent to prison (*Superman: War of the Supermen* #4, July 2010).

There was also Earth-11, which featured a young woman named Laurel who was that world's Superwoman. There gender roles were reversed, which meant she had a young cousin named Superlad (*Superman/Batman* #23, January 2006; *Search for Ray Palmer: Superwoman/Batwoman* #1, February 2008).

SUPREMO

Scientist and world traveler Jake Vale arrived in Smallville and gave his nephew Allan Vale a formula that temporarily bestowed the teen with "super-strength, invulnerability, and power of flight." The goal was to allow the boy to enjoy assisting Superboy before "the incurable disease he caught in Hong Kong" took his life.

Wearing a yellow costume with purple trunks,

boots, belt, cape and cowl, and a stylized purple S emblazoned on his chest, Supremo enjoyed several supercharged days (*Superboy* [first series] #132, September 1966).

SUPRO

When Superman was marooned on Morgu, the natives called him Supro, the name of the deliverer whom prophecies had promised to the impoverished slaves residing on the world (*Superman* [first series] #229, August 1970).

SURRUS

A Kryptonian city on the southern continent of Bolenth named after its tranquilizing Surrus Blossoms, seductive singing plants that had a tranquilizing effect (*Superman* [first series] #236, April 1971; others).

SURVIVAL ZONE, THE

When Argo City was rapidly dying as a result of a meteor strike that exposed the city's kryptonite core, Zor-El used a projector to send himself and his wife Alura to a limbo-like realm he called the Survival Zone. Like the Phantom Zone, which his brother Jor-El discovered, the Survival Zone allowed them to exist in immaterial form; they could manage limited telepathic contact with people in the corporeal world. When they contacted their daughter Kara Zor-El, she was able to free them, and they came to live in the bottle city of Kandor (*Action Comics* #309, February 1964).

SWAMI RAMA

A carnival performer, Swami Rama duped a gullible Jimmy Olsen into believing he had lived previous lives and had actually interacted with Samson, Thor, and Hercules. Jimmy wanted additional sessions, but the Swami explained that the device he used to help the process was losing energy. The reality was, the crooked performer wanted Jimmy to steal radium for Rama to sell at a fat profit. His scheme was exposed (*Superman's Pal, Jimmy Olsen* #16, October 1956).

SWIFTY

Superboy saved Swifty, a dark-colored dog, from the cruel fox hunter who owned him. The dog was drawn to the kindly hero and tracked him down "over hundreds of miles," arriving at the Kent home. Superboy decided to reward the dog by mixing up a serum based on a formula devised by Roz-Em that gave the dog temporary superpowers. He placed a cape on the canine and trained Swifty to be protective of Krypto. The Super-Dog, though, feared he was being replaced and left Smallville. When Swifty's powers faded and he was in danger of drowning, Krypto came to his rescue. Superboy finally explained that he saw the second dog as "a fitting playmate to romp through space with . . . a canine pal who could save [Krypto] from Green Kryptonite!" (*Superboy* [first series] #105, July 1963). Temporarily re-empowered, Swifty returned soon afterward as a pawn of Phantom Zone criminals (*Superboy* [first series] #109, December 1963).

SWORDFISH AND BARRACUDA

Temporarily catapulted from the late seventeenth century to the present, the Swordfish and his partner the Barracuda ended up back in their own time, locked in battle with the alien X'ult (*World's Finest Comics* #304–307, June–September 1984).

X'ult, the first mate aboard an alien vessel that landed in the Caribbean, chose to remain on Earth when the expedition ended and make himself a local king. However, X'ult wound up becoming stuck within molten rock when he tried to use some of his technology.

Some time later, the beautiful Abigail Kent had chosen to sail with a ship full of pirates rather than return to England. She wound up falling in love with a European swordsman they had captured. She helped him escape, and they fled together. The couple came upon locals worshipping an oddly marked stone obelisk, and when they touched it, each was imbued with incredible powers.

The man became the Swordfish, able to fly and wielding a deadly cutlass, while Abigail became the Barracuda, with the strength of a whale and other aquatic abilities. They eventually crossed paths with the Master Pirate, who turned out to be X'ult. During their battle, he employed his temporal device, but was caught in its wake. The three sank beneath the waves, lost to the ages.

While Superman and Batman sought the supervillains Null and Void, they encountered the time-lost trio. The recovery occurred near Cuba, which got the Communist nation interested. The three were awoken, and it was discovered Null and Void had gained their powers in the same way that the Swordfish and the Barracuda had. X'ult still wanted to rule the world, and now that he was free he quickly fled the scene, taking Abigail with him. Superman found a way to use X'ult's technology to return them all to their proper era. The chronicles never recorded what became of them.

SYLVIA; AKA SYLVIA VAN-ZEE

Living in the bottle city of Kandor, Sylvia DeWitt was married to Van-Zee and mother to twins Lyle and Lili. Much as Van-Zee was a remarkable lookalike to Kal-El, Sylvia bore an uncanny resemblance to Lois Lane.

For a period of time, Van-Zee was living in America, having been accidentally enlarged when Superman used a ray designed by renegade Kandorian scientist Zak-Kul. Van-Zee met Sylvia, a rich young heiress from a bustling midwestern city, and fell head over heels in love with the human. He revealed his extraterrestrial origins, which did not bother her. Once they married, the couple briefly resided on Venus. When they were ready, Superman used Brainiac's ingenious reduction ray to turn the family microscopic, and they returned to Van-Zee's native Kandor (*Superman's Girl Friend, Lois Lane* #15, February 1960). Appropriately, Sylvia later served as Lois Lane's double in the Lookalike Squad (*Superman's Pal, Jimmy Olsen* #70, July 1963).

SYNDICATE OF FIVE, THE

When Turk Kane rose to lead Metropolis's criminal underworld, he surrounded himself with a quintet of lieutenants known as the Syndicate of Five. In time, they murdered their boss and jointly ruled the lawless. They tried to subvert a charity appearance by the Man of Steel by making a series of requests for super-feats that were designed to reveal the whereabouts of ten million dollars that had reportedly been hidden away. Superman complied since each feat required a substantial contribution to the Worldwide Charities telethon. Superman found the money but apprehended the syndicate in addition to raising one hundred million dollars for the needy (*Action Comics* #180, May 1953).

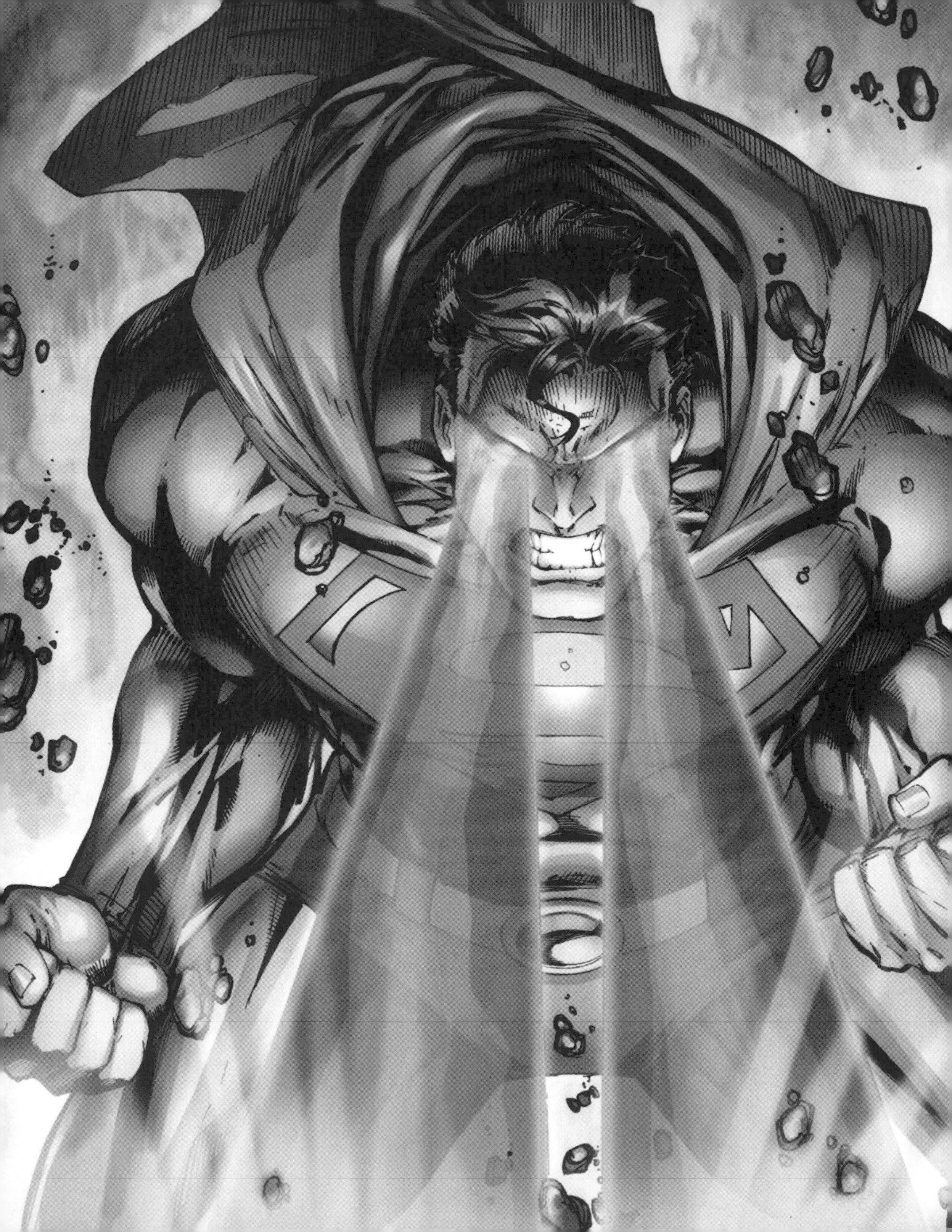

TAG-ALONG

When an explosion sent the Earth-1 Superman back in time, it temporarily robbed him of his memories. It also sent him to the European Theater of Operations during World War II, and he found a discarded army uniform and donned it in order to hide his colorful costume. He then hooked up with Easy Company, commanded by the legendary Sergeant Frank Rock. Since most of his soldiers had nicknames, Rock assigned the newcomer the name Tag-Along.

During a firefight, Superman's subconscious mind prevented him from taking a life, an act that caused trouble with Rock. He smacked the ground in frustration, his super-strength causing reverberations that opened a fissure beneath a German tank. Soon after, his memory returned, but the Man of Steel chose to lend the Rock a helping hand before returning to his own era (*DC Comics Presents* #10, June 1979).

TAIL TERRIER

A member of the Space Canine Patrol Agency, this canine could stretch his tail and perform feats as if it were a lariat (*Superboy* [first series] #131, July 1966).

TALA-EL

A member of the prestigious House of El who wrote the planetary constitution in 9852 and had two sons of his own, the architect Gam-El and the detective Pym-El, in the latter half of the 9800s (*Adventure Comics* #313, October 1963; *Krypton Chronicles* #3, November 1981).

TALLOW, OLIVIA

The tall, willowy girlfriend and later wife of Captain Horatio Strong, Olivia had just accepted a marriage proposal from her beloved sailor when the alien Carnox attacked and kidnapped her. Strong and Superman rescued her with ease, and the happy couple were finally wed (*Action Comics* #439, September 1974).

TALON

Albert Caldwell, president of Metropolis Subway Inc., was also a secret "Fascist sympathizer" and "fifth columnist" who called himself the Talon. In Superman's words, he "tried to sabotage the city's transport system, so that the conquest of our nation by the Axis would be that much simpler." The Talon's plans to destroy the Metropolis subway system were exposed by the Man of Steel (*Superman* [first series] #17, July–August 1942).

TANNER, SAMUEL

The aggressive president of the United Broadcasting Corporation, he was also once the super-villain Blackrock on Earth-1 (*Action Comics* #458–459, April–May 1976). He battled Superman on a few occasions and was also uncle to comedian Les Vegas (*Superman* [first series] #315, September 1977).

TARIK THE MUTE

After losing his voice during a conflict with the thirtieth century's Science Police, Tarik decided to form a team of villains in order to gain his vengeance. He blackmailed Colossal Boy from the Legion of Super-Heroes to help train the first generation of the Legion of Super-Villains. The two Legions would then clash repeatedly through the years and across the various incarnations of Earth (*Adventure Comics* #372, September 1968).

TAR-LU

The mythical Juliet who, along with her lover Ren-Re, inspired the ancient legend behind Krypton's twin "lovers' stars," which were seen as an omen of their planet's eventual destruction (*Superman* [first series] #255, August 1972).

TATE, ROGER

When the demigod Hercules briefly stayed in Metropolis, he disguised himself as Roger Tate and worked alongside Clark Kent at the *Daily Planet* (*Action Comics* #267, August 1960).

TAYLOR, FREDDIE

Upon learning of Nancy Thorgenson's fortune, Freddie Taylor decided that the two of them should elope. She accepted, seeing it as her best hope of leaving home and gaining independence, a plan that was stopped by Superman's intervention (*Action Comics* #40, September 1941).

TAYLOR, GEORGE

When Clark Kent arrived in Earth-2's Metropolis to find work as a reporter, he was hired by *Daily Star* editor George Taylor. The veteran newspaperman was impressed by Kent's ability to land the exclusive coverage of Superman's first public appearance, stopping an attempted lynching at a county jail (*Action Comics* #1, June 1938; *Superman* [first series] #1, Summer 1939). Upon Taylor's retirement in the early 1950s, he proposed a competition between Kent and veteran reporter Perry White for his job. Perry proved the better reporter by a nose but ironically lost out to Clark because Taylor believed the better reporter should remain as such rather than being cooped up behind a desk (*Superman Family* #196, November–December 1979).

Sadly, George Taylor had little time to enjoy his retirement. Discovering evidence that exposed Superman's true identity, Taylor winked at Clark that he would never divulge it. Overhearing the conversation, a corrupt reporter murdered the former editor to acquire that proof, a filmstrip depicting Kent changing to Superman. The Man of Steel ultimately debunked the images as a fraud and avenged George Taylor's death (*Superman Family* #209, August 1981).

On Earth-1, George Taylor succeeded a man named Morton as editor. During Clark Kent's junior year at Metropolis University, the sixty-five-year-old Taylor retired, naming Perry White as his successor (*Superman: The Secret Years* #4, May 1985). George Taylor's son became editor of the *Daily Star* in Star City and a general thorn in the side of Oliver Queen, as Taylor constantly tried to prove that Queen was Green Arrow. The younger Taylor's son George Taylor III, was a record-breaking pole vaulter (*World's Finest Comics* #244, April–May 1977).

In the reality formed after the Crisis on Infinite Earths, the *Daily Star* was a rival paper to the *Daily Planet* in Metropolis, with George Taylor still

in place as editor (*The Adventures of Superman* #451, February 1989) and not above needling his rival Perry White over stories (*Superman* [second series] #183, August 2002).

TEAM LUTHOR

Recognizing a need for security forces befitting LexCorp's reputation for producing cutting-edge technology, Lex Luthor created an armored outfit that in time was dubbed Team Luthor (*Superman* [second series] #31, May 1989). The first two appearances attributed to Team Luthor (*Man of Steel* #5, December 1986; *The Adventures of Superman* #446, November 1988) actually depicted Luthor's thugs in prototypes for the group's LX-20 armor (based on the suit the Earth-1 Luthor wore in his final appearances). When Superman exiled himself from Earth for a period of time, Luthor used his team to supplement Metropolis's police protection. On numerous occasions, they performed altruistic acts—even temporarily adventuring with Supergirl (*Supergirl/Lex Luthor Special* #1, 1993). In the wake of Luthor's seeming death, the team continued to function and proclaimed their loyalty when Alexander Luthor, Junior, appeared to run the company. This Luthor continued to use Team Luthor to polish the company's image, especially in the days following the Man of Steel's death at the hands of Doomsday. Given their performance, Luthor convinced Mayor Frank Berkowitz to have Team Luthor given full police powers.

Luthor had hoped that his romance with Supergirl would keep her loyal to Team Luthor, and she was coaxed into enticing Superman's clone Superboy to join the team (*The Adventures of Superman* #502, July 1993)—a ploy that did not work.

While Lex Luthor's personal fortunes rose and fell, Team Luthor continued to perform for the public good. The full team was deployed during the Battle for Metropolis when they aided the Metropolis S.C.U. in handling the Underworlders (*Superman: The Man of Steel* #34, June 1994). On the other hand, they also performed whatever Luthor bid, including a raid on Project Cadmus that left the facility in ruins (*The Adventures of Superman* #513, June 1994).

Weeks later, after LexCorp had been seized by Luthor's ex-wife the Contessa and seemingly channeled into a force for good, the disgraced Team Luthor was reactivated for a short time as the Centurions to complement the company's new champion, the Alpha Centurion (*Action Comics* #715, October 1995).

TEEN TITANS, THE

The teenage heroes Robin, Kid Flash, and Aqualad came together to combat the threat of Mister Twister (*The Brave and the Bold* [first series] #54, June–July 1964) and enjoyed the experience so much that, after defeating the menace of Antithesis alongside Wonder Girl and Speedy, they formed a group named the Teen Titans (*Teen Titans* [first series] #53, February 1978; *The Brave and the Bold* [first series] #60, June–July 1965). Over the next few years, they adventured, partied, and learned valuable lessons as their ranks grew. The team was rescued by the Man of Steel from an "alien thought control unit" (*World's Finest Comics* #205, September 1971) and returned the favor by helping Superman and the Justice League of America oppose Brainiac (*Action Comics* #546, August 1983).

Circumstances led to the team disbanding for a brief period, but galactic and supernatural threats brought a new incarnation together (*DC Comics Presents* #26, October 1980). The New Teen Titans had a longer and more distinguished career, surviving the Crisis on Infinite Earths as well as the loss of several members. While the team—now calling itself the New Titans—was being led by Arsenal (formerly Speedy), Supergirl had an unsettling encounter with the heroine Raven that left the Teen Titan implanted with a demon seed to help Raven's father Trigon the Terrible gain power on Earth (*Showcase '95* #2, February 1995). She managed to free herself and worked with Arsenal's Teen Titans to stop Raven. He offered Supergirl membership, which she accepted (*The New Titans* #121, May 1995). However, it was not long before the team disbanded (*Titans Secret Files* #1, March 1999).

Later, Titans veteran Cyborg also decided that the next generation of heroes needed time to bond, blow off steam, and train, so he invited them all to re-form the Teen Titans, initially limiting the gatherings to the weekend. Superman insisted Connor Kent join so he could make some friends with powerful peers (*Teen Titans* [third series] #1, September 2003). Conner relished being on the team, becoming best of friends with Robin and beginning a serious romance with Cassie Sandsmark, the second Wonder Girl.

Superboy returned from a jaunt to the thirty-first century just in time to see the Titans and Legion of Super-Heroes get caught up in an adventure that resulted in a vastly different reality for the future team and landed the Titans a decade ahead of their normal era (*Titans/Legion Special* #1, 2004). Conner Kent was at first thrilled to see that he had grown up and finally become Superman, his fondest wish come true. He was horrified, however, to see that his older counterpart helped sustain a police state, never learning that his other genetic father Lex Luthor was acting as his mentor (*Teen Titans* [third series] #17–19, December 2004–February 2005).

Everyone who had ever been a Titan rallied to the call "Titans Together!" during the events of Infinite Crisis, helping oppose Superboy-Prime, only to see Conner fall in battle. A statue commemorating the fallen teen was placed in front of Titans Tower in San Francisco.

The Titans endured his loss, and the team continued to fight for justice. During a battle between the United States and the Amazons of Themyscira, Wonder Girl and the latest incarnation of Supergirl formed a close bond. The Maid of Might's actions led Superman to approve of her joining the Titans (*Teen Titans* [third series] #50, October 2007). On her very first mission, she wound up battling a potential future version of the Titans, complete with a resurrected version of Conner Kent, her sort-of cousin Superboy. The exploit led to an argument between Supergirl and Wonder Girl, and the Kryptonian decided she was better off working separately from the team (*Teen Titans* [third series] #55, March 2008).

Given the belief that Batman was dead, Tim Drake left the team to assume the role of Red Robin and find out the truth. Team leadership fell to Wonder Girl, who tried to keep the Titans intact even though the core founders were missing. She was an able field commander and good friend to the still-gelling team. When they needed a power infusion, Cyborg recruited Kid Flash (the former Impulse) and Superboy back to active duty (*Teen Titan* [third series] #81, May 2010).

TELEPATHIC HOUNDS

Native to Krypton, these "strange beasts" were yellow in color and had tails like wolves and snouts like wild boars "that can locate people at any distance by reading their minds to learn where they are" (*Superman* [first series] #158, January 1963). Several members of the species survived the planet's destruction and resided within the bottle city of Kandor. When Superman and Jimmy Olsen became fugitives, telepathic hounds were used to help find the duo. Much as it shielded from kryptonite radiation, a lead cap somehow prevented the beasts from making telepathic contact. The pair later adopted a hound when they adventured as Nightwing and Flamebird; they called the pet Nighthound (*World's Finest Comics* #143, August 1964). In another Kandorian adventure, the Man of Steel used two of the hounds to help learn Batman and Robin's secret identities after an amnesia machine caused him to forget them. The Caped Crusader avoided detection by using an EEG machine to record his thoughts, and then leaving the vital information in Clark Kent's apartment (*World's Finest Comics* #149, May 1965).

TELLE

The Kryptonian god of wisdom was remembered with a statue maintained along the "Boulevard of Legendary Heroes" in the bottle city of Kandor (*Action Comics* #99, April 1963).

TERRA-MAN

Toby Manning was "born on Earth 100 years ago, but raised on a faraway world where he learned science far beyond what we know here." His bizarre story began when an alien visited Earth in 1888, which coincided with a visit by a time-traveling Superboy (*The New Adventures of Superboy* #23, November 1981). The alien known as the Collector encountered outlaw Jess Manning—Toby's father—who drew his six-gun and fired at the unknown entity; the extraterrestrial reflexively fired back with a weapon of his own, killing Jess. Guilt-ridden, the Collector erased young Toby's memories of his role in the killing and decided to take the boy on his exploration across the galaxy. During their time together, Toby Manning learned how to use advanced technology and weaponry. The Collector chose to model some of the weapons after nineteenth-century Old West guns and ammunition to comfort the boy, who had grown to miss his old life. The alien somehow altered Manning's body to withstand the vacuum of space without protection.

When he reached adulthood, Manning revealed that he had not forgotten who took his father's life. He avenged Jess by killing the alien and chose the life of an intergalactic outlaw, using the name Terra-Man to identify his origins. "By a paradox of space-travel, time [slowed] down while traveling near the speed of light. Thus, while Toby [had] aged 20 years in two decades of space-flight, 100 years [had] gone by on Earth." In time, Terra-Man found his way back to his homeworld, only to find that his criminal ways were opposed by Superman (*Superman* [first series] #249–250, March–April 1972).

Astride his winged Arguvian space-steed Nova, speaking with a cowboy's drawl, and wearing a cowboy hat and boots, yellow shirt, green cape, and brown trousers with chaps, the Crooked Cowboy seemed a man out of time—until he unholstered his weapons and fired energy blasts that packed a much greater wallop than a Colt .45. After being upstaged by the Man of Steel, Terra-Man lingered on Earth, repeatedly seeking opportunities to gain the upper hand in battle (*Superman* [first series] #259, December 1972; *Action Comics* #426, August 1973; *Superman* [first series] #278, August 1974; others). When the Collector's brother targeted him for revenge, Terra-Man even conspired to transform Superman into his double in the hope that he would die instead (*Action Comics* #468–470, February–April 1977).

As he reacclimated himself to Earth, Terra-Man began forging short-lived partnerships with other villains such as the Penguin (*World's Finest Comics* #261, February–March 1981) and Lex Luthor (*Superman Spectacular* #1, 1982). He even discovered a parallel Earth governed by magic rather than science and joined forces with its enchanted Terra-Man in an effort to overpower Earth-1's Superman (*Superman* [first series] #377, November 1982).

After reality was altered by the Crisis on Infinite Earths, Tobias Manning was a twentieth-century resident on Earth deeply concerned about Earth's degrading ecology. In order to force companies to change environmentally destructive practices, he attacked firms he considered dangerous. While still resembling an old-time cowboy, Terra-Man employed sophisticated weaponry and even had a robotic army, named the Terra-Men, constructed (*Superman* [second series] #46, August 1990).

Using his jetpacks and armor, the criminal could fashion a teleportation vortex similar to a small tornado. His pistol could cause seismic activity or fire specially designed flora. The plants—bred for his ecological battle to save the planet—were able to drain any energy derived from sunlight away from living beings, including Superman. Terra-Man

felt ambivalently toward the hero, seeing in him a desire to also preserve the ecosphere but finding his methods of crime fighting questionable given the rampant destruction left in his wake. Terra-Man's own methods made him an ally or enemy depending upon the circumstances, so he was as likely to fight Superman as he was to aid the METROPOLIS SPECIAL CRIMES UNIT (*Metropolis S.C.U.* #1–4, November 1994–February 1995). Despite all that, he was enticed into joining ALEXANDER LUTHOR JUNIOR's Secret Society of Super-Villains.

Terra-Man returned to his own path once INFINITE CRISIS ended, but the temporary absence of Superman only meant that he was opposed instead by POWER GIRL when they fought over Ferris Air Flight 456. When he sought refuge in Khandaq, it was granted by its sovereign Black Adam. However, when Adam addressed the media in front of Khandaq's embassy in New York City, he ripped the Crooked Cowboy in half (*52* #3, July 2006).

TERRIBLE TRIO, THE

When LEX LUTHOR, TOYMAN, and the PRANKSTER combined forces, the media dubbed them the Terrible Trio. Even together, they were no match for the Man of Steel (*Superman* [first series] #88, March 1954).

THAN-AR

Than-Ar was a Kandorian official and brother to Jhan-Ar (*World's Finest Comics* #143, August 1964). Than-Ar used a special "force-radiating instrument" capable of transforming human flesh into "invulnerable metal." In this METALLOID form, he committed a series of crimes throughout the bottle city as part of a ruse on Superman's part to restore BATMAN's self-confidence after he was wounded during a case. The plan almost worked until Jhan-Ar, his criminal brother, also used the device to become a metalloid and caused much havoc. Not only did the Dynamic Duo swing into action, but Superman and JIMMY OLSEN, in their guises of NIGHTWING and FLAMEBIRD, partnered up and brought Jhan-Ar to justice (*World's Finest Comics* #143, August 1964).

THAN-OL

A reactionary Kryptonian scientist who devised an ultimately unsuccessful method of enlarging KANDOR. When he attempted the enlargement of the city, he was unaware that the apparatus he'd built contained a fatal drawback that would bring doomsday to the bottle city and its inhabitants by weakening the bonds among atoms and causing the city to disintegrate completely within three hours.

THE FANATIC SCIENTIST GLADLY WELCOMES "VAN ZEE", NOT KNOWING HE IS REALLY HIS DOUBLE... SUPERMAN!
SO YOU'VE CHANGED YOUR MIND, VAN ZEE? YOU'RE GOING TO HELP US IN THE GREAT TASK OF MAKING KANDOR NORMAL-SIZED?
FIRST I'D LIKE TO SEE THE PROCESS YOU INTEND TO USE! I MAY BE ABLE TO MAKE SOME SUGGESTION, THAN OL!

Superman opposed the experiment and was accused of being jealous that someone had found a way to save the city before he could. The city was enlarged as expected—but just at the three-hour mark, the Man of Steel's concerns became a grim reality. He then combined with NOR-KAN, VAN-ZEE, the SUPERMAN EMERGENCY SQUAD, and his pal JIMMY OLSEN to prevent a deadly catastrophe (*Superman* [first series] #158, January 1963). This also marked the first time Superman and Jimmy became NIGHTWING and FLAMEBIRD.

THARB-EL

Tharb-El of the famed HOUSE OF EL was a scientist devoted to finding a cure for VIRUS X, the fatal Kryptonian disease. He thought that "Element 202," discovered during his work with the pathologic microorganism, was the answer, but KRYPTON exploded before he could be certain (*Superman* [first series] #156, October 1962).

THARKA

Hailing from the planet ZOR, Tharka was a superhero on her homeworld. In her orange minidress, green cape, and green gloves, with the white letter T on a black background emblazoned on her chest, the attractive blonde once visited Earth in the name of interplanetary goodwill. While in METROPOLIS, she was determined to apprehend "Bowtie" Barris and his criminal gang. When she arrived, the thieves were helping themselves to the city's riches thanks to a hijacked experimental tank. Her efforts were hampered when she realized Earth's heavier gravity robbed her of many of her abilities, and Superman secretly aided Tharka so as not to hurt her feelings. When the mission was accomplished, she happily returned to Zor (*Superman* [first series] #81, March–April 1953).

THARN

The boy from the planet Kormo who became known as SKYBOY.

THAROK

When SUPERBOY and the LEGION OF SUPER-HEROES needed help to save Earth's star from the SUN-EATER, they turned to a quintet of deadly villains. Tharok was a cyborg, neatly divided vertically in half, with his left side automated and supplementing his human right side. He was initially a petty thief from ZARON, but his body suffered damage during a botched theft of a nuclear device. The one benefit that Tharok received from his computerized upgrades was an increased intellect. When he was recruited to help, he wound up taking control of the other criminals—the PERSUADER, VALIDUS, Emerald Empress, and MANO—and forming the dangerous FATAL FIVE (*Adventure Comics* #352–353, January–February 1967).

Tharok's background was modified in the wake of ZERO HOUR in that it was a powerful solvent that had destroyed half his body (*Legionnaires* #34, February 1996).

THE ZADRONIANS DID NOT REALIZE THAT THE LINKAGE OF HALF A HUMAN BRAIN TO HALF A ROBOT BRAIN GAVE THAROK A MENTALITY BEYOND MEASURE AND INCREASED HIS LUST FOR EVIL!
IT WAS A LAWMAN WHO DOOMED ME TO BE A HALF-METAL FREAK FOR LIFE! BUT I'LL HAVE MY REVENGE AGAINST ALL LAWMEN... EVERYWHERE!

THING, THE

"A shapeless protoplasm" that was capable of assuming any form it pleased, mimicking the characteristics of its target and menacing the people on a world in the year AD 40,000. They banished it to the past, and the creature arrived on twentieth-century Earth. There it survived by imitating various people in its quest to return to its normal era. Superman intervened and was also imitated, leading to a battle of the doubles. The creature's goal was not simply to go home but also to gain revenge by becoming the world's dictator, something the Man of Steel was determined to prevent. He thought the Thing had been destroyed when it was caught in a hydrogen bomb explosion (*Superman* [first series] #87, February 1954).

The creature, however, survived and landed on the planet Kuraq in a delusional state: It believed itself to be Superman himself and treated the Vegan star system's Omega Men as if they were the villains. Reminded of the heroic qualities that the true Man of Steel possessed, the Thing appeared to sacrifice its life to save the Omegans it had endangered. Now reduced to a disembodied state, the Thing joined similar energy beings in seeking a more altruistic existence (*DC Comics Presents* #89, January 1986).

THINKER, THE

There were two men who considered themselves smart enough to take the name the Thinker. The first was considered the "master strategist of the underworld," a brilliant "gang chieftain whose name has become legendary in underworld circles" for the "cunning generalship" with which he led his men and the "clockwork precision" that characterized his crimes in METROPOLIS. Despite all his vaunted brilliance, the Thinker was stopped and apprehended by Superman while still in his guise as mild-mannered reporter CLARK KENT (*Action Comics* #70, March 1944).

Sometime later, a second Thinker arrived in Metropolis's underworld. The "big brain of gangdom," he led his own gang that kidnapped JIMMY OLSEN.

Jimmy was replaced with Baby-Face, a thug who happened to resemble the cub reporter. The imitator fulfilled Jimmy's duties at the *Daily Planet* while gleaning information that could prove valuable to the criminals. He stumbled across evidence suggesting Clark Kent was also Superman, resulting in a ruse that revealed Baby-Face. Superman then apprehended him, the Thinker, and the gang while freeing Jimmy Olsen (*Superman* [first series] #93, November 1954).

THIRTEEN, TRACI

Daughter to Terrence Thirteen, the celebrated Ghost Breaker, Traci was actually born a member of the *homo magi*, a race of humans with the ability to wield magical energies. Since magic resulted in his wife's death, Dr. Thirteen forbade his teenage daughter from using her gifts. However, she worked on magical spells in private, with the Elongated Man and his wife Sue Dibny acting as mentors (*Blue Beetle* [second series] #16, August 2007). As a result of tensions at home, she and her pet iguana Leeroy left her father's home and rented an apartment in the Suicide Slum section of Metropolis. She found a way to use the city's "urban magic" and operated under the name Girl 13, taking on the supernatural forces in the city's shadows.

When she discovered a situation beyond her experience, she wound up writing a letter to Lana Lang asking for her help. Ignoring her husband Pete Ross's advice, Lana went to Metropolis only to suddenly vanish, prompting Superman to go undercover, against Batman's advice, in search of his friend. He encountered a mystical beast known as the Heartbreaker and its parasitic underlings, which fed on people's emotions, increasing their sense of despair. Just before Lana could commit suicide, Clark Kent rescued her and used memories of their childhood together to break the creature's hold on her. He then freed Dr. Thirteen and the others in its thrall before finally vanquishing the being (*Superman* [second series] #189; *The Adventures of Superman* #611; *Superman: The Man of Steel* #133; *Action Comics* #798—all February 2003).

Traci then met Superboy. While the Clone of Steel was attracted to the dark-haired beauty, she did not reciprocate his feelings.

Later, Traci met Natasha Irons when she was operating as Steel, and Cir-El, the futuristic Supergirl, forming an instant bond of friendship. They teamed up to assist Superman when he was injured in battle with the ghostly ninja Byakko (*Action Comics* #806–808, October–December 2003).

Traci survived the Spectre's assault on all magic users during the Day of Vengeance, and worked with the elder statesmen among magicians to perform cleanup duties (*Day of Vengeance: Infinite Crisis Special,* March 2006). At one point, at the invitation of the Elongated Man, she became a member of the Croatoan Society, a group of paranormal detectives. When not solving mystical crimes, she was actively dating Jaime Reyes, the third Blue Beetle. In time, he became a member of the Teen Titans; she flirted with the notion of also joining but decided to remain a free agent instead.

THOMPKINS, TOMMY

A member of the famed Newsboy Legion, this two-fisted adventurer was nicknamed Tommy.

THON

Superman visited the tiny planet of Thon when he was invited to compete against other super-Olympic contestants and thwarted a scheme by a pair of evil aliens to win. Their goal was to obtain the prize: a "giant power crystal," a glowing, "limitless source of energy," by employing a "powerful, remote-controlled robot" named Bronno in lieu of the legitimate contestant (*Action Comics* #220, September 1956).

THOR

The Man of Steel thought he might be dealing with the Norse god of thunder when Thor, Loki, and Odin publicly challenged him to several feats of strength. As he investigated, it turned out to be a publicity ploy from Miracle Movies for the forthcoming release of their film *Northern Lights* (*Superman* [first series] #52, May–June 1948).

Jimmy Olsen later had a series of dreams that implied he'd lived previous lives. In one, he was a Viking pal to the red-bearded god. "Jimmy the Red" would call upon the Thunderer's aid by using a "signal gong," hoping to write about their search for "Viking pirate treasure." When he awoke, the cub reporter realized he was being manipulated by the crooked Swami Rama (*Superman's Pal, Jimmy Olsen* #16, October 1956). "Jimmy the Red" later experienced an apparently genuine meeting with the god of thunder when a spell accidentally drew him into the past. Freeing Thor from imprisonment, Jimmy earned the hero's undying gratitude and ultimately helped him outwit Loki, whom the young reporter deduced was an imp from Fifth Dimensional Zrfff and could be returned there if he could be tricked into saying his name backward (*Superman's Pal, Jimmy Olsen* #55, September 1961).

In post-Crisis history, Thor summoned Superman and Wonder Woman to Valhalla to join him and other warriors in battling the demonic Vrgtsmyth for one thousand years even as only minutes passed on the Earthly plane (*Action Comics* #761, January 2000).

THORGENSON, MORGAN

Billionaire Morgan Thorgenson placed an ad in the *Daily Planet* seeking the Man of Steel's help with his willful daughter Nancy Thorgenson. As Superman arrived at the mansion, located by the Cathel River, the wealthy man was endangered when the nearby Dixon Dam broke (*Action Comics* #40, September 1941).

THORGENSON, NANCY

The spoiled daughter of billionaire Morgan Thorgenson, Nancy had planned to elope with Freddie Taylor before Morgan called on Superman for help. She also found herself in over her head when she visited an illegal gambling parlor run by a man named Parello (*Action Comics* #40, September 1941).

THORNTON, COLIN

Lord Satanus worked in the guise of Colin Thornton to further his goals of gathering souls—and therefore power—within Hell. As Thornton, he became a successful businessman, eventually owning and publishing *Newstime Magazine,* where Clark Kent briefly worked.

THORON

Located in the same solar system as Krypton, Thoron was a "smaller world than mighty Krypton—but still much larger than Earth!" The world was the home planet of the alien Halk Kar (*Superman* [first series] #80, January–February 1953).

THORONES

People living on the planet Thoron developed superpowers from their native star, but lost these abilities in darkness. Superman learned of this when he tracked the Four Galactic Thiefmasters to the world and was stranded there. On the planet's dark side, where no one developed powers, the Man of Steel built an army of robots and outwitted the Thorones, who harbored a desire to conquer Earth. While there, Superman fended off the amorous intentions of Lahla, who realized she preferred her men more mild-mannered than Superman (*Action Comics* #321, February 1965).

THORUL

When Jules and Arlene Luthor saw their teenage son Lex Luthor turn into a dangerous juvenile delinquent, the disgraced couple left Smallville and altered their surname to Thorul. Their younger daughter Lena Thorul grew up unaware that her sibling was a criminal genius. While Lena was still a toddler, her parents were killed in an automobile accident (*Superman's Girl Friend, Lois Lane* #23, February 1961).

THORUL, LENA

Young Lena Luthor grew up unaware that her significantly older brother Lex Luthor was not only a genius, but also a criminal. All she recalled was that at some point, the family relocated from Smallville, and she thought of herself as Lena Thorul, an only child, after her parents Jules and Arlene told her that Lex had died in a mountain-climbing accident (*Superman's Girl Friend, Lois Lane* #23, February 1961). Thanks to an electrical shock from an alien brain that her brother was studying before he

LINDA! SOMEHOW I SENSE JEFF IS IN DANGER! HE'S IN A PLANE... ABOUT TO CRASH...
RELAX! IT'S JUST YOUR IMAGINATION. I'M GOING TO LOOK FOR MORE FIREWOOD.
LENA'S E.S.P. POWERS ALWAYS WARN HER OF TROUBLE! I'D BETTER CHECK.

turned to crime, Lena also developed limited telepathic abilities. After her parents were killed in a car accident, the toddler Lena was raised in an orphanage (*Action Comics* #295, December 1962).

Growing into a beautiful blond teenager, Lena was also unaware that her older brother, still alive, kept a distant eye on her, ensuring her welfare through covert means. After graduating with a degree, Lena went to work as a librarian in the New England town of Cardiff. There she happened to meet Lois Lane, who thought Lena's uncanny resemblance to the witch Louella Thompson made her worthy of a feature story. Every effort she made to cover the story was thwarted, and she began to suspect that Lena was the witch reincarnated until she and Clark Kent began investigating. Then Lois and Superman confronted the escaped Lex Luthor and learned he had been perpetrating the weird events in the hope of protecting his sister's true identity. "Let me continue to protect Lena from the stigma of being exposed as Luthor's sister! It's the only decent thing I've ever done!" Please . . . !!" he asked of the reporters, who agreed not to file the story.

After her foster parents moved to Midvale, Lena quickly formed a friendship with Linda Danvers in their senior year of high school, unaware that the teen was also Supergirl. Intent on joining the FBI after graduation, Lena was heartbroken when she was rejected. Supergirl then looked into the matter and discovered that Lena's lack of birth records and basic background data made her a security risk. Digging deeper, the Girl of Steel learned of her friend's unsuspected relationship to Lex Luthor, but vowed never to tell her. Given Lena's extrasensory perception, Linda had to be doubly cautious around her friend lest a stray thought reveal either her alter ego or Lena's kinship to Lex (*Action Comics* #295, December 1962).

Lena subsequently became ensnared in a plot of the evil Lesla-Lar, who exchanged places with the teen as she once had with Supergirl. Working with Supergirl to thwart the plot of the villainess and her Phantom Zone partners, Lex Luthor agreed to return to prison peacefully once his sister was freed from her captivity from the bottle city of Kandor (*Action Comics* #296–298, January–March 1963).

Despite the best efforts of all involved, Lena's ESP ultimately picked up the truth from Lex himself while she was interviewing him for a criminology paper. In a state of shock, Lena fled Midvale and drifted from job to job until her brother escaped prison long enough to expose her to a rare plant whose scent stripped away her recent memories (*Action Comics* #313, June 1964).

As she neared graduation, Lena married Jeff Colby, an FBI agent who, to her brother's dismay, had once arrested Lex Luthor (*Action Comics* #317, October 1964). The couple became the parents of a son named Val (*Adventure Comics* #387–388, December 1969–January 1970), but their happiness turned to sorrow when Jeff was killed in the line of duty.

Moving to New York City with Val and her mother-in-law, Lena was reunited with Linda Danvers. When her mental powers were temporarily boosted by a psychic villain called the Mind-Bomber, Lena discovered conclusively that her old friend was, in fact, Supergirl, and promised to keep her secret (*Superman Family* #211, October 1981).

Soon after, however, Lena collapsed from a cerebral hemorrhage. As she underwent surgery, her mother-in-law resolved to share with her an FBI dossier that Jeff had "appropriated" before his death—files that revealed Lex Luthor as her brother. Lena's anger with Supergirl for withholding the secret was compounded when a rival of Lex's tried to strike at the villain through his sister. Ultimately, however, the siblings began to take the first tentative steps at reconciliation. Ironically, the surgery had stripped Lena of another secret, that of Supergirl's true identity (*Superman Family* #213–214, December 1981–January 1982).

In the realities after the Crisis on Infinite Earths, Lex Luthor had no sister until the events of Final Crisis restored the younger Lena to Lex's life (*Superman: Secret Origin* #2, December 2009; *Adventure Comics* #509, March 2010).

THOUGHT-BEAST

Found in the Scarlet Jungle of Krypton, this rhinoceros-sized beast also had a head frill not dissimilar to the triceratops on Earth. On its frill, a beast could project images that would show a third person's view of what was on its mind. The carnivorous creatures tended to see Kryptonians as a meal and were fairly aggressive.

One Thought-Beast survived the destruction of Krypton in the possession of an alien zoo, but it escaped and arrived on Earth, where it gained superpowers under the lighter gravity and yellow solar radiation. As a result, it fell to Superboy to

OW-W-W!!... MY SUPER-STRENGTH IS USELESS AGAINST THIS THOUGHT-MONSTER I ONCE ENCOUNTERED ON KRYPTON! AND JUDGING BY THE PICTURE ON HIS HEAD-SCREEN, I'M TO BE HIS NEXT MEAL!

capture the beast before it harmed any humans (*Superboy* [first series] #87, March 1961; others).

Later, as Superman, Kal-El traveled back in time with Jax-Ur, temporarily paroled from the Phantom Zone, to locate a rare fungal spore within the Scarlet Jungle. The pair used a mushroom to distract the beast that found them, and the impact on its frill broke the animal's concentration (*Action Comics* #310, March 1964).

In the history that developed following the Infinite Crisis, Superman had a living Thought-Beast in his Fortress of Solitude's Interplanetary Zoo (*Action Comics Annual* #10, March 2007), while others survived in Kandor (*Superman: World of New Krypton* #2, June 2009).

THRAXX

In another dimension resided the world of Thraxx. There the inhabitants' technology allowed them to pierce the dimensional veil and observe life elsewhere. The people were fascinated by the exploits of Earth's Superboy, and he became a popular media sensation. When an audience survey revealed Jonathan and Martha Kent were considered too old to care for the teen, Jolax and Mya traveled to Earth and exposed the Kents to a rejuvenation serum that made them appear to be in their thirties (*Superboy* [first series] #145, March 1968).

THREE MUSKETEERS, THE

On one of the many time-travel trips Superman took courtesy of Professor Carter Nichols, he and the Dynamic Duo wound up in France in the year 1696, during the reign of Louis XIV. As a result, they shared an unexpected adventure alongside the legendary Musketeers Athos, Porthos, and Aramis, along with D'Artagnan, bringing about the downfall of the king's "evil chancellor" Bourdet (*World's Finest Comics* #82, May–June 1956).

THUMB, TOM

Tom and Tina Thumb were a husband-and-wife team of midget actors who were hired to star in *The Super-Rescue of Lois Lane, Girl Reporter*. In the melodrama, Tom donned a Superman costume and was called Super-Midget. During shooting of the feature film, Tom was accidentally exposed to an enlarging ray by the real Man of Steel, and production was disrupted. To salvage the schedule, Superman flew back in time and collected himself when he was a mere Superbaby. His younger self performed opposite Tina, who played Lois Lane, and rescued her from the clutches of the evil Goliath the Giant. The villain's unscrupulous press agent Joe Trent tried to murder Tom in a publicity frenzy but was apprehended by Superman. In time, Tom was restored to his proper size (*Superman* [first series] #115, August 1957).

THWISTLE, HECTOR

This scatterbrained inventor created useless devices such as skis on rollers for skiers who also liked to roller skate, and an alarm clock that woke you up by tickling the soles of your feet. He wound up aiding the Man of Steel after the criminal Joe Jipper used his inventions to commit crimes, all

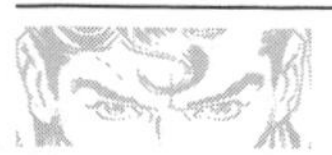

the while passing himself off as the inventor's agent and part of the Joe Jipper Promotion Company (*Superman* [first series] #43, November-December 1946).

TIELLI, CLAUDIO

A member of the Supermen of America who adventured under the name Pyrogen.

TIGER GANG, THE

A Metropolis criminal gang attired in striped costumes and masks that was apprehended by Superman at a "swank millionaire country club" while the Man of Steel was under the hypnotic compulsion of a comet (*Action Comics* #337, May 1966).

TIME-AND-SPACE WARPER, THE

When Jimmy Olsen wanted to make a film, he used Professor Phineas Potter's Time-and-Space Warper to summon both Titano the super-ape and a flame dragon from Krypton. He placed both on a remote Pacific island, where the two predators battled each other, which proved dangerous to the island's native inhabitants. Jimmy used a gas gun to calm the beasts down, and then used the time machine to send them back to their proper places. When Jimmy despaired that the fight had destroyed his camera, Superman revealed he had a satellite in place to record the battle for his friend (*Superman's Pal, Jimmy Olsen* #84, April 1965).

TIME-BUBBLE

When R. J. Brande suggested that Cosmic Boy, Saturn Girl, and Lightning Lad form the Legion of Super-Heroes, it was a moment of inspiration, recalling Superboy's classic exploits. Soon after they formed, Brande provided them with a Time-Bubble that allowed them to visit the past and invite the Teen of Steel to actually join the team. There was just the one Time-Bubble, although others were added until they were all replaced by the more sophisticated Time-Cubes (*Adventure Comics* #247, April 1958).

TIME TRAPPER, THE

Somewhere at the end point of the timestream resided the cloaked figure known only as the Time Trapper. While he could play with time to his heart's content, he seemed to single out the Legion of Super-Heroes in multiple versions of the universe and relished altering events to toy with or even destroy them (*Adventure Comics* #317, February 1964).

The Legion first became aware of him when he formed an Iron Curtain of Time that prevented the Legion's Time-Bubbles from traveling forward in time.

Over their encounters, the Legion came to learn that he had secreted away many slaves through the years, although he always kept one particular slave, a woman named Glorith, at his side. At that point, he tasked her with a scheme to revert the Legionnaires to their infant selves. When his machine was wrecked, he punished her failure by de-aging her back to a zygote (*Adventure Comics* #338, October 1965).

At one point, he did manage to trap Superman so far into the future that the Man of Steel had to struggle to loop around and return to his proper era (*Action Comics* #385–386, March–April 1970). On another occasion, the Time Trapper negated all future time lines that might lead to the creation of the Legion of Super-Heroes, leaving only an apocalyptic one where Kamandi once existed. A thirtieth-century Green Lantern named Xenofobe used Superman as the catalyst for restoring the infinite futures (*Superman* [first series] #295, January 1976).

During another time, a rogue member of the Controllers operated as the Time Trapper (*All-New Collector's Edition* #55, 1978), losing one match after another with the Legion until the Great Darkness Saga. There, even the Trapper proved no match for Darkseid, who wound up stripping him of his temporal abilities (*Legion of Super-Heroes* [third series] #291, September 1982). In fact, the Controller turned out to be an imposter later executed by the vastly more powerful genuine article (*Legionnaires Three* #1, February 1986).

While he did focus on the Legion, the Time Trapper apparently also interfered with other major figures through time, such as appearing to Wonder Woman under the name Time Master. He had the Amazon Princess and her friend Steve

Trevor travel through various eras dealing with disasters before she finally ended his game (*Wonder Woman* [first series] #101, October 1958). When he reappeared before her and Superman, Wonder Woman realized that the Time Master and the Time Trapper were one and the same, with the Man of Steel theorizing that the Trapper's plan was to wipe out heroes from throughout history (*Super Friends* #17, February 1979).

When the Crisis on Infinite Earths began a series of reality-altering events, the Time Trapper, perhaps because of his position at the end of all time, was most severely affected, so differing incarnations of the Legion found him to be an adult Cosmic Boy (*Legion of Super-Heroes* [third series] #36, July 1987), Glorith herself, Lori Morning (*Legion of Super-Heroes* [fourth series] #91, April 1997), the living embodiment of Entropy, and perhaps even Superboy-Prime (*Final Crisis: Legion of 3 Worlds* #4, April 2009).

During the First Crisis, the Time Trapper stole a sliver of time before it was altered and saved it as a Pocket Universe, one that resembled Earth-1 before reality changed. In the reordered universe, Kal-El became Superman without adventuring first as a Teen of Steel. In the Pocket Universe, however, Superboy continued to grow and learn how to use his amazing abilities. Every time the Legion journeyed back in time to visit Superboy, the Time Trapper diverted them to the Pocket Universe, with none of them the wiser. Superboy eventually found his way into the real universe and met Superman, setting in motion a series of events that exposed the Trapper's ploy and finally ended when Superboy sacrificed himself (*Action Comics* #591; *Superman* [second series] #8; *Legion of Super-Heroes* [third series] #37–38—all August–September 1987).

In the wake of these events, Duo Damsel, Brainiac 5, Saturn Girl, and Mon-El decided to violate the Legion charter and find a way to kill the Time Trapper. When they hunted him down at his lair, they used the Infinite Man as their weapon. While it seemingly worked, it came at a terrible price, as Duo Damsel lost her second self and Mon-El was placed in a coma (*Legion of Super-Heroes* [third series] #50, September 1988). It was later learned that the Trapper's essence survived and was hiding in Mon-El's mind. The absence of the Trapper also altered events that let the sorcerer Mordru the Merciless control the universe (*Legion of Super-Heroes* [fourth series] #5, March 1990). Glorith, alive in the post-Crisis reality, assumed his role, altering time so that the magician was stopped (*Legion of Super-Heroes* [fourth series] *Annual* #1, 1990).

During the reality-altering events of Zero Hour, the Time Trapper continued to function and seemed to be killed by Parallax—but as events played out, he ultimately survived. Although he had promised Cosmic Boy that he would not interfere with time and let the Legion form, he cheated and bedeviled the team in the new reality that was created. At this stage, he also recalled all his previous selves (*Legionnaires* #60–61 and *Legion of Super-Heroes* [fourth series] #104–105—both May–June 1998).

Recognizing Superman as the World's Greatest Super Hero, the Time Trapper made it clear that if he could, he would arrange events to prevent Kal-El from ever arriving on Earth. However, the fates seemed to thwart his every effort (*Action Comics* #864, June 2008), so he did what he could to complicate matters. He claimed to be responsible for the crystal tablet that led the post-Infinite Crisis thirty-first-century citizens of Earth to believe that Superman was actually born on Earth, resulting in a xenophobic backlash (*Action Comics* #858–863, December 2007–May 2008).

When the Time Trapper intervened in the battle among the Legions culled from three parallel universes to fight Superboy-Prime's ultimate Legion of Super-Villains, he was revealed to be an older incarnation of the angry teen. When the two versions of Superboy-Prime were brought together, the younger form was disgusted at what he was destined to become and delivered a mighty blow that knocked out his older self. It also resulted in the creation of a time paradox that removed both versions from reality (*Final Crisis: Legion of 3 Worlds* #1–5, October 2008–September 2009).

There is little doubt a new version of the Time Trapper will appear to plague the Legion.

TITANO

Toto was an ape considered by many to be the smartest simian alive, and was a media celebrity as a result. He was also being trained to test a space capsule for NASA, an event covered by Lois Lane for the *Daily Planet*. When Toto was hit with a cream pie as part of an appearance, he was scared but comforted by the sympathetic reporter. Soon after, Toto was launched into space for a week's duration. While he orbited the Earth, the capsule was irradiated as a result of two meteors colliding—one largely made from radium, the other from kryptonite. The unique combination altered Toto's physiology, and when the capsule landed days later, he emerged a towering giant of an ape, measuring forty feet tall. He was scared but recognized Lois and picked her up with a massive hand, and she took to calling him Titano.

Superman arrived soon after and tried to rescue Lois from what he thought was imminent danger. Instead, he was knocked from the sky by a blast of kryptonite vision, something new for the ape. The confused beast and the reporter wended their way through Metropolis, inadvertently leaving massive damage in their wake. Lois was inspired to have the Man of Steel fashion a pair of lead-lined glasses, then had Titano don them in imitation of herself putting on sunglasses. With his eyes covered, Superman was able to grab Titano and whisk him away from the city. Once Lois was freed, Superman decided the most humane thing to do was send the giant ape to the Mesozoic era (*Superman* [first series] #127, February 1959).

At a later date, Superman was studying an alien Time-Viewer and checked in on Titano, unaware the device could bring objects forward through time—and suddenly the ape was back. Lois returned to try to calm Titano down, but she was snatched up and placed within a cage he wore around his neck. Titano seemed to be attracted to large round objects, such as the Daily Planet globe, leading Superman to conclude that the ape was hungry and seeking the prehistoric equivalent of coconuts. He flew through time and gathered several of the familiar objects; while Titano was eating, he then saved Lois and returned the ape to the past (*Superman* [first series] #142, January 1961).

On a visit to the past to take measurements of a gigantosaur, Superman encountered the giant ape a third time. Weakened from a blast of kryptonite vision, Superman's return journey home fell short. He wound up in the near-past, encountering the likes of Perry White and mobster Al Capone (*Superman* [first series] #142, January 1961).

The next recorded encounter was between ape and dog. Krypto began a playful feud with the ape when the Canine of Steel discovered that a favorite bone had been crushed by the ape's last visit to the present. They made peace after Krypto brought the ape some bananas. Titano returned the favor, saving the heroic pup from aliens (*Superman* [first series] #147, August 1961).

Bizarro found Titano fascinating and created a Bizarro Titano, complete with blue kryptonite vision, for a television program on Bizarro World (*Adventure Comics* #289, October 1961). Stranded in the prehistoric past, Jimmy Olsen had a terrifying encounter of his own with Titano (*Superman's Pal, Jimmy Olsen* #59, March 1962). Jimmy had other encounters with the ape when Titano miraculously reappeared in Metropolis and grabbed Lucy Lane rather than Lois, but he was removed from Earth by the alien princess Allura; the simians on her world were the same size as Titano (*Superman's Pal, Jimmy Olsen* #77, June 1964). The ape made a brief return from the planet of giants when Jimmy used Phineas Potter's Time-and-Space Warper to bring Titano to the present to appear in a film (*Superman's Pal, Jimmy Olsen* #84, March 1965).

Superman brought Titano briefly back to Earth as a means of dealing with a red-kryptonite-induced incident when he wound up forty feet tall as well (*Superman* [first series] #226, May 1970). He made a final visit to Earth-1 when the Atomic Skull recruited him to stand watch over a kryptonite pipeline that was fueling a rocket designed by Skull as a weapon against the Man of Steel. Superman broke the nuclear villain's hold over Titano, accomplished through an electronic implant, and then lured him away from the pipe-

PARRRHGHH?
JUST HOLD STILL, TITANO...
...AND I'LL MAKE THIS AS PAINLESS AS POSSIBLE!

line by using a one-hundred-foot-tall marionette of a television cameraman to lead him safely into a cage. Superman then transported Titano back to Allura's world (*Superman* [first series] #324, June 1978).

In the world formed in the wake of the Crisis on Infinite Earths, Titano was a normal chimpanzee subjected to horrific experiments at the hands of the U.S. government. An accident led Titano to grow in size, with predictably disastrous results. Titano tried to kill the project director Dr. Thomas Moyers for inflicting such cruelty on him, but Superman arrived to contain the chimp until Moyers found a way to reverse the growth. The radical changes to his body, while reversed, also sadly proved fatal. The whimpering Titano died in reporter Lois Lane's compassionate arms. Her column "Tears for Titano" poignantly covered the event (*Superman* [second series] *Annual* #1, 1987).

The chimp was memorialized as the mascot and namesake to Titano's Pizza, with television ads featuring the ape, now in a chef's hat, in battle with the evil Turtle Boy, which was at one time played by Jimmy Olsen (*The Adventures of Superman* #487, February 1992).

A different ape was subjected to experiments by the Kryptonite Man that enabled the animal to emit kryptonite radiation, but he was ably handled by a superpowered Jimmy, then calling himself Mr. Action. The monkey was turned over to S.T.A.R. Labs for safekeeping (*Action Comics* #854, October 2007).

TNT TRIO, THE

Ted Grand, Nat Tryon, and Tim Moore worked in tandem as the TNT Trio when they were in the employ of Lex Luthor (*Action Comics* #525, November 1981).

TODD, TOMMY

When the Jimmy Olsen Fan Club decided to hold a competition to pick its next president, all the members began building their own projects. Tommy Todd, though, noted that a girl named Jackie seemed to have personal objects that could have been provided only by the Man of Steel—and so Jimmy's masquerade as Jackie was exposed. Such deductive reasoning led Tommy to be named president (*Superman's Pal, Jimmy Olsen* #84, April 1965).

TOLOS

Tolos was a legendary figure throughout certain sectors of space, seen as a wise man or healing magician. When Superman's intergalactic companion Mope was injured, they sought out Tolos on the planet Haven. While Tolos happily used his abilities to aid Mope, he wanted payment in the form of possessing the Man of Steel's body. Tolos needed a new host body from time to time and saw Superman as an ideal candidate (*Superman* [second series] #107, December 1995). He possessed a bottle containing miniaturized people who could serve as potential hosts, which is how the Man of Steel first discovered the existence of Kandor in the world after the Crisis on Infinite Earths.

In time, Tolos found Superman on Earth and attacked him in the hope of adding him to the collection (*Action Comics* #725, September 1996), going so far as to possess Cil-Gand, a Daxamite whose powers rivaled those of the Man of Steel (*Superman: The Man of Steel* #60, September 1996). Given a Daxamite's vulnerability to lead, Superman and Professor Emil Hamilton devised a lead-based gas to incapacitate Tolos. When the entity fled Cil-Gand's body, it left the man near death, but he managed to use his "mind goggles" to destroy the entity before it could possess another (*Superman* [second series] #116, Pre-October 1996). While he was presumed dead, Tolos managed to survive within Faern, a Kandorian woman, and when she casually touched the unsuspecting hero, she possessed Superman at last. Thanks to the Atom and Hamilton, Tolos was removed from Superman's body and trapped within the phase barrier that kept Kandor captive (*Superman: The Man of Steel* #69, July 1997).

TOMAR-RE

This beaked, crested, orange-skinned native of Xudar was one of the most celebrated members of the legendary Green Lantern Corps by the time Hal Jordan joined, assigned to neighboring Space Sector 2814. Tomar-Re was one of the first Lanterns to befriend Jordan. As he became a veteran, he began training new recruits such as Arisia before being promoted to the Honor Guard.

He ably protected Sector 2813, but one failed mission gnawed at him until the day of his retirement. Tomar-Re was assigned by the Guardians of the Universe to prevent Krypton from exploding. The Lantern sought the rare compound stellarium to relieve the tectonic pressures threatening to blow up the planet. As he was en route to Krypton, a solar flare briefly blinded him, and he arrived too late to prevent the world's destruction. When he retired, he mentioned this regret, although the Guardians assured him that the fates had something different in mind for the child Kal-El, whom they foresaw as a great member of the Corps. Instead, he grew up to become Superman and aid the known universe in ways they never could have imagined (*Superman* [first series] #257, October

1972). Personally meeting the Man of Steel years later, Tomar-Re observed that Superman's existence redeemed his failure (*DC Comics Presents* #60, August 1983).

TOMPKINS, LUCILLE LANE

See Lane, Lucy.

TOMPKINS, SUSIE

The pigtailed eight-year-old niece of Lois Lane, Susie made the Earth-2 Superman's life complicated as her elaborate storytelling propelled the trio into numerous escapades. The freckle-faced daughter of Lucy Lane and her husband George Tompkins, Susie lived in the country and visited Metropolis with regularity (*Action Comics* #59, April 1943).

She was regularly described in the chronicles as "Lois Lane's problem-niece" (*Action Comics* #98, July 1946), "Lois Lane's ultra-imaginative niece" (*Superman* [first series] #47, July–August 1947), "Lois Lane's ever-fibbing niece" (*Superman* #95, February 1955), and "the girl who loves to tell whoppers" (*Superman* [first series] #40, May–June 1946).

Clark Kent met Susie before his heroic alter ego did, when he agreed to babysit the child one afternoon. Her vivid imagination resulted in his having an elaborate dream after reading her Cinderella, with a variation of the fairy tale featuring him and Susie (*Action Comics* #59, April 1943).

When the Fifth Dimensional imp found her, Mr. Mxyztplk and Susie formed an alliance that left Metropolis almost unrecognizable until Superman could finally restore order by tricking the imp into saying his name backward, which sent him back to the Fifth Dimension. Susie was returned to her apartment and punished for misbehaving (*Superman* [first series] #40, May–June 1946).

Susie actually aided the Man of Steel in apprehending criminals who posed as performers during a visit to Thimble's Department Stores' Children's Theater (*Action Comics* #110, July 1947).

An attempt to reform from telling fibs almost led to Susie being crushed by an elephant that had been plucked from a circus by a dirigible, proving she did indeed see the animals flying through the air. Fortunately, Superman saved her from the falling pachyderm (*Superman* [first series] #47, July–August 1947).

I WON IT AND TEN DOLLARS --FIRST PRIZE IN THE JUNIOR LIARS' CLUB CONTEST!
GOOD HEAVENS!
AT LEAST THAT'S A LEGITIMATE WAY TO CASH IN ON HER--UH--TALENT!

When Susie accidentally touched a time machine, she was transported back in time to the era of the Arabian Nights. The Sultan was enchanted with Susie's fanciful stories and confiscated the machine to prevent her from using her "magic powers" to leave. Superman followed her into the past and played the part of her magic genie to free her without trouble and bring her back to a frantic Lois (*Superman* [first series] #95, February 1955).

Susie was present when Clark Kent and Lois Lane finally married (*Action Comics* #484, June 1977). As she grew up, her creative skills came in handy: She won prize money from the Junior Liars Club. Soon after, though, she had to convince Lois that she was talking with invisible aliens stranded in Metropolis Park. Superman was convinced and helped them before their damaged craft exploded and endangered the city (*Superman Family* #199, January–February 1980).

TONN

The legendary space explorer who, along with Kryp, was said to be the parent of the Kryptonian race (*Superman* [first series] #238, June 1971).

TOPSY-TURVY LAND

See Zrfff.

TORAN

An aggressive European nation, it was engaged in a long-standing struggle with neighboring Galonia. "The armed battalions of Toran unexpectedly swoops down upon a lesser nation, Galonia," fueling fears across Earth that "once again the world is being flung into a terrible conflagration!" Lois Lane and Clark Kent were dispatched as war correspondents to cover the conflict for the *Daily Star,* which enabled Superman to thwart a sinister plot to win "the sympathy of the democracies" for the Toranian cause. Sometime later, the Man of Steel realized that the war had been deliberately provoked by "a fiend named [Lex] Luthor . . . for evil purposes" as part of his heinous scheme "to engulf the entire [European] continent in bloody warfare." Neither man realized this was the beginning of a decades-long struggle between the two (*Action Comics* #22–23, March–April 1940).

TORQUASM-VO

A Kryptonian meditation technique or theta-state "practiced by certain legendary warrior sects many millennia ago . . . It was a kind of consciousness-control which allowed the practicing warrior to hone his mind into a perfect weapon. The adept could enter and maintain a hyper-calm, hyper-alert state of consciousness that would allow for perfect control and supremacy in battle" (*The Spectre* [fourth series] #3, May 2001; *Superman: The Man of Steel* #89, June 1999).

TORR THE TERRIBLE

A power-hungry emperor, Torr was the ruler of Duplor and earned his nickname given the large number of worlds he vanquished and subsequently looted. Using their advanced technology, he and his people developed starships and weapons that enabled them to terrorize their portion of the Milky Way galaxy with impunity. All inhabitants of Duplor were identical to one another given a quirk in their world's genetic codes.

Torr the Terrible's empire dwindled in size after he recklessly gambled away whole planets with other galactic conquerors. He concocted a scheme of conquest called "Project Earth-Doom," intending to kidnap the Earth and a dozen other planets by harnessing their geothermal energies to power gigantic atomic engines designed to propel the captive planets out of their respective solar systems. Each planet would therefore be transported to a new galaxy being prepared by Torr's minions in the outer reaches of space—an artificially created galaxy that would enable the power-mad Torr to rule unchallenged.

Instead, Torr encountered resistance in the form of Superman, who flew to Duplor and confronted the Terrible ruler on his home turf. Ready for a fight, he was surprised to see the mentally shattered ruler standing alone on a balcony, deserted by his followers, pathetically shouting orders to an army of inanimate robots, his only remaining subjects (*Superman* [first series] #178 July 1965).

TOTO

The original name of a gentle performing chimpanzee before he was accidentally turned into Titano.

TOWBEE

Called the "minstrel of space," Towbee was seemingly a carefree and "happy wanderer among the stars" who visited Earth, orbiting twenty-two thousand miles above Metropolis to lure the Man of Steel to him. Towbee told Superman that he had exhausted his repertoire of stories and was hoping to find tales of the hero to "sing to lonely

WELCOME, FAMOUS MAN OF STEEL!
WHO... ARE YOU?--
ARE YOU THE ONE RESPONSIBLE FOR THE MONSTER THAT'S INVADED THE CITY BELOW?

space-voyagers." To compose and perform, he used a "screensong," which could cast solid images and sounds that apparently took on a life of their own.

Seeking inspiration, he created a "drooling little monster," Artnig, a repulsive winged flying lizard that soared over the Metropolis skyline. The creature managed to grab Clark Kent and dangled the reporter over the city, preventing an opportunity for him to change into Superman. That changed when his super-breath attracted smokestack fumes to obscure his image. Recognizing the man's dilemma, Towbee created a Clark Kent apparition to cover the identity change. Superman traced the flying creature back to Towbee and asked why "these interplanetary meddlers can't understand that messing around with the lives of humans isn't right!" He then molded a "big wad of molten plastic" into a giant lens consisting of a series of prisms that focused the sun's rays on the lizard, dissolving the creation.

The minstrel left the Sol system with his "tale to sing across the galaxy," and eventually wrote his own equivalent of an epic poem about the incident (*Action Comics* #420, January 1973).

He later took the guise of the Master, aspiring to become an intergalactic conqueror. This brought him to Earth in search of papers written by Albert Einstein that had been suppressed but were reportedly involved with a new science theory. The papers, though, were stolen by Lex Luthor. When the Master arrived on Earth, Superman had already arrested Luthor and returned him to prison without securing the documents. Towbee stole them and fled for the stars. When Superman realized what was now at stake, he decided he needed Luthor's scientific genius and brought the criminal with him to a world populated by representatives of countless alien races, complicating the search for the Master. Fortunately, they found him before the Einstein documents could be used to launch the power-grabbing scheme. Superman retrieved the papers, stranding Towbee on the far-distant world. He returned to Earth, placing Lex back in jail and the papers back under lock and key (*Superman: Last Son of Krypton,* 1978).

TOYMAN, THE

Three different men used the name Toyman, all three bedeviling the Man of Steel throughout his legendary career. On Earth-2, Superman had to fight only one of these men, the bespectacled, bulbous-nosed villain who "invents weird automatic toys . . . to help him execute bizarre crimes" (*Action Comics* #64, September 1943).

In his striped suit and shoulder-length hair, the Toyman was an otherwise unnamed older gentleman who used his fascination with toys to turn them into tools to commit spectacular crimes.

The Toyman operated a secret workshop, tooled with the latest precision machinery to craft his weapons (*Action Comics* #64, September 1943). He apparently was seeking revenge against people who saw him as an odd old man, an eccentric who still played with toys. His toys proved very successful as tools of crime. His first two robberies made headlines and aroused the Man of Steel's

interest. Superman arrived in time to stop a third crime, but Toyman escaped to his hidden workshop. When Lois Lane stumbled upon it, she became his captive until rescued by the Action Ace.

Toyman escaped from prison and resumed his criminal ways, wasting his genius on crimes and vexing the Metropolis Marvel. Toyman even managed to capture Lois a second time, luring her to his workshop when she investigated his latest scheme, a crooked dollar arcade (*Superman* [first series] #27, March–April 1944). He managed to escape once more, in a model airplane, and set out to recover jewels hidden during the French Revolution by the wealthy Count du Rochette and now possessed by three wealthy Metropolis families (*Superman* [first series] #32, January–February 1945).

After another rapid escape from jail, the Toyman obtained pieces of jade that when assembled, provided a map to a hidden cache of stolen property. This escapade resulted in Lois once more being held by the criminal until Superman intervened (*Action Comics* #85, June 1945). That set the pattern for many of their subsequent encounters through the years, with the criminal genius never managing to stay imprisoned for long or successful at his crimes despite the fascinating creations he designed to accomplish them (*World's Finest Comics* #20, Winter 1945; *Superman* [first series] #47, July–August 1947; *Superman* [first series] #63, March–April 1950; others).

To change his fortunes, he once partnered with the Prankster and Lex Luthor to kill Superman as the Terrible Trio, but that failed as well (*Superman* [first series] #88, March 1954).

On Earth-1, the Toyman's background was essentially the same (*Superman's Pal, Jimmy Olsen* #9, December 1955), although he was now identified as Winslow P. Schott and finally recognized the futility of his criminal career and wanted to try reforming his ways. Jack Nimball, a younger and trimmer man, donned a black-and-yellow outfit styled after a court jester and became the new Toyman (*Action Comics* #432, February 1974). This new Toyman used high-tech gadgets and toys to commit crimes in the same manner as his predecessor, with about as much success (*Action Comics* #454, December 1975; *Superman* [first series] #299, May 1976).

When one of Schott's exhibits was accidentally destroyed by Bizarro Superman, he returned to crime, mistakenly targeting Superman as the cause. His first act, however, was to eliminate the competition, and he killed Nimball with an explosive cuckoo clock (*Superman* [first series] #305, November 1976).

Throwing himself fully into crime again, the Toyman briefly acquired a kid sidekick named Toyboy as part of the Super Foes (*Super Friends* #1–2, November–December 1976), collaborating with the Prankster (*Superman Family* #184, July–August 1977) and fighting allies of Superman such as the Justice League of America (*Super Friends* #41, February 1981), Plastic Man (*DC Comics Presents* #39, November 1981), Blue Devil (*Blue Devil* #24, May 1986), and, most incredibly, Santa Claus (*DC Comics Presents* #67, March 1984).

On the world after the Crisis on Infinite Earths, Winslow Percival Schott was an electronics genius, one of England's premier toy inventors. There were even reports that in nineteenth-century New York City, a Schott Toy Company was run by the crooked Archimedes Schott (*Speed Force* #1, November 1997). Given the resemblance to Winslow Schott, this may have been an ancestor.

A change in company ownership saw Schott get fired for being out of step with modern children's tastes, and he decided to gain revenge by devising a unique set of toys that killed the company's key shareholders, eluding capture by the country's heroine Godiva.

Successful, Schott then targeted LexCorp and its owner Lex Luthor, blaming them for instigating the corporate takeover that had cost him his job (*Superman* [second series] #13, January 1988). Arriving in Metropolis, Schott allied himself with Intergang and studied the technology from Apokolips that made the criminal organization so formidable (*Action Comics* #657, September 1990). Before he

could strike at Luthor, Intergang was exposed by DAILY PLANET reporter CATHERINE GRANT, so Schott targeted her instead for spoiling his plans. Schott remained a deadly threat, eventually shaving his head and hearing voices from "Mother" that prompted him into villainous acts. He kidnapped several children, blaming them rather than Luthor for costing him his job—by not appreciating his toys—until he was apprehended by Superman. Schott managed to gain his freedom and resumed kidnapping children, but by then it was clear he had become a child-abducting psychopath. This time he killed the children, among them Adam Grant, Cat's son. He explained that he was sent over the edge when a manufacturer released a set of toys based on the Man of Steel and his enemies—but there was no Toyman figure included (*Superman* [second series] #84, December 1993, and #98, March 1995). While Cat grieved, Superman attempted to find a rehabilitation program for the psychologically fragile man. The efforts failed, and Schott remained a deadly threat to children everywhere (*Superman* [second series] #146, July 1999).

Schott continued his criminal ways, helping to organize a mass escape from GOTHAM CITY'S Blackgate Penitentiary, adding the serums Venom and Velocity 9 to the evening's dinner stew, which caused not only the inmates but also several of the guards to temporarily gain super-strength and vastly more aggressive natures. Several members of the Justice League were required to quell the riot (*Villains United: Infinite Crisis Special*, 2006). He also served with Luthor's Injustice Gang, which attacked the League right before Green Arrow and Black Canary's nuptials (*Justice League of America Wedding Special*, 2007).

In Japan, a mechanical genius named Hiro Okamura came from a family known for manufacturing prowess. In fact, his grandfather had developed the metallic alloy that was stolen and used to fashion METALLO'S cyborg body (*Superman* [second series] #177, February 2002). Hiro encountered Superman and BATMAN when he built a giant Mecha robot combining their features to fly into space and shatter a deadly KRYPTONITE meteor that was rapidly approaching Earth. While he was successful, he also set off a chain of events that led KARA ZOR-EL'S long-trapped rocket to finally reach its intended destination and give the world a SUPERGIRL (*Superman/Batman* #1–6, October 2003–March 2004). Batman recognized Okamura's brilliance and subcontracted him—now nicknamed the Toyman—to build devices and equipment the Dark Knight needed in his never-ending battle against evil (*Superman/Batman* #7, April 2004). Okamura came to the heroes' aid on several occasions.

Okamura was a genius but also a socially lonely teen, so he faked his kidnapping at the hands of Winslow Schott, prompting a rescue by SUPERBOY and ROBIN (*Superman/Batman* #26, June 2006). When they learned the reason behind the event, they extended an offer of friendship, and Okamura began spending time at Titans Tower in San Francisco. He was also present for Conner Kent's funeral, holding a Superboy action figure in tribute. When the TEEN TITANS encountered a potential future version of themselves, Hiro was also among them (*Teen Titans* [third series] #52, January 2008).

In an apocryphal story, Superman and Batman attempted to collect all the kryptonite on Earth, and Hiro offered his assistance. He built spider-like nanobots to gather kryptonite molecules from the air. As his reward for helping, Superman arranged a dinner date in Paris for Hiro and Supergirl, the teen he'd helped rescue, and he was given honorary member status in the Justice League (*Superman/Batman* #45, March 2008).

A robot Toyman, looking like a child's marionette, later arrived in Metropolis and briefly worked with Lex Luthor (*Action Comics* #837–839; *Superman* #651–652—both May–July 2006).

After reality was modified by the events of INFINITE CRISIS, Winslow Schott was a successful toymaker who lived in America with his wife Mary. He owned a thriving independent toy shop in Metropolis and refused offers to sell and franchise his business. Mary died in a car accident a short while later, and the despondent Schott finally agreed to sell. When Schott learned that the buyer was selling his technology not for toys but munitions, he gained revenge via a bomb-stuffed teddy bear. He was also approached by the Prankster, who wanted to partner with him, but Schott refused. Schott also admitted to reporter JIMMY OLSEN that the Toyman that had killed Adam Grant was a cleverly crafted android that developed a glitch in its programming. While the android believed it was hearing "Mother," what it actually heard was Schott's attempts to contact it via remote control. Schott claimed credit for the creation of other androids, including ones that resembled the Jack Nimball incarnation, the marionette version, and even Hiro Okamura. In fact, he said that Mary was artificial, too—created to be his lifelong companion (*Action Comics* #865, July 2008).

Schott later partnered with the KRYPTONITE MAN and Mister Freeze to build a colossal robot that was based on both the Man of Steel and the Dark Knight and designed to destroy NEW KRYPTON and its inhabitants. While Red Robin, NIGHTWING, FLAMEBIRD, and Robin (Damian Wayne) began piecing together clues about the villains behind the scheme, Supergirl and the current BATGIRL were captured. Oracle had Batman (Dick Grayson) summon Superman back to Earth from New Krypton to help deal with the robot. Schott's monstrosity had not even been fully completed when it was put into operation by General SAMUEL LANE, and the machine's self-defense program was activated without its proper navigational controls. The giant robot quickly spun out of control, the KRYPTONITE MAN trapped inside and serving as its power source. Supergirl had also been trapped inside the robot as a prisoner, and while Batman was rescuing the Maid of Might and Batgirl, as well as the severely weakened Kryptonite Man, Superman hurled the giant robot into space, where it detonated harmlessly. Batgirl and Robin then captured Schott, who told the heroes that he had built the robot as part of General Lane's Project 7734. But before they could take the Toyman into custody, it was revealed that the Schott the heroes had captured was actually a sophisticated android. The real Schott was working for General Lane in exchange for having a deadly chemical removed from his brain that had been injected into him by Batman's mercurial foe, Black Mask (*World's Finest* #1–4, December 2009–March 2010).

Some of the latter incarnations of the Toyman were actually the primary representations of the villain in parallel universes. The Jack Nimball version, for instance, was part of the LEGION OF DOOM on Earth-22 (*Justice* #1, October 2005; others).

TRANSFORMOFLUX PACK

Created by the Kryptonian surgeon Dahr-Nel, this energy device was a type of battery that he used during procedures on KRYPTON. Superman used it to power the PLASTIMOLD, another of his inventions, on several occasions (*Superman's Girl Friend, Lois Lane* #90, February 1969, and #106, November 1970).

TRENT, LARRY

The former heavyweight champion of the world, Trent was saved from suicide by Superman. After learning that Trent was being drugged by thugs,

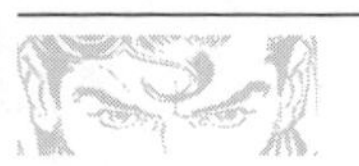

the Man of Steel helped him regain his boxing title (*Superman* [first series] #2, September 1939).

TRIBUNAL, THE

The Cyborg Superman allied himself with the Galactic Tribunal, influencing them to apprehend the Man of Steel and try him for Krypton's destruction because of actions committed by his ancestors. The impartial intergalactic entity agreed, but its notions of justice and adherence to the law differed from what was practiced on Earth. During the trial, the malevolent Cyborg sought to usurp the Tribunal Planet, altering it into a new Warworld. The Superman Rescue Squad, composed of Superboy, Supergirl, Steel, the Eradicator, and Alpha Centurion, arrived in time to thwart the Cyborg's deadly plans. Learning of the Cyborg's perfidy, they suspended Superman's trial in favor of arresting the Cyborg (*Superman: The Man of Steel* #50–52; *Superman* [second series] #106–108; *The Adventures of Superman* #529–531—all November 1995–January 1996; *Action Comics* #716–717, December 1995–January 1996; *Superman: The Man of Tomorrow* #3, Winter 1995).

TRICKY TOM

Tricky Tom, of the Black Cat World, led "a gang of cunning cats" against Tail Terrier's home planet the Green Dog World. After the Space Canine Patrol Agency defeated the "black-furred brigands," Tom was advised telepathically by the phanty-cats, "pet cats of Kryptonian criminals . . . exiled with them in the Phantom Zone," in a plan to kill Superboy and Krypto by booby-trapping statues of Superboy's ancestors (*Superboy* [first series] #136, March 1967).

TRITONIS

When ancient Atlantis sank beneath the waves, two cities survived: Tritonis and Poseidonis (first revealed in *Action Comics* #475, September 1977). While the population of each city found means of surviving underwater, the people of Tritonis did so only through a transformation into mer-people via a formula created by Nar Lemaris, an ancestor of Lori Lemaris (*Action Comics* #269, October 1960). One of the most sacred shrines in Tritonis was the Temple of Ilena, a monument of a torch-bearing "mermaid-goddess" reclining on a seashell (*Superman* [first series] #154, July 1962).

Lori Lemaris excepted, the Atlanteans' "telepathic powers [to communicate with undersea life] have weakened over the centuries," and technology was developed to assume that task (*Superman's Girl Friend, Lois Lane* #72, February 1967). The Atlantean Protective Squad dealt with attacks by aquatic life-forms, using sonic weapons or, as a last resort, force (*Action Comics* #269, October 1960) via weapons such as electric-spears (*Action Comics* #270, November 1960). Some criminals were deemed such major threats that they were exiled to the surface world, among them Goxo, who later used a growth ray that inadvertently transformed Jimmy Olsen into a giant turtle-man (*Superman's Pal, Jimmy Olsen* #53, June 1961).

Atlantis included a number of marine farms where they raised "food created especially for

THOUGH ROH-TUL'S PALACE WAS ENGULFED, OUR HISTORY SAYS THAT THE REST OF ATLANTIS SANK MORE SLOWLY, ENABLING OUR SCIENTISTS TO TURN ATLANTEANS INTO MERMEN AND MERMAIDS!

[their] unique needs. [Their] scientists developed food products that can thrive at the sea bottom." An artificially created metal "sun" provided heat and light, though "it is nowhere as hot or bright as the solar system's sun" (*Action Comics* #269, October 1960). A "chemical plant reduces the amount of salt in the water so that the Atlantides . . . can continue to survive in these oceanic depths" (*Superman* [first series] #154, July 1962).

A short-lived Fortress of Solitude once used by Superman (*Action Comics* #244, September 1958) was located at 28° North, 50° West in the Sargasso Sea. "The people of Atlantis use it as a showplace and tourist attraction" (*Superman* [first series] #176, June 1965).

The United States ultimately began the process of setting up diplomatic relations with Atlantis (*Action Comics* #420, January 1973). "Only Poseidonis, the city of Aquaman, is officially recognized by the United Nations, while Tritonis, the Atlantis of the mer-people is not" (*Action Comics* #475, September 1977). Nonetheless, perhaps as a result of the city nearly being destroyed by an atomic bomb test (*Superman* [first series] #146, July 1961), the UN declared the general area as "Zone X" and issued a fishing ban (*Action Comics* #302, July 1963).

Other inhabitants of Earth-1's Tritonis included Lori Lemaris's husband Ronal and Supergirl's one-time sweetheart Jerro.

In the reality formed after the Crisis on Infinite Earths, Tritonis and Poseidonis were ruled by the brothers Orin and Shalako, respectively, at the time Atlantis sank. According to the legendary Atlantis Chronicles, there was the account of a curse Shalako put on the rival Tritonians, causing them to develop fins in place of their legs and spawning a race of "mer-people" (*The Atlantis Chronicles* #1–5, March–July 1990).

TROLIUM

Some two thousand years in the past, the Kryptonian metal Trolium was used by Dol-Nd to create flying wings. The wings worked at keeping people aloft, but the metal left particles that were known as "death-trails," destroying any object or living being that entered the wake. While Dol-Nd destroyed the wings after they were misused by criminals, the metallic particles in the air remained, and the "death-trails" entered the planet's lore (*Superman* [first series] #243, October 1971).

TROMBUS

The Hyper-Family hailed from this far-distant planet orbiting a red sun that was described as "a close duplicate of Earth" (*Superboy* [first series] #144, January 1968).

TROUPE, RON

Ronald Troupe graduated with a BA in journalism from Howard University and then interned at *The Washington Post* for three years. He was refused a job at the *Daily Planet* by acting editor Sam Foswell before he moved to Metropolis to work as an editorial assistant at *Newstime Magazine*. After being laid off, he found work at the *Daily Planet* as a general assignment reporter, under the resumed editorship of Perry White (*The Adventures of Superman* #480, July 1991). Troupe's writing impressed White, who compared his stories about the Cyborg Superman to Clark Kent's and Lois Lane's initial reports on the newly arrived Superman. Troupe was said to be the best-educated reporter on the staff, having earned accolades for his political editorials (*Action Comics Annual* #11, 2008).

Perhaps given his temperament or training, Troupe rarely found himself in danger from costumed fanatics as his colleagues did. He was, however, in danger during a rampage from the second Bloodsport (*The Adventures of Superman* #507 and *Action Comics* #694—both December 1994). Troupe got on well with everyone at the paper, with the noteworthy exception of sports editor Steve Lombard.

MISS LANE. HI! DID YOU SAY SOMETHING?
OH... RON! HI!
YOU WERE WORKING LATE TOO, HUH?
LIKE THE HAT? MY SISTER GAVE IT TO ME WHEN I GOT MY PROMOTION.
SAID IT MADE ME LOOK LIKE A CLASSIC NEWSPAPER REPORTER.

At the time when the *Daily Planet* was sold to LexCorp, Troupe entered into a passionate romance with Lucy Lane. In time, Lucy wound up pregnant (*Superman: The Man of Steel* #83, September 1998). General Samuel Lane, exceptionally conservative in his worldview, made her life stressful, although relations improved when the couple was married and a healthy child, named Samuel Christopher, was born (*The Adventures of Superman* #487, February 2001).

When Lucy joined the military and was posted to Washington, Ron remained in Metropolis, raising Samuel on his own. He was devastated when Lucy, in her guise as Superwoman, was seemingly killed. After her miraculous resurrection she never got in touch with her husband, and when she was jailed, a crushed Ron had to raise their toddler as a single parent.

TRUGGS, NYLOR

In the thirtieth century, small-time crook Nylor Truggs robbed the Museum of Heroes and Legends and stole the alien H-dial that allowed the user to become a superpowered being for an hour. With the device, Truggs traveled back a thousand years to Smallville, where he worked with a teenage Lex Luthor. Using his advanced know-how, Truggs altered the device so that the personae were able to express evil intent as opposed to their natural inclinations. As the Cyclone (wind), Landslide (able to destroy material barriers), Unstoppable Smasher, and High-Roller (speed and agility), Truggs caused devastation across the town.

He also used the dial to transform other teens into villains under his control. As a result, Bash Bashford became Man-Mountain, Lana Lang was the Wisp (who could control molecular density), Lisa Davis morphed into the Blizzard, and Pete Ross was Megaton (who could explode and reassemble himself).

It took Superboy, aided by Chameleon Boy, Colossal Boy, Element Lad, Star Boy, and Wildfire of the Legion of Super-Heroes, to track Truggs. The Teen of Steel and Krypto the Super-Dog managed to apprehend the future foe, but only after a titanic battle with the superpowered teens (*The New Adventures of Superboy* #50, February 1984).

TRYON, NATHANIEL

This small-time criminal worked with Ted Grand and Tim Moore as the TNT Trio. When Lex Luthor sent them on a job, an accident turned Tryon into the nuclear-powered Neutron.

TURLOCK THE BERZERKER

When Zatara the Magician performed in Smallville, he wound up partnering with the Teen of Steel to stop the extra-dimensional conqueror named Turlock the Berzerker. The magically powered Turlock used a mystical sword and mace and rode on a chariot pulled by a pair of dog-like beings, making him quite the challenge for Superboy, who realized by then that magic could harm him.

The pair required the assistance of Johnny Webber, a local working as the magician's assistant, to trick the invader back to his proper realm (*The New Adventures of Superboy* #49, January 1984).

TURPIN, "TERRIBLE" DAN

On Earth-2, Dan Turpin fought in World War II as a member of Rip Carter's Boy Commandos. Known only as Brooklyn at the time, the tough-talking New Yorker used his fists with powerful precision (*Detective Comics* #64, June 1942).

On Earth-1, Turpin grew to adulthood and became a New York City cop whose brutal approach to criminals led to the nickname "Terrible." He got caught up in Darkseid's search for the Anti-Life Equation on Earth and found himself fighting criminals and creatures alongside the New God Orion (*The New Gods* #5, October–November 1971).

After the Crisis on Infinite Earths, Dan Turpin was an inspector working for the Metropolis Police Department and was one of the first assigned

Dan Turpin

to its newly formed Metropolis Special Crimes Unit when the rising tide of superpowered individuals required extra effort (*Superman* [second series] #7, July 1987). He was at first attracted to his superior, Captain Maggie Sawyer, until he learned she was a lesbian, then became her most loyal supporter and fierce friend. Though he still mourned for his wife Rosie, Dan took great pride in their daughter Maisie (*Superman* [second series] *Annual* #2, 1988).

The Metropolis S.C.U.'s success led to other cities asking for consultants to determine if they needed their own unit. Turpin was dispatched to Hawaii to consult, and there he met and adventured alongside Superboy, the Clone of Steel (*Superboy* [third series] #20, October 1995). Once the Female Furies arrived from Apokolips, Terrible Turpin agreed that the state could benefit from such a unit, which was then led by Sam Makoa.

In time, Turpin retired from active duty, but he returned to action when the New God Orion was found dead (*Final Crisis* #1, May 2008). The investigation led Turpin to the Dark Side Club, which featured mobsterized versions of the New Gods from Apokolips. In time, Turpin discovered his body was being used to house the essence of Darkseid, who avoided being killed by Infinity-Man, working on behalf of the Source (*Final Crisis* #4, August 2008).

To stop Darkseid, Batman shot Turpin with a Radion bullet, letting the Black Racer claim the New God and freeing Turpin (*Final Crisis* #6, January 2009).

TUSKY HUSKY

Able to elongate a canine tooth into a tusk, Tusky Husky was a noble member of the Space Canine Patrol Agency (*Superboy* [first series] #131, July 1966).

TWILIGHT

Twins Molly and Jane were born on the flame-pitted world of Apokolips and were being trained to join the Female Furies when they managed to escape Granny Goodness's orphanage. They made their way to Earth during the Middle Ages. Molly used her healing abilities to resurrect those who died during the Black Plague, but Jane, who had no special powers, died from the insidious disease, and all of Molly's power could not revive her sibling. She rejected God and decided to spend her waking time on Earth plotting ways to gain vengeance against the Creator (*Supergirl* [fourth series] #15, November 1997).

In the twentieth century, Jane, known now as Twilight, encountered Supergirl, who was one of the Earth-born angels, and saw destroying the teen as her way to finally get revenge. By this time, she had mastered the ability to summon shadow creatures from the blackened pit of her soul. She unleashed an army of these entities at the Maid of Steel. During their conflicts, it was revealed that Jane had not died but was possessed by the mother of demons Queen Lilith. Lilith seduced Twilight to join her, and when Supergirl was split into her two original components—Matrix and Linda Danvers—the Earth angel Matrix was captured, with Twilight assigned to guard the being.

Linda managed to rescue Jane but found herself confronted by Twilight when she tried to free Matrix. When Molly learned Jane had been freed, she switched allegiances, aiding Linda in her fight against Lilith. Twilight was mortally wounded at last by Lilith, so Matrix chose to sacrifice herself once more by merging with Twilight. The reborn being was the new Angel of Fire. With her healing abilities, she rejuvenated Linda and then left to wander the world on her own (*Supergirl* [fourth series] #74, November 2002).

U-BAN

U-Ban was one of three sibling criminals (along with Kizo and Mala) known as the Evil Three, despite their original careers as scientists on Krypton. They were among the ten leading scientists to serve on the planet's ruling Council, until they broke the Krypton Code of Honor. They intended to use their combined intellect to conquer the planet and rule it as they saw fit. To accomplish this, they built a device designed to extract all the moisture from the atmosphere, making it unfit to breathe. When Jor-El learned of their scheme, he was apprehended and held hostage while the brothers threatened the populace. In time, Jor-El freed himself and reversed the machine's devastating effects, thereby ending the danger. He even saved the criminals from a mob that wished to see them killed, instead placing them in a transparent tube that was rocketed into orbit, with the occupants placed in suspended animation until they could be rehabilitated.

The ship was thrown free when Krypton exploded, and the craft tumbled through the stars until a collision with a meteor awoke the men. They soon arrived on Earth and gained superpowers under the planet's lighter gravity and yellow solar radiation. Superman confronted them and saw that they, too, possessed superpowers. U-Ban noted, "Where I come from, everyone has see-through vision, extra-strength, and extra-speed!"

The trio explained their background and declared their intention of conquering Earth. To prove his point, U-Ban used what he called his Ultra-Voice to destroy a transmission tower; as the Man of Steel responded to the damage, the men escaped. In secret, they quickly conceived and built a device that would hypnotize all of Earth's population as well as a new moisture-sapping device dubbed the Z-2.

Superman found the men, destroyed the hypnosis machine, and reluctantly battled the fellow survivors of his doomed world. To protect his adopted home, Superman told the trio he would fight them where no one could get hurt, and the fierce battle in space wore out all four men. Superman, however, was the better trained and the more experienced tactician, and he used his ventriloquism skills to convince the others to fight among themselves. As they fought, Superman was able to gather the exhausted men into a new version of his father's rocket and return the criminals to a life in space (*Superman* [first series] #65, July–August 1950).

The outlaws from Krypton did find their way back to Earth once more, but again they met defeat at the hands of the World's Greatest Super Hero (*Action Comics* #194, July 1954).

UBC

The United Broadcasting Company was a nationwide network in all forms of mass media. Under president Samuel Tanner, they rivaled Galaxy Broadcasting System for the best ratings in television and radio. Noteworthy members of the UBC staff have included gossip reporter Lola Barnett, comedian Les Vegas, and Dr. Peter Silverstone, before he became the villainous Blackrock (*Action Comics* #458, April 1976). Its flagship channel was Metropolis's WUBC.

UGLY SUPERMAN

A professional wrestler with an unattractive face gained notoriety using the ring name of Ugly Superman. Covering an evening's set of matches for the *Daily Planet,* Lois Lane encountered the man, and her heart went out to him for enduring the fans' constant jeers. She decided to focus on the man in the Superman costume and made

him the subject of her story, hoping to win him some sympathy the next time he appeared at the Metropolis Arena.

On the day of publication, however, Lois was surprised when the dim-witted wrestler showed up at the *Daily Planet* offices, in full costume, misinterpreting the column as a declaration of her affection for him. She wound up agreeing to date him after the athlete made threats to Clark Kent. The outings were disasters, as he had little to say and displayed poor manners.

Superman tried to help by disguising himself behind a beard, and—calling himself Methuselah—he challenged the Ugly Superman to several tests of strength. At the Metropolis Gym, the two men entered the squared circle. It was clear the professional could not best the newcomer. Superman revealed himself, but that did not daunt the lug in his intention of winning Lois's heart for real.

When Lois next saw the man two months later, she was astonished to see that he was now handsome. He had undergone plastic surgery and renamed himself the Gorgeous Superman, but Lois still rejected his advances (*Superman's Girl Friend, Lois Lane* #8, April 1959).

The Ugly Superman name was still a draw for fans, and a new wrestler quickly assumed it, facing off against Elastic Lad when Jimmy Olsen used the serum to become a pliable professional wrestler (*Superman's Pal, Jimmy Olsen* #54, July 1961).

ULTRA BOY

Jo Nah was born and raised on the harsh, mostly criminal world of Rimbor, and he was naturally a borderline juvenile delinquent when his life changed forever. His parents Crav and Mytra Nah (*Adventure Comics* #356, May 1967) did what they could to educate the teen and teach him proper morals, but he was a numbers runner and a gang member. Jo Nah was flying a "space-speedster," the thirtieth-century equivalent of a hot rod, when his vehicle was swallowed by one of the Space Dragons that clustered near Rimbor.

While within the beast, something altered his physiology. When Jo Nah emerged, he suddenly had a fantastic array of powers, including flight, strength, invulnerability, and various forms of enhanced vision. Largely, his powers resembled Superboy's, although Jo Nah had penetra-vision, which could see through any object, even lead. He also had what he called "flash vision," which seemed to be a more instant version of heat vision. As he quickly learned, the powers could be used only one at a time, so he had to practice being able to rapidly switch from power to power. Jo Nah wound up rescuing Phantom Girl from Sugyn and chose to abandon both Rimbor and his girlfriend An Ryd to seek membership in the Legion of Super-Heroes (*Secret Origins* #42, July 1989).

Before gaining admittance, he had to pass a test, which was to travel back in time and discover Superboy's secret identity. Accompanied by Marla Latham, the Legion's adult adviser and a fellow Rimborian, he visited twentieth-century Smallville. The two settled in town, and Jo began attending Smallville High until he could learn the Teen of Steel's secret. Eventually successful, he and Latham first bestowed honorary membership on Pete Ross and then returned to their era and to membership as the fourteenth Legionnaire (*Superboy* [first series] #98, July 1962).

Soon after, Ultra Boy returned to Smallville to help Pete with a malfunctioning Superboy Robot (*Superboy* [first series] #100, October 1962). He also visited the past to bring Jimmy Olsen a wedding gift from the Legion when it appeared the cub reporter was about to marry Rona, a woman from another dimension (*Superman's Pal, Jimmy Olsen* #73, December 1963).

As one of the most powerful members of the Legion, Ultra Boy was often used in the vanguard of battles, flying into action flanked by Mon-El and Superboy. Given his rough upbringing, he proved himself a capable actor, playing dumber than he actually was, therefore becoming a valuable member of the Legion Espionage Squad for cover missions. He was a popular member, twice elected as Legion Leader (*Adventure Comics* #371, August 1968; *Superboy* [first series] #184, April 1972). Ultra Boy also had a lengthy romance with fellow Legionnaire Phantom Girl.

Superboy and honorary Legionnaire Lana Lang once visited the thirtieth century as part of her birthday celebration. There Lana became the Insect Queen, aiding the Teen of Steel and Ultra Boy in freeing the Legionnaires when they were taken over by a would-be conqueror who called himself the Master (*Superboy* [first series] #205, November–December 1974).

Later, An Ryd was killed by Pulsar Stargrave, who forced the insane Brainiac 5 to frame Jo Nah for the crime (*Superboy and the Legion of Super-Heroes* #239, May 1978). It was sometime later that Chameleon Boy revealed that he knew it was a frame-up, and much later before Stargrave's involvement was learned (*Superboy and the Legion of Super-Heroes* #273, March 1981).

Ultra Boy not only wound up being sent back to the twentieth century, but was also trapped in the Bgztl Buffer Zone, a realm that was theorized to also have been the Phantom Zone. Ultra Boy's mind was transferred into Superboy's body, and he adopted the new persona of Reflecto while the Legion presumed Jo Nah was dead (*Superboy and the Legion of Super-Heroes* #275, May 1981). Reflecto's true identity was revealed, however, and the confused Superboy then claimed to be Ultra Boy. As the Legion sought the truth, they confronted the Time Trapper (*Superboy and the Legion of Super-Heroes* #279–282, September–December 1981).

Not long after this was resolved, Ultra Boy was joined by Phantom Girl, Element Lad, Chameleon Boy, and Shrinking Violet in aiding Superman in his battle against Brainiac (*DC Comics Presents* #80, April 1985).

During the period when time had been altered and Superboy was removed from the Legion's history, the team actually disbanded. Ultra Boy proposed to Phantom Girl, but she seemingly died before they could wed (*Legion of Super-Heroes* [fourth series] *Annual* #1, 1990). Following this, Ultra Boy returned to Rimbor and worked as a smuggler and an outlaw. He eventually returned to the re-formed Legion after assassins targeting him for unspecified reasons wound up killing the occupants of an apartment building (*Legion of Super-Heroes* [fourth series] #3, January 1990).

Various opponents underestimated Jo Nah through the years, none more than Glorith, who took out any Legionnaires who might discover her attempts to manipulate the Legion's history. Ultra Boy exposed her scheme by tricking Mordru the Merciless into attacking her, weakening both opponents and allowing the Legion to defeat them both (*Legion of Super-Heroes* [third series] #50, September 1988; *Legion of Super-Heroes* [fourth series] *Annual* #1, 1990).

The reality after Zero Hour presented Jo Nah as the teen leader of the Emerald Dragons on the largely lawless Rimbor. He was nearly consumed by an Ultra Energy Beast, but Jo killed and ate the beast, resulting in his gaining powers. Jo Nah chose to profit from his newfound skills and served with the professional team Work Force. He was romantically involved with teammate Spider Girl (*Legion of Super-Heroes* [fourth series] #64,

January 1995), but he lost his heart to Apparition when the Legion and Work Force wound up stranded together. Ultra Boy and other members of Work Force were subsequently accepted into the Legion (*Legion of Super-Heroes* [fourth series] #72, September 1995). At one point, Apparition was believed dead, but it was learned that her essence resided within Ultra Boy's mind (*Legion of Super-Heroes* [fourth series] #82, July 1996). This deep connection led them to marry when her body was restored (*Legion of Super-Heroes* [fourth series] #96–100, September 1997–January 1998). Ultra Boy served with distinction and was part of the team that wound up lost in space (*Legion Lost* #1–12, May 2000–April 2001).

What Ultra Boy did not know at the time was that Apparition was already pregnant with their child, a fact she shared with Jo's family back on Rimbor. While there, she gave birth to a boy, who was named Cub (*Legion Worlds* #6, November 2001). During this time, Ultra Boy and Legion cofounder Saturn Girl almost gave in to their physical attraction (*Legion Lost* #9, January 2001). Fortunately, circumstances prevented anything from happening, and they were soon reunited with the remainder of the team. Ultra Boy finally got to reunite with his wife and meet his baby son (*The Legion* #14, January 2003).

In the wake of Infinite Crisis, Jo Nah's upbringing on Rimbor was largely unrevealed, but it was said "he is charged for a crime he never committed." It was later learned that the vehicular homicide charge was dismissed. When he joined the Legion in this reality, Jo wound up falling for Shadow Lass. Karate Kid was asked to train Jo in the best use of his one-power-at-a-time limitation, making him a more effective Legionnaire (*Legion of Super-Heroes* [fifth series] #6, July 2005). He also had a brief tryst with Saturn Girl that left both feeling guilty (*Legion of Super-Heroes* [fifth series] #45, October 2008).

Three versions of Ultra Boy, each coming from a different parallel world, participated in the Legion's battle against Superboy-Prime and the Legion of Super-Villains (*Final Crisis: Legion of 3 Worlds* #1–5, October 2008–September 2009).

ULTRA-HUMANITE, THE

Superman faced more than his fair share of mad scientists, but the most fiendish of them all may have been the unnamed man who found a way to repeatedly transfer his brain into other bodies, avoiding easy detection and capable of a virtual form of immortality.

The bald scientist was considered a genius and controlled an interconnected group of enterprises that brought in cash to further his scientific research, all with an eye toward global domination. He looked down on humankind, despite being paralyzed and confined to a wheelchair, and felt only he was fit to rule the world (*Action Comics* #13, June 1939). The man was called the Ultra-Humanite, or Ultra for short, since "a scientific experiment resulted in [his] possessing the most agile and learned brain on Earth!"

The Earth-2 Man of Steel first learned of Ultra when Jackie Reynolds, a racketeer arrested for trying to control Metropolis's taxi business, used a specially prepared cigarette to emit knockout gas that allowed him to escape the police. When Superman found him in a remote cabin safe house, the man was in a wheelchair. Ultra fired enough electricity at Superman to render the hero unconscious. Ultra then tried to kill Superman by using a buzz saw, until the criminal watched the blade shatter against his impenetrable skin, just before a jagged piece killed the mobster. A weakened Superman was unable to prevent Ultra's thugs from whisking their leader away. Somewhat recovered, he leapt into the air to pursue the fleeing aircraft but watched as it plummeted to Earth, seeming to end Ultra's menace.

A short time later, Superman was investigating Star, Inc., and its president Lyons for defrauding Metropolis by building its subways with substandard materials. The hunt led to a car chase that ended when Lyons's automobile seemingly vanished. Superman eventually managed to find the vehicle, and it led him to another meeting with Ultra, who had been biding his time, awaiting the Man of Steel. He quickly encased the hero in a block of crystal, unaware that a mere flex of Superman's mighty muscles would shatter the trap. Quickly, the master criminal activated an escape plan and vanished before the hero could apprehend him, but it had become clear that the threat the Ultra-Humanite posed had to be contained (*Action Comics* #14, July 1939).

To continue his costly subversive activities, the Ultra-Humanite extorted the owners of the Deering Lines, threatening to destroy their fleet of steamships if they did not pay five million dollars.

ONLY ONE OBSTACLE CONFRONTS ME — SUPERMAN! HE MUST BE WIPED OUT! IT'S A TERRIFIC TASK... BUT MY TREMENDOUS BRAIN CAN DEVISE SOME WAY TO TRICK HIM!
THE END

Superman stopped the attacks but Ultra outwitted him, using a projection of himself to deal with the Man of Steel from a remote location (*Action Comics* #17, October 1939).

Ultra's next attack came from a different direction: an epidemic modeled after the Purple Plague from the Middle Ages. This time, Ultra told the Man of Tomorrow, "The human race shall be blotted out so that I can launch a race of my own." A unique energy weapon was used against Superman, knocking him out, but the Man of Steel proved resistant to Ultra's attempt to hypnotize and control him. Ultra escaped and boarded an airship, ready to spread his disease farther, but Superman followed him and wound up placing the villain in front of a machine gun, seemingly ending the criminal's life (*Action Comics* #19, December 1939).

The dying Ultra was saved when his assistant used adrenaline to revive him. Ultra then changed tactics and had his underlings kidnap actress Dolores Winters, placing his own brain in her young body. Dolores then told the press she was retiring from acting and hosted a lavish farewell party aboard her yacht, the *Sea-Serpent*. Once they were out at sea, Winters shot one of the guests and told the others they were her captives. She then asked for five million dollars in exchange for their lives. Superman traced the ransom payment and found an underground cavern where the hostages were wearing helmets wired to a wicked-looking machine. He threw a stalagmite at the device and destroyed it. During the explosion, Dolores Winters dived into the water and was—erroneously—presumed dead (*Action Comics* #20, January 1940).

More than two years later, in February 1942, Superman and members of the All-Star Squadron were in his Secret Citadel, securing the Powerstone, when they were attacked by Ultra, who was now aided by the powerful Deathbolt and Cyclotron. Ultra managed to merge with the Powerstone and gained extraordinary abilities. He also obtained the Hammer of Thor and the helmet of the mystic Doctor Fate, then captured Robotman, intending to use the automaton as a permanent new host for his brain. Ultra's plans were thwarted by the combined efforts of the All-Star Squadron and the time-tossed members of the original Infinity, Inc. Before admitting defeat, Ultra tried to kill Superman one final time, but failed again. Instead, a vengeful Cyclotron—who'd been coerced into helping the villain—appeared to destroy both himself and Ultra in an atomic explosion (*All-Star Squadron* #21–26, May–October 1983; *All-Star Squadron Annual* #2, 1983).

In the early 1950s, Winters reappeared with new plans to conquer humanity and wipe out the Man of Steel (*Superman Family* #201, May–June 1980). Soon after, Ultra gave up the Winters body in exchange for one resembling that of a giant insect, and worked with the Insect Queen to conquer humanity and kill the Man of Steel (*Superman Family* #213–215, December 1981–February 1982).

Unfortunately, his age was causing Ultra to need to swap bodies more rapidly than ever, and the length he could keep each new host was dwindling, so he sought a more powerful and permanent form to use. Ultra mutated an albino ape to house his brain and formed a new incarnation of the Secret Society of Super-Villains. Despite the combined efforts of the Justice Society of America and the Justice League of America, Ultra succeeded in successfully having the transplant performed (*Justice League of America* [first series] #195–197, October–December 1981).

In the one world that remained after the events of Crisis on Infinite Earths, Ultra's history was much the same, with the exception of his opponents, who were now various members of the JSA. The Ultra-Humanite still sampled other bodies in his attempt to find the right vessel with which to eradicate humankind. He tried the form of a tyrannosaur but met defeat by the combined forces of the All-Star Squadron and their sidekicks, the Young All-Stars (*Young All-Stars* #13–14, June–July 1988).

Early in his career Superman encountered scientist Morgan Wilde, who wanted vengeance against Lex Luthor, blaming him for his wife's death. Wilde constructed a machine and transferred his mind to it, dubbing it the U.L.T.R.A. Humanite. His rampage was halted by Superman, with an assist from the first Blue Beetle (*Legends of the DC Universe* #1–3, February–April 1998).

The real Ultra-Humanite continued to plot humanity's downfall in his albino ape body (*Infinity, Inc.* #45, December 1987; *Teen Titans* #38, September 2006). When the ape form finally aged, Ultra began using new human hosts and built a company called Ultra-Gen. Through the firm's resources, Ultra created a series of genetic innovations, including a new body for himself, but he was stopped by the Justice Society (*Justice Society of America* [second series] #3–5, June–August 1991).

Ultra genetically grew an albino ape body and returned to it until he executed a daring new scheme. He took possession of Johnny Thunder's elderly body and tricked Jakeem Thunder into handing over the magic pen that could summon the Fifth Dimensional Thunderbolt. Now able to command the pink being, Ultra had Johnny's body restored to its youthful vigor and finally achieved his goal of global domination. He extended his essence into the body of every active meta-human; only a handful of costumed champions remained to oppose him. Ultra was apparently killed by the mystic Crimson Avenger, who was seeking vengeance on behalf of her predecessor (*JSA* [first series] #34–37, May–August 2002).

The Infinite Crisis reordered reality, creating fifty-two parallel universes, and on New Earth, Delores Winters became the host to the Ultra-Humanite, but her brain was placed in a different body, sparing her life but driving her mad. Obsessed with eternal youth, Winters endured countless surgeries over the years, ultimately stealing organs from other meta-humans (*JSA Classified* #19–20, January–February 2007).

Apparently in 1948, the time-traveling Per Degaton worked with the alien Despero to rescue Ultra, in Winters's body, from a hospital. Ultra pledged loyalty to Per Degaton in exchange for a new body, which was that of the albino ape from Gorilla City (*Justice League of America* [second series] #8–9, June–July 2007). The team, calling themselves the Time Stealers, worked with the Venusian menace Mister Mind, Rex Hunter, Black Beetle, and Supernova, Booster Gold's father. Their attempts to manipulate time in their favor were stopped by Booster and the second Blue Beetle, whom Booster plucked from the past moments before his death (*Booster Gold* [second series] #7–10, May–August 2008).

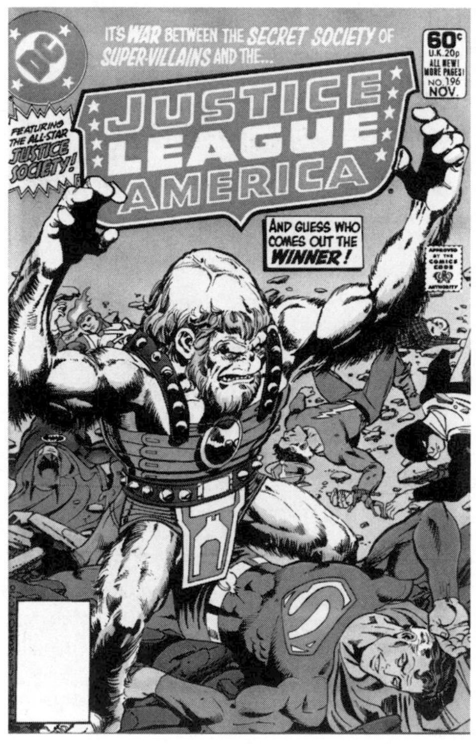

Ultra remained at large in the present, claiming to possess Mento's mind-controlling helmet (*Justice League of America* [second series] #1 October 2007). He may have tired of inhabiting an ape's form, as he threatened to destroy New York City unless Power Girl surrendered her body for his use (*Power Girl* [second series] #1–3, July–September 2009). When he obtained the heroine, he revealed that his true name was Gerard Shugel; he was cursed to be born both a genius and possessing a degenerative disease that threatened to shorten his life. He did manage to find ways to stem the disease's effects while seeking a way to perfect transplanting his mind into a healthier body. His research in college was aided by Satanna, who also romanced the man. Their research led them to study human-animal hybridization, which violated the school's ethics guidelines and resulted in their expulsion. They fled to the Congo, where they found the white ape body to be used as a temporary stopgap until a human form could be found for Ultra. Satanna helped perform the transplant but then left to seek her own fortunes. Power Girl found a way to free herself and prevent the villain from killing anyone—but he managed to escape.

Across the multiverse, there were other versions of the Ultra-Humanite. On one such world, Ultra's brain was in the body of Tex Thomson, known to most as the Americommando (*The Golden Age* #1–4, 1993).

Earth-3839's Ultra also fought Superman beginning in 1939, but his body nearly perished. He placed his brain into the body of his underling, a man named Lex Luthor. When Luthor managed to incapacitate the Man of Steel, he tried to appropriate his body but was killed when Superman's escape attempt led to a computer explosion (*Superman & Batman: Generations* #1–4, 1999).

When the new multiverse was created after the Infinite Crisis, Earth-9 featured an Ultra-Humanite who was a living weapon designed by the Russians that escaped their control. Superman stopped Ultra and then reprogrammed him, turning the weapon into a lackey (*Tangent: Superman's Reign* #3, July 2008, and #11–12, March–April 2009).

ULTRAMAN

In the original multiverse, Earth-3 was a world without heroes, a world that was terrorized by a quintet of superpowered villains who banded together and formed the Crime Syndicate of America. The most powerful of the group was Ultraman, who had steel-gray hair, an all-blue costume, and a red cape (*Justice League of America* [first series] #29, August 1964).

Ultraman's many powers, fueled by contact with kryptonite, included the ability to see through dimensional barriers. Spotting new worlds to conquer, the CSA launched an assault on Earth-1 and its Justice League of America, as well as Earth-2 with its Justice Society of America. The combined forces vanquished the CSA, and the criminals were stranded between realities within an emerald force field, formed by the twin Green Lantern rings with signs in multiple languages warning people to stay away (*Justice League of America* [first series] #30, September 1964).

Over time, the CSA managed to escape, and Ultraman sought revenge against Superman. Kryptonite provided the evil man with his enhanced powers and abilities, a new one acquired with each prolonged contact to the substance. He was approached by Lex Luthor and Alexei Luthor to threaten Earth-1 and Earth-2 with destruction and confront their Men of Steel. In turn, Superman-1 and Superman-2 partnered with Alexander Luthor, Senior, of Earth-3, the planet's first super hero, to save the multiverse (*DC Comics Presents Annual* #1, 1982).

Ultraman and the CSA continued to visit the parallel Earths, seeking revenge for their initial defeat years earlier. When the skies turned red and the wave of anti-matter reached Earth-3, Ultraman's powers proved useless; still, he flew toward the wave, fighting until the very end (*Crisis on Infinite Earths* #1, April 1985). When the Crisis on Infinite Earths came to a close, there was a positive-matter universe with its sole Earth and the anti-matter universe of Qward.

In that opposite reality, the JLA's doppelgängers were the Crime Syndicate of Amerika, complete with a new incarnation of Ultraman (*JLA: Earth-2,* 2000). This super-powerful man was Lieutenant Clark Kent, an astronaut whose space capsule was nearly lost in an accident. The man's badly damaged body was found by an unnamed alien race that reconstructed him, enhancing his abilities with "ultra" powers similar to those of Superman. When he returned, not only was Kent the most powerful man on Earth, but his mind was twisted, making him one of the cruelest individuals as well. He discovered that his powers waxed and waned given his proximity and prolonged exposure to an alien element known only as anti-kryptonite.

As he rose in power and influence on that Earth, he married the only woman close to his power level: the Amazon Princess known as Superwoman. In their civilian guises of Clark Kent and Lois Lane, they appeared a successful married couple, but with familiarity came contempt. The two fought alongside each other, grinding the world beneath the CSA's heel, but whenever possible Superwoman carried on a torrid affair with Owlman, flaunting it before her husband. Ultraman, for his part, delighted in interrupting their assignations.

Despite their woes, the couple did conceive a child, who wound up on the positive Earth but had also been targeted as the new host for Brainiac's consciousness. Inhabiting the infant, Brainiac seized control of the Fortress of Solitude, and the supermen allied briefly to force the baby into the Phantom Zone, where Superwoman managed to suffocate the child, forcing Brainiac to flee (*The Adventures of Superman* #603–605, June–August 2002).

Superman and Ultraman battled frequently until the day Ultraman journeyed to New Earth to seek Superman's assistance in preventing an entity called Megistus from mutating humanity into monsters in some warped alchemical experiment. The Earth-3 version of Mr. Mxyzptlk, Mixyezpitelik, also provided help as the threat grew and involved Green Lantern and the Challengers of the Unknown when the alchemist managed to alter Earth's sun from yellow to red, robbing Superman of his abilities. Superman taunted Megistus into attacking him by transforming himself into kryptonite, which powered Ultraman, who delivered the final blow, mutating into a grotesque shape in the process. He then uttered "Numartlu"—a magical word provided to him by the imp so he could return home (*The Brave and the Bold* [third series] #11–12, May–June 2008).

Their conflict continued when Ultraman returned to Earth and partnered with Saturn Queen, whom he rescued from the Phantom Zone, in an attempt to take over Kandor. The villainess also took possession of his mind and his sheer brawn and tried to wed him to Supergirl, who was also in her thrall. The Maid of Steel broke from the mind control and pummeled Ultraman, then threatened Saturn Queen—who won her freedom with information Supergirl wanted (*Supergirl* [fifth series] #6–8, April–September 2006). Ultraman remained in Kandor with Saturn Queen until they realized it was not the real Kryptonian city (*Superman* #670, January 2008).

Ultraman and the other members of the CSA continued to target Earth, seeking slave labor to help repair damage done to their world (*Trinity* #9, July 30, 2008). They were stopped by Superman, Batman, and Wonder Woman, only to watch their world fall into chaos without the CSA there to maintain strict order. The Trinity dispatched Ultraman, Owlman, and Superwoman to a "subdimension" (*Trinity* #13, August 27, 2008). This "subdimension" may have been a form of limbo where other alternate versions of the Man of Steel resided (*Final Crisis: Superman Beyond* #1, October 2008, and #2, March 2009). One was turned into a powerful vampire but was ultimately killed by the Green Lantern Corps (*Final Crisis* #7, March 2009).

In the wake of Infinite Crisis, the multiverse was re-formed with fifty-two parallel universes, and a Crime Syndicate of America separate from the anti-matter universe team operated on Earth-3. Shortly after the multiverse was re-formed, Mon-

arch sought to rule the new worlds. Ultraman saw himself as the cosmic despot's right-hand man, a role that was instead filled by Lord Havok. In a fight on Earth-51, Ultraman wound up killing that world's Batman (*Countdown to Final Crisis* #13, January 30, 2008).

An apocryphal account found Ultraman fighting the Man of Steel early in their careers when they accidentally met on a cruise ship, which also had Lois Lane, Bruce Wayne, and their Earth-3 counterparts aboard (*Superman/Batman Annual* #1, December 2006).

UNDERWORLDERS, THE

Created within Project Cadmus by the crazed scientist Dabney Donovan, these misshapen beings were considered errors and ultimately abandoned. They left the project and wound up living in the sewers of Metropolis (*Superman: The Man of Steel* #12, June 1992). Their existence became known during the Battle for Metropolis when they exhibited the same genetic breakdown that other Cadmus entities were suffering from. Blaming Cadmus for their fate, the Underworlders, led by Clawster, stole AmerTek Toastmaster weapons and declared war, assaulting the Man of Steel, the Guardian, the Metropolis S.C.U., and even Team Luthor (*Action Comics* #699, May 1994).

The fierce battle was quickly ended when the DNAlien Dubbilex arrived and used his telepathic abilities to shut down Clawster's own psionic powers. He was then shot and killed by a member of the Cadmus security team (*Superman: The Man of Steel* #34, June 1994).

UNIFORM GANG, THE

When Jimmy Olsen was visiting the thirtieth century to help the Legion of Super-Heroes with their official newsletter, he also stumbled into a robbery committed by a group called the Uniform Gang. After he described the incident to the Science Police, they determined the gang had posed as museum security guards to gain access and were quickly thwarted (*Superman's Pal, Jimmy Olsen* #106, October 1967).

UNITED PLANETS, THE

By the thirtieth century, many of the inhabited planets of the various solar systems had banded together as the United Planets. The exact scope of the UP's reach was modified with each iteration of the universe, but at one time the population governed by this body totaled three hundred billion (*Adventure Comics* #366, March 1968).

The UP ruling body—known as the United Planets Inner Council—consisted of Earth and the rulers from four other worlds (*Adventure Comics* #349, October 1966). Presidency was rotated among the five, and at different times and in separate time lines, the UP was led by Legion of Super-Heroes founder R. J. Brande; Marte Allon, mother to Colossal Boy; and Phantom Girl's mother Winema Wazzo.

Their law enforcement division was the Science Police, and more often than not, they officially sanctioned the Legion's activities. Prisoners were

maintained on Takron-Galtos (*Adventure Comics* #359, August 1967; others).

While the UP's capital was located in Metropolis, in honor of Superman, much of the actual bureaucracy occurred on Weber's World, an artificial satellite built as neutral territory for member worlds (*Superboy and the Legion of Super-Heroes* #241, July 1978; others). There was also the medical planet Quarantine (*Adventure Comics* #313, October 1963; others).

One reason the UP was formed was to ensure peace among the civilized worlds, as well as protection against aggressive races such as the Khunds.

UNIVERSAL INSURANCE COMPANY, THE

This seemingly respectable insurance firm was actually the front for a gang of protection racketeers who offered "insurance" to business firms and then vandalized those refusing to buy it. They were eventually apprehended by the Man of Steel (*Superman* [first series] #72, September–October 1951).

URANIUM

The heavy metal called uranium was discovered in 1789 by Martin Klaproth, a German chemist, and he named it after the planet Uranus, which had been discovered eight years earlier.

Krypton's uranium core, which for "untold ages [had] been building a cycle of chain-reactions," was on the verge of unleashing a planetary cataclysm such that "soon every atom on [the] planet would explode like one colossal atomic bomb!" (*Superman* [first series] #61, November–December 1949). Only Jor-El seemed to realize this, while everyone else was focused on the upcoming anniversary of the ten thousandth year of Kryptonian civilization (*Action Comics* #223, December 1956).

An unstable uranium core also doomed Krypton's twin world Xenon (*Superman* [first series] #119, February 1958).

The Man of Steel actually saved the planet Vergo by gathering up floating asteroids laced with uranium and hurling them into the system's star, thereby revitalizing it (*Superman* [first series] #113, May 1957).

On the other hand, when a uranium-based me-

teor collided with a kryptonite meteor, the resulting radiation turned the gentle Toto into the colossal Titano (*Superman* [first series] #127, February 1959).

Uranium became a much-sought-after power source on twentieth-century Earth, requiring Superman's intervention on several occasions. He stopped R24 from illegally mining the material at Grass Mountain (*Superman* [first series] #71, July–August 1951).

The powerful element also provided the energy to temporarily imbue people with superpowers for a twenty-four-hour period through a device designed by Professor Weirton (*Action Comics* #163, December 1951).

URANUS

When the first terrestrial "gods" appeared, the Earth spirit Gaea emerged and mated with the sky god Uranus, and the Titans of Myth were born (*The New Titans* #51, Winter 1988). Millennia later, in 1781, when humans began to study the stars, they learned of other planets in the solar system, naming the seventh planet Uranus.

In the parallel universe known as Earth-2, Uranus was a world inhabited by an advanced race of mechanical robots. They were space explorers and were well armed in case of a conflict. When they arrived to study Earth, they obtained a book, *Children's Picture Book of Animals,* and decided to collect a specimen found on each page, including a man and a woman. Superman led them to conclude that all humans were robots like themselves, making them less interesting to study, so the aliens left (*World's Finest Comics* #49, September–October 1949).

When the Man of Steel sought items for the Metropolis Museum's time capsule for the people of the fiftieth century, he visited Uranus and collected the fossil of an extinct six-legged horse; he later went to Ariel, one of Uranus's moons, to obtain an exotic rainbow-hued flower (*Superman* [first series] #122, July 1958).

By the 853rd century, Uranus was no longer a planet, its fate shrouded from the chronicles. In its place stood a space station manned by Ferris Knight, a direct descendant of the first Starman, Ted Knight. It fell to him to monitor the artificial sun Solaris (*DC One Million* #1, November 1999).

URSA

Ursa served under General Zod in Krypton's security forces and was responsible for arresting the scientists Non and Jor-El as heretics and delivering them to the Kryptonian Science Council. After the two scientists received a warning, they were set free, but Non refused the Council's directive and spoke of their planet's impending doom to the public (*Action Comics* #845, November 2006).

The coldly beautiful Ursa and the cruel Zod came to believe Non and defected to join his side. Non wound up captured and lobotomized, an act that turned Zod into a militant. He and Ursa launched an insurrection, which was violently and swiftly quashed, with the Council calling for their deaths. Jor-El pleaded their case and got the Council to agree that exile to the Phantom Zone was punishment enough for the insurrectionists (*Action Comics Annual* #10, 2007).

While trapped in the Zone, Zod and Ursa became lovers—with the result being their son Lor-Zod. When the boy was about ten, he managed to escape to Earth and came to reside with Clark Kent and Lois Lane in the human guise of Christopher Kent. Soon after, Zod, Ursa, and Non escaped the Phantom Zone and wanted Lor-Zod back. Ursa attacked the Daily Planet Building and took her son from Lois Lane, injuring the woman with a mere flick of her finger (*Action Comics* #846, February 2007). In time, Superman corralled all the escaped Phantom Zone criminals back into exile, with Christopher sadly sacrificing himself to ensure that there would never be a breach in the Zone again.

Later, when Kandor regained its proper size, albeit on Earth, Alura saw to it that all the Phantom Zone inhabitants were pardoned and freed. Ursa once more served Zod in the reconstituted Military Guild, but something had changed. Within the Phantom Zone neither Ursa nor Zod held rank and could easily become lovers and conceive a child. But once freed from the Zone, Zod was once more Ursa's commanding officer, and there was no place for emotions in the Military Guild (*Superman Secret Files 2009,* October 2009). Before Ursa served Zod without question, but after coming to love him, Ursa was a different person. This was true physically as well as emotionally, as Ursa's eyes were damaged during her transition from the Phantom Zone to Earth's atmosphere. She could not tolerate Earth's natural sunlight and continued to wear her goggles to filter the light, but this also further distanced her from her Kryptonian bretheren.

She was then assigned to plant sleeper agents around Earth, preparing against attack from the humans. Instead, her son Lor-Zod and security chief Thara Ak-Var began hunting and exposing them, disguised as Nightwing and Flamebird (*Action Comics* #875, May 2009). Ursa, never close to her son, declared she no longer considered him a part of her family. She blamed his rebellious streak on Lois Lane's influence, promising vengeance (*Action Comics* #876, June 2009).

Ursa continued to operate on Earth for a while, performing as if she once more commanded Black Zero. Instead, it now felt like she was doing Zod's dirtywork, such as killing the train Tor-An rather than let General Samuel Lane's Project 7734 interrogate him (*Action Comics* #877, July 2009).

Despite any misgivings she may have felt, Ursa remained loyal to Zod and was by his side when New Krypton was attacked by Brainiac, and while they witnessed their world be destroyed by Reactron's detonation. They were among the Kryptonian survivors who attacked Earth afterward, but Ursa was consigned once more to the newly reconstructed Phantom Zone after being bested by Supergirl and Superboy (*Superman*: *War of the Supermen* #1–4, July 2010).

URTHLO

A lead-masked being named Urthlo, who possessed an amazing array of powers, once nearly crippled the Legion of Super-Heroes. Superboy was summoned to help the Legion confront this man, who seemed to possess the ability to turn their innate powers on and off. Their erratic performance led Earth's World-Wide Police to demand they vacate the planet.

Superboy attempted to fight the green-and-purple-clad villain, but Urthlo used his kryptonite vision to weaken the Teen of Steel.

Just before the team admitted defeat, Saturn Girl freed Mon-El from the Phantom Zone and provided him with a temporary cure to his vulnerability to lead, allowing the Daxamite to battle Urthlo. Defeated, Urthlo had his mask removed, revealing the face of an adult Lex Luthor. Urthlo turned out to be a robot, programmed by Lex Luthor and sent to the future, with instructions to disband the Legion (*Adventure Comics* #300, September 1962).

USJAK, CAL

A member of the Supermen of America who operated under the code name Brahma.

UUZ

The homeworld of the super hero Regor and his archenemy Bantor was an intensely cold undiscovered world beyond Pluto's distant orbit, where gravity was far weaker than Earth's and where the buildings and automobiles were made out of glass (*Superman* [first series] #58, May–June 1949).

VAIL, VINSON

In a potential Earth-1 future, Vinson Vail was one of Earth's leading scientists and also the secret leader of a gang of "mystery-thieves" who had perpetrated a rash of spectacular scientific thefts. Their goal was the most titanic theft of all time: stealing the world's power supply, the great atomic plant outside thirtieth-century METROPOLIS, which "supplies power, by wireless, to every machine, car and plane on Earth." Deprived of energy, the technology-dependent people would be vulnerable to being taken over by the would-be world leader. Superman flew through time at the behest of his descendant, the Superman of 2956, and together they thwarted the plan, exposing Vail as the culprit (*Action Comics* #215, April 1956).

VALDEMAR OF THE FLAME

At one point in his career, Superman discovered a hidden valley in northern Maine where isolated Vikings still practiced their ancient customs shielded from the rest of the world by a fortifying Eternal Flame. Standing guard over them was the powerful, bearded Valdemar, who wielded a flaming sword and rode a giant falcon. The Man of Steel promised to keep their existence a secret (*Superman* [first series] #260, January 1973).

Sometime later, Valdemar visited METROPOLIS, but the city's thick pollution caused the Viking to experience violent hallucinations. He inadvertently threatened the citizens until Superman calmed him down (*Superman* [first series] #270, December 1973).

The Viking, always seeking a good fight, joined Superman in dealing with industrial polluters and joined his new friend in dealing with a political

group, the Compatriots, who were prone to violence (*Superman* [first series] #394–395, April–May 1984).

After the CRISIS ON INFINITE EARTHS, Valdemar did not appear in the chronicles.

VALDEZ, GENERAL PEDRO

The tiny South American republic of El Salmado was a country in turmoil. Its president clung to power while General Pedro Valdez, head of the country's Secret Police, planned a bloodless coup that would leave him in charge.

One Christmas season, Valdez tried to hire reporter CLARK KENT to impersonate the Man of Steel and act as the president's bodyguard. He explained to the American that no one would dare threaten the president if they saw Superman standing close by. Meantime, Valdez convinced the president he had actually engaged the real hero's services, letting him relax his guard.

When it became clear that Superman was posing as Kent and threatened the conspirators' assassination plans, they rigged a KRYPTONITE death trap, which the Man of Steel avoided. He then apprehended Valdez and his followers, keeping the country safe (*Action Comics* #306, November 1963).

VALE, ALLAN

This SMALLVILLE High School student was briefly the hero called SUPREMO.

VAL-EL

A member of the great HOUSE OF EL on KRYPTON, Val-El was an explorer, considered the moving force behind Krypton's great Age of Exploration (*Adventure Comics* #313, October 1963).

VALIDUS

Once described as "the strangest of all living beings," this towering creature had a transparent skull and emitted powerful lightning bolts from his brain. With his clawed hands and massive body, his very presence caused people to flee in terror. When his lightning struck, destruction was vast. The creature thought in the simplest of terms and was highly susceptible to suggestion—which made acquiring his services a fairly easy

Validus

task for the Legion of Super-Heroes. They were seeking help to defend Sol from the approach of a Sun-Eater, and Validus was one of a quintet added to the Legion's thin ranks during the crisis. Validus, though, was lured to work with a group of villains against the Legion. They formed the Fatal Five and attempted to kill the teen heroes once the crisis had ended. Princess Projectra managed to convince Validus to turn on the other four (*Adventure Comics* #352–353, January–February 1967).

Validus remained with the Fatal Five, falling under the sway of their cyborg leader Tharok. His mind blasts proved decisive on more than one occasion. It took time before the Legion learned that the fantastic metal Inertron was the one thing those blasts could not shatter. During his fights, Validus wound up killing Lyle Norg, the first Invisible Kid (*Superboy* [first series] #203, July–August 1974).

It was even later before the Legion's founders learned the horrible secret behind Validus's origins. During a battle against Darkseid, the conqueror from Apokolips took one of the twins born to Saturn Girl and Lightning Lad and sent the infant back in time, altering his form and turning him into Validus, who was raised without either parent's love. Darkseid presumed the child would kill the parents or the parents would be forced to slay their son (*Legion of Super-Heroes* [third series] *Annual* #3, 1984).

Later, Darkseid returned and manipulated events so Lightning Lad was in a position where he had to kill Validus or watch his grotesque son kill his twin brother Graym. Saturn Girl found a way to prevent either event from occurring and then forced Darkseid to undo his machinations. The restored child was named Garridan and reunited with his family (*Legion of Super-Heroes* [third series] *Annual* #2, 1986).

Garridan was also cursed with the Validus Plague, a fatal disease to which only natives of Winath and Titan were susceptible. This left Garridan permanently in a containment suit and in quarantine, isolated from his family (*Legion of Super-Heroes* [fourth series] #3, January 1990).

The events of Zero Hour changed Validus's background, removing his connection to the Ranzz family. His new origins were never recorded, however.

In one reality formed circa Infinite Crisis, Validus was the name of a nature spirit, the Lord of Lightning, in Winath's folklore (*Supergirl and the Legion of Super-Heroes* #32, September 2007). A Validus more in keeping with his original portrayal was recruited by Superboy-Prime to join his ultimate Legion of Super-Villains as he attempted to wipe out the Legion (*Final Crisis: Legion of 3 Worlds* #1–5, October 2008–September 2009).

VALL, VICTOR

The Vall family journeyed to Earth to see if Clark Kent was actually their cousin, who was an astronaut lost in space. With their special technology, they had followed Superman's exploits on Earth and theorized that he might be their relative, missing the last ten years. After Vall, his wife, their two children, and his elderly parents arrived on Earth, much like the Last Son of KRYPTON they developed powers and abilities.

It didn't take long for them to learn that Clark was a Kryptonian and not a relative, but they decided to visit for a while. Superman, though, was concerned anyone seeing these superpowered people spending time with mild-mannered Clark might expose his alter ego.

When they were sightseeing, Superman scoured the stars to find the missing astronaut, who was still alive but stranded on an alien world. Armed with this information, the Valls quickly departed Earth to rescue their cousin (*Superman* [first series] #104, March 1956).

VALLEYHO DAM

Located above Valleyho, this dam was "cracking under the strain of a huge downpour" and threatened to inundate the valley below it with a "great, irresistible flood of onrushing water," "killing thousands and destroying the fertile land." Superman rushed to repair the damage and protect the people below by diverting the raging "mountain of water" away from the town (*Action Comics* #5, October 1938).

VAL-LOR

All Kryptonians honored Val-Lor with a holiday known as the Day of Truth. Legend held that Val-Lor had courageously spoken out during a period when KRYPTON had been invaded by the VRANGS, and its people enslaved. Refusing to pay homage to his captors, he publicly declared his hatred for them—and was murdered for his words. The incident inspired his fellow Kryptonians to revolt against their oppressors and drive the aliens from their planet. Ever since, Val-Lor's honesty was emulated for a full day, which usually carried unintended consequences (*Superman* [first series] #176, April 1965).

VANCE, SHARON

A childhood friend of CLARK KENT's, as an adult she merged with the cosmic entity KISMET to become STRANGE VISITOR.

VANDYRE UNIVERSITY

After graduating from college, LINDA DANVERS worked in television for a time before enrolling at this California institution's famed School of Drama (*Supergirl* [first series] #1, November 1972). Completing the acting course, Linda moved on to become a student adviser at the New Athens Experimental School in Florida (*Superman Family* #165, June–July 1974).

VANISHING, THE

While Superman was rescuing GREEN LANTERN John Stewart in space, one million residents of METROPOLIS, including his wife LOIS LANE, disappeared in an instant, leaving just ghostly impressions where they'd once stood. The event came to be known as The Vanishing and sent the Man of Steel on a physical and spiritual quest to find his missing people (*Superman* [second series] #204–215, June 2004–May 2005).

His investigations led the Man of Steel to an unnamed country in the Middle East, where he encountered General Nox and his underling, the powerful EQUUS. The subsequent battle resulted in Nox activating the Vanishing Device a second time, causing another three hundred thousand people—including Nox and Equus—to leave Earth.

Superman took the device to the FORTRESS OF SOLITUDE for study, hoping to find a way to learn where the machine had sent everyone. He followed it into the PHANTOM ZONE where he found the Earthlings living on the artificial world he had once created. Metropia was a place where he thought he could rescue humanity in case KRYPTON's fate repeated itself on Earth. When he thought better of it, he consigned the city to the Zone and was surprised to see it now in use.

After Superman rescued the trapped people from Metropia, he destroyed the device.

VAN JONES, RUFFINGTON

CLARK KENT suspected that this boarding school teacher was behind a series of robberies all linked by wealth and the school. Sure enough, the teacher assigned essays that allowed him to assess the value of each student's home, then used a gang of thugs to burgle the houses. Kent enrolled in disguise and exposed the entire plot (*Superboy* [first series] #17, November–December 1951).

VAN-ZEE

Van-Zee was a scientist in KANDOR when the city was stolen by BRAINIAC. A cousin of JOR-EL, he bore a remarkable resemblance to KAL-EL, and after the city was rescued by Superman he proved a staunch ally. Unfortunately, he also met and fell in love with the Man of Steel's girlfriend LOIS LANE. As a result, Van-Zee was determined to find a woman just like her. He managed that during a period when he was

at his proper height and wandering through the American Midwest. There, he met Lois's look-alike, Sylvia DeWitt, and their whirlwind courtship led to marriage. In time, they briefly lived on VENUS and had twin children, Lyle and Lili Van-Zee. Sylvia became the first human immigrant welcomed into the bottle city when Superman reduced the entire family in size and returned them to Kandor (*Superman's Girl Friend, Lois Lane* #15, February 1960).

In addition to his research, Van-Zee served, along with VOL-DON, as the Man of Steel's stand-in in the LOOKALIKE SQUAD and was a member of the SUPERMAN EMERGENCY SQUAD (*Superman* [first series] #158, January 1963). Later, he partnered with Ak-Var to work as the crime-fighting duo NIGHTWING and FLAMEBIRD (*Superman Family* #183, May–June 1977; others).

Van-Zee's father NIM-ZEE served as "a distinguished member of the Kandorian Council," Kandor's governing body (*Superman* [first series] #151, February 1962). Dik-Zee was Van-Zee's identical twin bother (*Superman's Girl Friend, Lois Lane* #21, November 1960).

VARTOX

Vartox was a legendary champion of justice, his name known across the Earth-1 universe. Hailing from Valeron in the Sombrero Hat galaxy, he was—as Superman noted—"a force for good in the universe when I was still a super-tot" (*Superman* [first series] #281, November 1974). The two legends met for the first time when Vartox came to Earth in the wake of his wife's "psychic twin" being killed, which resulted in his own wife Elyra's demise. Quickly, his hyper-powers helped him locate Frank Sykes (who'd gotten away with the murder he committed on Earth), who was whisked away to Valeron to stand trial. Sentenced to sixty years for the murder, Sykes was instantly aged six decades via the planet's alien technology and subsequently returned to Earth by the Man of Steel.

Vartox's hyper-powers were "psychic in nature" and mostly directed through his hands. Aside from the powers of super-strength, flight, super-vision, intangibility, teleportation, and telekinesis, he was capable of generating blasts of heat and cold and could place his adversaries in suspended animation. His "hyper-charge" amounted to a virtual death-bolt. He could also manipulate his

hyper-energy into forming nets, ropes, force bubbles, or other basic objects. With hyper-hypnosis, he could manipulate crowds into seeing whatever he wished. At one point, he even "defied all the laws of physics and turned a three-dimensional object into a two-dimensional one." His ultimate exploitation of his abilities temporarily "converted [his] molecular structure into pure hyper-energy," generating a staggering burst of destructive force.

Superman and Vartox met again when the aging hero sought to recharge his weakening powers through an encounter with Karb-Brak, an alien exiled on Earth (*Action Comics* #475–476, September–October 1977). Tragically, Vartox would soon call Earth his home when Valeron was destroyed, the indirect result of a space element that he'd unwittingly introduced into its atmosphere. Adopting the guise of Vernon O'Valeron and going to work at Galaxy Communications, he fell in love with Lana Lang. Perhaps in penance for his role in Valeron's destruction, Vartox denied himself happiness and returned to the stars in search of a world more in need of a super hero than Earth (*Action Comics* #498–499, August–September 1979).

He found it in the form of the planet Tynola, where he remained as resident hero even after discovering that its people had originally planned to sacrifice him to an entity called Moxumbra (*Superman* [first series] #356–357, February–March 1981). Returning for Lana, Vartox proposed marriage and intended to bring her to Tynola, shielding her from its poisonous atmosphere with a protective aura. After Lana was turned to stone by a jealous former lover of Vartox's named Syreena, the hyper-man opted to cancel the wedding rather than put his beloved at risk once more (*Superman* [first series] #373–375, July–September 1982).

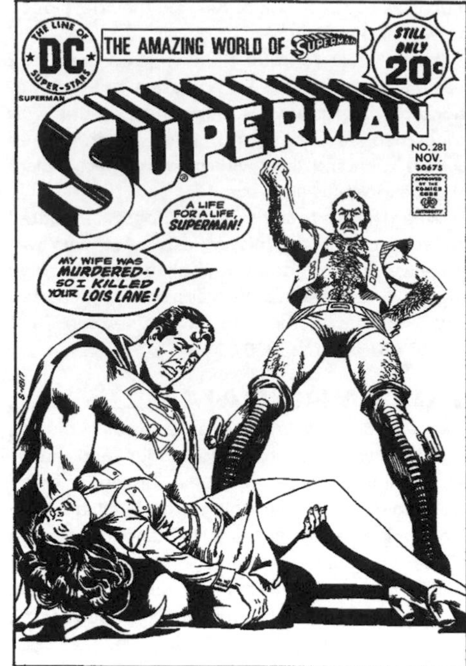

More tragedy lay ahead for Vartox. A parasite named Srakka that fed on super-beings destroyed Tynola, triggering outrage in the hyper-man that allowed the entity to enter his body. Working with Superman, Vartox was able to expel Srakka but opted not to linger on Earth after learning that Lana was now dating Clark Kent (*Superman* [first series] #390–392, December 1983–February 1984).

After the Crisis on Infinite Earths, Vartox was forced, along with other alien heroes, to do the bidding of Brainiac lest their respective homeworlds be destroyed. Having developed a deep respect for Superman in the short time that they'd known each other, Vartox used his "invisible hyper-shield" to protect the Man of Steel from a lethal blast from Brainiac. On Earth, Vartox and fellow heroes Paz and Vestion drew a line in the sand and sent the villain into space as they pursued him. "Remain here and take care of your home and your loved ones, Superman," the hyper-man shouted as they teleported away, "for the day may come when you might *lose* them" (*Superman* [second series] #148, September 1999, and #150, November 1999).

It was later revealed that Vartox's homeworld of Valeron suffered from the aftereffects of a contraceptive bomb that had left all the women on the planet sterile. The vain Vartox decided that he needed a genetically compatible and desirable mate to help him propogate his species. He selected Earth's Power Girl for this task and arrived on the planet intent on impressing her. To do so he summoned an Ix Negaspike, an indestructible creature native to Valeron, and battled it before Power Girl's disbelieving eyes. When the creature got out of control, Power Girl accidentally broke the Ix Negaspike's containment device, thereby preventing Vartox from returning it to its natural habitat back on Valeron. Power Girl and Vartox wound up breaking the creature into several pieces and froze them before each piece could regenerate into a new Ix Negaspike. The frozen "space cows" were then tossed into the vacuum of space. Vartox then explained his planet's dire fertility circumstances to Power Girl over dinner, and she agreed to help him. She entered a fertility chamber on Valeron and technologically combined her life force with Vartox's, which was then compressed into a "pregno-ray." Once the beam of energy from the ray bathed the planet, all the women of child-bearing age on Valeron found themselves pregnant (*Power Girl* [second series] #7–8, February–March 2010).

VATHGAR

Vathgar was a ruthless criminal on a dimensional world known as Xeron who wanted to take over as ruler. He intended to use skrans, native lower life-forms, as his shock troops, turning them into raging monsters by injecting them with the precious element iron. To amass the necessary quantities of ore, he sent a skran through the dimensional barrier to Earth to see how pure the planet's iron ore was, and if it was sufficient for his needs. The creature rampaged across Metropolis until Superman, Batman, and Robin managed to contain it. They then went to Xeron and ended Vathgar's plans for conquest (*World's Finest Comics* #118, June 1961).

VATHLO ISLAND

An island populated by a black race in the Dandahu Ocean on Krypton. They retained their independence throughout history, and did not join the planetary federation, though maintaining good relations with it (*Action Comics* #793, September 2002; *Krypton Chronicles* #2, October 1981; *Superman* [first series] #234, February 1971; *The World of Krypton* #1, July 1979).

VEGAS, LES

The nephew of United Broadcasting Company president Samuel Tanner, Les Vegas was the star of the network's *Friday Night Revue.* He gained audience acceptance when he began doing a dead-on impression of former president Gerald R. Ford, leading to his hosting the fake-news portion of the show, *Evening News Update.* When he was briefly transformed into the super-villain Black-rock, he also imitated Clark Kent (*Superman* [first series] #315, September 1977).

VELLUM, BARNEY

Barney Vellum turned bookbinding into an artform by matching the book's case-binding to the book's contents. After using horsehide for *The Jockey* and others, his friends in the field began ordering specialty bindings out of impossible materials in order to mock him. Instead, the Man of Steel came to his aid, locating objects from Atlantis for *The Lost Continent* and others. As a thank-you, Vellum bound Lois Lane's scrapbook of Superman photos out of the hero's cape (*World's Finest Comics* #29, July–August 1947).

VEL QUENNAR

When Superman was on trial for the murder of Lexor's hero, Lex Luthor, he was assigned the highly esteemed attorney Vel Quennar. Aided by his younger partner Garn Abu, the legal counsel began preparing a vigorous defense despite recognizing the hopelessness of the case. He tried to convince the Man of Steel to allow him to use a defense of temporary insanity, one Superman refused to accept. The trial was going as Quennar feared until Luthor appeared alive, having been in a death-like trance induced by a coma drug. Superman was eventually acquitted of all charges (*Action Comics* #318–319, November–December 1964).

VENTURA

The notorious intergalactic gambling world ruled by Rokk and Sorban (*Superman* [first series] #171, August 1964).

VENUS

While Venus was a gaseous planet that was inhospitable to human life, it did give birth to life-forms, most notably the would-be conqueror Mister Mind (*Captain Marvel Adventures* #26, August 1943), who tried to consume the fifty-two parallel universes in the reality formed after Infinite Crisis (*52* #52, May 2, 2007).

In the pre-Crisis reality, Venus was said to be home to humanoids that adopted English as a primary language (*Action Comics* #152, January 1951). A conflicting account showed that the world hosted cute "tomato girls," "pumpkin men," "cucumber men," and other comical "plant-beings" (*Superman* [first series] #151, February 1962).

Superboy once visited Venus after deflecting a meteor that could have shattered it. He stopped for a drink and accidentally brought back a Venusian spore that grew into a tree, emitting an invisible toxin that compelled people to act out of character (*Superboy* [first series] #29, December 1953).

At some point in a potential Earth-1 future, Venus was inhabited by humans and was the homeworld to Cosmic King of the Legion of Super-Villains (*Superman* [first series] #147, August 1961). It was also where Van-Zee and Sylvia lived prior to relocating with their children to Kandor (*Superman's Girl Friend, Lois Lane* #15, February 1960). Superman also once threatened to exile a juvenile delinquent to the planet (*Superman* [first series] #151, February 1962). He also visited the planet to collect a flower as a gift for Lois Lane (*Superman* [first series] #55, November-December 1948).

SUPERMAN FLIES TO THE PLANET VENUS...
I'VE VISITED THIS WORLD BEFORE! IT'S PERFECT FOR WHAT I HAVE IN MIND!

In the 853rd century, Venus was protected by Justice Legion A member Wonder Woman, a marble statue given life by the goddess of truth (*DC One Million* #1, November 1999).

VILLAIN, DR. ARTHUR

Described as a "dysfunctional" Lex Luthor, the enigmatic and eccentric Arthur Villain tirelessly corrected the pronunciation of his last name. "It is WILL-hayne. It's French." Villain was chief of staff at Garden State Medical Center and would go to any lengths to raise money for his cash-strapped hospital, which at one time employed John Henry Irons. Villain, who kept a hired assassin, Skorpio, on staff, had vaporized a crack addict, shut down a trauma procedure (because it was cheaper to settle a lawsuit than pay two star surgeons to save the uninsured patient), had himself kidnapped, conducted genetic experimentation in the sub-basement, and committed a host of other cheerily eccentric pseudo-villainous activities. He eventually received his comeuppance at the hands of Steel (*Steel* #34–52, January 1997–July 1998).

VINDEN, JOHN

While John Vinden was considered brilliant, he used his scientific gifts for criminal ends. As a result he served a five-year prison sentence and, after his parole, immediately returned to his old habits. He used his warped scientific genius to give four ordinary criminals artificial superpowers in an effort to beat the Man of Steel and loot the scientific world of Metropolis. His plan for seeking revenge against the scientific community, which he blamed for his incarceration, was thwarted by Superman (*Action Comics* #175, December 1952).

VINE, MORNA

Cub reporter Jimmy Olsen was joined on the *Daily Planet*'s staff by this attractive brunette, who was niece to Mark Vine, the paper's biggest stockholder. She had managed to obtain the head of a Superman Robot after the body was destroyed during a battle with an undersea monster. She had her father take circuits and energy cells from the optical center and build her a pair of super-spectacles and earrings allowing her to replicate the Man of Steel's optical and auditory abilities. Morna then wrangled her way on to the *Planet*'s staff in the hope of meeting and wooing Superman. She used her newfound tools to scoop her peers and jump from cub to star reporter. When the Man of Steel learned of her efforts, rather than being flattered, he scolded her for using his technology for selfish purposes. He then took back the devices, leaving her crushed (*Superman* [first series] #181, November 1965).

VIRUS X

Virus X was said to be a fatal contagion that could kill any native of Krypton in thirty days. No cure had been discovered for this disease by the time the planet was destroyed. Continuing research in the bottle city of Kandor also proved fruitless. It was theorized that any disease to survive the explosion would evolve to super-virulence, able to kill even superpowered Kryptonians such as Kal-El, Superman. His relative Tharb-El theorized that El-

Virus X

ement 202, discovered during his work with the pathologic microorganism, could be the elusive cure, but never could prove it (*Superman* [first series] #156, October 1962).

The Man of Steel once appeared to have contracted the disease, which left his skin bloated, distorted, and green-colored. It was later believed that the evolved disease was also fatal to human beings. The cure proved to be a dose of white KRYPTONITE, which eradicated plant life and therefore the organism (*Action Comics* #362–366, April–August 1968).

VITAR

Vitar, a scientist residing in KANDOR, won "many scientific and scholarly awards" as well as at least nine medals in the "Kandorian Games," the Kryptonian Olympics. His athletic prowess made him a natural candidate to serve in the SUPERMAN EMERGENCY SQUAD.

"One of the most promising young men in Kandor," Vitar was engaged to a woman named Serena. Rather than marry her, he instead brought LOIS LANE and LANA LANG to the bottle city and proclaimed his love to both women. He offered the woman who best exemplified the Kandorian way a serum for invulnerability. Lois was prepared as a detective, and Lana was trained to be an archaeologist. Together they tracked down the Sky Thief, who stole "a rare jewel-mask of the Kvorn period" from the Kandor art museum. When they proved triumphant, Vitar admitted the serum had side effects on humans. The humans were miffed and returned to Earth, prompting Vitar to return

to Serena's waiting arms (*Superman's Girl Friend, Lois Lane* #78, October 1967).

VIVANIUM

Vivanium was an ultra-rare element that could power a machine imbuing humans with superpowers. LEX LUTHOR created the machine and LOIS LANE tried it on herself, earning herself eight hours of superpowered experience. Superman decided the machine was too dangerous and destroyed it, then used his heat vision to burn the remaining vivanium on Earth (*Action Comics* #156, May 1951).

VIXON, JANE

This world-renowned psychic also had telepathic skills and used them on Superman, learning his secret identity. She then went to work for a female gangster and attempted to forge a mental connection with the Man of Steel, which caused mental feedback. As a result, LOIS LANE was inadvertently given the secret name, but also absorbed the gangster's desire to kill Superman. The effects proved temporary, and the criminal was caught while both Jane and Lois forgot Superman's alter ego (*Superman's Girl Friend, Lois Lane* #130, April 1973).

VOHC

According to Kryptonian mythology, when the Big Bang spread fiery matter across the universe, a consciousness was formed and took the name RAO. He then gathered up some of the cooling universal matter and formed stars and planets. One such solar system became a favorite, and Rao gave life to a world and dubbed it KRYPTON. Rao then took part of its essence and created children: FLAMEBIRD, who stood for renewal and rebirth, and Vohc, "whose hands are guided by endless curiosity and a boundless desire to create, to craft, to improve upon that which he has built before, and to inscribe Ra the Father's signature upon the material world."

Vohc, toiling in the twilight, came to love Flamebird, and as she destroyed his creations, Vohc strove to create even more perfect landscapes and sunsets. They worked in perfect harmony as the planet took shape across the eons. In time, Rao created another sibling he named NIGHTWING, to be

his "Eyes in the Night." With Flamebird dwelling in the day, Vohc in twilight, and Nightwing in the night, everything seemed to be in perfect alignment. To celebrate Flamebird's love for Nightwing, Vohc created a gift as "an expression of the pure, unselfish love" he had for his muse Flamebird. Flamebird was pleased with the gift, and after she admired it she destroyed it, as was her wont. She believed that it would only inspire greater things in Vohc, but for the first time, he disagreed. Hurt beyond imagining, Vohc created a spire of pure crystal that the Flamebird destroyed after admiring it, as was Vohc's plan. Flamebird's destroying the crystal tore asunder the fabric of reality and created a "new space for phantoms and emptiness" that trapped Nighwing, depriving Flamebird of her true love. To regain access to Nightwing, Vohc asked that the Flamebird renounce her love for her dark sibling. She refused and Vohc cursed her. He then broke free from Rao's family and became known as Krypton's first heretic, Vohc the Breaker (*Action Comics* #886, April 2010).

Much as the spirit of the Flamebird resided in Thara Ak-Var and the Nightwing nestled deep within the soul of Lor-Zod, Vohc found purchase within the corrupted soul of Kandorian villain Jax-Ur. All three operated on Earth, with Jax-Ur disguised as the Canadian scientist Dr. Pillings. He used his time on Earth to build a massive engine of destruction in the shape of Rao. When it became clear just who the benevolent Dr. Pillings really was and what his true plans for Earth were, Nightwing and Flamebird confronted Jax-Ur. Using the final shard of Vohc's crystal, Jax-Ur trapped Lor-Zod in the Phantom Zone, while the soulless clone of Rao began traversing the globe and leaving a path of destruction in its wake. Vohc and Flamebird then fought, continuing a conflict that dated back to the dawn of Krypton. Jax-Ur flew up into Earth's orbit to construct a staff called the Void of Shadows Projector, but before it could be activated, Jax-Ur broke free of Vohc's control and the Nightwing was freed of its imprisonment. Rao fulfilled its artificial programming by attempting to become an enormous gravity well that would crush Earth and all its surrounding celestial bodies. Vohc then left Jax-Ur's body, and Nightwing stopped the lethal gravity well from forming. With Rao's threat seemingly ended and Vohc consigned to the stars, Jax-Ur was remanded to the Justice Society of America (*Action Comics* #887–889, May–June 2010).

VOL-DON

Along with Van-Zee, Vol-Don was a double for Clark Kent and served on the Lookalike Squad based in the bottle city of Kandor (*Superman's Pal, Jimmy Olsen* #70, July 1963). Vol-Don was a Kandorian representative on WMET's inaugural episode of *Our American Heroes,* which shone the spotlight on the Superman (*Action Comics* #309, February 1964). His son Varn-Don was a look-alike for Superboy (*Superboy* [first series] #118, January 1965).

VON KAMP

This onetime Nazi scientist was also considered a ruthless crime dictator. He was clad in a medal-bedecked officer's uniform and wore a monocle over one eye. The mastermind behind Project X—a mysterious underworld operation—he oversaw the work performed on a remote, uncharted island using shipwrecked seamen as slave laborers. His ultimate goal was to launch a "criminal eye in the sky," an artificial satellite equipped with a TV camera, with a telescopic lens, intended to observe bank truck routes, police activities, and other information. The data would then be sent from the remote island to the international crime syndicate that financed Project X. Instead, Von Kamp and his henchmen were apprehended by Superman (*Action Comics* #248, January 1959).

VRANGS

A race of gray-furred alien conquerors. Thousands of years ago, the Vrangs invaded Krypton and enslaved its population. Sul-El, an ancestor to Kal-El, was the first to warn against the invaders—but his warning came too late (*Krypton Chronicles* #2, October 1981). It fell to Val-Lor to speak out in defiance of the feral beasts, rallying the citizens to overthrow the yoke of slavery and win back their world. The Day of Truth was ever after observed in Val-Lor's honor (*Superman* [first series] #176, April 1965).

The Vrangs' ancestral hatred of Kryptonians led them to seek revenge on anyone who survived that world's destruction. When the marauders attacked Earth, Superman and the Phantom Zone criminals put aside their differences to destroy them using jewel kryptonite, whose qualities were uniquely toxic to the Vrangs (*Action Comics* #548–549, October–November 1983).

VULCAN

The Roman god of fire, he provided weapons to Hercules, who used them in his efforts to defeat Superman and win the heart of Lois Lane (*Action Comics* #267–268, August–September 1960).

Later, he lent his powers, along with Zeus, Hercules, Apollo, Achilles, and Mercury, to a clay being named Zha-Vam, given life and intended to make certain the gods would be remembered in the future. This came about from fear after the Oracle of Delphi said a Man of Steel would one day be world-famous (*Action Comics* # 353, August 1967).

WAFFLE, WILMINGTON

A famed Hollywood comic, Wilmington Waffle wore a Superman costume and performed spoofs of the Man of Steel's exploits. He used a seltzer bottle, for example, to quash a theater-prop bomb. He performed these stunts all to promote a forthcoming motion picture. Aliens studying Earth mistakenly targeted Waffle, thinking him the genuine Superman. Their study would indicate whether or not Earth was ripe for conquest. Upon learning of this threat, Superman had Waffle halt the comedic stunts and perform some true superfeats to dissuade the malevolent aliens (*Superman* [first series] #93, November 1954).

WALKER, EBENEEZER

Somehow this eccentric millionaire learned that aliens intended to conquer Earth, weakening the populace by using their technology to transform key buildings into atomic constructions. Rather than alert the authorities, he merely bought up each building targeted and then had the Man of Steel demolish it in exchange for a million-dollar contribution to charity. Fearing that his reputation would keep people from taking the threat seriously, Walker kept the dire information to himself. Once the Man of Steel learned the truth, he made certain the entire planet's appreciation was extended to the wealthy savior (*Action Comics* #214, March 1956).

WALLER, AMANDA

Some people hide in the wake of adversity; others turn it into a form of strength. For Amanda Waller, the loss of her husband and son became defining moments, turning her into one of the most formidable nonpowered people in Superman's life (*Legends* #1, November 1986). Life was hard for her in the Cabrini-Green section of Chicago, but she and her husband Joseph tried to make the best of it, raising their six children. However, gang violence turned young Damita into a victim and Joseph snapped, seeking vengeance, only to die in a hail of gunfire. Determined that her remaining children would have a better chance at living, Amanda returned to school and obtained a degree, becoming an aide to a congressman from Illinois. In time, she earned a doctorate in political science (*Checkmate* [second series] #1, June 2006). While doing basic research, she uncovered government documents alluding to Task Force X, a covert team of operatives working both domestically (Argent) and internationally (Suicide Squad). In time, the international team was disbanded, and Argent went silent after John F. Kennedy was assassinated (*Suicide Squad Annual* #1, 1988).

Waller worked to revive the project for modern times, using people with special talents to perform missions on behalf of the federal government. In her mind, the ends justified the means, and if it meant using super-villains or janitors, it made no difference to her. To Waller's surprise, the government not only accepted her proposal, but placed her in charge of the new division. They refurbished Belle Reve prison in Louisiana to work as a super-villain containment facility in addition to the Squad's base of operations. She staffed the prison with people to not only operate the facility but also lend logistics support, including her cousin Flo Crawley.

Waller's work also saw remnants of other operations coalesced into a new uniformed branch for national security. Under the guidance of former Doom Patrol member Valentina Vostok, later replaced by Harry Stein, Checkmate became

another force for good. Superman was among the first heroes to know of its existence (*Action Comics* #598, March 1988).

Waller's take-no-prisoners attitude earned her the nickname of "the Wall," and she shouted, wheedled, cajoled, and blackmailed to get what she needed in order to serve her country. The Squad was first placed into action to deal with the threat of Brimstone, a creature from Apokolips that threatened to demolish the carvings at Mount Rushmore. In exchange for amnesty, a collection of villains were joined by several super heroes, and all were under the command of Rick Flagg, Junior, son of the original Squad's field commander.

After this, the Suicide Squad endured various government administrations, political threats, and a very high loss rate among those serving on missions. When the Squad needed a team in the Pacific, Superboy and Knockout were recruited for a brief time that saw the Clone of Steel working side by side with his foe King Shark (*Superboy* [third series] #13–15, March–May 1995). Steel also served on one mission that nearly killed him (*The Adventures of Superman* #594, September 2001).

Waller's control of the Squad grew challenging, and when the public learned of its existence, she was required to resign. Instead, an actor was hired to portray the new leader, with Waller still controlling things. When that was exposed, she was tried and imprisoned, although the country's needs saw to it that she was exonerated and returned to command the team when the Oval Office needed her.

The Squad's missions were more successful than not, but the high fatality rate gnawed at Waller's conscience. Eventually, she was reassigned as southeastern regional director for the Department of Extranormal Operations.

When Lex Luthor became president, Waller was elevated to Secretary of Meta-Human Affairs, continuing to oversee Task Force X but casting a jaundiced eye over the entire super-community (*Superman* [second series] #166, March 2001). When Luthor's criminal activities led him to leave office, she was arrested for complicit actions on the president's behalf. President Jonathan Vincent Horne, though, granted her a pardon and named her the Black King to Checkmate, the government operation that had been reconstituted into an international agency (*Checkmate* [second series] #1, June 2006).

The Wall continued to covertly run the Suicide Squad for her own missions, such as re-forming the Squad to take down Black Adam, then ruling the Middle Eastern country of Khandaq (*52* #33–34, December 20–27, 2006). The United Nations reorganized Checkmate once more, asking her to serve as its White Queen, responsible for policy-making decisions but taking her out of operational issues. She continued using the Squad when she saw the need, including rounding up as many super-villains as possible and exiling them to an alien world to save humanity (*Salvation Run* #1–7, January–July 2008). When the villains returned and her participation was exposed, she was forced to resign her seat before Checkmate informed the U.S. government what had been done.

Her suspicion of super heroes may have led her to hoard kryptonite on behalf of the government, as part of the Last Line, an anti-Superman defensive group in case the Man of Steel ever went out of control. She lost control of the operation when her trump card, the All-American Boy—built to resemble Doomsday, complete with green k shards growing from his colossal body—went berserk. After Superman and Batman shut down the operation, Waller agreed to personally pay for repairs to Smallville, which had been damaged during the confrontation (*Superman/Batman* #47–49, June–August 2008).

Waller's devotion to duty and troubles with various administrations strained her relationship with her surviving children—Odalys Milagro Valdez, Joseph, Junior, Martin, Jesse, and Coretta.

WALTERS, BROCK

After a series of gold shipments between the mine and the local bank were hijacked, the news prompted Lois Lane to investigate. When she went missing, Superman got involved. Over the course of rescuing her five different times, he managed to expose Brock Walters, owner of the Walters Mine, as the secret leader of a gang of criminals (*Action Comics* #35, April 1941).

WALTERS, CYRUS

Citizens were alarmed when the Man of Steel appeared to be committing a series of gaffes, calling his trustworthiness into question. It turned out to be an elaborate plot on the part of jewel thieves who wanted to steal Cyrus Walters's fabulous gem collection before Superman personally escorted it to a charity exhibition. Superman determined who was behind his problems and apprehended them before they could steal the jewels (*Superman* [first series] #87, February 1954).

WARBOW, NATHAN

A purebred Apache Indian who was also a top-notch industrial engineer, Nathan Warbow lived at 344 Clinton Avenue, the same Metropolis apartment building as Clark Kent (*Superman* [first series] #246, December 1971). Warbow was one of the neighbors endangered when the Quakerer, a lizard-like being from the 420th century, revealed himself after posing as neighbor Martin Thorpe. Clark had to save his neighbors without revealing his secret identity. When that proved impossible, he stopped the alien threat and then had Batman use a hypnotic device to remove his secret from everyone's mind (*Action Comics* #430–431, December 1973–January 1974).

WARREN, KATHY

When this small blonde child briefly lived with Jonathan and Martha Kent, she encountered an alien device that Superboy had recently collected. The device irradiated her, and for a time she developed an ultra-intellect. Kathy Warren used the newfound knowledge to help the Teen of Steel thwart an impending alien invasion (*Superboy* [first series] #176, July 1971). Kathy retained most of her new brain processing power even after leaving the Kents, complete with the knowledge of Superboy's secret identity (*Superboy* [first series] #191, October 1972).

WARWORLD

A long-extinct race known in legend as the Warzoon had built an artificial satellite the size of a planet and named it Warworld. Despite this formidable weapon, the Warzoon died out, leaving one last guardian in the control room. He eventually died, too, and the doomsday machine was found by the peaceful Largas, who deactivated the construct and kept the activating key in their posses-

Warworld

sion. As they died off, the key was entrusted to the Martians. Eons later, the galactic conqueror MONGUL began a quest to obtain the artifact that would grant him access to the long-defunct satellite. He managed to gain this object despite confrontations with Superman and the MARTIAN MANHUNTER. Mongul then located the satellite and found it still intact. After activating it, Mongul was poised to impose his will on the known galaxy until Superman appeared once more. Seated in the control chair, Mongul neurologically fired off its impressive arsenal, to no avail. It took SUPERGIRL flying through the satellite to finally overtax Mongul's mind and force him unconscious, rendering Warworld ineffective. Superman found the self-destruct mechanism, but by then Mongul had revived and fled (*DC Comics Presents* #27–29, November–January 1981).

In the reality after the CRISIS ON INFINITE EARTHS, Mongul obtained Warworld from three aliens, who approved of his notion of conquering planets to form his own empire. When Superman traveled among the stars during a self-imposed exile, he discovered Mongul's growing empire in addition to the powerful weapon he used for conquest. The Man of Steel wound up fighting Mongul's champion DRAAGA before he could confront Mongul directly, and it was during this adventure that he found the Kryptonian device known as the ERADICATOR (*Action Comics Annual* #2, 1989).

Sometime after Superman defeated Mongul and shattered the empire, BRAINIAC gained control of Warworld and used it to cause panic in the sky when the satellite appeared over METROPOLIS. Superman, aided by many of the World's Greatest Super Heroes, kept the populace safe and destroyed Warworld (*The Adventures of Superman* #488; *Action Comics* #674–675; *Superman: The Man of Steel* #9–10; *Superman* [second series] #65–66—all March–April 1992).

Mongul returned and partnered with the CYBORG SUPERMAN with a scheme to convert Earth into an organic Warworld, beginning with the destruction of Coast City and its six million inhabitants. This became the first Engine City—with Metropolis, on the opposite coast, scheduled to be next—until the villains were stopped by Supergirl, SUPERBOY, STEEL, the Eradicator, GREEN LANTERN, and the surprise arrival of Superman, recently revived after being killed by DOOMSDAY (*Superman* [second series] #82, October 1993).

Later, Brainiac 13 adapted that plan and turned PLUTO into a new version of Warworld. To destroy it, Superman amped up his powers by flying first through Sol and then through the planetoid (*Action Comics* #780–782; *The Adventures of Superman* #593–595; *Superboy* [third series] #89–91; *Supergirl* [fourth series] #59–61; *Superman* [second series] #171–173; *Superman: The Man of Steel* #115–117; *World's Finest Comics: Our Worlds at War* #1—all August–October 2001). Apparently, the planetary construct was repaired, since it was seen intact in the thirty-first century (*Legion* #5, October 2001).

WASHINGTON MONUMENT, THE

Standing more than 555 feet high, the obelisk dedicated to President George Washington featured an observatory and was completed in 1884. Superman thwarted EMIL LORING's attempts to destroy it and other world-famous landmarks (*Action Comics* #56, January 1943).

A Kryptonian named MALA once stole many famous monuments, including this one, in an attempt to gain vengeance against Superman (*Action Comics* #194, July 1954). It was taken from the Washington Mall again by the Four Galactic Thiefmasters as part of their elaborate plan to lure the Man of Steel into a diabolical "red-sun trap" (*Action Comics* #321, February 1965).

WATER SPRITE, THE

Described as part man, part fish, this green-colored beast appeared unexpectedly and broke the Annisdale levee—later attempting to demolish the Annisdale dam—without success. He later explained that he intended to "choke off the free flow of nature's water."

As Superman investigated, the Water Sprite was revealed to be Kenneth Darby, an advocate for a new dam who found his pleas going unheeded. He created his hideous-looking outfit in an attempt to force people to see things his way as well as to profit from the new construction by selling the town substandard materials. Had he been successful, he would have let Annisdale build the dam, then destroyed it before his shoddy work materials could be discovered. Instead, he wound up apprehended by the Man of Steel (*Action Comics* #82, March 1945).

WATKINS

"I am one of 'the human bombs,'" a man told a stunned CLARK KENT and PERRY WHITE. He and his cohorts made up a criminal gang that declared death held no threat for them, so they felt free to rob as they pleased; anyone interfering, they continued, would become a potential fatality as they detonated their suicide explosives. As Superman investigated, he learned that Watkins, "a hawk-faced man of utterly ruthless features," was an evil "master hypnotist" who had hypnotized a group of innocent men into becoming human bombs to serve his criminal will. The crimes were successful until the Action Ace finally located Watkins and knocked him unconscious, breaking his hold over the bombers (*Superman* [first series] #17, July–August 1942).

WATUGI TRIBE

Living on the South Sea island of Pajor-Pajor, members of the Watugi tribe were unwitting "extras" in a monster movie that JIMMY OLSEN attempted to film. He had used PROFESSOR PHINEAS POTTER's device to bring TITANO and a Kryptonian FLAME DRAGON to the island, which endangered the peaceful tribe when the monstrous battle ignited the dormant volcano they worshipped. Olsen sent the "stars" back before anyone was harmed (*Superman's Pal, Jimmy Olsen* #84, April 1965).

WAVERIDER

In a potential future, Earth's super heroes had been wiped out, killed by one of their own who

had turned traitor. That traitor, clad in armor and now called Monarch, turned the Earth into a depressing dictatorship by 2030. There were few pockets of resistance—although one was scientist Matthew Ryder, who wanted to alter time and eradicate Monarch's existence. As Monarch surreptitiously observed, the experiments were failures, killing the subjects sent through time. The despot made his presence known and made modifications to the device, then tried it on Ryder himself. The trip through the quantum field wound up not killing him, but transforming him into a living temporal being. Taking the name Waverider, he sought to collect allies from the twentieth century to help free his era.

Young Matthew Ryder was trapped by the cave-in of a METROPOLIS subway tunnel triggered during Captain Atom's battle with Monarch (*Armageddon 2001* #2, October 1991). The boy was rescued from the rubble by the time-traveling being known as Waverider, the beginning of an odd relationship since both were actually the same person.

As Superman and the METAL MEN removed an experimental quantum field generator from the ruin of S.T.A.R. LABS, the unstable generator exploded. Again, Waverider arrived to save the citizenry, including Matt and his parents. Ironically, Waverider had once been a future Matthew Ryder who had journeyed to the past from a divergent time line to prevent the machinations of the Monarch. In the Waverider's personal past, his parents had been killed by the explosion, which he alone had survived. In changing his past, Waverider created a new future for Matt Ryder—and yet, due to his having become part of the timestream, Waverider's existence was not disrupted.

Monarch was surprised to see that Ryder had not only survived but actually thrived. He divined the man's intentions and followed him through time, leading to a struggle that then threatened two eras. Hawk, an agent for the Lords of Chaos, wound up killing and replacing Monarch, who turned out to be his older self. This mentally unhinged the adventurer and he went wild, causing Superman to lead the JUSTICE LEAGUE OF AMERICA, the TEEN TITANS, and the Metal Men into pitched battle. Waverider was an active participant and worked with the quantum-powered Captain Atom to finally end the threat (*Armageddon 2001* #1–2, May–October 1991).

Ryder grew up and studied with the noted time researcher Ripley Hunter. As an adult, he began his own time experiments under the patronage of LEX LUTHOR. When something went wrong, Ryder found himself and his equipment projected to a

strange plane beyond time and space (*Superman* [second series] #73, November 1992).

After that, Waverider chose to spend his time with the Linear Men, traversing the timestream in an effort to keep all eras safe from tampering.

Superman met the Linear Men at their base, known as the Vanishing Point, in the midst of Waverider's attempt to change history by preventing the catastrophic explosion that had killed his parents. Stealing member Liri Lee's wrist control, Waverider succeeded in doing just that, never realizing that he had actually fulfilled destiny by creating the time line that belonged to the Linear Men's founder . . . Matthew Ryder (*Superman* [second series] #61, November 1991). Soon after, Waverider was chosen to replace Travis O'Connell in the group (*Superman* [second series] #73, November 1992).

WAYNE, BRUCE

Bruce Wayne was the tragically driven man who achieved the peak of perfection across multiple disciplines to fight crime as Batman.

(For a detailed biography of Bruce Wayne and his caped alter ego, see *The Essential Batman Encyclopedia,* 2008.)

WEAPON-MASTER, THE

The Weapon-Master was an alien who employed weapons taken from across time and space in his quest to plunder Earth. Several of his devices proved potent enough to affect even the Man of Steel. It took Batman, temporarily imbuing himself with super-strength from a device maintained at the Fortress of Solitude, to risk his life to free his friend and the rest of humanity (*World's Finest Comics* #272–274, October–December 1981).

He reappeared, this time using his equipment to enslave the entire Green Lantern Corps, prompting the Guardians of the Universe to summon Superman for help (*DC Comics Presents* #60, August 1983).

The Weapon-Master

He is not to be confused with Xotar, the time-traveling villain known as the similarly named Weapons Master who traveled from the year 11,960 to steal weapons, only to be opposed by the newly formed Justice League of America (*The Brave and the Bold* [first series] #29, April–May 1960). There have been other Weapons Masters as well, including one who managed to sap Superman of his powers for a time (*Action Comics* #817–818, September–October 2004).

WEBBER, JOHNNY

Smallville High School's resident class clown, Johnny Webber adopted the guise of Dyna-Mind, a would-be super-villain, after gaining psychokinetic powers when a passing meteor shower exposed him to radiation. With his newfound intelligence and mental skills, he tried his hand at crime, opposed by the town's Teen of Steel (*The New Adventures of Superboy* #42–44, June–August 1983).

Johnny was apprehended and remanded to a juvenile detention facility. Upon his release, and still possessing his formidable skills, he covertly lent Superboy and Zatara the Magician his help when they had to stop the interdimensional threat of Turlock the Berzerker. Somehow the confrontation left him devoid of his mental powers (*The New Adventures of Superboy* #49, January 1984).

Johnny was reunited with Clark Kent years later at their high school reunion, where he revealed that he was now vice president of the Smallville National Bank and that his subconscious had held

the secret of Superman's alter ego ever since his brief foray as Dyna-Mind (*Superman* [first series] #403, January 1985).

WEGTHOR

Wegthor was one of the three moons orbiting Krypton and sustained colonies. The moon was visited by exploring astronauts including Lara, the future wife of Jor-El. He had designed an antigravity vessel that took her to the satellite. However, she was stranded there, requiring Jor-El to take a standard rocket to rescue her (*Superman* [first series] #233, January 1971).

Tragically, the moon was destroyed by the scientist Jax-Ur, an act that earned him a lengthy sentence within the Phantom Zone (*Action Comics* #310, March 1964). Its loss may have also led to the planet's increasing instability, hastening its destruction ahead of Jor-El's estimates.

WELLINS, BART

One never knows what will happen when one goes out to sea. Bart Wellins never expected to gain superpowers that rivaled the Man of Tomorrow's when he was exposed to artifacts—still carrying experimental radiation—that had surfaced from ancient Atlantis after a seaquake dislodged them. The unscrupulous man used his newfound abilities not to imitate Superman but to oppose him by robbing Metropolis with delight. As they fought, Superman was also exposed to the radiation, which temporarily increased his powers "a thousand fold." Once Wellins was in jail, Superman stopped functioning for fear his out-of-control abilities would come to harm people (*Action Comics* #230, July 1957).

WELLS, KRISTIN

A student from the twenty-ninth century who visited Earth-1's past and became the heroine Superwoman.

WESTFIELD, PAUL

A well-respected geneticist, Paul Westfield was placed in charge of Project Cadmus. However, his zeal for the unknown led him to approve experiments that crossed the ethical threshold and often led to bizarre creations (*Superman* [second series] #58, August 1991). He became obsessed with finding a way to clone Superman so that Earth could retain a champion in the event of his death. He was surreptitiously aided in his work on occasion by Lex Luthor, who lent his own genetic material to the project. After discovering that a pure Kryptonian clone was impossible, Westfield began combining human and Kryptonian DNA, using Luthor's material, and wound up creating a successful life-form. It was under rapid development when Superman was killed by Doomsday, so the new hero emerged still in the form of a teenager. Following Westfield's death, Superboy was told that it was the geneticist's own DNA matched with the Man of Steel's that gave him life (*Superboy* [second series] *Annual* #2, 1995).

Westfield took advantage of the Battle for Metropolis that allowed him to direct a missile at Cadmus, destroying the Underworlders, bizarre creatures manufactured by the mad Dabney Donovan. To gain revenge, Donovan disguised himself as a janitor and killed Westfield, keeping his right ear as a souvenir (*Superman* [second series] #90, June 1994).

When Superboy was traveling through Hypertime, there was an incident that wiped all versions of Westfield from the myriad realities (*Superboy* [third series] #63, June 1999).

Westfield was also the father of Amanda Spence, an agent for the Agenda, which used his genetic research to clone Superboy and create the malformed duplicate Match (*Superboy* [third series] #73, April 2000).

WGBS

The flagship television station for Morgan Edge's Galaxy Communications' Galaxy Broadcasting

System was based in Metropolis. Its employees through the years included Clark Kent, Lana Lang, Steve Lombard, Catherine Grant, Oscar Asherman, and Jimmy Olsen (*Superman* [first series] #233, January 1971).

Field reporters included Lauren Bradley (*Haven: The Broken City* #5, June 2002), Emma Bradshaw (*Supermen of America* #1, March 1999), Misty Brink (*Swamp Thing* [second series] #79, December 1988), Jim Brody (*Superman Family* #176, April–May 1976), Carl Brookman (*The Adventures of Superman* #535, June 1996), Jorge Buenitez (*Superman* [second series] #134, April 1998), Ross Chapman (*The Adventures of Superman* #526, August 1995), Nora Cheung (*JLA-Superman: The Never-Ending Story,* 2004), Walter Conrad (*The Sandman* #6, December 1975–January 1976), Lyla Dean (*Action Comics* #670, October 1991), Quentin Fairacre (*Justice League Quarterly* #1, Winter 1990), Don Friedman (*Animal Man* #13, July 1989), Grant Gibson (*Aquaman* [fifth series] #63, January 2000), Walter Haines (*The Adventures of Superman* #492, July 1992), Roger Harp (*Detective Comics* #498, January 1981), Lisa Haymore (*JLA* #2, February 1997), Roland Headley (*Fury of Firestorm* #16, September 1983), Gary Hoffman (*Superman* [second series] *Annual* #12, 2000), Steve Jones (*Secret Origins Special* #1, 1989), Richard Kovacs (*JLA Classified* #29, January 2007), Hugh Langley (*Action Comics* #700, June 1994), Wes Lesman (*The Adventures of Superman* #603, May 2002), Walter Lewis (*Booster Gold* [first series] #12, January 1987), Bill Logan (*Action Comics* #513, November 1980), Melba Manton (*Superman's Girl Friend, Lois Lane* #131, June 1973; others), Gary McCraw (*52* #7, June 21, 2006), Bob McGinnis (*Superboy* [second series] #100, July 2002), Tiffany Mellon (*Titans* #48, February 2003), Cindy Miles (*Booster Gold* [first series] #1, February 1986), Allen Miller (*Superman: The Man of Steel* #71, September 1997), Taylor Mills (*JLA* #2, February 1997), Morrie Morris (*Superboy* [third series] #73, April 2000), Bob Nenno (*The Adven-*

tures of Superman #451, February 1989), Davida Perkins (*Action Comics* #699, May 1994), Amanda Trellace (*JLA* #16, March 1998), David Trimble (*JLA* #2, February 1997), Frank Weeks (*The Adventures of Superman* #568, June 1999), Dan Whether (*Fury of Firestorm* #7, December 1982), and Bill Wultzer (*The L.A.W.* #1, September 1999).

Tim McCready was one of the station's sports reporters (*Superman* #673, April 2008), and Carolyn Waters (*Action Comics* #561, November 1984) was the consumer advocate.

Kelly Johansen and Rick Raymond were the newsreaders on WGBS's *AM Metropolis* morning broadcast (*JLA–Superman: The Never-Ending Story*, 2004), and Betsy Lord read the news on *Good Morning, Metropolis* (*Detective Comics* #740, January 2000). David Rowlands anchored the GBS Evening News (*JLA–Superman: The Never-Ending Story*, 2004).

Dave Burnside (*Detective Comics* #511, February 1982) and Caitlin Callahan (*Detective Comics* #798, November 2004) were the Gotham City correspondents, while Desiree Busch (*The Flash Annual* #3, 1989), and "Doc" Dockerty (*Titans* #26, April 2001) worked the New York City beat. San Francisco was covered by Patricia Niles (*Showcase '95* #3, March 1995). Lisa Abernathy was a long-standing Washington correspondent (*Wonder Woman* [first series] #306, August 1983), while Fran Farmer was also a national correspondent in Washington (*Captain Atom* [third series] #14, April 1988).

Cal Emery (*Booster Gold* [first series] #11, December 1986) was a reporter for WGBS's radio station.

Superboy's girlfriend Tana Moon briefly worked for WGBS before relocating to Hawaii.

WHIRLICANE

Emilio Storn was a brilliant S.T.A.R. Labs scientist specializing in biotechnology and climate-control research but also mentally unstable. His delusion led him to decide to conquer the world by building a "storm-bomb" that would alter the elements at his command and threaten countries that did not capitulate. He left his employment and donned a garish green, purple, and white costume, as well as a pointed mask and striped leggings, becoming Whirlicane.

While hideous to look at, Whirlicane's outfit was laced with technology that allowed him to create powerful whirlwinds with concussive force. With his hired henchmen, he began committing robberies throughout Metropolis to fund his plans for conquest. When confronted by the Man of Steel, he managed a wall of force that momentarily stunned even Superman. He fled after spraying molten lead over the hero's eyes, preventing his vision powers from locating his getaway. It took the Man of Steel only a little longer to find and apprehend him (*Action Comics* #457, March 1976).

Whirlicane next appeared—after his release from prison—back at S.T.A.R. with a robotic creation called Thunder and Lightning that could shift between shapes, each with different powers (Thunder generated shock waves, and Lightning had electrical powers). The android believed itself human and teamed up with Storn to steal meteorological equipment that would allow them to complete their plans for conquest. Superman trailed the automated menace back to Storn's lab. During the battle, the android learned the truth about its nature and detonated itself, apparently killing Storn in the process (*Superman* [first series] #303, September 1976).

WHITE, ALICE

On Earth-1, Alice White was the wife of *Daily Planet* editor Perry White (*Superman's Pal, Jimmy Olsen* #42, January 1960). A full-time homemaker, Alice raised their children Hank White, Will White, and Perry White, Junior, while gracefully enduring the long hours that came with her spouse's demanding job. They made their home in a one-story ranch-style house "on the outskirts of Metropolis" (*Action Comics* #278, July 1961).

Alice was also the grandmother of Perry White, III, Jeremy White, Matthew White, Gretchen White, and two unnamed granddaughters (*Action Comics* #461, July 1976).

The Earth-2 Perry and Alice White apparently had only one son, Perry White, Junior (*Superman Family* #196, July–August 1979).

WHITE, ALICE SPENCER

After the Crisis on Infinite Earths, *Daily Planet* reporter Perry White married Alice Spencer. Previously, while her then-boyfriend Perry was overseas in the army, she and Lex Luthor had had a brief affair, resulting in her pregnancy (*World of Metropolis* #1, August 1988). It was years before her husband learned that their only son Jerry White was not his (*Superman* [second series] #47, September 1990). Alice and Perry reconciled and grew even closer after Jerry's troubled life ended at the hands of the satanic Blaze.

In the wake of Jerry's death, Perry took a leave of absence to be with Alice, and in time they decided to open their home once more. They adopted Keith Steven Parks, an orphaned African American youth who added the surname *White* to his legal name (*Superman: The Man of Steel* #39–40, December 1994–January 1995).

Alice stood by Perry's side as he battled lung cancer, a result of his seemingly hourly cigar habit, and was delighted when it went into remission.

In the New Earth after the Infinite Crisis, there is no record of Alice White.

WHITE, HANK

The youngest son of *Daily Planet* editor Perry White and his wife Alice White, Hank White also had two brothers, Will White and Perry White, Junior (*Superman's Pal, Jimmy Olsen* #40, October 1959). As a teen, Hank joined the biker gang the Kings, a secret only learned when cub reporter Jimmy Olsen disguised himself to infiltrate the juvenile delinquent band and report from within. In fact, Hank had infiltrated the gang himself, taking notes to demonstrate to his father that he had the makings of a good reporter. He eventually married an unnamed woman and had several children with her (*Action Comics* #461, July 1976).

WHITE, JERRY

Perry Jerome White, Junior, grew up a troubled boy, unaware his biological father was not *Daily Planet* editor Perry White, but the criminal genius Lex Luthor. He frequently got into trouble as a teen, and even when he reached young adulthood, Perry was bailing his son Jerry out of jail (*The Adventures of Superman* #433, October 1987).

Perry made every effort to help his son, showing tremendous patience, but Jerry continued to make mistakes and find himself in trouble with drugs and gangs. The intervention of and growing friendship between Jerry and community activist Jose Delgado, who was secretly the hero Gangbuster, began to show Jerry a safer path (*The Adventures of Superman* #451, February 1989). In time, Jerry even found a steady girlfriend, a woman named Tammy Brown (*Superman* [second series] #36, October 1989). Soon after, he took a job at a new nightclub, unaware it was a front for the demon Blaze, who was seeking new souls to enhance her power within Hell (*Superman* [second series] #45, July 1990). Jerry wound up getting into trouble anew, shot along with Jimmy Olsen by Intergang (*The Adventures of Superman* #469, August 1990).

As Luthor learned the news about his son's grave condition, he confronted Perry and revealed the truth. Superman, meantime, had been taken to limbo by the Black Racer to confront Blaze, who intended to keep their souls, something Superman was ready to fight for. Instead, Jerry sacrificed his immortal soul to Blaze to free Jimmy and Superman. That act, the Black Racer told the Man of Steel, ensured that Jerry would not spend eternity in Hell (*Action Comics* #656, August 1990; *Superman* [second series] #47 and *The Adventures of Superman* #470—both September 1990).

WHITE, JOYCE

To capture the "crime chief" Coup Colby, Superman created a pretty blonde female robot whom he introduced as *Daily Planet* editor Perry White's niece Joyce. Working the remote control from behind his cape, Superman faked a romance in order to lure Colby into the open and apprehend him (*Superman* [first series] #120, March 1958).

WHITE, PERRY

Perry White was gruff and irascible, but he was also a dedicated professional journalist who made sure that the DAILY PLANET lived up to the ideals of journalism, offering fair and objective coverage of the news (first appearance in *Superman* [first series] #7, November–December 1940; first name revealed in *Superman* [first series] #10, May–June 1941).

On Earth-2, Perry White was a reporter for the *Daily Star* in METROPOLIS. He was a rival to CLARK KENT and LOIS LANE, but it was a friendly competition for scoops. Upon GEORGE TAYLOR's retirement in the early 1950s, he proposed a competition between Clark Kent and veteran reporter Perry White for his job. Perry proved the better reporter by a nose and ironically lost out to Clark because Taylor believed the better reporter should remain such rather than being cooped up behind a desk (*Superman Family* #196, November–December 1979). The Earth-2 Perry and ALICE WHITE apparently had only one son, PERRY WHITE, JUNIOR (*Superman Family* #196, July–August 1979).

On Earth-1, Perry White came from a distinguished Metropolis family, begun by his grandfather Josiah and his father Judge White (*Superman's Pal, Jimmy Olsen* #70, July 1963). Other chronicles indicated that he was raised by steamboat captain Josiah White in 1906 San Francisco (*Superman* [first series] #168, April 1964) or was the operator of a shoeshine stand in 1920s Chicago (*Superman* [first series] #142, January 1961). He attended Metropolis Public School No. 84 (*Superman* [first series] #84, February 1962).

ALL MY HARD-WORKING REPORTERS DESERVE A BONUS!
REPORTERS HAD TO FIGHT BEFORE FOR RAISES! NOW PERRY HAS TURNED GENEROUS! LOIS, THAT PROVES THIS JEWEL'S RAYS TURNED JIMMY FROM MY FRIEND INTO MY ENEMY!

He was drawn to journalism and began working as a freelance reporter for newspapers based around the country, including Chicago. He also wrote for the GOTHAM CITY's lead paper the *Gazette* (*World's Finest Comics* #80, January–February 1956). A plaque commemorated Perry White's coverage of the "Secret Olympics" held in 1941 during World War II, an event the editor did not recall. This prompted Superman to travel back in time to learn the truth. Posing as John Clinton, he met the foreign correspondent and, as Superman, aided the Blackhawks in saving the life of Albert Einstein (*DC Comics Presents* #69, May 1984).

White served in the Korean War as commander of a firing squad that executed deserters—although one, Victor Stark, escaped accidentally. Years later, Stark sought revenge by killing members of the firing squad, including White. The newsman was saved, though, through the efforts of Superman, BATMAN, and ROBIN (*World's Finest Comics* #171, November 1967).

When he met SUPERBOY in SMALLVILLE, White's exclusive coverage revealing the hero's extraterrestrial origins won him a job at Metropolis's *Daily Planet* (*Adventure Comics* #120, September 1947; *The New Adventures of Superboy* #12, December 1980). It was White who noted that the boy had become a man and was operating out of Metropolis, a fact Clark Kent was trying to keep quiet while the reporter established himself before his alter ego (*Superman* [first series] #366, December 1981). Such coverage led White to being promoted to editor in chief of the paper upon the retirement of George Taylor, while Kent was a college junior (*Superman: The Secret Years* #4, May 1985).

Perry White surrounded himself with a staff of bright, eager reporters, including Lois Lane and Clark Kent. He also created the position of cub reporter to train the next generation of journalists. JIMMY OLSEN was the first to hold the position and did so for quite some time. As editor of the *Planet,* White was described as "gruff" (*Action Comics* #302, July 1963), "irascible" (*Superman* [first series] #49, September 1947), "hard-boiled" (*Superman* [first series] #16, May–June 1942), "tough" (*Superman* [first series] #72, September–October 1951), "dynamic" (*Superman* [first series] #73, November–December 1951), "sentimental" (*Superman* [first series] #16, May–June 1942), warmhearted (*Action Comics* #269, October 1960), and a "two-fisted crusading editor" (*Superman* [first series] #72, September–October 1951).

He was also described as "the best editor in the business," a man whose unique "brand of slam-bang, no-holds-barred journalism has made the *Daily Planet* the biggest paper in Metropolis!" (*Superman* [first series] #73, November–December 1951).

Perry was considered one of Superman's best friends (*Action Comics* #243, August 1958). In fact, the Man of Steel dedicated a room to Perry White in the FORTRESS OF SOLITUDE (*Action Comics* #268, July 1961).

Perry White had the opportunity to experience what it was like to possess superpowers. The first time came when XASNU, a plant intelligence, possessed Perry's body, merging to produce a superpowered person who masqueraded as MASTERMAN until he was stopped by a piece of white KRYPTONITE tossed at the invader by SUPERGIRL (*Action Comics* #278, July 1961). There was an occasion when Perry and Gotham police commissioner James W. Gordon were exposed to a gas at the Fortress of Solitude. The gas altered their minds, turning the duo evil, and they used costumes and serums to provide them temporary superpowers to wage war against the World's Finest team as ANTI-SUPERMAN and Anti-Batman (*World's Finest Comics* #159, August 1966).

The final time came in the form of a gift as four-thumbed mutants from another world presented Perry with a box of cigars. Lighting each one gave him powers and abilities on a par with the Man

of Tomorrow's, although these wore off when each cigar burned up. The adventure coincided with Perry's appearance at Columbia University to receive his third Pulitzer Prize, this particular honor bestowed due to his coverage of those selfsame mutants and the Army of Tomorrow (*Action Comics* #436, June 1974).

Perry assumed dual identities to assist Superman in two criminal sting operations, taking the guise of the Black Knight in one instance (*Superman* [first series] #124, September 1958) and posing as Mento the Great in another (*Superman* [first series] #147, August 1961). The Man of Steel also worked out scenarios that JIMMY OLSEN ("Plan J"), Lois Lane ("Plan L"), and Perry White ("Plan P") would each carry out in specific crisis situations. "Plan P" required Perry to bind Superman with fake kryptonite chains to dupe the SUPERMAN REVENGE SQUAD (*Action Comics* #295, December 1962).

In addition to being the editor of the *Daily Planet,* Perry White was also president of the Magazine and News Association (*Action Comics* #155, August 1958). A Native American tribe made him an honorary chief, bestowing upon him the tribal name Chief Stony Voice (*Action Comics* #200, January 1955).

The paper prospered, and eventually MORGAN EDGE purchased it to make it a part of his Galaxy Communications media empire. Edge's first act was to take Clark from the *Planet* staff and make him a television reporter (*Superman* [first series #133, January 1971). Edge later attempted to force the sixty-five-year-old editor to retire, citing Galaxy Broadcasting's mandatory retirement rule. When the entire *Daily Planet* staff threatened to quit alongside Perry, Edge reversed his decision (*Superman* [first series] #280, December 1974).

At some point, Perry married a woman named Alice, and together they raised their children HANK WHITE, WILL WHITE, and Perry WHITE, Junior. They

made their home in a one-story ranch-style house on the outskirts of Metropolis (*Action Comics* #278, July 1961).

Perry was also the grandfather of Perry White, III, Jeremy White, Matthew White, Gretchen White, and two unnamed granddaughters (*Action Comics* #461, July 1976).

As Earth-1's history was ending, Perry began to display the early symptoms of Alzheimer's disease, although it was never formally diagnosed.

After the Crisis on Infinite Earths reordered reality, Perry Jerome White was born in the Suicide Slum section of Metropolis, having lost his father to an overseas war. Growing up, he and fellow urchin Lex Luthor were boyhood pals, with Perry seeing Lex as his only friend. One day, Perry innocently coaxed Lex to attend a high school football game with him, preventing Lex from being on hand when his adoptive father Casey Briggs killed Lex's sister Lena. Luthor hated Perry for this and planned to seek revenge in the future (*Superman* [second series] #131, January 1998).

Driven to be a journalist, White began his career at a tender age as a *Daily Planet* copy boy and worked his way up to reporter, then editor, then editor in chief. When he reached general assignment reporting, Perry was dispatched to Melonville to investigate a string of racially motivated deaths. There he met Franklin Stern, who'd seen several family members go missing, and at first they did not get along. When Perry saved Franklin from a beating by the Aryan Brotherhood, however, the two forged a friendship that endured. Together they discovered that the Brotherhood had been kidnapping people in order to experiment on them in the hope of creating a genetically perfect master race. Perry's reporting earned him his first Pulitzer Prize. Later, Stern graduated from Harvard Business School, went on to a successful career, and wound up buying the *Daily Planet* as a favor to a friend, despite their differing political philosophies (*Superman: The Man of Steel* #47, August 1995).

While Perry White was rising up the *Planet*'s ladder of success, Luthor burst onto the scene with his successful LexWing and then LexCorp; soon he was the preeminent figure in Metropolis. In time, that meant his owning the *Daily Planet* for a while. Upon purchasing it, Lex asked Perry to join WLEX, his newly acquired television station, but White had printer's ink in his veins and refused. Instead, Perry found a man named David Ling to buy the paper, including the condition that the sale would mean his promotion to editor in chief. The entire business left Perry feeling sour toward Lex without knowing the hatred Luthor felt for his onetime friend. As Luthor prepared to sell the *Daily Planet* to Ling, Lex went so far as to seduce editor Perry White's wife Alice White (*World of Metropolis* #1, August 1988) in revenge for being at the football game when Lena was murdered by their adoptive father.

When Perry rose to become the paper's editor, one of his first moves was to hire Lois Lane, a fiery reporter he'd first met when she was just fifteen—but who'd made a memorable impression. The paper prospered thanks to her coverage, but circulation really soared when Clark Kent got himself hired by providing White with the first coverage featuring the Man of Steel (*Man of Steel* #2, October 1986). Perry built a powerhouse team of reporters that kept the paper among the nation's elite.

He and Alice raised their only child Jerry White, who wound up having a troubled youth, until he died from gunshots suffered at the hands of Intergang (*The Adventures of Superman* #469–470, August–September 1990). Only then did he learn of Alice's affair and the truth of Jerry's parentage (*Superman* [second series] #47, September 1990). In the wake of Jerry's death, Perry took a leave of absence to be with Alice, and in time they decided to open their home to children once more. They adopted Keith Steven Parks, an orphaned African American youth who eventually added the surname White to his legal name (*Superman: The Man of Steel* #39–40, December 1994–January 1995).

Alice stood by Perry's side as he battled lung cancer, a result of his seemingly hourly cigar habit, and was delighted when it went into remission (*The Adventures of Superman* #538, September 1996; *Superman* [second series] #124, June 1997; others). As White fought the disease, Clark Kent oversaw the paper. Perry emerged from convalescence to sit beside Lois's parents when she walked down the aisle to marry Clark (*Superman: The Wedding Album,* December 1996).

His return to the *Planet* came as its circulation was embattled by the rise of television and the Internet. Franklin Stern wound up selling the paper, meaning that Perry could no longer count on his friend for support. Luthor bought the paper once more, this time firing the staff with the exception of Lois and Jimmy, who were transferred to LexCom. Perry was immediately hired to lecture about journalism at Metropolis University (*Superman* [second series] #151, December 1999). This proved temporary, and the paper was sold once more, thanks to some behind-the-scenes engineering from Lois. Even so, the *Planet* had to reinvent itself repeatedly to remain relevant in a time of intense competition.

Lois and Perry were caught in an explosion triggered by Clayface at the *Daily Planet* offices. While Lois recovered with Superman's help, Perry was on life support for a time before recovering and returning to work (*Final Crisis* #2–3, August–September 2008).

Perry was deeply upset when he believed Jimmy Olsen had died while investigating General Samuel Lane's Project 7734. He was the first to discover that Olsen was actually in hiding, and White began surreptitiously working with the photographer to build the story. Later, as Lois Lane also began assembling the facts to doom the operation her father had masterminded, the Federal Government pressured Perry not to run the incendiary stories. White then suggested Lois "quit" the *Planet* and publish the facts elsewhere, something she did with a network of bloggers (*Action Comics* #884, February 2010). In the wake of Project 7734's downfall, Perry was only too glad to have his core staff back in place.

After reality was shuffled by the Infinite Crisis, Perry White's background was modified, including the reason for his enmity with Luthor. He'd once defied Luthor by running an exposé on LexCorp's seemingly corrupt business practices that left many competing companies out of business and drove many competing businessmen to an early

grave. He had been punished by Luthor ever since and struggled to keep the *Daily Planet* afloat. Perry was on the verge of shutting the paper down when Superman first flew over Metropolis. The fire this event set in his reporters, including oddballs such as Catherine Grant, Steve Lombard, and Ron Troupe, motivated Perry to keep the paper running. He knew then that Luthor's days as a free man were numbered (*Superman: Secret Origin* #3, January 2010).

Perry White was always considered a shrewd observer, so there was always speculation about whether he knew Clark Kent's secret. Bruce Wayne once had the opinion, "Perry White is too good of a reporter not to have discovered Clark's identity, but he acts otherwise. It reminds me of Commissioner Gordon back home . . ." (*Batman* #612, April 2003).

In a potential thirtieth century, Parri Wyte was a remote descendant who edited the *Daily Solar System* (*Action Comics* #215, April 1958). Also in the thirtieth century, the Legion of Super-Heroes employed a Perry White robot as part of an elaborate hoax they played on Superman and Supergirl (*Superman* [first series] #152, April 1962). Superman encountered a life-like android of Perry White during a time journey to Metropolis one million years in the future (*Action Comics* #300, May 1963).

Throughout the galaxy and across the myriad parallel universes, Perry White and the *Daily Planet* appeared to be the template for imitators, doppelgängers, and variants. Examples included the *Daily Zorian,* a so-called telenewspaper on the planet Zor (*Action Comics* #168, May 1952); Ar-Rone, the reformed criminal who was Perry White's double in the Lookalike Squad (*Action Comics* #309, February 1964); and the Perry White lookalike who was also named Perry White, whom Superman and Batman encountered during a visit to an extra-dimensional "parallel world" (*World's Finest Comics* #148, March 1965). On the planet Oceania, Chester King's editor at the Oceania Network bore a striking resemblance to Perry White (*Action Comics* #265, June 1960).

On Earth-988, Perry's son Trevor Jenkins "T. J." White was an aspiring stand-up comic who attended Shuster University alongside a young Clark Kent (*Superboy* [second series] #1–4, February–May 1990).

WHITE, PERRY, JUNIOR

Perry White, Junior, was the Earth-1 son of Alice and Perry White, along with his siblings Hank White and Will White. The younger Perry had graduated from journalism school and was immediately hired at the prestigious *Daily Planet*. Despite his inexperience in the field, growing up at the knee of the editor in chief taught him investigative skills that gave him a head start. Unfortunately, young Perry took a series of clues and erroneously concluded that fellow reporter Clark Kent was the criminal known as Mister Wheels. Kent knew the truth but could not expose the real Mister Wheels without revealing his own true identity to Perry, Junior. Superman managed to apprehend the criminal while teaching Perry something about investigation. Perry apologized to Clark and realized experience would be the true teacher (*Superman* [first series] #108, September 1956).

He later married and had children including Perry White III (*Action Comics* #461, July 1976).

On Earth-2, Perry White, Junior, was the only son to that world's Alice and Perry White (*Superman Family* #196, June–July 1979).

In the reality formed after the Crisis on Infinite Earths, Perry White, Junior, was better known as Jerry White (*The Adventures of Superman* #428, May 1987; others).

WHITE, WILL

The son of Perry and Alice White, Will White grew up with his brothers Hank White and Perry White, Junior.

In an attempt to work as a reporter without seeming to be employed as an act of patronage on the part of his father, *Daily Planet* editor in chief Perry White, redheaded Will White used the alias Will Whitman. He agreed to a true test: report on a major news story within twenty-four hours. He managed that by providing Superman with the information the hero needed to apprehend a gang of protection racketeers posing as the Universal Insurance Company (*Superman* [first series] #72, September–October 1951).

He later married and had children (*Action Comics* #461, July 1976).

WHITE LOTUS

Nona Lin-Baker was a member of the Supermen of America, able to generate a malleable force field as the White Lotus.

WHIZ WAGON, THE

When the clones of the Newsboy Legion were ready to leave the DNA Project, they did so in style. Big Words, one of the members, designed a futuristic vehicle that put motor homes to shame. Morgan Edge agreed to build the amazing Whiz Wagon, which comfortably fit the Legion along with reporter Jimmy Olsen (*Superman's Pal, Jimmy Olsen* #133, October 1970).

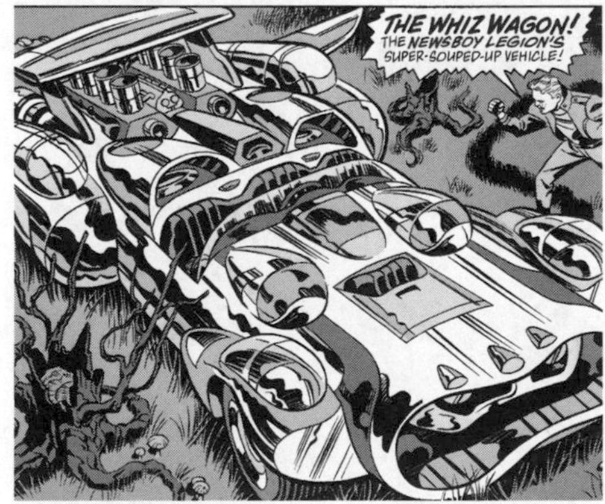

THE WHIZ WAGON!
THE NEWSBOY LEGION'S SUPER-SOUPED-UP VEHICLE!

WHIZZY

Streaky the Supercat had good genes, which were passed on through countless generations of offspring, resulting in the birth of the thirtieth-century identical-looking cat called Whizzy. The orange cat feline was noteworthy for the twin white lightning-shaped marks on his sides and the red cape he sported, although the cape had a yellow W-shield rather than the traditional S-shield. After helping the Legion of Super-Heroes defeat the Positive Man, Supergirl was surprised to find the cat, who possessed telepathic abilities. The feline's collar said, whizzy, descendant of famed supercat streaky. The super-cat came to the rescue when he and Supergirl were trapped in the Phantom Zone by the Chameleon Men Gang and used his telepathy to instruct a manufacturer of androids to free them (*Action Comics* #287, April 1962). Despite his powers, Whizzy was not a member of that era's Legion of Super-Pets.

WILDE, JACK

There were many odd coincidences on Earth-2, and one of the oddest may have been the fact that the *Daily Planet* employed Jack Wilde, a reporter who looked exactly like Clark Kent, sans glasses, and was therefore also a duplicate for Superman (*Action Comics* #171, August 1952).

WILD MEN, THE

In the hidden Wild Lands ruled by King Caesar, three anthropomorphic bodyguards accompanied the king's son Prince Tuftan: the leader Howler, a wolf archer; Gorr, a bull-man; and Growler, a bear-man with a keen intellect. They shared several adventures with the Clone of Steel when Superboy stumbled upon the Wild Lands, temporarily suffering from amnesia. The trio debated whether or not Superboy fit a legend that foretold a Mighty One given his unusual ability to speak. To the Roamans, only mutated animals were thought capable of speech.

Superboy joined them in a mission to end a threat from the malevolent snake Sacker. They then accompanied him back to Hawaii for some adventures (*Superboy* [third series] #50–54, April–August 1998; others).

WILD WORLD

Farlow Knurd was a scientist who designed a World Duplicator and experimented with it while Superman was away from Earth. When the Man of Steel returned, he discovered that his familiar homeworld had been replaced by a multicolored duplicate—an imperfect one where his friends and foes were mashed-up versions of their normal selves. For example, Mr. Mxyzptlk wore Brainiac's traditional togs, while Bizarro was surprisingly articulate. Krypto looked like Streaky and the Kryptonians were suddenly susceptible to chocolate, brussels sprouts, and old garbage. Oddly, Superman on this wacky world was about to marry Lois Lane, something that Sergeant Frank Rock, still fighting World War II, was trying to stop.

In the end, Superman reversed the scientist's machine and restored Earth to its proper orbit, consigning Wild World to another dimension (*Action Comics* #388, May 1970).

WILLIAMS, MAXWELL

A superpowered costumed champion known as Maximum, Maxwell Williams was a member of the Supermen of America.

WILLIAMS, NICK

A huckster who claimed to be the Man of Steel's personal manager, Williams attempted to cash in on the hero's popularity by booking personal appearances and collecting fees (*Superman* [first series] #3, Winter 1939).

WILLIAMS, TOBIAS

A self-proclaimed mystic, Tobias Williams was able to place himself in a trance and access his "prana"—life force. Shirley Adams discovered Williams and learned how to access his prana for her own personal gain. She absorbed his prana, becoming extremely powerful, then emerged clad in LEAD armor and sacked METROPOLIS. After she was defeated by the Action Ace, Superman erased Williams's memories of his having had powers (*Action Comics* #504, February 1980).

WILLIS, FRED

Working on a formula for super-accelerated growth, a biologist named Willis prematurely died during an unexpected volcanic explosion. Soon after, his toddler son Fred accidentally ingested the untested formula, growing to colossal size. Unable to control his actions, the toddler threatened all of SMALLVILLE until SUPERBOY devised a giant robotic version of himself to distract the titan until scientists could design a cure. After he was restored to normal, the boy was adopted by Mayor George Dean (*Superboy* [first series] #30, January 1954).

WILLIS, LESLIE

The shock jock who became the electrically charged LIVE WIRE.

WIMMER, J.

A onetime publisher of the *DAILY PLANET*, Wimmer ordered editor PERRY WHITE to fire his star reporter CLARK KENT. White was instructed to hire a man considered more charismatic, since "the newspaper business is no place for shrinking violets!" The mild-mannered Kent worked to appear more energetic, changing Wimmer's mind. As a result, Kent remained with the *Planet*, which he considered essential to his role as Superman (*Action Comics* #139, December 1949).

WINGED ONES, THE

Known in the Kryptonian tongue as Tanthuo Flez, the Winged Ones were stark-white flying reptiles considered sacred by the planet's inhabitants (*Superman* [first series] #164, October 1963). Legend had it that Dakar-Ra rode one to warn of a coming alien invasion (*Superman's Pal, Jimmy Olsen* #101, April 1967). Only one specimen of the race was known to exist in KANDOR (*Superman* [first series] #164, October 1963).

WINKI LAMM

The mild-mannered television reporter on the planet UUZ who was secretly the super-champion REGOR.

WINTERBOURNE, COLONEL ADAM

When MICKEY "THE MECHANIC" CANNON was hired to take over PROJECT CADMUS, he brought in an entirely new administrative staff, including Colonel Adam Winterbourne, who served as a government-appointed military liaison. He had previously met SUPERBOY when the Clone of Steel was in the Wild Lands (*Superboy* [third series] #52–53, June-July 1998) and had developed a good rapport. The military man ensured that all field operations were executed by the book and minimized civilian safety issues (*Superboy* [third series] #57, December 1998).

WINTERS, DOLORES

The leading lady of Colossal Films, Dolores Winters was kidnapped and had her brain removed in favor of the ULTRA-HUMANITE's. She then spent the next several decades as his vessel (*Action Comics* #20, January 1940).

While the Ultra-Humanite inhabited Winters's body, he did not realize that Doctor Marten, the scientist who performed the surgery, was a fan of the actress and had preserved her brain. In time, Marten sought out and found a new body for Winters to inhabit again. A suicide victim's body was taken from Our Lady of Snows' General Hospital, and the successful surgery managed to bring the woman back to life. Winters, however, was disgusted she no longer had her former beauty and underwent a series of plastic surgeries to alter her appearance. As she aged, though, she saw further reconstructive surgery would be useless, so she conspired with Marten to abduct her daughter, who was now a beautiful adult. Winters cruelly had her own brain placed in her daughter's body and then underwent a new round of surgeries to "perfect" her appearance. When she decided she needed an entirely new body once more, she selected attractive heroine Icemaiden, from the Global Guardians. She hired the mercenary Warp to have Icemaiden kidnapped and brought to Marten. The doctor then flayed her alive, transplanting the hero's pale white skin to Winters. The heroine did not die, and her body was rescued and placed in a hydration womb at a branch of S.T.A.R. LABS. Now calling herself Endless Winter, Dolores partnered with the criminal Roulette who took the losers of the gambler's bouts and used them to sell for spare parts. Doctor Mid-Nite infiltrated Roulette's headquarters and brought down the operation, but not before Endless Winter had her body frozen and her right arm snapped off (*JSA Classified* #20, February 2007). Marten then grafted a replacement arm onto the villain, and she was then somehow forced by PROMETHEUS to attack the new Batwoman in GOTHAM CITY. After being defeated, Winters seemingly died (*Justice League: Cry for Justice* #5, January 2010).

DOLORES WINTERS-- THE ACTRESS! ONLY...
...ONLY I, THE ULTRA-HUMANITE, HAD MY BRAIN TRANSPLANTED INTO HER BODY!

WINTERS, HARRY

Considered an "average American," his resemblance to the Man of Steel was close enough that when he wore a Superman costume for a party, Winters was confused for the real hero. In the end, the Man of Steel and Harry Winters worked together to apprehend a team of criminals (*Superman* [first series] #127, February 1959).

WMET

WMET was a popular television station in Metropolis, rivaled only by WGBS. At one time, it aired a popular series, *Our American Heroes*, which debuted with an episode focusing on Superman and featured many of his friends and allies appearing on camera (*Action Comics* #309, February 1964).

LANA LANG spent a few years as a television reporter with WMET (*Superman's Girl Friend, Lois Lane* #21, November 1960) before ultimately going to work as one of the station's European consultants (*Superman's Girl Friend, Lois Lane* #109, April 1971).

Brett Bradley (*Superman* [first series] #199, August 1967), Ms. Lanpher (*52* #6, June 14, 2006), Dale Smith (*Superman* [first series] #280, October 1974), Rock Steele (*Superboy and the Ravers* #9, May 1997), Madeline Wade (*The Adventures of Superman* #425, February 1987), and Lance Armstrong (*The Weird* #2, May 1988) all worked for WMET at one time or another.

There was also a WMET radio station.

WOLFINGHAM, J. WILBUR

One of the slickest and most devious hucksters on Earth-2, J. Wilbur Wolfingham always saw an angle and a sucker. Operating in METROPOLIS, as far as the king of old-time confidence men was concerned, even the Man of Tomorrow was just another mark (*Superman* [first series] #35, July-August 1945).

Superman once described the overweight Wolfingham as "one of the most notorious flimflam artists of our century" (*Action Comics* #79, De-

cember 1944) and as "a notorious con-man with a long record of arrests" (*World's Finest Comics* #43, December 1949–January 1950). Superman saw the potential in Wolfingham to be a top-notch salesman had he the desire to go straight (*Superman* [first series] #35, July—August 1945).

Sporting a monocle over his right eye and an ever-present cigar, despite his crooked ways Wolfingham always appeared to do good to everyone but himself (*Superman* [first series] #28, May-June 1944). All too often, the scams intended to enrich Wolfingham actually improved the lives of his intended victims, leaving the con artist empty-handed—but free to plot again.

On Earth-1, Wolfingham was an infrequent pain in the neck for the Man of Steel, first selling amulets, promising buyers they would teleport the owner to a place of safety (*Superman* [first series] #341, November 1979). He later tried to sell Earth to an alien real estate agent; Superman had to dissuade the being when he came to take possession of his "purchase" (*Action Comics* #573, November 1985).

WONDER MAN

The Superman Robots were all built for different functions, but the mightiest of them all was given the name Ajax. While the Man of Steel was dealing with an earthquake, he dispatched Ajax to deal with an impending meteor shower. While in space, the robot was captured by the Superman Revenge Squad. Their leader Attal had an organically based android prepared and then placed the robot's command center within the android. Looking unlike the Man of Steel, the new creation was dubbed Wonder Man and sent to Earth in the hope he would first replace and ultimately kill Superman. Unknown to them, Ajax understood what was being done and intended to thwart their plans.

Wonder Man arrived in Metropolis and began performing feats and displaying an array of powers equal to the Man of Steel's. To his credit, Wonder Man played up his jealousy of the hero and showed an interest in Lois Lane, all part of the plan. This climaxed in a battle for possession of the Fortress of Solitude. Hoping to lure the Squad into the open, Wonder Man employed a piece of green kryptonite, secreted in his artificial body by the Revenge Squad. When the ploy worked, Wonder Man suddenly partnered with the Man of Steel, and they made short work of the alien enemies. Once they were sent back into deep space, a fail-safe device, intended to kill the android when Superman had been destroyed, took the nascent hero's life. Superman honored Ajax's sacrifice by placing his remains in a grave marked with a large tombstone reading WONDER-MAN, FORMERLY CALLED AJAX. HE WAS BORN A ROBOT . . . BUT HE DIED A MAN (*Superman* [first series] #163, August 1963).

WONDER WOMAN

Wonder Woman was Diana, daughter of Queen Hippolyta. The Amazons of Earth-2 lived on fabled Paradise Island, protected by the Greek gods; men were forbidden there. Bereft of a child, Hippolyta begged the gods for a daughter and was instructed to fashion one out of clay. One by one, the gods and goddesses bestowed the clay form with abilities and finally life. Diana grew up training to be a warrior, as was the Amazon way, until army intelligence officer Steve Trevor's plane crashed and he washed ashore. The Amazons learned of the world war that threatened freedom itself, and they decided a champion would go to "Man's World" to preach peace. A Contest was held and Diana, wearing a mask to fool her forbidding mother, handily won. Outfitted in a red, white, and blue costume to appeal to Americans, she took Trevor back home and remained as a symbol of peace. Wonder Woman's exploits throughout World War II earned her a spot as secretary and then full-fledged member of the fabled Justice Society of America. She and Superman also served side by side on the All-Star Squadron (*All Star Comics* #8, December 1941). In time, Wonder Woman and Steve Trevor married and raised a daughter, Lyta.

On Earth-1, Wonder Woman's origins were much the same, but she arrived during the age of heroes and was a charter member of the Justice League of America. At one point, the Amazons chose to leave the plane of reality for another realm, and Diana was cut off from her gods-given powers. She continued to fight for justice using her warrior training

in addition to martial arts. When she regained her powers, she put herself through a series of trials to assure herself that she belonged once more with the JLA.

In the wake of the Crisis on Infinite Earths, Diana was given life during the second age of heroes. At one point, Hippolyta traveled through time and assumed the Wonder Woman identity to adventure alongside the JSA during World War II, where she enjoyed a brief romance with Wildcat.

With her bulletproof bracelets and Lasso of Truth, Wonder Woman managed to fight all manner of criminals in addition to continuing her mission as Themyscira's ambassador to the world. She made her public debut, coming to the aid of Superman and other heroes during a battle with the forces of Apokolips (*Legends* #6, April 1987). Almost immediately, the media made a match between the Amazon Princess and the Man of Steel.

Superman began dreaming about the statuesque woman (*Superman* [second series] #5, May 1987), and after several such nights, Clark Kent began making calls, trying to find a way of contacting this enticing female. Clark's efforts intrigued the Princess, and she finally agreed they should meet (*Wonder Woman* [second series] #16, May 1988) to explore their mutual feelings (*The Adventures of Superman* #440, May 1988).

That meeting turned out to be less than social, however, when the heroes got caught up in a conflict between Darkseid, with his Apokoliptian acolytes, and the gods of Olympus. The sexual tension between the two proved distracting, and by the battle's end they agreed it would be best if they remained "just friends" (*Action Comics* #600, May 1988). In time, they became the best of friends, confiding in each other when they needed a sympathetic ear.

They were once magically transported to Valhalla, fighting alongside the Norse gods to protect their home for the glorious dead. In subjective time, they were gone for a millennium—and even so, Superman resisted the obvious chemistry between the champions. He told Wonder Woman, "Even if she is . . . gone . . . a thousand years and another world past . . . Lois is still the only one" (*Action Comics* #761, January 2000).

Despite hearing of his steadfast loyalty, Lois Lane could not resist feeling jealous of the Princess and insecure as a mere mortal in competition with her. Diana allayed her fears by letting the reporter spend a day with her, the two of them getting to speak as both women and friends (*Wonder Woman* [second series] #170, July 2001).

When the Joker was convinced by a doctor at the Slab, a super-prison, that he was dying, he released a strain of his Joker Venom. Many of the world's criminals were infected, their abilities amped up by the poison. In one case, the evil sorceress Circe used her magic to transform the Man of Steel into a gargantuan monster, out to destroy New York City. Wonder Woman had to stop her friend and find a way to undo the spell (*Wonder Woman* [second series] #175, December 2001).

Wonder Woman, Superman, and Batman were seen as the triumvirate of heroes that all others modeled themselves after, especially considering their close friendship, forged through battle, adversity, and timing (*Batman/Superman/Wonder Woman: Trinity* #1–3, June–November 2003). As a result, they oversaw the combined heroes' efforts during cosmic battles or earth-shattering disasters. When Wonder Woman found herself killing Maxwell Lord to end Lord's mental hold over Superman, rather than let the Man of Steel kill Batman, the world's faith in her was challenged and the triumvirate shattered (*Superman* [second series] #219, September 2005). As the events triggered by Infinite Crisis came to an end, Wonder Woman worked hard to restore her reputation and assure the world she did what her warrior training demanded. The three spent time carefully selecting the next iteration of the JLA after the heroes took a year to put their personal lives back in order.

When Morgaine Le Fey gathered a dark trinity of her own, she cast a spell that created a world in which Superman, Wonder Woman, and Batman did not exist. This alternate reality became the sorceress's plaything, and reality kept shifting until the super-trinity returned, this time in the form of gods without the spark of humanity that made them the heroes they were (*Trinity* #1–52, June 2008–May 2009).

(For a detailed account of Wonder Woman, consult *The Essential Wonder Woman Encyclopedia,* 2010.)

WONG, RICHARD

This Chinese youngster in Metropolis's Chinatown was forbidden by his grandfather to attend Chinese New Year festivities until he repaid a three-dollar debt to a friend. He earned the money he needed

in the nick of time when Clark Kent graciously gave him an odd job to do at the *Daily Planet*. "Golly . . . ," beamed a grateful Richard, "you're just as good as Superman, Mr. Kent!" (*Superman* [first series] #54, September–October 1948).

WORD-BRINGER, THE

Hfuhruhurr the Word-Bringer led a cult known as The Union, but he was actually an alien being who came to Earth and collected human brains to allow him to "become one with a higher power." Superman learned of him after the president asked him to visit the Canadian town of Trudeau to learn where its people had gone. He found their brains encased in the Word-Bringer's ship, buried beneath the city. Their bodies were used to fashion a greenish creature that obeyed his commands. The alien thought he was doing them a favor, freeing "them from their prisons of the flesh." The Man of Steel attempted to beat the alien, but the pair's psionic powers proved a match; rather than prolong a battle, Hfuhruhurr fled Earth. The collective brains of the Trudeau victims begged Superman to end their torment, but the hero refused to take lives so they telepathically forced him into the equipment, bringing them the peace they deserved (*The Adventures of Superman Annual* #1, 1987).

Superman encountered the Word-Bringer a second time while he was traveling through the stars in self-imposed exile. He came across a world devoid of its inhabitants, then soon after found Hfuhruhurr's ship filled with brains taken from races around the galaxy. The two fought another evenly matched battle, so Word-Bringer tipped the scales by activating a device that collected The Union's brain power into a being known as Eon. This powerful being managed to generate powerful energy blasts that hurled the Man of Steel through the ship and into space. In time, though, Superman convinced Eon it was as much a victim as the individual brains it comprised. Seeing the truth in his words, Eon teamed with Superman to crush Hfuhruhurr (*Superman* [second series] #29, February 1987; *The Adventures of Superman* #425, February 1987).

WOR-UL, KARSTA

This Kryptonian once resided in the town of Ansom. A deserter from the scuttled stellar navy, she eventually made her way to Earth and established the alias of Kristin Wells, living a long life of quiet solitude until Superman learned that there was another Kryptonian on Earth besides Kara Zor-El and himself (*Superman* #668–670, December 2007–January 2008).

WRECKER, THE

This criminal, known as the "dictator of destruction," had a reputation for the devastation left in his wake after the "sensational crimes" he committed with his villainous gang. After blowing a hole in Empire Dam and flooding the valley beneath in order to loot the local bank by submarine, the Wrecker and his henchmen were apprehended by the Action Ace (*Superman* [first series] #54, September–October 1948).

WRIGHT, WILLIAM

William Wright was a high school teacher who discovered that he had the telepathic ability to tap into others' brains and gain tremendous power. In time, he determined that teenagers, such as his students, provided the optimum fuel, so he relocated to Smallville—home of the most powerful teen of all, Superboy. The mild Wright also learned the power flowed best when he had the strongest belief in himself, which was not easy to come by.

In Smallville, he intended to obtain power from Superboy and then use it to become a figure to be feared. As he began the school term, he gave his students a test designed to determine which teens offered him the best choice of power and hoped to find Superboy in the mix. Clark Kent, though, noticed the anomalous questions and was on the alert.

Bash Bashford, Lana Lang, and Pete Ross were among those to score well, so Wright tapped their power to gain mental control over Police Chief Douglas Parker and the Smallville Savings and Loan's manager Wallach. He then robbed the bank, only to be opposed by the Teen of Steel. By tapping the teens, Wright made himself more powerful than Superboy and bested him in battle.

The following day, Wright tapped their minds once more and managed to trap Smallville citizens within buildings, clearing the streets in a demonstration of power. Jonathan Kent pointed out to his son that Wright required not only others' minds but also the conviction that he was capable. Rattle that belief, he told his adoptive son, and Wright's powers would weaken.

At the top of Maynard's Hill just outside of town, Superboy used a form of super-hypnosis on himself, and then confronted the teacher. Believing that Wright's mental powers couldn't adversely affect him, he managed to break the man's concentration and defeat him, freeing his fellow students (*The New Adventures of Superboy* #36–37, December 1982–January 1983).

X-156-99F

Lexor, the world that hailed Lex Luthor as a hero, orbited this red star (*Action Comics* #318, November 1964).

XADU, DR.

Xadu was a Kryptonian doctor who, with his wife Erndine Ze-Da, was consigned to the Phantom Zone for conducting suspended animation experiments (*Adventure Comics* #283, April 1961). The pair managed to escape when a volcanic explosion on Earth tore a hole between the dimensions. Adjusting to their newfound superpowers, they decided to torment Superboy by impersonating Jonathan and Martha Kent, but the Teen of Steel saw through their masquerade and exiled them to a planet orbiting a red sun, where they became mere mortals (*Superboy* [first series] #100, October 1962).

BUT AFTER THE BOY OF STEEL STREAKS OFF...
¡CHUCKLE¡ IT'S SAFE TO UNMASK NOW, ERNDINE! LITTLE DOES SUPERBOY SUSPECT THAT WE'RE REALLY TWO KRYPTONIAN CRIMINALS WHO ESCAPED FROM EXILE IN THE PHANTOM ZONE...
...TO WHICH WE WERE SENTENCED FOR OUR CRIMES, BEFORE KRYPTON EXPLODED, DR. XADU!

Years later, the duo found their way back to Earth, this time posing as a dentist and his nurse after tricking Clark Kent into consuming candy that managed to give the Kryptonian a toothache. Once in the dentist's chair, Clark was brainwashed and sent out to destroy the world. Superman managed to overcome the hypnotic command and apprehend the criminals. Because the husband and wife could now unleash the shattering power of a "cosmic power-grip" when they held hands, the Man of Steel ensured that they were imprisoned "in separate cells—in separate galaxies" (*Action Comics* #434–435, April–May 1974).

XAN

Xan didn't intend to become a killer, but he acquiesced to his father's deathbed request that his son seek out and kill Superman and Batman, the heroes who had apprehended him and consigned him to a space prison where he fell ill. Xan arrived on Earth and decided to use Joe Meach as his weapon, reactivating his combined powers of the Legion of Super Heroes and unleashing the Composite Superman once more. Just as the villain was ready to crush the heroes, Xan removed the powers so he could deliver the killing blow with his Magna-Gun. Meach sacrificed himself to spare the World's Finest heroes, allowing them to apprehend Xan, who was then incarcerated on his own world (*World's Finest Comics* #168, August 1967).

Xan escaped conferment and returned seeking personal vengeance, becoming the Composite Superman but using the name Amalgamax. To stop him, Superman requested assistance from

MY NEW INVENTION, THE MAGNA-GUN, COULD PROBABLY DESTROY THEM BOTH IN AN INSTANT...
BUT THAT WOULD BE TOO SWIFT... TOO MERCIFUL!

the Legion (*World's Finest Comics* #283–284, September–October 1982).

XAN CITY

An ancient, abandoned city in northern Urrika on Krypton that was devastated by a two-hundred-year war with the city of Erkol, once that world's oldest (*Superman* [first series] #239, June–July 1971). Both cities were bombed-out ruins some five hundred years prior to the planet's destruction, and the refugees from Erkol wound up founding

the city of Kryptonopolis. Nam-Ek once sought refuge in Xan City when he was a fugitive (*Superman* [first series] #282, December 1974).

XANTHRO, JARL

Superboy once visited the thirty-fifth century and was amused by the Metropolis "Museum of the 20th Century," owned and operated by Jarl Xanthro. When the Teen of Steel saw that the business was doing poorly, he performed for the public to generate interest. The rival owner of the Superman Museum, ironically a descendant of Lex Luthor, decided to use a three-dimensional projector helmet to generate an image that made Superboy believe his descendant was about to be executed for breaking the law. Returning to his own era, the upset teen saw Lex building a two-dimensional projector, concluding that he'd been duped (*Superboy* [first series] #120, April 1965).

XANU

There was an ancient mirror imbued with magical powers that was the sole entry point between Earth and a weird mirror dimension. How and why the mirror was crafted remained a mystery, but Xanu was a dictator who desired power, including dominion over Earth. Batman and Robin wound up in the odd realm, with Batman physically distorted by the transit. Superman came to their aid, defeating Xanu in the process. The Man of Steel found a way to return Batman to his normal form, and the mystic passageway was then sealed (*World's Finest Comics* #121, November 1961).

XARIANS

Jimmy Olsen came to the aid of these pacifist aliens when they arrived on Earth, warning of an out-of-control artificial intelligence they'd created. Jimmy tried to lead them in a vigorous defense, but was inexperienced in these matters and was thankful that Superman and Supergirl returned from a space mission in time to stop the threat (*Superman's Pal, Jimmy Olsen* #60, April 1962).

XASNU

This native of the planet Zelm was in the vanguard of an invasion force targeting Earth. The "plant intelligence" possessed Perry White's body, merging to produce a superpowered person who masqueraded as Masterman until he was stopped by a piece of white kryptonite tossed at the invader by Supergirl (*Action Comics* #278, July 1961).

XAVIER, MR.

Clark Kent was somewhat suspicious of his neighbor Mr. Xavier at 344 Clinton Avenue, going so far as to trail him for a while without finding anything menacing about the man (*Superman* [first series] #258, November 1972).

It was sometime later before he realized that Xavier was actually Xviar, an alien sent from Homeworld to Earth. The planet had been contracted to eradicate Earth since it posed a problem for a proposed intergalactic teleportation route. Xviar actually followed Kal-El's rocket to Earth and shadowed the growing hero as Clark Kent grew to

adulthood, moving next door to Kent in order to execute his plan.

Xviar began manipulating Kent's psyche and his powers by treating his clothes so they would no longer allow solar radiation to pass through them and recharge the Man of Steel. As a result, Clark had to decide whether or not to live full-time as Superman or the mild-mannered reporter. He experimented with both personae, going so far as to finally consummate Clark's long-simmering romance with Lois Lane. He was a more assertive Kent, no longer holding himself back, which led to him exposing an Intergang plot.

As Superman, he defeated the onetime foe Solarman and then faced nine of his old enemies, finally becoming aware that the efforts were also turning him into a super-charged living bomb designed to detonate and eradiate his adopted world. When he thwarted Xviar's plan, the alien tried to flee, disguised as one of the defeated enemies, Amalak (*Superman* [first series] #296–299, February–May 1976).

XENON

Once, millennia ago, Krypton's moon, Xenon, left its orbit and became known as the "twin world of Krypton." Xenon was smaller than Krypton but identical in many other attributes, complete with humanoid life. One day, Zoll Orr, a scientist who closely resembled Jor-El, discovered a series of earthquakes and volcanic eruptions that heralded the instability of Xenon's uranium-based core. Superman came to the planet's aid, refusing to let it be destroyed like his homeworld. He fought natural disasters while finding a solution that stabilized the core and allowed life to flourish again on the world (*Superman* [first series] #119, February 1958).

XERON

The extra-dimensional world that was home to the villainous Vathgar (*World's Finest Comics* #118, June 1961).

XI-PI-HI-FI

Known for its vicious hazing practices, this Stanhope College sorority prompted Supergirl to demand admittance in order to reform its practices. The members suspected the Maid of Steel might also be Linda Lee Danvers, so they tried to learn the truth—a plan she thwarted thanks to the clever use of a Supergirl Robot. In the end, her efforts proved successful and the club changed its practices (*Action Comics* #359, February 1968).

XIUM

The unworldly element Xium was used by Lex Luthor, who secreted a minute amount in a hollow tooth to "furnish super-energy" to a super-ray projector he had made out of radio parts. The device was designed to imbue others with superpowers, but the criminal scientist tried it out first on Clark Kent. Fortunately, the observant reporter noted that a fly had been caught in the beam and had enhanced abilities, so he faked gaining powers to protect his secret identity (*Action Comics* #257, November 1959).

XL-49

In a potential future, XL-49 was a Superman scholar who desired to learn if the Man of Tomorrow ever married Lois Lane, a fact that eluded him. He traveled back in time via a machine and gave himself a set of abilities identical to those of Superman. In the twentieth century, XL-49 concluded that even if the couple did not marry, they should, and he intended to influence events to get the desired outcome. He masqueraded as Futureman, a new super hero, and courted Lois in an attempt to provoke feelings of jealousy from Superman. Lois also wanted Superman for herself, so she accepted Futureman's proposal, hoping for the appropriate outcome. She wound up calling off the engagement when Futureman created the belief that her true love was about to finally propose. Satisfied, XL-49 returned to his era and told a friend that he had put Superman on the path toward matrimony (*Superman* [first series] #121, May 1958).

XLYM

People on Earth were astonished to see Batman display powers that rivaled those of Superman. They were stunned to watch the World's Finest heroes become bitter rivals as they performed miraculous feats. The truth was that the Caped Crusader's newfound powers were the result of a wager among some residents of the far-flung planet Xlym. They had used their superior technology to bring Batman and the Man of Steel to their planet, granted Batman mighty abilities, and then altered the heroes' emotional makeup so friends became enemies. As the two battled on Earth, the Xlymians' superiors discovered what had been done and reversed the modifications made to the super heroes. As a result, Batman's powers faded, and the men's personalities returned to normal (*World's Finest Comics* #95, July–August 1958).

XONAR

Khai-Zor was a Kryptonian scientist whose intent to join Jor-El's exodus to Earth-1 masked his plans to conquer the planet with his new superpowers. Exposed and imprisoned, Khai-Zor perished in Krypton's explosion before he could stand trial (*Action Comics* #223, December 1956). In the universe of pre-Crisis Earth-32 he escaped in a rocket, eventually taking the alias of Xonar. He found space "coffins" that Dr. Krylo had designed to allow others, including Jor-El and Lara, to survive Krypton's destruction. Xonar revived Krylo and used a tape of Jor-El to lure Superboy into space. During the battle, Xonar and Krylo perished (*Superboy* [first series] #158, July 1969).

XON-UR

When the Man of Steel and Lois Lane managed to visit a false version of Krypton created by Brainiac 13, they got caught up in a conflict involving a Raoist cult—led by the cruel Xon-Ur—that had overthrown the Science Council. Superman wound up partnering with a duplicate of his father Jor-El to help keep the peace. When Xon-Ur nearly beat Kal-El to death, he was saved by Kru-El, once a Phantom Zone prisoner (*The Adventures of Superman* #606, and *Superman: The Man of Steel* #128—both September 2002).

Xon-Ur

X-PLAM

Hailing from the mid-twenty-fourth century, the handsome X-Plam came back in time with one goal: marry Lois Lane and bring her joy. To convince the skeptical reporter of his intentions, he showed her a yellowing copy of the Daily Planet that announced their wedding, proving it was destined to occur. Lois, tired of waiting for the Man of Steel to pop the question, decided to wed the kindly man. X-Plam, though, could tell she was not at all happy, married to someone other than her true love. He chose to return her home, ending the marriage, but he wound up sacrificing his life by fatally overexposing himself to the "radioactive fuel that powers [his] time machine" (*Superman* [first series] #136, April 1960).

XVIAR

The alien menace who masqueraded as Clark Kent's neighbor, Mr. Xavier.

XYTH, THE

When a Xyth spacecraft was damaged by a meteor near the Sol system, Superboy flew to their rescue, saving two of the green-skinned travelers. Only after he ensured the vessel's safety did he learn that the Xyth were sorcerers and could have magically repaired the damage themselves. His generous act earned him one wish, which he used to have his foster parents Jonathan and Martha Kent turned invulnerable. Their safety was on his mind after he had recently revealed his true identity to his neighbor Lana Lang. They agreed, and the Teen of Steel returned home and announced his secret to the general populace.

While the Kents were safe from violence, their lives were still complicated by the revelation—Jonathan was suddenly mobbed for autographs, for instance. Clark was expelled from Smallville High School for creating an impediment to learning, and Lana, who'd thought she was special as the only one he'd told, now dumped Clark as a friend. The escalating turmoil his news caused led Superboy to abandon his adopted world and wish to himself that none of this had ever happened. In his mind, he heard the master sorcerer tell him, "It is not too late to change it, if you like."

In a blink, Superboy realized he was still on the Xyth spacecraft and the master sorcerer had shown him what his wish *might* cause if he went through with it. With a shake of his head, he altered the wish to remove the knowledge from Lana's mind (*Superman Family* #195, June 1979).

WE HAVE USED OUR MAGIC TO RESTORE THE MYSTIC DEFLECTOR-AURA THAT ENVELOPED OUR CRAFT-- PROTECTING IT FROM COLLISION!
I HAD BEEN INSTRUCTING MY APPRENTICE HERE IN THE ART OF CREATING SUCH AN AURA...

YANGO THE SUPER-APE

Professor An-Kal, a Kryptonian anthropologist, experimented on the young ape Yango, raising him from birth and subjecting him to conditional-cybernetic brain programming. Upon hearing from Jor-El that Krypton was doomed, he asked the Science Council to allow him to save Yango in one of the space arks being considered. They refused, so the bitter scientist used a small craft to launch Yango toward Earth much as Jor-El had sent Kal-El to the same world, with the ape landing in Kenya.

Some fifteen years later, game preserve officials radioed Superboy for help. Reports indicated that an ivory poacher and his freshly killed elephant had been carried off by a giant ape. All the native guides could tell them was that Yango, a powerful simian, was responsible. While Superboy was hearing the report, two hunters trying to capture a gorilla for a zoo were also carried off. To find the ape responsible, Superboy hid under a gorilla in the hope of being found.

In time, the Teen of Steel was taken and was astonished to discover a cave with an elaborate carving of a gorilla's head, wearing a crown containing a glowing red-sun symbol. Deeper within, he found a giant statue of a garbed ape, again wearing a glowing red-sun crown, standing over a large throne. Before he could identify the familiar markings, he heard a commotion as the trapped humans tried to escape. The apes, though, called out for Yango, and the giant beast arrived, speaking Kryptonese. Superboy and Yango tangled briefly before it became obvious they were super-powered and evenly matched. Yango then threw Superboy out of the cave and into orbit. Using that momentum, the hero sped up and pierced the time barrier, traveling back to Krypton's past to learn Yango's story.

Upon returning to the present, Superboy addressed Yango respectfully and said that he now understood what had occurred and that, as protector of the jungle wildlife, Yango would not harm the humans. He had clearly surpassed his conditioning and was more an ally than an enemy, a sentiment with which Yango agreed (*Superboy* [first series] #172, March 1971).

Y'BAR

The homeworld of the evil sorcerer Zerno (*World's Finest Comics* #127, August 1962).

YEAST-MEN, THE

Superman found himself in the custody of the humanoids he dubbed the yeast-men after ren-

dering himself unconscious by trying to build up immunity to KRYPTONITE via donning a green kryptonite collar. His prone form was discovered by the extraterrestrials and brought home for study; he was presumed to be a typical Terran, not the Last Son of KRYPTON. Once awake, Superman found himself poked and prodded by the aliens, weakened by the collar still around his neck. The "strange hissing speech" of his captors was impossible for him to master, so he could not make himself understood. Instead, he was treated more like a curiosity until he finally managed to burn off the collar and regain his might. He finally managed to communicate that he was not a lower life-form but actually an intelligent being that deserved his freedom, and they agreed (*Superman* [first series] #84, September–October 1953).

YELLOW PERI, THE

Loretta York was an average teen living in Apple Creek, Oregon, interested in many fantastical things, including magic. Still fascinated by the occult as she grew up, she found an abandoned burned-out bookstore and located the one untouched tome in the entire building. In time, she began to master the spells contained in the book and transformed herself into a magician dubbed the Yellow Peri. Attired in a white-and-gold costume, the attractive young adult wanted to cast spells to aid people—but clearly she had not fully mastered them given the frequently marred results.

She left home and worked with a traveling carnival, which brought her to SMALLVILLE, Kansas. Her spells proved obstacles to the Teen of Steel as he tried to perform his duties, so SUPERBOY took Loretta's book and tossed it into outer space. The loss of this volume seemed to rob Loretta not only of her supernatural abilities but also of any memory of operating as the Yellow Peri (*The New Adventures of Superboy* #34–35, October–November 1982).

After being returned to Apple Creek, Loretta remained there, attending college and eventually marrying Alvin Grant. As an adult, she was astounded to find the book once more in her possession after it crashed through the roof of her home. One touch and Loretta was transformed into the Yellow Peri again. Alvin saw this as a chance to improve their fortunes—he wanted her magic to help him con others out of their money. To build up her reputation, he asked her to remove all the dirt from their hometown, but her inexperience showed once more: The dirt did not vanish but merely relocated to another town. Her husband determined that if they moved from locale to locale, he could sell towns on her cleaning prowess, a scam that brought them to Superman's attention. Recognizing his nemesis, he decided to let Loretta keep the book but suggested she find more altruistic uses for her skills (*Action Comics* #559, September 1984).

LORETTA YORK IS GREETED WITH OPEN ARMS BY HER PARENTS, HAPPY THAT SHE HAS RETURNED HOME, BUT THEY ARE UNAWARE OF HER DUAL IDENTITY AND AWESOME POWERS--
--POWERS WHICH BECOME EVIDENT TO ALL 1703 RESIDENTS OF THE TOWN IN THE WEEKS THAT FOLLOW--
"'I WANT TO HELP ALL MY FRIENDS EVERY WAY I CAN', SAID THE MYSTERIOUS YELLOW PERI AFTER HER MOST RECENT FEAT. BUT ONE WONDERS, FROM HER ACTIONS, IF SHE ISN'T TRYING TO ATONE FOR SOME WRONG SHE HAS DONE... SOMEWHERE... SOMETIME!" -- APPLE CREEK JOURNAL EDITORIAL

Time passed, and Loretta was talked into helping Alvin sell a vacation development in Pennsylvania's Pocono Mountains, using her magic to enhance its appeal, once again with poor results. Her magic, now beyond her control, required intervention from the Man of Steel, who this time took the spell book and covered it with LEAD (*Action Comics* #567, May 1985).

The Yellow Peri survived the CRISIS ON INFINITE EARTHS and INFINITE CRISIS, regaining access to her spell book at some point. She was seen at the funeral of Booster Gold, acting as a pallbearer alongside other obscure heroes including Mind-Grabber Kid, the Blimp, the Beefeater, and Odd Man (*52* #18, September 6, 2006).

She next was chronicled coming to Doctor Occult's aid in Hell during Neron's war with LORD SATANUS and his sister BLAZE. Occult referred to her as a spirit guide, implying that her affinity with the spell book was greater than previously chronicled. Her skill with spells was by then markedly improved, although she lost both legs below the knees after an attack by demons (*Reign in Hell* #2–5, October 2008–January 2009).

YUDA

One of the chief goddesses of ancient KRYPTON, Yuda was the patron of love and also of Krypton's two remaining moons, which, when they came together in the night sky, were believed to represent marriage. Though her worship ended with the flood, she was remembered in folklore, and at one time a mechanical statue of her was used at certain festivals in Superman's home city, KRYPTONOPOLIS (*Krypton Chronicles* #3, November 1981).

Z

ZAHARA

Wife to the feline-like Prana, a member of the mysterious organization known only as the Circle, she feared that the telepathic backlash of attempting to co-opt the Man of Steel would kill her husband. When that happened, she and the Circle left Earth (*The Adventures of Superman* #427, April 1987).

ZAK-KUL

Considered a renegade scientist, he once escaped the bottle city of Kandor and used an electronic plastic surgery machine to impersonate Superman, then used the radioactive element Illium-349 to enlarge himself. Lois Lane mistook the Man of Steel for the impostor, and so Superman wound up imprisoned in Kandor. As a result, Zak-Kul literally replaced Superman on Earth, performing good deeds and enjoying the adulation of the people. Unlike the original Man of Tomorrow, Zak-Kul became Lois's ardent suitor. She wound up accepting his proposal and they quickly married, with Lois coming to live with the criminal. Zak-Kul concluded that sooner or later the reporter would discover his ruse since he did not possess Superman's memories or habits; thus he would have to kill her. Before he could carry out the deed, Superman, freshly escaped from Kandor, arrived in the nick of time, saving Lois and apprehending the impostor. He was returned to the bottle city and presumably sentenced to the Phantom Zone (*Action Comics* #245, October 1958).

ZAORA

On Earth-1, she was known as Faora Hu-Ul, a man-hating Kryptonian criminal who was consigned to the Phantom Zone.

After the Crisis on Infinite Earths, reality was altered and she was known simply as Zaora, trapped in a sliver of time preserved by the Time Trapper and living in a Pocket Universe. When that reality's Superboy died, there was no one to stop her, Zod, and Quex-Ul from devastating Earth when they managed to escape their spectral confinement by tricking Lex Luthor (*The Adventures of Superman* #444, September 1988).

With few people left alive, Luthor managed to send Matrix, an artificial life-form, to the real universe to summon Superman for help. The Man of Steel arrived to confront the trio of Kryptonian villains. Their struggle was titanic, but in the end

Luthor provided Superman with gold kryptonite, which he used to rob them of their powers. They then threatened to find a way to his world and to kill him and his people. Feeling he had no choice, the Last Son of Krypton reluctantly exposed them to green kryptonite, executing them for their crimes against humanity (*Superman* [second series] #22, October 1988).

ZAR-AL

The Kryptonian name of the Krypton Kid.

ZARON

Ten evil scientists from the world Zaron chose to conquer Earth. Upon arriving, they hid in Smallville until they could execute their plan. When the law enforcement agency from Zaron sent what appeared to be a monster, Superboy confronted it until he could learn the truth and then aided it in apprehending the criminals (*Adventure Comics* #274, July 1960).

A thousand years in the future, Zaron was the homeworld of Tharok, the cyborg leader of the Fatal Five.

ZATANNA

Zatanna Zatara was the daughter of the famed magician-turned-crime-fighter Giovanni "John" Zatara. Her mother was Sindella, a Queen in a magical dimension of *homo magi*. The Zatara family traced its lineage back to Nostradamus, Leonardo da Vinci, Alessandro di Cagliostro, alchemist Nicholas Flamel, and Arion, Lord High Mage of Atlantis. She had a younger cousin also named Zatara, who eventually became a hero after the events of Infinite Crisis and joined Robin in the Teen Titans (*Hawkman* [first series] #4, October-November 1964).

Zatanna herself followed her father to a successful stage career and became a popular attraction around the world. When her father vanished, she sought out several super heroes—Hawkman, Hawkgirl, Atom, Green Lantern, Elongated Man, and Batman—for help. He was recovered safe and sound, and Zatanna was on her way to becoming a next-generation super hero (*Justice League of America* [first series] #51, February 1967). On Earth-1, she befriended Supergirl, agreeing to perform a show for the residents of the Midvale Orphanage (*Supergirl* [first series] #3, February 1973).

In time, she joined the Justice League of America, and shortly thereafter was finally reunited with her mother. She was also the pivotal player in the darkest period of the JLA's history (*Justice League of America* [first series] #161–165, December 1978–April 1979). When Dr. Light raped Sue Dibny, he was taken by the JLA and the team was split over what should be done. It was decided that Zatanna should use her magic to alter Dr. Light's memories and personality. Just after the decision had been made but before she performed the spell, Batman arrived at their satellite headquarters. He objected to the decision; she then cast a spell erasing ten minutes from the Dark Knight's memory, and the remaining Leaguers kept the secret (*Identity Crisis* #2, September 2004). After that incident, she used her abilities time and again, altering memories to protect the heroes' secret identities and their loved ones from super-villains.

Her powers and her dedication to crime fighting waxed and waned through the years, but she always found her way back to the fight for justice. She worked as one of the principals coming to help Superman rebuild the damaged Metropolis in the wake of Lex Luthor's destructive swath (*The Adventures of Superman* #522, April 1995). Finally, her role in mindwiping the villains became common knowledge among the heroes and villains in the wake of Sue Dibny's death (*Identity Crisis* #1–7, August 2004–February 2005). Worse, Batman came to remember what she had done to him, and their friendship deteriorated. It was that betrayal that prompted him to construct Brother I to keep an eye on meta-humans around the world. The revelation also was used to form the Society, the first truly unified, powerful organization of super-villains.

Catwoman was one of Zatanna's most frequent victims, and when she learned the truth, she was furious. When she needed help, she insisted the Maid of Magic owed her big time. For what Zatanna hoped was the last time, she mindwiped Angle Man and Film Freak, who had come to learn Catwoman's identity.

In the period surrounding the Infinite Crisis, Zatanna sought to make amends, working alongside Superman (*The Adventures of Superman* #644, November 2005) and the Gotham Guardian to repair relationships. She briefly lost her abilities when trying to deal with the guilt, thanks in part to her new apprentice Misty Kilgore. She also learned that she possessed within her her father's magical spell books, enhancing her confidence and skills (*Seven Soldiers: Zatanna* #1–4, June–December 2005).

When Earth-26 suffered a cataclysm, the super-powered anthropomorphic refugees came to New Earth. Zatanna adopted Captain Carrot, unaware of his heroic nature, using him in her performances (*Captain Carrot and the Final Ark* #3, February 2008). They were restored to their proper forms and returned to their world during the Final Crisis (*Final Crisis* #7, March 2009). She also worked with the Phantom Stranger to help Superman battle creatures of darkness, part of Arion's prophecy come true (*Superman* #667, November 2007).

She journeyed to Hell with other mystic heroes during Neron's war with Lord Satanus and Blaze. There she found her father's soul—only to watch in horror as Lobo destroyed it, consign-

ing the spirit to the Abyss, the worst possible fate (*Reign in Hell* #1–8, September 2008–April 2009). Zatanna remained a staunch member of the Justice League, which proved pivotal when they were attacked anew by Amazo. When the league believed their ally, the female Doctor Light, had been kidnapped in Metropolis, Zatanna was among those to investigate. In the end, Kimiyo Hoshi was safely recovered, and a new threat from the alien conqueror Starbreaker was thwarted (*Justice League of America* [second series] #32–34, June–August 2009). Just as others confronted the undead forms of their loved ones during the cosmic event Blackest Night, Zatanna matched black magic with Zatara. Once more she had to witness his destruction, leaving her devastated (*Justice League of America* [second series] #40, December 2009).

ZE-DA, ERNDINE

The spouse and co-conspirator to Krypton's Xadu.

ZEELIUM

While Jor-El was preparing to build rockets to evacuate Krypton, fellow scientist Zol-Zu sent his son Zar-Al to Earth in a "time ship" to bring back the incredibly rare element zeelium, which would prevent the uranium core of Krypton from exploding. The Teen of Steel found his fellow countryman and assisted in the search, without success. In time, Zar-Al told Superboy he'd found a quantity hidden under deep layers of ocean ooze, and returned to Krypton. This was actually a lie told to keep Kal-El from returning home to die alongside his biological parents (*Adventure Comics* #242, November 1957).

ZEENA

Clark Kent was at a circus performance when he saw the star attraction Zeena hypnotized by one of the sideshow mentalists. Unfortunately, the spell was difficult to break, and Zeena endangered the audience until the quick-thinking reporter filled his hat with water and used the reflection to help show Zeena the truth. The reality broke the spell (*Superman* [first series] #256, August 1972).

ZELL-EX

A Kandorian scientist and father of Kull-Ex who falsely believed that Jor-El had stolen designs for a multipurpose transportation device he independently created (*Superman* [first series] #134, January 1960).

ZELM

The home planet of the evil "plant alien" Xasnu (*Action Comics* #278, July 1961).

ZENIUM

Zenium was an ultra-rare element used to power an exchange ray that could switch objects through the X-dimension. The Kandorian scientist Kull-Ex used it to exchange places with Superman. Supergirl had to locate another sample of Zenium to restore the men to their proper worlds (*Superman* [first series] #134, January 1960).

ZERNO

Zerno was a warlock who possessed a powerful crystal that channeled his powers and was able to summon forth weapons and life-forms from other planets. He left his native world of Y'bar, journeying to Earth in order to accumulate a large quantity of bronze, an ore that would render his fellow Y'barians insensate. The sorcerer and his aide Sborg discovered resistance then defeat at the hands of Batman, Robin, and Superman (*World's Finest Comics* #127, August 1962).

ZERO HOUR

Not long after the Crisis on Infinite Earths came a crisis in time that Earth's costumed champions called Zero Hour. At the center of the event was Hal Jordan, Earth's Green Lantern, who was grief-stricken after being unable to prevent the Cyborg Superman and Mongul from destroying his home of Coast City. This allowed a being known as Parallax to corrupt his soul. In time, Jordan became Parallax, a power-mad figure who was determined to alter time and reality in an attempt to restore Coast City and its inhabitants.

Parallax's efforts brought numerous odd iterations of people, places, and objects as reality shifted through the time line, from the days of cavemen to the future of the Legion of Super heroes. Each era experienced a compression time and a whiteout event that seemed to herald a reordered reality. Parallax's attempts at altering reality were hampered by the intervention of Extant, who was once Hawk, an agent of the Lords of Chaos, who had operated as a hero on Earth along with a female partner, Dove. The super heroic community worked together to prevent Extant and Parallax from changing time to suit their needs and were largely successful, although some people saw aspects of their lives changed. Superman and his friends appeared largely unaffected by these events, while Legionnaires suffered substantive alterations (*Zero Hour: Crisis in Time* #4–0, November 1994).

ZEUS

The leader of the Olympian pantheon of gods, Zeus sat on the throne of Mount Olympus, periodically toying with mortals on Earth, either hurling thunderbolts at those who displeased him or sleeping with women he found attractive. On Earth-1, Zeus—along with other gods—lent his powers to create the being Zha-Vam (*Action Comics* #267, August 1960), while on Earth-S he provided the power to create Captain Marvel, represented by the *Z* in the word Shazam (*Whiz Comics* #2, February 1940).

After the Crisis on Infinite Earths, Zeus continued to lend his power to the wizard Shazam and his champions Captain Marvel, Captain Marvel, Junior, and Mary Marvel. He also worked alongside other cosmic beings to form the Quintessence, periodically meddling in human affairs (*JLA* #29, May 1999).

Zeus may have been worshipped by Wonder Woman and the other Amazons of Themyscira, but it was questionable if they respected him.

ZHA-VAM

The gods of Olympus proved themselves awe inspiring, petty, and jealous, so when the Oracle of Delphi told them of the coming of the Earth-1 Superman, they objected to the thought of anyone being so powerful. Fearing humans would forget them, they conspired to create a figure who could humble the Man of Tomorrow. Prometheus was urged to shape a man from clay, and Zeus, Hercules, Achilles, Vulcan, Apollo, and Mercury all gifted the form with a measure of their powers.

The being came to life and was named Zha-Vam, the ultimate champion. The gods gave him a magic belt that would allow their agent to sum-

mon powers from other immortal beings in time of great need. He also fashioned himself a sock from KRYPTONITE to protect the weak heel he had inherited from Achilles. Zha-Vam was then sent into the future to battle the Man of Steel. Given his magic-sourced abilities, he proved more than a match for Superman. To learn about his opponent, Superman traveled back in time and saw how the Olympic gods were once more meddling in mortal affairs.

To even the odds, Superman gained support from PLUTO, Neptune, and ATLAS—all rivals to Zeus. They gifted him with a magic belt that gave the Man of Steel a fighting chance. When he returned to his era, he managed to vanquish Zha-Vam, proving the Oracle correct after all (*Action Comics* #351–353, June–August 1967; *Superman* [first series] #214, February 1969).

ZHOR

Explorers from Zhor, a planet with a chlorine atmosphere, were stranded on an uninhabited Pacific island until they were found by the Man of Steel. Learning of their dilemma, Superman repaired their craft—which had suffered meteor damage—and let them return to the stars and their home (*Superman* [first series] #161, May 1963).

ZIGI AND ZAGI

Hailing from a planet far more scientifically advanced than Earth, located in the Alpha Centauri system, siblings Zigi and Zagi came to Earth in search of fun and excitement—only to get more than they bargained for when they encountered the Man of Steel.

The boys were somewhat alike, although Zigi had honey-blond hair while Zagi's was black. In time, Superman came to describe them as "two of the nicest kids I've ever met!" They left behind their parents and sister Zyra after accidentally activating a control on their father's space-runabout in Centauri City. Arriving in METROPOLIS, the pair found human culture confusing. When they tried to fit in or use their "weird scientific powers," things went awry—such as the time criminals talked them into melting prison bars with Zigi's pocket blaster.

Superman found them and learned of their plight, but the boys were having such a good time on Earth that they were in no rush to return home, oblivious to the chaos they were causing. In time, the Man of Steel had to trick the boys into thinking one of them was homesick so they would leave the planet. An unintended consequence was that SLASH SABRE, a psychopathic killer, had stowed aboard their craft.

Sabre was found and taken captive, only to escape. While seeking refuge, he wound up fiddling with a gravity master, which tore an asteroid from its celestial path and sent it hurtling toward the boys' planet until it was deflected by the Man of Steel, who was seeking the dangerous villain. The thankful Zigi and Zagi returned Sabre to his prison on Earth via a teleport bubble (*Action Comics* #315–316, August–September 1964).

ZIMBA, ROLF

The head of the Gold Badge Organization, a secret terrorist organization determined to smash the government and seize control of the United States. The group blew up the METROPOLIS suburb of Metrodale in retaliation for the recent arrest of some GBO members. The power-mad Zimba then tried to extort a bank president, warning that his institution would be "leveled to ashes in a few minutes." The Man of Steel worked with the U.S. Army on a massive sweep, collecting the GBO's members. Rolf Zimba and a few stragglers tried to flee in an airplane, but Superman interfered. The plane crashed, killing all aboard (*Superman* [first series] #11, July–August 1941).

ZIM-RA

A legendary archer who "died hundreds of years ago" saving KRYPTON from aliens (*Action Comics* #336, April 1966) had his name used by the leader of a separatist movement that preferred to live on Earth rather than the bottle city of KANDOR. NIGHTWING and FLAMEBIRD had to quell the movement before it turned into a civil war, arresting the violent Zim-Ra in the process (*Superman Family* #184, July–August 1977).

ZKOR

While flying through space, SUPERBOY found a zkor that had been trapped. The grateful animal, which was somewhat of a combined dragon and dog, followed his savior back to Earth. Once in SMALLVILLE, the zkor and KRYPTO the Super-Dog grew jealous of each other, and the Teen of Steel had difficulty figuring out how to keep the newcomer from terrorizing the citizens given his natural teleportation and force-field abilities. In time, though, the zkor realized how miserable his presence was making the Canine of Steel, so he faked a weakness to rainwater and used it as an excuse to return to space (*Superboy* [first series] #148, June 1968).

ZOD, GENERAL; AKA DRU-ZOD

Of all the criminals residing in the PHANTOM ZONE, the one that proved the most dangerous was Dru-Zod, who plagued the Earth-1 Superman when he was still a teen and continued to be a threat through adulthood and across the myriad parallel universes.

KAL-EL first learned of Zod, a respected military man who commanded the armed forces on the

planet KRYPTON. When he prevented ZO-MAR from executing a coup, he was promoted to general (*DC Comics Presents* #84, August 1985). While he was military director (*Superman* [first series] #233, January 1971) of the Kryptonian Space Center, Zod met a promising young scientist named JOR-EL who was just joining the staff. Zod welcomed him with, "A young man with your talents can make quite a name for himself in rocketry!" (*World of Krypton* #1, July 1979).

The space program was abolished in reaction to JAX-UR destroying the moon WEGTHOR, leaving General Zod with nothing to command. The megalomaniacal man attempted to create a private army of duplicates in an attempt to usurp control of Krypton. The imperfect robot duplicates led to his downfall and arrest, with Zod sentenced to forty years in the Phantom Zone, which was how he survived the destruction of his homeworld. When the time was up, SUPERBOY used the PHANTOM ZONE PROJECTOR to release him, but Zod returned the favor by attempting to conquer Earth. They battled for a time, although the Teen of Steel was more experienced in the use of his superpowers and managed to return the would-be conqueror to the Phantom Zone (*Adventure Comics* #283, April 1961).

Zod tormented Superboy and later Superman through the years, seeking ways to escape and taunting MON-EL, Superboy's friend who lived in the Zone until a cure for his vulnerability to LEAD was discovered. With his telepathic powers, Zod proved a continued threat to the Last Son of Krypton, usually the de facto leader whenever criminals did manage to escape, however briefly.

After the CRISIS ON INFINITE EARTHS, reality was altered. There now existed a sliver of time preserved by the TIME TRAPPER, a POCKET UNIVERSE that resembled Earth-1 complete with a Phantom Zone. When that reality's Superboy died, there was no one to stop Zod, ZAORA, and QUEX-UL from devastating Earth when they managed to escape their spectral confinement by tricking LEX LUTHOR (*The Adventures of Superman* #444, September 1988).

With few people left alive, Luthor managed to send MATRIX, an artificial life-form, to the real universe to summon Superman for help. The Man of Steel arrived to confront the trio of Kryptonian villains. Their struggle was titanic, but in the end Superman secured gold KRYPTONITE from a dying

Luthor, which he used to rob the criminals of their powers, knowing that this other reality's kryptonite would not affect him. The crazed criminals threatened to find a way to his world and kill him and his people. Feeling he had no choice, the Last Son of Krypton exposed them to green kryptonite, reluctantly executing them for their crimes against humanity (*Superman* [second series] #22, October 1988).

The Man of Steel met a different General Zod in a reality crafted as part of a plot by Brainiac 13. This version still worked on Krypton as the leader of the planet's military and was dictatorial and harsh in his manner. Again, this Zod attempted to take over the planet by allying himself with aliens, but he was beaten by the combined efforts of Kal-El and his father Jor-El (*Superman* [second series] #166, March 2001).

On Earth, Superman encountered a Russian general also named Zod. His destiny was intertwined with the Man of Steel's given that his cosmonaut parents were exposed to kryptonite radiation as Kal-El's rocket passed close to their orbiting capsule. He became a scientific curiosity and was studied by the KGB, which learned that Sol's radiation actually weakened the man whereas a red giant's rays would empower him. His mind was slowly twisted; he claimed that a voice from beyond was urging him to seek out and destroy Superman, which may have been the Phantom Zone Zod from one reality or another. Regardless, the Russian took the name General Zod for himself (*Action Comics* #803, July 2003).

The general wound up creating a suit of crimson armor to manipulate the extant sunlight and took charge of Pokolistan, a former USSR state.

YOU WOULD
KNEEL
BEFORE
ZOD!

Slowly, Zod worked to undermine the Man of Steel, infecting him with a kryptonite-based cancer and then finding a way to animate the tumor, which became the creature Kancer. Aided by Ignition and Faora, this General Zod and Superman finally battled in person as the Kryptonian tried to prevent Zod from altering Sol into a red giant, effectively replacing him as the world's mightiest mortal. After Superman's jaw was broken, the computerized Kelex declared the general a "Doomsday level threat" and had the hero retreat. Superman was actually saved by Lex Luthor, who used a device to revivify his powers and allow him to defeat General Zod. The Russian resisted and died for his troubles (*Action Comics* #779, August 2001).

There was yet another Zod, one who resided in an alternate version of the Phantom Zone, Metropia, a world that Superman had created in the belief he needed someplace to rescue humanity in case of disaster. Zod had come to hate the surviving Kal-El. This version of the chronicles indicated that Jor-El created the Phantom Zone as a way to contain the threat posed by his power-hungry enemy—a man who saw himself as "Krypton's greatest visionary and its greatest threat," and was rather honored that the Phantom Zone had been created specifically for him (*Superman* [second series] #204–#215, June 2004–May 2005).

After Infinite Crisis reordered reality, General Zod, descendant of the legendary Kryptonian conqueror Admiral Dru-Zod, ruled Krypton's security forces. When the scientists Non and Jor-El were ordered arrested for heresy, he dispatched Ursa to deliver them to the Kryptonian Science Council. After receiving a warning, the scientists were set free, but Non refused the Council's directive and spoke of their planet's impending doom to the public (*Action Comics* #845, November 2006).

The coldly beautiful Ursa and Zod came to be-

lieve Non and defected to join his side. Non wound up recaptured and lobotomized, an act that turned Zod into a militant. He and Ursa launched an insurrection, which was violently and swiftly quashed, with the Council calling for their deaths. Jor-El pleaded their case and got the Council to agree that exile to the Phantom Zone was punishment enough (*Action Comics Annual* #10, 2007).

While trapped in the Zone, Zod and Ursa became lovers—with the result being their son Lor-Zod. When the boy was about ten, he found his way to freedom and came to reside with Clark Kent and Lois Lane in the human guise of Christopher Kent. Soon after, Zod, Ursa, and Non escaped the Phantom Zone and wanted Lor-Zod returned. Zod was actually surprised to be recognized by Kal-El, who explained that he'd learned of Zod from the Sunstone recordings left him by Jor-El. Superman wound up exiled to the Phantom Zone until Mon-El helped him escape. The Man of Steel then formed an unlikely pact with Luthor, Metallo, Parasite, and Bizarro to corral the Phantom Zone criminals and return them to exile. While these efforts were successful, nearly half a dozen Kryptonians died in the battle.

Later, when Kandor regained its proper size, albeit on Earth, Alura saw to it that the Phantom Zone inhabitants were pardoned and freed. Zod was restored to his rightful place as head of the Military Guild while Ursa, armed with her pole-arm and a laser baton, once more served at his side. Those who recalled his great achievements hailed

the move cementing his place in government and the hearts of the Kandorians now living on New Krypton (*Action Comics* #875, May 2009).

When Superman decided to investigate the real motivations of the Kandorians living on the world in orbit opposite Earth, Alura had him assigned to the Military Guild, where he could train Zod's forces in the proper use of their newfound powers and abilities. Zod welcomed him and named him Commander El (*Superman: World of New Krypton* #1, May 2009).

Zod spared no time in getting his forces in order and introducing the Archer-Class assault weapons that his army would be using. Their red-sun energy would prove fatal to fellow Kryptonians; it was intended to be used only to maintain the peace. He named Kal-El leader of his Red Shard assault forces, counting on the hero's greater tactical experience to help his countrymen adapt to their newfound superpowers. Despite this, Zod and Kal-El continued to clash over ideologies and methods of dealing with problems, as witnessed by the violent Labor Guild protest (*Superman: World of New Krypton* #2–3, June–July 2009).

As leader of the Military Guild, Zod was the first to deal with external threats to the young planet, such as an investigation from the Green Lantern Corps (*Superman: World of New Krypton* #3, July 2009), who expressed their concern over the number of munitions already built and stockpiled. When a fugitive, Val-Ty, was arrested, it was learned that he was also wanted by the Corps, but Zod wouldn't turn him over, ordering the man's death instead. Commander El aided the Corps, resulting in his arrest and trial for treason, with Zod leading the prosecution (*Superman: World of New Krypton* #5, September 2009). When he tried to engineer Kal-El's escape, turning him from the accused into an escapee, Zod was surprised to see his opponent remain in place. As a result, Zod arranged for the Religious Guild to pardon the man. Soon after, during the Nova celebration, a lone gunman fired on the general (*Superman: World of New Krypton* #5, September 2009). While Zod hovered between life and death, Kal-El donned his Superman uniform and pursued the shooter, Ral-Dar, to Earth, where he was apprehended. It was learned Ral-Dar was in league with General Samuel Lane, who continued to mistrust the solar system's new neighbors (*Superman: World of New Krypton* #6, October 2009).

As Zod recovered, he named Kal-El as acting commander of the Guild, continuing the unexpected evolution of the men's relationship (*Superman: World of New Krypton* #7, November 2009). Soon after, New Krypton and its Military Guild had to deal with the arrival of a Thanagarian army (*Superman: World of New Krypton* #8, December 2009), and then a visit from Jemm and his fellow Saturnians (*Superman: World of New Krypton* #9, January 2010).

After several Kryptonian Council members were murdered, Superman was joined by Adam Strange, who aided the Man of Steel in investigating the crimes. The pair stumbled upon Zod's secret base on New Krypton, where hundreds of silver-skinned aliens were being tested and stripped of their metallic skins. The fully recovered Zod explained to a horrified Kal-El that he was preparing to defend New Krypton from a war with Earth, something he felt certain was coming. Zod and Kal-El then discovered that General Samuel Lane had promised Council member Wri-Qin that he and his supporters would rule over the Earth-conquered New Krypton if they helped disrupt the nascent New Kryptonian society. Lane's scheme was exposed,

and before Wri-Qin could kill Kal-El, the Red Shard elite security team arrived and arrested the traitor. "Speaking as your adversary, even at times as your enemy, you have changed New Krypton for the better," General Zod told a conflicted Kal-El (*Superman: World of New Krypton* #11–12, March–April 2010).

When Brainiac arrived to reclaim New Krypton, Zod and Kal-El put aside lingering differences to come to their peoples' aid. After his Global Defense Cannons proved ineffectual against Brainiac's ship, Zod was seemingly left without options. Ursa urged him to protect the surviving Council members, but Zod felt it was pointless. When members of the Legion of Super-Heroes arrived on New Krypton pledging assistance, Zod disbelieved them and had them arrested. Alura interceded on the Legionnaires' behalf, informing Zod that roughly one-tenth of the Kandorians had been killed. Brainiac managed to rebottle Kandor as Superboy confronted Zod. The general defeated Superboy and reverse-engineered Brainiac's technology with his Red Shard soldiers. Working in concert, they were able to stop Brainiac and save the remaining Kandorians (*Superman: Last Stand of New Krypton* #1–3, May–June 2010; *Superman* #698, May 2010; *Adventure Comics* #513, June 2010).

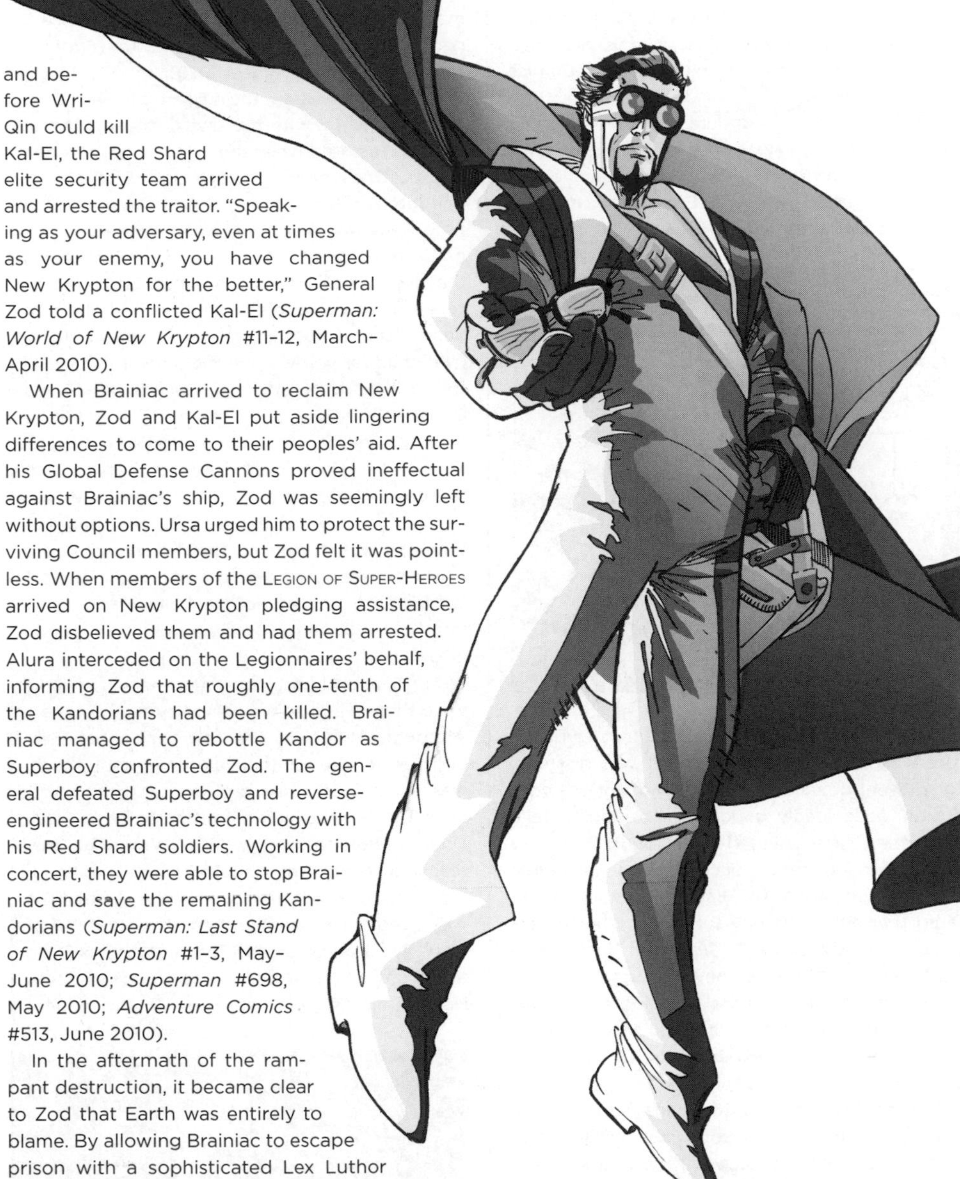

In the aftermath of the rampant destruction, it became clear to Zod that Earth was entirely to blame. By allowing Brainiac to escape prison with a sophisticated Lex Luthor android, General Lane earned Zod's undying enmity. From a secret military installation one mile beneath New Krypton's surface, Zod ordered his guild to launch an all-out assault on Earth, igniting the very war he anticipated. Superman arrived at the installation too late to prevent the invasion of Earth, and the two Kryptonians battled. Zod explained to Kal-El that he continued to harbor deep hatred for the son of Jor-El but had let Superman train the Red Shard anyway, turning them into the very elite force he needed to invade Earth. "I haven't changed, particularly in one regard," Zod told his sworn enemy, "I'm still the man who swore revenge on Jor-El's house and yours. The House of El. So don't for a moment think this isn't personal as well."

What Zod never anticipated was that General Lane had allowed the criminal Reactron to be captured and brought to New Krypton so that he could destroy the planet. When thousands of Kryptonians died in the devastating explosion, an enraged Zod traveled to Earth with Ursa and Non to wreak havoc on Superman's adopted world. The inevitable final confrontation between Superman and Zod occurred in the skies over Metropolis, and the two fought to a near stand- still until Superboy arrived with the Phantom Zone Projector. Before Zod could be returned to the Zone he attempted to kill Superboy, but Krypto saved his master. Zod's actions damaged the projector, which opened a rift between Earth and the endless void. At that moment, Zod's son Lor-Zod arrived and sacrificed himself to maintain the Zone's stability forevermore. Lor-Zod took his father back into the limbo-like realm with him, ending the threat to humanity, hopefully once and for all (*Superman: War of the Supermen* #0–4, June–July 2010).

Across the multiverse, there was a General Zod on Earth-15 who became Superman instead of Kal-El, only to die at the hands of Superboy-Prime (*Countdown to Final Crisis* #30, October 3, 2007, and #24, November 14, 2007).

ZO-GAR

Zo-Gar and his companion Jan-Dex were Durlans who traveled from the thirtieth century to expose Superman to a piece of red kryptonite. This altered the hero's abilities for forty-eight hours to include conjuring, fire breathing, and telepathy. When the shape-shifting aliens impersonated President John F. Kennedy and Soviet premier Nikita Khrushchev, Superman read their thoughts and prevented a diplomatic disaster before returning them to their proper era (*Action Comics* #283, December 1961).

ZOHTT

Superman was once taken to a potential future against his will and infected with this microorganism, which survived in the bloodstream of living beings. He attempted blood transfusions to rid himself of the alien invader, to no avail. Instead, he had to trick Zohtt into transferring itself to another body, that of a Superman replica, where it was finally trapped, allowing the Man of Steel to return to his own era (*Action Comics* #403, August 1971).

ZOLAR

Somewhere in the Middle East lived Zolar, the leader of a sinister band who sought quantities of radium to fuel his weapons and experiments. In addition to his globe-gun, which emitted forceful blinding rays, he created a meteorological device and tested it by causing a snowfall during a Metropolis summer.

From their hidden base in the Sahara Desert, the horde attacked the lost city of Ulonda in heavily armed sky-ships, in the hope of stealing their vast supply of the element. This path of destruction cost the peaceful city many lives, but the devastation was halted by the arrival of the Man of Steel. While crushing the armada of sky-ships, Superman was rendered unconscious by a blast from the power weapon, but he recovered to confront Zolar one final time. An acolyte fired his globe-gun, but the fiery energy sphere rebounded off the hero's chest and killed Zolar and his woman (*Action Comics* #30, November 1940).

ZOLIUM

The "density of the atmosphere" in addition to the "peculiar refraction of rays and light intensity" on the world of Zolium gifted Jimmy Olsen with superpowers after he arrived in an experimental rocket tossed by the Man of Steel. Jimmy's accidental journey provided many an exploit before

the powers faded and he was returned to Earth (*Superman's Pal, Jimmy Olsen* #39, September 1959).

ZOL-LAR

Jimmy Olsen's Kandorian double and a member of the Lookalike Squad (*Superman's Pal, Jimmy Olsen* #70, July 1963).

ZOLL ORR

Zoll Orr, a scientist who closely resembled Jor-El, discovered a series of earthquakes and volcanic eruptions that heralded the instability of Xenon's uranium-based core. Superman came to the planet's aid, refusing to let it be destroyed like his homeworld. He fought natural disasters while finding a solution that stabilized the core and allowed life to flourish on the world. During this time, Zoll's son Kell Orr, who looked like Superman, filled in for the Man of Steel on Earth (*Superman* [first series] #119, February 1958).

ZOL-ZU

This scientist sent his son Zar-Al to Earth to seek the rare element zeelium in an attempt to prevent Krypton from exploding (*Adventure Comics* #242, November 1957).

ZO-MAR

Zo-Mar created a will-controlling symbol that he used in an attempt to seize Fort Rozz in his first step toward conquering Krypton. This symbol, according to Jor-El, somehow gave the Kryptonian "mastery over any and all people he showed it to." Condemned to a lifetime in satellite orbit, Zo-Mar's craft eventually drifted to Earth, where he escaped and attempted to use the symbol to conquer Earth. It fell to Superman and the Challengers of the Unknown to protect all life on Earth from the powerful weapon. Zo-Mar was eventually captured and sent to the Phantom Zone by the Man of Steel (*DC Comics Presents* #84, August 1985).

ZOR

Superman battled an alien named Olav on the planet Zor, a world almost devoid of metal (*Action Comics* #168, May 1952). A different world named Zor was the home to the heroine Tharka (*Superman* [first series] #81, March–April 1953).

ZORA VI-LAR

A Kandorian devotee of Lesla-Lar who was sentenced to the Phantom Zone after menacing Supergirl as Black Flame.

ZOR-EL

Born into the famed House of El, Zor-El was the younger brother to twins Jor-El and Nim-El. All three brothers went into the sciences, with Zor-El concentrating on climatography. In time, he married Alura In-Ze. They had one child, Kara Zor-El, and settled in Krypton's Argo City (*Action Comics* #252, May 1959).

On Earth-2, Zor-L and Alura were Kara's parents and lived in Kandor. He was an expert psychologist and designed a virtual reality to educate and entertain Kara when he sent her to Earth before Krypton exploded (*Showcase* #97, February 1978).

When his brother began warning that Krypton's core was unstable and the planet was doomed, Zor-El went on record agreeing with Jor-El's conclusion, a decidedly unpopular position to take (*Superman* [first series] #146, July 1961). Their city was thrown intact into space when the inevitable explosion occurred. The Earth-1 chronicles indicated that either the city survived by being "enclosed in a bubble of air" (*Superman* [first series] #150, January 1962), or they managed to cover the entire chunk of planet by using an airtight plastic "weather dome" on hand to accommodate Zor-El's "atmospheric experiments" (*Action Comics* #316, September 1964).

The residents of Argo City managed to survive with sufficient air and a food machine for their basic needs until the piece of Krypton they were atop began to glow green with kryptonite radiation, threatening everyone. Zor-El had the ground covered with sheets of lead, shielding the people. The temporary solution worked until a meteor shower shattered the weather dome and punctured the lead sheets, exposing everyone to the deadly radiation.

Zor-El decided to save his teenage daughter by placing her in a small rocket. Like his brother, he then sent her to Earth, where she arrived to greet her cousin. While Kara lamented her parents' sacrifice, she was unaware that before they were poisoned to death, Zor-El and Alura managed to escape to a limbo-like realm known as the Survival Zone, which was similar to the Phantom Zone (*Action Comics* #309, February 1964). Some years later, Supergirl managed to rescue her parents. They were reduced in size to live with their brethren in the bottle city of Kandor, which resided within the Fortress of Solitude (*Action Comics* #310, March 1964).

When Superman finally found a way to restore Kandor's proper size, Kara's parents chose to remain on their new homeworld of Rokyn while Supergirl decided to remain on Earth (*Superman* [first series] #338, August 1979).

In the reality after the Crisis on Infinite Earths, Zor-El perished with the rest of the Kryptonians but was restored when the Infinite Crisis reordered events. Once more, Zor-El decided to send his daughter to Earth, encouraged by Alura, but this time Kara was older and was intended to arrive on Earth before Kal-El to help the infant grow on the alien planet. Her ship was inscribed, "This vessel carries my daughter, Kara Zor-El from the now dead planet Krypton. Treat her as you would your own child for you will see the treasure she will be for your world" (*Superman/Batman* #8–13, May–October 2004).

Unfortunately, prolonged exposure to green kryptonite—which had trapped Kara's vessel, thereby letting her cousin arrive on Earth years before her—altered her perceptions, and for a time she was convinced that her father had actually programmed her to come to Earth to kill Kal-El. That proved both a hallucination and a falsehood (*Supergirl* [fifth series] #35, January 2009).

Zor-El and Alura, along with others in Argo City, were thrown into space when Krypton detonated. Although Alura was the family scientist, Zor-El engineered the protective dome until the city was taken by Brainiac and grafted onto Kandor, allowing his specimen collection to grow (*Action Comics* #869, November 2008). When Superman rescued Kandor from the Coluan, he managed to restore it to its normal size in the Arctic. There were suddenly one hundred thousand Kryptonians living on Earth and Zor-El, given his Ranger training, was thrust into a position of leadership. He was also happily reunited with his daughter

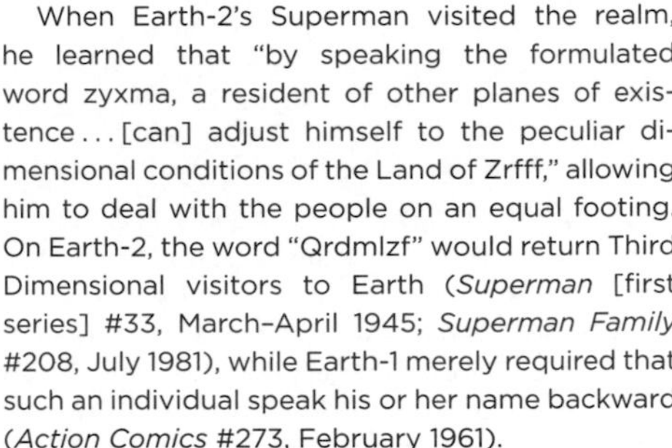

Zor-El

and his nephew (*Superman: New Krypton Special* #1, December 2008).

Sadly, some of the humans were not so welcoming to the intergalactic immigrants, and General Samuel Lane dispatched the criminal Reactron to destabilize things by having Zor-El assassinated. Alura assumed command of her people and saw to it that they used Brainiac's technology to form a planet of their own—and New Krypton was born. Zor-El was lovingly memorialized on the new world (*Action Comics* #872, February 2009).

ZORON

The homeworld of the man who would be rocketed to Oceania as an infant and grow up to be that world's champion Hyper-Man. Remnants of the planet turned radioactive and emitted a deadly blue radiation known as zoronite (*Action Comics* #265, June 1960).

There was another world named Zoron, which suffered under the rule of Chorn and his fellow Baxians until the timely arrival of Batman, Robin, and Superman (*World's Finest Comics* #114, December 1960).

ZORONITE

Much as remnants of Krypton turned radioactive and poisonous to Kryptonians, the same held true for the pieces of the planet Zoron that survived its destruction. The only difference was that zoronite was blue and had no other variations to confound the hero Hyper-Man (*Action Comics* #265, June 1960).

ZRFFF; AKA THE FIFTH DIMENSION

For each parallel universe, there came countless unique dimensions. Particular to Superman was the Fifth Dimension, which its residents called Zrfff. There the inhabitants possessed magical abilities.

On Earth-2, Zrfff was home to the derby-wearing Mr. Mxyztplk (*Superman* [first series] #33, March–April 1945), while the Earth-1 Zrfff provided Superman with Mr. Mxyzptlk (*Superboy* [first series] #78, January 1960). In both cases, the imps' magical abilities were subject to rules. For one, anyone leaving the Fifth Dimension would automatically be returned and trapped there for ninety days if that resident said his or her name backward.

The Land of Zrfff was ruled by King Brpxz (*Superman* [first series] #33, March–April 1945), or Bprxz (*Superman* [first series] #40, May–June 1946). Mister Mxyztplk was apparently the court jester to both leaders whenever he was not on Earth bedeviling the Man of Steel.

The society of Zrfff seemed to be built around pranks, plots, stunts, and other amusements, with practical jokes considered the highest form of art. The Academy of Practical Joking had an annual award for the year's best practical joke (*Superman* [first series] #154, July 1962). The chronicles appeared contradictory, though, with one indicating that Mxyzptlk's gags meant he "had to spend some time in jail in [his] own dimension—for playing a few practical jokes!" (*Superman* [first series] #131, May 1964).

When Earth-2's Superman visited the realm, he learned that "by speaking the formulated word zyxma, a resident of other planes of existence . . . [can] adjust himself to the peculiar dimensional conditions of the Land of Zrfff," allowing him to deal with the people on an equal footing. On Earth-2, the word "Qrdmlzf" would return Third Dimensional visitors to Earth (*Superman* [first series] #33, March–April 1945; *Superman Family* #208, July 1981), while Earth-1 merely required that such an individual speak his or her name backward (*Action Comics* #273, February 1961).

After the Crisis on Infinite Earths reordered all reality, it seemed to affect the dimensions as well. Other magical beings were now said to reside there, including Mxyzptlk's girlfriend Miss Gzptlsnz (*Superman's Pal, Jimmy Olsen* #52, April 1961), but also Quisp (Qwsp), Lkz, and Yz the Thunderbolt. As a result, multiple magical beings from Zrfff operated on Earth mistaken for imps and genies, with Yz remaining on the planet for decades, working as an aide to various people who belonged to the legendary Justice Society of America. Rules governing the use of their magic were well defined, including that the magical feat had to be considered a trick or prank in some way.

The djinn Lkz was possessed by the now powerless Triumph; he had given the Zrfffian free rein in exchange for regaining his powers. This brought a wave of chaos to the world, requiring the combined efforts of the JSA and Justice League of America to be quelled. Things grew worse when it appeared Lkz and Yz were being manipulated by Qwsp, who used to spend time with Aquaman and sought to ruin Earth to avenge being ignored. Captain Marvel and Green Lantern Kyle Rayner journeyed to the Fifth Dimension to elicit Gzptlsnz's help. She agreed, concluding that her beloved might be sad if Earth was destroyed. The two djinn merged into a new being while Gzptlsnz had Qwsp arrested, thereby restoring peace to the two realms (*JLA* #28–31, April–July 1999).

On Earth-3, the Fifth Dimensional troublemaker who plagued Ultraman was named Mixyezpitelik (*The Brave and the Bold* [third series] #11–12, May–June 2008).

ZUMOOR

The home planet to Mighty Boy and Rovo the Mighty Dog.

ZYNTHIA

When Thom Kallor (Star Boy) first met Superboy in Smallville, he had been dating the lovely blonde haired teenager named Zynthia. She joined the Teen of Steel and the Stellar Sentinel in teaching Lana Lang a lesson about jealousy (*Adventure Comics* #282, March 1961).

Zrfff

ARTIST CREDITS

Jack Abel, Dusty Abell, Art Adams, Neil Adams, Dan Adkins, Christian Alamy, Gerry Alanguilan, Oclair Albert, Marlo Alquiza, Murphy Anderson, Ross Andru, Derec Aucoin, Terry Austin, Ramon F. Bachs, Brandon Badeaux, Michael Bair, Darryl Banks, Matt Banning, Eddy Barrows, Chris Batista, Howard Bender, Ed Benes, Mariah Benes, Ramon Bernado, Bit, Tex Blaisdell, Jon Bogdanove, Brian Bolland, Wayne Boring, Doug Braithwaite, Brett Breeding, Bob Brown, Rick Bryant, Rich Buckler, Rich Burchett, John Byrne, Cafu, Talent Caldwell, Matt Camp, Marc Campos, Nick Cardy, Keith Champagne, Bernard Chang, Howard Chaykin, Frank Chiaramonte, Vicente Cifuentes, Sam Citron, Matthew Clark, Dave Cockrum, Vince Colletta, Paris Cullins, Fernando Dagnino, Tony S. Daniel, Alan Davis, Dan Davis, Shane Davis, Mike DeCarlo, Jose Delbo, John Dell, Jesse Delperding, Wellington Dias, Dick Dillin, Ed Dobrotka, Rachel Dodson, Terry Dodson, Kieron Dwyer, Scot Eaton, Mark Farmer, Raul Fernandez, Pascual Ferry, John Fischetti, John Forte, Gary Frank, Ron Frenz, Kerry Gammill, German Garcia, Jose Luis Garcia-Lopez, Ron Garney, Carlos Garzon, Frank Giacoia, Joe Giella, Keith Giffen, Dick Giordano, Alan Goldman, Adrian Gonzales, Jason Gorder, Al Gordon, Jamie Grant, Mick Gray, Dan Green, Sid Greene, Tom Grummett, Renato Guedes, Jackson Guice, Yves Guichet, Matt Haley, Ed Hannigan, Doug Hazelwood, Clayton Henry, Adam Hughes, Dave Hunt, Jamal Igle, Stuart Immonen, India Inc., Carmine Infantino, Jack Jadson, Dennis Janke, Klaus Janson, Phil Jimenez, Dave Johnson, J. G. Jones, Dan Jurgens, Gil Kane, Kano, Stan Kaye, Karl Kerschl, Karl Kesel, Jack Kirby, Leonard Kirk, Barry Kitson, George Klein, Scott Koblish, Adam Kubert, Andy Kubert, Ray Lago, Ken Landgraf, Andy Lanning, Erik Larsen, Jim Lee, Rick Leonardi, Steve Lightle, Livesay, Aluaro Lopez, Julian Lopez, Aaron Lopresti, Mike Machlan, Jose Wilson Magalhaes, Larry Mahlstedt, Doug Mahnke, Francis Manapul, Tom Mandrake, Jose F. Marzan, J. P. Mayer, Ray McCarthy, John McCrea, Scott McDaniel, Luke McDonnell, Todd McFarlane, Ed McGuinness, Mike McKone, Bob McLeod, Jesus Merino, Joshua Middleton, Mike Mignola, Al Milgrom, Steve Mitchell, Steve Montano, Jim Mooney, Mark Morales, Rags Morales, Nelson, Diogenes Neves, Tom Nguyen, Phil Noto, Irv Novick, Leo Nowak, Kevin Nowlan, Bob Oksner, Ariel Olivetti, Jerry Ordway, Andy Owens, Carlos Pacheco, Jimmy Palmiotti, George Papp, Charles Paris, Paul Pelletier, Mark Pennington, George Perez, Pere Perez, Al Plastino, Keith Pollard, Carl Potts, Eric Powell, Frank Quitely, Rodney Ramos, Ron Randall, Tom Raney, Bill Reinhold, Albert Reis, Ivan Reis, Robin Riggs, Eduardo Risso, Denis Rodier, Alex Ross, Werner Roth, Duncan Rouleau, George Roussos, Stephane Roux, Mike Royer, Joe Rubinstein, Steve Rude, Jose Ruy, Paul Ryan, Bernard Sachs, Tim Sale, Alex Saviuk, Kurt Schaffenberger, Ethan van Sciver, Bart Sears, Mike Sekowsky, James Sherman, Curt Shiln, Jim Shooter, Joe Shuster, John Sibal, John Sikela, Tom Simmons, Walter Simonson, Bob Smith, Cam Smith, Ryan Sook, Dick Sprang, Jim Starlin, Joe Staton, Curt Swan, Romeo Tanghal, Greg Theakston, Art Thibert, Michael Turner, Peter Vale, Rick Veitch, Al Vey, Ricardo Villagran, Dexter Vines, Mike Wieringo, Scott Williams, Al Williamson, Stan Woch, Walden Wong, Wally Wood, Pete Woods, Eric Wright, Ira Yarbrough, Leinil Francis Yu

ABOUT THE AUTHORS

Robert Greenberger was given his first comic, *Superman,* at age six. Since then, he has been a passionate fan of the medium. He wrote and edited for his various school newspapers, serving as editor in chief of *Pipe Dream* at Binghamton University.

Bob's professional career began at Starlog Press, where he created *Comics Scene,* the first nationally distributed magazine to cover comic books, comic strips, and animation. He then joined DC Comics as assistant editor, working on the seminal *Crisis on Infinite Earths* and *Who's Who.* He rose to full editor and eventually switched to the administrative side of the company, rising to the role of manager, editorial operations.

In 2000, Bob left DC for a job as producer at Gist Communications and then returned to comics in 2001, as Marvel Comics' director, publishing operations. In 2002, he went back to DC Comics as a senior editor in its collected editions department. Bob joined *Weekly World News* as managing editor until its demise in 2007. Since then he has been a full-time freelance writer and editor including news editor at ComicMix.com.

As a freelancer, Bob has written numerous *Star Trek* novels and short fiction in addition to short works of science fiction and fantasy. His adult nonfiction includes Del Rey's 2008 release *The Essential Batman Encyclopedia* and Running Press's 2009 *The Batman Vault.* Also for Del Rey, he penned *Iron Man: Femmes Fatales.* He won the Scribe Award in 2009 for his novelization of *Hellboy II: the Golden Army.*

He has served his hometown of Fairfield, Connecticut, as an elected member of its representative town meeting and most recently represented the town on the Greater Bridgeport Regional Planning Agency. Bob makes his home with is wife, Deb, and their dogs, Dixie and Ginger. Their daughter, Kate lives in Maryland.

For more information, see his website, www.bobgreenberger.com.

Martin Pasko is a veteran writer and story editor in a diverse array of media, including comics, nonfiction, children's fiction, and television, both animated and live-action, working on such shows as *Roseanne* and cult favorites *The Twilight Zone* and *Max Headroom.*

During his long career in comics, he moved to Los Angeles to begin working simultaneously in television, during which time he helped translate many comics properties to TV animation. These include *The Tick, Cadillacs and Dinosaurs,* and *Batman: The Animated Series,* for which he won a 1993 Daytime Emmy Award. He is also a co-writer of the animated feature *Batman: Mask of the Phantasm.*

Pasko has worked for many comics publishers, but is best known for his work with DC, most recently as liaise with Warner Bros., assisting the studio's development of DC content for the screen. Since leaving his staff position at DC, he has continued his association with the publisher as he concentrates on nonfiction about popular culture. *The Essential Superman Encyclopedia,* as well as the recent *DC Vault,* are products of that association.

Pasko has been on close terms with Superman for many years, having written the character in many media, including TV animation, webisodes, and a syndicated newspaper strip, as well as in comics. He also co-created the enduring DC villain Kobra and the revamp of *Dr. Fate* that is the basis of the character's current, long-lived incarnation. He lives outside Manhattan with his wife, Judith, a realtor and seminar instructor, and their daughter, Laura.

He blogs at http://martinpasko.blogspot.com/.

DAILY